INTERMEDIATE STATISTICS AND ECONOMETRICS

INTERMEDIATE STATISTICS AND ECONOMETRICS

A Comparative Approach

Dale J. Poirier

The MIT Press
Cambridge, Massachusetts
London, England

This book was set in Times Roman by Asco Trade Typesetting Ltd., Hong Kong and was printed and bound in the United States of America.

Library of Congress Cataloging-in-Publication Data
Poirier, Dale J.
Intermediate statistics and econometrics : a comparative approach / Dale J. Poirier.
p. cm.
Includes bibliographical references and index.
ISBN 0-262-16149-4
1. Economics—Statistical methods. 2. Econometrics. 3. Mathematical statistics. I. Title.
HB137.P645 1995
330'.01'5195—dc20 94-28184
CIP

To my parents,
for showing me the meaning of commitment.

Contents

	Words of Wisdom		xi
	Preface		xiii
1	**Introduction**		
	1.1	The Origin of Econometrics	1
	1.2	Realism Versus Instrumentalism	1
	1.3	The Shuttle Disaster	4
2	**Basic Concepts**		
	2.1	Probability	9
	2.2	Random Variables	29
	2.3	Univariate Mathematical Expectation	36
	2.4	Joint and Conditional Distributions	43
	2.5	Stochastic Independence	52
	2.6	Multivariate Mathematical Expectation	55
	2.7	Population Regression and Partial Correlation	64
	2.8	Inequalities	76
3	**Special Distributions**		
	3.1	Introduction	81
	3.2	Discrete Univariate Distributions	81
	3.3	Continuous Univariate Distributions	93
	3.4	Multivariate Distributions I	117
	3.5	Multivariate Distributions II	136
4	**Distributions of Functions of Random Variables**		
	4.1	Introduction	143
	4.2	Cumulative Distribution Function Technique	143
	4.3	Moment Generating Function Technique	147
	4.4	Change-of-Variable Technique	149
	4.5	Quadratic-Form Technique	155
5	**Sampling Theory**		
	5.1	Basic Concepts	165
	5.2	Statistics and Sample Moments	168
	5.3	Sampling Distributions	176
	5.4	Order Statistics	181
	5.5	Stochastic Convergence	185
	5.6	Laws of Large Numbers	199
	5.7	Central Limit Theorems	201
	5.8	Subjectivist View of Sampling	210

6 **Estimation**
6.1 Likelihood and Sufficiency 219
6.2 Likelihood and Stopping Rule Principles 226
6.3 Sampling Properties of Point Estimators in Finite Samples 233
6.4 Sampling Properties of Point Estimators in Large Samples 250
6.5 An Overview of Frequentist Point Estimation 259
6.6 Classical Point Estimation Methods 271
6.7 Bayesian Point Estimation 288
6.8 Choice of Prior and Bayesian Sensitivity Analysis 318
6.9 Interval Estimation 334
6.10 Reflections on Conditioning 343

7 **Hypothesis Testing**
7.1 Introduction 351
7.2 Sampling Theory Approach 354
7.3 Asymptotic Tests 367
7.4 Bayesian Posterior Odds 376
7.5 *P*-values 396
7.6 Postscript 400

8 **Prediction**
8.1 Introduction 405
8.2 The Simplest Case: Known Parameters 411
8.3 Structural Modelling 418
8.4 Predictive Likelihood 425
8.5 Classical Point and Interval Prediction 429
8.6 Bayesian Point and Interval Prediction 432
8.7 Combination of Forecasts 439

9 **The Linear Regression Model**
9.1 A Tale of Two Regressions 445
9.2 Classical Estimation in Multiple Linear Normal Regression 460
9.3 Estimation Subject to Exact Restrictions on Regression Coefficients 482
9.4 Distribution Theory for Classical Estimation 490
9.5 Confidence Intervals 494
9.6 Classical Hypothesis Testing 498
9.7 Dummy Variables 509

	9.8	Pretest Estimators	519
	9.9	Bayesian Estimation in Multiple Linear Normal Regression	524
	9.10	Bayesian Hypothesis Testing	540
	9.11	Prediction	551
	9.12	Goodness-of-Fit	559
	9.13	Sample Partial Correlation	563
	9.14	Multicollinearity	567
10	**Other Windows on the World**		
	10.1	Introduction	585
	10.2	The Initial Window	586
	10.3	Examples of Larger Worlds	590
	10.4	Pragmatic Principles of Model Building	601
	10.5	Statistical Framework	602
	10.6	Pure Significance Tests	607
	10.7	Diagnostic Checking of the Maintained Hypothesis	609
	10.8	Data-Instigated Hypotheses	613
	10.9	Reconciliation	615
Appendix A	**Matrix Algebra Review I**		
	A.1	Elementary Definitions	619
	A.2	Vector Spaces	621
	A.3	Determinants and Ranks	624
	A.4	Inverses	626
	A.5	Systems of Linear Equations and Generalized Inverses	629
	A.6	Idempotent Matrices	633
	A.7	Characteristic Roots and Vectors	634
	A.8	Quadratic Forms and Definite Matrices	638
Appendix B	**Matrix Algebra Review II**		
	B.1	Kronecker Products	645
	B.2	Vectorization of Matrices	646
	B.3	Matrix Differentiation	649
Appendix C	**Computation**		
	C.1	Maximization	653
	C.2	Monte Carlo Integration	654
	C.3	Gibbs sampling	659

Appendix D Statistical Tables
D.1 Cumulative Normal Distribution 661
D.2 Cumulative Chi-Squared Distribution 662
D.3 Cumulative *F*-Distribution 663
D.4 Cumulative Student *t*-Distribution 666

References 667
Author Index 699
Subject Index 705

Words of Wisdom

Doing econometrics is like trying to learn the laws of electricity by playing the radio.
—G. Orcutt

All *the laws of physics are wrong, at least in some ultimate detail, though many are awfully good approximations.*
—J. Tukey

All theories are born refuted.
—I. Lakatos

All models are wrong but some are useful.
—G. E. P. Box

Models do not represent truth. Rather they are ways of viewing a system, its problems and their contexts.
—M. West and J. Harrison (1989, p. 1)

Hence, in econometrics we are not searching for the "truth," but rather trying to find statistically and economically sound models that are of value for the problem in hand, and that are congruent with the available information.
—G. J. Anderson and G. E. Mizon (1989, p. 6)

A model *is a simplified representation intended to capture the salient features of some group of phenomena. Intrinsically, therefore, models embody the notions of design and a corresponding focus of interest, but are inherently approximations and inevitably 'false.'*
—D. F. Hendry and G. E. Mizon (1990, p. 124)

If it is, as the Bible tells us, that the truth will make us free, as researchers it is the surprising truth that will make us famous.
—J. B. Kadane and T. Seidenfeld (1990, p. 338)

A new scientific truth does not triumph by convincing the opponents and making them see the light, but rather because its opponents eventually die, and a new generation grows up that is familiar with it.
—M. Planck (1949, pp. 33–34)

Therefore, it is one thing to build a theoretical model, it is another thing to give rules for choosing the facts to which the theoretical model is to be applied.
—T. Haavelmo (1944, p. 4)

Far better an approximate answer to the right *question, which is often vague, than an* exact *answer to the wrong question, which can always be made precise.*
—J. Tukey (1962, pp. 13–14)

In the past, advances in econometrics were usually motivated by a desire to answer specific empirical questions. This symbiosis of theory and practice is less common today.
—C. F. Manski (1991, p. 49)

Fisher's fiducial argument is a gallant but unsuccessful attempt to make the Bayesian omelette without breaking the Bayesian egg.
—L. J. Savage (1981)

Bayesianism is the only view presently in the offing that holds out the hope for a comprehensive and unified treatment of inductive reasoning.... Whatever one's ultimate decision about Bayesian confirmation theory, it possesses the one unmistakable characteristic of a worthy philosophical doctrine: the harder it is pressed, the more interesting results it yields.
—J. Earman (1992, p. 2)

one of the most attractive features of the Bayesian approach is its recognition of the legitimacy of a plurality of (coherently constrained) responses to data. Any approach to scientific inference which seeks to legitimise an *answer in response to complex uncertainty is, for me, a totalitarian parody of a would-be rational learning process.*
—A. F. M. Smith (1984)

The objection to classical statistical inference is that it's nonsense. But everybody knows that. So if you follow the style I use, which would be classical statistical inference, you don't take it too seriously—you don't take it literally. If you use a Bayesian procedure, I get the impression you really have to believe the implications—you've already committed yourself to everything. You don't have the opportunity for waffling afterwards because you've already put everything in, and you have to take it literally from there on out. That may not be a virtue, but a disadvantage. Of course, a deeper reason for my *not adopting a Bayesian approach was the computational and mathematical complexity of incorporating prior information.*
—A. S. Goldberger (1989, p. 152)

Preface

Statistical thinking will one day be as necessary for efficient citizenship as the ability to read and write.
—H. G. Wells in Rao (1989, pp. 100–111)

All sensible graduate students should have a catholic approach to econometric methodology.
—Johnston (1991, p. 56)

This text is an introduction to mathematical statistics and the linear regression model for students pursuing research careers in economics. *Its distinguishing feature is its broad perspective that develops in parallel both classical and Bayesian treatments of topics.* Because this approach is rarely followed in other texts or in the classroom, let me say a few words about its motivation. By way of analogy, consider the situation in macroeconomics. Macroeconomics can scarcely be described as a homogeneous field. The nature of macroeconomics courses varies widely across universities, and for that matter, often widely across professors at the same university. The reasons are simple enough: one only has to reflect on the labels that characterize the field (e.g., Keynesian, monetarist, classical, new classical, post-Keynesian, etc.). Such adjectives are seldom added to the title of the course (e.g., "Keynesian Macroeconomics"); rather, I believe most professors try to give students an appreciation of a few of these viewpoints, with their own preference serving as a unifying theme. I realize there are some professors who teach macroeconomics courses exclusively from one perspective, but I do not believe this approach is widespread, and I certainly do not believe it is appreciated by students.

The state of affairs in econometrics is decidedly different. Although there are again different approaches, the standard introductory course is almost entirely based more or less on the frequentist (i.e., sampling theory) approach. The Bayesian approach, if taught at all, is generally relegated to an advanced topics course to be taken only after it is assured that the student has made a substantial investment in human capital in the classical approach. This "ghettoizing" of Bayesian statistics gives the impression that it consists solely of a few unrelated techniques appropriate only in special circumstances. Implicitly it is put on a par with other candidates for topics in an econometrics course (e.g., panel data techniques). Of course nothing could be further from reality. This book enables instructors to change this state of affairs.

Gigerenzer (1987) laments the fact that the diametrically opposed positions of Fisher and Neyman/Pearson over testing and statistical induction are covered up in the teaching of statistics in psychology. The attempt to present a hybrid and the anonymous presentation of ideas has done a disservice to students. This text attempts to rectify similar problems that I see in econometrics.

The primary intended reader is a first-year Ph.D. student in economics. It is important that a text is immediately accessible to its primary intended audience. This text assumes the minimal mathematical background demanded for admittance to most graduate programs in economics: elementary calculus, set theory, and linear algebra. For students feeling shaky in the latter area, Appendix A provides a concise refresher in elementary matrix algebra, leaving more advanced topics to Appendix B.

Typically, first-year graduate students in economics are very heterogenous in their statistical background. Most graduate programs offer a course in the first semester that attempts to bring students with the weakest statistical backgrounds up to the level of introductory mathematical statistics, and to provide a refresher for students who already have a mathematical statistics background. The comparative approach of this book will likely bring new material to the attention of both groups. The assumed minimal statistical background is only a standard introductory business statistics course—presumably not very rigorous—and narrowly taught from a classical perspective.

Notably, no background in measure theory is required for readers of this text. The need for measure theory in providing a firm foundation in probability theory and statistics goes back at least to Kolmogorov (1950) and Cramér (1946), respectively. Fortunately, although measure theory is often required for rigorous development of a result, once the measure theoretic "dust" has settled, the result can usually be understood and used without knowledge of the measure theory (see Cabanis and Simons 1977). The real world is finite, and finite sample spaces require few measure-theoretic concepts. Mathematical convenience often suggests superficial simplifications if continuity is assumed, but lingering in the background there is usually the need for measure-theoretic foundational material. Students planning to specialize in econometrics will eventually need more advanced treatments of the material contained herein. However, the primary intended audience is *not* the specialist, but rather potential empirical researchers looking for more than a cookbook terminal treatment of topics. The treatment here provides a solid foundation for subsequent courses in econometrics.

Near the end of the first-term course described, or possibly in a second term, students are introduced to the standard linear regression model under ideal conditions. Some generalizations beyond the ideal case might be discussed, but detailed discussion of the myriad of topics (e.g., time series analysis, multiple equation models, limited dependent variable models etc.) are usually left to later courses, as are the details of the more sophisticated statistical tools (i.e., asymptotic theory) they require. Except for a few limited excursions in Section 9.1 and 10.3, this text leaves such topics to existing texts, but in the future I hope that texts will exist that treat these topics from a broad perspective.

Over the last dozen or so years that I have been distributing lecture notes in my econometrics classes, I have received numerous helpful comments from students and others regarding this material as it progressed toward the current text. Many people must regrettably remain anonymous, including some helpful reviewers of earlier drafts. I wish, however, to note some of the helpful contributors: Jeffrey Amato, Pierre-Pascal Gendron, John Geweke, W. E. Griffiths, H. S. Konijn, Jacek Osiewalski, and Denise Young. Jeffrey Amato's help with the graphics for this text is particularly appreciated.

1 Introduction

Econometric research aims, essentially, at a conjunction of economic theory and actual measurements, using the theory and technique of statistical inference as a bridge pier.
—Haavelmo in Morgan (1989, p. 242)

Statistics is the study of how information should be employed to reflect on, and give guidance for action in a practical situation involving uncertainty.
—Barnett (1982)

1.1 The Origin of Econometrics

When the term "econometrics" was first used it conveyed both (i) the development of pure economic theory from a mathematical viewpoint, and (ii) the development of empirical estimation and inference techniques for economic relationships. This is reflected in the constitution of the Econometric Society, founded 29 December 1930, which defined the society's primary objective as "the advancement of economic theory in its relation to statistics and mathematics" (Frisch (1933, p. 1)). Today, the term "econometrics" signifies primarily (ii), and (i) is called *mathematical economics*. Tintner (1953) quotes the following definition of Wassily Leontief that is adequate for our purposes: *econometrics* is "a special type of economic analysis in which the general theoretical approach—often formulated in explicitly mathematical terms—is combined frequently through the medium of intricate statistical procedures—with empirical measurement of economic phenomena."[1]

1.2 Realism versus Instrumentalism

To be sure, the object of the scientist's attention may well be an assumed external, objective reality: but the actual reality of the scientific process consists in the evolution of scientists beliefs *about that reality.*
—Smith (1984, p. 245)

The philosophy of science literature seems continually engulfed in conflict. Particularly notable is the clash between proponents of *realism* and proponents of *instrumentalism* (e.g., Cartwright 1983 or Morgenbesser 1969).[2]

1. No attempt is made here to go into an excursion of the history of econometrics nor the history of econometrics thought. The scholarly works of Christ (1985), Epstein (1987), Morgan (1987, 1989), and Qin (1989) are valuable guides to these two areas.

2. I suggest that interested readers consult Granger (1990a), Kloek and Haitovsky (1988), De Marchi and Gilbert (1989), and the symposium discussed in Phillips (1988), Stigum (1990), Swamy, Conway and von zur Muehlen (1985), and especially Poirier (ed., 1994).

Space constraints also do not permit detailed methodological discussion, but the clash between these two views (see Dempster 1990, pp. 264–265; Lawson 1989; Poirier 1994b) warrants brief discussion.

Realists believe that science should not only enable us to make accurate and reliable predictions, but it should also enable us to discover new "truths" about the world and to "explain" phenomena. Realists believe the objects mentioned in theories (e.g., black holes, quarks, production frontiers, etc.) exist independently of the enquiry in question. Realists who use models are in a difficult position. In particular the ubiquitous phrase "true model" in econometrics raises problems, as by definition models are abstractions from reality. Models do not represent literal truth. Rather they are tools for viewing the world, its problems, and contexts.

In contrast to realists, *instrumentalists* believe that the primary goal of science is to develop tools (models) that enable us to make reliable and useful predictions of future observables. Instrumentalists need not believe the literal "truth" of any theory or model, and they may view entities appearing in theories as merely valuable intellectual fictions. The problems and peculiarities of quantum mechanics have led many physicists to an instrumentalist view of science. Instrumentalism also has a strong toehold in economics—much to the chagrin of some. For example, the widely cited essay by Friedman (1953) is best appreciated from the instrumentalist perspective (see Boland 1979).

Being asked to choose between realism and instrumentalism is like being asked to choose between "nature" and "nurture" in explaining human behavior. Can we be eclectic without being wishy-washy? I believe the answer is yes. In practice the realist versus instrumentalist distinction is more a question of emphasis than inescapable conflict. I know of no realist embarrassed by predictive success. Only an extreme instrumentalist could be described as worshipping prediction *and only prediction.*

The instrumentalist's concern for predictive success is not meant to favor mere black-box projection of history into the future. It is necessary to peer inside the box in an attempt to understand the inner workings. Predictions must be intellectually compelling in order to address the *problem of induction*, that is, in the absence of deductive proof, why should any empirical prediction about the world be believed? Realist arguments can sometimes provide reasons to find a prediction compelling. Causal explanations, which describe an empirical regularity in terms of an instance of broader or deeper regularity, are often compelling, but the concept of causality remains elusive.

The need for "compelling" predictions should not be underestimated. Academic research is a public exercise, and the "compellingness" of predictions must meet the market test of colleague approval. Granger (1990b,

p. 2) argues: "The basic objective of a modelling exercise is to affect the beliefs—and hence the behavior—of other research workers and possibly other economic agents." The way to convince others of the worthiness of a model is to communicate its content by means of an evaluation exercise. Granger (1990b, p. 3) refers to such models as being *transferable*. One component of an evaluation exercise is an accounting of past predictive performance.

Instrumentalists downplay the literal "truth" of assumptions; realists are concerned with their literal accuracy. Even before Friedman (1953), economists were perplexed over what to demand of a model's assumptions (economic, statistical, or otherwise). Curiously, the distinction between assumptions and predictions is not always clear-cut. Trivially, assumptions imply themselves. Hence, false assumptions yield at least some false predictions, namely themselves. This requires instrumentalists to be concerned with the descriptive accuracy of predictions. The escape from this trap for instrumentalists is to remember the purpose of the theory. An instrumentalist defense of a theory is offered only for particular uses of the theory—for other uses the theory may be totally inappropriate.

The realist/instrumentalist distinction arises in the difference between "objective" and "subjective" interpretations of probability covered in Section 2.1, and which underlie many debates in statistics. Although objective interpretations have dominated econometrics, ironically, early writers offered interpretations suspiciously close to modern subjectivist/instrumentalist thinking (e.g., see Haavelmo 1944, p. 43). Bayesians' preoccupation with prediction and frequentists' preoccupation with diagnostic testing are not unrelated to their instrumentalist/realist differences in attitudes.

The early days of econometrics were not without controversy. The controversy revolved around the need to distinguish between fundamental laws and mere empirical regularities. The controversy began in the late 1940s, and it continues in the contemporary literature. Lawson (1989, p. 240) offers a view of these two early debates from the realism versus instrumentalism perspective.

It can be argued, convincingly in the opinion of this author, that the defining essence of econometrics, distinguishing it from statistics at large, is its literature on *structure*. Frisch developed the idea of "structure," and Haavelmo developed a statistical framework for studying it. The need for structure arises from the need to address the essence of economic policy analysis—prediction in the face of intervention. The source of structure is economic theory. The essential idea of a "structure" is invariance. The components of a structure warrant a degree of autonomy (detachability or projectibility) in the face of change elsewhere in the statistical model. Structural equations have a "life of their own" and can be discussed without reference to other parts of the model. Section 8.3 expands on the idea of structure.

Aldrich (1989) nicely ties together numerous strands of the literature on policy analysis and structure. Poirier (ed., 1993, Parts II and III) contains many of the original and still relevant articles.

1.3 The Shuttle Disaster

This text does not provide much in the way of empirical examples. Nonetheless we close this first chapter with an example that motivates much of the theoretical discussion that follows. This example is a manageable real world data set involving a fairly well known event: the space shuttle *Challenger* disaster of January 28, 1986, in which the entire crew was lost because of an explosion shortly after takeoff. Anyone who saw the television coverage of this disaster will have it etched in their memories for life. As a result of the disaster, President Ronald Reagan appointed a commission headed by former Secretary of State William Rogers and including numerous renowned researchers in the scientific and space communities. The resulting report by the Presidential Commission on the Space Shuttle *Challenger* Accident (1986, p. 70) concluded that the cause of the accident was as follows: "A combustion gas leak through the right Solid Rocket Motor aft field joint initiated at or shortly after ignition eventually weakened and/or penetrated the External Tank initiating vehicle structure breakup and loss of the Space Shuttle *Challenger* during mission 61-L."

What makes this example so interesting is that the night before the flight there was extensive discussion whether the flight should be postponed. These discussions are well documented, involved data, and appear to have included some dubious statistical analysis. With the hindsight of the Roger's Commission and subsequent statistical analysis by the National Research Council's Shuttle Criticality Review Hazard Analysis Audit Committee (1988), Dalal et al. (1989), Lavine (1991b), and Martz and Zimmer (1992), we now describe the statistical problem facing launch officials the night before the disaster.

The space shuttle is launched by two solid rocket motors. The solid rocket motors are shipped in four pieces and assembled at the Kennedy Space Center. These four pieces are connected by three *field joints* on each rocket. Hence there are a total of six field joints. O-rings are used to seal the joint formed by the "tang segment" fitting into the "clevis segment." For redundancy, two O-rings (primary and secondary) are used. The O-rings measure 37.5 feet in diameter and are .28 inches thick. Catastrophic failure occurs when both the primary and secondary O-rings of a particular field joint fail.

Table 1.1
Shuttle data for twenty-three previous launches

Flight	Date (day/month/year)	Number of O-rings exhibiting some distress	Temperature
1	12/4/81	0	66
2	12/11/81	1	70
3	22/3/82	0	69
5	11/11/82	0	68
6	4/4/83	2	67
7	18/6/83	0	72
8	30/8/83	0	73
9	28/11/83	0	70
41-B	3/2/84	1	57
41-C	6/4/84	1	63
41-D	30/8/84	1	70
41-G	5/10/84	0	78
51-A	8/11/84	0	67
51-C	24/1/85	3	53
51-D	12/4/85	0	67
51-B	29/4/85	0	75
51-G	17/6/85	0	70
51-F	29/7/85	0	81
51-I	27/8/85	0	76
51-J	3/10/85	0	79
61-A	30/10/85	2	75
61-B	26/11/85	0	76
61-C	12/1/86	1	58

Source: Dalal et al. (1989, p. 950, Table 1).

O-rings do not always seal properly at low temperatures. As a result of a forecast launch temperature of 31°F, which was far lower than any of the previous shuttle flights, the discussion the night before the flight focused on the potential effects of low temperature on O-ring performance, and how such performance might affect the probability p_{31} of a catastrophic failure of a field joint when launching at 31°F.

Like many researchers, the launch officials had only limited data available on which to base a decision. Table 1.1 contains the launch temperatures for 23 previous shuttle launches for which motor rocket data are available.[3] Although no catastrophic field-joint O-ring failures had occurred previously, there was evidence of O-ring thermal distress on seven

3. After each launch the rocket motors are recovered from the ocean for inspection and possible reuse. There was a twenty-fourth launch, but the rocket motors were lost at sea and not inspected.

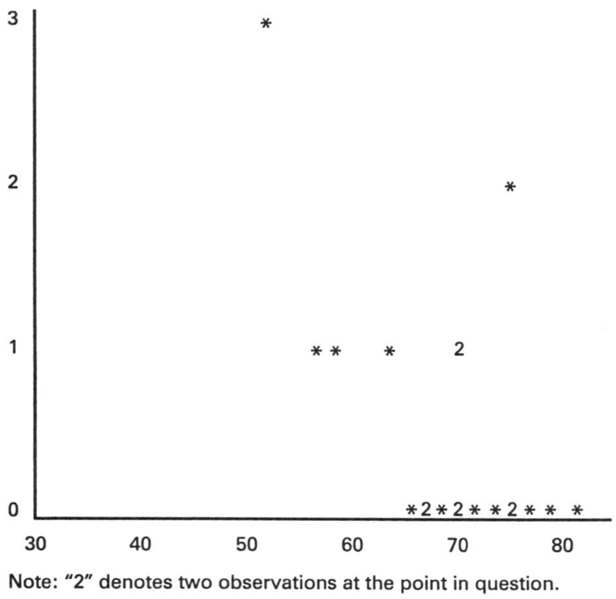

Figure 1.1
Number of O-ring failures versus temperature

previous flights. There are two kinds of thermal distress: "erosion" caused by excessive heat burning up the O-ring, and "blow-by," which occurs when gases rush by the O-ring. The number of O-rings exhibiting some thermal distress ranged from one to three on these flights. In all but one of the seven cases, the O-rings exhibiting thermal distress were the primary O-rings. The O-ring distress data are also included in Table 1.1. Figure 1.1 graphs the number of O-rings exhibiting some distress as a function of launch temperature. Notice that Flight 51-C had the largest number of O-ring problems (3) and corresponds to the lowest previous launch temperature (53°F).

It is useful to note a few key points. First, the launch officials were faced with a prediction problem, that is, predict the number of O-rings that will exhibit some distress if the launch goes ahead at an ambient temperature of 31°F, and the probability p_{31} of a catastrophic failure of a field joint. This text emphasizes the importance of prediction; Chapter 8 is devoted to this topic.

Second, the launch officials drew on a body of knowledge (i.e., theory) that linked O-ring performance to another variable, namely, temperature. This theory was not air-tight and complete. It suggested the two variables might be systematically related because of subject matter considerations, but the link was neither deterministic nor was its direction fully understood. Empirical researchers in economics should be able to identify with launch officials; economic theory seldom delivers a tight statistical model to their doorsteps.

Third, the prediction of O-ring performance was to be made at a temperature (31°F) far different than all previous launch temperatures. The temperature at the time of the preceding 23 launches ranged from 53°F to 81°F, and averaged 69.6°F. This substantial extrapolation outside of the existing data suggests the importance of using all available prior information in connection with the data. Sensible extrapolation to a 31°F launch requires engineering (subject matter) considerations that go beyond the data in Table 1.1.

The most disturbing part of the statistical analysis by launch officials was that they asked the wrong question. Records show that the night of January 27, 1986, there was a three-hour teleconference call among people at Morton Thiokol (manufacturer of the solid rocket motor), Marshall Space Flight Center (the National Aeronautics and Space Administration center for motor design control), and Kennedy Space Center. In formulating the predictive question of interest, officials asked whether the number of O-rings exhibiting distress and launch temperature were related *on any of the previous launches that exhibited at least one O-ring distress.* This led to consideration of the seven data points in the upper part of Figure 1.1. Although there was some dissent, the "U-configuration" of these points led officials to conclude that there was no evidence of a temperature effect. In the terminology of Chapters 8 to 10, the "distribution of interest" implicit in the choice of these seven observations, namely, the number of O-rings exhibiting distress given launch temperature *and that the number of O-rings exhibiting distress is at least one*, is not very interesting for purposes of the predictive questions at hand. A better choice of distribution of interest would have simply been the number of O-rings exhibiting distress, given launch temperature. Using only these seven observations to make inference regarding this latter distribution of interest is an example of the *sample selection* problem commonly encountered in economic analysis. The picture that emerges from casual examination of all twenty-three observations in Figure 1.1 suggests that O-ring performance is inversely related to launch temperature.

No formal statistical analyses of these data are presented here because the analyses that have been performed are beyond the scope of this text, however, some comments regarding others analyses are in order.

Dalal et al. (1989) consider different ways of relating the probability of O-ring distress as a function of temperature. In the language of Chapter 6, these correspond to different windows for viewing the observed data. They also consider related data on other joints, additional variables (pressure leak-tests of the O-rings after assembly). The bottom-line of Dalal et al. (1989) was that at 31°F they expected five of the primary O-rings to suffer "blow-by" or "erosion" damage. Of course primary O-ring failure alone does not mean catastrophic failure because there are secondary O-rings to back them up. Catastrophic failure occurs when both the primary and secondary O-rings of a field joint fail.

The meaning of probability is discussed in Chapter 2. For now note that because there had been previously no catastrophic failures, it is difficult to think of an empirically based relative frequency interpretation of this concept. Rather, a "degree of belief" interpretation seems necessary.

Given the small data set in Table 1.1, Maritz and Zimmer (1992) consider additional data from five military solid rocket programs and post-*Challenger* space shuttle data. Incorporation of such diverse data raises a variety of problems demanding a Bayesian analysis. They apply their results to predicting the probability of catastrophic failure on a later shuttle mission (*Galileo* in October, 1989).

Lavine (1991b) focuses on the robustness or sensitivity in any prediction of distressed O-rings for a launch at 31°F. In particular he notes the sensitivity of results to omission of key influential data points, particularly the observations corresponding to Flights 51-C (the coldest previous launch, which also suffered from the most O-ring distress) and 61-A (for which two O-rings suffered thermal distress despite the relatively warm launch temperature of 75°F).

Lavine (1991b) also poses a relevant decision theoretic interpretation of the task facing launch officials the night before the launch. Decision theoretic perspectives often cut right to the heart of the matter and identify the primary issues of importance. Hence, they will often be adopted in this text. Specifically, suppose we ask whether the launch should have been postponed until the launch temperature was 60°F. Let c be the cost of postponing the launch, C the cost of a launch failure, and normalize the cost of a successful launch at 0. Distressed O-rings are not sufficient to cause failure of a launch. If p_t is the probability of catastrophic failure at temperature t, then the expected cost of launching at 31°F is $p_{31}C$ and the cost of postponement to 60°F is $c + p_{60}C$. Dalal et al. (1989) estimate $p_{60} = .019$. Therefore, the launch should have been postponed if $p_{31} > .019 + (c/C)$. Although an appealing formulation, this leaves open the values of c/C and p_{31} (the probability of launch failure at a temperature of 31°F) while launch failure had never been observed before. No sensible researcher would envy the difficult question faced by launch officials the night before the *Challenger* disaster.

2 Basic Concepts

2.1 Probability

Probability is the very guide to life.
—Cicero

Probability does not exist.
—de Finetti (1974, p. x)

As these two quotations suggest, there exist widely varying opinions on the concept of "probability." Despite the differences in the tones of these comments, however, these two quotations are not necessarily incompatible. Such irony is also reflected in the following comments of Savage (1954, p. 2):

> It is unanimously agreed that statistics depends somehow on probability. But, as to what probability is and how it is connected with statistics, there has seldom been such complete disagreement and breakdown of communication since the Tower of Babel.... Considering the confusion about the foundations of statistics, it is surprising, and certainly gratifying, to find that almost everyone is agreed on what the purely mathematical properties of probability are. Virtually all controversy therefore centers on questions of interpreting the generally accepted axiomatic concept of probability, that is, of determining the extramathematical properties of probability.

Differences in the interpretations of this concept, are not just of academic interest. The existence of competing paradigms of statistical inference can be explained in part by the different definitions of probability that each employs. Before expanding on these differences, however, their mathematical similarities will first be discussed. We begin with a few preliminary definitions and uncontested theorems. The elementary background in probability theory assumed in this text should be adequate motivation for these formalities.

Definition 2.1.1 An *experiment* is a process whose outcome is not known in advance with certainty. The *sample space*, denoted by $\mathscr{S}$, is the set of all possible outcomes of the experiment under consideration.

As will be seen momentarily, "probability" is a numerical measure defined over subsets of the sample space. However, not all subsets are permissible candidates because some subsets are too "irregular," particularly when dealing with uncountably infinite sample spaces.[1] Therefore, the following definition provides a restricted family of subsets.

1. For example, DeGroot (1970, p. 9) considers a case in which an arrow is aimed at a two-dimensional target. It is often reasonable to assume that the probability of the arrow

Definition 2.1.2 A family $\tilde{A}$ of sets, each element of which is a subset of the sample space $\mathcal{S}$, is a *Boolean algebra* (alternatively, simply an *algebra* or a *field*) iff:

(a) $\mathcal{S} \in \tilde{A}$.

(b) If $A \in \tilde{A}$, then $A^c \in \tilde{A}$.[2]

(c) If $A_1, A_2 \in \tilde{A}$, then $A_1 \cup A_2 \in \tilde{A}$.

In other words, $\tilde{A}$ is an algebra iff the sample space is contained in $\tilde{A}$, the complement of any set in $\tilde{A}$ is itself in $\tilde{A}$, and the union of two sets from $\tilde{A}$ is also contained in $\tilde{A}$. This is reasonable: If A occurs, then $A \cup B$ occurs for all $B \in \tilde{A}$, and if A does not occur, then certainly A^c does occur. An algebra also satisfies the following properties.

Theorem 2.1.1 Suppose $\tilde{A}$ is an algebra. Then:

(a) $\emptyset \in \tilde{A}$, where $\emptyset$ is the null set.

(b) If $A_1, A_2 \in \tilde{A}$, then $A_1 \cap A_2 \in \tilde{A}$.

(c) If $A_1, A_2, \ldots, A_N \in \tilde{A}$, then $A_1 \cup A_2 \cup \cdots \cup A_N \in \tilde{A}$ and $A_1 \cap A_2 \cap \cdots \cap A_N \in \tilde{A}$.

Proof Because $\mathcal{S}^c = \emptyset$, (a) follows directly from parts (a) and (b) of Definition 2.1.2. Because $(A_1 \cup A_2)^c = A_1^c \cap A_2^c$, (b) follows directly from parts (b) and (c) of Definition 2.1.2. Finally, (c) follows from (b) and Definition 2.1.2(c) upon use of mathematical induction.

To illustrate concepts discussed so far, note the following standard example.

Example 2.1.1 Consider the experiment of tossing a two-sided coin twice. The sides of the coin are denoted H and T, for "heads" and "tails," respectively. Then the sample space is $\mathcal{S} = \{(H, H), (H, T), (T, H), (T, T)\}$, where the first component of each ordered pair refers to the outcome of the first toss and the second element refers to the outcome of the second toss. There are many possible subsets of $\mathcal{S}$. The set of all possible subsets is known as the *power set of* $\mathcal{S}$, and here it contains $2^4 = 16$ elements. Can you list them? Clearly, $\mathcal{S}$ is an algebra. The set $\tilde{A} \equiv \{\emptyset, \mathcal{S}, \{(T, H)\}, \{(H, H), (H, T), (T, T)\}\}$ is also an algebra. The set $C \equiv \{\emptyset, \mathcal{S}, \{(H, H), (T, T)\}\}$, however, is *not* an algebra since $\{(H, H), (T, T)\}^c \notin C$.

---

hitting in any given subset of the target is proportional to the area of the subset. Certain subsets of the plane are so irregular, however, that no meaningful definition of area can be applied to them.

2. A^c denotes the *complement of* A in $\mathcal{S}$, i.e. the set of points in $\mathcal{S}$ but not in A.

Most treatments of probability further restrict the domain of events from an algebra to a subset satisfying the following definition.

Definition 2.1.3 A Boolean algebra $\tilde{A}$ is called a *sigma-algebra* (denoted σ-algebra), or alternatively a *sigma-field*, iff condition (c) in Definition 2.1.2 is strengthened to hold for countable unions, that is, (c) is replaced by

(c*) If $A_1, A_2, \ldots, A_n \ldots, \in \tilde{A}$, then $A_1 \cup A_2 \cup \cdots \cup A_n \cup \cdots \in \tilde{A}$.

In this case the pair $(\mathscr{S}, \tilde{A})$ is said to be a *measurable space*, and the sets in $\tilde{A}$ are referred to as *measurable sets*.

Clearly, a σ-algebra is an algebra, but not conversely. Thus, Theorem 2.1.1 holds for σ-algebras as well. Furthermore, in the case of a σ-algebra, part (c) of Theorem 2.1.1 can be extended to cover countable unions and intersections. If the sample space is finite, then every algebra is also a σ-algebra. Differences arise when considering infinite sample spaces. The reason for delineating between an algebra and a σ-algebra is discussed momentarily.

If $\tilde{A} \subseteq \mathscr{S}$ is not a σ-algebra, then it is always possible to generate from it another subset of the sample space that is a σ-algebra by taking all possible set unions, intersections and complements of the elements in $\tilde{A}$. The resulting σ-algebra is known as the *minimal σ-algebra* generated by $\tilde{A}$. This is most important in cases involving uncountable sample spaces. See Exercise 2.1.21 for an important example.

Now some more important concepts must be defined.

Definition 2.1.4 Consider an experiment with sample space $\mathscr{S}$ and let $\tilde{A}$ denote an appropriately chosen algebra. The sets in $\tilde{A}$ are *events*. If $A \in \tilde{A}$ consists of a single point, then A is an *elementary event*. An event A *occurs* iff the experiment results in an outcome that belongs to A. Two events $A, B \in \tilde{A}$ are *mutually exclusive* (*disjoint*) iff $A \cap B = \varnothing$. The *pairwise disjoint sets* A_n $(n = 1, 2, \ldots, N)$, i.e., $A_i \cap A_j = \varnothing$ for $i \neq j$, comprise a *finite partition* of A iff

$$A = \bigcup_{n=1}^{N} A_n, \tag{2.1.1}$$

The countably infinite sequence A_n $(n = 1, 2, \ldots)$ of *pairwise disjoint sets* comprise a *σ-partition* of A iff

$$A = \bigcup_{n=1}^{\infty} A_n. \tag{2.1.2}$$

A mathematical definition of probability can now be provided. For any experiment with a sample space $\mathscr{S}$, probabilities are defined for all sets in an appropriately chosen σ-field $\tilde{A}$. If $\mathscr{S}$ is finite or countable, then $\tilde{A}$ is chosen to be the power set of $\mathscr{S}$. If $\mathscr{S}$ is the n-dimensional Euclidean space $\Re^n$, then $\tilde{A}$ is usually chosen to be the *Borel field* $\mathring{A}^n$, i.e. the smallest σ-field containing all n-dimensional intervals. (See Exercise 2.1.21 for construction of the Borel field in the case $n = 1$.) The axiomatic treatment that follows was developed by Kolmogorov (1950) in the 1930s.

Definition 2.1.5 A *finitely additive probability function*, denoted $P(\cdot)$, is a real-valued set function $P\colon \tilde{A} \to \Re$ satisfying the following axioms:

(a) $P(A) \geq 0$ for all $A \in \tilde{A}$.

(b) $P(\mathscr{S}) = 1$.

(c) If A_1 and A_2 are *mutually exclusive* events in $\tilde{A}$, then
$P(A_1 \cup A_2) = P(A_1) + P(A_2)$.

A *countably additive probability function* is a set function with domain equalling a σ-algebra $\tilde{A}$ that satisfies the axioms (a) and (b) and the following strengthened version of (c):

(c*) If $A_1, A_2, \ldots,$ is a sequence of pairwise mutually exclusive events in $\tilde{A}$, then

$$P\left(\bigcup_{n=1}^{\infty} A_n\right) = \sum_{n=1}^{\infty} P(A_n).$$

Definition 2.1.6 A *finitely additive probability space* is the triplet $[\mathscr{S}, \tilde{A}, P(\cdot)]$, where $\mathscr{S}$ is the sample space, $\tilde{A}$ is an algebra associated with $\mathscr{S}$, and $P(\cdot)$ is a finitely additive probability function with domain $\tilde{A}$. A *countably additive probability space* is the triplet $[\mathscr{S}, \tilde{A}, P(\cdot)]$, where $\mathscr{S}$ is the sample space, $\tilde{A}$ is a σ-algebra associated with $\mathscr{S}$, and $P(\cdot)$ is a countably additive probability function with domain $\tilde{A}$.[3]

From Definition 2.1.5, the following results arise.

Theorem 2.1.2 Let $P(\cdot)$ be a probability function over the algebra $\tilde{A}$. Then

(a) $P(\varnothing) = 0$.

(b) If $A \in \tilde{A}$, then $P(A^c) = 1 - P(A)$.

(c) If $A, B \in \tilde{A}$ are mutually exclusive, then $P(A \cap B) = 0$.

(d) If $A, B \in \tilde{A}$, then $P(A) = P(A \cap B) + P(A \cap B^c)$.

(e) If $A, B \in \tilde{A}$, then $P(A \cup B) = P(A) + P(B) - P(A \cap B)$.

3. If a set function satisfies (a) and (c) of Definition 2.1.5 and $|P(\varnothing)| = 0$, then it is a *measure*, and the triplet in Definition 2.1.6 is a *measure space*. For further discussion see Dhrymes (1989, Chapter 1). A probability measure on an algebra $\tilde{A}$ has a unique extension to a generated σ-algebra (the intersection of all σ-algebras containing $\tilde{A}$) (see Billingsley 1986, Chapter 1).

(f) If $A, B \in \tilde{A}$, then $P(A \cap B^c) = P(A) - P(A \cap B)$.

(g) If $A, B \in \tilde{A}$ and $A \subseteq B$, then $P(A) \leq P(B)$.

(h) If $A_n \in \tilde{A}$ $(n = 1, 2, \ldots, N)$ are mutually exclusive, then

$$P\left[\bigcup_{n=1}^{N} A_n\right] = \sum_{n=1}^{N} P(A_n).$$

(i) If $\tilde{A}$ is a σ-algebra and $A_n \in \tilde{A}$ $(n = 1, 2, 3, \ldots)$ (not necessarily mutually exclusive), then

$$P\left(\bigcup_{n=1}^{\infty} A_n\right) \leq \sum_{n=1}^{\infty} P(A_n).$$

Proof Left to the reader.

Although Kolmogorov's classic treatment of probability justified a finitely additive probability, he assumed countable additivity "for expedience." In contrast, Bayesian statisticians Bruno de Finetti and Jimmie Savage, and even fiducialist Ronald A. Fisher, argued in favor of finitely additive probability. Many foundational issues and resolution of alleged paradoxes in probability theory involve the distinction between finitely additive and countably additive probability functions. For lucid discussions of some implications of adopting finite additivity axiom (c), but not countable additivity axiom (c^*) in Definition 2.1.5, see Kadane, Schervish, and Seidenfeld (1986) and Walley (1991, pp. 323–327). *In this text, as all texts at this level, countable additivity is assumed unless stated otherwise.*

In practical problems, it is often desirable to consider the probability of an event A given another event B has occurred. Thus the following definition is introduced.

Definition 2.1.7 Let A and B be two events in $\tilde{A}$ of the given probability space $[\mathscr{S}, \tilde{A}, P(\cdot)]$. The *conditional probability* of the event A, denoted $P(A|B)$, is defined by

$$P(A|B) = \frac{P(A \cap B)}{P(B)} \quad \text{if } P(B) > 0, \tag{2.1.3}$$

and is left undefined if $P(B) = 0$.

In conditional probability the "frame of reference" is shifted from the entire sample space $\mathscr{S}$ to the event B, and then to that part of the event A that overlaps with B (i.e., $A \cap B$).[4] Division of $P(A \cap B)$ by $P(B)$ ensures the probability of the new frame of reference is unity.[5]

4. Rényi (1970) provides an axiomatic development of conditional probability.

5. A probability distribution is *conglomerable* iff for any partition (possibly infinite) of events, if the conditional probability of another event given each element in the partition lies between the two bounds, then the unconditional probability of the event must also lie between

It is easy to show that the conditional probability of an event satisfies the axioms of Definition 2.1.5. In addition conditional probabilities satisfy properties analogous to those contained in Theorem 2.1.2. Of particular interest is the case where the conditional probability $P(A|B)$ equals the unconditional probability $P(A)$, and hence does not depend on B. The following definition is concerned with this case.

Definition 2.1.8 Consider the probability space $[\mathscr{S}, \tilde{A}, P(\cdot)]$. Events A and B in $\tilde{A}$, are *independent* iff any one the following conditions is satisfied:

(a) $P(A \cap B) = P(A)P(B)$.

(b) $P(A|B) = P(A), \quad \text{if} \quad P(B) > 0$.

(c) $P(B|A) = P(B), \quad \text{if} \quad P(A) > 0$.

The reader should keep clear the distinction between independent and mutually exclusive events. If both events have positive probability of occurring, then independence implies that the events are *not* mutually exclusive. If two events are mutually exclusive, then they are *dependent* (i.e., not independent), because if one event occurs the other cannot. For additional discussion, see Wang et al. (1993).

The next definition extends Definition 2.1.8 to more than two events.

Definition 2.1.9 Consider the probability space $[\mathscr{S}, \tilde{A}, P(\cdot)]$ and let $A_n \in \tilde{A}\ (n = 1, 2, \ldots, N)$. The events $A_1, A_2, \ldots, A_N$ are *mutually independent* (or simply *independent*) iff all of the following conditions are satisfied for $i, j, n = 1, 2, \ldots, N$:

$$P(A_i \cap A_j) = P(A_i)P(A_j) \qquad (i \neq j), \tag{2.1.4}$$

$$P(A_i \cap A_j \cap A_n) = P(A_i)P(A_j)P(A_n) \qquad (i \neq j, j \neq n, i \neq n), \tag{2.1.5}$$

$$\vdots \qquad \qquad \vdots$$

$$P(A_1 \cap A_2 \cap \cdots \cap A_N) = P(A_1)P(A_2)\ldots P(A_N). \tag{2.1.6}$$

Note that all of conditions (2.1.4) to (2.1.6) are required. For example, (2.1.5) holds if $P(A_n) = 0$, but (2.1.4) does not hold if A_i and A_j are dependent. Furthermore, as Exercise 2.1.6 illustrates, pairwise independence does *not* imply mutual independence.

Related to the idea of independent events is the idea of conditionally independent events (for detailed study see Dawid 1979).

---

these bounds. For countable sample spaces, conglomerability and countable additivity are equivalent. Probability distributions that are finitely additive, but not countably additive, are *nonconglomerable*. See Schervish et al. (1984) and Hill and Lane (1986) for detailed discussions.

Definition 2.1.10 Consider three events A, B, and C with $P(C) > 0$. Then *A and B are conditionally independent given C* iff $P(A \cap B|C) = P(A|C)P(B|C)$.

There are a number of useful theorems involving conditional probabilities whose validity is not a matter of controversy, although their applicability may be. Before turning towards controversial matters, two important theorems are stated.[6]

Theorem 2.1.3 (Bayes' Theorem for Events) Consider a probability space $[\mathscr{S}, \tilde{A}, P(\cdot)]$ and a collection $B_n \in \tilde{A}$ $(n = 1, 2, \ldots, N)$ of mutually disjoint events such that $P(B_n) > 0$ $(n = 1, 2, \ldots, N)$ and $B_1 \cup B_2 \cup \cdots \cup B_N = \mathscr{S}$. Then

$$P(B_n|A) = \frac{P(A|B_n)P(B_n)}{\sum_{j=1}^{N} P(A|B_j)P(B_j)} \qquad (n = 1, 2, \ldots, N) \tag{2.1.7}$$

for every $A \in \tilde{A}$ such that $P(A) > 0$.

Proof Follows directly from Definition 2.1.7 after noting that the denominator in (2.1.7) is $P(A)$; see Theorem 2.1.2(d).

Theorem 2.1.4 (Multiplication Rule) Consider a probability space $[\mathscr{S}, \tilde{A}, P(\cdot)]$ and a collection $A_i \in \tilde{A}$ $(n = 1, 2, \ldots, N)$ such that $P(A_1 \cap A_2 \cap \cdots \cap A_{N-1}) \neq 0$. Then

$$P(A_1 \cap A_2 \cap \cdots \cap A_N) = P(A_1) \cdot P(A_2|A_1) \cdot P(A_3|A_1 \cap A_2) \cdot \ldots \cdot P(A_N|A_1 \cap A_2 \cap \ldots A_{N-1}). \tag{2.1.8}$$

Proof By mathematical induction.

There is broad agreement among competing views of probability on the preceding mathematical properties. There is, however, wide disagreement concerning the *interpretation* and application of the concept "probability" that satisfies these properties. Carnap (1962) argues that this is a *problem of explication*, that is, a problem where a concept already in use (the *explicandum*) is to be replaced by a more exact new concept (the *explicatum*). The explicandum for every view of probability is a prescientific concept of probability that characterizes its everyday usage (e.g., "it will probably rain tomorrow," or "the probability of obtaining a head on the next flip of a coin is one-half"). The fact that there are many explicata is a simple matter of historical record, and as the preceding two examples of usages suggest, there may be more than one explicandum. Acknowledging more than one explicandum suggests multiple explicata to the eclectic mind

6. For stimulating applications of Theorem 2.1.3 (Bayes' Theorem), see Salop (1987).

and less religious fervor for a single explicatum. Proponents who believe in a single explicandum usually view competing explicata as mutually incompatible.[7]

In the ensuing discussion four basic explicata or interpretations of "probability" will be identified: classical (symmetric), objective (frequency), logical (necessary), and subjective (personal).[8] In practice the boundaries between these interpretations are somewhat blurred. Sometimes more than one interpretation is appropriate; other times only one interpretation is possible. Rather than view these interpretations or explicata as competitors, it is more appropriate to view them as reflecting different explicanda arising from the application of "probability" to different entities.

The first correct probability calculations are usually attributed to the Italian mathematician Geralmo Cardano in the sixteenth century. A flourish of activity occurred in the 1650s involving the Frenchmen Blaise Pascal and Pierre de Fermat, and the Dutchman Christian Huygens. Important contributions by the Swiss Jacob Bernoulli in the seventeenth century, the London-based French expatriate Abraham de Moivre in the eighteenth century, and the Frenchman Pierre Simon Laplace in the late eighteenth and early nineteenth century produced the following classical interpretation.

Definition 2.1.11 (Classical or Symmetric) The *probability* of an event A is the number of equally likely outcomes that lead to the event A divided by the total number of equally likely outcomes.

Definition 2.1.11 has obvious deficiencies (see Barnett 1982, pp. 73–75). For example, two flips of a coin can lead to one of three events: two heads, two tails, or a head and a tail. Thus the classical interpretation of probability suggests that the probability of two heads is one-third. Opponents of the classical definition argue there are four equally likely outcomes: two heads, two tails, a head followed by a tail, and a tail followed by a head. The issue is how is one to know which events are equally likely? If "equally

7. An example is the alleged distinction of Knight (1921) between risk and uncertainty: the former warranting an objective interpretation of probability, and the latter being inherently unknowable. The risk-uncertainty distinction supports the frequentist view that probability is not applicable to all cases of uncertainty. A reflection of the controversial nature of Knight's proposition is that two of the best known Chicago economists are in disagreement over the matter: Robert Lucas is a proponent of the distinction and Milton Friedman an opponent. For further discussion, see Pelloni (1991), and particularly, LeRoy and Singell (1987) who dispute that Knight made this distinction.

8. For a more complete discussion see Barnett (1982, Chapter 3), de Finetti (1972), Fine (1973), Jeffreys (1961), Savage (1954), Howson and Urbach (1989, Chapters 2 and 3), and Walley (1991, esp. Chapters 1 and 2). Kyburg and Smokler (1964) contains original contributions of many early writers. For a detailed historical discussion see David (1962), Hacking (1975), Maistrov (1974), and Stigler (1986).

likely" means "equally probable," then a rather circular definition arises. To avoid such circularity, two distinct principles have been proposed for recognizing "equally likely" outcomes.

First, according to the *Principle of Cogent Reason*, physical symmetry suggests equiprobability. Second, according to the *Principle of Insufficient Reason*, if the researcher has no reason to believe one outcome is more likely to occur than any other, then the researcher should act as if all outcomes are "equally likely." The appeal to "symmetry" underlying these two principles reflects the realist-instrumentalist distinction made in the Section 1.2. The *Principle of Cogent Reason* is a realist notion that appeals to objective physical symmetry in the observable world. In contrast the *Principle of Insufficient Reason* is an instrumentalist notion that appeals to a subjective symmetry of opinion in an individual's perception of the world. Although modern interpretations of probability have found both these principles deficient, refinements of this embryonic interpretation of probability have yielded other interpretations that also reflect the realist-instrumentalist conflict.

If the grounds for the Principle of Cogent Reason rest on the performance of a symmetric object under repeated trials (e.g., ten rolls of a standard six-sided die), then the argument leads to the following objective (frequency) interpretation of probability.

Definition 2.1.12 (Objective or Frequentist) Let N be the number of trials of an experiment, and let $m(N)$ be the number of occurrences of an event A in the N trials. Then the *probability* of A is defined to be (assuming the limit exists):

$$P(A) = \operatorname*{Limit}_{N \to \infty} \frac{m(N)}{N}. \tag{2.1.9}$$

The early traces of the frequency approach can be found in the work of Simon Pierre Laplace, Siméon Denis Poisson, and John Venn in the nineteenth century. The construction of a sound mathematical basis did not occur, however, before the work of von Mises in the 1920s. To calculate a frequency it is necessary to consider a repetitive phenomenon of a standardized variety. The appropriate meaning of "repetitive" and "standardized" is not obvious. In a trivial sense, repetition of the same experiment must lead to the same outcome. To calculate a relative frequency it is necessary to subjectively define (possibly only conceptually) a class of events (known as a *collective*) over which to count the frequency. The relative frequency of the event A should also tend to the same limit for all subsequences that can be picked out in advance. To the extent that individuals agree on a class of events, they share an objective frequency. The objectivity, however, is in themselves, not in nature.

Some argue that the concept of a collective is untenable because it is never possible to assert that an unlimited sequence of essentially identical situations exist. In this sense the relative frequency interpretation is a *conceptual* interpretation, not an *operational* interpretation. Indeed, because Definition 2.1.12 is a limiting process, it cannot serve as an empirical basis for measuring probability: a finite number of terms in the sequence $m(N)/N$ can be changed without affecting the limit.

Strict frequentists argue that situations that do not admit repetition under essentially identical conditions are not within the realm of statistical enquiry. Unlike the classical interpretation of probability that only seems appropriate for artificial problems involving flipping coins, rolling dice, and so on, the frequency interpretation is appropriate for many real-world substantive problems involving repetition of physical processes (e.g., quality-control of a production process). The frequency interpretation, however, cannot be applied: (i) to unique, once-and-for-all type of phenomenon (e.g., elections), (ii) to theories (e.g., "monetarist" or "Keynesian" economics), or (iii) to uncertain past events (e.g., whether the Cleveland Indians won the 1954 World Series).[9] Logical and subjective interpretations of probability permit such applications.

The frequency and the classical interpretations of probability are *not* devoid of nonobjective elements.[10] Such elements are implicit in the construction of a collective. Also, the Principle of Insufficient Reason, which is based on the work of Jacob Bernoulli, Simon Pierre Laplace, and Reverend Thomas Bayes, describes a state of ignorance involving failure to distinguish asymmetry among outcomes. The ability to distinguish asymmetries that imply unequal probabilities brings nonobjective information into play.

The desire to expand the set of relevant events over which the concept of probability may be applied, and the willingness to entertain the formal introduction of "nonobjective" information into the analysis, led to the logical and subjective interpretations of probability. These interpretations are defined as follows.

Definition 2.1.13 (Logical or Necessary) Let κ denote the body of knowledge, experience or information accumulated about the situation of con-

9. Some frequentists apply probability to individual members of a class when there are no "recognizable" subsets within the class (a subset is said to be *recognizable* if its frequency is known to differ from the frequency of the complete class of events). The existence of recognizable subsets is personal, however, and somewhat subjective. The *propensity* interpretation of Popper (1959) is an example of this quasi-Frequentist interpretation.

10. The connotations involved with words such as "objective" or "subjective" are unfortunate. Applied statistical analysis along the lines of any interpretation of probability involves inherently subjective elements. Objectivists do not seriously deny this; rather they deny any *formal* role to such subjective elements in the theory of statistical inference.

cern, and let A denote an uncertain event (not necessarily repetitive). Then the *probability* of A afforded by κ is the "rational degree-of-belief" or "credibility" of A in the face of κ.

Definition 2.1.14 (Subjective or Personal) Let κ denote the body of knowledge, experience or information that *an individual* has accumulated about the situation of concern, and let A denote an uncertain event (not necessarily repetitive). Then the *probability* of A afforded by κ is the "degree of belief" in A held *by the individual* in the face of κ.

Barnett (1982, pp. 80–84) notes that the logical interpretation straddles the subjective and frequency interpretations in being "objective" but expressing "degree-of-belief." The subjective interpretation reflects an individual's personal assessment of the situation, whereas the logical interpretation reflects a "rational" (inevitable, unique, and correct) degree-of-belief induced by, and logically stemming from, a certain body of evidence—a degree-of-belief any rational person should have, justified by the evidence and unrelated to the personal makeup of the individual. In both cases probabilities are conditional on the state of knowledge, although the notation usually suppresses this conditioning. Again reminiscent of the realist-instrumentalist distinction discussed earlier, *according to the subjective and logical interpretations, probability is a property of an individual's perception of reality, whereas according to the classical and frequency interpretations, probability is a property of reality itself.* For the subjectivist there are no "true unknown probabilities" in the world out there to be discovered. Instead, "probability" is in the eye of the beholder. This view underlies the quotation by de Finetti at the beginning of this section: "Probability does not exist." Given such fundamental differences in the interpretation of probability, it should not be surprising in later chapters to find that statistical reasoning based on different conceptions can lead to very different answers to questions, and in fact, to very different questions being asked.

The *logical* interpretation of probability arose out of the work of Keynes (1921), Jeffreys (1961), and Carnap (1962).[11] It was motivated by the desire to expand deductive inference to allow for a "degree of implication." If A is some propositional information describing a particular situation and B is another statement relating to that situation, then logical probability is intended to measure the *extent* to which A supports B, which is intermediate between the extremes of logical implication, or complete denial. This degree of implication is a formal property of A and B similar to the mass or velocity of a physical object. Acceptance of the

11. There has been some debate over whether Jeffreys would be better classified as subjectivist. See Zellner (1982a, 1982b) and Kass (1982) for details.

logical interpretation of probability is tantamount to acceptance of inductive inference, and all the methodological controversy that surrounds the latter.

The *subjective* interpretation of probability was informally introduced by Bernoulli and Bayes in the eighteenth century, discussed by Augustus de Morgan in the nineteenth century, and refined by Ramsey (1931), de Finetti (1937), Savage (1954), Anscombe and Aumann (1963), Pratt et al. (1964), DeGroot (1970), Fishburn (1981, 1986), Karni et al. (1983), Karni (1985), and Machina and Schmeidler (1992) in the twentieth century.[12] In contrast to logicalists who sought criteria for the extent to which one proposition provides evidence for another, subjectivists argue that the appropriate desiderata is a set of criteria for deciding upon appropriate courses of action in the face of uncertainty.[13] Such a viewpoint requires the decision maker to make subjective probability assessments. The fact that such assessments can differ among individuals, or among circumstances involving the same individual under different states of information, is not considered embarrassing by subjectivists.

One essential question that subjectivists must face is why "degrees of belief" should satisfy the mathematical properties of probability given in Definition 2.1.5. Numerous axiom systems have been developed describing how a rational individual's judgments of uncertainty for events, preferences for consequences, and choice of action fit together in a consistent fashion (e.g., see Fishburn 1981, 1986). Two strands of answers are noted here.

The first strand asserts the primitive concept that individuals, when faced with two uncertain events, can decide which is more likely to occur or whether they are equally likely to occur. Given this assertion and four additional assumptions, it can be shown (see DeGroot 1970, Chapter 5, or Lindley 1985, Chapter 2) that a probability measure exists. A crucial assumption in this derivation is the existence of a reference standard or canonical experiment capable of generating all possible probabilities. Such a reference standard is based on a classical interpretation of probability (e.g., flipping a fair coin) and is assumed to be intuitively compelling. The assumed existence of this standard allows the axiomatic construction of subjective probability without reference to preferences.

12. Press (1989, pp. 18–19) provides a convenient summary of Savage's Axioms as well as a reprint of Bayes (1763).

13. It should be emphasized that these researchers put forth subjective probability, and the resulting implication of decision making based on maximization of expected utility, as a *normative* proposition, that is, "rational" people *ought* to behave in this manner. The *descriptive* accuracy of the subjective probability-expected utility maximization package has come under numerous attacks. For a good review of this extensive literature, see Machina (1987).

The second strand asserts that anyone who makes decisions under uncertainty in a "rational" way will act as if he or she has degrees of belief that obey axioms (a) and (b) of Definition 2.1.5. An early answer along these lines was offered by Ramsey (1931). Other answers were given by de Finetti (1937, 1974, 1975) in terms of betting odds and scoring rules (see also Bernardo and Smith (1994, Chapter 2), Lindley 1982b, 1985), and Savage (1971). The former can be outlined as follows, and latter is illustrated by Exercise 2.1.32. De Finetti considered a situation in which an individual was asked to quote betting odds on a set of uncertain events and accept any wagers others may decide to make about these events. According to his *coherence principle* the individual should never assign "probabilities" so that someone else can select stakes that guarantee a sure loss (known as a "Dutch book") for the individual whatever the eventual outcome. This simple principle implies axioms (a) through (c) in Definition 2.1.5 (see Exercise 2.1.22). The following example illustrates the unfortunate consequences of incoherent probabilities.

Example 2.1.2 When baseball pitcher Don Sutton was negotiating on the free-agent market his agent was quoted in a UPI story as follows: "Chances are 50-50 that Don will sign with the Astros and 50-50 for the New York Yankees. Those are the leading candidates. We're waiting for revised proposals from Minnesota (Twins) and Montreal (Expos), so I wouldn't rule them out, but I rate their chances only about 40-60."

Clearly, the agent is not coherent. Let A, Y, T, and E denote Sutton signing with the Astros, Yankees, Twins, and Expos, respectively. These events are mutually exclusive. Suppose they are also exhaustive. Then the agent's statements suggest

$$\frac{P(A)}{1-P(A)} = \frac{P(Y)}{1-P(Y)} = \frac{50}{50} \Rightarrow P(A) = P(Y) = \frac{1}{2},$$

$$\frac{P(T)}{1-P(T)} = \frac{P(E)}{1-P(E)} = \frac{40}{60} \Rightarrow P(T) = P(E) = \frac{2}{5}.$$

Note: $P(A) + P(Y) + P(T) + P(E) = 9/5 > 1$. If the agent was a bettor it would be profitable to make a wager with him such as the following. For example, bet \$50 on A^c, \$20 on Y^c, and \$60 on E^c. Table 2.1.1 contains the payoffs for each of these three bets corresponding to the four possible outcomes (i.e., "states of nature"). Note that the first two bets on A^c and Y^c are at 1:1 odds. The bet on E^c is at the favorable 3:2 odds, and hence it returns less than the amount bet when E^c occurs. The net winnings are \$10 if A occurs, \$10 if E occurs, \$70 if Y occurs, and \$110 if T occurs. Therefore, the initial probability assignments are incoherent.

At least four criticisms of de Finetti's answer have arisen. First, some authors are bothered by the gambling orientation, believing probability

Table 2.1.1
Payoffs for example 2.1.2

Bet	State of nature			
	A occurs	*Y* occurs	*T* occurs	*E* occurs
\$50 on A^c	−\$50	+\$50	+\$50	+\$50
\$20 on Y^c	+\$20	−\$20	+\$20	+\$20
\$60 on E^c	+\$40	+\$40	+40	−\$60
Net winnings	+\$10	+\$70	+\$110	+\$10

should be applicable in wider circumstances. This criticism is fairly specious because the gambling context is based on pragmatic grounds: It provides a context in which we often observe behavior in the face of uncertainty. Second, utility is likely a nonlinear function of money and so the size of the stakes (independent of the probabilities) can influence the acceptability of a gamble. Third, different information among the participants may lead an individual to quote a different probability than he or she truly believes, either to take advantage of the other player or to avoid being taken advantage of. Fourth, some authors do not find Dutch book arguments compelling as they presuppose a situation in which the individual is forced to accept any side of a bet (see Border and Segal 1990; Earman 1992, pp. 38–44; Eells 1991; and Maher 1993). Researchers sympathetic to Dutch book arguments often respond that degrees of belief should be independent of the institutional setting (though not, of course, the state of knowledge), and that willingness to accept both sides of a bet acts to signal the credibility of the beliefs to be used in a variety of circumstances.

These latter three issues involve the difficult problem of separating probability elicitation from utility. For the economist, such separation is particularly interesting because beliefs are typically treated as transient whereas preferences or tastes are usually taken as fixed. In seminal work, Savage (1954) provided one axiomatic system in which such separation was possible and which did not depend on auxiliary randomization, but his axiom system has not earned universal approval (e.g., see Machina and Schmeidler 1992). Such issues are not explored here, but the reader is urged to consult Fishburn (1982), Gardenfors and Sahlin (1988), Geweke (1992), Kadane (1992), Kadane and Winkler (1988), Karni (1985), Rubin (1987), and Schervish et al. (1990, 1992).

An important philosophical topic is whether the conditionalization in Bayes Theorem (see equation 2.1.7) warrants an unquestioned position as the model of learning in the face of knowledge of the event *A* (e.g., see Diaconis and Zabell 1982; Earman 1992, pp. 46–51; Eells 1991, pp. 11–24;

Goldstein 1985; Jeffrey 1983; Kyburg 1980; and Levi 1978). One justification for such conditioning can be made in terms of Dutch book arguments, but as noted previously, such arguments are not convincing to all. Also note that such Dutch book arguments refer to *ex ante* agreements to payoffs conditional on events not yet decided. *Ex post* experience of an event can sometimes have striking influence on the probability assessor (e.g., experiencing events like unemployment, stock market crashes, etc.), and the experience can bring with it more information than originally anticipated in the event (see Shafer 1985). *In this text we simply adopt such conditionalization as a basic principle.*

Because the paradigm of the subjectivist views the scientist in a decision-making context (e.g., see Lindley 1985), a few words seem warranted now regarding this text's adoption of a decision-making orientation as the basis for statistical activity. Some researchers (e.g., Birnbaum 1977; Tukey 1960; and Walley 1991, p. 21) emphasize a distinction between inference and decision: Decision, unlike inference requires a utility function. Others argue that the decision-making perspective is not warranted because most statisticians or econometricians engage in professional activities that do *not* require them to make actual decisions as do, say, business managers. Such attitudes seem to miss a few important points.

First, they overlook the valuable organizational features of the decision-making perspective. As will be seen later, through variation in the prior distribution or loss function, many seemingly dissociate statistical techniques can be viewed from a common perspective.

Second, whether statisticians actually act professionally as decision makers is really no more relevant than whether economic agents are literally utility maximizers. The "as if" argument of Friedman (1953) is applicable here as well. It is especially surprising that the decision-making perspective has not been more widely accepted among econometricians. The economist in such researchers rarely objects to postulating utility maximizing behavior for a representative economic agent, and this is essentially what is being advocated here for the representative researcher. As in economic theory, relatively few general results are available for arbitrary utility functions, and often an interesting simplifying assumption (e.g., separability assumptions) is made to sharpen the results. Most economists find it difficult to describe their own indifference curves, yet this does not stop them from adopting the optimizing framework as a basis for most economic analyses. Should difficulties in eliciting priors be anymore damaging to the status of the Bayesian framework as a basis for statistical analysis? In short, *what is good for the agents in economists' theories, is good for themselves as empirical researchers.*

Most introductory statistics courses give students the impression that there is little controversy among statisticians about statistical methods. Unfortunately, such an agreeable picture is *not* accurate. The realist-instrumentalist distinction discussed in Chapter 1 underlies many debates in statistics. Heated debate continues concerning the foundations of statistical inference, and the controversies are unlikely to be resolved to everyone's satisfaction. Interpretations of probability are the central issues in this debate. Although objective interpretations have dominated econometrics, ironically, early writers offered interpretations suspiciously close to modern subjectivist thinking. For example, Haavelmo (1944, p. 43) remarked "The question is not whether probabilities exist or not, but whether—if we proceed as if they existed—we are able to make statements about real phenomena that are 'correct for practical purposes'."

There are many other interpretations of probability that have not been mentioned here and for which the resulting "probabilities" even possess different mathematical properties. For example, according to Keynes (1921) probabilities are only partially ordered. Many authors (e.g., Koopman 1940; C. A. B. Smith 1961; Good 1962; Dempster 1968; Walley 1991; and Williams 1976) have discussed "probabilities" that do not necessarily give single numerical measures to degree of belief, but rather yielding intervals of upper and lower probabilities.

This section has briefly outlined some differences in interpretations of "probability." These differences will not be important again, however, until statistical estimation, hypothesis testing, and prediction are discussed in Chapters 6, 7, and 8.

Exercises

2.1.1 Show: $P(A \cup B \cup C) = P(A) + P(B) + P(C) - P(A \cap B) - P(A \cap C) - P(B \cap C) + P(A \cap B \cap C)$.

2.1.2 Prove or disprove the following, assuming all events have positive probability:

(a) If $P(A|B) > P(A)$, then $P(B|A) > P(B)$.

(b) If $P(A) > P(B)$, then $P(A|C) > P(B|C)$ for all C.

(c) If A and B are independent, then $P(A \cap B|C) = P(A|C) \cdot P(B|C)$.

(d) If $P(A|B) = P(B)$, then A and B are independent.

(e) If $P(A|B^c) = P(A|B)$, then A and B are independent.

(f) If $P(A|B) = P(B|A)$ and $P(A \cap B) \neq 0$, then $P(A) = P(B)$.

(g) A and B are independent iff A^c and B^c are independent.

2.1.3 Suppose A, B, and C are three events such that A is independent of B and B is independent of C. Is A independent of C?

2.1.4 Suppose each of four people A, B, C, and D tell the truth with probability $\frac{1}{2}$. Suppose A makes a statement, and then D says that C says that B says that A is telling the truth. What is the probability that A is lying? Repeat the problem in the case where each tells the truth with probability $\frac{1}{3}$.

2.1.5 The game of craps is played as follows. A player tosses two dice until the player either wins or loses. The player wins on the first toss if the player gets a total of 7 or 11; the player loses if the total is 2, 3, or 12. If the player gets any other total on the first toss, then that total is called the *point*. The player then tosses the dice repeatedly until either a total of 7 or the point is obtained. The player wins if the player gets the point and loses if the player gets a 7. What is the player's probability of winning?

2.1.6 Consider the experiment of tossing two dice. Let A_1 denote the event of an even face on the first die, A_2 denote the event of an even face on the second die, and A_3 denote the event of an even total. Show that A_1, A_2, and A_3 are pairwise independent but not mutually independent.

2.1.7 Assume that a student is taking a multiple-choice test. On a given question involving four alternate answers, the student either knows the answer, in which case the student answers it correctly, or does not know the answer, in which case the student guesses. Suppose the probability of these two events are p and $1 - p$, respectively. Further suppose that one answer is obviously false, and that when guessing, the student randomly chooses among the remaining three alternatives. Given that student answers the question correctly, what is the probability that the student guessed?

2.1.8 In 1693 Samuel Pepys asked Sir Isaac Newton whether it is more likely to get at least one six when six dice are rolled, at least two sixes when twelve dice are rolled, or at least three sixes when eighteen dice are rolled. Assume the dice are fair and find the answer to Pepys' question.

2.1.9 The so-called gambler's fallacy goes like this. In a dice game seven has not turned up in quite a few rolls of a pair of fair dice. Thus a seven is said to be "due" to come up. Why is this a fallacy?

2.1.10 Consider two events, A and B, such that $P(A) = .7$, $P(B) = .6$ and $P(A \cap B) = .2$. Are the beliefs coherent?

2.1.11 In a three-horse race the odds against the favorite are even (one to one), against the second horse two to one, against the third horse three to one. Is the bookie who quoted these odds coherent? Justify your answer.

2.1.12 Suppose you had \$100 to bet with Mr. Harcourt in Example 2.1.1. What would be the optimal bet?

2.1.13 Suppose you announce $P(A) = .7$ and $P(A^c) = .6$. Show that if someone bets against you with \$75 on A and \$100 on A^c, then they stake \$175 and receive \$250 no matter the outcome.

2.1.14 (Birthday Problem) Consider a group of $N < 365$ unrelated people none of whom were born on a Leap Year Day (February 29). Suppose the probability of being born on any particular day of the year is 1/365. (For a detailed discussion of the case in which not all days are equally likely, see Nunnikhoven 1992.)

(a) What is the probability p that at least two people have the same birthday?

(b) What is the minimum value of N for which $p > \frac{1}{2}$?

2.1.15 (Collector's Problem) Suppose that each package of a certain bubble gum contains the picture of a baseball player. Further suppose that the pictures of r players are used and that the picture of each player is equally likely to be placed in any given package of gum. Finally, suppose that pictures are placed in different packages independently of each other. What is the probability that a person who purchases n packages of gum $(n \geq r)$ will obtain a complete set of the r different pictures?

2.1.16 Assume that on a Monday morning you receive a letter in the mail from a new forecasting firm that predicts a certain stock will either rise or fall in the upcoming week. Suppose the prediction turns out correctly. Then on the next Monday you receive another letter from the same firm with another prediction for the upcoming week and it also turns out to be correct. This continues for five more weeks, and each week the firm's prediction turns out correctly. On the eighth Monday the firm calls you and offers to sell you their prediction for the upcoming week for \$100. How do you evaluate this proposal?

2.1.17 (Gambler's Ruin) Suppose two gamblers A and B are playing a game against each other. Let p be a given number $(0 < p < 1)$, and suppose that on each play of the game, the probability that A wins one dollar from B is p and that the probability that gambler B wins one dollar from A is $q = 1 - p$. Suppose that the initial fortune of A is $I > 0$ dollars and the initial fortune of B is $K - I > 0$ dollars. The game continues until the fortune of one gambler is reduced to zero. What is the probability that A wins?

2.1.18 Consider the television game show "Let's Make a Deal" in which Host Monty Hall asks contestants to choose the prize behind one of three curtains. Behind one curtain lies the "grand prize"; the other two curtains conceal only relatively small gifts. Assume Monty knows what is behind every curtain. Once the contestant has made a choice, Monty Hall reveals what is behind one of the two curtains that were not chosen. Having been shown one of the lesser prizes, the contestant is offered a chance to switch curtains. Should the contestant switch? (See Morgan et al. 1991; Klein 1993; Nalebuff 1987; and Page 1991.)

2.1.19 Consider three prisoners: Alan, Bernard, and Charles. Alan knows that two of them are to be executed and the other set free, and he concludes that each of them is equally likely to be the lucky one that goes free. Let A denote the event that Alan goes free, and B and C similarly for Bernard and Charles. Alan says to the jailer: "Because either Bernard or Charles is certain to be executed, you will give me no information about my own chances if you give me the name of one man, Bernard or Charles, who is going to be executed with certainty." Accepting this argument, the jailer truthfully says, "Bernard will be executed" (denoted b). Alan chuckles to himself, because he thinks he has tricked the jailer into giving him some information. Alan reasons that because he now knows that either he or Charles will go free and, as before, he has no reason to think it is more likely to be Charles, his chance of going free is now $\frac{1}{2}$, not $\frac{1}{3}$, as before.

Is Alan acting consistently with the usual rules of probability to update his probability of going free from $\frac{1}{3}$ to $\frac{1}{2}$? If so, then show it. If not, then why not? Precisely what probability, or range of probabilities, for A is it coherent for Alan to entertain after he speaks with the jailer [Lindley 1985, pp. 41–43)?

2.1.20 Let A, B, and C be events such that the following hold:

(a) $P(A \cap B|C) = P(A|C)P(B|C)$

(b) $P(A \cap B|C^c) = P(A|C^c)P(B|C^c)$

(c) $P(A|C) > P(A|C^c)$

(d) $P(B|C) > P(B|C^c)$

Show that $P(A \cap B) > P(A)P(B)$. Do you think that the event C warrants the title of a "cause" of the events A and B? (See van Fraassen 1980, p. 28.)

2.1.21 Let $\mathscr{S} = \Re$ (the set of real numbers) and consider the set of events $B = \{B_y | y \in \Re\}$, where $B_y = \{r | r \leq y\} = (-\infty, y]$. Suppose we wish to generate a σ-algebra $\tilde{A}$ from B. Let $B \in \tilde{A}$ and $B_y^c = \{r | r > y\} = (y, \infty) \in \tilde{A}$. Also require countable unions of intervals of the form $(-\infty, y - (1/n)]$ $(n = 1, 2, 3, \ldots)$ to be in $\tilde{A}$.

(a) Show: $\bigcup_{n=1}^{\infty} (-\infty, y - (1/n)] = (-\infty, y)$.

(b) Show that $\tilde{A}$ so defined is a σ-algebra. $\tilde{A}$ is known as the *Borel field* on $\Re$ and will be denoted $\tilde{B}$. Elements of $\tilde{B}$ are known as *Borel sets.*

(c) Show that each of the following sets are in $\tilde{B}$: (y, ∞), $[y, \infty)$, $\{y\}$ and (x, y), where $x < y$ and $x, y \in \Re$.

2.1.22 Suppose you are asked to quote betting odds on a set of uncertain events $A, B, \ldots$ and accept any wagers others may desire to make about these events. In other words you must assign to each A a "probability" $P(A)$ indicating a willingness to sell lottery tickets that pay $\$S_a$ if A occurs for the price $\$P(A)S_a$, where S_a is the "stake" (positive or negative) selected by your opponent. Show that de Finetti's coherence principle implies axioms (a) through (c) of probability in Definition 2.1.5.

2.1.23 Consider the experiment of selecting a positive integer in some way. Show that if the underlying probabilities exhibit countable additivity, then it is impossible for each integer to have the same probability of being selected. Also show that no such inconsistency arises if the underlying probabilities are only finitely additive.

2.1.24 (Allais 1953, Paradox) Consider two situations both involving two choices. In Situation 1 you are asked to choose between

Choice A: $500,000 with certainty.

Choice B: $500,000 with probability .89, $2,500,000 with probability .10, and the status quo ($0) with probability .01.

In Situation 2 you are asked to choose between

Choice C: $500,000 with probability .11 and status quo ($0) with probability .89.

Choice D: $2,500,000 with probability .10 and the status quo ($0) with probability .90.

(a) Which do you prefer in Situation 1, A or B?

(b) Which do you prefer in Situation 2, C or D?

(c) Let U_1 = Utility of $0, U_2 = Utility of $500,000, and U_3 = Utility of $2,500,000. What is the expected payout for each of the four choices?

(d) Allais argued that many people are inclined to prefer A over B, and D over C. Does this agree with expected utility maximization?

2.1.25 (Ellsberg 1961, Paradox) Consider two urns containing red and black balls from which one ball is chosen at random. Urn 1 contains 100 red and black balls in a ratio entirely unknown to you. Urn 2 contains 50 red and 50 black balls. To "bet on Red i" means you choose to draw from Urn i, and you will win $100 if a ball from Urn i is red, and $0 otherwise. "To bet on Black i" is defined similarly. Answer each of the following five questions:

(a) Do you prefer to bet on Red 1 or Black 1, or are you indifferent?

(b) Do you prefer to bet on Red 2 or Black 2, or are you indifferent?

(c) Do you prefer to bet on Red 1 or Red 2, or are you indifferent?

(d) Do you prefer to bet on Black 1 or Black 2, or are you indifferent?

(e) Many people are indifferent in (a) and (b), prefer Red 2 to Red 1, and prefer Black 2 to Black 1. Show that such preferences violate the laws of probability.

2.1.26 A healthy forty-two-year-old woman suddenly dies the afternoon following a midday visit to her dentist to have a wisdom tooth extracted. The coroner's report showed there was no evidence of violence. The most likely cause is an allergic reaction caused by an adverse drug reaction. Before visiting the dentist, the patient took a penicillin tablet (because of a history of heart murmur), denoted P. The dentist prescribed a pain medication, zomepirac (denoted Z), which she was to take if needed. From the local pharmacy it is known that the patient did indeed fill the prescription, but it is unknown whether she ever took this medication. Besides P and Z, a third suspect is the novocaine (denoted N) used during the tooth extraction procedure. Take as fact Dr. Kramer's observation that if she took Z, then the probability that Z was responsible for her death (denoted) is .95. But you do not know for sure if she took Z. You do know, however, that among patients who had similar operations, 60 percent had sufficient post-operative pain that they took the pain medication Z. What is the probability that zomepirac was responsible for the woman's death? (Nalebuff 1990, p. 180)

2.1.27 Following Jeffreys (1961, pp. 43–44) and Huzurbazar (1955), let H be a hypothesis, κ the previous information, and y_1 an observed fact.

(a) Show:

$$P(H|y_1, \kappa) = \frac{P(y_1|H, \kappa)P(H|\kappa)}{P(y_1|\kappa)}. \tag{2.1.10}$$

(b) If y_1 is a consequence of H, that is, $P(y_1|H) = 1$, then (2.1.10) implies

$$P(H|y_1, \kappa) = \frac{P(H|\kappa)}{P(y_1|\kappa)}.$$

If y_t $(t = 2, 3, \ldots, T)$ are further consequences of H found to be true, show:

$$P(H|y_1, \ldots, y_T, \kappa) = \frac{P(H|\kappa)}{P(y_1|\kappa) \prod_{t=2}^{T} P(y_t|y_{t-1}, \ldots, y_1, \kappa)}. \tag{2.1.11}$$

In words, each verification divides the probability of the hypothesis by the probability of the verification given the previous information.

(c) Suppose that $P(H|\kappa) > 0$ and that

$$\operatorname*{Limit}_{T\to\infty} P(H|y_1, y_2, \ldots, y_T, \kappa) = \alpha.$$

Show that for any T such that $P(H|y_1, \ldots, y_T, \kappa) > \alpha - \varepsilon$, for some $\varepsilon > 0$, it follows that $P(y_T, \ldots, y_{T+m})|y_1, \ldots, y_{T-1}, \kappa) > (\alpha - \varepsilon)/\alpha$. Hence, the probability that all future inferences will be verified tends to unity.

(d) Comment on whether the result in (c) serves as a solution to the Riddle of Induction (i.e., Is there any deductive validity to induction?). (See also Hesse 1974, p. 117; and Glymour 1980, p. 73.)

2.1.28 Let X and Y be two statements whose truth is represented by the probabilities $P(X) \neq 0$ and $P(Y) \neq 0$, respectively.

(a) Show: $P(X|Y) > P(X)$ iff $P(Y|X) > P(Y)$.

(b) Let $\overline{C}(X, Y)$ denote "X is supported or corroborated or confirmed by Y," and define $\overline{C}(X, Y)$ as holding iff $P(X|Y) > P(X)$, or equivalently in light of (a), iff $P(Y|X) > P(Y)$. For example, if X is a universal law and Y is empirical evidence that can be deduced from X, then $P(Y|X) = 1$, $P(Y) < 1$, and hence $\overline{C}(X, Y)$ is true. Prove that there are cases in which X is strongly supported by Z while Y is strongly undermined by Z and, at the same time X is corroborated by Z to a lesser degree than is Y. (Hint: Consider a throw with a fair, six-sided die. Let X be the statement "six will turn up," let Y be the negation of X, and let Z be the information "an even number will turn up.")

2.1.29 Popper interprets the preceding problem as implying that identification of degree of corroboration with probability is self-contradictory. He then goes on to offer the following alternate measure. Let X be consistent and $P(Y) \neq 0$, and define

$$C(X, Y) = \left[\frac{P(Y|X) - P(Y)}{P(y|X) + P(y)}\right][1 + P(X)P(X|Y)]. \tag{2.1.12}$$

We say: Y supports X iff $C(X, Y) > 0$; Y is independent of X iff $C(X, Y) = 0$; Y undermines X iff $C(X, Y) < 0$. Prove each of the following:

(a) $-1 = C(Y^c, Y) \leq C(X, Y) \leq C(X, X) \leq 1$, where Y^c is the negation of Y.

(b) $0 \leq C(X, X) = P(X^c) \leq 1$.

(c) If $P(X|Y) = 1$, then $C(X, Y) = C(X, X) = 1 - P(X^c)$.

(d) If $P(X^c|Y) = 1$, then $C(X, Y) = C(X, Y) = C(Y^c, Y) = -1$.

(e) If $C(X, Y) > 0$, then $C(X^c, Y) < 0$ and $C(X, Y^c) < 0$.

2.1.30 Consider the following two games. Game 1 consists of betting \$1 on "heads" in the flip of a fair two-sided coin. Game 2 consists of betting \$1 on "red" on a roulette wheel in which the probability of "red" is $18/38 \approx .474$. Suppose that in Game 1 the gambler has \$900 and the goal is to reach \$1,000,000, and that in Game 2 the gambler has \$900 but the goal is to reach \$1000. In which game is the gambler more likely to achieve the stated goal? Why (Coyle and Wang 1993)?

2.1.31 At a British parliamentary election a firm of bookmakers offered odds of 4:7 against Labour and 5:4 against the Conservatives. Equating utility to money, show that one should bet unless one's personal probability of Labour's chances of winning lies between .56 and .64 (Lindley 1985, p. 70, Exercise 4.7).

2.1.32 Consider an event A with a known probability p. You are required to assess it by a probability q of your choice. Your score will be $(q-1)^2$ if the event occurs, and q^2 if the event does not occur (Lindley 1985, pp. 162–165).

(a) Show that the expected score if you state q is $(q-p)^2 + p(1-p)$.

(b) Treating the score as negative utility, show that $q = p$ maximizes your expected utility. Such a scoring rule which motivates you to be "honest" (i.e., choose $p = q$) is known as a *proper scoring rule*.

(c) Show that the scoring rule $-l(p)$ if A occurs, and $-ln(1-p)$ if A does not occur, is also a proper scoring rule.

(d) Show that the scoring rule $1 - q$ if A occurs and q if A does not occur is *not* a proper scoring rule.

2.2 Random Variables

A random variable is the soul of an observation.... An observation is the birth of a random variable.
—Watts (1991, p. 291)

The sample space can be tedious to work with if its elements cannot be directly manipulated mathematically. Fortunately, it is often possible to assign quantifiable attributes to the outcomes of an experiment, and so it is convenient to formulate a set of rules by which the elements of the sample space can be represented by numbers. This leads us to consider mappings (i.e., functions) from the sample space $\mathscr{S}$ onto the set $\Re$ of real numbers. The possible functions, however, must be restricted so that (i) the event structure of a countably additive probability space $[\mathscr{S}, \tilde{A}, P(\cdot)]$ is preserved, and (ii) so that the probability function $P(\cdot)$ defined over the σ-algebra $\tilde{A}$ can be used later to induce probabilities for the mapping.[14] In other words, for a candidate function $Y: \mathscr{S} \to \Re$ with image $\Re_Y$, the inverse mapping $Y^{-1}: \Re \to \mathscr{S}$ must reflect the algebraic structure of the domain $\tilde{A}$ of the countably additive probability function $P(\cdot)$, that is, for any $B \subseteq \Re_Y$, the inverse image $Y^{-1}(B) \equiv \{s | s = Y^{-1}(y), y \in B\}$ must be an

14. A *function* $Y: \mathscr{S} \to \Re$ is a relation that associates with each $s \in \mathscr{S}$ a unique element $Y(s) \in \Re$. The *image* of $A \subseteq \mathscr{S}$ is the set $Y(A) \equiv \{y | y = Y(s), s \in A\} \subseteq \Re$. The image of $\mathscr{S}$ under Y is sometimes denoted by $\Re_Y$, that is, $Y(\mathscr{S}) = \Re_Y$. The *inverse image* of $B \subseteq \Re_Y$ is the set $Y^{-1}(B) \equiv \{s | s = Y^{-1}(y), y \in B\} \subseteq \mathscr{S}$. If $(\mathscr{S}_i, \tilde{A}_i)$ $(i = 1, 2)$ are measure spaces, then $Y: \mathscr{S}_1 \to \mathscr{S}_2$ is a *measurable function* provided $Y^{-1}(\tilde{A}_2) \subseteq \tilde{A}_1$.

event in $\tilde{A}$. This "event preserving condition" can be imposed by restricting attention to a σ-field defined on $\mathfrak{R}_Y$. The next definition formalizes these notions in terms of the Borel field (see Exercise 2.1.21).

Definition 2.2.1 Consider the probability space $[\mathscr{S}, \tilde{A}, P(\cdot)]$. The function $Y = Y(\cdot)$ is a *random variable relative to the σ-field $\tilde{A}$* iff it is a function with domain $\mathscr{S}$ and range $\mathfrak{R}$ such that $\{s \mid Y(s) \le y, s \in \mathscr{S}\} \in \tilde{A}$ for every $y \in \mathfrak{R}_Y$.[15] (Note that the probability function $P(\cdot)$ plays no role in this definition, but that the σ-field $\tilde{A}$ is essential.)

In other words, a random variable is a function from the sample space onto the real line such that for any real number y the set of points in the sample space mapped into real numbers less than or equal to y belongs to the σ-field $\tilde{A}$. The terminology "random variable" is a somewhat unfortunate historical accident since Y is neither random nor a variable. Nonetheless this terminology is so established that it is followed here as well.

Example 2.2.1 Reconsider the coin tossing experiment in Example 2.1.1. Define the σ-algebra $\tilde{A} = \{\phi, \mathscr{S}, \{(H,H)\}, \{(T,T)\}, \{(H,H),(T,T)\}, \{(H,T),(T,H)\}, \{(H,T),(T,H),(H,H)\}, \{(H,T),(T,H),(T,T)\}\}$. Consider the function $Y\colon \mathscr{S} \to \mathfrak{R}$ defined by

$$Y(s) = \left\{\begin{array}{ll} 0, & \text{if } s = \{(T,T)\} \\ 1, & \text{if } s \in \{(H,T),(T,H)\} \\ 2, & \text{if } s = \{(H,H)\} \end{array}\right\}.$$

In words, Y is the number of "heads" in two tosses of the coin. To decide whether Y is a random variable, it is necessary to determine whether the inverse images of half-open intervals of the form $(-\infty, y]$, $y \in \mathfrak{R}$, are in $\tilde{A}$ since these half-open intervals generate the Borel field $\tilde{B}$. In other words, if $Y^{-1}((-\infty, y]) \in \tilde{A}$ for all $(-\infty, y] \in \tilde{B}$, then $Y^{-1}(B) \in \tilde{A}$ for all $B \in \tilde{B}$. From the definition of $Y(s)$ it is straightforward to see

$$\begin{aligned} Y^{-1}((-\infty, y)] &= \{s \mid Y(s) \le y, s \in \mathscr{S}\} \\ &= \left\{\begin{array}{ll} \phi, & \text{if } y < 0 \\ \{(T,T)\}, & \text{if } 0 \le y < 1 \\ \{(T,T),(T,H),(H,T)\}, & \text{if } 1 \le y < 2 \\ \mathscr{S}, & \text{if } y \ge 2 \end{array}\right\} \end{aligned}$$

is in $\tilde{A}$ for all $y \in \mathfrak{R}$, and hence Y is a random variable.

Example 2.2.2 Continuing Example 2.2.1, define:

$$X(s) = \left\{\begin{array}{ll} 0, & \text{if } s \in \{(T,T),(T,H)\} \\ 1, & \text{if } s \in \{(H,T),(H,H)\} \end{array}\right\}.$$

15. In measure theoretic terms, a random variable is a real-valued *measurable* function defined on a probability space. See, for example, Dhrymes (1989) for further discussion.

In words, $X = 1$ iff a "head" is obtained on the first flip; $X = 0$ otherwise. Then

$$X^{-1}((-\infty, x]) = \{s | X(s) \leq x, s \in \mathscr{S}\}$$

$$= \left\{ \begin{array}{ll} \phi, & \text{if } x < 0 \\ \{(T,T),(T,H)\}, & \text{if } 0 \leq x < 1 \\ \mathscr{S}, & \text{if } y \geq 2 \end{array} \right\}.$$

But $X^{-1}((-\infty, x]) \notin \tilde{A}$ for $x = 0$. Therefore, X is not a random variable with respect to the σ-algebra $\tilde{A}$. It is possible, however, to choose a new σ-field $\tilde{A}_X$ relative to which X is a random variable. This new field is known as the *minimal σ-field generated by X*. Its construction is straightforward. Start with $X^{-1}(0) = \{(T,T),(T,H)\}$ and $X^{-1}(1) = \{(H,T),(H,H)\}$, and generate a σ-field by taking unions, intersections and complements. The resulting σ-field is $\tilde{A}_X = \{\phi, \{(T,T),(T,H)\}, \{(H,T),(H,H)\}, \mathscr{S}\}$ and X is a random variable relative to $\tilde{A}_X$.

A random variable Y relative to the σ-algebra $\tilde{A}$ maps $\mathscr{S}$ into a subset of $\Re$ and the Borel field $\tilde{B}$ plays the role of $\tilde{A}$. Now we wish to assign probabilities to the elements in $\tilde{B}$ consistent with the probabilities assigned to the corresponding events in $\tilde{A}$ by defining the set function P_Y: $\tilde{B} \rightarrow [0, 1]$ such that $P_Y(B) = P[Y^{-1}(B)] = P\{s | Y(s) \in B, s \in \mathscr{S}\}$ for all $B \in \tilde{B}$. This gives rise to a probability space $[\Re, \tilde{B}, P_Y(\cdot)]$ induced by Y that is equivalent to the original probability space $[\mathscr{S}, \tilde{A}, P(\cdot)]$, and is much easier to manipulate mathematically.

Further simplification is possible by replacing the set function $P_Y(\cdot)$ by an ordinary function $F_Y(\cdot)$ with domain $\Re$, as is now defined.

Definition 2.2.2 Consider the probability space $[\mathscr{S}, \tilde{A}, P(\cdot)]$. The *(cumulative) distribution function* (c.d.f.) of a random variable Y, denoted $F_Y(y)$ or simply $F(y)$, is the function with domain the real line and range the interval $[0, 1]$ which satisfies

$$F(y) = P_Y(Y \leq y) = P[\{s | Y(s) \leq y, s \in \mathscr{S}\}] \tag{2.2.1}$$

for any real number y. An *atom* of Y is a real number y such that $P(Y = y) > 0$. [Note: (2.2.1) needs $\{s | Y(s) \leq y, s \in \mathscr{S}\} \in \tilde{A}$ (as required in Definition 2.2.1) in order to use probability function $P(\cdot)$.]

In Definitions 2.2.1 and 2.2.2 the difference between Y and y should be emphasized. The random variable Y is a function $\mathscr{S} \rightarrow \Re$; $y \in \Re$ is a particular value that Y can obtain. Unless noted otherwise, capital letters (usually toward the end of the alphabet) denote random variables and the corresponding small letters denote values of the random variable. The notation $Y = y$, or more properly, $Y(s) = y$, denotes that for a "realized" or "revealed" outcome s of the experiment the random variable Y takes the value y.

Example 2.2.3 Consider again the coin tossing experiment in Examples 2.2.1 and 2.2.2 and the random variable Y (the number of "heads" in two tosses). Suppose the coin is "fair" in the sense that on any toss H and T are equally likely, and that the two tosses are independent. Then the appropriate probability function is defined by $P[(H,H)] = P[(H,T)] = P[(T,H)] = P[(T,T)] = \frac{1}{4}$, and the corresponding cumulative distribution function is

$$F(y) = \left\{ \begin{array}{ll} 0, & \text{if } y < 0 \\ \frac{1}{4}, & \text{if } 0 \leq y < 1 \\ \frac{3}{4}, & \text{if } 1 \leq y < 2 \\ 1, & \text{if } y \geq 2 \end{array} \right\}.$$

The atoms of Y are 0, 1, and 2.

Based on Definition 2.2.2 it is straightforward to prove the following.

Theorem 2.2.1 Let Y be a random variable with distribution function $F(\cdot)$. Then

(a) $F(-\infty) \equiv \operatorname*{Limit}_{y \to -\infty} F(y) = 0.$

(b) $F(\infty) \equiv \operatorname*{Limit}_{y \to \infty} F(y) = 1.$

(c) $F(\cdot)$ *is a monotonic nondecreasing function, that is,* $F(y_1) \leq F(y_2)$ for $y_1 < y_2$.

(d) $F(\cdot)$ *is continuous to the right, that is,* $\text{Limit}_{h \to 0^+} F(y + h) = F(y)$.

(e) *The real number y is an atom of Y iff $F(\cdot)$ is discontinuous at y. Y can have at most a countable number of atoms.*

Proof Left to the reader.

It should be emphasized that the distribution function $F(\cdot)$ contains all the relevant probabilistic information about the random variable Y. Every random variable Y has a c.d.f. and, for any function $F(\cdot)$ satisfying properties (a) through (e) of Theorem 2.2.1, there exists a random variable having $F(\cdot)$ as its c.d.f..

An important class of random variables is described in the following two definitions.

Definition 2.2.3 A random variable Y is *discrete* iff Y has a countable number (i.e., finite or in a one-to-one correspondence with the positive integers) of atoms y_i $(i = 1, 2, 3, \ldots)$ such that

$$\sum_i P(Y = y_i) = \sum_i f(y_i) = 1. \qquad (2.2.2)$$

Equivalently, a random variable is discrete iff its distribution function is a step function.

Definition 2.2.4 Let Y be a discrete random variable with distinct values y_i $(i = 1, 2, 3, \ldots)$ in its range. Then the *probability mass function* (p.m.f.) of Y, denoted $f(y)$, is

$$f(y) = \begin{Bmatrix} P(y_i), & \text{if } y = y_i & \text{for some } i \\ 0, & \text{otherwise} & \end{Bmatrix} \tag{2.2.3}$$

for any real number y.

Based on Definitions 2.2.3 and 2.2.4, it is straightforward to prove the following.

Theorem 2.2.2 Let $f(\cdot)$ be the p.m.f. of a discrete random variable Y with atoms y_i $(i = 1, 2, 3, \ldots)$.

(a) $f(y_i) > 0$ $(i = 1, 2, 3, \ldots)$.

(b) $f(y_i) = 0$ for $y \neq y_i$ $(i = 1, 2, 3, \ldots)$.

(c) $F(y) = \sum_{j \in J} f(y_i)$, where $J \equiv \{j | y_i \leq y\}$ and $y \in \mathfrak{R}$.

(d) $\sum_{i=1}^{\infty} f(y_i) = 1$.

Proof Left to the reader.

In contrast to Definition 2.2.3, a second class of random variables is now introduced.

Definition 2.2.5 A random variable Y is *continuous* iff its distribution function $F(\cdot)$ is absolutely continuous, that is, if there exists a function $f(\cdot)$ such that

$$F(y) = \int_{-\infty}^{y} f(t)\,dt \qquad \text{for all} \qquad y \in \mathfrak{R}. \tag{2.2.4}$$

The function $f(\cdot)$ is the *probability density function (p.d.f.)* of the continuous random variable Y.[16]

From Definition 2.2.5 the following results can be easily derived.

Theorem 2.2.3 Let $f(y)$ be the p.d.f. of a continuous random variable Y. Then

(a) $f(y) \geq 0$ for all y.

16. Strictly speaking the p.d.f. of a continuous random variable is not uniquely defined by (2.2.4) because it can be redefined at a countable number of points without affecting the value of integral (2.2.4). Continuous random variables are best thought of as mathematical idealizations of discrete random variables. In reality, all measurement devices yield discrete values, but a continuous random variable may serve as a convenient idealization.

(b) $f(y) = \dfrac{dF(y)}{dy}$ except at most a countable number of points.

(c) $\int_{-\infty}^{\infty} f(t)\,dt = 1.$

Proof Left to the reader. Part (b) follows from the Fundamental Theorem of Calculus.

Example 2.2.4 Consider the continuous random variable Y with c.d.f.

$$F(y) = \begin{Bmatrix} 0, & \text{if } y \leq 0 \\ 1 - \exp(-y), & \text{if } y > 0 \end{Bmatrix}.$$

The corresponding p.d.f. is

$$f(y) = \begin{Bmatrix} 0, & \text{if } y \leq 0 \\ \exp(-y), & \text{if } y > 0 \end{Bmatrix}.$$

Note that $F(y)$ satisfies Definition 2.2.5 and $f(y)$ satisfies Theorem 2.2.3.

It is convenient to have terminology and notation that make it possible to discuss discrete distributions and absolutely continuous distributions simultaneously. Accordingly, to designate a function $f(\cdot)$ that may be either a probability mass function (p.m.f.) or a probability density function (p.d.f.), we shall use the term *probability function* (p.f.). Despite this common notation, p.m.f.s and p.d.f.s have quite different interpretations. For discrete random variables, $f(y)$ is the probability that Y equals y. This is not true for a continuous random variable. Indeed $f(y)$ may take on any value in the interval $[0, \infty)$ for continuous random variables. In fact the probability that a continuous random variable takes on the value of any particular value in its range is zero! However, the probability that a continuous random variable Y takes a value in the interval $[a, b]$—equivalently (a, b), $[a, b)$ or $(a, b]$, where $a < b$, can be positive and is given by

$$P(a \leq Y \leq b) = F(b) - F(a) = \int_a^b f(t)\,dt. \tag{2.2.5}$$

Similarly, the notation $F(\cdot)$ is used to designate c.d.f.s for both discrete and continuous random variables, and the following integral notation [see Exercise 2.3.11] is now introduced:

$$F(y) = \int_{-\infty}^{y} dF_Y(t) \equiv \begin{Bmatrix} \sum_{t \leq y} f(t), & \text{if } Y \text{ is discrete} \\ \int_{-\infty}^{y} f(t)\,dt, & \text{if } Y \text{ is continuous} \end{Bmatrix}. \tag{2.2.6}$$

In general, random variables need not have continuous nor discrete p.f.s associated with them (see Exercise 2.2.6). However, a distribution function can always be written as the sum of a step function and a function differentiable almost everywhere.

Theorem 2.2.4 Let $F(y)$ be a distribution function. Then $F(y) = q_1F_1(y) + q_2F_2(y) + q_3F_3(y)$, where $q_i \geq 0$ $(i = 1, 2, 3)$, $q_1 + q_2 + q_3 = 1$, $F_i(y)$ $(i = 1, 2, 3)$ are distribution functions, $F_1(y)$ is a step function, $F_2(y)$ is absolutely continuous, and $F_3(y)$ has a derivative equal to zero almost everywhere.

Proof Mood et al. (1974, pp. 63–64) or Laha and Rohatgi (1979, pp. 10–14).

A final piece of terminology is given in the following definition.

Definition 2.2.6 Let Y be a random variable with p.d.f. $f(\cdot)$. The *support* of Y is the set $\{y|f(y) > 0\}$, i.e., the support of Y is the set of all $y \in \Re$ having positive density.

Example 2.2.5 The support of Y in Example 2.2.4 is $(0, \infty)$.

In closing note that it is often required to state that a random variable has a particular distribution. For ease of exposition we will make such statements by giving either the c.d.f. *or* the p.f.. Detailed discussion of numerous discrete and continuous distributions are provided in Sections 3.2 and 3.3, respectively.

Exercises

2.2.1 Let Y be a random variable with p.f. $f(y)$. The *mode* of the distribution of Y, assuming it exists and is unique, is that value of y that maximizes $f(y)$. Find the mode in each of the following cases:

(a) $$f(y) = \begin{cases} 2^{-y}, & \text{if } y = 1, 2, 3, \ldots \\ 0, & \text{otherwise} \end{cases}.$$

(b) $$f(y) = \begin{cases} 12y^2(1 - y), & \text{if } 0 < y < 1 \\ 0, & \text{otherwise} \end{cases}.$$

(c) $$f(y) = \begin{cases} \frac{1}{2}y^2 \exp(-y), & \text{if } 0 < y < \infty \\ 0, & \text{otherwise} \end{cases}.$$

2.2.2 The *qth quantile* (or *percentile*), $0 < q < 1$, of a random variable Y with distribution function $F(y)$, denoted ξ_q, is defined as the smallest number ξ satisfying $F(\xi) \geq q$. Find $\xi_{.20}$ corresponding to the p.d.f.

$$f(y) = \begin{cases} 3y^2, & \text{if } 0 < y < 1 \\ 0, & \text{otherwise} \end{cases}.$$

2.2.3 A *median* of a random variable Y, denoted med(Y), is defined to be any number satisfying: $P[Y \leq \text{med}(Y)] \geq \frac{1}{2}$ and $P[Y \geq \text{med}(Y)] \geq \frac{1}{2}$. The set of medians is always a closed interval (possibly a single point). Find the median corresponding to the random variable with p.d.f.

$$f(y) = \begin{cases} 4y^3, & \text{if } 0 < y < 1 \\ 0, & \text{otherwise} \end{cases}.$$

2.2.4 Let $f(y)$ be a p.d.f. and let α be a number such that for all $\varepsilon > 0$, $f(\alpha - \varepsilon) = f(\alpha + \varepsilon)$. Then $f(\cdot)$ is *symmetric around* $y = \alpha$. Show:

(a) α is the median of Y.

(b) If $f(\cdot)$ is unimodal, then $y = \alpha$ is the mode.

2.2.5 Let Y be a random variable with p.d.f. $f(\cdot)$ and c.d.f. $F(\cdot)$. Given a scalar y_0, the conditional p.d.f. of Y, given $Y > y_0$, is $g(y|Y > y_0) = f(y)/[1 - F(y_0)]$ if $y > y_0$, zero elsewhere. This is an example of a *truncated distribution*. Find $P(Y > 2|Y > 1)$, where $f(y) = \exp(-y)$, $0 < y < \infty$, zero elsewhere.

2.2.6 Let Y be a random variable with p.d.f. $f(\cdot)$ and c.d.f. $F(\cdot)$, and define

$$Z = \begin{Bmatrix} Y, & 1 < Y < \infty \\ 1, & 0 < Y \leq 1 \end{Bmatrix}.$$

The random variable Y is *censored*. It yields the random variable Z which is *mixed* since its p.d.f. consists of a continuous segment and a spike reflecting the fact that $Z = 1$ with positive probability, i.e. $Z = 1$ is an atom. Find the p.f. of Z and graph it.

2.2.7 Show that $\alpha = \beta$, where Y is a random variable with p.d.f.

$$f(y) = \begin{Bmatrix} 2(\beta - y)/(\alpha\beta), & \text{if } 0 < y < \beta \\ 0, & \text{otherwise} \end{Bmatrix}.$$

2.3 Univariate Mathematical Expectation

A useful concept related to distributions of random variables is mathematical expectation. It is defined as follows.

Definition 2.3.1 Let Y be a random variable with c.d.f. $F(\cdot)$ and p.f. $f(\cdot)$, and let $g(\cdot)$ be a function with domain and range equal to the real line. The *expected value* of the function $g(\cdot)$ of the random variable Y, denoted $E[g(Y)]$, or $E_Y[g(Y)]$, is defined by

$$E[g(Y)] = \sum_i g(y_i)f(y_i), \tag{2.3.1}$$

if Y is discrete with atoms y_i $(i = 1, 2, 3, \ldots)$ [provided (2.3.1) is absolutely convergent], and by

$$E[g(Y)] = \int_{-\infty}^{\infty} g(y)f(y)\,dy \tag{2.3.2}$$

if Y is continuous (provided $\int_{-\infty}^{\infty} |g(y)f(y)\,dy < \infty$). For an arbitrary random variable, see Exercise 2.3.11.

Note that the "expected value" need not be a possible outcome of the experiment. For example, let $g(Y) = Y$ and suppose that Y is the number of dots on the top side of a fair die. It is easy to show that $E(Y) = 3.5$, which is not a possible outcome. Although we would never "expect" to see 3.5 dots after a single roll, the average number of dots appearing after a large number of rolls is 3.5.

Particular choices of $g(\cdot)$ deserve special attention and are covered in the following definition.

Definition 2.3.2 Let Y be a random variable for which the following expectations exist. If r is a positive integer, the expectation $E[(Y-b)^r]$, where b is a real number, is called the *rth moment of the distribution of Y around the point b.* The first moment around zero, $\mu \equiv E(Y)$, is the *mean* of Y. The second moment around the mean, $\sigma^2 \equiv E[(Y-\mu)^2] = \text{Var}(Y)$, is the *variance* of Y. The *standard deviation* is $\sigma \equiv +(\sigma^2)^{1/2}$. The reciprocal σ^{-2} of the variance is the *precision.* In general, the rth moment around the mean will be denoted by $\mu_r \equiv E[(Y-\mu)^r]$ and the rth moment around zero will be denoted $\mu_r' \equiv E(Y^r)$. Note $\mu = \mu_1'$ and $\sigma^2 = \mu_2$.

Given Definitions 2.3.1 and 2.3.2 the following properties are easily derived.

Theorem 2.3.1 Let Y be a random variable and assume all expectations below exist.

(a) $E(c) = c$ for a constant c.

(b) $E[cg(Y)] = cE[g(Y)]$ for a constant c and any function $g(\cdot)$.

(c) $E[c_1 g_1(Y) + c_2 g_2(Y)] = c_1 E[g_1(Y)] + c_2 E[g_2(Y)]$ for constants c_1 and c_2, and functions $g_1(Y)$ and $g_2(Y)$.

(d) $E[g_1(Y)] \leq E[g_2(Y)]$ if $g_1(y) \leq g_2(y)$ for all y.

(e) $\text{Var}(Y) = E(Y^2) - [E(Y)]^2$.

Proof Left to the reader.

The *mean* is the most common measure of "central tendency" of a random variable. Other frequently used measures are the *median* (Exercise 2.2.3) and the *mode* (Exercise 2.2.2). The *variance* is the most common measure of "dispersion" of a random variable. Another measure is the *interquartile range*: $\xi_{.75} - \xi_{.25}$ (Exercise 2.2.3). It is important to note that such quantitative measures of central tendency and dispersion are somewhat arbitrary and different measures of the same concept can often give conflicting results. Similar remarks are appropriate for other quantitative measures of the shape of p.d.f.s, for example, *skewness* or *asymmetry* (Exercise 2.3.5) and *kurtosis* or *peakedness* (Exercise 2.3.6).

The question of existence of the rth moment is addressed in the following theorem.

Theorem 2.3.2 Let Y be a random variable and $r > 0$. Then $E(|Y|^r) < \infty$ iff

$$\sum_{n=1}^{\infty} P[|Y| \geq n^{1/r}] < \infty.$$

Proof Left to the reader.

The following two examples illustrate various issues related to mathematical expectation. For the sake of brevity only continuous random variables are considered.

Example 2.3.1 Let Y have the p.d.f.

$$f(y) = \begin{Bmatrix} \frac{1}{2}(y+1), & \text{if } -1 < y < 1 \\ 0, & \text{otherwise} \end{Bmatrix}.$$

Then the mean of Y is

$$\mu = \int_{-1}^{1} \tfrac{1}{2}y(y+1)\,dy = \left[\frac{y^3}{6} + \frac{y^2}{4}\right]_{-1}^{1} = \frac{1}{6} + \frac{1}{4} + \frac{1}{6} - \frac{1}{4} = \frac{1}{3},$$

and the variance of Y, using Theorem 2.3.2(e), is

$$\sigma^2 = \int_{-1}^{1} \tfrac{1}{2}y^2(y+1)\,dy - \mu^2 = \left[\frac{y^4}{8} + \frac{y^3}{6}\right]_{-1}^{1} - \frac{1}{9}$$

$$= \frac{1}{8} + \frac{1}{6} - \frac{1}{8} + \frac{1}{6} - \frac{1}{9} = \frac{2}{9}.$$

Example 2.3.2 Let Y have the p.d.f.

$$f(y) = \begin{Bmatrix} y^{-2}, & \text{if } 1 < y < \infty \\ 0, & \text{otherwise} \end{Bmatrix}.$$

Then the mean of Y does not exist, since the following integral diverges:

$$\int_1^{\infty} y(y^{-2})\,dy = \operatorname*{Limit}_{c\to\infty} \int_1^{c} y^{-1}\,dy = \operatorname*{Limit}_{c\to\infty} ln(c) \to \infty.$$

Using Theorem 2.3.2, this nonexistence is confirmed since for $r = 1$:

$$P(|Y| \geq n) = P(Y \geq n) = \int_n^{\infty} y^{-2}\,dy = [-y^{-1}]_n^{\infty} = n^{-1},$$

and hence,

$$\sum_{n=1}^{\infty} n^{-1} \to \infty.$$

The moments (see Definition 2.3.2) of a random variable play an important role in statistics since, in *some cases*, if all the moments are known, then the distribution can be uniquely determined.[17] In such cases it is useful to have a simple way of generating all such moments. Such considerations motivate the following definition.

Definition 2.3.3 Let Y be a random variable with p.d.f. $f(\cdot)$. The *moment generating function* (m.g.f.) of Y, denoted $M_Y(t)$ or simply $M(t)$, is defined

17. This is known as the *problem of moments*. For further discussion, see Chung (1974), Feller (1968), Rao (1973, p. 106) or Serfling (1980, p. 46). For examples in which the moments do not identify a unique distribution, see Exercise 2.3.14 and Rao (1973, p. 152, Exercise 17).

to be $E[\exp(tY)]$ provided this expectation exists for every value of t in an open interval around zero.[18]

If a m.g.f. exists, then it is continuously differentiable in some neighborhood of the origin. Differentiating $M(t)$ r times with respect to t yields

$$\frac{d^r}{dt^r}[M(t)] = \int_{-\infty}^{\infty} y^r \exp(ty) f(y)\, dy. \tag{2.3.3}$$

Letting $t \to 0$ in (2.3.3) implies

$$\frac{d^r}{dt^r}[M(0)] = E(Y^r). \tag{2.3.4}$$

Thus, as its name suggests, the moments of a distribution may be obtained from differentiating $M(t)$ and evaluating the derivative at zero. Similar results hold for discrete random variables.

Let $\mu_r' \equiv E(Y^r)$ and replace $\exp(ty)$ in (2.3.3) by its MacLaurin's series expansion:

$$M(t) = E\left[1 + tY + \frac{1}{2!}(tY)^2 + \frac{1}{3!}(tY)^3 + \cdots\right] = \sum_{r=0}^{\infty} \frac{1}{r!}\mu_r' t^r. \tag{2.3.5}$$

Then the coefficient of $t^r/r!$ in the MacLaurin's series representation of $\mu(t)$ is μ_r'.[19]

We now turn to a simple example.

Example 2.3.3 Let Y be a random variable with p.d.f.

$$f(y) = \begin{Bmatrix} y\exp(-y), & \text{if } 0 < y < \infty \\ 0, & \text{otherwise} \end{Bmatrix}. \tag{2.3.6}$$

Then the m.g.f. of Y is

$$\begin{aligned} M(t) \equiv E[\exp(ty)] &= \int_0^{\infty} \exp(ty)[y\exp(-y)]\, dy \\ &= \int_0^{\infty} y\exp[y(t-1)]\, dy. \end{aligned}$$

Let $u = y$ and $v\,dv = \exp[y(t-1)]\,dy$. Then $du = dy$ and $v = (t-1)^{-1}\exp[y(t-1)]$, where we also assume $t < 1$. Hence,

18. When the m.g.f. exists in an open interval containing zero, then the moment sequence determines the distribution uniquely (see Feller 1971). Note: $M_Y(t)$ is the *Laplace transform* of $f_Y(t)$.

19. The *cumulant generating function* of Y is defined to be $\ln[M_Y(t)]$. The *rth cumulant* of Y is the coefficient of $t^r/r!$ in the Taylor series expansion of the cumulant generating function. Cumulants (except the first) are invariant to translations of random variables. For a summary discussion of various generating functions, see Johnson et al (1992, pp. 40–51) or Stuart and Ord (1987).

$$
\begin{aligned}
M(t) &= [y(t-1)^{-1}\exp(t-1)]]_0^\infty - \int_0^\infty (t-1)^{-1}\exp[y(t-1)]\,dy \\
&= 0 - 0 - [(t-1)^{-2}\exp[y(t-1)]]_0^\infty \\
&= -[0 - (t-1)^{-2}\exp(0)] = (t-1)^{-2}.
\end{aligned}
$$

Because $M'(t) = 2(1-t)^{-3}$ and $M''(t) = 6(1-t)^{-4}$, if follows that $\mu = \sigma^2 = 2$.

Unfortunately, in many common cases the m.g.f. does not exist. This motivates consideration of the *characteristic function* defined to be $\phi(t) \equiv E[\exp(itY)] = E[\cos(tY)] + iE[\sin(tY)]$, where i is the imaginary number defined by $i^2 = -1$. The characteristic function always exists since $|\exp(ity)| = |\cos(ty) + i\sin(ty)| = 1$ is bounded for all y. Furthermore, if the density $f(y)$ is symmetric around zero, then $\phi(t)$ is real. If the m.g.f. also exists, $\phi(t) = M(it)$. Every distribution has a unique characteristic function, and to each characteristic function there corresponds a unique distribution function. Whereas $M(t)$ is the Laplace transform of the density $f(\cdot)$, $\phi(t)$ is the Fourier transform. For further discussion of characteristic functions, see Chung (1974), Dhrymes (1989, pp. 246–257), and Shephard (1991).

Exercises

2.3.1 Let Y be a random variable with mean μ and variance σ^2. Find the value of c that minimizes: $E[(Y-c)^2]$.

2.3.2 Alice has two pennies; Bob has one. They match pennies until one of them has all three. Let Y denote the number of trials required to end the game.

(a) Find the p.d.f. of Y.

(b) Find the mean and variance of Y.

(c) What is the probability that Bob will win the game?

2.3.3 Consider a random variable Y with p.d.f.

$$
f(y) = \begin{Bmatrix} c\exp(-|y-\alpha|/\beta), & \text{if } \alpha-\beta < y < \alpha+\beta \\ 0, & \text{otherwise} \end{Bmatrix},
$$

where $-\infty < \alpha < \infty$, $\beta > 0$ and $c > 0$ are constants.

(a) Find c so that $f(\cdot)$ is a valid p.d.f. and sketch it.

(b) Find $F(\cdot)$.

(c) Find the mean and variance of Y.

(d) Find the qth quantile of Y.

2.3.4 Let Y be a random variable with p.d.f.

$$
f(y) = \begin{Bmatrix} \alpha + \beta y^2, & \text{if } 0 \le y \le 1 \\ 0, & \text{otherwise} \end{Bmatrix},
$$

and $E(Y) = \frac{2}{3}$. Find α and β.

2.3.5 Let Y be a random variable with mean μ, median $\xi_{.50}$, variance σ^2 and suppose $E[(Y-\mu)^3]$ exists. The unit-free ratios $r_1 = E[(Y-\mu)^3]/\sigma^3$ and $r_2 = (\mu - \xi_{.50})/\sigma$ are often used as measures of *skewness* (*asymmetry*) in the p.d.f. of Y. Graph each of the following p.d.f.s and show that r_1 is negative, zero, and positive for these respective distributions (said to be skewed to the left, not skewed, and skewed to the right, respectively). Does the sign of r_2 agree with the sign of r_1? What can you say in general?

(a) $f(y) = \begin{cases} \frac{1}{2}(y+1), & \text{if } -1 < y < 1 \\ 0, & \text{otherwise} \end{cases}.$

(b) $f(y) = \begin{cases} \frac{1}{2}, & \text{if } -1 < y < 1 \\ 0, & \text{otherwise} \end{cases}.$

(c) $f(y) = \begin{cases} \frac{1}{2}(y-1), & \text{if } -1 < y < 1 \\ 0, & \text{otherwise} \end{cases}.$

2.3.6 Let Y be a random variable with mean μ and variance σ^2 such that $E[(Y-\mu)^4]$ exists. The value of $K = E[(Y-\mu)^4]/\sigma^4 - 3$ is often used as a measure of *kurtosis* (peakedness or flatness) of the density near its center (see Balanda and MacGillivray 1987, 1990 and Ruppert 1987). Because $K = 0$ for the normal p.d.f. (see Equation 3.3.11), negative values of K are sometimes used to indicate that a p.d.f. is more flat near its center than a bell-shaped normal density, and positive values that it is more peaked near its center than a normal density. (Such conclusions are often, but not always, warranted.) Densities with $K < 0$, $K = 0$, $K > 0$ are defined to be *platykurtic*, *mesokurtic*, and *leptokurtic*, respectively. Graph the following p.d.f.s. Show: K is smaller for (a).

(a) Same as $f(y)$ in Exercise 2.3.5(b).

(b) $f(y) = \begin{cases} 3(1-y^2)/4, & \text{if } -1 < y < 1 \\ 0, & \text{otherwise} \end{cases}.$

2.3.7 The *rth factorial moment of* Y (r a positive integer) is $E[Y(Y-1)\dots(Y-r+1)]$. The *factorial* moment generating function is $M^*(t) \equiv E(t^Y)$ if it exists. The factorial moment generating function is used to generate factorial moments in the same way as raw moments are obtained from $M(t)$ except that $t \to 1$ instead of $t \to 0$. $M^*(t)$ is often useful in finding moments of discrete random variables. For example, consider the random variable Y with p.m.f.

$$f(y) = \begin{cases} \exp(-\lambda)\lambda^y/y!, & \text{if } y = 0, 1, 2, \dots \\ 0, & \text{otherwise} \end{cases},$$

where $\lambda > 0$. [Y is known as a Poisson random variable (see Definition 3.2.8)].

(a) Show: $E(t^Y) = \exp[\lambda\{\exp(t) - 1\}]$.

(b) Use (a) to show $E(Y) = \text{Var}(Y) = \lambda$.

2.3.8 Let c be a constant and let Y be a random variable with p.d.f.

$$f(y) = \begin{cases} c\exp(-y), & \text{if } y > 0 \\ 0, & \text{if } y \leq 0 \end{cases}.$$

(a) Find c.

(b) Find the m.g.f. of Y and use it to find the mean and variance of Y.

2.3.9 Let Y be a continuous random variable with a p.d.f. $f(\cdot)$, which is *symmetric* with respect to $y = \alpha$, i.e. $f(\alpha - \varepsilon) = f(\alpha + \varepsilon)$ for all $\varepsilon > 0$.

(a) Show: $E(Y) = \alpha$, provided the expectation exists.

(b) Median$(Y) = \alpha$.

(c) If $f(\cdot)$ is unimodal, then α is the mode.

2.3.10 Let Y be a continuous random variable with support $(0, \infty)$ such that $E(|Y|) < \infty$. Using integration by parts, show:

$$E(Y) = \int_0^\infty [1 - F(y)]\,dy. \tag{2.3.7}$$

2.3.11 Consider the following generalization of Definition 2.3.1:

$$E[g(y)] \equiv \int_{-\infty}^{\infty} g(y)\,dF(y) \equiv \operatorname*{Limit}_{\varepsilon \to 0} \sum_{k=-\infty}^{\infty} g(t_k)[F(y_k) - F(y_{k-1})] \tag{2.3.8}$$

provided the limit exists, where $y_{k-1} < t_k \leq y_k$, $\varepsilon \equiv \max_k |y_k - y_{k-1}|$, k is an integer, and $\{y_k\}$ is a sequence of strictly increasing real numbers. The integral in (2.3.8) is known as *Stieltjes integral*. If $F(y)$ is absolutely continuous, then $dF(y) = f(y)\,dy$ and (2.3.8) reduces to (2.3.2), which is known as a *Riemann integral*. (Also see Equation 2.2.6). If Y is a discrete random variable, then (2.3.8) reduces to (2.3.1). Suppose $g(Y) = \exp(tY)$ and $F(y) = F_1(y) + F_2(y)$, where

$$F_1(y) = \begin{cases} \exp(-y), & \text{if } y \geq 1 \\ 0, & \text{if } y < 1 \end{cases},$$

$$F_2(y) = \begin{cases} 0, & \text{if } y \geq 1 \\ 1 - \exp(-1), & \text{if } y < 1 \end{cases}.$$

Show: $E[g(Y)] = -(t-1)\exp(t-1) + [1 - \exp(-1)]\exp(t)$.

2.3.12 Let Y be a random variable with p.d.f.

$$f(y) = \begin{cases} y, & \text{if } 0 \leq y \leq 1 \\ 2 - y, & \text{if } 1 \leq y \leq 2 \\ 0, & \text{otherwise} \end{cases}.$$

(a) Find the c.d.f. $F(y)$.

(b) Find the m.g.f. $M(t)$.

2.3.13 (a) Verify the following relationship between the rth moment around the mean, μ_r, and the first r moments μ_i' $(i = 1, 2, \ldots, r)$ around the origin:

$$\begin{aligned}\mu_r &= \sum_{j=0}^{r} (-1)^j \binom{r}{j} (\mu_1')^j \mu_{r-j}' \\ &= \mu_r' - \binom{r}{1}\mu_1'\mu_{r-1}' + \binom{r}{2}(\mu_1')^2\mu_{r-2}' + \cdots + (-1)^{r-1}(r-1)(\mu_1')^r,\end{aligned} \tag{2.3.9}$$

where $\binom{r}{k} \equiv \dfrac{r!}{(r-k)!\,k!}$.

Hint: Use the Binomial Theorem:

$$(x + y)^n = \sum_{k=0}^{n} \binom{n}{k} x^k y^{n-k}. \tag{2.3.10}$$

Note that $0! = 1$, and

$$\binom{n}{0} = \binom{n}{n} = 1, \tag{2.3.11}$$

$$\binom{n}{k} = \binom{n}{n-k}. \tag{2.3.12}$$

(b) Also verify the analogous relationship:

$$\mu'_r = \sum_{j=0}^{r} (-1)^j \binom{r}{j} (\mu'_1) \mu_{r-j}. \tag{2.3.13}$$

2.3.14 Consider the random variables X and Y with respective p.d.f.s:

$$f_x(x) = \frac{1}{x(2\pi)^{1/2}} \exp[-\tfrac{1}{2}\{ln(x)\}^2], \tag{2.3.14}$$

$$f_Y(y) = \left[\frac{1 + \alpha \sin[2\pi\, ln(y)]}{y(2\pi)^{1/2}}\right] \exp\{-\tfrac{1}{2}[ln(y)]^2\}, -1 \le \alpha \le 1. \tag{2.3.15}$$

Show that X and Y have the same moments. (Hence, as noted in footnote 17, moments alone do not uniquely define a distribution.)

2.3.15 Given a scalar random variable Y, show that $E[|Y - c|]$ is minimized by any median of Y (see Exercise 2.2.3). Unlike Exercise 2.3.1, the objective function here is not everywhere differentiable, and so calculus arguments are not appropriate. Instead, let the closed interval $[m_1, m_2]$ be the set of medians. Suppose $c > m_2$. Show $E[|Y - c|] - E[|Y - \text{med}(Y)|] > 0$ (Lehmann 1983, Exercise 1.10).

2.4 Joint and Conditional Distributions

In econometrics the researcher is usually interested in relationships involving more than one random variable. Hence, it is necessary to extend the definitions of distribution and density functions of one random variable (the univariate case) to those of several random variables (the multivariate case). These random variables are stacked to form a vector. The distribution of a vector random variable corresponds to the joint distribution of all of its elements. Formally, we have the following definition.

Definition 2.4.1 Let Y_n $(n = 1, 2, \ldots, N)$ be N random variables defined on the same probability space $[\mathscr{S}, \tilde{A}, P(\cdot)]$, and define $Y \equiv [Y_1, Y_2, \ldots, Y_N]'$. The *joint (cumulative)* distribution function of $Y_1, Y_2, \ldots, Y_N$ is

$$F(y) = P(Y_1 \le y_1, Y_2 \le y_2, \ldots, Y_N \le y_N), \tag{2.4.1}$$

where $y \equiv [y_1, y_2, \ldots, y_N]'$ is an arbitrary element in N-dimensional real space $\Re^N$.

Based on Definition 2.4.1 properties of joint distribution functions may be derived. These are given in the following theorem, which for notational simplicity, is restricted to the bivariate case, that is, $N = 2$.

Theorem 2.4.1 Let $F(y_1, y_2)$ be a joint distribution function. Then

(a) $F(-\infty, y_2) = \underset{y_1 \to -\infty}{\text{Limit}}\, F(y_1, y_2) = 0.$

(b) $F(y_1, -\infty) = \underset{y_2 \to -\infty}{\text{Limit}}\, F(y_1, y_2) = 0.$

(c) $F(\infty, \infty) = \underset{\substack{y_1 \to \infty \\ y_2 \to \infty}}{\text{Limit}}\, F(y_1, y_2) = 1.$

(d) If $a_1 < b_1$ and $a_2 < b_2$, then

$$P(a_1 \le Y_1 \le b_1, a_2 \le Y_2 \le b_2) = F(b_1, b_2) - F(b_1, a_2) - F(a_1, b_2) + F(a_1, a_2). \tag{2.4.2}$$

(e) $F(\cdot, \cdot)$ is right continuous in each argument, that is,

$$\operatorname*{Limit}_{h_1 \to 0^+} F(y_1 + h_1, y_2) = \operatorname*{Limit}_{h_2 \to 0^+} F(y_1, y_2 + h_2) = F(y_1, y_2).$$

Proof Left to the reader.

In this section and subsequent sections, it is necessary to work with numerous distribution and density functions pertaining to subsets of Y_n $(n = 1, 2, \ldots, N)$. For notational convenience, we use $F(\cdot)$ to denote any c.d.f., $f(\cdot)$ to denote any p.f., and the argument lists to denote a particular function. If this convention causes confusion in a particular context, then more explicit notation is introduced as needed.

In the multivariate setting the distribution of subsets are often required. Such distributions are referred to as *marginal distributions*. The following theorem relates these distributions to the overall joint distribution.

Theorem 2.4.2 Let Y_n $(n = 1, 2, \ldots, N)$ have joint distribution function $F(y_1, \ldots, y_N)$. Then the marginal distribution of $Y_n, F(y_n)$, is related to $F(y_1, \ldots, y_N)$ by

$$F(y_n) = F(\infty, \ldots, y_n, \ldots, \infty) = \operatorname*{Limit}_{y_i \to \infty} F(y_1, \ldots, y_{n-1}, y_n, y_{n+1}, \ldots, y_N) \quad (\text{for all } i \neq n). \tag{2.4.3}$$

Given J $(1 \le J < N)$, the joint marginal distribution function of Y_j $(j = 1, 2, \ldots, J)$ is

$$F(y_1, \ldots, y_J) = F(y_1, \ldots, y_J, \infty, \ldots, \infty). \tag{2.4.4}$$

Joint marginal distribution functions of other subsets may similarly be obtained by rearrangement of Y_n $(n = 1, 2, \ldots, N)$.

Proof Left to the reader.

Definitions 2.2.3 and 2.2.5 were concerned with discrete univariate random variables. Their multivariate counterparts will now be introduced. For ease in exposition we consider only the cases in which the random variables in question are either all discrete or all continuous.

Definition 2.4.2 The N-dimensional random variable $Y = [Y_1, Y_2, \ldots, Y_N]'$ is defined to be a *N-dimensional discrete random variable* if it can assume values only at a countable number of points $y = [y_1, y_2, \ldots, y_N]'$ in $\Re^N$.

Definition 2.4.3 If Y is a N-dimensional discrete random variable, then the *joint probability mass function* of Y, denoted $f(y)$, is defined by

$$f(y) = P(Y_1 = y_1, Y_2 = y_2, \ldots, Y_N = y_N) \tag{2.4.5}$$

for $y = [y_1, y_2, \ldots, y_N]' \in \Re^N$.

Applying Definition 2.4.3. directly to marginal joint distribution function (2.4.4) yields a *joint probability mass function* for Y_j ($j = 1, \ldots, J$). Alternatively, it is easy to show

$$f(y_1, \ldots, y_J) = \sum_{j_{J+1}} \cdots \sum_{y_N} f(y_1, \ldots, y_J, y_{J+1}, \ldots, y_N), \tag{2.4.6}$$

where the summations in (2.4.6) are over all permissible values of y_n ($n = J + 1, \ldots, N$).

Definition 2.2.5 was concerned with continuous univariate random variables. Its multivariate counterpart is now introduced.

Definition 2.4.4 A N-dimensional random variable $Y = [Y_1, Y_2, \ldots, Y_N]'$ is (*absolutely*) *continuous* iff there exists a function $f(y) \geq 0$ such that

$$F(y) = \int_{-\infty}^{y_N} \cdots \int_{-\infty}^{y_1} f(t_1, \ldots, t_N)\, dt_1 \ldots dt_N \tag{2.4.7}$$

for all $y = [y_1, y_2, \ldots, y_N]' \in \Re^N$, where $f(y)$ is the *joint probability density function* of Y.

From Definition 2.4.4 the following results can be easily derived.

Theorem 2.4.3 Let $f(y)$ be the joint p.d.f. of the N-dimensional random variable Y. Then

(a) $f(y) \geq 0$ for all y.

(b) $f(y) = \dfrac{\partial^N F(y)}{\partial y_1\, \partial y_2 \cdots \partial y_N}$ except at most a countable number of points.

(c) $\displaystyle\int_{-\infty}^{\infty} \cdots \int_{-\infty}^{\infty} f(t_1, \ldots, t_N)\, dt_1 \ldots dt_N = 1.$

Proof Left to the reader.

Analogous to (2.4.6) in the discrete case, the marginal joint density of Y_j ($j = 1, 2, \ldots, J$) in the continuous case is

$$f(y_1, \ldots, y_J) = \int_{-\infty}^{\infty} \cdots \int_{-\infty}^{\infty} f(y_1, \ldots, y_J, y_{J+1}, \ldots, y_N)\, dy_{J+1} \ldots dy_N. \tag{2.4.8}$$

Other marginal densities can be computed in an analogous fashion.

The marginal distribution of Y_j ($j = 1, 2, \ldots, J$) (in either the continuous or discrete cases) characterizes the probability structure after the effects of Y_n ($n = J + 1, \ldots, N$) have been "allowed for" or "integrated-out."

The marginal distribution of Y_j $(j = 1, 2, \ldots, J)$ does not depend on Y_n $(n = J + 1, \ldots, N)$. If such dependency is desired and interest focuses on the subjunctive case "were $Y_n = y_n$ $(n = J + 1, \ldots, N)$ to be known," then the concept of a conditional distribution is appropriate.

The basic idea of conditional probability for events (Definition 2.1.7) is fairly easily transferred to discrete random variables, but its transferring to the case of continuous random variables involves some nontrivial mathematics requiring careful measure-theoretic details. These complications also spill over to the discussion of independence and conditional expectation in the next two sections, but they are not be discussed in any great detail here (the interested reader can consult any standard advanced probability text or more friendly texts such as Dhrymes 1989, pp. 110–132, and Walley 1991, pp. 306–308, 330–333, 436–440). Instead conditional probability functions are introduced as follows.

Definition 2.4.5 Let Y_n $(n = 1, 2, \ldots, N)$ have joint p.f. $f(y_1, \ldots, y_N)$. Given J $(1 \leq J < N)$, let $f(y_{J+1}, \ldots, y_N)$ be the marginal p.f. of Y_n $(n = J + 1, \ldots, N)$. Then the *conditional p.d.f.* of Y_j $(j = 1, 2, \ldots, J)$ given Y_i $(i = J + 1, J + 2, \ldots, N)$ is defined by

$$f(y_1, \ldots, y_J | y_{J+1}, \ldots, y_N) = \frac{f(y_1, \ldots, y_{J+1}, \ldots, y_N)}{f(y_{J+1}, \ldots, y_N)} \tag{2.4.9}$$

for $f(y_{J+1}, \ldots, y_N) > 0$. If Y_n $(1, 2, \ldots, N)$ are discrete random variables, then (2.4.8) is referred to as a conditional p.m.f. In this case the *conditional (cumulative) distribution function* of Y_j $(j = 1, 2, \ldots, J)$ given $Y_n = y_n$ $(n = J + 1, \ldots, N)$ is defined by

$$F(y_1, \ldots, y_J | y_{J+1}, \ldots, y_N) \equiv \sum_{t_1 \leq y_1} \cdots \sum_{t_J \leq y_J} f(t_1, \ldots, t_J | y_{J+1}, \ldots, y_N), \tag{2.4.10}$$

where t_j ranges over atoms of Y_j $(j = 1, 2, \ldots, J)$. If Y_N $(n = 1, 2, \ldots, N)$ are absolutely continuous random variables, then (2.4.9) is referred to as a conditional p.d.f. In this case the *conditional (cumulative) distribution function* of Y_j $(j = 1, 2, \ldots, J)$ given $Y_n = y_n$ $(n = J + 1, \ldots, N)$ is defined by

$$\begin{aligned} &F(y_1, \ldots, y_J | y_{J+1}, \ldots, y_N) \\ &\quad = P(Y_1 \leq y_1, \ldots, Y_J \leq y_J | Y_{J+1} = y_{J+1}, \ldots, Y_N = y_N) \\ &\quad = \int_{-\infty}^{y_1} \cdots \int_{-\infty}^{y_J} f(t_1, \ldots, t_J | y_{J+1}, \ldots, y_N)\, dt_1 \ldots dt_J. \end{aligned} \tag{2.4.11}$$

The reader can appreciate some of the formal problems that arise in rigorous development of (2.4.9) by noting that in the case of continuous random variables, $P(Y_{J+1} = y_{J+1}, \ldots, Y_N = y_N) = 0$, and so extension from (2.1.3) is nontrivial. A heuristic solution is to first consider $P[A_1 | A_2(\varepsilon)]$, where $\varepsilon > 0$ is given, A_1 is the event $\{s | Y_1(s) \le y_1, \ldots, Y_J(s) \le y_J\} \in \tilde{A}$ and $A_2(\varepsilon)$ is an event such as $\{s | y_{J+1} - \varepsilon < Y_{J+1} < y_{J+1} + \varepsilon, \ldots, y_N - \varepsilon < Y_N < y_N + \varepsilon\} \in \tilde{A}$, use (2.1.3) to obtain $P[A_1 | A_2(\varepsilon)] = P[A_1 \cap A_2(\varepsilon)]/P[A_2(\varepsilon)]$, and then to define (2.4.11) as the limit of $P[A_1 | A_2(\varepsilon)]$ as $\varepsilon \to 0$. Of course there are many different ways of defining the conditioning event $A_2(\varepsilon)$, and different choices can have material effect on the resulting (2.4.9) and (2.4.11). For example, see Exercise 2.5.7 or Stuart and Ord (1987, pp. 278–279, Exercise 7.22). *The main point the reader needs to keep in mind for immediate purposes is that conditional probability depends intricately on the conditioning random variables* Y_n $(n = J + 1, J + 2, \ldots, N)$ *and not just on the values* y_n $(n = J + 1, J + 2, \ldots, N)$. The notation of Definition 2.4.5 could have been changed to add subscripts to f and F involving "$Y_1, \ldots, Y_J | Y_{J+1} = y_{J+1}, \ldots, Y_N = y_N$" to emphasize this fact, but it would seem to unnecessarily complicate matters. For readers interested in further introductory discussion, see DeGroot (1987, pp. 171–174), Lindley (1982a, pp. 68–69, 74–77) and Rao (1989).

The next two examples illustrate the concepts discussed so far in this section: Example 2.4.1 involves bivariate discrete random variables and Example 2.4.2 involves bivariate continuous random variables. More examples of multivariate random variables are given in Section 3.3.

Example 2.4.1 Let Y_1 and Y_2 be discrete random variables with bivariate p.d.f.

$$f(y_1, y_2) = \begin{Bmatrix} (y_1 + y_2)/9, & y_1 = 0, 1, 2 \text{ and } y_2 = 0, 1 \\ 0, & \text{otherwise} \end{Bmatrix}.$$

Then the marginal p.d.f. of Y_1 is

$$f(y_1) = \sum_{y_2=0}^{1} f(y_1, y_2) = \frac{y_1}{9} + \frac{y_1 + 1}{9} = \frac{(2y_1 + 1)}{9}, \qquad y_1 = 0, 1, 2$$

and zero elsewhere. The marginal p.d.f. of Y_2 is

$$f(y_2) = \sum_{y_1=0}^{2} f(y_1, y_2) = \frac{y_2}{9} + \frac{1 + y_2}{9} + \frac{2 + y_2}{9} = \frac{(1 + y_2)}{3}, \qquad y_2 = 0, 1$$

and zero elsewhere. The conditional p.d.f. of Y_1 given $Y_2 = y_2$ is

$$f(y_1 | y_2) = \frac{f(y_1, y_2)}{f(y_2)} = \frac{y_1 + y_2}{3(1 + y_2)}, \qquad y_1 = 0, 1, 2$$

and zero elsewhere. The conditional p.d.f. of Y_2 given $Y_1 = y_1$ is

$$f(y_2 | y_1) = \frac{f(y_1, y_2)}{f(y_1)} = \frac{y_1 + y_2}{2y_1 + 1}, \qquad y_2 = 0, 1$$

and zero elsewhere.

The marginal distribution function of Y_1 is

$$F(y_1) = \begin{cases} 0, & \text{if } y_1 < 0 \\ 1/9, & \text{if } 0 \leq y_1 < 1 \\ 4/9, & \text{if } 1 \leq y_1 < 2 \\ 1, & \text{if } y_1 \geq 2 \end{cases},$$

and the marginal distribution function of Y_2 is

$$F(y_2) = \begin{cases} 0, & \text{if } y_2 < 0, \\ \frac{1}{3}, & \text{if } 0 \leq y_2 < 1 \\ 1, & \text{if } y_2 \geq 1 \end{cases}.$$

Finally, the conditional distribution function of Y_1 given $Y_2 = y_2$ is

$$F(y_1|y_2) = \begin{cases} 0, & \text{if } y_1 < 0 \\ \dfrac{y_2}{3(1 + y_2)}, & \text{if } 0 \leq y_1 < 1 \\ \dfrac{(1 + 2y_2)}{3(1 + y_2)}, & \text{if } 1 \leq y_1 < 2 \\ 1, & \text{if } y_1 \geq 2 \end{cases},$$

and the conditional distribution function of Y_2 given $Y_1 = y_1$ is

$$F(y_2|y_1) = \begin{cases} 0, & \text{if } y_2 < 0 \\ \dfrac{y_1}{2y_1 + 1}, & \text{if } 0 \leq y_2 < 1 \\ 1, & \text{if } y_2 \geq 1 \end{cases}.$$

Example 2.4.2 (Hogg and Craig 1978, p. 68). Let Y_1 and Y_2 be continuous random variables with bivariate p.d.f.

$$f(y_1, y_2) = \begin{cases} 2, & \text{if } 0 < y_1 < y_2 < 1 \\ 0, & \text{otherwise} \end{cases}.$$

Then the marginal p.d.f.s are, respectively,

$$f(y_1) = \int_{y_1}^{1} 2\, dy_2 = 2(1 - y_1), \qquad 0 < y_1 < 1,$$

zero elsewhere, and

$$f(y_2) = \int_{0}^{y_2} 2\, dy_1 = 2y_2, \qquad 0 < y_2 < 1,$$

zero elsewhere. The conditional p.d.f. of Y_1 given $Y_2 = y_2$ is

$$f(y_1|y_2) = \begin{cases} (y_2)^{-1}, & \text{if } 0 < y_1 < y_2 \\ 0, & \text{otherwise} \end{cases}.$$

and the conditional p.d.f. of Y_2 given $Y_1 = y_1$ is

$$f(y_2|y_1) = \begin{cases} (1 - y_1)^{-1}, & \text{if } y_1 < y_2 < 1 \\ 0, & \text{otherwise} \end{cases}.$$

The marginal distribution function of Y_1 is

$$F(y_1) = \begin{Bmatrix} 0, & \text{if } y_1 \leq 0 \\ y_1(2 - y_1), & \text{if } 0 < y_1 < 1 \\ 1, & \text{if } y_1 \geq 1 \end{Bmatrix},$$

and the marginal distribution function of Y_2 is

$$F(y_2) = \begin{Bmatrix} 0, & \text{if } y_2 \leq 0 \\ y_2^2, & \text{if } 0 < y_2 < 1 \\ 1, & \text{if } y_2 \geq 1 \end{Bmatrix}.$$

Finally, the conditional distribution function of Y_1 given $Y_2 = y_2$ is

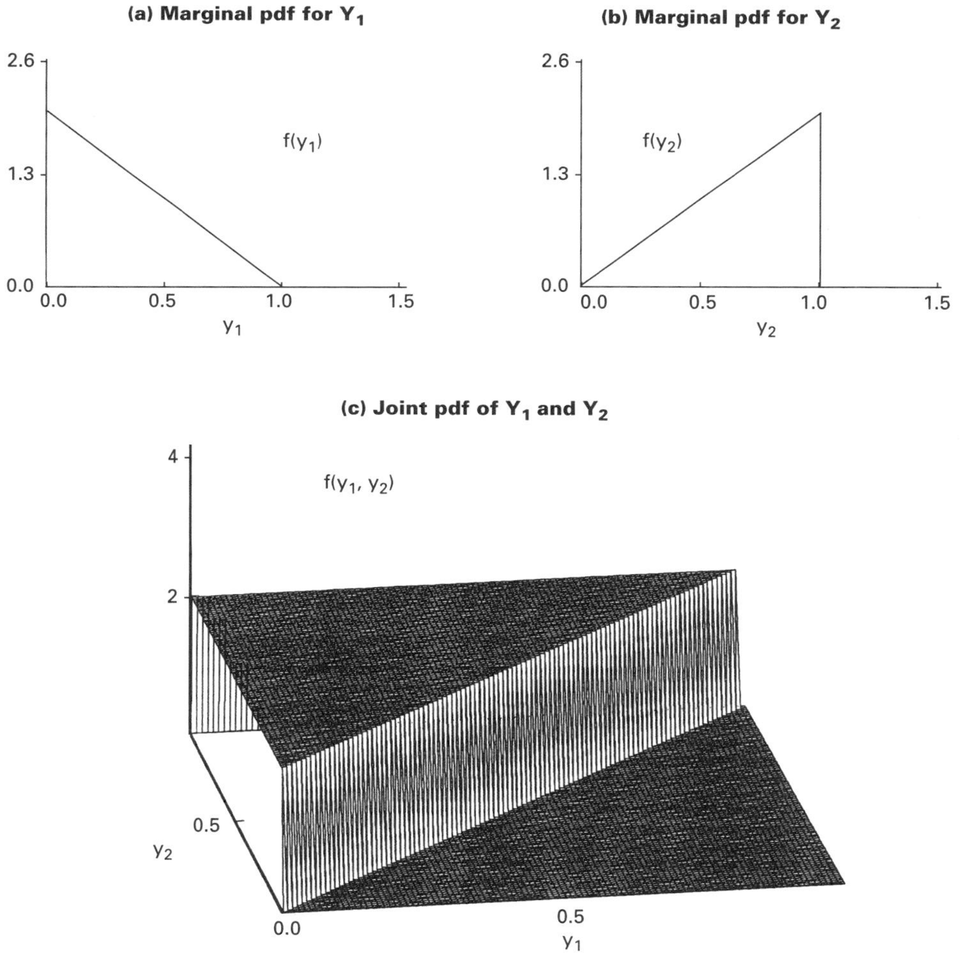

Figure 2.4.1
Densities corresponding to Example 2.4.2

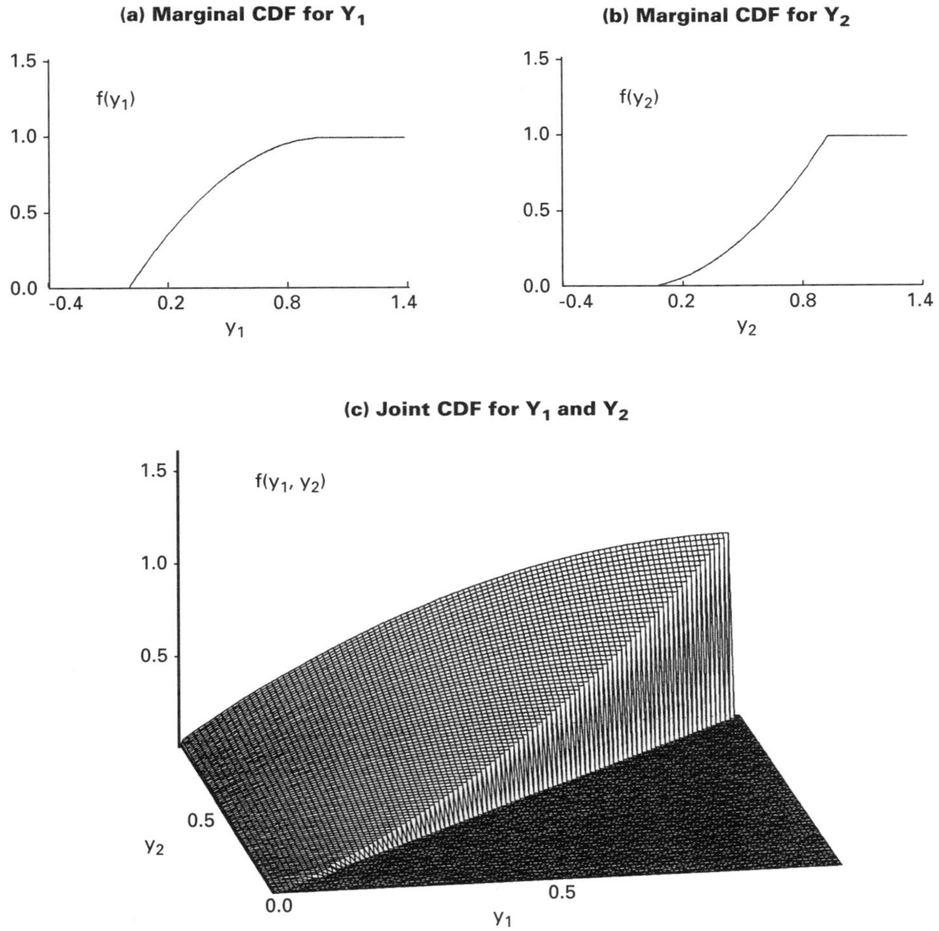

Figure 2.4.2
Cumulative distributions corresponding to Example 2.4.2

$$F(y_1|y_2) = \begin{cases} 0, & \text{if } y_1 \leq 0 \\ y_1/y_2, & \text{if } 0 < y_1 < y_2 \\ 1, & \text{if } y_2 \leq y_1 \end{cases},$$

and the conditional distribution function of Y_2 given $Y_1 = y_1$ is

$$F(y_2|y_1) = \begin{cases} 0, & \text{if } y_2 \leq y_1 \\ y_2/(1 - y_1), & \text{if } y_1 < y_2 < 1 \\ 1, & \text{if } y_2 \geq 1 \end{cases}.$$

Figure 2.4.1 provides graphs of the marginal and joint p.d.f.s, and Figure 2.4.2 provides graphs of the marginal and joint c.d.f.s.

This section closes with a theorem that is often useful in breaking down the joint p.f. of a large number of random variables into more manageable components. This result parallels Theorem 2.1.4 in the case of events.

Theorem 2.4.4 Let Y_n $(n = 1, 2, \ldots, N)$ have joint p.f. $f(y_1, \ldots, y_N)$. Then provided all conditional p.f.s exist:

$$f(y_1, \ldots, y_N) = f(y_1)f(y_2|y_1)f(y_3|y_1, y_2)\ldots f(y_N|y_1, \ldots, y_{N-1}). \qquad (2.4.12)$$

Exercises

2.4.1 Let $F(x, y)$ be the distribution function of X and Y. Show that

$$P(a < X \leq b, c < Y \leq d) = F(b, d) - F(b, c) - F(a, d) + F(a, c)$$

for all real numbers $a < b, c < d$.

2.4.2 Let $f(y_1, y_2, y_3) \equiv \exp[-(y_1 + y_2 + y_3)]$, $0 < y_n < \infty$ $(n = 1, 2, 3)$, zero otherwise, be the p.d.f. of Y_1, Y_2, Y_3.

(a) Find $F(y_1, y_2, y_3)$.

(b) Find $P(Y_1 < Y_2 < Y_3)$.

(c) Find $P(Y_1 = Y_2 < Y_3)$.

2.4.3 Consider the p.d.f. $f(x, y) = (r - 1)(r - 2)(1 + x + y)^{-r}$, $x > 0$, $y > 0$, zero elsewhere, where $r > 2$. Find

(a) $F(x, y)$

(b) $f(x)$

(c) $F(x)$

(d) $f(y|x)$

2.4.4 Consider the p.d.f. $f(x, y) = 3x$, $0 < y < x$, $0 < x < 1$, zero elsewhere.

(a) Verify that $f(x, y)$ is a valid joint p.d.f.

(b) Find $f(x|y)$.

2.4.5 In general, two random variables can each have the same marginal distribution, even when their joint distributions are different. Verify this for

$$f(y_1, y_2) = \begin{Bmatrix} 1, & \text{if } 0 < y_1 < 1, 0 < y_2 < 1 \\ 0, & \text{otherwise} \end{Bmatrix},$$

and

$$h(y_1, y_2) = \begin{Bmatrix} 1 + \alpha(2y_1 - 1)(2y_2 - 1), & \text{if } 0 < y_1 < 1, 0 < y_2 < 1 \\ 0, & \text{otherwise} \end{Bmatrix},$$

where $-1 \leq \alpha \leq 1$. Note, however, that the Cramér-Wold Theorem implies that a multivariate distribution can be uniquely defined by specifying the distribution of *all* linear combinations of its component random variables.

2.4.6 Consider the p.d.f.

$$f(x, y) = \begin{Bmatrix} 15x^2y, & \text{if } 0 < x < y \text{ and } 0 < y < 1 \\ 0, & \text{otherwise} \end{Bmatrix}.$$

(a) Find $f(x)$.

(b) Find $P(X > .75)$.

2.4.7 Consider the joint p.d.f.

$$f(y_1, y_2) = [2\pi(1-\alpha)]^{-1}\exp[-\tfrac{1}{2}(y_1^2 + 2\alpha y_1 y_2 + y_2^2)]$$

for $-\infty < y_i < \infty$ $(i = 1, 2)$ and $-1 < \alpha < 1$.

(a) Find the marginal p.d.f. of y_i $(i = 1, 2)$.

(b) Find the conditional p.d.f.s $f(y_1|y_2)$ and $f(y_2|y_1)$.

2.4.8 Consider the joint p.d.f. $(\beta, \theta > 0)$

$$f(x, y) = \frac{\theta\exp[-(\beta+\theta)y](\beta y)^x}{x!}, \quad y \geq 0, \quad x = 0, 1, 2, \ldots$$

(a) Show: $f(x) = \alpha(1-\alpha)^x$ $(x = 0, 1, 2, \ldots)$ for suitably defined α.

(b) Show: $f(y) = \theta\exp(-y)$ $y \geq 0$.

(c) Show: $f(y|x) = \dfrac{\lambda\exp(-\lambda y)(\lambda y)^x}{x!}$ $(y \geq 0)$ for suitably chosen λ.

(d) Show: $f(x|y) = \dfrac{\exp(-\beta y)(\beta y)^x}{x!}$ $(x = 0, 1, 2, \ldots)$.

(e) Show: $E(x|y) = \beta y$.

(f) Show: $E(y|x) = \delta x$ for suitably chosen δ.

2.4.9 Consider two random variables X and Y with joint c.d.f $F(x, y)$ and conditional c.d.f $F(y|x) = P(Y \leq y|x \leq X)$. Show:

$$F(x, y) = E_X[F(y|X)], \tag{2.4.13}$$

where $E_X[\cdot]$ denotes expectation with respect to X.

2.5 Stochastic Independence

In the preceding section, concepts discussed in Section 2.1 in terms of events were extended in an obvious fashion to random variables. For example, the definition of a conditional distribution (Definition 2.4.5) is based on the definition of the probability of an event conditional on the occurrence of another event (Definition 2.1.5). In this section, Definition 2.1.6 of independent events serves as a basis for the following definition of stochastically independent random variables.

Definition 2.5.1 Let $Y = [Y_1, Y_2, \ldots, Y_N]'$ be a N-dimensional vector of random variables with c.d.f. $F(y_1, \ldots, y_N)$ and p.f. $f(y_1, \ldots, y_n)$. Y_n $(n = 1, 2, \ldots, N)$ are defined to be *mutually stochastically (or statistically) independent* iff

$$F(y) = \prod_{n=1}^{N} F(y_n) \tag{2.5.1}$$

for all $y = [y_1, y_2, \ldots, y_N]' \in R^N$. Alternatively, a condition equivalent to (2.5.1) is

$$f(y) = \prod_{n=1}^{N} f(y_n), \tag{2.5.2}$$

where (2.5.2) is required to hold for all $y \in R^N$ in the case of continuous random variables, and to hold for all atoms of y of Y in the case of discrete random variables. Random variables that are not stochastically independent are said to be *stochastically dependent*. Often the word "stochastically" is omitted.

Examples of stochastically independent and dependent random variables, respectively, are given in the following examples.

Example 2.5.1 Consider two random variables Y_1 and Y_2 with joint p.d.f.

$$f(y_1, y_2) = \begin{Bmatrix} 12y_1y_2(1 - y_2), & \text{if } 0 < y_1 < 1 \text{ and } 0 < y_2 < 1 \\ 0, & \text{otherwise} \end{Bmatrix}.$$

It is easy to show that the marginal p.d.f.s are

$$f(y_1) = \begin{Bmatrix} 2y_1, & \text{if } 0 < y_1 < 1 \\ 0, & \text{otherwise} \end{Bmatrix},$$

$$f(y_2) = \begin{Bmatrix} 6y_2(1 - y_2), & \text{if } 0 < y_2 < 1 \\ 0, & \text{otherwise} \end{Bmatrix}.$$

Because $f(y_1, y_2) = f(y_1)f(y_2)$ for all y_1 and y_2, Y_1 and Y_2 are stochastically independent.

Example 2.5.2 Consider two random variables Y and X with joint p.d.f.

$$f(y, x) = \begin{Bmatrix} y + x, & \text{if } 0 \leq y \leq 1 \text{ and } 0 \leq x \leq 1 \\ 0, & \text{otherwise} \end{Bmatrix}.$$

The marginal p.d.f.s are

$$f(y) = \begin{Bmatrix} y + \tfrac{1}{2}, & \text{if } 0 \leq y \leq 1 \\ 0, & \text{otherwise} \end{Bmatrix},$$

$$f(x) = \begin{Bmatrix} x + \tfrac{1}{2}, & \text{if } 0 \leq x \leq 1 \\ 0, & \text{otherwise} \end{Bmatrix}.$$

Because $f_{Y,X}(0,0) = 0 \neq f_Y(0)f_X(0) = \tfrac{1}{4}$, Y and X are stochastically dependent.

As in the case of events, pairwise independence of random variables does not, in general, imply mutual independence. See Exercise 2.5.2 for an example.

Finally, it should be noted that independence is preserved under univariate transformations of random variables. Specifically, the following result can be easily derived.

Theorem 2.5.1 If Y_n $(n = 1, 2, \ldots, N)$ are independent random variables and $Z_n = g_n(Y_n)$ $(n = 1, 2, \ldots, N)$ are transformed variables, then Z_n $(n = 1, 2, \ldots, N)$ are also independent.

Proof Left to the reader.

Exercises

2.5.1 Let Y_1 and Y_2 have p.d.f.

$$f(y_1, y_2) = \begin{Bmatrix} 2\exp[-(y_1 + y_2)], & \text{if } 0 < y_1 < y_2 < \infty \\ 0, & \text{otherwise} \end{Bmatrix}.$$

Are Y_1 and Y_2 independent?

2.5.2 Let Y_1, Y_2, Y_3 have p.d.f.

$$f_Y(y) = \begin{Bmatrix} \frac{1}{4}, & \text{if } y \in [1,0,0]', [0,1,0]', [0,1,1]', [1,1,1]' \\ 0, & \text{otherwise} \end{Bmatrix}.$$

(a) Find the joint p.d.f. of Y_i and Y_j $(i \neq j)$.

(b) Are Y_i and Y_j $(i \neq j; i, j = 1, 2, 3)$ independent?

(c) Are Y_1, Y_2 and Y_3 independent?

2.5.3 Let Y_1 and Y_2 be discrete random variables with the following joint p.d.f.s. In each case determine whether the variables are independent.

(a) $$f(y_1, y_2) = \begin{Bmatrix} \dfrac{y_1^2 + y_2^2}{13}, & \text{if } y_1 = 0, 1, 2 \text{ and } y_2 = 0, 1 \\ 0, & \text{otherwise} \end{Bmatrix}.$$

(b) $$f(y_1, y_2) = \begin{Bmatrix} \dfrac{(y_1 + 1)(y_2 + 1)^2}{30}, & \text{if } y_1 = 0, 1, 2 \text{ and } y_2 = 0, 1 \\ 0, & \text{otherwise} \end{Bmatrix}.$$

(c) $$f(y_1, y_2) = \begin{Bmatrix} \dfrac{36}{121 y_1 y_2}, & \text{if } y_1 = 0, 1, 2 \text{ and } y_2 = 0, 1 \\ 0, & \text{otherwise} \end{Bmatrix}.$$

2.5.4 Let Y_1, Y_2, Y_3 have p.d.f.

$$f(y_1, y_2, y_3) = \begin{Bmatrix} \dfrac{1 + y_1 y_2 y_3}{8}, & \text{if } -1 \le y_n \le 1 \ (n = 1, 2, 3) \\ 0, & \text{otherwise} \end{Bmatrix}.$$

Are Y_n $(n = 1, 2, 3)$ pairwise independent? Mutually independent?

2.5.5 Let Y_1, Y_2, Y_3 have p.d.f.

$$f(y_1, y_2, y_3) = \begin{Bmatrix} (y_1 + y_2)\exp(-y_3), & \text{if } 0 < y_1 < 1, 0 < y_2 < 1, y_3 > 0 \\ 0, & \text{otherwise} \end{Bmatrix}.$$

Show each of the following.

(a) Y_1 and Y_3 are independent.

(b) Y_2 and Y_3 are independent.

(c) Y_1 and Y_2 are dependent.

(d) Y_1, Y_2 and Y_3 are not independent.

2.5.6 Consider Exercise 2.4.7. Under what conditions are Y_1 and Y_2 independent?

2.5.7 Suppose Y_1 and Y_2 are independent and identically distributed random variables each with p.d.f. $f(y) = \exp(-y)$ for $y > 0$, and $f(y) = 0$ otherwise. Define $Z = (Y_2 - 1)/Y_1$. Using the techniques of Section 4.4 it can be shown that $f(y_1|z = 0) = y_1\exp(-y_1)$ for $y_1 > 0$. Note: $Z = 0$ is equivalent to $Y_2 = 1$. Since Y_1 and Y_2 are independent, $f(y_1|y_2) = f(y_1) = \exp(-y_1)$ for $y_1 > 0$, and $f(y_1) = 0$ otherwise. The fact that this gives a different answer reflects the well known *Borel-Kolmogorov Paradox* (see DeGroot 1987, pp. 171–174; Kolmogorov 1950, pp. 50–51; and Walley 1991, pp. 330–333, 436–440). This paradox arises because it is not possible to define a conditional distribution in a meaningful manner for just a single event having probability zero. The Borel-Kolmogorov Paradox also illustrates that countably additive distributions may fail to be conglomerable for nondenumerable (uncountable) partitions (see Kadane et al. 1986, pp. 70–75).

2.5.8 Assume that among families with two children the four sex distributions are equally likely. Suppose you are introduced to one of the two children in such a family, and that the child is a girl. What is the conditional probability that the other child in this family is also a girl?

2.5.9 (Dawid 1979b). Let X, Y and Z be random variables such that *X and Y are conditionally independent given Z*, that is, $f(x, y|z) = f(x|z)\cdot f(y|z)$. Also suppose X and Z are conditionally independent given Y. Is X independent of $[Y, Z]$, that is, is $f(x, y, z) = f(x)f(y, z)$?

2.5.10 Prove Theorem 2.5.1.

2.6 Multivariate Mathematical Expectation

In Section 2.3 mathematical expectation for univariate random variables was introduced. This section extends this concept to N-dimensional random variables.

Definition 2.6.1 Let $Y = [Y_1, Y_2, \ldots, Y_N]'$ have p.f. $f(y_1, \ldots, y_N)$. The *expected value* of a function $g(\cdot)$ of the N-dimensional random variable Y, denoted $E[g(Y)]$ or $E_Y[g(Y)]$, is defined to be

$$E[g(Y)] = \sum_{y} g(y)f(y) = \sum_{y_1} \cdots \sum_{y_N} g(y_1, \ldots, y_N)f(y_1, \ldots, y_N), \tag{2.6.1}$$

if the random variable is discrete where the summation is over all possible values of y, and

$$E[g(Y)] \equiv \int_{-\infty}^{\infty} g(y)f(y)\,dy \equiv \int_{-\infty}^{\infty} \cdots \int_{-\infty}^{\infty} g(y)f(y)\,dy_1 \ldots dy_N, \tag{2.6.2}$$

if the random variable is continuous. In order for the expected value to be defined, it is understood that sum (2.6.1) and multiple integral (2.6.2) exist.

Properties of the expected value of functions of N-dimensional random variables can be easily derived analogous to Theorem 2.3.1. Here we mention only the following.

Theorem 2.6.1 Let Y be a N-dimensional random variable, let $g_j(Y)$ $(j = 1, 2, \ldots, J)$ be given functions, and let c_j $(j = 1, 2, \ldots, J)$ be given constants. Then

$$E\left[\sum_{j=1}^{J} c_j g_j(Y)\right] = \sum_{j=1}^{J} c_j E[g_j(Y)]. \tag{2.6.3}$$

Proof Consider the case of continuous random variables. Let

$$g(y) = \sum_{j=1}^{J} c_j g_j(y).$$

Then from (2.6.2) it follows:

$$\begin{aligned} E[g(Y)] &= \int_{-\infty}^{\infty} \left[\sum_{j=1}^{J} c_j g_j(y)\right] f(y)\,dy \\ &= \sum_{j=1}^{J} c_j \int_{-\infty}^{\infty} g_j(y) f(y)\,dy \\ &= \sum_{j=1}^{J} c_j E[g_j(Y)]. \end{aligned}$$

The discrete case follows in an analogous fashion.

Particular choices of $g(\cdot)$ commonly arise in practice and hence the following definitions are introduced.

Definition 2.6.2 Let $Y = [Y_1, Y_2]'$ and consider Definition 2.6.1. The *covariance* of Y_1 and Y_2, denoted σ_{12} or $\mathrm{Cov}(Y_1, Y_2)$, is defined to be

$$\sigma_{12} \equiv \mathrm{Cov}(Y_1, Y_2) \equiv E[(Y - \mu_1)(Y_2 - \mu_2)], \tag{2.6.4}$$

where $g(Y) = (Y_1 - \mu_1)(Y_2 - \mu_2)$ and $\mu_n \equiv E(Y_n)$ $(n = 1, 2)$. The *correlation coefficient* of Y_1 and Y_2, denoted ρ_{12} or $\rho(Y_1, Y_2)$, is defined by

$$\rho_{12} \equiv \rho(Y_1, Y_2) = \frac{\sigma_{12}}{\sigma_1 \sigma_2}, \tag{2.6.5}$$

where σ_n $(n = 1, 2)$ is the standard deviation of Y_n. In (2.6.5) σ_{12}, σ_1 and σ_2 are assumed to exist and it is also assumed that $\sigma_n > 0$ $(n = 1, 2)$.

Example 2.6.1 Reconsider the bivariate distribution in Example 2.4.2. Then it is straightforward to calculate the following moments: $E(Y_1) = \frac{1}{3}$, $E(Y_2) = \frac{2}{3}, E(Y_1^2) = 1/6, E(Y_2^2) = \frac{1}{2}$ and $E(Y_1 Y_2) = \frac{1}{4}$. These moments in turn imply: $\mathrm{Var}(Y_1) = \mathrm{Var}(Y_2) = 1/18$, $\mathrm{Cov}(Y_1, Y_2) = 1/36$ and $\rho = \rho(Y_1, Y_2) = \frac{1}{2}$.

Both the covariance and the correlation are measures of the *linear* relationship of Y_1 and Y_2. If $Y_1 - \mu_1$ and $Y_2 - \mu_2$ tend to have the same sign with high probability, then $\sigma_{12} > 0$; if $Y_1 - \mu_1$ and $Y_2 - \mu_2$ tend to have opposite signs with high probability, then $\sigma_{12} < 0$. The magnitude of σ_{12} does not have much meaning since it depends on the units of measurement of Y_1 and Y_2. In contrast ρ_{12} is a unit free measure, and it is shown in

Section 2.8 that $-1 \leq \rho_{12} \leq 1$. In passing it is important to note the following result (cf. Theorem 2.3.2e).

Theorem 2.6.2 Provided all quantities exist,

$$\mathrm{Cov}(Y_1, Y_2) = E(Y_1, Y_2) - \mu_1\mu_2. \tag{2.6.6}$$

Proof Using Theorem 2.6.1, it follows:

$$\begin{aligned}\mathrm{Cov}(Y_1, Y_2) &= E[(Y_1 - \mu_1)(Y_2 - \mu_2)] \\ &= E(Y_1 Y_2 - Y_1\mu_2 - \mu_1 Y_2 + \mu_1\mu_2) \\ &= E(Y_1 Y_2) - \mu_2 E(Y_1) - \mu_1 E(Y_2) + \mu_1\mu_2 \\ &= E(Y_1 Y_2) - \mu_1\mu_2.\end{aligned}$$

When the covariance between two random variables is zero then on the average they exhibit no *linear* relationship between each other. Zero covariance, or equivalently, zero correlation is of sufficient importance that we introduce the following terminology.

Definition 2.6.3 Random variables Y_1 and Y_2 are defined to be *uncorrelated* iff $\sigma_{12} = \rho_{12} = 0$ (assuming the expectation exists).

It is important to clarify the relationship between independent random variables and uncorrelated random variables. The following two theorems do so.

Theorem 2.6.3 If Y_1 and Y_2 are independent and $g_1(\cdot)$ and $g_2(\cdot)$ are two functions, each of a single argument, then

$$E[g_1(Y_1)g_2(Y_2)] = E[g_1(Y_1)]E[g_2(Y_2)]. \tag{2.6.7}$$

Proof First, consider the case of jointly continuous random variables:

$$\begin{aligned}E[g_1(Y_1)g_2(Y_2)] &= \int_{-\infty}^{\infty}\int_{-\infty}^{\infty} g_1(y_1)g_2(y_2)f_Y(y_1, y_2)\,dy_1\,dy_2 \\ &= \int_{-\infty}^{\infty}\int_{-\infty}^{\infty} g_1(y_1)g_2(y_2)f_1(y_1)f_2(y_2)\,dy_1\,dy_2 \\ &= \int_{-\infty}^{\infty} g_1(y_1)f_1(y_1)\,dy_1 \int_{-\infty}^{\infty} g_2(y_2)f_2(y_2)\,dy_2 \\ &= E[g_1(y_1)]E[g_2(y_2)]. \end{aligned} \tag{2.6.8}$$

The case of jointly discrete random variables follows analogously.

Theorem 2.6.4 If Y_1 and Y_2 are independent, then $\mathrm{Cov}(Y_1, Y_2) = 0$.

Proof Follows directly from Theorem 2.6.3 with $g_n(Y_n) = Y_n - \mu_n$ $(n = 1, 2)$.

It is very important to note that the converse of Theorem 2.6.4 is not always true, that is, $\text{Cov}(Y_1, Y_2) = 0$ does not necessarily imply that Y_1 and Y_2 are independent. (This is discussed in some detail in Section 2.7.) Zero correlation between Y_1 and Y_2 is equivalent to stating that every *linear* function of Y_1 is uncorrelated with every *linear* function of Y_2. Independence between Y_1 and Y_2 is equivalent to stating that *every* function of Y_1 with finite variance (not just linear functions) is uncorrelated with *every* function of Y_2 with finite variance.

In the N-dimensional case there can obviously be many means, variances, covariances and correlations. For notational convenience, these quantities are stacked into vector and matrix forms. Letting $Y \equiv [Y_1, Y_2, \ldots, Y_N]'$, the *mean of* Y is understood to refer to the vector of means:

$$\mu \equiv E(Y) = [E(Y_1), E(Y_2), \ldots, E(Y_N)]'. \tag{2.6.9}$$

Variances and covariances of the components of Y are arranged into the $N \times N$ *variance-covariance matrix* (or simply, *covariance matrix* or *variance matrix*):

$$\Sigma \equiv \text{Var}(Y) = E[(Y-\mu)(Y-\mu)'] = \begin{bmatrix} \sigma_{11} & \sigma_{12} & \cdots & \sigma_{1N} \\ \sigma_{12} & \sigma_{12} & \cdots & \sigma_{2N} \\ \vdots & \vdots & & \vdots \\ \sigma_{1N} & \sigma_{2N} & \cdots & \sigma_{NN} \end{bmatrix}. \tag{2.6.10}$$

The diagonal elements in (2.6.10) are the variance of the components of Y, i.e.,

$$\sigma_{nn} \equiv \text{Var}(Y_n) \text{ (also denoted } \sigma_n^2) \qquad (n = 1, 2, \ldots, N). \tag{2.6.11}$$

The off-diagonal elements in (2.6.10) are all the covariances of the components of Y:

$$\sigma_{ij} \equiv \text{Cov}(Y_i, Y_j) \qquad (i < j; j = 2, 3, \ldots, N). \tag{2.6.12}$$

Because $\text{Cov}(Y_i, Y_j) = \text{Cov}(Y_j, Y_i)$, the variance-covariance matrix is symmetric, as the notation in (2.6.10) suggests. There are $\frac{1}{2}N(N-1)$ covariances in (2.6.10). From Theorem 2.6.2 it follows immediately that (2.6.10) can also be written

$$\Sigma \equiv E(YY') - \mu\mu'. \tag{2.6.13}$$

The determinant $|\Sigma|$ is known as the *generalized variance* of Y.

Given the variance-covariance matrix, the so-called correlation matrix can be easily constructed. Let D be a diagonal $N \times N$ matrix (i.e., a $N \times N$ matrix with all off-diagonal elements equalling zero) with all diagonal elements equalling $+(\sigma_{nn})^{-1/2}$ $(n = 1, 2, \ldots, N)$. Then the *correlation matrix* is defined to be

$$\rho(Y) \equiv D\Sigma D = \begin{bmatrix} 1 & \rho_{12} & \cdots & \rho_{1N} \\ \rho_{12} & 1 & \cdots & \rho_{2N} \\ \vdots & \vdots & & \vdots \\ \rho_{1N} & \rho_{2N} & \cdots & 1 \end{bmatrix}. \tag{2.6.14}$$

Like variance-covariance matrix (2.6.10), correlation matrix (2.6.14) is symmetric.

Theorem 2.6.1 suggests that the operation of mathematical expectation is a linear operator. This means that it is particularly easy to develop rules for manipulating many matrix expressions. The following theorem is used repeatedly throughout this text.

Theorem 2.6.5 Let Y be a $N \times 1$ random vector with mean $\mu = E(Y)$ and covariance matrix $\Sigma = E[(Y - \mu)(Y - \mu)']$. Let A be a fixed $M \times N$ matrix, and define $X = AY$.

(a) $E(X) = A\mu$.

(b) $\text{Var}(X) = A\Sigma A'$.

Proof

(a) Let $a_m = [a_{m1}, \ldots, a_{mN}]'$ be row m of A, that is, $A = [a_1, \ldots, a_M]'$. Then

$$X_m = \sum_{n=1}^{N} a_{mn} Y_n \qquad (m = 1, 2, \ldots, M).$$

By Theorem 2.6.1 with $J = N$, $g_j(Y) = a_{mj} Y_j$ $(j = 1, 2, \ldots, M)$ and

$$E(X_m) = \sum_{n=1}^{N} a_{mn} E(Y_n) = a_m' \mu \qquad (m = 1, 2, \ldots, M).$$

Therefore, $E(X) = [a_1'\mu, \ldots, a_M'\mu]' = A\mu$.

(b)
$$\begin{aligned} \text{Var}(X) &= E\{[X - E(X)][X - E(X)]'\} \\ &= E\{[A(Y - \mu)][A(Y - \mu)]'\} \\ &= E\{A[(Y - \mu)(Y - \mu)'A']\} \\ &= A\{E[\{A(Y - \mu)(Y - \mu)'\}']\} \\ &= A\{A[E\{(Y - \mu)(Y - \mu)'\}]\}' = A\{A\Sigma\}' = A\Sigma A'. \end{aligned}$$

Often in econometrics the need arises to evaluate the expected value of a function of random variables *given* the value of some of the random variables. Such conditional expectations are defined as follows.

Definition 2.6.4 Let $Y = [Y_1, \ldots, Y_N]'$ be a N-dimensional random variable, let $g(Y)$ be a given (possibly a matrix) function, and let

$f(y_1,\ldots,y_J|y_{J+1},\ldots,y_N)$ be a given conditional probability function. If Y_n $(n = 1,2,\ldots,N)$ are discrete random variables, then the *conditional expectation* of $g(Y)$ given $Y_n = y_n$ $(n = J+1,\ldots,N)$, denoted $E[g(Y)Y_{J+1} = y_{J+1},\ldots,Y_N = y_N]$, is

$$E[g(Y)|Y_{J+1} = y_{J+1},\ldots,Y_N = y_N] = \sum_{y_1}\cdots\sum_{y_J} g(y_1,\ldots,y_N)f(y_1,\ldots,y_J|y_{J+1},\ldots,y_N), \tag{2.6.15}$$

where the summations are over all possible values of Y_j $(j = 1,2,\ldots,J)$. If Y_n $(n = 1,2,\ldots,N)$ are continuous random variables, then the *conditional expectation* of $g(Y)$, given $Y_n = y_n$ $(n = J+1,\ldots,N)$, is

$$E[g(Y)|Y_{J+1} = y_{J+1},\ldots,Y_N = y_N] = \int_{-\infty}^{\infty}\cdots\int_{-\infty}^{\infty} g(y_1,\ldots,y_N)f(y_1,\ldots,y_J|y_{J+1},\ldots,y_N)\,dy_1\ldots dy_J. \tag{2.6.16}$$

All expectations are, of course, assumed to exist.

The notation $E[g(Y)|Y_{J+1} = y_{J+1},\ldots,Y_N = y_N]$ is somewhat cumbersome and so it will often be shortened to $E[g(Y)|y_{J+1},\ldots,y_N)$. Because (2.6.16) depends on the conditional p.d.f. $f(y_1,\ldots,y_J|y_{J+1},\ldots,y_N)$, however, *it is important to remember that the random variables Y_j $(j = J+1,\ldots,N)$, and not just their realized values y_j $(j = J+1,\ldots,N)$, play a crucial role in Definition 2.6.4.*

Conditional expectation admits many properties similar to those for unconditional expectation. Some such properties are given in the following two theorems.

Theorem 2.6.6 Let $Y = [Y_1,\ldots,Y_N]'$ be a N-dimensional random variable, and let $g_j(Y_1,\ldots,Y_N)$ $(j = 1,2)$ be functions for which the expectations below exist. Then

$$E[g_1(Y_1,\ldots,Y_N) + g_2(Y_1,\ldots,Y_N)|y_{J+1},\ldots,y_N] = E[g_1(Y_1,\ldots,Y_N)|y_{J+1},\ldots,y_N] + E[g_2(Y_1,\ldots,Y_N)|y_{J+1},\ldots,y_N]. \tag{2.6.17}$$

Proof Left to the reader.

Theorem 2.6.7 Let $Y = [Y_1,\ldots,Y_N]'$ be a N-dimensional random variable, and let $g_1(Y_1,\ldots,Y_N)$ and $g_2(y_{J+1},\ldots,y_N)$ be functions for which the required expectations exists. Then

$$E[g_1(Y_1,\ldots,Y_N)g_2(Y_{J+1},\ldots,Y_N)|y_{J+1},\ldots,y_N] = g_2(y_{J+1},\ldots,y_N)E[g_1(Y_1,\ldots,Y_N)|y_{J+1},\ldots,y_N]. \tag{2.6.18}$$

Proof Left to the reader.

The conditional expectation $E[g(Y)| Y_{J+1} = y_{J+1}, \ldots, Y_N = y_N]$ of Definition 2.6.4 is a non-stochastic function of y_j ($j = J + 1, \ldots, N$). A related concept is the random variable now defined. The righthand side of (2.6.15) and (2.6.16) define a random variable, denoted $E[g(Y)| Y_{J+1}, \ldots, Y_N]$, that is a function

$$h(Y_{J+1}, \ldots, Y_N) \equiv E[g(Y)| Y_{J+1}, \ldots, Y_N]. \tag{2.6.19}$$

of the conditioning variables. This random variable takes on realized values $E[g(Y)| Y_{J+1} = y_{J+1}, \ldots, Y_N = y_N]$. The question immediately arises: what is the expectation of $h(Y_{J+1}, \ldots, Y_N)$ with respect to Y_n ($n = J + 1, \ldots, N$)? The following theorem provides the answer. Extensions of Theorems 2.6.6 and 2.6.7 to cover the case of (2.6.19) are straightforward. This is not to suggest, however, that there are no subtleties involved. Rigorous discussion of conditional expectations can be found in advanced texts such as Billingsley (1986, pp. 466–476) or Dhrymes (1989, pp. 110–125).

Theorem 2.6.8 (Iterated Expectations) Let $Y = [Y_1, \ldots, Y_N]'$ be a N-dimensional random variable. Let $g(Y)$ be a given function for which *all the expectations below exist.* Then

$$E[g(Y)] = E_2\langle E_{1|2}[g(Y)| Y_{J+1}, \ldots, Y_N]\rangle, \tag{2.6.20}$$

where $E_{1|2}$ denotes expectation taken with respect to Y_n ($n = 1, 2, \ldots, J$) given Y_n ($n = J + 1, \ldots, N$), and E_2 denotes expectation with respect to Y_n ($n = J + 1, \ldots, N$). (To appreciate the importance of *all* expectations existing, see Exercise 2.6.6.)

Proof Using (2.6.17) and assuming continuous random variables,

$$\begin{aligned}
&E_2(E_{1|2}[g(Y)| Y_{J+1}, \ldots, Y_N]) \\
&\quad = E[h(Y_{J+1}, \ldots, Y_N)] \\
&= \int_{-\infty}^{\infty} \cdots \int_{-\infty}^{\infty} h(y_{J+1}, \ldots, y_N) f(y_{J+1}, \ldots, y_N)\, dy_{J+1} \ldots dy_N \\
&= \int_{-\infty}^{\infty} \cdots \int_{-\infty}^{\infty} \left[\int_{-\infty}^{\infty} \cdots \int_{-\infty}^{\infty} g(y_1, \ldots, y_N) f(y_1, \ldots, y_N | y_{J+1}, \ldots, y_N) \right. \\
&\quad \left. \times\, dy_1 \ldots dy_J \right] f(y_{J+1}, \ldots, y_N)\, dy_{J+1} \ldots dy_N \\
&= \int_{-\infty}^{\infty} \cdots \int_{-\infty}^{\infty} g(y_1, \ldots, y_N) f(y_1, \ldots, y_N)\, dy_1 \ldots dy_N \\
&= E[g(Y)].
\end{aligned}$$

Cases in which $g(y) = [Y_1, \ldots, Y_J]'$ and $E[g(Y)| Y_{J+1}, \ldots, Y_N]$ do not depend on Y_n ($n = J + 1, \ldots, N$) warrant special attention, and are discussed in detail in Section 2.7.

Finally, we can use the concept of expected value contained in Definition 2.6.1 to extend the notion of a moment generating function in Definition 2.3.3 to include cases involving more than one random variable.

Definition 2.6.5 The *(joint) moment generating function* of $Y = [Y_1, Y_2, \ldots, Y_N]'$ is

$$M_Y(t) = E[\exp(t'Y)] = E\left(\exp\left[\sum_{n=1}^{N} t_n Y_n\right]\right) \tag{2.6.21}$$

if the expectation exists for all values of $t \equiv [t_1, t_2, \ldots, t_N]'$ such that $-h < t_n < h$ for some $h > 0$ $(n = 1, 2, \ldots, N)$.

As in the case of a single random variable, the m.g.f. in (2.6.19), *if it exists*, completely determines the joint distribution of Y. The following theorem summarizes many useful properties of $M_Y(t)$. For notational simplicity only the bivariate case ($N = 2$) is considered, although generalization to the case $N > 2$ is straightforward.

Theorem 2.6.9 Let $Y = [Y_1, Y_2]'$ have joint m.g.f. $M_Y(t), t = [t_1, t_2]'$, and marginal m.g.f. $M_n(t_n) \equiv E[\exp(t_n Y_n)]$ $(n = 1, 2)$. Then

(a) $M_Y(t_1, 0) = M_1(t_1)$

(b) $M_Y(0, t_2) = M_2(t_2)$

(c) $E(Y_1^i Y_2^j] = \left[\dfrac{\partial^{i+j} M_Y(t_1, t_2)}{\partial t_1^i \partial t_2^j}\right]_{t_2 = t_2 = 0} \qquad (i \geq 0, j \geq 0)$

(d) Y_1 and Y_2 are stochastically independent iff $M_Y(t) = M_1(t_1)M_2(t_2)$ for all t.

Proof Left to the reader.

Example 2.6.2 Let Y_1, Y_2 be continuous random variables with joint p.d.f.

$$f(y_1, y_2) = \begin{cases} \exp(-y_2), & \text{if } 0 < y_1 < y_2 < \infty \\ 0, & \text{otherwise} \end{cases}.$$

It is straightforward to show that the m.g.f. of Y is $M_Y(t) = [(1 - t_1 - t_2) \times (1 - t_2)]^{-1}$ for $t_1 + t_2 < 1$ and $t_2 < 1$. Furthermore, (a) and (b) in Theorem 2.6.9 imply, respectively, that $M_1(t_1) = (1 - t_1)^{-1}$ for $t_1 < 1$ and $M_2(t_2) = (1 - t_2)^{-2}$ for $t_2 < 1$. Using Theorem 2.6.9(c) it is straightforward to show: $E(Y_1) = 1, E(Y_2) = 2, \text{Var}(Y_1) = 2$ and $\text{Cov}(Y_1, Y_2) = 1$. Finally, because $M_Y(t) \neq M_1(t_1)M_2(t_2)$ for all t, Theorem 2.6.9(d) implies Y_1 and Y_2 are dependent.

Exercises

2.6.1 Let Y_1 and Y_2 be random variables with the same variance. Show that $Y_1 + Y_2$ and $Y_1 - Y_2$ are uncorrelated.

2.6.2 Let Y_1 and Y_2 be discrete binary random variables such that $P(Y_1 = i, Y_2 = j) = p_{ij}$ for $i, j = 0, 1$. Prove: Y_1 and Y_2 are independent iff $\text{Cov}(Y_1, Y_2) = 0$.

2.6.3 Let Y be a random variable with a symmetric p.d.f. $f(\cdot)$, around zero [i.e., $f(y) = f(-y)$], and let $E(Y) = 0$. Show that $\text{Cov}(Y, Y^2) = 0$.

2.6.4 Use Theorem 2.6.5 to prove:

$$\begin{aligned}&\text{Cov}[\alpha_0 + \alpha_1 Y_1 + \alpha_2 Y_2, \beta_0 + \beta_1 Y_1 + \beta_2 Y_2]\\ &\quad = \alpha_1\beta_1 \text{Var}(Y_1) + \alpha_2\beta_2 \text{Var}(Y_2) + (\alpha_1\beta_2 + \alpha_2\beta_1)\text{Cov}(Y_1, Y_2),\end{aligned} \tag{2.6.22}$$

where Y_1 and Y_2 are random variables, and the αs and βs are constants.

2.6.5 Let Y_1 and Y_2 have bivariate p.d.f.

$$f(y) = \begin{Bmatrix} 1, & \text{if } |y_1| < y_2 \text{ and } 0 < y_2 < 1 \\ 0, & \text{otherwise} \end{Bmatrix}.$$

(a) Show that $f(y)$ is a valid p.d.f.

(b) Are Y_1 and Y_2 independent?

(c) Are Y_1 and Y_2 uncorrelated?

2.6.6 Let X and Y be random variables such that the marginal p.d.f. of X is

$$f(x) = \begin{Bmatrix} (2x)^{-1/2}\exp(-\tfrac{1}{2}x), & \text{if } x > 0 \\ 0, & \text{if } x \le 0 \end{Bmatrix},$$

and the conditional p.d.f. of Y given $X = x$ is $f(y|x) = (2\pi)^{-1/2}x^{1/2}\exp(-xy^2/2)$ for $-\infty < y < \infty$. Show that $E(Y|x) = 0$ and hence that $E[E(Y|x)] = 0$, but that $E(Y)$ does not exist.

2.6.7 Prove each of the following.

(a) Let Y_n $(n = 1, 2, \ldots, N)$ be random variables, and let a_n $(n = 1, 2, \ldots, N)$ be constants. Then

$$\text{Var}\left(\sum_{n=1}^{N} a_n Y_n\right) = \sum_{n=1}^{N} a_n^2 \text{Var}(Y_n) + 2\sum_{i=1}^{N}\sum_{j=i+1}^{N} a_i a_j \text{Cov}(Y_i, Y_j). \tag{2.6.23}$$

(b) $\text{Var}(Y_1 \pm Y_2) = \text{Var}(Y_1) + \text{Var}(Y_2) \pm 2\text{Cov}(Y_1, Y_2)$.

(c) If Y_1 and Y_2 are independent random variables, then

$$\text{Var}(Y_1 Y_2) = \mu_2^2 \text{Var}(Y_1) + \mu_1^2 \text{Var}(Y_2) + \text{Var}(Y_1)\text{Var}(Y_2). \tag{2.6.24}$$

2.6.8 Let Y be a $N \times 1$ random variable with mean μ and variance Σ. Y is a *degenerate* iff there exists a $N \times N$ non-zero matrix R such that

$$R[Y - \mu] = 0_N \tag{2.6.25}$$

for all values of Y. Show that (2.6.25) is equivalent to $R\Sigma = 0$.

2.6.9 Let Y_n $(n = 1, 2, 3)$ be random variables with finite second moments. Given the correlations ρ_{12} and ρ_{23}, show [see *IMS Bulletin* (1990, pp. 213–215)]:

$$\rho_{12}\sigma_{23} - [(1 - \rho_{12}^2)(1 - \rho_{23}^2)]^{1/2} \le \rho_{13} \le \rho_{12}\rho_{23} + [(1 - \rho_{12}^2)(1 - \rho_{23}^2)]^{1/2}. \tag{2.6.26}$$

2.6.10 Let Y be a $T \times 1$ vector such that $E(Y) = \mu$ and $\text{Var}(Y) = \Sigma$. Also let A be a $T \times T$ matrix of constants and let c be a $T \times 1$ vector of constants. Show:

(a) $E(Y'AY) = \text{tr}(A\Sigma) + \mu' A\mu$

(b) $E[(Y - c)'A(Y - c)] = \text{tr}(A\Sigma) + (\mu - c)'A(\mu - c)$

2.6.11 Let Y_t $(t = 1, 2, \ldots, T)$ be independent and identically distributed random variables with $E(Y_t) = \mu$ and $\text{Var}(Y_t) = \sigma^2$ for $t = 1, 2, \ldots, T$. Define $Q \equiv (Y_1 - Y_2)^2 + (Y_2 - Y_3)^2 + \cdots + (Y_{T-1} - Y_T)^2$. Show $E(Q) = 2(T-1)\sigma^2$.

2.6.12 Verify all the moments reported in Example 2.6.1.

2.6.13 Show: $\text{Cov}(Y_1, Y_2) = E[(Y_1 - \mu_1)Y_2] = E[Y_1(Y_2 - \mu_2)]$.

2.6.14 Let U, X and Y be random variables such that $\text{Median}(U) = \text{Median}(U|X) = 0$, and define:

$$Y = \begin{Bmatrix} -1, & \text{if } U < 0 \\ 0, & \text{if } U = 0 \\ 1, & \text{if } U > 0 \end{Bmatrix}.$$

Find $\text{Cov}(X, Y)$.

2.6.15 Show: $\text{Cov}(X, Y) = \text{Cov}[X, E(Y|X)]$.

2.6.16 Show: $\text{Cov}(X, Y) = 0$ implies $E_Z[\text{Cov}(X, Y|Z)] = -\text{Cov}[E(X|Z), E(Y|Z)]$.

2.7 Population Regression and Partial Correlation

Some may wish to postpone reading this section until getting to Chapter 9's discussion of regression analysis. I recommend covering it now because it involves only the concepts discussed so far and a little matrix algebra, which, in any case, will be introduced in Chapter 3. The rewards are primarily four-fold: (i) Algebraic properties of the multivariate expectation operation discussed in the preceding section are developed and reinforced, (ii) the types of regressions implied by numerous multivariate distributions discussed in Chapter 3 serve as a valuable distinguishing characteristic for these distributions, (iii) a population counterpart is presented for the estimation discussion of Chapter 9, and (iv) prediction is introduced where it belongs, logically prior to estimation and hypothesis testing.

For some mysterious reason discussion of population regression models and their properties has largely vanished from econometrics textbooks. Some researchers (e.g., Kiviet and Ridder 1987) would seem to nod approvingly. Notable exceptions are Goldberger (1968, 1991).

Often in econometrics the need arises to evaluate the expected value of a function of random variables *given* the value of some of the random variables. Such conditional expectations were defined in Definition 2.6.4. Two particular choices for $g(\cdot)$ in Definition 2.6.4 that commonly occur in practice are given in the following definition. In order to coincide with later discussion, the notation in this section is slightly different than in Section 2.6: Here we work in terms of a $K \times 1$ vector $Z = [Y, X']'$, where X is a $(K - 1) \times 1$ vector. Throughout this section all expectations are assumed to exist.

Definition 2.7.1 The *conditional mean* of Y given $X = x$, denoted $E(Y|X = x) = E_{Y|X=x}(Y)$, is the mean of the conditional distribution of Y given $X = x$. The random variable $E(Y|X)$ is commonly called the *popula-*

tion regression function (or *conditional expectation function*) of Y given X. A graph of $E(Y|X)$ versus $X = x$ is the *population regression curve* of Y on X. The *conditional variance* of Y given $X = x$, $\mathrm{Var}(Y|X = x) = E_{Y|x}[\{Y - E(Y|X = x)\}^2]$, is the variance of the conditional distribution of Y given $X = x$, and measures the expected squared deviations of Y from $E(Y|X = x)$. The random variable $\mathrm{Var}(Y|X)$ is the *conditional variance function* of Y given X. Sometimes the shorthand notation $E(Y|x)$ and $\mathrm{Var}(Y|x)$ is used for $E(Y|X = x)$ and $\mathrm{Var}(Y|X = x)$, respectively.

The relationship between $E(Y|X)$ and $E(Y)$ was described in the Iterated Expectations Theorem (Theorem 2.6.8), that is, the random variable $E(Y|X)$ has mean $E(Y)$. The relationship between $\mathrm{Var}(Y|X)$ and $\mathrm{Var}(Y)$ is discussed later in this section.

Regression functions are a primary topic of interest in econometrics. The concepts introduced in Definition 2.7.1 provide the population counterparts that are the goals of the estimation and inference methods discussed in Chapter 8. These concepts are illustrated in the following example. See Goldberger (1991, Chapter 5) for a valuable alternative treatment of material contained in this section.

Example 2.7.1 Consider Example 2.5.2. The conditional density of Y, given $X = x$, is for $0 \le x \le 1$. Hence

$$f(y|x) = \begin{Bmatrix} \dfrac{y + x}{x + \frac{1}{2}}, & \text{if } 0 \le y \le 1 \\ 0, & \text{otherwise} \end{Bmatrix}$$

$$E(Y|X = x) = \int_0^1 y\left[\frac{y + x}{x + \frac{1}{2}}\right]dy = \left[\frac{2y^3 + 3xy^2}{6x + 3}\right]_0^1 = \frac{2 + 3x}{3 + 6x}, \tag{2.7.1}$$

and analogous to Theorem 2.3.1(e),

$$\begin{aligned} \mathrm{Var}(Y|X = x) &= E(Y^2|X = x) - [E(Y|X = x)]^2 \\ &= \int_0^1 y^2\left[\frac{y + x}{x + \frac{1}{2}}\right]dy - \left[\frac{2 + 3x}{3 + 6x}\right]^2 \\ &= \frac{(1 + x)(1 + 12x)}{18(1 + 2x)^2}. \end{aligned} \tag{2.7.2}$$

Regression function (2.7.1) links the expected valued of Y to conditioning on $X = x$. Conditional variance (2.7.2) describes variability of Y around its conditional mean (2.7.1), given $X = x$. In the present case both (2.7.1) and (2.7.2) are nonlinear functions of the conditioning variable x. Chapter 9 considers the case in which the regression function is linear in x and any unknown quantities (i.e., parameters), and in which the conditional variance is an unknown constant (i.e., does not vary with x). Linear regressions play a sufficiently important role in econometrics that the following theorem is offered now linking the parameters of a linear regression to population moments. Examples of joint distributions for which such linear regressions hold are provided in Section 3.4.

Theorem 2.7.1 Let $Z = [Y, X']'$ be a $K \times 1$ vector with mean $\mu = [\mu_Y, \mu_X']'$ and nonsingular covariance matrix

$$\mathrm{Var}(Z) = \begin{bmatrix} \mathrm{Var}(Y) & \mathrm{Cov}(Y, X') \\ \mathrm{Cov}(X, Y) & \mathrm{Var}(X) \end{bmatrix} = \begin{bmatrix} \sigma_{YY} & \sigma_{XY}' \\ \sigma_{XY} & \Sigma_{XX} \end{bmatrix}. \tag{2.7.3}$$

Suppose $E(Y|X) = \alpha + X'\beta$. Then

$$\beta = \Sigma_{XX}^{-1}\sigma_{XY}, \tag{2.7.4}$$

$$\alpha = \mu_Y - \mu_x'\beta. \tag{2.7.5}$$

Proof $E(Y) = E_X[E(Y|X)] = E_X[\alpha + X'\beta] = \alpha + \mu_X'\beta$, and hence (2.7.5) follows immediately. Also, using Definition 2.6.2 and Theorem 2.6.8:

$$\begin{aligned} \sigma_{XY} = \mathrm{Cov}(X, Y) &= E_X E_{Y|X}[(X - \mu_X)(Y - \mu_Y)] \\ &= E_X[(X - \mu_X)(\alpha + X'\beta - \mu_Y)] \\ &= E_X[(X - \mu_X)(X - \mu_X)'\beta] \\ &= \Sigma_{XX}\beta. \end{aligned} \tag{2.7.6}$$

Therefore, (2.7.4) follows directly from (2.7.6) and the assumed nonsingularity of Σ_{xx}.

One explanation for the popularity of regression functions lies in their properties in conditional prediction. Suppose a researcher wishes to predict Y, given X, using a general function $g(X)$ of the conditioning variables. What function $g(\cdot)$ should the researcher use? The answer, of course, depends on the criteria employed to judge the quality of predictions. One popular criteria is: Choose $g(\cdot)$ so as to minimize the expected squared error of prediction. The following theorem shows that this criterion implies that the population regression function is in fact the optimal function.

Theorem 2.7.2 Let Y be a random variable and X a random vector such that $E(Y|X)$ and $E(\varepsilon^2)$ exist, where $\varepsilon \equiv Y - g(X)$ and $g(\cdot)$ is an arbitrary function. Then $E(\varepsilon^2) = E_{Y,X}(\varepsilon^2)$ is minimized by the choice $g(X) = E(Y|X)$.

Proof[20] Define $U \equiv Y - E(Y|X)$ and rewrite ε as $\varepsilon \equiv Y - g(X) = Y - E(Y|X) + E(Y|X) - g(X) = U + [E(Y|X) - g(X)]$. Then

20. The strategy of "adding zero in a judicious fashion," as in this proof, is an approach that is often followed in proofs. Another useful strategy that will be used in other proofs is "multiplying by unity in a judicious fashion."

$$E(\varepsilon^2) = E(U^2) + 2E\{U[E(Y|X) - g(X)]\} + E\{[E(Y|X) - g(X)]^2\}. \tag{2.7.7}$$

The middle term in (2.7.7) equals

$$\begin{aligned} &2E_X[E_{Y|X}\{U[E(Y|X) - g(X)]\}] \\ &\quad = 2E_X[\{E(U|X)\}\{E(Y|X) - g(X)\}] = 0, \end{aligned} \tag{2.7.8}$$

because

$$E(U|X) = E_{Y|X}[Y - E(Y|X)] = E(Y|X) - E(Y|X) = 0. \tag{2.7.9}$$

Hence,

$$E(\varepsilon^2) = E(U^2) + [E(Y|X) - g(X)]^2. \tag{2.7.10}$$

Because $g(X)$ appears only in the last term of (2.7.10) and this term is clearly non-negative, (2.7.10) is minimized by the choice $g(X) = E(Y|X)$ in which case $E(\varepsilon^2) = E(U^2)$.

As promised in Section 2.6, cases in which the population regression function $E(Y|X)$ does not depend on X warrant special attention. Such cases are discussed in the following definition and theorem.

Definition 2.7.2 Suppose $E(Y|X)$ exists. Y is said to be *mean-independent* of X iff $E(Y|X)$ does not depend on X.

Theorem 2.7.3 Y is mean-independent of X iff $E(Y|X) = E(Y)$.

Proof (a) Suppose Y is mean-independent of X. Then taking iterated expectations [see Theorem 2.6.8], $E(Y) = E_X[E(Y|X)] = E(Y|X)$. (b) If $E(Y|X) = E(Y)$, then $E(Y|X)$ does not depend on X. Therefore, Y is mean-independent of X.

Unlike independence and uncorrelatedness, which are symmetric relationships, mean-independence is asymmetric, that is, "Y is mean-independent of X" neither implies nor is implied by "X is mean-independent of Y." Also, mean-independence is a weaker condition than stochastic independence. If Y and X are independent, then $f(y|x) = f(y)$, and thus all the moments of Y which exist equal the conditional moments of Y given $X = x$. Mean-independence only requires equality of conditional and unconditional *first* moments. The relationships among stochastic independence, mean-independence, and uncorrelatedness are given in the following theorem.

Theorem 2.7.4 Let Y and X be random variables (possibly vectors).

(a) If Y and X are stochastically independent, then Y is mean-independent of X and X is mean-independent of Y.

(b) If Y is mean-independent of X, or if X is mean-independent of Y, then $\text{Cov}(Y, X) = 0$.

Proof For simplicity only the case of continuous variables is considered. The case of discrete random variables follows analogously.

(a) If Y and X are independent, then $f(y|x) = f(y)$. Thus

$$E(Y|X = x) = \int_{-\infty}^{\infty} yf(y|x)\,dy$$

$$= \int_{-\infty}^{\infty} yf(y)\,dy = E(Y).$$

Similarly, $E(X|Y) = E(X)$.

(b) Using Theorems 2.6.6 through 2.6.8,

$$\text{Cov}(X, Y) = E_X E_{Y|X}[(X - \mu_X)(Y - \mu_Y)']$$

$$= E_X\{(X - \mu_X)[E(Y|X) - \mu_Y]'\}. \tag{2.7.11}$$

If Y is mean-independent of X, then by Theorem 2.7.3, $E(Y|X) = \mu_Y$, and hence $\text{Cov}(X, Y) = 0$ follows immediately from (2.7.11). Similarly, $E(X|Y) = E(X)$ implies $\text{Cov}(X, Y) = 0$.

Theorem 2.7.4 suggests that mean-independence is "between" two other measures of "unrelatedness": independence and uncorrelatedness. This reinforces the result noted in Section 2.6 that uncorrelatedness does *not* imply independence.[21] Mean-independence plays an important role in regression analysis. In particular, deviations of Y from $E(Y|X)$ are mean-independent of the conditioning variables X.

Theorem 2.7.5 Suppose the regression function $E(Y|X)$ exists. Define the difference $U \equiv Y - E(Y|X)$.

(a) $E(U|X) = 0$

(b) U is mean-independent of X.

(c) $\text{Cov}(X, U) = 0$

(d) $E(U) = 0$

Proof (a) See (2.7.9). (b) Given (a), Definition 2.7.2 implies U is mean-independent of X. (c) See Theorem 2.7.4(b). (d) $E(U) = E_X[E(U|X)] = E_X(0) = 0$.

In cases where $E(Y|X)$ is not linear (e.g., Example 2.7.1), it may be of interest to consider a linear approximation to $E(Y|X)$. The following theorem states that the best linear approximation, in the sense of expected

21. To further reinforce these points, the following exercises are recommended. Exercise 2.7.4 illustrates that the converse of Theorem 2.7.4(a) is not necessarily true. Exerxcise 2.5.7–2.7.7 illustrate that the converse Theorem 2.7.4(b) also need not be true. Exercise 2.7.12 introduces the additional concept of "variance independence."

squared error, is in fact given by the intercept and slopes defined in Theorem 2.7.1.

Theorem 2.7.6 Let $V \equiv V(a,b) \equiv E(Y|X) - [a + X'b]$ measure the difference between $E(Y|X)$ and the approximation $a + X'b$, where a is scalar and b is $(K-1) \times 1$. The values of a and b that minimize $E(V^2)$ are given by α and β in (2.7.4) and (2.7.5).

Proof Proceeding as suggested in footnote 20, write

$$V(a,b) = W + Z(a,b), \tag{2.7.12}$$

where $W \equiv E(Y|X) - [\alpha + X'\beta]$ and $Z \equiv Z(a,b) \equiv [\alpha + X'\beta] - [a + X'b]$. Then

$$E(V^2) = E(W^2) + E(Z^2) \tag{2.7.13}$$

because $E(WZ) = 0$ [Exercise 2.7.15]. Since W does not depend on a and b, and $Z(\alpha, \beta) = 0$, it follows from (2.7.12) that $a = \alpha$ and $b = \beta$ minimize $E[\{V(a,b)\}^2]$.

Because the best linear approximation to $E(Y|X)$ in Theorem 2.7.6 is of wide interest, we shall adopt a particular notation for it [identical to Goldberger (1991)]: $E^*(Y|X) \equiv \alpha + X'\beta$. $E^*(Y|X)$ is also known as the *linear projection of* Y *on* X. One pragmatic reason for being interested in $E^*(Y|X)$ is its usefulness as a predictor of Y when X is available. As a result of the following theorem, $E^*(Y|X)$ also warrants the label *best linear predictor of* Y *given* X.

Theorem 2.7.7 Let $\varepsilon \equiv \varepsilon(a,b) \equiv Y - [a + X'b]$ measures the difference between Y and the approximation $a + X'b$, where a is scalar and b is $(K-1) \times 1$. Then the values of a and b that minimize $E(\varepsilon^2)$ are given by α and β in (2.7.4) and (2.7.5).

Proof Write $\varepsilon = U + V$, where U and $V = V(a,b)$ are defined in Theorems 2.7.5 and 2.7.6, respectively. Note that $E_{Y|X}(V) = V$, and by (2.7.9), $E(U|X) = 0$. Hence, $E(UV) = E_X E_{Y|X}(UV) = E_X[VE(U|X)] = 0$. Therefore, $E(\varepsilon^2) = E(U^2) + E(V^2)$, and by Theorem 2.7.6, $E(V^2)$ is minimized by (2.7.4) and (2.7.5).

In general, the difference $U^* \equiv Y - E^*(Y|X)$ is *not* mean-independent of X as is $U \equiv Y - E(Y|X)$ [recall Theorem 2.7.5(b)]. However, the following theorem shows that U^* has zero mean and is uncorrelated with X.

Theorem 2.7.8 Let $U^* \equiv Y - E^*(Y|X)$.

(a) $E(U^*) = 0$

(b) $\text{Cov}(U^*, X') = 0'_{K-1}$.

Proof

(a) $E(U^*) = E[Y - \alpha - X'\beta]$

$$= E(Y) - E(Y) + E[X - E(X)]'\beta = 0.$$

(b) $\text{Cov}(U^*, X') = E\{[Y - \alpha - X'\beta][X - E(X)]'\}$

$$= E\{[Y - E(Y) - \{X - E(X)\}'\beta][X - E(X)]'\}$$

$$= \sigma'_{XY} - \sigma'_{XY}\Sigma_{XX}^{-1}\Sigma_{XX} = 0.$$

Although the concept of correlation plays an important role in the study of regression analysis, and even more important concept when more than two variables are involved is that of *partial correlation*, which depends on $E^*(Y|X)$.

Definition 2.7.3 Let V and W denote random variables and let Z denote a $(K - 2) \times 1$ vector such that the joint covariance matrix

$$\Gamma = \begin{bmatrix} \gamma_{vv} & \gamma_{vw} & \gamma'_{vz} \\ \gamma_{vw} & \gamma_{ww} & \gamma'_{wz} \\ \gamma_{vz} & \gamma_{wz} & \Gamma_{zz} \end{bmatrix} \tag{2.7.14}$$

exists and is positive definite. Let μ_v, μ_w and μ_z denote the respective means. Also let $E^*(V|Z)$ denote the linear regression of V on Z defined in Theorem 2.7.6:

$$E^*(V|Z) = \mu_v + (Z - \mu_Z)'\Gamma_{zz}^{-1}\gamma_{vz}, \tag{2.7.15}$$

and correspondingly,

$$E^*(W|Z) = \mu_w + (Z - \mu_z)'\Gamma_{zz}^{-1}\gamma_{wz}. \tag{2.7.16}$$

Then the *population partial correlation between V and W, adjusted for Z*, denoted $\rho_{wv \cdot z}$, is

$$\rho_{wv \cdot z} \equiv \text{Corr}[V - E^*(V|Z), W - E^*(W|Z)]. \tag{2.7.17}$$

Yule (1897, 1907) introduced $\rho_{vw \cdot z}$ into the statistics literature, but referred to it as the *net correlation coefficient*. The term *partial correlation coefficient* was later introduced by Pearson (1920a). In words, $\rho_{vw \cdot z}$ is the simple correlation between the residuals from the linear regression of V on Z with the residuals from the linear regression of W on Z. Thus, $\rho_{vw \cdot z}$ measures the correlation between V and W after removing the linear effect of Z on both variables.[22]

The following two theorems give alternative expressions for calculating $\rho_{vw \cdot z}$.

22. The term "adjusted for" in Definition 2.7.3 is often replaced with "controlling for," "holding constant," "allowing or accounting for the influence of," "in the presence of," or "correcting for the influence of" without any change in meaning. As Lewis and Styan (1981, p. 57) note, Sverdrup (1967, p. 18) replaces $E^*(V|Z)$ and $E^*(W|Z)$ in (2.7.17) with $E(V|Z)$ and $E(W|Z)$. Unless these conditional means are in fact linear, this gives rise to an alternative definition of partial correlation.

Theorem 2.7.9 Consider Definition 2.7.3. Then

$$\rho_{vw\cdot z} = \frac{\gamma_{vw} - \gamma_{vz}'\Gamma_{zz}^{-1}\gamma_{wz}}{(\gamma_{vv} - \gamma_{vz}'\Gamma_{zz}^{-1}\gamma_{vz})^{1/2}(\gamma_{ww} - \gamma_{wz}'\Gamma_{zz}^{-1}\gamma_{wz})^{1/2}}. \tag{2.7.18}$$

Proof Noting that $E[V - E^*(V|Z)] = E[W - E^*(W|Z)] = 0$, it follows that

$$\begin{aligned}
\mathrm{Var}&[V - E^*(V|Z)] \\
&= E[\{V - \gamma_{vz}'\Gamma_{zz}^{-1}(Z - \mu_z)\}\{V - \gamma_{vz}'\Gamma_{zz}^{-1}(Z - \mu_z)\}'] \\
&= \gamma_{vv} - 2\gamma_{vz}'\Gamma_{zz}^{-1}\gamma_{vz} + \gamma_{vz}'\Gamma_{zz}^{-1}\gamma_{vz} \\
&= \gamma_{vv} - \gamma_{vz}'\Gamma_{zz}^{-1}\gamma_{vz}, \qquad (2.7.19)
\end{aligned}$$

$$\mathrm{Var}[W - E^*(W|Z)] = \gamma_{ww} - \gamma_{wz}'\Gamma_{zz}^{-1}\gamma_{wz}, \tag{2.7.20}$$

$$\begin{aligned}
\mathrm{Cov}&[V - E^*(V|Z), W - E^*(W|Z)] \\
&= E[\{V - \gamma_{vz}'\Gamma_{zz}^{-1}(Z - \mu_z)\}\{W - \gamma_{wz}'\Gamma_{zz}^{-1}(Z - \mu_z)\}'] \\
&= \gamma_{vw} - \gamma_{vz}'\Gamma_{zz}^{-1}\gamma_{wz}. \qquad (2.7.21)
\end{aligned}$$

Hence, from (2.7.17),

$$\rho_{vw\cdot z} = \frac{\gamma_{vw} - \gamma_{vz}'\Gamma_{zz}^{-1}\gamma_{wz}}{(\gamma_{vv} - \gamma_{vz}'\Gamma_{zz}^{-1}\gamma_{vz})^{1/2}(\gamma_{ww} - \gamma_{wz}'\Gamma_{zz}^{-1}\gamma_{wz})^{1/2}}. \tag{2.7.22}$$

Theorem 2.7.10 Consider Definition 2.7.3. Let

$$\tilde{P} = \begin{bmatrix} 1 & \rho_{vw} & \rho_{vz}' \\ \rho_{vw} & 1 & \rho_{wz}' \\ \rho_{vz}' & \rho_{wz}' & P_{zz} \end{bmatrix} \tag{2.7.23}$$

denote the correlation matrix corresponding to covariance matrix (2.7.14). Then

$$\rho_{vw\cdot z} = \frac{\rho_{vw} - \rho_{vz}'P_{zz}^{-1}\rho_{wz}}{(\rho_{vv} - \rho_{vz}'P_{zz}^{-1}\rho_{vz})^{1/2}(\rho_{ww} - \rho_{wz}'P_{zz}^{-1}\rho_{wz})^{1/2}}. \tag{2.7.24}$$

Proof The result (2.7.24) follows from dividing numerator and denominator of (2.7.18) by the square root of the product of (2.7.19) and (2.7.20).

The case $K = 3$ arises sufficiently often that it warrants singling out in the following corollary.

Corollary 2.7.11 Consider Theorem 2.7.10 with $K = 3, P_{zz} = 1$. Then:

$$\rho_{vw\cdot z} = \frac{\rho_{vw} - \rho_{vz}\rho_{wz}}{(1 - \rho_{vz}^2)^{1/2}(1 - \rho_{wz}^2)^{1/2}}. \tag{2.7.25}$$

Proof Follows directly from (2.7.24).

In general the partial correlation coefficient $\rho_{vw\cdot z}$ is *not* equal to the correlation between V and W in the conditional distribution of V and W

given Z. Such equality holds if $E(V|Z)$ and $E(W|Z)$ are both linear in Z and if $\text{Var}(V|Z)$ and $\text{Var}(W|Z)$ do not depend on Z, as in the case where V, W and Z have a multivariate normal distribution, but not in general. See Gokhale (1976), Lawrance (1976), and Lewis and Styan (1981) for more details.

The relevance of the preceding development of population regression functions and best linear predictors will be best appreciated in the study of regression analysis in Chapter 9. Goldberger (1991, p. 54) notes the ambiguous nature of a "linear relationship" such as

$$Y = a + X'b + \varepsilon. \tag{2.7.26}$$

Without further information, (2.7.26) is *vacuous*, that is, the components $a + Xb'$ and ε are not identified in any meaningful sense. If $E(\varepsilon) = 0$, then it follows that $E(Y) = a + [E(X)]'b$, and so, $\varepsilon = Y - E(Y)$. If in addition, $\text{Cov}(X, \varepsilon) = 0_{K-1}$, then it is straightforward to show that $a + X'b = E^*(Y|X)$ and $\varepsilon = Y - E^*(Y|X)$. Neither $E(\varepsilon) = 0$ nor $\text{Cov}(X, \varepsilon) = 0_{K-1}$, however, really amount to a substantive assumption. Rather they only serve to identify (2.7.26) as a decomposition of Y into its projection of Y given X and a deviation from this projection. In contrast, $E(\varepsilon|X) = 0$ is substantive since it implies that $E(Y|X)$ is linear and equal to $a + X'b$.

Before concluding this section, there remains one loose end: As promised in the beginning of this section, we now provide an important theorem relating conditional and unconditional variances.

Theorem 2.7.12 Let Y and X be random variables for which the expectations below exist. Then:

$$\text{Var}(Y) = E_X[\text{Var}(Y|X)] + \text{Var}_X[E(Y|X)]. \tag{2.7.27}$$

Proof Define $U \equiv Y - E(Y|X)$ and $V \equiv E(Y|X) - E(Y)$. Considering $Y - E(Y) = [Y - E(Y|X)] + [E(Y|X) - E(Y)] = U + V$, recalling $E_X[E(Y|X)] = E(Y)$ and noting $E_{Y|X}(UV) = 0$, it follows:

$$\begin{aligned}\text{Var}(Y) &= E_X E_{Y|X}[(U + V)(U + V)'] \\ &= E_X E_{Y|X}(UU') + E_X E_{Y|X}(VV') \\ &= E_X(\text{Var}(Y|X)] + E_X(VV') \\ &= E_X(\text{Var}(Y|X)] + \text{Var}_X[E(Y|X)].\end{aligned} \tag{2.7.28}$$

In summary, we have now arrived at the following point regarding minimizing expected squared prediction error. For the univariate case, Exercise 2.3.1(a) implies the best constant predictor of Y is the marginal mean $E(Y)$, yielding the predictive error variance $E\{[Y - E(Y)]^2\} = \text{Var}(Y)$. In the multivariate case, Theorem 2.7.2 implies that the conditional expectation function $E(Y|X)$ is the best predictor, and it yields a prediction error with variance no larger than in the univariate case [see (2.7.27)]: $E\{[Y - E(Y|X)]^2\} = E_X[\mathrm{Var}(Y|X)] = \mathrm{Var}(Y) - \mathrm{Var}[E(Y|X)]$. If attention focuses only on linear predictors in the multivariate case, then Theorem 2.7.7 implies that $E^*(Y|X) = \alpha + X'\beta$ is the best linear predictor, yielding the intermediate prediction error variance: $E\{[Y - E^*(Y|X)]^2\} = E\{(Y - E(Y) - E[X - E(X)]'\beta)^2\} = \mathrm{Var}(Y) - \beta'\Sigma_{XX}\beta$.

Exercises

2.7.1 Suppose $f(y|x)$ is defined by

$$f(y = -1|x = -1) = f(y = 3|x = -1) = \tfrac{1}{2}$$

$$f(y = 0|x = 0) = f(y = 4|x = 0) = \tfrac{1}{2}$$

$$f(y = 0|x = 1) = f(y = 2|x = 1) = \tfrac{1}{2}.$$

and that $f(x = -1) = f(x = 0) = f(x = 1) = \tfrac{1}{3}$.

(a) Find $E(Y|x = -1)$, $E(Y|x = 0)$ and $E(Y|x = 1)$.

(b) Find $E(YX|x = -1)$, $E(YX|x = 0)$ and $E(YX|x = 1)$.

(c) Find $E(X)$, $E(Y)$ and $E(YX)$.

(d) Is Y independent of X?

(e) Is Y mean-independent of X?

(f) Are Y and X uncorrelated?

2.7.2 Suppose that the joint p.d.f. of Y_1 and Y_2 is

$$f(y) = \begin{cases} \dfrac{3y_1 + y_2}{7}, & \text{if } 0 < y_1 < 2 \text{ and } 0 < y_2 < 1 \\ 0, & \text{otherwise} \end{cases}.$$

Verify that $f(y)$ is a legitimate bivariate density.

(a) Find the marginal density of Y_1.

(b) Find the conditional density of Y_2 given $Y_1 = y_1$.

(c) Find the regression curve $E(Y_2|Y_1 = y_1)$.

(d) Find $\mathrm{Var}(Y_2|Y_1 = y_1)$.

2.7.3 Let X, Y, and Z be random variables taking on only the values 0 and 1. Given the parameter β, $0 < \beta < 1$, suppose the joint p.m.f. is

$$f(x, y, z) = \begin{cases} \dfrac{\beta}{9}, & \text{if } (x, y, z) = (1, 1, 0) \\ \dfrac{2\beta}{9}, & \text{if } (x, y, z) \in \{(1, 0, 0), (0, 1, 0), (0, 0, 0)\} \\ \dfrac{4(1-\beta)}{9}, & \text{if } (x, y, z) = (1, 1, 1) \\ \dfrac{2(1-\beta)}{9}, & \text{if } (x, y, z) \in \{(1, 0, 1), (0, 1, 1)\} \\ \dfrac{1-\beta}{9}, & \text{if } (x, y, z) = (0, 0, 1) \end{cases}.$$

(a) Show $\rho_{XY} \neq 0$.

(b) Show $\mathrm{Corr}(X, Y|Z = z) = 0$ for all z.

(c) Show $\rho_{XY \cdot Z} \neq 0$ for $\beta \neq \frac{1}{2}$.

2.7.4 Consider the following four bivariate p.d.f.'s

(a) $$f(y_1, y_2) = \begin{Bmatrix} \frac{1}{2}, & \text{if } |y_1| + |y_2| \leq 1 \\ 0, & \text{otherwise} \end{Bmatrix}$$

(b) $$f(y_1, y_2) = \begin{Bmatrix} \frac{1}{4}(1 + [\cos(\pi y_1)][\cos(\pi y_2)]), & \text{if } |y_1| \leq 1, |y_2| \leq 1 \\ 0, & \text{otherwise} \end{Bmatrix}$$

In each case show:

(c) $$f(y_1, y_2) = \begin{Bmatrix} \frac{1}{8}(1 + 9y_1^2 y_2^2), & \text{if } |y_1| \leq 1 \text{ and } |y_2| \leq 1 \\ 0, & \text{otherwise} \end{Bmatrix}$$

(d) $$f(y_1, y_2) = \begin{Bmatrix} \frac{1}{8}, & \text{if } (y_1, y_2) \in \{(1, 1), (1, -1), (-1, 1), (-1, -1)\} \\ \frac{1}{2}, & \text{if } y_1 = y_2 = 0 \\ 0, & \text{otherwise} \end{Bmatrix}$$

(1) Y_1 is mean-independent of Y_2.

(2) Y_2 is mean-independent of Y_1.

(3) Y_1 and Y_2 are uncorrelated.

(4) Y_1 and Y_2 are *not* independent.

2.7.5 Let Y_1 be a random variable with p.d.f.

$$f(y_1) = \begin{Bmatrix} \frac{1}{3}, & \text{if } y_1 = -1, 0, 1 \\ 0, & \text{otherwise} \end{Bmatrix}.$$

Let $Y_2 = Y_1^2$. Answer each of the following:

(a) If Y_1 independent of Y_2?

(b) Is Y_1 mean-independent of Y_2?

(c) Is Y_2 mean-independent of Y_1?

(d) Are Y_1 and Y_2 uncorrelated?

2.7.6 Consider the bivariate p.d.f.:

(a) If Y_1 independent of Y_2?

(b) Is Y_1 mean-independent of Y_2?

$$f(y_1, y_2) = \begin{Bmatrix} 3y_1^2 - y_2^2, & \text{if } 0 < y_1 < 1 \text{ and } -y_1 < y_2 < y_1 \\ 0, & \text{otherwise} \end{Bmatrix}.$$

(c) Is Y_2 mean-independent of Y_1?

(d) Are Y_1 and Y_2 uncorrelated?

2.7.7 Repeat Exercise 2.7.6 for

$$f(y_1, y_2) = \begin{Bmatrix} \frac{1}{2}, & \text{if } y_1 = y_2 = 1 \\ \frac{1}{4}, & \text{if } y_1 = y_2 = 0 \\ \frac{1}{8}, & \text{if } (y_1, y_2) \in \{(1, -1), (-1, 1)\} \\ \frac{1}{2}, & \text{if } y_1 = y_2 = 0 \\ 0, & \text{otherwise} \end{Bmatrix}.$$

2.7.8 Repeat Exercise 2.7.6 for

$$f(y_1, y_2) = \begin{Bmatrix} \frac{3}{8}(y_1^2 + y_2^2), & \text{if } -1 < y_1 < 1 \text{ and } -1 < y_2 < 1 \\ 0, & \text{otherwise} \end{Bmatrix}.$$

2.7.9 Prove that if $E(Y_1 | Y_2 = y_2)$ is constant, then Y_1 is mean-independent of Y_2. Use this result to find $E(U)$, where $U \equiv Y_1 - E(Y_1 | Y_2 = y_2)$.

2.7.10 Consider Exercise 2.6.7(c). Does (2.6.24) still hold if the assumption of independence is weakened to only mutual mean-independence?

2.7.11 Verify each of the following:

(a) "Y mean-independent of X" does *not* imply "X is mean-independent of Y."

(b) If Y and X are independent and $E(X) = 0$, then $\text{Cov}(YX, Y) = 0$.

2.7.12 Y is *variance-independent* of X iff $\text{Var}(Y|X)$ is constant over X.

(a) Show: Y independent of X implies Y is variance-independent of X.

(b) Show: Y variance-independent of X does *not* imply $\text{Var}(Y|X) = \text{Var}(Y)$.

(c) Suppose $E(Y^r|X)$ is constant for $r \in \mathfrak{R}$. Does $E(Y^r|X) = E(Y^r)$?

2.7.13 Suppose Z_1, Z_2, and Z_3 are random variables with zero means, unit variances, $\text{Corr}(Z_1, Z_2) = \rho$ and $\text{Corr}(Z_1, Z_3) = \text{Corr}(Z_2, Z_3) = 0$. Define $X_1 = Z_1 + cZ_3$, $X_2 = Z_2 + cZ_3$ and $X_3 = Z_3$.

(a) Find $\rho_{12} = \text{Corr}(X_1, X_2)$.

(b) Find $\rho_{12 \cdot 3}$.

2.7.14 Using Example 2.7.1, demonstrate Theorem 2.7.6.

2.7.15 Using Exercises 2.6.13 and 2.7.11(a), show that the cross-product term omitted from (2.7.12) does in fact equal zero.

2.7.16 Suppose the bivariate distribution of X and Y is uniform over the region bounded by the ellipse $ax^2 + 2hxy + by^2 = c$, where $h \neq 0, h^2 < ab, a > 0$, and $b > 0$. Show that the regression of each variable on the other is linear and that the conditional variances are parabolas (Kendall and Stuart 1979, p. 394, Exercise 28.1).

2.7.17 Suppose the bivariate distribution of X and Y is uniform over the parallelogram bounded by the lines $x = 3(y - 1), x = 3(y + 1), x = y + 1$, and $x = y - 1$. Show that the regression of Y on X is linear, but that the regression of X on Y consists of sections of three straight lines joined together (Kendall and Stuart 1979, p. 394, Exercise 28.2).

2.7.18 (Generalization of Goldberger 1991, p. 57, Exercise 5.8) Let $E^{**}(Y|X) = X'\beta^{**}$ be the *best proportional predictor* of Y given X, where β^{**} is the constrained estimate of b in Theorem 2.7.7, which minimizes $E(\varepsilon^2)$ subject to $a = 0$.

(a) Show: $\beta^{**} = [E(XX')]^{-1}E(XY)$.

(b) Let $\varepsilon^{**} \equiv Y - X'\beta^{**}$. Find $E(\varepsilon^{**})$.

(c) Find $\text{Cov}(X, \varepsilon^{**})$.

(d) Find $E[(\varepsilon^{**})^2]$.

2.7.19 Let $R^2_{Y \cdot X}$ be the squared correlation between Y and $\alpha + X'\beta$, where α and β are given by (2.7.4) and (2.7.5). Show:

$$R^2_{Y \cdot X} = \frac{\beta' \Sigma_{XX} \beta}{\sigma_{YY}}. \tag{2.7.29}$$

2.7.20 Suppose Y is mean-independent of X. Let $Z = h(X)$ be a strictly increasing function of X. Is Y mean-independent of Z?

2.7.21 Let X and Y be random variables for which all expectations below exist.

(a) Suppose Y is mean-independent of X. Show: $E(X^r Y) = E(X^r)E(Y)$ for any $r \in \mathfrak{R}$.

(b) Suppose Y is mean-independent of X. Does $E(X^r Y^s) = E(X^r)E(Y^s)$ for any r, $s \in \mathfrak{R}$?

2.8 Inequalities

Lawrence Klein "If the Devil promised you a theorem in return for your immortal soul, would you accept the bargain?"

Harold Freeman "No. But I would for an inequality."

—Reported in Klein (1991)

This section presents some inequalities that are often useful in statistical proofs.

Theorem 2.8.1 (Markov's Inequality) Let Y be a random variable and consider a function $g(\cdot)$ such that $g(y) \geq 0$ for all $y \in R$. Assume that $E[g(Y)]$ exists. Then

$$P[g(Y) \geq c] \leq c^{-1}E[g(Y)], \qquad \text{for all } c > 0. \tag{2.8.1}$$

Proof Assume that Y is continuous random variable (the discrete case follows analogously) with p.d.f. $f(\cdot)$. Define $A_1 = \{y | g(y) \geq c\}$ and $A_2 = \{y | g(y) < c\}$. Then

$$\begin{aligned} E[g(Y)] &= \int_{A_1} g(y)f(y)\,dy + \int_{A_2} g(y)f(y)\,dy \\ &\geq \int_{A_1} g(y)f(y)\,dy \\ &\geq \int_{A_1} cf(y)\,dy \\ &= cP[g(Y) \geq c], \end{aligned}$$

and (2.8.1) follows immediately.

A well-known result that follows directly from Theorem 2.8.1 is the following. It will be used later in proving the *law of large numbers*.

Corollary (Chebyshev's Inequality) Let Y be a random variable with finite mean μ and variance σ^2. Then

$$P[|Y - \mu| \geq r\sigma] \leq r^{-2} \qquad \text{for all } r > 0. \tag{2.8.2}$$

Proof Put $g(y) = (y - \mu)^2$ and $c = r^2\sigma^2$ in Theorem 2.8.1.

Sometimes Chebyshev's inequality is stated in the equivalent form

$$P[|Y - \mu| < r\sigma] \geq 1 - r^{-2} \qquad \text{for all r} > 0. \tag{2.8.3}$$

In words, (2.8.3) says that the probability of Y falling within r standard deviations of its mean is at least $1 - r^{-2}$. Thus, for example, for *any* random variable with finite variance the probability of it falling within two standard deviations of its mean is at least $\frac{3}{4}$.

Chebyshev's inequality often provides bounds which are far from accurate, and in fact, useless for $0 < r \leq 1$. It cannot be improved without further assumptions about the distribution of the random variable, however, because there are distributions for which it holds with equality for some $r > 1$. See Exercise 2.8.3 for an example.

Another famous result is the following theorem.

Theorem 2.8.2 (Cauchy-Schwarz Inequality) If Y_n $(n = 1, 2)$ have finite second moments, then

$$[E(Y_1 Y_2)]^2 \leq E(Y_1^2) \cdot E(Y_2^2), \tag{2.8.4}$$

with equality holding if $\text{Prob}(Y_2 = cY_1) = 1$ for some constant c.

Proof The existence of $E(Y_n)$ $(n = 1, 2)$ and $E(Y_1 Y_2)$ follows from the existence of expectations $E(Y_n^2)$ $(n = 1, 2)$. Consider

$$h(t) \equiv E[(tY_1 - Y_2)^2] = E(Y_1^2)t^2 - 2tE(Y_1 Y_2) + E(Y_2^2) \geq 0.$$

If $h(t) > 0$, then its roots are not real numbers. This implies that the quantity under the square root sign in the familiar quadratic roots formula must be negative, and hence $[2E(Y_1 Y_2)]^2 - 4E(Y_1^2)E(Y_2^2) < 0$. Inequality (2.8.4) then follows directly. If $h(t_0) = 0$ for some t_0, then $E[(t_0 Y_1 - Y_2)^2] = 0$ which implies $\text{Prob}(t_0 Y_1 = Y_2) = 1$.

An immediate consequence of the Cauchy-Schwarz inequality is that ρ_{12}, the coefficient of correlation between Y_1 and Y_2 defined in (2.6.5), must satisfy

$$-1 \leq \rho_{12} \leq 1, \tag{2.8.5}$$

if $\sigma_n^2 > 0$ $(n = 1, 2)$. In addition it follows that the variance-covariance matrix

$$V(Y) = \begin{bmatrix} \sigma_1^2 & \sigma_{12} \\ \sigma_{12} & \sigma_2^2 \end{bmatrix} \tag{2.8.6}$$

defined in (2.6.9) is positive definite, unless $|\rho_{12}| = 1$, in which case (2.8.6) is positive semidefinite.

A generalization of the Cauchy-Schwarz inequality is now given.

Theorem 2.8.3 (Holder's Inequality) Let c and d be two real numbers such that $c > 1, d > 1$ and $c^{-1} + d^{-1} = 1$. Let Y_1 and Y_2 be two random variables such that $E(|Y_1|^c) < \infty$ and $E(|Y_2|^d) < \infty$. Then

$$E[|Y_1 Y_2|] \leq [E(|Y_1|^c]^{1/c} \cdot E[|Y_2|^d]^{1/d}. \tag{2.8.7}$$

Proof See Lukâcs (1975, p. 11). The Cauchy-Schwarz inequality corresponds to the case $c = d = 2$.

Mathematical expectation is a linear operator in the sense that the expectation of a linear function equals the linear function of the expectation. In general, such equality does not hold for nonlinear functions. Inequality information is, however, sometimes available.

Definition 2.8.1 A continuous function $g(\cdot)$ is defined to be *convex* iff for all $x, y \in R$ and $0 \leq \lambda \leq 1, g[\lambda x + (1 - \lambda)y] \leq \lambda g(x) + (1 - \lambda)g(y)$. If the inequality is strict, then $g(\cdot)$ is *strictly convex*. $g(\cdot)$ is *concave* iff $-g(x)$ is convex, and $g(\cdot)$ is *strictly concave* iff $-g(x)$ is strictly convex. Note: If $g(\cdot)$ is twice differentiable, then $g(\cdot)$ is convex iff its *Hessian* (i.e., the matrix of second-order partial derivatives) is positive semidefinite, and $g(\cdot)$ is concave iff its Hessian is negative semidefinite.

Theorem 2.8.4 (Jensen's Inequality) Let Y be a random variable and let $g(\cdot)$ be a convex function. If $E(Y)$ and $E[g(Y)]$ exist, then

$$E[g(Y)] \geq g[E(Y)]. \tag{2.8.8}$$

If $g(\cdot)$ is strictly convex, the inequality is strict unless Y is a constant with probability one.

Proof Lehmann (1983, p. 50).

Example 2.8.1 Because $g(y) = y^2$ is convex, Jensen's inequality implies $E(Y^2) \geq [E(Y)]^2$. Furthermore, it follows immediately that $\text{Var}(Y) = E(Y^2) - [E(Y)]^2 \geq 0$.

Example 2.8.2 Let Y be a nonconstant positive random variable with finite mean. Then Jensen's inequality implies:

(a) $E(Y^{-1}) > [E(Y)]^{-1}$,

(b) $E[ln(Y)] < ln[E(Y)]$.

Finally, the following sometimes useful theorems are stated without proof.

Theorem 2.8.5 Let Y be a positive random variable such that the required expectations exist.

(a) $E(Y^\alpha) \leq [E(Y)]^\alpha, \qquad 0 \leq \alpha \leq 1.$

(b) $E(Y^\alpha) \geq [E(Y)]^\alpha, \qquad \alpha \leq 0 \text{ or } \alpha \geq 1.$

(c) $h(\alpha) \equiv \dfrac{E(Y^{\alpha-1})}{E(Y^\alpha)}$ is a nonincreasing function of $\alpha > 0$.

Proof Left to the reader. Hint: use Jensen's inequality (2.8.8).

Theorem 2.8.6 Let Y and Z be independent random variables such that the required expectations exist.

(a) $E\left[\left(\dfrac{Y}{Z}\right)^{\alpha}\right] \geq \dfrac{E(Y^{\alpha})}{E(Z^{\alpha})}$ for all α.

(b) If $E(Y) = E(Z) = 0$ and $E(Z^{-1})$ exists, then $\operatorname{Var}\left(\dfrac{Y}{Z}\right) \geq \dfrac{\operatorname{Var}(Y)}{\operatorname{Var}(Z)}$.

Proof Mullen (1967).

Theorem 2.8.7 Suppose Y is a random variable with $E(|Y|^{\alpha}) < \infty$ for some $\alpha > 0$. Then $E[|Y|^{\beta}] < \infty$ for $0 \leq \beta \leq \alpha$.

Proof Laha and Rohatgi (1979, p. 33).

Theorem 2.8.8 (Minkowski Inequality) Let Y and Z be random variables such that $E(|Y|^{\alpha}) < \infty$ and $E(|Z|^{\alpha}) < \infty$ for some $1 \leq \alpha < \infty$. Then

$$[E(|Y + Z|^{\alpha})]^{1/\alpha} \leq [E(|Y|^{\alpha})]^{1/\alpha} + [E(|Z|^{\alpha})]^{1/\alpha}. \tag{2.8.9}$$

Proof See Lukâcs (1975, p. 11).

Theorem 2.8.9 Let Y be a random variable such that $E[|Y|^{\alpha}] < \infty$. Then

$$\operatorname*{Limit}_{y \to \infty} y^{\alpha} P(|Y| \geq y) = 0. \tag{2.8.10}$$

Proof Laha and Rohatgi (1979, pp. 36–37).

Theorem 2.8.10 (Information Inequality) Let $\Sigma_i a_i$ and $\Sigma_i b_i$ be convergent series of positive numbers such that $\Sigma_i a_i \ \Sigma_i b_i$. Then

$$\sum_{i=1}^{\infty} a_i \, ln\left(\frac{b_i}{a_i}\right) \leq 0, \tag{2.8.11}$$

and (2.8.11) is sharp unless $a_i = b_i$ $(i = 1, 2, 3, \ldots)$.

Proof Rao (1973, pp. 58–59).

Exercises

2.8.1 Let A and B be arbitrary events. Prove *Booles' inequality*: $P(A \cap B) \geq P(A) - P(B^c) = 1 - P(A^c) - P(B^c)$.

2.8.2 Let A, B, and C be events such that $A \cap B \subset C$. Prove $P(C^c) \leq P(A^c) + P(B^c)$.

2.8.3 Let Y be a discrete random variable such that $P(Y = -1) = \frac{1}{8}$, $P(Y = 0) = \frac{3}{4}$ and $P(Y = 1) = \frac{1}{8}$. Show that Chebyshev's inequality holds exactly for $r = 2$.

2.8.4 Consider Theorem 2.8.4. Show: if $g(\cdot)$ is concave, then $E[g(Y)] \leq g[E(Y)]$.

2.8.5 If $\mu = E(Y) < \infty$ and $g(y)$ is a nondecreasing function, then use Jensen's inequality to show:

$$E[g(Y)(Y - \mu)] \geq 0. \tag{2.8.12}$$

2.8.6 Let Y be a random variable and $g(y)$ and $h(y)$ functions such that $E[g(Y)], E[h(y)]$ and $E[g(Y)h(Y)]$ exist. See Casella and Berger 1990, p. 184), show:

(a) If $g(y)$ is a nondecreasing function and $h(y)$ is a nonincreasing function, then $E[g(Y)h(Y)] \leq \{E[g(Y)]\}\{E[h(Y)]\}$.

(b) If $g(y)$ and $h(y)$ are both nonincreasing or both nondecreasing functions, then $E[g(Y)h(Y)] \geq \{E[g(Y)]\}\{E[h(Y)]\}$.

2.8.7 Suppose y_t $(t = 1, 2, \ldots, T)$ are positive numbers. Define:

$$\text{Arithmetic mean: } \bar{y} = \frac{1}{T}\sum_{t=1}^{T} y_t, \tag{2.8.13}$$

$$\text{Geometric mean: } \bar{y}_G = \left[\prod_{t=1}^{T} y_t\right]^{1/T}, \tag{2.8.14}$$

$$\text{Harmonic mean: } \bar{y}_H = \left[\frac{1}{T}\sum_{t=1}^{T}\frac{1}{y_t}\right]^{-1}. \tag{2.8.15}$$

Use Jensen's inequality (Theorem 2.8.4) to show: $\bar{y}_H \leq \bar{y}_G \leq \bar{y}$.

2.8.8 Let Y_n $(n = 1, 2, \ldots, N)$ be jointly distributed with $E(Y_n) = \mu_n$ and $\text{Var}(Y_n) = \sigma_n^2$ $(n = 1, 2, \ldots, N)$. Define $A_n \equiv \{Y_n | Y_n - \mu_n| \leq N^{1/2} r \rho_n\}$, where $r > 0$. Prove the following *multivariate Chebyshev inequality*:

$$P(A_1 \cap A_2 \cap \cdots \cap A_N) \geq 1 - r^{-2}. \tag{2.8.16}$$

2.8.9 Use Jensen's inequality to prove *Liapounov's inequality*: if $E[|Y|^r]$ exists and $0 < s < r < \infty$, then

$$[E(|Y|^s)]^{1/s} \leq [E(|Y|^r)]^{1/r}. \tag{2.8.17}$$

2.8.10 Suppose the m.g.f. $M_Y(t)$ exists for a random variable Y. Show:

$$P(Y \geq c) \leq \exp(-ct) M_Y(t) \qquad \text{for } 0 < t < h < \infty. \tag{2.8.18}$$

3 Special Distributions

3.1 Introduction

A *parametric family* of probability functions is a collection of probability functions indexed by quantities called *parameters.* This chapter discusses several parametric families of probability functions: univariate discrete p.m.f.s in Section 3.2, univariate continuous p.d.f.s in Section 3.3, and multivariate p.f.s in Sections 3.4 and 3.5. In each case summary information (e.g., moments and m.g.f.s) are provided and examples of random experiments for which the defined parametric family might provide a reasonable model are included. Memorization of such summary information should *not* be the reader's first priority. *It is more important to get a grasp of the interrelationships among the distributions, and the types of experiments for which each may be appropriate.*

In this chapter the interpretation of the parameters is left aside. For now they are simply known quantities, and to emphasize this fact, they appear as arguments of p.f.s or c.d.f.s after a vertical line "|" indicating conditioning, for example, $f(y|\theta)$ where θ is a parameter. A researcher's attitude toward parameters when they are unknown, however, reflects the researcher's basic viewpoint toward probability. Is θ merely an index (i.e., a mathematical fiction), or is θ a "real" quantity? These matters are addressed in detail at the appropriate time, that is, when dealing with estimation and inference in later chapters.

Finally, it is useful to introduce terminology for two types of parameters that frequently arise in practice, especially in connection with continuous random variables.

Definition 3.1.1 Suppose the c.d.f. of Y is $F(y)$, and let θ and α be parameters such that $-\infty < \theta < \infty$ and $\alpha > 0$. If $X = Y + \theta$ has c.d.f. $F(x - \theta)$, then θ is a *location parameter* and the family of distributions $\{F(x - \theta)\}$ is a *location family.* If $X = \alpha Y$ has c.d.f $F(x/\alpha)$, then α is a *scale parameter* and the family of distributions $\{F(x/\alpha)\}$ is a *scale family.* Finally, if $X = \theta + \alpha Y$ has c.d.f $F[(x - \theta)/\alpha]$, then θ is a *location parameter,* α is a *scale parameter* and the family $\{F[(x - \theta/\alpha)\}$ is a *location-scale family.* If Y has density $f(y)$, then in the location-scale case the density of X is $\alpha^{-1}f[(x - \theta)/\alpha]$.

3.2 Discrete Univariate Distributions

Before discussing discrete univariate distributions, we review a few counting formulae and definitions.

Definition 3.2.1 If the elements of a set are aligned in a specific order, then such an arrangement is defined to be a *permutation* of the elements of the set.

Example 3.2.1 A permutation of the first three positive integers is 213 and is distinct from the permutation 123.

Theorem 3.2.1 The number of ways in which r distinct elements can be selected from a set of N elements, that is, the number of permutations of r distinct elements selected from a set of N elements is

$$N^{P_r} \equiv N(N-1)(N-2)\ldots(N-r+1) = \frac{N!}{(N-r)!}, \qquad (3.2.1)$$

where $N!$ denotes N *factorial* (the product of the first N positive integers).

Proof There are N choices for the first element, $N-1$ choices for the second element, ..., $N-r+1$ choices for the rth element. Multiplying these possibilities together gives the total number of possible permutations, and this is precisely what (3.2.1) does.

Theorem 3.2.2 The number of arrangements of N symbols of which r_1 are alike, r_2 others are alike, ..., and r_k others are alike is

$$\frac{N!}{r} \qquad (3.2.2)$$

Proof Left to the reader.

Example 3.2.2 The number of distinct arrangements of the seven letters in “success” is $7!/(3!\,2!\,1!\,1!) = 420$.

Permutations are concerned with the order in which the elements of subsets of r elements are selected from a set of N elements. Thus, there are the following six permutations of two of the first three letters of the alphabet:

ab ba
ac ca
bc cb

If we are interested only in the number of distinct subsets and not in the order in which their elements are arranged, however, each of the above three rows constitutes the permutations of the elements of one subset. The distinction between permutations and combinations is analogous to the distinction between sets and ordered pairs. In general we have the following definition and theorem.

Definition 3.2.2 The number of *combinations* of N elements taken r at a time, denoted ${}_N C_r$, is the number of ways in which distinct subsets of r elements can be selected from a set of N elements (without regard to order).

Theorem 3.2.3

$$
\begin{aligned}
{}_N C_r &\equiv \binom{N}{r} = \frac{N!}{(N-r)!\,r!} = \frac{{}_N P_r}{r!} \\
&= \frac{\text{number of ways } r \text{ distinct elements can be selected from a set of } N \text{ elements}}{\text{number of arrangements of } r \text{ distinct elements}}
\end{aligned}
\tag{3.2.3}
$$

Proof Left to the reader.

We begin our discussion of discrete univariate distributions with the simplest case.

Definition 3.2.3 A random variable Y has a *discrete uniform distribution* over the first N integers iff its p.m.f. is

$$
f_U(y|N) \equiv \begin{cases} N^{-1}, & \text{if } y = 1, 2, \ldots, N \\ 0, & \text{otherwise} \end{cases}, \tag{3.2.4}
$$

where N is a positive integer.

The moment generating function of the discrete uniform distribution, and some explicit moment formulae, are given in the following theorem.

Theorem 3.2.4 If Y has discrete uniform mass function (3.2.4), then its moment generating function (m.g.f.) is

$$
M(t) = E[\exp(tY)] = \frac{1}{N}\sum_{n=1}^{N}\exp(nt). \tag{3.2.5}
$$

Using (3.2.5) the following moments can be found:

$$
\mu = \frac{N+1}{2}, \tag{3.2.6}
$$

$$
\sigma^2 = \frac{N^2-1}{12}, \tag{3.2.7}
$$

$$
E(Y^3) = \frac{N(N+1)^2}{4}, \tag{3.2.8}
$$

$$
E(Y^4) = \frac{(N+1)(2N+1)(3N^2+3N-1)}{30}. \tag{3.2.9}
$$

Proof Moment generating function (3.2.5) follows immediately from Definition 2.3.3. Using (3.2.5) and (2.3.4), derivation of (3.2.6) through (3.2.9) is straightforward.

Example 3.2.3 Let Y be the number of dots on the top side of a fair six-sided die when it is rolled. Then Y has a uniform distribution with $N = 6$, $E(Y) = 3.5$.

Often in statistics we encounter a random experiment whose outcomes can be classified into two categories, called "success" and "failure". Such an experiment is called a *Bernoulli trial.* A Bernoulli distribution arises by considering a random variable Y defined to equal unity if a Bernoulli trial results in a "success", and zero if it results in a "failure."

Definition 3.2.4 A random variable Y has a *Bernoulli distribution* iff its p.m.f. is

$$f_b(y|\theta) = \begin{Bmatrix} \theta^y(1-\theta)^{1-y}, & \text{if } y = 0, 1 \\ 0, & \text{otherwise} \end{Bmatrix}, \tag{3.2.10}$$

where $0 \le \theta \le 1$.

The moment generating function of the Bernoulli distribution, and some explicit moment formulae, are given in the following theorem.

Theorem 3.2.5 If Y has a Bernoulli distribution, then its m.g.f. is

$$M(t) = \theta[\exp(t)] + 1 - \theta. \tag{3.2.11}$$

Using (3.2.11) the following moments can be found:

$$\mu = \theta, \tag{3.2.12}$$

$$\sigma^2 = \theta(1 - \theta), \tag{3.2.13}$$

$$E(Y^r) = \theta, \quad \text{for all } r. \tag{3.2.14}$$

Proof Moment generating function (3.2.11) follows directly from Definition 2.3.3. Using (3.2.11) and (2.3.4), derivation of (3.2.12) through (3.2.14) are straightforward.

Consider now a random experiment consisting of T independent Bernoulli trials, where the probability of a "success" is θ. The term "repeated" is used to indicate that the probability of a success remains the same from trial to trial. Let Y be the random variable representing the number of successes in the T repeated independent Bernoulli trials. Because the number of configurations of trials yielding y successes is ${}_TC_y$, this gives rise to the following definition.

Definition 3.2.5 A random variable Y has a *binomial distribution*, denoted $Y \sim B(T, \theta)$, iff its p.m.f. is

$$f_B(y|T,\theta) = \begin{Bmatrix} \binom{T}{y}\theta^y(1-\theta)^{T-y}, & \text{if } y = 0, 1, \ldots, T \\ 0, & \text{otherwise} \end{Bmatrix}, \tag{3.2.15}$$

where $0 \leq \theta \leq 1$ and T is a positive integer.

Using the notation of Definition 3.2.5, with $T = 1$, the Bernoulli distribution (Definition 3.2.4) is denoted $B(1, \theta)$.

The moment generating function of the binomial distribution, and some explicit moment formulae, are given in the following theorem.

Theorem 3.2.6 If Y has a binomial distribution, then its m.g.f. is

$$M(t) = [1 - \theta + \theta[\exp(t)]]^T. \tag{3.2.16}$$

Using (3.2.16) the following moments can be found:

$$\mu = T\theta, \tag{3.2.17}$$

$$\sigma^2 = T\theta(1-\theta), \tag{3.2.18}$$

$$E[(Y-\mu)^3] = T\theta(1-\theta)(1-2\theta), \tag{3.2.19}$$

$$E[(Y-\mu)^4] = 3T^2\theta^2(1-\theta)^2 + T\theta(1-\theta)[1-6\theta(1-\theta)]. \tag{3.2.20}$$

Proof According to Definition 2.3.3 the moment generating function is

$$\begin{aligned} M(t) = E[\exp(tY)] &= \sum_{y=0}^{N} \exp(ty)\binom{N}{y}(\theta)^y(1-\theta)^{N-y} \\ &= \sum_{y=0}^{N} \binom{N}{y}[\theta\exp(t)]^y(1-\theta)^{N-y} \end{aligned}$$

Using the Binomial Theorem:

$$(r+s)^N = \sum_{n=0}^{N} \binom{N}{n} r^n s^{N-n}, \tag{3.2.21}$$

(3.2.16) follows immediately. Using (2.3.4) and (3.2.16), derivation of (3.2.17) through (3.2.20) are straightforward.

Example 3.2.4 The number of heads Y in seven independent flips of a fair coin follows the binomial $B(7, \frac{1}{2})$ $(y = 0, 1, \ldots, 7)$. The probability of five heads in seven flips is

$$f_B(5|7, \tfrac{1}{2}) = \binom{7}{5}(\tfrac{1}{2})^5(1-\tfrac{1}{2})^2 = \frac{21}{128}.$$

The probability of getting *at least* five heads in seven flips is

$$P(Y \geq 5) = \sum_{y=5}^{7} f_B(y|7, \tfrac{1}{2}) = \frac{29}{128}.$$

The expected number of heads in seven flips is $\mu = 7(\frac{1}{2}) = 3.5$.

Two requirements of the binomial distribution, given θ, are: (i) the Bernoulli trials are independent, and (ii) the probability of success remains constant from trial to trial.[1] If there are only a finite number of objects (e.g., draws from a deck of 52 cards in which a success is defined as choosing a red card), then it is necessary to sample *with replacement* in order to satisfy the above two requirements, that is, after an object is chosen on a trial it is replaced before the next trial in such a way that the probability of a success remains constant (e.g., by shuffling the deck of cards). Note that this permits the number of trials to be arbitrarily large even though the number of objects is finite. Cases in which sampling is done *without replacement* can be handled using the hypergeometric distribution. The hypergeometric distribution gives the probability of drawing Y "successes" and $T - Y$ "failures" when sampling without replacement from a finite population containing K "successes" and $M - K$ "failures." It is defined as follows.

Definition 3.2.6 A random variable Y has a *hypergeometric distribution*, $Y \sim H(M, T, K)$, iff its p.m.f. is

$$f_H(y|M, K, T) \equiv \begin{Bmatrix} \dfrac{\dbinom{K}{y}\dbinom{M-K}{T-y}}{\dbinom{M}{T}}, & \text{if } y = 0, 1, 2, \ldots, N \\ 0, & \text{otherwise} \end{Bmatrix}, \tag{3.2.22}$$

where T and M are positive integers, $T \leq M$, and $K \leq M$ is a nonnegative integer.

Some moments of the hypergeometric distribution are given in the following theorem.

Theorem 3.2.7 Suppose $Y \sim H(M, K, T)$, and let $\theta \equiv K/M$. Y has the moments:

$$\mu = T\theta, \tag{3.2.23}$$

$$\sigma^2 = \left(\frac{M-T}{M-1}\right)[T\theta(1-\theta)], \tag{3.2.24}$$

$$E[Y(Y-1)\ldots(Y-r+1)] = r!\left[\frac{\dbinom{K}{r}\dbinom{T}{r}}{\dbinom{M}{T}}\right]. \tag{3.2.25}$$

Proof For a proof of (3.2.23), (3.2.24), and (3.2.25) in the case $r = 2$, see

1. From a subjectivist standpoint, de Finetti argued that independence may not be a phenomenon about which we have very useful intuition. In place of independence, he recommended the concept of *exchangeability*, which is discussed in Chapter 5.

Mood, Graybill, and Boes (1974, pp. 91–92). Proof of (3.2.25) for $r > 2$ is left to the reader.

To illustrate the use of the hypergeometric distribution, consider the next example.

Example 3.2.5 A university committee consists of six faculty members and four students. If a subcommittee of four persons is to be chosen randomly from the committee, what is the probability that the subcommittee will consist of three faculty members? Let Y be the number of faculty members chosen for the subcommittee of $T = 4$ individuals. Of the $M = 10$ committee members, $K = 6$ are faculty members. Applying the hypergeometric p.m.f. (3.2.22) it follows:

$$P(Y = 3) = f_H(3; 10, 6, 4) = \frac{\binom{6}{3}\binom{10-6}{4-3}}{\binom{10}{4}} = \frac{\left(\frac{6!}{3!3!}\right)\left(\frac{4!}{1!3!}\right)}{\left(\frac{10!}{6!4!}\right)} = \frac{8}{21}.$$

The appropriateness of the hypergeometric distribution in Example 3.2.5 can be seen as follows. There are a total of ${}_MC_T$ ways of choosing a subcommittee of size T from an overall committee size M. The number of ways of choosing y faculty members from the K on the committee is ${}_KC_y$, and corresponding to each of these choices there are ${}_{M-K}C_{T-y}$ ways of choosing $T - y$ students from the $M - K$ students on the committee. Out of ${}_MC_T$ committees of size $T = 4$, ${}_KC_y \cdot {}_{M-K}C_{T-Y}$ correspond to three faculty members and one student. Thus, the relative frequency of four-member subcommittees with three faculty members is given by $({}_6C_3 \cdot {}_4C_1)/{}_{10}C_4 = 8/21$.

Note also that by defining $\theta \equiv K/M$ in Theorem 3.2.7, the mean (3.2.23) of the hypergeometric distribution is of the same algebraic form as for the binomial distribution (see Equation 3.2.17). This definition of θ corresponds to the probability of a "success" on the first trial. When sampling *without replacement*, however, this probability changes from trial to trial. For example, given a success on the first trial, the probability of a success on the second trial drops to $(K - 1)/(M - 1)$. Note also that comparison of (3.2.24) and (3.2.18) implies that given T and θ, the variance of the hypergeometric distribution cannot be larger than that of the binomial distribution. The ratio $(M - T)/(M - 1)$ of (3.2.24) to (3.2.18) is sometimes referred to as a *finite population correction factor*. The motivation for this terminology will become clear later.

There are other distributions besides the hypergeometric that are closely related to the binomial distribution. For example, consider a sequence of independent repetitions of a random experiment with constant probability θ of success. Let the random variable Y denote the number of failures in the sequence before the Jth success (i.e., $Y + J$ trials are necessary to produce J successes), where J is a fixed positive integer. Then the distribution of Y is given by the following.

Definition 3.2.7 A random variable Y has a *negative binomial (or Pascal) distribution*, denoted $Y \sim NB(\theta, J)$, $\theta > 0$, iff its p.m.f. is

$$f_{NB}(y|\theta, J) \equiv \begin{cases} \binom{y+J-1}{J-1}\theta^J(1-\theta)^y, & \text{if } y = 0, 1, 2, \ldots \\ 0, & \text{otherwise} \end{cases}. \tag{3.2.26}$$

When $J = 1$, Y has a *geometric distribution*, denoted $Y \sim g(\theta)$ or $Y \sim NB(\theta, 1)$:

$$f_g(y|\theta) \equiv f_{NB}(y|\theta, 1) = \begin{cases} \theta(1-\theta)^y, & \text{if } y = 0, 1, 2, \ldots \\ 0, & \text{otherwise} \end{cases}. \tag{3.2.27}$$

The negative binomial distribution derives its name from the fact that $f_{NB}(y|\theta, J)$ $(y = 0, 1, 2, \ldots)$ is a general term in the expansion of $\theta^J[1 - (1-\theta)]^{-J}$. Similarly, in the case of the binomial distribution, $f_B(y|T, \theta)$ $(y = 0, 1, \ldots, T)$ is a general term in the expansion of $[(1-\theta) + \theta]^T$.

The moment generating function of the negative binomial distribution, and some explicit moment formulae, are given in the following theorem.

Theorem 3.2.8 Suppose $Y \sim NB(\theta, J)$. Then its m.g.f. is

$$M(t) = \theta^J[1 - (1-\theta)\exp(t)]^{-J} \tag{3.2.28}$$

for $t < -\ln(1-\theta)$. Using (3.2.28) the following moments can be found:

$$\mu = \frac{J(1-\theta)}{\theta}, \tag{3.2.29}$$

$$\sigma^2 = \frac{J(1-\theta)}{\theta^2}, \tag{3.2.30}$$

$$E[(Y-\mu)^3] = \frac{J(1-\theta)(2-\theta)}{\theta^3}, \tag{3.2.31}$$

$$E[(Y-\mu)^4] = \frac{J[1-\theta+(3J+4)\theta^2+(1-\theta)^3]}{\theta^4}. \tag{3.2.32}$$

Proof According to Definition 2.3.3 the moment generating function is

$$\begin{aligned} M(t) = E[\exp(tY)] &= \sum_{y=0}^{\infty} \exp(ty)\binom{y+J-1}{y}\theta^J(1-\theta)^y \\ &= \sum_{y=0}^{\infty} \binom{y+J-1}{y}\theta^J[(1-\theta)\exp(t)]^y. \end{aligned} \tag{3.2.33}$$

Using the following result [see Mood et al. (1974, p. 533, eq. (33))]:

$$(1-x)^{-J} = \sum_{y=0}^{\infty} \binom{y+J-1}{y} x^y, \qquad -1 < x < 1, \tag{3.2.34}$$

(3.2.28) follows immediately from (3.2.33). Using (3.2.28) and (2.3.4), derivation of (3.2.29) through (3.2.32) are straightforward.

The special case of the geometric distribution is well-named since its p.m.f. assumes values that are the terms of a geometric series. A random variable with a geometric distribution is often referred to as a *discrete waiting-time* random variable because it represents how long (measured in terms of the number of failures) one has to wait for a success.[2] The following theorem states that the geometric distribution possesses a "memoryless property" in the sense that the probability at least $i + k$ trials are required before the first success, given there have been i successive failures, equals the unconditional probability at least k trials are needed before the first success.

Theorem 3.2.9 If Y has the geometric distribution with parameter θ, then

$$P(Y \geq i + k \mid Y \geq i) = P(Y \geq k) \qquad (k = 0, 1, 2, 3, \ldots). \tag{3.2.25}$$

Proof Mood et al. (1974, p. 101).

The final discrete univariate distribution that we consider is one of the most important. Recalling that

$$\exp(\lambda) = \sum_{y=0}^{\infty} \frac{\lambda^y}{y!} \qquad \text{for } \lambda > 0, \tag{3.2.36}$$

consider the following definition.

Definition 3.2.8 A random variable Y has a *Poisson distribution*, denoted $Y \sim Po(\lambda)$, iff its p.m.f. is

$$f_{Po}(y \mid \lambda) \equiv \begin{cases} \dfrac{\lambda^y \exp(-\lambda)}{y!}, & \text{if } y = 0, 1, 2, 3, \ldots \\ 0, & \text{otherwise} \end{cases}, \tag{3.2.37}$$

where λ is a positive real number.

The moment generating function of the Poisson distribution, and some explicit moment formulae, are given in the following theorem.

Theorem 3.2.10 Suppose $Y \sim Po(\lambda)$. Then its m.g.f. is

$$M(t) = \exp[\lambda\{\exp(t) - 1\}]. \tag{3.2.38}$$

2. A random variable with a negative binomial distribution describes how long one waits for the jth success. The geometric distribution is simply the case $j = 1$.

Using (3.2.38) the following moments can be found:

$$\mu = \lambda, \tag{3.2.39}$$

$$\sigma^2 = \lambda, \tag{3.2.40}$$

$$E[(Y - \mu)^3] = \lambda, \tag{3.2.41}$$

$$E[(Y - \mu)^4] = \lambda + 3\lambda^2. \tag{3.2.42}$$

Proof According to Definition 2.3.3 the moment generating function is

$$\begin{aligned} M(t) = E[\exp(tY)] &= \sum_{y=0}^{N} \exp(ty)\left[\frac{\exp(-\lambda)\lambda^y}{y!}\right] \\ &= \exp(-\lambda)\sum_{y=0}^{N} \frac{[\lambda\exp(t)]^y}{y!} = \exp(-\lambda)\exp[\lambda\exp(t)] \\ &= \exp(\lambda[\exp(t) - 1]), \end{aligned} \tag{3.2.43}$$

where use is made of the Taylor series expansion of the exponential function:

$$\exp(x) = \sum_{j=0}^{\infty} \frac{x^j}{j!}. \tag{3.2.44}$$

Using (3.2.38) and (2.3.4), derivation of (3.2.39)–(3.2.42) is straightforward.

Some claim that the Poisson distribution became famous because it fit extremely well the frequency of deaths from the kick of a horse in the Prussian Army Corps in the last quarter of the nineteenth century. More importantly, the Poisson distribution has proved valuable as the p.m.f. of phenomena such as product demand, number of calls coming into a telephone switchboard, number of passenger cars arriving at a toll booth, and so on. In all such cases, there is a rate in terms of number of occurrences per interval of time or space that characterizes a process. A more formal characterization is given in the following theorem.

Theorem 3.2.11 Let $Y(t)$ denote the number of occurrences of a certain happening in a time interval of length t. Further suppose:

(a) The probability that exactly one happening occurs in a small time interval of length h is approximately equal to vh. Formally,

$$\operatorname*{Limit}_{h\to 0} P\begin{pmatrix}\text{one happening in an} \\ \text{interval of length } h\end{pmatrix} = vh + o(h), \tag{3.2.45}$$

where $o(h)$ (read "some function of smaller order than h") denotes an unspecified function such that

$$\operatorname*{Limit}_{h\to 0} \frac{o(h)}{h} = 0. \tag{3.2.46}$$

Note that v can be interpreted as the mean rate at which happenings occur per unit of time, that is, v is the mean rate of occurrence.

(b) The probability of more than one happening in a small interval of length h is negligible compared to the probability of just one happening in the same time interval. Formally,

$$\operatorname*{Limit}_{h\to 0} P\begin{pmatrix}\text{two or more happenings}\\ \text{in an interval of length } h\end{pmatrix} = o(h), \tag{3.2.47}$$

(c) The number of happenings in non-overlapping time intervals are independent.

Then $Y(t)$ has a Poisson distribution with parameter $\lambda = vt$.

Proof Mood et al. (1974, pp. 95–96).

Example 3.2.6 Suppose the number of customers arriving at a retail store has a Poisson distribution such that on the average thirty customers per hour arrive. Let Y denote the number of customers arriving in a three-minute period. What is the probability no customers arrive in a three-minute period? Because thirty customers per hour is equivalent to $v = .5$ customers per minute, the expected number of customers in a three minute period is $\lambda = vt = .5(3) = 1.5$. Hence:

$$P(Y = 0) = \frac{\exp(-\lambda)\lambda^y}{y!} = \frac{\exp(-1.5)(1.5)^0}{0!} = \exp(-1.5) = .223.$$

The Poisson distribution can also be viewed as a limiting form of the binomial distribution, and this motivates its use as a computational aid when working with the binomial distribution. This connection is described in the following theorem.

Theorem 3.2.12 The Poisson distribution is a limiting form of the binomial distribution as $\theta \to 0$, $T \to \infty$ and $\lambda = T\theta$ remains constant.

Proof Suppose $X \sim B(T, \theta)$ and $Y \sim Po(\lambda)$ with $\lambda = T\theta$. From (3.2.16) the m.g.f. of X is $M_X(t) = [1 - \theta + \theta\exp(t)]^T = [1 + T^{-1}\lambda\{\exp(t) - 1\}]^T$. Then as $T \to \infty$, $M_X(t) \to \exp[\lambda\{\exp(t) - 1\}]$, which by (3.2.28), is $M_Y(t)$.[3]

For a detailed and complete discussion of discrete univariate distributions, see Johnson et al. (1992).

3. Let $c = \lambda[\exp(t) - 1]$ and use the well-known result

$$\operatorname*{Limit}_{T\to\infty}\left[1 + \frac{c}{T}\right]^T = \exp(c),$$

Exercises

3.2.1 Let Y be a discrete random variable with p.m.f.

$$f(y) = P(Y = y) = \begin{Bmatrix} \dfrac{6}{(\theta y)^2}, & \text{if } y = 1, 2, 3, \ldots \\ 0, & \text{otherwise} \end{Bmatrix}.$$

Show that the mean of Y does not exist.

3.2.2 Suppose the outcome of each baseball game (win or lose) between teams A and B is a Bernoulli trial with probability of team A winning equally θ. Suppose the outcomes of two games in a doubleheader are independent. What is the probability of either team winning both games (i.e., "sweeping" the doubleheader)?

3.2.3 Consider the seven-game World Series of baseball. Suppose the probability of the American League team winning a particular game is θ. Further suppose this probability is constant over games and the outcome of each game is independent of all other games. The Series is over as soon as a team wins four games. No games end in ties. What is the p.m.f. for the number of games played?

3.2.4 Suppose that incoming telephone calls behave according to a Poisson process with intensity of twelve per hour. What is the probability that more than eighteen calls will occur in any given one-hour period? If the phone operator takes a fifteen-minute coffee break, what is the probability that at least one call will come in during the break?

3.2.5 Let y_{mode} be the unique mode of the binomial distribution with p.m.f. $f_B(y|T, \theta)$. Show: $(T + 1)\theta - 1 < y_{\text{mode}} < (T + 1)\theta$.

3.2.6 If someone gives you \$8 each time you roll 1 with a fair die, how much should you pay the person when you role a 2, 3, 4, 5, or 6 in order to make the game "fair," that is, so that your expected winnings are zero? Now suppose somebody asks you to toss a fair coin and offers to pay you \$2 if you get a head on the first toss but not on the second, \$4 if you get a head on the first two tosses but not on the third, \$8 if you get a head on the first three tosses but not the fourth, and so on. How much would you be willing to pay to play this game? This game illustrates the so-called St. Petersburg paradox. What is the nature of this "paradox"?

3.2.7 Show that the hypergeometric distribution can be approximated by the binomial distribution as $M \to \infty$, $K \to \infty$ and $K/M \to p$.

3.2.8 In the city of Redneck there are 800 white citizens registered to vote and 400 nonwhite citizens registered. Trial juries of twelve people are allegedly selected at random from the list of registered voters with the possibility that a person can serve more than once. In the last five trials the composition of each jury was eleven white citizens and one nonwhite citizen. Do you believe that these juries were randomly selected? Fully justify your answer and state all assumptions.

3.2.9 Find the mode of a Poisson distribution. When is it unique? Also compute measures of skewness and kurtosis for the Poisson distribution.

3.2.10 Suppose $Y \sim Po(\lambda)$. Show:

$$f_{Po}(y + 1|\lambda) = \frac{\lambda f_{Po}(y|\lambda)}{y + 1} \quad (y = 0, 1, 2, \ldots). \tag{3.2.48}$$

3.2.11 Suppose $Y \sim Po(\lambda)$, and let $g(\cdot)$ be a function such that $-\infty < E[g(Y)] < \infty$ and $-\infty < g(-1) < \infty$.

(a) Show: $E[\lambda g(Y)] = E[Yg(Y - 1)]$.

(b) Show: $E(Y^3) = \lambda^3 + 3\lambda^2 + \lambda$. [Hint: use (a) with $g(Y) = Y^2$.]

3.2.12 Suppose $Y \sim NB(\theta, J)$, and let $g(\cdot)$ be a function such that $-\infty < E[g(Y)] < \infty$ and $-\infty < g(-1) < \infty$. Show: $E[(1-\theta)g(Y)] = E[\{Y/(J+Y-1)\}g(Y-1)]$.

3.2.13 (Imelda's Problem) A closet contains N pairs of shoes. Suppose $2r$ shoes are chosen at random, where $2r < N$. Find each of these probabilities.

(a) P(no pairs)

(b) P(exactly one complete pair)

(c) P(exactly two complete pairs)

3.2.14 (Banach's Match Problem) The mathematician Banach kept two match boxes, one in each pocket of his pants. Each box contained N matches. Whenever he wanted a match he reached at random into one of his pockets. Show that the moment he found that the box he picked was empty, the distribution of the number R of matches left in the other box is (see Feller 1973, p. 157):

$$P(R = r) = \binom{2N - r}{N} 2^{-2N+r}, \quad (r = 1, 2, \ldots, R). \tag{3.2.49}$$

3.2.15 Consider the random variables X and Y with means μ_X and μ_Y, variances σ_X^2 and σ_Y^2, and covariance σ_{XY}. Suppose Y is the return on a stock and X is the return on a bond such that $\mu_Y > \mu_X$ and $\sigma_Y^2 > \sigma_X^2$. Finally, let W be a Bernoulli random variable distributed independently of X and Y, where $P(W = 1) = p$, $P(W = 0) = 1 - p$, and $0 < p < 1$. Consider the random portfolio $Z = WX + (1 - W)Y$.

(a) Find μ_Z.

(b) Which is larger, μ_Z or μ_Y?

(c) Find σ_Z^2.

(d) How large must $\mu_Y - \mu_X$ be in order for $\sigma_Z^2 > \sigma_Y^2$?

3.3 Continuous Univariate Distributions

Although all measurement is inherently discrete, continuous random variables are, nonetheless, useful for various conceptual reasons. In fact they play a dominant role in econometrics. This section presents six important families of univariate continuous distributions: (i) uniform, (ii) normal, (iii) gamma, (iv) beta, (v) t, and (vi) F. Special cases of each that warrant particular attention due to their frequency of occurring in practice are noted. Also, nine additional continuous distributions are presented in summary form in Table 3.3.1. More distributions are introduced in the exercises.

As in Section 3.2 we begin the discussion with the simplest case.

Definition 3.3.1 A continuous random variable Y has a *uniform distribution*, or a *rectangular distribution*, over the interval $[\alpha, \beta]$, denoted $Y \sim U[\alpha, \beta]$, iff its p.d.f. is

$$f_U(y|\alpha,\beta) \equiv \begin{Bmatrix} \dfrac{1}{\beta - \alpha}, & \text{if } \alpha \le y \le \beta \\ 0, & \text{otherwise} \end{Bmatrix}, \tag{3.3.1}$$

where $-\infty < \alpha < \beta < \infty$. The distribution function of Y is

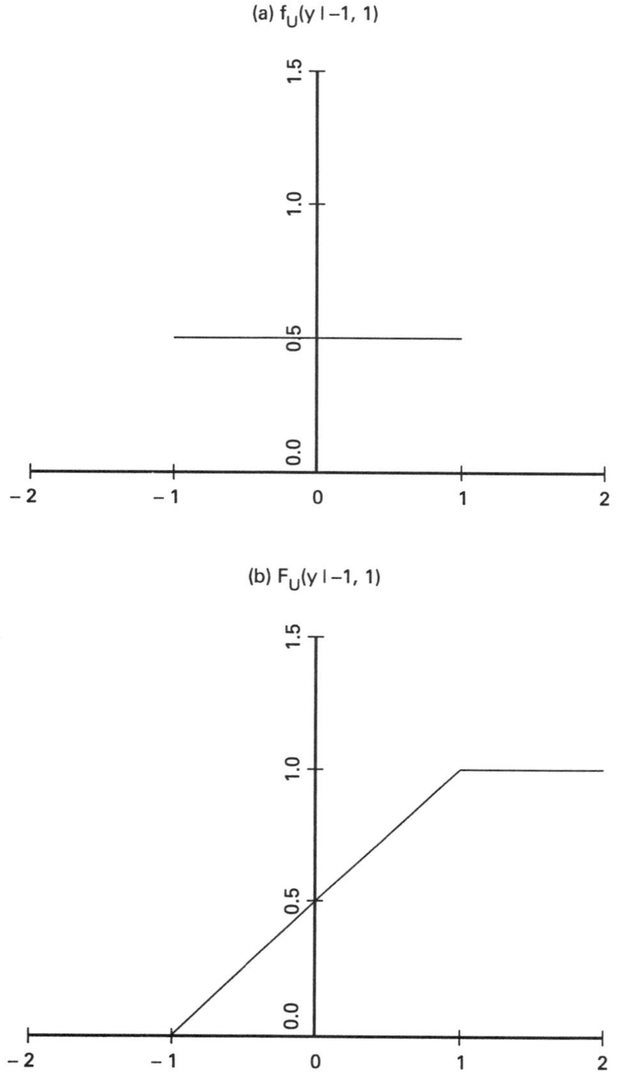

Figure 3.3.1
Uniform density and distribution functions over $[-1, 1]$

$$F_U(y|\alpha, \beta) \equiv P(Y \leq y|\alpha, \beta) = \begin{Bmatrix} 0, & \text{if } y < \alpha \\ \dfrac{y-\alpha}{\beta-\alpha}, & \text{if } \alpha \leq y \leq \beta \\ 1, & \text{if } y > \beta \end{Bmatrix}. \tag{3.3.2}$$

Figure 3.3.1 illustrates the uniform p.d.f. and its distribution function in the case $\alpha = -1$ and $\beta = 1$. The moment generating function of the uniform distribution, and some explicit moment formulae, are given in the following theorem.

Theorem 3.3.1 If $Y \sim U[\alpha, \beta]$, then its m.g.f. is

$$M(t) = \frac{\exp(\beta t) - \exp(\alpha t)}{(\beta - \alpha)t}. \tag{3.3.3}$$

The moments of Y are

$$\mu = \frac{\alpha + \beta}{2}, \tag{3.3.4}$$

$$\sigma^2 = \frac{(\beta - \alpha)^2}{12}, \tag{3.3.5}$$

$$E[(Y - \mu)^r] = 0 \quad \text{for } r \text{ odd}, \tag{3.3.6}$$

$$E[(Y - \mu)^r] = \frac{(\beta - \alpha)^r}{2^r(r + 1)} \quad \text{for } r \text{ even}. \tag{3.3.7}$$

Proof According to Definition 2.3.3 the moment generating function is

$$M(t) = E[\exp(tY)] = \int_\alpha^\beta \exp(ty)\left[\frac{1}{\beta - \alpha}\right]dy = \frac{\exp(\beta t) - \exp(\alpha t)}{(\beta - \alpha)t}.$$

Using (3.3.3) and (2.3.4), derivation of (3.3.4) through (3.3.7) are straightforward, and left to the reader.

Although the uniform distribution is the simplest continuous univariate distribution, it is not encountered as often as the following distribution.

Definition 3.3.2 A continuous random variable Y has a *normal distribution*, or a *Gaussian distribution*, denoted $Y \sim N(\mu, \sigma^2)$, iff its p.d.f. is

$$\phi(y|\mu, \sigma^2) = [2\pi\sigma^2]^{-1/2} \exp\left[-\frac{1}{2}\left(\frac{y - \mu}{\sigma}\right)^2\right], \quad -\infty < y < \infty. \tag{3.3.8}$$

The distribution function of Y is

$$\Phi(y|\mu, \sigma^2) = \int_{-\infty}^{y} [2\pi\sigma^2]^{-1/2} \exp\left[-\frac{1}{2}\left(\frac{t - \mu}{\sigma}\right)^2\right]dt, \quad -\infty < y < \infty. \tag{3.3.9}$$

Unfortunately, there is no closed-form expression for (3.3.9).

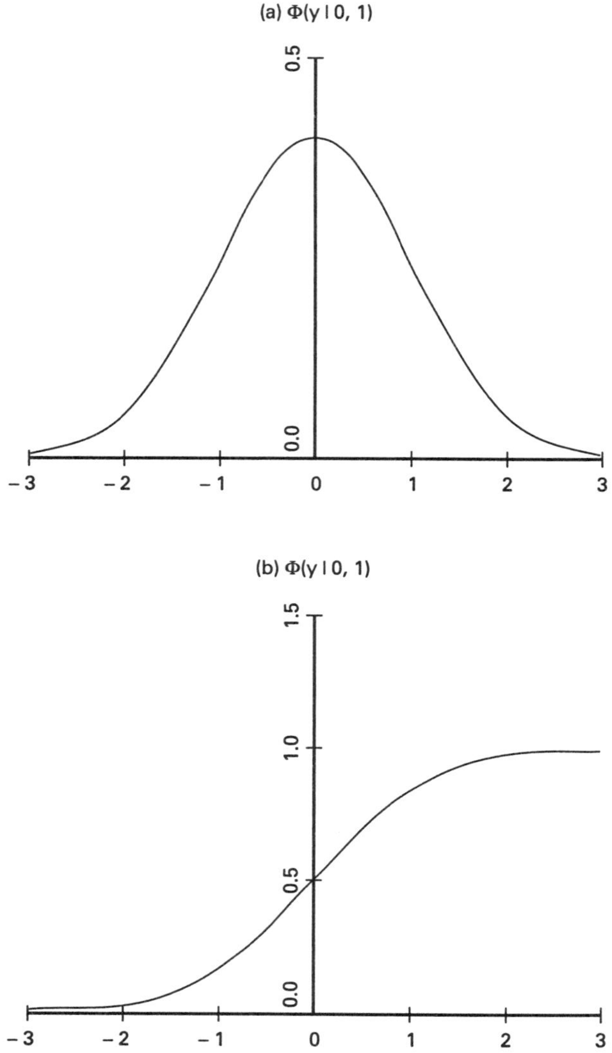

Figure 3.3.2
Standard normal density and distribution function

Definition 3.3.2 introduces specific notation $\phi(\cdot|\mu,\sigma^2)$ and $\Phi(\cdot|\mu,\sigma^2)$ for the density function and the distribution function, respectively, of a normally distributed random variable Y with mean μ and variance σ^2. This notation is used hereafter.

Figure 3.3.2 illustrates the normal p.d.f. and the distribution function in the case $\mu = 0$, $\sigma^2 = 1$. Just how "normal" is the normal distribution is open to debate. Its central role in statistics is in large part explained by the fact that it arises as the output of various limiting theorems discussed in Section 5.3. Many statisticians (and in fact an increasing number) do not think that such theorems justify, for example, a normality assumption for the disturbance term in a linear regression model. Their concern arises from the fact that many statistical estimation procedures discussed in Chapter 6 are not *robust* to the assumption of normality for the data-generating process. Such "robustnics" favor the robust estimation techniques (see Section 6.4), and usually prefer the less prejudicial name of a *Gaussian distribution.*

A standardized form of the normal distribution is described in the next definition.

Definition 3.3.3 A random variable Z has a *standard normal distribution,* denoted $Z \sim N(0,1)$, iff it has a normal distribution with mean zero and unit variance. The density and distribution functions in the standardized case are denoted by $\phi(\cdot) \equiv \phi(\cdot|0,1)$ and $\Phi(\cdot) \equiv \Phi(\cdot|0,1)$, respectively, and are shown in Figure 3.3.2.

The moment generating function of the normal distribution, and some explicit moment formulae, are given in the following theorem.

Theorem 3.3.2 If $Y \sim N(\mu,\sigma^2)$, then its m.g.f. is

$$M(t) = \exp[\mu t + \tfrac{1}{2}\sigma^2 t^2]. \tag{3.3.10}$$

The mean and variance of Y are μ and σ^2, respectively, explaining the choice of notation for the parameters of the normal distribution. It can also be shown that

$$E[(Y-\mu)^m] = 0, \qquad m = 3, 5, 7, \ldots \tag{3.3.11}$$

$$E[(Y-\mu)^{2r}] = (2\sigma^2)^r \pi^{-1/2}\Gamma(r + \tfrac{1}{2}), \tag{3.3.12}$$

where $\Gamma(\cdot)$ denotes the gamma function defined in (3.3.16). In particular,

$$E[(Y-\mu)^4] = 3\sigma^4. \tag{3.3.13}$$

Proof According to Definition 2.3.3 the moment generating function is

$$M(t) = E[\exp(tY)] = \int_{-\infty}^{\infty} \exp(ty)(2\pi\sigma^2)^{-1/2}\exp\left[-\frac{1}{2}\left(\frac{y-\mu}{\sigma}\right)^2\right]dy$$

$$= \exp\left(\mu t + \frac{1}{2}\sigma^2 t^2\right)\int_{-\infty}^{\infty} (2\pi\sigma^2)^{-1/2}$$

$$\times \exp\left[-\frac{1}{2}\left(\frac{y-\mu}{\sigma}\right)^2 + ty - \mu t - \frac{1}{2}\sigma^2 t^2\right] dy$$

$$= \exp\left(\mu t + \frac{1}{2}\sigma^2 t^2\right) \int_{-\infty}^{\infty} (2\pi\sigma^2)^{-1/2}$$

$$\times \exp\left[-\frac{1}{2\sigma^2}\{(y-\mu)^2 - 2\sigma^2 t(y-\mu) + \sigma^4 t^2\}\right] dy.$$

Noting that $(y-\mu)^2 - 2\sigma^2 t(y-\mu) + \sigma^4 t^2 = (y - \mu - \sigma^2 t)^2$, the above integrand is recognized as the density $\phi(y|\mu + \sigma^2 t, \sigma^2)$, and hence (3.3.10) follows immediately. Using (3.3.10) and (2.3.4) derivation of (3.3.11) through (3.3.13) are straightforward.

Theorem 3.3.3 Suppose $Y \sim N(\mu, \sigma^2)$ and define $Z \equiv (Y - \mu)/\sigma$. Then:

(a) $Z \sim N(0, 1)$,

(b) $P(a \leq Y \leq b) = \Phi[(b - \mu)/\sigma] - \Phi[(a - \mu)/\sigma]$,

(c) $\Phi(y) = 1 - \Phi(-y)$.

Proof Left to the reader. Note that without a normality assumption in (a), it is still true that $E(Z) = 0$ and $\text{Var}(Z) = 1$. Also note in (c) that a similar result holds for any distribution function whose p.d.f. is symmetric around zero.

We now turn to other important, albeit less commonly encountered, distributions.

Definition 3.3.4 A continuous random variable Y has a *gamma distribution*, denoted $Y \sim G(\alpha, \beta)$, iff its p.d.f. is

$$f_G(y|\alpha, \beta) \equiv \begin{Bmatrix} c_G^{-1} y^{\alpha-1} \exp(-y/\beta), & \text{if } 0 < y < \infty \\ 0, & \text{otherwise} \end{Bmatrix}, \tag{3.3.14}$$

where $\alpha > 0$, $\beta > 0$, the *integrating constant* is

$$c_G = c_G(\alpha, \beta) = \beta^\alpha \Gamma(\alpha), \tag{3.3.15}$$

and $\Gamma(\alpha)$ denotes the *gamma function*

$$\Gamma(\alpha) \equiv \int_0^\infty t^{\alpha-1} \exp(-t)\, dt. \tag{3.3.16}$$

When α is a positive integer, then the gamma c.d.f has a convenient closed-form given in the following theorem.

Theorem 3.3.4 If Y has a gamma distribution with parameters α and β, and if α is a positive integer, then the distribution function is

$$F(y) = 1 - \sum_{j=0}^{\alpha-1} \frac{(y/\beta)^j \exp(-y/\beta)}{j!}. \tag{3.3.17}$$

If $\beta = 1$, then (3.3.17) is referred to as the *incomplete gamma function*.

Proof Straightforward using successive integration by parts.

There are some interesting computational properties associated with the gamma distribution and these are given in the following three theorems.[4]

Theorem 3.3.5 Consider the gamma function $\Gamma(\cdot)$ defined by (3.3.16).

(a) $\Gamma(\alpha) = (\alpha - 1)\Gamma(\alpha - 1)$ for any positive real number.

(b) $\Gamma(\alpha) = (\alpha - 1)!$ if α is a positive integer greater than one.

(c) $\Gamma(\frac{1}{2}) = \pi^{1/2}$.

Proof DeGroot (1987, pp. 286–288).

The moment generating function of the gamma distribution, and some explicit moment formulae, are given in the following theorem.

Theorem 3.3.6 Suppose $Y \sim G(\alpha, \beta)$, where $\alpha > 0$, $\beta > 0$. Then the m.g.f. of Y is

$$M(t) = [1 - \beta t]^{-\alpha}, \qquad \text{for } t < \beta^{-1}. \tag{3.3.18}$$

The moments of Y are

$$\mu = \alpha\beta, \tag{3.3.19}$$

$$\sigma^2 = \alpha\beta^2, \tag{3.3.20}$$

$$E[(Y - \mu)^3] = 2\alpha\beta^3, \tag{3.3.21}$$

$$E[(Y - \mu)^4] = 3\alpha(\alpha + 2)\beta^4, \tag{3.3.22}$$

$$E(Y^r) = \frac{\Gamma(\alpha + r)\beta^r}{\Gamma(\alpha)}. \tag{3.3.23}$$

Proof According to Definition 2.3.3 the moment generating function is

$$\begin{aligned} M(t) = E[\exp(tY)] &= \int_0^\infty \exp(ty) f_y(y|\alpha, \beta)\, dy \\ &= [1 - \beta t]^{-\alpha} \int_0^\infty \left[\frac{(1 - \beta t)^\alpha}{\beta^\alpha \Gamma(\alpha)}\right] y^{\alpha - 1} \exp\left(-\frac{y}{\beta/(1 - \beta t)}\right) dy. \end{aligned}$$

Because this last integrand is recognized as the gamma density $f_y(y|\alpha, \beta/[1 - \beta t])$, the integral is unity. Hence, (3.3.18) follows. Using (3.3.18) and (2.3.4) derivation of (3.3.19) through (3.3.23) is straightforward.

4. Stirling's series provides an expansion of $\ln[\Gamma(\alpha + h)]$, which is asymptotic in α for bounded h. It provides a very good approximation when α is large. In particular,

$$\Gamma(\alpha) = (2\pi)^{1/2}\alpha^{\alpha - 1/2} \exp\left(1 + \frac{1}{12\alpha} + \frac{1}{288\alpha^2} - \frac{139}{51840\alpha^3} - \frac{571}{248320\alpha^4} \cdots\right).$$

See Box and Tiao (1973, pp. 146–148) for more details.

An alternative to the parameterization of the gamma distribution introduced in Definition 3.3.4 is often employed. Let $\mu = \alpha\beta$ and $\nu = 2\alpha$, and hence, $\alpha = \frac{1}{2}\nu$ and $\beta = 2\mu/\nu$. Then density (3.3.14) can be rewritten as

$$f_\gamma(y|\mu, \nu) \equiv \begin{Bmatrix} c_\gamma^{-1} y^{(\nu-2)/2} \exp\left(-\dfrac{y\nu}{2\mu}\right), & \text{if } 0 < y < \infty \\ 0, & \text{otherwise} \end{Bmatrix}, \tag{3.3.24}$$

where the integrating constant is

$$c_\gamma = c_\gamma(\mu, \nu) = (2\mu/\nu)^{\nu/2}\Gamma(\nu/2) = c_G(\alpha, \beta). \tag{3.3.25}$$

In terms of this new parameterization, variance (3.3.20) becomes $\sigma^2 = 2\mu^2/\nu$. The parameter ν is often referred to as the *degrees of freedom* (the motivation for this terminology will become clear later). When using the parameterization (3.3.24), $Y \sim G(\alpha, \beta)$ is replaced by $Y \sim \gamma(\mu, \nu)$.

Two special cases of the gamma distribution arise sufficiently often that they warrant special attention and terminology. The definition of each case is followed by a theorem giving relevant moments.

Definition 3.3.5 A gamma distribution with $\alpha = 1$ (equivalently $\nu = 2$) is an *exponential distribution*, denoted EXP(β), $G(1, \beta)$ or $\gamma(\frac{1}{2}\nu\beta, 2)$, with p.d.f. and c.d.f, respectively,

$$f_{\text{EXP}}(y|\beta) \equiv \begin{Bmatrix} \beta^{-1}\exp(-\beta^{-1}y), & \text{if } 0 < y < \infty \\ 0 & \text{otherwise} \end{Bmatrix}, \tag{3.3.26}$$

$$F_{\text{EXP}}(y|\beta) = \begin{Bmatrix} 1 - \exp(-\beta^{-1}y), & \text{if } 0 \le y < \infty \\ 0, & \text{otherwise} \end{Bmatrix}. \tag{3.3.27}$$

Theorem 3.3.7 Suppose $Y \sim \text{EXP}(\beta)$. Then Y has the following moments:

$$\mu = \beta, \tag{3.3.28}$$

$$\sigma^2 = \beta^2, \tag{3.3.29}$$

$$E[(Y - \mu)^3] = 2\beta^3, \tag{3.3.30}$$

$$E[(Y - \mu)^4] = 9\beta^4, \tag{3.3.31}$$

$$E[Y^r] = \Gamma(1 + r)\beta^r. \tag{3.3.32}$$

Proof Set $\alpha = 1$ in Theorem 3.3.6.

Definition 3.3.6 A gamma distribution with $\beta = 2$ (equivalently $\mu = \nu$) is defined to be a *chi-squared distribution*, denoted $\chi^2(\nu)$, with p.d.f.

$$f_\chi(y|\nu) = \begin{Bmatrix} c_\chi^{-1} y^{(\nu-2)/2}\exp(-\frac{1}{2}y), & \text{if } 0 < y < \infty \\ 0, & \text{otherwise} \end{Bmatrix}, \tag{3.3.33}$$

where the integrating constant is

$$c_\chi = c_\chi(\nu) = 2^{\nu/2}\Gamma(\nu/2) = c_\gamma(\nu, \nu). \tag{3.3.34}$$

Theorem 3.3.8 Suppose $Y \sim \chi^2(\nu)$. Then Y has the following moments:

$$\mu = \nu, \tag{3.3.35}$$

$$\sigma^2 = 2\nu, \tag{3.3.36}$$

$$E[(Y-\mu)^3] = 8\nu, \tag{3.3.37}$$

$$E[(Y-\mu)^4] = 12\nu(\nu+1), \tag{3.3.38}$$

$$E(Y^r) = \frac{2^r\Gamma\left(\frac{\nu}{2}+r\right)}{\Gamma\left(\frac{\nu}{2}\right)}. \tag{3.3.39}$$

Proof Set $\beta = 2$ in Theorem 3.3.6 and use the alternative parameterization in (3.3.24) with $\mu = \nu$.

For small values of α, the gamma p.d.f. has a long tail to the right (i.e., it is skewed to the right). As α grows in size for any given value of β, the p.d.f. becomes more symmetric and approaches the normal p.d.f. Some typical gamma p.d.f.s are shown in Figure 3.3.3. The second row corresponds to the exponential distribution ($\alpha = 1$). The second column corresponds to the chi-squared distribution ($\beta = 2$) for $\nu = 1, 2, 3, 4$ ($\alpha = \frac{1}{2}, 1, 3/2, 2$). The left-hand column and right-hand columns correspond to the same values of α (in any one row) but with $\beta = 1$ and $\beta = 4$, respectively.

The exponential distribution ($\alpha = 1$) is closely related to the Poisson distribution. If the number of "happenings" in a fixed time interval has a Poisson distribution with parameter λ, then it can be shown (e.g., Hogg and Craig 1978, pp. 104–105) that the length of time between successive happenings has an exponential distribution ($\alpha = 1$) with $\beta = \lambda^{-1}$. Also, the length of time needed to produce α happenings is a gamma distribution. The geometric and negative binomial random variables are discrete "waiting-time" random variables. Their continuous analogs are the exponential and gamma distributions, respectively. An interesting property of the exponential distribution, reminiscent of Theorem 3.2.9, is given in the following theorem.

Theorem 3.3.9 If Y has an exponential distribution, then

$$P(Y > c + b \mid Y > c) = P(Y > b) \tag{3.3.40}$$

for $c > 0$ and $b > 0$.

Proof Substituting (3.3.27) into the definition of conditional probability yields

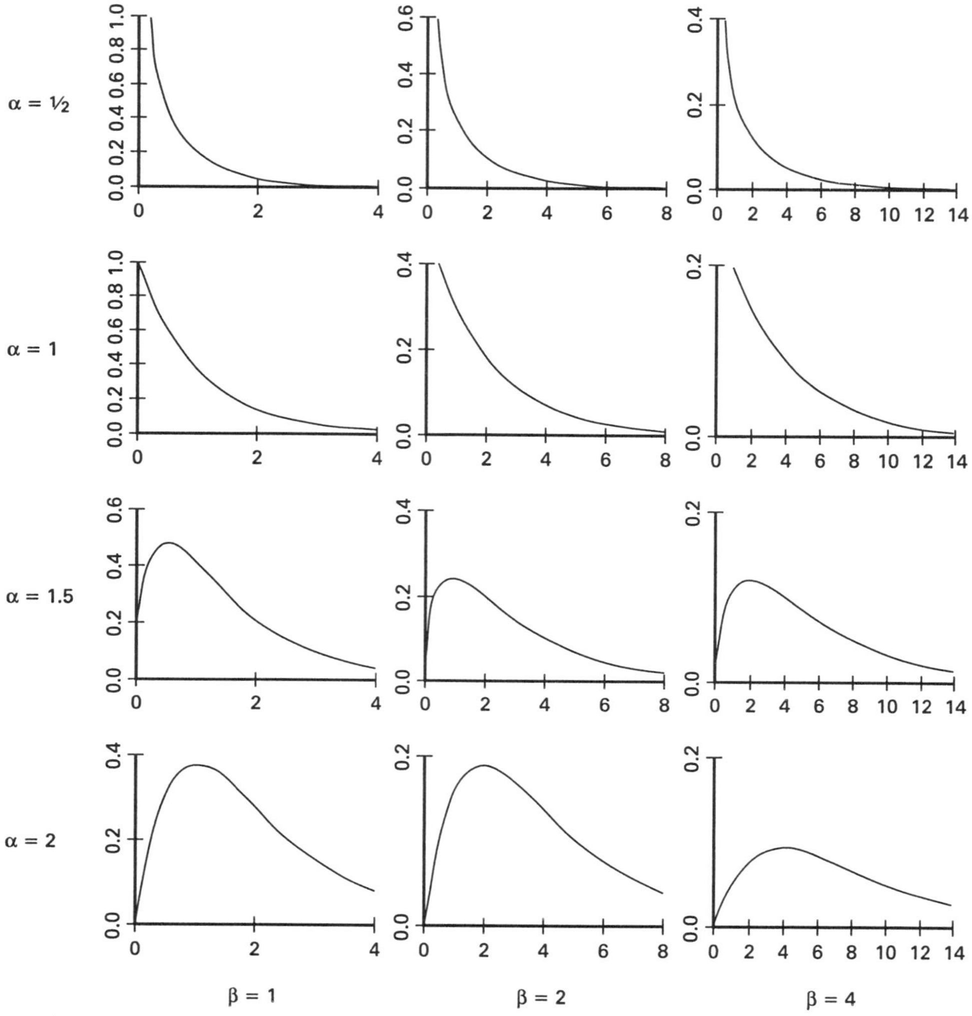

Figure 3.3.3
Gamma p.d.f.'s

$$P(Y > c + b | Y > c) = \frac{P(Y > c + b)}{P(Y > c)} = \frac{\exp[-(c + b)/-\beta]}{\exp[-c/\beta]}$$
$$= \exp[-b/\beta] = P(Y > b).$$

To help appreciate the importance of Theorem 3.3.9 consider the following. The exponential distribution is often used to describe the lifetimes of physical objects (e.g., transistors) or the duration of a state (e.g., unemployment). In context of unemployment, Theorem 3.3.9 implies the probability an unemployment spell will last $c + b$ days, given that it has lasted c days, is simply the probability of the spell lasting b days. Obviously, such *duration independence* can often be an overly restrictive condition, necessitating a more complicated distribution than the exponential (see Exercise 3.3.3).

Before introducing other continuous univariate distributions, we first relate the uniform, normal and gamma families in Theorems 3.3.10 through 3.3.12. Proofs are postponed until Chapter 4. For the present we are only trying to tie together different concepts so that they do not appear totally unrelated.

Theorem 3.3.10 Let Y be *any* continuous random variable with distribution function $F(\cdot)$. Then the random variable $X \equiv F(Y)$ has a uniform distribution over $[0, 1]$.

Proof See Example 4.4.3.

Theorem 3.3.11 Suppose $Y_t \sim G(\alpha_t, \beta)$ $(t = 1, 2, \ldots, T)$ are independent gamma random variables. Define

$$X \equiv \sum_{t=1}^{T} Y_t, \tag{3.3.41}$$

$$\alpha \equiv \sum_{t=1}^{T} \alpha_t. \tag{3.3.42}$$

Then $X \sim G(\alpha, \beta)$.

Proof See Exercise 4.3.3.

Theorem 3.3.12 Suppose $Y \sim N(\mu, \sigma^2)$, $\sigma^2 > 0$. Then $X \equiv [(Y - \mu)/\sigma]^2 \sim \chi^2(\nu)$, where $\nu = 1$.

Proof See Examples 4.2.1 or 4.3.2.

The next family of distributions comprises a flexible class of distributions with finite interval support. For convenience we introduce it in standardized form over the unit interval $[0, 1]$. Generalizations can be easily made when needed (see Johnson and Kotz 1970a).

Definition 3.3.7 A continuous random variable Y has a *beta distribution*, denoted $Y \sim \beta(\alpha, \delta)$, iff its p.d.f. is

$$f_\beta(y|\alpha,\delta) \equiv \begin{cases} [B(\alpha,\delta)]^{-1} y^{\alpha-1}(1-y)^{\delta-1}, & \text{if } 0 < y < 1 \\ 0, & \text{otherwise} \end{cases}, \tag{3.3.43}$$

where $\alpha > 0$, $\delta > 0$ and

$$B(\alpha,\delta) \equiv \frac{\Gamma(\alpha)\Gamma(\delta)}{\Gamma(\alpha+\delta)} \tag{3.3.44}$$

is the *beta function*. The distribution function of Y, denoted $F_\beta(y|\alpha,\delta)$, is called the *incomplete beta function* and it is widely tabulated.

Beta distributions comprise a two-parameter family of distributions which can assume a variety of shapes. If $\alpha > 1$, then (3.3.43) is tangential to the abscissa at $y = 0$, and if $\delta > 1$, then (3.3.43) is tangential at $y = 1$. If $\alpha = \delta = 1$, then (3.3.43) reduces to uniform density (3.3.1). Graphs of (3.3.43) for a variety of values of α and δ are given in Figure 3.3.4. Note that (3.3.43) is symmetric around $y = \frac{1}{2}$ *if* $\alpha = \delta$, positively skewed if $\alpha < \delta$, and negatively skewed if $\alpha > \delta$.

The m.g.f. for the beta distribution does not have a simple form (see John and Kotz 1970b, p. 40). Nonetheless, its moments can be easily computed from the following theorem.

Theorem 3.3.13 If Y has a beta distribution, then its mean and variance are, respectively,

$$\mu = \frac{\alpha}{\alpha+\delta}, \tag{3.3.45}$$

$$\sigma^2 = \frac{\alpha\delta}{(\alpha+\delta+1)(\alpha+\delta)^2}. \tag{3.3.46}$$

In addition, moments around the origin can be computed from

$$\begin{aligned} E(Y^m) &= \frac{\Gamma(m+\alpha)\Gamma(\alpha+\delta)}{\Gamma(\alpha)\Gamma(m+\alpha+\delta)} \\ &= \frac{B(m+\alpha,\delta)}{B(\alpha,\delta)}, \quad (m = 1, 2, 3, \ldots). \end{aligned} \tag{3.3.47}$$

The mode exists if $\alpha > 1$ and $\delta > 1$ is given by

$$y_{\text{mode}} = \frac{\alpha - 1}{\alpha + \beta - 2}. \tag{3.3.48}$$

Proof According to Definition 2.3.3,

$$\begin{aligned} E(Y^m) &= [B(\alpha,\delta)]^{-1} \int_0^1 y^{m+\alpha-1}(1-y)^{\delta-1}\,dy \\ &= \frac{B(m+\delta,\delta)}{B(\alpha,\delta)} \int_0^1 [B(m+\alpha,\delta)]^{-1} y^{m+\alpha-1}(1-y)^{\delta-1}\,dy. \end{aligned}$$

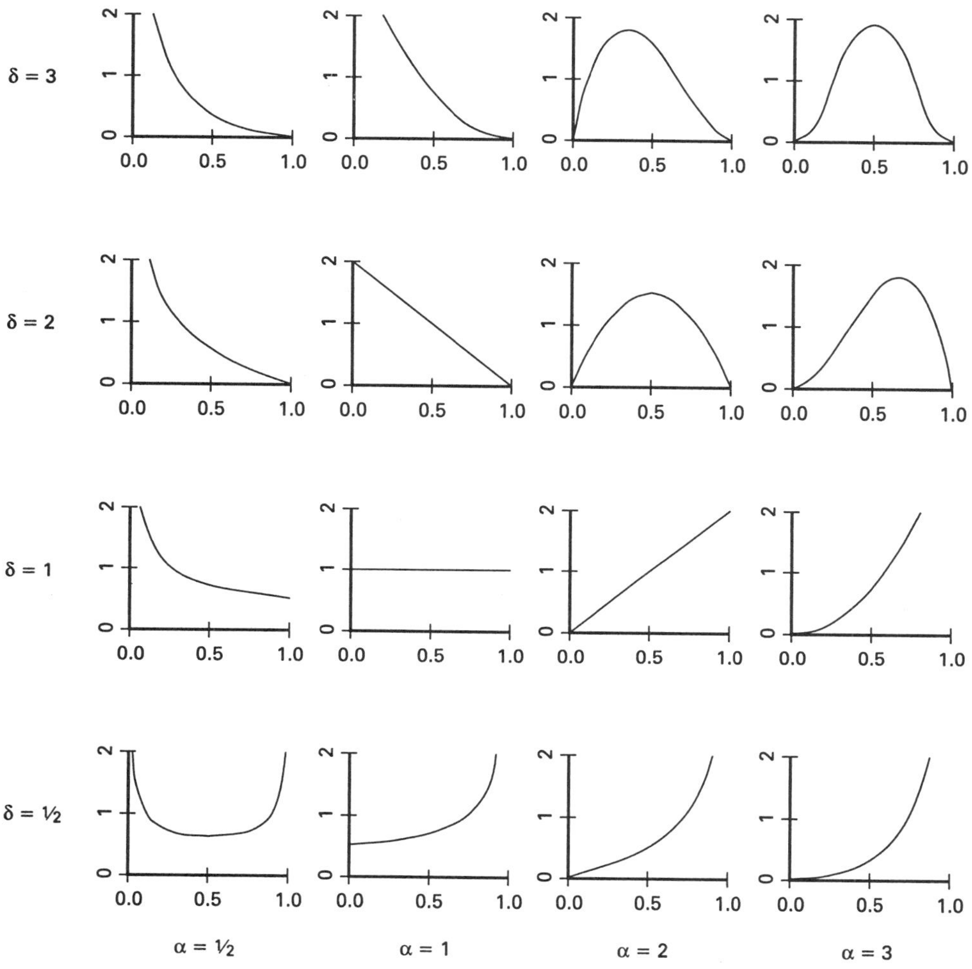

Figure 3.3.4
Beta p.d.f.'s

Because the integrand presented is the beta density $f_\beta(y|m + \alpha, \delta)$, the integral is unity and (3.3.47) follows immediately. Using (3.3.47) it is straightforward to derive (3.3.45) and (3.3.46). The mode (3.3.48) follows from straightforward differentiation of the beta p.d.f. in (3.3.43), equating the result to zero, and solving for y. Second order conditions can be checked to verify that a local maximum occurs at (3.3.48).

The following theorem gives a simple relationship between the beta and gamma distributions that worth noting.

Theorem 3.3.14 Let X have a gamma distribution with parameters α_1 and $\beta = 1$ and let Z have a gamma distribution with parameters α_2 and $\beta = 1$. Further suppose X and Z are independent. Then $Y \equiv X/(X + Z)$ has a beta distribution with parameters $\alpha = \alpha_1$ and $\delta = \alpha_2$.

Proof Postponed to Chapter 4.

The Student t-distribution is frequently encountered in applied work. The development of the Student t-distribution is attributed to W. S. Gosset, who at the time was employed by an Irish brewery. Because the brewery did not permit the publication of research by its staff, Gosset chose the pen name "Student." The following definition expands the Student t-distribution to the broader family of t-distributions.

Definition 3.3.8 A continuous random variable Y has a *t-distribution*, denoted $Y \sim t(\theta, \alpha, v)$, iff its p.d.f. is

$$f_t(y|\theta, \alpha, v) = c_t^{-1}\left[1 + \frac{1}{v}\left(\frac{y - \theta}{\alpha}\right)^2\right]^{-(v+1)/2}, \qquad -\infty < y < \infty, \tag{3.3.49}$$

where $-\infty < \theta < \infty$, $\alpha > 0$, $v > 0$, and the integrating constant is

$$c_t = c_t(v) = B(\tfrac{1}{2}v, \tfrac{1}{2}v)(v\alpha^2)^{1/2}. \tag{3.3.50}$$

The standardized random variable $Z \equiv (Y - \theta)/\alpha$ has a p.d.f. of the form (3.3.49) with $\theta = 0$ and $\alpha = 1$, known as a *Student t-distribution* with v degrees of freedom, denoted $Z \sim t(v)$. If $v = 1$ in (3.3.49), then Y has a *Cauchy distribution* in which case $c_t(1) = \pi\alpha$. The *standardized Cauchy distribution* has a p.d.f. of the form (3.3.49) with $\theta = 0$, $\alpha = 1$ and $v = 1$.

The p.d.f. of the t-distribution is a bell-shaped curve symmetric around $y = \theta$, which is also its mode and median. As $v \to \infty$ the t-distribution approaches a normal distribution with mean θ and variance α^2. For finite v the p.d.f. of the t-distribution is similar in appearance to the normal p.d.f. depicted in Figure 3.3.2 except that it has "fatter" tails. See Figure 3.3.5 for examples.

Moments of the t-distribution are given in the next theorem.

Theorem 3.3.15 If Y has a t-distribution, then its m.g.f. does *not* exist. However, it may have moments depending on the degrees of freedom v. For example, the mean is

$$E(Y) = \theta, \qquad \text{if } v > 1. \tag{3.3.51}$$

Even-ordered moments around the mean are:

$$E[(Y - \theta)^{2r}] = \frac{\Gamma(r + \frac{1}{2})\Gamma[(\frac{1}{2}v) - r](v\alpha^2)^r}{\Gamma(\frac{1}{2})\Gamma(\frac{1}{2}v)} \qquad (r = 1, 2, \ldots) \text{ if } v > 2r. \tag{3.3.52}$$

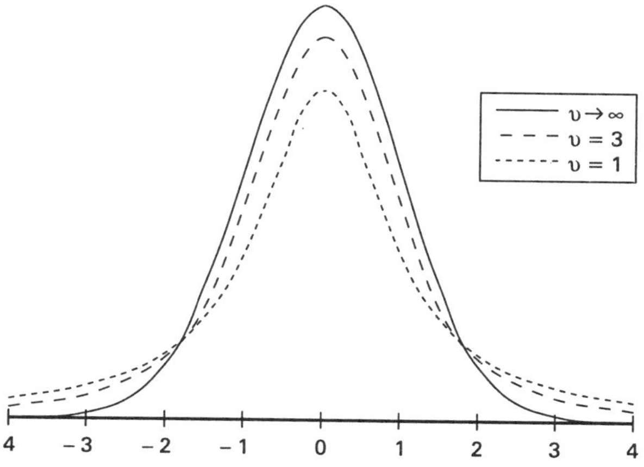

Figure 3.3.5
Standardized t-densities with $v = 1$, $v = 3$, and $v \to \infty$

In particular, the first two even-ordered moments around the mean are:

$$\operatorname{Var}(Y) = \alpha^2\left(\frac{v}{v-2}\right), \quad \text{if } v > 2, \tag{3.3.53}$$

$$E[(Y-\theta)^4] = \frac{3v^2\alpha^4}{(v-2)(v-4)}, \quad \text{if } v > 4. \tag{3.3.54}$$

All odd-ordered moments around the mean are zero (provided they exist):

$$E[(Y-\theta)^{2r+1}] = 0 \quad (r = 0, 1, 2, \ldots), \text{ if } v > 2r + 1. \tag{3.3.55}$$

In all cases, θ is the median and mode.

Proof Zellner (1971, pp. 366–369).

The t-distribution plays a central role in both classical and Bayesian statistics. In the case of the former it serves as the basis for many test statistics and confidence intervals. This basis is the result of the following important theorem which ties together normal, chi-squared and t-distributions.

Theorem 3.3.16 Let $Z \sim N(0, 1)$ and $X \sim \chi^2(v)$ be independent. Then

$$Y = \frac{Z}{[X/v]^{1/2}} \sim t(v). \tag{3.3.56}$$

Proof To be given in Section 4.4.

The final distribution we emphasize in this section is closely related to the chi-squared and t-distributions, and hence, also to the normal distribution. It is defined as follows.

Definition 3.3.9 A continuous random variable Y is said to have a *F-distribution*, denoted $F(\nu_1, \nu_2)$ iff its p.d.f. is

$$f_F(y|\nu_1, \nu_2) \equiv \begin{Bmatrix} \dfrac{c_F^{-1} y^{(\nu_1 - 2)/2}}{[1 + (\nu_1 y/\nu_2)]^{(\nu_1+\nu_2)/2}}, & \text{if } y > 0 \\ 0, & \text{if } y \le 0 \end{Bmatrix}, \tag{3.3.57}$$

where $\nu_1 > 0$, $\nu_2 > 0$, and the integrating constant is

$$c_F = c_F(\nu_1, \nu_2) = B\left(\frac{1}{2}\nu_1, \frac{1}{2}\nu_2\right)\left(\frac{\nu_1}{\nu_2}\right)^{-\nu_1/2}. \tag{3.3.58}$$

The parameters ν_1 and ν_2 are, respectively, *degrees of freedom in the numerator* and *degrees of freedom in the denominator*.

The p.d.f. of the F-distribution is skewed to the right. If $\nu_1 = 1$, (3.3.57) approaches zero as $y \to 0$. If $\nu_1 = 2$, (3.3.57) has a mode at zero. If

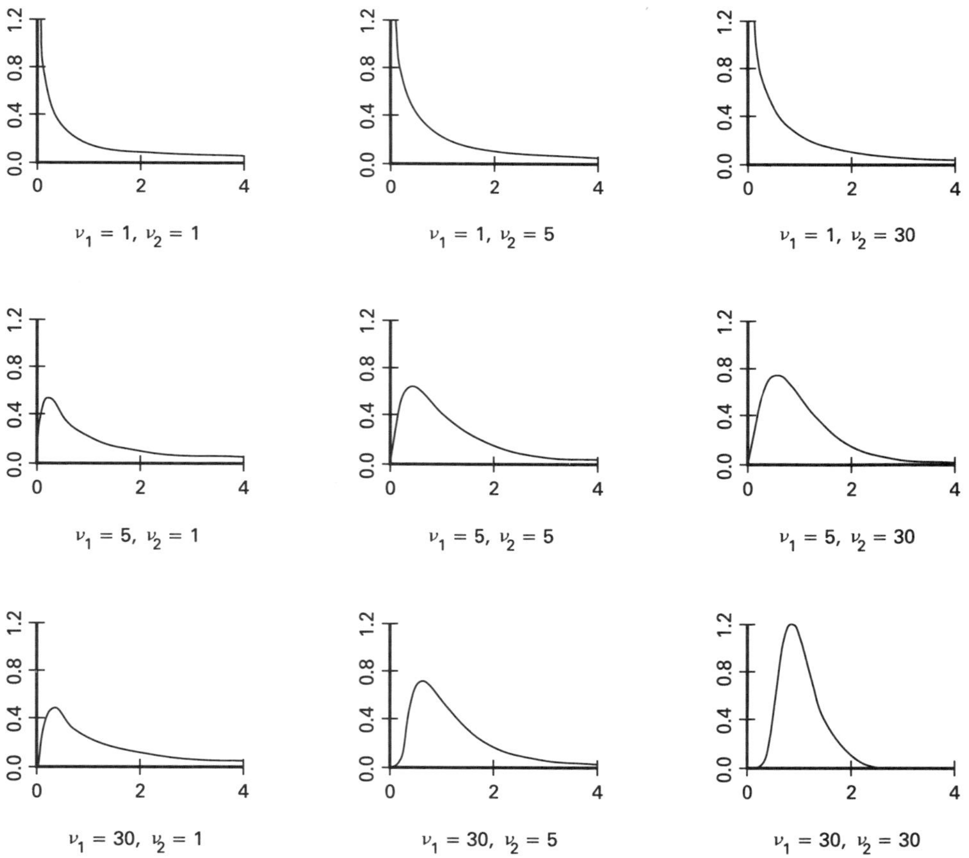

Figure 3.3.6
F-p.d.f.'s

$\nu_1 > 2$, then (3.3.57) has a mode at $y = \nu_2(\nu_1 - 2)/[\nu_1(\nu_2 + 2)]$. Like the t-distribution, the m.g.f. of the F-distribution does *not* exist. It does, however, possess moments for sufficiently large values of ν_2. Figure 3.3.6 illustrates numerous special cases of F-densities.

The moment generating function does not exist for the F-distribution, however, some explicit moment formulae are given in the following theorem. Note like in the earlier case of the Student t-distribution, only some lower order moments may exist.

Theorem 3.3.17 Suppose that the continuous random variable Y has an F-distribution with ν_1 and ν_2 degrees of freedom, that is, $Y \sim F(\nu_1, \nu_2)$, then

$$E(Y^m) = \left(\frac{\nu_2}{\nu_1}\right)^m \left[\frac{\Gamma(\frac{1}{2}\nu_1 + m)\Gamma(\frac{1}{2}\nu_2 - m)}{\Gamma(\frac{1}{2}\nu_1)\Gamma(\frac{1}{2}\nu_2)}\right], \quad \text{if } m < \frac{1}{2}\nu_2. \tag{3.3.59}$$

In particular the mean and variance are, respectively,

$$\mu = \frac{\nu_2}{\nu_2 - 2}, \quad \text{if } \nu_2 > 2, \tag{3.3.60}$$

$$\sigma^2 = \frac{2\nu_2^2(\nu_1 + \nu_2 - 2)}{\nu_1(\nu_2 - 2)^2(\nu_2 - 4)}, \quad \text{if } \nu_2 > 4. \tag{3.3.61}$$

When ν_2 does not satisfy these inequalities, then the respective moments do not exist.

Proof Mood et al. (1974, p. 248) derives (3.3.60).

Important relationships between the F-distribution and other distributions that we have considered are given in the following theorem.

Theorem 3.3.18 Let X and Y be random variables.

(a) Let $Y \sim t(\nu)$ and let $X \equiv Y^2$. Then $X \sim F(1, \nu)$.

(b) Let $Y_n \sim \chi^2(\nu_n)$ $(n = 1, 2)$ be independent. Then $X \equiv (Y_1/\nu_1)/(Y_2/\nu_2) \sim F(\nu_1, \nu_2)$.

(c) Let $Y \sim F(\nu_1, \nu_2)$ and $X \equiv (\nu_1 Y/\nu_2)/[1 + (\nu_1 Y/\nu_2)]$. Then $X \sim B(\frac{1}{2}\nu_1, \frac{1}{2}\nu_2)$.

(d) Let $Y \sim F(\nu_1, \nu_2)$ and let $X \equiv Y^{-1}$. Then $X \sim F(\nu_2, \nu_1)$. Thus, although the F-distribution is asymmetric, it is only necessary to tabulate, say, the upper tail of the cumulative distribution function because $P(Y \leq y) = P(X \geq y^{-1})$. See Table D.3.

(e) Let $Y \sim F(\nu_1, \nu_2)$. As $\nu_2 \to \infty$, $Y \to \nu_1^{-1}\chi^2(\nu_1)$.

Proof Postponed until Section 4.

The distributions discussed so far in this section are the most important continuous univariate distributions encountered in econometrics. Others are described in Table 3.3.1, together with helpful summary information.

Table 3.3.1
Other continuous univariate distributions

(a) Burr:* Bu(δ, λ)

$$F_{\mathrm{Bu}}(z|\gamma,\lambda) = \begin{cases} 1-(1+z^{\gamma})^{-\lambda}, & \text{if } z<0 \\ 1, & \text{if } z \geq 0 \end{cases} \qquad (\gamma>0, \lambda>0)$$

$$f_{\mathrm{Bu}}(z|\gamma,\lambda) = \begin{cases} \lambda\gamma z^{\gamma-1}(1+z^{\gamma})^{-(\lambda-1)}, & \text{if } z<0 \\ 0, & \text{if } z \geq 0 \end{cases}$$

$$E(Z^m) = \lambda B\left(1+\frac{m}{\gamma}, \lambda-\frac{m}{\gamma}\right), \quad \text{if } m<\gamma\lambda$$

Median: $\xi_{.50} = [(\tfrac{1}{2})^{-(1/\lambda)} - 1]^{1/\gamma}$

Note: Skewed to the right.

(b) Exponential power family:* EPF(λ)

$$f_{\mathrm{EPF}}(z|\lambda) = \frac{\exp(-\tfrac{1}{2}|z|^{[2/(1+\lambda)]})}{\Gamma\left(1+\dfrac{1+\lambda}{2}\right)2^{[1+1/2(1+\lambda)]}} \qquad (-\infty<z<\infty, -1<\lambda\leq 1)$$

$E(Z) = 0$

$\mathrm{Var}(Z) = 2^{(1+\lambda)}\Gamma[3(1+\lambda)/2]/\Gamma[(1+\lambda)/2]$

Median $\xi_{.50} = 0$

Mode: $z = 0$

Note: Symmetric around zero; $\lambda = 0$ if $N(0,1)$; $\lambda = 1$ is Laplace (double exponential); $\lambda \to -1$, $f(\cdot) \to$ uniform.

(c) Extreme value (Gumbel):* EV

$F_{\mathrm{EV}}(z) = \exp[-\exp(-z)], \; -\infty<z<\infty$

$f_{\mathrm{EV}}(z) = F(z)\exp(-z), \; -\infty<z<\infty$

$M(t) = \Gamma(1-t)$, if $t<1$

$E(Z) = .57722$

$\mathrm{Var}(Z) = \pi^2/6$

Median: $\xi_{.50} = .36611$

Mode: $z = 0$

Note: $\exp(-Z)$ has an exponential distribution skewed to the right.

(d) Inverse Gaussian: ig(λ)**

$$F_{\mathrm{ig}}(z|\lambda) = \begin{cases} \Phi\left[(z-1)\left(\dfrac{\lambda}{z}\right)^{1/2}\right] + \exp(2\lambda)\Phi\left[-(z+1)\left(\dfrac{\lambda}{z}\right)^{1/2}\right], & \text{if } z>0 \\ 0, & \text{if } z \leq 0 \end{cases}$$

$$f_{\mathrm{ig}}(z|\lambda) = \begin{cases} \left(\dfrac{2\pi z^3}{\lambda}\right)^{-1/2} \exp\left[-\dfrac{\lambda(z-1)^2}{2z}\right], & \text{if } z>0 \\ 0, & \text{if } z \leq 0 \end{cases} \qquad (\lambda>0)$$

$E(Z) = 1$

$\mathrm{Var}(Z) = \lambda^{-1}$

$E[\{Z-E(Z)\}^3] = 3\lambda^{-2}$

$E[\{Z-E(Z)\}^4] = 15\lambda^{-3} + 3\lambda^{-2}$

Mode: $z = [1+(9/4\lambda^2)]^{1/2} - (3/2\lambda)$

Note: $Z \to N(0,1)$ as $\lambda \to \infty$; skewed to the right.

Table 3.3.1 (cont.)

(e) Inverted gamma: $\mathbf{IG}(\alpha, \beta)$

$$f_{IG}(y|\alpha,\beta) = \begin{cases} [\Gamma(\alpha)]^{-1}\beta^{-\alpha}y^{-(\alpha+1)}\exp(-1/\beta y), & \text{if } 0 < y < \infty \\ 0, & \text{if } y \leq 0 \end{cases}$$

$E(Y) = [\beta(\alpha - 1)]^{-1}$, if $\alpha > 1$

$\text{Var}(Y) = [\beta^2(\alpha - 1)^2(\alpha - 2)]^{-1}$, if $\alpha > 2$

Mode: $y = [\beta(\alpha + \frac{1}{2})]^{-1/2}$

Notes: Skewed to the right; $Y^{-1} \sim G(\alpha, \beta)$.

(f) Logistic:* LOG

$F_{LOG}(z) = [1 + \exp(-z)]^{-1}, \ -\infty < z < \infty$

$f_{LOG}(z) = F_{LOG}(z)[1 - F_{LOG}(z)], \ -\infty < z < \infty$

$M(t) = B(1 - t, 1 + t)$

$E(Z) = 0$

$\text{Var}(Z) = \pi^2/3$

$E[(Z - E(z))^4] = 7\pi^4/15$

Median: $\xi_{.50} = 0$

Mode: $z = 0$

Note: Symmetric around $z = 0$.

(g) Lognormal: $\mathbf{LN}(\gamma, \delta)$

$$F_{LN}(z|\gamma,\delta) = \begin{cases} \Phi\left(\dfrac{\ln(z) - \gamma}{\delta}\right), & \text{if } z > 0 \\ 0, & \text{if } z \leq 0 \end{cases}$$

$$f_{LN}(z|\gamma,\delta) = \begin{cases} z^{-1}\phi(\ln(z)|\gamma,\delta), & \text{if } z > 0 \\ 0, & \text{if } z \leq 0 \end{cases}$$

$E(Z^m) = \exp(m^2\delta^2/2)$

$\text{Var}(Z) = \exp(\delta^2)[\exp(\delta^2) - 1]$

Median: $\xi_{.50} = 1$

Mode: $z = \exp(-\delta^2)$

Notes: Skewed to the right; $\ln Z \sim N(\gamma, \delta)$; m.g.f. does *not* exist.

(h) Pareto: $\mathbf{Pa}(\gamma, \lambda)$

$$F_{Pa}(z|\gamma,\lambda) = \begin{cases} 1 - \left(\dfrac{\gamma}{z}\right)^{\lambda}, & \text{if } z \geq \gamma \\ 0, & \text{if } z < \gamma \end{cases}$$

$$f_{Pa}(z|\gamma,\lambda) = \begin{cases} \dfrac{\lambda\gamma^{\lambda}}{z^{\lambda+1}}, & \text{if } z \geq \gamma \\ 0, & \text{if } z < \gamma \end{cases}$$

$E(Z^m) = \lambda\gamma^m/(\lambda - m)$, if $m < \lambda$

Median: $\xi_{.50} = \gamma 2^{1/\lambda}$

Mode: $z = \gamma$

Notes: Skewed to the right; m.g.f. does not exist.

Table 3.3.1 (Cont.)

(i) Weibull:* We(λ)

$$F_{\text{We}}(z|\lambda) = \begin{cases} 1 - \exp[-z^{\lambda}], & \text{if } z > 0 \\ 0, & \text{if } z \le 0 \end{cases} \qquad (\lambda > 0)$$

$$f_{\text{We}}(z|\lambda) = \begin{cases} \lambda z^{\lambda-1} \exp(-z^{\lambda}), & \text{if } z > 0 \\ 0, & \text{if } z \le 0 \end{cases}$$

$Z^{\lambda} \sim \text{EXP}(1)$

$E(Z^m) = \Gamma(m\lambda^{-1} + 1)$

$$\text{Mode: } z = \begin{cases} \gamma\left(\dfrac{\lambda - 1}{\lambda}\right)^{1/\lambda} + \delta, & \text{if } \lambda > 1 \\ 0, & \text{if } 0 < \lambda < 1 \end{cases}$$

Note: Skewed to the right.

* Stated in standardized form; can easily be extended to location-scale form by replacing Z with $Z = (Y - \theta)/\alpha$.

** Stated in standardized form; can easily be extended by replacing Z with $Z = Y/\alpha$.

Table 3.3.2
Variances and selected quantiles of some symmetric distributions

		Quantiles			
Distribution	Variance	$\xi_{.75}$	$\xi_{.90}$	$\xi_{.95}$	$\xi_{.99}$
Cauchy [$t(1)$]	∞	1.000	3.078	6.314	31.82
$t(2)$	∞	.816	1.886	2.920	6.965
$t(3)$	3.000	.765	1.638	2.353	4.541
$t(4)$	2.000	.741	1.533	2.132	3.747
$t(15)$	1.154	.691	1.341	1.753	2.602
$t(30)$	1.071	.683	1.310	1.697	2.457
$t(\infty) = N(0, 1)$	1.000	.674	1.282	1.645	2.326
$N(0, \pi^2/3)$	1.814	1.223	2.325	2.984	4.219
Laplace	2.000	.693	1.609	2.303	3.912
Logistic	1.814	1.098	2.197	2.944	4.595

Note: The t-distribution is defined in Definition 3.3.39. The $N(0, 1)$ distribution is defined in Definition 3.3.3. The Laplace and logistic distribution are defined in Table 3.3.1(b) and 3.3.1(f), respectively.

In order to help contrast tail behavior, the variance and the .75, .90, .95, and .99 quantiles (recall Exercise 2.2.3) for a variety of symmetric standardized distributions is given in Table 3.3.2. It is clear from Table 3.3.2 that as the degrees of freedom v of the Student t-distribution goes from one (Cauchy) to infinity (standard normal), the quantiles move toward the median of zero, and the variances go from infinity to unity. The quantiles of the *Laplace/double exponential distribution* (see Table 3.3.1b with $\lambda = 1$ and Exercise 3.3.22) are similar to a t(3)-distribution, although its variance is two rather than three. The .95 and .99 quantiles and the variance of the logistic distribution are very close to those of the $N(0, \pi^2/3)$ distribution.

Many of the distributions encountered in Section 3.2 and this section are members of the following family of distributions which are of significant theoretical importance.

Definition 3.3.10 Let $\gamma \in \Gamma$ be a $M \times 1$ vector of parameters. A random variable Y has a distribution belonging to the *K-parameter exponential family of distributions* iff its p.f. can be expressed as

$$f_{EXF}(y|\gamma) = \exp\left[a(\gamma) + b(y) + \sum_{k=1}^{K} \theta_k(\gamma)d_k(y)\right], \tag{3.3.62}$$

where $\theta = [\theta_1, \theta_2, \ldots, \theta_K]'$ and $a(\theta)$, $b(y)$ and $d_k(y)$ $(k = 1, 2, \ldots, K)$ are suitably chosen functions. Often it is more convenient to use the θ_ks as the parameters and write the density in its *canonical form*:

$$f_{EXFC}(y|\theta) = \exp\left[c(\theta) + b(y) + \sum_{k=1}^{K} \theta_k d_k(y)\right], \tag{3.3.63}$$

for some suitably chosen function $c(\theta)$. The set Θ of points for which (3.3.63) integrates to unity with respect to y is known as the *natural parameter space*. If $K = 1$ and $d_K(y) = y$ in either (3.3.62) or (3.3.63), then the family is referred to as the *linear exponential family*.

It can be shown that Θ is convex (see Lehmann 1986, p. 57). It is assumed that neither the θ_k's and d_k's satisfy any linear constraints in which case representation (3.3.63) is said to be *minimal*. If in addition Θ contains an open K-dimensional rectangle, then family (3.3.63) is said to be of *full rank*. For extensive discussion of the exponential family, see Barndorff-Nielsen (1978), Brown (1986), or Lehmann (1983, 1986).

Many of the distributions discussed in this section belong to the exponential family (see Exercise 3.3.10). Notable exceptions are distributions whose supports (recall Definition 2.2.6) depend on the unknown parameters, for example, the uniform distribution $U(0, \theta)$.

Generalizations of many of the distributions in this section are possible and sometimes important (see Exercises 3.3.8 and 3.3.10). For example, the importance of the chi-squared distribution, Student t-distribution, and F-distribution stems in large part from their role in hypothesis testing (Chapter 7) where they describe the distribution of test statistics under the *null* hypothesis. Under the *alternative* hypothesis, such test statistics have distributions which are generalizations of these distributions obtained by introducing so-called *noncentrality parameters* (which have nonzero values under the alternative hypothesis, and zero values under the null hypothesis). These noncentral distributions are discussed in Section 4.5 (see also Patnaik 1949).

For an extensive discussion of continuous univariate distributions, see Johnson and Kotz (1970a, 1970b). Finally, as a convenient summary of this section, the reader is urged to study Figure 3.3.7.

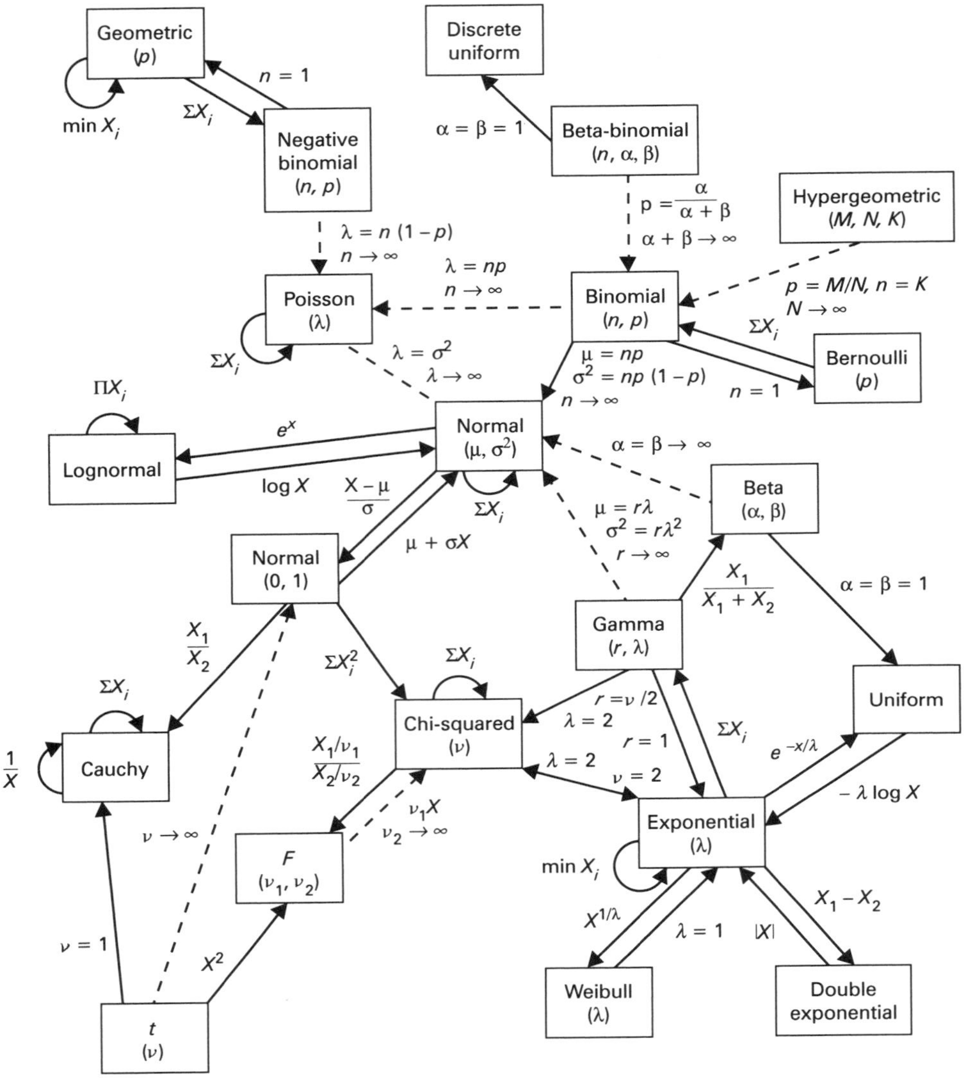

*Solid lines represent transformations and special cases, and dashed lines represent limits. [Adapted from Leemis (1986) and Casella and Berger (1991, p. 630).]

Figure 3.3.7
Relationships among common distributions

Exercises

3.3.1 Suppose $Y \sim N(\mu, \sigma^2)$. Show the following:

(a) $E(|Y - \mu|) = \sigma(2/\pi)^{1/2}$.

(b) $\phi(y|\mu, \sigma^2)$ has points of inflection at $y = \mu \pm \sigma$.

3.3.2 Recall Exercise 2.2.4 and consider the *truncated normal* random variable Z with p.d.f.

$$f_{TN}(z|\mu, \sigma^2) = \left\{ \begin{array}{ll} \dfrac{\phi(z|\mu, \sigma^2)}{\Phi(b|\mu, \sigma^2) - \Phi(a|\mu, \sigma^2)}, & \text{if } a < z < b \\ 0, & \text{otherwise} \end{array} \right\}. \tag{3.3.64}$$

Define $a^* \equiv (a - \mu)/\sigma$ and $b^* = (b - \mu)/\sigma$.

(a) Show: $E(Z) = \mu + \sigma\left[\dfrac{\phi(a^*) - \phi(b^*)}{\Phi(b^*) - \Phi(a^*)}\right]$.

(b) Show: $\mathrm{Var}(Z) = \sigma^2\left[1 + \dfrac{a^*\phi(a^*) - b^*\phi(b^*)}{\Phi(b^*) - \Phi(a^*)} - \left(\dfrac{\phi(a^*) - \phi(b^*)}{\Phi(b^*) - \Phi(a^*)}\right)^2\right]$.

3.3.3 Suppose the life-time of an individual is represented by a continuous random variable Y with p.d.f. $f(\cdot)$ and c.d.f. $F(\cdot)$. The probability of surviving until at least a time y is $P(Y > y) = 1 - F(y)$. The probability that an individual, having survived to time y, will survive a further time t is

$$P(Y > y + t|Y > y) = 1 - \left[\frac{F(y + t) - F(y)}{1 - F(y)}\right]. \tag{3.3.65}$$

The "death rate per unit time" is $t^{-1}P[Y > y + t|Y > y]$, and the instantaneous death rate as $t \to 0$ is known as the *hazard rate*:

$$h(y) \equiv \operatorname*{Limit}_{t \to 0} t^{-1}P(Y > y + t|Y > y] = \frac{f(y)}{1 - F(y)}. \tag{3.3.66}$$

(a) Show that the exponential distribution has a constant hazard rate.

(b) Show that the Weibull distribution (see Table 3.3.1i) has an increasing hazard rate for $\lambda > 1$, and a decreasing hazard rate for $\lambda < 1$.

3.3.4 Suppose $Y \sim N(20, \sigma^2)$ and that $P(Y > 15) = .90$. Use Table D.1 to find σ.

3.3.5 Suppose that the number of fatal car accidents in a particular region follows a Poisson distribution with an average of one per *day*.

(a) What is the probability of more than twelve such accidents in a *week*?

(b) What is the probability that more than three days will lapse between two such accidents?

3.3.6 Compute the measures of skewness and kurtosis discussed in Exercises 2.3.5 and 2.3.6 for the gamma distribution $G(\alpha, \beta)$. What happens to these measures as $\alpha \to \infty$? How do you interpret your result?

3.3.7 Show: the c.d.f. of the Cauchy random variable is $F(y) = \frac{1}{2} + \pi^{-1}\arctan[(y - \theta)/\alpha]$, $-\infty < y < \infty$.

3.3.8 Near the end of the nineteenth century Karl Pearson developed the *Pearson family* of distributions in which the p.d.f. $f(y)$ satisfies the differential equation

$$\frac{1}{f(y)}\frac{d[f(y)]}{dy} = -\frac{a + y}{b + cy + dy^2} \tag{3.3.67}$$

subject to the constraints that $f(y) \geq 0$ and $f(y)$ integrates to unity. If a formal solution to the differential equation does not satisfy $f(y) \geq 0$, then the range of values of y is restricted to those for which $f(y) > 0$, and $f(y) = 0$ is assigned when y is outside this family. For appropriate choices of a, b, c, and d, show that each of the following distributions is a member of the Pearson family (see Johnson and Kotz 1970a, pp. 9–15):

(a) normal distribution

(b) beta distribution

(c) gamma distribution

(d) t-distribution.

3.3.9 Suppose $X \sim t(\nu)$, $Y \sim F(1, \nu)$ and $E(X^{2r})$ exists. Show: $E(X^{2r}) = E(Y^r)$.

3.3.10 Show the following distributions belong to the exponential family: Bernoulli, binomial, Poisson, beta, exponential, gamma, normal (unknown mean, known variance) and normal (unknown mean and variance). In what sense is the negative binomial distribution a member? Identify any cases that belong to the linear exponential family.

3.3.11 Suppose $Y \sim N(\mu, \sigma^2)$ and let $g(\cdot)$ be a differentiable function satisfying $E|g'(Y)| < \infty$.

(a) Show: $E[g(Y)(Y - \mu)] = \sigma^2 E[g'(Y)]$.

(b) Use (a) to show: $E(Y^3) = 3\mu\sigma^2 + \mu^3$.

3.3.12 Suppose $Y \sim \Gamma(\alpha, \beta)$, $\alpha > 1$, and let a and b be constants. Use integration by parts to show: $P(a < Y < b) = \beta[f_y(a|\alpha, \beta) - f_y(b|\alpha, \beta)] + P(a < Z < b)$, where $Z \sim \Gamma(\alpha - 1, \beta)$. Note that if α is an integer, repeated use of this recursive formula leads to an integral that can be evaluated analytically (i.e., Z has an exponential distribution with $\alpha = 1$).

3.3.13 Suppose $Y|Z \sim B(T, Z)$ and $Z \sim \beta(\alpha, \delta)$. The marginal distribution of Y is known as the *beta-binomial distribution.*

(a) Show that the marginal p.m.f. of Y is:

$$P(Y = y) = \binom{T}{y}\left[\frac{\Gamma(\alpha + \delta)\Gamma(y + \alpha)\Gamma(T - y + \delta)}{\Gamma(\alpha)\Gamma(\delta)\Gamma(\alpha + \delta + T)}\right]. \tag{3.3.68}$$

(b) Show: $E(Y) = T\alpha/(\alpha + \delta)$.

(c) Show: $\text{Var}(Y) = [T\alpha\delta(T + \alpha + \delta)]/[(\alpha + \delta)^2(\alpha + \delta + 1)]$.

(d) What is the distribution of Y when $\alpha = \delta = 1$?

Note: For an extension to where Z is Dirichlet (Exercise 3.4.23) and $Y|Z$ is multinomial (Definition 3.4.1); see Johnson and Kotz (1969, pp. 308–311).

3.3.14 Suppose $Y|Z \sim P(Z)$ and $Z \sim \Gamma(\alpha, \delta)$. Show that the marginal p.m.f. of Y negative binomial.

3.3.15 Suppose $Y|N, Z \sim B(N, Z)$, $N|Z \sim P(Z)$ and $Z \sim \Gamma(\alpha, \delta)$. Show that the marginal p.m.f. of Y is the same as in Exercise 3.3.14.

3.3.16 Suppose X and Y be i.i.d. random variables with zero means, unit variances, and that $(X + Y)/2^{1/2}$ has the same distribution as X and Y. Show: $X \sim N(0, 1)$.

3.3.17 A useful property of the exponential family is that for any integrable function $h(y)$ and any θ in the interior of Θ, the integral

$$\int_{-\infty}^{\infty} h(y)\exp\left[c(\theta) + b(y) + \sum_{k=1}^{K} \theta_k d_k(y)\right] dy, \tag{3.3.69}$$

is continuous and has derivatives of all orders with respect to θ, and these can be obtained by differentiating under the integral sign (see Lehmann 1986, pp. 59–60). For k, $i = 1, 2, \ldots, K$ and $k \neq i$, use (3.3.69) with $h(y) = 1$ to show:

$$E[d_k(y)] = -\frac{\partial c(\theta)}{\partial \theta_k}, \tag{3.3.70}$$

$$\text{Cov}[d_k(y), d_i(y)] = -\frac{\partial^2 c(\theta)}{\partial \theta_k \, \partial \theta_i}. \tag{3.3.71}$$

3.3.18 The random vector $d(Y) = [d_1(Y), d_2(Y), \ldots, d_K(Y)]'$ plays a crucial role in the exponential family density (3.3.43). Show that the moment generating function of $d(Y)$ is

$$M_Y(t) = \exp[c(\theta + t) - c(\theta)]. \tag{3.3.72}$$

for some $t = [t_1, t_2, \ldots, t_K]'$ in the neighborhood of the origin.

3.3.19 Suppose $Y \sim t(1)$, i.e. standardized Cauchy.

(a) Show: $\int_0^c y(1 + y^2)^{-1}\, dy = \frac{1}{2}\ln(1 + c^2)$.

(b) Using (a), show: $E(|Y|) = \infty$.

3.3.20 A c.d.f. F_X is *stochastically greater* than a c.d.f. F_Y iff $F_X(t) \le F_Y(t)$ for all t and $F_X(t) < F_Y(t)$ for some t. Show that if $X \sim F_X$ and $Y \sim F_Y$, then $P(X > t) \ge P(Y > t)$ for all t, and $P(X > t) > P(Y > t)$ for some t. (In other words, X tends to be bigger than Y.)

3.3.21 A family of c.d.f.'s $\{F(x|\theta), \theta \in \Theta\}$ is *stochastically increasing in* θ iff $\theta_1 > \theta_2$ implies $F(x|\theta_1)$ is stochastically greater than $F(x|\theta_2)$. Show that the $N(\mu, \sigma^2)$ family is stochastically increasing in μ for fixed σ^2.

3.3.22 Consider the Laplace distribution that corresponds to the exponential power family (see Table 3.3.1b) with $\lambda = 1$. Because this distribution amounts to reflecting the exponential distribution around zero, it is also known as the *double exponential* distribution.

(a) Graph the p.d.f. of the Laplace distribution.

(b) Find the c.d.f. of the Laplace distribution.

3.3.23 Verify the entries in Table 3.3.2.

3.4 Multivariate Distributions: I

There have been many approaches to constructing multivariate distributions. One approach is based on generalizations of the univariate Pearson system of distributions (see Exercise 3.3.8). Other approaches are based on series expansions (e.g., Gram-Charlier or Edgeworth) or on transformations to a multivariate normal distribution. For a detailed discussion, see Johnson and Kotz (1972, pp. 1–31).

The need for such general approaches arises because marginal distributions do *not* uniquely define a joint distribution.[5] In other words, many joint distributions may have identical marginal distributions (see Exercises

5. Under fairly mild regularity conditions, it can be shown that *all* univariate *conditional* distributions do uniquely characterize the joint distribution (see Arnold et al. 1992 and Gourieroux and Monfort 1979). Also, according to a theorem due to Cramér and Wold, the multivariate distribution of any N-dimensional column vector Y is completely determined by the univariate distributions of linear functions $c'Y$ where c is an arbitrary $N \times 1$ vector of constants.

2.4.5, 3.4.4–3.4.6).[6] One way of restricting the class of possible joint distributions is to add the restriction that conditional distributions and marginal distributions are members of the same parametric family of distributions, but this is not always possible. For example, Seshadri and Patil (1964) show that no bivariate distribution exists having both marginal and conditional distributions of the Poisson form.

Although the marginal distributions do not uniquely determine the joint distribution, they do put limits on its behavior. For example, in the bivariate case, let Y_n $(n = 1, 2)$ be continuous random variables with marginal distribution functions $F_n(\cdot)$ $(n = 1, 2)$, respectively. Fréchet (1951) showed that the joint c.d.f. $F_Y(y_1, y_2)$ must satisfy

$$\max[F_1(y_1) + F_2(y_2) - 1, 0] \leq F_Y(y_1, y_2) \leq \min[F_1(y_1), F_2(y_2)]. \quad (3.4.1)$$

Plackett (1965) gave a one-parameter family of bivariate distributions, which included these boundary distributions and also permitted independent random variables (see Exercise 3.4.13). Mardia (1970) extended these results to include the bivariate normal distribution.

No attempt is made in this section to survey all the multivariate distributions found in the statistics literature. Interested readers are directed to Johnson and Kotz (1969, Chapter 11; 1972), Mardia (1970), and Ord (1972) for extensive discussions. Rather in this section I discuss only multivariate distributions that commonly arise in the econometrics literature. Other cases are introduced through exercises at the end of this section. Extensions to more complicated, yet common multivariate distributions, are provided in Section 3.5. The emphasis is on continuous, as opposed to discrete, multivariate distributions.

In this section we denote the $N \times 1$ vector of interest as Z instead of Y in order that we can partition it as $Z = [Y', X']'$ in correspondence with later use in regression analysis. We begin the discussion with a common discrete multivariate distribution.

Consider an experiment whose outcomes must belong to one of $N \geq 2$ mutually exclusive and exhaustive categories, and let θ_n $(0 < \theta_n < 1)$ be the probability that the outcome belongs to the nth category $(n = 1, 2, \ldots, N)$, where $\theta_1 + \theta_2 + \cdots + \theta_N = 1$. Suppose the experiment is performed T times and that the T outcomes are independent, given θ_n $(n = 1, 2, \ldots, N)$. Letting Z_n $(n = 1, 2, \ldots, N)$ denote the number of these outcomes belonging to category n, their joint distribution is given by the following definition.

Definition 3.4.1 The discrete N-dimensional random vector $Z = [Z_1, Z_2, \ldots, Z_N]'$ has a *multinomial distribution*, denoted $M_N(T, \theta)$, iff its

6. For examples of bivariate distributions with normal marginals, see Kowalski (1973).

p.m.f. is

$$f_M(z|T,\theta) = \begin{cases} \dfrac{T!}{z_1!z_2!\dots z_N!}\theta_1^{z_1}\theta_2^{z_2}\dots\theta_N^{z_N}, & \text{if } z_n = 0,1,\dots,T \text{ and } z_1 + z_2 + \cdots + z_N = T \\ 0, & \text{otherwise} \end{cases}. \tag{3.4.2}$$

where T is a positive integer, and $\theta = [\theta_1, \theta_2, \dots, \theta_N]'$ with $\theta_1 + \theta_2 + \cdots + \theta_N = 1$.

Because the probability that $Z_1 + Z_2 + \cdots + Z_N = T$ is unity, one of the N random variables $Z_1, Z_2, \dots, Z_N$ can be eliminated, and the multinomial p.d.f. defined by (3.4.2) can be written as a nonsingular, $(N-1)$-dimensional distribution. This reduction introduces an asymmetry among the N categories, similar to the binomial distribution in Section 3.2. (Note: If Z_1 has a binomial distribution with parameters T and p, then $Z = [Z_1, T - Z_1]$ has a multinomial distribution with parameters T and $[p, 1-p]'$.)

A few properties of the multinomial distribution are given in the following four theorems. Firstly, we investigate the marginal and conditional distributions.

Theorem 3.4.1 Suppose $Z = [Z_1, Z_2, \dots, Z_N]' \sim M_N(T, \theta)$.

(a) $Z_n \sim B(T, \theta_n)$ $(n = 1, 2, \dots, N)$

(b) Partition $Z = [Y', X']'$, where $Y = [Z_1, \dots, Z_m]'$ and $X = [Z_{m+1}, \dots, Z_N]'$. Also, partition $\theta = [\theta_Y', \theta_X']'$ accordingly. Let $\alpha = [\alpha_1, \dots, \alpha_m]'$, where $\alpha_i = \theta_i$ $(i = 1, 2, \dots, m-1)$ and $\alpha_m = 1 - (\theta_1 + \cdots + \theta_{m-1})$, and let $\delta = [\delta_1, \dots, \delta_m]'$, where $\delta_i = \theta_{i+m}$ $(i = 1, 2, \dots, N-m-1)$ and $\delta_{N-m} = 1 - (\theta_{m+1} + \cdots + \theta_{N-m-1})$. Then the marginal distributions of Y and X are: $Y \sim M_m(T, \alpha)$ and $X \sim M_{N-m}(T, \delta)$.

(c) Consider the partitioning in (b). Define $\beta = [\beta_1, \dots, \beta_m]'$, where $\beta_i = \theta_i/(1 - \psi_X)$ $(i = 1, 2, \dots, m-1)$, $\beta_m = 1 - [(\theta_1 + \cdots + \theta_{m-1})/(1 - \psi_X)]$ with $\psi_X = \theta_{m+1} + \cdots + \theta_N$. Let $T_Y = T - (z_{m+1} + \cdots + z_{N-m})$. Then $Y|X = x \sim M_m(T_Y, \beta)$.

(d) Consider the partition in (b). Define $\gamma = [\gamma_1, \dots, \gamma_{N-m}]'$, where $\gamma_i = \theta_{m+i}/(1 - \psi_Y)$ $(i = 1, 2, \dots, N-m)$, $\gamma_{N-m} = 1 - [(\theta_{m+1} + \cdots + \theta_{N-m-1})/(1 - \psi_Y)]$ with $\psi_Y = \theta_1 + \cdots + \theta_m$. Let $T_X = T - (z_1 + \cdots + z_m)$. Then $X|Y = y \sim M_{N-m}(T_X, \gamma)$.

Proof Left to reader.

Next we investigate the m.g.f. and moments of the multinomial distribution in the next two theorems.

Theorem 3.4.2 Suppose $Z = [Z_1, Z_2, \ldots, Z_N]' \sim M_N(T, \theta)$. The m.g.f. corresponding to the nonsingular distribution of $Z_1, Z_2, \ldots, Z_{N-1}$ is

$$M_Z(t_1, t_2, \ldots, t_{N-1}) = \left[\theta_N + \sum_{n=1}^{N-1} \theta_n \exp(t_n)\right]^T. \tag{3.4.3}$$

Proof Left to the reader.

Theorem 3.4.3 Suppose $Z = [Z_1, Z_2, \ldots, Z_N]' \sim M_N(T, \theta)$.

(a) $E(Z) = T\theta$

(b) $\mathrm{Var}(Z_n) = T\theta_n(1 - \theta_n)$ $(n = 1, 2, \ldots, N)$

(c) $\mathrm{Cov}(Z_i, Z_j) = -T\theta_i\theta_j$ $(i, j = 1, 2, \ldots, N; i \neq j)$

(d) $\mathrm{Var}(Z) = T^{-1}[\mathrm{diag}(\theta) - \theta\theta']$, where $\mathrm{diag}(\theta)$ denotes a $N \times N$ diagonal matrix with diagonal elements θ_n $(n = 1, 2, \ldots, N)$. Note that $\mathrm{Var}(Z)$ is a singular matrix.

Proof Follows straightforwardly from (2.3.4) and m.g.f. (3.4.3).

To demonstrate Theorems 3.4.1 and 3.4.3, we turn to the following example.

Example 3.4.1 Suppose $Z = [Y', X']' \sim M_3(T, \theta)$, where $Y = [Z_1, Z_2]'$, $X = Z_3$, and $\theta = [\theta_1, \theta_2, \theta_3]'$, with $\theta_1 + \theta_2 + \theta_3 = 1$. Then

$$\mathrm{Var}(Z) = \frac{1}{T}\begin{bmatrix} \theta_1(1-\theta_1) & -\theta_1\theta_2 & -\theta_1\theta_3 \\ -\theta_1\theta_2 & \theta_2(1-\theta_2) & -\theta_2\theta_3 \\ -\theta_1\theta_3 & -\theta_2\theta_3 & \theta_3(1-\theta_3) \end{bmatrix}.$$

The conditional distribution of Y given $X = x$ is $M_2(T_y, \beta)$, where $T_Y = T - z_3$, $\beta = (1 - \theta_3)^{-1}[\theta_1, \theta_2]'$. Therefore, $Z_1 | Z_3 = z_3 \sim B(T_y, \theta_1/[1 - \theta_3])$ with

$$E(Z_1 | Z_3 = z_3) = (T - z_3)\left(\frac{\theta_1}{1 - \theta_3}\right) = \frac{T\theta_1}{1 - \theta_3} - \left(\frac{\theta_1}{1 - \theta_3}\right)z_3,$$

$$\mathrm{Var}(Z_1 | Z_3 = z_3) = (T - z_3)\left(\frac{\theta_1(1 - \theta_1 - \theta_3)}{(1 - \theta_3)^2}\right).$$

Note that both the regression curve and the variance around it are linear in the conditioning variable z_3.

Finally, we note a useful theorem stating that the multinomial distribution is closed under sums of independent multinomial random variables.

Theorem 3.4.4 Suppose $Z_j \sim M_N(T_j, \theta)$ $(j = 1, 2, \ldots, J)$ are independent, and let $T \equiv T_1 + T_2 + \cdots + T_J$. Then $Z \equiv Z_1 + Z_2 + \cdots + Z_J \sim M_N(T, \theta)$.

Proof Postponed until Chapter 4.

The preeminent position of the multivariate normal distribution among multivariate continuous distributions is more marked than that of the normal among univariate continuous distributions. The bivariate normal distribution dates back to the early part of the nineteenth century, but it remained little noticed until the work of Galton on regression and correlation in the last quarter of that century. In part, the popularity of the multivariate normal distribution, as in the univariate case, is the result of central limit theorems to be described later. This popularity is also the result of many tractable characteristics of the multivariate normal distribution. For example, the N-dimensional multivariate normal distribution is uniquely characterized by its N first-order moments and its $N(N+1)/2$ second-order moments.

Definition 3.4.2 The N-dimensional random vector $Z = [Z_1, Z_2, \ldots, Z_N]'$ has a *multivariate normal distribution*, denoted $N(\mu, \Sigma)$, iff its p.d.f. is

$$\phi_N(z|\mu, \Sigma) \equiv (2\pi)^{-1/2N}|\Sigma|^{-1/2} \exp[-\tfrac{1}{2}(z-\mu)'\Sigma^{-1}(z-\mu)],\ z \in \Re^N, \tag{3.4.4}$$

where $\mu \in R^N$ and Σ is a $N \times N$ positive definite matrix. The *standardized multivariate normal distribution* corresponds to the case $\mu = 0$ and all diagonal elements of Σ equal to unity. If the dimensionality is unclear from the context, then it is emphasized by writing $Z \sim N_N(\mu, \Sigma)$.

As is obvious from parts (b) and (c) of the following theorem, the notation for the parameters of the multivariate normal distribution is self-explanatory.

Theorem 3.4.5 Suppose $Z = [Z_1, Z_2, \ldots, Z_N]' \sim N(\mu, \Sigma)$.

(a) The m.g.f. of Z is $M(t) = \exp(t'\mu + \tfrac{1}{2}t'\Sigma t)$, where $t = [t_1, t_2, \ldots, t_N]'$.

(b) $E(Z) = \mu$.

(c) $\text{Var}(Z) = \Sigma$.

Proof This is a straightforward generalization of Theorem 3.2.2.

As noted in the following theorem, an attractive property of the multivariate normal distribution is that all marginal and conditional distributions are also normal (see Exercise 2.4.7 for the bivariate case). Keep in mind, however, Exercises 3.4.10 through 3.4.12. (For further examples, see Arnold et al. 1992.)

Theorem 3.4.6 Consider the $N \times 1$ random vector Z partitioned as $Z = [Z_1', Z_2']'$, where Z_1 is $m \times 1$ and Z_2 is $(N-m) \times 1$. Suppose that $Z \sim N(\mu, \Sigma)$, where

$$\mu = \begin{bmatrix} \mu_1 \\ \mu_2 \end{bmatrix}, \qquad \Sigma = \begin{bmatrix} \Sigma_{11} & \Sigma_{12} \\ \Sigma'_{12} & \Sigma_{22} \end{bmatrix} \tag{3.4.5}$$

have been partitioned to conform with the partitioning of Z. Then the marginal and conditional distributions involving Z_1 and Z_2 are given as follows.

(a) The marginal distributions are: $Z_1 \sim N_m(\mu_1, \Sigma_{11})$ and $Z_2 \sim N_{N-m}(\mu_2, \Sigma_{22})$.

(b) The conditional distribution of Z_1, given $Z_2 = z_2$, is $Z_1|z_2 \sim N(\mu_{1|2}, \Sigma_{1|2})$, where[7]

$$\begin{aligned} \mu_{1|2} \equiv \mu_{1|2}(z_2) &\equiv E[Z_1|Z_2 = z_2] \\ &= \mu_1 + \Sigma_{12}\Sigma_{22}^{-1}[z_2 - \mu_2], \end{aligned} \tag{3.4.6}$$

$$\begin{aligned} \Sigma_{1|2} &\equiv \mathrm{Var}[Z_1|Z_2 = z_2] \\ &= \Sigma_{11} - \Sigma_{12}\Sigma_{22}^{-1}\Sigma'_{12}. \end{aligned} \tag{3.4.7}$$

(c) The conditional distribution of Z_2, given $Z_1 = z_1$, is $Z_2|z_1 \sim N(\mu_{2|1}, \Sigma_{2|1})$, where

$$\begin{aligned} \mu_{2|1} \equiv \mu_{2|1}(z_1) &\equiv E[Z_2|Z_1 = z_1] \\ &= \mu_2 + \Sigma'_{12}\Sigma_{11}^{-1}[z_1 - \mu_1], \end{aligned} \tag{3.4.8}$$

$$\begin{aligned} \Sigma_{2|1} &= \mathrm{Var}[Z_2|Z_1 = z_1] \\ &= \Sigma_{22} - \Sigma'_{12}\Sigma_{11}^{-1}\Sigma_{12}. \end{aligned} \tag{3.4.9}$$

Proof By Theorem A.4.4(a),

$$\Sigma^{-1} = \begin{bmatrix} \Sigma^{11} & \Sigma^{12} \\ \Sigma^{21} & \Sigma^{22} \end{bmatrix}, \tag{3.4.10}$$

where

$$\Sigma^{11} = [\Sigma_{1|2}]^{-1}, \tag{3.4.11}$$

$$\Sigma^{12} = -\Sigma^{11}\Sigma_{12}[\Sigma_{22}]^{-1}, \tag{3.4.12}$$

$$\Sigma^{22} = [\Sigma_{22}]^{-1} - [\Sigma^{12}]'[\Sigma^{11}]^{-1}\Sigma^{12}. \tag{3.4.13}$$

Using Theorem A.4.4(b),

$$|\Sigma| = |\Sigma_{22}||\Sigma_{11} - \Sigma_{12}\Sigma_{22}^{-1}\Sigma'_{12}| \tag{3.4.14a}$$

$$= |\Sigma_{22}||\Sigma_{1|2}|. \tag{3.4.14b}$$

Using (3.4.10), the quadratic form in the exponential term of (3.4.4) can be written as

$$\begin{aligned} (z - \mu)'\Sigma^{-1}(z - \mu) = {} & [z_1 - \mu_1]'\Sigma^{11}[z_1 - \mu_1] \\ & + 2[z_1 - \mu_1]'\Sigma^{12}[z_2 - \mu_2] \\ & + [z_2 - \mu_2]'\Sigma^{22}[z_2 - \mu_2]. \end{aligned} \tag{3.4.15}$$

7. For an extension of part (b) to the case of singular Σ, see Muirhead (1982, pp. 12–13).

Using (3.4.11)–(3.4.13) and "completing the square" on z_1, it follows that (3.4.15) can also be written as

$$(z - \mu)'\Sigma^{-1}(z - \mu) = [z_1 - \mu_{1|2}]'[\Sigma_{1|2}]^{-1}[z_1 - \mu_{1|2}] + [z_2 - \mu_2]'[\Sigma_{22}]^{-1}[z_2 - \mu_2]. \tag{3.4.16}$$

Collecting together (3.4.14b) and (3.4.16), it follows that multivariate normal density (3.4.4) can be written

$$\phi_N(z|\mu, \Sigma) = \phi_m(z_1|\mu_{1|2}(z_2), \Sigma_{1|2}) \cdot \phi_{N-m}(z_2|\mu_2, \Sigma_{22}). \tag{3.4.17}$$

Integrating-out z_1 from (3.4.17), it follows immediately that $Z_2 \sim N(\mu_2, \Sigma_{22})$, and hence (a) has been proved for Z_2. Dividing the left-hand side of (3.4.17) by the second factor on the righthand side implies $Z_1|Z_2 = z_2 \sim N(\mu_{1|2}, \Sigma_{1|2})$, and hence (b) is proved. By completing the square on z_2 in (3.4.15), instead of on z_1, it is straightforward to prove (c) and (a) for Z_1.

Example 3.4.2 Consider the case of the bivariate normal distribution (recall Exercise 2.4.7). Let $Z = [Y, X]'$, $\mu = [\mu_Y, \mu_X]'$ and

$$\Sigma = \begin{bmatrix} \sigma_Y^2 & \rho\sigma_Y\sigma_X \\ \rho\sigma_Y\sigma_X & \sigma_X^2 \end{bmatrix}, \qquad -1 < \rho < 1. \tag{3.4.18}$$

Then $Y \sim N(\mu_Y, \sigma_Y^2)$, $X \sim N(\mu_X, \sigma_X^2)$, $Y|X = x \sim N(\mu_{Y|X}, \sigma_{Y|X}^2)$, where

$$\mu_{Y|X} = \mu_Y + \rho(\sigma_Y/\sigma_X)(x - \mu_X), \tag{3.4.19}$$

$$\sigma_{Y|X}^2 = \sigma_Y^2(1 - \rho^2), \tag{3.4.20}$$

and $X|Y = y \sim N(\mu_{X|Y}, \sigma_{X|Y}^2)$, where

$$\mu_{X|Y} = \mu_X + \rho(\sigma_X/\sigma_Y)(y - \mu_Y), \tag{3.4.21}$$

$$\sigma_{X|Y}^2 = \sigma_X^2(1 - \rho^2). \tag{3.4.22}$$

Figure 3.4.1 depicts a standardized bivariate normal density using the notation of Example 3.4.2. Note its bell-shape and the normal density shapes (indicated by the slices parallel to the axes) for both conditional densities. Slicing this bivariate normal density by a plane parallel to the $x - y$ plane and projecting this intersection down to the $x - y$ plane produces an "isodensity" ellipse with a boundary containing points yielding the same value for the density. Figure 3.4.2 depicts the densities and isodensity ellipses for bivariate normal densities with zero means, unit variances, and correlations (a) $\rho = .5$ and (b) $\rho = -.5$.

Example 3.4.2 illustrates in the bivariate case a general result for the multivariate normal distribution, namely, its regression curves are linear functions of the conditioning variables (see Equations 3.4.6, 3.4.8, 3.4.19, and 3.4.21). The parameters of these regression functions relate to the covariance structure in precisely the manner described earlier in Theorem 2.7.1. Given the importance of linear regression, Example 3.4.3 gives details in the case $m = 1$ and $N \geq 2$. Theorem 3.4.7 adds details of later importance.

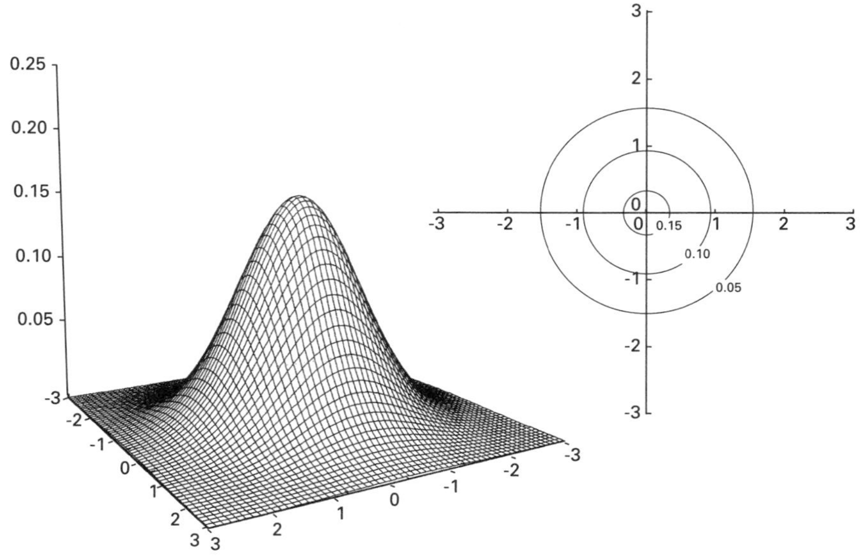

Figure 3.4.1
Standardized bivariate normal density with $\rho = 0$

Example 3.4.3 Consider Theorem 3.4.6 in the case $m = 1$, $N \geq 2$, and write $Z = [Y, X']'$, where X is $(N-1) \times 1$. Define:

$$\beta = [\Sigma_{12}\Sigma_{22}^{-1}]' = \Sigma_{22}^{-1}\Sigma_{21}, \tag{3.4.23}$$

$$\alpha = \mu_1 - \mu_2'\beta, \tag{3.4.24}$$

$$\sigma_{Y|X}^2 = \Sigma_{11} - \Sigma_{12}\Sigma_{22}^{-1}\Sigma_{12}'. \tag{3.4.25}$$

Then (3.4.6) and (3.4.7) imply

$$E(Y|X = x) = \alpha + X'\beta, \tag{3.4.26}$$

$$\mathrm{Var}(Y|X = x) = \sigma_{Y|X}^2. \tag{3.4.27}$$

Theorem 3.4.7 Consider Example 3.4.3. Let $R_{Y \cdot X}^2$ be the squared correlation coefficient between Y and $\alpha + X'\beta$. Then:

(a) $$R_{Y \cdot X}^2 = \frac{\beta'\Sigma_{22}\beta}{\sigma^2}. \tag{3.4.28}$$

(b) $$\sigma_{Y \cdot X}^2 = (1 - R_{Y \cdot X}^2)\Sigma_{11}. \tag{3.4.29}$$

Proof Part (a) follows immediately from Exercise 2.7.19. Part (b) follows immediately from Part (a), (3.4.23) and (3.4.25).

The following theorem gathers together miscellaneous results concerning the multivariate normal distribution. In particular, note that (a) implies linear combinations are also normally distributed, and (d) implies that the distinction of Section 2.7 among uncorrelated, mean-independent,

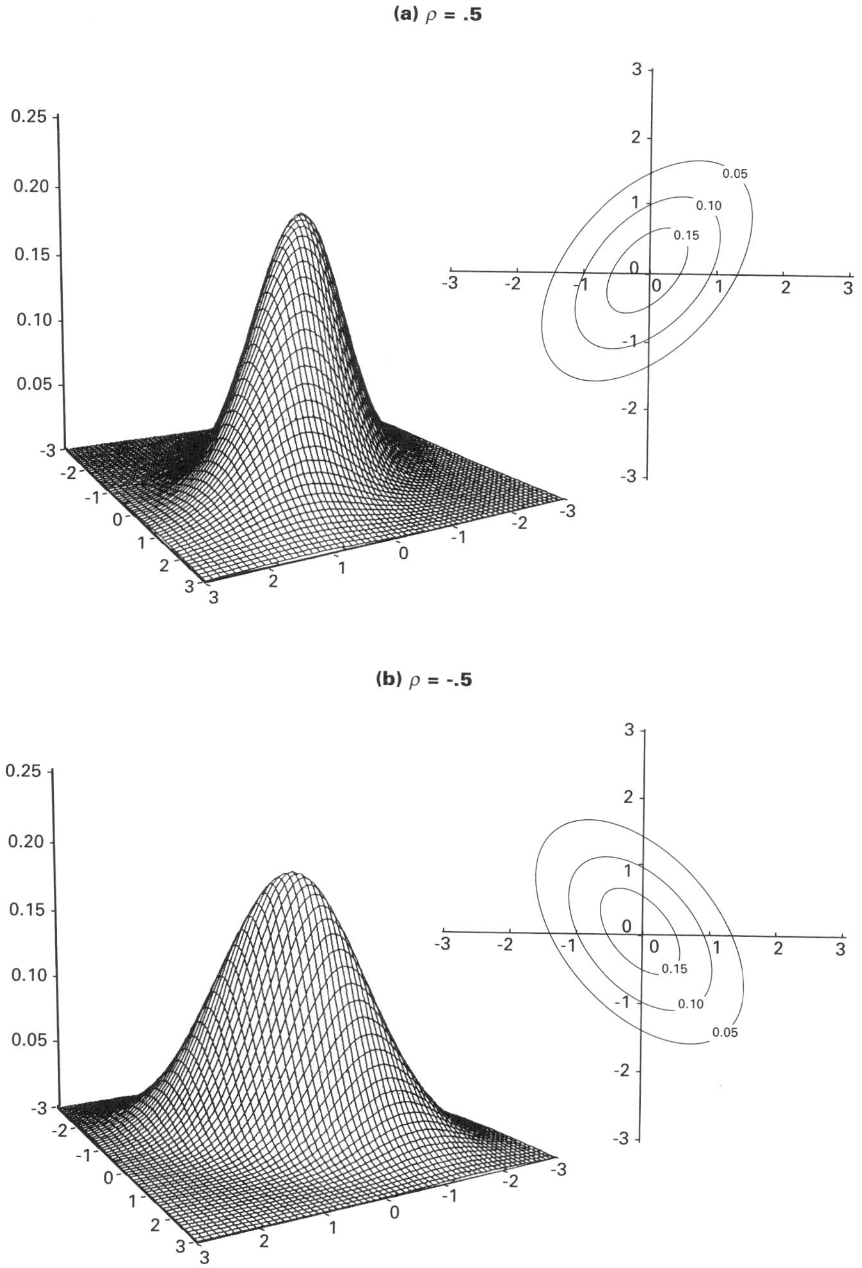

Figure 3.4.2
Bivariate normal densities and isodensity ellipses

and independent random variables is vacuous in the case of the multivariate normal distribution.

Theorem 3.4.8 Suppose $Z = [Z_1, Z_2, \ldots, Z_N]' \sim N(\mu, \Sigma)$.

(a) If A is a fixed $M \times N$ matrix with $\text{rank}(A) = M$, then $AZ \sim N_M(A\mu, A\Sigma A')$.

(b) $Z \sim N(\mu, \Sigma)$ iff $c'Z \sim N(c'\mu, c'\Sigma c)$ for every $N \times 1$ vector c of constants.

(c) The elements of Z are mutually independent iff the elements of Z are pairwise independent.

(d) Z_i and Z_j $(i, j = 1, 2, \ldots, N; i \neq j)$ are independent iff $\text{Cov}(Z_i, Z_j) = 0$.

(e) Suppose $\Sigma = \text{diag}\{\sigma_{11}, \sigma_{22}, \ldots, \sigma_{NN}\}$. Then

$$\phi_N(z|\mu, \Sigma) = \prod_{n=1}^{N} \phi_n(z_n|\mu_n, \sigma_{nn}). \tag{3.4.30}$$

(f) $E[(Z_i - \mu_i)(Z_j - \mu_j)(Z_k - \mu_k)(Z_l - \mu_l)] = \sigma_{ij}\sigma_{kl} + \sigma_{ik}\sigma_{jl} + \sigma_{il}\sigma_{jk}$, $1 \leq i, j, k, l \leq N$.

(g) Let A and B be symmetric matrices of order N. Then

$$\text{Cov}[(Z - \mu)'A(Z - \mu), (Z - \mu)'B(Z - \mu)] = 2\text{tr}(A\Sigma B\Sigma). \tag{3.4.31}$$

Proof Left to the reader.

As noted Section 3.3, an important univariate distribution in statistics is the t-distribution. We now introduce the multivariate counterpart.

Definition 3.4.3 The N-dimensional vector $Z = [Z_1, Z_2, \ldots, Z_N]'$ has elements distributed according to a *multivariate t distribution*, denoted $t_N(\theta, \Omega, \nu)$, iff their joint p.d.f. is

$$f_t(z|\theta, \Omega, \nu) = c_t^{-1}|\Omega|^{-1/2}[\nu + (z - \theta)'\Omega^{-1}(z - \theta)]^{-(\nu+N)/2}, \tag{3.4.32}$$

for $z = [z_1, z_2, \ldots, z_N]' \in R^N$, $\nu > 0$, $\theta = [\theta_1, \theta_2, \ldots, \theta_N]' \in R^N$, Ω is a $N \times N$ positive definite matrix, and the integrating constant is

$$c_t = c_t(\nu, N) = \frac{\pi^{N/2}\Gamma(\nu/2)}{\nu^{\nu/2}\Gamma[(\nu + N)/2]}. \tag{3.4.33}$$

The case $\nu = 1$ is known as the *multivariate Cauchy distribution.*

As in the univariate case, existence of moments for the multivariate t distribution depends on sufficient degrees of freedom. The following theorem provides the mean and covariance matrix (when they exist).

Theorem 3.4.9 Suppose $Z \sim t_N(\theta, \Omega, \nu)$. Then

$$E(Z) = \theta, \text{ if } \nu > 1, \tag{3.4.34}$$

$$\text{Var}(Z) = E[(Z - \theta)(Z - \theta)'] = [\nu/(\nu - 2)]\Omega, \text{ if } \nu > 2. \tag{3.4.35}$$

Proof Zellner (1971, pp. 385–386).

Note that (3.3.35) implies Ω is not quite the covariance matrix of Z. Lacking a widely accepted terminology for it, we simply refer to it as a *scale matrix*.

As in the case of the multivariate normal distribution, the multivariate t-distribution has the attractive property that all its marginal and conditional distributions are also multivariate t-distributions. This result is stated formally in the following theorem.

Theorem 3.4.10 Suppose $Z \sim t_N(\theta, \Omega, \nu)$. Partition Z as $Z = [Z_1, Z_2']'$, where Z_1 is $m \times 1$, Z_2 is $(N - m) \times 1$, and

$$\theta = \begin{bmatrix} \theta_1 \\ \theta_2 \end{bmatrix}, \qquad \Omega = \begin{bmatrix} \Omega_{11} & \Omega_{12} \\ \Omega_{12}' & \Omega_{22} \end{bmatrix} \tag{3.4.36}$$

have been partitioned to conform with the partitioning of Z.

(a) The marginal distributions are: $Z_1 \sim t_m(\theta_1, \Omega_{11}, \nu)$ and $Z_2 \sim t_{N-m}(\theta_2, \Omega_{22}, \nu)$.

(b) The conditional distribution of Z_1, given $Z_2 = z_2$, is $Z_1|Z_2 = z_2 \sim t_m(\theta_{1|2}, \Omega_{1|2}, \nu + m)$, where

$$\theta_{1|2} \equiv \theta_{1|2}(z_2) = \theta_1 + \Omega_{12}\Omega_{22}^{-1}[z_2 - \theta_2] \tag{3.4.37}$$

$$\Omega_{1|2} = h_{1|2}(\mu_2, \Omega_{22}, \nu)[\Omega_{11} - \Omega_{12}\Omega_{22}^{-1}\Omega_{12}'], \tag{3.4.38}$$

$$h_{1|2}(\mu_2, \Omega_{22}, \nu) = [\nu + (z_2 - \theta_2)'[\Omega_{22}]^{-1}(z_2 - \theta_2)]/(\nu + N - m). \tag{3.4.39}$$

(c) The conditional distribution of Z_2, given $Z_1 = z_1$, is $Z_2|Z_1 = z_1 \sim t_{N-m}(\theta_{2|1}, \Omega_{2|1}, \nu + N - m)$, where

$$\theta_{2|1} \equiv \theta_{2|1}(z_1) = \theta_2 + \Omega_{12}'\Omega_{11}^{-1}[z_1 - \theta_1], \tag{3.4.40}$$

$$\Omega_{2|1} = h_{2|1}(\mu_1, \Omega_{11}, \nu)[\Omega_{22} - \Omega_{12}'\Omega_{11}^{-1}\Omega_{12}], \tag{3.4.41}$$

$$h_{2|1}(\mu_1, \Omega_{11}, \nu) = [\nu + (z_1 - \theta_1)'[\Omega_{11}]^{-1}(z_1 - \theta_1)]/(\nu + N - m). \tag{3.4.42}$$

Proof Zellner (1971, pp. 383–388).

The close analogy between Theorems 3.4.10 and 3.4.6 is indicative of the close relationship between the multivariate t and normal distributions. Indeed, both are members of the *multivariate elliptical distribution* family described in Exercises 3.4.27 and 3.4.28. As $\nu \to \infty$, the multivariate t distribution converges to the multivariate normal distribution. Note that in both cases, regression curves (i.e. conditional means) are linear in the conditioning variables. In the case of the multivariate normal distribution, however, variation around the conditional mean does *not* depend on the conditioning variables (see Equations 3.4.7 and 3.4.9), whereas in the case of the multivariate t distribution, variation around the conditional means depends on the conditioning variables in a quadratic fashion (see 3.4.38 and 3.4.41). Recall from Example 3.4.1, in the case of the multinomial distribution, regression curves and variation around them are linear in conditioning variables.

The following theorem shows that the multivariate t-distribution, like the multivariate normal (see Theorem 3.4.8a), is closed under linear combinations.

Theorem 3.4.11 Suppose $Z \sim t_N(\theta, \Omega, v)$ and let A be a fixed $M \times N$ matrix with $\text{rank}(A) = M$. Then $AZ \sim t_M(A\theta, A\Omega A', v)$.

Proof Zellner (1971, p. 388).

In order to relate the multivariate t-distribution to another previously encountered distribution, consider the following generalization of Theorem 3.3.18(a) to $N > 1$.

Theorem 3.4.12 Suppose $Z \sim t_N(\theta, \Omega, v)$. Then $(Z - \theta)'\Omega^{-1}(Z - \theta)/N \sim F(N, v)$.

Proof DeGroot (1970, p. 2).

In order to relate the multivariate normal, gamma, and multivariate t-distributions, the following multivariate distribution is introduced. Further connections are explored in Section 4.5.

Definition 3.4.4 Let θ be $N \times 1$ and Σ be $N \times N$ be fixed matrices, and let m and v be positive scalars. Suppose $Y|W, \theta, \Sigma \sim N_N(\theta, W^{-1}\Sigma)$ and $W|m, v \sim \gamma(m, v)$. Then Y and W have a *normal-gamma distribution*, denoted $Y, W \sim NG_{N+1}(\theta, \Sigma, m, v)$. When $N = 1$, the normal-gamma distribution is usually denoted simply as $NG(\theta, \Sigma, m, v)$.

The multivariate normal-gamma and multivariate t-distributions are related in the following theorem.

Theorem 3.4.13 Suppose $Y, W \sim NG_{N+1}(\theta, \Sigma, m, v)$.

(a) The marginal distribution of Y is $Y \sim t_N(\theta, m^{-1}\Sigma, v)$.

(b) The conditional distribution of W, given $Y = y$, is $W|y \sim \gamma(m_*, v_*)$, where

$$m_* = (v_*^{-1}[vm^{-1} + (y - \theta)'\Sigma^{-1}(y - \theta)])^{-1}, \tag{3.4.43}$$

$$v_* = \underline{v} + N. \tag{3.4.44}$$

Proof Left to the reader.

Let $\phi_N(\cdot)$, $f_\gamma(\cdot)$, and $f_t(\cdot)$ denote multivariate normal density (3.4.4), univariate gamma density (3.3.24) and multivariate-t density (3.4.32), respectively. Then Definition 3.4.5 and Theorem 3.4.13 imply that the density

$f_{NG}(\cdot)$ of the $NG_{N+1}(\theta, \Sigma, m, v)$ distribution can be expressed as

$$\begin{aligned} f_{NG}(y, w|\theta, \Sigma, m, v) &= \phi_N(y|\theta, w^{-1}\Sigma)f_\gamma(w|m, v) \\ &= f_t(y|\theta, m^{-1}\Sigma, v)f_\gamma(w|m_*, v_*), \end{aligned} \tag{3.4.45}$$

where m_* and v_* are given by (3.4.43) and (3.4.44).

Exercises

3.4.1 Verify that Var(Z) in Theorem 3.4.2(d) is singular.

3.4.2 Suppose $Y \equiv [Y_1, Y_2, Y_3]' \sim M(T, \theta)$ and $\theta = [\theta_1, \theta_2, \theta_3]'$. This case is often referred to as a *trinomial distribution*. Show that the conditional distribution of Y_2 given $Y_1 = y_1$ is binomial and, in particular, $B(T - y_1, \theta_2/(1 - \theta_1))$ (i.e., prove Theorem 3.4.1a in the case $N = 3$, $n = 2$).

3.4.3 Let Y_1 and Y_2 have a bivariate normal distribution with $E(Y_1) = 5$, $E(Y_2) = 10$, $\text{Var}(Y_1) = 1$, $\text{Var}(Y_2) = 25$, and $\text{Cov}(Y_1, Y_2) = 5\rho$. Find $\rho > 0$ such that $P(4 < Y_2 < 1 | Y_1 = 5) = .954$.

3.4.4 Suppose $Y = [Y_1, Y_2, Y_3]' \sim N_3(\mu, \Sigma)$, where

$$\Sigma = \begin{bmatrix} 1 & \rho & \rho^2 \\ \rho & 1 & 0 \\ \rho^2 & 0 & 1 \end{bmatrix}.$$

Show: $[Y_1, Y_2]' | Y_3 = y_3 \sim N_2(\alpha, A)$, where $\alpha = [\mu_1 + \rho^2(y_3 - \mu_3), \mu_2]'$ and

$$A = \begin{bmatrix} 1 - \rho^4 & \rho \\ \rho & 1 \end{bmatrix}.$$

3.4.5 It is of interest to study the sentiment of people toward racially integrated neighborhoods. Let Y_1 denote the time an individual has lived in a given neighborhood, let Y_2 denote the individual's feelings toward an integrated neighborhood (measured on a scale along the real line where lower values denote more dissatisfaction with integrated neighborhoods), and let Y_3 denote the number of years of education of the individual. Define $Y = [Y_1, Y_2, Y_3]'$ and suppose $Y \sim N(\mu, \Sigma)$, where $\mu = [3, 10, 8]'$ and

$$\Sigma = \begin{bmatrix} 1 & 3 & 1 \\ 3 & 16 & 2 \\ 1 & 2 & 4 \end{bmatrix}.$$

Although, literally speaking, Y_1 and Y_2 cannot take on all values along the real line, their variances are such that virtually zero probability is assigned to such unreasonable values. Hence, a trivariate normal distribution may still be a reasonable approximation. (See Press 1982, p. 91.)

(a) Find the correlation matrix.

(b) Find the distribution of Y_1, given $Y_2 = y_2$ and $Y_3 = y_3$.

(c) Find the distribution of $[Y_1, Y_2]'$, given $Y_3 = y_3$.

3.4.6 Let $X = [X_1, X_2, \ldots, X_N]'$, with $X_n > 0$ $(n = 1, 2, \ldots, N)$. X has a *multivariate lognormal distribution* iff its p.d.f is

$$f_{LN}(x|\theta, \Sigma) = \frac{\exp[-\frac{1}{2}(\ln x - \theta)'\Sigma^{-1}(\ln x - \theta)]}{(2\pi)^{N/2}|\Sigma|^{1/2} \prod_{n=1}^{N} x_n}, \tag{3.4.46}$$

where $\ln(x) \equiv [\ln(x_1), \ln(x_2), \ldots, \ln(x_N)]'$, θ is $N \times 1$, and $\Sigma = [\sigma_{ij}]$ is a $N \times N$ positive definite matrix. Show:

(a) $E(X_n^r) = \exp(r\theta_i + \frac{1}{2}r^2\sigma_{nn})$ $(n = 1, 2, \ldots, N)$

(b) $\text{Var}(X_n^r) = \exp(2\theta_i + 2\sigma_{nn}) - \exp(2\theta_i + \sigma_{nn})$ $(n = 1, 2, \ldots, N)$

(c) $\text{Cov}(X_i, X_j) = \exp[\theta_i + \theta_j + \frac{1}{2}(\sigma_{ii} + \sigma_{jj}) + \sigma_{ij}] - \exp[\theta_i + \theta_j + \frac{1}{2}(\sigma_{ii} + \sigma_{jj})$ $(i, j = 1, 2, \ldots, N)$

3.4.7 Suppose $Y = [Y_1, Y_2, \ldots, Y_N]' \sim N(\mu, \Sigma)$, where $\Sigma = (1 - \alpha)I_N + \alpha\iota_N\iota_N'$ and ι is a $N \times 1$ vector with each element equal to unity and I_N is the $N \times N$ identity matrix. Given $1 \le m < N$, compute the distribution of Y_j $(j = 1, 2, \ldots, m)$ given Y_n $(n = m + 1, \ldots, N)$. Use (A.8.6) to simplify your answer.

3.4.8 Suppose $Y \sim N_N(\mu, \sigma^2(1 - \alpha)I_N)$. Given $1 \le m < N$, find the p.d.f. of Y_j $(j = 1, 2, \ldots, m)$ given Y_j $(j = m + 1, \ldots, N)$. Compare your answer to Exercise 3.4.7.

3.4.9 Suppose $Y \sim N_5(\mu, \Sigma)$, where $Y = [Y_1, Y_2, Y_3, Y_4, Y_5]'$, $\mu = [0, 0, 1, 1, 1]'$,

$$\Sigma = \begin{bmatrix} 1 & 1 & 0 & 0 & 0 \\ 1 & 4 & 0 & 0 & 0 \\ 0 & 0 & 9 & 0 & 3 \\ 0 & 0 & 0 & 9 & 0 \\ 0 & 0 & 3 & 0 & 9 \end{bmatrix}.$$

Using the elements of Y, construct random variables with the following distributions:

(a) Cauchy

(b) $\chi^2(3)$

(c) $F(1, 1)$

(d) $t(2)$

(e) $N_2(0_2, I_2)$

(f) $\beta(\frac{1}{2}, \frac{1}{2})$.

3.4.10 Let X_1 and X_2 be independent $N(0, 1)$ random variables. Let $Y_1 = X_1$ if $X_1X_2 \ge 0$ and $Y_1 = -X_1$ if $X_1X_2 < 0$, and let $Y_2 = X_2$.

(a) Show that Y_1 and Y_2 are each $N(0, 1)$, but that their joint distribution is not bivariate normal.

(b) Show that Y_1 and Y_2 are not independent.

(c) Show that Y_1^2 and Y_2^2 are independent.

3.4.11 Consider the *bivariate normal mixture density*

$$f(y_1, y_2) = w_1\phi(y_1, y_2|\rho_1) + w_2\phi(y_1, y_2|\rho_2), \tag{3.4.47}$$

where $w_1 + w_2 = 1$, $\phi(y_1, y_2|\rho_i)$ $(i = 1, 2)$ is the standardized bivariate normal density with zero means, unit variances and correlation ρ_i.

(a) Show: Y_1 and Y_2 have normal marginals but that $f(y_1, y_2)$ is not a bivariate normal density unless $\rho_1 = \rho_2$.

(b) Show: the correlation between Y_1 and Y_2 is $\rho = w_1\rho_1 + w_2\rho_2$.

(c) Show: the conditional density of Y_1 given $Y_2 = y_2$ is the mixture of the $N(\rho_1 y_2, 1 - \rho_1^2)$ and $N(\rho_2 y_2, 1 - \rho_2^2)$ densities with weights w_1 and w_2.

(d) Show: $E(Y_1|Y_2 = y_2) = \rho y_2$.

(e) Show: $\text{Var}(Y_1|Y_2 = y_2) = 1 - (w_1\rho_1^2 + w_2\rho_2^2) + [(w_1\rho_1^2 + w_2\rho_2^2) - \rho^2] - \rho^2]y_2^2$.

3.4.12 Let Y_1 and Y_2 be random variables such that $Y_1|Y_2 \sim N(c/(1 + y_2^2), (1 + y_2^2)^{-1})$ and $Y_2|Y_1 \sim N(c/(1 + y_1^2), [1 + y_1^2]^{-1})$. [Note: Y_1 and Y_2 are *not* bivariate normal.] Suppose $c > 2$. Show:

(a) The joint p.d.f. of Y_1 and Y_2 is

$$f(y_1, y_2) = d^{-1}\exp\{-\tfrac{1}{2}[y_1^2y_2^2 + y_1^2 + y_2^2 - 2c(y_1 + y_2)]\},$$

where d is the integrating constant.

(b) The p.d.f. in (a) is bimodal. (See Gelman and Meng 1991).

3.4.13 Let $Y = [Y_1, Y_2, Y_3]'$, and consider the trivariate p.d.f.

$$f(y) = (2\pi)^{-3/2}\exp[-\tfrac{1}{2}(y_1^2 + y_2^2 + y_3^2)][1 + y_1y_2y_3\exp\{-\tfrac{1}{2}(y_1^2 + y_2^2 + y_3^2)\}] \tag{3.4.48}$$

for $y = [y_1, y_2, y_3]' \in R^3$. Show that y_n $(n = 1, 2, 3)$ are pairwise stochastically independent and that each pair has a bivariate normal distribution. Note that for the N-dimensional case

$$f(y) = (2\pi)^{N/2}\exp\left[-\frac{1}{2}\sum_{n=1}^{N} y_n^2\right]\left[1 + \prod_{i=1}^{N} y_n\exp\left(\frac{1}{2}y_n^2\right)\right], \tag{3.4.49}$$

any proper subset of Y_n $(n = 1, 2, \ldots, N)$ is jointly normal and mutually independent, yet Y is not normal and Y_n $(n = 1, 2, \ldots, N)$ are dependent (see Pierce and Dykstra 1969).

3.4.14 Show that the correct answer to each of the following is "No" (see Melnick and Tenenbein 1982).

(a) Are two normally distributed random variables with zero correlation always independent?

(b) If n linear combinations of k $(k \leq n)$ random variables are normally distributed, do the k random variables have a multivariate normal distribution?

(c) Is a linear combination of normally distributed random variables always normally distributed?

3.4.15 Consider the bivariate distribution $F(y_1, y_2) = \Phi(y_2)\{1 + \alpha[1 - \Phi(y_1)][1 - \Phi(y_2)]\}$, where $|\alpha| < 1$ and $\Phi(\cdot)$ denotes the standard normal c.d.f.

(a) Show: the density corresponding to $F(y_1, y_2)$ is $f(y_1, y_2) = \phi(y_1)\phi(y_2) \times \{1 + \alpha[2\phi(y_1) - 1][2\phi(y_2) - 1]\}$, where $\phi(\cdot)$ is the standard normal p.d.f.

(b) Show: the conditional density of Y_1 given $Y_2 = y_2$ is $f(y_1|Y_2 = y_2) = \phi(y_1)\{2\Phi(y_1) - 1][2\Phi(y_2) - 1]\}$.

(c) Show: $E(Y_1|Y_2 = y_2) = \alpha[2\Phi(y_2) - 1]\pi^{1/2}$.

(d) Show: $\mathrm{Corr}(Y_1, Y_2) = \alpha/\pi$.

3.4.16 Let Y_n $(n = 1, 2)$ be continuous random variables with marginal c.d.f.'s $F_n(\cdot)$ $(n = 1, 2)$, respectively. Let $|\alpha| < 1$. Consider the bivariate c.d.f.:

$$\begin{aligned} F(y_1, y_2) = {} & \tfrac{1}{2}\alpha^2(1 - \alpha)\max[F_1(y_1) + F_2(y_2) - 1, 0] \\ & + (1 - \alpha^2)F_1(y_1)F_2(y_2) + \tfrac{1}{2}\alpha^2(1 + \alpha)\min[F_1(y_1), F_2(y_2)]. \end{aligned} \tag{3.4.50}$$

(a) Show that $F(y_1, y_2)$ is a valid joint distribution function.

(b) Show that for appropriate choices of α, $F(y_1, y_2)$ can equal either of Frechet's boundary distributions in (3.4.1).

(c) Choose α so that Y_1 and Y_2 are independent.

3.4.17 Let $Y = [Y_1, Y_2, \ldots, Y_N]'$ and suppose Y has the *linear exponential* distribution with p.d.f.

$$f(y|\theta) = \exp[a(\theta) + b(y) + \theta' y], \tag{3.4.51}$$

where θ is $N \times 1$ and $a(\cdot)$ and $b(\cdot)$ are appropriately chosen functions.

(a) Find the m.g.f. of Y.

(b) Show that all joint marginals are also members of the linear exponential type.

(c) Show that all conditionals are also members of the linear exponential type.

3.4.18 (a) Show: $N(\mu, \Sigma)$ is a member of the exponential family.

(b) Show: $N(\mu, \Sigma)$, Σ known, is a member of the linear exponential family.

(c) Show: the multinomial distribution is a member of the linear exponential family.

3.4.19 Suppose $V|W \sim N(W, \sigma^2)$ and $W \sim N(\mu, \tau^2)$. Show: $V \sim N(\mu, \sigma^2 + \tau^2)$.

3.4.20 Suppose $Y = [Y_1, Y_2]'$ has a standardized bivariate normal distribution with correlation ρ. Show: $\text{Corr}(Y_1^2, Y_2^2) = \rho^2$.

3.4.21 Verify Equation 3.4.15.

3.4.22 Suppose Y, X and Z have a trivariate normal distribution with zero means and covariance matrix Σ, where

$$\Sigma = \begin{bmatrix} 1 & \rho_{yx} & \rho_{yz} \\ \rho_{yx} & 1 & \rho_{xz} \\ \rho_{yz} & \rho_{xz} & 1 \end{bmatrix},$$

and $\rho_{yx} = \rho_{yz}\rho_{xz}$. Assume $\rho_{yz} \neq 0$ and $\rho_{xz} \neq 0$.

(a) Are X and Y independent?

(b) Find $f(y, x|z)$.

(c) Given $Z = z$, are X and Y independent?

(d) Compute the coefficient on X in the regression of Y on X.

(e) Compute the coefficient on X in the regression of Y on X and Z.

3.4.23 Let Y_n $(n = 1, 2, \ldots, N)$ be random variables such that $Y_1 + Y_2 + \cdots + Y_N = 1$. Y $(n = 1, 2, \ldots, N)$ have a *standardized multivariate Dirichlet distribution* (a generalization of the beta distribution) iff their p.d.f is

$$f_D(y|\alpha) = \left[\frac{\Gamma(a)}{\prod_{n=1}^{N} \Gamma(\alpha_n)}\right] \prod_{n=1}^{N} y_n^{\alpha_n - 1}, \tag{3.4.52}$$

where $\alpha_n > 0$ $(n = 1, 2, \ldots, N)$ and $a = \alpha_1 + \cdots + \alpha_N$. Show:

(a) $E(Y_n) = \alpha_n/a$ $(n = 1, 2, \ldots, N)$.

(b) $\text{Var}(Y) = \alpha_n(a - \alpha_n)/a^2(a + 1)$ $(n = 1, 2, \ldots, N)$.

(c) $\text{Cov}(Y_i, Y_j) = -\alpha_i\alpha_j/a^2(a + 1)$.

(d) The marginal distribution of $Y_1, Y_2, \ldots, Y_J$ $(J < N)$ have a standardized multivariate Dirichlet distribution with parameters $\alpha_1, \alpha_2, \ldots, \alpha_J$ and $a - (\alpha_1 + \alpha_2 + \cdots + \alpha_J)$.

(e) $Y_N/(1 - Y_1 - \cdots - Y_N) \sim \beta(v_N, 1 - v_1 - \cdots - v_N)$.

3.4.24 Consider the *bivariate Pareto distribution* with p.d.f.

$$f(y_1, y_2|\alpha) = \begin{cases} \alpha(\alpha + 1)(y_1 + y_2 - 1)^{-(\alpha+2)}, & \text{if } y_1 > 1, y_2 > 1 \\ 0, & \text{otherwise} \end{cases}. \tag{3.4.53}$$

(a) Calculate the marginal p.d.f. of Y_n $(n = 1, 2)$.

(b) Show: $E(Y_n) = \alpha/(\alpha - 1)$ if $\alpha > 1$.

(c) If $\alpha > 2$, show that the variance-covariance matrix of Y_1 and Y_2 is:

$$\text{Var}(Y) = \frac{1}{(\alpha - 1)^2(\alpha - 2)} \begin{bmatrix} \alpha & 1 \\ 1 & \alpha \end{bmatrix}.$$

3.4.25 Suppose Y_1 and Y_2 have the *truncated standardized bivariate normal distribution*:

$$f(y_1, y_2) = \begin{cases} \dfrac{\exp[-\frac{1}{2}(1-\rho^2)(y_1^2 - 2\rho y_1 y_2 + y_2^2)]}{1 - \Phi(c)}, & \text{if } y_1 \geq c, \\ 0, & \text{if } y_1 < 0 \end{cases}, \tag{3.4.54}$$

for all $y_2 \in \mathfrak{R}$. Prove each of the following:

(a) $E(Y_2) = \rho E(Y_1)$.

(b) $E(Y_1 Y_2) = \rho E(Y_1^2)$.

(c) $E(Y_2^2) = 1 + \rho^2[E(Y_1^2) - 1]$.

(d) $\text{Cov}(Y_1, Y_2) = \rho \,\text{Var}(Y_1)$.

(e) $\text{Corr}(Y_1, Y_2) = \rho[\rho^2 + (1-\rho^2)/\text{Var}(Y_1)]^{-1/2} < |\rho|$.

(f) $E(Y_1 | Y_2 = y_2) = \rho y_2 + (1-\rho^2)^{1/2} h(y_2, c, \rho)$, where

$$h(y_2, c, \rho) = \frac{\phi\left(\dfrac{c - \rho y_2}{1 - \rho^2}\right)}{1 - \Phi\left(\dfrac{c - \rho y_2}{1 - \rho^2}\right)}. \tag{3.4.55}$$

3.4.26 Suppose $Y = [Y_1, Y_2]'$ has the *bivariate Poisson* p.d.m. for $y_1, y_2 = 0, 1, 2, \ldots$ and zero otherwise, where $\alpha \equiv \exp(-\lambda_2 - \lambda_1 + \lambda_0)$, $m \equiv$

$$f_{Po}(y|\lambda) = \alpha(\lambda_1 - \lambda_0)^{y_1}(\lambda_2 - \lambda_0)^{y_2} \sum_{i=0}^{m} \frac{\{\lambda_0/[(\lambda_1 - \lambda_0)(\lambda_2 - \lambda_0)]\}^i}{i!(y_1 - i)!(y_2 - i)!}, \tag{3.4.56}$$

$\min(y_1, y_2)$, $\lambda_1 > \lambda_0 > 0$, and $\lambda_2 > \lambda_0 > 0$.

(a) Show: Y_1 and Y_2 have marginal Poisson distributions.

(b) Show: $E(Y_2 | Y_1 = y_1) = (\lambda_2 - \lambda_0) + (\lambda_0/\lambda_1)y_1$.

(c) Show: $\text{Var}(Y_2 | Y_1 = y_1) = (\lambda_2 - \lambda_0) + [(\lambda_1 - \lambda_0)\lambda_0/\lambda_1^2]y_1$.

Note: see Johnson and Kotz (1969, pp. 297–300) for further discussion.

3.4.27 A random vector $Y = [Y_1, Y_2, \ldots, Y_N]'$ has an *elliptically symmetric distribution*, denoted $\text{Elip}_N[\mu, A, g(\cdot)]$, iff its p.d.f. can be written in the form

$$f_E(y|\mu, A) = g[(y - \mu)'A^{-1}(y - \mu)], \tag{3.4.57}$$

where μ is $N \times 1$, A is a $N \times N$ positive definite matrix, and $g(\cdot)$ is such that (3.4.57) is a p.d.f..

(a) Explain geometrically the use of the adjective "elliptically."

(b) Show: the multivariate normal distribution is elliptically symmetric.

(c) Show: the characteristic function of Y has the form $E[\exp(it'Y)] = \exp(it'\mu)\psi(t'At)$ for some function $\psi(\cdot)$, where t is a N-dimensional column vector, and $i \equiv (-1)^{1/2}$.

(d) Show (provided they exist) that $E(Y) = \mu$ and $\text{Var}(Y) = 2\psi'(0)A$.

3.4.28 Suppose Y has an *elliptically symmetric distribution* (see Exercise 3.4.27) with parameters μ and A. Show each of the following (Muirhead 1982, pp. 35–36):

(a) Suppose A is diagonal. If Y_n $(n = 1, 2, \ldots, N)$ are independent, then Y is multivariate normal.

(b) Partition Y, μ and A as follows:

$$Y = \begin{bmatrix} Y_1 \\ Y_2 \end{bmatrix}, \quad \mu = \begin{bmatrix} \mu_1 \\ \mu_2 \end{bmatrix}, \quad A = \begin{bmatrix} A_{11} & A_{12} \\ A_{21} & A_{22} \end{bmatrix}.$$

Show (provided they exist) that

$$E(Y_1 | Y_2) = \mu_1 + A_{12}A_{22}^{-1}(Y_2 - \mu_2), \tag{3.4.58}$$

$$\text{Var}(Y_1 | Y_2) = g(Y_2)(A_{11} - A_{12}A_{11}^{-1}A_{12}'), \tag{3.4.59}$$

for some function $g(\cdot)$. Moreover, show that Y_1 given Y_2 is an elliptically symmetric distribution. [Note: If $\mathrm{Var}(Y_1|Y_2)$ does *not* depend on Y_2, then Y must be multivariate normal.]

3.4.29 A $N \times 1$ random vector Y has a *spherically symmetric distribution* if BY and Y have the same distribution for any $N \times N$ orthogonal matrix (i.e., $B^{-1} = B'$). Suppose $Y \sim \mathrm{Elip}_N[0_N, I_N, g(\cdot)]$.

(a) Show: Y has a spherically symmetric distribution.

(b) Let α be a $N \times 1$ vector such that $\alpha'\mu = 1$. Define $W \equiv \alpha'Y/Y'Y$, where it is assumed that $P(Y = 0_N) = 0$. Show (see Muirhead 1982, pp. 38–39):

$$X \equiv \frac{(N-1)^{1/2}W}{(1-W^2)^{1/2}} \sim t(N-1). \tag{3.4.60}$$

3.4.30 Suppose $Y \equiv [Y_1, Y_2, \ldots, Y_N]' \sim N(0, 1)$, where Σ is a correlation matrix. Let $A = [a_{ij}]$ and $B = [b_{ij}]$ be two positive semidefinite correlation matrices such that $a_{ij} \geq b_{ij}$ $(i, j = 1, 2, \ldots, N)$. Then it can be shown (e.g., Tong 1980, pp. 10–11) that

$$P\left[\bigcap_{n=1}^{N} Y_n \leq c_n | \Sigma = A\right] \geq P\left[\bigcap_{n=1}^{N} Y_n \leq c_n | \Sigma = B\right] \tag{3.4.61}$$

holds for all $c = [c_1, c_2, \ldots, c_N]'$. Furthermore, the inequality is strict if A and B are positive definite and if $a_{ij} > b_{ij}$ holds for some i and j.

(a) Show that the same inequality holds if $Y_n \leq c_n$ is replaced by $Y_n \geq c_n$.

(b) Describe this result geometrically in the case $N = 2$.

3.4.31 Let Y_n $(n = 1, 2, \ldots, N)$ be independent random variables with means μ_n $(n = 1, 2, \ldots, N)$, common variance σ^2, and common third and fourth moments about their respective means, i.e. $\alpha_i = E[(Y_n - \mu_n)^i]$ $(i = 3, 4; n = 1, 2, \ldots, N)$. Let A be a symmetric matrix of order N. Show:

$$\mathrm{Var}(Y'AY) = (\alpha_4 - 3\sigma^4)d'd + 2\sigma^4 \mathrm{tr}(A^2) + 4\sigma^2\mu'A^2\mu + 4\alpha_3\mu'Ad, \tag{3.4.62}$$

where d is the $N \times 1$ vector of diagonal elements of A.

3.4.32 Suppose $X = [X_1, X_2]' \sim N_2(\mu, \Sigma)$, where $\mu = [\mu_1, \mu_2]'$ and

$$\Sigma = \begin{bmatrix} \sigma_1^2 & \rho\sigma_1\sigma_2 \\ \rho\sigma_1\sigma_2 & \sigma_2^2 \end{bmatrix} \quad (-1 < \rho < 1).$$

Define $Y_1 \equiv X_1$ and $Y_2 \equiv X_2 - (\rho\sigma_2/\sigma_1)X_1$. Are Y_1 and Y_2 independent?

3.4.33 Let Y_t $(t = 1, 2, \ldots, T)$ be independent random variables with means $\mu_t = E(Y_t)$ $(t = 1, 2, \ldots, T)$ and common moments $\alpha_j \equiv E[(Y_t - \mu_t)^j]$ $(j = 2, 3, 4; t = 1, 2, \ldots, T)$. Let A be a $T \times T$ symmetric matrix with diagonal elements arranged in a $T \times 1$ vector d, and let $\mu = [\mu_1, \mu_2, \ldots, \mu_T]'$ (see Seber 1977, pp. 14–15).

(a) Show: $\mathrm{Var}(Y'AY) = (\alpha_4 - 3\alpha_2^2)d'd + 2\alpha_2^2 \mathrm{tr}(A^2) + 4\alpha_2\mu'A^2\mu + 4\alpha_3\mu'Ad$.

(b) Suppose $Y \sim N(\mu, \Sigma)$ in which case $\alpha_3 = 0$ and $\alpha_4 = 3\mu_2^2 = 3\sigma^4$. Show:

$$\mathrm{Var}(Y'AY) = 2\sigma^4 \mathrm{tr}(A^2) + 4\sigma^2\mu'A\mu. \tag{3.4.63}$$

3.4.34 Suppose $Y_t \sim N(\mu, \sigma^2)$ $(t = 1, 2, \ldots, T)$ are independent. Define

$$Q = [2(T-1)]^{-1} \sum_{t=1}^{T} (Y_{t+1} - Y_t)^2, \tag{3.4.64}$$

$$S^2 = (T-1)^{-1} \sum_{t=1}^{T} (Y_t - Y)^2. \tag{3.4.65}$$

Show:

(a) $E(Q) = \sigma^2$.

(b) As $T \to \infty$, $\mathrm{Var}(S^2)/\mathrm{Var}(Q) \to 2/3$.

3.4.35 Suppose $Y \sim N_T(\mu, \Sigma)$ and let A be a $T \times T$ symmetric matrix. Show:

(a) $\text{Cov}(Y, Y'AY) = 2\Sigma A\mu$

(b) $\text{Var}(Y'AY) = 2\,\text{tr}(A\Sigma A\Sigma) + 4\mu' A\Sigma A\mu$

3.4.36 Let x, a and b be $K \times 1$ vectors, let A be a $K \times K$ symmetric matrix, let B be a $K \times K$ positive definite matrix, and let a_0 and b_0 be scalars. Show:

$$\int_{-\infty}^{\infty} \cdots \int_{-\infty}^{\infty} [x'Ax + x'a + a_0] \exp[-(x'Bx + x'b + b_0)]\, dx_1 \ldots dx_K$$
$$= \tfrac{1}{2}\pi^{K/2}|B|^{-1/2} \exp[\tfrac{1}{4}b'B^{-1}b - b_0][\text{tr}(AB^{-1}) - b'B^{-1}a + \tfrac{1}{2}b'B^{-1}AB^{-1}b + 2a_0]. \tag{3.4.66}$$

For details, see Graybill (1969, pp. 16–17).

3.4.37 Consider a multivariate normal distribution and Theorem 3.4.6. Let B be the $m \times (N - m)$ matrix $B = \Sigma_{12}\Sigma_{22}^{-1}$. Using the notation of Section 2.7, the element in the ith row and kth column of B, denoted as $\beta_{ik\cdot m+1,\ldots,k-1,k+1,\ldots,N}$, is the coefficient on Z_k $(m + 1 \le k \le N)$ in a regression of Z_i $(1 \le i \le m)$ on $Z_{m+1}, \ldots, Z_N$. Also let the element in the ith row and jth column of $\Sigma_{1|2} = \Sigma_{11} - \Sigma_{12}\Sigma_{22}^{-1}\Sigma_{12}'$ be denoted by $\sigma_{ij\cdot m+1,\ldots,N}$. Verify each of the following (see Anderson 1984, Chapter 2):

(a) $$\rho_{ij\cdot m+1,\ldots,N} = \frac{\sigma_{ij\cdot m+1,\ldots,N}}{[\sigma_{ii\cdot m+1,\ldots,N}]^{1/2}[\sigma_{jj\cdot m+1,\ldots,N}]^{1/2}} \tag{3.4.67}$$

(b) $$\sigma_{ij\cdot m+1,\ldots,N} = \sigma_{ij\cdot m+2,\ldots,N} - \frac{\sigma_{i,m+1\cdot m+2,\ldots,N}\sigma_{j,m+1\cdot m+2,\ldots,N}}{\sigma_{m+1,m+1\cdot m+2,\ldots,N}} \quad (i,j = 1,\ldots,m) \tag{3.4.68}$$

(c) $$\sigma_{ii\cdot m+1,\ldots,N} = \sigma_{ii\cdot m+2,\ldots,N}[1 - \rho^2_{i,m+1\cdot m+2,\ldots,N}] \quad (i = 1,\ldots,m) \tag{3.4.69}$$

(d) $$\rho_{ij\cdot m+1,\ldots,N} = \frac{\rho_{ij\cdot m+2,\ldots,N} - \rho_{i,m+1\cdot m+2,\ldots,N}\rho_{j,m+1\cdot m+2,\ldots,N}}{[1 - \rho^2_{i,m+1\cdot m+2,\ldots,N}]^{1/2}[1 - \rho^2_{j,m+1\cdot m+1,\ldots,N}]} \quad (i,j = 1,\ldots,m). \tag{3.4.70}$$

(e) $$\beta_{ik\cdot m+1,\ldots,k-1,k+1,\ldots,N} = \frac{\sigma_{ik\cdot m+1,\ldots,k-1,k+1,\ldots,N}}{\sigma_{kk\cdot m+1,\ldots,k-1,k+1,\ldots,N}}.$$
$$= \rho_{i,k\cdot m+1,\ldots,k-1,k+1,\ldots,N}\left[\frac{\sigma_{ii\cdot m+1,\ldots,k-1,k+1,\ldots,N}}{\sigma_{kk\cdot m+1,\ldots,k-1,k+1,\ldots,N}}\right]^{1/2}$$
$$(i = 1,\ldots,m; k = m + 1,\ldots,N). \tag{3.4.71}$$

(f) $$\rho^2_{ij\cdot m+1,\ldots,N} = \beta_{ij\cdot m+1,\ldots,N}\beta_{ji\cdot m+1,\ldots,N}. \tag{3.4.72}$$

(g) $$1 - R^2_{i\cdot m+1,\ldots,N} = (1 - \rho^2_{iN})(1 - \rho^2_{i,N-1\cdot N})\ldots(1 - \rho^2_{i,m+1\cdot m+2,\ldots,N}). \tag{3.4.73}$$

3.4.38 Is the distinction among uncorrelated, mean-independent, and independent random variables vacuous in the case of the multivariate t-distribution?

3.4.39 Suppose $Y = [Y_1, Y_2, \ldots, Y_J]' \sim N_J(\mu, \Sigma)$. Let $Z = [Z_1, Z_2, \ldots, Z_J]'$, where

$$Z_j = \frac{\exp(Y_j)}{1 + \sum_{i=1}^{J-1} \exp(Y_i)} \quad (j = 1, 2, \ldots, J - 1),$$

$$Z_J = 1 - \sum_{i=1}^{J-1} Z_i. \tag{3.4.74}$$

The transformation in (3.4.75) is known as the *logistic transformation* and the distribution of Z is the *logistic-normal* distribution (e.g., see Aitchison and Shen 1980).

(a) What is the support of Z?

(b) Find the p.d.f. of Z.

3.5 Multivariate Distributions: II

Consideration of multiple equation models necessitates extension of the multivariate distributions in Section 3.4 related to the multivariate normal distribution.[8] We begin by introducing a multivariate generalization of the chi-square (and hence, also the gamma) distribution: the Wishart distribution. The Wishart distribution arises naturally when drawing independent, identically distributed random vectors from a multivariate normal population. This motivation is discussed in more detail in Chapter 5. Although its p.d.f. is somewhat cumbersome, the Wishart distribution nonetheless has attractive properties.

Definition 3.5.1 Let $Z = [z_{ij}]$ be a symmetric $M \times M$ positive definite matrix with random elements.[9] Let $\omega \geq M$ and A be a symmetric $M \times M$ positive definite matrix. Z has a *Wishart distribution*, denoted $Z \sim W_M(A, \omega)$, iff its p.d.f. is

$$f_{W,M}(Z|A,\omega) = c_{W,M}^{-1}|Z|^{(\omega-M-1)/2}|A|^{-\omega/2}\exp[-\tfrac{1}{2}\operatorname{tr}(A^{-1}Z)], \tag{3.5.1}$$

over all regions for which Z is p.d., and equal to zero over all regions for which Z is not p.d., where

$$c_{W,M} = c_{W,M}(\omega) = 2^{\omega M/2}\pi^{M(M-1)/4}\prod_{m=1}^{M}\Gamma\left[\frac{1}{2}(\omega + 1 - m)\right]. \tag{3.5.2}$$

When $A = I_M$, the distribution is in *standard form*.[10]

When $M = 1$, the Wishart distribution $W_1(A, \omega)$ reduces to the gamma distribution $G(\omega/2, 2A)$, equivalently $\gamma(\omega A, \omega)$, which is $A\chi^2(\omega)$. The first two moments of the Wishart distribution are given in the following theorem.

Theorem 3.5.1 Let $Z = [z_{ij}]$ be a symmetric $M \times M$ positive definite matrix such that $Z \sim W_M(A, \omega)$, where $A = [a_{ij}]$.

(a) $E(z_{ij}) = \omega a_{ij} \quad (i = 1, 2, \ldots, M; j = 2, 3, \ldots, M)$ (3.5.3)

(b) $\operatorname{Var}(z_{ij}) = \omega(a_{ij}^2 + a_{ii}a_{jj}) \quad (i = 1, 2, \ldots, M; j = 2, 3, \ldots, M)$ (3.5.4)

8. No proofs of theorems are included in this section. The interested reader can consult standard multivariate statistics texts (e.g., see Anderson 1984; Muirhead 1982; Press 1982) or Zellner (1971, Appendix B).

9. Note the lower case z denotes elements in the random matrix Z rather than realizations of Z. This convention is continued throughout this section.

10. The distribution of Z is singular since, as a result of its symmetry, it has only $M(M + 1)/2$ distinct elements V. Thus, more appropriately, (3.5.1) is the p.d.f. of V. In terms of the vech($\cdot$) operator discussed in Appendix B, $V = \operatorname{vech}(Z)$.

(c) $\text{Cov}(z_{ij}, z_{km}) = \omega(a_{ik}a_{jm} + a_{im}a_{jk})$
$(i, k = 1, 2, \ldots, M; j, m = 2, 3, \ldots, M)$ (3.5.5)

Marginal and conditional distributions for the Wishart distribution are considered in the following theorem.

Theorem 3.5.2 Consider Definition 3.4.3 and partition the matrices Z and Ω as

$$Z = \begin{bmatrix} Z_{11} & Z_{12} \\ Z_{21} & Z_{22} \end{bmatrix} \quad \text{and } A = \begin{bmatrix} A_{11} & A_{12} \\ A_{21} & A_{22} \end{bmatrix} \tag{3.5.6}$$

where Z_{11} and A_{11} are $J \times J$, Z_{22} and A_{22} are $(M - J) \times (M - J)$, Z_{12} and A_{12} are $J \times (M - J)$, Z_{21} and A_{21} are $(M - J) \times J$, $Z_{21} = Z'_{12}$ and $J_{21} = J'_{12}$. Define

$$Z_{22\cdot 1} \equiv Z_{22} - Z_{21}[Z_{11}]^{-1}Z_{12}, \tag{3.5.7}$$

$$A_{22\cdot 1} \equiv A_{22} - A_{21}[A_{11}]^{-1}A_{12}. \tag{3.5.8}$$

Then:

(a) $z_{mm}/a_{mm} \sim \chi^2(\omega)$ $(m = 1, 2, \ldots, M)$.

(b) $Z_{11} \sim W_J(A_{11}, \omega)$

(c) $Z_{22} \sim W_{M-J}(A_{22}, \omega)$

(d) Z_{11} and Z_{12} are independent iff $A_{12} = 0_{J\times(M-J)}$.

(e) If $\omega > J$, then $Z_{22\cdot 1} \sim W_{M-J}(A_{22\cdot 1}, \omega - J)$ and $Z_{22\cdot 1}$ is independent of Z_{11} and Z_{22}.

(f) If $\omega > J$ and $A_{12} = 0_{J\times(M-m)}$, then $Z_{22} - Z_{22\cdot 1} = Z_{21}[Z_{11}]^{-1}Z_{12} \sim W_{M-J}(A_{22}, \omega - J)$ and $Z_{21}[Z_{11}]^{-1}Z_{12}$, Z_{11} and $Z_{22\cdot 1}$ are jointly independent.

The computational attractiveness of the Wishart distribution is illustrated by the following two theorems.

Theorem 3.5.3 Let $Z \sim W_M(A, \omega)$. Let G be a $K \times M$ matrix of constants. Then $GZG' \sim W_K(GAG', \omega)$. If $K = 1$, then $GZG'/GAG' \sim \chi^2(\omega)$.

Theorem 3.5.4 Let $V_t \sim W_M(A, \omega_t)$ $(t = 1, 2, \ldots, T)$ be independent. Define $V \equiv V_1 + V_2 + \cdots + V_T$ and $\omega = \omega_1 + \omega_2 + \cdots + \omega_T$. Then $V \sim W_M(A, \omega)$.

Because Z is p.d., Z^{-1} exists and the question arises as to its distribution. The next definition and theorem provide the answer.

Definition 3.5.2 The $M \times M$ positive definite matrix $X = [x_{ij}]$ has an *inverted Wishart distribution*, denoted $X \sim IW_M(H, \omega)$, iff its p.d.f. is

$$f_{IW}(X|H,\omega) = c_W^{-1}|X|^{-(\omega+M+1)/2}|H|^{\omega/2}\exp[-\tfrac{1}{2}\text{tr}(H^{-1}X^{-1})],\ X \text{ is p.d.,} \tag{3.5.9}$$

and equal to zero over all regions for which X is not p.d., where $\omega \geq M$, H is a $M \times M$ positive definite matrix, and c_W is given by (3.5.2).

Theorem 3.5.5 Suppose $Z \sim W_M(A,\omega)$. Then $Z^{-1} \sim IW_M(A^{-1},\omega)$.

Theorem 3.5.6 Suppose $Z^{-1} \sim IW_M(A^{-1},\omega)$, where $Z^{-1} = [z^{ii}]$ and $A^{-1} = [a^{ij}]$.

(a) $E(Z^{-1}) = (\omega - M - 1)^{-1}A^{-1}$, if $\omega > M + 1$.

(b) $\text{Var}(z^{ii}) = 2a^{ii}/(\omega - M - 1)^2(\omega - M - 3)$, if $\omega > M + 3$.

(c) $\text{Var}(z^{ij}) = [(\omega - M - 1)a^{ii}a^{jj} + (a^{ij})^2]/$
$[(\omega - M)(\omega - M - 1)^2(\omega - M - 3)]$, if $\omega - 2M > 4$, $i \neq j$.

(d) $\text{Cov}(z^{ij}, z^{km}) = [2a^{ij}a^{km} + (\omega - M - 1)(a^{ik}a^{jm} + a^{im}a^{kj})]/$
$[(\omega - M)(\omega - M - 1)^2(\omega - M - 3)]$, if $\omega - 2M > 4$.

(e) Analogous to (3.5.6), partition Z^{-1} as

$$Z^{-1} = \begin{bmatrix} Z^{11} & Z^{12} \\ Z^{21} & Z^{22} \end{bmatrix} \text{ and } A^{-1} = \begin{bmatrix} A^{11} & A^{12} \\ A^{21} & A^{22} \end{bmatrix}, \tag{3.5.10}$$

where Z^{11} and A^{11} are $J \times J$, Z^{22} and A^{22} are $(M - J) \times (M - J)$, Z^{12} and A^{12} are $J \times (M - J)$, Z^{21} and A^{21} are $(M - J) \times J$, $Z^{21} = (Z^{12})'$ and $A^{21} = (A^{12})'$. Then $Z^{11} \sim IW_J(A^{11}, \omega - N + J)$.

In order to relate Wishart and inverted Wishart distributions to the multivariate normal and other multivariate distributions, it is helpful to consider a particular subset of multivariate normal distributions. The resulting distributions are known by a variety of names. Here we assign the adjective "matric" to the root distribution of Section 3.4. We begin by discussing the *matric-normal distribution*, which unlike subsequent distributions in this section, is a special case of its parent multivariate normal distribution of Section 3.4.

Definition 3.5.3 Let Y be a $N \times M$ matrix of random variables, and let Ψ, C and Z be $N \times M$, $N \times N$ and $M \times M$ matrices, respectively, where C and Z are symmetric and positive definite. Given Ψ, C and Z, Y has a *matric-normal distribution*, denoted $Y \sim MN_{N \times M}(\Psi, C, Z)$, iff $\text{vec}(Y) \sim N_{NM}(\mu, \Sigma)$ where $\mu = \text{vec}(\Psi)$ and $\Sigma = Z^{-1} \otimes C^{-1}$.[11]

Using the commutation matrix defined in Definition B.2.2 and Theorems B.2.3–B.2.4, it is easy to show the following result.

11. vec(·) denotes the operator which converts a matrix into a vector by stacking its columns. The notation "⊗" denotes Kronecker product. Both notations are discussed in Appendix B.

Theorem 3.5.7 $Y \sim MN_{N \times M}(\Psi, C, Z)$ iff $Y' \sim MN_{M \times N}(\Psi', Z, C)$.

The matric-normal distribution arises naturally as a particular conditional distribution from a Wishart distribution as the next theorem illustrates.

Theorem 3.5.8 Suppose $Z \sim W_M(\Omega, \omega)$, and consider the partitioning introduced in Theorem 3.5.2. Then $Z_{12}|Z_{22} \sim N_{J \times (M-J)}(A_{12}A_{22}^{-1}Z_{22}, A_{11\cdot 2} \otimes Z_{22})$.[12]

The special structure of the matric-normal distribution proves most valuable when discussing multivariate sampling from normal distributions. In particular we are interested in cases where the marginal distribution of the $M \times M$ matrix Z in Definition 3.5.3 has a Wishart distribution. This leads to the following distribution.

Definition 3.5.4 Let Y be a $N \times M$ matrix of random variables, and let Ψ, C, Z and $\underline{A}$ be $N \times M$, $N \times N$, $M \times M$ and $M \times M$ matrices, respectively, where C, Z and A are positive definite. The $N \times M$ matrix Y and the $M \times M$ matrix Z have a *matric-normal-Wishart distribution*, denoted $Y, Z \sim MNW_{NM}(\Psi, C, A, \omega)$, iff $Y|Z \sim MN_{N \times M}(\Psi, C, Z)$ and $Z \sim W_M(A, \omega)$. The p.d.f. of the normal-Wishart distribution is

$$f_{MNW}(Y, Z) = \phi_{NM}(\text{vec}(Y)|\mu, Z^{-1} \otimes C^{-1}) f_W(Z|A, \omega), \tag{3.5.11}$$

where $\mu = \text{vec}(\Psi)$.

In the case $N = 1$, the $MNW_{1 \times M}(\Psi, C, A, \omega)$ is simply referred to as the *Normal-Wishart distribution*, and is denoted as $NW_M(\Psi', C, A, \omega)$. Note that Ψ' is $M \times 1$, C is a scalar, and $Y'|Z \sim N_M[\Psi', (CZ)^{-1}]$. In the case $M = 1$, the normal-Wishart distribution $MNW_{N \times 1}(\Psi, C, A, \omega)$ reduces to the normal-gamma distribution $NG_{N+1}(\Psi, C, \omega A, \omega)$ of Definition 3.4.5. Note in this case Ψ is $N \times 1$, A is a scalar, and $Y|Z \sim N_N[\Psi, (ZA)^{-1}]$.

Before stating the multivariate analog of Theorem 3.4.12, however, it is necessary to introduce a new distribution.[13]

Definition 3.5.5 Let Y be a $N \times M$ matrix of random variables, and let Ψ, C, and A be $N \times M$, $N \times N$ and $M \times M$ matrices, respectively, where C and A are positive definite. Let $\omega > 0$ be a scalar. Given Ψ, C, A and ω, Y has a *matric-t distribution*, denoted $Y \sim mt_{N \times M}(\Psi, C, A, \omega)$, iff

$$f_{mt}(Y|\Psi, C, A, \omega) = \frac{c_{mt}^{-1}|C|^{M/2}|A|^{(\omega+M-1)/2}}{|A + (Y - \Psi)'C(Y - \Psi)|^{(\omega+N+M-1)/2}}, \tag{3.5.12}$$

12. Note: the regression $E(Z_{12}|Z_{22})$ is once again linear in the conditioning variables.

13. The matric-t distribution is also known as the matrix t, matrix variate t, and generalized multivariate Student t distribution. In addition to the texts cited earlier, good references to the matric-t distribution are Box and Tiao (1973, pp. 441–453) and Dickey (1967).

where

$$c_{mt} = c_{mt}(N, M, \omega) = \frac{\pi^{NM/2} \prod_{i=1}^{M} \Gamma[(\omega + i - 1)/2]}{\prod_{j=1}^{M} \Gamma[(\omega + N + j - 1)/2]}. \tag{3.5.13}$$

The parameter ω is known as *degrees of freedom.*

Marginal and conditional distributions for the matric-t distribution are considered in the following theorem.

Theorem 3.5.9 Suppose $Y \sim mt_{N \times M}(\Psi, C, A, \omega)$. Partition Y as $Y = [Y_1, Y_2]$, where Y_1 is $N \times J$ and Y_2 is $N \times (M - J)$, and partition A as in Theorem 3.5.2.

(a) The marginal distributions of Y_1 and Y_2 are: $Y_1 \sim mt_{N \times J}(\Psi_1, C, A_{11}, \omega)$ and $Y_2 \sim mt_{N \times m}(\Psi_2, C, A_{22}, \omega)$.

(b) $Y_2 | Y_1 \sim mt_{N \times (M-J)}(d, D, A_{22 \cdot 1}, \omega + J)$, where $A_{22 \cdot 1}$ is given by (3.5.8) and

$$d = \Psi_2 + (Y_1 - \Psi_1) A_{11}^{-1} A_{12}, \tag{3.5.14}$$

$$D = [C^{-1} + (Y_1 - \Psi_1) A_{11}^{-1} (Y_1 - \Psi_1)']^{-1}. \tag{3.5.15}$$

(c) Let Y_i and Ψ_i be the ith columns of Y and Ψ, respectively, and let $A = [a_{ij}]$. Then $Y_i \sim t_N(\Psi_i, a_{ii} C, v)$, where $v = \omega - (M - 1)$.

(d) Joint density $f_{mt}(Y | \Psi, C, A, \omega)$ can be written as a product of multivariate t densities.

(e) $Y' \sim mt_{M \times N}(\Psi', A, C, \omega)$

(f) Partition Y and C as

$$Y = \begin{bmatrix} Y_{11} & Y_{12} \\ Y_{21} & Y_{22} \end{bmatrix} \text{ and } C = \begin{bmatrix} C_{11} & C_{12} \\ C_{21} & C_{22} \end{bmatrix}, \tag{3.5.16}$$

where Y_{11} is $n \times m$, Y_{22} is $(N - n) \times (M - m)$, Y_{12} is $n \times (M - m)$, Y_{21} is $(N - n) \times m$, C_{11} is $m \times m$, C_{22} is $(M - m) \times (M - m)$, C_{12} is $m \times (M - m)$, C_{21} is $(M - m) \times m$, and $C_{21} = C_{12}'$. Then $Y_{11} \sim mt_{n \times m}(\Psi_{11}, C_{11}, A_{11}, \omega)$.[14]

As a result of (e), (a)–(d) hold in analogous fashion for the rows of Y. Note that in general the matric-t distribution is distinct from the multivariate t distribution of Definition 3.4.4, although particular marginal and conditional distributions from the matric t-distribution resulting in a

14. Note that (*f*) extends directly for Y_{22}, Y_{12}, or Y_{21} taken separately. This is *not* true in general. For example, the marginal distribution of Y_{11} and Y_{22} is not matric-t, nor is the conditional distribution of Y_{12} and Y_{21}, given Y_{11} and Y_{22}.

single column (or row) are in fact multivariate-t. Part (c) provides an example. Another example is provided by the Normal-Wishart case ($N = 1$) for which $Y \sim t_M(\Psi', (CZ)^{-1}, \omega)$.

The following two theorems describe some properties of the matric-variate t-distribution.

Theorem 3.5.10 Suppose $Y \sim mt_{N \times M}(\Psi, C, A, \omega)$, and let $A = [a_{ij}]$.

(a) $E(Y) = \Psi$, if $\omega > 1$.

(b) Let Y_i be the ith column of Y. Then $\mathrm{Var}(Y_i) = [a_{ii}/(\omega - 2)]C$ ($i = 1, 2, \ldots, M$) if $\omega > 2$.

(c) Let Y_i and Y_j be the ith and jth columns of Y. Then $\mathrm{Var}(Y_i) = [a_{ii}/(\omega - 2)]C$ ($i, j = 1, 2, \ldots, M$) if $\omega > 2$.

(d) $\mathrm{Var}[\mathrm{vec}(Y)] = (\omega - 2)^{-1}[C \otimes A]$

(e) Let G be $n \times N$ ($n \leq N$) and H be $M \times m$ ($m \leq M$). Suppose $\mathrm{rank}(G) = n$ and $\mathrm{rank}(H) = m$. Define $X \equiv GYH$. Then $X \sim mt_{n \times m}(G\Psi H, GCG', HAH', \omega)$.

(f) Suppose $\omega^{-1}A \to A^*$ as $\omega \to \infty$. Then $Y \xrightarrow{d} MN_{N \times M}(\Psi, C, A^*)$ as $\omega \to \infty$.

Theorem 3.5.11 Reconsider Theorem 3.5.2. Then $Z_{11}^{-1}Z_{12} \sim mt_{J \times (N-J)}(A_{11}^{-1}A_{12}, A_{11}^{-1}, A_{22 \cdot 1}, \omega + J)$.

We close this section with the promised analog of Theorem 3.4.12.

Theorem 3.5.12 Let Y be a $N \times M$ matrix of random variables, and let Ψ, C, Z and $\underline{A}$ be $N \times M$, $N \times N$, $M \times M$ and $M \times M$ matrices, respectively, where C, Z and $\underline{A}$ are positive definite. Suppose $Y, Z \sim NW(\Psi, C, A, \omega)$. Then:

(a) $Y \sim mt_{N \times M}(\Psi, C, A, \omega)$

(b) $Z | Y \sim W(\overline{A}, \overline{\omega})$, where

$$\overline{A} = [A^{-1} + (Y - \Psi)'C(Y - \Psi)]^{-1}, \tag{3.5.17}$$

$$\overline{\omega} = \omega + N. \tag{3.5.18}$$

Exercises

3.5.1 Verify Theorem 3.5.9(e).

3.5.2 Verify Theorem 3.5.9(c).

3.5.3 Suppose $Z \sim N_T(\mu, \Sigma)$. Let e_i be a $T \times 1$ vector with all elements equal to zero except the ith which equals unity. Show:

$$E(ZZ' \otimes ZZ') = (I + K)(\Sigma \otimes \Sigma) + \mathrm{vec}(\Sigma)[\mathrm{vec}(\Sigma)]', \tag{3.5.19}$$

where

$$K = \begin{bmatrix} e_1 e_1' & \cdots & e_T e_1' \\ \vdots & & \vdots \\ e_1 e_T' & \cdots & e_T e_T' \end{bmatrix}. \tag{3.5.20}$$

3.5.4 The matric-t p.d.f. is a monotonic increasing function of

$$U(Y) = \frac{|A|}{|A + (Y - \Psi)' C (Y - \Psi)|}$$
$$= |I_M + A^{-1}(Y - \Psi)' C (Y - \Psi)|^{-1}. \tag{3.5.21}$$

Show each of the following:

(a) $$E[U(Y)^r] = \prod_{m=1}^{M} \frac{B\left(\frac{v-1+i}{2} + r, \frac{M}{2}\right)}{B\left(\frac{v-1+i}{2}, \frac{M}{2}\right)} \tag{3.5.22}$$

(b) If $M = 1$, then $v[1 - U(Y)]/[NU(y)] \sim F(N, v)$.

3.5.5 Prove Theorem 3.5.7.

4 Distributions of Functions of Random Variables

4.1 Introduction

This chapter investigates the following problem. Consider the random vector $X = [X_1, X_2, \ldots, X_N]'$ with distribution function $F_X(\cdot)$. Define the vector-valued function $g(\cdot)$ from $\Re^N$ to $\Re^J$ by $Y = g(X)$, where $Y = [Y_1, Y_2, \ldots, Y_J]'$ and $Y_j = g_j(X)$ $(j = 1, 2, \ldots, J)$. What is the distribution function $F_Y(y)$ of Y? This question is a very basic one. Its answer is a prerequisite for statistical estimation and inference. Its importance is obvious from Chapter 3, where various theorems linking together common distributions were stated without proof. This chapter develops the tools needed to prove these theorems.

Four approaches to the solution of this problem are discussed: (i) the cumulative distribution function technique (Section 4.2), (ii) the moment generating function technique (Section 4.3), (iii) the change-of-variable technique (Section 4.4), and (iv) the quadratic-form technique (Section 4.5). Each of these is now discussed in turn.

4.2 Cumulative Distribution Function Technique

For the problem described in Section 4.1, the joint cumulative distribution function of $Y_j \equiv g_j(X)$ $(j = 1, 2, \ldots, J)$ is

$$F_Y(y) \equiv P[Y_1 \le y_1, Y_2 \le y_2, \ldots, Y_J \le y_J] \tag{4.2.1a}$$

$$= P[g_1(X) \le y_1, g_2(X) \le y_2, \ldots, g_J(X) \le y_J]. \tag{4.2.1b}$$

Because $F_X(\cdot)$ is assumed given, (4.2.1b) can be computed, and hence $F_Y(\cdot)$ determined. The ease with which this can be accomplished, however, is highly problem specific.

Example 4.2.1 (Proof of Theorem 3.3.12) Suppose $J = N = 1$, $X \sim N(0, 1)$ and $Y = g(X) = X^2$. Then

$$F_Y(y) = P(Y \le y) = P(X^2 \le y) = P(-y^{1/2} \le X \le y^{1/2}). \tag{4.2.2a}$$

Using the symmetry of the normal density, (4.2.2a) equals

$$F_Y(y) = 2\int_0^{y^{1/2}} (2\pi)^{-1/2} \exp(-t^2/2)\,dt$$

$$= \int_0^{y} (2\pi u)^{-1/2} \exp(-u/2)\,du, \tag{4.2.2b}$$

where $u = t^2$. From Definition 3.3.7 it is seen that (4.2.2b) is the distribution function of a chi-squared random variable with one degree of freedom.

The cumulative distribution function technique is useful in deriving the distribution of maxima and minima of random variables. This is illustrated in the following theorem and Exercise 4.2.1.

Theorem 4.2.1 Suppose $J = 1$ and X_n $(n = 1, 2, \ldots, N)$ are *independent* random variables. Define

$$Y \equiv g(X) = \max\{X_1, X_2, \ldots, X_N\}. \tag{4.2.3}$$

Then

$$F_Y = (y) = \prod_{n=1}^{N} F_n(y), \tag{4.2.4}$$

where $F_n(\cdot)$ is the distribution function of X_n. If in addition X_n $(n = 1, 2, \ldots, N)$ are *identically* distributed, then

$$F_Y(y) = [F(y)]^N, \tag{4.2.5}$$

where $F(\cdot)$ is the common distribution function of X_n $(n = 1, 2, \ldots, N)$. If in the latter case, the independent and identically distributed (i.i.d.) X_ns have common p.d.f. $f(\cdot)$, then

$$f_Y(y) = N[F(y)]^{N-1} f(y). \tag{4.2.6}$$

Proof Because the largest of the X_ns is less than or equal to y iff all the X_ns are less than or equal to y, it follows that

$$F_Y(y) = P[X_1, \leq y, X_2 \leq y, \ldots, X_N \leq y].$$

The independence of the X_ns further implies

$$F_Y(y) = \prod_{n=1}^{N} P_n(y) = \prod_{n=1}^{N} F_n(y),$$

from which (4.2.4) follows. If the X_ns are also identically distributed, then let $F(y) \equiv F_1(y) = \cdots = F_N(y)$, and (4.2.5) follows immediately. Differentiating (4.2.5), (4.2.6) is obtained in the case where the common p.d.f. $f(\cdot)$ exists.

In many situations the cumulative distribution function technique is cumbersome due to the integrations required. It is, however, convenient for proving the following two handy theorems that deal with functions commonly encountered.

Theorem 4.2.2 (Convolution Theorem) Let X_1 and X_2 be continuous random variables with joint p.d.f. $f_X(x_1, x_2)$. Define $Y_1 = X_1 + X_2$ and $Y_2 = X_1 - X_2$. Then the marginal p.d.f.s of Y_1 and Y_2 (known as *convolutions*) are respectively,

$$g_1(y_1) = \int_{-\infty}^{\infty} f_X(x_1, y_1 - x_1)\, dx_1 = \int_{-\infty}^{\infty} f_X(y_1 - x_2, x_2)\, dx_2, \tag{4.2.7}$$

$$g_2(y_2) = \int_{-\infty}^{\infty} f_X(x_1, x_1 - y_2)\, dx_1 = \int_{-\infty}^{\infty} f_X(y_2 - x_2, x_2)\, dx_2. \tag{4.2.8}$$

If X_1 and X_2 are independent, then

$$g_2(y_1) = \int_{-\infty}^{\infty} f_1(x_1)f_2(y_1 - x_1)\,dx_1 = \int_{-\infty}^{\infty} f_1(y_1 - x_2)f_2(x_2)\,dx_2, \tag{4.2.9}$$

$$g_2(y_2) = \int_{-\infty}^{\infty} f_1(x_1)f_2(x_1 - y_2)\,dx_1 = \int_{-\infty}^{\infty} f_1(y_2 - x_2)f_2(x_2)\,dx_2. \tag{4.2.10}$$

Proof Mood et al. (1974, pp. 185–187).

Theorem 4.2.3 Let X_1 and X_2 be continuous random variables with joint p.d.f. $f_X(x_1, x_2)$. Define $Y_1 = X_1X_2$ and $Y_2 = X_1/X_2$. Then the marginal p.d.f.s of Y_1 and Y_2 are:

$$g_1(y_1) = \int_{-\infty}^{\infty} |x_1|^{-1} f_X\left(x_1, \frac{y_1}{x_1}\right) dx_1 = \int_{-\infty}^{\infty} |x_2|^{-1} f_X\left(\frac{y_1}{x_2}, x_2\right) dx_2, \tag{4.2.11}$$

$$g_2(y_2) = \int_{-\infty}^{\infty} |x_2|\, f_X(x_2y_2, x_2)\,dx_2. \tag{4.2.12}$$

Proof Mood et al. (1974, pp. 187–188).

The usefulness of Theorems 4.2.2 and 4.2.3 can be seen from the following two examples.

Example 4.2.2 Suppose X_1 and X_2 are random variables with joint p.d.f.

$$f(x_1, x_2) = \begin{Bmatrix} 8x_1x_2, & \text{if } 0 < x_1 < 1, \text{if } 0 < x_2 < x_1 < 1 \\ 0, & \text{otherwise} \end{Bmatrix}.$$

What is the p.d.f. of $Y \equiv X_1 + X_2$?

First note that if $0 < y \leq 1$, then the range of possible x_1 values is $x_1 = y/2$ to $x_1 = 1$. Hence, using (4.2.7), for $0 < y \leq 1$,

$$\begin{aligned} g(y) &= \int_{1/2y}^{y} 8x_1(y - x_1)\,dx_1 = 8\left[\frac{1}{2}(x_1^2 y) - \frac{1}{3}x_1^3\right]_{1/2y}^{y} \\ &= 8\left[\frac{1}{2}y^3 - \frac{1}{3}y^3 - \frac{1}{8}y^3 + \frac{1}{24}y^3\right] = \frac{8y^3(12 - 8 - 3 + 1)}{24} = \frac{2y^3}{3}. \end{aligned}$$

For $1 < y < 2$,

$$\begin{aligned} g(y) &= \int_{1/2y}^{1} 8x_1(y - x_1)\,dx_1 = 8\left[\frac{1}{2}x_1^2 y - \frac{1}{3}x_1^3\right]_{1/2y}^{1} \\ &= 8\left[\frac{1}{2}y - \frac{1}{3} - \frac{1}{8}y^3 + \frac{1}{24}y^3\right] = \frac{12y - 8 - 2y^3}{3}. \end{aligned}$$

Example 4.2.3 Suppose X_1 and X_2 are independent and identically distributed exponential ($\beta = 1$) random variables with common p.d.f.

$$f(x) = \begin{Bmatrix} \exp(-x), & \text{if } 0 < x < \infty \\ 0, & \text{if } -\infty < x \le 0 \end{Bmatrix}.$$

Find the p.d.f. of $y = x_1/x_2$. Using (4.2.12),

$$g(y) = \int_0^\infty x_2 \exp(-yx_2)\exp(-x_2)\,dx_2$$

$$= \int_0^\infty x_2 \exp[-(1+y)x_2]\,dx_2.$$

Let $u = x_2$, $du = dx_2$, $dv = \exp[-(1 + y)x_2\,dx_2$, $v = -(1+y)^{-1}\exp[-(1+y)x_2]$. Then:

$$g(y) = \left[\left(\frac{-x_2}{1+y}\right)\exp[-(1+y)x^2]\right]_0^\infty - \int_0^\infty$$

$$-(1+y)^{-1}\exp[-(1+y)x_2]\,dx_2$$

$$= 0 + (1+y)^{-1}\left[-\frac{\exp[-(1+y)x_2]}{(1+y)}\right]_0^\infty$$

$$= (1+y)^{-2} \quad \text{for } y > 0.$$

Hence, the p.d.f. of y is

$$g(y) = \begin{Bmatrix} (1+y)^{-2}, & \text{if } y > 0 \\ 0, & \text{if } y \le 0 \end{Bmatrix}.$$

Exercises

4.2.1 State and prove the analog of Theorem 4.2.1 for $Y \equiv \min\{X_1, X_2, \ldots, X_N\}$.

4.2.2 Let X_1 and X_2 be independent $U(0,1)$ random variables. Find the p.d.f.'s of the following random variables:

(a) $Y = X_1 + X_2$

(b) $Y = X_1 X_2$

(c) $Y = X_1/X_2$. In this case, does $E(Y) = E(X_1)/E(X_2)$?

4.2.3 Let X_1 and X_2 be independent random variables each with p.d.f. $f(x) = 2x$ for $0 < x < 1$, and zero otherwise. Define $Y = X_1/X_2$. Find $P(Y \ge \frac{1}{2})$.

4.2.4 Let X_n ($n = 1, 2, 3$) be i.i.d. each with p.d.f. $f(x) = 5x^4$, for $0 < x < 1$, and zero otherwise. Define $Y = \max\{X_1, X_2, X_3\}$. Find $P(Y \ge \frac{3}{4})$.

4.2.5 Suppose Y_1 and Y_2 are independent random variables with exponential distributions having parameters β_1 and β_2, respectively. Find $E[\max\{Y_1, Y_2\}]$.

4.2.6 Let X_t ($t = 1, 2, 3, \ldots$) be a sequence of independent and identically distributed random variables with mean μ_X and variance σ_X^2. Also let T be an integer-valued random variable, and define $S_T = X_1 + X_2 + \cdots + X_T$. Thus, S_T is a sum of a *random number* of *random variables*. Assume T is independent of X_t ($t = 1, 2, 3, \ldots$) and that $E(T) = \mu_T$ and $\mathrm{Var}(T) = \sigma_T^2$.

(a) Prove: $E(S_T) = \mu_T \mu_X$.

(b) Prove: $\text{Var}(S_T) = \mu_T \sigma_X^2 + \sigma_T^2 \mu_X^2$.

(c) Suppose T has a geometric distribution with parameter θ and that X_t has an exponential distribution with parameter λ. Prove that the distribution of S_T is exponential with parameter $\theta\lambda$.

4.3 Moment Generating Function Technique

As was noted in Sections 2.3 and 2.6, when the moment generating function (m.g.f.) of a random variable Y—denoted as $M_Y(\cdot)$—exists, it is unique and it uniquely determines the distribution function $F_Y(\cdot)$. Thus, one approach to solving the problem stated in Section 4.1 is to compute $M_Y(t) = E[\exp(t'Y)] = E[\exp\{t_1 g_1(X) + t_2 g_2(X) + \cdots + t_J g_J(X)\}]$, assuming it exists, and hopefully recognize it as the m.g.f. of a familiar distribution. Obviously, this approach can only be taken in particular situations (i.e. when $M_Y(\cdot)$ exists and is easily recognizable), and hence is less general than the cumulative distribution function technique. With the use of the following theorems, however, the moment generating function technique is often more convenient. In what follows we will only consider the case of one function ($J = 1$) and hence omit all subscripts "j". A case in which $J = 2$ is covered in Exercise 4.3.3.

We begin illustrating the m.g.f. technique by two simple examples.

Example 4.3.1 [Proof of Theorem 3.4.7(a) in the case M = 1] Suppose $X = [X_1, X_2, \ldots, X_N]' \sim N(\mu, \Sigma)$ and define $Y = a'X$, where $a = [a_1, a_2, \ldots, a_N]'$ is a N-dimensional column vector of constants. What is the distribution of Y?

By Theorem 3.4.5(a) the m.g.f. of X is $M_X(t) = \exp(t'\mu + \frac{1}{2}t'\Sigma t)$, where $t = [t_1, t_2, \ldots, t_N]'$. The m.g.f. of Y is $M_Y(c) = E[\exp(cY)] = E[\exp(ca'X)]$ for any real number c. Letting $t = ca$, it follows from the m.g.f. of X that $M_Y(c) = \exp[(ca)'\mu + \frac{1}{2}c(a'\Sigma a)c]$. Hence $Y \sim N(a'\mu, a'\Sigma a)$.

Example 4.3.2 (Second Proof of Theorem 3.3.12) Consider $W \sim N(\mu, \sigma^2)$ and $X \equiv (W - \mu)/\sigma \sim N(0, 1)$. Define $Y = X^2$. Then

$$
\begin{aligned}
M(t) = E[\exp(tX^2)] &= \int_{-\infty}^{\infty} (2\pi)^{-1/2} \exp(tx^2 - x^2/2)\,dx \\
&= (1 - 2t)^{-1/2} \int_{-\infty}^{\infty} [2\pi/(1 - 2t)]^{-1/2} \exp[-x^2/[2/(1 - 2t)]\,dx \\
&= (1 - 2t)^{-1/2} \quad \text{for } t < \tfrac{1}{2},
\end{aligned}
$$

which is recognized from (3.3.16) to be the m.g.f. of a chi-squared distribution with one degree of freedom. Note that Example 4.2.1 showed this result using the cumulative distribution function technique.

The moment generating function technique is particularly convenient in cases where Y is the sum of independent random variables each of which has a m.g.f. The following theorem illustrates this fact and Example 4.3.3 uses it to prove Theorem 3.3.4.

Theorem 4.3.1 Suppose X_n $(n = 1, 2, \ldots, N)$ are independent random variables, and that the moment generating function $M_n(t)$ $(n = 1, 2, \ldots, N)$ of each exists for all $-h < t < h$ for some $h > 0$. Define $Y \equiv X_1 + X_2 + \cdots + X_N$. Then the m.g.f. of Y is

$$M_Y(t) = \prod_{n=1}^{N} M_n(t). \tag{4.3.1}$$

Proof

$$\begin{aligned} M_Y(t) &= E[\exp(tY)] = E[\exp\{t(X_1 + X_2 + \cdots + X_N)\}] \\ &= E\left[\prod_{n=1}^{N} \exp(tX_n)\right] = \prod_{n=1}^{N} E[\exp(tX_n)] = \prod_{n=1}^{N} M_n(t). \end{aligned}$$

Example 4.3.3 [Proof of Theorem 3.4.4] Suppose $Y_j \sim M(T_j, \theta)$ $(j = 1, 2, \ldots, J)$ are independent, and let $Y = Y_1 + Y_2 + \cdots + Y_J$. Then by Theorems 3.4.2 and 4.3.1,

$$\begin{aligned} M_Y(t) = \prod_{n=1}^{J} M_n(t) &= \prod_{n=1}^{J} \left[\theta_N + \sum_{n=1}^{N-1} \theta_n \exp(t_n)\right]^{T_j} \\ &= \left[\theta_N + \sum_{n=1}^{N-1} \theta_n \exp(t_n)\right]^{T}, \end{aligned}$$

where $T \equiv T_1 + T_2 + \cdots + T_J$. Hence, using Theorem 3.3.4, $Y \sim M(T, \theta)$.

Exercises

4.3.1 Suppose X_n $(n = 1, 2, \ldots, N)$ are independent Poisson random variables with parameters λ_n $(n = 1, 2, \ldots, N)$. Define $Y = X_1 + X_2 + \cdots + X_N$ and $\lambda = \lambda_1 + \lambda_2 + \cdots + \lambda_N$. Show that Y has a Poisson distribution with parameter λ.

4.3.2 Suppose X_n $(n = 1, 2)$ each independent $N(0, 1)$. Find the joint distribution of $Y_1 = [\frac{1}{2}(X_1 + X_2)]^{1/2}$ and $Y_2 = [\frac{1}{2}(X_2 - X_1)]^{1/2}$.

4.3.3 Suppose X_n $(n = 1, 2, \ldots, N)$ are independent gamma random variables with parameters α_n and β $(n = 1, 2, \ldots, N)$, and let $Y = X_1 + X_2 + \cdots + X_N$. Find the distribution of Y. Note that this is a generalization of Theorem 3.3.11.

4.4 Change-of-Variable Technique

Probably the most common technique in econometrics for dealing with the general problem of finding the distribution of functions of random variables is the *change-of-variable technique.* We will first discuss this technique in terms of discrete random variables, and then devote the majority of our attention to continuous random variables.

Theorem 4.4.1 Let X be a discrete random variable with p.m.f. $f(\cdot)$ and support A. Consider $Y \equiv g(X)$, where $g(\cdot)$ is a one-to-one function that maps A onto a set B. Finally, let $g^{-1}(\cdot)$ denote the inverse mapping from B to A, that is, $X = g^{-1}(Y)$. Then the p.m.f. of Y is

$$h(y) \equiv P(Y = y) = P[X = g^{-1}(y)] = \begin{Bmatrix} f[g^{-1}(y)], & \text{if } y \in B \\ 0, & \text{otherwise} \end{Bmatrix}. \tag{4.4.1}$$

Proof Left to the reader.

Example 4.4.1 Suppose $X \sim B(4, \theta)$ and consider $Y \equiv g(X) = X^2$. Note that $g(\cdot)$ is one-to-one over $A = \{0, 1, 2, 3, 4\}$. Then $g^{-1}(y) = y^{1/2}$, $B = \{0, 1, 4, 9, 16\}$ and

$$h(y) = P(Y = y) = \begin{Bmatrix} \begin{pmatrix} 4 \\ y^{1/2} \end{pmatrix} \theta^{y^{1/2}}(1-\theta)^{4-y^{1/2}}, & \text{if } y \in B \\ 0, & \text{otherwise} \end{Bmatrix}.$$

Theorem 4.4.1 can be straightforwardly extended to cover joint transformations. See Exercise 4.4.1. We shall now discuss the analog of Theorem 4.4.1 for continuous random variables.

Theorem 4.4.2 Let X be a continuous random variable with p.d.f. $f(\cdot)$ and support A. Consider $Y \equiv g(X)$ where $g(\cdot)$ is a one-to-one function that maps A onto a set B. Let the inverse of $g(\cdot)$ be denoted $g^{-1}(\cdot)$ and assume that the derivative $d[g^{-1}(y)]/dy = dx/dy$ (known as the *Jacobian* of the inverse transformation) is continuous and does not equal zero for any point $y \in B$. Then the p.d.f. of Y is

$$h(y) = \begin{Bmatrix} \left| \left[\frac{dx}{dy} \right] \right| f[g^{-1}(y)], & \text{if } y \in B \\ 0, & \text{otherwise} \end{Bmatrix}. \tag{4.4.2}$$

Proof To minimize space we will consider only the case in which A is a finite interval $[a, b]$ and $g(\cdot)$ is monotonically increasing. For $y \in B$, $F_Y(y) = P(g(X) \le y) = P(X \le g^{-1}(y)] = F_X[g^{-1}(y)]$. By the chain rule of differentiation,

$$h(y) = \frac{d}{dy}[F_Y(y)] = \frac{d}{dy}(F_X[g^{-1}(y)])$$
$$= \left[\frac{d}{dy}[g^{-1}(y)]\right] f[g^{-1}(y)]$$
$$= \left[\frac{dx}{dy}\right] f[g^{-1}(y)]$$

for $y \in B$, and zero otherwise. Because $g(\cdot)$ is monotonically increasing, $dx/dy = |dx/dy|$ and (4.4.2) follows immediately.

Example 4.4.2 Suppose X has a uniform distribution over $[0, 1]$, and consider $Y \equiv g(X) = -2 \ln X$. Then $X = g^{-1}(Y) = \exp(-\frac{1}{2}Y)$, $A = [0, 1]$, $B = (0, \infty)$ and $|dx/dy| = \frac{1}{2}\exp(-\frac{1}{2}y)$. Hence, it follows from (4.4.2) that the p.d.f. of Y is

$$h(y) = \begin{cases} \frac{1}{2}\exp(-\frac{1}{2}y), & \text{if } 0 < y < \infty \\ 0, & \text{if } -\infty < y \leq 0 \end{cases}. \tag{4.4.3}$$

From (3.3.16), (4.4.3) is recognized as the p.d.f. of a chi-squared distribution with two degrees of freedom.

Example 4.4.3 (Proof of Theorem 3.3.10). Let X be any continuous random variable with distribution function $F(\cdot)$ and p.d.f. $f(\cdot)$. Define $Y = g(X) = F(X)$. This transformation is called the *probability integral transformation* and it plays an important role in goodness-of-fit tests and nonparametric tests. Then $X = F^{-1}(Y)$, $A = (-\infty, \infty)$, $B = [0, 1]$ and $|dx/dy| = \{f[F^{-1}(y)]\}^{-1}$. Because

$$\left|\frac{dx}{dy}\right| \cdot f[F^{-1}(y)] = \frac{1}{f[F^{-1}(y)]} \cdot f[F^{-1}(y)] = 1,$$

it follows that Y has a uniform distribution over $[0, 1]$.

We now extend Theorem 4.4.2 to cover the case of more than one function of the random vector X.

Theorem 4.4.3 Let $X = [X_1, X_2, \ldots, X_N]'$ be a N-dimensional random vector whose elements have the joint p.d.f. $f_X(x)$, $x = [x_1, x_2, \ldots, x_N]'$, with support A. Consider the one-to-one transformations

$$Y_n \equiv g_n(X) = g_n(X_1, X_2, \ldots, X_N) \qquad (n = 1, 2, \ldots, N), \tag{4.4.4}$$

which map A onto a set B. Also let the inverse transformation be denoted by

$$X_n = \psi_n(Y) = \psi_n(Y_1, Y_2, \ldots, Y_N) \qquad (n = 1, 2, \ldots, N) \tag{4.4.5}$$

and assume that the $N \times N$ determinant (called the *Jacobian*)

$$J \equiv \det \begin{bmatrix} \frac{\partial x_1}{\partial y_1} & \frac{\partial x_2}{\partial y_2} & \cdots & \frac{\partial x_1}{\partial y_N} \\ \frac{\partial x_2}{\partial y_1} & \frac{\partial x_2}{\partial y_2} & \cdots & \frac{\partial x_2}{\partial y_N} \\ \vdots & \vdots & & \vdots \\ \frac{\partial x_N}{\partial y_1} & \frac{\partial x_N}{\partial y_2} & \cdots & \frac{\partial x_N}{\partial y_N} \end{bmatrix} \tag{4.4.6}$$

does not equal zero for any $y = [y_1, y_2, \ldots, y_N]' \in B$. Then the joint p.d.f. is

$$h(y) = \begin{Bmatrix} |J| f_X[\psi_1(y), \psi_2(y), \ldots, \psi_N(y)], & \text{if } y \in B \\ 0, & \text{otherwise} \end{Bmatrix}, \tag{4.4.7}$$

where $|J|$ denotes the absolute value of determinant (4.4.6)

Proof Left to the reader.

Example 4.4.4 Suppose X_n $(n = 1, 2)$ are independent $\chi^2(2)$. Then the joint p.d.f. of X_1 and X_2 is

$$h(x_1, x_2) = \begin{Bmatrix} \exp[-\tfrac{1}{2}(x_1 + x_2)]/4, & \text{if } 0 < x_1 < \infty \text{ and } 0 < x_2 < \infty \\ 0, & \text{otherwise} \end{Bmatrix}.$$

Suppose we wish to find the p.d.f. of $Y_1 = g_1(X) = \tfrac{1}{2}(X_1 - X_2)$. In order to apply Theorem 4.4.3, we let $Y_2 = g_2(X) = X_2$ and seek the joint p.d.f. of Y_1 and Y_2. Then Y_2 can be integrated-out to obtain the marginal p.d.f. of Y_1.

The inverse transformation is given by

$$X_1 = \psi_1(Y) = 2Y_1 + Y_2,$$
$$X_2 = \psi_2(Y) = Y_2,$$

for which the Jacobian is

$$J = \det \begin{bmatrix} 2 & 1 \\ 0 & 1 \end{bmatrix} = 2.$$

Noting that $A = \{(x_1, x_2) | 0 < x_1 < \infty, 0 < x_2 < \infty\}$ and $B = \{(y_1, y_2) - 2y_1 < y_2, y_2 > 0, -\infty < y_1 < \infty\}$, (4.4.7) yields

$$|J| f([\psi(Y)]) = 2\{\exp[-\tfrac{1}{2}(2y_1 + y_2 + y_2)]\}/4$$
$$= \tfrac{1}{2}\exp[-(y_1 + y_2)].$$

Hence, the joint p.d.f. of Y_1 and Y_2 is

$$h(y_1, y_2) = \begin{Bmatrix} \tfrac{1}{2}\exp[-(y_1 + y_2)], & \text{if } -\infty < y_1 < \infty, y_2 > 0, y_2 > -2y_1 \\ 0, & \text{otherwise} \end{Bmatrix}.$$

If $-\infty < y_1 < 0$, the marginal p.d.f. of Y_1 is

$$h_1(y_1) = \int_{-2y_1}^{\infty} \tfrac{1}{2}\exp[-(y_1 + y_2)]\, dy_2$$
$$= \tfrac{1}{2}\exp(-y_1)\Big[-\exp(-y_2)\Big]_{-2y_1}^{\infty} = \tfrac{1}{2}\exp(y_1), \tag{4.4.8}$$

and if $0 < y_1 < \infty$, the marginal p.d.f. of Y_1 is

$$h_1(y_1) = \int_0^\infty \tfrac{1}{2}\exp[-(y_1 + y_2)]\,dy_2$$

$$= \tfrac{1}{2}\exp(-y_1)\Big[-\exp(-y_2)\Big]_0^\infty = \tfrac{1}{2}\exp(-y_1). \tag{4.4.9}$$

Putting together (4.4.8) and (4.4.9) yields the p.d.f.

$$h(y_1) = \tfrac{1}{2}\exp(-|y_1|), \qquad -\infty < y_1 < \infty. \tag{4.4.10}$$

Consulting Table 3.3.1(b) with $\lambda = 1$, (4.4.10) is recognized as the p.d.f. of the *Laplace* distribution (also see Exercise 3.4.22).

Cases in which the functions of interest (4.1.4) are not one-to-one can be easily handled by dividing their domain into disjoint sets over which these functions are one-to-one, applying (4.4.7) to each set, and then adding-up the results. See Hogg and Craig (1978, pp. 151–153) for details, and Exercise 4.4.10 for an example requiring such an extension.

This section closes with two more examples providing proofs promised in Section 3.3.

Example 4.4.5 (Proof of Theorem 3.3.16) Suppose $X_1 \sim N(0,1)$ and $X_2 \sim \chi^2(v)$ are independent. Then their joint p.d.f. is

$$f(x_1,x_2) = \begin{cases} \dfrac{(2\pi)^{-1/2}\exp(-\frac{1}{2}x_1^2)\exp(-\frac{1}{2}x_2)}{[\Gamma(v/2)2^{-1/2}]2^{1/2v-1}}, & \text{if } (y_1,y_2) \in B \\ 0, & \text{otherwise} \end{cases}.$$

where $A = \{(x_1,x_2)| -\infty < x_1 < \infty,\ 0 < x_2 < \infty\}$. Consider the one-to one transformation of A onto $B = \{(y_1,y_2)| -\infty < y_1 < \infty, 0 < y_2 < \infty\}$ defined by $Y_1 = g_1(X_1,X_2) = X_1(X_2/v)^{-1/2}$ and $Y_2 = g_2(X_1,X_2) = X_2$. Then the inverse transformation is $X_1 = \psi_1(Y_1,Y_2) = Y_1(Y_2/v)^{1/2}$ and $X_2 = \psi_2(Y_1,Y_2) = Y_2$, and the absolute value of the Jacobian is $|J| = (Y_2/v)^{1/2}$. By Theorem 4.4.3, the p.d.f. of Y_1 and Y_2 is

$$h(y_1,y_2) = \begin{cases} \dfrac{(y_2/v)^{1/2}y_2^{1/2v-1}\exp[-\frac{1}{2}y_2(1 + y_1^2/v)]}{(2\pi)^{1/2}[\Gamma(v/2)]2^{1/2v}}, & \text{if } (y_1,y_2) \in B \\ 0, & \text{otherwise} \end{cases}.$$

Employing the change-of variable $w = \frac{1}{2}y_2(1 + y_1^2/v)$ to integrate-out y_2 from $h(y_1,y_2)$, yields the marginal p.d.f. $h(y_1)$, which corresponds to (3.3.44) with $\theta = 0$ and $\alpha = 1$.

Example 4.4.6 (Proof of Theorem 3.3.18b) Suppose X_1 and X_2 are independent chi-squared random variables with v_1 and v_2 degrees of freedom, respectively. Then their joint p.d.f. is

$$f(x_1,x_2) = \begin{cases} \dfrac{(x_1^{(v_1/2)-1}x_2^{(v_2/2)-1}\exp[-(x_1+x_2)/2]}{\Gamma(v_1/2)\Gamma(v_2/2)2^{(v_1+v_2)/2}}, & (x_1,x_2)\in A \\ 0, & \text{otherwise} \end{cases}.$$

where $A = \{(x_1,x_2)|0 < x_1 < \infty, 0 < x_2 < \infty\}$. Consider the one-to-one transformation of A onto $B = \{(y_1,y_2)|0 < y_1 < \infty, 0 < y_2 < \infty\}$ defined by $Y_1 = g_1(X_1,X_2) = [(X_1/v_1)(X_2/v_2)^{-1}]$ and $Y_2 = g_2(X_1,X_2) = X_2$. Then the inverse transformation is $X_1 = \psi_1(Y_1, Y_2) = v_1 Y_1 Y_2/v_2$ and $X_2 = \psi_2(Y_1, Y_2) = Y_2$, and the absolute value of the Jacobian is $|J| = v_1 Y_2/v_2$. Thus by Theorem 4.4.3, the p.d.f. of Y_1 and Y_2 is

$$h(y_1,y_2) = \begin{cases} \dfrac{\left(\dfrac{v_1 y_2}{v_2}\right)\left(\dfrac{[v_1 y_1 y_2/v_2]^{(v_1/2)-1}}{y_2^{(1-v_2/2)}}\right)\exp\left[-\dfrac{1}{2}y_2\left(\dfrac{v_1 y_1}{2}+1\right)\right]}{\Gamma(v_1/2)\Gamma(v_2/2)2^{(v_1+v_2)/2}}, & \text{if } (y_1,y_2)\in B \\ 0, & \text{otherwise} \end{cases}.$$

Integrating-out y_2 from $h(y_1,y_2)$, by employing the change-of-variable $w = \frac{1}{2}y_2[(v_1 y_1/v_2)+1]$, yields the marginal p.d.f. $h_1(y_1)$ which corresponds to (3.3.52).

Exercises

4.4.1 Suppose X_1 and X_2 are independent random variables with binomial distributions $B(T_1,\theta)$ and $B(T_2,\theta)$, respectively, where T_1 and T_2 are positive integers. Using the fact that

$$\sum_{j=0}^{J}\binom{T_1}{J}\binom{T_2}{J-j} = \binom{T_1+T_2}{J}, \tag{4.4.11}$$

find the joint p.d.f. of $Y_1 = X_1 + X_2$ and $Y_2 = X_2$, and find the marginal p.d.f. of Y_1. Compare your answer to that obtained in Example 4.3.2.

4.4.2 Prove Theorem 3.3.18(c).

4.4.3 Prove Theorem 3.3.18(d).

4.4.4 Let X_1 and X_2 be two independent random variables each uniformly distributed over $[0,1]$. Define $Y_1 = X_1 + X_2$ and $Y_2 = X_1 - X_2$.

(a) Find the joint p.d.f. of Y_1 and Y_2.

(b) Find the marginal p.d.f. of Y_n $(n = 1,2)$.

4.4.5 Let X_1 and X_2 be independent random variables having gamma distributions with parameters α_n and β_n $(n = 1,2)$, respectively. Assume $\beta_1 = \beta_2 = 1$. Define $Y_1 = X_1 + X_2$ and $Y_2 = X_1/(X_1 + X_2)$.

(a) Find the joint p.d.f. of Y_1 and Y_2.

(b) Find the marginal p.d.f. of Y_n $(n = 1,2)$ and relate it to distributions discussed in Section 3.3).

4.4.6 Let X_1 and X_2 be independent $N(0,1)$. Show: $Y = X_1/X_2$ is Cauchy.

4.4.7 Let X_1 and X_2 be independent $N(0,1)$ random variables. Define

$Y_1 = \mu_1 + \sigma_1 X_1,$

$Y_2 = \mu_2 + \rho\sigma_2 X_1 + \sigma_2(1-\rho^2)^{1/2}X_2,$

where $\sigma_n > 0$ ($n = 1, 2$) and $0 < \rho < 1$. Find the joint p.d.f. of Y_1 and Y_2.

4.4.8 Suppose X_n ($n = 1, 2$) are independent $N(\mu, \sigma^2)$. Define $Y_1 = X_1 + X_2$ and $Y_2 = X_1 - X_2$. Find the joint p.d.f. of Y_1 and Y_2 and show that Y_1 and Y_2 are stochastically independent.

4.4.9 Suppose X_n ($n = 1, 2$) are independent random variables each uniformly distributed over $[0, 1]$. Consider the *Box-Muller transformation*

$Y_1 = [-2\ln(X_1)]^{1/2}\cos(2\pi X_2),$

$Y_2 = [-2\ln(X_1)]^{1/2}\sin(2\pi X_2),$

with inverse transformation $X_1 = \exp[-\frac{1}{2}(Y_1^2 + Y_2^2)]$ and $X_2 = (2\pi)^{-1}\arctan(Y_2/Y_1)$. Show: Y_1 and Y_2 are independent $N(0, 1)$ random variables.

4.4.10 Suppose $X \sim U[-1, 1]$. Find the p.d.f. of $Y \equiv X^2$.

4.4.11 Prove Theorem 4.4.2 in the case where A is a finite interval and $g(\cdot)$ is monotonically decreasing.

4.4.12 Suppose $X \sim N(\mu, \sigma^2)$. Find the distribution, mean and variance of $Y \equiv \exp(X)$. What is the name of this distribution?

4.4.13 Consider Exercise 3.4.27. Show the following:

(a) $X \equiv A^{-1/2}(Y - \mu)$ is spherically symmetric.

(b) If $Y = [Y_1, Y_2, \ldots, Y_N]'$ is spherically symmetric, then for $1 \le J < N$:

$$\frac{(N-1)\sum_{t=1}^{T} Y_t^2}{J\sum_{i=J+1}^{N} Y_i^2} \sim F(J, N-J).$$

4.4.14 Suppose $Y \sim Pa(\gamma, \lambda)$. Show: $\ln(Y/\gamma) \sim \text{EXP}(\lambda)$.

4.4.15 Suppose $Y \sim WE(0, \gamma, \lambda)$. Show: $Y^\lambda \sim \text{EXP}(\gamma^{-\lambda})$.

4.4.16 Suppose $X \sim \text{EXP}(\beta)$. Find the p.d.f. of $Y \equiv (2X/\beta)^{1/2}$ (*Raleigh distribution*).

4.4.17 Suppose $X \sim G(3/2, \beta)$. Find the p.d.f. of $Y \equiv (X/\beta)^{1/2}$ (*Maxwell distribution*).

4.4.18 Suppose $X_t \sim Po(\lambda_t)$ ($t = 1, 2, \ldots, T$) are independent, and define $Y \equiv X_1 + X_2 + \cdots + X_T$. Show: $Y \sim Po(\lambda)$, where $\lambda = \lambda_1 + \lambda_2 + \cdots + \lambda_T$.

4.4.19 Suppose $X = [X_1, X_2, \ldots, X_N]$, where $X_n \sim Po(\lambda_n)$ ($n = 1, 2, \ldots, N$) are independent, and define $Y \equiv X_1 + X_2 + \cdots + X_T$. Show: for any positive integer T, $X|T \sim M(T, \theta)$, where $\theta_n = \lambda_n/\lambda$ and $\lambda = \lambda_1 + \lambda_2 + \cdots + \lambda_T$.

4.4.20 Using the matrix differentiation theorems of Appendix B and the change of variable technique, demonstrate that Wishart density (3.5.1) implies inverted Wishart density (3.5.9).

4.4.21 Consider the vector $d(Y)$ defined in Exercise 3.3.18 when Y has an exponential family p.d.f. Show: the p.d.f. of $d(Y)$ also belongs to the exponential family.

4.4.22 Suppose $Y \sim \text{Elip}_N[\mu, \Sigma, g(\cdot)]$.

(a) Let $X = \Sigma^{-1/2}(Y - \mu)$. Show: X has a spherical symmetric distribution.

(b) Let A be a $K \times N$ matrix of constants with $\text{rank}(A) = K$, and let b be a $K \times 1$ vector of constants. Define $X = AY + b$. Show: $X \sim \text{Elip}[A\mu + b, A\Sigma A', g_*(\cdot)]$, where $g_*(\cdot)$ depends on $g(\cdot)$ and A.

(c) Suppose C is a nonsingular $N \times N$ matrix such that $C'\Sigma C = I_N$. Show: $C^{-1}(Y - \mu) \sim \text{Elip}_N[0_N, I_N, g(\cdot)]$.

4.4.23 Let Z be a $N \times 1$ random vector with p.d.f.:

$$f(z) = \alpha\phi(z|\mu, \sigma_1^2 I_N) + (1 - \alpha)\phi(z|\mu, \sigma_2^2 I_N), \tag{4.4.12}$$

where $0 < \alpha < 1$ and $\sigma_i^2 > 0$ $(1 = 1, 2)$. Z is said to have a *contaminated normal distribution*. Show that Z also has a spherically symmetric distribution.

4.4.24 Consider Theorem 4.4.2. Show: $E_X[g(X)] = E_Y(Y)$.

4.4.25 Suppose X_1 and X_2 are i.i.d. random variables with p.d.f.

$$f(x) = \left(\frac{\sqrt{2}}{2}\right)\left(\frac{x^2}{1 + x^4}\right), \qquad -\infty < x < \infty,$$

Show $Y = X_1/X_2$ has a standardized Cauchy distribution.

4.5 Quadratic-Form Technique

Unlike the other techniques that have been discussed so far, the quadratic-form technique has a limited range of application, namely, to finding the distribution of quadratic forms in multivariate normal random variables.[1] Because we frequently encounter test statistics that are functions (e.g., ratios) of quadratic forms, however, this technique can often be used together with other techniques. The discussion begins with a commonly encountered quadratic form.

Theorem 4.5.1 Suppose $Y = [Y_1, Y_2, \ldots, Y_N]' \sim N(\mu, \Sigma)$ and define the quadratic form $Q \equiv (Y - \mu)'\Sigma^{-1}(Y - \mu)$. Then $Q \sim \chi^2(N)$.

Proof The following proof uses the m.g.f. technique described in Section 4.3. By definition the m.g.f. of Q is

$$\begin{aligned}
M_Q(t) \equiv E[\exp(tQ)] &= \int_{-\infty}^{\infty} \cdots \int_{-\infty}^{\infty} \exp(tQ)\phi(y|\mu, \Sigma)\, dy_1 \ldots dy_N \\
&= \int_{-\infty}^{\infty} \cdots \int_{-\infty}^{\infty} [(2\pi)^N|\Sigma|]^{-1/2} \exp\left[-\frac{1}{2}(1 - 2t)Q\right] dy_1 \ldots dy_N \\
&= (1 - 2t)^{-1/2N} \int_{-\infty}^{\infty} \cdots \int_{-\infty}^{\infty} \left[\frac{(2\pi)^N|\Sigma|}{(1 - 2t)^N}\right]^{-1/2} \\
&\quad \times \exp[-\tfrac{1}{2}(Y - \mu)'\{\Sigma/(1 - 2t)\}^{-1}(Y - \mu)]\, dy_1 \ldots dy_N \\
&= (1 - 2t)^{-1/2N}, \qquad \text{for } t < \tfrac{1}{2},
\end{aligned}$$

where the last equality follows from the fact that the integral in the line above it is unity because its integrand is that of a N-dimensional normal density with mean μ and variance-covariance matrix $(1 - 2t)^{-1}\Sigma$. Recalling (3.3.18), (4.5.1) is immediately recognized as the m.g.f. corresponding to

1. For a general discussion of quadratic form in multivariate normal random variables, see Johnson and Kotz (1970b, Chapter 29). Mathai and Provost (1992) provide an extensive survey of quadratic forms of all types.

a chi-squared distribution with N degrees of freedom. Note that this is a generalization of Example 4.3.2.

Theorem 4.5.1 serves as a start for our investigation of the distribution of quadratic forms in multivariate normal random variables. In more general cases, such quadratics will not have central chi-squared distributions. Under appropriate conditions, however, a quadratic form in multivariate normal random variables may have a *noncentral chi-squared distribution* with v degrees of freedom and *noncentrality parameter* $\lambda \geq 0$, denoted $\chi^2(v, \lambda)$. The noncentral chi-squared distribution is described in Table 4.5.1(a).[2] Note that when $\lambda = 0$, the noncentral chi-squared distribution reduces to the ordinary central chi-squared distribution, that is, $\chi^2(v, \lambda = 0) = \chi^2(v)^3$. Noncentral distributions play a key role in the analysis of "power" of hypothesis tests. This is developed more fully in Chapter 7, but Example 4.5.1 indicates the basic point.

We can now extend Theorem 4.5.1 to obtain our desired general case.

Theorem 4.5.2 Suppose $Y = [Y_1, Y_2, \ldots, Y_N]' \sim N(\mu, \Sigma)$, where Σ is positive definite. Let A be a real symmetric matrix of order N with $\text{rank}(A) = v$. Define $Q \equiv Y'AY$ and $\mu' A\mu/2$. Then $Q \sim \chi^2(v, \lambda)$ for all μ iff $A\Sigma$ is idempotent.

Proof Hocking (1985, pp. 28–29, Theorem 2.3).

When $A\Sigma$ is not idempotent, then Q can be expressed as a linear combination of independent noncentral chi-squared random variables (see Exercises 4.5.16 and 4.5.17).

On the basis of Theorem 4.5.2 we are able to say in which cases quadratic forms in multivariate normal random variables have central or noncentral chi-squared distributions. Thus for example, when "sums of squares" are encountered later in our study of regression analysis, Theorems 4.5.2 and 4.5.5 prove quite useful. Because Theorem 3.3.18(b) (proved in Example 4.4.6) shows that a quotient of independent chi-squared random variables, each divided by their respective degrees of freedom, has a F-distribution, Theorem 4.5.2 will also prove useful as a stepping stone in deriving F-distributions. It is, however, necessary to determine when quadratic forms in normal random variables are independent. The following theorem provides the answer.

Theorem 4.5.3 Suppose $Y = [Y_1, Y_2, \ldots, Y_N]' \sim N(\mu, \Sigma)$, where Σ is positive definite. Let A_i $(i = 1, 2)$ be real symmetric matrices, and define $Q_i \equiv Y'A_iY$ $(i = 1, 2)$. Then Q_1 and Q_2 are stochastically independent for all μ iff

2. For a detailed discussion, see Johnson and Kotz (1970b, Chapter 28).

3. Interestingly, the c.d.f. $F(y|v, \lambda)$ is a discrete mixture of central chi-squared c.d.f.'s, $F(y|v, \lambda = 0)$, with weights equal to the Poisson p.m.f. $f_{Po}(j|\lambda)$ $(j = 0, 1, 3, \ldots)$.

Table 4.5.1

(a) Noncentral chi-squared distribution: $\chi^2(\nu, \lambda)$

$$F(y|\nu,\lambda) = \sum_{k=0}^{\infty}\left[\frac{\lambda^k \exp(-\lambda)}{k!}\right]F(y|\nu, \lambda = 0) \qquad (\lambda \neq 0)$$

$$F(y|\nu,\lambda = 0) = \int_0^y [\Gamma(\tfrac{1}{2}\nu)2^{1/2\nu}]^{-1} t^{(\nu/2)-1}\exp(-\tfrac{1}{2}t)\,dt$$

$$f(y|\nu,\lambda) = \left[\frac{\exp[-(y+2\lambda)/2]}{2^{\nu/2}}\right]\sum_{k=0}^{\infty}\frac{y^{(\nu/2)+k-1}(2\lambda)^k}{\Gamma(\frac{1}{2}\nu + k)2^{2k}k!}$$

$$= \sum_{k=0}^{\infty}\left[\frac{\lambda^k \exp(-\lambda)}{k!}\right]f(y|\nu + 2k, 0)$$

$M(t) = (1-2t)^{-\nu/2}\exp[2t\lambda/(1-2t)]$, for $t < \frac{1}{2}$

$E(Y) = \nu + 2\lambda$

$\text{Var}(Y) = 2\nu + 8\lambda$

$$E(Y^m) = 2^m\Gamma(\tfrac{1}{2}\nu + m)\sum_{k=0}^{\infty}\binom{m}{k}\frac{\lambda^k}{\Gamma(\frac{1}{2}\nu + k)}$$

Mode: at y^* such that $f(y^*|\nu,\lambda) = f(y^*|\nu - 2, \lambda)$

(b) Noncentral F-distribution: $F(\nu_1, \nu_2, \lambda)$

$$f(y|\nu_1,\nu_2,\lambda) = \left[\frac{y^{(\nu_1/2)-1}\exp(-\lambda/2)}{(1+y)^{(\nu_1+\nu_2)/2}}\right]\sum_{k=0}^{\infty}\frac{(\lambda y/[2(1+y)])^k}{B(\frac{1}{2}\nu_1 + k, \frac{1}{2}\nu_2)k!}$$

$$E(Y^m) = \left[\frac{\nu_2}{\nu_1}\right]^m\left[\frac{\Gamma(\frac{1}{2}\nu_1 + m)\Gamma(\frac{1}{2}\nu_2 - m)}{\Gamma(\nu_1/2)\Gamma(\nu_2/2)}\right]\sum_{k=0}^{M}\binom{m}{k}\left[\frac{\Gamma(m/2)(\lambda\nu_1/2)^k}{\Gamma(\frac{1}{2}m + k)}\right]$$

$$E(Y) = \frac{\nu_2(\nu_1 + \lambda)}{\nu_1(\nu_2 - 2)} \qquad (\nu_2 > 2)$$

$$\text{Var}(Y) = 2\left[\frac{\nu_2}{\nu_1}\right]^2\left[\frac{(\nu_1+\lambda)^2 + (\nu_1 + 2\lambda)(\nu_2 - 2)}{(\nu_2 - 2)^2(\nu_2 - 4)}\right] \qquad (\nu_2 > 4)$$

(c) Noncentral t-distribution: $nt(\nu, \lambda)$

$$F(y|\nu,\lambda) = \frac{1}{2^{1/2\nu - 1}\Gamma(\frac{1}{2}\nu)}\int_0^{\infty} x^{\nu-1}\exp(\tfrac{1}{2}x^2)\Phi\left[\left(\frac{yx}{\sqrt{\nu}}\right)|\lambda, 1\right]dx$$

$$f(y|\nu,\lambda) = \frac{\exp(\frac{1}{2}\lambda^2)}{2^{1/2\nu-1}\sqrt{\pi\nu}\Gamma(\frac{1}{2}\nu)}\int_0^{\infty} x^{\nu}\exp[-\tfrac{1}{2}(x^2[1 + (y^2/\nu)] - 2yx\sqrt{\nu}]\,dx$$

$$E(Y^m) = (\tfrac{1}{2}\nu)^{1/2m}\left[\frac{\Gamma[\frac{1}{2}(\nu - m)]}{\Gamma(\frac{1}{2}\nu)}\right]\sum_{0 \le k \le 1/2m}\binom{2}{2k}\left[\frac{(2k)!}{2^k k!}\right]\lambda^{m-2k}$$

$$E(Y) = \sqrt{\tfrac{1}{2}\nu}\left[\frac{\Gamma[\frac{1}{2}(\nu - 1)]}{\Gamma(\frac{1}{2}\nu)}\right]\lambda$$

$$\text{Var}(Y) = \frac{\nu}{\nu - 2}[1 + \lambda^2] - [E(Y)]^2$$

$$A_1 \Sigma A_2 = A_2 \Sigma A_1 = 0. \tag{4.5.2}$$

If $\Sigma = \sigma^2 I_N$, then (4.5.2) simplifies to

$$A_1 A_2 = A_2 A_1 = 0. \tag{4.5.3}$$

Proof Hocking (1985, p. 29, Theorem 2.4).

Thus Theorems 4.5.2, 4.5.3 and 3.3.18(b) taken together provided an easy way of recognizing when a ratio of quadratic forms in normal random variables has a F-distribution. In Chapter 7 when calculating the power function of a test statistic used in a hypothesis test, we will encounter ratios in which the numerator has a *noncentral* chi-squared distribution. In such cases the following theorem will prove useful.

Theorem 4.5.4 Suppose $X_1 \sim \chi^2(v_1, \lambda)$, $X_2 \sim \chi^2(v_2)$ are independent. Then

$$Y \equiv \frac{X_1/v_1}{X_2/v_2} \tag{4.5.4}$$

has a *noncentral F-distribution*, denoted $F(v_1, v_2, \lambda)$ as described in Table 4.5.1(b).[4]

Proof Muirhead (1982, pp. 24–25).

When $\lambda = 0$ in Theorem 4.5.4 then X_1 has a central chi-squared distribution and Y has a central F-distribution, that is, $Y \sim F(v_1, v_2) = F(v_1, v_2, \lambda = 0)$, as stated in Theorem 3.3.18(b). We will not discuss the case in which X_2 also has a noncentral chi-squared distribution, except to note that the resulting distribution for (4.5.4) in that case is known as a *doubly noncentral F-distribution.*[5]

In addition to encountering ratios of quadratic forms—as in Theorem 3.3.18(b)—we sometimes also encounter ratios of linear forms to functions of quadratic forms (as in Theorem 3.3.16). In such cases it is usually necessary to show the independence of the two forms. Thus analogous to Theorem 4.5.3 we state the following theorem.

Theorem 4.5.5 (Craig's Theorem) Suppose $Y = [Y_1, Y_2, \ldots, Y_N]' \sim N(\mu, \Sigma)$. Let A be a $N \times N$ matrix, and let B be a $M \times N$ matrix. Then the linear form $X = BY$ is distributed independently of the quadratic form $Q = Y'AY$ for all μ iff

$$B\Sigma A = 0_{M \times N}, \tag{4.5.5}$$

4. For a detailed discussion, see Johnson and Kotz (1970b, Chapter 30). Note that the c.d.f. $F(y|v_1, v_2, \lambda)$ is monotone increasing in λ, monotone decreasing in v_1, and monotone decreasing in v_2.

5. See Johnson and Kotz (1970b, pp. 196–198).

Proof Hocking (1985, p. 30, Theorem 2.5). For a detailed discussion see Driscoll and Gundberg (1986).

The following theorem uses Theorem 4.5.5 in conjunction with previously encountered theorems to derive the distribution of a random variable that plays a central role in later discussion. It is a special case of Theorem 3.3.16.

Theorem 4.5.6 Let $Y_t \sim N(\theta, \sigma^2)$ $(t = 1, 2, \ldots, T)$ be independent random variables, where neither θ nor σ^2 are known. Define $\nu \equiv T - 1$, and

$$\bar{Y} \equiv T^{-1} \sum_{t=1}^{T} Y_t, \tag{4.5.6}$$

$$S^2 \equiv \nu^{-1} \sum_{t=1}^{T} (Y_t - \bar{Y})^2. \tag{4.5.7}$$

Then $\tau \equiv T^{1/2}[(\bar{Y} - \theta)/S]$ has a Student t-distribution with ν degrees of freedom, that is, $\tau \sim t(\nu)$.

Proof Define $Z \equiv T^{1/2}[\bar{Y} - \theta)/\sigma]$, $X \equiv \nu S^2/\sigma^2$, and rewrite τ as

$$\tau = \frac{\sigma^{-1}}{\nu^{1/2}\sigma^{-1}/\nu^{1/2}} T^{1/2}\left[\frac{\bar{Y} - \theta}{S}\right] = \frac{Z}{(X - \nu)^{1/2}}. \tag{4.5.8}$$

By Theorem 3.3.3(a), $Z \sim N(0, 1)$. We now proceed to show: (i) $X \sim \chi^2(\nu)$, and (ii) Z and X are independent. It then follows immediately from Theorem 3.3.16 that $\tau \sim t(\nu)$.

In order to show (i), let $\iota \equiv [1, 1, \ldots, 1]'$ be a $T \times 1$ vector with all elements equalling unity, and define the $T \times T$ matrix $A \equiv I_T - T^{-1}\iota\iota'$. Exercise A.6.2(a) shows that A is idempotent with rank ν and Exercise 4.5.1 shows that $\nu S^2 = Y'AY$. Hence $\nu S^2/\sigma^2 = (Y/\sigma)'A(Y/\sigma)$. Applying Theorem 4.5.2 with $\Sigma = I_T$ and $\mu = \theta\iota$, it follows immediately that $\nu S^2/\sigma^2 \sim \chi^2(\nu, \lambda)$, where $\lambda = \theta^2\iota' A\iota/\sigma^2 = 0$.

To show (ii), define $B = T^{-1}\iota'$ and note that

$$\begin{aligned} B\Sigma A &= BA = T^{-1}\iota'(I_T - T^{-1}\iota\iota') \\ &= T^{-1}\iota' - T^{-2}(\iota'\iota)\iota' \\ &= T^{-1}\iota' - T^{2}(T)\iota' \\ &= T^{-1}\iota' - T^{-1}\iota' = 0_T. \end{aligned}$$

By Theorem 4.5.5, $\bar{Y} = BY$ and $\nu S^2 = Y'AY$ are independent. Hence, Z and X are independent.

As has been noted, Theorem 4.5.6 involves an application of Theorem 3.3.16. The following theorem provides a generalization of Theorem 3.3.16.

Theorem 4.5.7 Let $Z \sim N(0, 1)$ and $X \sim \chi^2(v)$ be independent. Then $Y \equiv (Z - \lambda)/[X/v]^{1/2}$, where $\lambda \in \Re$, has a *noncentral standardized Student t-distribution*, denoted $nt(v, \lambda)$, as described in Table 4.5.1(c).[6]

Proof Follows from Theorem 4.5.4 with $v_1 = 1$.

Example 4.5.1 To help understand Theorems 4.5.6 and 4.5.7, consider the following example. Although this example draws on hypothesis testing that is not covered until Chapter 7, it is assumed that the reader is sufficiently familiar with introductory statistics to appreciate the motivational purposes of the following.

Consider the observations Y_t $(t = 1, 2, \ldots, T)$ in Theorem 4.5.6 as a random sample drawn from a $N(\mu, \sigma^2)$ distribution with σ^2 known. Also consider testing H_0: $\mu = \mu_0$ versus H_1: $\mu \neq \mu_0$, where μ_0 is some specified value. Let $V_0 \equiv Y - \mu_0 \iota$. Under H_0, $V_0 \sim N(0_T, \sigma^2 I_T)$. The usual test statistic is

$$Z \equiv \frac{\overline{Y} - \mu_0}{\sigma/T^{1/2}} = \left[\frac{T^{1/2}}{\sigma}\right] B V_0, \tag{4.5.9}$$

where $B \equiv T^{-1}\iota'$. Under H_0, $Z \sim N(0, 1)$. Note also that

$$\begin{aligned} Z^2 &= \frac{T}{\sigma^2}(\overline{Y} - \mu_0)^2 \\ &= \frac{T}{\sigma^2} V_0' B' B V_0 \\ &= \frac{T}{\sigma^2} V_0' \left[\frac{\iota\iota'}{T^2}\right] V_0 \\ &= \frac{V_0'(I_T - A) V_0}{\sigma^2}, \end{aligned} \tag{4.5.10}$$

where $A \equiv I_T - T^{-1}\iota\iota'$. Under H_0, $Z^2 \sim \chi^2(1)$ by Theorem 4.5.2, where $\text{rank}(I_T - A) = 1$. Under H_1: $\mu = \mu_1 \neq \mu_0$, $V_0 \sim N([\mu_1 - \mu_0]\iota, \sigma^2 I)$ and $Z \sim N([T/\sigma^2]^{1/2}[\mu_0 - \mu_1], 1)$. Since $\text{tr}[\sigma^{-2}(I_T - A)\sigma^2 I] = \text{tr}(I_T - A) = T - (T - 1) = 1$, it follows from Theorem 4.5.2 that $Z^2 \sim \chi^2(1, \lambda)$, where

$$\lambda \equiv (\mu_0 - \mu_1)\iota' \left[\frac{I_T - A}{\sigma^2}\right](\mu_0 - \mu_1)\iota = \left[\frac{\mu_0 - \mu_1}{\sigma/T^{1/2}}\right]^2. \tag{4.5.11}$$

If σ^2 is unknown, then the appropriate test statistic is

$$\tau = \frac{\overline{Y} - \mu_0}{S/T^{1/2}}. \tag{4.5.12}$$

According to Theorem 4.5.6, $\tau \sim t(T - 1)$ under H_0: $\mu = \mu_0$. Under H_1: $\mu = \mu_1 \neq \mu_0$,

6. For a detailed discussion, see Johnson and Kotz (1970b, Chapter 31).

$$\tau = \frac{\dfrac{\bar{Y} - \mu_0}{\sigma/T^{1/2}}}{\left[\dfrac{(T-1)S^2/\sigma^2}{T-1}\right]^{1/2}} = \frac{\dfrac{\bar{Y} - \mu_1}{\sigma/T^{1/2}} - \dfrac{\mu_0 - \mu_1}{\sigma/T^{1/2}}}{\left[\dfrac{(T-1)S^2/\sigma^2}{T-1}\right]^{1/2}}, \tag{4.5.13}$$

and by Theorem 4.5.7, $\tau \sim nt(T-1, \lambda)$, where $\lambda = (\mu_0 - \mu_1)/(\sigma/T^{1/2})$ is the noncentrality parameter. Under H_0, $\tau^2 \sim F(1, T-1)$ by Theorem 3.3.18(a). Under H_1, $\tau^2 \sim F(1, T-1, \lambda^2)$ by Exercise 4.5.3.

Finally, we close this section by noting that Theorem 4.5.4 is used in the proof of the following three theorems that are important later.

Theorem 4.5.8 Suppose $Y = [Y_1, Y_2, \ldots, Y_N]' \sim N(0, \sigma^2 I_N)$. Let A_k $(k = 1, 2, \ldots, K)$ be real symmetric matrices and define $A \equiv A_1 + A_2 + \cdots + A_K$. Consider the quadratic forms $Q \equiv Y'AY/\sigma^2$ and $Q_k \equiv Y'A_kY/\sigma^2$ $(k = 1, 2, \ldots, K)$, and suppose that $Q \sim \chi^2(\nu)$, $Q_k = \chi^2(\nu_k)$ $(k = 1, 2, \ldots, K-1)$ and that Q_K is nonnegative. Then Q_k $(k = 1, 2, \ldots, K)$ are independent and $Q_K \sim \chi^2(\nu_K)$, where $\nu_K \equiv \nu - \nu_1 - \nu_2 - \cdots - \nu_{K-1}$.

Proof Hogg and Craig (1978, pp. 417–419).

Theorem 4.5.9 (Cochran's Theorem) Suppose $Y = [Y_1, Y_2, \ldots, Y_T]' \sim N(0, \sigma^2 I_T)$, and assume that $Y'Y = Q_1 + Q_2 + \cdots + Q_K$, where Q_k is a quadratic form in Y with $\text{rank}(A_k) = \nu_k$. Then Q_k $(k = 1, 2, \ldots, K)$ are independent and $Q_k/\sigma^2 \sim \chi^2(\nu_k)$ $(k = 1, 2, \ldots, K)$ iff $T = \nu_1 + \nu_2 + \cdots + \nu_k$.

Proof Hogg and Craig (1978, p. 419).

Theorem 4.5.10 Let $Y = [Y_1, Y_2, \ldots, Y_T]' \sim N(0, \sigma^2 I_T)$, and let A_1 and A_2 be $T \times T$ idempotent matrices of ranks ν_1 and ν_2, respectively. Suppose $A_1 \neq A_2$ and $A_1 A_2 = A_2$. Finally, define $Q_1 = Y'A_1Y$ and $Q_2 = Y'A_2Y$. Then

$$\frac{(Q_1 - Q_2)/(\nu_1 - \nu_2)}{Q_2/\nu_1} \sim F(\nu_1 - \nu_2, \nu_2). \tag{4.5.14}$$

Proof Fisher (1970, p. 362, Lemma 2.2).

Exercises

4.5.1 Let $Y = [Y_1, Y_2, \ldots, Y_T]'$, $\bar{Y} = T^{-1}\iota'Y$ and $\nu S^2 = (Y_1 - \bar{Y})^2 + (Y_2 - \bar{Y})^2 + \cdots + (Y_T - \bar{Y})^2$.

(a) Show that $\nu S^2 = Y'AY = W'AW = V'AV$, where A is the idempotent matrix defined in Exercise A.6.2, $W = AY$ and $V = Y - E(Y)$.

(b) Interpret $W = AY$.

4.5.2 Suppose Y_t $(t = 1, 2, \ldots, T)$ are independent $\chi^2(\nu_t, \lambda_t)$. Define $\bar{Y} = T^{-1}(Y_1 + Y_2 + \cdots + Y_T)$, $\nu = \nu_1 + \nu_2 + \cdots + \nu_T$ and $\lambda = \lambda_1 + \lambda_2 + \cdots + \lambda_T$. Show: $T\bar{Y} \sim \chi^2(\nu, \lambda)$.

4.5.3 Suppose $Y \sim t(\nu, \delta)$. Show: $Y^2 \sim F(1, \nu, \lambda)$, where $\lambda = \frac{1}{2}\delta^2$.

4.5.4 Suppose $Y \sim F(\nu_1, \nu_2, \lambda)$ and define $p \equiv \text{Prob}(Y > c)$ where, for $0 < \alpha < 1$, c is defined implicitly by $\alpha = \int_c^\infty dF(\nu_1, \nu_2, 0)$. Show each of the following:

(a) p is monotonically increasing in λ.

(b) p is monotonically increasing in α.

(c) p is monotonically increasing in ν_2.

(d) p is monotonically decreasing in ν_1.

4.5.5 Suppose Y is $T \times 1$ and $Y \sim N(\mu, \Sigma)$ and define $Q \equiv Y'AY$, where A is an arbitrary $N \times N$ symmetric matrix. Show that the moment generating function of Q is $M(t) = |I_T - 2tA\Sigma|^{-1/2} \exp\{-\frac{1}{2}\mu'[I_T - 2tA\Sigma)^{-1}]\Sigma^{-1}\mu\}$ for $t < t_0$, where t_0 is the smallest root of $|I_T - 2tA\Sigma| = 0$.

4.5.6 Suppose $Z = [Z_1, Z_2, \ldots, Z_T]' \sim N_T(\mu, \Sigma)$, where Σ is a positive definite matrix. Let A be a $T \times K$ matrix such that $\text{rank}(A) = K$. Show:

$$W = (Z - \mu)'A(A'\Sigma A)^{-1}A'(Z - \mu) \sim \chi^2(K). \tag{4.5.15}$$

4.5.7 Suppose $Y \sim N_K(\mu, \Sigma)$ and let $Q = Y'AY$ where A is a symmetric $K \times K$ matrix. Show that the moment generating function for Q is

$$M_Q(t) = |I_K - 2tA\Sigma|^{-1/2} \exp\left(-\frac{1}{2}\mu'[I_K - 2tA\Sigma)^{-1}]^{-1}\Sigma^{-1}\mu\right),$$

where $t < t_0$, and t_0 is the smallest root of $|I_K - 2tA\Sigma| = 0$.

4.5.8 Suppose $Y \sim N_K(\mu, \Sigma)$. Let $Q_1 = Y'A_1Y$, $Q_2 = Y'A_2Y$ and $X = BY$, where A_1 and A_2 are symmetric $K \times K$ matrices and B is $J \times K$. Prove each of the following (see Hocking 1985, p. 27).

(a) $E(Q_1) = \text{tr}(A_1\Sigma) + \mu'A_1\mu$

(b) $\text{Var}(Q_1) = 2\,\text{tr}(A_1\Sigma A_1\Sigma) + 4\mu'A_1\Sigma A_1\mu$

(c) $\text{Cov}(Q_1, Q_2) = 2\,\text{tr}(A_1\Sigma A_2\Sigma) + 4\mu'A_1\Sigma A_2\mu$

(d) $\text{Cov}(Y, Q_1) = 2\Sigma A_1\mu$

(e) $\text{Cov}(X, Q_1) = 2B\Sigma A_1\mu$.

4.5.9 Suppose $Y \sim N_K(\mu, \Sigma)$, where Σ is nonsingular. Partition X, μ and Σ:

$$Y = \begin{bmatrix} Y_1 \\ Y_2 \end{bmatrix}, \quad \mu = \begin{bmatrix} \mu_1 \\ \mu_2 \end{bmatrix}, \quad \Sigma = \begin{bmatrix} \Sigma_{11} & \Sigma_{12} \\ \Sigma_{21} & \Sigma_{22} \end{bmatrix}, \tag{4.5.16}$$

where Y_i and μ_i are $K_i \times 1$, $K_1 + K_2 = K$, and Σ_{ij} is $K_i \times K_j$ $(i,j = 1,2)$. Show:

$$Q \equiv (Y - \mu)'\Sigma^{-1}(Y - \mu) - (Y_1 - \mu_1)'\Sigma_{11}^{-1}(Y_1 - \mu_1) \sim X^2(K - K_1). \tag{4.5.17}$$

4.5.10 Consider Exercise 3.4.5. Let Y_{t1} $(t = 1, 2)$ denote two independent drawings on Y_1 (the time an individual has lived in the neighborhood) from the distribution of individuals who have $Y_2 = 10$ (attitude toward integration) and $Y_3 = 13$ (number of years of education). Define $\overline{U}_1 \equiv \frac{1}{2}(Y_{11} + Y_{21})$.

(a) What is the distribution of $\overline{Y}_1$?

(b) Define

$$W = \frac{\overline{Y}_1 - \theta}{[(Y_{11} - \overline{Y}_1)^2 + (Y_{21} - \overline{Y}_1)^2]^{1/2}/2^{1/2}}, \tag{4.5.18}$$

where $\theta \equiv E(\overline{Y}_1)$ from (a). What is the distribution of W?

(c) Suppose that *unknown* to you the individuals in your sample have eight years of education rather than thirteen. In this case what would be the distribution of W calculated from (b) using your previous choice of θ?

4.5.11 Let $Y \sim N_K(0_K, I_K)$, $Q_1 = Y'AY + 2a'Y + c$ and $Q_2 = Y'BY + 2b'Y + d$, where A and B are $K \times K$ matrices, a and b are $K \times 1$ vectors, and c and d are scalars. Show that Q_1 and Q_2 are independent iff all of the following hold: (*a*) $AB = 0_K$, (*b*) $Ab = 0_K$, (*c*) $Ba = 0_K$, and (*d*) $a'b = 0$.

4.5.12 Let Y_j be $K_j \times 1$ $(j = 1, 2, \ldots, J)$ vectors. Suppose Y_j $(j = 1, 2, \ldots, J)$ are independent with $Y_j \sim N(\mu_j, \Sigma_j)$. Find the distribution of

$$X = \sum_{j=1}^{J} Y_j' \Sigma_j^{-1} Y_j. \tag{4.5.19}$$

4.5.13 Suppose X and Y are independent $N(0, \sigma^2)$ random variables. Let $U = X^2 + Y^2$ and $V = X/U^{1/2}$. Show: U and V are independent.

4.5.14 Note that the density for a $\chi^2(v, \lambda)$ in Table 4.5.1(a) can be written as a mixture of central chi-squareds, where the mixing weights are given by a Poisson mass function. In other words, if $Y|\lambda, J \sim \chi^2(v + 2j)$ and $J|\lambda \sim Po(\lambda)$, then $Y|\lambda \sim \chi^2(v, \lambda)$. Using the law of iterated expectations, show that $E(Y) = v + 2\lambda$.

4.5.15 Compare and contrast the noncentral t-distribution with the t-distribution $t(\theta, \alpha, v)$ of Definition 3.3.8.

4.5.16 Let Y be a $N \times 1$ vector (not necessarily multivariate normal) with $E(Y) = \mu$ and $\text{Var}(Y) = \Sigma$, where Σ is positive definite. Let A be a $N \times N$ symmetric mtrix and define $Q \equiv Y'AY$. Let λ_n $(n = 1, 2, \ldots, N)$ be the eigenvalues of $\Sigma^{1/2} A \Sigma^{1/2}$ (or ΣA), and let P be the associated $N \times N$ orthogonal matrix such that $P'[\Sigma^{1/2} A \Sigma^{1/2}]P = \Lambda = \text{diag}\{\lambda_1, \ldots, \lambda_N\}$. Finally, define $X = P'Y$ and $\xi = P'\Sigma^{-1/2}\mu$. Show (see Mathai and Provost 1992):

(a) $E(X) = 0$.

(b) $\text{Var}(X) = I_N$.

(c) Q can be expressed as a linear combination of the squares of noncentral uncorrelated, unit-variance random variables, that is,

$$Q = \sum_{n=1}^{N} \lambda_n (X_n + \xi_n)^2. \tag{4.5.20}$$

4.5.17 Consider Exercises 4.5.15 with the additional assumptions that $Y \sim N(\mu, \Sigma)$. Show that X_n $(n = 1, 2, \ldots, N)$ are independent noncentral chi-squared random variables.

5 Sampling Theory

It would, then, seem to be prudent to recognize that the notion of long-run repeated sampling is a fiction of convenience, unless it is a physical fact.
—Hinkley (1980, p. 152)

5.1 Basic Concepts

The discussion of probability in Section 2.1 highlighted conflicting interpretations, in particular, *objective* (frequentist) versus *subjective* (Bayesian) interpretations. Such differences were set aside in Sections 2.2 through 4.5, but they will rise again in Chapter 6. This chapter is transitional: It continues to develop statistical tools to be applied in subsequent chapters, as did Sections 2.2 through 4.5, but it also prepares the reader for the conflicts of Chapter 6 and later chapters by previewing some of the basic differences in statistical viewpoints. In particular, Section 5.8 discusses conflicting attitudes towards the "parameters" of Chapters 3 and 4, which are the goals of Chapters 6 and 7.

We begin with a simple stylistic example that serves to introduce some important ideas. For generalizations see Exercise 5.3.9.

Example 5.1.1 Consider a bowl consisting of N balls identical in all noticeable ways except color: K are red and $N - K$ are blue. Assume the balls are distributed in the bowl in such a way that if you close your eyes, reach into the bowl and draw one of the N balls, the "probability" of it being red is simply K/N. T draws are to be made from the bowl, and the outcomes of the these draws are represented by a sequence Y_t $(t = 1, 2, \ldots, T)$ of Bernoulli random variables such that $Y_t = 1$ iff the ball on draw t is red, and $Y_t = 0$ iff the ball on draw t is blue.

A sequence of random variables, such as in Example 5.1.1, is referred to as a *sample*. Despite the simplicity of the present set-up, it still lacks sufficient structure for our purposes. More details concerning the sampling process are required in order to determine the joint distribution of Y_t $(t = 1, 2, \ldots, T)$. After a ball is drawn and its color noted, is the ball replaced and all balls mixed before drawing another ball? More formally, is the sampling performed *with replacement* or *without replacement*? In the former case, it may be reasonable to assume that Y_t $(t = 1, 2, \ldots, T)$ are statistically independent. In the latter case, Y_t $(t = 1, 2, \ldots, T)$ are clearly dependent because the number of balls and the breakdown between red and blue balls is changing from draw to draw.

Such questions also arose in Section 3.2 in connection with the sum $X_T = Y_1 + Y_2 + \cdots + Y_T$, which in the present context is the total number of red balls in T draws. Given a predetermined number T of draws, letting $\theta = K/N$, and replacing "draws" by "trials," the reader should recognize the distribution of X_T as binomial when sampling with replacement and hypergeometric when sampling without replacement. If the sample size T is not predetermined, but instead determined by the rule "continue sampling until obtaining J blue balls," then X_T has a negative binomial distribution.

As a reference case, we assume substantial structure, similar to that encountered in the binomial case. This structure is described formally in the following definition.

Definition 5.1.1 Consider the sample Y_t $(t = 1, 2, \ldots, T)$ with joint p.f. $g(y|\theta)$, where θ is a $K \times 1$ vector of parameters. Given θ, suppose Y_t $(t = 1, 2, \ldots, T)$ are independent and identically distributed each with p.f. $f(y_t|\theta)$ [denoted Y_t $(t = 1, 2, \ldots, T) \sim$ i.i.d. $f(\cdot|\theta)$], that is,

$$g(y_1, y_2, \ldots, y_T|\theta) = \prod_{t=1}^{T} f(y_t|\theta). \tag{5.1.1}$$

Then Y_t $(t = 1, 2, \ldots, T)$ is a *random sample* of size T from a population with p.f. $f(\cdot|\theta)$. The distribution corresponding to $f(y_t|\theta)$ is referred to as the underlying *population*.

The case in which the observations are independent, but not identically distributed, is denoted *i.n.i.d.*; the case in which the observations are not independent, but are identically distributed, is denoted *n.i.i.d.*; and the case in which the observations are neither independent nor identically distributed is denoted *n.i.n.i.d.* This section focuses on the i.i.d. case.

This chapter is concerned with *sampling distributions*, that is, the joint distribution of random variables comprising a sample, or random variables that are functions of such observations. The viewpoint is *ex ante* in the sense that the sampling distribution $F(Y_1 \le c_1, Y_2 \le c_2, \ldots, Y_T \le c_T|\theta)$, where c_t $(t = 1, 2, \ldots, T)$ are constants, describes what we expect to see when drawing a sequence of random variables Y_t $(t = 1, 2, \ldots, T)$ (referred to as a sample) *before we take the draws.* The interpretation of probability attached to a sampling distribution may be either frequentist or subjectivist. The crucial point is its *ex ante* nature. Once the draws are made and realizations $Y_t = y_t$ $(t = 1, 2, \ldots, T)$ are obtained, the relevance of the sampling distribution is debatable—a debate that will be discussed in Chapter 6.

Ex ante reasoning is clearly appropriate in some statistical activities. For example, *experimental design*, which by definition concerns planning strategies for drawing a sample, is necessarily an *ex ante* activity. An elementary example is a situation in which sampling is costly and the researcher chooses an "optimal" sample size, taking into account such costs. Experimental design, however, is not a topic discussed in this text because rarely are economists in a position to design their experiments.[1] Prediction of future observables also involves an *ex ante* perspective, and to many researchers, it is their most important activity. Because the concept of a random sample plays a fundamental role in classical statistics, let us look at its implications for prediction.

Example 5.1.2 Conditional on the known parameter suppose Y_t $(t = 1, 2, \ldots, T, T + 1) \sim$ i.i.d. $f(\cdot)$. After observing $Y_t = y_t$ $(t = 1, 2, \ldots, T)$, what is the sampling distribution of the yet to be observed Y_{T+1}? The answer is trivial. Since Y_t $(t = 1, 2, \ldots, T, T + 1)$ are assumed to be independent, the conditional distribution of Y_{T+1}, given $Y_t = y_t$ $(t = 1, 2, \ldots, T)$ and θ, is simply the marginal distribution of Y_{T+1} given θ. Hence, $f(y_{T+1}|y_1, y_2, \ldots, y_T, \theta) = f(y_{T+1}|\theta)$.

Example 5.1.2 may seem counterintuitive because it implies nothing is learned from observing the first T observations. Indeed, so long as we do not question that θ is known, nor question the basic i.i.d. assumption, nor the specification of $f(\cdot|\theta)$, there is nothing to be learned from experience. If the observations are independent, then nothing is learned from patterns in the observed data. Failure to appreciate this fact underlies the "gambler's fallacy" (recall Exercise 2.1.9). For example, after observing T i.i.d. flips of a coin known to be fair, no matter how many "heads" and "tails" are observed, the probability of a head on the next flip remains $\frac{1}{2}$. Once we remove the assumption that θ is known (i.e., the coin is known to be fair), then our original intuition regains some validity.

Naturally, to use a sampling distribution for an *ex ante* activity such as prediction, the researcher must know the distribution. There are few interesting statistical questions to be answered concerning random samples from *known* distributions: There is nothing to estimate, testing is trivial, and as just seen, prediction is straightforward.[2] Note, however, in the case of unknown parameters, a sampling distribution is of little *direct* use because it involves the unknown parameters. Prediction in this case involves

1. Notable exceptions are the numerous social experiments that have been performed in North America in the last twenty-five years (e.g., experiments involving negative income taxes, time-of-use pricing of electricity, and health and education vouchers). Also noteworthy is the growing use of laboratory experiments in analyzing, among other things, market structure.

2. In dynamic models the sample observations are dependent, and so prediction using a known distribution is less trivial than in the case of random samples, but still substantially easier than in the case of unknown distributions. Chapter 8 discusses prediction in more detail.

both *ex ante* and *ex post* perspectives (after seeing some data, predict other data yet to be observed).

The primary purpose of sampling is to "learn" about unknown quantities (parameters) that characterize the underlying distribution. By observing data from a particular sampling distribution, known up to a finite number of unknown parameters, we attempt to "invert" the process and learn what values of the unknown parameters may have reasonably given rise to such data. Such reasoning amounts to *estimation* and *inference*, and is discussed fully in later chapters. Note, however, that such reasoning is fundamentally different than the *ex ante* perspective of a sampling distribution. Rather than being *ex ante*, it asks an *ex post* question: *After* observing the data, what can be said about the possible parameter values that could have generated the data? The appropriate manner in which to engage in such *ex post* reasoning is highly debatable and underlies many of the controversies in statistics over how best to perform estimation, testing and prediction. *Ex ante* (sampling inferences) are the backbone of classical statistics, whereas *ex post* (posterior inferences) are the backbone of Bayesian statistics.

In part due to such considerations, some researchers question the fundamental role of the random sample. Recognizing when random variables (or more basically, events) are independent given an unknown parameter (referred to as *conditional independence*) is not something that is natural nor easy to do. For example, consider again Example 5.1.1. Although it is perfectly clear whether sampling is being performed with or without replacement, it is far less clear, after replacing a drawn ball and "mixing" all the balls in the bowl, whether the probability of drawing a red ball the next time is independent of drawing one on the previous draw, and whether the probability of drawing a red ball is the same as it was on the previous draw. Furthermore, such issues are conditional on the composition of balls in the bowl. If the latter is not known, how does a researcher assess these issues in practice?

In the final section of this chapter, we turn to Bruno de Finetti's subjectivist solution to these problems. Although his solution reassigns the fundamental role to a different concept, random sampling is provided an interesting interpretation in the process. Before exploring de Finetti's work, however, it is necessary to develop additional tools in the intervening sections.

5.2 Statistics and Sample Moments

The following definition introduces some terminology that is important in our discussion of estimation in Chapter 6.

Definition 5.2.1 A random variable is a *statistic* iff it can be expressed as a function, not involving any unknown quantities, of a sample Y_t ($t = 1, 2, \ldots, T$). If this statistic is intended to serve as a basis for learning about an unknown quantity θ, then the statistic is an *estimator* of θ, and it is often denoted by $\hat{\theta}$ or $\hat{\theta}_T$. A realized value of an estimator is an *estimate.*

By definition statistics do not involve unknown parameters, otherwise they could not be computed. The sampling distributions of statistics, however, depend (in general) on unknown parameters, and it is precisely such dependence that makes them potentially useful estimators. The special case in which the sampling distribution of a statistic does *not* depend on unknown parameters warrants a definition.

Definition 5.2.2 A statistic whose sampling distribution does not depend on unknown parameters is an *ancillary statistic.*

Because the sampling distributions of ancillary statistics do not depend on unknown parameters, their *ex ante* behavior is readily available. Although it may seem at first glance that ancillary statistics play little role in estimation (e.g., they cannot tell us about unknown parameters if their sampling distributions do not depend on such parameters?), it will be seen in Chapters 6 and 7 that they play a crucial role in frequentist reasoning.

Particular statistics occur so frequently in practice that they deserve special attention. These statistics are known as *moments* and they are the sample analogs of the population moments defined in Definition 2.3.2.

Definition 5.2.3 Consider the sample Y_t ($t = 1, 2, \ldots, T$). *The rth sample moment about zero*, denoted by M'_r, is defined to be the statistic

$$M'_r = \frac{1}{T}\sum_{t=1}^{T} Y_t^r. \tag{5.2.1}$$

If $r = 1$, then M'_r is the sample mean, denoted by $\overline{Y}$ or $\overline{Y}_T$. The *rth sample moment about* $\overline{Y}$, denoted by M_r, is defined to be the statistic

$$M_r = \frac{1}{T}\sum_{t=1}^{T} (Y_t - \overline{Y})^r. \tag{5.2.2}$$

The *sample variance* is defined as the statistic

$$S^2 = \frac{T}{T-1}M_2 = \frac{1}{T-1}\sum_{t=1}^{T} (Y_t - \overline{Y})^2. \tag{5.2.3}$$

Interest in sample moments (5.2.1) and (5.2.2) stems in part from their performance as estimators of unknown parameters using their respective population counterparts (assumed to exist):

$$\mu'_r \equiv \mu'_r(\theta) = E_{Y|\theta}(Y^r), \tag{5.2.4}$$

$$\mu_r \equiv \mu_r(\theta) = E_{Y|\theta}[(Y - \mu)^r], \tag{5.2.5}$$

where the notation in (5.2.4) and (5.2.5) emphasizes that population moments, unlike sample moments, depend explicitly on the (usually unknown) parameter vector θ. Also keep in mind that the expectations in (5.2.4) and (5.2.5) are taken with respect to the (sampling) distribution of Y given θ. Of course the *sampling distribution* of sample moments depends on θ, and this motivates using sample moments to estimate unknown parameters by equating the sample moments to the corresponding population moments and solving the implicit functions of θ to obtain point estimates of the unknown parameters. Such a procedure defines one of the oldest known methods of estimation, namely, the *method of moments.* A discussion of this method is given in Section 6.4.

This section derives moments of the sampling distribution of sample moments. Section 5.3 calculates the entire distribution (not just the moments) of the sample mean when sampling from some familiar distributions. Theorem 5.2.1 provides the mean and variance of (5.2.2), assuming only random sampling from a distribution in which given moments exist. Additional distributional assumptions are *not* required for the results of this section, but are required in Section 5.3.

Theorem 5.2.1 Let Y_t $(t = 1, 2, \ldots, T)$ be a random sample from a population for which the moments noted below exist.

(a) $E_{Y|\theta}(M_r') = \mu_r'$ (5.2.6)

(b) $\text{Var}(M_r') = T^{-1}[\mu_{2r}' - (\mu_r')^2]$. (5.2.7)

Proof

(a) Because the (sampling) expectation operator is linear:

$$E(M_r') = E\left[\frac{1}{T}\sum_{t=1}^{T} Y_t^r\right] = \frac{1}{T}\sum_{t=1}^{T} E(Y_t^r)$$

$$= \frac{1}{T}\sum_{t=1}^{T} \mu_T' = \frac{1}{T}(T\mu_r') = \mu_r'.$$

(b) Using (2.6.23) and noting that independent observations are also uncorrelated:

$$\text{Var}(M_r') = \text{Var}\left[\frac{1}{T}\sum_{t=1}^{T} Y_t^r\right] = \frac{1}{T^2}\sum_{t=1}^{T} \text{Var}(Y_t^r)$$

$$= \frac{1}{T^2}\sum_{t=1}^{T} [E(Y_t^{2r}) - [E(Y_t^r)]^2]$$

$$= \frac{1}{T^2}\sum_{t=1}^{T} [\mu_{2r}' - (\mu_r')^2] = \frac{1}{T}[\mu_{2r}' - (\mu_r')^2].$$

Note that both Parts (a) and (b) require Y_t $(t = 1, 2, \ldots, T)$ to be identically distributed. In addition, Part (b) requires Y_t $(t = 1, 2, \ldots, T)$ to be independent.

In the important case $r = 1$, Theorem 5.2.1 implies for a random sample from a population with finite mean μ and variance σ^2:

$$E(\overline{Y}) = \mu, \tag{5.2.8}$$

$$\operatorname{Var}(\overline{Y}) = \frac{\sigma^2}{T}. \tag{5.2.9}$$

In other words, (5.2.8) implies that the mean of the sample mean [i.e. $E(\overline{Y})$] equals the mean μ of the underlying population. The variance of the sample mean is inversely related to sample size (see Equation 5.2.9). Thus, for example, the distribution of the sample mean $\overline{Y}_{10}$ based on random samples of size $T = 10$ has the same mean as the distribution of the sample mean $\overline{Y}_{20}$ based on random samples of size $T = 20$ (namely the population mean μ), but in the latter case the dispersion of estimates around μ is tighter than in the former case. Intuitively this suggests that $\overline{Y}_{20}$ is a "better" estimate of μ than is $\overline{Y}_{10}$, and this intuition is formalized in the next chapter.

To help crystallize the ideas discussed so far, and also to provide a link to the next chapter, consider the following empirical example.

Example 5.2.1 Consider the following scenario. Suppose Y_t $(t = 1, 2, \ldots, T)$ represent the daily closing returns of the DOW Jones Industrial Average, and suppose that these observations are i.i.d $N(\mu, \sigma^2)$, where $\mu = .0010$ and $\sigma = .0098$. Given efficient markets it is plausible that daily returns [i.e., $(d_t - d_{t-1})/d_{t-1}$, where d_t is the level of the DOW at the close of day t] are independent. Ignoring any day-of-the-week anomalies, it is also plausible that daily returns are identically distributed. The normality assumption is largely one of convenience.[3]

Consider a sample of size $T = 16$ drawn from this distribution. It can be shown (see Theorems 3.3.10 and 5.3.5) that the sampling distribution of $\overline{Y}_{16}$ is $N(\mu, \sigma^2/16)$, or in other words, $\overline{Y}_{16} \sim N(.0010, [.00245]^2)$. Thus, a .95 probability interval for $\overline{Y}_{16}$ is

$$P[\mu - 1.96(.00245) < \overline{Y}_{16} < \mu + 1.96(.00245)] = .95, \tag{5.2.10a}$$

or

$$P[-.0038 < \overline{Y}_{16} < .0058] = .95. \tag{5.2.10b}$$

3. To give a real world context to this example, the assigned values of μ and σ are the observed sample moments on the Dow from March, 1987 to January, 1989. Keeping in the spirit of this chapter, we take these values as given.

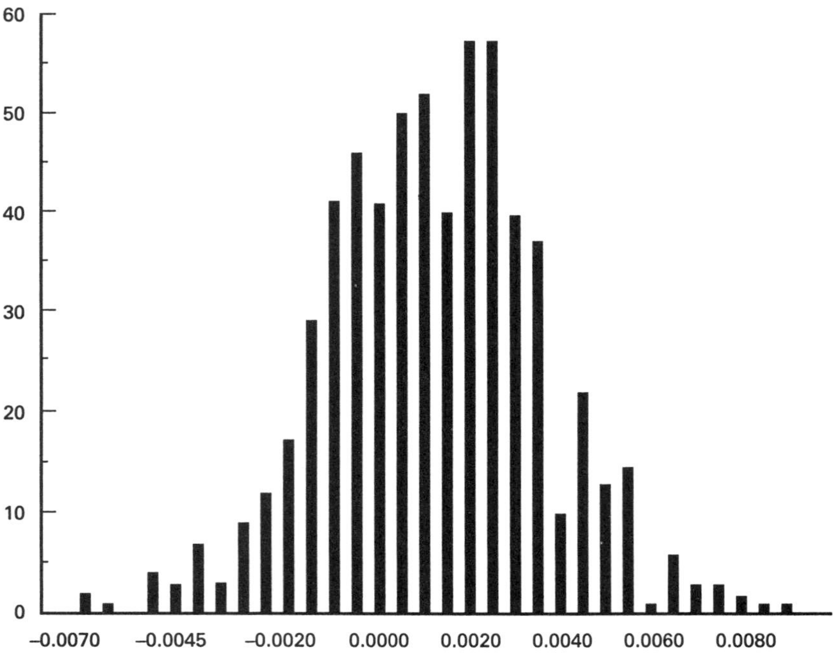

Figure 5.2.1
Histogram for 625 sample means based on samples of size 16 drawn from a $N(.0010, .0098^2)$

Now to illustrate some of the ideas involved with sampling distributions, 625 *pseudo-random samples* (samples generated on a computer) of size $T = 16$ were drawn from a $N(.0010, .0098^2)$ distribution, and the realized sample means $\overline{Y}_{16}$ were calculated for each. Figure 5.2.1 is a histogram of these 625 sample means, where 40 equally-spaced "bins" along the horizontal axis (based on the observed minimum and maximum) were used. As can roughly be seen from the histogram, approximately 566 (95.84%) out of the 625 realized sample means fall in the 95 percent interval (5.2.10b).

Of course, when dealing with "real-world" data we usually only have one sample available, and we do not know whether it is in one of the tails of the histogram or near the unknown μ. We like to think the data is representative of the middle of the histogram, but of course we cannot be certain. Even more crucially, however, note the need to reverse the inferential direction of the sampling distribution. *The sampling distribution starts with the parameter (unknown except in synthetic situations like the one here) and describes the behavior of repeated sampling from this distribution, whereas in practical situations, we start with an observed sample and wish to say something about the unknown parameter.*

This need to change the inferential direction leads to rewriting (5.2.10a) as

$$\bar{Y}_{16} - 1.96(.00245) < \mu < \bar{Y}_{16} + 1.96(.00245), \tag{5.2.11a}$$

or

$$\bar{Y}_{16} - .0048 < \mu < \bar{Y}_{16} + .0048. \tag{5.2.11b}$$

The sampling distribution of $\bar{Y}_{16}$ implies that (5.2.11) is also a 95 percent interval. Unlike (5.2.10) in which the interval is fixed and the quantity in the middle is random, interval (5.2.11) is random and, from the frequentist perspective, the quantity in the middle is fixed. We "use" (5.2.11) by taking a particular realized sample mean $\bar{y}_{16}$ and plugging it into (5.2.11b) to obtain the numerical interval

$$\bar{y}_{16} - .0048 < \mu < \bar{y}_{16} + .0048. \tag{5.2.12}$$

As will be seen in Section 6.9, (5.2.12) is called a *confidence interval*. Sampling interval (5.2.11) is *not* directly useful; it is indirectly useful in that it is the basis of a procedure for constructing a numerical interval like (5.2.12). But a large nagging question emerges: How should such a numerical interval be interpreted? Interesting frequentist probability statements *cannot* be made directly about *ex post* interval (5.2.12) because all quantities in it are constants.

Detailed discussion of the interpretation of (5.2.12) is left to Section 6.9. This example illustrates the very important point this section has tried to drive home. The direct use of sampling distribution-based inferences is of limited interest. Its value lies in its *indirect* use. As will become clearer in Section 6.3, frequentist based methods evaluate the performance in repeated sampling of *procedures* that give rise to numerical point and interval estimates that researchers actually use. Such methods are silent on whether these numerical estimates are accurate estimates of unknown parameters. *Instead, frequentist procedures focus on the expected (average) performance of the procedures used to produce the estimates in repeated data confrontations.*

We end this section with a theorem giving the first two moments of the sampling distribution of the sample variance S^2 defined in (5.2.3) (analogous to Equations 5.2.8 and 5.2.9 in the case of the sample mean). Note that we cannot use Theorem 5.2.1 directly, as we are now interested in sample moments around the sample mean.

Theorem 5.2.2 Let Y_t $(t = 1, 2, \ldots, T)$ be a random sample from a population with mean μ, variance σ^2 and $\mu_4 \equiv E(Y_t - \mu)^4 < \infty$. Then

(a) $E(S^2) = \sigma^2$ (5.2.13)

(b) $\text{Var}(S^2) = [\mu_4 - (T-1)^{-1}(T-3)^4]/T.$ (5.2.14)

Proof

(a) From Exercise 5.2.2 it follows that

$$\sum_{t=1}^{T} (Y_t - \mu) = \sum_{t=1}^{T} (Y_t - \overline{Y})^2 + T(\overline{Y} - \mu)^2. \tag{5.2.15}$$

Hence,

$$\begin{aligned} E(S^2) &= \frac{1}{T-1}\left[\sum_{t=1}^{T} E[(Y_t - \mu)^2] - TE[(\overline{Y} - \mu)^2]\right] \\ &= \frac{1}{T-1}[T\sigma^2 - T(\sigma^2/T)] \\ &= \frac{(T-1)\sigma^2}{T-1} = \sigma^2. \end{aligned}$$

(b) Adding zero judiciously in the form $-\mu - (-\mu)$, write

$$\begin{aligned} \operatorname{Var}(S^2) &= \frac{1}{(T-1)^2}\operatorname{Var}\left[\sum_{t=1}^{T} [(Y_t - \mu) - (\overline{Y} - \mu)]^2\right] \\ &= \frac{1}{(T-1)^2}\operatorname{Var}\left[\sum_{t=1}^{T} (X_t - \overline{X})^2\right], \end{aligned}$$

where $X_t = Y_t - \mu$, $\overline{X} = \overline{Y} - \mu$, $E(X_t) = 0$, $\operatorname{Var}(X_t) = \sigma^2$ and $E(X_t^4) = \mu_4$. Consider

$$\operatorname{Var}\left[\sum_{t=1}^{T} (X_t - \overline{X})^2\right] = E\left[\left(\sum_{t=1}^{T} (X_t - \overline{X})^2\right)^2\right] - \left[E\left(\sum_{t=1}^{T} (X_t - \overline{X})^2\right)\right]^2. \tag{5.2.16}$$

The first term in (5.2.16) can be written (using Exercise 5.2.4):

$$\begin{aligned} &E\left[\left(\sum_{t=1}^{T} (X_t - \overline{X})^2\right)^2\right] \\ &\quad = E\left[\left(\sum_{t=1}^{T} X_t^2\right)^2\right] - 2TE\left[\overline{X}^2 \sum_{t=1}^{T} X_t^2\right] + T^2 E(\overline{X}^4) \\ &\quad = [T\mu_4 + T(T-1)\sigma^4] - 2T\left(\frac{1}{T}[\mu_4 + (T-1)\sigma^4]\right) \\ &\qquad + T^2\left(\frac{1}{T^3}[\mu_4 + 3(T-1)\sigma^4]\right), \end{aligned} \tag{5.2.17}$$

and from (a), the second term in (5.2.16) equals

$$\left[E\left[\sum_{t=1}^{T} (X_t - \overline{X})^2\right)\right]^2 = (T-1)^2\sigma^4. \tag{5.2.18}$$

Therefore,

$$\text{Var}(S^2) = (T-1)^{-2}[T^{-1}(T-1)\{(T-1)\mu_4 + (T^2 - 2T + 3)\sigma^4\} \\ - (T-1)^2\sigma^4] \\ = T^{-1}[\mu_4 - (T-1)^{-1}(T-3)\sigma^4]. \tag{5.2.19}$$

Exercises

5.2.1 Consider the sample values Y_t $(t = 1, 2, \ldots, T)$. Show:

$$\max_{1 \le t \le T} |y_t - \bar{y}| \le \left(\frac{T-1}{T}\right)^{1/2} s, \tag{5.2.20}$$

where $\bar{y}$ and s denote the realized values of the sample mean and standard deviation, respectively.

5.2.2 Consider the sample Y_t $(t = 1, 2, \ldots, T)$ with sample mean $\bar{Y}$. Show:

$$\sum_{t=1}^{T} (Y_t - \mu)^2 = \sum_{t=1}^{T} (Y_t - \bar{Y})^2 + T(\bar{Y} - \mu)^2,$$

where μ is the population mean (assumed to exist) of the underlying population.

5.2.3 Suppose Y_t $(t = 1, 2, \ldots, T)$ are i.i.d. with finite moments $E(Y_t) = 0$, $E(Y_t^2) = \text{Var}(Y_t) = \sigma^2$ and $E(Y_t^4) = \mu_4' = \mu_4$. Prove each of the following:

(a) $E\left[\left(\sum_{t=1}^{T} Y_t^2\right)^2\right] = T\mu_4 + T(T-1)\sigma^4$

(b) $E\left[\bar{Y}^2 \sum_{t=1}^{T} Y_t^2\right] = T^{-1}[\mu_4 + (T-1)\sigma^4]$

(c) $E[\bar{Y}_t^4] = T^3[\mu_4 - 3(T-1)\sigma^4]$.

5.2.4 Let (x_t, y_t) $(t = 1, 2, \ldots, T)$ be a sample of T paired observations. Define $z_t = ax_t + cy_t$ $(t = 1, 2, \ldots, T)$, where a and c are constants.

(a) Show: $\bar{z} = a\bar{x} + c\bar{y}$.

(b) Show: $s_z^2 = a^2 s_x^2 + 2acs_{xy} + c^2 s_y^2$, where

$$s_x^2 = \frac{1}{T-1}\sum_{t=1}^{T} (x_t - \bar{x})^2, \tag{5.2.21}$$

$$s_y^2 = \frac{1}{T-1}\sum_{t=1}^{T} (y_t - \bar{y})^2, \tag{5.2.22}$$

$$s_{xy}^2 = \frac{1}{T-1}\sum_{t=1}^{T} (x_t - \bar{x})(y_t - \bar{y}). \tag{5.2.23}$$

(c) Define the *sample correlation* $r_{xy} \equiv s_{xy}/s_x s_y$. Geometrically, the sample correlation between $x = [x_1, x_2, \ldots, x_T]'$ and $y = [y_1, y_2, \ldots, y_T]'$ is the cosine of the angle between the T-dimensional vectors x and y. Noting $s_z^2 \ge 0$, show by two different judicious choices of a and c that $-1 \le r \le 1$ (see Koch 1985).

5.2.5 Let $\bar{Y}_T$ and S_T^2 be the sample mean and variance of Y_t $(t = 1, 2, \ldots, T)$. Suppose a new observation Y_{T+1} becomes available. Show (see Casella and Berger 1990, p. 244):

(a) $\bar{Y}_{T+1} = (T+1)^{-1}[Y_{T+1} + T\bar{Y}_T]$

(b) $TS_{T+1}^2 = (T-1)S_T^2 + [T/(T+1)][Y_{T+1} - \bar{Y}_T]^2$

(c) $\text{Cov}(\bar{Y}_{T+1}, Y_{T+1} - \bar{Y}_T) = 0$.

5.2.6 Let $\overline{Y}_T$ be the sample mean based on a random sample of size T from a population with finite moments to at least the fourth order. Let $m_r = E(Y^r)$ and $\mu_r = E[(Y - \mu)^r]$ ($r = 3, 4$). Show:

(a) $E(\overline{Y}_T^3) = T^{-2}[m_3 + 3(T-1)m_2\mu + 6(T-1)(T-2)\mu^3]$,

(b) $E(Y_T^4) = T^{-3}[m_4 + 4(T-1)m_3\mu + 6(T-1)(T-2)m_2\mu^2 + 3(T-1)m_2^2 + (T-1)(T-2)(T-3)\mu^4]$.

5.2.7 Let $\overline{Y}_T$ be the sample mean based on a random sample of size T from a population with finite moments to at least the fourth order. Define $\hat{\sigma}^2 = [(T-1)/T]S^2$. Show:

(a) $E(\hat{\sigma}^2) = [(T-1)/T]\sigma^2$

(b) $\text{Var}(\hat{\sigma}^2) = T^{-1}(\mu_4 - \mu_2^2) - 2T^{-2}(\mu_4 - 2\mu_2^2) + T^{-3}(\mu_4 - 3\mu_2^2)$

(c) $E[(\hat{\sigma}^2)^3] = T^{-2}(T-1)(T-2)\mu_3$

(d) $E[(\hat{\sigma}^2)^4] = T^{-3}(T-1)(T^2 - 3T + 3)\mu_4 + 3T^{-3}(T-1)(2T-3)\mu_2^2]$.

5.2.8 Suppose X_t ($t = 1, 2, \ldots, T$) are i.i.d. observations from a scale-parameter family with c.d.f. $F(x/\sigma)$, where $0 < \sigma < \infty$. Show any statistic depending on the sample only through the $T - 1$ values $X_1/X_T, X_2/X_T, \ldots, X_{T-1}/X_T$ is ancillary for σ.

5.2.9 Show that S^2 in (5.2.3) can be rewritten:

$$S^2 = \frac{1}{2(T-1)(T-2)} \sum_{i=1}^{T} \sum_{t=1}^{T} (Y_i - Y_t)^2. \tag{5.2.24}$$

5.2.10 Let Y_t ($t = 1, 2, \ldots, T$) be i.i.d. with finite fourth moment. Show:

$$E[(Y - \mu)^2] = 0 \Rightarrow \text{Cov}(\overline{Y}, S^2) = 0. \tag{5.2.25}$$

5.2.11 Let Y_t ($t = 1, 2, \ldots, T$) be random variables (not necessarily independently distributed) with mean μ and variance σ^2.

(a) Show: $(T-1)E(S^2) = T\sigma^2 - T\,\text{Var}(\overline{Y})$

(b) Using (a), show:

$$0 \le E(S^2) \le \left(\frac{T}{T-1}\right)\sigma^2. \tag{5.2.26}$$

5.2.12 Assuming the moments below exist, show:

(a) $E[(\overline{Y}_T - \mu)^3] = T^{-2}\mu_3$

(b) $E[(\overline{Y}_T - \mu)^4] = T^{-3}\mu_4 + 3T^{-3}\mu_2^2$.

5.3 Sampling Distributions

Because statistics are nothing more than transformations of random variables, it is possible to use the techniques of Chapter 4 to derive their sampling distributions. In this section the distribution of the sample mean is derived for random sampling from some commonly encountered distributions. These results are stated in Theorems 5.3.1 through 5.3.7.

Theorem 5.3.1 Let Y_t ($t = 1, 2, \ldots, T$) be a random sample from an exponential distribution with mean β. The distribution of $\overline{Y}_T$ is a gamma distribution with parameters T and $T\beta$.

Proof Follows immediately from the fact that $T\overline{Y}_T = Y_1 + Y_2 + \cdots + Y_T$

has a gamma distribution with parameters T and β (straightforward extension of Theorem 3.3.11).

Theorem 5.3.2 Let Y_t $(t = 1, 2, \ldots, T)$ be a random sample from a uniform distribution on the interval (0, 1). Then the p.d.f. of $\bar{Y}_T$ is

$$f(\bar{y}_t) = \sum_{k=0}^{T-1} \frac{T}{(T-1)!}\left[(T\bar{y}_T)^{T-1} - \binom{T}{1}(T\bar{y}_T - 1)^{T-1} + \cdots \right.$$
$$\left. + (-1)^k \binom{T}{k}(T\bar{y}_T - k)^{T-1} I_{(k/T, (k+1)/T]}(\bar{y}_T)\right], \tag{5.3.1}$$

where

$$I_{(k/T, (k+1)/T]}(\bar{y}_T) = \begin{Bmatrix} 1, & \text{if } k/T < \bar{y}_T \le (k+1)/T \\ 0, & \text{otherwise} \end{Bmatrix}. \tag{5.3.2}$$

Proof See Mood et al. (1974, p. 238) for the cases $T = 1, 2, 3$. Remaining cases can be shown by mathematical induction.

Theorem 5.3.3 Let Y_t $(t = 1, 2, \ldots, T)$ be a random sample from a Bernoulli distribution with parameter θ. Then the distribution of the sample mean is

$$P\left(\bar{Y}_T = \frac{k}{T}\right) = \begin{Bmatrix} \binom{T}{k}\theta^k(1-\theta)^{T-k}, & \text{if } k = 0, 1, \ldots, T \\ 0, & \text{otherwise} \end{Bmatrix}. \tag{5.3.3}$$

Proof Follows from the fact that $T\bar{Y}_T = Y_1 + Y_2 + \cdots + Y_T$ has a $B(T, \theta)$ distribution.

Theorem 5.3.4 Let Y_t $(t = 1, 2, \ldots, T)$ be a random sample from a Poisson distribution with mean λ. Then the distribution of the sample sum is Poisson with mean $T\lambda$, and the distribution of the sample mean is

$$f\left(\bar{Y}_T = \frac{k}{T}\right) = \begin{Bmatrix} \dfrac{(T\lambda)^k \exp(-T\lambda)}{k!}, & \text{if } k = 0, 1, \ldots, T \\ 0, & \text{otherwise} \end{Bmatrix}. \tag{5.3.4}$$

Proof From (3.1.34) and (4.3.1) it follows that the moment generating function of the sample sum is

$$M_{T\bar{Y}_T}(t) = \prod_{i=1}^{T} \exp(\lambda[\exp(t) - 1])$$
$$= \exp(T\lambda[\exp(t) - 1]),$$

which is the m.g.f. of a Poisson random variable with mean $T\lambda$. Therefore, (5.3.4) follows.

The next theorem, covering random sampling from a normal distribution, is probably the most useful of all the sampling distributions in this section.

Theorem 5.3.5 Let Y_t $(t = 1, 2, \ldots, T)$ be a random sample from a $N(\mu, \sigma^2)$ distribution.

(a) $\bar{Y}_T \sim N(\mu, \sigma^2/T)$

(b) $(T-1)S^2/\sigma^2 \sim \chi^2(T-1)$

(c) $\bar{Y}_T$ and S^2 are stochastically independent.

Proof (a) The m.g.f. of $\bar{Y}_T$ is, for any real number v,

$$
\begin{aligned}
M_{\bar{Y}_T}(v) = E_{Y|\mu,\sigma^2}[\exp(v\bar{Y}_T)] &= E_{Y|\mu,\sigma^2}\left[\prod_{t=1}^{T} \exp(vY_t/T)\right] \\
&= \prod_{t=1}^{T} E_{Y_t|\mu,\sigma^2}[\exp(vY_t/T)] && \text{(Theorem 4.4.1)} \\
&= \prod_{t=1}^{T} M_{Y_t}(v/T) \\
&= \prod_{t=1}^{T} \exp[\mu(v/T) + \sigma^2(v/T)^2/2] && \text{(Theorem 3.3.2)} \\
&= \exp[\mu v + (\sigma^2/T)v^2/2].
\end{aligned}
$$

From Theorem 3.2.2, $\bar{Y}_T \sim N(\mu, \sigma^2/T)$. For proofs of (b) and (c), see the proof of Theorem 4.5.6.

In light of Theorem 5.3.5(b), it should be noted that the phrase "degrees of freedom" for the parameter of a chi-squared distribution reflects the fact that $(T-1)S^2 = (Y_1 - \bar{Y})^2 + (Y_2 - \bar{Y})^2 + \cdots + (Y_T - \bar{Y})^2$ contains only $T-1$ independent terms since

$$
\sum_{t=1}^{T} (Y_t - \bar{Y}) = 0. \tag{5.3.5}
$$

Theorem 5.3.5 implies that as sample size T increases, the distribution of $\bar{Y}_T$ remains centered over μ, but its variance (spread) decreases. Such desirable behavior on the part of the sample depends, however, on the underlying population distribution. The following theorem illustrates that when sampling from "fat-tail" distributions such as the Cauchy, the sampling distribution of the sample mean need not "collapse" upon the population location parameter. In fact, in the case of the Cauchy, the sampling distribution does *not* even depend on sample size T.

Theorem 5.3.6 Let Y_t $(t = 1, 2, \ldots, T)$ be a random sample from the Cauchy distribution $t(\theta, \alpha, 1)$. Then $\bar{Y}_T$ has the same distribution, $t(\theta, \alpha, 1)$, regardless of sample size.

Proof This theorem can be easily proved using characteristic functions and proceeding in the same fashion as in the proof of Theorem 5.3.5(a) which involved moment generating functions. Noting that the characteristic function (CF) of $t(\theta, \alpha, 1)$ is $\text{CF}(v) = \exp[i\theta v - \alpha|v|]$, where $i = (-1)^{1/2}$, it follows immediately:

$$
\begin{aligned}
CF_{\bar{Y}_T}(v) &= \prod_{t=1}^{T} CF_{Y_t}(v/T) \\
&= \prod_{t=1}^{T} \exp[i\theta(v/T) - \alpha|v/T|] \\
&= \exp[Ti\theta(v/T) - T\alpha|v/T|] \\
&= \exp[i\theta v - \alpha|v|].
\end{aligned}
$$

Extension of Theorem 5.3.5 to the case of random sampling from a multivariate normal distribution is straightforward, and is provided in the following theorem. In the process this extension provides strong motivation for the Wishart distribution of Section 3.5.

Theorem 5.3.7 Let the $M \times 1$ vectors $Y_t = [Y_{t1}, Y_{t2}, \ldots, Y_{tM}]'$ $(t = 1, 2, \ldots, T)$ be i.i.d. $N_M(\mu, \Sigma)$. Suppose $T > M$ and define

$$\bar{Y} = \frac{1}{T}\sum_{t=1}^{T} Y_t, \tag{5.3.6}$$

$$Z = \sum_{t=1}^{T} (Y_t - \bar{Y})(Y_t - \bar{Y})'. \tag{5.3.7}$$

Then,

(a) $\bar{Y}$ and Z are independent.

(b) $\bar{Y} \sim N_M(\mu, T^{-1}\Sigma)$

(c) $Z \sim W_M(\Sigma, T-1)$

(d) Let A be a symmetric matrix and define the $T \times M$ matrix $R = [r_{tm}]$, where $r_{tm} = y_{tm} - \mu_m$. Then the unique elements of $R'AR$ have a Wishart distribution (see Definition 3.5.1) iff A is idempotent, in which case their distribution is $W_M(\Sigma, r)$ where $r = \text{rank}(A)$.

(e) $[(T-M)/M](\bar{Y} - \mu)'Z^{-1}(\bar{Y} - \mu) \sim F(M, T-M)$.

(f) If the mean μ varies across observations, then the unique elements of Z have a *noncentral* Wishart distribution.

Proof See Press (1982).

In other words, Theorem 5.3.7(c) implies that the Wishart distribution arises quite naturally as the joint distribution of the distinct sample variations and sample covariations when drawing i.i.d. random vectors from a multivariate normal distribution.

Exercises

5.3.1 Consider a random sample Y_t $(t = 1, 2, \ldots, T)$ from a $N(\mu, \sigma^2)$ population. Find the minimum value of T such that the probability is .95 that the sample mean will not differ from the population mean by more than 25 percent of the standard deviation.

5.3.2 Let Y_t $(t = 1, 2, \ldots, T)$ be a random sample from a distribution which has a finite fourth central moment, that is, μ_4 exists. Show that $\text{Cov}(\overline{Y}, S^2) = 0$ if $\mu_3 = 0$.

5.3.3 Consider an urn containing N chips numbered from one to N, and consider a sample of size T drawn *without* replacement from this urn such that all possible subsets of size T have an equal chance to be drawn.

(a) What is the expected value of the sample mean (the sum of the numbers on the T chips divided by T)?

(b) What is the variance of the sample mean?

5.3.4 Consider Theorem 5.3.7. The quantity $T\overline{Y}'Z^{-1}\overline{Y}$ is known as Hotelling's T^2 statistic (see Muirhead 1982, pp. 98–99 or Press 1982, pp. 132–135). Show that $X \equiv (T - M)T\overline{Y}'Z^{-1}\overline{Y}/[M(T-1)] \sim F(M, T - M, \lambda)$, where $\lambda = T\mu'\Sigma^{-1}\mu/2$.

5.3.5 If $Z \sim W_M(\Sigma, N)$ $[N \geq M$ an integer$]$, then $|Z|/|\Sigma|$ has the same distribution as a product of M independent chi-squared random variables with degrees of freedom $v = N - +1, N - +2, \ldots, N$, respectively (see Muirhead 1982, pp. 100–101).

(a) Show:

$$E[|Z|^r] = |\Sigma|^r \prod_{m=1}^{M} \frac{2^r\Gamma[\frac{1}{2}(N - m + 1) + r]}{\Gamma[\frac{1}{2}(N - m + 1)]}. \tag{5.3.8}$$

(b) Consider Theorem 5.3.7. Let $S = T^{-1}Z$. Find: $E[|S|]$ and $\text{Var}[|S|]$.

5.3.6 Let Y_t $(t = 1, 2, \ldots, T)$ be random variables with common mean $\mu \equiv E(Y_t)$ $(t = 1, 2, \ldots, T)$. Suppose $\text{Cov}(Y_t, Y_i) = 0$ for all $t > i + 1$. Define:

$$Q_1 = \sum_{t=1}^{T} (Y_t - \overline{Y})^2, \tag{5.3.9}$$

$$Q_2 = \sum_{t=1}^{T-1} (Y_t - Y_{t+1})^2 - (Y_T - Y_1)^2. \tag{5.3.10}$$

Show: $E[\{T(T-3)\}^{-1}(3Q_1 - Q_2)] = \text{Var}(\overline{Y})$.

5.3.7 Derive the exact distribution of S^2 for a random sample of size T from a Bernoulli distribution with parameter θ.

5.3.8 Let Y_t $(t = 1, 2, \ldots, T)$ be a random sample from the exponential family of distributions defined in (3.3.62), where $T \geq K$. Consider the statistics

$$X_k = \sum_{t=1}^{T} d_k(Y_t) \qquad (k = 1, 2, \ldots, K). \tag{5.3.11}$$

Show that the sampling distribution of X_k $(k = 1, 2, \ldots, K)$ is also a member of the exponential family of distributions.

5.3.9 Example 5.1.1 is an *urn model*. More generally, suppose that sampling occurs with replacement, and after a ball is drawn it is replaced and in addition X balls of the color drawn and Z balls of the opposite color are also added to the urn. A new ball is then drawn from the urn containing $N + X + Z$ balls, and the procedure is repeated. X and Z are arbitrary integers, with the proviso that if they are negative, then the procedure may terminate after a finite number of draws. For example, if $X = -1$ and $Z = 0$ we have the case of sampling without replacement. In general it is difficult to describe sampling probabilities explicitly, except in special cases such as the following. A *Polya urn* is characterized by $X > 0$ and $Z = 0$.

(a) The Polya urn is sometimes used to describe the spread of contagious diseases. Why might it be appropriate?

(b) Find an expression describing the probability of drawing r red balls and b blue balls from a Polya urn.

5.4 Order Statistics

This section briefly discusses statistics based on rankings of sample observations. These statistics play an important role in nonparametric analysis.[4] For a detailed discussion see Arnold et al. (1992).

Definition 5.4.1 Let X_t $(t = 1, 2, \ldots, T)$ be i.i.d. random variables with common cumulative distribution function $F_X(\cdot)$, and let $Y_1 \leq Y_2 \leq \cdots \leq Y_T$ be the X_t's arranged in order of increasing magnitudes. Then Y_t $(t = 1, 2, \ldots, T)$ are defined to be the *order statistics* corresponding to X_t $(t = 1, 2, \ldots, T)$.

Order statistics are themselves random variables and their marginal cumulative distribution functions are given in the following theorem.

Theorem 5.4.1 Let X_t $(t = 1, 2, \ldots, T)$ be i.i.d. random variables with common cumulative distribution function $F_X(\cdot)$, and let Y_t $(t = 1, 2, \ldots, T)$ be the corresponding order statistics defined in Definition 5.4.1. Then the marginal cumulative distribution function of Y_i is

$$F_{Y_i}(y) = \sum_{j=i}^{T} \binom{T}{j} [F_x(y)]^j [1 - F_X(y)]^{T-j}. \tag{5.4.1}$$

Proof For given y, define

$$Z_i = \begin{Bmatrix} 1, & \text{if } Y_i \leq y \\ 0, & \text{if } Y_i > y \end{Bmatrix} = I_{(-\infty, y]}(Y_i) \qquad (i = 1, 2, \ldots, T), \tag{5.4.2}$$

where, in general,

$$I_{(a,b]}(Y_t) = \begin{Bmatrix} 1, & \text{if } a < Y_i \leq b \\ 0, & \text{if } Y_i < a \text{ or } Y_i > b \end{Bmatrix} \qquad (a < b) \tag{5.4.3}$$

is the *indicator function*—$I_{(a,b)}(Y_i)$, $I_{[a,b)}(Y_i)$ and $I_{[a,b]}(Y_i)$ are similarly defined. Then $Z \equiv Z_1 + Z_2 + \cdots + Z_T$ is the number of the Y_i's less than or equal to y. Note that Z has a binomial distribution with parameters T and

4. Nonparametric methods are statistical procedures designed to be applicable for large classes of distributions, and for which relevant probability statements are independent of the actual population distribution. It is often useful to think of nonparametric techniques as modeling the underlying distribution in a parametric fashion, but in which there are an infinite number of unknown parameters.

$\theta = F_X(y)$, that is, $Z \sim B(T, \theta)$. Because the ith order statistic Y_i is less than or equal to y iff the number of X_ts less than or equal to y is greater than or equal than i, it follows that

$$F_{Y_i}(y) = P(Y_i \le y) = \sum_{j=i}^{T} P(Z = j) = \sum_{j=i}^{T} [F_X(y)]^j [1 - F_X(y)]^{T-j}. \tag{5.4.4}$$

Example 5.4.1 Letting $i = T$ in Theorem 5.4.1 and noting that $Y_T = \max\{X_1, X_2, \ldots, X_T\}$, it immediately follows that

$$F_{Y_T}(y) = [F_X(y)]^T \tag{5.4.5}$$

as in Theorem 4.2.1. Letting $i = 1$ and noting $Y_1 = \min\{X_1, X_2, \ldots, X_N\}$, it follows immediately that

$$F_{Y_1}(y) = 1 - [1 - F_X(y)]^T. \tag{5.4.6}$$

Marginal and joint density functions corresponding to the c.d.f. given in Theorem 5.4.1 are given in the following theorem.

Theorem 5.4.2 Let X_t $(t = 1, 2, \ldots, T)$ be i.i.d. random variables with common c.d.f. $F_X(\cdot)$ and p.d.f. $f_X(\cdot)$, and let $Y_1 \le Y_2 \le \cdots \le Y_T$ denote the corresponding order statistics. Then

(a) $$f_{Y_t}(y) = \frac{T!}{(t-1)!\,(T-t)!}[F_X(y)]^{t-1}[1 - F_X(y)]^{T-t} f_X(y)$$

(b) $$f_{Y_t, Y_i}(y_t, y_i) = \frac{T![F_X(y_n)]^{t-1}[F_X(y_i) - F_X(y_t)]^{i-t-1}[1 - F_X(y_i)]^{T-i} f_X(y_t) f_X(y_i)}{(t-1)!\,(i-t-1)!\,(T-i)!}$$

if $y_t < y_i$, and equals zero otherwise.

(c) $$f_Y(y) = \left\{\begin{array}{ll} T! \prod_{t=1}^{T} f_X(y_t), & \text{if } y_1 < y_2 < \cdots < y_T \\ 0, & \text{otherwise} \end{array}\right\}.$$

Proof Mood et al. (1974, pp. 253–254).

Some commonly used order statistics, and functions thereof, are introduced in the following definition.

Definition 5.4.2 Let $Y_1 \le Y_2 \le \cdots \le Y_T$ denote the order statistics of the i.i.d. random variables X_t $(t = 1, 2, \ldots, T)$ with p.d.f. $F_X(\cdot)$. The *median* of X_t $(t = 1, 2, \ldots, T)$ is defined to be the middle order statistic, Y_k, if T is the odd integer $T = 2k - 1$, and to be the average of the middle two order statistics, $\frac{1}{2}(Y_k + Y_{k+1})$, if T is the even integer $T = 2k$. The *range* of X_t $(t = 1, 2, \ldots, T)$ is $Y_T - Y_1$. The *midrange* is $\frac{1}{2}(Y_1 + Y_T)$.

If T is odd, say $T = 2k + 1$, then the p.d.f. of the median is given by the p.d.f. of Y_k defined in Theorem 5.4.2(a). If T is even, say $T = 2k$, then the p.d.f. of the median $(Y_k + Y_{k+1})/2$ can be obtained by a transformation of the bivariate density of Y_k and Y_{k+1} in Theorem 5.4.2(b). The joint p.d.f. of the range and midrange is given in the next theorem.

Theorem 5.4.3 Consider Definition 5.4.2 and let R and M be the range and midrange of X_t $(t = 1, 2, \ldots, T)$ with common p.d.f. $f_X(\cdot)$ and distribution function $F_X(\cdot)$. Then the joint p.d.f. of R and M is

$$f_{R,M}(r, m) = \begin{cases} T(T-1)\{F_X[\tfrac{1}{2}(m+r)] - F_X[\tfrac{1}{2}(m-r)]\}^{T-2} \\ \quad f_X[\tfrac{1}{2}(m-r)]f_X[\tfrac{1}{2}(m+r)], & \text{if } r > 0 \\ 0, & \text{otherwise} \end{cases}. \tag{5.4.7}$$

Proof Left to the reader.

Example 5.4.2 Let X_t $(t = 1, 2, \ldots, T)$ be independent random variables each with a uniform distribution over $(a, b) = (\mu - \{3\sigma^2\}^{1/2}, \mu + \{3\sigma^2\}^{1/2})$. As the notation suggests, it follows from Theorem 3.3.1:

$$E(X_t) = \tfrac{1}{2}(b + a) = \tfrac{1}{2}(\mu + \{3\sigma^2\}^{1/2} + \mu - \{3\sigma^2\}^{1/2}) = \mu, \tag{5.4.8}$$

$$\text{Var}(X_t) = (b - a)^2/12 = (\mu + \{3\sigma^2\}^{1/2} - \mu + \{3\sigma^2\}^{1/2})^2/12 = \sigma^2, \tag{5.4.9}$$

for $t = 1, 2, \ldots, T$. The common p.d.f. is

$$f(x_t) = \begin{cases} \dfrac{1}{2(3\sigma^2)^{1/2}}, & \text{if } \mu - (3\sigma^2)^{1/2} < x_t < \mu + (3\sigma^2)^{1/2} \\ 0, & \text{otherwise} \end{cases}, \tag{5.4.10}$$

and the common cumulative distribution function is

$$F(x) = \begin{cases} 0, & \text{if } x \leq \mu - (3\sigma) \\ \dfrac{x - \mu + (3\sigma)^{1/2}}{2(3\sigma)^{1/2}}, & \text{if } \mu - (3\sigma)^{1/2} < x < \mu + (3\sigma)^{1/2} \\ 1, & \text{if } x > \mu + (3\sigma)^{1/2} \end{cases}. \tag{5.4.11}$$

From (5.4.11) it follows that the joint p.d.f. of the range and midrange is

$$f_{R,M}(r, m) = \begin{cases} \dfrac{T(T-1)r^{T-2}}{[2(3\sigma)^{1/2}]^T}, & \text{if } 0 < r < 2(3\sigma)^{1/2} \text{ and } \mu - (3\sigma)^{1/2} \\ & \quad + \tfrac{1}{2}r < m < \mu + (3\sigma)^{1/2} - \tfrac{1}{2}r \\ 0, & \text{otherwise} \end{cases}. \tag{5.4.12}$$

Integrating (5.4.12) with respect to m yields the marginal p.d.f. for the range:

$$f_R(r) = \begin{cases} \dfrac{T(T-1)r^{T-2}[2(3\sigma)^{1/2} - r]}{[2(3\sigma)^{1/2}]^T}, & \text{if } 0 < r < 2(3\sigma)^{1/2} \\ 0, & \text{otherwise} \end{cases}. \tag{5.4.13}$$

Note that (5.4.13) is independent of the parameter μ and that

$$E(R) = \frac{2(T-1)(3\sigma)^{1/2}}{T+1}. \tag{5.4.14}$$

Integrating (5.4.12) with respect to r yields the marginal p.d.f. for the midrange:

$$f_M(m) = \begin{cases} \dfrac{T\left[1 + \left(\dfrac{m-\mu}{(3\sigma)^{1/2}}\right)\right]^{T-1}}{2(3\sigma)^{1/2}}, & \text{if } \mu - (3\sigma)^{1/2} < m < \mu \\ \dfrac{T\left[1 - \left(\dfrac{m-\mu}{(3\sigma)^{1/2}}\right)\right]^{T-1}}{2(3\sigma)^{1/2}}, & \text{if } \mu < m < \mu + (3\sigma)^{1/2} \\ 0, & \text{otherwise} \end{cases}. \tag{5.4.15}$$

Related to order statistics is the concept introduced in the next definition and subsequent theorems.

Definition 5.4.3 Consider the Definition 5.4.1. The *sample (or empirical) cumulative distribution function*, denoted by $F_T(X)$, is the statistic defined by

$$F_T(y) = T^{-1}(\text{number of } X_t \leq y) = T^{-1}(\text{number of } Y_t \leq y)$$
$$= T^{-1} \sum_{t=1}^{T} Z_t, \tag{5.4.16}$$

where Z_t is defined by (5.4.2).

Theorem 5.4.4 Let $F_T(y)$ denote the sample cumulative distribution function of a random sample of size T from a population with cumulative distribution function $F(y)$. Then

$$P\left[F_T(y) = \frac{k}{T}\right] = \binom{T}{k}[F(y)]^k[1 - F(y)]^{T-k} \qquad (k = 0, 1, \ldots, T)$$
$$= T^{-1} \sum_{t=1}^{T} Z_t. \tag{5.4.17}$$

Proof Z_t $(t = 1, 2, \ldots, T)$ are i.i.d. Bernoulli random variables with the probability $P(Z_t = 1) = F(y)$. Therefore, the number W of Y_t less than or equal to y,

$$W = \sum_{t=1}^{T} Z_t, \tag{5.4.18}$$

has the binomial distribution $B[T, F(y)]$. Since $F_T(y) = T^{-1}W$, (5.4.17) holds.

Finally, the mean and variance of p.m.f. (5.4.17) is given in the next theorem.

Theorem 5.4.5 Let $F_T(y)$ be the sample c.d.f. with p.m.f. (5.4.17). Then

$$E[F_T(y)] = F(y), \tag{5.4.19}$$

$$\mathrm{Var}[F_T(y)] = T^{-1}F(y)[1 - F(y)]. \tag{5.4.20}$$

Proof Follows directly using (5.4.17).

Exercises

5.4.1 Consider Example 5.4.2. Prove each of the following.

(a) $E(R) = [(T-1)/(T+1)]2(3\sigma)^{1/2}$

(b) $\mathrm{Var}(R) = 24\sigma^2(T-1)/[(T+1)^2(T+2)]$

(c) $E(M) = \mu$

(d) $\mathrm{Var}(M) = 6\sigma^2/[(T+1)(T+2)]$.

5.4.2 Let $Y_1 \le Y_2 \le \cdots \le Y_T$ be the order statistics corresponding to Example 5.4.2. Suppose $T = 2k + 1$ $(k = 0, 1, 2, \ldots)$. Prove:

(a) $E(Y_k) = \mu$

(b) $\mathrm{Var}(Y_k) = 3\sigma^2/(2k+3)$.

5.4.3 Let X_t $(t = 1, 2, 3, 4)$ be independent random variables each with p.d.f.

$$f(x) = \begin{Bmatrix} \exp(-x), & \text{if } 0 < x < \infty \\ 0, & \text{otherwise} \end{Bmatrix}.$$

Find $P(\max\{X_1, X_2, X_3, X_4\} \ge 2)$.

5.4.4 Let X_t $(t = 1, 2, 3)$ be independent random variables each with p.d.f.

$$f(x) = \begin{Bmatrix} 2x, & \text{if } 0 < x < 1 \\ 0, & \text{otherwise} \end{Bmatrix}.$$

Compute the probability that $\min(X_1, X_2, X_3)$ exceeds the median.

5.4.5 Let X_t $(t = 1, 2, \ldots, T)$ be independent random variables each having a $N(\mu, \sigma^2)$ distribution. Suppose T is odd, that is, $T = 2k + 1$ for some positive integer k, and let Y denote the median of X_t $(t = 1, 2, \ldots, T)$. Show that the p.d.f. of Y is symmetric with respect to μ and that $E(Y) = \mu$.

5.4.6 Suppose X_t $(t = 1, 2, \ldots, T)$ are i.i.d $U[\theta, \theta + 1]$ given θ, where $-\infty < \theta < \infty$.

(a) Show: $R \sim B(T - 1, 2)$, where R is the sample range.

(b) Show that R is ancillary for θ.

5.4.7 Suppose X_t $(t = 1, 2, \ldots, T)$ are i.i.d. observations from a location-parameter family with c.d.f. $F(x - \theta)$, where $-\infty < \theta < \infty$. Show that the sample range R is ancillary for θ.

5.4.8 Let X_t $(t = 1, 2, \ldots, T)$ be a random sample from a uniform $U(\theta, 2\theta)$ distribution, where $\theta > 0$, and let Y_t $(t = 1, 2, \ldots, T)$ be the corresponding order statistics. Show that $W \equiv Y_T/Y_1$ is ancillary for θ (Basu 1992).

5.4.9 Consider Theorem 5.4.4. Suppose $y_1 < y_2$. Show: $\mathrm{Cov}[F_T(y_1), F_T(y_1)] = T^{-1}\{F(y_1)[1 - F(y_2)]\}$ (see Davidson and MacKinnon 1993, pp. 507–508).

5.5 Stochastic Convergence

If you need to use asymptotic arguments, do not forget to let the number of observations tend to infinity.
—Le Cam (1990, p.165)

Functions of the natural numbers (i.e., positive integers) are known as *sequences*. This section considers sequences of random variables: Z_1, $Z_2, \ldots, Z_T, \ldots$ For notational simplicity, such sequences are denoted $\{Z_T\}$. The nature of the elements in the sequence are left unspecified here.[5] The primary question of interest regarding such sequences is whether the elements are in any sense "converging" to a limit Z. The limit can be a random variable or a constant (i.e., a degenerate random variable). Determination of the rate of convergence of the sequence may lead to consideration of another sequence of the form $\{T^\delta Z_T\}$ for some scalar δ.

As with any limit analysis, a primary motivation here is the use of the limit Z, assuming it exists, as a proxy for terms far out in the sequence. In such instances it is important to keep in mind one point that is often easily forgotten: the limit is not of direct interest, rather its approximating role is of primary interest. In order to evaluate the quality of the limit as a tool of approximation, it is essential to identify the quantity being approximated. Many distinct sequences may have the same limit, but the quality of the limit in approximating Z_T for given T may be quite different across the sequences.

Before addressing sequences of random variables, we first review some basic concepts involving limits of sequences of constants.

Definition 5.5.1 Let $\{c_T\}$ be a sequence of constants. If there exists is a real number c such that for any positive real number ε, there exists a positive integer $\tau(\varepsilon)$ such that $|c_T - c| < \varepsilon$ for all $T > \tau(\varepsilon)$, then c is defined to be the *limit* of the sequence, and is denoted $c_T \to c$ or

$$c \equiv \operatorname*{Limit}_{T \to \infty} c_T, \tag{5.5.1}$$

If the elements in the sequence $\{c_T\}$ are vectors or matrices, then a vector or matrix is its limit iff every element in the latter is the limit of the corresponding element in the sequence.

In other words, the sequence $\{c_T\}$ has a limit iff for any degree of precision ε specifying "closeness" between sequence elements and the limit, it is possible to choose an element in the sequence (namely the τth element) beyond which all elements in the sequence are within a distance of ε of the limit. Limits of vectors (or matrices) of real numbers are defined in terms of the corresponding vectors (or matrices) of the component limits. The reader should be able to show the results in the following example.

5. For the reader seeking motivation and has some familiarity with estimation (Chapter 6), let $\hat{\theta}_T$ be an estimator of an unknown scalar parameter θ based on a sample of size T, and define $Z_T \equiv \hat{\theta}_T - \theta$. Then $\{Z_T\}$ comprises a sequence of sampling errors as sample size increases.

Example 5.5.1 Let $c_T = 5 + (2/T)$. Then $\{c_T\} \to 5$ as $T \to \infty$. On the other hand, the sequence $\{(-1)^T\}$ does *not* have a limit.

Given that a sequence possesses a limit, attention often focuses on a related sequence, and the question arises whether the latter sequence has a limit. Such a question is intimately related to the concept of a continuous function as is now defined.

Definition 5.5.2 Consider a function $g: \Re^K \to \Re^N$, and let $c \in \Re^K$. Then the function $g(\cdot)$ is *continuous at a point* c iff for any sequence $\{c_T\}$ such that $c_T \to c$, $g(c_T) \to g(c)$. Equivalently, $g(\cdot)$ is continuous at c iff for every $\varepsilon > 0$, there exists $\delta(\varepsilon, c) > 0$ such that if $b \in \Re^K$ and $|b_k - c_k| < \delta(\varepsilon, c)$ $(k = 1, 2, \ldots, K)$, then $|g_n(b) - g_n(c)| < \varepsilon$ $(n = 1, 2, \ldots, N)$. The function $g(\cdot)$ is *(pointwise) continuous over a set* C iff it is continuous at every point $c \in C$. Finally, the function $g(\cdot)$ is *uniformly continuous over the set* C iff for all $\varepsilon > 0$ and b, $c \in \Re^K$ there exists $\delta(\varepsilon) > 0$ such that if $|b_k - c_k| < \delta(\varepsilon)$ $(k = 1, 2, \ldots, K)$, then $|g_n(b) - g_n(c)| < \varepsilon$ $(n = 1, 2, \ldots, N)$.

Uniform continuity implies continuity on C, but not conversely. The important extra ingredient of uniform continuity is that δ depends only on ε, but *not* on c. If C is compact (i.e., closed and bounded), then continuity of $g(\cdot)$ on C implies $g(\cdot)$ is uniformly continuous on C (see Bartle 1976, p. 160).

To illustrate Definition 5.5.2, consider the following important application.

Example 5.5.2 Let M be a positive integer and define $K = M^2$. Let A be a $M \times M$ nonsingular matrix, and consider the function $g: \Re^K \to \Re^K$ defined by $g(A) = A^{-1}$. It can be shown that $g(\cdot)$ is continuous at every point in $\Re^K$ that represents a nonsingular matrix. Now consider a sequence $\{A_T\}$ of nonsingular matrices such that $A_T \to A$, where A is a nonsingular matrix. Then $\{A_T^{-1}\} \to A^{-1}$.

In assessing whether the limit of a sequence is a good indicator of terms far out in the sequence, it is helpful to have measures of the size of such terms. The following definition provides some useful measures.

Definition 5.5.3 Let k be a nonnegative scalar and $\{a_T\}$ a sequence of constants. $\{a_T\}$ is *at most of order* T^k, denoted $a_T = O(T^k)$, iff there exists a real number r such that

$$T^{-k}|a_T| \le r \tag{5.5.2}$$

for all T. $\{a_T\}$ is *of smaller order than* T^k, denoted $a_T = o(T^k)$, iff

$$\operatorname*{Limit}_{T \to \infty} T^{-k} a_T = 0. \tag{5.5.3}$$

Definition 5.5.3 extends to vectors and matrices by applying the conditions to every element in the relevant vector or matrix. For other extensions, see Spanos (1986, p. 196).

Note that if a_T is $O(T^0) = O(1)$, then a_T is eventually bounded (it may or may not have a limit). On the other hand if a_T is $o(1)$, then $a_T \to 0$. The following theorem provides means for assessing the order of sequences that are algebraic functions of component sequences.

Theorem 5.5.1 Suppose $a_T = O(T^k)$, $b_T = O(T^i)$, $c_T = o(T^j)$ and $d_T = o(T^m)$. Then each of the following hold:

(a) $a_T = o(T^{k+\delta})$, where $\delta > 0$.

(b) $a_T b_T = O(T^{k+i})$

(c) $c_T d_T = o(T^{j+m})$

(d) $|a_T|^s = O(T^{ks})$ for all $s > 0$.

(e) $|c_T|^s = o(T^{js})$ for all $s > 0$.

(f) $a_T + b_T = O(T^{\max\{k,i\}})$

(g) $c_T + d_T = o(T^{\max\{j,m\}})$

(h) $a_T c_T = o(T^{k+j})$

(i) $a_T + c_T = O(T^{\max\{k,j\}})$

Proof White (1984, p. 15).

With this background, we can now consider convergence of stochastic sequences. Although Definition 5.5.2 provides a clear cut meaning to the concept of convergence of a sequence of constants, the question of the convergence of a sequence of random variables is less straightforward. In fact there are many modes of convergence discussed in the statistics literature, and this section discusses four of the most important modes. For a discussion of other modes, see Lukacs (1975, pp. 50–57).

Definition 5.5.4 Let $\{Z_T\}$ denote a sequence of random variables (not necessarily i.i.d.), and let $\{F_T(\cdot)\}$ be the corresponding sequence of distribution functions. Also, let Z be a random variable (possibly degenerate) with distribution function $F(z)$.

(a) $\{Z_T\}$ *converges weakly in probability* (or simply *in probability*) to Z, denoted plim $Z_T = Z$ or $Z_T \xrightarrow{p} Z$, iff for every positive real number ε,

$$\operatorname*{Limit}_{T\to\infty} P(|Z_T - Z| > \varepsilon) = 0, \tag{5.5.4a}$$

or equivalently,

$$\operatorname*{Limit}_{T\to\infty} P(|Z_T - Z| \le \varepsilon) = 1. \tag{5.5.4b}$$

(b) $\{Z_T\}$ *converges strongly in probability* (also termed *convergence almost surely, convergence almost everywhere*, or *convergence with probability one*) to Z, denoted $Z_T \xrightarrow{a.s.} Z$, iff for every positive real number ε,

$$\operatorname*{Limit}_{T\to\infty} P\left(\bigcup_{\tau>T} |Z_\tau - Z| > \varepsilon\right) = 0, \tag{5.5.5a}$$

or equivalently,

$$\operatorname*{Limit}_{T\to\infty} P\left(\bigcap_{\tau>T} |Z_\tau - Z| \le \varepsilon\right) = 1. \tag{5.5.5b}$$

Lukacs (1975, pp. 28–30) shows that (5.5.5) can also be equivalently expressed as

$$P\left(\operatorname*{Limit}_{T\to\infty} Z_T = Z\right) = 1, \tag{5.5.5c}$$

where the limit inside (5.5.5c) implies that for all $\varepsilon > 0$ and any element $s \in \mathscr{S}$ of the relevant sample space (except perhaps for $s \in \mathscr{S}_0$, where $\mathscr{S}_0 \subseteq \mathscr{S}$ and $P(\mathscr{S}_0) = 0$), there exists $\tau = \tau(\varepsilon, s)$ such that $|Z_T(s) - Z(s)| < \varepsilon$ for all $T > \tau$.

(c) $\{Z_T\}$ *converges in rth moment* to Z, denoted $Z_T \xrightarrow{Lr} Z$, iff

$$\operatorname*{Limit}_{T\to\infty} E[|Z_T - Z|^r] = 0, \tag{5.5.6}$$

where it is assumed that the elements in the sequence and Z posses finite rth moments. The case $r = 2$ often occurs in practice and is termed *convergence in mean square*, and is denoted $Z_T \xrightarrow{m.s.} Z$.

(d) $\{Z_T\}$ *converges in distribution* (or *convergence in law*) to Z, denoted $Z_T \xrightarrow{d} Z$, iff

$$\operatorname*{Limit}_{T\to\infty} F_T(z) = F(z) \tag{5.5.7}$$

at all points z of continuity of $F(z)$. $F(\cdot)$ is the *limiting distribution* of Z_T.

It should be clear from Definition 5.5.1 that the different modes of convergence of a stochastic sequence $\{Z_T\}$ involve convergence of different characteristics of the sequence. Weak convergence involves convergence of a sequence of probabilities, convergence in rth moment involves convergence of a sequence of rth absolute moments, and convergence in distribution involves convergence of a sequence of distribution functions. Only strong convergence involves actual convergence of a sequence of random variables (see Equation 5.5.5c), that is, convergence of real-valued functions defined over the sample space. Let us consider some other differences in these convergence concepts.

According to weak convergence as given in (5.5.4b), for any given $\varepsilon > 0$ and $\delta > 0$, there exists an index τ such that for all $T > \tau$,

$$P[|Z_T - Z| \leq \varepsilon] > 1 - \delta. \tag{5.5.8}$$

In words, (5.5.8) implies that beyond a certain point τ in the sequence, any element Z_T is arbitrarily close (as determined by ε) to the limit Z with probability arbitrarily close (as determined by δ) to unity. In contrast, according to strong convergence as given in (5.5.5b), for any $\varepsilon > 0$ and $\delta > 0$, there exists an index τ such that

$$P[|Z_{\tau+1} - Z| \leq \varepsilon, |Z_{\tau+2} - Z| \leq \varepsilon, \ldots] > 1 - \delta. \tag{5.5.9}$$

Clearly, (5.5.9) is stronger than (5.5.8) since (5.5.9) implies the probability that all Z_T ($T > \tau$) are *simultaneously* within ε of Z is arbitrarily close to unity. In contrast (5.5.8) only involves the probability of a single event. Thus, (5.5.9) implies (5.5.8), but not conversely.[6]

To gain another perspective on strong convergence, consider the following. Random variables are real-valued functions defined on the sample space $\mathscr{S}$. Let $s \in \mathscr{S}$, and consider $Z_T(s)$ and $Z(s)$. According to Definition 5.5.4(b), $Z_T \xrightarrow{a.s.} Z$ if the functions $Z_t(s)$ converge to $Z(s)$ for all $s \in \mathscr{S}$, except perhaps for $s \in \mathscr{S}_0$, where $\mathscr{S}_0 \subseteq \mathscr{S}$ and $P(\mathscr{S}_0) = 0$. This is illustrated in the following simple example.

Example 5.5.3 (Casella and Berger 1990, p. 215) Consider the sample space $\mathscr{S} = [0, 1]$ and the uniform distribution over the unit interval, that is, $U[0, 1]$. Define the random variables $Z_T(s) = s + s^T$ and $Z(s) = s$. For every $s \in [0, 1)$, $s^T \to 0$ as $T \to \infty$, and $Z_T(s) \to Z(s)$. However, $Z_T(1) = 2$ for all T, and so $Z_T(1)$ does *not* converge to $Z(1) = 1$. But since $P(\mathscr{S}_0) = 0$ where $\mathscr{S}_0 = \{1\}$, Z_T converges "almost surely" to Z.

Similarly, convergence in mean square is also stronger than weak convergence. For simplicity, consider the case in which Z equals a constant c (see Exercise 5.5.3 for the case in which Z is a random variable). Writing

$$E[(Z_T - Z)^2] = \text{Var}(Z_T) + [E(Z_T) - c]^2, \tag{5.5.10}$$

it is clear that (5.5.6), for $Z = c$ and $\tau = 2$, implies

$$\text{Limit}_{T \to \infty} \text{Var}(Z_T) = 0, \tag{5.5.11}$$

6. It should be noted, however, that if $\{Z_T\}$ converges weakly in probability to Z, then there always exists a subsequence of $\{Z_T\}$, which converges strongly in probability to Z. For a proof, see Lukacs (1975, pp. 48–49). Strong convergence is the stochastic convergence concept most closely related to the concept of nonstochastic convergence in Definition 5.5.1.

$$\operatorname*{Limit}_{T\to\infty} E(Z_T) = c. \tag{5.5.12}$$

In words, (5.5.11) and (5.5.12) imply that beyond a point τ, the distribution of any element in the sequence is arbitrarily close to a degenerate distribution which has collapsed to a spike at c. Because, using Markov's inequality (2.8.1) we can deduce that

$$P[|Z_T - c| > \varepsilon] = P[|Z_T - c|^2 > \varepsilon^2] \leq \varepsilon^{-2}E[|Z_T - c|^2], \tag{5.5.13}$$

it follows immediately that convergence in mean square implies convergence in probability, but not conversely.

In general, without further assumptions no definite relationship holds between strong convergence and mean square convergence; however, these modes of convergence are compatible (see Lukacs 1975, p. 36). Under additional sufficient conditions, Rao (1973, p. 111) shows that mean square convergence implies strong convergence.

It is sometimes mistakenly believed that convergence in probability of Z_T to a constant c as $T \to \infty$ implies convergence of $E(Z_T)$ to c as $T \to \infty$. To see that this is *not* the case, consider the following example. Also see Exercise 5.5.8.

Example 5.5.4 Let $\{Z_T\}$ be a sequence of univariate random variables such that $P(Z_T = c) = 1 - T^{-1}$ and $P(Z_T = T) = T^{-1}$. Clearly, as $T \to \infty$, $Z_T \xrightarrow{p} c$. However, because $E(Z_T) = c(1 - T^{-1}) + T(T^{-1}) = c + cT^{-1} + 1$, it is clear that $E(Z_T) \to c + 1$ as $T \to \infty$. In addition, since $E[(Z_T - c)^2] = T^{-1}(T - c)^2$, it follows that $E[(Z_T - c)^2] \to \infty$ as $T \to \infty$. Thus this example also illustrates that convergence in probability does *not* imply convergence in mean square.

The mistaken belief above is predicated on the belief that $Z_T \xrightarrow{p} c$ implies the distribution of Z_T is "collapsing" on c as $T \to \infty$, and hence c must be the limit of the expected values. This of course is not true. $E(Z_T)$ is a weighted sum (in the discrete case) of the values taken by Z_T, with the weights being the corresponding probabilities. While $Z_T \xrightarrow{p} c$ implies that the sum of probability weights lying outside an arbitrarily small neighborhood of c tend to zero as $T \to \infty$, this implies nothing about the sum of products of these weights and values taken by Z_T. The following theorem provides an additional condition that guarantees the desired result.

Theorem 5.5.2 Let $\{Z_T\}$ be a sequence of random variables such that Z_T converges to Z in rth moment. If $0 < s < r$, then Z_T converges to Z in the sth moment. In particular if $r > 1$ and $s = 1$, then

$$\operatorname*{Limit}_{T\to\infty} E(Z_T) = \operatorname*{plim}_{T\to\infty} Z_T = Z. \tag{5.5.14}$$

Proof Lukacs (1975, p. 34).

Convergence in distribution is very different than the other forms of stochastic convergence. Recall that for convergence in distribution, it is the sequence of cumulative distribution functions, not the random variables themselves, which is converging to something. For example, any i.i.d. sequence converges in distribution to a random variable with the common distribution function. Convergence in distribution is the weakest form of convergence in the sense that it is implied by the three other modes of convergence. In particular $Z_T \xrightarrow{p} Z$ implies $Z_T \xrightarrow{d} Z$ (Rao 1973, p. 122), and by earlier arguments, strong convergence and mean square convergence must also imply convergence in distribution since they both imply weak convergence. In general, $Z_T \xrightarrow{d} Z$ does *not* imply $Z_T \xrightarrow{p} Z$ as the following example shows. In fact, $Z_T \xrightarrow{d} Z$ is defined on $\Re$, whereas $Z_T \xrightarrow{p} Z$ refers to random variables defined over sample spaces. If Z is a constant, however, then convergence in distribution and weak convergence both hold (see Exercise 5.5.11).

Example 5.5.5 (Lukacs 1975, p. 37) Let Z be a Bernoulli random variable that takes on the values 0 and 1 each with probability $\frac{1}{2}$. Define $Z_T = 1 - Z$ for all $T > 0$. Since all the Z_T, and also Z, have the same distribution, it is obvious that Z_T converges in distribution to Z as $T \to \infty$. But since $|Z_T - Z| = |1 - 2Z| = 1$ regardless of the value of Z, it is clear that (5.5.4) cannot be satisfied, and hence that Z_T does *not* converge in probability to Z.

Convergence "weakly in probability" and "almost surely" will serve as the modes of convergence relevant to the laws of large numbers discussed in Section 5.6. Convergence "in distribution" is the relevant mode of convergence for the central limit theorem discussed in Section 5.7.

Before introducing new material, the relationships among the various modes of convergence are summarized in the following theorem and Figure 5.5.1.

Theorem 5.5.3 Consider a sequence $\{Z_T\}$ of random variables.

(a) $Z_T \xrightarrow{a.s.} Z$ implies $Z_T \xrightarrow{p} Z$.

(b) $Z_T \xrightarrow{m.s.} Z$ implies $Z_T \xrightarrow{p} Z$.

(c) $Z_T \xrightarrow{p} Z$ implies $Z_T \xrightarrow{d} Z$.

(d) $Z_T \xrightarrow{L_s} Z$ implies $Z_T \xrightarrow{L_r} Z$, provided $s > r$.

Proof Lukacs (1975, pp. 33–34).

The behavior of *continuous* functions of sequences that converge weakly, strongly, or in distribution is analogous to the nonstochastic case.

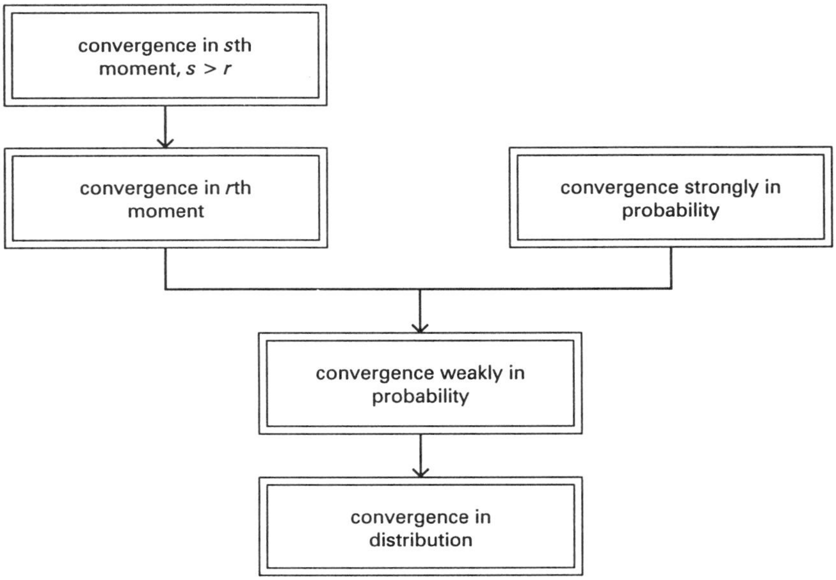

Figure 5.5.1
Relationships among modes of convergence

The following theorem states the precise results. Since existence of moments is not guaranteed when taking continuous functions of random variables, no general result is available for convergence in rth moment.

Theorem 5.5.4 Consider the function g: $\mathfrak{R}^K \to \mathfrak{R}^N$ such that $g(\cdot)$ is continuous and $g(\cdot)$ is a fixed function not depending on T. Let $\{Z_T\}$ be a sequence of random variables.

(a) $Z_T \xrightarrow{a.s.} Z$ implies $g(Z_T) \xrightarrow{a.s.} g(Z)$.

(b) $Z_T \xrightarrow{p} Z$ implies $g(Z_T) \xrightarrow{p} g(Z)$.

(c) $Z_T \xrightarrow{d} Z$ implies $g(Z_T) \xrightarrow{d} g(Z)$.

Proof Note: some weakening of the continuity requirement is possible.

(a) White (1984, p. 17),

(b) White (1984, p. 23–24),

(c) Mann and Wald (1943).

Another theorem of considerable importance is the following.

Theorem 5.5.5 (Helly-Bray) Let $\{F_T(\cdot)\}$ be a sequence of distribution functions converging to the distribution function $F(\cdot)$, and let $g(\cdot)$ be a *bounded continuous* function. Then

$$\underset{T\to\infty}{\text{Limit}} \int_{-\infty}^{\infty} g(z_T)dF_T(z_T) = \int_{-\infty}^{\infty} g(z)dF(z). \tag{5.5.15}$$

Proof Rao (1973, pp. 117–118).

Econometrics often deals with estimators in which limits of sequences of moments and moments of the limiting distribution do *not* coincide. In fact, often the former do not even exist! The Helly-Bray Theorem, in general, is *not* sufficient to deal with such problems because the function $g(\cdot)$ is not bounded in such cases. Of course, if the random variable Z has a finite range, then Theorem 5.5.5 implies in such cases that small sample moments always converge to the moments of the limiting distribution.

Similarly, when $g(Z_T) = \exp(vZ_T)$ and $v \in \Re$, the Helly-Bray Theorem cannot be used to say that the sequence of moment generating functions converges to the moment generating function of the limiting distribution. Indeed the latter need not exist. Because the characteristic function is bounded (see Hogg and Craig 1978, p. 54), however, the Helly-Bray Theorem can be used to show the following convergence results.

Theorem 5.5.6 (Continuity Theorem) Consider a sequence $\{Z_T\}$ of random variables with characteristic functions $\{c_T(v)\}$. If $Z_T \overset{d}{\to} Z$, then $\{c_T(v)\} \to c(v)$, where $c(v)$ is the characteristic function of Z. If $\{c_T(v)\} \to c(v)$ and $c(v)$ is continuous at $v = 0$, then $Z_T \overset{d}{\to} Z$.

Proof Pollock (1979, pp. 330–331).

In the case where convergence in rth moment occurs, then the following theorem is of interest.

Theorem 5.5.7 Consider a sequence $\{Z_T\}$ converges in distribution to a random variable Z. Suppose the sth absolute moment of Z exists. If $\{Z_T\}$ converges in sth moment to Z, then the rth absolute moment of Z_T exists for $0 \le r \le s$, and

$$\underset{T\to\infty}{\text{Limit}}\, E[|Z_T|^r] = E[|Z|^r], \quad 0 < r \le s. \tag{5.5.16}$$

Proof Dhrymes (1974, p. 97).

It should be realized that unless the limiting distribution F has a finite rth absolute moment, then (5.5.16) does *not* guarantee that the rth absolute moment of F_t exists. A counter example is provided by Exercise 5.5.5(c).

In general there is no correspondence between the existence of moments of members of a sequence $Z_T \overset{d}{\to} Z$ and moments of the limiting random variable Z (known as *asymptotic moments*). The following result, however, holds. For further discussion, see Serfling (1980).

Theorem 5.5.8 Suppose $E(Z_T)$ and $\text{Var}(Z_T)$ exist, and $Z_T \xrightarrow{d} Z$. Then:

(a) $\underset{T\to\infty}{\text{Limit}} \{\inf E[|Z_T|]\} \geq E[|Z|]$

(b) $\underset{T\to\infty}{\text{Limit}} \{\inf \text{Var}(Z_t)\} \geq \text{Var}(Z)$

Proof Chung (1974).

The following three theorems prove useful in practice.

Theorem 5.5.9 (Glivenko-Cantelli) The empirical distribution function (see Definition 5.4.3) $F_T^*(y)$ converges uniformly to $F(y)$, that is,

$$\underset{T\to\infty}{\text{Limit}}\, P\left(\sup_{-\infty<y<\infty} |F_T^*(y) - F(y)| > \varepsilon\right) = 0. \tag{5.5.17}$$

Proof See Loéve (1963, pp. 20–21).

Theorem 5.5.10 Let $\{X_T\}$ and $\{Y_T\}$ be sequences of random variables.

(a) Suppose $X_T \xrightarrow{d} X$ and $Y_T \xrightarrow{p} c$, where c is a constant. Then

(1) $X_T + Y_T \xrightarrow{d} X + c$,

(2) $X_T Y_T \xrightarrow{d} cX$,

(3) $X_T/Y_T \xrightarrow{d} X/c$ (provided $c \neq 0$).

(b) Suppose $X_T \xrightarrow{d} X$ and $Y_T \xrightarrow{p} 0$. Then $X_T Y_T \xrightarrow{p} 0$.

(c) Suppose $X_T - Y_T \xrightarrow{p} 0$ and $X_T \xrightarrow{d} X$. Then $Y_T \xrightarrow{d} X$.

Proof Rao (1973, pp. 122–123).

Theorem 5.5.10(a) or Theorem 5.5.4(b) are commonly called *Slutsky's Theorem*. Note that in the case $c = 0$, part (b) of Theorem 5.5.10 is more powerful than part (a), subpart (2). The following important generalization of Theorem 5.5.10 holds in the case of rational functions of X_T and Y_T.

Theorem 5.5.11 If $g(\cdot)$ is a rational function, plim $Y_{ti} = \alpha_i$ $(i = 1, 2, \ldots, J)$, and $X_{tk} \xrightarrow{d} X_k$ $(k = 1, 2, \ldots, K)$, then the limiting distribution of $g(X_{t1}, \ldots, X_{tK}, Y_{t1}, \ldots, Y_{tJ})$ is the same as the distribution of $g(X_1, \ldots, X_K, \alpha_1, \ldots, \alpha_J)$.

Proof Follows from repeated application of Theorem 5.5.10. See Amemiya (1985, p. 89).

The concept of "order" of a sequence, given in Definition 5.5.3 for nonstochastic sequences, can be generalized to the case of stochastic sequences (see Mann and Wald 1943). We will do so here for convergence in probability. For extension to "order almost surely" see White (1984, pp. 21–22).

Definition 5.5.5 Let k be a nonnegative scalar and $\{Z_T\}$ a sequence of random variables. $\{Z_T\}$ is *at most of order T^k in probability*, denoted $Z_T = O_p(T^k)$, iff for every $\varepsilon > 0$ there exists a real number r such that

$$P(T^{-k}|Z_T| \geq r) \leq \varepsilon \tag{5.5.18}$$

for all T. $\{Z_T\}$ is *of smaller order in probability than T^k*, denoted $Z_T = o_p(T^k)$, iff

$$\text{plim}(T^{-k}Z_T) = 0. \tag{5.5.19}$$

As before these definitions extend to vectors and matrices by applying the conditions to every element in the relevant vector or matrix.

Note that Theorem 5.5.1 generalizes directly to cover O_p and o_p. For completeness we repeat it here again in the present context.

Theorem 5.5.12 Suppose $W_T = O_p(T^k)$, $X_T = O_p(T^i)$, $Y_T = o_p(T^j)$ and $Z_T = o_p(T^m)$. Then each of the following hold:

(a) $W_T = o_p(T^{k+\delta})$, where $\delta > 0$.

(b) $W_T X_T = O_p(T^{k+i})$.

(c) $Y_T Z_T = o_p(T^{j+m})$.

(d) $|W_T|^s = O_p(T^{ks})$ for all $s > 0$.

(e) $|Y_T|^s = o_p(T^{js})$ for all $s > 0$.

(f) $W_T + X_T = O_p(T^{\max\{k,i\}})$.

(g) $Y_T + Z_T = o_p(T^{\max\{j,m\}})$.

(h) $W_T Y_T = o_p(T^{k+j})$.

(i) $W_T + Y_T = O_p(T^{\max\{k,j\}})$.

Proof Left to the reader.

The following theorem connects convergence in distribution with the order in probability concept.

Theorem 5.5.13 If $Z_T \xrightarrow{d} Z$, then $Z_T = O_p(1)$.

Proof White (1984, p. 63).

Later in Section 6.6 it will be convenient to employ a slightly stronger mode of convergence that has been discussed so far. Therefore, we introduce the following two extensions of the concepts of convergence in probability and almost sure convergence.

Definition 5.5.6 Consider a sequence $\{X_T(\theta)\}$ of random variables depending on a parameter vector $\theta \in \Theta$. Let $X(\theta)$ be the candidate limit, which may or may not be a random variable.

(a) $\{X_T(\theta)\}$ converges *uniformly in probability* to $X(\theta)$ as $T \to \infty$

iff

$$\underset{T\to\infty}{\text{Limit}}\ \text{Prob}\left[\sup_{\theta\in\Theta}|X_T(\theta) - X(\theta)| < \varepsilon\right] = 1, \qquad \text{for all } \varepsilon > 0. \tag{5.5.20}$$

(b) $\{X_T(\theta)\}$ converges *almost surely uniformly* to $X(\theta)$ as $T \to \infty$ iff

$$\text{Prob}\left[\underset{T\to\infty}{\text{Limit}}\ \sup_{\theta\in\Theta}|X_T(\theta) - X(\theta)| < \varepsilon\right] = 1, \qquad \text{for all } \varepsilon > 0. \tag{5.5.21}$$

It is straightforward to show that (b) implies (a), but not conversely. Amemiya (1985, p. 106) provides an example demonstrating that the converse fails. Uniform stochastic convergence proves valuable in demonstrating that extremal estimators are "consistent" (see Section 6.6). Sufficient conditions for the maximum of a limit to be the limit of the maximum are that the convergence is uniform in the sense of (a) or (b) and that θ is compact. For connections between uniform convergence in probability and *stochastic continuity*, see Newey and McFadden (1993, Section 2.8).

For purposes of convenience, the discussion of this section has been in terms of univariate random variables. All definitions and theorems, however, extend straightforwardly to vectors of random variables provided the vectors are of finite fixed dimension, and provided $|Z_T - Z|$ is interpreted as Euclidean distance rather than absolute value. For further discussion of stochastic convergence, see Dhrymes (1989, Chapters 3 and 4).

Exercises

5.5.1 Let $\{Z_T\}$ be a sequence of random variables such that $P(Z_T = 0) = 1 - T^{-1}$ and $P(Z_T = T^2) = T^{-1}$.

(a) Find plim Z_T.

(b) $\text{Limit}_{T\to\infty} E(Z_T)$.

5.5.2 Suppose $X \sim N(0, \sigma^2)$ and consider the sequence $\{Z_T\}$ of random variables, each independent of X, where $P(Z_T = 0) = 1 - T^{-1}$ and $P(Z_T = T) = T^{-1}$. Define $Y_T = X + Z_T$.

(a) Find $E(Y_T)$.

(b) Find $\text{Limit}_{T\to\infty} E(Y_T)$.

(c) Find $E(Y_T^2)$.

(d) Find $\text{Limit}_{T\to\infty} E(Y_T^2)$.

(e) Find plim Y_T.

5.5.3 Suppose $X \sim N(0, \sigma^2)$ and consider the sequence $\{Z_T\}$ of random variables, each independent of X, where $P(Z_T = 1) = 1 - T^{-1}$ and $P(Z_T = 0) = T^{-1}$. Define $Y_T = X + Z_T^{-1}$.

(a) Find plim Z_T^{-1}.

(b) Find $E(Y_T^2)$.

(c) Find plim Y_T.

5.5.4 Let $c \neq 0$ be a constant. Consider the sequence $\{Z_T\}$ of random variables where $P(Z_T = 0) = 1 - T^{-1}$ and $P(Z_T = cT) = T^{-1}$. Define $Y_T = X + Z_T^{-1}$.

(a) Find $E(Z_T^2)$.

(b) Find plim Z_T.

5.5.5 Suppose X has a Cauchy distribution. Let $\overline{Y}_T$ be the sample mean of a random sample of size T from a population with mean zero and finite variance σ^2. Define $Z_T = X + \overline{Y}_T$ and consider the sequence $\{Z_T\}$.

(a) Find $E(Z_T)$.

(b) Find $E(Z_T^2)$.

(c) Find plim Z_T.

5.5.6 Let $\{Z_T\}$ be i.i.d. random variables such that (see Lukacs 1975, pp. 34–35):

$$P(Z_T = j) = \begin{Bmatrix} \frac{1}{2}T^{-1/4}, & \text{if } j = -1, 1 \\ 1 - T^{-1/4}, & \text{if } j = 0 \\ 0, & \text{otherwise} \end{Bmatrix}.$$

(a) Use this sequence to show mean-square convergence does not imply almost sure convergence.

(b) Use this sequence to show weak convergence in probability does not imply strong convergence.

5.5.7 Let $\{Z_T\}$ be i.i.d. random variables such that (see Lukacs 1975, p. 36):

$$P(Z_T = j) = \begin{Bmatrix} \frac{1}{2}T^{2}, & \text{if } j = -T^{2/r} \text{ or } j = T^{2/r} \\ 1 - T^{-2}, & \text{if } j = 0 \\ 0, & \text{otherwise} \end{Bmatrix}.$$

(a) Use this sequence to show that Z_T converges to zero almost surely, but not in rth moment.

(b) Use this sequence to show Z_T converges to zero in probability but not in rth moment.

5.5.8 Let $\{Z_T\}$ be i.i.d. random variables such that (see Lukacs 1975, p. 41)

$$P(Z_T = j) = \begin{Bmatrix} \dfrac{1}{T+4}, & \text{if } j = -(T+4) \\ 1 - \left(\dfrac{4}{T+4}\right), & \text{if } j = -1 \\ \dfrac{3}{T+4}, & \text{if } j = T+4 \\ 0, & \text{otherwise} \end{Bmatrix}$$

(a) Show: plim $Z_T = -1$.

(b) Show: $\text{Limit}_{T\to\infty} E(Z_T) = 1$.

5.5.9 Let X, Y and Z be mutually independent scalar random variables such that

$P(X = 1) = \alpha$, $P(X = 0) = 1 - \alpha$, $0 < \alpha < 1$,

$P(Y = 1) = P(X = 0) = \frac{1}{2}$,

and $Z \sim U[-\frac{1}{2}, \frac{1}{2}]$. Consider the sequence $\{W_T\}$, where

$$W_T = TXY + \frac{(1 - X)Z}{T} \qquad (T = 1, 2, 3, \ldots).$$

Discuss the limiting behavior of $\{W_T\}$ as $T \to \infty$. (see Dhrymes 1974, p. 91).

5.5.10 In cases where all the required moment generating functions exist, Theorem 5.5.7 implies that the limiting distribution of a sequence can be derived from the limit of the moment generating functions. Show the following.

(a) Let $Y_T \sim B(T, \theta)$ and suppose that $\lambda = T\theta$ is constant for all T. Show that the limiting distribution of Y_T as T is a Poisson distribution with parameter λ. (Note: This proves Theorem 3.2.12.)

(b) Let $X_T \sim \chi^2(T)$ and define $Y_T = (X_T - T)/(2T)^{1/2}$. Show that the limiting distribution of Y_T as $T \to \infty$ is $N(0, 1)$.

5.5.11 Show: if $Z_T \xrightarrow{d} c$, where c is a constant, then $Z_T \xrightarrow{p} c$. (see Dhrymes 1989, pp. 262–263).

5.5.12 Suppose $X_T \xrightarrow{m.s.} X$ and $Y_T \xrightarrow{m.s.} Y$. Show:

$\text{Limit}_{T \to \infty} E(X_T Y_T) = E(XY)$.

5.5.13 Let $Y \sim B(T, \theta)$. Using the normal approximation to the binomial distribution, prove that for any $\varepsilon < \infty$, $\text{Limit}_{T \to \infty} P(|Y - T\theta| > c) = 1$. Interpret this result.

5.5.14 Show the following:

(a) If $\text{Var}(Z_T) \equiv \sigma_T^2 < \infty$, then $(Z_T/\sigma_T) = O_p(1)$.

(b) $Z_T = O_p(T^{-1/2})$ implies $Z_T = o_p(1)$.

(c) $Z_T \xrightarrow{d} Z$ implies $Z_T + o_p(1) \xrightarrow{d} Z$.

5.5.15 Let Y be a random variable such that $E[|Y|^r] < \infty$ for some $r > 0$. Show: $P(|Y| \geq y) = o(y^{-r})$ (Serfling 1980).

5.5.16 Consider Exercise 5.4.9. Show: $F_T(y_2) - F_T(y_1)$ converges in mean-square to $F(y_2) - F(y_1)$.

5.5.17 Show each of the following.

(a) The sum and difference of uniformly continuous functions are uniformly continuous.

(b) If a uniformly continuous function is multiplied by a constant, then the resulting function is uniformly continuous.

(c) The product of uniformly continuous functions over closed *bounded* sets is uniformly continuous.

(d) Show that the "bounded" requirement in (c) is important by considering $g(x) = x$ over $\Re$, that is, show $g(x)$ is uniformly continuous, but $h(x) = [g(x)]^2 = x^2$ is *not* uniformly continuous.

5.6 Laws of Large Numbers

The concepts of weak and strong convergence in probability introduced in Section 5.5 will now be used to determine the asymptotic behavior of particular functions of sums of random variables. We begin by defining what is meant by the laws of large numbers.

Definition 5.6.1 Let $\{Y_T\}$ be a sequence of random variables with finite means (not necessarily identical) arranged in the sequence $\{\mu_T\}$, where $\mu_T \equiv E(Y_T)$. Define

$$\overline{Y}_T = \frac{1}{T} \sum_{t=1}^{T} Y_t, \tag{5.6.1}$$

$$\bar{\mu}_T = \frac{1}{T}\sum_{t=1}^{T} \mu_t. \tag{5.6.2}$$

$\overline{Y}_T$ obeys the *weak law of large numbers (WLLN)* iff $\overline{Y}_T - \bar{\mu}_T \xrightarrow{p} 0$. $\overline{Y}_T$ obeys the *strong law of large numbers (SLLN)* iff $\overline{Y}_T - \bar{\mu}_T \xrightarrow{a.s.} 0$.

The laws of large numbers capture the essential basics for the frequentist concept of probability. This is most easily (but not necessarily) discussed in terms of the case where the $\overline{Y}_T$'s are Bernoulli random variables with common mean (i.e., probability of a "success") μ. In this case $\bar{\mu}_T = \mu$ and $\overline{Y}_T$ constitutes the relative frequency of successes in T trials. The laws of large numbers assert the existence of a limiting relative frequency μ that is interpreted as the "probability of a success."

In determining the circumstances under which the WLLN and SLLN hold, we begin with the simplest case, namely, that of a random sample. This case represents the ideal situation of replication for interpreting "probability" in a frequentist sense. The following theorem, due to Kolmogorov, fully characterizes this case.

Theorem 5.6.1 (Kolmogorov) Let $\{Y_T\}$ be a sequence of i.i.d. random variables. Then a necessary and sufficient condition that $\overline{Y}_T \xrightarrow{a.s.} \mu$ is $E(Y_T)$ exists and is equal to μ.

Proof Rao (1973, pp. 115–116).

Because almost sure convergence implies convergence in probability, Theorem 5.6.1 implies that both the SLLN and the WLLN hold in the case of i.i.d. random variables. As we depart from the i.i.d. case, restrictions on the degree of heterogeneity and/or dependence in the sequence are introduced in order for a WLLN or a SLLN to survive.

Consider first the case of a WLLN with some heterogeneity permitted.

Theorem 5.6.2 (Chebyshev) Let $\{Y_T\}$ be a sequence of random variables with associated sequences of means $\{\mu_T\}$ and variances $\{\sigma_T^2\}$ assumed to exist. Further suppose:

(a) $\operatorname{Cov}(Y_t, Y_s) = 0$ for all $t \neq s$.

(b) $\displaystyle\operatorname*{Limit}_{T\to\infty} \frac{1}{T^2}\sum_{t=1}^{T} \sigma_t^2 = 0$.

Then $\overline{Y}_T - \bar{\mu}_T \xrightarrow{p} 0$.

Proof Using Chebyshev's Inequality (Corollary to Theorem 2.8.1), simply note

$$P(|\overline{Y}_T - \bar{\mu}_T| > \varepsilon) \leq \frac{1}{T^2\varepsilon^2}\sum_{t=1}^{T} \sigma_t^2 \to 0.$$

Therefore, $\overline{Y}_T - \bar{\mu}_T \xrightarrow{p} 0$.

Theorem 5.6.2 is more general than Theorem 5.6.1 in the sense that it does not require the elements in $\{Y_T\}$ to be independent (but rather only uncorrelated) nor that they be identically distributed (in particular they may have different means). On the other hand Theorem 5.6.2 is more restrictive than Theorem 5.6.1 in that it requires variances to exist and to satisfy (b) of Theorem 5.6.2.

Of course the mode of convergence in Theorem 5.6.2 is weaker than that of Theorem 5.6.1. The following theorem gives conditions under which the SLLN holds for i.n.i.d. sequences.

Theorem 5.6.3 (Markov) Let $\{Y_T\}$ be a sequence of independent random variables with finite means $\{\mu_T\}$. Suppose $E[|Y_T - \mu_T|^{1+\delta}]$ exists for all T for some $\delta > 0$, and

(a) the elements in $\{Y_T\}$ are independent,

(b) $\underset{T\to\infty}{\text{Limit}} \sum_{t=1}^{T} t^{-(1+\delta)}E[|Y_t - \mu_t|^{1+\delta}] < \infty$ (Markov condition).

Then $\overline{Y}_T - \mu_T \xrightarrow{a.s.} 0$.

Proof Chung (1974, pp. 125–126).

When $\delta = 1$, Theorem 5.6.3 corresponds to the case studied by Kolmogorov (see Rao 1973, p. 114). In this case, the independence condition can be weakened to that of uncorrelatedness as in Theorem 5.6.2 provided condition (b) of Theorem 5.6.3 is suitably strengthened (see Rao 1973, p. 114, eq. [2c.3.10]).

Further discussion of laws of large numbers for sequences of correlated and heterogeneous elements will not be pursued here. The reason is simple. It is a matter of complexity; numerous mathematically demanding concepts must be introduced (e.g., stochastic processes, martingales, mixing processes) in order to handle dependency. The scope of this text does not require extensive use of limiting behavior of dependent stochastic sequences. Readers interested in laws of large numbers for the n.i.i.d. and n.i.n.i.d. cases are urged to consult an advanced probability text. Good discussions intended for econometrics audiences are contained in Andrews (1988), Dhrymes (1989, Chapter 5), Hamilton (1994), Spanos (1986, pp. 168–173), and White (1984, pp. 36–60).

5.7 Central Limit Theorems

In this section we are concerned with the convergence of sequences of sample moments (and functions thereof) standardized by sample size in such a way so that the sequences converge in distribution to nondegenerate random variables. Such convergence is described by various *central limit theorems (CLTs)* that extend the preceding limit theorems by investigating the rate of convergence. These theorems explain in part the central role played by the normal distribution in statistics.[7]

We begin with the most familiar CLT.

Theorem 5.7.1 (Lindeberg-Levy CLT) Let $\{Y_T\}$ be a sequence of i.i.d. random variables with mean μ and variance $\sigma^2 > 0$. Consider the sequence $\{Z_T\}$, where

$$Z_T = \frac{T^{1/2}(\overline{Y}_T - \mu)}{\sigma}, \tag{5.7.1}$$

and $\overline{Y}_T$ is the sample mean defined by (5.6.2). Then $Z_T \xrightarrow{d} Z$, where $Z \sim N(0, 1)$.

Proof Elementary proofs based on moment generating functions (when they exist) are given in Hogg and Craig (1978, pp. 193–194) and Mood et al. (1974, pp. 234–235). A more general proof involving characteristic functions, and based on Theorem 5.5.6, is given by Amemiya (1985, pp. 91–92).

Speaking loosely, Theorem 5.7.1 is often expressed: The asymptotic distribution as $T \to \infty$ of the sample mean of a random sample of size T from any population with finite mean and positive finite variance is $N(\mu, \sigma^2/T)$. As $T \to \infty$, $\overline{Y}_T - \mu$ is converging to zero and $T^{1/2}$ is approaching infinity. Each is approaching its respective limit at the same rate so that their product approaches in the limit a nondegenerate random variable. By standardizing $\overline{Y}_T$ in (5.7.1) we are able to say something about the distribution of $\overline{Y}_T$ as it approaches a degenerate distribution by studying the nondegenerate limiting distribution of Z_T.

Note that given that the sample is random, the only restrictions Theorem 5.7.1 puts on the underlying distribution are that μ and $\sigma^2 > 0$ exist. Otherwise, this underlying distribution may be discrete or continuous, symmetric or skewed, or anything else. Not surprisingly the "more nearly" normal are the Y_ts, the closer is Z_T to normality for small T. The approximation is often surprisingly good, however, for fairly small sample sizes. The following example illustrates his latter point.

Example 5.7.1 (Wonnacott and Wonnacott 1980) Consider Figure 5.7.1. Reading from left to right in the first row, the first two columns display uniform discrete probability mass functions with three and six elements, respectively. The right-hand graph depicts a nonuniform discrete probability mass function with three elements. Reading down each of the three

7. "Robustnic" statisticians are fond of pointing out common cases when the conditions of these theorems are not satisfied, and thus when appeals to normality are inappropriate. Their main point can be put quite succinctly: there is nothing "normal" about the normal distribution. To emphasize this belief, they often use the less familiar term "Gaussian."

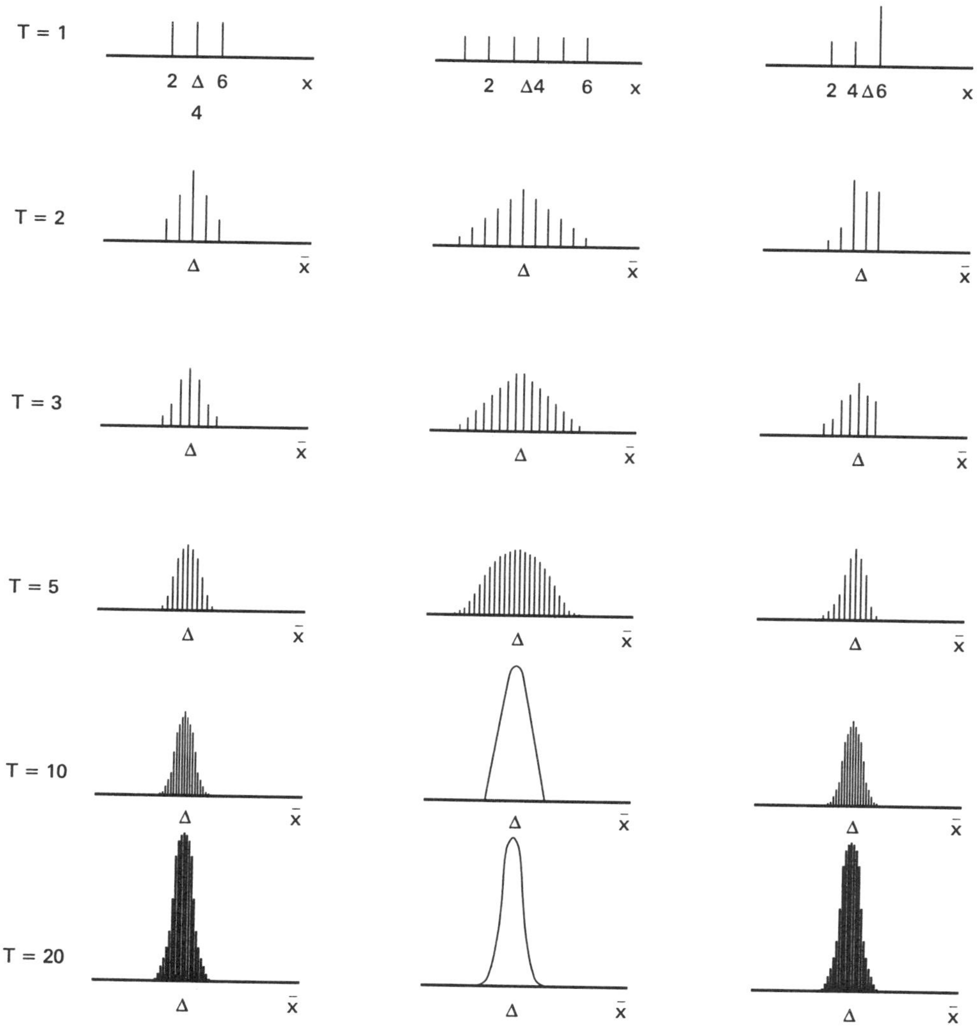

Figure 5.7.1
Three examples of probability functions of $\overline{Y}_T$

columns, the probability mass functions of sample means based on sample sizes of $T = 2, 3, 5, 10$, and 20, respectively, are displayed. A fairly reasonable degree of normality is obtained with a sample size $T = 10$, and certainly, in the case $T = 20$.

Example 5.7.1, however, should *not* be interpreted as illustrative of all possible cases. For example, if a random sample is drawn from an underlying Cauchy distribution (recall Theorem 5.3.6), then the Lindeberg-Levy CLT does not apply because μ does not exist.

Often attention focuses not just on the sample mean, but also on functions of the sample mean. Under the appropriate conditions, the following theorem can be applied in such cases.

Theorem 5.7.2 Let $\{Y_T\}$ be a sequence of i.i.d. random variables with finite mean μ and variance σ^2. Let $g(\cdot)$ be a function possessing continuous derivatives of order $n \geq 2$. Then the sequence $\{Z_T\}$, where

$$Z_T = T^{1/2}[g(\overline{Y}_T) - g(\mu)] \tag{5.7.2}$$

converges to $Z \sim N(0, \sigma^2[g'(\mu)]^2)$ provided the derivative $g'(\mu) \neq 0$.

Proof Consider a nth order Taylor series expansion of $g(\cdot)$ around μ, evaluated at $\overline{Y}_T$:

$$g(\overline{Y}_T) = g(\mu) + \sum_{m=1}^{n+1} \frac{1}{m!}\left[\frac{\partial^m g(\mu)}{\partial \overline{Y}_T}\right](\overline{Y} - \mu)^m + \frac{1}{n!}\left[\frac{\partial^n g(\xi)}{\partial \overline{Y}_T}\right](\overline{Y}_T - \mu)^n,$$

where ξ is a point on the interior of the line segment joining $\overline{Y}_T$ and μ. For $n = 1$ this expansion reduces to simply

$$g(\overline{Y}_T) = g(\mu) + g'(\xi)(\overline{Y}_T - \mu). \tag{5.7.3}$$

Thus (5.7.2) equals

$$Z_T = g'(\xi)T^{1/2}(\overline{Y}_T - \mu). \tag{5.7.4}$$

According to Theorem 5.7.1 $T^{1/2}(\overline{Y}_T - \mu)$ converges to a random variable distributed as $N(0, \sigma^2)$. Because $g'(\cdot)$ is continuous and $|\xi - \mu| \leq |\overline{Y}_T - \mu|$, it follows from Theorem 5.5.4(b) that $g'(\xi) \xrightarrow{p} g(\mu)$. Hence, Theorem 5.5.10(a2) implies that Z_T converges to $Z \sim N(0, \sigma^2[g'(\mu)]^2)$.

Example 5.7.2 Let $\{Y_T\}$ be a sequence of i.i.d. random variables from a distribution with finite mean $\mu \neq 0$, finite variance σ^2, and density $f(\cdot)$ with $f(0) > 0$. Let $g(\overline{Y}_T) = 1/\overline{Y}_T$. Then according to Theorem 5.7.2, $T^{1/2}/\overline{Y}_T$ converges to a $N(\mu^{-1}, \sigma^2\mu^{-4})$ random variable as $T \to \infty$. Note that $T^{1/2}/\overline{Y}_T$ has no finite moments for any finite value of T since there is always a positive probability that $\overline{Y}_T$ falls in an open interval around zero.

As with laws of large numbers, the assumptions of Theorem 5.7.1 can be altered to permit i.n.i.d. observations. The following well known theorem provides one such modification of the Lindeberg-Levy CLT (Theorem 5.7.1).

Theorem 5.7.3 (Lindeberg-Feller CLT) Let $\{Y_T\}$ be a sequence of independent random variables with corresponding cumulative distribution functions $\{F_T(\cdot)\}$. Suppose $E(Y_T) = \mu_T$ and $0 < \text{Var}(Y_T) \equiv \sigma_T^2 < r$ for finite r $(T = 1, 2, \ldots)$. Let

$$Z_T = D_T^{-1} \sum_{t=1}^{T} (Y_t - \mu_t) = \frac{\overline{Y}_T - \overline{\mu}_T}{T^{-1} D_T}, \tag{5.7.5}$$

where $\overline{Y}_T$ and $\overline{\mu}_T$ are defined by (5.6.1) and (5.6.2), respectively, and

$$D_T \equiv \left[\sum_{t=1}^{T} \sigma_t^2\right]^{1/2}. \tag{5.7.6}$$

Then $\{Z_T\}$ converges in distribution to $Z \sim N(0, 1)$ and

$$\underset{T\to\infty}{\text{Limit}} \left[\max_{1 \le t \le T} \left(\frac{\sigma_t}{D_T}\right)\right] = 0, \tag{5.7.7}$$

iff for every $\varepsilon > 0$,

$$\underset{T\to\infty}{\text{Limit}} \frac{1}{D_T^2} \sum_{t=1}^{r} \left[\int_{|y_t - \mu_t| > \varepsilon D_T} (y - \mu_t)^2 \, dF_t(y)\right] = 0. \tag{5.7.8}$$

Proof See Cramér (1937, pp. 57–61) or Loéve (1963).

Condition (5.7.8) assures that no single element in $\{Y_T\}$ dominates $\text{Var}(\overline{Y}_T) = T^{-2} D_T$. Without some condition of this type, the distribution of Z_T could possibly be dominated by the distribution of one of the elements of $\{Y_T\}$. Condition (5.7.8) is the *Lindeberg condition*.[8] To interpret it, first define

$$\sigma_t^2 = \int_{-\infty}^{\infty} (y - \mu_t)^2 \, dF_t(y) \qquad (t = 1, 2, \ldots, T). \tag{5.7.9}$$

The integral appearing in (5.7.9) differs from the integral in (5.7.8) only with respect to the region of integration. As T increases, each term in the sum contained in (5.7.8) must eventually decrease. Lindeberg condition (5.7.8) requires that the sum of such terms increases at a slower rate than D_T^2 defined by (5.7.6).[9] If the elements in $\{Y_T\}$ are i.i.d. or if each element

8. For a detailed advanced treatment of the Lindeberg condition, see Dhrymes (1989, pp. 265–276).

9. The essence of the Lindeberg condition is to limit the effect of any one term in a sequence of sums of random variables so as to ascertain the asymptotic behavior of such sums. Spanos (1986, p. 175) draws an analogy from economic theory where under the assumption of perfect competition (no individual agent dominates the aggregate) the existence of a general equilibrium is proved. Spanos also draws analogy with the theory of gas in physics.

has a finite moment of order $2 + \alpha$, $\alpha > 0$, then the Lindeberg condition is satisfied.

Helpful in deriving multivariate extensions of Theorem 5.7.3 is the following theorem.

Theorem 5.7.4 Let $\{Y_T\}$ be a sequence of $K \times 1$ vectors of random variables and let $\{F_T(\cdot)\}$ be a sequence of their associated c.d.f.s. Let $F_{\lambda T}(\cdot)$ be the distribution of the *scalar* random variable

$$\mu_{\lambda T} = \lambda' Y_T, \tag{5.7.10}$$

where λ is a $K \times 1$ vector of constants. A necessary and sufficient condition that the sequence $\{F_T(\cdot)\}$ converges to the distribution function $F(\cdot)$ is that $\{F_{\lambda T}(\cdot)\}$ converges to a limit for every λ. Furthermore, $\{F_T(\cdot)\}$ converges to a multivariate normal distribution function $F(\cdot)$ iff $\{F_{\lambda T}(\cdot)\}$ converges to a univariate normal distribution for any λ.

Proof Rao (1973, p. 128).

The importance of Theorem 5.7.4 is that it reduces problems of multivariate convergence in distribution to those of univariate convergence in distribution. For example, Theorem 5.7.4 plays a central role in proving the following three useful theorems.

Theorem 5.7.5 Let $\{Y_T\}$ be an i.i.d. sequence of $K \times 1$ vectors having finite mean μ and covariance matrix Σ. Then the sequence $\{Z_T\}$ of vectors, where

$$Z_T = T^{-1/2} \sum_{t=1}^{T} (Y_T - \mu) = \sqrt{T}(\overline{Y}_T - \mu), \tag{5.7.11}$$

converges to a vector $Z \sim N_K(0, \Sigma)$.

Proof Apply Theorem 5.7.4 to Theorem 5.7.1.

Theorem 5.7.6 (Lindeberg-Feller Multivariate CLT) Let $\{Y_T\}$ be a sequence of independent vector random variables with means $\{\mu_T\}$ and finite covariance matrices $\{\Omega_T\}$. Suppose

$$\operatorname*{Limit}_{T \to \infty} \frac{1}{T} \sum_{t=1}^{T} \Omega_t = \Omega \neq 0, \tag{5.7.12}$$

and for every $\varepsilon > 0$

$$\operatorname*{Limit}_{T \to \infty} \frac{1}{T} \sum_{t=1}^{T} \left[\int_{\|y_t - \mu_t\| > \varepsilon T^{1/2}} \|y - \mu_t\|^2 \, dF_t(y) \right] = 0, \tag{5.7.13}$$

where $\|y_t\| = [y_{t1}^2 + y_{t2}^2 + \cdots + y_{tK}^2]^{1/2}$ is the length of the vector y_t, and $F_T(\cdot)$ is the c.d.f. of Y_T. Consider the sequence $\{Z_T\}$, where

$$Z_T = T^{-1/2} \sum_{t=1}^{T} (Y_t - \mu_t) = \sqrt{T}\,(\overline{Y}_T - \overline{\mu}_T). \tag{5.7.14}$$

Then $Z_T \xrightarrow{d} Z$, where $Z \sim N(0, \Omega)$.

Proof Dhrymes (1974, p. 104) proves the slightly simplified version in which the elements of $\{Y_T\}$ are assumed to have zero mean. Note that Theorem 5.7.4 is used to reduce the problem to one in which Theorem 5.7.6 can be applied. The crucial step is to show that (5.7.13) can be used to establish Lindeberg condition (5.7.8).

The following theorem is useful in a wide variety of problems and it is commonly known as the *δ-method*. Theorems 5.7.2 is a special case of it.

Theorem 5.7.7 Let $\{Y_T\}$ be a sequence of independent $K \times 1$ random vectors such that $T^{1/2}(\overline{Y}_T - \mu) \xrightarrow{d} N_K(0_K, \Omega)$ as $T \to \infty$. Let $g(\cdot) = [g_1(\cdot), g_2(\cdot), \ldots, g_J(\cdot)]'$ be a $J \times 1$ vector function with continuous second-order derivatives in an open interval around μ, and define

$$A = \begin{bmatrix} \frac{\partial g_1(\mu)}{\partial y_1} & \frac{\partial g_1(\mu)}{\partial y_2} & \cdots & \frac{\partial g_1(\mu)}{\partial y_K} \\ \frac{\partial g_2(\mu)}{\partial y_1} & \frac{\partial g_2(\mu)}{\partial y_2} & \cdots & \frac{\partial g_2(\mu)}{\partial y_K} \\ \vdots & \vdots & & \vdots \\ \frac{\partial g_J(\mu)}{\partial y_1} & \frac{\partial g_J(\mu)}{\partial y_2} & \cdots & \frac{\partial g_J(\mu)}{\partial y_K} \end{bmatrix}, \tag{5.7.15}$$

where $\partial g_i(\mu)/\partial y_j$ denotes $\partial g_i(y_j)/\partial y_j$ evaluated at $y_j = \mu$, and $y = [y_1, y_2, \ldots, y_K]'$. Then $T^{1/2}[g(\overline{Y}) - g(\mu)] \xrightarrow{d} N_J(0_J, A\Omega A')$.

Proof See Theil (1971, p. 383, Problems 3.6 and 3.7) or Bhattacharya (1977).

The following theorem gives the limiting distribution of the order statistics discussed in Section 5.4.

Theorem 5.7.8 Let $\{X_T\}$ be a sequence of independent vector random variables with common p.d.f. $f(\cdot)$ and c.d.f. $F(\cdot)$. Assume $F(\cdot)$ is strictly increasing for $0 < F(x) < 1$, and let ξ_q be the qth quantile, that is, $F(\xi_q) = q$ for $0 < q < 1$. Let q_T be such that Tq_T is an integer and $T|q_T - q|$ is bounded, and let $Z(T, q_T)$ denote the (Tq_T)th order statistic for a random sample of size T. As $T \to \infty$, $Z(T, q_T)$ is asymptotically distributed as $N(\xi_q, q(1-q)/T[f(\xi_q)]^2)$, that is

$$\underset{T\to\infty}{\text{Limit}} \left[\frac{\sqrt{T}[Z(T, q_t) - \xi_q]}{(q(1-q)/[f(\xi_q)]^2)^{1/2}} - Z \right] = 0, \tag{5.7.16}$$

where $Z \sim N(0, 1)$.

Proof See Cox and Hinkley (1974, pp. 468–469).

Example 5.7.3 Consider Theorem 5.7.9 in the case $q = \frac{1}{2}$ so that ξ_q is the population median and $Z(T, \frac{1}{2})$ is the sample median. Then the asymptotic variance of $T^{1/2}[Z(T, \frac{1}{2}) - \xi_{.5}]$ is $(4[f(0)]^2)^{-1}$. Thus, if $f(\cdot)$ is a normal p.d.f. with mean $\mu = \xi_{.50}$ and variance σ^2, i.e. $f(x) = \phi(x|\mu, \sigma^2)$, then the sample median is asymptotically normally distributed with mean μ and variance $\pi\sigma^2/2$. For evidence of the good quality of this asymptotic approximation when $T = 20$, across a variety of underlying distributions, see Lehmann (1983, p. 358).

CLTs provide no information as to how large is the approximation error made by using the asymptotic c.d.f. instead of the actual c.d.f. of the Tth term in the sequence. At the turn of the twentieth century, Liapounov derived an upper bound on the approximation error when random sampling from an underlying population with finite third moments. This result was later sharpened in the 1940s by Berry (1941) and Esseen (1945), and is given in the following theorem.

Theorem 5.7.9 (Berry-Esseen Theorem) For random samples from populations with finite third-order moments,

$$\sup_y |F_T(y) - \Phi(y)| \leq \frac{33E[(Y-\mu)^3]}{4\sigma^3\sqrt{T}} \quad \textit{for all } T. \tag{5.7.17}$$

Proof Chow and Teicher (1988).

The constant 33/4 in (5.7.16) was sharpened by van Beeck (1972) to .7975. Extensions of the Berry-Esseen Theorem to cover cases involving i.n.i.d. observations and nonuniform (in y) bounds are available (e.g., see Dufour and Hallin 1992). Extensions to permit y to vary with T have been provided by Ibragimov and Linnik (1971). An alternative approach is to consider *Edgeworth expansions* (see Phillips 1977; Rothenberg 1984; or Sargan 1976). Of course pragmatic use of Theorem 5.7.9 requires knowledge of the third moment.

Complementing CLTs is the following theorem, which characterizes the extreme fluctuations in a sequence of averages or partial sums from i.i.d. observations.

Theorem 5.7.10 (Law of Iterated Logarithm [LIL]) Let Y_t $(t = 1, 2, \ldots, T)$ be i.i.d. with mean μ and finite variance σ^2. Define $c_T \equiv \sigma[2T\ln\{\ln(T)\}]^{1/2}$. Then:

$$\sup\left(c_T^{-1}\sum_{t=1}^{T}(Y_t - \mu)\right) \xrightarrow{a.s.} 1, \quad \text{as } T \to \infty, \tag{5.7.18}$$

$$\inf\left(c_T^{-1}\sum_{t=1}^{T}(Y_t-\mu)\right)\xrightarrow{a.s.}-1, \quad \text{as } T\to\infty. \tag{5.7.19}$$

Proof Loéve (1963).

Recall that a CLT suggests that the sequence of random variables

$$\frac{\sum_{t=1}^{T}(Y_t-\mu)}{\sigma/\sqrt{T}} \quad (T=1,2,3,\ldots) \tag{5.7.20}$$

converges in distribution to $N(0,1)$, but does not provide any additional description regarding fluctuations of these random variables around their mean of zero. The LIL asserts that these fluctuations, that is (5.7.20), are of order $[2\ln\{\ln(T)\}]^{1/2}$. In other words, with probability unity (i.e. almost surely), for any $\varepsilon>0$, all but finitely many if these fluctuations fall within the boundaries $\pm(1+\varepsilon)[2\ln\{\ln(T)\}]^{1/2}$. Furthermore, the boundaries $\pm(1-\varepsilon)[2\ln\{\ln(T)\}]^{1/2}$ are reached infinitely often (see Serfling 1980, pp. 35–37). For extension to the i.n.i.d. case, see Rao (1973, p. 130).

For the same reasons indicated at the end of the previous section in connection with laws of large numbers, further discussion of central limit theorems for sequences of correlated and heterogeneous elements are not pursued here. Again the reader is encouraged to consult Dhrymes (1989), Hamilton (1994), Spanos (1986), White (1984), or an advanced probability text for details.

Exercises

5.7.1 Theorem 5.7.1 was not applicable when the underlying population is Cauchy. Provide another distribution for which this is also the case.

5.7.2 Compare the asymptotic distribution of the sample mean and sample median of a random sample from a double exponential distribution.

5.7.3 Let $\overline{Y}_T$ denote the mean of a random sample if size T from a gamma distribution with parameters $\alpha>0$ and $\beta=1$. Show that the limiting distribution of $T^{1/2}(\overline{Y}_T-\alpha)/\overline{Y}_T^{1/2}$ is $N(0,1)$.

5.7.4 Let $\{Y_T\}$ be a sequence of independent random variables with finite means $\{\mu_T\}$, variances $\{\sigma_T^2\}$, and third absolute moments $\{c_T\}$, where $c_T=E[|Y_T-\mu_T|^3]$. *Liapounov's Theorem* states (see Chung 1974) that if

$$\operatorname*{Limit}_{T\to\infty}\frac{C_T}{D_T}=0, \tag{5.7.21}$$

where

$$C_T=\left[\sum_{t=1}^{T}c_t\right]^{1/3}, \tag{5.7.22}$$

and D_T is defined by (5.7.6), then $Z_T=[T^{-1}D_T]^{-1}(\overline{Y}_T-\overline{\mu}_T)\xrightarrow{d}N(0,1)$.

(a) Prove that (5.7.21) holds if the Y_T's are i.i.d..

(b) Is the Lindeberg-Levy Theorem a special case of Liapounov's Theorem?

5.7.5 Suppose $X_T \xrightarrow{d} X$ and $Y_T \xrightarrow{p} c$, where c is a constant. Suppose $E(X_T Y_T)$ $(T = 1, 2, 3, \ldots)$ and $E(X)$ exist, and $E(X_T^2)$ and $E(X_T Y_T^2)$ are bounded for all T. Show:

$$\operatorname*{Limit}_{T\to\infty} E(X_T Y_T) = \left[\operatorname*{plim}_{T\to\infty} Y_T\right]\left[\operatorname*{Limit}_{T\to\infty} E(X_T)\right] = cE(X). \tag{5.7.23}$$

5.7.6 Show that for a random sample, the empirical cumulative distribution function converges (uniformly) in quadratic mean to the population distribution function.

5.7.7 Suppose $Z_T \xrightarrow{d} Z$ and that there exist s and M such that for all T, $E[|Z_T|^s] \le M$. Show (Rao 1973, p. 121): for all $r < s$,

$$\operatorname*{Limit}_{T\to\infty} E[|Z_T|^r] = E[|Z|^r]. \tag{5.7.24}$$

5.7.8 A *variance stabilizing transformation* $g(\cdot)$ is a continuous function such that if $Z_T \xrightarrow{d} Z$, then the variance of the limiting distribution of $g(Z_T)$, as $T \to \infty$, does not depend on unknown parameters.

(a) Suppose Y_t $(t = 1, 2, \ldots, T) \sim$ i.i.d. $\beta(1, \theta)$. Define $X_T = g(\overline{Y}_T) = \sin^{-1}(\overline{Y}_T)$. Show: $T^{1/2}[X_T - \sin^{-1}(\lambda^{1/2})] \xrightarrow{d} N(0, \frac{1}{4})$ as $T \to \infty$.

(b) Suppose Y_t $(t = 1, 2, \ldots, T) \sim$ i.i.d. Po(λ). Define $X_T = g(\overline{Y}_T) = (\overline{Y}_T)^{1/2}$. Show: $T^{1/2}(X_T - \lambda^{1/2}) \xrightarrow{d} N(0, \frac{1}{4})$ as $T \to \infty$.

5.8 Subjectivist View of Sampling

It is the model itself, as a more or less suitable approximation to reality, which is of primary interest. The problems of estimation of its parameters or testing of its features have a derived interest only.
—Koopmans (1949, pp. 89–90)

An objectivist is concerned with modelling literal reality—an oxymoron if there ever was one. To an objectivist the idea of random sampling applies to the actual process that generates the data. This process is commonly called the *data generating process* (DGP). Its characteristics reflect the underlying population and the sampling process from it which gives rise to the data. In some special instances (e.g., when sampling from an extant finite population like the bowl of balls in Example 5.8.1, or in pure measurement error problems—location/scale families—where the measured quantity is a tangible feature of reality like the length of a table) the DGP and the parameters would seem to have an agreed upon existence in the eyes of most researchers. But in economics, typical cases involve hypothetical sampling and the meaning of the parameters is less clear.

In Section 5.1 we raised questions of how one ascertains the validity of the i.i.d. assumption that characterizes a random sample. Answers to these questions from the objectivist standpoint are most difficult since they involve properties of the real world which do not seem to be the matter of everyday experience. The literal "truth" of the i.i.d. assumptions is at issue in the physical repetitive process whose long run behavior forms the basis for probabilistic reasoning. How does one discover such "truths" in our finite experience? Both the answer and the relevance of this question have plagued the history of science for centuries.

Proponents of a subjective interpretation of probability emphasize that probability reflects an individual's beliefs about reality, rather than a property of reality itself. Ironically, subjectivists emphasize observables (i.e., data) and objectivists usually focus on unobservables, namely, parameters. The i.i.d. assumption of a random sample are conditioned upon the unknown parameters of the underlying population. In a heavenly world where a deity makes these parameters known to the researcher, most statistical activities lose their importance. There is no estimation nor testing to perform since the goals of such activities are presumed known. As seen in Section 5.1, prediction takes on a fairly trivial form since nothing is learned from random sampling. And why would a researcher ever be interested in experimental design? It is paradoxical that an alleged fundamental building block such as random sampling virtually eliminates the statistical activities it purports to motivate.

Fortunately, Bruno de Finetti provided a subjectivist solution to this perplexing state of affairs. Although his solution reassigns the fundamental role to a different concept, ironically random sampling is provided an interesting interpretation in the process. De Finetti favored assigning the fundamental role to the concept of *exchangeability* defined as follows. See McCall (1991) for a discussion of the importance of exchangeability in economics.

Definition 5.8.1 A finite sequence Y_t $(t = 1, 2, \ldots, T)$ of random variables (or events) is *exchangeable* iff the joint distribution of the sequence, or any subsequence, is invariant under permutations of the subscripts, that is, the distribution and probability functions satisfy

$$F(y_1, y_2, \ldots, y_T) = F(y_{\pi(1)}, y_{\pi(2)}, \ldots, y_{\pi(T)}), \tag{5.8.1}$$

$$f(y_1, y_2, \ldots, y_T) = f(y_{\pi(1)}, y_{\pi(2)}, \ldots, y_{\pi(T)}), \tag{5.8.2}$$

where $\pi(t)$ $(t = 1, 2, \ldots, T)$ is a permutation of the elements in $\{1, 2, \ldots, T\}$. A finite sequence A_t $(t = 1, 2, \ldots, T)$ of events is *exchangeable* iff the joint probability of the sequence, or any subsequence, is invariant under permutations of the subscripts. An infinite sequence is *exchangeable* iff any finite subsequence is exchangeable.

Exchangeability provides an operational meaning to the weakest possible notion of a sequence of "similar" random quantities. It is "operational" in the sense that it requires probability assignments involving only *observable* quantities. The case of Bernoulli sequences is considered in the following example.

Example 5.8.1 A sequence of Bernoulli trials is *exchangeable* iff the probability assigned to particular sequences does not depend on the order of "successes" and "failures." For example, let S denote the event "success" and let F denote the event "failure." If the trials are exchangeable, then the sequences FSS, SFS, and SSF are assigned the same probability.

Exchangeability involves recognizing symmetry in degrees of belief concerning only observables, and presumably this is something about which a researcher may have more intuition. de Finetti's Representation Theorem (Theorem 5.8.1, later in this chapter) and its generalizations are especially interesting because they provide conditions under which exchangeability gives rise to an isomorphic world in which we have i.i.d. observations given a mathematical construct, namely, a parameter. Furthermore, exchangeable events are *not* necessarily independent, and the predictive implications of such dependence is demonstrated in Example 5.8.3. Finally, de Finetti's theorem provides an interpretation of parameters that differs substantively from the interpretation of an objectivist.

As in the case of i.i.d. sequences, the individual elements in an exchangeable sequence are identically distributed. In the case of exchangeability, however, the individual elements need *not* be independent, as the following example demonstrates.

Example 5.8.2 Suppose $Y = [Y_1, Y_2, \ldots, Y_T]' \sim N_T(0_T, \Sigma)$, where $\Sigma_T \equiv I_T - \alpha\iota_T\iota_T'$ is positive definite for some scalar α and ι_T is a $T \times 1$ vector with each element equal to unity (see Exercise A.8.1). Let $\pi(t)$ $(t = 1, 2, \ldots, T)$ be a permutation of $\{1, 2, \ldots, T\}$ and suppose $[Y_{\pi(1)}, Y_{\pi(2)}, \ldots, Y_{\pi(T)}] = AY$, where A is a $T \times T$ selection matrix such that for $t = 1, 2, \ldots, T$, row t in A consists of all zeroes except column $\pi(t)$, which is unity. Note that $AA' = I_T$ and $A\iota_T = \iota_T$. Then $AY \sim N_T(0_T, \Sigma)$. Hence, beliefs regarding Y_t $(t = 1, 2, \ldots, T)$ are exchangeable, but if $\alpha \neq 0$, then Y_t $(t = 1, 2, \ldots, T)$ are *not* independent.

The importance of the concept of exchangeability is due to the following remarkable theorem by de Finetti (1937).

Theorem 5.8.1 (de Finetti's Representation Theorem) Let Y_t $(t = 1, 2, 3, \ldots)$ be an infinite sequence of Bernoulli random variables indicating the occurrence or nonoccurrence of some event of interest. For any finite sequence Y_t $(t = 1, 2, \ldots, T)$, define the average number of occurrences:

$$\overline{Y}_T = \frac{1}{T}\sum_{t=1}^{T} Y_t. \tag{5.8.3}$$

Let $g(y_1, y_2, \ldots, y_T) = P(Y_1 = y_1, Y_2 = y_2, \ldots, Y_T = y_T)$ denote a probability mass function reflecting *exchangeable* beliefs for an arbitrarily long finite sequence Y_t $(t = 1, 2, \ldots, T)$ [i.e. beliefs are exchangeable for an infinite sequence Y_t $(t = 1, 2, 3, \ldots)$], and let $G(y) \equiv P(Y \leq y)$ denote its associated c.d.f.. Then $g(\cdot)$ has the representation:[10]

$$g(y_1, y_2, \ldots, y_T) = \int_0^1 \mathscr{L}(\theta; y)\, dF(\theta), \tag{5.8.4}$$

where

$$\mathscr{L}(\theta; y) = \sum_{t=1}^{T} \theta^{y_t}(1-\theta)^{1-y_t}, \tag{5.8.5}$$

$$F(\theta) \equiv \operatorname*{Limit}_{T\to\infty} P_G(\bar{Y}_T \leq \theta), \tag{5.8.6}$$

and $P_G(\cdot)$ denotes probability with respect to the distribution with c.d.f. $G(\cdot)$ corresponding to p.m.f. (5.8.4).

Proof See de Finetti (1937) or the simpler exposition of Heath and Sudderth (1976).

In other words, Theorem 5.8.1 implies it is *as if*, given θ, Y_t $(t = 1, 2, \ldots, T)$ are i.i.d. Bernoulli trials where the probability of a success is θ, and the "parameter" θ is assigned a probability distribution with c.d.f. $F(\cdot)$ that can be interpreted as belief about the long-run relative frequency of $\bar{Y}_T \leq \theta$ as $T \to \infty$. From de Finetti's standpoint, both the quantity θ and the notion of independence are "mathematical fictions" implicit in the researcher's subjective assessment of arbitrarily long *observable* sequences of successes and failures. The parameter θ is of interest primarily because it constitutes a limiting form of predictive inference (Chapter 8) about the observable $\bar{Y}_T$ via (5.8.6). The mathematical construct θ may nonetheless be useful. Note, however, that Theorem 5.8.1 implies that the subjective probability distribution need not apply to the "fictitious θ" but only to the *observable* exchangeable sequence of successes and failures.

When the c.d.f. $F(\theta)$ is absolutely continuous, so that the density $f(\theta) = dF(\theta)/d\theta$ exists, then (5.8.4) can be rewritten as

$$g(y_1, y_2, \ldots, y_T) = \int_0^1 \prod_{t=1}^{T} \theta^{y_t}(1-\theta)^{1-y_t} f(\theta)\, d\theta. \tag{5.8.7}$$

It is clear from both (5.8.4) and (5.8.7) that exchangeable beliefs assign probabilities acting *as if* the Y_ts are i.i.d. Bernoulli random variables given θ, and then average over values of θ using the weight $f(\theta)$ to obtain a marginal density for the Y_ts.

Let $S_T = T\bar{Y}_T$ be the number of successes in T trials. Because there are $\binom{T}{r}$ ways in which to obtain $S_T = \mathrm{r}$ successes in T trials, it follows

10. Integral (5.8.4) is a Stieltjes integral; see (2.3.7) and Exercise 2.3.11.

immediately from (5.8.4) and (5.8.5):

$$\text{Prob}(S_T = r) = \binom{T}{r} \int_0^1 \theta^r (1-\theta)^{T-r}\, dF(\theta) \qquad (r = 0, 1, \ldots, T), \quad (5.8.8)$$

where

$$F(\theta) \equiv \underset{T\to\infty}{\text{Limit}}\; P(T^{-1} S_T \leq \theta). \quad (5.8.9)$$

Thus, given θ, it follows from (5.8.8) that exchangeable beliefs assign probabilities acting as if S_T has a Binomial distribution given θ, and then average over values of θ using the weight $f(\theta) = dF(\theta)/d\theta$. Bayes and Laplace suggest choosing the "mixing" distribution $F(\theta)$ for θ to be uniform over $[0, 1]$, in which case (5.8.8) reduces to

$$\text{Prob}(S_T = r) = \frac{1}{T+1} \qquad (r = 0, 1, \ldots, T). \quad (5.8.10)$$

In words, (5.8.10) describes beliefs that in T trials, any number r of successes are equally likely.[11] In the degenerate case in which the distribution of θ assigns probability one to some value θ_o, then de Finetti's Theorem implies that S_T follows the standard Binomial distribution (see Definition 3.2.5).

$$\text{Prob}(S_T = r) = \binom{T}{r} \theta_o^r (1-\theta_o)^{T-r}, \quad (5.8.11)$$

and (5.8.9) implies

$$\underset{T\to\infty}{\text{Limit}}\; \overline{Y}_T = \theta \quad (5.8.12)$$

with "probability one." This last result, a special case of de Finetti's Theorem, is equivalent to the "strong law of large numbers."

De Finetti's Representation Theorem has been extended to cover exchangeable beliefs involving random variables more complicated than

11. The definition of the Beta function—see (3.3.44)—and Theorem 3.3.5(a) imply:

$$B(r, T-r) = \int_0^1 \theta^r (1-\theta)^{T-r}\, d\theta = \frac{\Gamma(r+1)\Gamma(T-r+1)}{\Gamma(T+2)}$$

$$= \frac{r!\,(T-r)!}{(T+1)!}.$$

Therefore,

$$\binom{T}{r} B(r, T-r) = \frac{T!\,r!\,(T-r)!}{r!\,(T-r)!\,(T+1)!} = \frac{1}{T+1}.$$

Bernoulli random variables.[12] Theorem 5.8.1 requires exchangeability over an infinite or potentially infinite number of exchangeable random variables. In a sense this implies in our finite world that de Finetti's Theorem does not completely qualify as operational. Although the theorem does not hold exactly for finite sequences, it does hold approximately for sufficiently large finite sequences (see Diaconis 1977 and Diaconis and Freedman 1980).

The pragmatic value of de Finetti's Theorem depends on whether it is easier to assess the lefthand side of (5.8.4), which involves only observable quantities, or instead, the integrand on the righthand side of (5.8.4), which involves two distributions and the mathematical fiction θ. Most statisticians think in terms of the righthand side. As will become clear in Chapter 6, frequentists implicitly do so with a degenerate distribution for θ that in effect treats θ as a constant, and Bayesians do so with a nondegenerate "prior" distribution for θ. What is important to note here, however, is the isomorphism de Finetti's theorem suggests between two worlds, one involving only observables and the other involving the parameter θ. de Finetti put parameters in their proper perspective: (i) They are mathematical constructs that provide a convenient index for a probability distribution, and (ii) they induce conditional independence for a sequence of observables.

The following example demonstrates the usefulness of de Finetti's Theorem.

12. For discussions of exchangeability and extensions of de Finetti's Representation Theorem, see Aldous (1983), Bernardo and Smith (1994), Dawid (1982), de Finetti (1937; 1972, pp. 209–225; 1975, Chapter 11), Diaconis (1977, 1988), Diaconis and Freedman (1980, 1984), Diaconis et al. (1990), Draper et al. (1993), Heath and Sudderth (1978), Hewitt and Savage (1955), Jaynes (1986), Kingman (1978), Koch and Spizzichino (1982), Lauritzen (1984), Lindley and Novick (1981), Skyrms (1984), Walley (1991, pp. 460–467), and the references cited therein.

In the general case of real-valued random quantities, A. F. M. Smith (1984, p. 252) succinctly summarizes the corresponding result as follows. The joint distribution function for exchangeable $Z_1, Z_2, \ldots, Z_T$ has the representation

$$G(z_1, z_2, \ldots, z_T) = \int_{\mathscr{F}} \prod_{t=1}^{T} F(z_t)\, d\mu(F),$$

where $\mathscr{F}$ is the space of all distribution functions on $\mathfrak{R}$, and μ is a measure on $\mathscr{F}$ representing, as $T \to \infty$, prior opinion—induced by exchangeable beliefs—about the empirical distribution function

$$F_T(z) = T^{-1}[I(Z_1 \le z) + I(Z_2 \le z) + \cdots + I(Z_T \le z)],$$

where $I(\cdot)$ is the indicator function equaling unity if the argument inequality holds, and zero otherwise. In the words of A. F. M. Smith (1984, p. 252); "in this setting, it is again *as if* we have an independent sample, conditional on F, an 'unknown' distribution function, beliefs about which have an operational interpretation in terms of 'what we think the empirical distribution would look like for a large sample'." See Bernardo and Smith (1994, pp. 177–181) for further discussion.

Example 5.8.3 Suppose a researcher makes a coherent probability assignment to an infinite sequence Y_t $(t = 1, 2, 3, \ldots)$ of exchangeable Bernoulli random variables. Given an observed sequence of T trials with r successes, the probability of the next outcome is

$$
\begin{aligned}
P(Y_{T+1} = y_{T+1} | T\overline{Y}_T = r) &= \frac{P(T\overline{Y}_T = r, Y_{T+1} = y_{T+1})}{P(T\overline{Y}_T = r)} \\
&= \frac{\int_0^1 \theta^{r+y_{T+1}}(1-\theta)^{T+1-r-y_{T+1}} f(\theta)\, d\theta}{\int_0^1 \theta^r (1-\theta)^{T-r} f(\theta)\, d\theta} \\
&= \frac{\int_0^1 \theta^{y_{T+1}}(1-\theta)^{1-y_{T+1}} f(\theta)\mathscr{L}(\theta; y)\, d\theta}{\int_0^1 \mathscr{L}(\theta; y) f(\theta)\, d\theta} \\
&= \int_0^1 \theta^{y_{T+1}}(1-\theta)^{1-y_{T+1}} f(\theta | y)\, d\theta \\
&= \begin{Bmatrix} E(\theta | y), & \text{if } y_{T+1} = 1 \\ 1 - E(\theta | y), & \text{if } y_{T+1} = 0 \end{Bmatrix},
\end{aligned} \tag{5.8.13}
$$

where

$$
f(\theta | y) = \frac{f(\theta)\mathscr{L}(\theta; y)}{f(y)}. \tag{5.8.14}
$$

The simplicity of Example 5.8.3 does not reflect its importance because it demonstrates most of the essential operations that characterize the Bayesian approach to statistics. This will become clear in subsequent chapters. For now we simply note the following. First, we introduce some terminology: $f(\theta)$ is the *prior density*, $\mathscr{L}(\theta; y)$ is the *likelihood function*, and $f(\theta | y)$ is the *posterior density*. Second, the existence of the prior density is a result of Theorem 5.8.1, *not* an assumption. Third, the updating of prior beliefs captured in (5.8.14) amounts to nothing more than Bayes Theorem. Fourth, although Y_t $(t = 1, 2, \ldots, T)$ are independent conditional on θ, unconditional of θ they are dependent. Finally, the parameter θ is merely a mathematical entity indexing the integration in (5.8.13). Its "real-world existence" is a question only of metaphysical importance.[13]

13. For an intriguing discussion of possible subjectivist interpretations of the "true value" of a parameter, see Jones (1982). To whet the readers appetite, consider the following provoking arguments (Jones 1982, p. 152):

> The usual 3-dimensional Euclidean model of space was once a well established model with no obvious need for further data collection to improve it. Parameters such as length or height were accurately measurable and so were regarded as true values. The

The representation theorem of de Finetti has also been generalized in the direction of seeking more stringent forms of "symmetry" than exchangeability that would rationalize other sampling models than the binomial. This has been accomplished in a variety of cases. Smith (1984, pp. 252–253) cites the following two theorems covering familiar cases. See Berger and Bernardo (1994, Chapter 4) for a fine survey of other cases.

Theorem 5.8.2 Consider a sequence Y_t $(t = 1, 2, \ldots, T)$ and let $\bar{Y}_T$ denote the sample mean. Suppose for all T that beliefs about $Y_1 - \bar{Y}_T$, $Y_2 - \bar{Y}_T, \ldots, Y_T - \bar{Y}_T$ are invariant under orthogonal linear transformations.[14] Then such beliefs are equivalent to proceeding *as if* Y_t $(t = 1, 2, \ldots, T)$ are i.i.d. $N(\mu, \sigma^2)$ with a prior distribution for μ and σ^2.

Proof Smith (1981).

Theorem 5.8.3 Consider a sequence Y_t $(t = 1, 2, \ldots, T)$ and let $M_T \equiv \max(Y_1, Y_2, \ldots, Y_T\}$. Suppose for all T that beliefs about $Y_1, Y_2, \ldots, Y_T$, given M_T, are independent and uniform over the interval $[0, M_T]$. Then such beliefs are equivalent to proceeding *as if* Y_t $(t = 1, 2, \ldots, T)$ are i.i.d. $U[0, \theta]$ with a prior distribution for θ.

Proof Smith (1984).

Exercises

5.8.1 Consider a random sample Y_t $(t = 1, 2, \ldots, T)$ from a distribution with finite mean. Define $Z_t = Y_t - \bar{Y}_T$ $(t = 1, 2, \ldots, T)$.

(a) Are Z_t $(t = 1, 2, \ldots, T)$ i.i.d.?

(b) Are Z_t $(t = 1, 2, \ldots, T)$ exchangeable?

---

theory of relativity however changed all this, an object no longer having an absolute 'length', but a 'length' dependent on its relative speed to the observer. This perhaps provides one of the most striking illustrations of the temporary nature of the notion of 'true value' or 'correct model.'

14. Equivalently, a judgment of identical beliefs for all outcomes $Y_1, Y_2, \ldots, Y_T$ leading to same values of $(Y_1 - \bar{Y}_T)^2 + (Y_2 - \bar{Y}_T)^2 + \cdots + (Y_T - \bar{Y}_T)^2$.

6 Estimation

There are two things you are better off not watching in the making: sausages and econometric estimates.
—Leamer (1983, p. 37)

6.1 Likelihood and Sufficiency

Likelihood is the single most important concept of statistics.
—Barndorff-Nielsen (1991, p. 232)

This chapter considers the following problem of estimation. Suppose attention focuses on a sample $Y = [Y_1, Y_2, \ldots, Y_T]' \in \mathscr{S}_T$ with joint p.f. $f(\cdot|\theta)$, where $\theta = [\theta_1, \theta_2, \ldots, \theta_K]'$ is an unknown parameter vector. Based on the observed (realized) sample values $y \equiv [y_1, y_2, \ldots, y_T]'$, it is desired to estimate θ, or more generally, some function of θ, say $g(\theta)$. This estimation may proceed in two distinct ways: point estimation or interval estimation. *Point estimation* seeks a single numerical estimate of $g(\theta)$, whereas *interval estimation* seeks a range of numerical values (e.g. an interval) for $g(\theta)$. In both cases statistical theory will be used to produce estimators, and subsequently, the required numerical values (estimates).

Before developing point and interval estimation in later sections, this section and the next section provide foundational discussion for competing statistical paradigms designed for such tasks. In the ensuing discussion it is convenient to have terms to describe some of the more important competing paradigms. For simplicity we employ the dichotomy: classical versus Bayesian.[1] These two approaches can be distinguished in many ways. The distinction usually emphasized by classical researchers is that Bayesian analysis involves *formal* consideration of prior information and loss, whereas classical analysis involves only *informal* consideration of

1. The terminology "classical" is somewhat unfortunate (although widely accepted) since it is predated in history by the Bayesian approach. A more accurate label for "classical" is "non-Bayesian," but the implicit importance it suggests for the Bayesian reference point is likely to offend many "non-Bayesians." Admittedly, neither component of the dichotomy represents a homogeneous viewpoint. Both can be further subdivided according to the probability concept they employ. Frequentism comes in many guises involving different degrees of conditioning in order to define the appropriate sample space over to perform averaging. Although frequentist reasoning permeates classical inference, among classicists there are also many modes of inference that are employed: *conditional frequentist* (see Kiefer 1977a, 1977b), *conditional likelihood* (see Hinkley 1981; Cox and Reid 1987), *fiducial* (see Fisher 1956; Wilkinson 1977), *pivotal* (see Barnard 1977, 1980a, 1981), *structural* (see Fraser 1963, 1968, 1972, 1979) and *plausibility* (see Barndorff-Nielson 1976). The influence of R. A. Fisher (especially, Fisher 1934) underlies many of these classical modes. Among Bayesians, there are: *necessarists* (see Jeffreys 1961; Keynes 1921), and *subjectivists* (see de Finetti 1974; Savage 1954). Barnett (1982) and Bernardo and Smith (1994, Appendix B) are an excellent introductory source to many of these different approaches.

such concepts. The issue is whether such concepts play a central role. An even more crucial distinction is the criterion of accuracy that each type of analysis employs.

This latter distinction is one of initial precision versus final precision. *Initial precision* is concerned with the accuracy of procedures (i.e., estimators) viewed *ex ante*, before the sample is taken. The appropriate vehicle for evaluation of the expected performance of a procedure is the sampling distribution (recall Chapter 5), and usually the frequency interpretation of probability (i.e., performance in a long series of identical experiments) is attached to such evaluation. *Final precision*, on the other hand, is concerned with the accuracy of an estimate *after* the sample information is observed. The vehicle for assessing such *ex post* accuracy is a subjective (i.e., degree of belief) interpretation of probability.

One important characteristic of this text is that it emphasizes a *likelihood* approach to the topic of estimation. Such an approach requires a complete specification (up to a finite number of unknown parameters) of the underlying probabilistic structure of the problem at hand. The likelihood approach is consistent with both classical and Bayesian paradigms. It is demanding in the sense that it requires a great deal of input from the researcher. This seems especially demanding to many researchers of the frequentist (objective) persuasion because they must specify *the* probability structure characterizing the data. Subjectivists need only specify *a* coherent set of degrees of belief. The former must be able to answer the question: how do you know that the data come from, say, a normal distribution? The latter need only rationalize why their degrees of belief can be characterized by a normal distribution, and implicitly, why such a characterization is likely to be of interest to other researchers.

The likelihood approach is characterized by the central role of the likelihood function as now defined.[2]

Definition 6.1.1 Suppose Y_t $(t = 1, 2, \ldots, T)$ comprise a sample from a population such that $Y \equiv [Y_1, Y_2, \ldots, Y_T]'$ has the joint density $f(y|\theta)$, where $y = [y_1, y_2, \ldots, y_T]'$ and $\theta = [\theta_1, \theta_2, \ldots, \theta_K]'$ is a vector of unknown parameters belonging to a known set Θ called the *permissible parameter*

2. For a history of the concept of likelihood, see Edwards (1972, 1974). The concept owes much to the lifelong work of R. A. Fisher: particularly, Fisher (1922, 1924, 1934, 1956). The fertility of the likelihood concept is evidenced by its numerous offspring. Hinkley (1981) identifies a dozen: bootstrap, canonical, composite, conditional, empirical, marginal, partial, penalized, pivotal, predictive, profile, and quasi. Some authors prefer to define the likelihood function as any function of θ proportional to $f(y|\theta)$, where the constant of proportionality may depend on y but *not* on θ. As will be seen in Section 6.2, to believers in the Likelihood Principle, such factors of proportionality are irrelevant for determining the evidence in the data concerning θ. Definition 6.1.1 is without ambiguity. See Exercises 6.1.11 and 6.7.34 for introductions to the stimulating paper by Bayarri et al. (1988).

space. The *likelihood function* $\mathscr{L}(\theta; y) = f(y|\theta)$ is simply the joint density function of the sample viewed as a function of the parameter vector θ *given* the data $Y = y$. In contrast, the sampling density $f(y|\theta)$ is viewed as a function of y given θ. The *log-likelihood function* is $L(\theta; y) \equiv \ln[\mathscr{L}(\theta; y)]$.

Because the likelihood is *not* a density for θ, we do *not* denote it as $\mathscr{L}(\theta|Y)$ or $\mathscr{L}(\theta|y)$. When the likelihood function $\mathscr{L}(\theta; y)$ is viewed as a function of the θ for the observed value of the data y, it is natural to take a final precision approach to likelihood inference. Bayesians do so, and so did the originator of maximum likelihood estimation, Sir Ronald A. Fisher in his fiducial methods. Nonetheless, it is also possible to take an initial precision approach, express the likelihood as $\mathscr{L}(\theta; Y)$, and view likelihood-based methods as procedures whose *ex ante* sampling properties should be investigated. In fact the latter approach is the most popular in econometrics. Such approaches, however, are in direct conflict with one of the most important and far-reaching principles in statistics: the *Likelihood Principle*. Discussion of this principle is postponed until the next section.

In general the likelihood and log-likelihood functions are given by

$$\begin{aligned}\mathscr{L}(\theta; y) &= f(y_1|\theta) \prod_{t=2}^{T} f(y_t|y_{t-1}, \ldots, y_1, \theta)\\ &= f(y_1|\theta) f(y_2|y_1, \theta) \ldots f(y_T|y_{T-1}, \ldots, y_1, \theta),\end{aligned} \tag{6.1.1}$$

$$\begin{aligned}L(\theta; y) &= \ln[f(y_1|\theta)] + \sum_{t=2}^{T} \ln[f(y_t|y_{t-1}, \ldots, y_1, \theta)]\\ &= \ln[f(y_1|\theta)] + \ln[f(y_2|y_1, \theta)] + \cdots + \ln[f(y_T|y_{T-1}, \ldots, y_1, \theta)],\end{aligned} \tag{6.1.2}$$

respectively. If the sample is random, then the likelihood function is

$$\mathscr{L}(\theta; y) = \prod_{t=1}^{T} f(y_t|\theta), \tag{6.1.3}$$

where $f(\cdot;\theta)$ is the common p.d.f. of Y_t $(t = 1, 2, \ldots, T)$. Similarly, if the sample is random, then the log-likelihood can be written as

$$L(\theta; y) = \sum_{t=1}^{T} \ln[f(y_t|\theta)]. \tag{6.1.4}$$

Example 6.1.1 Consider the random sample Y_t $(t = 1, 2, \ldots, T) \sim$ i.i.d. $N(\mu, \sigma^2)$, where σ^2 is assumed known. Then the likelihood function is

$$\mathscr{L}(\mu; y) = \prod_{t=1}^{T} \phi(y_t|\mu, \sigma^2) = (2\pi\sigma^2)^{-T/2} \exp\left[-\frac{1}{2\sigma^2} \sum_{t=1}^{T} (y_t - \mu)^2\right]. \tag{6.1.5}$$

Example 6.1.2 Generalizing Example 6.1.1, the likelihood function for a random sample from the exponential family of distributions (3.3.62) is

$$\mathscr{L}(\gamma; y) = \prod_{t=1}^{T} f_{EXF}(y_t|\gamma) = \exp\left[Ta(\gamma) + \sum_{t=1}^{T} b(y_t) + \sum_{k=1}^{K} \theta_k(\gamma) W_k(y) \right], \quad (6.1.6)$$

where the following statistics will soon be seen to play a fundamental role:

$$W_k(y) = \sum_{t=1}^{T} d_k(y), \qquad (k = 1, 2, \ldots, k). \quad (6.1.7)$$

Note that (6.1.6) is a member of the exponential family.

Recall that a "statistic" is merely a (measurable) function of Y not depending on any unknown quantities (see Definition 5.2.2). Since statistics do not involve unknown quantities, they can be computed from data. An important role in any likelihood method is assigned to "sufficient statistics." Sufficient statistics are now defined, and the remainder of this section develops this concept. Full appreciation of sufficient statistics, however, awaits mastery of additional concepts to be developed later in this chapter. For surveys of the many refinements of the concept of sufficiency, see Huzurbazar (1976) and Yamada and Morimoto (1992).

Definition 6.1.2 Let Y_t $(t = 1, 2, \ldots, T)$ be a random sample from a population characterized by the density $f(y_t|\theta)$. Let $V = v(Y_1, Y_2, \ldots, Y_T)$ be an arbitrary statistic. A statistic $W = \omega(Y_1, Y_2, \ldots, Y_T)$ is a *sufficient statistic* iff the conditional distribution of V given $W = w$ does not depend on θ for all values w of W. The statistics $W_j = \omega_j(Y_1, Y_2, \ldots, Y_T)(j = 1, 2, \ldots, J)$ are *jointly sufficient* iff the conditional distribution of V given $W_j = w_j$ $(j = 1, 2, \ldots, J)$ does not depend on θ for all values of w_j of W_j $(j = 1, 2, \ldots, J)$. A set of $J \leq T$ jointly sufficient statistics is *minimal sufficient* iff it is a function of every other set of sufficient statistics.

Intuitively, a statistic is sufficient if given it, the distribution of any other statistic does not involve θ. Thus it is "sufficient" to consider only the sufficient statistic, because given it, no other statistic can contribute any additional information for estimating θ because its distribution does not involve θ.

A minimal sufficient statistic is a statistic that has achieved the maximal amount of data reduction possible while retaining all the sample information about the parameter θ. A minimal sufficient statistic eliminates all "extraneous" sample information about θ. Let X and Y be two samples. If W is minimally sufficient and V is any other sufficient statistic, then $V(Y) = V(X)$ implies $W(Y) = W(X)$.

In some cases, no sufficient statistic exists. However, there always exist jointly sufficient statistics (but not necessarily minimal) because the sample itself and the order statistics (Section 5.4) are jointly sufficient. Also, any one-to-one function of jointly sufficient statistics is jointly sufficient.

Fortunately, it is relatively easy to determine whether a given statistic is sufficient or a set of statistics is jointly sufficient by using the following theorem.[3]

Theorem 6.1.1 (Factorization Theorem) Let Y_t $(t = 1, 2, \ldots, T)$ be a random sample from a population characterized by the density $f(y_t; \theta)$. A set of statistics $W_j = \omega_j(Y_1, Y_2, \ldots, Y_T)(j = 1, 2, \ldots, J)$ is jointly sufficient iff

$$\mathscr{L}(\theta; y) = f(y|\theta) = d(w_1, w_2, \ldots, w_J; \theta)h(y), \tag{6.1.8}$$

where $W = w$ is the realized statistic corresponding to $y \equiv [y_1, y_2, \ldots, y_T]'$, $h(y)$ is a nonnegative function not depending on θ, and $d(W_1, W_2, \ldots, W_J; \theta)$ is a nonnegative function depending on y only through W_j $(j = 1, 2, \ldots, J)$. In the case $J = 1$, (6.1.6) provides a condition for W_1 to be a sufficient statistic.

Proof For a proof in the discrete case, see DeGroot (1987, p. 359); for a proof in the continuous case, see Hogg and Craig (1978, pp. 344–345).

To illustrate Theorem 6.1.1, consider the following two examples.

Example 6.1.3 Consider Example 6.1.1 where σ^2 is assumed known. Recalling (5.2.15),

$$\sum_{t=1}^{T} (y_t - \mu)^2 = \sum_{t=1}^{T} (y_t - \bar{y})^2 + T(\bar{y} - \mu)^2, \tag{6.1.9}$$

likelihood function (6.1.5) can be rewritten

$$\begin{aligned}\mathscr{L}(\mu; y) &= \left((2\pi\sigma^2)^{-T/2} \exp\left[-\frac{T}{2\sigma^2}(\bar{y} - \mu)^2\right]\right)\left(\exp\left[-\frac{1}{2\sigma^2}\sum_{t=1}^{T}(y_t - \bar{y})^2\right]\right) \\ &= d(w; \mu)h(y).\end{aligned} \tag{6.6.10}$$

Therefore, $W = \bar{Y}$ is a sufficient statistic for μ. In this case, $d(w; \theta) = \phi(\bar{y}|\mu, \sigma^2/T)$.

Example 6.1.4 In the case of random sampling from the exponential family of distributions considered in Example 6.1.2, likelihood (6.1.6) factorizes according to (6.1.8) with

$$d(w; \theta) = \exp\left[Ta(\gamma) + \sum_{k=1}^{K} \theta_k(\gamma) W_k(y)\right], \tag{6.1.11}$$

$$h(y) = \exp\left[\sum_{t=1}^{T} b(y_t)\right], \tag{6.1.12}$$

3. Theorem 6.1.1 is not very useful in showing that a statistic is *not* sufficient because it requires showing failure of (6.1.1) for all possible factorizations.

where $W_k(Y)$ $(k = 1, 2, \ldots, K)$ are the jointly sufficient statistics given by (6.1.7).

If $J \ll T$, then the sufficient statistic provides a convenient data summarization device in the sense that (6.1.5) implies the likelihood of θ is proportional to the function $d(w; \theta)$ involving simply θ and the sufficient statistic w. The function $h(y)$ of the data merely serves as a factor of proportionality. For a variety of purposes involving $\mathscr{L}(\theta; y)$ (e.g., maximizing or integrating it with respect to θ), only $d(w; \theta)$ is important. The perspective reader will note the suggestive form of $d(w; \theta)$ in Example 6.1.3.

Just as Theorem 6.1.1 was introduced in place of Definition 6.1.2 as a vehicle for determining whether a statistic was sufficient, the following theorem of Lehmann and Scheffé is introduced as a convenient vehicle for determining whether a statistic is minimally sufficient.

Theorem 6.1.2 Let $f(y|\theta)$ be the p.f. of a sample y, and suppose there exists a function $W(\cdot)$ such that, for two $T \times 1$ sample points y and x, the ratio $f(y|\theta)/f(x|\theta)$ is constant as a function of θ iff $W(y) = W(x)$. Then $W(Y)$ is a minimal sufficient statistic for θ.

Proof Lehmann and Scheffé (1950) or Casella and Berger (1990, pp. 255–256).

The following two examples use Theorem 6.1.2 to demonstrate that the sufficient statistics derived in Examples 6.1.3 and 6.1.4 are also minimally sufficient.

Example 6.1.5 Consider a random sample of size T from a $N(\mu, \sigma^2)$ distribution, where both μ and σ^2 are unknown. For two $T \times 1$ sample points y and x, let the respective sample means and variances be denoted $(\bar{x}, s_x^2)$ and $(\bar{y}, s_y^2)$. Using (6.1.9),

$$\frac{f(y|\mu, \sigma^2)}{f(x|\mu, \sigma^2)} = \frac{(2\pi\sigma^2)^{-T/2}\exp(-[T(\bar{y} - \mu)^2 + (T - 1)s_y^2]/(2\sigma^2))}{(2\pi\sigma^2)^{-T/2}\exp(-[T(\bar{x} - \mu)^2 + (T - 1)s_x^2]/(2\sigma^2))}$$
$$= \exp([-T(\bar{y}^2 - \bar{x}^2) + 2T\mu(\bar{y} - \bar{x}) - (T - 1)(s_y^2 - s_x^2)/(2\sigma^2)]). \tag{6.1.13}$$

This ratio is a constant function of μ and σ^2 iff $\bar{y} = \bar{x}$ and $s_y^2 = s_x^2$. Therefore, by Theorem 6.1.2, $(\bar{Y}, S_y^2)$ is a minimal sufficient statistic for (μ, σ^2).

Example 6.1.6 Consider a random sample of size T from the exponential family of distributions discussed in Examples 6.1.2 and 6.1.4. Consider two $T \times 1$ sample points y and x. Then it follows immediately:

$$\frac{f_{EXF}(y|\gamma)}{f_{EXF}(x|\gamma)} = \exp\left(\sum_{k=1}^{K} \theta_k(\gamma)[W_k(y) - W_k(x)]\right)\cdot\exp[h(y) - h(x)]. \tag{6.1.14}$$

This ratio is a constant function of γ iff $W_k(y) = W_k(x)$ $(k = 1, 2, \ldots, K)$. Hence, by Theorem 6.1.2, sufficient statistics (6.1.7) are minimally sufficient for γ.

Sufficient statistics are closely linked to the exponential family of p.d.f.s (recall Definition 3.3.13). Examples 6.1.4 and 6.1.6 show that minimal sufficient statistics exist for members of the exponential family. Loosely speaking, among "smooth" absolutely continuous distributions with fixed support not depending on unknown parameters, exponential families contain the only p.d.f.s that permit dimensional reduction of the sample through sufficiency (see Lehmann 1983, pp. 44–45, and the references cited therein for further discussion). Requiring the support to be free of unknown parameters rules out cases such as the $U(0, \theta)$ distribution, which has a one-dimensional sufficient statistic (see Exercise 6.1.5), but which is not a member of the exponential family.

Because the distribution of an ancillary statistic (recall Definition 5.2.2) does not depend on θ, it might seem reasonable to expect that a minimal sufficient statistic is unrelated or statistically independent of an ancillary statistic, but this is not necessarily the case (e.g., Exercise 5.4.6 shows that the range is ancillary, and it is straightforward to show that the sample range and midrange are minimally sufficient). Situations in which this intuition is valid are discussed later in connection with Basu's Theorem 6.5.7.

The demands of likelihood approaches have led many to alternative approaches. Such alternatives, however, are not really substitutes. They require less of the researcher, but they also deliver less. With the exception of a few nonparametric techniques in the simplest of problems, finite-sample based probabilistic statements cannot be made without first assuming a probabilistic structure for the data up to a finite number of unknown parameters. Nonlikelihood methods eschew making probabilistic inferences in finite samples, and instead move the discussion to the asymptotic arena (Section 6.4) where such information is not required. The quality of an asymptotic approximation to the finite sample case at hand, however, cannot be judged without a full specification of the probabilistic specification of the problem. *In other words, although many asymptotic methods do not require a complete statement of the sampling distribution up to a finite number of unknown parameters, in order to evaluate the* quality of an asymptotic approximation, *it is first necessary to identify the thing being approximated in finite samples, and in general the latter requires a complete statement of the distribution of the underlying data up to a finite number of unknown parameters.* This point will become clearer as the chapter proceeds, but is sufficiently important to warrant mention now. The bottom line is: like in economics and real life, there is no free lunch in econometrics.

Exercises

6.1.1 Let Y_t $(t = 1, 2, \ldots, T) \sim$ i.i.d. $N(0, \theta)$, where $0 < \theta < \infty$. Show that $W = Y_1^2 + Y_2^2 + \cdots + Y_T^2$ is a sufficient statistic for θ.

6.1.2 Let Y_t $(t = 1, 2, \ldots, T)$ be a random sample from a Bernoulli density with parameter θ. Show that $\overline{Y}$ is a sufficient statistic.

6.1.3 Let Y_t $(t = 1, 2, \ldots, T) \sim$ i.i.d. $N(\mu, \sigma^2)$. Show that $\overline{Y}$ and S^2 defined by (5.2.3) are jointly sufficient for μ and σ^2.

6.1.4 Let Y_t $(t = 1, 2, \ldots, T) \sim$ i.i.d. $\text{Po}(\theta)$, where $0 < \theta < \infty$. Show that $W = Y_1 + Y_2 + \cdots + Y_T$ is a sufficient statistic for θ.

6.1.5 Let Y_t $(t = 1, 2, \ldots, T) \sim$ i.i.d. $U(0, \theta)$, where $0 < \theta < \infty$. Show that $W = \max\{Y_1, Y_2, \ldots, Y_T\}$ is a sufficient statistic for θ.

6.1.6 Let Y_t $(t = 1, 2, \ldots, T)$ be i.i.d. $g(\theta)$ (i.e., the geometric distribution defined in Definition 3.2.7). Show: $W = Y_1 + Y_2 + \cdots + Y_T$ is a sufficient statistic for θ.

6.1.7 Let Y_t $(t = 1, 2, \ldots, T) \sim$ i.i.d. $\beta(\theta, 2)$, where $0 < \theta < \infty$. Show that the product $W = Y_1 Y_2 \ldots Y_T$ is a sufficient statistic for θ.

6.1.8 Given θ, suppose X_t $(t = 1, 2, \ldots, T)$ is a random sample from the uniform distribution $U(\theta, \theta + 1)$, $-\infty < \theta < \infty$. Let Y_t $(t = 1, 2, \ldots, T)$ be the corresponding order statistics.

(a) Show that $W \equiv [Y_1, Y_T]'$ is a minimal sufficient statistic for θ.

(b) Is $V \equiv [(Y_T - Y_1, (Y_1 + Y_T)/2]'$ a minimal sufficient statistic for θ. Note that the first component of V is ancillary for θ. Why?

6.1.9 Reconsider Exercise 5.4.8 in which X_t $(t = 1, 2, \ldots, T)$ is a random sample from a uniform $U(\theta, 2\theta)$ distribution, where $\theta > 0$, and let Y_t $(t = 1, 2, \ldots, T)$ be the corresponding order statistics. Show that $W \equiv [Y_1, Y_T]'$ is a minimal sufficient statistic for θ (Basu 1992). (Note: as in Exercise 6.1.8, the dimension of the minimal sufficient statistic does *not* equal the dimension of θ.)

6.1.10 Let Y_t $(t = 1, 2, \ldots, T) \sim$ i.i.d. $U(\theta_1, \theta_2)$ distribution. Show that the first and last order statistics are jointly sufficient for θ_1 and θ_2.

6.1.11 Consider two random variables X and Y and the scalar parameter θ related by $f(x|\theta) = \theta\exp(-\theta x)$ for $x > 0$ and $\theta > 0$, $f(y|x, \theta) = f(y|x) = x\exp(-xy)$ for $y > 0$ and $x > 0$. [Note that Y and θ are conditionally independent given x.] Suppose the researcher wishes to estimate θ, observes Y, but does not observe X. What is the appropriate likelihood function? Obtain analytical expressions for each of the following three possibilities (see Bayarri et al. 1988, pp. 6–7):

(a) $\mathscr{L}_1(\theta; y) = f(y|\theta) = \displaystyle\int_0^\infty f(y|x) f(x|\theta)\, dx$,

(b) $\mathscr{L}_2(\theta; x, y) = f(\text{random variables}|\text{parameters}) = f(y, x|\theta)$,

(c) $\mathscr{L}_3(\theta, x; y) = f(\text{observed}|\text{unobserved}) = f(\theta, x|y)$.

6.2 Likelihood and Stopping Rule Principles

I learned the stopping rule principle from Professor Barnard, in conversation in the summer of 1952. Frankly, I then thought it a scandal that anyone in the profession

could advance an idea so patently wrong, as even today I can scarcely believe that some people resist an idea so patently right.
—L. J. Savage (in Savage et al. 1962)

There is no principle in statistics that has as far-reaching consequences as the *Likelihood Principle (LP)*. Despite its simplicity and importance, it is rarely discussed in statistics texts and is virtually unheard of in econometrics texts.[4] Slightly simplified, the LP can be informally stated as follows.

Definition 6.2.1 (Informal LP) All the evidence obtained from an experiment about an unknown quantity θ is contained in the likelihood $\mathscr{L}(\theta; y)$ for the observed data y.

Although the informal statement of the LP in Definition 6.2.1 is straightforward, it is difficult to appreciate the significance and implications of the LP without further elaboration. Readers are free to agree or disagree with the LP, but readers are not free to disregard the profound implications of their decisions. Depending on the reader's decision, large parts of the statistics literature can be labeled "interesting" or "uninteresting." Those areas labeled uninteresting, however, should not be ignored. The result of that action would be to cut oneself off from a sizeable proportion of the statistics profession.

Early versions of the LP were developed and promoted by Barnard (1947a, 1947b, 1949). Fisher (1956) came close to giving it his approval. The major impetus to the LP came from the seminal work of Birnbaum (1962).[5] Although each of these authors later had reservations regarding the LP, others have since taken over its promotion. The definitive discussion of the matter to date is Berger and Wolpert (1988) who have resurrected the LP from undeserved oblivion and once again confronted the statistics profession with it. Despite some efforts, the econometrics profession has to date found it convenient to ignore the issues involved.[6]

Before formally stating the LP it is instructive to first discuss two other principles about which the reader is likely to find it easier to form an opinion. These two principles are the *Weak Sufficiency Principle (WSP)* (i.e., observations independent of sufficient statistics are irrelevant) and the *Weak Conditionality Principle (WCP)* (i.e., experiments not actually

4. Evidence regarding the latter is provided in Poirier (1989).

5. Admittedly, Birnbaum later appeared to have second thoughts (see Berger and Wolpert 1988, Section 4.1.5).

6. For exceptions to this general rule, see Hendry et al. (1990), Hill (1985–1986), Leamer (1978, pp. 292–295), Malinvaud (1980), Phillips (1991), Poirier (1988c, 1991d), and Zellner (1971).

performed are irrelevant).[7] Both principles involve the concept of evidence as now defined.

Definition 6.2.2 Consider an experiment $\mathscr{E}$ characterized by the triplet $\{Y, \theta, f(y|\theta)\}$, where the random variable Y, defined over the sample space $\mathscr{S}$ and having a probability function $f(y|\theta)$ for some $\theta \in \Theta$, is observed.[8] Then the *evidence about* θ *arising from* $\mathscr{E}$ *and the data* $Y = y$, denoted $Ev(\mathscr{E}, y)$, is broadly defined to be any inference, conclusion or report concerning θ based on $\mathscr{E}$ and y.

Common examples of "evidence" are point estimates, interval estimates or the results of hypothesis tests involving θ. The emphasis in what follows is how the evidence depends on $\mathscr{E}$ and y. The WSP is based on the earlier mentioned intuition underlying a sufficient statistic. Formally, it may be stated as follows.

Definition 6.2.3 (Weak Sufficiency Principle) Consider an experiment $\mathscr{E} = \{Y, \theta, f(y|\theta)\}$, and suppose $W(Y)$ is a sufficient statistic for θ with realized value $w(y)$. Let two runs of the experiment result in the data $Y = y_1$ and $Y = y_2$, respectively, and suppose $w(y_1) = w(y_2)$. Then $Ev(\mathscr{E}, y_1) = Ev(\mathscr{E}, y_2)$.

In other words, the WSP states that when a sufficient statistic exists, then two samples which yield the same observed value for the sufficient statistic provide the same evidence regarding θ.

In developing the WCP we require the notion of a mixed experiment defined next.

Definition 6.2.4 Consider two experiments $\mathscr{E}_j = \{Y_j, \theta, f_j(y_j|\theta)\}$ $(j = 1, 2)$ involving the same parameter θ. A *mixed experiment based on* $\mathscr{E}_1$ *and* $\mathscr{E}_2$ is an experiment of the form $\mathscr{E}_* = \{Y_*, \theta, f_*(j, y_j|\theta)\}$, where $Y_* = [J, Y_J]$ and $f_*(j, y_j|\theta) = .5 f_j(y_j|\theta)$.

In words, a mixed experiment based on $\mathscr{E}_1$ and $\mathscr{E}_2$ is a randomly chosen experiment from the set $\{\mathscr{E}_1, \mathscr{E}_2\}$, where the random variable $J = 1, 2$ denotes which of the two equally likely experiments is chosen.[9] An example of a mixed experiment is the following.

7. As the adjective "weak" suggests, there are stronger versions of the WSP and WCP principles, but they will not concern us here. See Basu (1975) for details.

8. For notational convenience, $\mathscr{S}$ and Θ are suppressed in the description of $\mathscr{E}$. Most statistical methodologies require only this triplet of information. Exceptions are the "structural theory" of Fraser and the "pivotal theory" of Barnard.

9. The assumption that $J = 1$ and $J = 2$ are equally likely is made for the sake of simplicity. The essential characteristic is that $P(J = j|\theta)$ $(j = 1, 2)$ does not depend on θ.

Example 6.2.1 Suppose a physician is contemplating sending out a blood sample to test for the presence ($\theta = 1$) or absence ($\theta = 0$) of AIDS. There are two possible laboratories: one in Toronto and one in Montreal. The physician decides to flip a coin and if "heads" obtains, then the sample is sent to the laboratory in Toronto; if "tails" obtains, then the sample is sent to the laboratory in Montreal.

The WCP asserts that the evidence about θ from a mixed experiment corresponds to the experiment actually performed. Formally, the WCP may be stated as follows.

Definition 6.2.5 (Weak Conditionality Principle) Consider two experiments $\mathscr{E}_j = \{Y_j, \theta, f_j(y_j|\theta)\}$ $(j = 1, 2)$ involving the same parameter θ, and the *mixed experiment based on* $\mathscr{E}_1$ *and* $\mathscr{E}_2$, $\mathscr{E}_* = \{Y_*, \theta, f_*(j, y_j|\theta)\}$, where $Y_* = [J, Y_J]$ and $f_*(j, y_j|\theta) = .5f_j(y_j|\theta)$. Then $Ev[\mathscr{E}_*, (j, y_j)] = Ev[\mathscr{E}_j, y_j]$.

In other words, according to the WCP, when confronted with a mixed experiment in which one of two possible experiments involving the same parameter θ can be performed, and when it is known that one experiment —say the first—was actually performed and yielded the data y_1, then the entire evidence about θ provided by the mixed experiment is given by the first experiment. The second experiment, which could have been performed but was not, provides no evidence regarding θ. In short, outcomes not observed are irrelevant once the data are observed.

Example 6.2.2 Reconsider Example 6.2.1. The physician flips the coin, "heads" obtains, the sample is sent to the laboratory in Toronto, and a "positive" result is obtained for the presence of AIDS. According to the WCP, the evidence in the mixed experiment equals the evidence from the experiment actually run in Toronto. The fact that the blood sample would have been sent to Montreal if "tails" were obtained is irrelevant.

We are now ready to formally state the LP, which was informally stated in Definition 6.2.1.

Definition 6.2.6 (Formal LP) Consider two experiments $\mathscr{E}_j = \{Y_j, \theta, f_j(y_j|\theta)\}$ $(j = 1, 2)$, where all the unknowns in the experiments are contained in the same parameter θ. Suppose that for particular realizations y_1 and y_2 of the data, the respective likelihood functions satisfy $\mathscr{L}_1(\theta; y_1) = c\mathscr{L}_2(\theta; y_2)$ for some constant c possibly depending on y_1 and y_2, but not depending on θ. Then $Ev[\mathscr{E}_1, y_1] = Ev[\mathscr{E}_2, y_2]$.

The connection between the WSP, WCP, and the LP is now provided.

Theorem 6.2.1 The LP holds iff both the WSP and the WCP hold.

Proof Birnbaum (1962) provided a proof in the discrete case under stronger formulations of the WSP and the WCP (see also Basu 1975; Berger and Wolpert 1988, pp. 27–28; or Casella and Berger 1990, pp. 269–271). For a discussion of extensions beyond the discrete case, see Berger and Wolpert (1988, pp. 28–36). Basu (1975) argues that the sample space in any physically realizable experiment must be finite, due to our inability to measure with infinite precision, and hence, from a philosophical standpoint, only a discrete version of the LP is needed. Also see Bjornstad (1992, pp. 470–471) for introductory discussion and other relevant references.

Therefore, according to Theorem 6.2.1, if the researcher does not have an intuitive feeling regarding the validity of the LP, then the researcher can instead consider the WSP and the WCP to decide on the validity of the LP. Although most readers will find it difficult to directly decide on the validity of the LP, I trust most readers will find both the WSP and the WCP intuitively acceptable, and hence logically compelled to accept the LP. Such logic also implies acceptance of the following corollary.

Corollary 6.2.1 (Likelihood Principle Corollary) Consider the experiment $\mathscr{E} = \{Y, \theta, f(y|\theta)\}$ involving the parameter θ. Suppose that for a particular realization y of the data, the likelihood function $\mathscr{L}(\theta; y)$ is obtained. Then $Ev[\mathscr{E}, y]$ depends on $\mathscr{E}$ and y only through $\mathscr{L}(\theta; y)$.

As the monograph by Berger and Wolpert (1988) attests, there is a great deal of controversy surrounding the LP. The discussion comes from all directions, even some Bayesians have argued that further refinements in its statement are necessary.[10] Rather than devote sizeable space to a discussion of some of the issues involved, we instead cut directly to the heart of the matter. *The basic thrust of the LP is to get the researcher thinking conditionally on the observed data and eschewing any consideration of data that could have been observed, but were not observed.* In other words, stop worrying about the sample space for the observed data. It may come as a surprise to the reader to hear that reputable scientists take into consideration data not observed in interpreting evidence from an experiment about unknown quantities. (What could be less "scientific?") But, frequentist statistics is built upon techniques whose validity is judged in a manner that does precisely this. This will become clear in the next section when frequentist properties of estimators are discussed. Furthermore, as

10. For some of the notable dissenters from the LP, see Durbin (1970a), Evans et al. (1986), and Kalbfleisch (1975). For refutations of their arguments, see Berger and Wolpert (1988, esp. pp. 45–46). Hill (1987) offers a restricted version of the LP that emphasizes only *marginal* inferences about θ are encompassed by $\text{Ev}[\mathscr{E}, y]$.

will be seen in later sections, Bayesians obey the main thrust of the LP (conditioning on all the data) even in cases where the LP is not applicable (e.g., because the two experiments do not involve the same unknowns).

The LP is intended to apply to situations in which the likelihood is given beforehand. Any uncertainty over the specification of the likelihood must be incorporated into the unknown parameter vector. In the case of a discrete sample space, a fully nonparametric approach is straightforward (see Berger and Wolpert 1988, pp. 43–44), and according to Basu's argument noted earlier, that is all that is necessary philosophically. Extensions to nonparametric, nondiscrete situations are possible (see Berger and Wolpert 1988, p. 44). Also, the choice of experiment to perform must be noninformative with regard to θ (see Berger and Wolpert 1988, pp. 88–90).

An important point regarding the LP is to note that the LP does *not* say how exactly to go about estimating θ or testing hypotheses involving θ. It only provides restrictions on the evidence about θ provided by the experiment and the realized data. The LP says nothing about the relevance of nonexperimental information regarding θ or how the latter should be combined with data.

There are many implications of the LP. An important example concerns the relevance of rules governing when to stop collecting data. Although such data collection decisions may not be relevant in a largely observational science such as economics, they are of prime importance in experimental sciences, particularly in biometrics (see Example 6.2.3). Consider the following formal definition.

Definition 6.2.7 Let Y_t $(t = 1, 2, \ldots)$ be an observable sequence of random variables from a sequential experiment. A *stopping rule* is a sequence $\tau = \{\tau_0, \tau_1, \tau_2, \ldots\}$ in which $\tau_0 \in [0, 1]$ is a constant, and τ_m $(m = 1, 2, \ldots)$ is a measurable function of $Y_1, Y_2, \ldots, Y_m$ taking values in the interval $[0, 1]$.

As the name suggests, the stopping rule determines when to stop collecting data: τ_0 is the probability of stopping the experiment before collecting any data; $\tau_1(y_1)$ is the probability of stopping after observing $Y_1 = y_1$, conditional on having taken one observation; $\tau_2(y_1, y_2)$ is the probability of stopping after observing $Y_1 = y_1$ and $Y_2 = y_2$, conditional on having taken two observations; and so on. When using a stopping rule the sample size is itself a random variable, giving rise to the following definition.

Definition 6.2.8 The *stopping time* T, depending on the stopping rule and the observed data, is the (random) sample size taken in a sequential experiment. A stopping rule is *proper* iff $P(T < \infty | \theta) = 1$ for all $\theta \in \Theta$.

Because the stopping rule is permitted to depend on the data already observed, it might be thought that such stopping rules are important in interpreting the evidence an experiment contains about θ. The following principle addresses this point, and provides perhaps a surprising answer.

Definition 6.2.9 Consider a sequential experiment with observed data $y = [y_1, y_2, \ldots, y_T]'$. Then according to the *Stopping Rule Principle (SRP)* all experimental information about θ is contained in the observed likelihood $\mathscr{L}(\theta; y)$. The stopping rule τ that was used provides no *additional* information about θ.

The SRP can be shown to follow from the LP, although it predates the LP historically.[11] To many the SRP at first sounds like scientific heresy since it seems to condone sampling to a foregone conclusion, for example, by looking at the data and deciding when to stop sampling, a researcher could conclusively prove or disprove any hypothesis desired. Such possibilities are indeed possible for some statistical hypothesis testing techniques, but that fact should draw into doubt the techniques involved (classical techniques) rather than the SRP itself.[12] The SRP is a matter of everyday experience, and in fact, ignoring it is sometimes judged to be "unethical" as the following example indicates.

Example 6.2.3 The August 14, 1991, issue of the *New York Times* (p. A10) reported a story that received international attention due to its medical importance. The story concerned a surgical technique designed to clear clogged neck arteries leading to the brain that was found to be effective in preventing strokes in patients suffering from a severe case of blockage. The research team was led by Dr. Henry J. M. Barnett of the John P. Robarts Research Institute in London, Ontario. Patients, all of whom had symptoms suggestive of blockage, were randomly split into two groups: 331 patients were treated with aspirin and the anticoagulant warfarin, and 328 patients underwent the surgical technique known as carotoid endarerectomy. In the first group 26 percent of the patients had a subsequent stroke compared to only 9 percent in the second group. The length of the initial experiment was terminated early because preliminary results indicated that "the patients receiving the surgery were doing so well that it would be unethical to continue to endorse conventional medical therapy."

As Edwards et al. (1963) note, the irrelevance of stopping rules is one respect in which Bayesian procedures are more "objective" than classical ones. Classical procedures insist that the intentions of the researcher are crucial to the interpretation of data. According to the LP, the intentions

11. See Berger and Wolpert (1988, pp. 74–90) or Berger and Berry (1988) for details.

12. See Cornfield (1966a, 1966b, 1969, 1970).

are irrelevant once the data are collected, although of course they are crucial to the design of experiments.

We conclude this discussion of the LP with the following example.

Example 6.2.4 Let θ be an unknown parameter satisfying $0 \leq \theta \leq 1$. Consider the following two experiments involving θ. $\mathscr{E}_1 = \{Y_1, \theta, f_1(y_1|\theta)\}$ is a binomial experiment in which a coin is flipped T_1 times, where T_1 is predetermined, and Y_1 is the number of "heads" obtained in the T_1 flips. From Definition 3.2.5 we know the p.m.f. of Y_1 is

$$f_1(y_1|\theta) = \left[\frac{T_1!}{y_1!(T_1 - y_1)!}\right]\theta^{y_1}(1-\theta)^{T_1 - y_1}, \qquad (y = 0, 1, \ldots, T_1), \quad (6.2.1)$$

and zero otherwise. $\mathscr{E}_2 = \{Y_2, \theta, f_2(y_2|\theta)\}$ is a negative binomial experiment in which a coin is flipped until m "tails" are obtained, where $m > 0$ is predetermined, and Y_2 is defined to be the number of "heads" obtained in the process. From Definition 3.2.7 we know that the p.m.f. of Y_2 is

$$f_2(y_2|\theta) = \left[\frac{(y_2 + m - 1)!}{(m-1)!\,y_2!}\right]\theta^{y_2}(1-\theta)^m, \qquad (y_2 = 0, 1, 2, \ldots), \qquad (6.2.2)$$

and zero otherwise.

Suppose $T_1 = 12$ and $m = 3$, and that the two experiments yield the following results: $y_1 = y_2 = 9$. Then

$$\mathscr{L}_1(\theta; y_1) = \left[\frac{12!}{9!\,3!}\right]\theta^9(1-\theta)^3 = 220[\theta^9(1-\theta)^3], \qquad (6.2.3)$$

$$\mathscr{L}_2(\theta; y_2) = \left[\frac{11!}{2!\,9!}\right]\theta^9(1-\theta)^3 = 55[\theta^9(1-\theta)^3]. \qquad (6.2.4)$$

Because $\mathscr{L}_1(\theta; y_1) = c\mathscr{L}_2(\theta; y_2)$, where $c = 4$, the LP is applicable. Hence, the evidence in the data regarding θ is the same for both experiments.

Would you entertain any estimation or hypothesis testing technique that would not conclude that the evidence regarding θ is the same in both of the experiments in Example 6.2.4? This question is well worth dwelling upon. Section 6.10 will take it up again. The curious reader may also wish to jump ahead to Example 7.2.3.

6.3 Sampling Properties of Point Estimators in Finite Samples

I am reminded of the lawyer who remarked that 'when I was a young man I lost many cases that I should have won, but when I grew older I won many that I should have lost, so on the average justice was done.'
—Leamer (1983, p. 31)

Before discussing specific methods for generating classical point estimators in Section 6.6, it is first necessary to develop a language describing what constitutes a desirable point estimator. The criteria discussed in this section are based on the performance of an estimator in repeated samples. It is essential to keep in mind that the criteria developed here refer to *estimators* and not directly to their realized values called *estimates.* A primary goal of applied research is to obtain good estimates of unknown parameters and the implicit assumption underlying frequentist estimation is that a good estimate is obtained by plugging the data into a good estimator. To proponents of the LP this assumption is probably better described as a "leap of faith". Classical properties of estimators such as *bias* and *mean square error* defined below do *NOT* refer to how close the numerical estimate, produced by an estimator in a particular realized sample, is to the unknown value of the parameter, but rather to how close is the average numerical estimate over repeated samples of the same size. In the language of Section 6.1, this section considers *initial precision* as opposed to *final precision.* To reiterate, this section takes the point estimator as given.

We begin our discussion with the following definition of some basic concepts.

Definition 6.3.1 Let $Y = [Y_1, Y_2, \ldots, Y_T]'$ be a data vector consisting of T draws on a random variable Y whose probability density function $f(y|\theta)$ is characterized by the parameter vector $\theta = [\theta_1, \theta_2, \ldots, \theta_K]' \in \Theta$. The set $\mathcal{S}_T$ comprising all possible values of the data Y is called the *sample space.* A *point estimator* $\hat{\theta} = \hat{\theta}(Y)$ is a statistic which associates with each value in $\mathcal{S}_T$ a unique value in the permissible parameter space Θ. A *point estimate* $\hat{\theta}(y)$ is a realized value of a point estimator.

Example 6.3.1 Suppose Y_t $(t = 1, 2, \ldots, T) \sim N(\theta, \sigma^2)$, where θ is an unknown scalar, $\Theta = (-\infty, \infty)$ and σ^2 is known. Four examples of point estimators are:

$$\hat{\theta}_1 = \hat{\theta}_1(Y_1, Y_2, \ldots, Y_T) = \overline{Y} = T^{-1} \sum_{t=1}^{T} Y_t,$$

$$\hat{\theta}_2 = \hat{\theta}_2(Y_1, Y_2, \ldots, Y_T) = \left(\frac{\underline{T}}{\underline{T} + T}\right)\underline{\mu} + \left(\frac{T}{\underline{T} + T}\right)\overline{Y},$$

$$\hat{\theta}_3 = \hat{\theta}_3(Y_1, Y_2, \ldots, Y_T) = \underline{\mu},$$

$$\hat{\theta}_4 = \theta_4(Y_1, Y_2, \ldots, Y_T) = \overline{Y} + 1,$$

where $\underline{\mu}$ and $\underline{T}$ are known scalars satisfying $-\infty < \underline{\mu} < \infty$ and $\underline{T} > 0$. $\hat{\theta}_1$ is the familiar sample mean. $\hat{\theta}_4$ adds unity to $\hat{\theta}_1$. $\hat{\theta}_3$ is a degenerate estimator always equal to the known constant $\underline{\mu}$ regardless of the sample observations. $\hat{\theta}_2$ is a convex combination of $\hat{\theta}_1$ and $\hat{\theta}_3$. Substituting realized values $Y_t = y_t$ $(t = 1, 2, \ldots, T)$ into these estimators yields numerical estimates. Note that the estimator $\hat{\theta}_3$ and the estimate $\hat{\theta}_3 = \underline{\mu}$ are indistinguishable, that is, the estimator $\hat{\theta}_3$ equals $\underline{\mu}$ with probability one.

Since given μ and σ^2, $\hat{\theta}_1 = \bar{Y} \sim N(\theta, \sigma^2/T)$, it is straightforward to show:

$$\hat{\theta}_2 \sim N\left(\left[\frac{\underline{T}}{\underline{T}+T}\right]\underline{\mu} + \left[\frac{T}{\underline{T}+T}\right]\theta,\ \left[\frac{T}{\underline{T}+T}\right]^2\frac{\sigma^2}{T}\right),$$

$$\hat{\theta}_4 \sim N\left(\theta + 1, \frac{\sigma^2}{T}\right).$$

In characterizing the situations in which it is possible to make valid inferences about θ, distinct values of θ should lead to distinct probability density functions. Formally, this can be expressed as follows:

Definition 6.3.2 The parameter vector θ is *identified* at $\theta = \theta_o \in \Theta$ iff for all $\theta \in \Theta$, $\theta \neq \theta_o$ implies $f(y|\theta) \neq f(y|\theta_o)$ for all $y \in \mathscr{S}_*$, where $\mathscr{S}_* \subseteq \mathscr{S}_T$ and $\text{Prob}_{Y|\theta_o}(\mathscr{S}_*) > 0$. If θ is identified at all $\theta_o \in \Theta$, then θ is identified.

Identification at θ_o requires that values of θ distinct from θ_o yield values of $f(y|\theta)$ distinct from $f(y|\theta_o)$ over some subset $\mathscr{S}_*$ of the sample space $\mathscr{S}_T$ that has an *ex ante* positive probability of occurring. Whether this holds for the observed y is left open. If θ is identified in this sense at all $\theta_o \in \Theta$, then we simply say that θ is identified. Identification is a fairly weak condition. If a parameter is not identified, then it makes little sense to try to estimate it, that is, identification logically precedes estimation. In such cases, however, individual components of θ, or more generally vector-valued functions of θ, may be identified and these can be estimated. For additional discussion of identification, see Bowden (1973), Hsiao (1983), and Rothenberg (1971).

Example 6.3.2 For $t = 1, 2, \ldots, T$, let X_t and Z_t be independent random variables such that $X_t \sim$ i.i.d. $N(\alpha, 1)$ and $Z_t \sim$ i.i.d. $N(\beta, 1)$. Also let $Y_t = X_t + Z_t$ $(t = 1, 2, \ldots, T) \sim$ i.i.d. $N(\theta, 2)$, where $\theta \equiv \alpha + \beta$. Suppose Y_t is observed, but neither X_t nor Z_t are observable individually. Defining $\theta_o = \alpha_o + \beta_o \in \Theta \equiv \Re$ to be the "true" value of θ, note that $Y = [Y_1, Y_2, \ldots, Y_T]' \sim N_T(\theta_o \iota_T, 2I_T)$, where ι_T is a $T \times 1$ vector with all elements equal to unity. Although θ is identified at θ_o, neither α nor β are identified at α_o and β_o, respectively. To see this, let $c \neq 0 \in \Re$ and consider $\alpha = \alpha_o + c$ and $\beta = \beta_o - c$. Then for any $y \in \mathscr{S}$, $f(y|\alpha, \beta) = \phi_T(y|[\alpha + \beta]\iota_T, 2I_T) = \phi_T(y|[\alpha_o + \beta_o]\iota_T, 2I_T)$ even though $\alpha \neq \alpha_o$ and $\beta \neq \beta_o$.

Measuring the worth of an estimator requires a criterion, and the following definition satisfies this need.

Definition 6.3.3 A function $C(\hat{\theta}, \theta) \geq 0$ satisfying $C(\theta, \theta) = 0$ and which measures the consequences of using $\hat{\theta} = \hat{\theta}(Y)$ when the "state of nature" is

θ is called a *loss function or a cost function.* The *sampling error* of an estimator $\hat{\theta}$ is $\hat{\theta} - \theta$. Usually $C(\hat{\theta}, \theta)$ is a nondecreasing function of a norm of the sampling error, e.g. the Euclidean length $\|\hat{\theta} - \theta\| = [(\hat{\theta}_1 - \theta_1)^2 + \cdots + (\hat{\theta}_k - \theta_k)^2]^{1/2}$.

Example 6.3.3 Consider Example 6.3.1. Two common examples of loss functions are:

$C_1(\hat{\theta}, \theta) = (\hat{\theta} - \theta)^2,$

$C_2(\hat{\theta}, \theta) = |\hat{\theta} - \theta|,$

where $\hat{\theta}$ is an arbitrary estimator of the scalar θ. $C_1(\hat{\theta}, \theta)$ is strictly convex. $C_2(\hat{\theta}, \theta)$ is convex, but not strictly convex. Convex loss functions are convenient from a mathematical standpoint, and they yield many rich results (see Exercise 6.3.20). Various pragmatic considerations (e.g., financial), however, suggest that loss functions must ultimately be bounded, and if $\hat{\theta}$ can take on any values in $(-\infty, \infty)$ or $(0, \infty)$, then no nonconstant bounded loss function can be convex. See Lehmann (1983, pp. 55–56) for further discussion.

Unfortunately, frequentists sometimes argue that the need to specify a loss function is one of the shortcomings of the Bayesian approach. Such a state of affairs is most unfortunate. As is often the case, the Bayesian approach (Section 6.7) makes explicit what is left implicit in other approaches. The familiar concept of mean square error (defined in Definition 6.3.7) simply corresponds to a particular type of loss function, namely, quadratic loss. To the extent that loss functions (equivalently, disutility functions) are difficult to specify, both classicists and Bayesians encounter problems. It should be noted, however, that consumers' utility functions are also difficult to specify in microeconomic theory, and the latter field seems to flourish despite such difficulties.

Clearly, it is desired to "minimize" $C(\hat{\theta}, \theta)$ in some sense, but its randomness must first be eliminated. From the sampling theory point of view, θ is nonstochastic but $C(\hat{\theta}, \theta)$ is nonetheless stochastic because the estimator $\hat{\theta} = \hat{\theta}(Y)$ is a random variable.[13] An obvious way to circumscribe the randomness of $C(\hat{\theta}, \theta)$ is to focus attention on its expected value, assuming it exists.[14] The following definition provides the necessary terminology.

13. In the Bayesian approach developed in Section 6.7, loss is a final precision concept in which the estimator $\hat{\theta}(Y)$ is replaced by the estimate $\hat{\theta}(y)$. Although $\hat{\theta}(y)$ is non-stochastic (because the analysis is conditioned on $Y = y$ in agreement with the Likelihood Principle), loss is nonetheless stochastic because uncertainty about θ is treated probabilistically via the posterior distribution for θ.

14. Of course other candidates are possible, for example, the median of the distribution of $C(\hat{\theta}, \theta)$. The median loss, unlike (6.3.1) is guaranteed to exist, and in the case of continuous random variables, is unique.

Definition 6.3.4 Let $\hat{\theta} = \hat{\theta}(Y)$ be an estimator of θ and consider the loss function $C(\hat{\theta}, \theta)$. Then the *risk function* (or simply *risk*) is the nonstochastic function

$$R(\hat{\theta}|\theta) \equiv E_{Y|\theta}[C(\hat{\theta}(Y), \theta)], \tag{6.3.1}$$

where the expectation (assumed to exist) is taken with respect to the sampling p.f. $f(y|\theta)$.

Example 6.3.4 Consider Example 6.3.1 and the quadratic loss function $(\hat{\theta} - \theta)^2$. Then the risk functions for the four estimators in Example 6.3.1 are:

$$R(\hat{\theta}_1|\theta) = E_{Y|\theta}[(\hat{\theta}_1 - \theta)^2] = E_{Y|\theta}[(\overline{Y} - \theta)^2] = \mathrm{Var}(\overline{Y}) = \frac{\sigma^2}{T},$$

$$\begin{aligned}
R(\hat{\theta}_2|\theta) &= E_{Y|\theta}[(\hat{\theta}_2 - \theta)^2] \\
&= E_{Y|\theta}\left(\left[\left(\frac{\underline{T}}{\underline{T} + T}\right)(\underline{\mu} - \theta) + \left(\frac{T}{\underline{T} + T}\right)(\overline{Y} - \theta)\right]^2\right) \\
&= \left(\frac{\underline{T}}{\underline{T} + T}\right)^2 (\underline{\mu} - \theta)^2 + 2\left(\frac{\underline{T}T}{(\underline{T} + T)^2}\right)(\underline{\mu} - \theta)E_{Y|\theta}(\overline{Y} - \theta) \\
&\quad + \left(\frac{T}{\underline{T} + T}\right)^2 E_{Y|\theta}[(\overline{Y} - \theta)^2] \\
&= \left(\frac{\underline{T}}{\underline{T} + T}\right)^2 (\underline{\mu} - \theta)^2 + \left(\frac{T}{\underline{T} + T}\right)^2 \frac{\sigma^2}{T} \\
&= \frac{T\sigma^2 + \underline{T}^2(\underline{\mu} - \theta)^2}{(\underline{T} + T)^2} = \frac{\sigma^2}{T}\left[\left(\frac{T}{\underline{T} + T}\right)^2 + \left(\frac{\underline{T}}{\underline{T} + T}\right)^2 \left(\frac{\underline{\mu} - \theta}{\sigma/\sqrt{T}}\right)^2\right],
\end{aligned}$$

$$R(\hat{\theta}_3|\theta) = E_{Y|\theta}[(\hat{\theta}_3 - \theta)^2] = E_{Y|\theta}[(\underline{\mu} - \theta)^2] = (\underline{\mu} - \theta)^2,$$

$$\begin{aligned}
R(\hat{\theta}_4|\theta) &= E_{Y|\theta}[(\hat{\theta}_4 - \theta)^2] = E_{Y|\theta}[(\overline{Y} + 1 - \theta)^2] \\
&= E_{Y|\theta}[(\overline{Y} - \theta)^2] + 2E_{Y|\theta}(\overline{Y} - \theta) + E_{Y|\theta}[(1 - \theta)^2] \\
&= \frac{\sigma^2}{T} + (1 - \theta)^2.
\end{aligned}$$

From an initial precision standpoint a "good" estimator is defined to be one for which the risk (6.3.1) is "small" for all possible value of $\theta \in \Theta$. This recommendation implies that procedures should be evaluated based on the "average" performance in repeated sampling. Obviously inferior estimators can be ruled out by adopting the following terminology.

Definition 6.3.5 Consider two estimators $\hat{\theta}_1$ and $\hat{\theta}_2$. Given a loss function $C(\hat{\theta}_i(Y), \theta)$ $(i = 1, 2)$, suppose that $R(\hat{\theta}_1|\theta) \leq R(\hat{\theta}_2|\theta)$ for all $\theta \in \Theta$, and $R(\hat{\theta}_1|\theta) < R(\hat{\theta}_2|\theta)$ for at least one $\theta \in \Theta$. Then $\hat{\theta}_1$ is a *relatively more efficient* estimator than $\hat{\theta}_2$ according to loss function $C(\hat{\theta}, \theta)$. The estimator $\hat{\theta}_2$ in this case is *inadmissible* with respect to the loss function $C(\hat{\theta}, \theta)$. An estimator is *admissible* with respect to the loss function $C(\hat{\theta}, \theta)$ iff there does not exist any estimator better than it in the preceding sense.

It must be emphasized that admissibility is defined with respect to a particular loss function. If a particular loss function captures all interesting aspects of the estimation problem at hand, then the researcher would seem compelled by intellectual honesty (at least from the standpoint of initial precision) to reject any inadmissible estimator in favor of any estimator available which dominates it in terms of risk. Choice of an inadmissible estimator is tantamount to rejection of the appropriateness of the loss function involved, or possibly implying that some additional constraints (e.g., invariance with respect to a group of transformations) needs to be added to the problem.

Particular choices of loss functions in Definition 6.3.4 warrant mention, and the following terminology is commonly employed.

Definition 6.3.6 Given a $K \times K$ positive definite matrix Q, the loss function

$$C(\hat{\theta}, \theta) = (\hat{\theta} - \theta)'Q(\hat{\theta} - \theta) \tag{6.3.2}$$

is *weighted squared error loss*. In the unweighted case $Q = I_K$, referred to simply as *squared error loss*, (6.3.2) is the squared Euclidian distance of sampling error, that is,

$$C(\hat{\theta}, \theta) = \sum_{k=1}^{K} (\hat{\theta}_k - \theta_k)^2. \tag{6.3.3}$$

Example 6.3.5 Consider Example 6.3.4. Under quadratic loss, estimator $\hat{\theta}_4$ is inadmissible as can be seen from a comparison of $R(\hat{\theta}_4|\theta)$ and $R(\hat{\theta}_1|\theta)$.

Often an unambiguous choice for the weighting matrix Q in (6.3.2) is not available. Fortunately, in some cases it may still be possible to compare two estimators for all possible choices of Q.

Definition 6.3.7 The *mean square error matrix* of an estimator $\hat{\theta}$ (assuming it exists) is

$$\text{MSE}(\hat{\theta}) \equiv \text{MSE}(\hat{\theta}|\theta) \equiv E_{Y|\theta}[(\hat{\theta} - \theta)(\hat{\theta} - \theta)']. \tag{6.3.4}$$

If $K = 1$, $\text{MSE}(\hat{\theta}) = E_{Y|\theta}[(\hat{\theta} - \theta)^2]$ is known simply as the *mean square error* of $\hat{\theta}$.

Example 6.3.6 In Example 6.3.4, $R(\hat{\theta}_j|\theta) = \text{MSE}(\hat{\theta}_j)$ $(j = 1, 2, 3, 4)$.

Ordering estimators according to whether differences in their MSE matrices are positive definite permits ordering risks for arbitrary weighted squared error loss. The following theorem makes the required connection.

Theorem 6.3.1 Let $\hat{\theta}_i$ $(i = 1, 2)$ be two estimators of θ. Denote their risks under weighted squared error loss by

$$R_i \equiv R(\hat{\theta}_i|\theta) = E_{Y|\theta}[(\hat{\theta} - \theta)'Q(\hat{\theta} - \theta)] \qquad (i = 1, 2) \tag{6.3.5}$$

for an arbitrary positive definite matrix Q. Then regardless of the choice of Q, $R_2 - R_1 > 0$ iff $\text{MSE}(\hat{\theta}_2) - \text{MSE}(\hat{\theta}_1)$ is a positive definite matrix for all $\theta \in \Theta$.

Proof Using Theorem A.1.4(c),

$$\begin{aligned} R_2 - R_1 &= E_{Y|\theta}[\text{tr}\{(\hat{\theta}_2 - \theta)'Q(\hat{\theta}_2 - \theta)\}] - E_{Y|\theta}[\text{tr}(\hat{\theta}_1 - \theta)'Q(\hat{\theta}_1 - \theta)] \\ &= \text{tr}\{QE_{Y|\theta}[(\hat{\theta}_2 - \theta)(\hat{\theta}_2 - \theta)']\} - \text{tr}\{QE_{Y|\theta}[(\hat{\theta}_1 - \theta)(\hat{\theta}_1 - \theta)']\} \\ &= \text{tr}\{Q[\text{MSE}(\hat{\theta}_2) - \text{MSE}(\hat{\theta}_1)]\}. \end{aligned} \tag{6.3.6}$$

Because Q is positive definite, according to Theorem A.7.14 there exists a matrix A such that $Q = AA'$. Letting a_k $(k = 1, 2, \ldots, K)$ denote the columns of A, (6.3.6) can be written [again using Theorem A.1.4(c)]:

$$\begin{aligned} R_2 - R_1 &= \text{tr}[A'[\text{MSE}(\hat{\theta}_2) - \text{MSE}(\hat{\theta}_1)]A] \\ &= \sum_{k=1}^{K} a_k'[\text{MSE}(\hat{\theta}_2) - \text{MSE}(\hat{\theta}_1)]a_k. \end{aligned} \tag{6.3.7}$$

Then the result of the theorem follows directly from (6.3.7).

Theorem 6.3.1 implies that if the difference in mean square error matrices of two estimators is positive (or negative) definite for all $\theta \in \Theta$, then the estimator with the "smaller" mean square error matrix is relatively more efficient according to arbitrarily weighted squared error loss. Note also that $\text{tr}[\text{MSE}(\hat{\theta})]$ corresponds to precisely the risk of $\hat{\theta}$ under simple squared error loss.

Yet another way of comparing the risk of two estimators under arbitrarily weighted squared error loss is provided by the following theorem.

Theorem 6.3.2 Let $\hat{\theta}_i$ $(i = 1, 2)$ be two estimators of θ and let c be a $K \times 1$ vector of constants. Define $\alpha \equiv c'\theta$ and consider the estimators $\hat{\alpha}_i \equiv c'\hat{\theta}_i$ $(i = 1, 2)$. Then $\text{MSE}(\hat{\theta}_2) - \text{MSE}(\hat{\theta}_1)$ is positive definite iff $\text{MSE}(\hat{\alpha}_2) > \text{MSE}(\hat{\alpha}_1)$ for arbitrary c.

Proof Consider

$$\begin{aligned} \text{MSE}(\hat{\alpha}_i) &\equiv E_{Y|\theta}[(\hat{\alpha}_i - \alpha)^2] \\ &= E_{Y|\theta}[c'(\hat{\theta}_i - \theta)(\hat{\theta}_i - \theta)'c] \\ &= c'[\text{MSE}(\hat{\theta}_i)]c \qquad (i = 1, 2). \end{aligned} \tag{6.3.8}$$

Then for arbitrary c,

$$\text{MSE}(\hat{\alpha}_2) - \text{MSE}(\hat{\alpha}_1) = c'[\text{MSE}(\hat{\theta}_2) - \text{MSE}(\hat{\theta}_1)]c, \tag{6.3.9}$$

and the conclusion of Theorem 6.3.2 follows immediately from (6.3.9).

Corollary If $\text{MSE}(\hat{\theta}_2) - \text{MSE}(\hat{\theta}_1)$ is positive definite, then

$$\text{MSE}(\hat{\theta}_{2k}) > \text{MSE}(\hat{\theta}_{1k}) \qquad (k = 1, 2, \ldots, K). \tag{6.3.10}$$

Proof Choose c in Theorem 6.3.2 so that all its elements equal zero except the kth which is set equal to unity, that is, set $c = e_{k,K}$, where $e_{k,K}$ is a $K \times 1$ vector with all elements equal to zero except the kth which equals unity. Then (6.3.10) follows directly from (6.3.9).

Returning to the general case of Definition 6.3.4, a major difficulty must be noted. As the notation $R(\hat{\theta}|\theta)$ makes clear, in general *the risk of an estimator* $\hat{\theta}$ *depends on* θ. This is explicit for $\hat{\theta}_j$ ($j = 2, 3, 4$) in Example 6.3.4; $\hat{\theta}_1$ is an exception in this regard. This dependency implies that without further structure it is not possible to find an estimator which is optimal according to (6.3.1) *for all values* of θ. To see that this is the case, consider the trivial admissible estimator $\hat{\theta}_3 = \underline{\mu}$ in Example 6.3.1, which cannot be beat by any estimator when $\theta = \underline{\mu}$, but which may be disastrous when θ is far from $\underline{\mu}$. When considering more interesting nontrivial admissible estimators, one is likely to find that their risk functions cross so that one estimator is preferred for some values of θ, and the other estimator is preferred for other values of θ.

Example 6.3.7 Consider Example 6.3.4. Define $z = [T(\underline{\mu} - \theta_o)^2/\sigma^2]^{1/2} > 0$, where θ_o is the unobserved "true" value of θ unknown to the researcher. Note the MSE ratios:

$$\frac{\text{MSE}_2}{\text{MSE}_1} = \frac{R(\hat{\theta}_2|\theta = \theta_o)}{R(\hat{\theta}_1|\theta = \theta_o)} = \left(1 + \frac{\underline{T}}{T}\right)^{-2}\left[1 + \left(\frac{\underline{T}}{T}\right)^2 z^2\right],$$

$$\frac{\text{MSE}_3}{\text{MSE}_1} = \frac{R(\hat{\theta}_3|\theta = \theta_o)}{R(\hat{\theta}_1|\theta = \theta_o)} = z^2,$$

$$\frac{\text{MSE}_4}{\text{MSE}_1} = \frac{R(\hat{\theta}_4|\theta = \theta_o)}{R(\hat{\theta}_1|\theta = \theta_o)} = 1 + \left(\frac{1 - \theta_o}{\sigma/\sqrt{T}}\right)^2.$$

As seen in Example 6.3.5, $\hat{\theta}_1$ implies $\hat{\theta}_4$ is inadmissible with respect to quadratic loss, and so we eliminate $\hat{\theta}_4$ from further consideration. Note, however, that $\hat{\theta}_4$ may dominate $\hat{\theta}_2$ and $\hat{\theta}_3$ for some values of θ_o.

Table 6.3.1 provides a numerical comparison of $\text{MSE}_2/\text{MSE}_1$ and $\text{MSE}_3/\text{MSE}_1$ for various values of z and $\underline{T}/T$. z measures the distance of the known constant $\underline{\mu}$ from the unknown "truth" θ_o in units $\sigma/T^{1/2}$ of the standard deviation of $\hat{\theta} = \hat{\theta}_1$. $\hat{\theta}_2$ is a compromise between $\hat{\theta}_1 - \overline{Y}$ and the dogmatic estimate $\hat{\theta}_3 = \underline{\mu}$. The ratio $\underline{T}/T$ reflects the relative weight attached to $\underline{\mu}$ in the compromise. As can be seen from Table 6.3.1, $\hat{\theta}_3$ dominates $\hat{\theta}_1$ when the prior guess $\underline{\mu}$ is close to θ_o, that is, $z < 1$. $\hat{\theta}_2$ dominates $\hat{\theta}_1$ over a wider range of values of $\underline{\mu}$ depending on $\underline{T}/T$. Figure 6.3.1 depicts

Table 6.3.1
MSE comparisons of example 6.3.7

		MSE$_2$/MSE$_1$			
z	MSE$_3$/MSE$_1$	$\underline{T}/T = .1$	$\underline{T}/T = .25$	$\underline{T}/T = .5$	$\underline{T}/T = 1$
.000	.000	.826	.640	.444	.250
.500	.250	.829	.650	.451	.313
1.000	1.000	.835	.680	.555	.500
2.000	4.000	.860	.800	.889	1.250
3.000	9.000	.901	1.000	2.080	2.500
4.000	16.000	.956	1.280	2.222	4.250
5.000	25.000	1.033	1.640	3.222	6.500

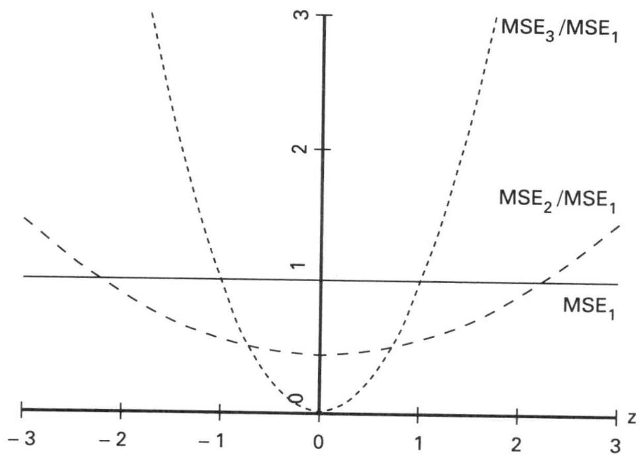

Figure 6.3.1
MSE comparisons from Table 6.3.1

these results for $\underline{T}/T = \frac{1}{2}$. Because z depends on θ_o, z is inherently unknown to the researcher, whereas $\underline{T}/T$ is under the control of the researcher in specifying $\hat{\theta}_2$.

Although the problem caused by the dependency of risk on the unknown θ_o is easy to comprehend, its resolution is far from easy. One obvious approach is to choose an estimator with small risk for those values of θ thought to be most likely. Such an approach may seem eminently reasonable, but it does not fit in well with classical statistics because it suggests the use of nondata based imperfect information concerning θ. Such information sounds embarrassingly close to a Bayesian's prior distribution for θ, and such discussion is postponed until Section 6.7.

Another approach is to appeal to some principle that will "remove θ" from the criterion function. One possibility is the *minimax principle*, which advocates selecting an estimator $\hat{\theta}^*$ satisfying

$$\underset{\theta}{\text{supremum}}\ R(\hat{\theta}^*|\theta) = \underset{\hat{\theta}}{\text{infinum}}\ \underset{\theta}{\text{supremum}}\ R(\hat{\theta}|\theta). \tag{6.3.11}$$

In other words, the minimax principle recommends choosing an estimator $\hat{\theta}^*$ that "minimizes" the "maximum" risk attainable under the least favorable state of nature. The existence or uniqueness of such an estimator is problem specific. If it exists, however, it does not depend on the true state of nature because the "supremum" operator in (6.3.11) removes θ from the criterion. The minimax principle is "conservative" because it recommends choosing an estimator based on its performance in the worst possible circumstances, regardless of its performance in other states of nature or the plausibility of the worse case scenario. The minimax principle has some attractiveness in game theory with two or more intelligent opponents. In contrast, in statistical decision theory the decision maker and "nature" are not cast in adversarial positions, and hence, the minimax principle is less attractive.

By far the most popular approach to removing the general dependency on θ of an estimator's risk is to restrict the class of estimators over which an optimal estimator is sought. The leading example of such cases is the class of unbiased estimators as defined in the following definition.

Definition 6.3.8 The *bias* of an estimator is defined to be the expected value (assuming it exists) of its sampling error, that is,

$$\text{Bias}(\hat{\theta}) \equiv \text{Bias}(\hat{\theta}|\theta) \equiv E_{Y|\theta}(\hat{\theta} - \theta) = E_{Y|\theta}(\hat{\theta}) - \theta. \tag{6.3.12}$$

If $\text{Bias}(\hat{\theta}) = 0$ for all $\theta \in \Theta$, then $E_{Y|\theta}(\hat{\theta}) = \theta$ and the estimator $\hat{\theta}$ is defined to be an *unbiased estimator* of θ. In the case $K = 1$, if $\text{Bias}(\hat{\theta}|\theta) > 0$ for all $\theta \in \Theta$, then $\hat{\theta}$ is said to be *positively biased*, and if $\text{Bias}(\hat{\theta}|\theta) < 0$ for all $\theta \in \Theta$, then $\hat{\theta}$ is said to be *negatively biased*.

Example 6.3.8 Consider Example 6.3.4. In deriving the risk function of the four estimators in Example 6.3.1, it was implicitly shown: $\text{Bias}(\hat{\theta}_1) = 0$, $\text{Bias}(\hat{\theta}_2) = \underline{T}(\underline{\mu} - \theta_o)/(\underline{T} + T)$, $\text{Bias}(\hat{\theta}_3) = \underline{\mu} - \theta_o$, and $\text{Bias}(\hat{\theta}_4) = 1$.

Lehmann (1983, p. 145) reports that Gauss (1823) introduced the concept of unbiasedness as "lack of systematic error." The attractiveness of the concept of bias upon which unbiasedness is based is in part due to the following theorem that relates $\text{Bias}(\hat{\theta})$ to $\text{MSE}(\hat{\theta})$.

Theorem 6.3.3 Let $\hat{\theta}$ be an estimator with finite first and second moments. Then

$$\text{MSE}(\hat{\theta}) = \text{Var}(\hat{\theta}) + [\text{Bias}(\hat{\theta})][\text{Bias}(\hat{\theta})]', \tag{6.3.13}$$

where

$$\text{Var}(\hat{\theta}) = E_{Y|\theta}\{[\hat{\theta} - E_{Y|\theta}(\hat{\theta})][\hat{\theta} - E_{Y|\theta}(\hat{\theta})]'\} \tag{6.3.14}$$

is the *variance-covariance matrix* of $\hat{\theta}$.

Proof Let $\mu \equiv E(\hat{\theta})$. Then

$$\begin{aligned}\text{MSE}(\hat{\theta}) &= E_{Y|\theta}[\{\hat{\theta} - \theta\}\{\hat{\theta} - \theta\}'] \\ &= E_{Y|\theta}[\{(\hat{\theta} - \mu) + (\mu - \theta)\}\{(\hat{\theta} - \mu) + (\mu - \theta)\}'] \\ &= E_{Y|\theta}[(\hat{\theta} - \mu)(\hat{\theta} - \mu)' + (\hat{\theta} - \mu)(\mu - \theta)' + (\mu - \theta)(\hat{\theta} - \mu)' \\ &\quad + (\mu - \theta)(\mu - \theta)'] \\ &= E_{Y|\theta}[(\hat{\theta} - \mu)(\hat{\theta} - \mu)'] - 0 - 0 + (\mu - \theta)(\mu - \theta)'] \\ &= \text{Var}(\hat{\theta}) + [\text{Bias}(\hat{\theta})][\text{Bias}(\hat{\theta})]'.\end{aligned}$$

Corollary 6.3.4 If $\hat{\theta}$ is an unbiased estimator of θ, then

$$\text{MSE}(\hat{\theta}) = \text{Var}(\hat{\theta}). \tag{6.3.15}$$

Proof Follows directly from (6.3.13) and the definition of an unbiased estimator.

It is instructive to view decomposition (6.3.13) as an equal weighting of the variance and squared bias of an estimator. Other weightings are possible of course (see Exercise 6.3.14), but MSE remains the most popular. MSE is especially attractive when comparing an unbiased estimator with a biased estimator with smaller variance since it permits "trading-off" bias for a reduction in variance. In the case $K = 1$, MSE is simply risk under the quadratic loss $C(\hat{\theta}, \theta) = (\hat{\theta} - \theta)^2$, and decomposition (6.3.13) permits a visualization of such risks directly in terms of the sampling distribution of an estimator.

Example 6.3.9 Figure 6.3.2 depicts graphically the sampling distributions of $\hat{\theta}_1$ and $\hat{\theta}_2$ in Example 6.3.1 for the case: $\theta = 0$, $\sigma^2 = 1$, $T = 10$, $\underline{\mu} > \theta_o$, $\underline{T} = .5$ and $z = 3/5^{1/2}$ (see Example 6.3.7). For these values $\text{MSE}(\hat{\theta}_1) = \text{MSE}(\hat{\theta}_2)$. As noted in Example 6.3.8, $\hat{\theta}_1$ is unbiased and $\hat{\theta}_2$ is biased. Given $\underline{T}$, further increase in $\text{Bias}(\hat{\theta}_2) = \underline{T}(\underline{\mu} - \theta_o)$ leads to $\text{MSE}(\hat{\theta}_1) < \text{MSE}(\hat{\theta}_2)$.

By restricting attention to the class (possibly empty) of unbiased estimators, it is possible to obtain a lower bound on the variance of such estimators, and as a result of the Corollary to Theorem 6.3.3, to obtain a lower bound on the MSE matrix of any unbiased estimator. Such a bound is known as the *Cramer-Rao lower bound* and it is derived in Theorem 6.5.2. Unfortunately, this bound is obtainable only in particular circumstances (see Theorem 6.5.3); fortunately, it is possible in such cases to describe a

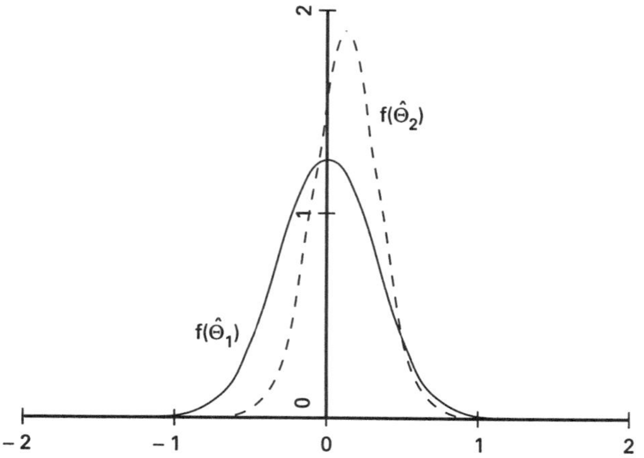

Figure 6.3.2
Sampling densities of $\hat{\theta}_1$ and $\hat{\theta}_2$ in Example 6.3.9

procedure for generating an estimator that achieves this bound (see Theorem 6.5.6).

The value of such derivations is dependent on the attractiveness of the class of unbiased estimators toward which attention is directed. Overlooking the value-loaded connotation of the term "unbiasedness", it is unclear whether the concept has any special primitive appeal. Recalling the quote by Leamer that opened this section, it would seem that most potential clients would not be interested in the lawyer's long-run relative performance, but rather the lawyer's actual performance in their own case. Clearly unbiasedness is a concept concerned with initial precision.

Even if unbiasedness has a primitive attractiveness, it should be noted that sometimes no unbiased estimator exists (e.g., see Cox and Hinkley 1974, p. 253; DeGroot 1987, p. 416; Lehmann 1983, pp. 75, 79; Kendall and Stuart 1979, p. 36, Problem 17.26; and Mood et al. 1974, pp. 330). For example, consider Y_t $(t = 1, 2, \ldots, T) \sim$ i.i.d. $B(1, \theta)$, $0 \leq \theta \leq 1$, then no unbiased estimator exists for $\theta^{1/2}$. Also, unbiasedness often requires "impossible" estimates (i.e., outside Θ, see Blyth 1993). Furthermore, such unbiased estimators are generally inadmissible (Lehmann 1983, p. 263, Lemma 3.1 and Exercise 6.3.8).

If the primitive notion is that an estimator should be "centered" over θ, then this does *not* necessarily lead to unbiasedness since other measures of central tendency can be employed. For example, consider the following definition.

Definition 6.3.9 An estimator $\hat{\theta}$ of the scalar θ is *median unbiased* for all $\theta \in \Theta$ iff $\text{Prob}(\hat{\theta} < \theta) = \text{Prob}(\hat{\theta} > \theta) = \frac{1}{2}$.

Because the median always exists, unlike the mean, the concept of median unbiasedness is always applicable, even when moments of $\hat{\theta}$ do not exist, as for example in the case of many "simultaneous equations estimators." A measure of efficiency sometimes used in such cases is the probability of nearness criterion of Pitman (1937). In the case of $K = 1$, this criterion is defined as follows.

Definition 6.3.10 Let $\hat{\theta}_i$ $(i = 1, 2)$ be two estimators of the scalar parameter θ. Then $\hat{\theta}_1$ is preferred to $\hat{\theta}_2$ according to the *probability of nearness (PN) criterion* iff

$$\text{Prob}(|\hat{\theta}_1 - \theta| \leq |\hat{\theta}_2 - \theta|) \geq .5. \tag{6.3.16}$$

In other words, $\hat{\theta}_1$ is preferred to $\hat{\theta}_2$ according to the PN criterion iff $\hat{\theta}_1$ is nearer to θ than $\hat{\theta}_2$ more frequently than $\hat{\theta}_2$ is nearer to θ than $\hat{\theta}_1$.

Rao (1981) provides examples in which $\hat{\theta}_1$ dominates $\hat{\theta}_2$ according to the PN criterion even though $\text{MSE}(\hat{\theta}_1) < \text{MSE}(\hat{\theta}_2)$. Thus the PN criterion and the MSE criterion can be in conflict. Although the PN criterion has more intuitive appeal than the MSE criterion, it has two major shortcomings: (i) rarely does there exist a PN closest estimator and (ii) the PN criterion is not always transitive (see Blyth 1972). For further discussion, see Blyth and Pathak (1985), Das Peddada (1985), Rao et al. (1986), and Sen (1992).

Another way of restricting the class of potential estimators is to restrict attention to the class of *linear estimators*, i.e. estimators which are linear functions of the data. For example, the sample mean

$$\overline{Y} = \frac{1}{T}\sum_{t=1}^{T} Y_t$$

is a linear estimator. Unfortunately, attempts to find the linear estimator with smallest MSE usually result in "estimators" which depend on θ (e.g., Theil 1971, pp. 125–126, Kmenta 1986, pp. 185–186) and Exercise 6.3.10b). If a different concept of efficiency is employed, however, a meaningful optimal linear estimator may exist (see Exercise 6.3.11).

When the class of potential estimators is limited to both linear and unbiased estimators, then it is usually possible to find an optimal estimator as defined next.

Definition 6.3.11 An estimator is the *best linear unbiased estimator (BLUE)* of θ iff it is relatively more efficient than any other linear unbiased estimator of θ.

For example, the sample mean from a random sample is the BLUE of the population mean (see Exercise 6.3.10). The imposition of both linearity and unbiasedness is very restrictive, however, and the resulting "optimal" estimator may not be even moderately good when compared to estimators outside this class. For example, when sampling from multivariate normal distributions it is often possible to construct nonlinear, biased estimators that are relatively more efficient than the sample mean, in the sense of Definition 6.3.4, for all values of the unknown parameters. Such estimators are members of the family of *Stein-like estimators* (see Example 6.6.8).

In summary, if one adopts an initial precision perspective, then the averaging over the sample space upon which the definition of risk is based seems reasonably palatable. Unfortunately, the risk of an estimator typically depends on the value of the unknown parameters, and as a result, the risk functions of different estimators usually cross. If they don't cross, then the inferior estimator is inadmissible and presumably should be abandoned if the superior estimator is available; otherwise the researcher is admitting the inappropriateness of the loss function involved. Embarrassingly, the classical approach finds it difficult to choose among competing estimators based on knowledge (possibly imperfect) of where θ lies.[15] Instead classical statisticians usually restrict the class of potential estimators by imposing a side condition that they be unbiased. The primitive appeal of this condition is at best unclear. Even if unbiasedness is deemed acceptable, it does not guarantee that the price in terms of risk of imposing unbiasedness is acceptable.

In Section 6.5 three questions will be addressed: (i) Is there a lower bound on the variance (and hence MSE) of an unbiased estimator? (ii) Is this bound attainable? (iii) How can one find an estimator that achieves this lower bound when it is attainable? It will be seen that fully satisfactory answers can only be obtained in special settings. Even accepting the initial precision perspective, such limited answers to questions which seem contrived (due to the unbiasedness restriction) to many statisticians is faint praise for the classical approach.

Exercises

6.3.1 Define

$$\overline{Y}_j = \frac{1}{T_j}\sum_{t=1}^{T_j} Y_{tj} \qquad (j = 1, 2),$$

where Y_{tj} $(t = 1, 2, \ldots, T_j; j = 1, 2)$ are independent and identically distributed observa-

15. One solution is to employ biased "shrinkage" estimators that concentrate risk reduction in that part of the parameter space thought to be most likely. An example is the James-Stein estimator discussed in Example 6.6.8. Although such estimators partially rescue classical statistics from total embarrassment, they also yield disturbing inadmissibility results for estimators (e.g., maximum likelihood estimators) commonly proposed as classical statistics.

tions with common mean and variance μ and σ^2, respectively. Consider the following two estimates of μ:

$$\hat{\mu}_1 = \frac{\bar{Y}_1 + \bar{Y}_2}{2}, \qquad \hat{\mu}_2 = \frac{T_1\bar{Y}_1 + T_2\bar{Y}_2}{T_1 + T_2},$$

(a) Find $E(\hat{\mu}_j)$ for $j = 1, 2$.

(b) Find $\text{Var}(\hat{\mu}_j)$ for $j = 1, 2$.

(c) Find $\text{MSE}(\hat{\mu}_j)$ for $j = 1, 2$.

(d) Which estimator is more efficient? Is either estimator BLUE?

6.3.2 Suppose $Y = [Y_1, Y_2, \ldots, Y_T]' \sim N_T(\mu, \Sigma)$, where $\mu = \theta$, $\Sigma = \sigma^2[(1-\alpha)I_T + \alpha\iota_T\iota_T']$ is a $T \times 1$ vector with each element equal to unity, and α is a scalar such that Σ is positive definite [i.e., $\alpha > -(T-1)^{-1}$].

(a) For what value of α does Y comprise a random sample?

(b) Find $\text{Var}(\bar{Y})$ and simplify your answer.

(c) Is S^2 an unbiased estimator of σ^2?

(d) Find $\text{Var}(S^2)$ and simplify your answer.

(e) Find Σ^{-1}. (Use Theorem A.4.3.)

(f) Find the distribution of Y_T given $Y_1, Y_2, \ldots, Y_{T-1}$. Simplify your answer.

6.3.3 Suppose Y_1 and Y_2 are independently distributed with the same variance σ^2, but with different means: $E(Y_1) = 2\theta$ and $E(Y_2) = 4\theta$. Consider the estimator $\hat{\theta} = w_1Y_1 + w_2Y_2$, where w_1 and w_2 are unknown "weights." Find w_1 and w_2 so that $\hat{\theta}$ has the smallest variance possible, and yet is unbiased.

6.3.4 Let $Y_1, Y_2, \ldots, Y_T$ be a random sample from a population with mean μ and variance σ^2. Consider the following estimator of σ^2:

$$\hat{\sigma}^2 = \frac{1}{T}\sum_{t=1}^{T}(Y_t - \bar{Y})^2 = \left(\frac{T-1}{T}\right)S^2. \tag{6.3.17}$$

Find $E_{Y|\theta}(\hat{\sigma}^2)$ and determine whether $\hat{\sigma}^2$ is an unbiased estimator of σ^2. If $\hat{\sigma}^2$ is biased, then find the bias. Is $\hat{\sigma}^2$ asymptotically unbiased?

6.3.5 Using Theorem 5.2.1, Exercise 6.3.4, and the result that $(T-1)S^2/\sigma^2 \sim \chi^2(T-1)$ when sampling from a normal population, answer each of the following:

(a) Find $\text{MSE}(S^2)$.

(b) Find $\text{MSE}(\hat{\sigma}^2)$.

(c) Which estimator is more efficient, S^2 or $\hat{\sigma}^2$? Explain.

6.3.6 Repeat Exercise 6.3.4 without assuming the underlying normal distribution.

6.3.7 Let Y_t $(t = 1, 2, \ldots, T)$ be i.i.d. with common mean and variance μ and σ^2, respectively. Consider the following three estimators of μ:

$$\hat{\mu}_1 = \bar{Y} = \frac{1}{T}\sum_{t=1}^{T} Y_t,$$

$$\hat{\mu}_2 = \frac{1}{T+1}\sum_{t=1}^{T} Y_t,$$

$$\hat{\mu}_3 = \frac{1}{2}Y_1 + \frac{1}{2T}\sum_{t=2}^{T} Y_t.$$

Compare these three estimators according to the following criteria:

(a) Unbiasedness.

(b) MSE.

6.3.8 Let $\hat{\theta}$ be an estimator of a parameter θ known to lie in the interval (a, b). Consider the estimator:

$$\tilde{\theta} = \begin{Bmatrix} a, & \text{if } \hat{\theta} \leq a \\ \hat{\theta}, & \text{if } a < \hat{\theta} < b \\ b, & \text{if } \hat{\theta} \geq b \end{Bmatrix}.$$

(a) Show: $\text{MSE}(\tilde{\theta}) < \text{MSE}(\hat{\theta})$.

(b) Suppose $E_{Y|\theta}(\hat{\theta}) = 0$. Show: $\text{Var}(\tilde{\theta}) < \text{Var}(\hat{\theta})$.

6.3.9 Let $\hat{\theta}$ be an unbiased estimator of the scalar $\theta (\theta \neq 0)$, and consider the estimator $\tilde{\theta} \equiv c\hat{\theta}$, where c is a constant. Let $v \equiv [\text{Var}(\hat{\theta})]^{1/2}/E(\hat{\theta})$ be the coefficient of variation in $\hat{\theta}$.

(a) Show: $\text{MSE}(\tilde{\theta}) < \text{MSE}(\hat{\theta})$ iff $1 > c > (1 - v^2)/(1 + v^2)$.

(b) Show: $\text{MSE}(\tilde{\theta})$ is minimized for $c = (1 + v^2)^{-1}$.

(c) Show: $\text{MSE}(\hat{\theta}) - \text{MSE}(\tilde{\theta}^*)$, where $\tilde{\theta}^*$ corresponds to the optimal value of c found in (*b*), is a monotonic function of v increasing from zero to $\text{Var}(\hat{\theta})$ as v increases from zero to infinity.

For further discussion of estimators of the form $\tilde{\theta}$, see Rao (1981, pp. 124–125).

6.3.10 Consider Exercise 6.3.9 and suppose that $\hat{\theta}$ is the sample mean based on T i.i.d. drawings from a $U[\theta, 2\theta]$ distribution. Demonstrate Exercise 6.3.9.

6.3.11 Consider Exercise 6.3.9 and suppose $\hat{\theta} = S$, where S^2 is the sample variance based on T i.i.d. drawings from a $N(\mu, \sigma^2)$ distribution. Demonstrate Exercise 6.3.9.

6.3.12 Consider Exercise 6.3.9 and suppose it is known that $a < v < b$, where $a < b$ are given positive scalars. Derive lower and upper bounds for the lower bound $(1 - v^2)/(1 + v^2)$ in Exercise 6.3.9(b).

6.3.13 Consider a random sample Y_t $(t = 1, 2, \ldots, T)$ from a distribution with finite mean μ and variance σ^2. Consider the linear estimator

$$\hat{\mu} = \sum_{t=1}^{T} a_t T_t,$$

where a_t $(t = 1, 2, \ldots, T)$ are constants to be determined. The BLUE of μ is the solution to

$$\underset{a_1, \ldots, a_T}{\text{minimize}} \ \text{Var}(\hat{\mu}) \text{ subject to } E_{Y|\mu,\sigma^2}(\hat{\mu}) = \mu.$$

(a) Show that the solution to this problem is $a_t = T^{-1}$ $(t = 1, 2, \ldots, T)$, that is, the BLUE of μ is $\bar{Y}$.

(b) Show that if the unbiasedness condition $E(\hat{\mu}) = \mu$ is dropped, then the resulting minimum MSE "estimator" depends on unknown parameters.

6.3.14 Reconsider Exercise 6.3.13, but with the following criterion:

$$\underset{a_1, \ldots, a_T}{\text{minimize}} \ \alpha \left[\frac{\text{Var}(\hat{\mu})}{\sigma^2}\right] + (1 - \alpha)\left[\frac{\text{Bias}(\hat{\mu})}{\mu}\right]^2, \tag{6.3.18}$$

where α is a scalar such that $0 < \alpha < 1$. Find $a_1, a_2, \ldots, a_T$ which solve (6.3.18). Note that $\hat{\mu}$ is *not* required to be unbiased. You need *not* verify the second-order conditions for a minimum. Hint: Derive the first-order conditions, add them up, and solve for $a \equiv a_1 + a_2 + \cdots + a_T$. Then go back and find the optimal values a_t $(t = 1, 2, \ldots, T)$.

6.3.15 Suppose a farmer has a square field with length μ and area $A \equiv \mu^2$ that the farmer wants to estimate. When measuring the length of the field, the farmer makes a random error such that the measured length $X_1 \sim N(\mu, \sigma^2)$, where σ^2 is known. Aware of the measurement error, the farmer decides to take a second independent measurement $X_2 \sim N(\mu, \sigma^2)$, Consider the following three estimators of A:

$$\hat{A}_1 = \left[\frac{X_1 + X_2}{2}\right]^2 = \overline{X}^2,$$

$$\hat{A}_2 = \frac{X_1^2 + X_2^2}{2},$$

$$\hat{A}_3 = X_1 X_2.$$

Note that $\hat{A}_3 = 2\hat{A}_1 - \hat{A}_2$. Also note:

$$E\left[\sum_{t=1}^{T} (X_t - \overline{X})^2\right] = E[X_1^2 + X_2^2 - 2\overline{X}^2], \tag{6.3.19}$$

$$\mathrm{Var}\left[\sum_{i=1}^{2} (X_i - \overline{X})^2\right] = 2\sigma^4, \tag{6.3.20}$$

$$E(Z^4) = \alpha^4 + 6\alpha^2\beta^2 + 3\beta^4, \quad \text{if } Z \sim N(\alpha, \beta^2). \tag{6.3.21}$$

(a) Which (if any) of $\hat{A}_i$ $(i = 1, 2, 3)$ are unbiased?

(b) Find $\mathrm{Var}(\hat{A}_j)$ $(j = 1, 2, 3)$.

(c) Compare $\mathrm{MSE}(\hat{A}_j)$ $(j = 1, 2, 3)$.

6.3.16 Suppose Y_t $(t = 1, 2, \ldots, T) \sim$ i.i.d. $N(\mu, \sigma^2)$. Define

$$\hat{\sigma}^r = \left[\frac{2^{-r/2}\Gamma[(T + r - 1)/2]}{\Gamma[(T - 1)/2}\right]^{-1} S^r, \tag{6.3.22}$$

$$S = \left[\frac{1}{T - 1}\sum_{t=1}^{T} (Y_t - \overline{Y})^2\right]^{1/2}. \tag{6.3.23}$$

(a) Show: $E(\hat{\sigma}^r) = \sigma^r$. [Hint: $(S^2/\sigma^2) \sim \chi^2(T - 1) = G[\frac{1}{2}(T - 1), \frac{1}{2}]$. Then use (3.3.23).]

(b) Let $\tilde{\sigma}^r \equiv c\hat{\sigma}^r$, where $c > 0$. Find c so as to minimize $\mathrm{MSE}(\tilde{\sigma}^r)$.

(c) Consider $p = P(T_t \leq \xi) = \Phi(\xi | \mu, \sigma^2)$ for given ξ, or $\xi = \mu + \sigma\Phi^{-1}(p)$ for given p. Find a minimum variance unbiased estimator of ξ.

6.3.17 Suppose Y_{it} $(t = 1, 2, \ldots, T_i) \sim$ i.i.d. $N(\mu_i, \sigma^2)$ $(i = 1, 2)$ represent two independent samples with sample means $\overline{Y}_i$ $(i = 1, 2)$. Ignoring the fact that $\overline{Y}_2$ reflects "contaminated" observations from the first population, consider

$$\hat{\mu}_1 = \frac{T_1\overline{Y}_1 + T_2\overline{Y}_2}{T_1 + T_2}. \tag{6.3.24}$$

(a) Let $\delta \equiv (\mu_2 - \mu_1)/\sigma$. Show that

$$\mathrm{MSE}(\hat{\mu}_1) = E[(\hat{\mu}_1 - \mu_1)^2] = \frac{\sigma^2}{T_1 + T_2}\left[1 + \frac{T_2^2\delta^2}{T_1 + T_2}\right]. \tag{6.3.25}$$

(b) Deduce that if $\delta^2 < T_1^{-1} + T_2^{-1}$, then $\mathrm{MSE}(\hat{\mu}_1) < \mathrm{MSE}(\overline{Y}_1)$.

(c) Compare and contrast the Exercise with Examples 6.3.1 through 6.3.7.

6.3.18 The *jackknife* is a general technique for reducing estimation bias (see Quenouille 1956). The simple case of a one-step jackknife can be defined as follows. Let Y_t $(t = 1, 2, \ldots, T)$ be a random sample and let $W_T = W_T(Y_1, Y_2, \ldots, Y_T)$ be an estimator of θ. Define $W_T^{(t)}$ to be the same estimator applied to all observations except observation t. For example, if $W_T = \overline{Y}_T$, then $W_T^{(t)}$ is the sample mean of the $T - 1$ observations after omitting observation t. The jackknife estimator $\hat{\theta}_{JK}$ of θ is defined by:

$$\hat{\theta}_{JK} = \hat{\theta}_{JK}(W_T) = TW_T - \left(\frac{T - 1}{T}\right)\sum_{t=1}^{T} W_T^{(t)}. \tag{6.3.26}$$

In general: $\text{Bias}[W_T^{(t)}] < \text{Bias}(W_T)$. Suppose the Y_t's are i.i.d. Bernoulli $B(1, \theta)$ and it is desired to estimate θ^2.

(a) Consider the estimator $W_T = \bar{Y}^2$ of θ^2. Show that W_T is biased.

(b) Find the one-step jackknife estimator $\hat{\theta}_{JK}$ based on W_T.

(c) Show that $\hat{\theta}_{JK}$ is an unbiased estimator of θ^2.

6.3.19 Discuss the convexity properties of the following two loss functions and compare them graphically with quadratic and absolute error loss functions:

(a) $C(\hat{\theta}, \theta) = |\hat{\theta} - \theta|^p, \quad 1 < p < 2,$

(b) $C(\hat{\theta}, \theta) = \begin{cases} (\hat{\theta} - \theta)^2, & \text{if } |\hat{\theta} - \theta| \leq k \\ 2k|\hat{\theta} - \theta| - k^2, & \text{if } |\hat{\theta} - \theta| > k \end{cases}$ $\quad (k > 0)$ (Huber 1964).

6.3.20 Let $C(\hat{\theta} - \theta)$ be a convex function defined on $(-\infty, \infty)$ and suppose $R(\hat{\theta}|\theta) = E[C(\hat{\theta} - \theta)]$ is finite. Show (Lehmann 1983, p. 54):

(a) If $C(\hat{\theta} - \theta)$ is not monotone, $R(\hat{\theta}|\theta)$ takes on its minimum value and the set on which this value is taken is a closed interval.

(b) If $C(\hat{\theta} - \theta)$ is strictly convex, then the minimizing value of $R(\hat{\theta}|\theta)$ is unique.

6.3.21 Suppose Y_t $(t = 1, 2, \ldots, T) \sim$ i.i.d. $N(\mu, \sigma^2)$. Consider the estimator

$$\hat{\sigma}^2 = \frac{1}{T+1} \sum_{t=1}^{T} (Y_t - \bar{Y})^2. \tag{6.3.27}$$

Show that $\hat{\sigma}^2$ is inadmissible, being dominated in MSE by

$$\tilde{\sigma}^2 = \min\left[\frac{1}{T+3}, \frac{1}{T+2} \sum_{t=1}^{T} (Y_t - \bar{Y})^2\right]. \tag{6.3.28}$$

See Zacks (1971, p. 397).

6.3.22 Suppose X_t $(t = 1, 2, \ldots, T) \sim N(\mu, \sigma^2)$ and Z_t $(t = 1, 2, \ldots, T) \sim N(\mu + \theta, k^2\sigma^2)$ be independent random variables. Define Y_t $(t = 1, 2, \ldots, T)$ by $P(Y_t = X_t) = 1 - \varepsilon$, $P(Y_t = Z_t) = \varepsilon$, where ε is a known constant, $0 \leq \varepsilon \leq 1$. Find $\text{MSE}(\bar{Y})$.

6.3.23 Consider T Bernoulli trials Y_t $(t = 1, 2, \ldots, T)$ with probability of a success θ, $0 < \theta < 1$. Let there be $X \geq 2$ successes and $T - X$ failures. (DeGroot 1985)

(a) Under binomial sampling, show $\hat{\theta} \equiv X/T$ is an unbiased estimator of θ.

(b) Under negative binomial sampling in which sampling continues until x successes are obtained, show $\tilde{\theta} \equiv (X - 1)/(T - 1)$ is an unbiased estimator of θ.

6.3.24 For $t = 1, 2, \ldots, T$, let X_t and Z_t be independent random variables such that $X_t \sim$ i.i.d. $N(\mu, \alpha)$ and $Z_t \sim$ i.i.d. $N(\mu, \beta)$. Also let $Y_t \sim X_t + Z_t$ $(t = 1, 2, \ldots, T) \sim N(2\mu, \theta)$, where $\theta = \alpha + \beta$. Suppose Y_t is observed, but neither X_t nor Z_t are observed separately.

(a) Show that μ and θ are identified.

(b) Show that α and β are not identified.

(c) What do (a) and (b) tell you about unbiased estimation and the LP?

6.4 Sampling Properties of Point Estimators in Large Samples

The traditional machinery of statistical processes is wholly unsuited to the needs of practical research. Not only does it takes a cannon to shoot a sparrow, but it misses the sparrow! The elaborate mechanism built on the theory of infinitely large samples is not accurate enough for simple laboratory data. Only by systematically tackling

small sample problems on their merits does it seem possible to apply accurate tests to practical data.
—Sir Ronald A. Fisher (in Agresti 1992, p. 132)

In Sections 6.5 and 6.6, it will be seen that classical statistics fails to provide a general finite-sample theory for point estimation that satisfies the risk minimization goals discussed in Section 6.3.[16] As a result proponents of classical statistics often appeal to methods of estimation which have desirable sampling properties as sample size $T \to \infty$. Before discussing such methods in Section 6.6, this section develops these asymptotic properties. These properties rely heavily on the discussion of stochastic convergence, laws of large numbers, and central limit theorems in Sections 5.5 through 5.7.

Consider the stochastic sequence $\{Z_T\}$, where $Z_T = \hat{\theta}_T - \theta$ is the sampling error (Definition 6.3.6) of the estimator $\hat{\theta}_T$ of θ based on a sample of size T. The parameter θ is a $K \times 1$ vector. Requiring that sampling error to converge as $T \to \infty$ to a zero vector (in the sense of weak, strong or mean-square convergence) would seem to be a minimal requirement for any estimator to be taken seriously. The following definition provides the necessary terminology. Note that all concepts involve convergence to a constant.

Definition 6.4.1 Let $\hat{\theta}_T$ be an estimator of θ based on a sample of size T.

(a) $\hat{\theta}_T$ is a *weakly consistent* (or simply *consistent*) estimator of θ iff $\hat{\theta}_T - \theta \xrightarrow{p} 0_K$.

(b) $\hat{\theta}_T$ is a *strongly consistent* estimator of θ iff $\hat{\theta}_T - \theta \xrightarrow{a.s.} 0_K$.

(c) $\hat{\theta}_T$ is a *mean-square consistent* estimator of θ iff $\hat{\theta}_T - \theta \xrightarrow{m.s.} 0_K$.

Unlike the case of the finite sample property of unbiasedness (Definition 6.3.8), continuous functions of consistent estimators consistently (weakly or strongly) estimate the corresponding function of the parameter (Theorem 5.5.4). Thus, for example in the case $K = 1$, if $\hat{\theta}_T \xrightarrow{p} \theta$ (a scalar), then $[\hat{\theta}_T]^{1/2} \xrightarrow{p} \theta^{1/2}$ and $[\hat{\theta}_T]^{-1} \xrightarrow{p} \theta^{-1}$ (provided $\theta \neq 0$). The corresponding results for unbiased estimators hold only in the case of linear functions.

The convergence $\hat{\theta}_T \xrightarrow{p} \theta$ is usually (but by no means always) at a rate such that the sequence of distribution functions of the random variable

16. For a controversial assessment of the relevance of finite sample distribution theory in classical econometrics, see Taylor (1983).

$Z_T \equiv T^{1/2}(\hat{\theta}_T - \theta)$ converges to a nondegenerate distribution variable as $T \to \infty$.[17] This leads to the following definition.

Definition 6.4.2 Let $\hat{\theta}_T$ be an estimator of θ based on a sample of size T. Define $Z_T \equiv T^{1/2}(\hat{\theta}_T - \theta)$. Suppose $Z_T \xrightarrow{d} Z$ as $T \to \infty$, where Z is a nondengerate random variable. The distribution of Z is the *limiting distribution* of Z_T. Usually, this limiting distribution is normal, say $N_K(\mu, \Omega)$, in which case $\hat{\theta}_T$ is said to be *asymptotically normal*. Approximating the distribution of Z_T by its limiting distribution $N_K(\mu, \Omega)$, suggests the approximate distribution $N_K(\mu + \theta, T^{-1}\Omega)$ for $\hat{\theta}_T$, known as the *asymptotic distribution* of $\hat{\theta}_T$. The mean of the limiting distribution is the *asymptotic expectation (mean)* of Z_T, denoted $AE(Z_T)$. Similarly, $\theta + \mu$ is the *asymptotic expectation (mean)* of $\hat{\theta}_T$, denoted $AE(\hat{\theta}_T)$. The estimator $\hat{\theta}_T$ is *asymptotically unbiased* iff $\mu = 0_K$, in which case $AE(\hat{\theta}_T) = \theta$. The *asymptotic bias* of $\hat{\theta}_T$ is $\text{Abias}(\hat{\theta}_T) \equiv \mu$. The variance of the limiting distribution of Z_T is the *asymptotic variance* of $\hat{\theta}_T$, denoted $\text{Avar}(\hat{\theta}_T)$.

If $E_{Y|\theta}[\hat{\theta}_T]$ exists for all T, then some authors prefer the alternative definition of asymptotic bias as

$$\operatorname*{Limit}_{T\to\infty} \text{Bias}(\hat{\theta}_T|\theta) = \left[\operatorname*{Limit}_{T\to\infty} E_{Y|\theta}(\hat{\theta}_T)\right] - \theta, \tag{6.4.1}$$

but this text does not do so. In general, (6.4.1) is not the same as $\text{Abias}(\hat{\theta}_T)$: (6.4.1) requires $E_{Y|\theta}(\hat{\theta}_T)$ exists for all finite T, and (6.4.1) says nothing about the rate of convergence (see Amemiya 1985, pp. 93–95, for a further discussion of the differences).

Although it is widely recognized that consistent estimators are not necessarily unbiased (their expectations may not even exist in any finite sample!), it must also be remembered that unbiased estimators need not be consistent (e.g. consider $\hat{\theta}_T = Y_1$ for all T). Thus, neither property implies the other. However, a consistent estimator whose asymptotic distribution has finite sample mean must be asymptotically unbiased. Clearly an unbiased estimator must yield a value of zero for (6.4.1), but it need not be asymptotically unbiased.

Consistency implies nothing about the rate of convergence of the sequence in question. Thus we seek an asymptotic analog of the efficiency discussed in the previous section. Given that asymptotic normality is commonly encountered, we identify the following class

17. Different normalizing factors occur with explosive time series. Lehmann (1983, pp. 338–339) provides an example that is not time series oriented. Also see Exercise 6.6.17.

of estimators over which we seek a measure of asymptotic efficiency.[18]

Definition 6.4.3 The class of all consistent estimators $\hat{\theta}_T$ of θ based on a sample of size T such that $T^{1/2}(\hat{\theta}_T - \theta) \xrightarrow{d} Z$, where $Z \sim N_K(0, \Omega)$ for some $K \times K$ positive definite matrix Ω, is known as the *consistent asymptotically normal (CAN)* class of estimators. Members of this class are called *CAN estimators.*

A natural way of defining asymptotic efficiency is to order CAN estimators in terms of their *asymptotic variances* Ω. A CAN estimator with an asymptotic variance less than the asymptotic variance of any other CAN estimator is the *best asymptotically normal (BAN)*. However, as the following example demonstrates it is necessary to first further restrict the class of CAN estimators.

Example 6.4.1 Let $\hat{\theta}_T$ be an estimator of a scalar θ based on a sample of size T, and suppose $T^{1/2}(\hat{\theta}_T - \theta) \xrightarrow{d} N(0, \omega)$ as $T \to \infty$. Consider the estimator

$$\tilde{\theta}_T = \begin{Bmatrix} \gamma\hat{\theta}_T, & \text{if } |\hat{\theta}_T| \le T^{-1/4} \\ \hat{\theta}_T, & \text{if } |\hat{\theta}_T| > T^{-1/4} \end{Bmatrix}, \tag{6.4.2}$$

for $0 < \gamma < 1$. Then as $\to \infty$, $T^{1/2}(\tilde{\theta}_T - \theta) \xrightarrow{d} N(0, \delta)$, where $\delta = \omega$ if $\theta \neq 0$, and $\delta = \gamma^2\omega < \omega$ if $\theta = 0$. Therefore, given a CAN estimator, it is always possible to construct another CAN estimator with variance smaller at one point in the parameter space, and the same elsewhere. Such estimators are referred to as *super efficient estimators.*

The difficulty encountered in Example 6.4.1 can be avoided by restricting the class of possible estimators such that in compact subsets of the admissible parameter space the convergence to normality is uniform. Such estimators are called *consistent uniformly normal (CUAN) estimators.* See Rao (1973, pp. 346–351) for more details. This leads to the following definition.

Definition 6.4.4 Omitting the sample size subscript, let $\hat{\theta}_1$ and $\hat{\theta}_2$ denote two CUAN estimators of the parameter vector θ based on a sample of size T, such that as $T \to \infty$, $T^{1/2}(\hat{\theta}_i - \theta) \xrightarrow{d} N(0, \Omega_i)$ $(i = 1, 2)$. Then $\hat{\theta}_1$ *is asymptotically efficient relative to* $\hat{\theta}_2$ iff $\Omega_2 - \Omega_1$ is positive semidefinite. If a CUAN estimator is asymptotically efficient relative to any CUAN estimator, then the estimator is *asymptotically efficient.*

18. For a discussion of asymptotic efficiency comparisons in cases in which the normalizing factor is T^α ($\alpha \neq \frac{1}{2}$) or the limiting distribution is not normal, see Lehmann (1983, pp. 349–351).

Example 6.4.2 Consider a random sample Y_t $(t = 1, 2, \ldots, T)$ from a unimodal symmetric distribution with finite mean/median θ and variance σ^2. Let $\overline{Y}_T$ and $\widetilde{Y}_T$ denote the sample mean and sample median, respectively. Then Theorems 5.7.1 and 5.7.9 (also see Example 5.7.3) imply that as $T \to \infty$:

$$T^{1/2}(\overline{Y}_T - \theta) \xrightarrow{d} N(0, \sigma^2), \tag{6.4.3}$$

$$T^{1/2}(\widetilde{Y}_T - \theta) \xrightarrow{d} N(0, [4\{f(0)\}^2]^{-1}), \tag{6.4.4}$$

where $f(\cdot)$ is the underlying population density of $Y - \theta$. *The relative asymptotic efficiency of the sample mean and median depends crucially on the underlying distribution in question.* Table 6.4.1 (see Lehmann 1983, p. 357) compares the asymptotic relative efficiency of the sample median to the sample mean, defined as

$$\frac{\text{asy. var. of the sample mean}}{\text{asy. var. of the sample median}} = \frac{\sigma^2}{[4\{f(0)\}^2]^{-1}} = 4[f(0)]^2\sigma^2, \tag{6.4.5}$$

for a variety of distributions, including standard normal, t, and uniform distributions. Also included are *contaminated normal distributions* (see Exercises 4.4.22 and 6.3.25) with c.d.f.s:

$$F(y) = (1 - \varepsilon)\Phi(y) + \varepsilon\Phi\left(\frac{y}{\tau}\right), \tag{6.4.6}$$

permitting large errors $(\tau > 1)$ with low probability ε. In the case of sampling from a $N(0, 1)$ distribution, (6.4.5) equals $4[(2\pi)^{1/2}]^2 \approx .6366$. Loosely speaking, this implies that the sample mean based on a sample of

Table 6.4.1
Asymptotic relative efficiency measure (6.4.6) comparing the performance of the sample mean to the sample median

Underlying distribution	(6.4.6)
Cauchy: $t(0, 1, 1)$	∞
Laplace	4.00
$t(0, 1, 3)$	1.62
$t(0, 1, 4)$	1.12
$t(0, 1, 5)$	.96
Logistic	.82
Standard normal: $N(0, 1) = t(0, 1, \infty)$	.64
Uniform: $U(-.5, .5)$	.33
Contaminated normal:	
$\varepsilon = .10$ and $\tau = 4$	1.36
$\varepsilon = .10$ and $\tau = 2$	1.00
$\varepsilon = .10$ and $\tau = 2$	.75
$\varepsilon = .01$ and $\tau = 4$	.72
$\varepsilon = .01$ and $\tau = 2$	.65

size .6366T is approximately as efficient as a sample median based on a sample of size T. For many other distributions, however, relative measure (6.4.5) is greater than unity. Fixing $f(0)$, the relative performance of the sample mean compared to the sample median deteriorates as the variance of the underlying distribution increases, or again loosely speaking, as the "tails" of the distribution increase.

The sample median is obviously insensitive to the values of outlying observations; the sample mean is obviously highly sensitive. Table 6.4.1 suggests that the sample median sometimes goes too far in discarding outlying observations. A natural compromise between the sample mean and the sample median is to discard only a few observations, and the next definition introduces such an estimator.

Definition 6.4.5 Consider a sample X_t $(t = 1, 2, \ldots, T)$, and denote the order statistics as Y_t $(t = 1, 2, \ldots, T)$. Given $\alpha < \frac{1}{2}$, define $k = [T\alpha]$ as the largest integer less than or equal to $T\alpha$. The *trimmed mean of order* α is defined to be the sample mean of the observations after discarding the k smallest and k largest observations:

$$\overline{Y}_\alpha \equiv \frac{1}{T - 2k} \sum_{t=k+1}^{T-k} Y_t. \tag{6.4.7}$$

The mean and median are two extreme cases of symmetric trimming in which either no observations are discarded or all observations except the one or two central observations.

The asymptotic distribution of the trimmed mean can be obtained from the next theorem.

Theorem 6.4.1 Let $F(\cdot)$ be symmetric around zero. Suppose there exists a constant c such that $F(-c) = 0$, $F(c) = 1$, and $0 < c \leq \infty$. Also suppose $F(\cdot)$ possess a density $f(\cdot)$ which is continuous and positive for all $-c < y < c$. If Y_t $(t = 1, 2, \ldots, T)$ are i.i.d. according to $F(y - \theta)$, then for any $0 < \alpha < \frac{1}{2}$, $\alpha = F[\xi(\alpha)]$, as $T \to \infty$:

$$\sqrt{T}(\overline{Y}_\alpha - \theta) \xrightarrow{d} N(0, \sigma_\alpha^2), \tag{6.4.8}$$

where

$$\sigma_\alpha^2 = \frac{2}{(1 - 2\alpha)^2}\left[\int_0^{\xi(1-\alpha)} t^2 f(t)\,dt + \alpha\xi^2(1 - \alpha)\right]. \tag{6.4.9}$$

Proof Bickel (1965) or Stigler (1973a).

It can be shown (e.g., see Lehmann 1983, pp. 361–368, esp. Table 4.4) that a moderate amount of trimming can provide a better estimator that the sample mean when drawing from a distribution with heavy tails. At the same time $\overline{Y}_\alpha$ gives up little when sampling from a normal distribution. A value in the neighborhood of $\alpha = .1$ is recommended. Choice of α based on the data leads to an *adaptive estimator* (see Manski 1984 for discussion, references and extensions).

Trimmed mean (6.4.7) can be viewed as a linear combination of order statistics with zero weight on the k smallest and k largest observations, and equal weight $(T - 2k)^{-1}$ on the $T - 2k$ middle observations. Estimators based on a smoother choice of weights are known as *L-estimators* (see Lehmann 1983, pp. 368–376). Another broad class of estimators, *R-estimators*, are based on ranks of the observations (see Lehmann 1983, pp. 382–388). Yet another compromise suggested by Huber (1964) is the estimator that minimizes risk for the loss function in Exercise 6.3.19(b). (Note that the sample mean and the sample median minimize the quadratic and absolute error components of the loss function in Exercise 6.3.19b). Other loss functions can be used (e.g., Exercise 6.3.19a) leading to a wide class of estimators, corresponding to solutions to different maximization problems, called *M-estimators* (for maximum-likelihood-based) by Huber (1981) (also see Lehmann 1983, pp. 376–382). In econometrics *M-estimators* are usually referred to as *extremal estimators* (see Amemiya 1985 and Newey and McFadden 1993). Examples of extremal estimators in econometrics are maximum likelihood, nonlinear least squares, generalized method of moments, minimum distance, and minimum chi-square estimators.

All of these classes of estimators share the common motivation that they are designed to have desirable properties when sampling from a wide variety of underlying distributions. Such estimators are examples of *robust estimators*, and their study comprises a sizeable area of statistics that began flourishing in the 1960s (see Stigler 1973b). For reviews of this literature, see Huber (1981) and Koenker (1982). The likelihood-based orientation of this text implies that these broad classes of estimators are not studied herein in any great detail. Some rationalizations for this decision are provided in the closing comments of this section.

A lower bound on how small the asymptotic covariance matrix of a CUAN estimator can become is provided by the Cramér-Rao Inequality discussed in the next section. The method of maximum likelihood, discussed in the subsequent section, provides a means for obtaining estimators that achieve this lower bound *asymptotically* in a wide variety of standard problems.

In closing this section on asymptotic properties of point estimators, a few comments seem warranted to keep matters in perspective.

First, desirable asymptotic properties (e.g., consistency and asymptotic efficiency) are at best necessary, and certainly not sufficient, characteristics for a desirable estimator. Inconsistent estimators have little to recommend themselves, and once an estimator is discovered to be inconsistent and the nature of the inconsistency derived, it is often possible to use the inconsistency to construct a consistent estimator.

Second, asymptotic analysis is a research tool (as opposed to a goal) designed to help in approximating the *ex ante* sampling distribution of an estimator based on the sample size T at hand. The class of CUAN estimators is large, and estimators with the same asymptotic distribution may have vastly different sampling distributions for finite T.

Third, as noted in Section 5.5, convergence in distribution is the weakest form of stochastic convergence. Suppose an estimator $\hat{\theta}_T(Y)$ of an unknown parameter vector θ is a member of the CUAN class. Then there exists a sequence of random variables $\{Z_T\}$, with $Z_T = T^{1/2}[\hat{\theta}_T(Y) - \theta]$, such that $Z_T \xrightarrow{d} Z$ and $Z \sim N_K(0_K, \Omega)$. The Z_Ts are not statistics because they depend on θ, and (ii) in general Ω depends on θ. The "convergence" is in terms of the sequence of distribution functions $\{F_T(z)\}$, where $F_T(z) \equiv \text{Prob}(Z_T \leq z|\theta)$, to the limiting normal distribution $\Phi(z|0_K, \Omega)$. For given finite T, $F_T(z)$ may be very different than the limiting distribution $\Phi(z|0_K, \Omega)$, implying that in repeated sampling the random variable Z_T does not behave very much like the limiting normal random variable Z. Also note that the quality of the asymptotic approximation depends on the unknown θ. In fact Z_T, $F_T(\cdot)$ and the limiting distribution $\Phi(z|0_K, \Omega)$ all depend on θ. For given finite T, the approximation may be good for some values of θ, but not others. Of course the "uniformity" of CUAN implies that for *arbitrarily large* T, the quality of the approximation is uniform in θ.

Fourth, Z_T is only of intermediary interest. Of primary interest is the estimator $\hat{\theta}_T(Y)$, and its finite sample distribution function, say $G_T(\cdot)$, is approximated by rewriting $Z_T = T^{1/2}[\hat{\theta}_T(Y) - \theta]$ as $\hat{\theta}_T(Y) = \theta + T^{-1/2}Z_T$, and using the asymptotic distribution of Z_T to obtain the following finite sample approximation: $G_T(\cdot) \approx \Phi(\cdot|\theta, T^{-1}\Omega)$. The preceding comments regarding the quality of the asymptotic approximation to the finite sample distribution of Z_T are again appropriate.

Fifth, the dependency of the sampling distribution of $\hat{\theta}_T(Y)$ on θ is both fortunate and unfortunate. It is fortunate in the sense that this dependency is what permits the researcher to "learn" about θ by computing the statistic $\hat{\theta}_T(Y)$. It is unfortunate in the sense that the marginal distribution of one component of the $K \times 1$ vector $\hat{\theta}_T(Y)$, say $\hat{\theta}_{T,k}(Y)$, in general depends on *all* elements of θ, not just θ_k. In general the asymptotic distribution for $\hat{\theta}_{T,k}(Y)$ also has a similar dependency, but by Theorem 5.5.11, such unknown "nuisance" parameters may be replaced with consistent estimators without changing the asymptotic distribution. In general there is no similar technique in classical analysis that can be applied in finite samples. It will be seen in subsequent discussions of interval estimation and hypothesis testing that *the nuisance parameter problem is a major shortcoming of classical statistics.*

Sixth and finally, the sampling distribution of an estimator for finite samples depends on the form of the underlying distribution from which the data are drawn. Indeed, sometimes so do asymptotic properties (see Table 6.4.1). Even when the asymptotic distribution of an estimator is the same over a broad family of underlying data distributions, the quality of the asymptotic distribution as an approximating tool will vary over members in this family because the thing being approximated, namely the estimator's sampling distribution in finite samples, will vary across members in the family. As hinted near the end of Section 6.1, although it may not be necessary to know exactly the underlying distribution of the data up to a finite number of unknown parameters in order to apply a CLT and obtain the asymptotic distribution of the estimator, in order to evaluate the *quality of an asymptotic approximation*, it is first necessary to identify the thing being approximated, namely the estimator's sampling distribution for finite T, and this requires a complete statement of the underlying data distribution up to a finite number of unknown parameters.

The area of robust estimation attempts to downplay the need to know the underlying distribution, but robustness with respect to all possible statistical assumptions is an unattainable goal in finite sample point estimation. Implicit when using any estimator, the researcher acts as if the underlying distributions for which the estimator performs well are "likely" to hold in the application at hand, and the underlying distributions for which the estimator performs poorly are "unlikely" to hold. Whether or not the researcher articulates such beliefs explicitly or not, they remain lingering in the background.

Exercises

6.4.1 Show that for unimodal symmetric densities around zero, asymptotic efficiency ratio (6.4.5) is always greater than $\frac{1}{3}$, and that this lower bound is attained for the uniform distribution and no other. (Lehmann 1983, p. 359)

6.4.2 Compute (6.4.5) when sampling from a contaminated normal distribution.

6.4.3 Verify the entries in Table 6.4.1.

6.4.4 Suppose $T^{1/2}(\hat{\theta}_T - \theta) \xrightarrow{d} N_K(0, \Omega)$. For some $i \neq j$, $1 \leq i, j \leq K$, where $\theta_j \neq 0$, define $\alpha_1 \equiv g_1(\theta) = \theta_i/\theta_j$, $\alpha_2 = g_2(\theta) = \theta_i\theta_j$, and $\alpha = [\alpha_1, \alpha_2]'$. Use Theorem 5.7.7 to find the asymptotic distribution of $\hat{\alpha}_T \equiv [g_1(\hat{\theta}_T), g_2(\hat{\theta}_T)]'$.

6.5 An Overview of Frequentist Point Estimation

This section discusses frequentist point estimation in "well-behaved" situations. Attention focuses on the sampling properties of the likelihood function and various related statistics. To emphasize the frequentist orientation we replace "$\mathcal{L}(\theta; y)$" by "$\mathcal{L}(\theta; Y)$."

We begin with the definition of regularity conditions describing an ideal sampling situation. These conditions are mutually consistent. They are not all necessary, however, for all the results that follow. No attempt will be made to give a minimal set of assumptions for each result derived.

Definition 6.5.1 The likelihood function $\mathcal{L}(\theta; Y)$, where $Y = [Y_1, Y_2, \ldots, Y_T]' \in \mathcal{S}_T$, $\theta = [\theta_1, \theta_2, \ldots, \theta_K]' \in \Theta$, is *regular* iff the following *regularity conditions* hold:

(a) The "true" value of θ, denoted θ_o, lies in an open subset Θ_* of Θ.

(b) θ is finite-dimensional and θ_o is identified in the sense of Definition 6.3.2.

(c) Θ is compact.

(d) The sample observations Y_t $(t = 1, 2, \ldots, T)$ are i.i.d. with common p.f. $f(\cdot|\theta)$ and common sample space $\mathcal{S}$, where $\mathcal{S}_T = \mathcal{S} \times \mathcal{S} \times \cdots \times \mathcal{S}$.

(e) The support of Y_t $(t = 1, 2, \ldots, T)$ does not depend on the parameter vector θ.

(f) $\ln[f(Y_t|\theta)]$ is continuous for all $\theta \in \Theta_*$ and almost all $Y_t \in \mathcal{S}$.

(g) The $\ln[f(Y_t|\theta)]$ possesses derivatives of at least the third order with respect to θ for all $\theta \in \Theta_*$ and almost all $Y_t \in \mathcal{S}$, and these derivatives are bounded by integrable functions of Y_t, i.e. there exists a function $M_{ijk}(Y_t)$ such that

$$-M_{ijk}(Y_t) < \frac{\partial^3 \ln[f(Y_t|\theta)]}{\partial\theta_i\,\partial\theta_j\,\partial\theta_k} \leq M_{ijk}(Y_t) \tag{6.5.1}$$

for all $\theta \in \Theta_*$ and all $1 \leq i, j, k \leq K$, and $E_{Y_t|\theta}[M_{ijk}(Y_t)] < \infty$.

(h) The following $K \times K$ matrix is positive definite in an open interval around θ_o:

$$E_{Y_t|\theta}\left[-\frac{\partial^2 \ln[f(Y_t|\theta)]}{\partial\theta\,\partial\theta'}\right]. \tag{6.5.2}$$

(i) $E_{Y_t|\theta}(\ln[f(Y_t|\theta)]) < \infty$ for all $\theta \in \Theta$.

A few brief comments seem warranted regarding these regularity conditions. Generally, they are motivated by demands of classical estimation rather than Bayesian estimation. It is convenient to think of two groups: (a) through (c) and (d) through (i).

First, consider conditions (a) through (c) involving the parameter space. The notion of a "true" value θ_o is introduced for purposes of classical discussion; no objective existence is intended. Assuming θ_o to lie in an open subset of the parameter space is required for later differentiability assumptions. Boundary values of θ_o cause problems for the asymptotic distribution theory in Section 6.6. Identifiability is logically precedent to estimation. Compactness of the parameter space is largely for mathematical convenience in proofs drawing on properties of extremal estimators in combination with uniform convergence results. Because it is equivalent to saying that the parameter space is closed and bounded, it asserts the existence of information concerning θ that is embarrassing to some objectivists.

Second, consider regularity conditions (d) through (i) involving the sampling density $f(\cdot|\theta)$. Assumption (d) of a random sample is a natural place to begin discussion, but it is questionable in many applications. Classical estimation theory (especially distribution theory) quickly becomes complicated without it, requiring moving the discussion to the asymptotic arena. But the LLNs and CLTs of Sections 5.6 and 5.7 quickly become non-elementary in such cases, and *in the hope of making connections to the fairly elementary discussion of those sections, random sampling is invoked here.* The remaining conditions, (e) through (i) are fairly technical in nature. Requiring the support to not depend on θ rules out, for example, sampling from the uniform distributions $U[0, \theta]$. Continuity and differentiability of $\ln[f(y_t|\theta)]$, together with the integrable bounds implied by (f) and (h) are purely technical assumptions that ensure a variety of Taylor series expansions. In the presence of other assumptions, less differentiability is often sufficient. Finally, nonsingularity of the matrix (6.5.2) is related to the identifiability assumption noted earlier.

The following quantities play important roles in subsequent developments.

Definition 6.5.2 Let Y_t $(t = 1, 2, \ldots, T)$ be a sample for which the likelihood function $\mathscr{L}(\theta; Y)$ satisfies the regularity conditions in Definition 6.5.1. Then

$$s_c(\theta; Y) = \frac{\partial L(\theta; Y)}{\partial \theta} \tag{6.5.3}$$

is the *score function*, where $L(\theta; Y)$ is the log-likelihood. The $K \times K$ matrix

$$H(\theta; Y) = \frac{\partial^2 L(\theta; Y)}{\partial \theta \, \partial \theta'} \tag{6.5.4}$$

is the *Hessian matrix* of the log-likelihood $L(\theta; Y)$. Finally, minus the sampling expectation of (6.5.4) is known as the *information matrix of a sample of size T*, and is denoted:

$$J_T(\theta) = -E_{Y|\theta}[H(\theta; Y)]. \tag{6.5.5}$$

Sometimes the prefix "expected" or "Fisher" is attached to "information matrix" (6.5.5). To differentiate it from (6.5.5), $-H(\theta; y)$ is often referred to as the *observed information in the realized sample y*. Hessian matrix (6.5.4) measures the curvature of the log-likelihood. Consider the case $K = 1$. If the log-likelihood has a sharp local maximum at the point θ_*, then θ_* is favored by $L(\theta; y)$ rather strongly and $H(\theta_*; y) \ll 0$. On the other hand, if $L(\theta; y)$ is fairly flat in the neighborhood of θ_*, then no value of θ in that neighborhood is much more "likely" than any other, and $H(\theta_*; y) \approx 0$. A positive measure of the "informativeness" of the log-likelihood at θ_* is $-H(\theta_*; y)$. Averaging $-H(\theta; Y)$ over Y yields the expected information defined in (6.5.5).

The following theorem is of fundamental importance in discussing the likelihood function.

Theorem 6.5.1 Let $s_c(\theta; Y)$ be the score function (6.5.3) defined in Definition 6.5.2. Then evaluating all quantities at θ_o:

$$E_{Y|\theta_o}[s_c(\theta_o; Y)] = E_{Y|\theta_o}\left[\frac{\partial L(\theta_o; Y)}{\partial \theta}\right] = 0_k, \tag{6.5.6}$$

$$\mathrm{Var}_{Y|\theta_o}[s_c(\theta_o; Y)] = E_{Y|\theta_o}\left(\left[\frac{\partial L(\theta_o; Y)}{\partial \theta}\right]\left[\frac{\partial L(\theta_o; Y)}{\partial \theta}\right]'\right) = J_T(\theta_o). \tag{6.5.7}$$

Proof We only consider the continuous case; the discrete case follows analogously. Because $\mathscr{L}(\theta; Y)$ is a legitimate joint density function for Y,

$$\int_{\mathscr{S}_T} \mathscr{L}(\theta_o; y)\, dy = \int_{\mathscr{S}_T} \exp[L(\theta_o; y)]\, dy = 1. \tag{6.5.8}$$

Differentiating (6.5.8) with respect to θ and evaluating at the value $\theta = \theta_o$ assumed to generate the data implies[19]

$$\int_{\mathscr{S}_T} \frac{\partial}{\partial \theta}[\mathscr{L}(\theta_o; y)]\, dy = \int_{\mathscr{S}_T} [s_c(\theta_o; y)]\mathscr{L}(\theta_o; y)\, dy = 0_K, \tag{6.5.9}$$

19. The interchange of the operations of differentiation and integration in (6.5.9) and (6.5.10) is permissible if the limits of integration are finite and independent of θ (a special case of Leibnitz's Rule), or if these limits are infinite, provided that the integral resulting from the interchange is uniformly convergent for all θ and its integrand is a continuous function of y and θ. These conditions are sufficient. (To see that they are not necessary, see Kendall and Stuart 1979, p. 35, Problems 17.21 and 17.22.) For an elementary, but fairly complete discussion including statistical applications, see Casella and Berger (1990, pp. 68–76), who also cover the interchange of summation and differentiation. Also see Newey and McFadden (1993).

and hence, (6.5.6). Differentiating (6.5.9) with respect to θ' and evaluating at $\theta = \theta_o$ yields

$$\int_{\mathscr{S}_T} \left(\left[\frac{\partial^2 L(\theta_o; y)}{\partial \theta \, \partial \theta'} \right] \mathscr{L}(\theta_o; y) + \left[\frac{\partial L(\theta_o; y)}{\partial \theta} \right] \left[\frac{\partial L(\theta_o; y)}{\partial \theta} \right]' \mathscr{L}(\theta_o; y) \right) dy = 0_{K \times K}. \tag{6.5.10}$$

Noting (6.5.6), it follows that

$$\mathrm{Var}[s_c(\theta_o; Y)] = E_{Y|\theta}([s_c(\theta_o; Y)][s_c(\theta_o; Y)]'), \tag{6.5.11}$$

and thus, (6.5.7) follows immediately from (6.5.11).

The celebrated Cramér-Rao inequality provides a lower bound for the variance of estimators of scalar parameters, irrespective of the method of estimation. Not surprisingly, the lower bound depends on the underlying distribution of the data. Following Dhrymes (1974, pp. 125–126) we shall prove the following more general multivariate result.[20]

Theorem 6.5.2 (Generalized Cramér-Rao Inequality) Let Y_t $(t = 1, 2, \ldots, T)$ be a sample from a population for which the likelihood function $\mathscr{L}(\theta; Y)$ is regular in the sense of Definition 6.5.1. Let $g(\theta) \equiv [g_1(\theta), g_2(\theta), \ldots, g_M(\theta)]'$ be a vector-valued function of $\theta = [\theta_1, \theta_2, \ldots, \theta_K]'$ such that the $M \times K$ matrix

$$\frac{\partial g(\theta)}{\partial \theta'} = \begin{bmatrix} \frac{\partial g_1(\theta)}{\partial \theta_1} & \frac{\partial g_1(\theta)}{\partial \theta_2} & \cdots & \frac{\partial g_1(\theta)}{\partial \theta_K} \\ \frac{\partial g_2(\theta)}{\partial \theta_1} & \frac{\partial g_2(\theta)}{\partial \theta_2} & \cdots & \frac{\partial g_2(\theta)}{\partial \theta_K} \\ \vdots & \vdots & & \vdots \\ \frac{\partial g_M(\theta)}{\partial \theta_1} & \frac{\partial g_M(\theta)}{\partial \theta_2} & \cdots & \frac{\partial g_M(\theta)}{\partial \theta_K} \end{bmatrix} \tag{6.5.12}$$

exists, and suppose there exists an estimator $\hat{g} \equiv \hat{g}(Y) = [\hat{g}_1(Y), \hat{g}_2(Y), \ldots, \hat{g}_M(Y)]'$ which is an unbiased estimator of $g(\theta)$, i.e.

$$E_{Y|\theta_o}[\hat{g}(Y)] = g(\theta_o). \tag{6.5.13}$$

Then the Generalized Cramér-Rao Inequality states that the $M \times M$ matrix

$$\mathrm{Var}(\hat{g}) - \left[\frac{\partial g(\theta_o)}{\partial \theta} \right] [J_T(\theta_o)]^{-1} \left[\frac{\partial g(\theta_o)}{\partial \theta} \right]', \tag{6.5.14}$$

20. In cases where the regularity conditions of Theorem 6.3.2 are not satisfied (e.g. when sampling from a $U[0, \theta]$ distribution), if the limits of integration are finite an alternative lower bound, the Chapman-Robbins lower bound, can be derived. See Krutchkoff (1970, pp. 210–213) for an introductory discussion. See also Casella and Berger (1990, pp. 312–313), Kendall and Stuart (1979, pp. 12–14), Lehmann (1983, pp. 115–130), and Mood et al (1974, p. 330).

is positive semidefinite, where $\operatorname{Var}(\hat{g})$ is the variance-covariance matrix of the estimator $\hat{g}$ and $J_T(\theta)$ is the information matrix of the sample of size T defined by (6.5.5).

Proof From (6.5.13) it follows immediately that

$$\int_{\mathscr{S}_T} \hat{g}(y)\mathscr{L}(\theta_o; y)\,dy = g(\theta_o). \tag{6.5.15}$$

Differentiating (6.5.15) with respect to θ yields

$$\frac{\partial g(\theta)}{\partial \theta} = \int_{\mathscr{S}_T} \hat{g}(y)[s_c(\theta_o; y)]\mathscr{L}(\theta_o; y)\,dy. \tag{6.5.16}$$

Because $E_{Y|\theta}[s_c(\theta; Y)] = 0_k$ by (6.5.6), if follows from (6.5.16) that

$$\operatorname{Cov}[\hat{g}(Y), s_c(\theta_o; Y)] = E_{Y|\theta}[\hat{g}(Y)s_c(\theta_o; Y)] = \frac{\partial g(\theta_o)}{\partial \theta}. \tag{6.5.17}$$

Defining $Z = [\hat{g}', s_c(\theta; Y)]'$ it follows from (6.5.7) and (6.5.17) that

$$\operatorname{Var}(Z) = \begin{bmatrix} \operatorname{Var}(\hat{g}) & \dfrac{\partial g(\theta_o)}{\partial \theta} \\ \dfrac{\partial g(\theta_o)}{\partial \theta'} & J_T(\theta_o) \end{bmatrix} \tag{6.5.18}$$

is a positive semidefinite matrix. Now define

$$C = \begin{bmatrix} I_M & -\left[\dfrac{\partial g(\theta_o)}{\partial \theta}\right][J_T(\theta_o)]^{-1} \\ 0_{K\times M} & I_k \end{bmatrix}, \tag{6.5.19}$$

and consider the positive semidefinite matrix

$$C\operatorname{Var}(Z)C' = \begin{bmatrix} \operatorname{Var}(\hat{g}) - \left[\dfrac{\partial g(\theta_o)}{\partial \theta}\right][J_T(\theta_o)]^{-1}\left[\dfrac{\partial g(\theta_o)}{\partial \theta}\right]' & 0_{M\times K} \\ 0_{K\times M} & J_T(\theta_o) \end{bmatrix}. \tag{6.5.20}$$

Using Theorem A.8.1, the implied positive semidefiniteness of the upper left hand block of (6.5.20) implies that (6.5.14) is positive semidefinite, completing the proof.

Theorem 6.5.2 implies that no matter what estimation method is used, the covariance matrix of an estimator $\hat{g}$ has a lower bound given by

$$\left[\frac{\partial g(\theta_o)}{\partial \theta}\right][J_T(\theta_o)]^{-1}\left[\frac{\partial g(\theta_o)}{\partial \theta}\right]'. \tag{6.5.21}$$

If $M = K$ and $\hat{g}(Y)$ is an unbiased estimator of θ [i.e. $E_{Y|\theta}[\hat{g}(Y)] = \theta$], then

$$\frac{\partial g(\theta_o)}{\partial \theta} = I_K, \tag{6.5.22}$$

and the bound (6.5.21) simplifies to

$$[J_T(\theta_o)]^{-1}. \tag{6.5.23}$$

If the sample is random, then (6.5.5) implies that lower bound (6.5.23) equals

$$[J_T(\theta_o)]^{-1} = [TJ_1(\theta_o)]^{-1}, \tag{6.5.24}$$

where

$$J_1(\theta) \equiv -E_{Y_t|\theta}\left[\frac{\partial^2 \ln[f(Y_t;\theta)]}{\partial\theta\,\partial\theta'}\right] \tag{6.5.25}$$

is the *information matrix for one observation* from the i.i.d. sample.

Part of the attractiveness of the Cramér-Rao lower bound is that it is sometimes attainable in cases of interest. For the remainder of this section we restrict attention to unbiased estimators so that the Cramer-Rao lower bound simplifies to the inverse of the information as given by (6.5.23). We now provide a name for unbiased estimators that achieve (6.5.23).

Definition 6.5.3 An unbiased estimator whose variance attains the Cramér-Rao lower bound (6.5.23) for all $\theta \in \Theta$ is defined to be a *minimum variance bound (MVB) estimator.*

Example 6.5.1 Consider a random sample from a $N(\mu, \sigma^2)$ population, σ^2 known. Then

$$\frac{\partial^2 \ln[\phi(y_t;\mu,\sigma^2)]}{\partial\mu^2} = \frac{\partial}{\partial\mu^2}\left[\ln(2\pi\sigma^2) - \frac{(y_t-\mu)^2}{2\sigma^2}\right] = -\sigma^{-2}. \tag{6.5.26}$$

Thus we see from (6.5.24) and (6.5.26) that the lower bound for any unbiased estimator of μ is σ^2/T. But $\text{Var}(\overline{Y}) = \sigma^2/T$, and so $\overline{Y}$ is the MVB estimator of μ.

The question immediately arises as to when a MVB estimator exists. Necessary and sufficient conditions for its existence in the scalar case $K = 1$ are given in the following theorem. Interestingly, these conditions refer to restrictions to be placed on the score function which also appears in lower bound (6.5.23) via (6.5.7).

Theorem 6.5.3 Let Y_t $(t = 1, 2, \ldots, T)$ be a sample from a population for which the likelihood function $\mathscr{L}(\theta; Y)$ satisfies the regularity conditions in Definition 6.5.1. The estimator $\hat{g} = \hat{g}(Y)$ of $g(\theta)$ in Theorem 6.5.2 is MVB iff

$$s_c(\theta; Y) = h(\theta)[\hat{g} - g(\theta)], \tag{6.5.27}$$

where $h(\theta)$ is a function not involving the data.

Proof Mood et al. (1974, p. 317).

Example 6.5.2 covers a familiar case in which a MVB estimator exists and in which this can be shown without appeal to Theorem 6.5.3. Example 6.5.2 provides an illustration in which a MVB estimator exists for one function of the unknown parameter, but *not* for a monotonic function of it.

Example 6.5.2 Consider a random sample from a $N(0, \sigma^2)$ population, with a known mean of zero and let $g(\sigma^2) = \sigma^2$. Then

$$\frac{\partial L(\sigma^2; Y)}{\partial \sigma^2} = \frac{T}{2\sigma^4}\left[\frac{1}{T}\left(\sum_{t=1}^{T} Y_t^2\right) - \sigma^2\right]. \tag{6.5.28}$$

Hence,

$$\tilde{\sigma}^2 = \frac{1}{T}\sum_{t=1}^{T} Y_t^2 \tag{6.5.29}$$

is the MVB estimator of σ^2. Note that if $g(\sigma^2) = \sigma$, then

$$\frac{\partial L(\sigma; Y)}{\partial \sigma} = \frac{T}{2\sigma^3}\left[\frac{1}{T}\left(\sum_{t=1}^{T} Y_t^2\right) - \sigma^2\right], \tag{6.5.30}$$

cannot be put in the form of (6.5.27). Hence no MVB of σ exists.

Returning to the general case in which $K > 1$, the following theorem is useful in developing properties connecting MVB estimators to other estimators.

Theorem 6.5.4 Let Y be a T-dimensional column vector of random variables with joint p.d.f. $f(y; \theta)$. Let U_g be the set of all unbiased estimators of a given function $g(\theta)$, and let U_0 be the set of all functions of Y having zero expectations. [Note: $\hat{g} \in U_g$ iff $E(\hat{g}|\theta) = g(\theta)$ for all $\theta \in \Theta$, and $f \in U_0$ iff $E(f|\theta) = 0$ for all $\theta \in \Theta$.] Then $\hat{g} \in U_g$ is a MVB estimator at $\theta = \theta_0$ iff $\text{Cov}(\hat{g}, f|\theta) = 0$ for all $f \in U_0$ such that $\text{Var}(f|\theta) < \infty$, provided $\text{Var}(\hat{g}|\theta_0) < \infty$.

Proof

(a) Necessity: If $\hat{g} \in U_g$, then $\hat{g} + \lambda f \in U_g$ for all scalar λ. Consider λ between zero and $-2\,\text{Cov}(g, f)/\text{Var}(f)$. Because $\text{Var}(\hat{g} + \lambda f) = \text{Var}(\hat{g}) + 2\lambda\,\text{Cov}(f, \hat{g}) + \lambda^2\,\text{Var}(f) \leq \text{Var}(\hat{g})$, $\hat{g}$ cannot be a MVB estimator unless $\text{Cov}(\hat{g}, f) = 0$.

(b) Sufficiency: Let $\tilde{g} \in U_g$ such that $\text{Var}(\tilde{g}) < \infty$. Then $f \equiv \hat{g} - \tilde{g} \in U_0$ and $\text{Cov}(\hat{g}, \tilde{g}) = 0$ implies

$$E(\hat{g}f) = E[\hat{g}(\hat{g} - \tilde{g})] = 0. \tag{6.5.31}$$

Hence, noting (6.5.31) and $E(\hat{g}) = E(\tilde{g}) = g(\theta)$, it follows that

$$\begin{aligned}\text{Var}(\hat{g}) &= E(\hat{g}^2) - [E(\hat{g})]^2 = E(\hat{g}\tilde{g}) - [E(\hat{g})E(\tilde{g})] \\ &= \text{Cov}(\hat{g}, \tilde{g}),\end{aligned} \tag{6.5.32}$$

or, letting $\rho \equiv \text{Corr}(\hat{g}, \tilde{g})$,

$$[\text{Var}(\hat{g})]^{1/2} = \rho[\text{Var}(\tilde{g})]^{1/2} \leq [\text{Var}(\tilde{g})]^{1/2}. \tag{6.5.33}$$

Thus $\hat{g}$ is a MVB estimator.

From Theorem 6.5.4, many interesting results flow. For example, (6.5.33) implies $\rho \geq 0$ and also that two unbiased estimators with the same minimum variance must be perfectly correlated. For further discussions, see Rao (1973, p. 318).

A concept closely related to MVB estimators is that of sufficient estimators as defined in Definition 6.1.1. In general it is *not* possible to find a MVB estimator since, as noted earlier, the Cramér-Rao lower bound need not be attainable. Often, however, it is possible to find an unbiased estimator whose variance, although not equal to the Cramér-Rao lower bound, is nonetheless no larger than the variance of any other unbiased estimator for all $\theta \in \Theta$. The following definition introduces the necessary terminology.

Definition 6.5.4 An unbiased estimator whose variance is less than or equal to the variance of any other unbiased estimator for all $\theta \in \Theta$ is known as a *uniform minimum variance unbiased (UMVU) estimator*.

Not only may MVB estimators fail to exist, UMVU estimators may also fail to exist. This is not too surprising, since as noted earlier in Section 6.3, unbiased estimators need not exist. Furthermore, Mood et al. (1974, pp. 330–331) provides an example where unbiased estimators exist, but none of them are uniformly better than all others. Thus, even in this less ambitious setting, restricting attention to unbiased estimators need not be sufficient to guarantee the existence of an "optimal estimator."

Fortunately, in cases where sufficient statistics exist, the situation is not so bleak. According to the following theorem, in our search for MVB estimators we need consider only unbiased estimators that are functions of sufficient statistics.

Theorem 6.5.5 (Rao-Blackwell) Let Y_t $(t = 1, 2, \ldots, T)$ be a random sample from a population characterized by the density $f(y_t; \theta)$, where $\theta = [\theta_1, \ldots, \theta_K]'$, and let $W_j = \omega_j(Y_1, Y_2, \ldots, Y_T)$ $(j = 1, 2, \ldots, J)$ be a set of jointly sufficient statistics. Suppose that $\hat{g}_i$ is an unbiased estimator of $g_i(\theta)$ $(i = 1, 2, \ldots, I)$, and define $\hat{g}_i^* \equiv E(\hat{g}_i | W_1, W_2, \ldots, W_J)$ $(i = 1, 2, \ldots, I)$. Then

(a) $E(\hat{g}_i^*) = g_i(\theta)$ $(i = 1, 2, \ldots, I)$

(b) $\text{Var}(\hat{g}_i^*) \leq \text{Var}(\hat{g}_i)$ $(i = 1, 2, \ldots, I)$

Proof See Mood et al. (1974, p. 322) for the case $K = 1$. Note that the ordering in (b) of variances (i.e., quadratic loss) can be extended to cover arbitrary convex loss functions (see Lehmann 1983, pp. 50–51).

Example 6.5.3 Consider a random sample Y_t $(t = 1, 2, \ldots, T)$ from a Bernoulli distribution with parameter θ. Set $I = J = 1$ in Theorem 6.5.5 and drop subscripts i and j. Clearly, $\hat{g} \equiv Y_1$ is an unbiased estimator of $g(\theta) \equiv \theta$. Also, $W \equiv T\overline{Y}$ is a sufficient statistic (see Exercise 6.5.3). It is straightforward to show (e.g., see Mood et al. 1974, p. 323) that the conditional p.d.f. of $\hat{g}$ given $W = w$ is

$$P(\hat{g} = i|w) = \left\{ \begin{array}{ll} \dfrac{T - w}{T}, & \text{if } i = 0 \\ \dfrac{w}{T}, & \text{if } i = 1 \\ 0, & \text{otherwise} \end{array} \right\}. \tag{6.5.34}$$

Thus according to Theorem 6.5.5,

$$\hat{g}^* \equiv E(\hat{g}|w) = 0 \cdot \left(\frac{T - W}{T}\right) + 1 \cdot \left(\frac{W}{T}\right) = \frac{W}{T} = \overline{Y} \tag{6.5.35}$$

is an unbiased estimator of θ with a variance not larger than that of $\hat{g} \equiv Y_1$. Clearly, this is the case if $T > 1$, because $\text{Var}(\hat{g}) = \theta(1 - \theta)$ and $\text{Var}(\hat{g}^*) = \theta(1 - \theta)/T$.

Theorem 6.5.5 describes how to possibly improve on unbiased estimators by conditioning on sufficient statistics. To determine when such estimators are MVB, the following concept is useful.

Definition 6.5.5 Let Y_t $(t = 1, 2, \ldots, T)$ be a random sample from a population characterized by the p.f. $f(y_t; \theta)$, where $\theta = [\theta_1, \theta_2, \ldots, \theta_K]'$. The set of statistics $W_j = \omega_j(Y_1, Y_2, \ldots, Y_T)$ $(j = 1, 2, \ldots, J)$ are defined to be *jointly complete* iff the only unbiased estimators of zero that are functions of W_j $(j = 1, 2, \ldots, J)$ are functions that are identically zero with probability one. If $J = 1$, W_1 is *complete*.

Mood et al. (1974, pp. 354–355) show that the first and last order statistics are jointly complete when a random sample is drawn from a $U[\theta_1, \theta_2]$ distribution. Also, if $f(y_t; \theta)$ is a member of the K-parameter exponential family with a K-dimensional parameter space defined in Exercise 3.3.10, then a minimal set of jointly complete and sufficient statistics can be found (e.g., see Lehmann 1986, 142–143). In general, showing completeness is difficult (see Lehmann 1983, pp. 46–48 for helpful discussion). It is, however, a rewarding exercise. For example, consider the simple case $K = 1$. If the p.f. in question admits a complete statistic, then there can be *at most* one unbiased estimator of 0. To see this, suppose W_1 and W_2 are unbiased estimators of θ and consider $W_3 \equiv W_1 - W_2$. Then $E(W_3) = 0$ and completeness implies $W_3 = 0$, or equivalently, $W_1 = W_2$. Also, in the case $J = 1$, if a complete sufficient statistic W_1 exists and if there is an unbiased estimator of $g_1(\theta)$, then there exists a MVB estimator of $g_1(\theta)$, and furthermore, the MVB estimator is the unique unbiased estimator of $g_1(\theta)$ which is a function of W_1. The formal statement in the case $J \geq 1$ is given in the following theorem.

Theorem 6.5.6 (Lehmann-Scheffé) Let Y_t $(t = 1, 2, \ldots, T)$ be a random sample from a population characterized by the density $f(y_t; \theta)$, where $\theta = [\theta_1, \theta_2, \ldots, \theta_K]'$. Suppose:

(a) $W_j = \omega_j(Y_1, Y_2, \ldots, Y_T)$ $(j = 1, 2, \ldots, J)$ are jointly complete sufficient statistics.

(b) There exists an unbiased estimator $\hat{g} \equiv [\hat{g}_1, \hat{g}_2, \ldots, \hat{g}_M]'$ of $g(\theta) \equiv [g_1(\theta), g_2(\theta), \ldots, g_M(\theta)]'$.

Then $\hat{g}^* \equiv E[\hat{g}_1^*, \hat{g}_2^*, \ldots, \hat{g}_M^*]'$, where

$$\hat{g}_M^* \equiv E(\hat{g}_m | W_1, W_2, \ldots, W_J) \qquad (m = 1, 2, \ldots, M) \tag{6.5.36}$$

is an UMVU estimator of $g(\theta)$.

Proof Lehmann and Scheffé (1950).

In summary, the connection between sufficient statistics and MVB estimators is as follows. If jointly complete sufficient statistics exist (as they generally do when sampling from the K-dimensional exponential family with a nondegenerate K-dimensional parameter space), then every function of them is a UMVU estimator of its expected value (assuming it exists). The importance of the Rao-Blackwell Theorem 6.5.6 is that it implies that the search for UMVU estimators can be restricted to the class of estimators that are functions of sufficient statistics. The concept of completeness implies that there is a unique function of sufficient statistics that is unbiased for any given parametric function.[21] In order to find the UMVU estimator, Theorem 6.5.7 (Lehmann-Scheffé) suggests starting with any unbiased estimator and then taking its conditional expectation, given the jointly complete sufficient statistics.[22]

Although a path to MVB estimators (when they exist) has now been described, the goal can be disappointing as the following example illustrates.

21. Recall from the discussion in Section 6.3, unbiased estimators my not exist for some parametric functions. For a readable discussion of MVB estimators, see Krutchkoff (1970, Chapter 11).

22. In cases where no unbiased estimator is available, a "jackknife" estimator (recall Exercise 6.3.18) may be used to obtain an estimator that is approximately unbiased.

Example 6.5.4 (Lehmann 1983, pp. 114–115) Suppose Y_t $(t = 1, 2, \ldots, T) \sim$ i.i.d. Po(θ). Then $W = Y_1 + Y_2 + \cdots + Y_T$ is a sufficient statistic and $W \sim$ Po$(T\theta)$ [recall Theorem 5.2.4]. Suppose interest focuses on estimating $g(\theta) \equiv \exp(-c\theta)$, where c is a known positive scalar. Clearly, $0 < g(\theta) < 1$ for $0 < \theta < \infty$. Consider the estimator

$$\hat{g} = \hat{g}(W) \equiv \left[1 - \frac{c}{T}\right]^W. \tag{6.5.37}$$

Then

$$\begin{aligned} E(\hat{g}) &= \sum_{w=0}^{\infty} \left(1 - \frac{c}{T}\right)^w \left[\frac{(T\theta)^w \exp(-T\theta)}{w!}\right] \\ &= \exp(-T\theta) \sum_{w=0}^{\infty} \frac{[(T-c)\theta]^w}{v!} = \exp[-T\theta + T\theta - c\theta] \\ &= \exp(-c\theta) = g(\theta), \end{aligned} \tag{6.5.38}$$

and hence $\hat{g}$ is an unbiased estimator of $g(\theta)$. Since the Poisson family is complete, $\hat{g}$ is the only unbiased estimator of $g(\theta)$. By Theorem 6.5.6, $\hat{g}$ is UMVU. Note, however, if $c > T$, then $\hat{g}$ oscillates wildly between positive and negative values and bears little relationship to $g(\theta)$. Of course as $T \to \infty$, this problem goes away.

Finally, consider the following theorem promised in Section 6.1. Complete sufficient statistics are particularly effective in reducing data because they are always minimal (see Lehmann and Scheffé 1950). Furthermore, completeness provides a sufficient condition for a sufficient statistic to be independent of an ancillary statistic. Part of the attractiveness of the following theorem is that it permits one to deduce the independence of two statistics *without* obtaining their joint distribution.

Theorem 6.5.7 (Basu) A complete sufficient statistic is independent of every ancillary statistic.

Proof Lehmann (1983, p. 46).

The converse of Basu's Theorem 6.5.7 does not hold. Intuitively, the reason is simple: ancillarity is concerned with the whole distribution of a statistic whereas completeness is a property dealing only with expectation. See Lehmann (1981) and Casella and Berger (1990, pp. 282–283) for further discussion.

Exercises

6.5.1 Let Y_t $(t = 1, 2, \ldots, T) \sim$ i.i.d. $U(\theta - \frac{1}{2}, \theta + \frac{1}{2})$ distribution.

(a) Show: $W = [\min\{Y_t\}, \max(Y_t\}]'$ is minimal sufficient for θ.

(b) Show: W is *not* complete [consider $\max\{Y_t\} - \min\{Y_t\} - \{(T-1)/(T+)\}$].

6.5.2 Let Y_t $(t = 1, 2, \ldots, T)$ be a random sample from the p.d.f. $f(y|\theta) = 2y/\theta^2$, if $0 < y < \theta$, and zero otherwise.

(a) Show: $W = 3\overline{Y}/2$ is an unbiased estimator for θ.

(b) Find the Cramér-Rao lower bound. Is it applicable?

6.5.3 Show that the ML estimator is asymptotically sufficient. You may assume $K = 1$.

6.5.4 Let Y_t $(t = 1, 2, \ldots, T)$ be a random sample from a distribution with p.d.f. $f(y;\theta)$ and $\theta \in \Re^K$. Suppose that θ is a *location parameter*, that is, the distribution of $Y - \theta$ does not depend on θ. Let $\hat{\theta}$ be a *location-invariant estimator*, i.e. $\hat{\theta}(Y + c) = \hat{\theta}(Y) + c$ for all Y and c. Pitman (1939) showed that

$$\tilde{\theta} = \frac{\int_{-\infty}^{\infty} \theta \mathscr{L}(\theta; y)\, d\theta}{\int_{-\infty}^{\infty} \mathscr{L}(\theta; y)\, d\theta}, \tag{6.5.39}$$

where $\mathscr{L}(\theta | Y)$ is the likelihood function, has uniformly smallest MSE within the class of location-invariant estimators.

(a) Show that $\tilde{\theta} = \overline{Y}$ when sampling from a $N(0, 1)$ distribution.

(b) Show that $\tilde{\theta}$ equals the midrange when sampling from the $U(\theta - \frac{1}{2}, \theta + \frac{1}{2})$ distribution.

6.5.5 Let Y_t $(t = 1, 2, \ldots, T)$ be a random sample from a distribution with p.d.f. $f(y; \theta)$ and $\theta \in \Re^K$. Suppose that $\theta > 0$ is a *scale parameter*, that is, the distribution of Y/θ does not depend on θ. Let $\hat{\theta}$ be a scale-invariant estimator, that is, $\hat{\theta}(cY) = c\hat{\theta}(Y)$ for all y and $c > 0$. Pitman (1939) showed that

$$\tilde{\theta} = \frac{\int_{0}^{\infty} \theta^{-2} \mathscr{L}(\theta; y)\, d\theta}{\int_{0}^{\infty} \theta^{-3} \mathscr{L}(\theta; y)\, d\theta}, \tag{6.5.40}$$

where $\mathscr{L}(\theta; y)$ is the likelihood function, minimizes $E[(\tilde{\theta} - \theta)^2/\theta^2]$ within the class of scale-invariant estimators.

(a) Show that $\tilde{\theta} = [(T + 2)/(T + 1)] \max\{Y_1, Y_2, \ldots, Y_T)$ when sampling from a $U(0, \theta)$ distribution.

(b) Show that $\tilde{\theta} = (Y_1 + Y_2 + \cdots + Y_T)/(T + 1)$ when sampling from an exponential distribution with mean θ.

6.5.6 Suppose that T independent binomial trials, each with probability θ of success, are carried out. In addition suppose trials are continued until an additional k successes are obtained, this requiring m additional trials (see Silvey 1975, pp. 34–35).

(a) Show that the likelihood function corresponding to the binary outcomes Y_i $(i = 1, 2, \ldots, T + m)$ is given by $\mathscr{L}(\theta; y) = \theta^{r+k}(1 - \theta)^{T+m-r-k}$, where $r \equiv Y_1 + Y_2 + \cdots + Y_m$.

(b) Show that $W \equiv [r, m]'$ is a minimal sufficient statistic for θ.

(c) Define $h(W) = (r/m) - [(k - 1)/(m - 1)]$. Show that $E[h(W)] = 0$ for all θ.

(d) Is W a complete statistic?

6.5.7 Suppose the statistic $W \sim b(T, \theta)$, where $0 < \theta < 1$. Show that W is complete.

6.5.8 Suppose Y_t $(t = 1, 2, \ldots, T) \sim$ i.i.d. $U(0, \theta)$. Show that $W \equiv \max\{Y_1, Y_2, \ldots, Y_T\}$ is a complete sufficient statistic for θ (Casella and Berger 1990, p. 261).

6.5.9 Show that the minimal sufficient statistic in Exercise 6.1.8 is *not* complete.

6.5.10 Let Y_t $(t = 1, 2, \ldots, T) \sim$ i.i.d. $N(\theta, \sigma^2)$. Define $\alpha = \theta^2$.

(a) Suppose σ^2 is known. Show: $\hat{\alpha}_1 = \overline{Y}^2 - (\sigma^2/T)$ is the UMVU unbiased estimator of α.

(b) Suppose σ^2 is unknown. Show: $\hat{\alpha}^2 = \overline{Y}^2 - [s^2/T(T-1)]$ is the UMVU unbiased estimator of α.

(c) Suppose σ^2 is known and consider $\hat{\alpha}_3 = \overline{Y}^2 - (c\sigma^2/T)$, where c is a constant. Find MSE($\hat{\alpha}_3$).

[Note that in each case the estimator can take on negative values although $\mu^2 \geq 0$.]

6.5.11 Suppose $Y|\alpha, \beta \sim G(\alpha, \beta)$. Show that the information matrix is

$$J_1(\alpha, \beta) = \begin{bmatrix} \psi'(\alpha) & \dfrac{1}{\beta} \\ \dfrac{1}{\beta} & \dfrac{\alpha}{\beta^2} \end{bmatrix}, \tag{6.5.41}$$

where $\psi(\alpha) \equiv \Gamma'(\alpha)/\Gamma(\alpha)$ (known as the *digamma function*), $\psi'(\alpha) = d\psi(\alpha)/d\alpha$ (known as the *trigamma function*), and $\Gamma'(\alpha) = d\Gamma(\alpha)/d\alpha$.

6.5.12 Suppose $Y|\alpha, \delta \sim \beta(\alpha, \delta)$. Show that the information matrix is

$$J_1(\alpha, \delta) = \begin{bmatrix} \psi'(\alpha) - \psi'(\alpha + \delta) & -\psi'(\alpha + \delta) \\ -\psi'(\alpha + \delta) & \psi'(\delta) - \psi'(\alpha + \delta) \end{bmatrix}, \tag{6.5.42}$$

where $\psi(\alpha)$ and $\psi'(\alpha)$ are defined in Exercise 6.5.11.

6.5.13 Consider a location/scale family (recall Definition 3.1.1) with density $\theta_2^{-1} f[(y - \theta_1)/\theta_2]$, $\theta_2 > 0$, and $f(\cdot) > 0$. Let $f'(y) = df(y)/dy$. Show that the elements of the information matrix $J_1(\theta)$ are given by:

(a) $$J_{1,11}(\theta) = \frac{1}{\theta_2^2}\int_{-\infty}^{\infty} \left[\frac{f'(y)}{f(y)}\right]^2 f(y)\,dy \tag{6.5.43}$$

(b) $$J_{1,22}(\theta) = \frac{1}{\theta_2^2}\int_{-\infty}^{\infty} \left[\frac{yf'(y)}{f(y)} + 1\right]^2 f(y)\,dy \tag{6.5.44}$$

(c) $$J_{1,12}(\theta) = \frac{1}{\theta_2^2}\int_{-\infty}^{\infty} y\left[\frac{f'(y)}{f(y)}\right]^2 f(y)\,dy \tag{6.5.45}$$

(d) If $f(\cdot)$ is symmetric around zero, then $J_{1,12}(\theta) = 0$.

6.5.14 Suppose Y_t $(t = 1, 2, \ldots, T) \sim$ i.i.d. $B(1, \theta)$. Show that $\hat{\alpha} = T\overline{Y}(1 - \overline{Y})/(T - 1)$ is the UMVU estimator of $\alpha = \theta(1 - \theta)$.

6.6 Classical Point Estimation Methods

In the discussion of properties of estimators in Section 6.3, we noted that in general minimum MSE estimators do not exist. One response to such circumstances is to restrict the class of potential estimators to only unbiased estimators, and then seek the estimator within this class having minimum variance. In the case $K = 1$ we saw in Theorem 6.5.3, however, that a MVB estimator $\hat{\theta}_T$, that is, an unbiased estimator achieving the Cramer-Rao lower bound (6.5.23), of θ is available only if the score function is proportional to $\hat{\theta} - \theta$. Generally in finite samples this condition does not hold. One response to this state of affairs is to further restrict the class of permissible estimators to also be linear and seek a BLUE (see Definition 6.3.11 and Exercise 6.3.13). A different response is to consider estimators which perform desirably in an asymptotic sense in the hope that such properties are approximately accurate in describing the estimator's behavior in small samples.

We will begin our discussion with one of the oldest known methods of estimation: the method of moments. This method, implicit in the discussion of Sections 5.1 and 5.2, is based on the simple principle that a researcher should estimate a moment of the population distribution by the corresponding moment of the sample.[23] Although *not* likelihood based, our discussion of classical estimation methods begins with method of moments estimation largely for historical reasons.

Definition 6.6.1 Let Y_t $(t = 1, 2, \ldots, T)$ be a random sample from a population where $\theta = [\theta_1, \theta_2, \ldots, \theta_K]'$. Suppose the first K moments around zero exist, and denote these by $\mu'_k \equiv \mu'_k(\theta_1, \theta_2, \ldots, \theta_K) = E(Y_t^k)$ $(k = 1, 2, \ldots, K; t = 1, 2, \ldots, T)$. Finally, let $M'_k \equiv T^{-1}(Y_1^k + Y_2^k + \cdots + Y_T^k)$ $(k = 1, 2, \ldots, K)$ denote the kth sample moment. Then a *method of moments (MM) estimator* $\hat{\theta} = [\hat{\theta}_1, \hat{\theta}_2, \ldots, \hat{\theta}_K]'$ is a solution to

$$M'_k = \mu'_k(\hat{\theta}) = \int_{\Re_k} y^k f(y|\hat{\theta})\,dy \qquad (k = 1, 2, \ldots, K). \tag{6.6.1}$$

We use "MME" to denote both the method of moments estimator and the method of moments estimate, leaving the context to distinguish between the two.

Before commenting in more detail on MMEs we consider the following example.

Example 6.6.1 Suppose $Y_t \sim$ i.i.d. $N(\theta_1, \theta_2)$ $(t = 1, 2, \ldots, T)$. Then the MM estimators $\hat{\theta}_1$ and $\hat{\theta}_2$ are defined to be the solutions to

$$M'_1 = \mu'_1(\hat{\theta}_1, \hat{\theta}_2) = \hat{\theta}_1,$$

$$M'_2 = \mu'_2(\hat{\theta}_1, \hat{\theta}_2) = \hat{\theta}_2 + (\hat{\theta}_1)^2,$$

where $M'_1 = \overline{Y}$ and $M'_2 = T^{-1}(Y_1^2 + Y_2^2 + \cdots + Y_T^2)$. In other words, $\hat{\theta}_1 = \overline{Y}$ and $\hat{\theta}_2 = M'_2 - \overline{Y}^2 = T^{-1}[(Y_1 - \overline{Y})^2 + (Y_2 - \overline{Y})^2 + \cdots + (Y_T - \overline{Y})^2]$.

Desirable properties for MM estimators rely on desirable behavior on the part of the sample moments M'_k $(k = 1, 2, \ldots, K)$ as given in the following theorem.

Theorem 6.6.1 Let Y_t $(t = 1, 2, \ldots, T)$ be a random sample from a distribution for which $\mu'_{2r} \equiv E(Y_t^{2r})$ exists.

23. This is an example of the more general guideline known as the *analogy principle*. See Manski (1988) for a detailed discussion.

(a) $M'_r \equiv T^{-1}[Y_1^r + Y_2^r + \cdots + Y_T^r]$ is a mean-square consistent estimator of μ'_r.

(b) Then the joint distribution of a finite number of random variables $T^{1/2}[M'_j - \mu'_j]$ $(j = 1, 2, \ldots, J)$ converges to $N_J(0_J, \Sigma)$, where $\Sigma = [\sigma_{ij}]$ and $\sigma_{ij} = \mu'_{i+j} - \mu'_j\mu'_j$ for $i, j = 1, 2, \ldots, J$. In particular, the asymptotic distribution of

$$Z_T = T^{1/2}\left[\frac{M'_r - \mu_r}{[\mu'_{2r} - (\mu'_r)^2]^{1/2}}\right], \tag{6.6.2}$$

as $T \to \infty$ is $N(0, 1)$.

Proof

(a) From Theorem 5.1.1 we see that M'_r is an unbiased estimator of μ'_r with variance $\mathrm{Var}(M'_r) = [\mu'_{2r} - (\mu'_r)^2]/T$. Thus $\mathrm{Var}(M'_r) \to 0$ as $T \to \infty$, and hence M'_r converges in mean square to μ'_r.

(b) Follows directly from (a) and a multivariate extension of Theorem 5.7.1 (Lindeberg-Levy CLT).

MME's inherit the desirable asymptotic properties of the sample moments provided a little more structure is placed on the problem as given in the following theorem.

Theorem 6.6.2 Suppose the functions $\mu'_k(\theta)$ $(k = 1, 2, \ldots, K)$ in (6.6.1) have continuous partial derivatives up to order K on Θ, and that the Jacobian $|\partial\mu(\theta)/\partial\theta| \neq 0$ for $\theta \in \Theta$. Also suppose equations (6.6.1) have a unique solution $\hat{\theta}_{MM}$ with probability approaching one as $T \to \infty$. Then as $T \to \infty$:

(a) $\hat{\theta}_{MM} \xrightarrow{p} \theta$.

(b) $T^{1/2}(\hat{\theta}_{MM} - \theta) \xrightarrow{d} N_K(0_K, \Omega)$, where $\Omega = [\partial\mu(\theta)/\partial\theta]'\Sigma[\partial\mu(\theta)/\partial\theta]$ and Σ is given in Theorem 6.6.1(b).

Proof (a) Follows from the consistency of sample moments for the corresponding population moments and Theorem 5.5.4(b). (b) Follows from Theorems 6.6.1 and 5.7.5.

In the 1980s, method of moments estimation received renewed attention. In a fundamentally important article, Hansen (1982) considered estimators based on population moment restrictions of the form

$$E[\psi(Y_t, \theta)] = 0, \qquad t = 1, 2, 3, \ldots \tag{6.6.3}$$

where ψ is a known function with $q > K$ components. For example in Definition 6.6.1 the implicit underlying relation corresponds to the choice

$$\psi_k(Y_t, \theta) = Y_t^k - \mu'_k(\theta) \qquad (k = 1, 2, \ldots, K) \tag{6.6.4}$$

with $\psi(Y_t, \theta) = [\psi_1(Y_t, \theta), \psi_2(Y_t, \theta)\psi_k(Y_t, \theta)]'$. Hansen (1982) defined *generalized method of moments (GMM)* estimators as a solution to the following problem:

$$\min_{\theta} \left[\frac{1}{T}\sum_{t=1}^{T} \psi(y_t, \theta)\right]' A_T \left[\frac{1}{T}\sum_{t=1}^{T} \psi(y_t, \theta)\right], \tag{6.6.5}$$

where A_T converges with probability one to a positive definite matrix A.[24] Under suitable regularity conditions, Hansen (1982) showed that the optimal choice of A is $A = [E\{\psi(Y, \theta)\psi(Y, \theta)'\}]^{-1}$, and that $T^{1/2}(\hat{\theta} - \theta) \xrightarrow{d} N(0, \Omega)$ as $T \to \infty$, where

$$\Omega^{-1} = \left[E\left(\frac{\partial \psi(Y, \theta)}{\partial \theta}\right)\right](E[\psi(Y, \theta)(\psi(Y, \theta))'])^{-1}\left[E\left(\frac{\partial \psi(Y, \theta)}{\partial \theta}\right)\right]', \tag{6.6.6}$$

and all expectations in (6.6.6) are taken with respect to the sampling distribution of Y given θ. See Burguette et al. (1982), Hamilton (1994, pp. 409–343), and Newey and McFadden (1993) for further discussion of GMM.

Despite Theorem 6.6.2, MMEs have some drawbacks. Firstly, they are not uniquely defined: central moments or higher order moments could also be used in (6.6.1). Secondly, MM cannot be applied in problems where the underlying distribution does not possess moments. Finally, no general claims for efficiency (even asymptotic) can be made for MMEs (but see Kendall and Stuart 1979, Section 18.36). The following example demonstrates the possible relative inefficiency of MMEs.

Example 6.6.2 Consider a random sample Y_t ($t = 1, 2, \ldots, T$) from a $U(\theta - \frac{1}{2}, \theta + \frac{1}{2})$ distribution. Then $E(\overline{Y}) = \theta$, $\text{Var}(\overline{Y}) = 1/12T$ and $\overline{Y}$ is mean-square consistent. Letting $Y_{(1)}$ and $Y_{(T)}$ be the sample minimum and maximum, respectively, the midrange $\hat{\theta} \equiv [Y_{(1)} + Y_{(T)}]/2$ is unbiased, has a variance $[2(T + 1)(T + 2)]^{-1}$, and is also mean-square consistent. Thus the midrange is more efficient than $\overline{Y}$ for all T by an order of magnitude. Asymptotically, $\overline{Y}$ has zero efficiency relative to the midrange. Note that $\hat{\theta}$ depends on the minimally sufficient statistic $[Y_{(1)}, Y_{(2)}]'$, but that $\overline{Y}$ is not sufficient.

The performance of MMEs relative to other estimators reflects in part that they do not always make use of all available information. Specifically, they are not likelihood based. Intuitively, it seems reasonable to expect that an estimator based on the joint p.d.f. of the data should utilize more effectively all the information in the data than an estimator based only on

24. For related work, see Burguette et al. (1982), Chamberlain (1987), Huber (1967), and Manski (1984).

population moment relationships. Furthermore, as seen in Section 6.5, the likelihood function (i.e., the joint p.d.f. of the data viewed as a function of the parameters θ given the data) is intimately related to the existence of MVB estimators, thus suggesting that estimators based on the likelihood function should be "good."

In classic papers R. A. Fisher (1921, 1922, 1925) introduced three important concepts into the statistics literature: consistency, efficiency and sufficiency. In addition he advocated estimation according to the method of maximum likelihood. This method is defined in Definition 6.6.2. For an extensive survey of the maximum likelihood method, see Norden (1972, 1973). A good textbook treatment of ML estimation is Lehmann (1983, pp. 409–454).

Definition 6.6.2 Let Y_t $(t = 1, 2, \ldots, T)$ be a sample with likelihood function $\mathscr{L}(\theta; Y)$, where θ is a vector of unknown parameters. The *maximum likelihood (ML) estimator* $\hat{\theta}_{\text{ML}} = \hat{\theta}_{\text{ML}}(Y)$ of θ is the point in Θ for which $\mathscr{L}(\theta; Y)$, or equivalently $L(\theta; Y)$, achieves a global maximum. For a realization $Y = y$, the resulting $\hat{\theta}_{\text{ML}}(y)$ is the *maximum likelihood estimate.* Both the maximum likelihood estimator and the maximum likelihood estimate are denoted by MLE, the context identifying the appropriate choice.

More formally, the ML estimator is the solution to the optimization problem:

$$\hat{\theta}_{\text{ML}} \equiv \underset{\theta \in \Theta}{\operatorname{argmax}}\ \mathscr{L}(\theta; Y) = \underset{\theta \in \Theta}{\operatorname{argmax}}\ L(\theta; Y). \tag{6.6.7}$$

Provided the regularity conditions in Definition 6.5.1 are satisfied, the ML estimator can be found by solving the *likelihood equations*

$$s_c(\hat{\theta}_{\text{ML}}; Y) = 0_K, \tag{6.6.8}$$

for the root corresponding to a global maximum of $L(\theta; Y)$. When the regularity conditions are not satisfied, then other procedures may be required (see Exercise 6.6.6). Appendix C provides a summary discussion of numerical optimization techniques.

Note that multiple solutions to (6.6.8) are common in econometrics. Dhrymes (1974, p. 117) cites an example that yields fifty roots. Multiple roots also commonly occur when estimating the location parameter of a Cauchy distribution. Note also that it is common in econometrics for there to be no "closed-form" explicit solution to the likelihood equations. In such cases, (6.6.8) must be solved by iterative nonlinear programming methods. Somewhat surprisingly, even when an explicit solution to (6.6.8) is *not* available, it is possible to derive the asymptotic properties of the ML estimator in a wide variety of settings. In other cases, however, the ML does not even exist (e.g., see Kendall and Stuart 1979, p. 77, Exercise 18.23; p. 80, Exercise 18.34) or is not unique (e.g., see Kendall and Stuart 1979, p. 76, Exercise 18.17; p. 80, Exercise 18.33).

Of critical importance in the discussion of ML estimation is the score function $s_c(\theta; Y) = \partial L(\theta; Y)/\partial\theta$ defined in Definition 6.5.1. Treated as a function of the random variables Y_t $(t = 1, 2, \ldots, T)$ and evaluated at θ_o, we saw in Theorem 6.5.1 that $s_c(\theta_o; Y)$ is a random variable with mean zero and variance-covariance matrix equalling information matrix $J_T(\theta)$ defined in (6.5.4). The method of ML takes the observed (realized) data $Y = y$ and considers estimates of θ, which equate the score function to its mean of zero; in words this is what likelihood equations (6.6.8) are doing.

We will now illustrate the method of ML with two examples.

Example 6.6.3 Suppose that a random sample Y_t $(t = 1, 2, \ldots, T)$ of size T is drawn from a Bernoulli population with probability mass function

$$f(y;\theta) = \begin{Bmatrix} \theta, & \text{if } y = 1 \\ 1-\theta, & \text{if } y = 0 \\ 0, & \text{otherwise} \end{Bmatrix}. \tag{6.6.9}$$

Then the log-likelihood function is

$$\begin{aligned} L(\theta; Y) &= \sum_{t=1}^{T} \ln[f(y_t;\theta)] = \left[\sum_{t=1}^{T} Y_t\right]\ln(\theta) + \left[T - \sum_{t=1}^{T} Y_t\right]\ln(1-\theta) \\ &= T\overline{Y}\ln(\theta) + T(1-\overline{Y})\ln(1-\theta), \end{aligned} \tag{6.6.10}$$

and the score function is

$$s_c(\theta; Y) = \frac{T\overline{Y}}{\theta} - \frac{T(1-\overline{Y})}{1-\theta}. \tag{6.6.11}$$

Setting (6.6.11) equal to zero and solving for θ yields the MLE $\hat{\theta}_{\text{ML}} = \overline{Y}$. Because

$$\frac{\partial^2 L(\theta; Y)}{\partial\theta^2} = -\frac{T\overline{Y}}{\theta^2} - \frac{T(1-\overline{Y})}{(1-\theta)^2} < 0 \tag{6.6.12}$$

for $0 < \overline{Y} < 1$ and all θ, it follows that $\hat{\theta}_{\text{ML}}$ is the global maximum of (6.6.10). Note that $\hat{\theta}_{\text{ML}} = \overline{Y}$ is also the method of moments estimator.

Example 6.6.4 Suppose that Y_t $(t = 1, 2, \ldots, T) \sim$ i.i.d. $N(\theta_1, \theta_2)$. Then the log-likelihood function is

$$L(\theta; Y) = -\frac{T}{2}\ln(2\pi) - \frac{T}{2}\ln(\theta_2) - \frac{1}{2\theta_2}\sum_{t=1}^{T}(Y_t - \theta_1)^2, \tag{6.6.13}$$

where $\theta = [\theta_1, \theta_2]'$. The score function contains two elements:

$$\frac{\partial L(\theta; Y)}{\partial\theta_1} = \frac{1}{\theta_2}\sum_{t=1}^{T}(Y_t - \theta_1), \tag{6.6.14}$$

$$\frac{\partial L(\theta; Y)}{\partial \theta_2} = -\frac{T}{2\theta_2} + \frac{1}{2\theta_2^2} \sum_{t=1}^{T} (Y_t - \theta_1)^2. \qquad (6.6.15)$$

Equating (6.6.14) and (6.6.15) to zero and solving for $\hat{\theta}_1$ and $\hat{\theta}_2$ yields the ML estimators

$$\hat{\theta}_1 = \bar{Y}, \qquad (6.6.16)$$

$$\hat{\theta}_2 = \frac{1}{T} \sum_{t=1}^{T} (Y_t - \bar{Y})^2. \qquad (6.6.17)$$

Verification of second order conditions is left to the reader. Note that once again the MLEs are the same as the method of moment estimators (see Example 6.6.1).

Note that choosing θ_1 to maximize log-likelihood (6.6.13) is equivalent to the *least squares estimator*:

$$\hat{\theta}_{1,\text{LS}} \equiv \underset{\theta_1}{\operatorname{argmin}} \sum_{t=1}^{T} [Y_t - g_t(\theta_1)]^2, \qquad (6.6.18)$$

where $g_t(\theta_1) = \theta_1$ $(t = 1, 2, \ldots, T)$ for the problem at hand. In the context of Example 6.6.4 the least squares estimator is simply the sample mean. Although the least squares estimator will receive detailed discussion in Chapter 9, we introduce here to emphasize minimizing squared errors is motivated by underlying normality even though (6.6.18) can be used in cases not involving normality.

Although the MLE $\hat{\theta}_1$ in (6.6.16) is an unbiased estimator of θ_1, the MLE $\hat{\theta}_2$ in (6.6.17) is a biased estimator of θ_2 (see Exercise 6.3.4). Typically, $\text{Bias}(\hat{\theta}_{\text{ML}}) = O(T^{-1})$ (Lehmann 1983, p. 426). The following theorem shows, however, that MLE's are consistent under fairly general conditions.[25]

Theorem 6.6.3 Let Y_t $(t = 1, 2, \ldots, T)$ be a sample for which the likelihood function $\mathscr{L}(\theta; Y)$ satisfies the regularity conditions in Definition 6.5.1. Then the MLE is a weakly consistent estimator of θ_o, that is, $\hat{\theta}_{\text{MLE}} \xrightarrow{p} \theta_o$ as $T \to \infty$.

Proof See Exercises 6.6.18 and 6.6.19.

There are many proofs in the literature of the consistency of the MLE with some variation in the nature of the regularity conditions required. Wald (1949) showed the consistency of the MLE without assuming compactness of the parameter space, but his conditions are not easy to verify.

25. There are many examples, however, in which the MLE is inconsistent: Bahadur (1958), Basu (1955), Ferguson (1982), Kraft and Le Cam (1956), Le Cam (1990), Lehmann (1983, pp. 410–412, 420–421), and Neyman and Scott (1948).

The proof strategy employed in Exercises 6.6.18 and 6.6.19 (and the important lemmas they contain) are based on the extremal estimator literature (see Amemiya (1985), Newey and McFadden (1993), Huber (1981) and Burguette, et al. 1982). This proof strategy is based on characterizing the MLE as a solution to maximizing the log-likelihood. Uniform convergence and either compactness of the parameter space or concavity of the log-likelihood (see Newey and McFadden 1993, Section 2.6) for a discussion of the trade-offs play crucial roles in these proofs.

In contrast a more established strategy is to focus on the MLE solving the likelihood equations (6.6.8). Such proofs do not require uniform convergence or compactness, but usually yield only the conclusion that there is a consistent root of the likelihood equations (e.g., Cramér 1946 provided seminal ideas). Huzurbazar (1948) showed that there is only one unique consistent root and this root corresponds to a local maximum of $L(\theta; Y)$ with probability one. This root, however, need not correspond to the global maximum defining the MLE. The addition of a concavity assumption may render the root unique, but in general these proofs do not fully solve the problem. Lehmann (1983, Chapter 6) is a good source for these strategies. Numerous references to other proofs are given by Lehmann (1983, esp. pp. 421, 430).

Extensions of either of these proof strategies to cover cases of non-i.i.d. sampling are numerous. The i.n.i.d. case usually hinges on the applicability of a LLN to the likelihood equations and that the information for the sample is $O(T)$ (e.g., see Hoadley 1971). The n.i.n.i.d. case is more difficult. Spanos (1986, pp. 272–276) provides a convenient summary discussion, and Crowder (1976) provides a proof. Strengthening the conclusion of Theorem 6.6.3 to almost sure convergence is usually possible with additional assumptions.

The limiting distribution of $T^{1/2}(\hat{\theta} - \theta_o)$, where $\hat{\theta}$ is the consistent root of the likelihood equations is given in the following theorem.

Theorem 6.6.4 Let Y_t $(t = 1, 2, \ldots, T)$ be a random sample from a population for which the likelihood function $\mathscr{L}(\theta; Y)$ satisfies the regularity conditions in Definition 6.5.1. Let $\hat{\theta}$ be a consistent root of (6.6.8), guaranteed to exist by Theorem 6.6.3, and define

$$Z_T = T^{1/2}(\hat{\theta} - \theta_o). \qquad (6.6.19)$$

Then $Z_T \overset{d}{\to} Z$ as $T \to \infty$, where$Z \sim N(0, [J_1(\theta_o)]^{-1})$.

Proof The proof below follows along the lines of the second strategy discussed after Theorem 6.6.3, similar to Lehmann (1983, pp. 429–434). Similar strategies exist in the extremal functional literature. Again see Amemiya (1985), Burguette et al. (1982), Huber (1981), and Newey and McFadden (1993).

A first-order Taylor series expansion (see Exercise 6.6.14 with $n = 2$) to the score function $s_c(\theta; Y)$ in (6.5.3), around the "true" value θ_o, evaluated at θ_T implies:

$$s_c(\hat{\theta}; Y) = s_c(\theta_o; Y) + H(\theta_o; Y)(\hat{\theta} - \theta_o) + r(\theta_o, \theta_*; Y), \tag{6.6.20}$$

where $H(\hat{\theta}; Y)$ is the Hessian matrix given in (6.5.4), θ_* is a point on the line segment connecting $\hat{\theta}$ and θ_o, and the remainder is

$$\begin{aligned} r(\theta_o, \theta_*; Y) &= \frac{1}{2}\sum_{i=1}^{K}\sum_{j=1}^{K}\left[\frac{\partial^3 L(\theta_*; Y)}{\partial\theta\,\partial\theta_i\,\partial\theta_j}\right](\hat{\theta}_i - \theta_{oi})(\hat{\theta}_j - \theta_{oj}) \\ &= [R(\theta_o; \theta_*; Y)](\hat{\theta} - \theta_o), \end{aligned} \tag{6.6.21}$$

where the $K \times K$ matrix R is given by

$$R(\theta_o, \theta_*; Y) = \frac{1}{2}\begin{bmatrix} (\hat{\theta} - \theta_o)' & \left(\dfrac{\partial H(\theta_*; Y)}{\partial\theta_1}\right) \\ \vdots & \vdots \\ (\hat{\theta} - \theta_o)' & \left(\dfrac{\partial H(\theta_*; Y)}{\partial\theta_K}\right) \end{bmatrix}. \tag{6.6.22}$$

Because $\hat{\theta}$ satisfies the likelihood equations (6.6.8), $s_c(\hat{\theta}; Y) = 0$. Dividing (6.6.20) by $T^{1/2}$ and rearranging yields:

$$T^{-1/2}s_c(\theta_o; Y) = \left[-\frac{1}{T}H(\theta_o; Y) - \frac{1}{T}R(\theta_o, \theta_*; Y)\right]\sqrt{T}(\hat{\theta} - \theta_o). \tag{6.6.23}$$

We now make three arguments. (i) Under random sampling, $\partial\ln[f(Y_t|\theta_o)/\partial\theta$ $(t = 1, 2, \ldots, T)$ are i.i.d. random vectors with mean 0_K and covariance matrix $J_1(\theta)$ (see Theorem 6.5.1 with $T = 1$). Therefore, central limit Theorem 5.7.5 implies that as $T \to \infty$ the left hand side of (6.6.21) converges to

$$T^{-1/2}s_c(\theta_o; Y) = \sqrt{T}\left[\frac{1}{T}\sum_{t=1}^{T}\frac{\partial f(Y_t; \theta_o)}{\partial\theta}\right] \xrightarrow{d} N_K[0, J_1(\theta_o)]. \tag{6.6.24}$$

(ii) The regularity condition on second-order derivatives of the log-likelihood (Definition 6.5.1g) imply the applicability of a LLN (e.g., Theorem 5.6.1) element by element so that

$$\frac{1}{T}H(\theta_o; Y) = \frac{1}{T}\sum_{t=1}^{T}\frac{\partial^2\ln[f(Y_t; \theta_o)]}{\partial\theta\,\partial\theta'} \xrightarrow{p} J_1(\theta_o). \tag{6.6.25}$$

By Definition 6.5.1(e), the limit in (6.6.25) is positive definite. (iii) Consider the kth row of (6.6.22):

$$T^{-1}R_k(\theta_o, \theta_*; Y) = \frac{1}{2}(\hat{\theta}_j - \theta_{oj})'\left[\frac{1}{T}\sum_{t=1}^{T}\frac{\partial^3\ln[f(Y_t|\theta_*)]}{\partial\theta_k\,\partial\theta_i\,\partial\theta_j}\right]. \tag{6.6.26}$$

The regularity condition on third-order derivatives of the log-likelihood (see Equation 6.5.1) implies that a LLN is applicable to the sum in (6.6.26), and so it converges to a finite number. The consistency of $\hat{\theta}$ implies $\hat{\theta}_* - \theta_o \xrightarrow{p} 0$, and hence, the kth row of $R(\theta_o, \theta_*; Y)$ converges to $0'_K$.

Together, (i) through (iii) imply

$$\left[-\frac{1}{T}H(\theta_o;Y)\right]\sqrt{T}(\hat{\theta}-\theta_o)\xrightarrow{d}N_K[0_K, J_1(\theta_o)]. \tag{6.6.27}$$

Therefore, noting that $[J_1(\theta_o)]^{-1}[J_1(\theta_o)][J_1(\theta_o)]^{-1} = [J_1(\theta_o)]^{-1}$, Theorem 5.5.11 implies:

$$\sqrt{T}(\hat{\theta}-\theta_o)\xrightarrow{d}N_K(0_K, [J_1(\theta_o)]^{-1}). \tag{6.6.28}$$

This completes the proof of Theorem 6.6.4.

For "reasonably large" T, Theorem 6.6.4 implies that the distribution of Z_T in finite samples should be fairly well approximated by

$$Z_T \sim N_K(0_K, [J_1(\theta_o)]^{-1}), \tag{6.6.29}$$

or solving for $\hat{\theta}$ in (6.6.19) and recalling that $J_T(\theta_o) = TJ_1(\theta_o)$,

$$\hat{\theta} \sim N_K(\theta, [J_T(\theta_o)]^{-1}). \tag{6.6.30}$$

Thus asymptotically speaking, the ML estimator achieves the Cramér-Rao lower bound (6.5.30). Hence, according to Definition 6.4.4, the ML estimator is asymptotically efficient within the class of CUAN estimators.

Example 6.6.5 Let Y_t $(t = 1, 2, \ldots, T)$ be a random sample from $N(\theta_1, \theta_2)$ distribution with both θ_1 and θ_2 unknown. The MLE $\hat{\theta}_{\text{ML}} = [\hat{\theta}_1, \hat{\theta}_2]'$ is given by (6.6.16) and (6.6.17), and it is the unique root of the likelihood equations. Differentiation of (6.6.14) and (6.6.15) yields the Hessian matrix

$$\frac{\partial^2 L(\theta;Y)}{\partial\theta\,\partial\theta'} = \begin{bmatrix} -\dfrac{T}{\theta_2} & -\dfrac{1}{\theta_2^2}\displaystyle\sum_{t=1}^{T}(Y_t-\theta_1) \\ -\dfrac{1}{\theta_2^2}\displaystyle\sum_{t=1}^{T}(Y_t-\theta_1) & \dfrac{T}{2\theta_2^2}-\dfrac{1}{\theta_2^3}\displaystyle\sum_{t=1}^{T}(Y_t-\theta_1)^2 \end{bmatrix}. \tag{6.6.31}$$

The asymptotic variance-covariance matrix of $\hat{\theta}_{\text{ML}}$ is

$$[J_T(\theta_o)]^{-1} = [TJ_1(\theta_o)]^{-1} = \left[-E_{Y|\theta_o}\left(\frac{\partial^2 L(\theta_o;Y)}{\partial\theta\,\partial\theta'}\right)\right]^{-1}$$

$$= \begin{bmatrix} \dfrac{\theta_{o2}}{T} & 0 \\ 0 & \dfrac{2\theta_{o2}^2}{T} \end{bmatrix}. \tag{6.6.32}$$

Example 6.6.5 demonstrates the standard result that the asymptotic variance-covariance matrix of $\hat{\theta}$ depends on the unknown θ_o. Replacing θ by $\hat{\theta}$ leads to consistent estimators of such variances and does not affect the validity of the asymptotic distribution derived (recall Theorem 5.5.11).

There are at least three obvious consistent estimators of $\Omega(\theta_o) \equiv [J_T(\theta_o)]^{-1}$ that can be used. Firstly, $\hat{\Omega}_1 = [J_T(\hat{\theta}_{ML})]^{-1}$ is consistent. However, $\hat{\Omega}_1$ requires taking the sampling expectation of the Hessian to obtain $J_T(\cdot)$, and this is often difficult if not impossible analytically. Such computation considerations suggest a second consistent estimator: $\hat{\Omega}_2 = [-H(\hat{\theta}_{ML})]^{-1}$. Computation of the second derivatives required in the Hessian $H(\cdot)$, however, can be a daunting task in some cases, and so a third consistent estimator (suggested by Berndt et al. 1974) based on (6.5.7) is often used:

$$\hat{\Omega}_3 = \sum_{t=1}^{T} \left[\frac{\partial \ln[f(y_t|\hat{\theta}_{ML})]}{\partial \theta}\right]\left[\frac{\partial \ln[f(y_t|\hat{\theta}_{ML})]}{\partial \theta'}\right]. \tag{6.6.33}$$

The performance of (6.6.33) is, however, often erratic (see MacKinnon and White 1985).[26]

When the regularity conditions in Definition 6.5.1 fail, the results of Theorem 6.6.4 may no longer hold. For example, if (b) fails and the support depends one or more of the unknown parameters, then often asymptotic normality is not obtained (see Lehmann 1983, pp. 452–454, and Exercise 6.6.17). If (c) fails and θ_o lies on the boundary of Θ, then while MLE is usually still consistent, the asymptotic distribution is usually a mixture of chi-squared distributions. Probably the most common violation of the regularity conditions involves the failure of the assumption of random sampling, in which case a CLT for n.i.n.i.d. processes must be invoked to show (6.6.24), and a suitable LLN must be invoked to show (6.6.25). A classic proof in general cases is Cramér (1946). A convenient reference for much econometric work is Crowder (1976) who deals with the n.i.n.i.d case.

The multivariate analog of Example 6.6.5 is given next.

Example 6.6.6 Suppose Z_t $(t = 1, 2, \ldots, T) \sim$ i.i.d. $N_K(\mu, \Sigma)$. Then the log-likelihood is

$$L(\mu, \Sigma) = -\left(\frac{TK}{2}\right)\ln(2\pi) + \frac{T}{2}\ln(|\Sigma^{-1}|) - \frac{1}{2}\sum_{t=1}^{T}(Z_t - \mu)'\Sigma^{-1}(Z_t - \mu). \tag{6.6.34}$$

Using fairly advanced matrix differentiation (see Magnus and Neudecker 1988, pp. 314–319, or Anderson 1984), it can be shown that the MLE's of μ and Σ are

$$\hat{\mu} = \bar{Z} = \frac{1}{T}\sum_{t=1}^{T} Z_t, \tag{6.6.35}$$

26. Use of $\hat{\Omega}_2$ or $\hat{\Omega}_3$ are favored by the arguments in Efron and Hinkley (1978) concerning conditioning on ancillary statistics. See Section 6.10 for related discussion.

$$\hat{\Sigma} = \frac{1}{T}\sum_{t=1}^{T}(Z_t - \hat{\mu})(Z_t - \hat{\mu})'. \tag{6.6.36}$$

The distribution of $\hat{\mu}$ and $\hat{\Sigma}$ is the normal-Wishart as given in Theorem 3.5.4.

Note that if interest focuses on some function $\alpha \equiv g(\theta)$ of the unknown parameter θ, then the following theorem shows that the ML estimator of α is $\hat{\alpha} = g(\hat{\theta})$.

Theorem 6.6.5 (Invariance of MLEs) Let $\alpha = g_j(\theta)$ $(j = 1, 2, \ldots, J)$ be J functions (not necessarily one-to-one) of the $K \times 1$ parameter vector θ, where $1 \leq J \leq K$, and let $\hat{\theta}_{\text{ML}}$ be the maximum likelihood estimator of θ based on the likelihood $\mathscr{L}(\theta; y)$. Then the maximum likelihood estimator of α is $\hat{\alpha} = g(\hat{\theta}_{\text{ML}})$.

Proof Consider the likelihood function induced by $g(\cdot)$:

$$\mathscr{L}_g(\alpha; y) \equiv \sup_{\theta: g(\theta) = \alpha} \mathscr{L}(\theta; y). \tag{6.6.37}$$

Because imposing constraints cannot lower the maximum of the objective function, it follows immediately from (6.6.37):

$$\begin{aligned}\mathscr{L}_g(\alpha; y) &\leq \sup_{\theta} \mathscr{L}(\theta; y) = \mathscr{L}(\hat{\theta}_{\text{ML}}; y)\\ &= \sup_{\theta: g(\theta) = g(\hat{\theta}_{\text{ML}})} \mathscr{L}(\theta; y)\\ &= \mathscr{L}_g(\hat{\alpha}; y).\end{aligned} \tag{6.6.38}$$

Hence, $\mathscr{L}_g(\alpha; y) \leq \mathscr{L}_g(\hat{\alpha}; y)$ for all α, and therefore $\hat{\alpha}$ is the ML of α.

Example 6.6.7 ML estimators are invariant to whether σ^2 or σ is as the parameter of interest. The asymptotic distribution for transformations follows from Theorem 5.4.13.

Although the ML estimator has desirable asymptotic properties, it is often computationally difficult to obtain. In cases where an alternative simple consistent estimator is available (e.g. from the method of moments), it is possible to compute a tractable estimator which has the same asymptotic distribution as the ML estimator.

Theorem 6.6.6 Let Y_t $(t = 1, 2, \ldots, T)$ be a random sample from a population for which the likelihood function $\mathscr{L}(\theta; Y)$ satisfies the regularity conditions in Definition 6.3.2. Let $\tilde{\theta}$ be any consistent estimator such that $T^{1/2}(\tilde{\theta} - \theta)$ has a proper limiting distribution, i.e. $\tilde{\theta}$ is $O_p(T^{-1/2})$. Then both

$$\hat{\theta}_1 = \tilde{\theta} - [H(\tilde{\theta}; Y)]^{-1}[s_c(\tilde{\theta}; Y)] \tag{6.6.39}$$

and

$$\hat{\theta}_2 = \tilde{\theta} + [J(\tilde{\theta})]^{-1}[s_c(\tilde{\theta}; Y)] \tag{6.6.40}$$

have the same asymptotic distribution as the ML estimator, that is, $T^{1/2}(\hat{\theta}_2 - \theta_o) \xrightarrow{d} N_K(0_K, [J_1(\theta_o)]^{-1})$.

Proof Rothenberg and Leenders (1964).

It cannot be overstressed that in general the efficiency results derived in this section for the ML estimator rest entirely on asymptotic arguments. There is no guarantee that the ML estimator will achieve the Cramér-Rao lower bound (6.3.22) in finite samples. Indeed even in cases where the ML estimator does achieve the Cramér-Rao lower bound, it may not be optimal in terms of other reasonable criteria. The following example illustrates this point in a dramatic fashion by showing the inadmissibility of ML under squared error loss in a standard setting.

Example 6.6.8 Let $\theta = [\theta_1, \theta_2, \ldots, \theta_K]'$ be an unknown parameter vector where $K \geq 3$. Suppose that for each θ_k we observe an independent random variable $Z_k | \theta_k \sim N(\theta_k, 1)$ $(k = 1, 2, \ldots, K)$. It may be helpful to think of $Z_k \equiv \overline{Y}_k$, where $\overline{Y}_k$ is the mean of T i.i.d. $N(\theta_k, \sigma^2)$ observations. Then $\overline{Y}_k \sim N(\theta_k, \sigma^2/T)$ and, assuming σ^2 is known, a change of scale transforms σ^2/T to the more convenient value of unity. Extensions to the case of unknown σ^2 can also be made, but for the sake of clarity are not considered here. Then the likelihood function

$$\mathscr{L}(\theta; Z) = (2\pi)^{-K/2} \exp[-\tfrac{1}{2}(Z - \theta)'(Z - \theta)], \tag{6.6.41}$$

and the MLE of θ is $\hat{\theta}_{\text{ML}} = Z \sim N_K(\theta, I_K)$.

Now consider the risk of the squared error loss function

$$R(\hat{\theta}|\theta) = E_{Z|\theta}[(\hat{\theta} - \theta)'(\hat{\theta} - \theta)] = \sum_{k=1}^{K} \text{MSE}(\hat{\theta}_k). \tag{6.6.42}$$

It is straightforward to show that

$$R(\hat{\theta}_{\text{ML}}|\theta) = K. \tag{6.6.43}$$

In a path-breaking paper Stein (1956) showed that if $K \geq 3$, then $\hat{\theta}_{\text{ML}}$ is *inadmissible* with respect to (6.6.32), i.e., if $K \geq 3$, then there exists an estimator $\tilde{\theta}$ such that $R(\tilde{\theta}|\theta) \leq R(\hat{\theta}_{\text{ML}}|\theta)$ for all θ and $R(\tilde{\theta}|\theta) < R(\hat{\theta}_{\text{ML}}|\theta)$ for at least one value of θ. Stein, however, showed only the existence of such a $\tilde{\theta}$, he did not actually provide an example of such a $\tilde{\theta}$. It was not until 1961 that an example of such an estimator was provided. James and Stein (1961) suggested the estimator

$$\hat{\theta}_{\text{JS}} = \left[1 - \frac{K-2}{\hat{\theta}_{\text{ML}}'\hat{\theta}_{\text{ML}}}\right]\hat{\theta}_{\text{ML}}, \tag{6.6.44}$$

and showed that

$$R(\hat{\theta}_{\text{JS}}|\theta) = K - (K-2)^2 E\left[\frac{1}{\chi^2(K, \lambda)}\right], \tag{6.6.45}$$

where $\lambda \equiv \theta'\theta/2$. Clearly, $R(\hat{\theta}_{JS}|\theta) < R(\hat{\theta}_{ML}|\theta)$ if $K \geq 3$. Note that $R(\hat{\theta}_{JS}|\theta) \to 2$ as $\theta \to 0$ and $R(\hat{\theta}_{JS}|\theta) \to R(\hat{\theta}_{ML}|\theta)$ as $\theta'\theta \to \infty$. Hence, near the origin $\hat{\theta}_{JS}$ enjoys considerable risk advantages [as defined by (6.6.42)] over $\hat{\theta}_{ML}$, especially when K is large. Such risk advantages can be transferred to other parts of the parameter space than the origin, if desired, such as in cases where a priori information suggests "more likely" parameter value. The Bayesian overtones of such an approach will become obvious in Section 6.7 if they are not already.

James-Stein estimator (6.6.44) is *nonlinear* and *biased*. Its mean and covariance matrix are complicated and involve θ. See Judge and Bock (1978, pp. 172–173) for details. Note that $R(\hat{\theta}_{JS}|\theta) < R(\hat{\theta}_{ML}|\theta)$ does not imply that $\text{MSE}(\hat{\theta}_{JS,k}) < \text{MSE}(\hat{\theta}_{ML,k})$ for all $k = 1, 2, \ldots, K$. While it may appear that $\hat{\theta}_{JS}$ is some sort of mathematical trick pulled out of the air, this is not the case. $\hat{\theta}_{JS}$ can in fact be given a Bayesian interpretation: see Judge and Bock (1978, pp. 173–176) and the references cited therein. The importance of the present example is to emphasize that the concept of MVB is somewhat arbitrary and that under other reasonable criterion, such as (6.6.42), MVB estimators may in fact be inadmissible. This example is *not* intended to serve necessarily as an advertisement for James-Stein estimators, because they are in fact also inadmissible with respect to (6.6.42). For a discussion of other estimators which dominate $\hat{\theta}_{JS}$ according to (6.6.42), see Judge and Bock (1978, Chapter 8). Rather than breed scepticism, it is hoped that Example 6.6.8 points out that even "supposedly pure classical statistics" also has its arbitrariness, although it is not always as easily identifiable as in other paradigms.

Exercises

6.6.1 Find the method of moments estimator for the unknown parameters of each of the following distributions.

(a) $\text{Po}(\lambda)$

(b) $\text{Exp}(\beta)$

(c) $U(\mu - 3^{1/2}\sigma, \mu + 3^{1/2}\sigma)$

6.6.2 Let Y_t $(t = 1, 2, \ldots, T)$ represent a random sample from each of the distributions having the p.d.f.'s listed below. In each case find the MLE $\hat{\theta}_{ML}$ of θ.

(a) $f(y;\theta) = \theta^y \exp(-\theta)/y!$, if $y = 0, 1, 2, \ldots$; $f(y;\theta) = 0$, otherwise, where $0 \leq \theta < \infty$.

(b) $f(y;\theta) = \theta y^{\theta-1}$, if $0 < y < 1$; $f(y;\theta) = 0$, otherwise, where $0 \leq \theta < \infty$.

(c) $f(y;\theta) = \theta^{-1}\exp(-y/\theta)$, if $0 < y < \infty$; $f(y;\theta) = 0$, otherwise, where $0 < \theta < \infty$.

(d) $f(y;\theta) = \frac{1}{2}\exp[-|y - \theta|]$, for $-\infty < y < \infty$ and $\theta \in \mathfrak{R}$.

(e) $f(y;\theta) = \exp[-(y - \theta)]$, if $\theta \leq y < \infty$; $f(y;\theta) = 0$, otherwise, where $\theta \in \mathfrak{R}$.

6.6.3 For each of the p.d.f.s in Exercise 6.6.2, find the MME of θ.

6.6.4 Let y_t $(t = 1, 2, \ldots, T)$ be a random sample from the distribution with p.d.f. $f(y;\theta) = \theta_2^{-1}\exp[-(y-\theta_1)/\theta_2]$, if $\theta_1 < y < \infty$; $f(y;\theta) = 0$, otherwise, where $-\infty < \theta_1 < \infty$ and $0 < \theta_2 < \infty$. Find MLE of $\theta = [\theta_1, \theta_2]'$.

6.6.5 Suppose Y_t $(t = 1, 2, \ldots, T)$ are i.i.d. Bernoulli random variables such that

$$P_t = P(Y_t = 1) = \Phi(\alpha), \tag{6.6.46}$$

$$1 - P_t = P(Y_t = 0) = 1 - \Phi(\alpha), \tag{6.6.47}$$

where $\Phi(\cdot)$ is the standard normal c.d.f. For purposes of concreteness, suppose that the above sample corresponds to a cross-section of individuals, and that the first m individuals are homeowners (i.e., $y_t = 1$ for $t = 1, 2, \ldots, m$), and the last $T - m$ individuals are renters (i.e., $y_t = 0$ for $t = m + 1, \ldots, T$). Find the MLE of α.

6.6.6 Suppose Y_t $(t = 1, 2, \ldots, T)$ are i.i.d. $U(0, \theta)$.

(a) Show: the ML estimator of θ is $\hat{\theta} = \max\{Y_1, Y_2, \ldots, Y_T\}$.

(b) Show: the p.d.f. of $\hat{\theta}$ is $g(\hat{\theta};\theta) = T\theta^{-T}\hat{\theta}^{T-1}$ if $0 < \hat{\theta} < \theta$; $g(\hat{\theta};\theta) = 0$, otherwise.

(c) Show: $\hat{\theta}$ is a biased estimator of θ and find its bias.

(d) Find MSE($\hat{\theta}$).

(e) Define $\tilde{\theta} = c\hat{\theta}$, where c is a scalar. Find c such that $\tilde{\theta}$ is an unbiased estimator of θ.

(f) Find MSE($\tilde{\theta}$).

(g) Is $\tilde{\theta}$ relatively more efficient than $\hat{\theta}$? Justify your answer.

(h) Is $\hat{\theta}$ a consistent estimator of θ?

6.6.7 Consider Exercise 6.6.6 involving a random sample from a $U(0, \theta)$ distribution. Define the estimator $\hat{\theta}^* = d\hat{\theta}$, where d is a constant and $\hat{\theta} = \max\{Y_1, Y_2, \ldots, Y_T\}$ is the ML estimator found in Exercise 6.6.6(a).

(a) Find d so as to minimize MSE($\hat{\theta}^*$).

(b) What does your answer in (a) imply for $\hat{\theta}$ and $\tilde{\theta}$ in Exercise 6.6.6(e)?

6.6.8 Consider Exercise 6.6.6 and define the estimator $\hat{\theta}^+ = (T + 1)\min\{Y_1, Y_2, \ldots, Y_T\}$.

(a) Find the p.d.f of $\hat{\theta}^+$.

(b) Show: $E(\hat{\theta}^+) = \theta$.

(c) Show: $\text{Var}(\hat{\theta}^+) = T\theta^2/(T + 2)$.

(d) Compare $\hat{\theta}^+$ with $\hat{\theta}$ in Exercise 6.6.6(a).

6.6.9 The method of *randomized response* is often used to construct surveys on sensitive topics (e.g., illegal or sexual activities). Suppose a random sample of T people are drawn from a large population. For each person in the sample there is a probability of $\frac{1}{2}$ that the person will be asked a standard question, and probability $\frac{1}{2}$ that the person will be asked a sensitive question. The selection of the standard or sensitive question is made independently across people in the sample, for example, each person flips a fair coin and answers the standard question if "heads" obtains and answers the sensitive question if "tails" appear. Suppose the standard question is chosen such that there is a probability of $\frac{1}{2}$ that any person will answer in the affirmative. The probability of answering the sensitive question in the affirmative is an unknown quantity θ, $0 < \theta < 1$. The researcher observes the number Y of affirmative responses by the T people in the sample. The researcher *cannot* observe which of these people were asked the standard question and which were asked the sensitive question. (See Winkler and Franklin 1979 and Moors 1981 for further discussion.)

(a) What is the MLE of θ?

(b) Is there any advantage to setting the probabilities of $\frac{1}{2}$ to something else.

6.6.10 Compute James-Stein estimate (6.6.34) when $K = 3$ and $\hat{\theta}_{ML} = [0, .01, .01]'$. Compare the James-Stein and ML estimators.

6.6.11 Let Y_t $(t = 1, 2, \ldots, n)$ be i.i.d. with density $f(\cdot|\theta)$, and let C_j $(j = 1, 2, \ldots, J)$ be a partition of the range of the Y_t's. Denote the probability that an observation falls in cell C_j

as

$$p_j(\theta) = P(Y_t \in C_j) = \int_{C_j} f(y|\theta)\,dy,$$

where

$$\sum_{j=1}^{J} p_j(\theta) = 1.$$

Finally, let the random variable N_j denote the number of the Y_ts that fall in cell j $(j = 1, 2, \ldots, J)$, where $T = N_1 + N_2 + \cdots + N_J$, and define

$$\chi^2(\theta) = \sum_{j=1}^{J} \frac{[n_j - np_j(\theta)]^2}{np_j(\theta)}, \tag{6.6.48}$$

where n_j is the observed value of N_j and $n = N_1 + N_2 + \cdots + N_J$. The *minimum-chi-squared* estimate θ is defined by

$$\hat{\theta} \equiv \underset{\theta}{\operatorname{argmin}}\, \chi^2(\theta). \tag{6.6.49}$$

In words, the minimum-chi-squared estimate $\hat{\theta}$ make the expected number $np_j(\theta)$ of observations in cell C_j "nearest" to the observed number n_j $(j = 1, 2, \ldots, J)$. When the denominator of (6.6.39) is changed to n_j the resulting estimate is called the *modified minimum-chi-squared estimate.* Now suppose the Y_ts are Bernoulli random variables taking on the values 0 and 1, where $\theta = P(Y_t = 1)$. Let $J = 2$, and define $C_1 = \{0\}$, $C_2 = \{1\}$. Find the minimum chi-squared-estimate of θ. (See Berkson 1980 for further discussion of minimum chi-squared estimation.)

6.6.12 Suppose $K = 1$. For any fixed θ, show that as $T \to \infty$:

$$\text{Prob}[\mathcal{L}(\theta_o; Y) > \mathcal{L}(\theta; Y)] \to 1. \tag{6.6.50}$$

Hint: use Jensen's inequality (Theorem 2.8.4) (Lehmann 1983, p. 409).

6.6.13 Suppose Y_t $(t = 1, 2, \ldots, T) \sim$ i.i.d. $U(\theta, 2\theta)$, $0 < \theta < \infty$.

(a) Find $\hat{\theta}_{\text{ML}}$.

(b) Find MSE$(\hat{\theta})$, where $\hat{\theta} = (T + 1)\hat{\theta}_{\text{ML}}/(2T + 1)$.

(c) Let $\tilde{\theta} = c_1 Y_{\min} + c_2 Y_{\max}$, where c_1 and c_2 are constants. Find c_1 and c_2 so as to minimize Var$(\tilde{\theta})$ subject to the constraint that $E(\tilde{\theta}) = \theta$.

6.6.14 Recall from calculus the following multivariate version of Taylor's Theorem (e.g., see Serfling 1980, p. 44). Consider a function $g(\cdot)$ defined on $\Re^K$ possessing partial derivatives of order n at each point of an open subset A of $\Re^K$. Let $x \in A$. For each point y, $y \neq x$, such that the line segment $L(x, y)$ joining x and y lies in A, there exists a point z in the interior of $L(x, y)$ such that the nth order Taylor series expansion of $g(y)$ around x is:

$$g(y) = g(x) + \sum_{m=1}^{n-1} \frac{1}{m!} \sum_{i_1=1}^{K} \cdots \sum_{i_m=1}^{K} \frac{\partial^m g(x_1, \ldots, x_K)}{\partial x_{i_1} \cdots \partial x_{i_m}} \prod_{j=1}^{m} (y_{i_j} - x_{i_j})$$

$$+ \frac{1}{n!} \sum_{i_1=1}^{K} \cdots \sum_{i_n=1}^{K} \frac{\partial^n g(z_1, \ldots, z_K)}{\partial x_1 \cdots \partial x_{i_n}} \prod_{j=1}^{n} (y_{i_j} - x_{i_j}). \tag{6.6.51}$$

Consider the constant elasticity of substitution (CES) production function (in logarithmic form):

$$\ln[Q(x_1, x_2)] = \beta_0 + \beta_1 \ln[\beta_2 x_1^{\beta_3} + (1 - \beta_2) x_2^{\beta_3}], \tag{6.6.52}$$

where x_1 and x_2 are inputs and $Q(x_1, x_2)$ is output. Find the Taylor Series approximation of (6.5.50) with $n = 2$.

6.6.15 Discuss ML estimation in the case of a random sample from the exponential family.

6.6.16 Partition $\theta = [\gamma', \alpha']'$ and consider the log-likelihood $L(\gamma, \alpha)$. Partition accordingly the MLE $\hat{\theta} = [\hat{\gamma}', \hat{\alpha}']'$, the Hessian

$$H(\theta; Y) = \begin{bmatrix} H_{\gamma\gamma}(\gamma, \alpha; Y) & H_{\gamma\alpha}(\gamma, \alpha; Y) \\ H_{\alpha\gamma}(\gamma, \alpha; Y) & H_{\alpha\alpha}(\gamma, \alpha; Y) \end{bmatrix}, \tag{6.6.53}$$

and the information matrix

$$J_T(\theta; Y) = \begin{bmatrix} J_{T,\gamma\gamma}(\gamma, \alpha; Y) & J_{T,\gamma\alpha}(\gamma, \alpha; Y) \\ J_{T,\alpha\gamma}(\gamma, \alpha; Y) & J_{T,\alpha\alpha}(\gamma, \alpha; Y) \end{bmatrix}. \tag{6.6.54}$$

Given γ, define

$$\hat{\alpha}(\gamma) \equiv \underset{\alpha}{\operatorname{argmax}}\, L(\gamma, \alpha), \tag{6.6.55}$$

and the *concentrated (or profile) log-likelihood*

$$L_*(\gamma) \equiv L[\gamma, \hat{\alpha}(\gamma)]. \tag{6.6.56}$$

Also define:

$$\hat{\gamma}_* \equiv \underset{\gamma}{\operatorname{argmax}}\, L_*(\gamma). \tag{6.6.57}$$

Show that $\hat{\gamma}$ and $\hat{\gamma}_*$ have the same asymptotic distribution (see Amemiya 1985, pp. 125–127). Does $\hat{\gamma} = \hat{\gamma}_*$?

6.6.17 Consider Exercise 6.6.6. Define the *translated exponential distribution* (cf. Definition 3.3.6), denoted TEXP(β, α), by the p.d.f. (Lehmann 1983, p. 452):

$$f_{\text{TEXP}}(y|\beta, \alpha) = \begin{cases} \beta^{-1} \exp - (y - \alpha)/\beta], & \text{if } y > \alpha \\ 0, & \text{if } y \leq \alpha \end{cases}. \tag{6.6.58}$$

(a) Show: $T(\theta - \hat{\theta}) \xrightarrow{d} \text{TEXP}(0, \theta)$ as $T \to \infty$.

(b) Show: $T(\theta - \tilde{\theta}) \xrightarrow{d} \text{TEXP}(-\theta, \theta)$ as $T \to \infty$.

(c) Show: $E[T^2(\theta - \hat{\theta})^2] \xrightarrow{p} 2\theta^2$ as $T \to \infty$.

(d) Show: $E[T^2(\tilde{\theta} - \theta)^2] \xrightarrow{p} \theta^2$ as $T \to \infty$.

(e) Is the MLE $\hat{\theta}$ asymptotically unbiased?

(f) Compare $\hat{\theta}$ and $\tilde{\theta}$ asymptotically. Which do you prefer?

6.6.18 **Information Inequality:** Suppose θ_o is identified (Definition 6.3.2) and regularity condition (*h*) of Definition 6.5.1 holds [i.e., $E_{Y|\theta}(\ln[f(Y_t|\theta)]) < \infty$ for all θ Θ.]. Show that $E_{Y|\theta}(\ln[f(Y_t|\theta)])$ has a unique maximum at θ_o. Hint: Note that $\ln(\cdot)$ is strictly concave, and use Jensen's Inequality (Theorem 2.8.4) on the random variable $X = f(Y_t|\theta)/f(Y_t|\theta_o)$.

6.6.19 Consider the following two important lemmas:

Lemma 1 Let $\{Q_T(\theta)\}$ be a sequence of continuous functions of $\theta \in \Theta$, and let $Q(\theta)$ be a function for which the following conditions hold:

(a) $Q(\theta)$ is uniquely maximized at θ_o.

(b) Θ is compact.

(c) $Q(\theta)$ is continuous.

(d) $\{Q_T(\theta)\}$ converges uniformly in probability to $Q(\theta)$.

Let $\hat{\theta}_T = \operatorname{argmax}_{\theta \in \Theta} Q_T(\theta)$. Then $\{\hat{\theta}_T\} \xrightarrow{p} \theta_o$.

Proof Newey and McFadden (1993, Theorem 2.1)

Lemma 2 [Uniform Law of Large Numbers for Matrices] Consider a random sample Y_t $(t = 1, 2, \ldots, T)$ with density depending on $\theta \in \theta$, where Θ is compact. Let

$A(Y_t, \theta) = [a_{mm}(Y_t, \theta)]$ be a $M \times N$ matrix of functions of Y_t and θ. Define the Euclidean norm:

$$\|A\| = \left(\sum_{m=1}^{M} \sum_{n=1}^{N} [a_{mn}(Y_t, \theta)]^2 \right)^{1/2}. \tag{6.6.59}$$

Suppose $a_{mn}(Y_t, \theta)$ is continuous almost surely for all $\theta \in \Theta$, and there exists a function $b(Y_t)$ such that $\|A(Y_t, \theta)\| \leq b(Y_t)$ for all $\theta \in \Theta$, and $E[b(Y_t)] < \infty$. Then $E[A(Y_t, \theta)]$ is continuous and

$$\underset{\theta \in \Theta}{\text{supremum}} \left\| T^{-1} \sum_{t=1}^{T} A(Y_t, \theta) - E[A(Y, \theta)] \right\| \xrightarrow{p} 0. \tag{6.6.60}$$

Proof Newey and McFadden (1993, Lemma 2.4).

These two lemmas together with the Information Inequality in Exercise 6.6.18 provide the basis for the proof of the consistency of the MLE. This approach emphasizes the MLE as a solution to an extremal problem rather than as a solution to the likelihood equations. Prove the following theorem.

Theorem 6.6.7 [Consistency of an Extremal Estimator] Consider a sample Y_t ($t = 1, 2, \ldots, T$) yielding a likelihood that satisfies regularity conditions (b), (c), (e), (h), (i) of Definition 6.5.1. Let $\hat{\theta}_T = \text{argmax}_{\theta \in \Theta} L(\theta; Y)$. Then $\{\hat{\theta}_T\} \xrightarrow{p} \theta_o$.

6.6.20 Let Y_t ($t = 1, 2, \ldots, T$) $\sim$ i.i.d. $t(v)$, where $v > 2$.

(a) Find the MME $\hat{v}$ of v based on the variance of the Y_t's.

(b) If the estimated sample variance exhibits less variability than that of a standard normal distribution, how is your answer in (a) affected?

6.7 Bayesian Point Estimation

The Bayesian outlook can be summarized in a single sentence: any inferential or decision process that does not follow from some likelihood function and some set of priors has objectively verifiable deficiencies.
—Cornfield (1969, p. 617)

Statistical estimation is concerned with learning about aspects of an unknown structure based on observing data. The regularity of the structure is conceived in terms of an invariant vector of unknown quantities called *parameters* that characterize the *likelihood function.* The viewpoint adopted in Sections 6.3 through 6.6 was based on the *frequency* interpretation of probability (Definition 2.1.10). The focal point of that discussion was the idealized repetition of a statistical experiment. The likelihood function was simply the *data generating process (DGP)* viewed as a function of the unknown parameters, and it was thought of as having an "objective existence" in the sense of a meaningful repetitive experiment. The parameters themselves, according to this view, also had an objective existence independent of the DGP.

The probabilistic basis in Section 6.3 for the discussion of what constituted "good" estimates of the parameters was couched in terms of the *procedures* (i.e., *estimators*) used to generate the estimates, and specifically, how these procedures performed on average in repeated samples. This "averaging" involved expectation over the *entire* sample space. Hence, not only were the observed data that gave rise to the *estimate* relevant, but also, *all* the data that could have arisen (i.e., the entire sample space) were critically relevant. *In other words, according to the frequentist view, the criteria for deciding what constitutes a desirable estimate, involved not just the observed data, but also all the data that could have been observed, but were not observed.*

The viewpoint adopted in this section is in sharp contrast to that just described. Although it is possible to adopt the so-called *objective Bayesian* viewpoint in which the parameters and the likelihood maintain their objective existence, and in which a *logical* interpretation of probability is adopted (see Definition 2.1.12), it is not necessary to do so. One can also adopt the *subjective Bayesian* viewpoint in which the likelihood and the parameters are both subjective concepts (i.e., useful mental constructs), and in which a *subjective* interpretation of probability (Definition 2.1.13) is adopted. In this case the meaningful distinction between the "prior" and the likelihood is that the latter represents a *window* for viewing the observable world shared by a group of researchers who agree to disagree in terms of possibly different prior distributions. Poirier (1988c) introduced the metaphor "window" for a likelihood function because *a "window" captures the essential role played by the likelihood, namely, as a parametric medium for viewing the observable world.* In the context of de Finetti's Representation Theorem 5.8.1, such intersubjective agreement over the window (likelihood) may result from agreed upon symmetries in probabilistic beliefs concerning observables. Disagreements over priors are addressed by sensitivity analysis evaluating the robustness of posterior quantities of interest to changes in the prior.

The distinction between the "objective" and "subjective" Bayesian positions does not imply the need for different Bayesian techniques of estimation. Rather it is reflected more in the emphasis placed on activities such as estimation and hypothesis testing compared to prediction. Once one adopts the attitude that the parameters are mental constructs that exist only in the mind of the researcher, they become less of an end in themselves and more of an intermediate step in the process of dealing with potentially observable quantities that are the goal of prediction. Economists for the most part are quite attached to their parameters, and so estimation and hypothesis testing receive more emphasis here than in a pure predictivist approach.

According to both the logical and the subjective interpretations of probability, it is meaningful to use probability to describe degrees of belief about unknown entities such as a K-dimensional parameter vector $\theta \in \Theta$.[27] Before observing the data y, these beliefs are described by a p.d.f. $f(\theta)$ known as the *prior density*. For any value of θ, the data are viewed as arising from the p.d.f. $f(y|\theta)$, which when viewed as a function of θ given y, is known as the likelihood function $\mathscr{L}(\theta; y)$. Manipulating density functions according to the rules of probability yields *Bayes' Theorem* for densities:

$$f(\theta|y) = \frac{f(\theta, y)}{f(y)} = \frac{f(\theta)\mathscr{L}(\theta; y)}{f(y)}$$

$$\propto f(\theta)\mathscr{L}(\theta; y), \tag{6.7.1}$$

where $f(y|\theta)$ is known as the *posterior* density, and the denominator in (6.7.1), known as the *marginal density of the data*, or *marginal likelihood*, is given by

$$f(y) = \int_{\Re^k} \mathscr{L}(\theta; y) f(\theta)\, d\theta, \tag{6.7.2}$$

and does not depend on θ. The corresponding prior and posterior c.d.f.s are denoted $F(\theta)$ and $F(\theta|y)$.

Bayesian analysis is truly a learning process in that prior beliefs $f(\theta)$ are updated by (6.7.1) in light of data y to obtain the posterior beliefs summarized by $f(\theta|y)$. The posterior density reflects prior beliefs and the data, and it serves as the basis for the point estimation discussed in this section. It is of crucial importance to note that this basis is grounded in the conditional distribution of beliefs about θ given the observed (i.e., realized) data $Y = y$. The distribution $\theta|y$ is in sharp contrast to the emphasis in Sections 6.3 through 6.6 on the sampling distribution $Y|\theta$. Use of posterior density (6.7.1) as a basis for estimation and inference is in agreement with the WCP and the LP discussed in Section 6.2.[28]

27. The idea of postulating probability distributions for parameters is not a monopoly of Bayesians. For example, in the 1920s R. A. Fisher proposed the idea of "fiducial distributions" for parameters, a not fully developed concept that remains somewhat of an enigma even today. See Barnett (1982, pp. 274–282) for a brief discussion. Of course from the perspective of de Finetti's Representation Theorem (Theorem 5.8.1), the prior beliefs about the unknown parameters are derived from beliefs about sequences of future observables. The latter beliefs are the ones pure subjectivists emphasize. The more common emphasis is on prior beliefs regarding unknown unobservables (i.e., parameters). This more traditional view is most tenable when such unobservables have interpretations that do not rely on the likelihood.

28. According to the traditional view that parameters θ have interpretations independent of the likelihood, and hence so do prior beliefs regarding θ, then the "objective Bayesian" considers it meaningful to consider two experiments involving the same unknown parameter θ. If such experiments yield proportional likelihoods $\mathscr{L}_1(\theta; y_1) = c\mathscr{L}_2(\theta; y_2)$, then use of (6.7.1) clearly leads to the same posterior density for θ.

Before discussing Bayesian point estimation, it is useful to consider some examples of (6.7.1) in practice. The ease with which Bayesian analysis can be applied is greatly enhanced when there exists *conjugate prior distributions* as now loosely defined.[29]

Definition 6.7.1 Given the likelihood $\mathscr{L}(\theta; y)$, if there exists a family of prior distributions with the property that no matter the data actually observed, the posterior distribution $f(\theta|y)$ is also member of this family, then this family of prior distributions is called a *conjugate family*, and any member of the family is said to be a *conjugate prior*. A conjugate prior that has the same functional form as the likelihood function is called a *natural conjugate prior*.

A few points regarding conjugate priors are worth noting. Firstly, the class of all distributions is trivially a conjugate family for all likelihood functions. For a given likelihood there may not exist a nontrivial conjugate family. The existence of a sufficient statistic of fixed dimension independent of sample size, however, insures the existence of a nontrivial conjugate family. For example, natural conjugate priors are available whenever the likelihood function belongs to the *exponential family*, as well as in other cases such as when sampling from a $U[0, \theta]$ distribution (see Exercise 6.7.6).

Second, conjugate priors are computationally attractive because usually it is not necessary to compute the K-dimensional integral (6.7.2) that serves as an *integrating constant* to insure that the posterior density (6.7.1) integrates to unity. Because the posterior must belong to the same family as the prior, such knowledge can usually be used to appropriately scale the numerator in (6.7.1) without any explicit integration. This is made clear in Example 6.7.4, although it is also implicit in Examples 6.7.1 through 6.7.3 as well. Furthermore, provided the conjugate family is familiar, analytical expressions for moments are often readily available.

Third, when conjugate families exist they are quite large. Mixtures of conjugate priors are also conjugate priors because the corresponding posterior distributions is a mixture of the component posteriors. Although mixture distributions tend to be "parameter-rich," they are capable of representing a wide range of prior beliefs (e.g., multimodal priors) while still enjoying the computational advantages of the component conjugate priors.

Fourth, Diaconis and Ylvisaker (1979) show that the characteristic feature of natural conjugate priors for likelihoods from the exponential

29. For a discussion of qualifications to keep in mind with respect to Definition 6.7.1, see Diaconis and Ylvisaker (1979, 1985).

family is that the resulting posterior means are linear in the observations. This result will become clear in the examples that follow.

Finally, examples of *natural conjugate priors* appear in Examples 6.7.1 through 6.7.4. As will be discussed later in this section, natural conjugate priors are especially attractive in situations where it is desired to interpret the prior information as arising from a fictitious sample from the same underlying population that gave rise to the likelihood.

First, however, consider some examples to illustrate the concepts discussed so far.

Example 6.7.1 Given the parameter θ, where $0 < \theta < 1$, consider T i.i.d. Bernoulli random variables Y_t $(t = 1, 2, \ldots, T)$ each with p.m.f.:

$$f(y_t|\theta) = \begin{Bmatrix} \theta, & \text{if } y_t = 1 \\ 1 - \theta, & \text{if } y_t = 0 \end{Bmatrix}. \tag{6.7.3}$$

Note, according to de Finetti's Representation Theorem (Theorem 5.8.1), this formulation of the problem has the alternative subjectivist interpretation in which subjective beliefs over arbitrarily long sequences of the Y_ts are assumed *exchangeable* (see Definition 5.8.1) as well as *coherent*. In either case the likelihood function (i.e. parametric window) through which the observables are viewed is

$$\mathscr{L}(\theta; y) = \theta^m (1 - \theta)^{T-m}, \tag{6.7.4}$$

where $m \equiv T\bar{y}$ is the number of successes (i.e. $y_t = 1$) in T trials.

Suppose that prior beliefs concerning θ are represented by a beta distribution (Definition 3.3.8) with p.d.f.

$$f(\theta|\underline{\alpha}, \underline{\delta}) = \left[\frac{\Gamma(\underline{\alpha} + \underline{\delta})}{\Gamma(\underline{\alpha})\Gamma(\underline{\delta})}\right] \theta^{\underline{\alpha}-1}(1 - \theta)^{\underline{\delta}-1}, \qquad 0 < \delta < 1, \tag{6.7.5}$$

where $\underline{\alpha} > 0$ and $\underline{d} > 0$ are known constants. Given the variety of shapes the beta p.d.f. can assume (see Figure 3.3.4), this class of priors can represent a wide range of prior opinions.

The denominator (6.7.2) of posterior density (6.7.1) is easy to compute in this instance. Define

$$\bar{\alpha} = \underline{\alpha} + m, \tag{6.7.6}$$

$$\bar{\delta} = \underline{\delta} + T - m, \tag{6.7.7}$$

and consider

$$\begin{aligned} f(y) &= \int_0^1 [B(\underline{\alpha}, \underline{\delta})]^{-1} \theta^{\underline{\alpha}-1}(1 - \delta)^{\underline{\delta}-1} \theta^m (1 - \theta)^{T-m}\, d\theta \\ &= \left[\frac{B(\bar{\alpha}, \bar{\delta})}{B(\underline{\alpha}, \underline{\delta})}\right] \int_0^1 [B(\bar{\alpha}, \bar{\delta})]^{-1} \theta^{\bar{\alpha}-1}(1 - \theta)^{\bar{\delta}-1}\, d\theta \\ &= \frac{B(\bar{\alpha}, \bar{\delta})}{B(\underline{\alpha}, \underline{\delta})}, \end{aligned} \tag{6.7.8}$$

where the integral in the middle line of (6.7.8) equals unity because the integrand is a beta p.d.f.. From (6.7.1), (6.7.5), and (6.7.8) it follows that the posterior density of θ is

$$\begin{aligned} f(\theta|y) &= \frac{[B(\underline{\alpha},\underline{\delta})]^{-1}\theta^{\underline{\alpha}-1}(1-\delta)^{\underline{\delta}-1}\theta^{m}(1-\theta)^{T-m}}{B(\overline{\alpha},\overline{\delta})/B(\underline{\alpha},\underline{\delta})} \\ &= [B(\overline{\alpha},\overline{\delta})]^{-1}\theta^{\overline{\alpha}-1}(1-\theta)^{\overline{\delta}-1}, \qquad 0<\theta<1. \end{aligned} \tag{6.7.9}$$

Therefore, because posterior density (6.7.9) is itself a beta p.d.f. with parameters $\overline{\alpha}$ and $\overline{\delta}$ given by (6.7.6) and (6.7.7), it follows that the conjugate family of prior distributions for a Bernoulli likelihood is the beta family of p.d.f.s.

Example 6.7.2 Given $\theta = [\theta_1, \theta_2]' \in \Re \times \Re^+$, consider a random sample y_t $(t = 1, 2, \ldots, T)$ from a $N(\theta_1, \theta_2^{-1})$ population. For reasons that will become clear as we proceed, it is convenient to work in terms of θ_2, the reciprocal of the variance (known as the *precision*). For now assume θ_2 is known; this assumption is dropped in Example 6.7.4. Suppose prior beliefs concerning the unknown mean θ_1 are represented by the normal distribution

$$\theta_1|\theta_2 \sim N(\underline{\mu}, \underline{h}^{-1}), \tag{6.7.10}$$

where $\underline{\mu}$ and $\underline{h} > 0$ are given. For later notational convenience, let

$$h = [\theta_2^{-1}/T]^{-1} = T\theta_2, \tag{6.7.11}$$

$$\overline{h} = \underline{h} + h, \tag{6.7.12}$$

$$\overline{\mu} = \overline{h}^{-1}(\underline{h}\underline{\mu} + h\overline{y}). \tag{6.7.13}$$

It is useful to employ two identities. The first identity appeared as Exercise 5.2.2:

$$\begin{aligned} \sum_{t=1}^{T}(y_t-\theta_1)^2 &= \sum_{t=1}^{T}(y_t-\overline{y})^2 + T(\overline{y}-\theta_1)^2 \\ &= \nu s^2 + T(\overline{y}-\theta_1)^2 \end{aligned} \tag{6.7.14}$$

for all θ_1, where

$$\nu \equiv T - 1. \tag{6.7.15}$$

$$s^2 = \nu^{-1}\sum_{t=1}^{T}(y_t-\overline{y})^2. \tag{6.7.16}$$

The second identity is left as an exercise for the reader:

$$\underline{h}(\theta_1-\underline{\mu})^2 + h(\overline{y}-\theta_1)^2 = \overline{h}(\theta_1-\overline{\mu})^2 + (\underline{h}^{-1}+h^{-1})^{-1}(\overline{y}-\underline{\mu})^2, \tag{6.7.17}$$

for all θ_1, $\underline{h}$ and h.

Now we are prepared to apply Bayes Theorem to find the posterior density of θ_1 (given θ_2). Using identity (6.7.14), write the likelihood function as

$$\begin{aligned}\mathscr{L}(\theta_1; y|\theta_2) &= \prod_{t=1}^{T} \phi(y_t|\theta_1, \theta_2^{-1}) \\ &= (2\pi\theta_2^{-1})^{-T/2} \exp\left[-\frac{\theta_2}{2}\sum_{t=1}^{T}(y_t - \theta_1)^2\right] \\ &= (2\pi\theta_2^{-1})^{-T/2} \exp\left[-\frac{h}{2T}[\nu s^2 + T(\bar{y} - \theta_1)^2]\right] \\ &= c_1(\theta_2)\phi(\bar{y}|\theta_1, h^{-1}),\end{aligned} \tag{6.7.18}$$

where

$$c_1(\theta_2) = (2\pi)^{-1/2\nu}T^{-1/2}\theta_2^{\nu/2}\exp(-\tfrac{1}{2}\theta_2 \nu s^2) \tag{6.7.19}$$

does *not* depend on θ_1. Note that the factorization in (6.7.18) demonstrates that $\bar{y}$ is a sufficient statistic for θ_1 (recall Example 6.1.3). Also note that density $\phi(\bar{y}|\theta_1, h^{-1})$ corresponds to the sampling distribution of the sample mean (see Theorem 5.3.5a), given θ.

Using identity (6.7.17) and factorization (6.7.18), the numerator of (6.7.1) is

$$\begin{aligned}f(\theta_1|\theta_2)\mathscr{L}(\theta_1; y|\theta_2) &= \phi(\theta_1|\underline{\mu}, \underline{h}^{-1})c_1(\theta_2)\phi(\bar{y}|\theta_1, h^{-1}) \\ &= c_1(\theta_2)(2\pi\underline{h}^{-1})^{-1/2}(2\pi h^{-1})^{-1/2}\exp[-\tfrac{1}{2}\{\underline{h}(\theta_1 - \underline{\mu})^2 \\ &\quad + h(\bar{y} - \theta_1)^2\}] \\ &= c_1(\theta_2)(2\pi\underline{h}^{-1})^{-1/2}(2\pi h^{-1})^{-1/2}\exp[-\tfrac{1}{2}\{\bar{h}(\theta_1 - \bar{\mu})^2 \\ &\quad + (\underline{h}^{-1} + h^{-1})^{-1}(\bar{y} - \underline{\mu})^2\}] \\ &= c_1(\theta_2)\phi(\bar{y}|\underline{\mu}, \underline{h}^{-1} + h^{-1})\phi(\theta_1|\bar{\mu}, \bar{h}^{-1}).\end{aligned} \tag{6.7.20}$$

The denominator of (6.7.1), the density of the data given θ_2, can then be easily obtained from (6.7.20):

$$\begin{aligned}f(y|\theta_2) &= \int_{-\infty}^{\infty} f(\theta_1|\theta_2)\mathscr{L}(\theta_1; y|\theta_2)\,d\theta_1 \\ &= c_1(\theta_2)\phi(\bar{y}|\underline{\mu}, \underline{h}^{-1} + h^{-1})\int_{-\infty}^{\infty}\phi(\theta_1|\bar{\mu}, \bar{h}^{-1})\,d\theta_1 \\ &= c_1(\theta_2)\phi(\bar{y}|\underline{\mu}, \underline{h}^{-1} + h^{-1}).\end{aligned} \tag{6.7.21a}$$

The density $\phi(\bar{y}|\underline{\mu}, \underline{h}^{-1} + h^{-1})$ in (6.7.21a) corresponds to the sampling distribution of the sample mean given θ_2. Using Exercise 6.7.50, the marginal density of the data (remember θ_2 is assumed known) in (6.7.21a) can alternatively be expressed as

$$f(y|\theta_2) = \phi_T(y|\underline{\mu}\iota_T, \theta_2^{-1}[I_T + \underline{h}^{-1}\iota_T\iota_T']). \tag{6.7.21b}$$

Dividing (6.7.20) by (6.7.21a) yields the posterior density of θ_1, given θ_2:

$$f(\theta_1|y, \theta_2) = \phi(\theta_1|\bar{\mu}, \bar{h}^{-1}). \tag{6.7.22}$$

The interpretation of quantities (6.7.12) and (6.7.13) is now clear from (6.7.22): They are the posterior precision and posterior mean, respectively.

Note that it is the additivity of precisions in (6.7.12) that motivates working with precisions rather than variances. Also note that since posterior density (6.7.22) and prior density (6.7.10) are both members of the normal family, it follows that the natural conjugate prior for the case of random sampling from a normal population with *known* variance is itself a normal density.

The following numerical example illustrates some of the concepts in Example 6.7.2.

Example 6.7.3 (Box and Tiao 1973, pp. 15–18) Consider two researchers, A and B, concerned with obtaining accurate estimates of a parameter θ. Suppose that the prior beliefs of A are $\theta \sim N(900, 20^2)$ and the prior beliefs of B are $\theta \sim N(800, 80^2)$. Note that researcher A is far more certain, a priori, than researcher B. Figure 6.7.1(a) depicts the respective prior p.d.f.s. Suppose that given θ an unbiased method of experimental measurement is available and one observation is taken from a $N(\theta, 40^2)$ distribution and it turns out to be $y_1 = 850$. Then based on this observation both researchers will update their prior beliefs as in Example 6.7.2 to obtain the posterior distributions $\theta|y_1 \sim N(890, [17.9]^2)$ and $\theta|y_1 \sim N(840, [35.7]^2)$ for researchers A and B, respectively. These posterior p.d.f.s are depicted in Figure 6.7.1(c) which suggests that the beliefs of the two researchers have become more similar, but remain distinct. If ninety-nine additional observations are gathered so that the sample mean based on all $T = 100$ observations is $\bar{y} = 870$, then the posterior distributions for researchers A and B become $\theta|\bar{y} \sim N(871.2, [3.9]^2)$ and $\theta|\bar{y} \sim N(869.8, [3.995]^2)$, respectively. These posterior p.d.f.'s are shown in Figure 6.7.1(e), and near total agreement is now evident. The moral of the story is that a sufficiently large sample will "swamp" the non-dogmatic prior.

Example 6.7.4 Consider Example 6.7.2, but suppose the population precision θ_2 is also unknown. Also suppose the joint prior distribution for $\theta = [\theta_1, \theta_2]'$ is the normal-gamma distribution (recall Definition 3.4.5), denoted $\theta \sim \text{NG}(\underline{\mu}, \underline{q}, \underline{s}^{-2}, \underline{\nu})$, with density

$$f_{\text{NG}}(\theta|\underline{\mu}, \underline{q}, \underline{s}^{-2}, \underline{\nu}) = \phi(\theta_1|\underline{\mu}, \theta_2^{-1}\underline{q})\gamma(\theta_2|\underline{s}^{-2}, \underline{\nu}) \tag{6.7.23a}$$

$$\propto \{\theta_2^{1/2}\exp[-\tfrac{1}{2}\theta_2\underline{q}^{-1}(\theta_1 - \underline{\mu})^2]\}\{\theta_2^{1/2(\underline{\nu}-2)}\exp(-\tfrac{1}{2}\theta_2\underline{\nu}\underline{s}^2)\} \tag{6.7.23b}$$

$$\propto \theta_2^{1/2(\underline{\nu}-1)}\exp[-\tfrac{1}{2}\theta_2\{\underline{\nu}\underline{s}^2 + \underline{q}^{-1}(\theta_1 - \underline{\mu})^2\}], \tag{6.7.23c}$$

where $\underline{\mu} \in \Re$ and $\underline{q}$, $\underline{s}^2$ and $\underline{\nu}$ are known positive constants. The normal density in (6.7.23a) represents the prior conditional density of θ_1 given θ_2, and the gamma density in (6.7.23a) represents the prior marginal density of θ_2.

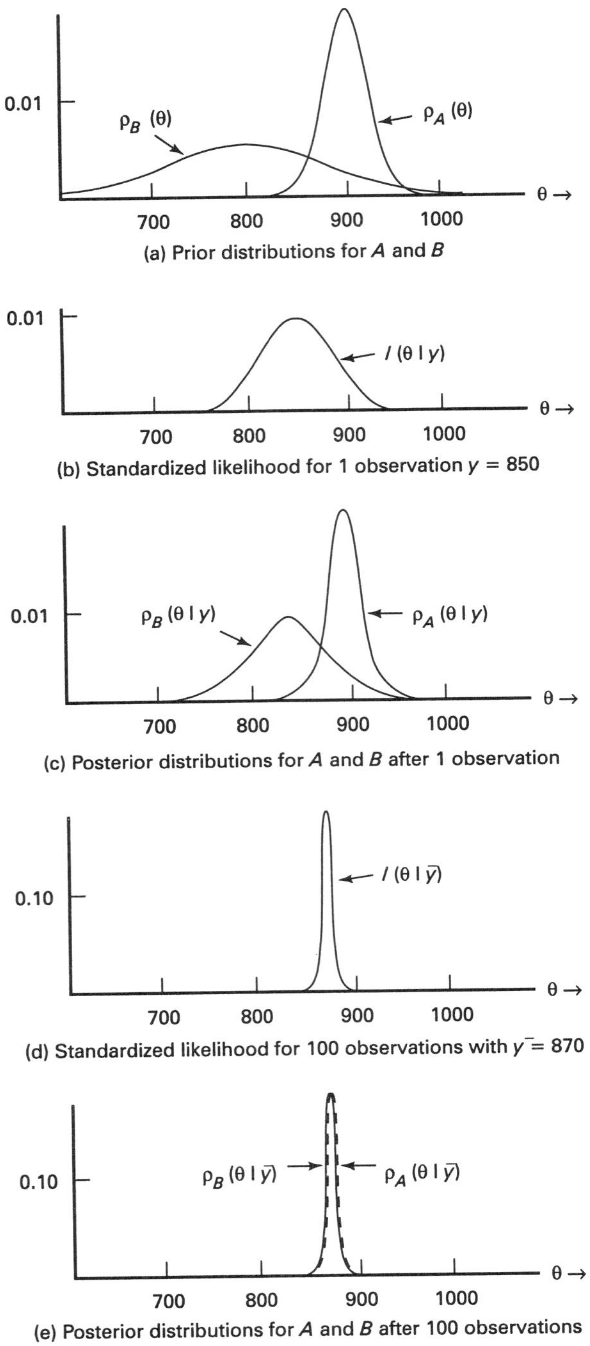
0.01
ρ_B (θ)
ρ_A (θ)
θ →
700
800
900
1000
(a) Prior distributions for A and B
0.01
l (θ | y)
θ →
700
800
900
1000
(b) Standardized likelihood for 1 observation y = 850
0.01
ρ_B (θ | y)
ρ_A (θ | y)
θ →
700
800
900
1000
(c) Posterior distributions for A and B after 1 observation
0.10
l (θ | $\bar{y}$)
θ →
700
800
900
1000
(d) Standardized likelihood for 100 observations with $\bar{y}$ = 870
0.10
ρ_B (θ | $\bar{y}$)
ρ_A (θ | $\bar{y}$)
θ →
700
800
900
1000
(e) Posterior distributions for A and B after 100 observations

Figure 6.7.1

Recall that the mean and variance of the gamma distribution $\gamma(\theta_2|\underline{s}^{-2}, \underline{\nu})$ are

$$E(\theta_2) = \underline{s}^{-2}, \tag{6.7.24}$$

$$\text{Var}(\theta_2) = \frac{2\underline{s}^{-4}}{\underline{\nu}}. \tag{6.7.25}$$

The implied prior distribution for the population variance θ_2^{-1} can be found using change-of-variable techniques (see Theorem 4.4.2). The distribution of θ_2^{-1} is the inverted gamma distribution (see Table 3.3.1.(e) or Zellner 1971, pp. 371–373). For later reference note that $\theta_2 = \sigma^{-2} \sim \gamma(\theta_2|\underline{s}^{-2}, \underline{\nu})$ implies

$$E(\sigma^2) = \underline{\nu}\underline{s}^2/(\underline{\nu} - 2), \quad \text{if } \underline{\nu} > 2, \tag{6.7.26}$$

$$E(\sigma) = \left[\frac{\Gamma[\frac{1}{2}(\underline{\nu} - 1)]}{\Gamma(\frac{1}{2}\underline{\nu})}\right]\left[\frac{1}{2}\underline{\nu}\right]^{1/2} \underline{s}, \quad \text{if } \underline{\nu} > 1. \tag{6.7.27}$$

Finally, note that the prior marginal distribution of θ_1 (see Theorem 3.4.13), obtained from (6.7.23) by integrating-out θ_2, is the t-distribution $t(\underline{\mu}, \underline{s}^2\underline{q}, \underline{\nu})$ with mean and variance

$$E(\theta_1) = \underline{\mu}, \quad \text{if } \underline{\nu} > 1, \tag{6.7.28}$$

$$\text{Var}(\theta_1) = \underline{\nu}\underline{s}^2\underline{q}/(\underline{\nu} - 2), \quad \text{if } \underline{\nu} > 2. \tag{6.7.29}$$

Dropping irrelevant constants not depending on θ_1 and θ_2, (6.7.1) implies posterior density $f(\theta|y)$ is proportional to the product of the kernels of (6.7.18) and (6.7.23):

$$\begin{aligned} f(\theta|y) &\propto f(\theta)\mathcal{L}(\theta; y) \\ &\propto [\phi(\theta_1|\underline{\mu}, \theta_2^{-1}\underline{q})\gamma(\theta_2|\underline{s}^{-2}, \underline{\nu})][c_1(\theta_2)\phi(\bar{y}|\theta_1, h^{-1})] \\ &\propto \theta_2^{1/2(\underline{\nu}-1)}\exp(-\tfrac{1}{2}\theta_2[\underline{\nu}\underline{s}^2 + \underline{q}^{-1}(\theta - \underline{\mu})^2])\theta_2^{1/2(\nu+1)} \\ &\quad \times \exp(-\tfrac{1}{2}\theta_2[\nu s^2 + T(\bar{y} - \theta_1)^2]) \\ &\propto \theta_2^{1/2\bar{\nu}}\exp(-\tfrac{1}{2}\theta_2[\underline{\nu}\underline{s}^2 + \nu s^2 + \underline{q}^{-1}(\theta_1 - \underline{\mu})^2 + T(\bar{y} - \theta_1)^2]), \end{aligned} \tag{6.7.30}$$

where

$$\bar{\nu} \equiv \underline{\nu} + T. \tag{6.7.31}$$

Using identity (6.7.17) with $\underline{h} = \underline{q}^{-1}\theta_2$ and $h = T\theta_2$, the last two terms in (6.7.30) can be written as

$$\begin{aligned} &\theta_2[\underline{q}^{-1}(\theta_1 - \underline{\mu})^2 + T(\bar{y} - \theta_1)^2] \\ &\quad = \theta_2[\bar{q}^{-1}(\theta_1 - \bar{\mu})^2 + (\underline{q} + T^{-1})^{-1}(\bar{y} - \underline{\mu})^2], \end{aligned} \tag{6.7.32}$$

where

$$\bar{q} \equiv (\underline{q}^{-1} + T)^{-1}, \tag{6.7.33}$$

$$\bar{\mu} \equiv \bar{q}(\underline{q}^{-1}\underline{\mu} + T\bar{y}). \tag{6.7.34}$$

Then letting

$$\bar{s}^2 \equiv \bar{\nu}^{-1}[\underline{\nu}\underline{s}^2 + \nu s^2 + (\underline{q} + T^{-1})^{-1}(\bar{y} - \underline{\mu})^2] \qquad (6.7.35a)$$

$$= \bar{\nu}^{-1}[\underline{\nu}\underline{s}^2 + \nu s^2 + \underline{q}^{-1}\bar{q}T(\bar{y} - \underline{\mu})^2], \qquad (6.7.35b)$$

it follows from (6.7.31) through (6.7.35) that posterior density (6.7.30) can be written

$$f(\theta|y) \propto \theta_2^{\bar{\nu}/2}\exp[-\tfrac{1}{2}\theta_2\{\bar{q}^{-1}(\theta_1 - \bar{\mu})^2 + \bar{\nu}\bar{s}^2\}] \qquad (6.7.36a)$$

$$\propto \theta_2^{1/2}\exp[-\tfrac{1}{2}\theta_2\bar{q}^{-1}(\theta_1 - \bar{\mu})^2]\theta_2^{(\bar{\nu}-2)/2}\exp(-\tfrac{1}{2}\theta_2\bar{\nu}\bar{s}^2). \qquad (6.7.36b)$$

Comparing (6.7.23) and (6.7.36b), it is seen that posterior density $f(\theta|y)$ corresponds to the kernel of a $NG(\bar{\mu}, \bar{q}, \bar{s}^{-2}, \bar{\nu})$ distribution, with updating formulas (6.7.31) and (6.7.33) through (6.7.35). Because both (6.7.23) and (6.7.36) are proportional to normal-gamma densities, prior density (6.7.23) is the natural conjugate prior when drawing a random sample from a normal population with *unknown mean and variance. Posterior* moments for θ_1 and θ_2 can be obtained from *prior* moments (6.7.24) through (6.7.29) simply by replacing $\underline{\mu}$, $\underline{q}$, $\underline{s}^{-2}$, $\underline{\nu}$ with $\bar{\mu}$, $\bar{q}$, $\bar{s}^2$, $\bar{\nu}$.

Also note that $f(y, \theta_2) = f(y|\theta_2)f(\theta_2)$ is a multivariate normal-Wishart density (recall Definition 3.5.4) and by Theorem 3.5.11(a) with $M = 1$, the marginal density of the data is the multivariate t-density

$$f(y) = t_T(y|\underline{\mu}\iota_T, \underline{s}^2[\underline{q} + T^{-1}]I_T, \underline{\nu}). \qquad (6.7.37)$$

Similarly, note that (6.7.21b) implies

$$f(\bar{y}|\theta_2) = \phi(\bar{y}|\underline{\mu}, \theta_2^{-1}[\underline{q} + T^{-1}]). \qquad (6.7.38)$$

Hence, $f(\bar{y}, \theta_2) = f(\bar{y}|\theta_2)f(\theta_2)$ is a (univariate) normal-gamma density, and the marginal density of the sample mean is the (univariate) t-density

$$f(\bar{y}) = t(\bar{y}|\underline{\mu}, \underline{s}^2[\underline{q} + T^{-1}], \underline{\nu}). \qquad (6.7.39)$$

Two issues implicit in Example 6.7.4 deserve comment. First, the normal-gamma conjugate prior family, does *not* permit prior information about θ_1 and θ_2 to be independent, that is, for no values of the prior parameters $\underline{\mu}$, $\underline{q}$, $\underline{s}^2$ and $\underline{\nu}$ does (6.7.23) factor into a product of marginal prior densities for θ_1 and θ_2. If such independence is desired, then a different prior must be used (see Dickey 1971). Second, (6.7.35) depends on *both* the prior and sample means. The greater the discrepancy between $\bar{y}$ and $\underline{\mu}$, the larger is $\bar{s}^2$. In fact, if the discrepancy is large enough then posterior uncertainty may exceed prior uncertainty, that is, $\bar{s}^2 > \underline{s}^2$.

Natural conjugate priors have the desirable feature that prior information can be viewed as "fictitious sample information" in that it is combined with the sample in exactly the same way that additional sample information would be combined. The only difference is that the prior information is "observed" in the mind of the researcher, not in the real world. To clarify this point, reconsider Examples 6.7.1, 6.7.2, and 6.7.4.

Example 6.7.5 In Example 6.7.1 a beta prior distribution with parameters $\underline{\alpha}$ and $\underline{\delta}$ can be interpreted as the information contained in a sample of size $\underline{T} = \underline{\alpha} + \underline{\delta} - 2$ with $\underline{\alpha} - 1$ successes from the Bernoulli process of interest. (Of course if $\underline{\alpha}$ and $\underline{\delta}$ are not integers, then this interpretation must be loosely made.) This does not mean that the researcher has actually observed such a sample, but rather only that the researcher imagines his/her prior information as being from such a sample. Such an interpretation follows directly from (6.7.6) and (6.7.7).

Example 6.7.6 In Example 6.7.2 (known variance) normal prior distribution (6.7.10) can be interpreted in terms of "equivalent sample information." To see this, define

$$\underline{T} \equiv \frac{\theta_2^{-1}}{\underline{h}^{-1}} = \frac{\underline{h}}{\theta_2}, \tag{6.7.40}$$

and write the prior variance as

$$\underline{h}^{-1} = \frac{\theta_2^{-1}}{\underline{T}}. \tag{6.7.41}$$

Similarly, using (6.7.12) define

$$\overline{T} \equiv \frac{\theta_2^{-1}}{\overline{h}^{-1}} = \frac{\overline{h}}{\theta_2} = \underline{T} + T, \tag{6.7.42}$$

and note that posterior mean (6.7.13) can be written

$$\overline{\mu} = \frac{\underline{T}\underline{\mu} + T\overline{y}}{\overline{T}}. \tag{6.7.43}$$

Hence, prior distribution (6.7.10) can be interpreted as the information contained in a sample of size $\underline{T}$ from the underlying $N(\theta_1, \theta_2^{-1})$ population yielding a "sample" mean $\underline{\mu}$ and a variance in this prior mean equalling (6.7.41). Given this interpretation, (6.7.42) and (6.7.43) can be viewed as formulae for pooling the information from the actual sample and the fictitious prior sample, where as noted in Exercise 6.3.1, the pooling in (6.7.43) is done in an efficient manner.

Example 6.7.7 A fictitious sample interpretation of prior (6.7.23) in Example 6.7.4 (unknown variance) can also be given. Simply let

$$\underline{T} \equiv \frac{1}{\underline{q}} \tag{6.7.44}$$

represent prior sample size, and let

$$\overline{T} \equiv \frac{1}{\overline{q}} = \underline{T} + T \tag{6.7.45}$$

represent total sample size. Then again posterior mean (6.7.34) can be written as the weighted average (6.7.43).

Table 6.7.1
Conjugate analysis: $Y_t\ (t = 1, 2, \ldots, T)|\mu, \sigma^{-2} \sim$ i.i.d. $N(\mu, \sigma^2)$

	Case	
Prior	Hyperparameter updating	Posterior
Case 1: μ unknown, σ^{-2} known		
$f(\mu) = \phi(\mu\|\underline{\mu}, \sigma^2/\underline{T})$	$\bar{\mu} = \bar{T}^{-1}(\underline{T}\underline{\mu} + T\bar{y})$ $\bar{T} = \underline{T} + T$	$f(\mu\|y) = \phi(\mu\|\bar{\mu}, \sigma^2/\bar{T})$
Case 2: μ known, σ^{-2} unknown		
$f(\sigma^{-2}) = \gamma(\sigma^{-2}\|\underline{s}^{-2}, \underline{\nu})$	$\bar{\nu}\bar{s}^2 = \underline{\nu}\underline{s}^2 + \nu s^2 + T(\bar{y} - \mu)^2$ $\bar{\nu} = \underline{\nu} + T$	$f(\sigma^{-2}\|y) = \gamma(\sigma^{-2}\|\bar{s}^{-2}, \bar{\nu})$
Case 3: μ unknown, σ^{-2} unknown		
$f(\mu, \sigma^{-2})$ $= \phi(\mu\|\underline{\mu}, \sigma^2/\underline{T})\gamma(\sigma^{-2}\|\underline{s}^{-2}, \underline{\nu})$ $= f_t(\mu\|\underline{\mu}, \underline{s}^2/\underline{T}, \underline{\nu})\gamma(\sigma^{-2}\|\underline{s}_*^{-2}, \underline{\nu}_*)$	$\underline{\nu}_* = \underline{\nu} + 1$ $\underline{\nu}_*\underline{s}_*^2 = \underline{\nu}\underline{s}^2 + \underline{T}(\mu - \underline{\mu})^2$ $\bar{\mu} = \bar{I}^{-1}(\underline{T}\underline{\mu} + T\bar{y})$ $\bar{T} = \underline{T} + T$ $\bar{\nu} = \underline{\nu} + T$ $\bar{\nu}\bar{s}^2 = \underline{\nu}\underline{s}^2 + \nu s^2 + (\underline{T}T/\bar{T})(\bar{y} - \underline{\mu})^2$ $\bar{\nu}_* = \bar{\nu} + 1$ $\bar{\nu}_*\bar{s}_*^2 = \bar{\nu}\bar{s}^2 + \bar{T}(\mu - \bar{\mu})^2$	$f(\mu, \sigma^{-2}\|y)$ $= \phi(\mu\|\bar{\mu}, \sigma^2/\bar{T})\gamma(\sigma^{-2}\|\bar{s}^{-2}, \bar{\nu})$ $= f_t(\mu\|\bar{\mu}, \bar{s}^2/\bar{T}, \bar{\nu})\gamma(\sigma^{-2}\|\bar{s}_*^{-2}, \bar{\nu}_*)$

Table 6.7.2
Conjugate analysis: $Y_t\ (t = 1, 2, \ldots, T)|\mu, \Sigma^{-1} \sim$ i.i.d. $N_M(\mu, \Sigma)$

	Case	
Prior	Hyperparameter updating	Posterior
Case 1: μ unknown, Σ^{-1} known		
$f(\mu) = \phi_M(\mu\|\underline{m}, \underline{\Sigma})$	$\bar{m} = \bar{\Sigma}^{-1}(\underline{\Sigma}^{-1}\underline{m} + T\underline{\Sigma}^{-1}\bar{y})$ $\bar{\Sigma}^{-1} = \underline{\Sigma}^{-1} + T\Sigma^{-1}$	$f(\mu\|y) = \phi_M(\mu\|\bar{m}, \bar{\Sigma})$
Case 2: μ known, Σ^{-1} unknown		
$f(\Sigma^{-1}) = W_M(\Sigma^{-1}\|\underline{S}^{-2}, \underline{\omega})$	$\bar{S} = \underline{S} + S + T(\bar{y} - \mu)(\bar{y} - \mu)'$ $\bar{\omega} = \underline{\omega} + T$	$f(\Sigma^{-1}\|y) = W_M(\Sigma^{-1}\|\bar{S}^{-1}, \bar{\omega})$
Case 3: μ unknown, Σ^{-1} unknown		
$f(\mu, \Sigma^{-1})$ $= \phi_M(\mu\|\underline{\mu}, \underline{T}^{-1}\Sigma)W_M(\Sigma^{-1}\|\underline{S}^{-1}, \underline{\omega})$ $= f_t(\mu\|\underline{\mu}, \underline{S}/\underline{T}, \underline{\omega})W_M(\Sigma^{-1}\|\underline{S}_*^{-1}, \underline{\omega}_*)$	$\underline{\omega}_* = \underline{\omega} + 1$ $\underline{S}_* = \underline{S} + \underline{T}(\mu - \underline{\mu})(\mu - \underline{\mu})'$ $\bar{\mu} = \bar{T}^{-1}(\underline{T}\underline{\mu} + T\bar{y})$ $\bar{T} = \underline{T} + T$ $\bar{\omega} = \underline{\omega} + T$ $\bar{S} = \underline{S} + S + (\underline{T}T/\bar{T})\cdot$ $(\bar{y} - \underline{\mu})(\bar{y} - \underline{\mu})'$ $\bar{\omega}_* = \bar{\omega} + 1$ $\bar{S}_* = \bar{S} + \bar{T}(\mu - \bar{\mu})(\mu - \bar{\mu})'$	$f(\mu, \bar{\Sigma}^{-1}\|y)$ $= \phi(\mu\|\bar{\mu}, \bar{T}^{-1}\Sigma)W_M(\Sigma^{-1}\|\bar{S}^{-1}, \bar{\omega})$ $= f_t(\mu\|\bar{\mu}, \bar{S}/\bar{T}, \bar{\omega})W_M(\Sigma^{-1}\|\bar{S}_*^{-1}, \bar{\omega}_*)$

Note: $S \equiv \sum_{t=1}^{T} (y_t - \bar{y})(y_t - \bar{y})'$.

Examples 6.7.1 through 6.7.7 illustrate the use of Bayes' Rule (6.7.1) in updating prior beliefs in light of sample evidence to obtain the posterior distribution for θ. Table 6.7.1 summarizes the results for sampling from a univariate normal distribution with a conjugate prior into three cases: in Case 1 the mean is unknown and the precision is known (Examples 6.7.2, 6.7.3, and 6.7.6), and in Case 3 both the mean and precision are unknown (Examples 6.7.4 and 6.7.7). Table 6.7.1 also includes a case not studied so far: In Case 2 the mean is known and the precision is unknown. Table 6.7.2 contains the analogous three cases for sampling from a *multivariate* normal distribution in which the conjugate priors involve a multivariate normal prior and a Wishart distribution (recall Definition 3.5.1).

Next we consider point estimation analogous to the classical (orthodox) methods of point estimation discussed in Section 6.6. Section 6.6 emphasized the method of moments and the method of maximum likelihood. Both methods were based on intuitive criteria and the question of statistical properties of the resulting estimators was addressed indirectly after-the-fact. In contrast Bayesian point estimation begins by announcing a criterion for determining what constitutes a good point estimate, and then derives a method for producing an "optimal" point estimate given the data at hand.

As before we presuppose a *loss (cost) function* $C \equiv C(\hat{\theta}, \theta)$ (recall Definition 6.3.3). The Bayesian perspective on estimation is entirely *ex post*: find a function $\hat{\theta} = \hat{\theta}(y)$ of the observed data to serve as a point estimate of the unknown parameter θ. Unlike the classical approach, no role is provided for data that could have been observed, but were not observed. Because θ is unknown the Bayesian perspective suggests formulation of subjective degrees of belief about it, given all the information at hand. Such information is fully contained in the *posterior* distribution of θ: it reflects both prior and sample information.

Thus, like in the classical approach, loss function $C(\hat{\theta}, \theta)$ is random from the Bayesian viewpoint, but the nature of *the randomness is fundamentally different*. From the Bayesian perspective $C(\hat{\theta}, \theta)$ is random because θ is unknown. From the classical perspective, although θ is also unknown, it is treated as a fixed constant. The *ex ante* perspective of the classical view implies that $C(\hat{\theta}, \theta)$ is random because $\hat{\theta} = \hat{\theta}(Y)$ is viewed as random variable with a sampling distribution in repeated samples.

The Bayesian solution to the randomness of the loss function is similar to the classical solution: take its expectation before minimization. The expectation, however, is with respect to the *posterior* distribution $\theta|y$, and not the sampling distribution $Y|\theta$ used to obtain risk function (6.3.1). The Bayesian prescription is equivalent to the principle usually advocated for economic agents acting in a world of uncertainty: using all available information, choose actions so as to maximize expected utility, or equivalently, minimize expected loss. This prescription is formalized in definition 6.7.2.

Definition 6.7.2 Given the posterior density $f(\theta|y)$ and the cost function $C(\hat{\theta}, \theta)$, the *Bayes estimate* (i.e. the Bayesian point estimate) $\hat{\theta}$ is obtained as the solution (assuming the expectation exists) to the following problem:

$$\min_{\theta} E_{\theta|y}[C(\hat{\theta}, \theta)], \tag{6.7.46}$$

where

$$E_{\theta|y}[C(\hat{\theta}, \theta)] = \int_{\Re^K} C(\hat{\theta}, \theta) f(\theta|y)\, d\theta. \tag{6.7.47}$$

Most importantly, note that the posterior expectation in (6.7.47) removes θ from the criterion function (6.7.46) unlike the case of risk function (6.3.1). Also note that if the researcher is interested only in a subset θ_1 of the parameter vector $\theta = [\theta_1', \theta_2']'$, and the remaining parameters θ_2 are nuisance parameters, then this preference can be reflected in the loss function specification: $C(\hat{\theta}, \theta) = C(\hat{\theta}_1, \theta_1)$. In this case the expected loss in (6.7.47) reduces to

$$\begin{aligned} E_{\theta|y}[C(\hat{\theta}, \theta)] &= \int_{\Re^{K_1}} \int_{\Re^{K_2}} C(\hat{\theta}, \theta) f(\theta|y)\, d\theta_2\, d\theta_1 \\ &= \int_{\Re^{K_1}} C(\hat{\theta}_1, \theta_1) \left[\int_{\Re^{K_2}} f(\theta_1, \theta_2|y)\, d\theta_2 \right] d\theta_1 \\ &= \int_{\Re^{K_1}} C(\hat{\theta}_1, \theta_1) f(\theta_1|y)\, d\theta_1. \end{aligned} \tag{6.7.48}$$

Thus, nuisance parameters are simply marginalized-out of the problem.

For concreteness we now define some particular loss functions that routinely arise in the case of a single parameter of interest.

Definition 6.7.3 Consider the case of a single parameter of interest θ. Let c, c_1, and c_2 be known constants. The loss (cost) function

$$C(\hat{\theta}, \theta) = c(\hat{\theta} - \theta)^2, \tag{6.7.49}$$

is known as a *quadratic loss function*. The loss function

$$C(\hat{\theta}, \theta) = \begin{cases} c_1|\hat{\theta} - \theta|, & \text{if } \hat{\theta} \leq \theta \\ c_2|\hat{\theta} - \theta|, & \text{if } \hat{\theta} > \theta \end{cases} \tag{6.7.50}$$

is known as an *asymmetric linear loss function*. The case $c_1 = c_2$, (6.7.50) is known as a *symmetric linear loss function*. The loss function

$$C(\hat{\theta}, \theta) = \begin{cases} c, & \text{if } \hat{\theta} \neq \theta \\ 0, & \text{if } \hat{\theta} = \theta \end{cases} \tag{6.7.51}$$

is known as an *all-or-nothing loss function*.

Bayesian point estimates corresponding to the loss functions defined in Definition 6.7.3 are given in the following theorem.

Theorem 6.7.1 Let $\hat{\theta}_j$ $(j = 1, 2, 3)$ denote the Bayesian point estimates obtained by solving (6.7.46) for loss functions (6.7.49) through (6.7.51). Then:

(a) $\hat{\theta}_1 = E(\theta | y)$.

(b) $\hat{\theta}_2 = \xi_q$, where $q = c_1/(c_1 + c_2)$ and ξ_q denotes the qth quantile of $f(\theta | y)$.

(c) $\hat{\theta}_3$ is the mode of $f(\theta | y)$.

Proof Left to the reader in Exercise 6.7.7.

Example 6.7.8 Consider the Bernoulli sampling problem considered in Example 6.7.1 with posterior p.d.f. given by (6.7.9). Then Theorem 6.7.1(a) and (3.3.45) imply that under quadratic loss function (6.7.49), the Bayesian point estimate of θ is given by

$$\hat{\theta}_1 = \frac{\bar{\alpha}}{\bar{\beta} + \bar{\delta}} = \frac{m + \underline{\alpha}}{T + \underline{\alpha} + \underline{\delta}} = \frac{T\bar{y} + \underline{T}(\underline{T}^{-1}\underline{\alpha})}{T + \underline{T} - 2}, \tag{6.7.52}$$

which in terms of the equivalent prior sample size $\underline{T} \equiv \underline{\alpha} + \underline{\delta}$, is a weighted average of the sample mean $\bar{y} = T^{-1}m$ and the effective prior mean $\underline{T}^{-1}\underline{\alpha}$. Theorem 6.7.1(b) implies that under loss function (6.7.50), the Bayesian point estimate of θ is that value of $\hat{\theta}_2$ which solves (recall Definition 3.3.8)

$$\frac{c_1}{c_1 + c_2} = \int_0^{\hat{\theta}_2} \frac{\theta^{\bar{\alpha}-1}(1 - \theta)^{\bar{\delta}-1}}{B(\bar{\alpha}, \bar{\delta})}\, d\theta. \tag{6.7.53}$$

If $c_1 = c_2$, then $\hat{\theta}_2$ equals the median of posterior p.d.f. (6.7.5). Finally, Theorem 6.7.1(c) implies that under loss function (6.7.51), the Bayesian point estimate of θ is the mode of posterior p.d.f. (6.7.5), which if $\bar{\alpha} > 1$ and $\bar{\delta} > 1$ is given by

$$\hat{\theta}_3 = \frac{\bar{\alpha} - 1}{\bar{\alpha} + \bar{\delta} - 2} = \frac{m + \underline{\alpha} - 1}{T + \underline{\alpha} + \underline{\delta} - 2}. \tag{6.7.54}$$

Example 6.7.9 Consider the normal sampling problem in Example 6.7.2. Then under either loss function (6.7.49) or (6.7.51), the Bayesian point estimate of θ is given by posterior mean-mode (6.7.13), or equivalently, (6.7.43). Under loss function (6.7.50) the Bayesian point estimate of θ is given by

$$\hat{\theta}_2 = \bar{\mu} + \bar{\sigma}\Phi^{-1}\left[\frac{c_1}{c_1 + c_2}\right], \tag{6.7.55}$$

where $\bar{\mu}$ and $\bar{\sigma}$ are the posterior mean and standard deviation, and $\Phi^{-1}(\cdot)$ is the inverse of the standard normal cumulative distribution function.

Note that when $c_1 = c_2$, $\Phi^{-1}(\frac{1}{2}) = 0$, and (6.7.55) also reduces to simply the posterior mean-median-mode $\bar{\mu}$.

When there is more than one parameter of interest, then the most popular loss function is the weighted squared error generalization of (6.7.49) defined in Definition 6.3.3. The all-or-nothing loss function in the case of more than one parameter is still defined by (6.7.51). The Bayesian point estimate in these cases are given in Theorem 6.7.2.

Theorem 6.7.2 Suppose $\theta \in \Re^K$.

(a) Consider weighted squared error loss function (6.3.2) and suppose its posterior expected value (6.7.47) exists. Then the Bayesian point estimate of θ is the posterior mean $\hat{\theta} = E_{\theta|y}(\theta) = E(\theta|y)$. Note that $\hat{\theta}$ does *not* depend on Q.

(b) Consider all-or-nothing loss function (6.7.51). Then the Bayesian point estimate of θ is its posterior mode.

Proof Exercise 6.7.8.

From the Bayesian standpoint, different estimates of θ may arise from solving (6.7.46) under different priors $f(\theta)$, which in turn alter the posterior $f(\theta|y)$. To the Bayesian statistician it is quite natural to change her/his point estimate under different situations of prior knowledge or having observed different data. What is quite *unnatural* to the Bayesian statistician, is to pick a point estimate that ignores all nondata based information (we will consider later the case when no such information exists or is weakly defined) and/or which is determined in part by *data that could conceivably have been observed but that were not in fact observed.* The classical sampling properties of estimators are concerned with precisely this latter situation.

Some statisticians attempt to walk a fine line between Bayesian and classical point estimation by taking risk function $R(\hat{\theta}|\theta)$ in (6.3.1) and "averaging" it over the permissible parameter space Θ to obtain a measure of the "average" performance of the estimator $\hat{\theta}(Y)$. The motivation behind such action is clear: to overcome the difficulty that risk functions of different estimators tend to cross each other at various points in Θ, it seems natural to weight the performance of an estimator in a particular region of the parameter space by an importance function. The interpretation of such an "importance function" would seem, however, perilously close to a prior distribution for θ that would weight heavily those regions of the parameter space that the researcher feels are most likely to be relevant. Given a weighting function $f(\theta)$, whatever its interpretation, that satisfies the properties of a proper p.d.f., consider the problem

$$\min_{\hat{\theta}} \bar{R}(\hat{\theta}), \tag{6.7.56}$$

where

$$\bar{R}(\hat{\theta}) \equiv \int_{\Theta} R(\hat{\theta}|\theta) f(\theta)\, d\theta, \tag{6.7.57}$$

and $f(\theta)$ is assumed to obey the mathematical properties of a p.d.f. Substituting risk function (6.3.1) into (6.7.56), where the sample space for Y is $\mathscr{S}_T$, yields

$$\bar{R} = \int_{\Theta} \left[\int_{\mathscr{S}_T} C[\hat{\theta}(y), \theta] f(y|\theta)\, dy \right] f(\theta)\, d\theta \tag{6.7.58a}$$

$$= \int_{\mathscr{S}_T} \left[\int_{\Theta} C[\hat{\theta}(y), \theta] f(y|\theta) f(\theta)\, d\theta \right] dy \tag{6.7.58b}$$

$$= \int_{\mathscr{S}_T} \left[\int_{\Theta} C[\hat{\theta}(y), \theta] \left(\frac{f(y|\theta) f(\theta)}{f(y)} \right) d\theta \right] f(y)\, dy \tag{6.7.58c}$$

provided it is permissible to switch the order of integration (see Exercise 6.7.16). From (6.7.58c) it is clear that the $\hat{\theta}$ that minimizes $\bar{R}$ must also minimize the quantity enclosed in square brackets in (6.7.58c). This quantity, however, is exactly the expected posterior loss (6.7.47) corresponding to the prior distribution $f(\theta)$. Hence, a researcher minimizing $\bar{R}$ behaves *as if* solving (6.7.46) with prior distribution $f(\theta)$. Therefore, *any* estimator that minimizes weighted risk *must* be a Bayesian point estimate.

The preceding analysis is rather damaging to the frequentist position because it shows that Bayesian point estimators have some desirable *frequentist* properties. Any Bayesian estimator based on a *proper prior* (i.e., a prior p.f. that integrates to unity) satisfies the minimal frequentist requirement of admissibility—more than can be said for MLE (recall Section 6.6). Furthermore, Wald (1950) showed, in most interesting settings, that *all* admissible rules are either Bayes or limits thereof known as generalized Bayes estimators (Wald 1950). A *generalized Bayes estimator* is a Bayes estimator based on an *improper prior*, i.e. a "prior" whose integral is unbounded. (Examples of improper priors will be considered in the discussion of "noninformative" priors in the next section.) In other words, preference for admissible decision rules implies a preference for Bayes rules. Also, if a Bayes estimator is unique, then it must be admissible. In short, Bayes estimators based on proper priors, have desirable properties in terms of "final precision" (by construction), and also have many desirable "initial precision" properties.[30] Bayes estimators corresponding to proper priors, however, are essentially never unbiased (Exercise 6.7.37). See Berger (1985, Chapter 8) for more details.

In nonconjugate situations the Bayesian approach can run into computational problems due to the need to evaluate multidimensional integrals such as the denominator in posterior p.d.f. (6.7.1). When $K = 1, 2$ it is easy to graph the numerator $f(\theta)\mathscr{L}(\theta; y)$ of (6.7.1) to get a feel for the its relative shape. More detailed information (e.g., moments), however, requires computation of the denominator in (6.7.2). In most situations the prior p.d.f. does not depend on sample size T, and so in large samples, the likelihood eventually dominates the prior density over their common support. This suggests that consideration of the behavior of posterior density (6.7.1) as $T \rightarrow \infty$ may provide useful analytical approximations when T is in fact large.

Such "Bayesian asymptotics" differ, however, from earlier discussed classical asymptotics in an important way. The thing being approximated in Bayesian asymptotics is conceptually well-defined in finite samples, namely posterior p.d.f. (6.7.1). "Nuisance" parameters can be addressed straightforwardly by marginalizing them out of (6.7.1) to obtain the exact marginal posterior p.d.f for the parameters of interest. As noted in Section 6.4, there is no general classical sampling distribution of estimators in finite samples free of nuisance parameters.[31]

The same way sampling distributions of MLEs in regular situations are asymptotically normal, posterior density (6.7.1) behaves similarly. This result is stated informally in the following theorem.

Theorem 6.7.3 Under suitable regularity conditions, posterior density (6.7.1) can be approximated as $T \rightarrow \infty$ by $\phi_K(\theta | \hat{\theta}_{ML}, [J_T(\hat{\theta}_{ML})]^{-1})$, where $\hat{\theta}_{ML}$ is the ML estimate and $J_T(\cdot)$ is the information matrix.

Proof Numerous proofs under a variety of regularity conditions exist in the literature. Notable references are Chen (1985), Dawid (1970), Heyde and Johnson (1979), Johnson (1970), Le Cam (1986), Sweeting (1980), Sweeting and Adekola (1987), and Walker (1969).

30. Kadane et al. (1986) note without apologies that Bayes estimators based on improper priors that are finitely additive, but not countably additive, can be inadmissible.

31. Because Bayesian analysis conditions on the observed data, asymptotic analysis which introduces "data" (as $T \rightarrow \infty$) that is never observed is somewhat "unnatural." As a result there have developed two strands of Bayesian asymptotics: (i) a conventional probabilistic one along classical lines, and (ii) a strand which is nonprobabilistic (e.g., Chen 1985). In the latter case, the given set of observations are imbedded into an infinite sequence of *Laplace regular* likelihoods (see Kass et al. 1988, 1990). Although the order of approximation errors in the latter case are stated nonprobabilistically, it is possible to state conditions so that the approximation error approach zero almost surely as $T \rightarrow \infty$ (see Kass et al. 1990).

The approximation in Theorem 6.7.3 does not depend on the prior, and is essentially numerically (but not conceptually) identical to the approximation offered by the asymptotic distribution theory for ML given in Theorem 6.6.4. Berger (1985, p. 224) argues informally that the quality of the approximation in Theorem 6.7.3 can usually be improved in finite samples by the following approximations that reflect the observed data and the prior.

Corollary 6.7.3 The following approximations offer increasingly improvements on the approximation in Theorem 6.7.3.

(a) $\phi_K(\theta|\hat{\theta}_{ML}, [-\bar{H}(\hat{\theta}_{ML})]^{-1})$, where $\bar{H}(\theta)$ is the Hessian of the log-posterior:

$$\bar{H}(\theta) = \frac{\partial^2 \ln[f(\theta)]}{\partial\theta\,\partial\theta'} + \frac{\partial^2 L(\theta; y)}{\partial\theta\,\partial\theta'}. \tag{6.7.59}$$

(b) $\phi_K(\theta|\hat{\theta}, [-\bar{H}(\hat{\theta})]^{-1})$, where $\hat{\theta}$ is the posterior mode.

(c) $\phi_K(\theta|E[\theta|y], \mathrm{Var}[\theta|y])$, where $E[\theta|y]$ and $\mathrm{Var}[\theta|y]$ are the posterior mean and posterior variance, respectively.

Unfortunately, (a) through (c) of Corollary 6.7.3 are increasingly demanding in terms of computation. In (c) the posterior mean and variance require computation of ratios of integrals of the form

$$G \equiv E[g(\theta)|y] = \frac{\int_{-\infty}^{\infty} g(\theta)f(\theta)\mathscr{L}(\theta; y)\,d\theta}{\int_{-\infty}^{\infty} f(\theta)\mathscr{L}(\theta; y)\,d\theta}, \tag{6.7.60}$$

for suitable choice of the function $g(\theta)$. For example: $g(\theta) = \theta_k^r$ in the calculation of the rth posterior moment of θ_k around the origin; $g(\theta) = \exp(v'\theta)$ in the case of the posterior m.g.f. of θ, where v is a $K \times 1$ vector of constants; and $g(\theta) = I_A(\theta)$, in the case $\mathrm{Prob}(\theta \in A|y)$, where A is a subset of Θ and $I_A(\theta)$ is the indicator function.

A famous technique in approximation theory for approximating integrals is *Laplace's method* (see Exercise 6.7.43). When $g(\theta) > 0$, Tierney and Kadane (1986) recommended writing the numerator and denominator integrands in (6.7.60) as $\exp[-Ta_N(\theta)]$ and $\exp[-Ta_D(\theta)]$, respectively, where

$$a_N(\theta) = -\frac{1}{T}(\ln[g(\theta)] + \ln[f(\theta)] + L(\theta; y)), \tag{6.7.61}$$

$$a_D(\theta) = -\frac{1}{T}(\ln[f(\theta)] + L(\theta; y)). \tag{6.7.62}$$

This way of applying Laplace's method is known as the *fully exponential form*. Applying Laplace's method [see (6.7.92)] separately to the numerator and denominator of (6.7.60) yields the Tierney-Kadane approximation:

$$\hat{G} = g(\hat{\theta}_N)\left[\frac{f(\hat{\theta}_N)\mathscr{L}(\hat{\theta}_N; y)}{f(\hat{\theta}_D)\mathscr{L}(\hat{\theta}_D; y)}\right]\left[\frac{|H_N(\hat{\theta}_N)|}{|H_D(\hat{\theta}_D)|}\right]^{-1/2}, \tag{6.7.63}$$

where the $\hat{\theta}_N$, $\hat{\theta}_D$ are modes, and $H_N(\cdot)$, $H_D(\cdot)$ the Hessians of $a_N(\theta)$ and $a_D(\theta)$, respectively. Approximation (6.7.63) is most attractive because it has converted an integration problem to two much easier maximization problems each with essentially the same level of difficulty as finding the MLE. Tierney and Kadane (1986) showed that the $O(T^{-1})$ terms in the Laplace approximation to the numerator and denominator cancel yielding the surprisingly accurate approximation result:[32]

$$G = \hat{G}[1 + O(T^{-2})]. \tag{6.7.64}$$

Tierney and Kadane (1986) also note the same order of approximation is obtained if the numerator in (6.7.63) is evaluated simply at one Newton-step away from $\hat{\theta}_D$, that is, at $\tilde{\theta} = \hat{\theta}_D - [H_D(\hat{\theta}_D)]^{-1}[\partial a_N(\hat{\theta}_D)/\partial\theta]$, eliminating the need for a second maximization. For a rigorous development, see Kass et al. (1990).

Numerous authors (Leonard 1982; Leonard et al. 1989; Phillips 1983; Tierney and Kadane 1986; Tierney et al. 1989a; and Wong and Li 1992) have also used Laplace's method to obtain marginal densities. For example, suppose $\theta = [\theta_1', \theta_2']' \in \Theta_1 \times \Theta_2$, where θ_i is $K_i \times 1$ $(i = 1, 2)$, and interest focuses on the marginal density:

$$f(\theta_1 | y) = \frac{1}{f(y)}\int_{\Theta_2} f(\theta_1, \theta_2)\mathscr{L}(\theta_1, \theta_2; y)\, d\theta_2. \tag{6.7.65}$$

Let $\hat{\theta}_2(\theta_1)$ denote the conditional posterior mode of θ_2 given θ_1, that is,

$$\hat{\theta}_2(\theta_1) \equiv \underset{\theta_2 \in \Theta_2}{\operatorname{argmax}} \ln[f(\theta_1, \theta_2)] + L(\theta_1, \theta_2; y). \tag{6.7.66}$$

Also let $\overline{H}_{22}(\theta_1, \theta_2)$ denote the lower righthand block of posterior Hessian (6.7.59). Then using Laplace's method to approximate the integral in

32. Earlier methods involving higher-order Taylor series expansions involving higher order derivatives were given by Mosteller and Wallace (1964, Section 4.6C) and Lindley (1961, 1980). When $g(\theta) \leq 0$, then the fully exponential method cannot be applied directly. Tierney et al. (1989a) discuss two alternatives. First, simply add a "large" positive constant to $g(\theta)$, apply the fully exponential method, and then subtracting the constant from the resulting answer. Second, apply the fully exponential method to estimate the m.g.f., which is positive, numerically differentiate the answer, and then evaluate at zero to obtain an estimate of G. This latter method turns out to be formally equivalent to methods used by Lindley (1961, 1980) and Mosteller and Wallace (1964).

(6.7.65) yields the approximate marginal density:

$$\hat{f}(\theta_1|y) = c|-T^{-1}\bar{H}_{22}[\theta_1,\hat{\theta}_2(\theta_1)]|^{-1/2}f[\theta_1,\hat{\theta}_2(\theta_1)]\mathscr{L}[\theta_1,\hat{\theta}_2(\theta_1)], \quad (6.7.67)$$

where c is an integrating constant. Tierney and Kadane (1986) note that $\hat{f}(\theta_1|y)$ has a relative error of order $O(T^{-3/2})$ on neighborhoods about the mode that shrink at the rate $T^{-1/2}$, and the approximation is of order $O(T^{-1})$ on bounded neighborhoods of the mode.

The approximations just discussed are merely meant to be intermediate stepping stones in the Bayesian analysis of data. Substantial progress, however, has been made recently in the area of Bayesian computation (e.g., see Smith 1992). "Final" results are best obtained using the "exact" results of the numerical methods discussed in Appendix C. For reviews of Bayesian computer packages, see Press (1980, 1989) and Goel (1988).

It is not at all clear that Bayesian and classical paradigms are direct competitors. Some would argue that they are not comparable since they do not have a common basis in probability. Rather than a kneejerk reaction pro or con, an eclectic view recognizing the strengths and weaknesses of both might be the most desirable outlook. Ignorance of either approach is, however, clearly an inadmissible state of affairs for any researcher.

Exercises

6.7.1 Suppose that a data-generating process is a normal process with unknown mean μ and with known variance $\theta_2^{-1} = 225$. A sample of size $T = 9$ is taken from this process with the sample results: 42, 56, 68, 56, 48, 36, 45, 71, 64. If your prior judgements about μ can be represented by a normal distribution with mean 50 and variance 14, what is your posterior distribution for μ? Using your posterior distribution, find $P(\mu > 50|y)$.

6.7.2 In reporting the results of a statistical investigation, a Bayesian researcher reports that the posterior distribution for μ is $N(52, 10)$, and that a sample of size 4 with sample mean 56 was taken from a $N(\mu, 100)$ population. What were the researcher's prior beliefs?

6.7.3 Consider a normal distribution in which the values of the mean θ_1 and the precision θ_2 are unknown, and suppose that a researcher wishes to select a conjugate prior such that $E(\theta_1) = 2$, $\text{Var}(\theta_1) = 5$, $E(\theta_2) = 3$ and $\text{Var}(\theta_2) = 3$.

(a) What values of $\underline{\mu}$, $\underline{T}$, $\underline{\nu}$ and $\underline{s}^2$ should be chosen?

(b) Suppose a random sample of size 10 from $N(\theta_1, [\theta_2]^{-1})$ yields $\bar{y} = 4.20$ and $\nu s^2 = 5.40$. Find the posterior moments $E(\theta_1|y)$, $\text{Var}(\theta_1|y)$, $E(\theta_2|y)$ and $\text{Var}(\theta_2|y)$.

6.7.4 Suppose Y_t $(t = 1, 2, \ldots, T)$ is a random sample from an exponential distribution with mean θ^{-1}, and that the prior distribution of θ is a gamma distribution with parameters $\underline{\alpha} > 0$ and $\underline{\beta} > 0$. Show that the posterior distribution of θ given the data is gamma with parameters $\bar{\alpha} = \underline{\alpha} + T$ and $\bar{\beta} = (\underline{\beta}^{-1} + T\bar{y})^{-1}$.

6.7.5 Suppose Y_t $(t = 1, 2, \ldots, T)$ is a random sample from a $U(0, \theta)$ distribution, where θ is unknown, and suppose the prior distribution of θ is Pareto with parameters $\underline{\gamma} > 0$ and $\underline{\lambda} > 0$. Show that the posterior distribution of θ given the data is a Pareto with parameters $\bar{\gamma} = \max(\underline{\gamma}, y_1, y_2, \ldots, y_T)$ and $\bar{\lambda} = \underline{\lambda} + T$.

6.7.6 Consider Example 6.7.2. Find the distribution of Y_t ($t = 1, 2, \ldots, T$) *unconditional* of θ, i.e. the marginal density of the data $f(y)$.

6.7.7 Prove Theorem 6.7.1 (a) and (b).

6.7.8 Prove Theorem 6.7.2.

6.7.9 Using the quadratic loss function in Exercise 6.7.9, find the Bayesian point estimate of θ in Example 6.7.4.

6.7.10 Using the cost function (6.7.50) with $c_1/(c_1 + c_2) = 3/4$, find the Bayesian point estimate of θ_1 in Example 6.7.4 when $\underline{\mu} = 1$, $\underline{T} = 3$, $\underline{\nu} = 6$, $\underline{s}^2 = 1$ and a sample of size $T = 11$ yields $\bar{y} = 2$ and $s^2 = \frac{1}{2}$.

6.7.11 Consider the weighted squared-error loss function $C(\hat{\theta}, \theta) = w(\theta)(\theta - \hat{\theta})^2$, where $w(\theta) > 0$ and θ is a single unknown parameter. Show that the Bayesian Point estimate corresponding to $C(\hat{\theta}, \theta)$ is given by

$$\hat{\theta} = \frac{E_{\theta|y}[\theta w(\theta)]}{E_{\theta|y}[w(\theta)]}. \tag{6.7.68}$$

Compare the role of $w(\theta)$ to that of the prior for θ.

6.7.12 Let θ be a single unknown parameter and suppose that $f(\theta|y)$ is unimodal and symmetric. Show for any loss of the form $C(|\hat{\theta} - \theta|)$ that is increasing in $|\hat{\theta} - \theta|$, the Bayes estimate $\hat{\theta}$ is the posterior median.

6.7.13 Let Y_t ($t = 1, \ldots, T$) be a random sample from a $N(\theta, \sigma^2)$ population with $\sigma^2 = 140$, $T = 25$ and $\bar{y} = 54$.

(a) Given a prior distribution which is equivalent to the evidence of a hypothetical sample of size 10 from the same distribution with a sample mean of 40, find the posterior distribution.

(b) Consider the loss function

$$C(\hat{\theta}, \theta) = \begin{Bmatrix} 0, & \text{if } \theta - 1 < \hat{\theta} < \theta + 1 \\ c, & \text{otherwise} \end{Bmatrix}, \tag{6.7.69}$$

where c is a known constant. Using the information in (a) and the sample information, find the Bayesian point estimate of θ.

6.7.14 Consider the p.d.f. $f(y|\theta) = \exp[-(y - \theta)]$ for $y > \theta$, and equal to zero, otherwise. Let the prior p.d.f. for θ be the Cauchy prior $f(\theta) = [\pi(1 + \theta^2)]^{-1}$. Given one observation y, find the posterior mode of θ.

6.7.15 The following example drawn from Cornfield (1969, pp. 630–631) shows that interchanging the order of integration is not universally valid. Let

$$f(x, y) = xy(2 - xy)\exp(-xy). \tag{6.7.70}$$

(a) Show:

$$\int_0^1 \int_0^\infty f(x, y)\,dy\,dx = 0.$$

(b) Show:

$$\int_0^\infty \int_0^1 f(x, y)\,dy\,dx = 1.$$

(c) Under what conditions is the interchange of the order of integration permissible?

6.7.16 Suppose Y_t ($t = 1, 2, \ldots, T$) comprise a random sample from an exponential family distribution with density

$$f(y_t|\theta) = a(\theta)b(\theta)\exp\left[\sum_{j=1}^{J} c_j(\theta)\,d_j(y_t)\right]. \tag{6.7.71}$$

Consider a prior density of the form

$$f(\theta) = f(\theta|\underline{\alpha}, \underline{\delta}) \propto [a(\theta)]^{\underline{\alpha}} b(\theta)\exp\left[\sum_{j=1}^{J} c_j(\theta)\underline{\delta}_j\right]. \tag{6.7.72}$$

where $\underline{\alpha}$ and $\underline{\delta} = [\underline{\delta}_1, \underline{\delta}_2, \ldots, \underline{\delta}_J]'$ are given.

(a) Show that the posterior distribution corresponding to (6.7.72) is of the form $f(\theta|\bar{\alpha}, \bar{\delta})$, where

$$\bar{\alpha} = \underline{\alpha} + T, \tag{6.7.73}$$

$$\bar{\delta}_j = \underline{\delta}_j + d_j(y) \qquad (j = 1, 2, \ldots, J). \tag{6.7.74}$$

$$\hat{d}_j = \hat{d}_j(y) = \sum_{t=1}^{T} d_j(y_t) \qquad (j = 1, 2, \ldots, J). \tag{6.7.75}$$

(b) Consider a mixture prior of the form

$$g(\theta) = \sum_{m=1}^{M} w_m f(\theta|\underline{\alpha}_m, \underline{\delta}_m), \tag{6.7.76}$$

where $w_m \geq 0\ (m = 1, 2, \ldots, M)$ are known weights satisfying: $w_1 + w_2 + \cdots + w_M = 1$, and $\underline{\alpha}_m, \underline{\delta}_m\ (m = 1, 2, \ldots, M)$ are given. Find the posterior density $g(\theta|y)$.

6.7.17 A *minimax estimator* (recall Section 6.3) is an estimator whose maximum risk is less than or equal to the maximum risk of any other estimator. Such an estimator is conservative because it protects against the worst that can happen. In other words, a minimax estimator minimizes the maximum risk. Show the following:

(a) If a Bayes estimator has constant risk, then it is a minimax estimator.

(b) For a random sample from a Bernoulli distribution, the estimator $\hat{\theta} = [T\bar{y} + T^{1/2}]/[T + T^{1/2}]$ is a minimax estimator under quadratic loss.

6.7.18 Consider a sampling situation in which a posterior distribution $p(\alpha|y)$ is obtained for a single parameter α. Suppose the parameter of interest is $\theta \equiv 1/\alpha$, and consider the relative squared error loss function

$$C(\hat{\theta}, \theta) = \left[\frac{\hat{\theta} - \theta}{\theta}\right]^2 = (\hat{\theta}\alpha - 1)^2, \tag{6.7.77}$$

where $\hat{\theta}$ is an estimate of θ. This loss function yields a greater loss for a given absolute error $|\hat{\theta} - \theta|$ when θ is small than when θ is large. See Zellner (1978) for more details.

(a) Show that if $p(\alpha|y)$ has finite first and second moments, then the Bayesian point estimate is

$$\hat{\theta} = \left(E(\alpha|y)\left[1 + \frac{\operatorname{Var}(\alpha|y)}{[E(\alpha|y)]^2}\right]\right)^{-1}. \tag{6.7.78}$$

Note that $\hat{\theta}$ is equal to the reciprocal of the posterior mean times a shrinking factor that assumes values between zero and one and is a function of the posterior squared coefficient of variation.

(b) Suppose $Y_t\ (t = 1, 2, \ldots, T)$ are i.i.d. $N(\mu, \sigma^2)$ and that the noninformative prior $p(\mu, \sigma) \propto \sigma^{-1}$ is used. Let $\alpha = \mu$. Show that (6.7.78) reduces to

$$\hat{\theta} = \left(\bar{y}\left[1 + \frac{\nu s^2}{T(\nu - 2)\bar{y}^2}\right]\right)^{-1}. \tag{6.7.79}$$

It can be shown that the sampling moments of the ML estimate $\bar{y}^{-1}$ of μ^{-1} do not exist, whereas the sampling moments of $\hat{\theta}$ are finite.

6.7.19 (Zellner 1978) Given the posterior density $f(\theta_1, \theta_2|y)$, suppose you wish to estimate $\alpha = \theta_1/\theta_2$ subject to the loss function $C(\hat{\alpha}, \alpha) = (\hat{\alpha} - \alpha)^2/\theta_2^2$. Show that the Bayesian point estimate is

$$\hat{\alpha} = \left[\frac{E(\theta_1|y)}{E(\theta_2|y)}\right]\left[\frac{1 + \dfrac{\text{Cov}(\theta_1, \theta_2|y)}{E(\theta_1|y)E(\theta_2|y)}}{1 + \dfrac{\text{Var}(\theta_2|y)}{[E(\theta_2|y)]^2}}\right]. \tag{6.7.80}$$

6.7.20 The *LINEX loss function* (see Varian 1975 and Zellner 1986b) is defined by

$$C(\hat{\theta}, \theta) = b[\exp\{a(\hat{\theta} - \theta)\} - a(\hat{\theta} - \theta) - 1], \tag{6.7.81}$$

where $a \neq 0$ and $b > 0$. Its name arises from the fact that if $a < 0$, $C(\hat{\theta}, \theta)$ rises almost linearly for $\hat{\theta} > \theta$, and almost exponentially for $\hat{\theta} < \theta$. For small values of $|a|$, the loss function is almost symmetric. For $a = 1$, the loss function is quite asymmetric with overestimation being more costly than underestimation.

(a) Show that the Bayesian point estimate of θ, given data y, is

$$\hat{\theta} = -a^{-1}\ln[M_{\theta|y}(-a)], \tag{6.7.82}$$

where $M_{\theta|y}(-a) = E[\exp(-a^{\theta})|y]$, the moment generating function of the posterior distribution of θ, is assumed to exist.

(b) Suppose $f(\theta|y) = \phi(\theta|c, d)$ and $Y \sim N(\theta, \sigma^2/T)$, where c and d are known.

(1) Show that (6.7.82) reduces to

$$\hat{\theta} = c - \tfrac{1}{2}ad. \tag{6.7.83}$$

(2) Using (6.7.81), show: $E_{Y|\theta}[R(\hat{\theta}|\theta)] = ba^2\sigma^2/2T$.

(3) Using (6.7.81), show: $E_{Y|\theta}[R(Y|\theta)] = b[\exp(a^2\sigma^2/2T) - 1]$.

(4) What do the results in (2) and (3) imply?

(5) Show: $\text{MSE}(\hat{\theta}) = \sigma^2 + (a^2d^2/4)$.

(6) Show: $\text{MSE}(Y) = \sigma^2$.

(7) What do the results in (5) and (6) imply?

6.7.21 Let Y_t $(t = 1, 2, \ldots, T) \sim$ i.i.d. $B(1, \theta)$. Consider a $U(0, 1)$ for θ. Define $\alpha \equiv \theta(1 - \theta)$ and the loss function $C(\hat{\alpha}, \alpha) = (\hat{\alpha} - \alpha)^2$. Show that the Bayesian point estimator of α is

$$\hat{\alpha} = \frac{(T\bar{y} + 1)(T - T\bar{y} + 1)}{(T + 3)(T + 2)}. \tag{6.7.84}$$

6.7.22 Suppose Y_t $(t = 1, 2, \ldots, T)$ comprise a random sample from $N(\mu, \sigma^2)$ distribution where μ and σ^2 are unknown parameters with prior distribution $\text{NG}(\underline{\mu}, \underline{T}, \underline{s}^2, \underline{\nu})$.

(a) Suppose you wish to estimate σ^{-2} under quadratic loss: $C(\hat{\sigma}^{-2}, \sigma^{-2}) = c(\hat{\sigma}^{-2} - \sigma^{-2})^2$, where c is a known constant. Find the Bayesian point estimate of $\hat{\sigma}^{-2}$.

(b) Consider the loss function $C(\hat{\mu}, \mu) = \mu^2(\hat{\mu} - \mu)^2$. Find the Bayesian point estimate $\hat{\mu}$.

(c) Let $\hat{\mu}_1 = E(\mu|y)$ and $\hat{\mu}_2 = \bar{Y}$.

(1) From the standpoint of *sampling theory*, compare $\text{MSE}(\hat{\mu}_1)$ with $\text{MSE}(\hat{\mu}_2)$.

(2) Under the loss function $C(\hat{\mu}, \mu) = (\hat{\mu} - \mu)^2$, compare the expected *posterior losses* of $\hat{\mu}_1$ and $\hat{\mu}_2$.

6.7.23 According to natural conjugate prior (6.7.23), the marginal distribution of θ_2^{-1} is the gamma distribution with mean and variance given by (6.7.24) and (6.7.25), respectively. The distribution of θ_2 is the inverted gamma distribution given in Table 3.3.1(e). Consider the standard deviation $\sigma \equiv \theta_2^{1/2}$.

(a) Show that the p.d.f. of σ is

$$f(\sigma|\underline{v}, \underline{s}) = 2(\tfrac{1}{2}\underline{v}\underline{s}^2)^{\underline{v}}[\Gamma(\tfrac{1}{2}\underline{v}))\sigma^{\underline{v}+1}]^{-1}\exp(-\tfrac{1}{2}\underline{v}\underline{s}^2/\sigma^2) \tag{6.7.85}$$

for $0 < \sigma < \infty$.

(b) Given that $E(\sigma^m) = \Gamma[\frac{1}{2}(\underline{v} - m)](\frac{1}{2}\underline{v}\underline{s}^2)^{1/2m}/\Gamma(\frac{1}{2}\underline{v})$, if $\underline{v} > m$ (see Zellner 1971, p. 372), show:

$$E(\sigma) = \Gamma[\tfrac{1}{2}(\underline{v} - 1)](\tfrac{1}{2}\underline{v})^{1/2}\underline{s}/\Gamma(\tfrac{1}{2}\underline{v}) \qquad (v > 1), \tag{6.7.86}$$

$$\mathrm{Var}(\sigma) = \underline{v}\underline{s}^2[(\underline{v} - 2)^{-1} - \tfrac{1}{2}\{\Gamma[\tfrac{1}{2}(\underline{v} - 1)]/\Gamma(\tfrac{1}{2}\underline{v})\}^2] \qquad (v > 2). \tag{6.7.87}$$

(c) Show that the mode of σ is $\underline{s}[\underline{v}/(\underline{v} + 1)]^{1/2}$.

6.7.24 Prove identity (6.7.17). You may use brute force or Exercise A.4.7.

6.7.25 Consider normal-gamma density (6.7.23). Show that the conditional distribution of θ_2, given θ_1, is $\gamma(\theta_2|[\underline{v}\underline{s}^2 + (\theta_1 - \underline{\mu})^2]/(\underline{v} + 1), \underline{v} + 1)$.

6.7.26 Consider Exercises 6.6.2(c) and 6.6.3(c) involving a random sample Y_t $(t = 1, 2, \ldots, T)$ from a distribution with p.d.f.

$$f(y_t|\theta) = \theta^{-1}\exp(-y_t/\theta), 0 < y_t < \infty, 0 < \theta < \infty. \tag{6.7.88}$$

These exercises showed that $\overline{Y}$ was both the maximum likelihood and the method of moments estimator of θ.

(a) Find $\mathrm{MSE}(\overline{Y})$.

(b) Consider the estimator $\hat{\theta} = T\overline{Y}/(T + 1)$. Find $\mathrm{MSE}(\hat{\theta})$.

(c) Compare the MSE's of $\overline{Y}$ and $\hat{\theta}$. Which estimator has the lower MSE?

(d) Let $\delta = \theta^{-1}$, and rewrite (6.7.88) as

$$f(y_t|\delta) = \delta[\exp(-\delta y_t)], 0 < y_t < \infty, 0 < \delta < \infty. \tag{6.7.89}$$

Suppose prior beliefs regarding δ have a gamma distribution with hyperparameters $\underline{\alpha}$ and $\underline{\beta}$, that is, $\delta \sim G(\underline{\alpha}, \underline{\beta})$. Find the posterior distribution of δ.

(e) Find the posterior distribution of θ corresponding to the answer in Part (d).

(f) Consider the loss function $C(\tilde{\theta}, \theta) = (\tilde{\theta} - \theta)^2$. What is the Bayesian point estimate $\tilde{\theta}$ of θ? Be specific!

(g) Find $\mathrm{MSE}(\tilde{\theta})$ and compare it to your answers in Parts (a) and (b). Which estimator do you prefer? Why?

(h) Compare $\overline{Y}$, $\hat{\theta}$ and $\tilde{\theta}$ according to expected posterior loss using the loss function in (f).

6.7.27 Derive the posterior distribution in Case 2 of Table 6.7.1.

6.7.28 Given $\theta = [\mu', \mathrm{vech}(\Sigma^{-1})']'$, where μ is $M \times 1$ and Σ is a $M \times M$ positive definite matrix, consider a random sample Y_t $(t = 1, 2, \ldots, T)$ from a $N_M(\mu, \Sigma)$ distribution. Define $Y = [Y_1, Y_2, \ldots, Y_T]'$ and

$$\overline{Y} = \sum_{t=1}^{T} Y_t, \tag{6.7.90}$$

$$S = \sum_{t=1}^{T} (Y_t - \overline{Y})(Y_t - \overline{Y})', \tag{6.7.91}$$

Suppose $\underline{m}$ and $\underline{\mu}$ are both $M \times 1$, $\underline{T} > 0$ and $\underline{\omega} > M$ are both scalars, and $\underline{S}$ is a $M \times M$ positive definite matrix. Recall Definitions 3.5.1 and 3.5.4 of the Wishart and normal-Wishart distributions. Consider the natural conjugate priors for the three multivariate cases in Table 6.7.2.

(a) Derive the posterior distribution for Case 1.

(b) Derive the posterior distribution for Case 2.

(c) Derive the posterior distribution for Case 3 and verify the marginal posterior distributions for μ and Σ^{-1}.

6.7.29 Suppose $Y \sim N(\theta, 1)$ and $f(\theta)$ is uniform over $\Re$. Let $\alpha \equiv \theta^2$ be the quantity of interest (see Walley 1991, p. 231).

(a) Find $f(\theta|y)$.

(b) Find $f(\alpha|y)$.

(c) Under the quadratic loss function $C(\hat{\alpha}, \alpha) = (\hat{\alpha} - \alpha)^2$, find the Bayesian point estimate $\hat{\alpha}$ of α.

(d) Find the risk function $R(\hat{\alpha}; \alpha) \equiv E_{Y|\alpha}[C(\hat{\alpha}; \alpha)]$.

(e) Let $\tilde{\alpha} = y^2 - 1$. Find $R(\tilde{\alpha}|\alpha)$.

(f) What do you conclude from (d) and (e)?

6.7.30 Suppose $Y_t \sim$ i.n.i.d. $N(\theta_t, 1)$ $(t = 1, 2, \ldots, T)$ and $\theta_t \sim$ i.i.d. $N(\mu, \sigma^2)$. Using the non-informative prior $f(\mu, \sigma) \propto \sigma^{-1}$, show that the joint posterior distribution for μ and σ^2 is proper whatever the observed data.

6.7.31 Let Y_t $(t = 1, 2, \ldots, T)$ be a random sample from a $N(\theta, \sigma^2)$ distribution with σ^2 *known*. Consider the *balanced loss function* (see Zellner 1994):

$$C(\hat{\theta}, \theta) = w\left[\sum_{t=1}^{T} (Y_t - \hat{\theta})^2\right] + (1 - w)(\hat{\theta} - \theta)^2$$

$$= w[\nu s^2 + (\hat{\theta} - \overline{Y})^2] + (1 - w)(\hat{\theta} - \theta)^2.$$

Suppose your prior distribution for θ is $N(\underline{\mu}, \sigma^2/T)$.

(a) Find the Bayesian point estimate of θ (denote it by $\hat{\theta}$).

(b) Find the risk function for $\hat{\theta}$.

6.7.32 Suppose $\theta \sim N_3(0_3, \underline{\omega} I_3)$ and $Y|\theta \sim N_3(\theta, I_3)$, where $\underline{\omega} > 0$ is given.

(a) Find the joint distribution of θ and Y.

(b) Find the conditional distribution of θ given $Y = y$.

(c) Let $\hat{\theta}_1 = Y$ and $\hat{\theta}_2 = E(\theta|Y)$ be two estimators of θ. Comment on the admissibility of $\hat{\theta}_1$ and $\hat{\theta}_2$ under the loss function

$C(\hat{\theta}, \theta) = (\hat{\theta} - \theta)'(\hat{\theta} - \theta)$.

(d) Find the following distributions:

(1) $X \equiv \theta'\theta/\underline{\omega}$

(2) $W \equiv Y'Y/(\underline{\omega} + 1)$

(3) $\omega^{-1}(\underline{\omega} + 1)\theta'\theta$ given $Y = y$

(4) $Y'Y$ given θ

(e) Define $Z \equiv \theta'\theta[(\underline{\omega} + 1)/\underline{\omega}] + Y'Y + 2\theta'Y$. Is $Z \sim \chi^2(6)$?

(f) Define $V \equiv X/W$. Is $V \sim F(3, 3)$?

6.7.33 Consider a test for the presence of a disease. A result "positive" (+) indicates that disease is present; a result "negative" (−) indicates that the disease is absent. Of course the test is not perfect. The *specificity* of the test is the probability of a "positive" result conditional on the disease being present; it is .98. The *sensitivity* of the test is the probability of a "negative" result conditional on the disease being absent; it is .90. The *incidence* of the disease is the probability that the disease is present in a randomly selected individual; it is .005. Denote specificity by p, sensitivity by q, and incidence by π. Suppose the test is administered to a randomly selected individual.

(a) Develop an expression for the probability of disease conditional on a "positive" outcome.

(b) Develop an expression for the probability of disease conditional on a "negative" outcome.

(c) Evaluate these expressions using the values given previously.

6.7.34 Consider Exercise 6.1.11.

(a) Find the MLE in (a) through (c).

(b) Find the $f(\theta, x|y)$. Does $f(\theta, x|y)$ depend on which definition of the likelihoods in Exercise 6.1.11 is used?

6.7.35 Suppose $Y_t|\theta, \tau$ $(t = 1, 2, \ldots, T) \sim$ i.i.d. $N(\theta, 1)$ and $f(\theta|\tau^2) = N(0, \tau^2)$.

(a) Find the marginal distribution of Y.

(b) The idea of using the marginal distribution in (a) to estimate τ underlies the so-called *empirical Bayes approach*. The related so-called *Type II maximum likelihood estimator* is defined to be the value of τ^2 that maximizes the marginal likelihood in (a). Find the Type II ML estimator of τ^2 and comment on its sampling properties.

6.7.36 (Hierarchical Modelling) Consider Exercise 6.7.35 and add the specification that $f(\tau)$ is an improper uniform distribution over $(0, \infty)$.

(a) Find $f(\theta|y, \tau^2)$

(b) Find $f(\theta|y)$.

6.7.37 Show that a scalar posterior mean based on a proper prior cannot be an unbiased estimator of θ (see Casella and Berger 1990, pp. 343–344 or Lehmann 1983, pp. 244–245) except in trivial problems in which the parameter can be estimated perfectly that is, when $E_\theta E_{Y|\theta}([E(\theta|y) - \theta]^2) = 0$.

6.7.38 Let Y_t $(t = 1, 2, \ldots, T) \sim$ i.i.d. $N(\theta, \sigma^2)$, where σ^2 is known. Hence, $\bar{Y} \sim N(\theta, \sigma^2/T)$ is sufficient for θ. Let $f(\theta)$ be an arbitrary prior for θ for which all the integrals below exist. Define:

$$m(y) = \int_{-\infty}^{\infty} \phi(\bar{y}|\theta, \sigma^2/T) f(\theta)\, d\bar{y}, \tag{6.7.92}$$

$$g(y) = -\frac{\partial \ln[m(y)]}{\partial y}. \tag{6.7.93}$$

Show (see Pericchi and Smith 1992):

(a) $E(\theta|y) = \bar{y} - \dfrac{\sigma^2 g(y)}{T}$

(b) $\mathrm{Var}(\theta|y) = \dfrac{\sigma^2}{T} - \dfrac{\sigma^4}{T^2}\left[\dfrac{\partial g(y)}{\partial y}\right]$

6.7.39 Given a prior density $f(\theta)$ and a likelihood $\mathscr{L}(\theta; y)$, where θ is a scalar, find the Bayesian point estimate corresponding to the loss function

$$C(\hat{\theta}, \theta) = \begin{Bmatrix} d, & \text{if } |\hat{\theta} - \theta| \geq c \\ 0, & \text{if } |\hat{\theta} - \theta| < c \end{Bmatrix}, \tag{6.7.94}$$

where c and d are known positive constants. (Note this is a generalization of Exercise 6.7.13 both in terms of the sampling distribution and the loss function.)

6.7.40 Suppose Y_t $(t = 1, 2, \ldots, T) \sim$ i.i.d. $N(\theta, 1)$. Consider the improper prior $f(\theta) \propto \exp(\theta^4)$. Show that $f(\theta|y)$ is improper for all $1 \leq T < \infty$ (Lehmann 1983, p. 481, Exercise 7.7).

6.7.41 Suppose the p.d.f. of Y given θ is $f(y|\theta)$. Let $W = [Z, X]'$ be a sufficient statistic for θ, and suppose X is ancillary for θ. If a statistic X is ancillary for a parameter θ, then $f(x|\theta) = f(x)$, and hence, $f(\theta|x) = f(\theta)$, where $f(\theta)$ is a prior density (Kadane and Seidenfeld 1990, p. 331).

(a) Show: $f(\theta|y) \propto f(z|x, \theta) f(\theta)$.

(b) The statistic Z is said to be *suppressible in the presence of X for θ* iff X is ancillary and $f(z|x, \theta) = f(z|\theta)$. Suppose Z is suppressible in the presence of X for θ. Show: $f(\theta|y) \propto f(\theta|z)$.

(c) Suppose Z is suppressible in the presence of X for θ. Show that Z is sufficient for θ.

6.7.42 Suppose $Y|\theta \sim N(\theta, 1)$, $\theta \sim N(0, 1)$, and $C(\hat{\theta}, \theta) = (\hat{\theta} - \theta)^2 \exp(3\theta^2/4)$. (Berger 1985, p. 254)

(a) Show: $f(\theta|y) = \phi(\theta|\frac{1}{2}y, \frac{1}{2})$.

(b) Show: the Bayesian point estimate is $\hat{\theta} = 2y$.

(c) Show: $E_{Y|\theta}[C(\hat{\theta}, \theta)] = (\theta^2 + 4)\exp(3\theta^2/4)$.

(d) Let $\tilde{\theta} = y$. Show: $E_{Y|\theta}[C(\tilde{\theta}, \theta)] = \exp(3\theta^2/4)$.

(e) What do you conclude from (c) and (d)? What is going on?

6.7.43 Consider an integral of the form:

$$i = \int_{-\infty}^{\infty} b(\theta)\exp[-Ta(\theta)]\,d\theta. \tag{6.7.95}$$

Taking a second-order Taylor series expansion of $a(\theta)$ around an (assumed) interior maximum $\hat{\theta} \equiv \operatorname{argmax}\{a(\theta)\}$, and noting that the first derivative of $a(\theta)$ vanishes at $\hat{\theta}$, yields the quadratic approximation:

$$a(\theta) \sim a(\hat{\theta}) + \tfrac{1}{2}(\theta - \hat{\theta})'[H(\hat{\theta})](\theta - \hat{\theta}), \tag{6.7.96}$$

where $H(\theta)$ is the Hessian of $a(\theta)$. Laplace (1847) suggested a method (see DeBruijn 1961, Chapter 4; and Wong 1989) to approximating integral (6.7.95) which amounts to substituting (6.7.96) into (6.7.95) and integrating to obtain an approximation $\hat{i}$. *Laplace's method* usually results in a reasonable approximation whenever the $-a(\theta)$ is unimodal or at least has a dominant peak at an interior maximum. Under fairly weak conditions, it can be shown that

$$\hat{i} = i[1 + O(T^{-1})]. \tag{6.7.97}$$

Using properties of the multivariate normal density, show:

$$\hat{i} = b(\hat{\theta})\exp[-Ta(\hat{\theta})]\left(\frac{2\pi}{T}\right)^{K/2}|-H(\hat{\theta})|^{-1/2}. \tag{6.7.98}$$

6.7.44 There are many ways of applying Laplace's method to integral (6.7.95) depending on the relevant definitions of $b(\theta)$ and $a(\theta)$, and the resulting approximation is *not* invariant to such changes. Demonstrate this lack of invariance by rewriting the integrand of (6.7.95) in the fully exponential form $\exp(-T[-T^{-1}\ln[b(\theta)] + a(\theta)])$, and then deriving the resulting Laplace approximation of (6.7.95). Broadly speaking, Laplace's Method performs best for a parameterization is which the posterior distribution is "nearly normal" (see Achcar and Smith 1990; Hills and Smith 1992, 1993; and Kass and Slate 1990, 1992). Also see Exercise 6.7.47.

6.7.45 Suppose $g(\theta) > 0$. How should you use the Tierney-Kadane method to approximate $\operatorname{Var}[g(\theta)|y]$? (Tierney et al. 1989b)

6.7.46 Suppose $g(\theta) > 0$ is monotonically increasing scalar function in θ. Use Laplace's method to obtain the marginal posterior density of $g(\theta)$. (Tierney et al. 1989a)

6.7.47 Suppose X_t $(t = 1, 2, \ldots, T) \sim \text{EXP}(\theta_1)$ and Y_t $(t = 1, 2, \ldots, T) \sim \text{EXP}(\theta_2)$. Let prior beliefs be represented by Jeffrey's prior: $f(\theta_1, \theta_2) \propto (\theta_1\theta_2)^{-1}$. Define $g(\theta_1, \theta_2) = \theta_1/\theta_2$. Show the following results of Achcar and Smith (1990).

(a) Show: $G \equiv E[g(\theta_1, \theta_2)|x, y] = T\bar{x}/[(T - 1)\bar{y}]$.

(b) Working in terms of the parameterization $\theta = [\theta_1, \theta_2]'$, show that the Tierney-Kadane approximation to G is

$$\hat{G}_\theta = \left(\frac{\bar{x}}{\bar{y}}\right)\left[\frac{T^{T-3/2}(T + 2)^{T+1/2}}{(T + 1)^{2T-1}}\right]. \tag{6.7.99}$$

(c) Define $\beta_i = \ln(\theta_i)$ $(i = 1, 2)$. The prior for θ implies $f(\beta_1, \beta_2) \propto$ constant. Working in terms of the parameterization $\beta = [\beta_1, \beta_2]'$, show that the Tierney-Kadane approximation to G is

$$\hat{G}_\beta = \left(\frac{\bar{x}}{\bar{y}}\right)\left[\frac{(T-1)^{T-3/2}(T+1)^{T+1/2}}{T^{2T-1}}\right]. \tag{6.7.100}$$

(d) Define $\lambda_1 = \theta_1/\theta_2$ and $\lambda_2 = \theta_1$. The prior for implies $f(\lambda_1, \lambda_2) \propto (\lambda_1\lambda_2)^{-1}$. Working in terms of the parameterization $\lambda = [\lambda_1, \lambda_2]'$, show that the Tierney-Kadane approximation to G is

$$\hat{G}_\lambda = \left(\frac{\bar{x}}{\bar{y}}\right)\left[\frac{T^{T+1/2}(T+1)^{T-3/2}}{(T-1)^{T-1/2}(T+2)^{T-1/2}}\right]. \tag{6.7.101}$$

(e) Cox and Reid (1987) advocate using parameterizations for which the information matrix is block diagonal. This recommendation leads to $\alpha_1 = \theta_1/\theta_2$ and $\alpha_2 = \theta_1^2/\alpha_1$. The prior for θ implies $f(\alpha_1, \alpha_2) \propto (\alpha_1\alpha_2)^{-1}$. Working in terms of the parameterization $\alpha = [\alpha_1, \alpha_2]'$, show that the Tierney-Kadane approximation to G is

$$\hat{G}_\alpha = \left(\frac{\bar{x}}{\bar{y}}\right)\left[\frac{(T+1)^{2T-1}}{T^{T-1/2}(T+2)^{T-1/2}}\right]. \tag{6.7.102}$$

(f) The relative quality of these approximations depends only on T, not on $\bar{x}/\bar{y}$. Tabulate the percentage error, that is, $(\hat{G} - G)/G$ of each for $T = 2, 3, \ldots, 10$. Note that $\hat{G}_\beta$, the parameterization for which Jeffreys' prior (6.8.2) is locally uniform, is best.

6.7.48 Derive each of the following indefinite integrals, where c is an arbitrary constant:

(a) $\displaystyle\int \exp(ax)\,dx = a^{-1}\exp(ax) + c.$

(b) $\displaystyle\int x\exp(ax)\,dx = \left(\frac{ax-1}{a^2}\right)\exp(ax) + c.$

(c) $\displaystyle\int x^2\exp(ax)\,dx = \left(\frac{ax^2-2x+2}{a^2}\right)\exp(ax) + c.$

(d) $\displaystyle\int x^3\exp(ax)\,dx = a^{-1}\left(x^3 - \left[\frac{3}{a}\right]x^2 + \left[\frac{6}{a^2}\right]x - \frac{6}{a^3}\right)\exp(ax) + c.$

6.7.49 For $a > 0$, $b > 0$, and $c > 0$, show:

(a) $\displaystyle\int_0^\infty x^{b-1}\exp(-ax^c)\,dx = \frac{1}{ca^{b/c}}\Gamma\left(\frac{b}{c}\right)$

(b) $\displaystyle\int_0^\infty x^{-(b+1)}\exp(-ax^{-c})\,dx = \frac{1}{ca^{b/c}}\Gamma\left(\frac{b}{c}\right)$

6.7.50 Consider Example 6.7.2 and define

$$z = \begin{bmatrix} \theta_1 - \underline{\mu} \\ y - \theta_1\iota_T \end{bmatrix}, \tag{6.7.103}$$

$$\Sigma = \begin{bmatrix} \underline{h}^{-1} & 0_T' \\ 0_T & \theta_2^{-1}I_T \end{bmatrix}, \tag{6.7.104}$$

$$A = \begin{bmatrix} \dfrac{\underline{h}}{\bar{h}} & -\left(\dfrac{\theta_2}{\bar{h}}\right)\iota_T' \\ \iota_T & I_T \end{bmatrix}. \tag{6.7.105}$$

(a) Show (see Hamilton 1994):

$$\underline{h}(\theta_1 - \underline{\mu})^2 + \theta_2(y - \theta_1 \iota_T)'(y - \theta_1 \iota_T) = z'\Sigma^{-1}z = z_*'\Sigma_*^{-1}z_*, \tag{6.7.106}$$

where

$$z_* = Az = \begin{bmatrix} \theta_1 - \overline{\mu} \\ y - \underline{\mu}\iota_T \end{bmatrix}, \tag{6.7.107}$$

$$\Sigma_* = A\Sigma A' = \begin{bmatrix} \overline{h}^{-1} & 0_T' \\ 0_T & \theta_2^{-1}(I_T + \underline{h}^{-1}\iota_T\iota_T) \end{bmatrix}. \tag{6.7.108}$$

(b) Use (6.7.106) to derive (6.7.21b).

6.8 Choice of Prior and Bayesian Sensitivity Analysis

The central formalization of ignorance thus remains the central object of a continuing quest by the knights of the Bayesian round table: inspiring them to imaginative feats of daring, while remaining, perhaps, forever unattainable.
—Dawid (1977b, p. 235)

No sensible absolute way to define noninformative is likely to ever be found, and often the most natural ways give the silliest answers.
—Berger and Bernardo (1992a, p. 38)

We have to learn ... that the prime virtue of any econometric procedure is robustness.
—Robert Solow in Klamer (1984, p. 145)

Many non-Bayesians admit that the Bayesian development of point estimation in the last section offers an attractive theoretical package. They remain skeptical, however, of whether pragmatic considerations of implementation render such an ideal unattainable, and hence, unsatisfactory as a goal for empirical researchers. Two elements of the Bayesian approach stand out for attack: the prior distribution and the loss function. Because the Bayesian approach provides explicit roles for both, these are obvious places to attack it. Because Section 6.7 took both these ingredients as given, it seems appropriate to address their choice now. The discussion of this section has six main points, the last of which is Bayesian sensitivity analysis.

First, a brief, general remark. Classical point estimates are often obtainable in a Bayesian framework by appropriate choice of prior distribution and loss function, possibly as limiting cases. In fact, usually there are many ways of doing it. (Of course the interpretation and conclusions to be drawn from these point estimates differ under the competing paradigms.) Loosely speaking, the point is that the classical estimates are nested within the Bayesian approach. This puts classical advocates in a decidedly disadvantageous position: They must argue against all other Bayesian estimates just to get back to equal footing between the common estimates being offered. In other words, rather than the Bayesián being forced to deal with justifying their choice of prior and loss function used to produced these estimates, the Bayesian can similarly confront the classical advocate with the issue of ruling out all the other Bayesian estimates that could arise from different choices of prior and/or loss function? Indeed, the choice of prior and loss function required to rationalize a classical point estimate is often embarrassing to advocates of the classical approach.

In Bayesian eyes classical researchers do not avoid the choice of prior and loss function; rather, classical researchers implicitly make unconscious, automatic selections without reference to the problem context. Making explicit what is implicit in classical analysis is hardly a shortcoming of the Bayesian approach. In fact, Bayesians argue it is one of their advantages. Actual choice of prior distribution and loss function are daunting tasks. In part this explains why many argue that it is much easier to do statistical or econometric theory than to do compelling empirical work. The Bayesian approach highlights why the latter can be so elusive.

Second, consider the question of choice of loss function. This can be dispensed with fairly quickly. As the development of this entire chapter has shown, loss functions are key ingredients to both risk and posterior loss minimization. Choice of a particular loss function, say, quadratic loss, may be difficult to justify as universally compelling, but this is a problem faced by both groups. Although as a result, some statisticians argue against adopting a decision-making framework (e.g., Birnbaum 1977; and Tukey 1960), their arguments are unlikely to be compelling to the economist-personality of an econometrician.[33] The major value of explicit loss functions is the overall structure they provide to the discussion and their role in defining what is meant by a "good estimate." The important distinction between Bayesians and classicists is how to average loss, that is, whether to minimize $E_{\theta|y}[C(\hat{\theta}, \theta)]$ or $E_{Y|\theta}[C(\hat{\theta}, \theta)]$, respectively. In other words, the debate is over

$$\theta | Y = y \qquad \text{versus} \qquad Y | \theta. \tag{6.8.1}$$

A major contention of this text is that the choice posed in (6.8.1) underlies most statistical debates. Section 6.10 discusses the matter further.

Third, unlike the choice of loss function underlying classical concepts such as MSE, there appears to be no *explicit* choice of prior distribution confronting the classical researcher. Indeed many classical proponents

33. Furthermore, even if one accepts that *inference* (i.e., drawing conclusions from premises or evidence as defined by Walley 1991, p. 21) does not require a loss functions as does a decision (or action), then the Bayesian posterior distribution appears to provide all the requisite ingredients for "inference."

champion their cause by arguing that nondata-based information has no role in "science." This author, among many, finds it difficult to take these arguments seriously. How else does a researcher choose a window (likelihood function)? Such arguments are particularly unconvincing to researchers who do empirical work. Empirical work is a humbling experience, and few if any engage in it for long before recognizing the many ways non-data based information enters the analysis. Furthermore, such information is not just the by-product of economic theory; indeed, the latter is often disappointingly quiet on matters of importance to the empirical researcher.

Fourth, although space does not permit a detailed investigation of one essential ingredient of applied Bayesian analysis, namely, the prior elicitation procedure, a few remarks are in order.[34] When conjugate priors are employed, prior elicitation amounts to choice of the hyperparameters that characterize the prior family (e.g., $\underline{\alpha}$ and $\underline{\delta}$ in Example 6.7.1, $\underline{\mu}$ and $\underline{h}$ in Example 6.7.2, and $\underline{\mu}$, $\underline{h}$, $\underline{s}^{-2}$, and $\underline{\nu}$ in Example 6.7.4). These hyperparameters can either be chosen by direct introspection of beliefs concerning unknown parameters (e.g., see Exercise 6.7.3) or, often more appropriately, indirect introspection in terms of the marginal data p.f. (6.7.2). The latter approach emphasizes observables in the pure subjectivist spirit of Section 5.8.

Conjugate priors are often criticized for being motivated largely by computational considerations. Why should prior beliefs conform to the conjugate prior form? One reason is that natural conjugate priors have an interpretation in terms of a prior fictitious sample from the same process that gives rise to the likelihood function (recall Examples 6.7.5–6.7.7), and use of a conjugate prior in such cases corresponds to organizing prior beliefs by viewing the observable world through the same window being used for viewing the data at hand. There is no obligation to use only conjugate priors, and if for the problem at hand the prior information does not conform to a conjugate prior (e.g., because in the context of Example 6.7.4 prior beliefs concerning θ_1 are independent of prior beliefs concerning θ_2), then by all means dispense with the conjugate prior. Little can be said in general, however, concerning elicitation in such nonconjugate cases, which tend to be very problem-specific. Furthermore, in problems with high-dimensional parameter spaces, prior elicitation tends to be

34. For detailed discussion see Crowder (1992), Dickey and Freeman (1975), Hogarth (1975), Kadane (1980), Kadane et al. (1980), Leamer (1992), Pilz (1991), Raiffa and Schlaifer (1961, pp. 58–69), Savage (1971), Walley (1991, especially pp. 167–206, 622–631), Winkler (1967; 1972, pp. 182–192) and Winkler et al. (1978). For an excellent example of a serious interrogation of prior beliefs in a substantive problem, see McCulloch and Rossi (1991).

both more difficult, and unfortunately, more important. Such considerations are strong motivation for use of parsimonious windows.

Fifth, although admitting the need to use nondata-based information in their research, many researchers (both Bayesian and non-Bayesian) argue that its role should in some sense be minimized. This has been particularly the case among "objective Bayesians," and has led to an immense literature on the development of "noninformative" (alternative synonyms are "diffuse," or "vague") priors. Some have treated "noninformative" in an absolute sense, but most tend to do so in a relative sense, relative to what the researcher expects to learn from the data.

The use of "noninformative" priors is probably the most controversial issue in Bayesian statistics with at least as much disagreement among Bayesians as between Bayesian and classical statisticians.[35] In a sense the issue turns on whether it is ever possible to be in a state of "total ignorance." As Leamer (1978, p. 61) notes regarding "ignorance": "Like the issue of original sin, this is a question that remains unresolved, that attracts a fair amount of theological interest, but that seems rather remote from the concerns of the man on the street."

The origin of this question goes back to Bayes and Laplace, who suggested the *Principle of Insufficient Reason*, that is, ignorance should be represented by a probability function that assigns equal probability to all events. Unfortunately, there can be no such probability function, because if mutually exclusive events A and B are assigned equal probability, the event $A \cup B$ is implicitly assigned twice the probability. Similarly, if a continuous random variable θ is assigned a uniform distribution as a reflection of ignorance, then $\gamma = \theta^{-1}$ has a nonuniform p.d.f. proportional to γ^{-2}. In other words, the "noninformative" prior for θ implies an "informative" prior for γ! In a situation of "real ignorance" there is insufficient reason to select one event space rather than another, or one parameterization rather than another. Thus, the Principle of Insufficient Reason is insufficient to determine probabilities.

One way of interpreting a state of prior ignorance is in a relative rather than absolute sense. In other words, a "noninformative" prior should yield a posterior distribution that reflects essentially only the sample information embodied in the likelihood function. This can happen (see Example 6.7.4) when faced with a "large" sample, but what constitutes a "large"

35. For example, see Akaike (1980), Barnett (1982, pp. 206–211), Berger and Bernardo (1992a), Bernardo (1979), Berger (1985), Box and Tiao (1973), Dawid (1977a), Dawid et al. (1973), DeGroot (1970), Fraser et al. (1985), Jaynes (1980), Jeffreys (1961), Kass (1990), Leamer (1978, pp. 61–63), Lindley (1965), Pericchi and Walley (1991), Walley (1991, pp. 226–235), Stone (1964), Winkler (1972, pp. 198–204) or Zellner (1971, pp. 41–53; 1977).

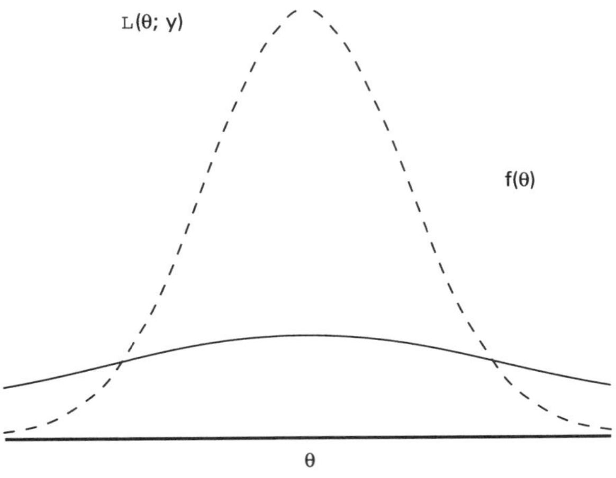

Figure 6.8.1
Example of a relatively "noninformative" prior

sample depends in part on how dogmatic is the prior.[36] What is really desired is a prior that is "flat" in the region where the likelihood is negligible so that the latter dominates in calculation of the posterior (see Figure 6.8.1). In such cases the prior can be treated as essentially uniform, and the dominance of the data is known as the *Principle of Stable Estimation.* Of course, presumably a prior is chosen before observing the data, and hence, strictly speaking the only way to guarantee that the likelihood will dominate is to choose again the prior to be flat everywhere.

As previously noted, if "noninformative" is interpreted as implying a uniform prior, then the implied prior for any nonlinear reparameterization is not uniform, suggesting an informative prior is being used for this alternative parameterization.[37] In an attempt to overcome such problems, Jeffreys sought a general rule to follow for choosing a prior so that the same posterior inferences were obtained regardless of the parameterization chosen. Jeffreys (1946, 1961) makes a general (but not dogmatic) argument in favor of choosing a "noninformative" prior proportional to the square root of the information matrix, that is,

36. Under fairly weak regularity conditions (e.g., the prior does not depend on sample size), in large samples (i.e. as $T \rightarrow \infty$), the likelihood dominates a nondogmatic prior. Because under general conditions the likelihood function assumes a normal shape as T gets large, with center at the ML estimate, tne posterior p.d.f. will be normal in large samples with mean equal to the ML estimate. See Blackwell and Dubins (1962), Edwards et al. (1963, pp. 201–208), Jeffreys (1961, Section 3.6), Lindley (1961), and Zellner (1971, pp. 31–34) for more details.

37. Lack of invariance to reparameterization plagues many areas of classical statistics as well as Bayesian statistics (e.g., unbiased estimation, efficient estimation and shortest confidence intervals). Invariance sounds nice, but it often entails unfortunate and unintended side consequences.

$$f(\theta) \propto |J(\theta)|^{1/2}, \tag{6.8.2}$$

where $J(\theta) \equiv E_{Y|\theta}[-\partial^2 L(\theta)/\partial\theta\,\partial\theta']$ is the *information matrix of the sample* defined in (6.5.5). Prior (6.8.2) has the desirable feature that if the model is reparameterized by a one-to-one transformation, say $\alpha = h(\theta)$, then choosing the "noninformative" prior

$$f(\alpha) \propto |E_{Y|\alpha}[-\partial^2 L(\alpha)/\partial\alpha\partial\alpha']|^{1/2} \tag{6.8.3}$$

will lead to identical posterior inferences as (6.8.2) (see Exercise 6.8.3). Priors adopted according to (6.8.3) or (6.8.2) are said to follow *Jeffreys' Rule*.

Jeffreys' prior has an established history (also see Hartigan 1964, 1965; Perks 1947; and Welsch and Peters 1963), but it is a history plagued with ambiguities. To some the associated invariance arguments are compelling, but the motivating arguments for invariance are not as sacrosanct as they appear at first. The claim to "noninformativeness" for Jeffreys' prior rests on various arguments using Shannon's information criterion as a measure of distance between densities (see Lindley 1961; and Zellner 1971, p. 50–53).[38] There is a fair amount of agreement that such priors may be reasonable in one-parameter problems, but substantially less agreement (including Jeffreys) in multiple parameter problems. Use of Jeffreys' prior in the case of dependent observations is fairly unusual. For an exception, see Zellner (1971, pp. 216–220) in the stationary case, and Phillips (1991), who dwells on the nonstationary case.[39] Note also that priors such as (6.8.2) are usually (but not always; see Example 6.8.1) *improper*, that is,

$$\int_{\Re^K} f(\theta)\, d\theta \to \infty. \tag{6.8.4}$$

Such impropriety can endow a posterior computed in the usual fashion using Bayes Theorem with a variety of disturbing properties (e.g., in some cases the posterior may also be improper). See Box and Tiao (1973, pp. 25–60), Jeffreys (1961), Phillips (1991), and Zellner (1971, pp. 41–53) for further discussion.

Because Jeffreys' prior is proportional to the square root of the information matrix, it depends on the *expected* information in the sample. The dependency of Jeffreys' prior on a sampling theory expectation makes it

38. See Zellner (1977) for other information formulations of "noninformative" priors.

39. Note that when the observations are i.i.d. it is not important whether Jeffreys prior is taken to be proportional to the square root of the information matrix of a single observation or of the entire sample. In the dependent case, the distinction is crucial because the latter choice makes the prior dependent on sample size.

sensitive to a host of problems related to the Likelihood Principle.[40] For example, if applied to different sampling experiments involving proportional likelihoods (e.g., binomial versus negative binomial as in Example 6.2.4), then different noninformative priors are suggested, and hence, different posteriors arise. For another example, suppose y_t corresponds to an asset price in a market subject to "circuit breakers" that activate whenever the cumulative price changes over some period exceed predetermined limits. The *ex ante* sampling distribution will change to take into account the potential censoring, and so (in general) Jeffreys' prior is different than when no potential censoring is present. Whether a market breaker is ever activated in the data at hand is *not* relevant. Rather the mere possibility of censoring, as opposed to its occurrence, is relevant. It is not hard to imagine that in almost any asset market, there is some finite change in price over the course of the day that would trigger market closure, if not catastrophe.

For the sake of concreteness, consider the following examples involving "noninformative" priors.

Example 6.8.1 Consider Example 6.7.1 and suppose prior p.d.f. (6.7.4) is uniform, i.e. $\underline{\alpha} = \underline{\delta} = 1$, or in terms of the equivalent prior sample information interpretation, $\underline{\alpha} - 1 = 0$ successes in a sample of $\underline{T} = \underline{\alpha} + \underline{\delta} - 2 = 0$. Combined with a sample in which m successes are observed in T trials, this prior implies a posterior mean (6.7.52) equalling $(m + 1)/(T + 2)$ and a posterior mode (6.7.54) equalling the ML estimate $\bar{y} = m/T$.

In contrast Villegas (1977) recommends setting $\underline{\alpha} = \underline{\delta} = 0$ in which case prior p.d.f. (6.7.4) is improper and equals

$$f(\theta) \propto \theta^{-1}(1 - \theta)^{-1}, \tag{6.8.5}$$

which is U-shaped with a minimum at $\theta = \frac{1}{2}$, and which approaches infinity as $\theta \to 0$ and as $\theta \to 1$. This prior is distinctly different than the uniform case. Note, however, that the corresponding posterior p.d.f. is a proper beta p.d.f. (provided $0 < m < T$) with $\bar{\alpha} = m$ and $\bar{\delta} = T - m$. Because in this case the posterior mean (6.7.52) equals the ML estimate $\bar{y} = m/T$, some might argue that prior (6.8.5) is "noninformative."

Box and Tiao (1973, pp. 34–36, 45) advocate a different "noninformative" prior: beta with $\underline{\alpha} = \underline{\delta} = \frac{1}{2}$. This yields a beta posterior for θ with $\bar{\alpha} = m + \frac{1}{2}$ and $\bar{\delta} = T - m + \frac{1}{2}$. In this case the posterior mean is $(m + \frac{1}{2})/(T + 1)$ and the posterior mode is $(m - \frac{1}{2})/(T - 1)$. The rationale for this prior being "noninformative" is that the likelihood is approximately *data translated* in $\alpha = \sin^{-1}(\theta^{1/2})$ (that is, the location but not the shape of the

40. For example, see the comments in Poirier (1991d) on Phillips (1991).

likelihood depends on α). This choice of prior also satisfies Jeffreys Rule. Finally, Zellner (1977) takes an information-theoretic approach which leads to the proper prior: $f(\theta) = 1.61856\ \theta^{\theta}(1-\theta)^{1-\theta}$, $0 \le \theta \le 1$. See Geisser (1984) for detailed discussion of the binary case, and see Berger and Bernardo (1992b) and Poirier (1994a) for discussions of the multinomial case.

Example 6.8.2 In the spirit of Example 6.7.6, if we use an "equivalent prior sample size" interpretation of a non-informative prior for the normal sampling problem (with known variance) in Example 6.7.2, then putting $\underline{T}$ in (6.7.40) equal to zero implies $\underline{h}^{-1} = \infty$ and an improper prior distribution $f(\theta) \propto$ constant, $-\infty < \theta < \infty$. In the limit, however, posterior distribution (6.7.22) is proper:

$$\theta|y \sim N(\bar{y}, h^{-1}). \tag{6.8.6}$$

Although (6.8.6) would imply a Bayesian point estimate of $\hat{\theta} = \bar{y}$ for θ under loss functions (6.7.49), (6.7.50) with $c_1 = c_2$, or (6.7.51), the interpretation of (6.8.6) is Bayesian. According to (6.8.6), θ is a normal random variable with fixed mean $\bar{y}$ and variance h^{-1}, whereas the standard classical view is that $\bar{y}$ is a normal random variable with fixed mean θ and variance h^{-1}. In other words, letting $Z \equiv h^{1/2}(\theta - \bar{y})$, according to Bayesian posterior analysis, $Z|y \sim N(0, 1)$, whereas according to standard classical analysis. $Z|\theta \sim N(0, 1)$. While the standard normal distribution $N(0, 1)$ is involved in both cases, Z is random for different reasons under the two paradigms.

Example 6.8.3 Reconsider Example 6.7.4 but with the normal-gamma prior distribution replaced by the "noninformative" prior

$$f(\theta_1, \theta_2) \propto \theta_2^{-1}. \tag{6.8.7}$$

Prior density (6.8.7) can be rationalized by: (a) arguing prior beliefs regarding θ_1 and θ_2 are independent, and (b) applying Jeffreys' Rule separately to θ_1 and θ_2.[41] Using (6.7.18) and (6.7.19), prior (6.8.7) implies the posterior density

$$f(\theta_1, \theta_2|y) \propto [\theta_2]^{2(T-3)/2} \exp(-\tfrac{1}{2}\theta_2 \nu s^2)\phi(\theta_1|\bar{y}, [T\theta_2]^{-1}), \tag{6.8.8a}$$

$$\propto [\theta_2]^{1/2[(T-1)-1]} \exp(-\tfrac{1}{2}\theta_2\{\nu s^2 + T(\theta_1 - \bar{y})^2\}, \tag{6.8.8b}$$

41. Because the information matrix in the case at hand is given by (6.6.22), applying Jeffreys' Rule jointly to θ_1 and θ_2 results in the improper prior density $f(\theta_1, \theta_2) \propto \theta_2$. This prior density gives the "wrong" (i.e., nonclassical) degrees of freedom and is not advocated by most "noninformative" Bayesians, including Jeffreys (see Zellner 1971, pp. 52–53). Yet another "noninformative" prior can be obtained by taking the limit of the informative normal-gamma natural conjugate prior density (6.7.23) as $\underline{T} \to 0$ (i.e., $\underline{q} \to \infty$) and $\underline{\nu} \to 0$, yielding the improper density $f(\theta_1, \theta_2) \propto \theta_2^{1/2}$. This prior is also seldom used, again in part because it gives the "wrong" degrees of freedom.

which is recognized (e.g., use Equation 6.7.23) as the kernel of the normal-gamma distribution $NG(\bar{y}, T^{-1}, s^2, T-1)$. The marginal posterior distribution of θ_1 corresponding to prior density (6.8.7) is $t(\bar{y}, s^2/T, T-1)$. Therefore, according to (6.8.8), θ_1 is a random variable with a t-distribution with fixed mean $\bar{y}$, variance h^{-1} and $T-1$ degrees of freedom, whereas the standard classical view would be that $\bar{Y}$ is a normal random variable with a t-distribution with fixed mean θ_1, variance h^{-1}, and $T-1$ degrees of freedom. In other words, letting $\tau \equiv T^{1/2}(\theta - \bar{y})/s$, according to Bayesian posterior analysis, $\tau | y \sim t(0, 1, \nu)$, whereas according to standard classical analysis. $\tau | \theta_1 \sim t(0, 1, \nu)$. Although the Student-$t$ distribution $t(0, 1, \nu)$ with ν degrees of freedom is involved in both cases, τ is random for different reasons under the two paradigms.

Some researchers view a prior as being noninformative if it yields a proper posterior which for "reasonable" loss functions yield a point estimate equal to the ML estimate. Such situations arose in Examples 6.8.1–6.8.3. Indeed a flat prior and an "all-or-nothing" loss function imply that the Bayesian point estimate, that is, posterior mode, is also the MLE. The motivation for such an interpretation of "noninformative" is that the classical ML point estimate is usually viewed as reflecting only "objective" sample information. A tongue-in-cheek Bayesian who held this view might further argue that a non-informative prior should reflect "ignorance," and what could be more ignorant than a prior that produces the point estimate of a maximum likelihoodlum?

Table 6.8.1 (like Table 6.7.1) summarizes the "noninformative" results for sampling from a univariate normal distribution with a "noninformative" prior: in Case 1 the mean is unknown and the precision is known (Example 6.8.2), in Case 2 the mean is known and the precision is unknown (not studied), and in Case 3 both the mean and precision are unknown (Example 6.8.3). Table 6.8.2 contains the analogous three cases for a *multivariate* normal distribution in which the "noninformative" Jeffreys' prior $f(\Sigma^{-1}) \propto |\Sigma|^{(M+1)/2}$ is used.

The next example involves the use of partial information that dogmatically rules out some parts of the permissible parameter space, but is "noninformative" over other parts.

Example 6.8.4 (Geweke 1986) Consider a random sample Y_t $(t = 1, 2, \ldots, T)$ from a $N(\theta, T)$ population, where it is known with certainty that $\theta \geq 0$. It is straightforward to show that the ML estimate of θ is

$$\hat{\theta}_{ML} = \begin{Bmatrix} \bar{y}, & \text{if } \bar{y} \geq 0 \\ 0, & \text{if } \bar{y} < 0 \end{Bmatrix}. \tag{6.8.9}$$

Consider the "noninformative prior" over $\Re^+$:

Table 6.8.1
"Noninformative" analysis: $Y_t\ (t = 1, 2, \ldots, T)|\mu, \sigma^{-2} \sim$ i.i.d. $N(\mu, \sigma^2)$

Prior	Hyperparameter updating	Posterior
Case 1: μ unknown, σ^{-2} known		
$f(\mu) \propto$ constant		$f(\mu\|y) = \phi(\mu\|\bar{y}, \sigma^2/T)$
Case 2: μ known, σ^{-2} unknown		
$f(\sigma^{-2}) \propto \sigma^2$	$\bar{v}\bar{s}^2 = vs^2 + T(\bar{y} - \mu)^2$ $\bar{v} = T$	$f(\sigma^{-2}\|y) = \gamma(\sigma^{-2}\|\bar{s}^{-2}, \bar{v})$
Case 3: μ unknown, σ^{-2} unknown		
$f(\mu, \sigma^{-2}) \propto \sigma^2$	$\bar{v}_* = \bar{v} + 1$ $\bar{v}_*\bar{s}_*^2 = \bar{v}\bar{s}^2 + \bar{T}(\mu - \bar{\mu})^2$	$f(\mu, \sigma^{-2}\|y) = \phi(\mu\|\bar{y}, \sigma^2/\bar{T})\gamma(\sigma^{-2}\|\bar{s}^{-2}, \bar{v})$ $= f_t(\mu\|\bar{y}, \bar{s}^2/\bar{T}, \bar{v})\gamma(\sigma^{-2}\|\bar{s}_*^{-2}, \bar{v}_*)$

Table 6.8.2
"Noninformative" analysis: $Y_t\ (t = 1, 2, \ldots, T)|\mu, \Sigma^{-1} \sim$ i.i.d. $N_M(\mu, \Sigma)$

Prior	Hyperparameter updating	Posterior
Case 1: μ unknown, Σ^{-1} known		
$f(\mu) \propto$ constant		$f(\mu\|y) = \phi_M(\mu\|\bar{y}, T^{-1}\Sigma)$
Case 2: μ known, Σ^{-1} unknown		
$f(\Sigma^{-1}) \propto \|\Sigma^{-1}\|^{-(M+1)/2}$	$\bar{S} = S + T(\bar{y} - \mu)(\bar{y} - \mu)'$	$f(\Sigma^{-1}\|y) = W_M(\Sigma^{-1}\|\bar{S}^{-1}, T)$
Case 3: μ unknown, Σ^{-1} unknown		
$f(\mu, \Sigma^{-1}) \propto \|\Sigma^{-1}\|^{-(M+1)/2}$	$\bar{v}_* = \bar{v} + 1$ $\bar{S}_* = vS + \bar{T}(\mu - \bar{\mu})(\mu - \bar{\mu})'$	$f(\mu, \bar{\Sigma}^{-1}\|y) = \phi(\mu\|\bar{y}, \bar{T}^{-1}\Sigma) W_M(\Sigma^{-1}\|\bar{S}^{-1}, \bar{\omega})$ $= f_t(\mu\|\bar{y}, \bar{S}/\bar{T}, \bar{\omega}) W_M(\Sigma^{-1}\|\bar{S}_*^{-1}, \bar{\omega}_*)$

$$f(\theta) = \begin{Bmatrix} 1, & \text{if } \theta \geq 0 \\ 0, & \text{if } \theta < 0 \end{Bmatrix}. \tag{6.8.10}$$

Then the posterior distribution of θ is a truncated (on the left at zero) $N(\bar{y}, 1)$ distribution:

$$f(\theta|y) = \begin{Bmatrix} \dfrac{\phi(\theta|\bar{y}, 1)}{1 - \Phi(\bar{y})}, & \text{if } \theta \geq 0 \\ 0, & \text{if } \theta < 0 \end{Bmatrix}. \tag{6.8.11}$$

Under quadratic loss the Bayesian point estimate of is the posterior mean (Theorem 6.7.1a) given by

$$E(\theta|y) = \bar{y} + \left[\frac{\phi(\bar{y})}{1 - \Phi(\bar{y})}\right]. \tag{6.8.12}$$

(See Exercise 3.3.2a). Estimates (6.8.9) and (6.8.12) differ appreciably as shown in Table 6.8.3. The reader can judge which are more reasonable.

Unfortunately, there are many candidates for "noninformative" priors. In fact one problem is that there are too many candidates (e.g., Example

Table 6.8.3
Maximum likelihood estimate and posterior mean based on a random sample from a truncated standard normal distribution

$\bar{y}$	$\hat{\theta}_{ML}$	$E(\theta\|y)$
−4	0	.22561
−3	0	.28310
−2	0	.37322
−1	0	.52514
0	0	.79788
1	1	1.28760
2	2	2.05525
3	3	3.00444
4	4	4.00013

6.8.1 in the case of a Bernoulli random variable, and Berger and Bernardo 1989 in the case of the product of two means.) Another problem is that "noninformative" priors often have properties that seem rather non-Bayesian (e.g., they are often improper). Most of the suggested "noninformative" priors depend on some or all of the following: (a) the likelihood, (b) the sample size, (c) an expectation with respect to the sampling distribution, (d) the parameters of interest, and (e) whether the researcher is engaging in estimation, testing or predicting. Regarding (a), dependency on the form of the likelihood is common (e.g., conjugate priors, informative or otherwise), but some of the other dependencies are less compelling and can have disturbing consequences. Furthermore, to an objectivist who envisions θ as having meaning on its own, it is disturbing that a "non-informative" prior for θ requires so much information regarding the experiment or purpose of the research.

In summary, attempts to employ "non-informative" priors raise problems in Bayesian point estimation. Caution is in order (see Berger 1985, pp. 90, 231; and Lee 1989, p. 93). For whom such a state of affairs should be embarrassing is another question. Classical statisticians like to question Bayesians about the interpretation of improper priors. Some Bayesians argue that improper priors are merely a mathematical convenience for producing a proper posterior which reflects only the sample information embodied in the likelihood. Other Bayesians refuse to consider non-informative priors arguing that in a theory of learning one cannot learn anything starting from a state of "total ignorance." Indeed, under total ignorance the sign of a point estimate cannot be "surprising." Such Bayesians further argue that we are never in a state of total ignorance in the first place. It is ironic to employ so much information in specifying the likelihood, and then go to the other extreme to claim "no information" about the parameters that characterize the likelihood. Just because priors may be difficult to specify does not mean one should pick a "noninformative" prior. Furthermore, because the motivation for picking a noninformative prior is often to obtain estimates numerically equal to classical point estimates, any embarrassment that arises in the process merely reflects the unsoundness of classical techniques.

My advice in these treacherous waters is to use a "noninformative" prior only with great care, and never alone. I sometimes employ "noninformative" priors (e.g., see Koop and Poirier 1990, 1991, 1993; or Poirier 1991c, 1992b) together with informative priors, because I anticipate that researchers will query me about the robustness of my results relative to standard "noninformative" priors. In other words, I include "noninformative" priors in the class of priors over which I perform my sensitivity analysis, leading to the final, and major, issue discussed in this section.

There have been many criticisms of the "over-precision" demanded by probability elicitors such as de Finetti or Savage. Many Bayesians adhere to the Savage/de Finetti idealism, but temper it with pragmatism in implementation that is commonly referred to as *Bayesian sensitivity analysis*.[42] This text follows this pragmatic approach and the Pragmatic Principles of Model Building offered in Poirier (1988c) (see Section 10.4). Anybody who takes seriously the question of choosing a particular loss function or prior distribution in a particular problem finds the matter difficult, evidence again of why compelling empirical work is so daunting a task. An obvious approach to mitigating this problem is to try out different prior distributions and loss functions and see if they materially matter, that is, conduct a Bayesian sensitivity analysis. Here the focus is on sensitivity analysis with respect to the prior. Because the window is defined as being an entity about which there is intersubjective agreement (i.e., the window is expanded until intersubjective agreement is reached), sensitivity analysis with respect to the likelihood is postponed until Chapter 10.

Keep in mind that academic research is a public exercise. Even a "Savage-like" researcher with an infinite amount of time who is able to elicit his/her own coherent prior distribution, must realize that readers are likely to want to see analysis incorporating other priors as well. Such prior sensitivity analysis has a well established tradition in the Bayesian literature, for example, numerous writings of I. J. Good (e.g. Good 1983; Edwards et al. 1963; and Berger 1984, 1985, 1990). The tradition continues to

42. In contrast many others, going back as least as far as Keynes (1921), have attempted to formalize theories of imprecise probabilities in which precise probabilities may not exist even in principle. For an extensive discussion, see Walley (1991, especially pp. 43–51). Despite a great deal of "Bayesian-bashing," Walley (1991, pp. 253–258) admits that Bayesian sensitivity analysis is close to what he advocates.

flourish (e.g., Berger and Sellke 1987; Berger and Delampady 1987; Kass et al. 1989; Lavine 1991a, 1991c; Leamer 1978, 1982, 1983, 1984, 1985; McCulloch 1989; Pericchi and Walley 1991; Wasserman 1992; and Wasserman and Kadane 1992). Sensitivity analyses may be local or global, depending on how far away the researcher is willing to wander from a maintained prior. Sensitivity analyses can also be performed in reference to all statistical activities: design, estimation, testing and prediction. Often it addresses more than one of these activities (e.g., Ramsay and Novick 1980).

Conceptually, sensitivity analysis of the prior in an estimation context proceeds as follows. Given the likelihood $\mathscr{L}(\theta; y)$, consider a family of prior p.f. $\mathscr{F} = \{f(\theta|\xi), \xi \in \Xi\}$ defined parametrically by a set Ξ, and a loss function $C(\hat{\theta}, \theta)$. Given $\xi \in \Xi$, the optimal Bayesian point estimate is

$$\hat{\theta}(\xi) \equiv \underset{\hat{\theta} \in \Theta}{\operatorname{argmin}} \int_{\Theta} C(\hat{\theta}, \theta) \left[\frac{f(\theta|\xi)\mathscr{L}(\theta; y)}{f(y|\xi)} \right] d\theta, \tag{6.8.13}$$

where the marginal density of the data is

$$f(y|\xi) = \int_{\Theta} \mathscr{L}(\theta; y) f(\theta|\xi)\, d\theta. \tag{6.8.14}$$

Bayesian sensitivity analysis is simply a study of the variability of $\hat{\theta}_{\Xi} \equiv \{\hat{\theta}(\xi), \xi \in \Xi\}$. Often a natural metric in which to measure such variability is expected posterior loss:

$$\min_{\xi \in \Xi} c(\xi) \leq c(\xi) \leq \max_{\xi \in \Xi} c(\xi), \tag{6.8.15}$$

where the minimum loss yielded by $\hat{\theta}(\xi)$ is

$$c(\xi) \equiv \int_{\Theta} C[\hat{\theta}(\xi), \theta] \left[\frac{f(\theta|\xi)\mathscr{L}(\theta; y)}{f(y|\xi)} \right] d\theta. \tag{6.8.16}$$

If the variability in $\hat{\theta}_{\Xi}$ or the range (6.8.15) is judged acceptable for the purposes at hand, then further interrogation of prior beliefs is not required and a point estimate $\hat{\theta}(\xi)$ may be chosen without much concern, say by choosing $\xi \in \Xi$ based on ease of interpretation or computational considerations. If the variability in $\hat{\theta}_{\Xi}$ or the range (6.8.15) is judged unacceptable for the purposes at hand, then further interrogation of prior beliefs is required in the hope of better articulating the prior family $\mathscr{F}$. If a prior p.f. $f(\xi)$ can be articulated, then the problem reduces to a standard case in which a single known prior

$$f(\theta) = \int_{\Xi} f(\theta|\xi) f(\xi)\, d\xi \tag{6.8.17}$$

can be used. Such situations are known as *Bayesian hierarchical analysis* (see the seminal work of Lindley and Smith (1972) and Exercise 6.8.6).

The following example demonstrates these points, albeit admittedly in a very elementary context. More complex situations, still yielding analytical results, are discussed in Chapter 9. Poirier (1991a, 1991c) illustrates a case in which more brute force is required.

Example 6.8.5 Consider Example 6.8.2 involving a random sample of size T from a normal distribution with unknown mean θ_1 and *known* precision θ_2. Suppose simple quadratic loss is appropriate: $C(\hat{\theta}_1, \theta_1) = (\hat{\theta}_1 - \theta_1)^2$. Suppose prior (6.7.10) can be only partially articulated. Specifically, prior beliefs are centered over $\underline{\mu}$, but the strength if these priors beliefs are unclear. This suggests a prior family $\mathscr{F} = \{\phi(\theta_1 | \underline{\mu}, \xi^{-1}), \xi \in \Xi\}$, where $\Xi = \{\xi | 0 \leq \xi < \infty\}$. Given $\xi \in \Xi$, Theorem 6.7.1(a) implies that the Bayesian point estimate of θ_1 is posterior mean (6.7.13) with ξ replacing $\underline{h}$, that is,

$$\hat{\theta}_1(\xi) = \frac{\xi\underline{\mu} + h\bar{y}}{\xi + h}, \tag{6.8.18}$$

where $h = T\theta_2$. Then it is easy to see that the set $\hat{\theta}_{1,\Xi}$ of possible posterior means is simply the interval $[\underline{\mu}, \bar{y})$ if $\underline{\mu} < \bar{y}$, or $(\bar{y}, \underline{\mu}]$ if $\underline{\mu} > \bar{y}$. Note, however, that if the prior location $\underline{\mu}$ is also uncertain, then the posterior mean can be any real number.

If the articulation in Example 6.8.5 is not possible or the prior family $\mathscr{F}$ cannot be reduced by some other means, then the researcher must accept the fact that for the data at hand the point estimate of θ cannot be agreed upon. Sometimes the conclusion that the data at hand have not "confessed," and unfortunately there remains an unacceptable level of ambiguity, is a valuable message to convey to consumers of research.

The facility of which a Bayesian sensitivity analysis can be conducted is somewhat problem specific, and the presentation of such results often relies on artistic merits. Conveying to consumers of research the posterior robustness of a point estimate (as judged by Equation 6.8.14 or $\hat{\theta}_\Xi$) is easy when analytical results are available and when the class of priors $\mathscr{F}$ is easy to envision, and challenging otherwise. There remains much to be learned in this art—and the obvious avenue for such learning is increased activity in performing serious Bayesian empirical studies (not just textbook illustrations) as contained in Poirier (1991a).

Exercises

6.8.1 Suppose Y_t $(t = 1, 2, \ldots, T) \sim$ i.i.d. $\text{Po}(\theta)$ and that the prior distribution of θ is a gamma distribution with parameters $\underline{\alpha} > 0$ and $\underline{\beta} > 0$.

(a) Show that the posterior distribution of θ given the data is a gamma distribution with parameters $\bar{\alpha} = \underline{\alpha} + T\bar{y}$ and $\bar{\beta} = (\underline{\beta}^{-1} + T)^{-1}$.

(b) Derive the posterior distribution of θ under the Box-Tiao (1973) "noninformative" prior $f(\theta) \propto \theta^{1/2}$.

(c) Repeat (b) under the "non-informative" prior $f(\theta) \propto \sigma^{-1}$.

6.8.2 (DeGroot 1987) Suppose you employ two researchers, A and B, each of whom must estimate an unknown parameter $\theta > 0$ subject to the loss function $C(\hat{\theta}, \theta)$. Researcher A can observe a random variable X having the gamma distribution $G(\alpha, \beta)$, where $\alpha = 3$ and $\beta = \theta^{-1}$. Researcher B can observe a random variable Y having the Poisson distribution $\text{Po}(2\theta)$. In collecting one observation each, Researcher A observes $X = 2$ and Researcher B observes $Y = 3$. Under what conditions would you expect the two researchers to provide you with the same point and interval estimates of θ? Provide a cogent discussion of the issues involved.

6.8.3 Let $J_\theta(\theta)$ and $J_\alpha(\alpha)$ denote the information matrices in (6.8.2) and (6.8.3), respectively, and let $\partial h/\partial h$ denote the $K \times K$ Jacobian matrix of the transformation $\alpha = h(\theta)$.

(a) Show: $J_\theta(\theta) = [\partial h/\partial\theta] J_\alpha(\alpha) [\partial h/\partial\theta]'$.

(b) Use (a) to show: $|J_\theta(\theta)|^{1/2}\, d\theta = |J_\alpha(\alpha)|^{1/2}\, d\alpha$.

(c) Use (b) to demonstrate the invariance of posterior inferences when using Jeffreys' prior. In other words, show that a researcher who parameterizes the problem in terms of α and uses prior density (6.8.3) obtains the same posterior density as a researcher who parameterizes the problem in terms of θ, uses prior density (6.8.2) to obtain a posterior density for θ, and then transforms this posterior density according to $\alpha = h(\theta)$ to obtain a posterior density for α.

6.8.4 Derive the posterior distribution in Case 2 of Table 6.7.1.

6.8.5 (Multivariate Analogue of Example 6.8.3) Given $\theta = [\beta', \text{vech}(\Sigma^{-1})']'$, where β is $M \times 1$ and Σ is a $M \times M$ positive definite matrix, consider a random sample Y_t $(t = 1, 2, \ldots, T)$ from a $N_M(\mu, \Sigma)$ distribution. Define $y = [y_1, y_2, \ldots, y_T]'$ and

$$\bar{y} = \sum_{t=1}^{T} y_t, \tag{6.8.19}$$

$$S = \sum_{t=1}^{T} (y_t - \bar{y})(y_t - \bar{y})', \tag{6.8.20}$$

Suppose the prior density $f(\theta)$ is the Jeffreys' prior density:

$$f(\theta) \propto |\Sigma|^{(M+1)/2}. \tag{6.8.21}$$

Recall Definitions 3.5.1 and 3.5.4 of the Wishart and normal-Wishart distributions. Consider the natural conjugate priors for the three multivariate cases in Table 6.8.2.

(a) Derive the posterior distribution for Case 1.

(b) Derive the posterior distribution for Case 2.

(c) Derive the posterior distribution for Case 3 and verify the marginal posterior distributions for μ and Σ^{-1}.

6.8.6 Reconsider Example 6.7.2 with the following hierarchical structure:

$$Y_1, Y_2, \ldots, Y_T | \theta_1, \theta_2, \xi \sim N(\theta_1, \theta_2^{-1}), \tag{6.8.22}$$

$$\theta_1, \theta_2, \xi \sim N(\xi, \underline{h}^{-1}), \tag{6.8.23}$$

$$\xi \sim N(\underline{a}, \underline{b}^{-1}), \tag{6.8.24}$$

where θ_2, $\underline{h}$, $\underline{a}$, and $\underline{b}$ are known constants: $-\infty < \underline{a} < \infty$ and $0 < \theta_2, \underline{h}, \underline{b} < \infty$.

(a) Express Example 6.7.2 as a limiting case of the above hierarchical structure.

(b) Using this hierarchical structure, give an example of conditionally independent random variables.

(c) Find $f(y|\xi)$.

(d) Find $f(y)$.

(e) Find $f(\theta_1)$.

(f) Find $f(\theta_1|y, \xi)$.

(g) Find $f(\theta_1|y)$.

(h) Find $f(\xi|y)$.

6.8.7 Consider Example 6.8.5 and suppose $\xi \sim \gamma(\underline{a}, \underline{v})$, where $\underline{a}$ and $\underline{v}$ are known positive constants.

(a) Find $f(\theta_1|\underline{\mu})$.

(b) Find $f(\theta_1|y, \underline{\mu})$.

6.8.8 Consider Example 6.8.1. Suppose $T = 2$ and $m = 1$. Find $\text{Prob}(\theta \geq \frac{1}{2}|y)$ using Jeffreys' prior under (see Walley 1991, p. 229):

(a) binomial sampling

(b) negative binomial sampling

6.8.9 Suppose the parameter space is finite, i.e. $\Theta = \{\theta_1, \theta_2, \ldots, \theta_N\}$, and let $f(\theta)$ be a probability density on Θ. The *entropy* of $f(\theta)$, denoted $\text{Ent}(f)$, is defined as

$$\text{Ent}(f) = -\sum_{n=1}^{N} f(\theta_n)\ln[f(\theta_n)]. \tag{6.8.25}$$

If $f(\theta_n) = 0$, then define $f(\theta_n)\ln[f(\theta_n)] = 0$. Entropy is a widely accepted measure of the amount of uncertainty in the p.m.f. $f(\cdot)$ (see Jaynes 1968).

(a) Show that $\text{Ent}(f)$ is maximized by the discrete uniform mass p.m.f. $f(\theta_n) = N^{-1}$ ($n = 1, 2, \ldots, N$), and that the maximized value of entropy in this case is $\ln(N)$.

(b) Show that $\text{Ent}(f)$ is minimized by the "dogmatic" mass p.m.f. $f(\theta_n) = 1$ and $f(\theta_i) = 0$ for $1 \leq n \leq N$ and $i \neq n$, and that the minimized value of entropy in this case is zero.

6.8.10 The *maximum entropy* approach suggests picking prior distributions by choosing among a given class of priors that prior which minimizes $\text{Ent}(f)$. Walley (1991, pp. 270–271) illustrates some disturbing properties of this approach in a simple experiment: the outcome of a football game in which there are three possibilities for the home team: win(W), lose(L) or draw(D).

(a) Suppose before the game you learn that the home team has won more than half the games between the two teams. Show that the p.m.f. $P(\text{W}) = \frac{1}{2}$, $P(\text{L}) = \frac{1}{4}$, $P(\text{D}) = \frac{1}{4}$ maximizes entropy subject to the available information.

(b) After the game suppose you learn only that the game was not a draw. Show that by updating the maximum entropy prior in (a) by Bayes Theorem yields the posterior probabilities: $P(\text{W}) = \frac{2}{3}$, $P(\text{L}) = \frac{1}{3}$ and $P(\text{D}) = 0$.

(c) Show that the p.m.f. over W, L, D that maximizes entropy subject to the information that the home team has won more than half the games between the two teams and that the game did not end in a draw is $P(\text{W}) = P(\text{L}) = \frac{1}{2}$ and $P(\text{D}) = 0$.

6.8.11 Let $\hat{G}$ be the Tierney-Kadane approximation (6.7.63) to $E[g(\theta)|y]$. Suppose the prior p.d.f. $f(\theta)$ is changed to $f_*(\theta)$. Define

$$\hat{G}_* = \left[\frac{f(\hat{\theta}_D)f_*(\hat{\theta}_N)}{f(\hat{\theta}_N)f_*(\hat{\theta}_D)}\right]\hat{G}. \tag{6.8.26}$$

Show that $\hat{G}_*$ has the same order of approximation (see Equation 6.7.64) as $\hat{G}$. Note that (6.8.32) does *not* require any new maximization (Kass, Tierney and Kadane 1989).

6.8.12 (Heath and Sudderth 1978) Suppose $Y \sim U[\theta/2, 3\theta/2]$, where $0 < \theta < \infty$. For any estimator $\hat{\theta}$, define the loss function $C(\hat{\theta}, \theta) = \min\{\hat{\theta}^{-1}|\theta - \hat{\theta}|, 3\}$.

(a) Consider estimators of the form $\tilde{\theta} = y/\beta$, where $2/3 \leq \beta \leq 2$. Show that the risk function is $R(\tilde{\theta}|\theta) = 2\{\beta[(\ln[2 \cdot 3^{-1/2}] - 1) + \ln(\beta)] + 1\}$.

(b) Show that the value of β in (a), which minimizes risk is $\beta_* = 2 \cdot 3^{-1/2}$.

(c) Consider the improper prior density $f(\theta) = 1$ for all θ. Show that the corresponding posterior density is $f(\theta|y) = (\theta \ln 3)^{-1}$ for $2y/3 \leq \theta \leq 2y$, $f(\theta|y) = 0$, otherwise.

(d) Show that the Bayesian point estimate of θ is $\hat{\theta} = 2y$.

(e) Use (b) to show that $\hat{\theta}$ in (d) is inadmissible with respect to $C(\hat{\theta}, \theta)$.

6.9 Interval Estimation

This section discusses interval estimation. It complements the discussion of point estimation in previous sections. Both classical and Bayesian interval estimation are discussed.[43] Classical interval estimation is closely aligned with classical hypothesis testing, and the latter is discussed in detail in Chapter 7. Bayesian interval estimation is not so closely tied to Bayesian hypothesis testing; it does, however, follow straightforwardly from a posterior distribution.

Discussion begins with classical interval estimation.

Definition 6.9.1 Let Y_t $(t = 1, 2, \ldots, T)$ be a sample with joint p.d.f. $f(\cdot;\theta)$ where θ is an unknown $K \times 1$ vector of parameters, and let $g(\theta)$ be a known function. Suppose $W_1 \equiv \omega_1(Y_1, Y_2, \ldots, Y_T)$ and $W_2 \equiv \omega_2(Y_1, Y_2, \ldots, Y_T)$ are two statistics such that

$$P(W_1 \leq g(\theta) < W_2) = 1 - \alpha, \tag{6.9.1}$$

for $0 < \alpha < 1$. Then (6.9.1) is a *100(1 − α) percent probability interval for g(θ)*. If W_1 and W_2 are replaced in (6.9.1) by their realized counterparts $w_1 = \omega_1(y_1, y_2, \ldots, y_T)$ and $w_2 = \omega_2(y_1, y_2, \ldots, y_T)$, then the resulting interval is a *100(1 − α) percent confidence interval for g(θ)* and is denoted by

$$C(w_1 \leq g(\theta) \leq w_2) = 1 - \alpha. \tag{6.9.2}$$

The numbers w_1 and w_2 are the *lower and upper confidence limits for g(θ)*, and $1 - \alpha$ is called the *confidence coefficient*.

The explanation for the dual terminology in Definition 6.9.1 is that because w_1, w_2 and $g(\theta)$ are all nonrandom, no objectivist probability statement can be made directly about confidence interval (6.9.2). A verbal interpretation for the statistical concept of "confidence" is best made in the context of an example, and hence will be momentarily postponed. We will note now, however, that because $g(\theta)$ is unknown it is meaningful to make

43. There are also nonstandard classical methods of interval estimation based on use of Stein-like estimators (recall Example 6.6.8). See Berger and Wolpert (1988, pp. 10–11) and the references cited therein for further details.

a subjectivist probability statement about the interval $w_1 \leq g(\theta) \leq w_2$. There is no need in Bayesian interval estimation to introduce the additional concept of "confidence."

In a wide variety of situations, confidence intervals can be constructed using pivotal quantities as will now be defined.

Definition 6.9.2 Let Y_t $(t = 1, 2, \ldots, T)$ be a sample with joint p.d.f. $f(\cdot; \theta)$, where θ is an unknown K-dimensional column vector of parameters. Then the function $Q = Q(Y; \theta)$ is a *pivotal quantity* iff the distribution of Q does not depend on θ.

Example 6.9.1 If θ is a location parameter (recall Definition 3.1.1), then by definition $Y_t - \theta$ is a pivotal quantity. Similarly, if θ is a scale parameter, then Y_t/θ is a pivotal quantity.

If Q is a pivotal quantity, then for any fixed $1 - \alpha$ there will exist $q_1 = q_1(1 - \alpha)$ and $q_2 = q_2(1 - \alpha)$ such that $P(q_1 \leq Q \leq q_2) = 1 - \alpha$.[44] If the sample is random and if the distribution function of the observations is monotonic in $g(\theta)$, then it is possible in theory to use a pivotal quantity to form a confidence interval for θ.[45] We will now use a series of examples to show this fact.[46]

Example 6.9.2 Let Y_t $(t = 1, 2, \ldots, T) \sim$ i.i.d. $N(\mu, \sigma^2)$, where $\theta = \mu$ and σ^2 is known. Then $Q = T^{1/2}(\overline{Y} - \theta)/\sigma \sim N(0, 1)$ is a pivotal quantity. If

$$P(q_1 \leq Q \leq q_2) = P(q_1 \leq T^{1/2}(\overline{Y} - \theta)/\sigma \leq q_2) = 1 - \alpha, \tag{6.9.3}$$

then

$$P(-q_1 \sigma T^{-1/2} \geq (\theta - \overline{Y}) \geq -q_2 \sigma T^{-1/2}) = 1 - \alpha, \tag{6.9.4a}$$

$$P(\overline{Y} - q_2 \sigma T^{-1/2} < \theta < \overline{Y} - q_1 \sigma T^{-1/2}) = 1 - \alpha. \tag{6.9.4b}$$

According to Exercise 6.9.1, the values q_1 and q_2 that minimize the length $(-q_1 + q_2)\sigma T^{-1/2}$ of (6.9.4b) subject to (6.9.3) imply $q_1 = -q_2$. Thus, it follows from (6.9.3) that $P(|Q| \leq q_2) = 1 - \alpha$, and hence $q_2 = z(1 - \frac{1}{2}\alpha)$ is the value which cuts off $\frac{1}{2}\alpha$ probability in the righthand tail of the $N(0, 1)$ distribution, i.e. $\Phi[z(1 - \frac{1}{2}\alpha)] = 1 - \frac{1}{2}\alpha$. Therefore, (6.9.46) can be written

$$P[\overline{Y} - z(1 - \tfrac{1}{2}\alpha)\{\sigma T^{-1/2}\} < \theta < \overline{Y} + z(1 - \tfrac{1}{2}\alpha)\{\sigma T^{-1/2}\}] = 1 - \alpha. \tag{6.9.5}$$

Given a realized value $\overline{Y} = \overline{y}$, a $100(1 - \alpha)$ percent confidence interval for

44. This statement need not be true in the case of finite samples from discrete distributions. Thus throughout this section we will consider only samples from continuous distributions.

45. See Mood et al. (1974, pp. 387–389).

46. If a pivotal quantity does not exist, it may still be possible to form a confidence interval for $g(\theta)$ by other means. See Mood et al. (1974, pp. 389–393).

μ is

$$C[\bar{y} - z(1 - \tfrac{1}{2}\alpha)\{\sigma T^{-1/2}\} < \mu < \bar{y} + z(1 - \tfrac{1}{2}\alpha)\{\sigma T^{-1/2}\}] = 1 - \alpha. \tag{6.9.6}$$

Example 6.9.3 Suppose a random sample of size $T = 9$ from a $N(\mu, 36)$ distribution yields $\bar{y} = 4$, and suppose that a 95% confidence interval for μ is desired. Then $\alpha = .05$ and $z(1 - \frac{1}{2}\alpha) = z(.975) = 1.96$. From (6.9.6) it follows that

$$C[4 - 1.96\{6/3\} \le \mu \le 4 + 1.96\{6/3\}] = C(.08 \le \mu \le 7.92) = .95. \tag{6.9.7}$$

Because μ is non-random, it is *NOT* permissible from a frequentist's standpoint to interpret (6.9.7) as implying that there is a probability of .95 that μ is between .08 and 7.92. The only frequentist's probability statement that can be made about this interval is trivial: the probability that μ is between .08 and 7.92 is either zero or unity, just as it was before observing any sample information.

What then is the interpretation of (6.9.7)? What does it mean to be 95 percent confident that μ is between .08 and 7.92? *The answer is that the confidence lies in the procedure used to construct (6.9.7).* If a large number of random samples of size $T = 9$ are taken from a $N(\mu, 36)$ distribution, then approximately 95 percent of the confidence intervals produced from these samples will contain μ, and 5 percent will not contain μ. The realized endpoints of these intervals will change from sample to sample, and when considering any particular interval, such as (6.9.7), it is not possible to decide whether or not it contains μ. All the researcher can say is that he/she is "confident" that the observed interval is one of the 95 percent that does contain μ. Note, as is always the case when employing a frequentist's interpretation of probability, it is necessary to consider all the possible samples of size T that could have been observed in repeated sampling, not just the sample actually observed.

The point here is again one of "initial" versus "final" precision. The "confidence" for the frequentist lies in the *procedure* and its performance under repetitive sampling. The degree to which such "confidence" should also be directed toward a realized interval such as (6.9.7) is, at best, unclear. Indeed, as the following example indicates, in some cases it is patently wrong to interpret such confidence as being a good approximation to what is known about the unknown parameter after seeing the data.

Example 6.9.4 (Berger 1980, p. 19) Let Y_t $(t = 1, 2, \ldots, T)$ be an independent sample from the $U(\theta - \frac{1}{2}, \theta + \frac{1}{2})$ distribution. It is desired to give a confidence interval for θ. It can be shown that a classical 95% confidence interval for θ, when $T = 25$, is $(\hat{\theta} - 0.056, \hat{\theta} + 0.056)$, where $\hat{\theta} = \frac{1}{2}(\min\{Y_t\} + \max\{Y_t\})$ is the sample midrange. Now suppose that when the experiment is conducted, the outcome is such that $\min\{Y_t\} = 3.1$ and $\max\{Y_t\} = 3.2$, yielding $\hat{\theta} = 3.15$. Since $\theta - \frac{1}{2} \le \min\{Y_t\}$ and $\max\{Y_t\} \le \theta + \frac{1}{2}$, all that is really now known about θ is that it lies somewhere between $[\max\{Y_t\} - \frac{1}{2}] = 2.7$ and $[\min\{Y_t\} + \frac{1}{2}] = 3.6$, with nothing in the sample giving information as to which of these possible values might be more "likely" than others. Thus to state that the classical confidence interval $(\hat{\theta} - 0.056, \hat{\theta} + 0.056) = (3.094, 3.206)$ has a precision of 95% is very misleading, in that if you had to state a true feeling of the "chance" that the interval contained θ, you might say it was $(3.206 - 3.094)/(3.6 - 2.7) = .124$. This "final precision" of 12.4 percent is vastly different from the initial precision of 95%. Of course, it was unlucky to obtain such an uninformative sample, but if we do, it seems silly to use initial precision as a measure of accuracy.

A similar problem can occur with "too accurate" a sample. For example, if $\min\{Y_t\} = 3.0$ and $\max\{Y_t\} = 3.96$, then we know for sure that $3.46 < \theta < 3.50$. The classical procedure states that $3.424 < \theta < 3.536$ with only 95 percent "confidence." This conclusion also seems ridiculous, in light of the *certain* knowledge that θ is in the smaller interval.

Having made the "initial" vs. "final" precision clear, we now continue with standard examples of confidence intervals.

Example 6.9.5 Consider Example 6.9.2 with $\theta = [\mu, \sigma^2]'$ unknown, and let S^2 be the sample variance defined by (4.5.7). Then $Q = T^{1/2}(\bar{Y} - \mu)/S$ is a pivotal quantity having a Student t-distribution with $\nu = T - 1$ degrees of freedom. Letting $t(1 - \frac{1}{2}\alpha, \nu)$ denote the value that cuts off $\frac{1}{2}\alpha$ probability in the righthand tail of a student t-distribution with ν degrees of freedom, it follows analogously to Example 6.9.2 that a $(1 - \alpha)100$ percent confidence interval for μ is

$$C(\bar{y} - t(1 - \tfrac{1}{2}\alpha, \nu)[sT^{-1/2}] \le \mu \le \bar{y} + t(1 - \tfrac{1}{2}\alpha, \nu)[sT^{-1/2}]) = 1 - \alpha. \tag{6.9.8}$$

Example 6.9.6 Consider Example 6.9.3 and suppose that σ^2 is unknown and a sample estimate of $s^2 = 32$ is obtained. Because $t(1 - \frac{1}{2}\alpha, \nu) = t(.975, 8)) = 2.306$, it follows from (6.9.8) that

$$C[4 - 2.306\{32/9\}^{1/2} < \mu < 4 + 2.306\{32/9\}^{1/2}] = C(-.35 < \mu < 8.35)$$
$$= .95. \tag{6.9.9}$$

Note that even though $s^2 = 32 < \sigma^2 = 36$, (6.9.9) is wider than (6.9.7) due to the added uncertainty of having to estimate σ^2.

Example 6.9.7 Let Y_t $(t = 1, 2, \ldots, T) \sim$ i.i.d. $N(\mu, \sigma^2)$, where $\theta = [\mu, \sigma^2]'$ is unknown, and let S^2 be the sample variance defined by (5.1.4). Then $Q = \nu S^2/\sigma^2 \sim \chi^2(\nu)$, where $\nu = T - 1$, and Q is a pivotal quantity for σ^2. If

$$P(q_1 \le Q \le q_2) = 1 - \alpha, \tag{6.9.10}$$

then

$$P\left(\frac{-q_1\sigma^2}{v} \le S^2 \le \frac{q_2\sigma^2}{v}\right) = 1 - \alpha, \tag{6.9.11a}$$

$$P\left(\frac{vS^2}{q_2} \le \sigma^2 \le \frac{vS^2}{q_1}\right) = 1 - \alpha. \tag{6.9.11b}$$

According to Exercise 6.9.2, the values of q_1 and q_2 that minimize the expected length $v\sigma^2(q_1^{-1} - q_2^{-1})$ of (6.9.11b) subject to (6.9.10) must satisfy (6.9.33). Because solution of (6.9.33) requires iterative methods or tables, nonoptimal values of q_1 and q_2, for example, values that cut off $\frac{1}{2}\alpha$ probability in each tail of a $\chi^2(v)$, are often used in the confidence interval

$$C\left(\frac{vs^2}{q_2} \le \sigma^2 \le \frac{vs^2}{q_1}\right) = 1 - \alpha. \tag{6.9.12}$$

Example 6.9.8 Consider Example 6.9.6. Using the nonoptimal values $q_1 = 1.34$ and $q_2 = 22.0$ which cut off .005 probability in the lefthand and righthand tails, respectively, of a $\chi^2(8)$ distribution, it follows from (6.9.12) that a 99 percent confidence interval for σ^2 is

$$C\left(\frac{8(32)}{22} \le \sigma^2 \le \frac{8(32)}{1.34}\right) = C(11.64 \le \sigma^2 \le 191.04) = .99. \tag{6.9.13}$$

Example 6.9.9 Let Y_{1t} $(t = 1, 2, \ldots, T_1) \sim$ i.i.d. $N(\mu_1, \sigma^2)$ and Y_{2t} $(t = 1, 2, \ldots, T_2) \sim$ i.i.d. $N(\mu_2, \sigma^2)$ be two independent samples from distributions with the *same* variance. It is straightforward to show that

$$(\bar{Y}_2 - \bar{Y}_1) \sim N(\mu_2 - \mu_1, \sigma^2[T_1^{-1} + T_2^{-1}]), \tag{6.9.14}$$

$$v_j S_j^2/\sigma^2 \sim \chi^2(v_j) \qquad (j = 1, 2), \tag{6.9.15}$$

$$vS^2/\sigma^2 \sim \chi^2(v) \tag{6.9.16}$$

where

$$\bar{Y}_j = T_j^{-1} \sum_{t=1}^{T} Y_{jt} \qquad (j = 1, 2), \tag{6.9.17}$$

$$v_j \equiv T_j - 1 \qquad (j = 1, 2), \tag{6.9.18}$$

$$S_j^2 = v_j^{-1} \sum_{t=1}^{T_j} (Y_{jt} - \bar{Y}_j)^2 \qquad (j = 1, 2), \tag{6.9.19}$$

$$v \equiv v_1 + v_2, \tag{6.9.20}$$

$$S^2 \equiv \frac{v_1 S_1^2 + v_2 S_2^2}{v}. \tag{6.9.21}$$

Furthermore,

$$Q = \frac{(\bar{Y}_2 - \bar{Y}_1) - (\mu_2 - \mu_1)}{S(T_1^{-1} + T_2^{-1})^{1/2}} \tag{6.9.22}$$

has a Student t-distribution with v degrees of freedom, and Q serves as a pivotal quantity for $\mu_2 - \mu_1$. Thus analogous to (6.9.8) the minimum expected length $100(1 - \alpha)$ percent confidence interval for $\mu_2 - \mu_1$ is

$$C[(\bar{y}_2 - \bar{y}_1) - t(1 - \tfrac{1}{2}\alpha, v)s(T_1^{-1} + T_2^{-1})^{1/2} < \mu_2 - \mu_1 < (\bar{y}_2 - \bar{y}_1) + t(1 - \tfrac{1}{2}\alpha, v)s(T_1^{-1} + T_2^{-1})^{1/2}] = 1 - \alpha. \tag{6.9.23}$$

Example 6.9.10 Consider Example 6.9.6 and suppose that a second sample of size $T = 16$ is taken from a possibly different $N(\mu_2, \sigma^2)$ distribution and yields $\bar{y}_2 = 8$ and $s_2^2 = 42$. Assume that the two samples are independent. Let μ_1 denote the mean of the population from which the first sample is drawn, and let $\bar{y}_1 = 4$ and $s_1^2 = 36$ be the corresponding sample statistics. It follows from (6.9.20) and (6.9.21) that $v = 8 + 15 = 23$ and $s^2 = [8(32) + 15(42)]/23 = 38.52$ and $t(.975, 23) = 2.069$. Thus from (6.9.23), a 95 percent confidence interval for $\mu_2 - \mu_1$ is

$$C[4 - 2.069\{38.52[(1/9) + (1/16)]\}^{1/2} < \mu_2 - \mu_1 < 4 + 2.069\{38.52[(1/9) + (1/16)]\}^{1/2}] = C(-1.35 < \mu_2 - \mu_1 < 9.35) = .95. \tag{6.9.24}$$

Example 6.9.11 Consider Example 6.9.9 but suppose that the variances of the two underlying distributions are not required to be the same. Letting σ_1^2 and σ_2^2 be these two variances, it follows that $v_j S_j^2/\sigma_j^2 \sim \chi^2(v_j)$ $(j = 1, 2)$. Hence from Theorem 3.2.16(b),

$$Q = \frac{S_1^2/\sigma_1^2}{S_2^2/\sigma_2^2} \sim F(v_1, v_2). \tag{6.9.25}$$

Given

$$P(q_1 \le Q \le q_2) = 1 - \alpha, \tag{6.9.26}$$

it follows that a $(1 - \alpha)100$ percent confidence interval for σ_2^2/σ_1^2 is

$$C\left(q_1\left[\frac{s_1^2}{s_2^2}\right] < \frac{\sigma_2^2}{\sigma_1^2} < q_2\left[\frac{s_1^2}{s_2^2}\right]\right) = 1 - \alpha. \tag{6.9.27}$$

For (6.9.27) to be of minimum expected length (assuming the mean exists) q_1 and q_2 should be chosen to satisfy (6.9.33) in Exercise 6.9.2.

Example 6.9.12 Consider Examples 6.9.10 and 6.9.11. Using the non-optimal values $q_1 = (5.52)^{-1}$ and $q_2 = 5.52$ which cut off .01 probability in the lefthand, and righthand tails, respectively, of a $F(v_1, v_2)$ distribution, then it follows from (6.9.27) that a 98 percent confidence interval for σ_2^2/σ_1^2 is

$$C\left(\frac{1}{5.52}\left[\frac{42}{36}\right] < \frac{\sigma_2^2}{\sigma_1^2} < 5.52\left[\frac{42}{36}\right]\right) = C\left(.21 < \frac{\sigma_2^2}{\sigma_1^2} < 6.44\right) = .98. \tag{6.9.28}$$

The reader may wonder why the two-sample situation of Examples 6.9.9–6.9.11 is not also extended to cover the derivation of a confidence interval for $\mu_2 - \mu_1$ when $\sigma_2^2 \neq \sigma_1^2$. The answer is quite simple, namely, there does not exist a pivotal quantity for $\mu_2 - \mu_1$ in this case. This problem is in fact a famous one in the statistics literature, and is known as the *Behrens-Fisher problem* (see Cox and Hinkley 1974). The central problem is simply the elimination of the "nuisance parameters" σ_1^2 and σ_2^2. *Classical statistics has no generally acceptable solution to this ubiquitous problem.*

In sharp contrast to this classical conundrum, the Bayesian solution is general and conceptually straightforward: nuisance parameters are "marginalized-out" (i.e., integrated-out) of the joint posterior density of the parameters of interest. This is not to suggest that this approach is always analytically possible (i.e., the integrals need not have closed-form expressions), but the fact that there is at least a conceptual solution is substantially more than the classical approach has to offer. The Bayesian solution with a given prior distribution is a natural extension of the classical "solution"—assuming a known value for the nuisance parameter—namely, averaging over all such possible known values.

From the Bayesian perspective, interval estimation is derived directly from the posterior density $f(\theta|y)$. Because opinions about the unknown parameter are treated in a probabilistic manner, there is no need to introduce the additional concept of "confidence." For example, given a K-dimensional region A, a subset of the parameter space, it is meaningful to ask: given the data, what is the *probability* that θ lies in A? The answer is direct:

$$P(\theta \in A|y) = \int_A f(\theta|y)\, d\theta. \tag{6.9.29}$$

Alternatively, given a desired probability content of $1 - \alpha$, it is possible to reverse this procedure and find a corresponding region A. From a mathematical standpoint, finding an "optimal" region that is in some sense the smallest region achieving a probability content of $1 - \alpha$, is identical to finding the HPD region A defined next.

Definition 6.9.3 Let $f(\theta|y)$ be a posterior density function. Let A be a subset of the parameter space Θ satisfying:

(a) $P(\theta \in A|y) = 1 - \alpha$,

(b) for all $\theta_1 \in A$ and $\theta_2 \notin A$, $f(\theta_1|y) \geq f(\theta_2|y)$.

Then A is a *highest posterior density (HPD) region of content* $(1 - \alpha)$ *for* θ.

The HPD region, given a probability content of $1 - \alpha$, has the smallest possible volume in the parameter space Θ. Also, if $f(\theta|y)$ is not uniform over every region in the parameter space of θ, then the HPD region of content $1 - \alpha$ is unique.

In standard cases, obtaining the HPD region is straightforward as the following example suggests.

Example 6.9.13 Consider Example 6.7.2 involving a random sample from a $N(\theta_1, \theta_2^{-1})$ distribution with known variance θ_2^{-1}, and a $N(\underline{\mu}, \underline{h}^{-1})$ prior for the unknown mean θ_1. The posterior density for θ_1 in this case is $f(\theta_1|y) = \phi(\theta_1|\bar{\mu}, \bar{h}^{-1})$, where $\bar{\mu}$ and $\bar{h}$ are given by (6.7.13) and (6.7.12), respectively. Then a $1 - \alpha$ *probability* interval for θ_1 is

$$P[\bar{\mu} - z(1 - \tfrac{1}{2}\alpha)(\theta_2 T)^{-1/2} < \theta_1 < \bar{\mu} + z(1 - \tfrac{1}{2}\alpha)(\theta_2 T)^{-1/2}] = 1 - \alpha, \tag{6.9.30}$$

From the standpoint of subjective probability, (6.9.30) yields the *posterior probability* of θ_1 lying between $\bar{\mu} \pm z(1 - \tfrac{1}{2}\alpha)h^{-1/2}$. If a diffuse prior is used as in Example 6.7.5, then (6.9.30) reduces to

$$P[\bar{y} - z(1 - \tfrac{1}{2}\alpha)(\theta_2 T)^{-1/2} < \theta_1 < \bar{y} + z(1 - \tfrac{1}{2}\alpha)(\theta_2 T)^{-1/2}] = 1 - \alpha, \tag{6.9.31}$$

which is numerically identical to confidence interval (6.9.6). The interpretation of (6.9.31) is, however, in terms of "probability" not "confidence". Note, however, that in this special case the common misinterpretation of a classical confidence interval in terms of final precision is fortuitously correct.

Exercises

6.9.1 Let Q be a pivotal quantity for the unknown scalar θ such that the length (or expected length) of a $100(1 - \alpha)$ percent confidence interval for θ is $c(q_2 - q_1)$, where c is a constant not depending on q_1 or q_2. If $f_Q(\cdot)$ is the p.d.f. of Q, then it must be the case that

$$\int_{q_1}^{q_2} f_Q(q)\, dq = 1 - \alpha. \tag{6.9.32}$$

Show that if $f_Q(\cdot)$ is symmetric around zero, then the values of q_1 and q_2 that minimize $c(q_2 - q_1)$ subject to (6.9.32) are such that $q_1 = -q_2$.

6.9.2 Let Q be a pivotal quantity for the unknown scalar θ such that the length (or expected length) of a $100(1 - \alpha)$ percent confidence interval for θ is $c(q_2^{-1} - q_1^{-1})$, where c is a constant not depending on q_1 or q_2. If $f_Q(\cdot)$ is the p.d.f. of Q, then (6.9.32) holds. Show that if $f_Q(\cdot)$ has support $(0, \infty)$, then the values of q_1 and q_2 that minimize $c(q_2^{-1} - q_1^{-1})$ subject to (6.9.32) satisfy

$$q_1^2 f_Q(q_1) = q_2^2 f_Q(q_2). \tag{6.9.33}$$

6.9.3 Prove (6.9.14) through (6.9.16) and (6.9.22).

6.9.4 In Example 6.9.4 the two samples were independent. Suppose instead the observations are *paired*. Let (Y_{1t}, Y_{2t}) $(t = 1, 2, \ldots, T)$ be i.i.d. bivariate normal with means μ_1 and μ_2, variances σ_1^2 and σ_2^2, and correlation ρ.

(a) Define $D_t = Y_{2t} - Y_{1t}$. Show that D_t $(t = 1, 2, \ldots, T)$ are i.i.d. $N(\mu_D, \sigma_D^2/T)$, where

$$\bar{D} = \frac{1}{T}\sum_{t=1}^{T} D_t, \tag{6.9.34}$$

$\mu_D = \mu_2 - \mu_1$, and $\sigma_D^2 = \sigma_1^2 + \sigma_2^2 - 2\rho\sigma_1\sigma_2$.

(b) Show that the minimum expected length $100(1-\alpha)$ percent confidence interval for μ_D is

$$C[\bar{D} - t(1-\tfrac{1}{2}\alpha, \nu)s_{\bar{D}} < \mu_D < \bar{D} + t(1-\tfrac{1}{2}\alpha, \nu)s_{\bar{D}}] = 1-\alpha, \tag{6.9.35}$$

where

$$S_D^2 = \frac{1}{\nu}\sum_{t=1}^{T}(D_t - \bar{D})^2, \tag{6.9.36}$$

$$S_{\bar{D}}^2 = \frac{S_D^2}{T}, \tag{6.9.37}$$

and $\nu \equiv T - 1$.

(c) Compare and contrast (6.9.35) with (6.9.23). How would you choose between them?

6.9.5 Suppose a random sample of size $T = 7$ from a $N(\mu, \sigma^2)$ yields $\bar{y} = 5$ and $s^2 = 1.96$. Find a 99 percent confidence interval for μ when:

(a) $\sigma^2 = 2$ is known.

(b) σ^2 is unknown.

6.9.6 What is the essential difference between a pivotal quantity and a statistic?

6.9.7 Consider K confidence intervals

$$C(q_{1k} < \theta_k < q_{2k}) = 1 - \alpha_k \qquad (k = 1, 2, \ldots, K), \tag{6.9.38}$$

and let $\alpha \equiv \alpha_1 + \alpha_2 + \cdots + \alpha_K$. Show that all K confidence intervals hold simultaneously at a confidence level of at least $1 - \alpha$. This method of constructing joint confidence intervals is known as the *Bonferroni method*. It is most useful when K is small. Why? Hint: Let A_k denote the event that the kth confidence interval does *not* contain θ_k, and let A_k^c denote its complement. Show that the probability that all K confidence intervals are correct equals $P(A_1^c \cap A_2^c \cap \cdots \cap A_K^c)$ and is greater than or equal to $1 - \alpha$.

6.9.8 Given θ, consider a random sample Y_t $(t = 1, 2, \ldots, T)$ from a $N(\theta, 25)$ distribution. Suppose $T = 25$ and that $\bar{y} = 0$ is observed.

(a) Construct a .95 confidence interval for θ.

(b) Construct a .95 HPD interval for θ based on Jeffreys' prior.

(c) *CAREFULLY* distinguish between the interpretations of the two numerical intervals in (a) and (b).

6.9.9 Let $f(y)$ be a unimodal p.d.f. Suppose the interval $[a, b]$ satisfies:

(a) $\int_a^b f(y)\,dy = 1 - \alpha$,

(b) $f(a) = f(b) > 0$,

(c) $a \leq \text{mode}(y) \leq b$.

Show: $[a, b]$ is the shortest interval among all intervals that satisfy (a) (Casella and Berger 1990, pp. 430–431).

6.9.10 Suppose Y_t $(t = 1, 2) \sim$ i.i.d. $U(\theta - \frac{1}{2}, \theta + \frac{1}{2})$. Let $X_1 = \min\{Y_1, Y_2\}$ and $X_2 = \max\{Y_1, Y_2\}$ (DeGroot 1987, pp. 400–401).

(a) Show: $P(X_1 < \theta < X_2) = \frac{1}{2}$.

(b) Show: $P(X_2 - \frac{1}{2} < \theta < X_1 + \frac{1}{2}) = 1$.

(c) Show: $P(X_1 < \theta < X_2 | X_2 - X_1 \geq \frac{1}{2}) = 1$.

(d) Show: $P(X_1 < \theta < X_2 | X_2 - X_1 < \frac{1}{2}) = 0$.

(e) Given (c) and (d), how do you interpret the interval in (a)?

6.9.11 Suppose Y_t $(t = 1, 2, \ldots, T) \sim$ i.i.d. $N_M(\mu, \Sigma)$, where both μ and Σ are unknown, and $T > M$. Define:

$$S = \frac{1}{T-1} \sum_{t=1}^{T} (Y_t - \overline{Y})(Y_t - \overline{Y})'. \tag{6.9.39}$$

(a) Using Theorems 3.5.1(a) and 5.3.7(c), show that S is an unbiased estimator of Σ.

(b) Let q be the value that cuts off α probability in the righthand tail of the $F(M, T-M)$ distribution, and define $c_\alpha = [M(T-1)/(T-M)]$. Show that a $1-\alpha$ confidence ellipsoid for μ is given by

$$C[T(\overline{Y} - \mu)'S^{-1}(\overline{Y} - \mu) \leq c_\alpha] = 1 - \alpha. \tag{6.9.40}$$

(c) The quantity $V \sim T\overline{Y}'S^{-1}\overline{Y}$ is commonly referred to as Hotelling's T^2 statistic. Show that $X = (T-M)V/[M(T-1)] \sim F(M, T-M, \lambda)$, where the noncentrality parameter is $\lambda = \frac{1}{2}T\mu'\Sigma^{-1}\mu$.

6.9.12 Suppose X_t $(t = 1, 2, \ldots, T_x) \sim$ i.i.d. $N_M(\mu_x, \Sigma)$ and Y_t $(t = 1, 2, \ldots, T_y) \sim$ i.i.d. $N_M(\mu_y, \Sigma)$ are independent samples, where μ_x, μ_y, and Σ are unknown, $T_x > M$, and $T_y > M$. Let $\overline{X}$ and $\overline{Y}$ be the sample means, and define

$$S = \frac{1}{T_x + T_y - 2}[(T_x - 1)S_x + (T_y - 1)S_y], \tag{6.9.41}$$

where

$$S_x = \frac{1}{T_x - 1} \sum_{t=1}^{T} (X_t - \overline{X})(X_t - \overline{X})'. \tag{6.9.42}$$

$$S_y = \frac{1}{T_y - 1} \sum_{t=1}^{T_y} (Y_t - \overline{Y})(Y_t - \overline{Y})'. \tag{6.9.43}$$

(a) Let $V \sim T_x T_y(\overline{X} - \overline{Y})'S^{-1}(\overline{X} - \overline{Y})/(T_x + T_y)$. Show that

$$\left(\frac{T_x + T_y - M - 1}{M}\right)\frac{V}{T_x + T_y} \sim F(M, T_x + T_y - M - 1, \lambda), \tag{6.9.44}$$

where the noncentrality parameter is

$$\lambda = \left(\frac{T_x T_y}{T_x + T_y}\right)(\mu_x - \mu_y)'\Sigma^{-1}(\mu_x - \mu_y). \tag{6.9.45}$$

(b) Construct a $1-\alpha$ confidence ellipsoid for $\mu_x - \mu_y$.

6.9.13 Consider Exercise 6.9.11. Let R be a $J \times M$ matrix of constants with rank$(R) = M$, and let r be a known $M \times 1$ vector of constants. Construct a $1-\alpha$ confidence ellipsoid for $R\mu - r$.

6.9.14 Given the likelihood $\mathcal{L}(\theta; y)$ and the prior p.d.f. $f(\theta)$, let $\gamma = g(\theta)$ be a one-to-one transformation of θ. Also let A be a $1-\alpha$ H.P.D. region for θ, and define $B = \{\gamma | \gamma = g(\theta), \theta \in A\}$. Is B a $1-\alpha$ H.P.D. region for γ?

6.10 Reflections on Conditioning

Should econometricians test $\theta = 1$ using the unconditional result, there will be a lot of random walks in econometric models.
—Hinkley (1983, p. 94)

The likelihood principle antithesis to the sample space based data analysis thesis of Pearson-Fisher-Neyman is indeed very strange. It is like stealing the big stick of the bully and hitting him over the head with it.
—Basu (1988, p. 78)

If statisticians could agree on conditioning, there would be far fewer controversies in statistics since it is the basis for most debates. A pure unconditional frequentist approach gets into all types of problems (recall Example 6.9.4). Here is another example.

Example 6.10.1 (Berger and Wolpert 1988, pp. 5–6) Given an unknown parameter $\theta(-\infty < \theta < \infty)$, suppose $Y_t = \theta + U_t$ $(t = 1, 2)$, where U_t $(t = 1, 2)$ are independent Bernoulli random variables such that $P(U_t = -1|\theta) = P(U_t = 1|\theta) = \frac{1}{2}$. Then Y_t $(t = 1, 2)$ are i.i.d. with p.m.f. $P(Y_t = \theta - 1|\theta) = P(Y_t = \theta + 1|\theta) = \frac{1}{2}$ $(t = 1, 2)$. It can be shown that a 75 percent confidence set of smallest size is

$$\begin{Bmatrix} \frac{1}{2}(y_1 + y_2), & \text{if } y_1 \neq y_2 \\ y_1 - 1, & \text{if } y_1 = y_2 \end{Bmatrix}. \tag{6.10.1}$$

In repeated sampling, (6.10.1) contains θ with a sampling probability of .75.

Note, however, when observing $y_1 \neq y_2$, it is *absolutely certain* that $\theta = \frac{1}{2}(y_1 + y_2)$, and when observing $y_1 = y_2$, it is *equally uncertain* that $\theta = y_1 - 1$ or $\theta = y_2 + 1$ (assuming no prior knowledge regarding θ). Therefore, *ex post* the "confidence" in using set (6.10.1) is either 100 percent or 50 percent, and depending on whether $y_1 \neq y_2$ or $y_1 = y_2$, we known which level it is. From the *ex ante* perspective, however, (6.10.1) is 75 percent confidence set: an average of the two *ex post* levels. The embarrassing question for the pure frequentist is: why use the realized value of (6.10.1) and report the *ex ante* confidence level 75 percent instead of the appropriate *ex post* measure of uncertainty?

Believers in the Likelihood Principle (LP) (recall Definition 6.2.6) condition on *all* the data. *Conditional frequentists* lie somewhere between LP proponents and pure frequentists, arguing that inference should be conditional on ancillary statistics (recall Definition 5.2.2), but otherwise unconditional.[47] Whether it is possible to sit on this fence is debatable. Partial conditional inference, however, goes a long way toward eliminating *some* of the embarrassing problems in the pure unconditional frequentist approach.

47. Given a likelihood function of an unknown parameter θ based on a sample vector y, recall that an *ancillary statistic* is any statistic whose distribution does *not* depend on θ. By definition an ancillary statistic contains no information about θ, but it may contain information on the precision of an estimator $\hat{\theta}$.

Any frequentist theory of inference requires the specification of a reference set—a (possibly hypothetical) set of repetitions to which an inference is referred. In order for orthodox frequentist theory to have wide applicability, it requires a principle to define the relevant subsets of the sample space over which to conceptualize the repeated sampling. Conditional frequentists argue that the observed value of an ancillary statistic should be used to define an appropriate reference set, and that inferences should be drawn conditional on ancillary statistics, which when combined with other statistics, comprise a sufficient statistic. According to Theorem 6.5.7 (Basu's Theorem), all ancillary statistics are independent of boundedly complete sufficient statistics. Hence, conditional and unconditional inferences based on boundedly complete sufficient statistics are the same. When boundedly complete sufficient statistics are not used, perhaps because they do not exist for the problem at hand, then conditional and unconditional inferences may differ.

Consider the following two examples.

Example 6.10.2 Reconsider Example 6.10.1. Define the Bernoulli random variable $Z \equiv |Y_1 - Y_2|$. Z is ancillary since its p.m.f. $P(Z = 0) = P(Z = 2) = \frac{1}{2}$ does not depend on θ. The conditional coverage probabilities of (6.10.1), given Z, are the appealing *ex post* probabilities .50 and 1.00, respectively, for $Z = 0$ and $Z = 2$.

Example 6.10.3 (Berger and Wolpert 1988, pp. 13–14) Reconsider Example 6.9.4. Note that $W = [W_1, W_2]' = [\min\{Y_t\}, \max\{Y_t\}]'$ is sufficient for θ, and $Z = W_2 - W_1$ is ancillary. The conditional distribution of W, given $Z = z$, is uniform on the set

$$S = \{(w_1, w_2) | w_2 - w_1 = z \text{ and } \theta - \tfrac{1}{2} < w_1 < \theta + \tfrac{1}{2} - z\}. \tag{6.10.2}$$

It can be shown that a $1 - \alpha$ confidence interval for θ is

$$C[w - \tfrac{1}{2}(1 - \alpha)(1 - z) < \theta < w - \tfrac{1}{2}(1 - \alpha)(1 - z)] = 1 - \alpha, \tag{6.10.3}$$

where $w = \frac{1}{2}(w_1 + w_2)$. Confidence interval (6.10.3) provides an alternative confidence interval to that considered in Example 6.9.4.

Unfortunately, there are no general constructive techniques for determining ancillary statistics. In fact they need not even exist as the following example shows.

Example 6.10.4 (Berger and Wolpert 1988, p. 17) Consider a measuring instrument which measures a parameter $\theta \in [0, \frac{1}{2})$ correctly $(1 - \theta) \times 100$ percent of the time, and which gives an erroneous measurement of zero $\theta \times 100\%$ of the time. Let Y denote such a measurement. The p.m.f. of Y is: $P(Y = \theta) = 1 - \theta$ and $P(Y = 0) = \theta$. The simple confidence set $\{y\}$ has an *ex ante* associated confidence level of $(1 - \theta) \times 100$ percent. If $y > 0$, however, $\{y\} = \theta$ with certainty. There is, however, no ancillary statistic to provide such conditioning.

Another problem with conditioning on ancillaries as a solution to such embarrassing examples is that ancillaries need not be unique. Consider the following example.

Example 6.10.5 (Basu 1964) Let (X_t, Y_t) $(t = 1, 2, \ldots, T)$ be a random sample from a bivariate normal distribution with both means equal to zero, both variances equal to unity and correlation θ. Both X_t $(t = 1, 2, \ldots, T)$ and Y_t $(t = 1, 2, \ldots, T)$ are ancillary individually, and taken together they exhaust the sample. Thus, if one tries to resolve the problem by conditioning on both, there is nothing left to be random. Should inference be conducted conditional on X or on Y? Some researchers try to avoid the problem by requiring the ancillary to be a function of the minimal sufficient statistic, in which case no ancillary is present here.

Besides existence and non-uniqueness, other problems also plague ancillary statistics. For example, ancillary statistics may not be functions of the minimal sufficient statistic and as a result conditioning upon them may lead to procedures incompatible with the Sufficiency Principle. Also, in general there are no unique maximal ancillaries. For more discussion see Buehler (1982) and Lehmann and Scholz (1992).

Nonetheless, conditioning on ancillary statistics often yield sensible classical inferences in cases where unconditional inferences are uniformly condemned. See Berger and Wolpert (1988, Chapter 2), Lehmann (1986, Chapter 10), and the references therein for further discussion. Such conditioning points the researcher down a path leading to conditioning on all the data. Once some conditioning is performed it is difficult to stop. Indeed the LP traps the advocate of partial conditioning into conditioning on all the data. A frequentist who conditions on all the data is left with nothing random. A smiling Bayesian stands at the end of this path with open arms.

Different choices for conditioning underlie the frequentist's concern with $Y|\theta$ and the Bayesian's concern with $\theta|y$. The following example dramatizes the degree to which sampling distributions and posterior distributions can differ.

Example 6.10.6 (Sims and Uhlig 1991) Let Y_0 be a given constant, and let U_t $(t = 1, 2, \ldots, T) \sim$ i.i.d. $N(0, 1)$. The assumption that the variance of U_t $(t = 1, 2, \ldots, T)$ is known and equal to unity is merely made for convenience. Consider the following *first-order Gaussian autoregression*:

$$Y_t = \theta Y_{t-1} + U_t \qquad (t = 1, 2, \ldots, T), \tag{6.10.4}$$

where θ is an unknown scalar parameter. Note that

$$Y_t | Y_{t-1}, \ldots, Y_0, \theta \sim N(\theta y_{t-1}, 1). \tag{6.10.5}$$

From (6.10.5) the likelihood function is seen to be:

$$\begin{aligned}\mathscr{L}(\theta; y) &= \prod_{t=1}^{T} \phi(y_t | \theta y_{t-1}, 1) \\ &= (2\pi)^{-T/2} \exp\left[-\tfrac{1}{2} \sum_{t=1}^{T} (y_t - \theta y_{t-1})^2 \right]\end{aligned} \tag{6.10.6}$$

Define the statistic

$$\hat{\theta} = \frac{\sum_{t=1}^{T} y_t y_{t-1}}{\sum_{t=1}^{T} y_{t-1}^2}, \tag{6.10.7}$$

and note:

$$\sum_{t=1}^{T} (y_t - \theta y_{t-1})^2 = \sum_{t=1}^{T} (y_t - \hat{\theta} y_{t-1})^2 + (\hat{\theta} - \theta)^2 w, \tag{6.10.8}$$

$$w \equiv \sum_{t=1}^{T} y_{t-1}^2. \tag{6.10.9}$$

Substituting (6.10.8) into (6.10.6), implies:

$$\begin{aligned}\mathscr{L}(\theta; y) &= (2\pi)^{-T/2} \exp\left[-\tfrac{1}{2}\left(\sum_{t=1}^{T} (y_{t-1} - \hat{\theta} y_{t-1})^2 + (\hat{\theta} - \theta)^2 w \right)\right] \\ &\propto \phi(\theta | \hat{\theta}, w^{-1}).\end{aligned} \tag{6.10.10}$$

It follows immediately from likelihood (6.10.10) that if an improper uniform prior for θ is used, then the posterior of θ given $y = [y_1, y_2, \ldots, y_T]'$ is $N(\hat{\theta}, w^{-1})$. In sharp contrast to $\theta | y$, the sampling distribution of the ML estimator (6.10.7) is quite complicated and its asymptotic distribution differs depending on whether $\theta < 1$, $\theta = 1$ or $\theta > 1$ (e.g., see Anderson 1959; White 1958; and Phillips 1987). Rather than discuss these complications associated with classical analysis, here we simply summarize the enlightening Monte Carlo experiment of Sims and Uhlig (1991).

Sims and Uhlig (1991) conducted the following experiment. Thirty-one values of θ ranging from .80 to 1.10 in steps of .01 were considered. For each value of θ, 10,000 random vectors $U = [U_1, U_2, \ldots, U_T]'$ with $T = 100$ were generated. In turn a vector y was generated according to (6.10.4). Thus, 310,000 data series on 100×1 vectors y were available: 10,000 series for each of the 31 values $(.80, .81, \ldots, 1.10)$ of θ. For each of these 310,000 series, MLE (6.10.6) was computed and a histogram was constructed with intervals $(-\infty, .795)$, $[.795, .805)$, $[.805, .815), \ldots, [1.095, 1.105)$, $[1.105, \infty)$ to categorize the resulting $\hat{\theta}$. Lining up these 31 histograms side by side, yields a surface which is the joint p.d.f. of θ and $\hat{\theta}$ under a $U[.80, 1.10]$

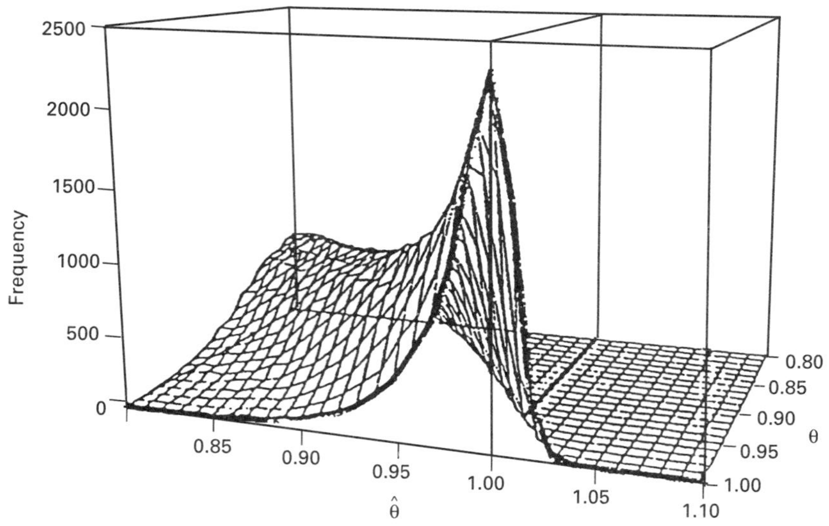

Figure 6.10.1
Joint p.d.f. of $\hat{\theta}$ and $\hat{\theta}$ sliced along $\theta = 1$

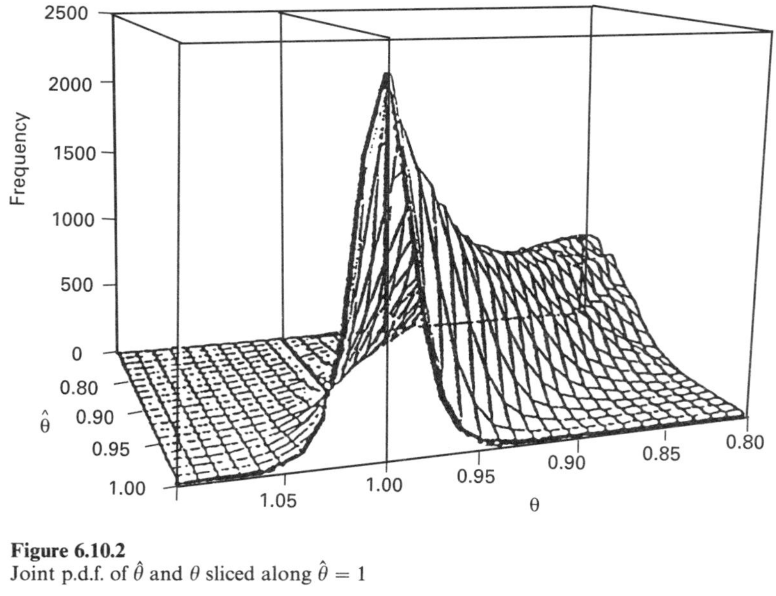

Figure 6.10.2
Joint p.d.f. of $\hat{\theta}$ and θ sliced along $\hat{\theta} = 1$

prior for θ. Figure 6.10.1 (Sims and Uhlig 1991, p. 1594, Figure 3) depicts the joint p.d.f. of $\hat{\theta}$ and θ sliced along $\theta = 1$. From this slice it can be seen that the sampling p.d.f. of $\hat{\theta}$ given $\theta = 1$ is decidedly skewed and the mean is less than unity. In contrast, Figure 6.10.2 (Sims and Uhlig 1991, p. 1595, Figure 4) depicts the joint p.d.f. of $\hat{\theta}$ and θ sliced along $\hat{\theta} = 1$. From this slice it can be seen that the posterior p.d.f. of θ given $\hat{\theta} = 1$ is symmetric around $\theta = 1$, as can be easily see from (6.10.10). See Sims and Uhlig (1991) for further enlightening discussion, in part foreshadowed by the insightful comment of David Hinkley opening this section.

Exercises

6.10.1 (Gleser 1990) Consider a baseball manager who must choose a pinch hitter in a crucial moment of a ball game. The opposing manager has just brought a left-handed pitcher into the game who must face the next batter. Two pinch hitters are available: A and B. Overall player A has a batting average of .300, and B has a batting average of .275. Player A bats lefthanded and averages only .260 against left-handed pitchers. Player B bats righthanded and while not as good a hitter overall as A, B bats .310 against lefthanded pitchers. How should the fans in the stands evaluate the manager's selection of a pinch hitter? (Interpret the type of pitcher—righthanded versus left-handed—as an ancillary statistic, and the two players are competing procedures with A dominating unconditionally and B dominating conditionally.)

6.10.2 (Brown 1967) Consider Example 6.9.5 and let $[a, b]$ denote the probability interval corresponding to denote confidence interval (6.9.8). Suppose $\alpha = \frac{1}{2}$ and $T = 2$. Show:

$$P_{\overline{Y},S^2|\mu,\sigma^2}[a \leq \mu \leq b] \geq \tfrac{2}{3}. \tag{6.10.11}$$

6.10.3 (Basu 1959) Let X and Y be independent $N(0, 1)$. Define $V = Y - X$ and

(a) Show both V and W are individually ancillary, but neither is a maximal ancillary. (Note: an ancillary statistic is a maximal ancillary iff every other ancillary statistic is a function of it.)

$$W = \begin{Bmatrix} Y - X, & \text{if } X + Y > 0 \\ X - Y, & \text{if } X + Y \leq 0 \end{Bmatrix}. \tag{6.10.12}$$

(b) Show $[V, W]'$ is not ancillary.

6.10.4 Let X and Y have joint p.d.f. $f(x, y) = 2g(x)g(y)G(\theta xy)$, where $g(\cdot)$ is a known p.d.f. symmetric around zero, and $G(\cdot)$ is its c.d.f.. (Dawid 1977a)

(a) Show that $f(x, y)$ is a legitimate bivariate p.d.f..

(b) The marginal p.d.f. of X is $g(x)$. Is X ancillary for θ?

(c) The marginal p.d.f. of Y is $g(y)$. Is Y ancillary for θ?

(d) Show that XY is sufficient for θ.

7 Hypothesis Testing

A model is a powerful device for organizing our thoughts; it is not literally true; indeed it derives its power from the very fact that it is not *literally true. Thus there is no reason to test it. Instead of testing, we should be determining its accuracy and usefulness. We should attempt to identify empirical circumstances in which the model is useful and other circumstances in which it is misleading.*
—Leamer (1981)

7.1 Introduction

Any model that is well enough articulated to give clear answers to the questions we put to it will necessarily be artificial, abstract, patently 'unreal'.
—Lucas (1980, p. 696)

This chapter deals with testing parametric hypotheses, both from the classical and Bayesian perspectives. Although hypothesis testing techniques are some of the most popular tools in econometricians' tool kits, outsiders (and a growing number of insiders) are perplexed by this popularity (e.g., Pratt 1965 and Roberts 1976). A major reason for this state of affairs is the failure of participants to agree on the goals of such activities. Let me try to explain.

Many subjective Bayesians question the importance of hypothesis testing, regardless of the techniques employed, because they view the object of the enterprise (i.e., the parameters) to be mental constructs whose objective existence is at best debatable. Such "predictivists" see the primary role of parameters as facilitating prediction of future observables, and hence, they question the amount of time that economists spend on the intermediary activity of hypothesis testing. As will be seen in the discussion of prediction in Chapter 8, the importance of hypothesis testing in prediction is diminished, although it may serve a role in the sensitivity analysis of prediction.

Even some objective Bayesians and frequentists are perplexed at the time spent on hypothesis testing, because they believe many researchers confuse the goals of the activity. In its usual form, hypothesis testing is cast as a decision problem where the researcher is confronted with a choice between two competing hypotheses. These hypotheses are "competing" because they impose mutually exclusive and exhaustive restrictions on the permissible parameter space. A question rarely asked, however, is whether there is really a need to make the choice.

Edwards et al. (1963, pp. 214–215) note that the appropriate action depends on what is at stake and offer the following pragmatic everyday example. You are unlikely not take an airplane if you believed it would crash, and you would not buy flight insurance if you believed it would not.

Seldom, however, must you choose between exactly two acts, one appropriate to the one hypothesis and the other to its alternative. Many intermediate or "hedging" acts are ordinarily possible, for example, flying after buying flight insurance.

An example more along statistical lines is *model selection*, that is, choosing among competing specifications for a likelihood. Such an activity is very much like hypothesis testing. The difficulty in developing a sensible loss structure in which to rationalize model selection was noted by Kadane and Dickey (1980). For example, the purpose of such activity is to obtain a specification to be used in prediction, then the choice is "forced" in the sense that most standard loss structures suggest particular weighted predictions (see Chapter 8 and Poirier 1991c) will dominate the prediction from any one specification alone.

Some researchers choose among hypotheses as an intermediary step in estimation. The motivation may be, for example, a "simplification search" in which a hypothesis asserting particular values for some of the parameters is entertained, and if not rejected, is imposed in the hope that the remaining parameters may be estimated more precisely. Such an activity is commonly called *pretesting* or *testimation*. It is most properly evaluated as a problem in estimation, and it is discussed in Section 9.8. Note now, however, that the resulting estimators are generally inferior (e.g., inadmissible) when compared to estimators which forego the discrete choice among hypotheses. Thus, once again the choice is "forced." Exercise 7.2.2 provides an introduction to the pretesting literature.

A hypothesis test provides a *qualitative* answer to what often is a *quantitative* question, especially because the hypotheses involved are usually composite. One time when a qualitative question is being asked and there is clearly a need to choose exactly one hypothesis is when the goal is a "truth search." By construction the problem is posed so that there is exactly one "true" hypothesis, and the assumed goal is to find it. For a discussion of other types of econometric searches, see Leamer (1978).

A distinguishing feature of hypothesis testing, compared to estimation, is the introduction of nondata-based information. This is most obvious for classicists because classical estimation purports to proceed in an "objective" fashion. Hypothesis testing requires a hypothesis to be tested, and for the activity to be interesting, the hypothesis must have some a priori credibility implying some information regarding possible values of unknown parameters. From where this information comes, and where it was when estimation was the only concern, are perplexing issues for non-Bayesian researchers. For Bayesians the need to introduce prior (nondata-based) information is hardly frightening. It will be seen in Section 7.4, however, unlike in estimation (point or interval) the prior information must assign nonzero prior probability to all hypotheses under consideration in order for the testing to be nontrivial.

In discussing the truth search problem (which is of relatively little interest to the pure subjectivist), it is helpful to note the manner in which the classical and Bayesian approaches address the following questions. First, because the problem is defined to be explicitly one of making a decision, how does each approach incorporate ingredients such as the costs of making incorrect decisions? Second, in what sense are the hypotheses posed believable to begin, that is, can some hypotheses be rejected out-of-hand as false without looking at any data? Third, how do the approaches behave as the sample size grows?

Before discussing the details of the classical and Bayesian approaches to hypothesis testing, we first formally set up the problem to be addressed. Basic vocabulary is introduced in Definition 7.1.1 and illustrated in Example 7.1.1.

Definition 7.1.1 A *statistical hypothesis* is an assertion about the distribution of one or more random variables. A *parametric hypothesis* is a statistical hypothesis that restricts some or all of the elements of the $K \times 1$ parameter vector θ that characterizes the likelihood function $\mathscr{L}(\theta; y)$. A *sharp hypothesis* is a parametric hypothesis that specifies a single value for at least one of the elements in θ. A *simple hypothesis* is a sharp hypothesis that specifies a single value for each of the elements in θ. A *composite hypothesis* is any hypothesis that is not simple.

Example 7.1.1 Suppose Y_t $(t = 1, 2, \ldots, T)$, given $\theta = [\mu, \sigma^2]'$, comprise a random sample from a $N(\mu, \sigma^2)$ population. If μ is unknown and σ^2 is known, then H_1: $\mu = 0$ is a simple hypothesis and H_2: $\mu > 0$ is a composite hypothesis. If both μ and σ^2 are unknown, then H_1 becomes a composite hypothesis, although it remains a sharp hypothesis. In this case H_1 is equivalent to H_1: $\mu = 0, 0 < \sigma^2 < \infty$.

We now introduce some additional terminology.

Definition 7.1.2 In the "truth searching" context, parameters restricted by the hypotheses under consideration are called the *parameters of interest*. Any remaining unknown parameters are called *nuisance parameters.*[1]

Example 7.1.2 Consider Example 7.1.1 in the case where both μ and σ^2 are unknown. Then under H_1 and H_2, μ is the parameter of interest and σ^2 is a nuisance parameter.

1. In pretesting (see Section 9.8) these roles are often reversed, that is, the hypotheses restrict the nuisance parameters rather than the parameters of interest.

As will be seen in subsequent sections, while all hypotheses are treated symmetrically in Bayesian testing, this is not the case in classical testing. A major reason for the asymmetry in the latter case is the implicit way decision theoretic elements are introduced in classical hypothesis testing. The terminology of the next definition is standard.

Definition 7.1.3 The statistical hypothesis of primary interest is referred to as the *null hypothesis.* The hypothesis tentatively adopted if the null is rejected is called the *alternative hypothesis.* Rejecting a true null hypothesis is called a *type I error*; failure to reject a false null hypothesis is called a *type II error.* The null hypothesis is usually chosen so that type I error is more serious than type II error.

We adopt the convention of letting H_1 denote the null hypothesis, and letting H_2 denote the alternative hypothesis. It should be kept in mind that null/alternative distinction is important only in classical testing. Also, while in principle the choice of the null hypothesis is based on consideration of the relative consequences of a type I error, in practice it is often based on other matters (e.g., mathematical expediency).

Finally, it should be noted that some classical statisticians and econometricians engage in hypothesis testing in situations even less structured than that outlined in this introductory section. Some researchers engage in "significance testing" of a null hypothesis. A *significance test* of a null hypothesis proceeds without a well specified alternative hypothesis. Given the asymmetry in classical hypothesis testing, it is possible to do this. Of course concepts such as "power" (discussed in the next section) cannot be investigated in such cases, Bayesians and most enlightened classical econometricians, eschew significance tests and so does this text. For further discussions of the author's opinions on significance tests, see Poirier (1991e, 1992a) and Hendry et al. (1990).

7.2 Sampling Theory Approach

We begin by partitioning the parameter space Θ according to $\Theta = \Theta_1 \cup \Theta_2$, where $\Theta_1 \cap \Theta_2$ is null. Consider testing $H_1\colon \theta \in \Theta_1$ versus $H_2\colon \theta \in \Theta_2$ based on a sample Y yielding the likelihood $\mathscr{L}(\theta; Y)$. Partition the sample space $\mathscr{S} = \mathscr{S}_1 \cup \mathscr{S}_2$, with $\mathscr{S}_1 \cap \mathscr{S}_2$ is null, in order to define the decisions: $d_j = d_j(Y) \equiv$ choose H_j iff $Y \in \mathscr{S}_j$ $(j = 1, 2)$. This leads to the following terminology.

Definition 7.2.1 Consider testing the null hypothesis $H_1\colon \theta \in \Theta_1$ versus the alternative hypothesis $H_2\colon\theta \in \Theta_2$. Then the subset $\mathscr{S}_2$ of the sample space $\mathscr{S}$ leading to the decision $d_2 \equiv$ choose H_2 is called the *critical region* (or the *rejection region*) of the test of H_1 versus H_2.

Choice of a critical region $\mathscr{S}_2$ is tantamount to the choice of a procedure for making a decision. From the classical standpoint, procedures are judged based on their expected performance in repeated samples. In the preceding hypothesis testing framework, good performance corresponds to avoiding incorrect decisions.[2] The frequency with which such errors occur in repeated sampling gives rise to the following concepts.

Definition 7.2.2 The upper limit α to the probability of incorrectly rejecting H_1 (i.e., a type I error) is called the *significance level of a test* and satisfies

$$\text{Prob}(Y \in \mathscr{S}_2 | \theta) \leq \alpha \text{ for all } \theta \in \Theta_1. \tag{7.2.1}$$

A test with critical region $\mathscr{S}_2$ that satisfies (7.2.1) is called a *level-α test*. A level-α test is said to have *size* ξ iff

$$\xi = \underset{\theta \in \Theta_1}{\text{supremum}} \text{ Prob}(Y \in \mathscr{S}_2 | \theta). \tag{7.2.2}$$

The *power of the test* with critical region $\mathscr{S}_2$ is defined by

$$\mathscr{P}(\theta) \equiv \text{Prob}(Y \in \mathscr{S}_2 | \theta), \text{ for all } \theta \in \Theta_2, \tag{7.2.3a}$$

$$= 1 - \text{Prob}(\text{type II error} | \theta), \text{ for all } \theta \in \Theta_2, \tag{7.2.3b}$$

and corresponds to the probability of correctly rejecting H_1 when it is false.

Because the righthand side of inequality (7.2.1) may not be attainable in some settings (e.g., when the random variable under consideration is discrete), the concept of test size defined by (7.2.2) is often useful. Although ideally we would like a test to have size zero and power unity for all $\theta \in \Theta_2$, such an ideal is not attainable in finite samples. For a fixed sample size, it is not possible to reduce the probabilities of type I and type II errors simultaneously. There is an inevitable trade-off that must be faced: Reducing the probability of a type I error increases the probability of a type II error, and vice versa.

The conventional sampling theory approach to hypothesis testing advocates a lexicographic preference ordering to deal with this trade-off. Between two tests of different size, the test with the smaller size is preferred. Between two tests of the same size, with power functions $\mathscr{P}_1(\cdot)$ and $\mathscr{P}_2(\cdot)$ respectively, the first test is preferred to the second at some point $\theta \in \Theta_2$ iff $\mathscr{P}_1(\theta) > \mathscr{P}_2(\theta)$.

2. For a detailed discussion of classical hypothesis testing, see Lehmann (1986, 1993) or Cox and Hinkley (1974).

A primary goal of this approach is to find a test that enjoys this power advantage for all $\theta \in \Theta_2$. This ideal is defined formally as follows.

Definition 7.2.3 A level-α test for which the power function $\mathscr{P}(\theta)$ is maximized simultaneously for all $\theta \in \Theta_2$ among all level-α tests is an *uniformly most powerful (UMP) level-α test* of H_1 versus H_2. If Θ_2 consists of a single point, then the test is a *most powerful test*.

Unfortunately, the situations in which an UMP test exists are extremely rare. Thus in order to make the basically sound idea of UMP operational, it is necessary to further restrict the class of tests under consideration. Before discussing such restrictions, however, we first consider a situation in which an UMP test exists. This situation is described in the celebrated lemma of Neyman and Pearson (1933) (Theorem 7.2.1) and involves the important concept of a likelihood ratio test defined as follows.

Definition 7.2.4 Let Y_t $(t = 1, 2, \ldots, T)$ be a random sample. Let $f(\cdot|\theta)$ denote a known p.d.f., and consider the two simple hypotheses $H_1: \theta = \theta_1$ and $H_2: \theta = \theta_2$, where θ_1 and θ_2 are two known distinct values of the parameter vector θ. Let $\mathscr{L}(\theta_j; Y)$ denote the likelihood function under H_j $(j = 1, 2)$ and define the *likelihood ratio*

$$\lambda = \lambda(\theta_1, \theta_2 | Y) = \frac{\mathscr{L}(\theta_1; Y)}{\mathscr{L}(\theta_2; Y)}. \tag{7.2.4}$$

Then a *simple likelihood ratio test* of H_1 versus H_2 is defined to be a test with a critical region of the form $\mathscr{S}_2 = \{Y | \lambda < c\}$ for some nonnegative scalar c.

Theorem 7.2.1 (Neyman-Pearson Lemma) Let Y_t $(t = 1, 2, \ldots, T)$ be a sample yielding likelihood $\mathscr{L}(\theta; y)$, where the permissible parameter space is simply two points: $\Theta = \{\theta_1, \theta_2\}$. Consider the two simple hypotheses $H_1: \theta = \theta_1$ versus $H_2: \theta = \theta_2$ and the likelihood ratio λ given by (7.2.4). Given $\alpha (0 < \alpha < 1)$, suppose there exists a critical region for rejecting H_1 in favor of H_2 of the form $\mathscr{S}_2 = \{Y | \lambda \leq d_\alpha\}$, where d_α is chosen so that $\text{Prob}(Y \in \mathscr{S}_2 | H_1) = \alpha$. Then $\mathscr{S}_2$ defines a UMP test of size α of H_1 versus H_2.

Proof Mood et al. (1974, p. 412) or Lehmann (1986, pp. 74–76).

In words the Neyman-Pearson Lemma suggests that it is reasonable to reject H_1 iff the likelihood ratio of H_1 versus H_2 is sufficiently small. This is equivalent to rejecting H_1 only if the sample data Y are sufficiently more probable *ex ante* under H_2 than under H_1. Most importantly in this context, the likelihood ratio is *not* intended to measure the relative probabilities of H_1 and H_2. From the classical perspective, it is not meaningful to assign probabilities other than zero or unity to hypotheses.

The following example illustrates the use of the Neyman-Pearson Lemma.

Example 7.2.1 Let $Y = [Y_1, Y_2, \ldots, Y_T]'$ be a random sample from a $N(\mu, \sigma^2)$ distribution with σ^2 known. Suppose $\mu_2 > \mu_1$, and consider testing H_1: $\mu = \mu_1$ versus H_2: $\mu = \mu_2$ at a level of significance α. Letting $\overline{Y}$ and S^2 denote the sample mean and variance, respectively, the likelihood function conditional on H_j $(j = 1, 2)$ is

$$\mathscr{L}(\mu_j | Y) = (2\pi\sigma^2)^{-T/2} \exp[-T\{S^2 + (\overline{Y} - \mu_j)^2\}/2\sigma^2].$$

The likelihood ratio (7.2.4) of H_1 versus H_2 is

$$\begin{aligned} \lambda &= \exp[-T\{(\overline{Y} - \mu_1)^2 - (\overline{Y} - \mu_2)^2\}/2\sigma^2] \\ &= \exp[T\{2(\mu_1 - \mu_2)\overline{Y} + (\mu_2^2 - \mu_1^2)\}/2\sigma^2]. \end{aligned} \tag{7.2.5}$$

According to the Neyman-Pearson Lemma (Theorem 7.2.1), the MP level-α test of H_1 versus H_2 has a critical region of the form $\lambda < d_\alpha$. But this implies $\overline{Y} > c_\alpha$, where

$$c_\alpha = \tfrac{1}{2}(\mu_1 + \mu_2) + [T^{-1}\sigma^2 \ln(d_\alpha)]/(\mu_1 - \mu_2). \tag{7.2.6a}$$

Under H_1, $\overline{Y} \sim N(\mu_1, \sigma^2/T)$. In order for the test to be of size α, c_α must satisfy

$$\alpha = \int_{c_\alpha}^{\infty} \phi(\bar{y} | \mu, \sigma^2/T)\, d\bar{y} = 1 - \Phi\left[\frac{c_\alpha - \mu_1}{\sigma/T^{1/2}}\right],$$

and hence,

$$c_\alpha = \mu_1 + \sigma T^{-1/2} \Phi^{-1}(1 - \alpha). \tag{7.2.6b}$$

Note that the best critical region $\overline{Y} > c_\alpha$ can also be written

$$\frac{\overline{Y} - \mu_1}{\sigma/T^{1/2}} > \Phi^{-1}(1 - \alpha). \tag{7.2.7}$$

The power of a test with critical region (7.2.7) is

$$\begin{aligned} \mathscr{P}(\mu_2) &= \int_{c_\alpha}^{\infty} \phi(\bar{y} | \mu_2, \sigma^2/T)\, d\bar{y} = 1 - \Phi\left[\frac{c_\alpha - \mu_2}{\sigma/T^{1/2}}\right] \\ &= 1 - \Phi\left[\frac{\mu_1 - \mu_2}{\sigma/T^{1/2}} + \Phi^{-1}(1 - \alpha)\right]. \end{aligned} \tag{7.2.8}$$

Note that $\mathscr{P}(\mu_2) \to 1$ as $\mu_2 \to \infty$. Also, $\mathscr{P}(\mu_2)$ is an increasing function of sample size T and an increasing function of α.

If $\mu_2 < \mu_1$, then critical region (7.2.7) is replaced by

$$\frac{\overline{Y} - \mu_1}{\sigma/T^{1/2}} < \Phi^{-1}(\alpha), \tag{7.2.9}$$

and power function (7.2.8) is replaced by

$$\mathscr{P}(\mu_2) = \Phi\left[\frac{\mu_1 - \mu_2}{\sigma/T^{1/2}} + \Phi^{-1}(\alpha)\right]. \tag{7.2.10}$$

In the Neyman-Pearson Lemma there is no question of *uniformly* greatest power since the alternative hypothesis H_2 is simple. This lemma can, however, be used to demonstrate the existence of UMP tests is more complicated situations in which H_2 is composite. For example, in Example 7.2.1 the critical value c_α in (7.2.6b) does *not* depend on μ_2, and hence the test defined by (7.2.7) is a UMP level-α test of H_1: $\mu = \mu_1$ versus H_2: $\mu > \mu_1$. Obviously, the test defined by (7.2.9) is UMP level-α test of H_1: $\mu = \mu_1$ versus H_2: $\mu < \mu_1$. However, there is no UMP level-α test of H: $\mu = \mu_1$ versus the two-sided alternative H_2: $\mu \neq \mu_1$; since the two UMP tests over the regions $\mu < \mu_1$ and $\mu > \mu_1$ are different and hence cannot be UMP over the entire region defined by H_2: $\mu \neq \mu_1$. This point is sufficiently important to warrant emphasis in the following example.

Example 7.2.2 Reconsider Example 7.2.1. Define the three standard critical regions for testing H_1: $\mu = \mu_1$ against the hypotheses H_2: $\mu > \mu_1$, H_3: $\mu < \mu_1$ and H_4: $\mu \neq \mu_1$:

$$\mathscr{S}_2 \equiv \{Y | \overline{Y} > \mu_1 + (\sigma/T^{1/2})\Phi^{-1}(1-\alpha)\}, \tag{7.2.11}$$

$$\mathscr{S}_3 \equiv \{Y | \overline{Y} < \mu_1 + (\sigma/T^{1/2})\Phi^{-1}(\alpha)\}, \tag{7.2.12}$$

$$\mathscr{S}_4 \equiv \{Y | \overline{Y} > \mu_1 + (\sigma/T^{1/2})\Phi^{-1}(1-\tfrac{1}{2}\alpha) \text{ or } \overline{Y} < \mu_1 - (\sigma/T^{1/2})\Phi^{-1}(\tfrac{1}{2}\alpha)\}. \tag{7.2.13}$$

The power functions corresponding to each of these critical regions are depicted in Figure 7.2.1. It is clear from Figure 7.2.1 that none of these critical regions yield UMP tests.

Example 7.2.3 Consider Example 6.9.3 in which Y_t $(t = 1, 2, \ldots, 9) \sim$ i.i.d. $N(\mu, 36)$. Suppose $\mu_1 = \frac{1}{2}$. Then rejection regions (7.2.11)–(7.2.13) for testing H_1: $\mu = \mu_1$ at the $\alpha = .05$ level of significance versus H_2: $\mu > \frac{1}{2}$, H_3: $\mu < \frac{1}{2}$ and H_4: $\mu \neq \frac{1}{2}$, respectively, are:

$$\mathscr{S}_2 \equiv \{Y | \overline{Y} > \tfrac{1}{2} + (6/3)\Phi^{-1}(.95)\} \tag{7.2.14a}$$

$$\equiv \{Y | \overline{Y} > 3.79\}, \tag{7.2.14b}$$

$$\mathscr{S}_3 \equiv \{Y | \overline{Y} < \tfrac{1}{2} + (6/3)\Phi^{-1}(.05)\} \tag{7.2.15a}$$

$$\equiv \{Y | \overline{Y} < -2.79\}, \tag{7.2.15a}$$

$$\mathscr{S}_4 \equiv \{Y | \overline{Y} > \tfrac{1}{2} + (6/3)\Phi^{-1}(.975) \text{ or } \overline{Y} < \tfrac{1}{2} - (6/3)\Phi^{-1}(.025)\} \tag{7.2.16a}$$

$$\equiv \{Y | \overline{Y} > 4.42 \text{ or } \overline{Y} < -3.42\}, \tag{7.2.16b}$$

where $\Phi(.95) = 1.645$, $\Phi(.05) = -1.645$, $\Phi(.975) = 1.96$ and $\Phi(.025) = -1.96$. Observing $\overline{y} = 4$ leads to rejecting H_1 in favor of H_2, but not rejecting H_1 in favor of H_3 or H_4.

The preceding results should not be interpreted as suggesting that UMP tests fail to exist only in the presence of two-sided alternative hypotheses. *In general when testing a simple null hypothesis against a one-sided alterna-*

tive, no UMP test is guaranteed to exist. For example, in Example 7.2.1 with unknown variance, but known coefficient of variation, Cox and Hinkley (1974, p. 98) show that no UMP test exists for testing $H_1: \mu = \mu_1$ versus $H_1: \mu > \mu_1$.[3] Also UMP tests usually do not exist when the hypotheses involve more than one parameter. Lehmann (1986, pp. 108–111, 192–203) summarizes the failures in the familiar case of a normal distribution with unknown mean and variance.

Because UMP tests do not generally exist, it is necessary to restrict the cases in which to seek such tests. Two types of restrictions can be imposed. Either (i) additional assumptions about the probability model can be considered, or (ii) the class of tests under consideration can be restricted. The need for some restrictions is obvious and should not be surprising since similar restrictions were required in seeking optimal estimators in Chapter 6.[4]

Under restrictions of type (i), the most commonly encountered restriction is to consider the case of a single parameter and require that the likelihood emits a monotone likelihood ratio. For example, when drawing a random sample from the exponential family with a single natural parameter θ, the likelihood ratio is in fact monotone. In such cases a UMP test of $H_1: \theta = \theta_1$ versus $H_2: \theta > \theta_1$ is available (see Lehmann 1986, pp. 78–81). More generally, Lehmann (1986, p. 509) notes that a necessary and sufficient condition for the single parameter density $f(y - \theta)$ to have a monotone likelihood ratio is that $-\ln[f(y - \theta)]$ is convex.

Under restrictions of type (ii), three restricted classes of tests are usually considered: unbiased, invariant and local tests. The first class of tests is defined as follows.

Definition 7.2.5 A statistical test of $H_1: \theta \in \Theta_1$ versus $H_2: \theta \in \Theta_2$ is *unbiased* iff

$$\text{Prob(rejecting } H_1|H_2) \geq \text{Prob(rejecting } H_1|H_1). \tag{7.2.17}$$

Otherwise the test is *biased.*

In words, (7.2.14) requires that the probability of falling in the rejection region is never larger under H_1 than under H_2. Unbiasedness of a test is an intuitively appealing restriction to impose, *ceteris paribus.* Like unbiased estimators, unbiased tests do not favor any particular regions of the

3. For another example, see Kendall and Stuart (1979, pp. 186–191). Note also that the existence of a UMP test is neither necessary nor sufficient for the existence of sufficient statistics. See Kendall and Stuart (1979, pp. 191–193) for more details.

4. For example, in seeking minimum MSE estimators, attention was restricted to unbiased estimators, and it was seen that a minimum variance estimator existed only when an unbiased estimator and a complete sufficient statistic existed (Theorem 6.5.6).

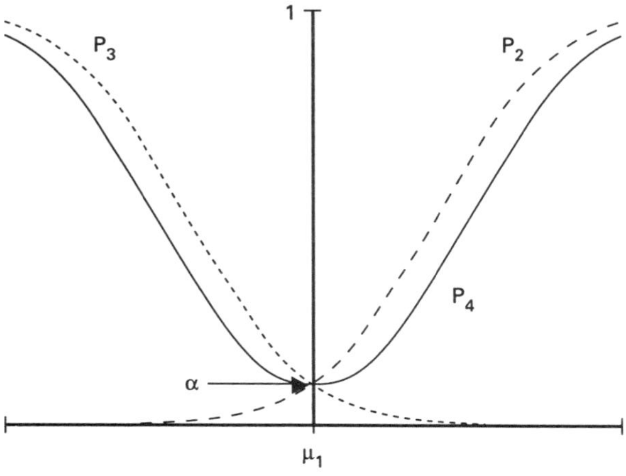

Figure 7.2.1
Power functions for Example 7.2.2

parameter space. For example, consider Example 7.2.2 and Figure 7.2.1. The tests corresponding to critical regions $\mathcal{S}_2$ and $\mathcal{S}_3$ are not unbiased, but critical region $\mathcal{S}_4$ is unbiased, as is clear from Figure 7.2.1. In fact the test corresponding to critical region $\mathcal{S}_4$ is UMP among all unbiased tests for this problem. Such a test is said to be *uniformly most powerful unbiased* (*UMPU*) in this case.

As in the case of unbiased estimators, unbiased tests lose their attractiveness when prior information is available. For example, if the researcher believes H_3: $\mu < \mu_1$ is most unlikely in a particular application of Example 7.2.2, then the test with critical region $\mathcal{S}_2$ may be more attractive than the test corresponding to $\mathcal{S}_4$. Certainly, in the limit when the prior information is so strong that H_2 replaces H_4 as the alternative, critical region $\mathcal{S}_2$ is preferable to $\mathcal{S}_4$. For *e* detailed discussion of unbiased tests, see Lehmann (1986, Chapters 4 and 5).

The second type (ii) restriction to place on a test is to require the test statistic to be *invariant* to certain transformations of the sample space (e.g., changes of scale or origin in the observations).[5] Within this restricted class, there may exist an optimum test: a *uniformly most powerful invariant* (*UMPI*) *test*. Sometimes UMPI tests exist when UMPU do not exist, and vice versa. Other times both UMPI and UMPU tests exist and coincide. For more discussion, see Lehmann (1986, pp. 302–305) and Cox and Hinkley (1974, pp. 157–174).

5. Invariance criteria are particularly useful in multidimensional problems in which there are no preferred directions. Sometimes, however, the invariance principle leads to a useless test (e.g., see Cox and Hinkley 1974, pp. 170–171).

A third type (ii) restriction that is sometimes invoked when the first two fail, is to consider tests that maximize power for alternatives "close" to the null hypothesis. Such tests are said to be *locally most powerful* (*LMP*). The LMP restriction is commonly invoked when considering power behavior as $T \to \infty$. See Section 7.3 for further discussion.

Three connections between hypothesis testing and estimation should be noted. First, consider point estimation. As noted in Section 6.3, even with the restrictive assumption of unbiasedness, the search for "optimal" point estimators (i.e., minimum variance) led at best to questionable estimators, even in those highly restricted cases for which they existed. Similar remarks hold in searching for optimal tests, whether they be UMP, UMPU, UMPI, or LMP, and so we will not pursue the matter here.

Second, consider interval estimation. The reader has probably already noticed the close connection between interval estimation and hypothesis testing: generally speaking, confidence intervals are the complements of the critical regions introduced in this section. This provides yet another interpretation of a confidence interval. *For example, in the context of a confidence interval for the mean of a normal distribution, the observed confidence interval is the set of all null hypotheses that the usual two-sided hypothesis test would not be able to reject with the data at hand.*

Example 7.2.4 Consider Examples 6.9.3 and 7.2.3. After observing $\bar{y} = 4$, then for any μ_1 in the .95 confidence interval $.08 \le \mu_1 \le 7.92$, the hypothesis $H_1\colon \mu = \mu_1$ versus $H_4\colon \mu \ne \mu_1$ cannot be rejected at the .05 level of significance.

Finally, again in connection with interval estimation, the presence of nuisance parameters causes problems. Analogous to the search for a "pivotal" quantity in interval estimation, there is a search for a test statistic in classical hypothesis testing with a known distribution (at least under the null and preferably under both hypotheses). This leads to the search for so-called *similar critical regions*, that is, critical regions of the same size for all values of the nuisance parameters. In general such similar critical regions exist only in special cases involving boundedly complete sufficient statistics (see Cox and Hinkley 1974, pp. 134–156; Hillier 1987; or Kendall and Stuart 1979, Chapter 23). Given our interest in general procedures, we will not pursue the matter further here.

If the reader draws on economic intuition, some light might be shed on the classical choice of a critical region. Consider the researcher in the position of a consumer choosing a bundle of two "bad" commodities, namely, a point in $\alpha \equiv$ Prob(type I error) versus $\beta \equiv$ Prob(type II error) space as depicted in Figure 7.2.2. The origin is the point of highest utility (minimum loss), but is not likely to be obtainable. In the case of no data

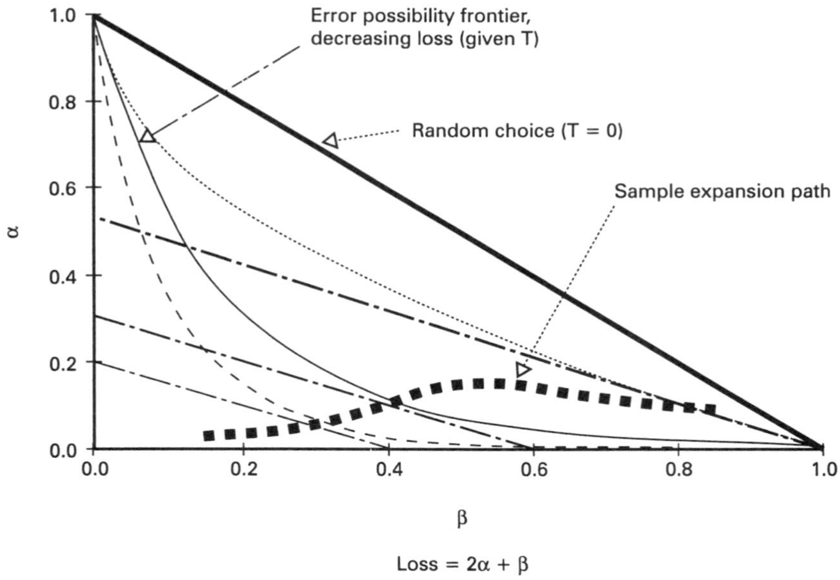

Figure 7.2.2
Error preferences for type I and type II errors

($T = 0$), any point on the line segment joining (0, 1) and (1, 0) is obtainable by appropriate randomization of choice. As sample size T increases, points closer to the origin become attainable. The curve of preferred points is the *error possibility frontier* (see Figure 7.2.2) and is analogous to the consumer's budget constraint.

How should one choose a point on the error possibility frontier? The answer, of course, depends on the researcher's preferences. Savage (1954), however, makes a convincing argument (at least for some researchers) that indifference curves should be straight lines. Here is the argument. Identify two points (α_0, β_0) and (α_1, β_1) between which you are indifferent. By assumption you are indifferent between these two points, so suppose someone chooses for you by randomly selecting (α_0, β_0) with probability p and selecting (α_1, β_1) with probability $1 - p$. Acceptance of this proposition implies indifference to the error probabilities given by the point $(p\alpha_0 + [1 - p]\alpha_1, p\beta_0 + [1 - p]\beta_1)$. By varying p, all points on the line segment joining (α_0, β_0) and (α_1, β_1) are generated. Therefore, you have revealed that your indifference curves are straight lines. Savage (1962, p. 67) notes the irony in the strength of the subjectivist's possible indifference curves compared to the objectivist's indifference curves for α versus β: "The subjectivist's position is more objective than the objectivist's, for the subjectivist finds the range of coherent or reasonable preference patterns much narrower than the objectivist thought it to be. How confusing and dangerous big words are!"

Figure 7.2.2 is based on Leamer (1978, pp. 94–98). It provides a means for an economist faced with testing two simple hypotheses to use his/her microeconomic training to choosing (α, β). Note that the usual classical procedure corresponds to *lexicographic preferences*: prefer tests with low probability of a type I error (the error assumed more serious), and between two tests with the same probability of a type I error, prefer the test with the lower type II error. Economists may wish to recall how much serious attention was devoted to lexicographic preferences in their microeconomic courses.

As $T \rightarrow \infty$, the level of the test remains at α, and the increased sample information is employed to reduce the probability of a type II error. Thus the "expansion path" in Figure 7.2.2 does *not* go through the origin. One implication of this path is that in large samples sharp null hypotheses are almost surely rejected when they are literally false since it becomes possible to discriminate hypotheses arbitrarily close to the null. This fact has been deplored often in the literature (e.g., Leamer 1978 and McCloskey 1985), but there have been few classical guidelines as to exactly how to decrease α with sample size. Exceptions are Bauer et al. (1988), Hendry et al. (1989, p. 233), and Pötscher (1983). Another exception is Hald (1971) who recommends that α should be decreasing at least as fast as $[T^{-1}(\ln T)]^{1/2}$. *In large samples (e.g., when using census data) everything becomes "significant" in the statistical sense, and the difference between "statistical significance" and "significance in the sense of a meaningful economic difference" diverge.*

An exception, but remaining within the sampling theory framework, is given in a fairly obscure article by Nobel Laureate Kenneth Arrow. Arrow (1960) advocates fixing a difference in the parameter space that is "significant" or "meaningful" in the sense that the cost of type I and type II errors are equal. This leads to an "equal-probability test." Unlike the usual situation described earlier, the probability of both types of errors approach zero as $T \rightarrow \infty$ under a equal-probability test. See Arrow (1960) for details. Similarly, Kunte (1992) argues that a weighted (by a prior density) average of the probability of type II error should never be less than the probability of type I error.

Finally, it should be repeated that the testing procedures discussed in this section are all founded in the sampling theory mode of inference. The following two examples provides a reminder of some of the frailties of such inferences.

Example 7.2.5 Recall the case of the binomial (Y_1 is the number of "heads" in $T_1 = 12$ flips) and the negative binomial (Y_2 is the number of "heads" before obtaining $m = 3$ "tails") experiments in Example 6.2.4. Adopt a significance level of $\alpha = .05$ for testing $H_1: \theta = \frac{1}{2}$ versus $H_2: \theta > \frac{1}{2}$. The data consist of nine "heads" and three "tails." Under binomial sampling, $P(Y_1 \geq 9|H_1) = .0730 > .05$, and hence, H_1 should not be rejected. Under negative binomial sampling, however, $P(Y_1 \geq 9|H_1) = .0337 < .05$, and hence, H_1 should be rejected. These conflicting recommendations depending on the sampling plan stand in sharp contrast to the conclusion reached in Example 6.2.4 that according to the LP, the evidence in the data regarding θ is the same in both experiments. This example illustrates the fact that the LP is of pragmatic, and not just theoretical, importance. See Lindley and Phillips (1976) for further discussion.

Example 7.2.6 recalls the Stopping Rule Principle (SRP) of Section 6.2 and bridges the discussion to the Bayesian testing techniques discussed in Section 7.4.

Example 7.2.6 (Adapted from Berger and Berry 1988, pp. 30–31) An experimental economist enters the office of an econometrician of the frequentist persuasion with $T = 100$ observations, assumed to be independent and from a $N(\theta, 1)$ distribution. The experimentalist wants to test $H_1: \theta = 0$ versus $H_1: \theta \neq 0$. The current sample mean is $\bar{y}_T = 0.2$, so the standardized test statistic is $z = T^{1/2}|\bar{y}_T - 0| = 2$. A careless classical econometrician might simply conclude that there is "significant" evidence against H_1 at the .05 level. But this econometrician asks the experimentalist: "Why did you cease experimentation after 100 observations?" The experimentalist replies: "I just decided to take a batch of 100 observations."

The classical econometrician seems satisfied, but continues to probe: "What would you have done had the first 100 observations not yielded significance?" The experimentalist replies: "I would have taken another batch of 100 observations." Further interrogation uncovers the following strategy implicit in the experimentalist mind:

(a) Take 100 observations.

(b) If $100^{1/2}|\bar{y}_{100}| \geq c_*$, then stop and reject H_1.

(c) If $100^{1/2}|\bar{y}_{100}| < c_*$, then take another 100 observations and reject H_1 if $200^{1/2}|\bar{y}_{200}| \geq c_*$.

Pocock (1977) shows that in order for this procedure to have level $\alpha = .05$, c_* must be 2.18. Because the actual data had $100^{1/2}|\bar{y}_{100}| = 2 < 2.18$, the experimentalist could not actually conclude significance, and hence would have to take another 100 observations.

This strikes many people as peculiar. The interpretation of the results of an experiment depends not only on the data obtained and the way it was obtained, but *also upon the thoughts of the experimenter concerning future plans*.

This analysis may be taken further. Suppose the puzzled experimentalist leaves and returns with 100 more observations. Consider two cases. If $200^{1/2}|\bar{y}_{200}| = 2.1 < 2.18$, then the results are not significant. *But they would have been significant had the experimentalist not paused halfway through the study to calculate* z. If, however, $200^{1/2}|\bar{y}_{200}| = 2.20 > 2.18$, then "significance" is obtained. But wait! Again the econometrician asks what the experimentalist would have done had the results not been significant. The experimentalist replies: "If my grant renewal were to be approved, I would then take another 100 observations; if the grant renewal were rejected, I would have no more funds and would have to stop the experiment in any case. The classical econometrician then offers the "wisdom": "I cannot make a conclusion until we find out the outcome of your grant renewal; if it is not renewed, you can claim significant evidence against H_1, while if it is renewed, you cannot claim significance and must take another 100 observations."

The value of such advice seems worthless, and the econometrician might be lucky to avoid death at the hands of the irate experimentalist. Nonetheless, the advice is entirely appropriate from the frequentist standpoint. *The moral is simple: The sample space is defined by the researcher's intentions and plans. To the extent that such plans or intentions are unclear, or to the extent that they are not shared by other researchers, ambiguity arises in the interpretation of the data at hand.* The false idol of "objectivity" has been exposed.

Example 7.2.6 also demonstrates a point made in Section 6.2. Suppose the researcher simply picks a fixed critical value c_*, and then decides to continue sampling until achieving a test statistic $z = T^{1/2}|\bar{y}_T| > c_*$. Once such a "significant" test statistic is achieved, the researcher then rejects the null hypothesis. What is the *ex ante* probability that a researcher following such a strategy can in fact sample to such a foregone conclusion? Using the "Law of Integrated Logarithm" (Theorem 5.7.10), it can in fact be shown that with "probability one" the researcher will find a finite sample which rejects the null hypothesis (see Robbins 1952 or Anscombe 1954). Because the SRP permits such a sampling strategy, isn't this evidence that something is suspect with the SRP, and hence, also the LP? The answer is an emphatic NO! Such "sampling to a foregone conclusion" results cast into question the testing procedure being employed, namely, classical hypothesis testing. As will be seen in Section 7.4, Bayesian posterior odds analysis is immune from such condemnation.

Exercises

7.2.1 (See Cornfield 1970 and Cox 1958b). Consider testing the simple null hypothesis $H_1\colon \theta = 1$ versus the simple alternative hypothesis $H_2\colon \theta = 10$. Two devices are available for measuring θ: device R produces a single observation $y \sim N(\theta, 100)$ and device U produces a single observation $y \sim N(\theta, 1)$. Clearly, device U is far more accurate than device R. Unfortunately, which device is available is determined by a random event J (independent of θ): device J is available with

$$\text{Prob}(J = R) = .05 - \varepsilon, \tag{7.2.18}$$

$$\text{Prob}(J = U) = .95 + \varepsilon, \tag{7.2.19}$$

where

$$\varepsilon = \frac{.95[1 - \Phi(4.5)]}{\Phi(4.5)} \doteq .0000003. \tag{7.2.20}$$

Fortunately, the probability $.95 + \varepsilon$ for the more accurate device is quite high.

For the pragmatic-minded researcher, let us give a little concreteness to this setting. Let device R be a testing device in a *rural* laboratory, and let device U be a testing device in an *urban* laboratory such as the federal government's laboratory in the capital. The randomization event J may reflect a "rural development program" which is intended to provide the rural laboratory some small fraction of government projects in order to enhance the training of government scientists stationed in rural areas.

Now consider the classical hypothesis test defined by the following rejection region. For device R, which is very inaccurate, H_1 is *always* rejected regardless of the observation y. (Note: This rejection rule may reflect urban researcher's distrust of the rural device R, that is, "better to ignore results and simply reject H_1.") For device U, H_1 is rejected iff $y > 4.5$.

(a) Compute the level of significance of this testing procedure, that is, compute:

(1) Prob(rejecting $H_1 | H_1, R$)

(2) Prob(rejecting $H_1 | H_1, U$)

(3) Prob(rejecting $H_1 | H_1$)

(b) Consider the power of the test. Compute Prob(rejecting $H_1 | H_2$).

(c) Suppose $J = R$ is observed, and then subsequently, $y = 1$ is observed. What do you conclude?

(d) How do you reconcile your "desirable" results in (a) and (b) with your "counter-intuitive" result in (c)?

7.2.2 (Goldberger 1991, pp. 262–263) Suppose $Y \sim N(\mu, 1)$ and that μ is believed to be near zero. Consider three estimators of μ based on a single observation Y: $\hat{\mu}_1 = Y$, $\hat{\mu}_2 = 0$, and

$$\hat{\mu}_3 = \begin{Bmatrix} \hat{\mu}_2, & \text{if } Y \leq 1 \\ \hat{\mu}_1, & \text{if } Y > 1 \end{Bmatrix}. \tag{7.2.21}$$

(a) Show: $E_{Y|\mu}(\hat{\mu}_3) = \pi_0 \mu + \pi_1$, where $\pi_0 = \Phi(-c_1) + \Phi(-c_2)$, $\pi_1 = \phi(c_2) - \phi(c_1)$, $c_1 = 1 + \mu$, *and* $c_2 = 1 - \mu$.

(b) Show: $\text{Var}(\hat{\mu}_3) = \pi_0(1 - \pi_0)\mu^2 + (\pi_2 - \pi_1^2) + 2\mu\pi_1(1 - \pi_0)$, where $\pi_2 = \pi_0 - \mu\pi_1 + \phi(c_1) + \phi(c_2)$.

(c) Compare the MSE's of $\hat{\mu}_i$ $(i = 1, 2, 3)$.

7.2.3 (Berger and Wolpert 1988, p. 7) Suppose $Y \sim N(0, .25)$ and consider the hypotheses $H_1\colon \theta = -1$ and $H_2\colon \theta = 1$.

(a) Show that the critical region $Y \geq 0$ yields error probabilities $\alpha = \beta = .0228$.

(b) Suppose $Y = 0$ is observed. Intuitively, which hypothesis does this observation favor?

(c) Suppose $Y = 1$ is observed. Intuitively, which hypothesis does this observation favor?

(d) Perform formal hypothesis testing of H_1 versus H_2 at the .05 level of significance in the case of both (b) and (c). What do you conclude? Do you obtain similar results?

7.2.4 Consider Example 6.9.8. Test $H_1\colon \sigma^2 = 40$ versus $H_2\colon \sigma^2 \neq 40$ at the .01 level of significance.

7.2.5 Consider Example 6.9.10. Test $H_1\colon \mu_1 = \mu_2$ versus $H_2\colon \mu_1 \neq \mu_2$ at the .05 level of significance.

7.2.6 Consider Example 6.9.12. Test $H_1\colon \sigma_1^2 = \sigma_2^2$ versus $H_2\colon \sigma_1^2 \neq \sigma_2^2$ at the .02 level of significance.

7.2.7 Consider Exercise 6.9.11.

(a) Use confidence ellipsoid (6.9.40) to construct a test of $H_1\colon \mu = 0_M$ versus $H_2\colon \mu \neq 0_M$ at the .05 level of significance.

(b) Discuss the power properties of your test in (a) (see Muirhead 1982, pp. 213–215, 218–219). In what sense is your test optimal?

7.2.8 Consider Exercise 6.9.12.

(a) Test $H_1\colon \mu_x = \mu_y$ versus $H_2\colon \mu_x \neq \mu_y$ at the .05 level of significance.

(b) Discuss the power properties of your test in (a) (see Muirhead 1982, pp. 216–218).

7.2.9 Let R be a $J \times M$ matrix of constants with $\text{rank}(R) = M$, and let r be a known $M \times 1$ vector of constants.

(a) Use your answer to Exercise 6.9.13 to test $H_1\colon R\mu = r$ versus $H_2\colon R\mu \neq r$ at the .05 level of significance.

(b) Discuss the power properties of your test in (a) (see Muirhead 1982, p. 218).

7.2.10 Suppose you have M null hypotheses each of which is tested at the significance level α. Further suppose all the tests are independent, and that all the null hypotheses are valid.

(a) Show that the probability of getting at least one rejection is $q = 1 - (1 - \alpha)^M$.

(b) Find q when $\alpha = .01, .05, .10$ and $M = 5, 10, 15$.

7.3 Asymptotic Tests

In our discussion of asymptotic tests we begin with a fairly weak property that any sensible test is presumed to satisfy in a truth search.

Definition 7.3.1 If the power of test approaches unity under all values of the alternative hypothesis, then the test is *consistent.*

In other words a consistent test is one for which the probability of a type II error goes to zero as $T \to \infty$. Note that consistency does *not* require that the probability of a type I error goes to zero as $T \to \infty$; this latter requirement can be achieved by picking the level of the test to be a decreasing function of sample size (see Bauer et al. 1988; Pötscher 1983; and Hald 1971). Because most tests are consistent it is necessary to impose more stringent conditions in order to eliminate "inefficient" tests. The most popular approach in econometrics is to consider the power of a test as the value of the parameter under the alternative hypothesis becomes closer to the null hypothesis as sample size increases. Such alternatives are known as *local alternatives*, and the ability to detect such violations of the null hypothesis is one grounds for comparing tests (for another criteria, see Bahadur 1960).

For detailed, but readable, accounts of classical testing procedures, see Godfrey (1988) and Engle (1984). Here only a brief introduction is provided, concentrating on three families of tests: Wald, likelihood ratio and score/Lagrange multiplier.

Suppose $\theta = [\lambda', \omega']'$ and $\Theta_j = \Lambda_j \times \Omega$ $(j = 1, 2)$. The dimension of λ is $K_\lambda \times 1$, and the dimension of ω is $K_\omega \times 1$, where $K = K_\lambda + K_\omega$. Consider testing $H_1: \lambda = \lambda_*$ versus $H_2: \lambda \neq \lambda_*$, where $\lambda_* \in \Lambda_1$ is given. Let $\hat{\theta}_* = [\lambda_*', \hat{\omega}_*']'$ and $\hat{\theta} = [\hat{\lambda}', \hat{\omega}']'$ denote the MLE's under H_1 and H_2, respectively. To simplify subscript notation, the information matrix in the sample, $J_T(\theta)$, is denoted here as $J(\theta)$, and the information matrix in a single observation, $J_1(\theta)$, is denoted here as $T^{-1}J(\theta)$. Partition the score, Hessian and information matrices accordingly:

$$s_{c,\theta}(\theta; Y) = \begin{bmatrix} s_{c,\lambda}(\lambda, \omega; Y) \\ s_{c,\omega}(\lambda, \omega; Y) \end{bmatrix} = \begin{bmatrix} \dfrac{\partial L(\lambda, \omega; Y)}{\partial \lambda} \\ \dfrac{\partial L(\lambda, \omega; Y)}{\partial \omega} \end{bmatrix}, \tag{7.3.1}$$

$$H(\theta; Y) = \begin{bmatrix} H_{\lambda\lambda}(\lambda, \omega; Y) & H_{\lambda\omega}(\lambda, \omega; Y) \\ H_{\omega\lambda}(\lambda, \omega; Y) & H_{\omega\omega}(\lambda, \omega; Y) \end{bmatrix}$$

$$= \begin{bmatrix} \dfrac{\partial^2 L(\lambda, \omega; Y)}{\partial \lambda \, \partial \lambda'} & \dfrac{\partial^2 L(\lambda, \omega; Y)}{\partial \lambda \, \partial \omega'} \\ \dfrac{\partial^2 L(\lambda, \omega; Y)}{\partial \omega \, \partial \lambda'} & \dfrac{\partial^2 L(\lambda, \omega; Y)}{\partial \omega \, \partial \omega'} \end{bmatrix}, \tag{7.3.2}$$

$$J(\theta; Y) = \begin{bmatrix} J_{\lambda\lambda}(\lambda, \omega; Y) & J_{\lambda\omega}(\lambda, \omega; Y) \\ J_{\omega\lambda}(\lambda, \omega; Y) & J_{\omega\omega}(\lambda, \omega; Y) \end{bmatrix}$$

$$= -E_{Y|\lambda,\omega} \begin{bmatrix} \dfrac{\partial^2 L(\lambda, \omega; Y)}{\partial \lambda \, \partial \lambda'} & \dfrac{\partial^2 L(\lambda, \omega; Y)}{\partial \lambda \, \partial \omega'} \\ \dfrac{\partial^2 L(\lambda, \omega; Y)}{\partial \omega \, \partial \lambda'} & \dfrac{\partial^2 L(\lambda, \omega; Y)}{\partial \omega \, \partial \omega'} \end{bmatrix}. \tag{7.3.3}$$

The partitioned inverses of (7.3.2) and (7.3.3) are denoted

$$[H(\theta; Y)]^{-1} = \begin{bmatrix} H^{\lambda\lambda}(\lambda, \omega; Y) & H^{\lambda\omega}(\lambda, \omega; Y) \\ H^{\omega\lambda}(\lambda, \omega; Y) & H^{\omega\omega}(\lambda, \omega; Y) \end{bmatrix}$$

$$= \begin{bmatrix} \dfrac{\partial^2 L(\lambda, \omega; Y)}{\partial\lambda\,\partial\lambda'} & \dfrac{\partial^2 L(\lambda, \omega; Y)}{\partial\lambda\,\partial\omega'} \\ \dfrac{\partial^2 L(\lambda, \omega; Y)}{\partial\omega\,\partial\lambda'} & \dfrac{\partial^2 L(\lambda, \omega; Y)}{\partial\omega\,\partial\omega'} \end{bmatrix}^{-1}, \tag{7.3.4}$$

$$[J(\theta; Y)]^{-1} = \begin{bmatrix} J^{\lambda\lambda}(\lambda, \omega; Y) & J^{\lambda\omega}(\lambda, \omega; Y) \\ J^{\omega\lambda}(\lambda, \omega; Y) & J^{\omega\omega}(\lambda, \omega; Y) \end{bmatrix}$$

$$= \left[-E_{Y|\lambda,\omega} \begin{bmatrix} \dfrac{\partial^2 L(\lambda, \omega; Y)}{\partial\lambda\,\partial\lambda'} & \dfrac{\partial^2 L(\lambda, \omega; Y)}{\partial\lambda\,\partial\omega'} \\ \dfrac{\partial^2 L(\lambda, \omega; Y)}{\partial\omega\,\partial\lambda'} & \dfrac{\partial^2 L(\lambda, \omega; Y)}{\partial\omega\,\partial\omega'} \end{bmatrix} \right]^{-1}. \tag{7.3.5}$$

We now consider a trinity of asymptotic tests. First, from the asymptotic normality of the unrestricted ML estimator $\hat{\theta}$, that is, $T^{1/2}(\hat{\theta} - \theta) \xrightarrow{d} N_K(0_K, [T^{-1}J(\theta)]^{-1})$ as $T \to \infty$, it follows immediately that under H_1,

$$T^{1/2}(\hat{\lambda} - \lambda_*) \xrightarrow{d} N(0, TJ^{\lambda\lambda}(\theta)) \text{ as } T \to \infty, \tag{7.3.6}$$

where using Theorem A.4.4 (Partitioned Inverse Theorem):

$$J^{\lambda\lambda}(\theta) = [J_{\lambda\lambda}(\theta) - J_{\lambda\omega}(\theta)\{J_{\omega\omega}(\theta)\}^{-1}J_{\omega\lambda}(\theta)]^{-1}. \tag{7.3.7}$$

Therefore, "squaring" (7.3.6) implies that under H_1,

$$\xi_W = (\hat{\lambda} - \lambda_*)'[J^{\lambda\lambda}(\theta)]^{-1}(\hat{\lambda} - \lambda_*) \xrightarrow{d} \chi^2(K_\lambda) \text{ as } T \to \infty. \tag{7.3.8}$$

Test statistic (7.3.8) is known as the *Wald (W) statistic* after Wald (1943). The intuition behind (7.3.8) is simple: ξ_W measures the distance of the null hypothesis value λ_* from the unrestricted estimator of $\hat{\lambda}$ relative to the asymptotic variability in $\hat{\lambda}$. Because in general $J^{\lambda\lambda}(\theta)$ involves unknown parameters, the following three operational versions, with the same asymptotic behavior as (7.3.8), can be used (recall Theorem 5.5.11 and similar discussion in Section 6.6):

$$\xi_{W,1} = (\hat{\lambda} - \lambda_*)'[J^{\lambda\lambda}(\hat{\theta})]^{-1}(\hat{\lambda} - \lambda_*), \tag{7.3.9}$$

$$\xi_{W,2} = (\hat{\lambda} - \lambda_*)'[-H^{\lambda\lambda}(\hat{\theta})]^{-1}(\hat{\lambda} - \lambda_*), \tag{7.3.10}$$

$$\xi_{W,3} = (\hat{\lambda} - \lambda_*)'[\tilde{J}^{\lambda\lambda}(\hat{\theta})]^{-1}(\hat{\lambda} - \lambda_*), \tag{7.3.11}$$

where analogous to (6.6.31),

$$\tilde{J}(\hat{\theta}) = \begin{bmatrix} \tilde{J}_{\lambda\lambda}(\hat{\theta}) & \tilde{J}_{\lambda\omega}(\hat{\theta}) \\ \tilde{J}_{\omega\lambda}(\hat{\theta}) & \tilde{J}_{\omega\omega}(\hat{\theta}) \end{bmatrix} = \sum_{t=1}^{T} \left[\frac{\partial \ln[f(y_t|\hat{\theta})]}{\partial\theta}\right]\left[\frac{\partial \ln[f(y_t|\hat{\theta})]}{\partial\theta'}\right], \tag{7.3.12}$$

$$\tilde{J}^{\lambda\lambda} = [\tilde{J}_{\lambda\lambda}(\hat{\theta}) - \tilde{J}_{\lambda\omega}(\hat{\theta})[\tilde{J}_{\omega\omega}(\hat{\theta})]^{-1}\tilde{J}_{\omega\lambda}(\hat{\theta})]^{-1}. \tag{7.3.13}$$

Under H_1, consistent estimators of $J^{\lambda\lambda}(\theta)$ are also obtained if $\hat{\theta}$ is replaced by $\hat{\theta}_*$ in (7.3.6)–(7.3.13). Estimation of $J(\theta)$ by $\tilde{J}(\hat{\theta})$, popularized by Berndt et al. (1974), is based on the equivalence $E_{Y|\theta}\{[s_c(\theta; Y)][s_c(\theta; Y)]'\} = -E_{Y|\theta}[H(\theta; Y)]$ noted in (6.5.7). Estimator (7.3.12) is commonly referred to as the *outer product of the score*.

Second, Wilks (1938) suggested the *likelihood-ratio (LR)* test statistic:

$$\xi_{\text{LR}} = -2\ln\left(\frac{\mathscr{L}(\hat{\theta}_*; Y)}{\mathscr{L}(\hat{\theta}; Y)}\right) = -2[L(\hat{\theta}_*; Y) - L(\hat{\theta}; Y)], \tag{7.3.14}$$

in which the assumed known values of θ in (7.2.4) are replaced by consistent estimators under H_1 and H_2. Under H_1, as $T \to \infty$, $\xi_{\text{LR}} \xrightarrow{d} \chi^2(K_\lambda)$. The LR test statistic is predicated on the simple intuition that the value of H_1 should be measured in terms of the costs it imposes on the criterion function $L(\theta; y)$.

Finally, the *score test statistic* (Rao 1948) is

$$\xi_{\text{LM}} = [s_{c,\lambda}(\hat{\theta}_*; Y)]'[J^{\lambda\lambda}(\theta)][s_{c,\lambda}(\hat{\theta}_*; Y)]. \tag{7.3.15}$$

The limiting asymptotic normality of the score (used in proving Theorem 6.6.4) implies under H_1, $\xi_{\text{LM}} \xrightarrow{d} \chi^2(K_\lambda)$ as $T \to \infty$. Operational versions of (7.3.15), with the same asymptotic behavior, are:

$$\xi_{\text{LM},1} = [s_{c,\lambda}(\hat{\theta}_*; Y)]'[J^{\lambda\lambda}(\hat{\theta}_*)][s_{c,\lambda}(\hat{\theta}_*; Y)], \tag{7.3.16}$$

$$\xi_{\text{LM},2} = [s_{c,\lambda}(\hat{\theta}_*; Y)]'[-H^{\lambda\lambda}(\hat{\theta}_*)][s_{c,\lambda}(\hat{\theta}_*; Y)], \tag{7.3.17}$$

$$\xi_{\text{LM},3} = [s_{c,\lambda}(\hat{\theta}_*; Y)]'[\tilde{J}^{\lambda\lambda}(\hat{\theta}_*)][s_{c,\lambda}(\hat{\theta}_*; Y)]. \tag{7.3.18}$$

An alternative development of the score test due to Aitchison and Silvey (1958) and Silvey (1959), and popularized in econometrics by Breusch and Pagan (1980), is based on the maximization of the Lagrangian function to derive the constrained maximum likelihood estimator:

$$[\hat{\lambda}_*', \hat{\omega}_*', \hat{\mu}_*']' = \underset{\lambda, \omega, \mu}{\text{argmax}}\ L(\lambda, \omega; Y) + \mu'(\lambda - \lambda_*). \tag{7.3.19}$$

The first-order condition for λ evaluated at the solution is simply $s_c(\lambda_*, \hat{\omega}_*) = -\hat{\mu}_*$. Economists refer to $\hat{\mu}_*$ as the *Lagrange multiplier* and interpret it as shadow prices measuring the "value" of H_1. In terms of the Lagrange multipliers, test statistic (7.3.15) can be rewritten as

$$\xi_{\text{LM}} = \hat{\mu}_*'[J^{\lambda\lambda}(\theta)]\hat{\mu}_*. \tag{7.3.20}$$

Intuitively, (7.3.20) is measuring the distance of the Lagrange multipliers from zero. Operational test statistics (7.3.16) through (7.3.18) can be written similarly.

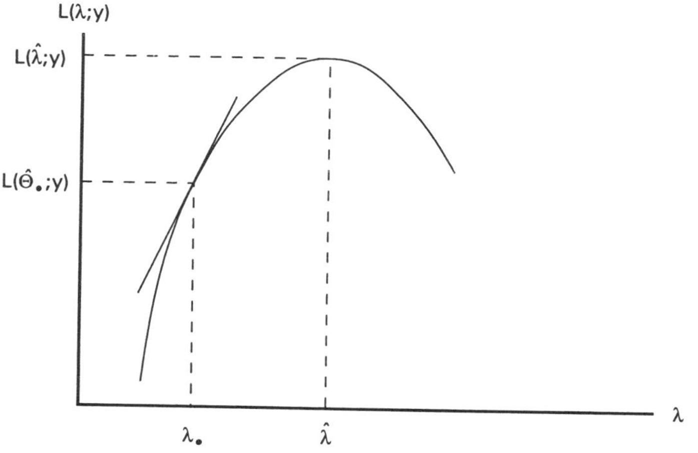

Figure 7.3.1
Test comparisons

Figure 7.3.1 (also see Buse 1982) provides a graphical interpretation of the Wald, likelihood-ratio and Lagrange multiplier test statistics when $K_\lambda = 1$. The Wald test is based on the horizontal distance $\hat{\lambda} - \lambda_*$, the LR test is based on the vertical distance $L(\hat{\theta}; Y) - L(\hat{\theta}_*; Y)$, and the LM test is based on the slope $s_c(\hat{\theta}_*; Y)$ of the log-likelihood at $\theta = \hat{\theta}_*$. For another geometrical interpretation of these three tests focusing on the score function, see Exercise 7.3.3. Engle (1984, pp. 782–784) shows that when the log-likelihood is quadratic, $\xi_W = \xi_{LR} = \xi_{LM}$.

So far we have seen that ξ_W, ξ_{LR}, and ξ_{LM} all have identical asymptotic $\chi^2(K_\lambda)$ distributions under the null hypothesis H_1. Thus an asymptotic test at the α level of significance can be constructed by employing a critical region equal to all values exceeding the value that cuts off α probability in the right hand tail of a $\chi^2(K_\lambda)$ distribution. The asymptotic power of these tests is also easy to derive. For example, consider the Wald test. Suppose under H_2: $\lambda = \lambda_{**} \neq \lambda_*$. Then under H_2, $\hat{\lambda} - \hat{\lambda}_*$ is $O_p(1)$ as opposed to $o_p(1)$ under H_1. Since by assumption $J(\theta)$ is $O_p(T)$, $[J^{\lambda\lambda}(\theta)]^{-1}$ is also $O_p(T)$, and hence, ξ_W is $O_p(T)$ under H_2. Therefore, ξ_W can exceed any pre-set finite critical value for the $\chi^2(K_\lambda)$ distribution with probability one as $T \to \infty$, implying that the asymptotic power of the Wald test is unity under H_2. A similar development is possible for the LR and LM tests (see Silvey 1959). Hence, Wald, LR, and LM tests are all consistent.

In an attempt to obtain a power ranking among these three tests, a common approach is to consider alternatives arbitrarily close to H_1, i.e. local alternatives, which will be challenging exercises for all three tests. This is usually accomplished by considering *Pitman drift*, that is, a sequence of alternative hypotheses H_{2T}: $\lambda = \lambda_* + T^{-1/2}\bar{\lambda}$, where $\bar{\lambda}$ is a fixed

$K_\lambda \times 1$ vector. As $T \to \infty$, $H_{2T} \to H_1$. For large T, H_{2T} is a stringent test case for seeing whether a test can correctly reject the false H_1 when H_{2T} is close to H_1. The popularity of these three tests is due in part to their common desirable asymptotic properties summarized in the following theorem.[6]

Theorem 7.3.1 Under the regularity assumptions in Crowder (1976), Wald, likelihood-ratio and Lagrange-multiplier test statistics have the same limiting distribution $\chi^2(K_\lambda)$ under the null hypothesis H_1, and $\chi^2(K_\lambda, \frac{1}{2}\bar{\lambda}'[J^{\lambda\lambda}(\theta)]\bar{\lambda}])$ under alternatives H_{2T}: $\lambda = \lambda_* + T^{-1/2}\bar{\lambda}$. In fact all three tests are asymptotically uniformly most powerful invariant against local hypotheses of this form.

Proof Silvey (1959).

Thus, these three tests are essentially asymptotically equivalent under the null hypothesis or local alternatives. They can, however, be distinguished on two other criteria. First, there is the matter of invariance in finite samples, and in particular, three types of such invariance: (i) invariance to the representation of the null hypothesis, invariance to one-to-one transformations of the parameters space (i.e., reparameterization), and (iii) invariance to one-to-one transformations of the model variables (e.g., changes in the units of measurement). Dagenais and Dufour (1991; also see Davidson and MacKinnon 1993, pp. 473–471) show that the LR test is invariant to all these transformations, the Wald test is not invariant to any of these transformations, and the LM test is invariant to (i), and invariant to (ii) and (iii) when the information matrix is used but not when the Hessian is used.

Second, there are computational considerations. Because the LR test requires solving two optimization problems (constrained and unconstrained), whereas the LM and Wald tests require only one (constrained in the case of the LM, and unconstrained in the case of the Wald), the LR appears at a computational disadvantage. But because the LR test requires only the maximized constrained and unconstrained function values, rather than first and second derivatives, the LR test is sometimes preferable on computational grounds: it is usually easier to achieve reliable estimates of the function than its derivatives at the maximum. When the constrained model is simpler than the unconstrained, the LM test has a computational advantage over the Wald test; when the unconstrained model is simpler, then the Wald test holds an advantage over the LM test. When many different hypotheses are to be tested individually (which usu-

6. Small sample comparisons of these three tests based on Edgeworth expansions have made by Rothenberg (1984), but few definitive results emerge.

ally is not appropriate), the Wald test has an advantage over both the LR and the LM tests since it does not require a new maximization for each hypothesis. In short, computational considerations may favor any of the three tests; it depends on the situation at hand.

For further discussion of these three tests as well as other tests, see Davidson and MacKinnon (1993), Durbin (1970b), Engle (1984), Godfrey (1988), Holly (1982), Neyman (1959), Ruud (1984), and Sargan and Mehta (1983).

Exercises

7.3.1 Consider T observations on a Bernoulli random variable with mass function:

$$\text{Prob}(Y_t = 1|\theta) = \theta, \tag{7.3.21}$$

$$\text{Prob}(Y_t = 0|\theta) = 1 - \theta, \tag{7.3.22}$$

where $0 < \theta < 1$. Consider $H_1: \theta = \theta_*$ versus $H_2: \theta \neq \theta_*$. Derive the following test statistics (see Engle 1984, pp. 785–786):

$$\xi_{\text{LR}} = 2T\left[\bar{Y}\ln\left(\frac{\bar{Y}}{\theta_*}\right) + (1-\bar{Y})\ln\left(\frac{1-\bar{Y}}{1-\theta_*}\right)\right], \tag{7.3.23}$$

$$\xi_{W,1} = \frac{T(\bar{Y}-\theta_*)^2}{\bar{Y}(1-\bar{Y})}, \tag{7.3.24}$$

$$\xi_{\text{LM},1} = \frac{T(\bar{Y}-\theta_*)^2}{\theta_*(1-\theta_*)}. \tag{7.3.25}$$

7.3.2 The idea underlying the LM/score test is that $E_{z|\gamma,H_*}[s_*(\lambda_*, \omega)] = 0$. In general, however, $E_{z|\gamma,H_*}[s_c(\lambda_*, \hat{\omega}_*)] \neq 0$. This fact led Conniffe (1990) to recommend "correcting" $s_c(\lambda_*, \hat{\omega}_*)$ to obtain a zero mean vector in finite samples under H_1, and also to make a corresponding correction to $J^{\omega\omega}(\lambda_*, \hat{\omega}_*)$ to reflect the finite sample variance of the corrected score under H_1. Unfortunately, making such corrections is not always a simple task. The root of this problem is a common one in classical inference, namely, the nuisance (from the standpoint of testing of H_1) parameter vector ω under H_1. If H_1 completely restricts ω as well as λ, then under H_1 the score evaluated at H_1 has a mean zero—in effect under H_1 the score is being evaluated at the "true" θ.

Suppose the prior densities $f(\lambda|H_1)$ and $f(\omega|H_2, \lambda)$ satisfy $f(\omega|H_2, \lambda) \to f(\omega|H_1)$ as $\lambda \to \lambda_*$. If $f(\omega|H_2, \lambda)$ is proper, then the *marginal likelihood* is

$$f(z|H, \alpha) = \int_\Gamma f(\gamma|H, \alpha)L(\gamma, \alpha)\,d\gamma. \tag{7.3.26}$$

As $\lambda \to \lambda_*$, $f(z|H_2, \lambda) \to f(z|H_1)$. Assuming it is permissible to interchange the differentiation and integration, consider the *Bayesian score*

$$\begin{aligned} s_B(\lambda) &\equiv \frac{\partial \ln[f(z|H_2, \lambda)]}{\partial \lambda} \\ &= [f(z|H_2, \lambda)]^{-1}\int_\Omega f(\omega|H_2, \lambda)L(\omega, \lambda)s_f(\omega, \lambda)\,d\omega \\ &= E_{\omega|z,H_2,\lambda}[s_f(\omega, \lambda)], \end{aligned} \tag{7.3.27}$$

where

$$s_f(\lambda, \omega) \equiv D_\lambda\{\ln[f(\omega|H, \lambda)]\} + s(\lambda, \omega). \tag{7.3.28}$$

Show:

(a) $E_{z|H_1}[s_B(\lambda_*)] = E_{z,\omega|H_1}[s_f(\lambda_*, \omega)] = 0_{K_\lambda}$.

(b) $\text{Var}_{z|H_1}[s_B(\lambda_*)] = -E_{z|H_1}[h_f(\lambda_*, \omega) + h(\lambda_*, \omega)]$

$= \text{Var}_{z,\omega|H_1}[s_f(\lambda_*, \omega)]$

$= -E_{z,\omega|H_1}[h_f(\lambda_*, \omega) + h(\lambda_*, \omega)]$,

where

$$h_f(\lambda_*, \omega) = \frac{\partial^2 \ln[f(\omega|H_2, \lambda_*)]}{\partial\lambda\,\partial\lambda'}. \tag{7.3.29}$$

(c) Under H_1, show:

$$\xi = [s_B(\lambda_*)]'(\text{Var}_{z|H_1}[s_B(\lambda_*)])^{-1}[s_B(\lambda_*)] \sim \chi^2(K_\lambda). \tag{7.3.30}$$

7.3.3 Pagan (1982) suggested the following geometrical interpretation of the LR, Wald and LM tests. Figure 7.3.2 shows a graph of a score function $s_c(\theta; y)$ in the case $K = 1$. At the MLE $\hat{\theta}$, $s_c(\hat{\theta}; y) = 0$ at the point C. The null hypothesis to be tested is $\theta = \theta_*$ (point A). Point B corresponds to $s_c(\theta_*; y)$. Noting that the antiderivative of the score is the log-likelihood, show:

(a) LR = 2 × (area of the triangle BAC).

(b) W = 2 × (area of triangle ADC).

(c) LM = 2 × (area of triangle BAE).

7.3.4 Under H_1 and the regularity conditions of this section show each of the following:

(a) $\hat{\mu}_* \sim N(0, [J^{\lambda\lambda}(\theta)]^{-1})$

(b) $H(\hat{\theta}_*)(\hat{\theta} - \hat{\theta}_*) \sim N[0, J(\theta)]$

(c) ξ_{LR} is asymptotically equivalent to $-(\hat{\theta} - \hat{\theta}_*)' H(\hat{\theta}_*)(\hat{\theta} - \hat{\theta}_*)$.

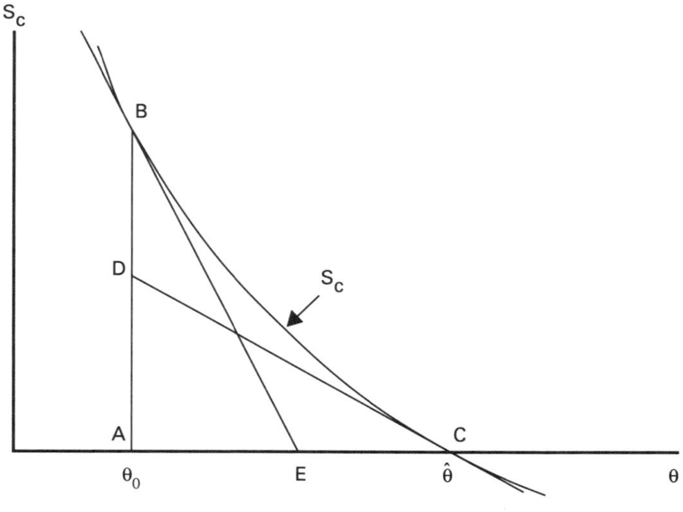

Figure 7.3.2
Score function

7.3.5 What computational advantages arise in Wald, LR, and LM tests when the following matrices are block diagonal?

(a) $J(\theta)$ for all $\theta \in \Theta$.

(b) $J(\lambda_*, \omega)$ for all $\omega \in \Omega$.

(c) $J(\lambda_*, \hat{\omega})$.

(d) $H(\theta)$ for all $\theta \in \Theta$.

(e) $H(\lambda_*, \omega)$ for all $\omega \in \Omega$.

(f) $H(\lambda_*, \hat{\omega})$.

7.3.6 Consider testing the linear hypothesis H_1: $R\theta = r$ versus H_2: $R\theta \neq r$, where R is a known $J \times K$ matrix of constants with rank$(R) = J$, and r is a $J \times 1$ known vector of constants. Show how to reparameterize these restrictions so that they are in the form H_1: $\lambda = \lambda_*$ versus H_2: $\lambda = \lambda_*$ as discussed in this section.

7.3.7 Consider testing the nonlinear hypotheses H_1: $g(\theta) = 0_J$, where $g(\theta)$ is a continuous $J \times 1$ vector function of the $K \times 1$ vector $\theta \in \Theta$. Suppose $g(\theta)$ has continuous first derivatives. Let θ_o be the "true" value of θ under H_1, and consider local alternative hypotheses described by $\theta = \theta_o + T^{-1/2}\delta$, where δ is a given fixed K-dimensional vector. Show that from the standpoint of testing H_1 versus local alternatives, the nonlinear restrictions $g(\theta) = 0_J$ are equivalent to the linear restrictions H_1^*: $R\theta = r$, where $r = R\theta_o$ and $R = [\partial g(\theta_o)/\partial\theta]$. (Hint: Start with a first-order Taylor series expansion of $g(\theta)$ around θ_o.)

7.3.8 Suppose Y_t $(t = 1, 2, \ldots, T) \sim$ i.i.d. $N_M(\mu, \Sigma)$, where both μ and Σ are unknown, and $T > M$. Define:

$$S = \frac{1}{T-1}\sum_{t=1}^{T}(Y_t - \bar{Y})(Y_t - \bar{Y})' \tag{7.3.31}$$

(a) Show: the LR test statistic for testing H_1: $\mu = 0_M$ versus H_2: $\mu \neq 0_M$ is

$$\xi_{LR} = T\ln\left(1 + \frac{V}{T-1}\right) \tag{7.3.32}$$

where V is Hotelling's statistic given in Exercise 6.9.11(c).

(b) Use your test statistic in (a) to construct a critical region corresponding to a .05 level of significance.

(c) Compare your results in (b) to Exercise 7.2.7(b).

7.3.9 Let Y_t $(t = 1, 2, \ldots, T) \sim$ i.i.d. $N(0, \exp[2\gamma])$, and consider testing H_1: $\gamma = 0$ versus H_2: $\gamma \neq 0$. Let $\hat{\gamma}$ be the MLE of γ (see Davidson and MacKinnon 1993, pp. 458–462).

(a) Show that the LR test statistic is $\xi_{LR} = T[\exp(2\hat{\gamma}) - 1 - 2\hat{\gamma}]$.

(b) Show that the 1×1 information matrix for a single observation is 2.

(c) Show that the score function satisfies $s_c(\hat{\gamma}; y) = T[\exp(2\hat{\gamma}) - 1]$.

(d) Using the information matrix, show that the LM test statistic is $\xi_{LM,1} = T[\exp(2\hat{\gamma}) - 1]^2/2$.

(e) Using the minus the Hessian, show that the LM test statistic is $\xi_{LM,2} = T\exp(-2\hat{\gamma})[\exp(2\hat{\gamma}) - 1]^2$.

(f) Using the outer product of the score, show that the LM test statistic is

$$\xi_{LM,3} = \frac{T^2[\exp(2\hat{\gamma}) - 1]^2}{\sum_{t=1}^{T}(y_t^2 - 1)^2}$$

(g) Using the information matrix, show that the Wald test statistic is $\xi_{W,1} = 2T\hat{\gamma}^2$.

(h) Using the minus the Hessian, show that the Wald test statistic is $\xi_{W,2} = 2T\hat{\gamma}^2$.

(i) Using the outer product of the score, show that the Wald test statistic is

$$\xi_{W,3} = \hat{\gamma}^2 \sum_{t=1}^{T} [y_t^2 \exp(-2\hat{\gamma}) - 1]^2.$$

7.3.10 Repeat Exercise 7.3.9 working in terms of the parameterization $\sigma^2 = 1$.

7.4 Bayesian Posterior Odds

The language of hypothesis testing (e.g., reject H_1) is inherently decision theoretic in nature, and thus it is ideally suited for Bayesian analysis. Unlike classical analysis, there is not the close connection between interval estimation and hypothesis testing in the approach recommended in most Bayesian circles. Also while interval estimation can proceed straightforwardly under "noninformative" priors, this is not so for hypothesis testing. Indeed, if prior beliefs were really "noninformative," then the value under the null hypothesis would have no special significance, violating the distinguishing feature between estimation and hypothesis testing noted in Section 7.1.

Before getting to the preferred Bayesian approach to hypothesis testing, we briefly consider and dismiss an obvious "Bayesian" approach which has much in common with classical techniques.

As seen in Section 7.2, when testing a sharp null hypothesis involving a single parameter, a confidence region of level $1 - \alpha$ comprises the set of possible null hypotheses not rejected by the data when using a two-tailed test of level α. In principle one could follow the same procedure with a Bayesian HPD interval of level $1 - \alpha$. For example, at one time Lindley (1965) advocated such a hybrid procedure, but long ago he renounced it, and it has largely vanished from the Bayesian literature in statistics in favor of the posterior odds analysis of Jeffreys (1961) discussed later in this section. Nonetheless, in Bayesian econometrics this hybrid is still sometimes used (e.g., see Florens and Mouchart 1993), despite the fact that it suffers from one of the major shortcomings of the classical approach—unless the level of significance α is made a decreasing function of sample size, most hypotheses are rejected in large samples (see Novick and Grizzle 1965).

Another shortcoming of the confidence interval or HPD interval approach to hypothesis testing is given in the following example.

Example 7.4.1 (Berger 1986, p. 26) A HPD interval only gives a set of points "most supported" by the data, but does not indicate the degree to which other points are ruled out by the data. For example, suppose the random variable Y has density

$$f(y) = \frac{1 - .01|y - \theta|}{1.99}, \quad \text{if } \theta - 1 \leq y \leq \theta + 1,$$

where $-\infty < \theta < \infty$. The shortest 95 percent confidence interval (or HPD interval if the "noninformative" prior $f(\theta) \propto$ constant is used) is $(y - .95, y + .95)$. Suppose there is reason to seriously consider the hypotheses H_1: $\theta = 0$ versus H_2: $\theta \neq 0$, and that $y = .97$ is observed. Using this interval one would be led to reject H_1. But really the only thing $y = .97$ helps conclude is that $-.03 \leq \theta \leq 1.97$. Since the likelihood varies by only 1 percent over the interval $[-.03, 1.97]$, virtually every value of θ is supported as well as any other, there is no evidence against H_1.

The remainder of this section develops the posterior odds analysis approach of Jeffreys (1961), which is widely accepted as the major hypothesis testing approach among Bayesians. The approach is distinctly different that the HPD interval testing approach just discussed.

Suppose the relevant *decision space* is the set $D = \{d_1, d_2\}$, where

$$d_j \equiv \text{choose } H_j \qquad (j = 1, 2). \tag{7.4.1}$$

Let the unsubscripted d denote a generic decision (i.e. either d_1 or d_2). Extensions to cases involving more than two hypotheses are straightforward. Let $C(d; \theta) \geq 0$ denote the relevant *loss function* describing the consequences of decision d when the unknown state of nature is θ. From the subjectivist perspective, $C(d; \theta)$ is random because uncertainty regarding θ is expressed by a distribution function. Before observing the data, this distribution is referred to as the *prior* distribution, denoted $F(\theta)$, and after observing the data it is referred to as the *posterior distribution*, denoted $F(\theta|y)$.

According to subjectivist canon, the optimal decision d_* minimizes expected cost. After observing the data y, the relevant distribution is the posterior distribution $F(\theta|y)$ since it reflects both prior and sample information. Therefore, d_* is defined by

$$d_* = \operatorname*{argmin}_d c(d|y), \tag{7.4.2}$$

where

$$c(d|y) \equiv E_{\theta|y}[C(d; \theta)] \tag{7.4.3a}$$

$$= E[C(d; \theta)|y] \tag{7.4.3b}$$

is the *posterior expected cost (loss) of taking decision d*.

In order to solve (7.4.2), it is first necessary to obtain the posterior distribution $F(\theta|y)$ so that the expectation in (7.4.3) can be obtained. As will become clear shortly (see Equation 7.4.8), from the Bayesian perspective a hypothesis is of interest only if the prior distribution $F(\theta)$ assigns it positive probability. Therefore, assume

$$\underline{\pi}_j \equiv \text{Prob}(H_j) = \text{Prob}(\theta \in \Theta) > 0 \qquad (j = 1, 2) \tag{7.4.4}$$

with[7]

$$\underline{\pi}_1 + \underline{\pi}_2 = 1. \tag{7.4.5}$$

The prior probability function (density/mass function) can be decomposed as

$$f(\theta) = \begin{Bmatrix} \underline{\pi}_1 f(\theta|H_1), & \text{if } \theta \in \Theta_1 \\ \underline{\pi}_2 f(\theta|H_2), & \text{if } \theta \in \Theta_2 \end{Bmatrix}, \tag{7.4.6}$$

where $f(\theta|H_j)$ is simply the prior probability function under H_j $(j = 1, 2)$. Note that the prior distribution can be "mixed" (see Exercise 2.2.5) with a positive atom $\underline{\pi}_j$ assigned to the point θ_j corresponding to the simple hypothesis H_j with $\Theta_j = \{\theta_j\}$. Also, in the case of a sharp hypothesis that is not simple [e.g. $\theta = [\lambda', \omega']'$ and $\Theta_j = \{\lambda_j\} \times \Omega_j$, where Ω_j is the parameter subspace (assumed to be non-singleton) for ω], a positive prior probability $\underline{\pi}_j$ is assigned to Θ_j.

Under H_j, the probability function of the data, marginal of all parameters, is

$$f(y|H_j) = \int_{\Theta_j} \mathscr{L}(\theta; y)\, dF(\theta|H_j) \tag{7.4.7a}$$

$$= E_{\theta|H_j}[\mathscr{L}(\theta; y)] \qquad (j = 1, 2). \tag{7.4.7b}$$

For the reader not familiar with Riemann-Stieltjes integration, (7.4.7a) can be thought of as short-hand notation for

$$f(y|H_j) = \mathscr{L}(\theta_j; y), \tag{7.4.7c}$$

if H_j is simple; for

$$f(y|H_j) = \int_{\Theta_j} f(\theta|H_j)\mathscr{L}(\theta; y)\, d\theta, \tag{7.4.7d}$$

if H_j is not sharp; and for

$$f(y|H_j) = \int_{\Omega_j} f(\lambda_j, \omega|H_j)\mathscr{L}(\lambda_j, \omega; y)\, d\omega, \tag{7.4.7e}$$

7. There is little guidance in the literature on elicitation of prior probabilities in (7.4.4). An exception is the *model occurrence* framework [developed in Poirier (1988b) and Poirier and Klepper (1981), and applied in Koop and Poirier (1990)] in which (7.4.4) is specified up to an unknown hyperparameter.

if H_j is sharp but not simple. From Bayes Theorem it follows immediately that the posterior probability of H_j is

$$\bar{\pi}_j = \text{Prob}(H_j|y) = \frac{\underline{\pi}_j f(y|H_j)}{f(y)} \qquad (j = 1, 2), \tag{7.4.8}$$

where the marginal probability function of the data (marginal of *both* parameters and hypotheses) is

$$f(y) = \underline{\pi}_1 f(y|H_1) + \underline{\pi}_2 f(y|H_2). \tag{7.4.9}$$

Clearly, $\bar{\pi}_1 + \bar{\pi}_2 = 1$.

With these preliminaries out of the way, we can now derive the posterior distribution for θ to be used in (7.4.3). Under H_j, the posterior probability function of θ is (according to Bayes Theorem):

$$f(\theta|y, H_j) = \frac{f(\theta|H_j)\mathscr{L}(\theta; y)}{f(y|H_j)}, \ \theta \in \Theta_j \ (j = 1, 2). \tag{7.4.10}$$

Using posterior probabilities $\bar{\pi}_j$ $(j = 1, 2)$ given by (7.4.8), the posterior probability function of θ (marginal of H_1 and H_2) is

$$f(\theta|y) = \begin{Bmatrix} \bar{\pi}_1 f(\theta|y, H_1), & \text{if } \theta \in \Theta_1 \\ \bar{\pi}_2 f(\theta|y, H_2), & \text{if } \theta \in \Theta_2 \end{Bmatrix}. \tag{7.4.11}$$

Using (7.4.11) and defining the expected posterior loss of decision d, given H_j,

$$c(d|y, H_j) = E_{\theta|y, H_j}[C(d; \theta)] \qquad (j = 1, 2), \tag{7.4.12}$$

posterior expected loss (7.4.3) can be written

$$c(d|y) = \bar{\pi}_1 c(d|y, H_1) + \bar{\pi}_2 c(d|y, H_2). \tag{7.4.13}$$

Without loss of generality, assume that correct decisions yield zero loss:

$$C(d_1; \theta) = 0, \quad \text{if } \theta \in \Theta_1, \tag{7.4.14}$$

$$C(d_2; \theta) = 0, \quad \text{if } \theta \in \Theta_2. \tag{7.4.15}$$

Under (7.4.14) and (7.4.15), it follows from (7.4.13) that

$$c(d_1|y) = \bar{\pi}_2 c(d_1|y, H_2), \tag{7.4.16}$$

$$c(d_2|y) = \bar{\pi}_1 c(d_2|y, H_1). \tag{7.4.17}$$

Therefore, from (7.4.16) and (7.4.17) it is optimal to choose H_2 (i.e., reject H_1), denoted $d_* = d_2$, iff

$$c(d_2|y) < c(d_1|y), \tag{7.4.18a}$$

or equivalently,

$$d_* = d_2 \text{ iff } \frac{\bar{\pi}_1}{\bar{\pi}_2} < \frac{c(d_1|y, H_2)}{c(d_2|y, H_1)}. \tag{7.4.18b}$$

Because $\bar{\pi}_2 = 1 - \bar{\pi}_1$, (7.4.18b) can also be written equivalently as

$$d_* = d_2 \text{ iff } \bar{\pi}_1 < \frac{c(d_1|y, H_2)}{c(d_1|y, H_2) + c(d_2|y, H_1)}, \tag{7.4.18c}$$

or

$$d_* = d_2 \text{ iff } \bar{\pi}_1 < \left[1 + \frac{c(d_2|y, H_1)}{c(d_1|y, H_2)}\right]^{-1}. \tag{7.4.18d}$$

The quantities $\underline{\pi}_1/\underline{\pi}_2$ and $\bar{\pi}_1/\bar{\pi}_2$ are the *prior odds* and *posterior odds*, respectively, of H_1 versus H_2. From (7.4.8) it follows immediately that these two odds are related by

$$\frac{\bar{\pi}_1}{\bar{\pi}_2} = B_{12}\left[\frac{\underline{\pi}_1}{\underline{\pi}_2}\right], \tag{7.4.19}$$

where

$$B_{12} = \frac{f(y|H_1)}{f(y|H_2)} \tag{7.4.20}$$

is the *Bayes factor for H_1 versus H_2*. Equivalently,

$$\frac{\bar{\pi}_2}{\bar{\pi}_1} = B_{21}\left[\frac{\underline{\pi}_2}{\underline{\pi}_1}\right], \tag{7.4.21}$$

where

$$B_{21} = \frac{f(y|H_2)}{f(y|H_1)} = B_{12}^{-1} \tag{7.4.22}$$

is the *Bayes factor for H_2 versus H_1*. Bayes factors (7.4.20) and (7.4.22) are ratios of marginalized or expected likelihoods. These Bayes factors summarize the effect of the data in modifying the prior odds to obtain posterior odds.[8] Also note that (7.4.19) and (7.4.21) imply the posterior

8. Jeffreys (1961, Appendix B); also see Kass and Raferty 1993) suggests $\ln(B_{12})$ serves as a measure of the *weight of evidence* provided by the data for H_1 against H_2, and he recommends the following "order of magnitude" interpretation of B_{12}:

$B_{12} > 1$,	evidence supports H_1,
$10^{-1/2} < B_{12} < 1$,	very slight evidence against H_1,
$10^{-1} < B_{12} < 10^{-1/2}$,	slight evidence against H_1,
$10^{-2} < B_{12} < 10^{-1}$,	strong to very strong evidence against H_1,
$B_{12} < 10^{-2}$,	decisive evidence against H_1,

probabilities:

$$\bar{\pi}_1 = \left[1 + B_{21}\left(\frac{\underline{\pi}_2}{\underline{\pi}_1}\right)\right]^{-1}, \tag{7.4.23}$$

$$\bar{\pi}_2 = \left[1 + B_{12}\left(\frac{\underline{\pi}_1}{\underline{\pi}_2}\right)\right]^{-1}. \tag{7.4.24}$$

Finally, substituting (7.4.19) into (7.4.18b) and rearranging, it follows that

$$d_* = d_2 \text{ iff } B_{12} < \left[\frac{c(d_1|y, H_2)}{c(d_2|y, H_1)}\right]\left[\frac{\underline{\pi}_2}{\underline{\pi}_1}\right], \tag{7.4.18e}$$

or equivalently,

$$d_* = d_2 \text{ iff } B_{21} \geq \left[\frac{c(d_2|y, H_1)}{c(d_1|y, H_2)}\right]\left[\frac{\underline{\pi}_1}{\underline{\pi}_2}\right]. \tag{7.4.18f}$$

To illustrate the concepts developed so far, consider the following examples.

Example 7.4.2 (Two Simple Hypotheses) Suppose H_1 and H_2 are both simple hypotheses with $\Theta_j = \{\theta_j\}$ $(j = 1, 2)$. Then prior probability function (7.4.6) reduces to the simple two-point mass function

$$f(\theta) = \begin{cases} \underline{\pi}_1, & \text{if } \theta = \theta_1 \\ \underline{\pi}_2, & \text{if } \theta = \theta_2 \end{cases}. \tag{7.4.25}$$

Noting (7.4.7b), posterior probability function (7.4.11) reduces to the two-point mass function

$$f(\theta|y) = \begin{cases} \bar{\pi}_1, & \text{if } \theta = \theta_1 \\ \bar{\pi}_2, & \text{if } \theta = \theta_2 \end{cases}, \tag{7.4.26}$$

where the posterior probabilities of each hypothesis (see Equation 7.4.8) are simply

$$\bar{\pi}_j = \frac{\underline{\pi}_j \mathcal{L}(\theta_j; y)}{f(y)} \qquad (j = 1, 2), \tag{7.4.27}$$

and the marginal p.f. of the data is

$$f(y) = \underline{\pi}_1 \mathcal{L}(\theta_1; y) + \underline{\pi}_2 \mathcal{L}(\theta_2; y). \tag{7.4.28}$$

Also note that Bayes factor (7.4.22) reduces to the familiar simple likelihood ratio

$$B_{21} = \frac{\mathcal{L}(\theta_2; y)}{\mathcal{L}(\theta_1; y)}. \tag{7.4.29}$$

---

where $10^{-1/2} \approx .3162$. For further discussion of the concept of weight of evidence, see Good (1985).

Finally, note that in the case of simple hypotheses,

$$c(d_1|y,H_2) = C(d_1;H_2), \tag{7.4.30}$$

$$c(d_2|y,H_1) = C(d_2;H_1). \tag{7.4.31}$$

Therefore, from (7.4.18f) and (7.4.29) through (7.4.31) it follows that

$$d_* = d_2 \text{ iff } \frac{\mathscr{L}(\theta_2;y)}{\mathscr{L}(\theta_1;y)} > \left[\frac{C(d_2;\theta_1)}{C(d_1;\theta_2)}\right]\left[\frac{\underline{\pi}_1}{\underline{\pi}_2}\right]. \tag{7.4.32}$$

In other words, choose H_2 iff the likelihood ratio of H_2 versus H_1 is greater than the ratio of the prior expected loss from choosing d_2 relative to the prior expected loss from choosing d_1, that is, the ratio

$$\frac{E_{\theta|H_1}[C(d_2;\theta)]}{E_{\theta|H_2}[C(d_1;\theta)]} = \frac{\underline{\pi}_1 C(d_2;\theta_1)}{\underline{\pi}_2 C(d_1;\theta_2)}. \tag{7.4.33}$$

Example 7.4.3 (Two Non-Sharp Hypotheses) Suppose that neither H_1 nor H_2 is sharp (and hence neither is simple). In this case (7.4.7d) applies and there is little simplification in the notation developed in (7.4.8) through (7.4.18f). There are two important distinctions from Example 7.4.2, however, to keep in mind. First, unlike (7.4.29), Bayes factor (7.4.20) does not simplify to a simple likelihood ratio. Instead the Bayes factor is a ratio of marginalized or expected likelihoods. Second, unlike (7.4.32), data appear on the righthand side of the inequality in (7.4.18e) and (7.4.18f). Thus, in general, the Bayes factor alone does *not* summarize the relevant aspects of the data. We will return to this second point again later.

Example 7.4.4 (Simple Null and Non-Sharp Alternative) Consider a combination of Example 7.4.2 and 7.4.3 where H_1 is simple with $\Theta_1 = \{\theta_1\}$ and H_2 is not sharp. Then the prior probability function of θ is of the mixed form

$$f(\theta) = \begin{cases} \underline{\pi}_1, & \text{if } \theta = \theta_1 \\ \underline{\pi}_2 f(\theta|H_2), & \text{if } \theta \in \Theta_2 \end{cases}, \tag{7.4.34}$$

with a "spike" of height $\underline{\pi}_1$ at $\theta = \theta_1$. Drawing on Examples 7.4.2 and 7.4.3, it is clear that the posterior probability function is also of mixed form:

$$f(\theta|y) = \begin{cases} \overline{\pi}_1, & \text{if } \theta = \theta_1 \\ \overline{\pi}_2 f(\theta|y,H_2), & \text{if } \theta \in \Theta_2 \end{cases}, \tag{7.4.35}$$

where

$$\overline{\pi}_1 = \text{Prob}(H_1|y) = \frac{\underline{\pi}_1 \mathscr{L}(\theta_1;y)}{f(y)}, \tag{7.4.36}$$

$$\overline{\pi}_2 = \text{Prob}(H_2|y) = \frac{\underline{\pi}_2 f(y|H_2)}{f(y)}, \tag{7.4.37}$$

$$f(y) = \underline{\pi}_1 \mathscr{L}(\theta_1; y) + \underline{\pi}_2 f(y|H_2). \tag{7.4.38}$$

Also note that Bayes factor (7.4.22) equals

$$B_{21} = \frac{\int_{\Theta_2} f(\theta|H_2)\mathscr{L}(\theta; y)\, d\theta}{\mathscr{L}(\theta_1; y)}. \tag{7.4.39}$$

Compared to the numerator in (7.4.29), the numerator in (7.4.39) marginalizes the likelihood $\mathscr{L}(\theta; y)$ using the prior density $f(\theta|H_2)$. Finally, the righthand side of the inequality in decision rule (7.4.18e) once again depends on data.

Next, consider the following example in which Example 7.4.4 is augmented to include nuisance parameters.

Example 7.4.5 (Two Non-Sharp Hypotheses with Nuisance Parameters) Suppose $\theta = [\lambda', \omega']'$ and $\Theta_j = \Lambda_j \times \Omega\ (j = 1, 2)$, where $\Lambda_1 = \{\lambda_*\}$ and Λ_2 is not sharp. Then the prior probability function can be written in the mixed form

$$f(\lambda, \omega) = \begin{Bmatrix} \underline{\pi}_1 f(\omega|H_1), & \text{if } \lambda = \lambda_* \text{ and } \omega \in \Omega \\ \underline{\pi}_2 f(\lambda, \omega|H_2), & \text{if } \lambda \in \Lambda_2 \text{ and } \omega \in \Omega \end{Bmatrix}. \tag{7.4.40}$$

Noting that $f(y|H_1)$ is given by (7.4.7e) and

$$f(y|H_2) = \int_{\Lambda_2}\int_{\Omega} f(\lambda, \omega)\mathscr{L}(\lambda, \omega; y)\, d\omega\, d\lambda, \tag{7.4.41}$$

posterior probabilities $\bar{\pi}_j\ (j = 1, 2)$ are given by (7.4.8), and the posterior probability function of θ is given by (7.4.10) and (7.4.11) with

$$f(\lambda, \omega|y, H_1) = \frac{f(\omega|H_1)\mathscr{L}(\lambda_1, \omega; y)}{f(y|H_1)}. \tag{7.4.42}$$

Bayes factors and posterior probabilities can be calculated in the usual fashion.

In the case of Examples 7.4.3 through 7.4.5, expected posterior loss $c(d|y, H_j)$ defined by (7.4.12) depends (in general) on the data, and hence, Bayes factors (7.4.20) and (7.4.22) do *not* serve as complete data summaries. In other words, since the righthand side of the inequalities in (7.4.18) depend on the data, they do *not* serve as "critical values" analogous to those that appear in classical testing. One exception is when both hypotheses are simple (Example 7.4.2). Here is another exception.

Suppose the loss resulting from decision d_i when $\theta \in \Theta_j$, $i \neq j$, is constant for all $\theta \in \Theta_j$:

$$C(d_1; \theta) = \bar{C}_1 \text{ for all } \theta \in \Theta_2, \tag{7.4.43a}$$

$$C(d_2; \theta) = \bar{C}_2 \text{ for all } \theta \in \Theta_1, \tag{7.4.43b}$$

Table 7.4.1
"All-or-nothing" loss structure

	State of nature	
Decisions	H_1	H_2
d_1	0	$\overline{C}_1$
d_2	$\overline{C}_2$	0

where $\overline{C}_1$ and $\overline{C}_2$ are given constants. This "all or nothing" loss structure is depicted in Table 7.4.1. Under (7.4.43), expected posterior losses (7.4.12) depends neither on the data nor on the prior for θ:

$$c(d_i|y, H_j) = E_{\theta|y,H_j}[C(d;\theta)] = \int_{\Theta_j} \overline{C}_i f(\theta|y, H_j)\, d\theta = \overline{C}_i \tag{7.4.44}$$

for $i \neq j$. Therefore, under (7.4.43) decision rule (7.4.18) reduces to

$$d_* = d_2 \text{ iff } B_{21} > \left[\frac{\overline{C}_2}{\overline{C}_1}\right]\left[\frac{\underline{\pi}_1}{\underline{\pi}_2}\right]. \tag{7.4.18g}$$

The righthand side of the inequality in (7.4.18g) is a known constant that serves as a *Bayesian critical value.*

How reasonable is loss structure (7.4.43)? It holds trivially when both hypotheses are simple (see Example 7.4.2). In the case of composite hypotheses, however, its appropriateness is suspect. For example, when testing H_1: $\theta = 0$ versus H_2: $\theta > 0$, should not the loss associated with d_1 depend on how far θ under H_2 deviates from $\theta = 0$? Kadane and Dickey (1980, p. 251) show that when dealing with at least one composite hypothesis, loss structure (7.4.43) is not only sufficient, but it is also necessary in order for the righthand sides of the inequalities (7.4.18) to be data-free.

To further illustrate the results of Examples 7.4.2–7.4.5, some more detailed examples are now considered. Each example is based on Example 6.5.2, which involves a random sample $Y = [Y_1, Y_2, \ldots, Y_T]'$ from a $N(\theta, \sigma^2)$ population in which θ is unknown and σ^2 is *known.* (Note the slight change in notation.) The case in which the nuisance parameter σ^2 is unknown is addressed in a straightforward manner as in Example 7.4.5: a prior is specified for σ^2 and then σ^2 is simply integrated-out of the marginal data densities below.

Analogous to (6.7.18) and (6.7.19), factor the likelihood as

$$\mathscr{L}(\theta; y) = c_1(\sigma^2)\phi(\bar{y}|\theta, h^{-1}), \tag{7.4.45}$$

where

$$c_1(\sigma^2) = (2\pi\sigma^2)^{-\nu/2} T^{-1/2} \exp\left(-\frac{\nu s^2}{2\sigma^2}\right), \tag{7.4.46}$$

$$h = \frac{T}{\sigma^2}, \tag{7.4.47}$$

$$v = T - 1, \tag{7.4.48}$$

$$vs^2 = \sum_{t=1}^{T} (y_t - \bar{y})^2. \tag{7.4.49}$$

Because $c_1(\sigma^2)$ does *not* depend on the unknown θ, (7.4.45) shows that $\bar{y}$ is sufficient for θ. According to the Likelihood Principle, no information is lost by ignoring $c_1(\sigma^2)$ and merely considering

$$\mathscr{L}(\theta; \bar{y}) = \phi(\bar{y}|\theta, h^{-1}). \tag{7.4.50}$$

Similarly, we can work with $c(d|\bar{y}, H_j)$ instead of $c(d|y, H_j)$.

First consider the case of two simple hypotheses.

Example 7.4.6 (Two Simple Hypotheses and Normal Likelihoods) Consider Example 7.4.2 where it is desired to test the simple hypothesis H_1: $\theta = \theta_1$ versus the simple hypothesis H_2: $\theta = \theta_2$, with $\theta_1 < \theta_2$. Under random sampling from a normal population, the Bayes factor for H_2 versus H_1 is

$$\begin{aligned} B_{21} &= \frac{\mathscr{L}(\theta_2; \bar{y})}{\mathscr{L}(\theta_1; \bar{y})} = \frac{(2\pi\sigma^2/T)^{-1/2} \exp[-T(\bar{y} - \theta_2)^2/2\sigma^2]}{(2\pi\sigma^2/T)^{-1/2} \exp[-T(\bar{y} - \theta_1)^2/2\sigma^2]} \\ &= \exp\{-\tfrac{1}{2}h[(\bar{y} - \theta_2)^2 - (\bar{y} - \theta_1)^2]\} \\ &= \exp\{\tfrac{1}{2}h[2\bar{y}(\theta_2 - \theta_1) + (\theta_1^2 - \theta_2^2)]\}. \end{aligned} \tag{7.4.51}$$

According to (7.4.32), H_1 should be rejected if

$$\exp[\tfrac{1}{2}h\{2\bar{y}(\theta_2 - \theta_1) + (\theta_1^2 - \theta_2^2)\}] > (\overline{C}_2\underline{\pi}_1/\overline{C}_1\underline{\pi}_2), \tag{7.4.52a}$$

or equivalently,

$$\bar{y} > \tfrac{1}{2}(\theta_1 + \theta_2) + [h(\theta_2 - \theta_1)]^{-1} \ln[(\overline{C}_2\underline{\pi}_1/\overline{C}_1\underline{\pi}_2)]. \tag{7.4.52b}$$

Note that when

$$\overline{C}_2\underline{\pi}_1 = \overline{C}_1\underline{\pi}_2, \tag{7.4.53}$$

that is, $E_{\theta|y}[C(d_2; \theta)] = E_{\theta|y}[C(d_1; \theta)]$, (7.4.52b) reduces simply to reject H_1 iff

$$\bar{y} > \tfrac{1}{2}(\theta_1 + \theta_2). \tag{7.4.54}$$

Thus, under (7.4.53) (i.e., equal expected posterior losses for d_1 and d_2), the critical value for $\bar{y}$ is simply the half-way point between θ_1 and θ_2. When (7.4.53) does not hold, (7.4.52b) implies adjustment of the critical point up or down depending on the relative posterior expected losses for the two types of errors.

Next consider the case of two one-sided hypotheses.

Example 7.4.7 (Two One-Sided Hypotheses and Normal Likelihoods) Consider Example 7.4.3, where $H_1\colon \theta \le \theta_*$ versus $H_2\colon \theta > \theta_*$, and θ_* is a given constant. In this situation, $\Theta_1 = \{\theta | \theta \le \theta_*\}$ and $\Theta_2 = \{\theta | \theta > \theta_*\}$. A convenient prior distribution for θ is the split-normal distribution given by (7.4.6) with

$$f(\theta|H_1) = [\Phi(\theta_*|\underline{\mu}_1, \underline{h}_1^{-1})]^{-1}\phi(\theta|\underline{\mu}_1, \underline{h}_1^{-1}),\ \theta \in \Theta_1, \tag{7.4.55}$$

$$f(\theta|H_2) = [1 - \Phi(\theta_*|\underline{\mu}_2, \underline{h}_2^{-1})]^{-1}\phi(\theta|\underline{\mu}_2, \underline{h}_2^{-1}),\ \theta \in \Theta_2. \tag{7.4.56}$$

Densities (7.4.55) and (7.4.56) are *truncated normal* densities, examples of which are shown in Figures 7.4.1 and 7.4.2.. The special case in which

$$\underline{\mu} = \underline{\mu}_1 = \underline{\mu}_2, \tag{7.4.57}$$

$$\underline{h} = \underline{h}_1 = \underline{h}_2, \tag{7.4.58}$$

$$\underline{\pi}_1 = \Phi(\theta_*|\underline{\mu}, \underline{h}^{-1}), \tag{7.4.59}$$

$$\underline{\pi}_2 = 1 - \Phi(\theta_*|\mu, \underline{h}^{-1}), \tag{7.4.60}$$

is shown in Figure 7.4.1 by replacing $f(\theta|H_2)$ with the density indicated by the dashed line. Under (7.4.57)–(7.4.60), $f(\theta) = \phi(\theta|\underline{\mu}, \underline{h}^{-1})$ as in the standard estimation problem. The case in which (7.4.57) holds with

$$\underline{\mu} = \theta_*, \tag{7.4.61}$$

but not (7.4.58)–(7.4.60), is shown in Figure 7.4.2. Prior specification (7.4.55) and (7.4.56) with all of (7.4.57)–(7.4.61) holding, that is, $f(\theta) = \phi(\theta|\theta_*, \underline{h}^{-1})$, is attractive in many settings and requires elicitation only of $\underline{h}$.

Analogous to (6.7.20), it is straightforward to show that

$$\phi(\theta|\underline{\mu}_j, \underline{h}_j^{-1})\mathscr{L}(\theta; \bar{y}) = \phi(\theta|\bar{\mu}_j, \bar{h}_j^{-1})\phi(\bar{y}|\underline{\mu}_j, \underline{h}_j^{-1} + h^{-1})\ (j = 1, 2), \tag{7.4.62}$$

where

$$\bar{h}_j = \underline{h}_j + h \qquad (j = 1, 2), \tag{7.4.63}$$

$$\bar{\mu}_j = (\bar{h}_j)^{-1}(\underline{h}_j\underline{\mu}_j + h\bar{y}) \qquad (j = 1, 2). \tag{7.4.64}$$

From (7.4.55), (7.4.56) and (7.4.62) it follows that

$$f(y|H_1) = \int_{\Theta_1} f(\theta|H_1)\mathscr{L}(\theta; \bar{y})\,d\theta$$

$$= \left[\frac{\Phi(\theta_*|\bar{\mu}_1, \bar{h}_1^{-1})}{\Phi(\theta_*|\underline{\mu}_1, \underline{h}_1^{-1})}\right]\phi(\bar{y}|\underline{\mu}_1, \underline{h}_1^{-1} + h^{-1}), \tag{7.4.65}$$

and

$$f(y|H_2) = \int_{\Theta_2} f(\theta|H_2)\mathscr{L}(\theta; \bar{y})\,d\theta$$

$$= \left[\frac{1 - \Phi(\theta_*|\bar{\mu}_1, \bar{h}_1^{-1})}{1 - \Phi(\theta_*|\underline{\mu}_2, \underline{h}_2^{-1})}\right]\phi(\bar{y}|\underline{\mu}_2, \underline{h}_2^{-1} + h^{-1}). \tag{7.4.66}$$

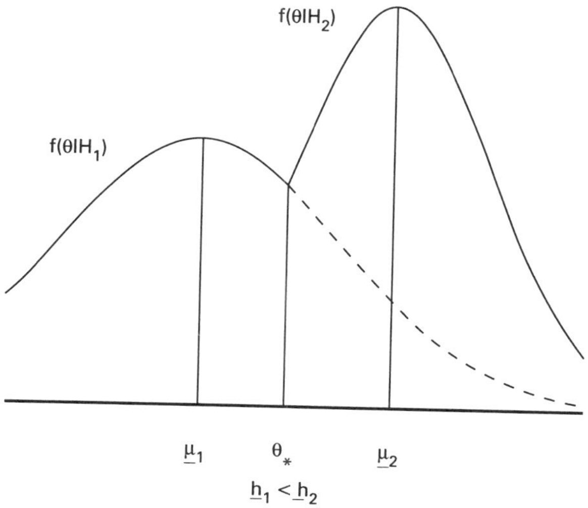

Figure 7.4.1
Prior densities under (7.4.57)–(7.4.60)

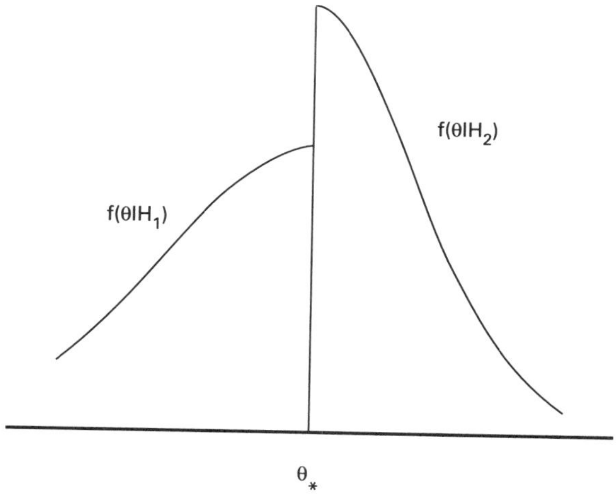

Figure 7.4.2
Prior densities under (7.4.57)–(7.4.61)

Therefore, the conditional posterior densities under each hypothesis are

$$f(\theta|\bar{y}, H_1) = [\Phi(\theta_*|\bar{\mu}_1, \bar{h}_1^{-1})]^{-1}\phi(\theta|\bar{\mu}_1, \bar{h}_1^{-1}),\ \theta \in \Theta_1, \tag{7.4.67}$$

$$f(\theta|\bar{y}, H_2) = [1 - \Phi(\theta_*|\bar{\mu}_2, \bar{h}_2^{-1})]^{-1}\phi(\theta|\bar{\mu}_2, \bar{h}_2^{-1}),\ \theta \in \Theta_2. \tag{7.4.68}$$

The hyperparameters $\bar{\mu}_j$ and $\bar{h}_j$ ($j = 1, 2$) of conditional posterior densities (7.4.67) and (7.4.68) are updated (see Equations 7.4.63 and 7.4.64) in the usual fashion from the prior hyperparameter values $\underline{\mu}_j$, $\underline{h}_j$ ($j = 1, 2$), since (7.4.67) and (7.4.68), like (7.4.55) and (7.4.56), form yet another conjugate prior for a random sample from a $N(\theta, \sigma^2)$ distribution with σ^2 known.

The Bayes factor B_{21} for H_2 versus H_1 is simply the ratio of (7.4.66) to (7.4.65). Posterior probabilities $\bar{\pi}_j = \text{Prob}(H_j|y)$ ($j = 1, 2$) can be easily calculated from (7.4.27) using (7.4.65) and (7.4.66). In general, however, no cancellations occur in forming these quantities, and hence decision rule (7.4.18) involves complex functions of the data $\bar{y}$ [through $\bar{\mu}_j$ ($j = 1, 2$)].

The unconstrained split-normal density implied by (7.4.55) and (7.4.56) is quite flexible, but fairly "parameter-rich": it requires specification of five hyperparameters ($\underline{\mu}_1, \underline{h}_1, \underline{\mu}_2, \underline{h}_2$ and $\underline{\pi}_1 = 1 - \underline{\pi}_2$). Restrictions (7.4.57) through (7.4.60) impose continuity on the prior $f(\theta)$ (see the dashed line in Figure 7.4.1) and reduce the number of hyperparameters to be specified down to two ($\underline{\mu}$ and $\underline{h}$). Under (7.4.57) through (7.4.60), the Bayes factor for H_2 versus H_1 simplifies to

$$B_{21} = \left[\frac{1 - \Phi(\theta_*|\bar{\mu}, \bar{h}_1^{-1})}{\Phi(\theta_*|\bar{\mu}, \bar{h}^{-1})}\right]\left[\frac{\underline{\pi}_1}{\underline{\pi}_2}\right], \tag{7.4.69}$$

where $\bar{\mu}$ and $\bar{h}$ are given by the common values across $j = 1, 2$ of (7.4.63) and (7.4.64). Bayes factor (7.4.69) implies (see Equation 7.4.23) that the posterior probability $\bar{\pi}_1 = \text{Prob}(H_1|y)$ equals simply

$$\bar{\pi}_1 = \Phi(\theta_*|\bar{\mu}, \bar{h}^{-1}). \tag{7.4.70}$$

Under "all-or-nothing" loss function (7.4.43), (7.4.69) implies that decision rule (7.4.18d) reduces to reject H_1 iff

$$\bar{y} > \theta_* + (\underline{h}/h)(\theta_* - \underline{\mu}) + \gamma h^{-1/2}, \tag{7.4.71}$$

where

$$\gamma \equiv -[1 + (\underline{h}/h)]^{1/2}\Phi^{-1}[\{1 + (\bar{C}_2/\bar{C}_1)\}^{-1}]. \tag{7.4.72}$$

The second term in (7.4.71) serves as an additive adjustment to θ_*: requiring $\bar{y}$ to be larger in order to reject H_1 when the prior mean $\underline{\mu}$ lies to the left of θ_*. Under (7.4.61) this adjustment term vanishes.

The constant γ defined by (7.4.72) plays the role of the tabulated critical value used in classical testing. However, it is an explicit function of the relative costs of a type I error and a type II error. Usually, the problem is posed so that this ratio, $\bar{C}_2/\bar{C}_1$, is greater than unity. Letting

$$\alpha \equiv \left[1 - \left(\frac{\overline{C}_2}{\overline{C}_1}\right)\right]^{-1}, \tag{7.4.73}$$

it is seen in this case that $\Phi^{-1}(\alpha) < 0$, and hence, $\gamma > 0$. The quantity α is like the level of significance in a classical test. Provided the prior is informative (i.e. $0 < \underline{h} < \infty$), γ is a function of sample size T through $h = T/\sigma^2$ and the first factor in (7.4.72) is greater than unity. As prior information becomes diffuse (i.e., $\underline{h} \to 0$), the second term in (7.4.71) vanishes independently of (7.4.61) holding, and the first factor in (7.4.72) approaches unity. Therefore, if prior information is diffuse and $\overline{C}_2/\overline{C}_1 = 19$, then $\alpha = .05$, $\gamma = \Phi^{-1}(.05) = 1.645$, and (7.4.71) is identical to the rejection region of a classical one-sided test at the .05 level of significance.

Finally, consider the case of a sharp null hypothesis and a two-sided alternative hypothesis. In this case the conflict between standard classical hypothesis testing and Bayesian posterior odds analysis is most striking.

Example 7.4.8 (Simple Null Hypothesis, Two-Sided Alternative, and Normal Likelihoods) Consider Example 7.4.4, where $H_1\colon \theta = \theta_*$ versus $H_2\colon \theta \neq \theta_*$ and θ_* is a given constant. In this case $\Theta_1 = \{\theta_*\}$ and $\Theta_2 = \Theta - \{\theta_*\} = \{\theta | \theta \in \Theta \text{ and } \theta \neq \theta_*\}$. Suppose the conditional prior density $p(\theta|H_2)$ in mixed prior density (7.4.34) is

$$f(\theta|H_2) = \phi(\theta|\underline{\mu}, \underline{h}^{-1}). \tag{7.4.74}$$

From (7.4.66), and also noting that the integral over Θ_2 is equivalent to the integral over $-\infty$ to ∞, it follows that

$$f(y|H_2) = \phi(\bar{y}|\underline{\mu}, \underline{h}^{-1} + h^{-1}), \tag{7.4.75}$$

and the Bayes factor for H_2 versus H_1 is

$$B_{21} = \frac{\phi(\bar{y}|\underline{\mu}, \underline{h}^{-1} + h^{-1})}{\phi(\bar{y}|\theta_*, h^{-1})} \tag{7.4.76a}$$

$$= \left[\frac{h^{-1}}{\underline{h}^{-1} + h^{-1}}\right]^{1/2} \exp[-\tfrac{1}{2}\{(\underline{h}^{-1} + h^{-1})^{-1}(\bar{y} - \underline{\mu})^2 - h(\bar{y} - \theta_*)^2\}]. \tag{7.4.76b}$$

Using identity (6.7.17) with $\theta_1 = \theta_*$, it follows from (7.4.76b) that

$$B_{21} = (\underline{h}/\bar{h})^{1/2} \exp[-\tfrac{1}{2}\{\underline{h}(\theta_* - \underline{\mu})^2 - \bar{h}(\theta_* - \bar{\mu})^2\}], \tag{7.4.76c}$$

where $\bar{h} = \underline{h} + h$ is the posterior precision. Then (7.4.18g) implies that $d_* = d_2$ iff

$$\ln(B_{21}) > \ln(\overline{C}_2\underline{\pi}_1/\overline{C}_1\underline{\pi}_2), \tag{7.4.77a}$$

or equivalently, using (7.4.76c),

$$|\bar{h}^{1/2}(\bar{\mu} - \theta_*)| > \{\underline{h}(\theta_* - \underline{\mu})^2 + 2\ln[(\overline{C}_2\underline{\pi}_1/\overline{C}_1\underline{\pi}_2)(\bar{h}/\underline{h})^{1/2}]\}^{1/2}, \tag{7.4.77b}$$

with

$$\bar{\mu} - \theta_* = [\underline{h}(\underline{\mu} - \theta_*) + h(\bar{y} - \theta_*)]/\bar{h}. \tag{7.4.78}$$

Numerous comments regarding (7.4.77b) are in order. First, in the noninformative case ($\underline{h} \rightarrow 0$), inequality (7.4.77b) becomes $|h^{1/2}(\bar{y} - \theta_*)| > \infty$, which cannot be satisfied. Hence, with a noninformative prior, H_1 is *never* rejected. This result, sometimes referred to as *Bartlett's paradox* after Bartlett (1957), is in sharp contrast to the one-sided testing problem of Example 7.4.7 in which the classical test emerges under a noninformative prior. The intuition behind this difference is as follows. In the two-sided case, mixed prior (7.4.34) assigns *positive* probability to $H_1: \theta = \theta_*$. Under $H_2: \theta \neq \theta^*$, as $\underline{h} \rightarrow 0$, the relative probability of θ being in any finite interval approaches zero. Thus, H_1 is favored. In the one-sided case, as $\underline{h} \rightarrow 0$ the relative probability of θ being in any finite interval approaches zero under *both* H_1 and H_2, leading at first glance to an indeterminate form. As shown in Example 7.4.7, however, this indeterminacy can be reconciled and the standard classical result emerges with one caveat: the critical value is an explicit function of the costs of two types of errors. We will return to the noninformative case in Section 9.10.

Second, consider the usual case in which $f(\theta|H_2)$ is "centered" over H_1, that is $\underline{\mu} = \theta_*$ as in (7.4.61). Then (7.4.77b) reduces to reject H_1 iff

$$|z| > (\bar{h}/h)\{2\ln[\bar{C}_2\underline{\pi}_1/\bar{C}_1\underline{\pi}_2)(h/\underline{h})^{1/2}]\}^{1/2}, \tag{7.4.79}$$

where

$$z = h^{1/2}(\bar{y} - \theta_*) \tag{7.4.80}$$

is the familiar classical test statistic. The righthand side of (7.4.79) serves as a "critical value". Not only does this Bayesian "critical value" depend on the relative expected costs of type I and type II errors, more importantly it is an *increasing* function of sample size T through $\bar{h} = \underline{h} + (T/\sigma^2)$. This latter fact is reminiscent of the common dictum shared by all good classical statisticians that the level of significance should be chosen to be a decreasing function of sample size. Because the level of significance is usually chosen on the basis of "convention," however, this warning is seldom operationalized.

Rejection rule (7.4.79) can also be interpreted in terms of the effect on the posterior probability $\bar{\pi}_1$ of H_1. Using (7.4.76c), (7.4.23) and again assuming the prior is centered over H_1, it follows:

$$\bar{\pi}_1 = \left[1 + \left(\frac{\underline{\pi}_1}{1 - \underline{\pi}_1}\right)\left(\frac{\underline{h}\sigma^2}{\underline{h}\sigma^2 + T}\right)^{1/2} \exp\left\{\frac{1}{2}\left(\frac{T}{\underline{h}\sigma^2 + T}\right)z^2\right]^{-1}. \tag{7.4.81}$$

From (7.4.81) it is easy to see that the classical test statistic z can be large (suggesting to a classicist with a fixed level of significance that H_1 should be rejected), while at the same time the posterior probability of H_1 is also close to unity. In fact, letting $T \rightarrow \infty$ in such a way that z (which also depends on T) is held fixed, it is easy to see that $\bar{\pi}_1 \to 1$. In other words, for any large finite value of the test statistic z, there is a sample size T for which the posterior probability $\bar{\pi}_1$ can be made arbitrarily close to unity. This conflict between sampling theory and Bayesian inference is known as *Jeffreys' Paradox* or *Lindley's Paradox*.[9]

Third, reconsider Example 7.2.5 in which it was seen that it is possible for a classical researcher with a constant fixed level significance level to sample to a forgone conclusion. There it was stated that this should not cast doubt on the SRP (with permits such sampling), but rather on the particular method of testing. A natural question that arises here is whether a Bayesian can sample to a foregone conclusion with probability of unity. Specifically consider the following example.

Example 7.4.9 (Effect of Optional Stopping on Bayesian Testing) Consider Example 7.4.8 with the following sampling rule. Pick p, $0 < p < \underline{\pi}_1$, and continue sampling until obtaining $\bar{\pi}_1 < p$, at which point sampling ceases and H_1 is deemed rejected since its posterior probability is "sufficiently small." Cornfield (1966, p. 581) and Edwards et al. (1963, p. 239) note that the probability q of ever stopping (i.e. sampling to a foregone conclusion) when in fact H_1 holds satisfies:

$$q \leq \frac{p/(1-p)}{\underline{\pi}_1/(1-\underline{\pi}_1)} = \frac{p(1-\underline{\pi}_1)}{\underline{\pi}_1(1-p)}. \tag{7.4.82}$$

In other words, if a Bayesian researcher sets out to disprove H_1 by continuing observation until the posterior odds in favor of H_1 are only $100q$ percent of the prior odds, then the probability q of succeeding is bounded above by (7.4.82). Furthermore, this upper bound is small when the prior probability assigned to H_1 is large and the critical probability p below which sampling ceases is small. Therefore, as a result of the introduction of a prior probability $\underline{\pi}_1 > 0$, it is by no means certain (fortunately) that the Bayesian researcher can sample to a foregone conclusion. See Cornfield (1966a, 1966b, 1970) for further discussion.

Finally, it is clear from (7.4.79) and (7.4.80) that choice of $\underline{h}$ can play an important role in reaching a final conclusion. It will be seen in the next section, however, that often it is possible to obtain a lower bound on $\bar{\pi}_1$—even in some cases involving more general families of prior distributions than considered in Example 7.4.8. Nonetheless, there will always be

9. See Shafer (1982). Hill (1992, p. 7) offers the following interpretation. Despite the fact that the data may be at some tiny level of significance, the departure of z from the null value is so small in real terms, namely $O(T^{-1/2})$, that the data are much less probable under H_2 than under H_1. Hill (1992) also notes that if the null hypothesis is an interval rather than sharp, then the paradox no longer holds.

some degree of nonrobustness in Bayesian testing (see Hill 1992). As a result it is important to take seriously prior elicitation, and a suggestion will be made in this regard.

Cornfield (1970, pp. 21–22) suggests one way of thinking about the choice of $\underline{h}$ and $\underline{\pi}_1$ that is often useful. In (7.4.81) the ratio

$$\psi = \frac{\underline{\pi}_1}{\underline{h}^{1/2}(1 - \underline{\pi}_1)} \tag{7.4.83}$$

critically determines $\bar{\pi}_1$ in the neighborhood of H_1. Suppose $\underline{h} \to 0$ and $\underline{\pi}_1 \to 0$ in such a way that ψ remains constant, i.e. let the prior precision under H_2 go to zero (favoring H_1) and let the probability of H_1 go to zero (favoring H_2). Under this limiting procedure posterior probability (7.4.81) reduces to

$$\begin{aligned}\bar{\pi}_{1*}(\psi, T) &\equiv \underset{\psi \text{ constant}}{\overset{\text{limit}}{\underline{h}, \underline{\pi}_1 \to 0}} \bar{\pi}_1 \\ &= \left[1 + (\psi T)^{-1/2} \exp\left(-\frac{1}{2}\left[\frac{\sigma^2}{T}\right] z^2\right)\right]^{-1},\end{aligned} \tag{7.4.84}$$

which involves only a single prior input ψ. Suppose H_1 is deemed acceptable if its posterior probability is greater than some critical probability c_* as determined by loss considerations, for example, see (7.4.18c). Now ask the researcher the question: what would be the smallest number of observations yielding a test statistic $z = 0$, which would lead to acceptance of H_1 at posterior probability c_*? Suppose the answer is T_*. Then solve $\bar{\pi}_{1*}(\psi, T_*) = c_*$ for ψ to obtain

$$\psi_* = \frac{c_*}{T_*(1 - c_*)}. \tag{7.4.85}$$

By using the limiting procedure in (7.4.84) and then asking the crucial interrogation question in terms of a critical sample size T_* it is hoped that the researcher can confidently complete the prior elicitation demands of Bayesian analysis. As suggested in Section 6.8, however, to make the eventual post data conclusion compelling to a wide range of consumers of the research, it may still be necessary to engage in a Bayesian sensitivity analysis (e.g., see Example 7.5.3).

Exercises

7.4.1 Consider Exercise 7.2.1. Let $\delta \equiv \bar{C}_2\underline{\pi}_1/\bar{C}_1\underline{\pi}_2$. Fill out Table 7.4.2.

7.4.2 In the preceding exercise, show that the Bayesian decision minimizes $\alpha + \delta\beta$.

Table 7.4.2
Table of Exercise 7.4.1

δ	Bayesian critical value		Unconditional probabilities of error	
	$J = R$	$J = U$	α	β
.50				
.67				
1.00				
1.50				
2.00				

7.4.3 Consider mixed prior (7.4.34) in Example 7.4.4, and suppose you wish to *estimate* θ under quadratic loss. Find the Bayesian point estimate of θ.

7.4.4 Consider the likelihood $\mathscr{L}(\theta; y)$ and the hypotheses $H_1: \theta_2 = 0$ versus $H_2: \theta_2 \neq 0$, where $\theta = [\theta_1', \theta_2']'$. Let $g(\theta_1, \theta_2) = g(\theta_1 | \theta_2) g(\theta_2)$ be a continuous density defined over $\Re^K$, and consider the prior densities $f(\theta_1 | H_1) = g(\theta_1 | \theta_2 = 0)$ and $f(\theta_1, \theta_2 | H_2) = g(\theta_1, \theta_2)$. Show that the Bayes factor for H_1 versus H_2 can be written as the ratio (known as the *Savage density ratio*) of the marginal *posterior* density of θ_2 to the marginal *prior* density of θ_2 each evaluated at $\theta_2 = 0$ and computed using $g(\theta_1, \theta_2)$ as the prior, that is,

$$B_{12} = \frac{g(\theta_2 = 0 | y)}{g(\theta_2 = 0)}, \tag{7.4.86}$$

where

$$g(\theta_1, \theta_2 | y) = \frac{g(\theta_1, \theta_2)\mathscr{L}(\theta_1, \theta_2; y)}{g(y)}. \tag{7.4.87}$$

7.4.5 In general, computation of $f(y|H_j)$ using (7.4.7a) through (7.4.7e) can be difficult. Laplace's method (see Exercise 6.7.43) offers an attractive approximation. Show that the Laplace (fully exponential) approximation to (7.4.7d) is

$$\hat{f}(y|H_j) = f(\hat{\theta}_j | H_j)\mathscr{L}(\hat{\theta}_j; y)\left(\frac{2\pi}{T}\right)^{K_j/2} |-\overline{D}_j(\hat{\theta}_j; y)|^{-1/2}, \tag{7.4.88}$$

where $\hat{\theta}_j$ is the posterior mode of θ under H_j, and $\overline{D}_j(\hat{\theta}_j; y)$ is the Hessian of the log-posterior. Under conditions outlined in Kass et al. (1990), it can be shown:

$$f(y|H_j) = \hat{f}(y|H_j)[1 + O(T^{-1})]. \tag{7.4.89}$$

7.4.6 Consider Example 7.4.5 and the Bayes factor $B_{21} = f(y|H_2)/f(y|H_1)$. Using the fully exponential form of Laplace's method (see Equation 7.4.88) in both the numerator and the denominator, derive the approximation

$$\begin{aligned}\hat{B}_{21} &= \frac{\hat{f}(y|H_2)}{\hat{f}(y|H_1)} \\ &= \left(\frac{2\pi}{T}\right)^{-(K_2-K_1)/2}\left[\frac{f(\hat{\theta}_2|H_2)\mathscr{L}(\hat{\theta}_2; y)|-\overline{D}_2(\hat{\theta}_2; y)|^{-1/2}}{f(\hat{\theta}_1|H_1)\mathscr{L}(\hat{\theta}_1; y)|-\overline{D}_1(\hat{\theta}_1; y)|^{-1/2}}\right],\end{aligned} \tag{7.4.90}$$

where $\hat{\theta}_j$ is the posterior mode of θ under H_j, and $\overline{D}_j(\hat{\theta}_j; y)$ is the Hessian of the log-posterior ($j = 1, 2$). Under conditions outlined in Kass et al. (1990), it can be shown:

$$B_{21} = \hat{B}_{21}[1 + O(T^{-1})]. \tag{7.4.91}$$

Kass and Raferty (1993) recommend against these asymptotic guidelines when $T < 5K_j$, and lend support to them when $T > 20K_j$.

7.4.7 Chow (1981, p. 29) suggests the asymptotic approximation

$$\ln[\tilde{f}(y|H_j)] \equiv L(\hat{\theta}_j; y) - \tfrac{1}{2}K_j\ln(T) - \tfrac{1}{2}\ln(|R_j|) + \tfrac{1}{2}K_j\ln(2\pi) + \ln[f(\hat{\theta}|H_j)], \tag{7.4.92}$$

where $\hat{\theta}_j$ is the MLE of θ under H_j, K_j is the number of elements unrestricted by H_j, $R_j = -T^{-1}\{\partial^2 \ln[\mathscr{L}(\hat{\theta}; y)]/\partial\theta\,\partial\theta'\}$ and $f(\hat{\theta}_j|H_j)$ is the prior density for θ under H_j evaluated at $\theta = \hat{\theta}_j$. Under conditions outlined in Kass et al. (1990), it can be shown:

$$f(y|H_j) = \tilde{f}(y|H_j)[1 + O(T^{-1})]. \tag{7.4.93}$$

Kass and Raferty (1993) note that when Fisher's expected information matrix is used in (7.4.92) in place of the observed information, the order of the approximation drops to $O(T^{-1/2})$. Rationalize $\tilde{f}(y|H_j)$ as a Laplace approximation (but not of fully exponential form) to $f(y|H_j)$.

7.4.8 The first two terms of (7.4.92),

$$\ln[\bar{f}(y|H_j)] = L(\hat{\theta}_j; y) - \tfrac{1}{2}K_j\ln(T), \tag{7.4.94}$$

correspond to the widely used approximation suggested by Schwarz (1978) for exponential families, and further generalized by Haughton (1988) for curved exponential families. Criterion (7.4.94) is a special case of the more general model selection criterion

$$L(\hat{\theta}_j; y) - c(K_j, T). \tag{7.4.95}$$

Besides $c(K_j; T) = \tfrac{1}{2}K_j\ln(T)$ in the case of Schwarz (1978) and Haughton (1988), the following choices for $c(K_j; T)$ have appeared (not necessarily from a Bayesian standpoint) in the literature: 0 in the case of ML, $\tfrac{1}{2}K_j$ by Akaike (1973), $\tfrac{3}{4}K_j$ by Smith and Spiegelhalter (1980), $3K_j/2$ and $2K_j$ by Bhansali and Downham (1977), $\tfrac{1}{2}$ by Nelder and Wedderburn (1972), ln(2) by Aitkin (1991), $\beta K_j\ln[\ln(T)]$ with $\beta > 2$ by Hannan and Quinn (1979), and $T\ln(T + 2K_j)$. Stone (1977, 1979) offers helpful perspective. Under fairly weak conditions, the change in (7.4.94) across hypotheses, that is,

$$\begin{aligned} SC &\equiv \ln[\bar{f}(y|H_2)] - \ln[\bar{f}(y|H_1)] \\ &= L(\hat{\theta}_2; y) - L(\hat{\theta}_1; y) - \tfrac{1}{2}(K_2 - K_1)\ln(T), \end{aligned} \tag{7.4.96}$$

serves as a consistent indicator of model choice under *both* H_1 and H_2. Contrast these choices of $c(K_j, T)$ in (7.4.95) with Schwarz's criterion, Akaike's criterion, and the conventional likelihood ratio tests as a model choice criterion. Hint: Think of the various criteria as penalized likelihood ratios.

7.4.9 Rewrite (7.4.90) as

$$\begin{aligned} 2\ln(\hat{B}_{12}) &= 2[L(\hat{\theta}_1; y) - L(\hat{\theta}_2; y)] + (K_2 - K_1)\ln(T) \\ &\quad - (K_2 - K_1)\ln(2\pi) + 2\ln[f(\hat{\theta}_1|H_1)] - 2\ln[f(\hat{\theta}_2|H_2)] \\ &\quad - \ln(|-T^{-1}\bar{D}_1(\hat{\theta}_1; y)|) - \ln(|-T^{-1}\bar{D}_2(\hat{\theta}_2; y)|). \end{aligned} \tag{7.4.97}$$

The first line of (7.4.97) is similar to minus twice (7.4.96), except that (7.4.95) is evaluated at the MLE's rather than the posterior modes. The latter two lines of (7.4.97) are important since these terms are all $O(1)$. Note that because part of these lines involves differences in prior densities at the respective modes, priors are seen to have more effect on posterior odds analysis than in ordinary estimation problems. Show each of the following results of Kass and Vaidyanathan (1992):

(a) The reciprocal of approximation (7.4.90) has multiplicative errors of size $O(T^{-1})$, i.e. $B_{12} = \hat{B}_{12}[1 + O(T^{-1})]$.

(b) $\ln(B_{12}) = \ln(\hat{B}_{12}) + O(T^{-1})$.

(c) $\ln(B_{12}) = SC + O(1)$, the larger approximation error arising from neglect of the last two lines in (7.4.97). Kass and Wasserman (1992) note cases in which the order of the approximation can be improved to $O(T^{-1/2})$.

(d) Under H_1, $B_{12} = O(T^{-\delta})$ where $\delta = (K_2 - K_1)/2$.

(e) Under H_2, $B_{12} = \exp[-O(T)]$.

7.4.10 As a diagnostic, the drawback of (7.4.88) or (7.4.90) is the need to compute the mode under H_2. In order to avoid possibly onerous computations under H_2, consider an expansion of $b(\theta) \equiv \ln[f(\theta|H_2)] + L(\theta)$ around the restricted posterior mode $\hat{\theta}_1$ instead of around the mode $\hat{\theta}_2$:

$$b(\theta) = b(\hat{\theta}_1) + [s(\hat{\theta}_1)]'(\theta - \hat{\theta}_1) + \tfrac{1}{2}(\theta - \hat{\theta}_1)'[\bar{D}_2(\hat{\theta}_1)](\hat{\theta}_1)(\theta - \hat{\theta}_1) + r(\theta, \hat{\theta}_1), \tag{7.4.98}$$

where $r(\theta, \hat{\theta}_*)$ is the remainder, and

$$s(\theta) \equiv \begin{bmatrix} s_\omega(\omega, \lambda) \\ s_\lambda(\omega, \lambda) \end{bmatrix} = \begin{bmatrix} \dfrac{\partial b(\omega, \lambda)}{\partial \omega} \\ \dfrac{\partial b(\omega, \lambda)}{\partial \lambda} \end{bmatrix} \tag{7.4.99}$$

is the score of $b(\theta)$.

(a) Dropping the remainder, substituting (7.4.98) into (7.4.7d), and making use of the moment generating function of the multivariate normal distribution to aid in the integration, derive the approximation (c.f., Poirier 1991b)

$$\tilde{f}(y|H_2) = \exp[b(\hat{\theta}_1)]\left(\frac{2\pi}{T}\right)^{K_2/2} |-\bar{D}_2(\hat{\theta}_1)|^{-1/2} \exp\left[\frac{1}{2} q(\hat{\theta}_1)\right], \tag{7.4.100}$$

where

$$q(\hat{\theta}_1) \equiv [s(\hat{\theta}_1)]'[-\bar{D}_2(\hat{\theta}_1)]^{-1}[s(\hat{\theta}_1)]. \tag{7.4.101}$$

(b) Suppose $f(\omega|H_2) = f(\omega|H_1)$. Note that

$$|\bar{D}_2(\theta)| = |\bar{D}_{\omega\omega,2}(\theta)| \cdot |\bar{D}_{\lambda\lambda,2}(\theta) - \bar{D}_{\lambda\omega,2}(\theta)[\bar{D}_{\omega\omega,2}(\theta)]^{-1}\bar{D}_{\omega\lambda,2}(\theta)|. \tag{7.4.102}$$

Using (7.4.100) to replace Laplace approximation $\hat{f}(y|H_2)$ in (7.4.90) by $\tilde{f}(y|H_2)$, derive the Bayes factor approximation:

$$\tilde{B}_{21} \equiv \frac{\tilde{f}(y|H_2)}{\hat{f}(y|H_1)} = (2\pi)^{K_\lambda/2} f(\lambda_*|\hat{\omega}_1, H_2)|-\bar{D}_{\lambda|\omega,2}(\hat{\theta}_1)|^{-1/2}\exp[\tfrac{1}{2}q(\hat{\theta}_1)], \tag{7.4.103}$$

where $f(\lambda_*|\hat{\omega}_1, H_2)$ denotes $f(\lambda|\omega, H_2)$ evaluated at $\lambda = \lambda_*$, $\omega = \hat{\omega}_1$, and

$$\bar{D}_{\lambda|\omega,2}(\theta) = \bar{D}_{\lambda\lambda,2}(\theta) - \bar{D}_{\lambda\omega,2}(\theta)[\bar{D}_{\omega\omega,2}(\theta)]^{-1}\bar{D}_{\omega\lambda,2}(\theta). \tag{7.4.104}$$

(c) Show that (7.4.103) implies:

$$2\ln(\tilde{B}_{12}) = q(\hat{\theta}_1) - K_\lambda \ln(T) + K_\lambda \ln(2\pi) + 2\ln[f(\lambda_*|\hat{\omega}_1, H_2)] - \ln(|-T^{-1}\bar{D}_{\lambda|\omega,2}(\hat{\theta}_1)|). \tag{7.4.105}$$

The first two terms in (7.4.105) are reminiscent of twice the difference in Schwarz criteria under H_2 and H_1 (see Equation 7.4.96), but with -2 times the log-likelihood ratio replaced by score statistic (7.4.101). The remaining terms in (7.4.105) are corrections analogous to (7.4.97). Note that (7.4.101) is a Bayesian analogue of a classical score/LM test statistic (using observed rather than expected sample information).

7.4.11 Assume i.i.d. observations. Let $\tau \subseteq \{1, 2, \ldots, T\}$ and partition y accordingly into a subvector $y_{(\tau)}$ containing those elements y_t for which $t \in \tau$, and into the subvector $y_{(-\tau)}$

containing those elements of y_t for which $t \notin \tau$. Consider the predictive density for $y_{(-\tau)}$ given $y_{(\tau)}$ under H_j:

$$f(y_{(-\tau)}|y_{(\tau)}, H_j) = \int_{\Theta} f(y_{(-\tau)}|y_{(\tau)}, \theta, H_j) f(\theta|y_{(\tau)}, H_j)\, d\theta. \tag{7.4.106}$$

Many Bayesian model selection criteria involve (7.4.106) (see Gelfand and Dey 1992). Approximate (7.4.106) by forming a ratio of Laplace approximations to its numerator and denominator.

7.4.12 Suppose Y_t $(t = 1, 2, \ldots, T) \sim N(\mu, \sigma^2)$, where both μ and σ^2 are unknown. Consider testing $H_1\colon \mu = 0$ versus $H_1\colon \mu \neq 0$. Jeffreys (1961) recommends the prior densities $f(\sigma|H_1) \propto \sigma^{-1}$ and $f(\mu, \sigma|H_2) \propto \sigma^{-1} f_t(\mu/\sigma|0, 1, 1)$, where $f_t(\mu/\sigma|0, 1, 1)$ denotes a proper standardized Cauchy density for μ/σ. Show that the Bayes factor $B_{12} \approx (\frac{1}{2}\pi v)^{1/2}/[1 + (t^2/v)]^{(v-1)/2}$, where $v = T - 1$ and t is the standard t-statistic $t = T^{-1/2}\bar{y}/s$.

7.5 *P*-values

I have always considered the arguments for the use of P (p-value) absurd. They amount to saying that a hypothesis that may or may not be true is rejected because a greater departure from the trial value was improbable: that is, that it has not predicted something that has not happened.
—Jeffreys (1980, p. 453)

Many researchers are reluctant to view themselves as decision makers, and as a result avoid making a choice between H_1 and H_2. Instead they seek merely to provide a summary measure of the evidence in favor of the null hypothesis, and let the reader decide on the course of action to follow. Recognition of the ad hoc selection of significance levels in classical testing can easily produce such a desire. For the Bayesian a similar problem may arise due to ambiguity in defining the appropriate loss function. Such Bayesians, however, have an obvious solution when faced with the class of all-or-nothing loss functions (7.4.43): Simply report, say, the posterior probability $\bar{\pi}_1$ (or alternatively, B_{12} or B_{21}) that serves to completely summarize the data's input into the decision in the case of "all-or-nothing" loss structures. But what should the non-Bayesian do? One observes many applied non-Bayesian researchers using *p-values* as a potential solution. This section defines this concept and relates this "solution" to the Bayesian alternative of reporting $\bar{\pi}_1$.

A p-value is *not* a pure frequentist concept. Rather it mixes together different notions of what constitutes appropriate conditioning. A formal definition follows for the case of a sharp null hypothesis.

Definition 7.5.1 Let $t(Y)$ be a test statistic, extreme values of which are deemed to be evidence against $H_1\colon \theta = \theta_1$. If $Y = y$ is observed, with corresponding $t(y)$, the *p-value* (or observed significance level) is

$$\alpha_p = \text{Prob}_{Y|\theta_1}[|t(Y)| \geq t(y)]. \tag{7.5.1}$$

In words, given the null hypothesis $H_1: \theta = \theta_1$, the p-value α_p is the probability of observing in repeated samples values of the test statistic as least as extreme as the value of the test statistic for the data actually observed. It conditions on the observed data in choosing the number $t(y)$, and then computes a frequentist type probability by making reference to all the possible data that could have been observed, but were not observed. *The first step is immediately suspect to the frequentist, and the second step violates the Likelihood Principle.* The "appeal" is that α_p gives the level of significance, if it had been selected before seeing the data, at which the observed data would have produced a test statistic exactly at that value which divides the rejection region from the acceptance region. No reference to the alternative hypothesis is made in Definition 7.5.1. At this point an example is worth many words.

Example 7.5.1 Consider once again the prototype of a random sample from a $N(\theta, \sigma^2)$ distribution with σ^2 known. The hypotheses of interest are $H_1: \theta = \theta_*$ versus $H_2: \theta \neq \theta_*$. Standard classical reasoning suggests the appropriate rejection region is defined by values of $|t(\overline{Y})| \equiv |h^{1/2}(\overline{Y} - \theta^*)|$ in excess of the critical value $z_{\alpha/2} \equiv \Phi^{-1}(1 - \frac{1}{2}\alpha)$. For example, if $\alpha = .05$, then $z_{\alpha/2} = 1.96$. Suppose $\overline{Y} = \overline{y}$ is observed yielding say the realized test statistic $h^{1/2}(\overline{y} - \theta_*) = 2$, which lies just above the critical value of 1.96. Then

$$\alpha_p = \text{Prob}_{\overline{Y}|\theta_*}[|h^{1/2}(\overline{Y} - \theta_*)| > 2] = .04.$$

If α had been chosen equal to α_p, the realized test statistic would lie on the border between the rejection and acceptance regions. For any $\alpha > \alpha_p$ (say $\alpha = .10$), the realized data would have led to rejection of H_1; for and $\alpha < \alpha_p$ (say $\alpha = .01$), the realized data would not have led to rejection of H_1.

Similar definitions and examples can be constructed for one-sided testing situations. Clearly, the idea underlying the use of p-values is that if α_p is very small, then this casts doubt on H_1 because only if the pre-assigned level of significance α was very small, would H_1 have survived rejection by the observed data. Similarly, if α_p is fairly large, say greater than highest level of most conventionally chosen significance levels (often .10), then this is taken as support for H_1 because at conventional levels of significance the realized data would not have led to rejection of H_1.

Whatever other merits of p-values, they certainly should *not* be equated with a measure of the *evidence* in favor of H_1. The father of frequentist hypothesis testing, Jerzy Neyman, argued fervently (although not necessarily consistently according to Johnstone 1987) that a hypothesis test was a rule of behavior or course of action, not necessarily an inference or belief. For example, according to Neyman, "rejecting" H_1 does *not* suggest it is false, but rather it is only a rule of action. Neyman was a pure frequentist —he was not concerned with any single case; rather he was concerned with the long-run frequencies of type I and type II errors. E. S. Pearson seems to have broken his ties with Neyman and Pearson (1933) in Pearson (1955).[10] Lehmann (1986) also seems to depart from the extreme frequentist stance of Neyman as do most researchers when interpreting the outcome of statistical hypothesis test. *As in the case of conffidence intervals, pragmatic interpretation seems to get in the way of "correct" frequentist reasoning.*

For these reasons low values of α_p need not cast doubt on H_1 in the same way low values of the Bayesian posterior probability $\bar{\pi}_1 = \text{Prob}(H_1|y)$ do. Posterior probabilities are decidedly evidential. In fact, $\bar{\pi}_1$ often is an order of magnitude larger than α_p. The work of Berger and Sellke (1987) and Berger and Delampady (1987) make this point very clear. In the one-sided case, Casella and Berger (1987) argue this distinction no longer holds (with some justification) and go on to argue that p-values may thus have some worth as measures of evidence in support of H_1. They have not won many Bayesian converts to the latter position.

Note α_p only measures the probability *under* H_1 of observing something more extreme than what was observed. The same probability can be computed under H_2 (or a range thereof if H_2 is composite) and it will often also be small. Is this evidence against H_1? Why not also against H_2? Consider the following example.

Example 7.5.2 (Edwards et al. 1963, pp. 221–222) Consider once again Example 7.5.1. Given H_1, the value of the test statistic $z = |h^{1/2}(\bar{y} - \theta)|$ will exceed 1.960 with probability .025 and will exceed 2.576 with probability .005. Hence, $\text{Prob}(1.960 < z < 2.576|H_1) = .020$. Suppose that under H_2 it is believed that all values of z between -20 and 20 are equally likely. In this case

$$\text{Prob}(1.960 < Z < 2.576) = \frac{2.576 - 1.1960}{20 - (-20)} = \frac{.616}{40} = .015.$$

Because $.015 < .020$, observing $1.960 < z < 2.576$ is mild evidence *in favor of* H_1, *not against* H_1.

Lest the reader think the conflict between $\bar{\pi}_1 = \text{Prob}(H_1|y)$ and non-Bayesian measures of evidence like α_p are specific to the choice $p(\theta|H_2) = \phi(\theta|\theta_*, \sigma^2)$, Table 7.5.1 reports the infinum of $\text{Prob}(H_1|y)$ over other classes of $f(\theta|H_2)$. First consider the last line of the table which only

10. The debate between Fisher and Neyman/Pearson is legendary (see Lehmann 1993 and references cited therein).

Table 7.5.1
$\underset{f(\theta|H_2)}{\text{infinum}}\ \bar{\pi}_1 = \text{Prob}(H_1|y)$ with $\underline{\pi}_1 = \underline{\pi}_2 = \frac{1}{2}$

	Test statistic/(p-value)			
$f(\theta\|H_2)$	1.645 (.100)	1.960 (.050)	2.576 (.010)	3.291 (.001)
1. $\phi(\theta\|\theta_*, \sigma^2)$				
$T = 1$	.42	.35	.21	.09
$T = 5$	.44	.33	.13	.03
$T = 10$	.47	.37	.14	.02
$T = 20$	.56	.42	.16	.03
$T = 50$	.65	.52	.22	.03
$T = 100$	.72	.60	.27	.05
$T = 1000$	.89	.82	.53	.12
2. $\phi(\theta\|\theta_*, \underline{h}^{-1}), 0 \le \underline{h} < \infty$	.41	.32	.13	.02
3. Any unimodal distribution symmetric around θ_*	.39	.29	.11	.02
4. Any distribution symmetric around θ_*	.34	.23	.07	.01
5. Any proper distribution	.21	.13	.04	.004

Source: Berger and Sellke (1987).
Note: Case 1 is exact.

restricts $p(\theta|H_2)$ to be proper. At first it may seem surprising that bounds are available in this case, but in fact the basic result was noted a quarter of a century ago in the seminal work of Edwards et al. (1963). The following theorem of Berger and Sellke (1987) provides the necessary background.

Theorem 7.5.1 Consider a two-sided test of $H_1\colon \theta = \theta_*$ versus $H_2\colon \theta \neq \theta_*$, where θ is a scalar. An observation y is drawn from a distribution with density $f(y|\theta)$. Suppose the maximum likelihood estimate $\hat{\theta}_{\text{ML}}$ exists. Then

$$\left\{\underset{f(\theta|H_2)}{\text{infinum}}\ B_{12}\right\} = \frac{f(y|\theta_*)}{f(y|\hat{\theta}_{\text{ML}})}, \tag{7.5.2}$$

and

$$\left\{\underset{f(\theta|H_2)}{\text{infinum}}\ \bar{\pi}_1\right\} = \left[1 + \left(\frac{1-\underline{\pi}_1}{\underline{\pi}_1}\right)\left(\frac{f(y|\hat{\theta}_{\text{ML}})}{f(y|\theta_*)}\right)\right]^{-1}, \tag{7.5.3}$$

where the infinum is taken over all possible proper prior distributions.

The intuition behind the theorem is simple. The $\inf\{B_{12} = f(y|\theta_*)/f(y|H_2)\}$ is clearly obtained by considering

$$\left\{\underset{f(\theta|H_2)}{\text{supremum}}\ f(y|H_2)\right\} = \int_{\Theta_2} f(y|\theta)\, dF(\theta|H_2), \tag{7.5.4}$$

and (7.5.4) is reached when a unitary point mass is assigned to that value of θ most preferred by the data, namely, $\hat{\theta}_{\text{ML}}$ which maximizes $f(y|\theta)$ by definition. The same argument works for $\bar{\pi}_1 = \text{Prob}(H_1|y)$.

Example 7.5.3 Suppose $f(y|\theta) = \phi(y|\theta, \sigma^2)$ with σ^2 known. Then $\hat{\theta}_{ML} = y$, $f(y|\hat{\theta}_{ML}) = (2\pi\sigma^2)^{-1/2}$, and (7.5.2)–(7.5.3) imply

$$\left\{\underset{f(\theta|H_2)}{\text{infinum}}\ B_{12}\right\} = \exp[-z^2], \tag{7.5.5}$$

$$\left\{\underset{f(\theta|H_2)}{\text{infinum}}\ \bar{\pi}_1\right\} = \left[1 + \left(\frac{\underline{\pi}_2}{\underline{\pi}_1}\right)\exp[-z^2]\right]^{-1}, \tag{7.5.6}$$

where $z^2 = (y - \theta_*)^2/\sigma^2$. Values of (7.5.6) are given in the last line of Table 7.5.1 assuming that H_1 and H_2 are treated on equal ground, that is, $\underline{\pi}_1 = \underline{\pi}_2 = \frac{1}{2}$. Strikingly, even in the case which is most unfavorable to H_1, $\bar{\pi}_1$ is still much greater than α_p.

Clearly, the class of all possible prior distributions is too broad to be widely interesting. By restricting the class of distributions for prior $f(\theta|H_2)$ over which the infinum is computed, the lower bounds in the last line of Table 7.5.1 are raised considerably.

Table 7.5.1 also considers three interesting intermediate cases between a completely free choice of $f(\theta|H_2)$ and restricting $f(\theta|H_2) = \phi(\theta|\theta_*, \sigma^2)$. These three intermediate cases involve imposing at least symmetry about θ_* on $f(\theta|H_2)$, a restriction most researchers are likely to feel is "objective." The moral is simple. The non-Bayesian response that $\bar{\pi}_1$ is a useless measure of the evidence provided by the data in favor of H_1 because it involves an "arbitrary" choice of prior for θ under H_2 does not hold water. Furthermore, $\bar{\pi}_1$ provides a very different measure of evidence than the commonly encountered non-Bayesian measure α_p. From the Bayesian viewpoint, classical researchers are far too inclined to reject sharp null hypotheses.

For generalizations of these results to other cases such as non-scalar θ, see Berger and Sellke (1987, pp. 120–122), Berger (1985, 1986), Berger and Delampady (1987, pp. 323–326), Berger and Mortera (1991), Delampady (1989a, 1989b), Delampady and Berger (1990), Dickey (1977), Edwards et al. (1963, pp. 232–235), and Good (1950, 1958, 1967).

7.6 Postscript

Basu, you either believe in what I say or you don't, but never ever try to make fun of my theories.
—R. A. Fisher in Basu (1988, p. 60)

A useful question to ask oneself is whether the world is simple. I do not wish to define simplicity in any precise way here. Rather I will take it as a "primitive" that I hope the reader can understand. The context in which the question is intended is to cover those aspects of the world about which economics has something useful to say. I conjecture that most economists feel this set of aspects is rather large (at least countable), and although I fear outsiders might be inclined to suggest that this set may be null, as an economist I vote for the former. Although I believe the answer to the question must be subjective, and hence the reader is free to disagree with me, I think the answer is easy: the world is *not* simple, in fact, it is incredibly complex.

Why do I ask this question? Well, if the world is simple, then the stated purpose of this chapter (i.e., finding true hypotheses) may appear obtainable. If the world is simple, then maybe we can find true DGP's whose parameters "exist" in the everyday sense of the word. Also the mixed priors used in this chapter, when analyzing sharp hypotheses, may in fact be plausible to those believing in a simple world. Nevertheless, I think such individuals are not without problems.

One of the often cited hallmarks of science is the willingness of scientists to continually subject their theories to possible falsification. While this falsificationist role is noble in principle, its implementation is another matter. There are two reasons why the falsificationist's sword need not cut as deeply as it might first appear.

First, even the "Father of Falsification," Karl Popper, emphasizes that we should never "accept" a hypothesis; rather we may fail to reject it in a particular situation. Because of the Problem of Induction, Popper believes we can never prove a hypothesis; at best we can fail to reject it.

Second, in economics we are rarely, if ever, in the position of exerting sufficient control on an experiment so as to be sure we are in fact testing the hypothesis of interest in isolation from other hypotheses whose validity is equally in question. Rejection of the conjunction "H_1 and H_2" is "not H_1 *or* not H_2." Therefore, failure of a hypothesis to fit the data can always be blamed *ex post* on the failure of some other hypothesis. In fact practicing scientists, from both the social and natural sciences, routinely cling to cherished theories in the face of conflicting evidence. "Rules of the game" to prevent such ad hoc fix-ups are one of the major objectives of philosophers of science such as Imre Lakatos.

Let me move on to those readers who believe, like myself, that the world is complex, but who, unlike myself, are attracted to the stated goal of this chapter (i.e., truth searching). Such readers will likely find the latest fashions in econometrics (namely, nonparametrics and semiparametrics) most attractive. The fare for traveling these fashionable roads, however, is very high, not just in terms of the technical virtuosity required, but also in terms of the complexity of the models at the end of the journey. Even if such travelers decide the price of the journey is worthwhile, however, they are still faced with the falsificationists' dilemmas discussed earlier. Readers inclined toward such journeys will find this text unattractive, because the road it travels points in a different direction.

Although I believe the world is complex, I steadfastly believe we want simple ways of viewing the world. In the language of Poirier (1988c), we want simple windows (likelihoods) through which to view the complex world outside. Thus, I am willing to accept the "heresy" that we are not interested in the literal truth. The heresy, however, is really not as disturbing as it first sounds. By this time the reader has probably asked the question: What do we mean by "truth"? As I have noted elsewhere (see Poirier 1988c, pp. 138–139), many respected economists readily admit to being unclear of the meaning of "truth". A widely accepted pragmatic interpretation would seem to be "correspondence of the facts sufficient for the purposes at hand," and I believe that is all that is required in econometrics.

Sharp hypotheses are of interest, not because they are true, but because they are useful. Useful hypotheses are often abstractions from reality that are best thought of as literally false. What is important for scientific inquiry is to determine whether the abstraction represented by the hypothesis is sufficiently accurate for the purposes at hand.[11] One role for econometrics in economic science is to develop procedures for judging when a hypothesis implied by a theory is in "disagreement" with the empirical evidence, and hence, both the hypothesis and the background theory warrant "rejection." Unfortunately, assessing such accuracy is often not accorded much attention, and mechanical procedures are often adopted. One explanation is the reluctance of researchers to state precisely the pragmatic purposes of their analyses.

Objectivists who believe the world is complex, but wish to use simple likelihoods to capture it are in a difficult position. By definition the entertained likelihood cannot be the true DGP. The parameters of those likelihoods no longer have an existence independently of the likelihood. Why estimate them or test hypotheses about them? What can such researchers do? If researchers are not interested in the literal "truth," in what should they be interested?

I believe there is a fairly clear answer. Rather than seeking the "truth" one can turn attention toward the possibly less noble, but certainly a more pragmatic, goal of *prediction of future observables*. Thus we return to meet our subjective Bayesian friends and their modest predictivist goals. Note,

11. For example, Berger and Delampady (1987) show that the sharp hypothesis $H_1\colon \theta = \theta_*$ is a good approximation to $H_2\colon |\theta - \theta_*| \le \varepsilon$, provided $\varepsilon < \frac{1}{2}\sigma$, where σ is the standard error associated with $\hat{\theta}_{\mathrm{ML}}$.

however, we cannot solve the "Problem of Induction," and so we can never be assured that our predictions will turn out to be accurate. Nonetheless, we must decide whether or not the prediction of a particular model can be utilized, say, for policy purposes. The answer will depend crucially on the underlying theory and whether we think it is appropriate for the policy question being asked (e.g., does it suffer from the so-called "Lucas Critique"; (see the articles in Poirier 1993, Chapter 4). This instrumentalist orientation leaves plenty of room for economic theory. I am not suggesting "black box" prediction.

8 Prediction

Prediction is difficult especially with regard to the future.
—Chinese proverb

It is the model itself, as a more or less suitable approximation to reality, which is of primary interest. The problems of estimation of its parameters or testing of its features have a derived interest only.
—Koopmans (1949, pp. 89–90)

8.1 Introduction

It is trite that specification of the purpose of a statistical analysis is important.
—Cox (1984, p. 309)

Prediction provides discipline and pragmatic importance to empirical research. Suppose a deity told you the values of all unknown parameters in your model, that is, you were completely successful in the activities of estimation (Chapter 6) and hypothesis testing (Chapter 7). What would you "do" with your model? The obvious answer is to use it for what it is intended to do: make *ex ante* probability statements about future observables.[1]

Prediction receives an inexplicable low priority in most econometrics texts.[2] The overwhelming emphasis in modern econometrics texts is on estimation and testing of parameters. This orientation is surprising because prediction has a long history in statistics: certainly going back to Laplace (1774), and in opinion of Stigler (1982), even back to Bayes (1763). Over seventy years ago, Pearson (1920b) offered a clear enunciation of its importance in terms of the simple case of Bernoulli trials (also recall Example 5.8.3). Statistical prediction attempts to provide some rationale for the inductive inference that permeates science despite numerous philosophers' attempts to banish it.

The primary goal of the statistical literature on prediction is defined next.

Definition 8.1.1 Consider a future observable random variable Y_* of interest, and let κ denote an available information set. Given a statistical experiment that generates Y_*, the generically specified distribution function $F(y_*|\kappa) = \text{Prob}(Y_* \leq y_*|\kappa)$ is referred to as the *distribution of interest (DOI)*. A precise specification of the distribution of interest, that is, a choice of functional form for $F(\cdot)$, is a *predictive distribution* for Y_* given

1. In this chapter the terms "predicting"/"forecasting" and "prediction"/"forecast" are used interchangeably.

2. Goldberger (1991, esp. Section 31.5) is a refreshing exception.

κ. The related probability function, $f(y_*|\kappa)$, is a *predictive probability function.* The set $\mathscr{S}_*$ of all possible values that Y_* can assume is the *predictive sample space.*

In Definition 8.1.1 Y_* may be a scalar or a vector random variable. The use of "future" does not necessarily imply a time series context; rather the important issue is that Y_* is observable in principle, but not yet observed. The information set κ may include such things as past data on the random variable of interest, data on related random variables, other forecasts of Y_*, or subject matter information (i.e., theory). Different information sets give rise to different DOIs and different predictive distributions.[3] To be of pragmatic importance, an information set must be based on *known* information. Linking the known κ to the unknown Y_* constitutes a form of inductive inference.

Definition 8.1.1 presupposes that Y_* is of interest, but unfortunately unknown. Because the distribution of Y_* given κ summarizes what the researcher knows about the unknown quantity of interest, everyday parlance suggests referring to $F(y_*|\kappa)$ as the *distribution of interest.* Like any distribution, the DOI reflects a statistical experiment, that is, a process whose outcome Y_* is not known with certainty (Definition 2.1.1). Complete articulation of the details of this experiment (even if it is only conceptual) includes describing the environment in which the quantity of interest, Y_*, is generated. Different environments are likely to give rise to different DOIs. The DOI is tantamount to announcing in statistical terms the purpose of the analysis, that is, how the statistical model is to be used. The DOI logically precedes all other activities. It answers the question; "why was the analysis performed?" Unfortunately, many researchers are more interested in answering the question "what techniques did you use to do the analysis?"

Statistical analyses motivated by different DOIs are not direct competitors. Rather competing statistical analyses agree on a DOI in terms of the quantity of interest Y_*, a statistical experiment envisioned to generate Y_*, and the available information set κ. What makes competing statistical analyses different is how these components merge together into a fully specified *predictive distribution.* Statistical analyses with the same DOI, and which offer the same predictive distribution, are identical for predictive purposes. The following examples will, it is hoped, clarify the preceding terminology.

Example 8.1.1 Consider an experiment in which a two-sided coin is

3. The discussion of Granger (1990b, Sections 9 and 10) concerning choice of the information set in forecasting as opposed to policy analysis is germane here.

flipped ten times under known conditions that the researcher assumes are i.i.d. with probability θ of a "head." Suppose the researcher is interested in determining the number Y_* of "heads" obtained. The DOI here is simply the binomial distribution $B(10, \theta)$. Different choices of θ lead to different predictive distributions, all of which are particular binomial distributions, e.g. $B(10, \frac{1}{2})$ in the case where the coin is assumed to be fair. Changing the experiment to consist of repeating trials until five "tails" are obtained changes the DOI to the negative binomial distribution $NB(\theta, 5)$. The variable of interest Y_* (the number of heads obtained) is the same in both cases, but the experiments and the resulting DOI's are different. The predictive distribution $NB(\frac{1}{2}, 5)$ is not a direct competitor to $B(10, \frac{1}{2})$—they are predicated on different DOIs, although they both involve the same unknown quantity of interest. Also note that unlike the discussion of the LP and Example 6.2.4 involving two experiments, one binomial and one negative binomial yielding proportional observed likelihoods, the *ex ante* difference between the binomial and negative binomial distributions is important here.

Example 8.1.2 Over the past twenty-five years numerous social experiments have been conducted in North America involving work incentives, job training, health concerns, education vouchers, and time-of-use pricing of electricity and telephone service, to name a few. Specifically, suppose the quantity of interest Y_* is a binary variable indicating the labor force participation decision of an individual (defined in terms of socio-economic characteristics) in period $T + 2$. One potential DOI is the distribution of Y_* given the individual voluntarily undergoes job-training in period $T + 1$. The distribution of Y_* unconditional of job-training status in period $T + 1$ is a different potential DOI.

Usually governments are reluctant to force people to participate in social experiments, requiring all participants to be volunteers. Governments are often interested, however, in drawing inferences in environments in which participation is mandatory. The distribution of Y_* given that the individual undergoes mandatory job-training in period $T + 1$ is likely to be quite different than both of the preceding DOIs. Indeed the evidence from a voluntary experiment is unlikely to be of much help in the case of this third DOI.

Given a predictive distribution, it is conceptually straightforward how to proceed with point and interval prediction. Indeed there is widespread agreement on the matter among both classical and Bayesian researchers. The basis of this agreement is the *ex ante* nature of prediction. There is considerably less agreement on the question of how to go about determining a predictive distribution. Casual introspection suggests that what is to be observed in the future is likely connected with what has been observed in the past. Let $Y = [Y_1, Y_2, \ldots, Y_T]'$ represent observable data, and let $y = [y_1, y_2, \ldots, y_T]'$ be their realized values. If the joint distribution for past data $Y = y$ and Y_* is known, then the obvious candidate for a predictive p.f. is simply the condition p.f. of Y_* given $Y = y$, that is,

$$f(y_*|\kappa) = f(y_*|y) = \frac{f(y_*, y)}{f(y)}. \tag{8.1.1}$$

The joint distribution of Y and Y_* "connects" the "in-sample" variables Y with the "out-of-sample" variable Y_*. The nature of this connection warrants some comment. In classical random sampling from a known distribution, then this common parent provides no usable link: Y and Y_* are independent! (recall Examples 5.1.2, 5.2.1 and Exercise 2.1.9). Ironically, a link is provided when the parent distribution depends on an *unknown* parameter θ—the intuitive link is to use the observed data y to learn about θ, and then use this knowledge to predict Y_*. It will be seen, however, that implementation of this strategy is far from being straightforward. An alternative and more direct connection is provided if Y_t $(t = 1, 2, \ldots, T)$ and Y_* are *exchangeable* (recall Section 5.8) since then Y and Y_* may be dependent.[4] Indeed, Example 5.8.3 provided a derivation of (8.1.1) in the case of Bernoulli trials. The importance of exchangeability in predictive questions is brought out quite clearly in Lindley and Novick (1981), and is developed in Exercise 8.3.6.

The "cleanest" way to derive a predictive distribution is to proceed as in the Bayesian case discussed in Example 5.8.3. Although not all researchers agree with the Bayesian approach, honesty requires most researchers at least to admit that the Bayesian approach offers the conceptually most attractive solution. The tools of the trade are nothing more than the ordinary rules of probability. Leaving a more detailed discussion to Section 8.6, it is worth describing now the Bayesian approach so that its stark simplicity is in the reader's mind when reading the accounts to follow of the classical struggle to provide a fully satisfactory answer to the fundamental question of prediction.

Suppose the information set κ consists of the union of past data $Y = y$, yielding the parametric likelihood function $\mathscr{L}(\theta; y)$, and other information in the form of a prior distribution $f(\theta)$. The sampling distribution of Y_* given $Y = y$ and θ, would be an acceptable predictive distribution if θ was

4. For notational convenience, let $Y_{T+1} = Y_*$. The observations $t = 1, 2, \ldots, T+1$ are *exchangeable in Y* iff the joint p.f. $f(y_1, y_2, \ldots, y_{T+1})$ is invariant under permutation of its subscripts. The observations $t = 1, 2, \ldots, T+1$ are *exchangeable in Y given X = x*, iff the conditional p.f. $f(y_1, y_2, \ldots, y_{T+1}|X_1 = x_1, X_2 = x_2, \ldots, X_{T+1} = x_{T+1})$ is invariant under permutation of the subscripts. For further discussion, see Lindley and Novick (1981).

known, but without such knowledge it cannot be used. Using standard results of probability theory and proceeding as in Example 5.8.3, the Bayesian predictive probability function $f(y_*|y)$ can be computed as follows:

$$\begin{aligned} f(y_*|y) &= \frac{f(y_*, y)}{f(y)} \\ &= \int_\Theta \frac{f(y_*, y, \theta)}{f(y)}\, d\theta \\ &= \int_\Theta f(y_*|y, \theta)\left[\frac{f(\theta)f(y|\theta)}{f(y)}\right] d\theta \\ &= \int_\Theta f(y_*|y, \theta) f(\theta|y)\, d\theta \\ &= E_{\theta|y}[f(y_*|y, \theta)]. \end{aligned} \tag{8.1.2}$$

In other words, the Bayesian predictive p.f. is the posterior expectation of the sampling p.f. $f(y_*|y, \theta)$, which involves the unknown θ. $\mathscr{L}(\theta; y)$ serves as an *in-sample window* on the world, and $\mathscr{L}_*(\theta; y, y_*) = f(y_*|y, \theta)$ serves as an *out-of-sample window*. Given the prior and both in-sample and out-of-sample windows, predictive density (8.1.2) is completely known. If the past and future are independent conditional on unknown parameters (e.g., as in random sampling), then $f(y_*|y, \theta) = f(y_*|\theta)$.

The crucial component of (8.1.2) is $f(y_*, y|\theta) = f(y_*|y, \theta)f(y|\theta)$. In particular, note that the out-of-sample window $f(y_*|y, \theta)$ is characterized by the same parameters that characterize the in-sample window $f(y|\theta)$. The plausibility of this feature depends on the similarity between the out-of-sample and in-sample environments. Two prototypes of statistical environments should be noted. First, there are passive environments in which the researcher merely observes data without taking any action to affect the environment. Such environments lead to *observational studies*, typical of non-laboratory sciences. Second, there are non-passive environments in which the researcher plays an active role, leading to *experimental studies*. The classic treatments of Cox (1958a) and Fisher (1951) address design of such experimental studies. A crucial issue in designing experiments is the use of randomization to assign "treatments" to some in-sample observational units in order to make inferences about out-of-sample units under different hypothetical states of the world that may occur. Consideration of the hypothetical or counterfactual states is an important characteristic of most notions of the exclusive concept of *causality*.

Experimental laboratory studies are relatively rare in most social sciences—psychology and particular areas of economics (e.g., market structure) are exceptions. Experimental laboratory experiments are common in the natural sciences, but there are exceptions (e.g., astronomy). Somewhere between pure observational and pure experimental studies are *social experiments* (recall Example 8.1.2), which involve control over some aspects of the environment, but are passive with respect to most aspects. Most important, in social experiments the units of observations involve humans rather than plots of land that Fisher often discussed. Humans act purposely, and may react to the randomization itself rather than to the treatment. Such effects are often called *Hawthorne effects* (e.g., see Cook and Campbell 1979). Less than perfect control is almost an inherent feature of social experiments, and economics is not alone in this regard. For example, in medical clinical trials control is less than perfect—drugs may be prescribed but it remains for individuals to taken them on a regular basis. This issue is known as the problem of *compliance* (see Efron and Feldman 1991). The efficacy of randomization in social experimentation is a controversial matter (see Heckman and Hotz 1989 and Heckman 1992 and the articles cited therein).

The importance of the observational versus experimental study dichotomy is that often the DOIs for observational studies involve hypothetical or real interventions on the part of the researcher in the out-of-sample environment. As Lindley (1982a, p. 77) notes, to appreciate what happens when control is exercised, it is necessary to experiment with control. When controlling one variable in a study it is crucial to understand not only the effect of the controlled variable on the variable of interest, but also the effect of the controlled variable on other variables involved in the study. There are many ways out-of-sample and in-sample environments may differ no matter how the data are generated. *The important point to be drawn from this discussion is that whenever drawing an inductive predictive inference, a compelling case must be made for invariance in* $f(y_*|y)$, *via the out-of-sample window* $\mathscr{L}_*(\theta; y, y_*) = f(y_*|y, \theta)$, *or a component derived thereof, for example, a marginal or conditional distribution.*

Other than Section 8.6 and part of Section 8.7, this chapter is about the struggle of non-Bayesian statistics to provide a compelling general alternative to (8.1.2). Section 8.2 begins with the unrealistic/idealistic, but pedagogically useful, situation in which the parameters take known values $\theta = \theta_0$. This can be thought of as a limiting case of (8.1.2) in which the posterior distribution of θ is a spike at $\theta = \theta_0$. Although there may be differences regarding the interpretation of probability (i.e., objective versus subjective interpretations), the mathematics of Section 8.2 is agreed upon by Bayesian and non-Bayesians. Section 8.3 discusses the important concept of a statistical structure. Often the researcher wishes to engage in prediction in which tomorrow is known not to be exactly like today because an "intervention" or some change in the environment is envisioned. If the DOI and predictive distribution are not affected by the change, then they are said to be "structural." Section 8.4 considers a classical likelihood-based attempt, known as predictive likelihood, to provide a direct alternative to (8.1.2) in the case of unknown parameters. Section 8.5 presents conventional ad hoc classical approaches to point and interval prediction. Finally, Section 8.7 considers the situation in which multiple predictive distributions are available.

The primary statistical text on prediction is Aitchison and Dunsmore (1975). The many contributions by Seymour Geisser have carried the predictivists' banner (e.g., Geisser 1971, 1980, 1982, 1985, 1993) admirably. An important early contribution was Roberts (1965). As noted at the start of this section, the predictivist tradition is well-established in Bayesian circles.

8.2 The Simplest Case: Known Parameters

This section assumes a state of nirvana: all parameters values are known, say $\theta = \theta_0$. Hence, $f(y_*|y, \theta_0)$ is available. All the artillery of sampling theory in Chapter 5 is readily available for describing random draws from $f(y_*|y, \theta_o)$. In the following it is assumed that a sample (not necessarily) random Y_t $(t = 1, 2, \ldots, T)$ is available, where the Y_ts and Y_* are $M \times 1$ vectors. The case $M = 1$, however, receives the majority of attention.

There is little disagreement about how to engage in point prediction in such a situation: use all available information to pick point predictions to minimize expected costs. The expectation is taken with respect to all uncertainty, which in this case is simply the uncertainty in future observables as described by the c.d.f $F(y_*|y, \theta_o)$. Letting $C(\hat{Y}_*, Y_*)$ denote a predictive cost (loss) function measuring the performance of a predictor $\hat{Y}_* = \hat{Y}_*(Y, \theta_o)$, the optimal point predictor $\hat{Y}_{**} = \hat{Y}_{**}(Y, \theta_o)$ is given by the solution

$$\hat{Y}_{**} \equiv \underset{\hat{Y}_*}{\operatorname{argmin}}\, E_{Y_*|Y,\theta_o}[C(\hat{Y}_*, Y_*)]. \tag{8.2.1}$$

If predictive loss is quadratic in the $M \times 1$ prediction (forecast) error

$$\hat{U}_* = \hat{Y}_* - Y_*, \tag{8.2.2}$$

that is,

$$C(\hat{Y}_*, Y_*) = (\hat{Y}_* - Y_*)'A_*(\hat{Y}_* - Y_*), \tag{8.2.3}$$

where A_* a known positive definite matrix of order M satisfying the normalization $\operatorname{tr}(A_*) = 1$, then the *optimal* point estimate according to

(8.2.1) is

$$\hat{Y}_{**} = E(Y_* | Y, \theta_o). \tag{8.2.4}$$

Predictor (8.2.4) is also optimal in more general settings (see Exercise 8.2.1). Results analogous to those in Section 6.7 (e.g., Theorem 6.7.1) can be derived for generating point predictions for other familiar loss functions (see Exercise 8.2.2).

With quadratic predictive loss in mind, the following terminology is introduced.

Definition 8.2.1 A predictor $\hat{Y}_*$ of Y_* is *unbiased* iff $E_{Y_*|Y,\theta}(\hat{Y}_* - Y_*) = E_{Y_*|Y,\theta}(\hat{U}_*) = 0$. The *predictive bias* of the predictor $\hat{Y}_*$ is $E_{Y_*|Y,\theta}(\hat{Y}_* - Y_*)$. The *predictive covariance matrix* of the predictor $\hat{Y}_*$ is $\text{Var}_{Y_*|Y,\theta}(\hat{Y}_* - Y_*) = \text{Var}_{Y_*|Y,\theta}(\hat{U}_*)$. The *predictive mean square error (MSEP) matrix* of the predictor $\hat{Y}_*$ is $\text{MSEP}(\hat{Y}_*|Y,\theta_o) \equiv E_{Y_*|Y,\theta}[(\hat{Y}_* - Y_*)(\hat{Y}_* - Y_*)'] = E_{Y_*|Y,\theta}(\hat{U}_*\hat{U}_*')$. To emphasize that these concepts are conditional on $Y = y$, the adjective "conditional" may be added as a prefix.

Patterned after Theorem 6.3.3, the following theorem is straightforward to prove.

Theorem 8.2.1 Let $\hat{Y}_*$ be a predictor of Y_*. Then:

$$\begin{aligned}\text{MSEP}(\hat{Y}_*|Y,\theta_o) &= \text{Var}_{Y_*|Y,\theta}(\hat{Y}_* - Y_*) \\ &\quad + [E_{Y_*|Y,\theta}(\hat{Y}_* - Y_*)][E_{Y_*|Y,\theta}[(\hat{Y}_* - Y_*)]' \qquad (8.2.5a) \\ &= \text{Var}_{Y_*|Y,\theta}(\hat{U}_*|Y,\theta_o) + [E_{Y_*|Y,\theta}(\hat{U}_*)][E_{Y_*|Y,\theta}(\hat{U}_*)]'. \qquad (8.2.5b)\end{aligned}$$

Proof Exercise 8.2.4.

Example 8.2.1 Predictor (8.2.4) is an unbiased predictor. Denoting its prediction error by $\hat{U}_{**} = \hat{Y}_{**} - Y_*$, (8.2.5b) implies $\text{MSEP}(\hat{Y}_{**}|Y,\theta_o) = \text{Var}(\hat{U}_{**}|Y,\theta_o)$.

If Y_* and Y are independent given θ (as in random sampling), then Y can be ignored and (8.2.4) simplifies to

$$\hat{Y}_{**} = E(Y_*|\theta_o). \tag{8.2.6}$$

Example 8.2.1 involves random sampling in which case (8.2.6) is relevant. Example 8.2.2 considers a case not involving random sampling and in which (8.2.4) is relevant.

Example 8.2.2 Suppose Y_t $(t = 1, 2, \ldots, T, T+1) \sim$ i.i.d. $N(\mu_o, \sigma_o^2)$, and let $Y = [Y_1, Y_2, \ldots, Y_{T+1}]'$.[5] Here $M = 1$, sampling is random, observa-

5. For a reformulation of this set-up in terms of exchangeability, see Theorem 5.8.2.

tions Y_t $(t = 1, 2, \ldots, T)$ are available, $Y_* = T_{T+1}$ is the quantity of interest, and $\theta_o = [\mu_o, \sigma_o^2]'$. Assume quadratic squared error loss (8.2.3) is relevant. Because $M = 1$, the normalization $\text{tr}(A_*) = 1$ implies $A_* = 1$. If θ_o is known, then the optimal point predictor of Y_* is the unbiased predictor $\hat{Y}_{**} = \mu_o$. The prediction error in this case is $\hat{U}_{**} = \mu_o - Y_*$, and $\hat{U}_{**} | Y, \theta_o \sim N(0, \sigma_o^2)$. The expected loss from using this predictor is

$$\begin{aligned} E_{Y_*|Y,\theta_o}[C(\hat{Y}_{**}, Y_*)] &= E_{Y_*|Y,\theta_o}[(\mu_o - Y_*)^2] \\ &= \text{MSEP}(\hat{Y}_{**} | Y, \theta_o)] \\ &= \text{Var}(\hat{U}_{**} | Y, \theta_o)] \\ &= \sigma_o^2. \end{aligned} \tag{8.2.7}$$

Note that knowledge of σ_o^2 is immaterial for computing point prediction in this case, as a result of the quadratic loss structure employed.

Example 8.2.3 Consider the Gaussian AR(1) in Example 6.10.6 with $M = 1$ and $A_* = 1$ in quadratic cost function (8.2.3). Sampling is not random in this case. Suppose that it is known that $\theta = \theta_o$. Then $f(y_* | y, \theta_o) = \phi(y_* | \theta_o y_T, 1)$. In this case, point predictor (8.2.4) is $\hat{Y}_{**} = \theta_o y_T$, the prediction error is $\hat{U}_{**} = \theta_o y_T - Y_*$, and $\hat{U}_{**} | Y, \theta_o \sim N(0, 1)$. The expected loss from this predictor is unity.

A multivariate analog of Example 8.2.2 is provided in the next example.

Example 8.2.4 Suppose Z_t $(t = 1, 2, \ldots, T, T + 1) \sim$ i.i.d. $N_M(\theta_o, \Sigma_o)$. Here $M > 1$, sampling is random, observations $Z_t = z_t$ $(t = 1, 2, \ldots, T)$ are available, the $M \times 1$ vector $Z_* = Z_{T+1}$ is the quantity of interest, and $\theta_o = [\mu_o', \{\text{vech}(\Sigma_o)\}']'$. Assume quadratic squared error loss (8.2.3) subject to the normalization $\text{tr}(A_*) = 1$. If θ_o is known, then as in Example 8.2.2 the optimal point predictor of Y_* is the unbiased predictor $\hat{Z}_{**} = \mu_o$. The prediction error in this case is $\hat{U}_{**} = \mu_o - Z_*$, and $\hat{U}_{**} | Z, \theta_o \sim N_M(0_M, \Sigma_o)$. The expected loss from using this predictor is

$$\begin{aligned} E_{Z_*|Z,\theta_o}[C(\hat{Z}_{**}, Z_*)] &= \text{tr}(A_* E_{Z_*|Z,\mu_o}[(\mu_o - Z_*)(\theta_o - Z_*)']) \\ &= \text{tr}[A_* \text{MSEP}(\hat{Z}_{**} | Z, \theta_o)] \\ &= \text{tr}[A_* \text{Var}(\hat{U}_{**} | Z, \theta_o)] \\ &= \text{tr}(A_* \Sigma_o). \end{aligned} \tag{8.2.8}$$

The preceding approach to point estimation is widely supported by both Bayesians and non-Bayesians. Both would also find it meaningful to make a probability statement like

$$\text{Prob}(Y_* \in \bar{\mathscr{S}}_* | Y = y, \theta_o) = 1 - \alpha, \tag{8.2.9}$$

where $\bar{\mathscr{S}}_*$ is a subset of the sample space $\mathscr{S}_*$ for Y_*. The region described by (8.2.9) is known as a *prediction (forecast) region* (interval when

$M = 1$). Note that while construction of (8.2.9) proceeds analogous to the construction of confidence intervals in Section 6.9, it is possible to make a *probability* (as opposed to confidence) statement because the quantity Y_* being captured by the region is a random variable. Furthermore, (8.2.9) can be used in either of two ways: given $\bar{\mathscr{S}}_*$, find α; or given α, find the smallest region $\bar{\mathscr{S}}_*$. Of course proponents of each camp interpret these probability statements differently. The former case is covered in the following example.

Example 8.2.5 In Example 8.2.2 a $1 - \alpha$ prediction (forecast) interval for Y_* is given by $\bar{\mathscr{S}}_* = \{Y_* | \theta_o - z_{\alpha/2}\sigma_o < Y_* < \theta_o + z_{\alpha/2}\sigma_o\}$, where $z_{\alpha/2}$ satisfies $\Phi(z_{\alpha/2}) = 1 - \alpha$.

Example 8.2.6 In Example 8.2.3 a $1 - \alpha$ prediction (forecast) interval for Y_* is given by $\bar{\mathscr{S}}_* = \{Y_* | \theta_o y_T - z_{\alpha/2}\sigma_o < Y_* < \theta_o y_T + z_{\alpha/2}\}$.

Example 8.2.7 In Example 8.2.4, Theorem 4.5.1 implies that a $1 - \alpha$ prediction (forecast) ellipsoid for Z_* is given by $\bar{\mathscr{S}}_* = \{Z_* | (Z_* - \mu_o)'\Sigma_o^{-1}(Z_* - \mu_o) \le c_\alpha\}$, where c_α cuts off $1 - \alpha$ probability in the righthand tail of the chi-squared distribution with M degrees of freedom.

In the remaining examples of this section we return to Section 2.7 and its predictive motivation for discussing regression functions.

Example 8.2.8 Consider Example 8.2.4 and the partitioning $Z_* = [X'_*, Y_*]'$, where $X_* = [Z_{*1}, Z_{*2}, \ldots, Z_{*M-1}]'$ and $Y_* = Z_{*M}$. Also partition μ_o and Σ_o accordingly:

$$\mu_o = \begin{bmatrix} \mu_x \\ \mu_y \end{bmatrix}, \Sigma_o = \begin{bmatrix} \Sigma_{xx} & \sigma_{xy} \\ \sigma_{yx} & \sigma_{yy} \end{bmatrix}. \tag{8.2.10}$$

Suppose the information set implicit in Example 8.2.4, $\kappa = \{Z_1, Z_2, \ldots, Z_T, \theta_o, \Sigma_o\}$, is expanded to include X_* as well. If $M = 1$ and θ_o is known, then under quadratic loss with $A_* = 1$, Theorem 2.7.2 implies that the optimal point estimate of Y_* is $\hat{Y}_{**} = E(Y_* | X_*, \mu_o, \Sigma_o) = \beta_1 + X'_*\tilde{\beta}_2$, where

$$\tilde{\beta}_2 = \Sigma_{xx}^{-1}\sigma_{xy}, \tag{8.2.11}$$

$$\beta_1 = \mu_y - \mu'_x\tilde{\beta}_2. \tag{8.2.12}$$

The prediction error in this case is $\hat{U}_{**y} = \hat{Y}_{**} - Y_* \sim N(0, \sigma_{yy|x})$, where

$$\sigma_{yy|x} = \sigma_{yy} - \sigma_{yx}\Sigma_{xx}^{-1}\sigma_{xy}. \tag{8.2.13}$$

The expected loss from using this predictor is

$$\begin{aligned} E_{Y_*|X_*, Z, \theta_o}[C(\hat{Y}_{**}, Y_*)] &= E_{Y_*|X_*, Z, \theta_o}[(\hat{Y}_{**} - Y_*)(\hat{Y}_{**} - Y_*)'] \\ &= \text{MSEP}(\hat{Y}_{**} | X_*, Z, \theta_o) \\ &= \text{Var}(\hat{U}_{**y} | X_*, Z, \theta_o) \\ &= \sigma_{yy|x}. \end{aligned} \tag{8.2.14}$$

Example 8.2.9 Consider Example 8.2.8. Using $\hat{Y}_{**}$, a $1-\alpha$ prediction (forecast) interval for Y_* is given by $\bar{\mathscr{S}}_* = \{Y | \hat{Y}_{**} - z_{\alpha/2}(\sigma_{yy|x})^{1/2} < Y_* < \hat{Y}_{**} + z_{\alpha/2}(\sigma_{yy|x})^{1/2}\}$.

An important, but somewhat subtle point, in using the optimal point predictor $\hat{Y}_{**} = \tilde{\beta}_1 + X'_* \tilde{\beta}_2$ is the nature of X_*. This point highlights the difference between observational and experimental studies. As Lindley (1982b, p. 77) notes, to appreciate what happens when control is exercised, it is necessary to experiment with control. Free and controlled variations differ not in the realized X_*, but rather in the random variable realized to be X_*. As noted in Chapter 2, conditional probability critically involves the random variable being conditioned upon, not just the realized value.

Exercises

8.2.1 (Granger 1969) Let $\hat{Y}_*$ be a predictor of the scalar random variable Y_* given the observed data $Y = y$ and cost function $C(\hat{Y}_*, Y_*) = C_*(U_*)$ depending only on the prediction (forecast) error $\hat{U}_* = Y_* - \hat{Y}_*$.

(a) Suppose $C_*(\hat{U}_*)$ is symmetric about zero, almost surely differentiable, and strictly monotonically increasing in the prediction error $\hat{U}_*$. Also suppose that $f(y_*|y, \theta_0)$ is symmetric about its mean $E(Y_*|y, \theta_0)$. Show that the optimal predictor is $\hat{Y}_{**} = E(Y_*|y, \theta_0)$.

(b) Suppose $C_*(\hat{U}_*)$ is symmetric about zero. Also suppose $f(y_*|y, \theta_0)$ is symmetric around its mean $E(Y_*|y, \theta_0)$, continuous and unimodal. Show that the optimal predictor is $\hat{Y}_{**} = E(Y_*|y, \theta_0)$.

8.2.2 Find the point predictions for the loss functions in the following exercises:

(a) Exercise 6.7.13(b)

(b) Exercise 6.7.18

(c) Exercise 6.7.19

(d) Exercise 6.7.20

8.2.3 Derive (8.2.4) from expected cost minimization of (8.2.3).

8.2.4 Prove Theorem 8.2.1.

8.2.5 Consider Example 8.2.2 with $Y_* = [Y_{T+1}, Y_{T+2}]'$. Find $f(y_*|y, \theta_o)$. Is $f(y_*|y, \theta_o)$ a bivariate normal density? Under squared error loss (8.2.3), what is the optimal point prediction of Y_*?

8.2.6 (Simpson's paradox) Let X_t, Y_t and Z_t $(t = 1, 2, \ldots, T+1)$ be a sequence of three Bernoulli random variables. We will take T as large, say, $T = 80{,}000$. The following numbers are drawn from Lindley and Novick (1981), but put into a context of more interest to economists. Table 8.2.1 provides a cross-classification summary of Y versus Z, where all quantities are measured in thousands. Tables 8.2.2 and 8.2.3 provide analogous cross-classifications summaries of Y versus Z for $X = 1$ and $X = 0$, respectively.

(a) Consider a one-year job training experiment involving T low-skilled individuals not in the labor force (i.e., not employed nor actively looking for work). Suppose $Y_t = 1$ denotes that individual t is in the labor force sometime during the post-training year, and $Y_t = 0$ denotes that the individual is *not* in the labor force during the entire post-training year. Suppose $Z_t = 1$ denotes that individual t received training during the experiment, and $Z_t = 0$ denotes that individual t was a member of the control

Table 8.2.1
Cross-classification of Y versus Z in Exercise 8.2.6

	$Y = 1$	$Y = 2$	Row total	Row proportion of $Y = 1$
$Z = 1$	20	20	40	.50
$Z = 0$	16	24	40	.40
Column sum	36	44	80	

Table 8.2.2
Cross-classification of Y versus Z for $X = 1$ in Exercise 8.2.6

	$Y = 1$	$Y = 0$	Row total	Row proportion of $Y = 1$
$Z = 1$	18	12	30	.60
$Z = 0$	7	3	10	.70
Column sum	25	15	40	

Table 8.2.3
Cross-classification of Y versus Z for $X = 0$ in Exercise 8.2.6

	$Y = 1$	$Y = 0$	Row total	Row proportion of $Y = 1$
$Z = 1$	2	8	10	.20
$Z = 0$	9	21	30	.30
Column sum	11	29	40	

group and did not receive training. Also suppose $X_t = 1$ denotes that individual t is male, and $X_t = 0$ denotes that individual t is female. Table 8.2.1 suggests the individuals who received the "treatment" (i.e., job training) were *more* likely to be employed in the post-training year than those who were "controls" (i.e., received no job training): .50 versus .40. Tables 8.2.2 and 8.2.3, however, suggest that males and females, respectively, who received the job training were *less* likely to be employed in the post-training year than those who were received no job training: .60 versus .70 for males, and .20 versus .30 for females. Therefore, it appears that job training helps the employment possibilities for the population as a whole, but neither for males nor females individually! This apparent paradox is known in the statistics literature as *Simpson's paradox*.[6] Would you recommend job training for individual $T + 1$ if you did not know the individual's gender at the time you made your decision? Would your answer change if you knew the individual's gender at the time of your recommendation?

(b) Consider an agricultural experiment involving planting corn in $T + 1$ plots of land. Suppose Z_t denotes two varieties of plants: Variety A ($Z_t = 1$) and Variety B ($Z_t = 0$); Y_t denotes crop yield: high ($Y_t = 1$) and low ($Y_t = 0$); and X_t denotes plant height: high ($X_t = 1$) and low ($X_t = 0$). Would you recommend planting Variety A on plot $T + 1$?

6. The name is due to Simpson (1951), but it was noticed earlier. A good flavor of the literature can be obtained from Basset (1989), Blyth (1972), Dawid (1979), Goddard (1991), Kaigh (1989), Kotz and Stroup (1983), Lindley and Novick (1981), Meier and DiNardo (1990), Mittal (1991), Samuels (1993), and Wagner (1982).

(c) Many people reach different recommendations in (a) and (b). Lindley and Novick suggest exchangeability considerations may offer a resolution. Consider case (a), and suppose your beliefs about individuals are exchangeable in Y, given Z and X. Such a belief is consistent with the belief that training and gender affect labor force status. The quantities of interest are of the form $P(Y_{T+1} = 1 | Z_{T+1}, X_{T+1}, Y_T, Z_T, X_T, \ldots, Y_1, Z_1, X_1)$, and given that $T = 80{,}000$, this probability will be approximately equal to the frequency for which $Y_{T+1} = 1$ occurred in the data with the same values of Z_{T+1} and X_{T+1}.

(1) Find each of the following:

(i) $P(Y_{T+1} = 1 | Z_{T+1} = 1, X_{T+1} = 1)$

(ii) $P(Y_{T+1} = 1 | Z_{T+1} = 0, X_{T+1} = 1)$

(iii) $P(Y_{T+1} = 1 | Z_{T+1} = 1, X_{T+1} = 0)$

(iv) $P(Y_{T+1} = 1 | Z_{T+1} = 0, X_{T+1} = 0)$

Table 8.2.4
Cross-classification of Y versus Z for $W = 1$ and $X = 1$ in Exercise 8.2.6

	$Y = 1$	$Y = 0$	Row total	Row proportion of $Y = 1$
$Z = 1$	11	4	15	.73
$Z = 0$	3	2	5	.60
Column sum	14	6	20	

Table 8.2.5
Cross-classification of Y versus Z for $W = 1$ and $X = 0$ in Exercise 8.2.6

	$Y = 1$	$Y = 0$	Row total	Row proportion of $Y = 1$
$Z = 1$	2	3	5	.40
$Z = 0$	5	10	15	.33
Column sum	7	13	20	

Table 8.2.6
Cross-classification of Y versus Z for $W = 0$ and $X = 1$ in Exercise 8.2.6

	$Y = 1$	$Y = 0$	Row total	Row proportion of $Y = 1$
$Z = 1$	10	5	15	.67
$Z = 0$	1	4	5	.20
Column sum	11	9	20	

Table 8.2.7
Cross-classification of Y versus Z for $W = 0$ and $X = 0$ in Exercise 8.2.6

	$Y = 1$	$Y = 0$	Row total	Row proportion of $Y = 1$
$Z = 1$	3	2	5	.60
$Z = 0$	1	14	15	.07
Column sum	4	16	20	

(2) Given your answers in (1), would you recommend job training for individual $T + 1$ if you know the individual's gender at the time you made your decision? Is your answer the same for males and females?

(3) If you do not known the gender of individual $T + 1$, consider

$$\begin{aligned} P(Y_{T+1} = 1|Z_{T+1} = 1) &= P(Y_{T+1} = 1|Z_{T+1} = 1, X_{T+1} = 1)P(X_{T+1} = 1|Z_{T+1} = 1) \\ &\quad + P(Y_{T+1} = 1|Z_{T+1} = 1, X_{T+1} = 0)P(X_{T+1} = 0|Z_{T+1} = 1) \\ &= .6P(X_{T+1} = 1|Z_{T+1} = 1) + .2[1 - P(X_{T+1} = 1|Z_{T+1} = 1)]. \end{aligned}$$

The data alone do *not* provide $P(X_{T+1} = 1|Z_{T+1} = 1)$.

(i) Suppose you judge individuals exchangeable in X given Z. Find $P(X_{T+1} = 1| Z_{T+1} = 1)$, $P(Y_{T+1} = 1|Z_{T+1} = 1)$, and $P(Y_{T+1} = 1|Z_{T+1} = 0)$. Would you recommend treatment for individual $T + 1$?

(ii) Suppose you judge X and Z to be independent, individual $T + 1$ exchangeable in X with the rest of the population, and that males and females are equally likely in this population. Find $P(X_{T+1} = 1|Z_{T+1} = 1)$, $P(Y_{T+1} = 1|Z_{T+1} = 1)$, and $P(Y_{T+1} = 1|Z_{T+1} = 0)$. Would you recommend treatment for individual $T + 1$?

(d) Consider the case in (a). Let W_t be another binary characteristic of individual t. Tables 8.2.4 through 8.2.7 provide cross-classification summaries of Y versus Z for $X = 1, 0$ and $W = 1, 0$. How does Simpson's paradox relate to these additional data?

(e) Is Simpson's paradox really a paradox? What connections does this exercise have with Exercise 3.4.22?

8.3 Structural Modelling

There would not be much purpose in devising a model ... if we did not have some hope that at least some features of our model would be invariant with respect to some changes in circumstances.... If all the model is good for is to describe a particular set of data ... then we might as well forego the effort of devising the model....
—Duncan (1975)

Prediction also played a fundamental role for the founders of the Econometric Society (e.g., the quote by Koopmans 1949 at the opening of this chapter plays down estimation and testing). It can be argued, that the defining essence of econometrics distinguishing it from statistics at large, is its literature on *structure*. Frisch (1938) developed the idea of "structure," and Haavelmo (1944) developed a statistical framework for studying it.

Definition 8.3.1 A distribution is a *structural distribution* iff it is invariant (i.e., does not change) with respect to a contemplated class of interventions. A set of parameters of a distribution are *structural parameters* iff it is meaningful (plausible) to contemplate each one separately with the rest remaining unchanged.

For example, "demand" and "supply" curves are entities that economists often shift individually assuming the other remains fixed. The validity of such analyses rests on whether such curves capture structural relationships, and whether their parameters are structural parameters. The components of a structure warrant a degree of autonomy (detachability or projectibility) in the face of change elsewhere in the statistical model. Structural relationships have a "life of their own" and can be discussed without reference to other parts of the model.

The need for structural interpretations is widespread (see the earlier quote by Duncan 1975). In economics the need for structure arises from the need to address *the essence of economic policy analysis–prediction in the face of intervention.* Numerous econometricians, however, have been pessimistic about our abilities to uncover structural relations with passive observational data sets—notably Frisch himself. One of the most influential attacks was by Lucas (1976), building on earlier efforts by Marschak (1953). Lucas demonstrated that an economy's theoretical Phillips curve relating inflation and real activity does not serve as a *usable* menu for policy choice. Basically, Lucas questioned whether econometricians were focusing on the invariants of the economy, starting an industry of excavation to find the "deep parameters" characterizing agents' preferences and the economy's technology. Favero and Hendry (1992) discuss how the empirical relevance of the Lucas Critique can be evaluated. Aldrich (1989) nicely ties together numerous strands of the literature on policy analysis and structure. See Poirier (ed. 1994) for many of the original contributions.

A detailed discussion of structure at this point is handicapped by the limited nature of the windows discussed so far. The issue needs raising now, however, because whenever out-of-sample observations are viewed through the same window as in-sample observations, the researcher is asserting, at least implicitly, the validity of the same window for the new data. The following discussion is intended only as a brief introduction.

Consider a $K \times 1$ vector $Z = [Y', X', W']'$, where Y is $K_y \times 1$, X is $K_x \times 1$, W is $K_w \times 1$, and $K = K_y + K_x + K_w$. There are many ways to factor the joint p.f. of Z into marginals and conditionals. Even without breaking apart the three subvectors Y, X and W, there are twelve factorizations:

$$f(y_*, x_*, w_*) = f(y_*|x_*, w_*)f(x_*, w_*) \tag{8.3.1a}$$

$$= f(y_*|x_*, w_*)f(x_*|w_*)f(w_*) \tag{8.3.1b}$$

$$= f(y_*|x_*, w_*)f(w_*|x_*)f(x_*) \tag{8.3.1c}$$

$$= f(y_*, x_* | w_*) f(w_*) \tag{8.3.1d}$$

$$= f(y_*, w_* | x_*) f(x_*) \tag{8.3.1e}$$

$$= f(x_* | y_*, w_*) f(y_*, w_*) \tag{8.3.1f}$$

$$= f(x_* | y_*, w_*) f(y_* | w_*) f(w_*) \tag{8.3.1g}$$

$$= f(x_* | y_*, w_*) f(w_* | y_*) f(y_*) \tag{8.3.1h}$$

$$= f(x_*, w_* | y_*) f(y_*) \tag{8.3.1i}$$

$$= f(w_* | y_*, x_*) f(y_*, x_*) \tag{8.3.1j}$$

$$= f(w_* | y_*, x_*) f(y_* | x_*) f(x_*) \tag{8.3.1k}$$

$$= f(w_* | y_*, x_*) f(x_* | y_*) f(y_*) \tag{8.3.1l}$$

As in Section 8.2, suppose that $f(y_*, x_*, w_*)$ is known, and hence all of the above twelve factorizations are also available. Finally, suppose the quantity of predictive interest is Y_*.

In this situation four candidates for the DOI suggest themselves. These candidates are the distributions corresponding to the following four p.f.s: $f(y_*)$, $f(y_*|x_*)$, $f(y_*|w_*)$ and $f(y_*|x_*, w_*)$. Before discussing choice among these candidates, for purposes of concreteness consider the following extension of Example 8.2.8.

Example 8.3.1 Suppose $Z_* \sim N_K(\mu, \Sigma)$. Corresponding to the partitioning $Z_* = [Y_*', X_*', W_*']'$, write

$$\mu = \begin{bmatrix} \mu_y \\ \mu_x \\ \mu_w \end{bmatrix}, \Sigma = \begin{bmatrix} \Sigma_{yy} & \Sigma_{yx} & \Sigma_{yw} \\ \Sigma_{yx}' & \Sigma_{xx} & \Sigma_{xw} \\ \Sigma_{yw}' & \Sigma_{xw}' & \Sigma_{ww} \end{bmatrix}. \tag{8.3.2}$$

Using Theorem 3.4.6, the four densities above are given by

$$f(y_*) = \phi_{K_y}(y_* | \mu_y, \Sigma_{yy}), \tag{8.3.3}$$

$$f(y_* | x_*) = \phi_{K_y}(y_* | \mu_{y \cdot x}, \Sigma_{yy \cdot x}), \tag{8.3.4}$$

$$f(y_* | w_*) = \phi_{K_y}(y_* | \mu_{y \cdot w}, \Sigma_{yy \cdot w}), \tag{8.3.5}$$

$$f(y_* | x_*, w_*) = \phi_{K_y}(y_* | \mu_{y \cdot xw}, \Sigma_{yy \cdot xw}), \tag{8.3.6}$$

where $f(y_* | x_*)$ involves

$$\mu_{y \cdot x} = \alpha_{y \cdot x} + B_{yx}' X_*, \tag{8.3.7}$$

$$B_{yx} = [\Sigma_{xx}]^{-1} \Sigma_{xy}, \tag{8.3.8}$$

$$\alpha_{y \cdot x} = \mu_y - B_{yx}' \mu_x, \tag{8.3.9}$$

$$\Sigma_{yy \cdot x} = \Sigma_{yy} - \Sigma_{yx} [\Sigma_{xx}]^{-1} \Sigma_{yx}', \tag{8.3.10}$$

$f(y_* | w_*)$ involves

$$\mu_{y \cdot w} = \alpha_{y \cdot w} + B'_{yw} W_*, \tag{8.3.11}$$

$$B_{yw} = [\Sigma_{ww}]^{-1} \Sigma_{wy}, \tag{8.3.12}$$

$$\alpha_{y \cdot w} = \mu_y - B'_{yw} \mu_w, \tag{8.3.13}$$

$$\Sigma_{yy \cdot w} = \Sigma_{yy} - \Sigma_{yw} [\Sigma_{ww}]^{-1} \Sigma'_{yw}, \tag{8.3.14}$$

and $f(y_* | x_*, w_*)$ involves

$$\mu_{y \cdot xw} = \alpha_{y \cdot xw} + B'_{yx \cdot w} X_* + B'_{yw \cdot x} W_*, \tag{8.3.15}$$

$$\begin{bmatrix} B_{yx \cdot w} \\ B_{yw \cdot x} \end{bmatrix} = \begin{bmatrix} \Sigma_{xx} & \Sigma_{xw} \\ \Sigma'_{xw} & \Sigma_{ww} \end{bmatrix}^{-1} \begin{bmatrix} \Sigma'_{yx} \\ \Sigma'_{yw} \end{bmatrix}, \tag{8.3.16}$$

$$\alpha_{y \cdot w} = \mu_y - B'_{yx \cdot w} \mu_x - B'_{yw \cdot x} \mu_w, \tag{8.3.17}$$

$$\Sigma_{yy \cdot xw} = \Sigma_{yy} - [\Sigma_{yx}, \Sigma_{yw}] \begin{bmatrix} \Sigma_{xx} & \Sigma_{xw} \\ \Sigma'_{xw} & \Sigma_{ww} \end{bmatrix}^{-1} \begin{bmatrix} \Sigma'_{yx} \\ \Sigma'_{yw} \end{bmatrix}. \tag{8.3.18}$$

Two useful relationships tying together (8.3.8), (8.3.12) and (8.3.16) are

$$B_{yx \cdot w} = B_{yx} - B_{wx} B_{yw \cdot x}, \tag{8.3.19}$$

$$B_{yw \cdot x} = B_{yw} - B_{xw} B_{yx \cdot w}, \tag{8.3.20}$$

where

$$B_{wx} = [\Sigma_{xx}]^{-1} \Sigma_{xw}, \tag{8.3.21}$$

$$B_{xw} = [\Sigma_{ww}]^{-1} \Sigma'_{xw}. \tag{8.3.22}$$

Interest in $f(y_*)$, $f(y_* | x_*)$, $f(y_* | w_*)$ and $f(y_* | x_*, w_*)$ motivates reparameterization of $\theta = [\mu', \{\text{vech}(\Sigma)\}']'$, where vech($\Sigma$) denotes the stacking operator, which stacks the columns of Σ on or below the main diagonal, that is, the unique elements of the symmetric matrix Σ (see Appendix B). Such reparameterizations are in part defined by (8.3.3) through (8.3.22), which contain the means, variances and covariances characterizing $f(y_*)$, $f(y_* | x_*)$, $f(y_* | w_*)$ and $f(y_* | x_*, w_*)$.

Table 8.3.1 compiles four complete and equivalent reparameterizations of θ corresponding to these four factorizations. The factorizations (8.3.1i), (8.3.1k), (8.3.1g) and (8.3.1a) involving $f(y_*)$, $f(y_* | x_*)$, $f(y_* | w_*)$ and $f(y_* | x_*, w_*)$, also involve other densities suggesting additional factorizations. New quantities appearing in Table 8.3.1 are given here:

$$\mu_{x \cdot y} = \alpha_{x \cdot y} + B'_{xy} y, \tag{8.3.23}$$

$$B_{xy} = [\Sigma_{yy}]^{-1} \Sigma_{yx}, \tag{8.3.24}$$

$$\alpha_{x \cdot y} = \mu_x - B'_{xy} \mu_y, \tag{8.3.25}$$

$$\Sigma_{xx \cdot y} = \Sigma_{xx} - \Sigma'_{yx} [\Sigma_{yy}]^{-1} \Sigma_{yx}, \tag{8.3.26}$$

$$\mu_{w \cdot y} = \alpha_{w \cdot y} + B_{wy} y, \tag{8.3.27}$$

$$B_{wy} = [\Sigma_{yy}]^{-1} \Sigma_{yw}, \tag{8.3.28}$$

$$\alpha_{w \cdot y} = \mu_w - B_{wy} \mu_y, \tag{8.3.29}$$

Table 8.3.1
Alternative parameterizations of $f(z_*)$

(I) $f(y_*, x_*, w_*)$	(IIa) $f(y_*\|x_*)$ $f(x_*)f(w_*\|y_*, x_*)$	(IIb) $f(y_*\|x_*)$ $f(x_*)f(w_*\|y_*, x_*)$	(IIIa) $f(y_*\|x_*, w_*)$ $f(x_*, w_*)$	(IIIb) $f(y_*\|x_*, w_*)$ $f(x_*, w_*)$
μ_y	$\alpha_{y \cdot x}$	$\alpha_{y \cdot w}$	$\alpha_{y \cdot xw}$	$\alpha_{y \cdot xw}$
μ_x	μ_x	α_x	μ_x	$\alpha_{x \cdot x}$
μ_w	$\alpha_{w \cdot yx}$	μ_w	μ_w	μ_w
$\text{vech}(\Sigma_{yy})$	$\text{vech}(\Sigma_{yy \cdot x})$	$\text{vech}(\Sigma_{yy \cdot x})$	$\text{vech}(\Sigma_{yy \cdot xw})$	$\text{vech}(\Sigma_{yy \cdot xw})$
Σ_{yx}	B_{yx}	B_{yx}	$B_{yx \cdot w}$	B_{yx}
$\text{vech}(\Sigma_{xx})$	$\text{vech}(\Sigma_{xx})$	$\text{vech}(\Sigma_{xx})$	$\text{vech}(\Sigma_{xx})$	$\text{vech}(\Sigma_{xx})$
Σ_{yw}	$B_{wy \cdot x}$	Σ_{yw}	$B_{yw \cdot x}$	$B_{yw \cdot x}$
Σ_{xw}	$B_{wx \cdot y}$	Σ_{xw}	Σ_{xw}	B_{wx}
$\text{vech}(\Sigma_{ww})$	$\text{vech}(\Sigma_{ww \cdot yx})$	$\text{vech}(\Sigma_{ww})$	$\text{vech}(\Sigma_{ww})$	$\text{vech}(\Sigma_{ww})$

$$\Sigma_{xw \cdot y} = \Sigma_{xw} - \Sigma_{yx}'[\Sigma_{yy}]^{-1}\Sigma_{yw}, \tag{8.3.30}$$

$$\Sigma_{ww \cdot y} = \Sigma_{ww} - \Sigma_{yw}'[\Sigma_{yy}]^{-1}\Sigma_{yw}, \tag{8.3.31}$$

$$\begin{bmatrix} B_{wy \cdot x} \\ B_{wx \cdot y} \end{bmatrix} = \begin{bmatrix} \Sigma_{yy} & \Sigma_{yx} \\ \Sigma_{yx}' & \Sigma_{xx} \end{bmatrix}^{-1} \begin{bmatrix} \Sigma_{yw}' \\ \Sigma_{xw}' \end{bmatrix}, \tag{8.3.32}$$

$$\alpha_{w \cdot yx} = \mu_w - B_{wy \cdot x}'\mu_y - B_{wx \cdot y}'\mu_x, \tag{8.3.33}$$

$$\Sigma_{ww \cdot yx} = \Sigma_{ww} - [\Sigma_{yw}', \Sigma_{xw}'] \begin{bmatrix} \Sigma_{yy} & \Sigma_{yx} \\ \Sigma_{yx}' & \Sigma_{xx} \end{bmatrix}^{-1} \begin{bmatrix} \Sigma_{yw} \\ \Sigma_{xw} \end{bmatrix}, \tag{8.3.34}$$

$$\begin{bmatrix} B_{xy \cdot w} \\ B_{xw \cdot y} \end{bmatrix} = \begin{bmatrix} \Sigma_{yy} & \Sigma_{yw} \\ \Sigma_{yw}' & \Sigma_{ww} \end{bmatrix}^{-1} \begin{bmatrix} \Sigma_{yx}' \\ \Sigma_{wx}' \end{bmatrix}, \tag{8.3.35}$$

$$\alpha_{x \cdot yw} = \mu_w - B_{wy \cdot w}'\mu_y - B_{xw \cdot y}'\mu_w, \tag{8.3.36}$$

$$\Sigma_{xx \cdot yw} = \Sigma_{xx} - [\Sigma_{yx}', \Sigma_{wx}'] \begin{bmatrix} \Sigma_{yy} & \Sigma_{yw} \\ \Sigma_{yw}' & \Sigma_{ww} \end{bmatrix}^{-1} \begin{bmatrix} \Sigma_{yx} \\ \Sigma_{wx} \end{bmatrix}. \tag{8.3.37}$$

Choice among $f(y_*)$, $f(y_*|x_*)$, $f(y_*|w_*)$ and $f(y_*|x_*, w_*)$ as the DOI is not a matter of which one "exists." They all exist! A more meaningful distinction is the different information each requires. If the information set κ contains X_* and W_*, then $f(y_*|x_*, w_*)$ is preferred because its mean $\mu_{y \cdot xw}$ is no worse in a mean square predictive sense than μ_y, $\mu_{y \cdot x}$ and $\mu_{y \cdot w}$. Recall that it was seen back in Section 2.7 that $\mu_{y \cdot xw}$ comprises the optimal linear combination of X_* and W_*. Therefore, such arguments favor $f(y_*|x_*, w_*)$ over $f(y)$, $f(y_*|x_*)$ or $f(y_*|w_*)$ as the DOI provided κ contains X_* and W_*.

Other considerations, however, can also enter into the choice of DOI. The various factorizations in Table 8.3.1 share the attractive feature that they are *variation-free*, that is, one component can be changed while holding all other components constant. The only qualification that needs to be added is that when changing components of Σ, the positive definiteness of Σ must be maintained. As previously noted, a hallmark of econometrics is asking predictive questions in the face of interventions. Depending on the nature of the intervention, some of the previously listed DOI candidates may change while others remain invariant to the intervention. Interventions that change μ_y or Σ_{yx} or Σ_{yw} are not particularly interesting since they will affect all of these distributions. Of more interest are interventions that change the distribution of X and W without changing some of these distributions. Invariance is attractive: It means that knowing a particular type of structural change has occurred without knowing its magnitude, need not hamper prediction. Consider the following examples of interventions.

Example 8.3.2 Trivially, $f(y_*)$ is structural with respect to changes in μ_x, μ_y, Σ_{yx}, Σ_{yw}, Σ_{xx}, Σ_{xw}, or Σ_{ww}. In particular changes in the bivariate distribution of X_* and W_* have no effect on the marginal distribution of Y_*.

Example 8.3.3 Consider parameterization (IIa) in Table 8.3.1. Then $f(y_*|x_*)$ is structural with respect to changes in μ_x, Σ_{xx}, $\alpha_{w\cdot yx}$, $B_{wy\cdot x}$, $B_{wx\cdot y}$, or $\Sigma_{ww\cdot yx}$. In particular changes in the regression slopes $B_{wy\cdot x}$ and $B_{wx\cdot y}$ have no effect on the conditional distribution of Y_* given X_*.

Example 8.3.4 Consider parameterization (IIb) in Table 8.3.1. Then $f(y_*|x_*)$ is structural with respect to changes in μ_x, Σ_{xx}, μ_w, Σ_{ww}, Σ_{yw}, or Σ_{xw}. In particular changes in the marginal distribution of W_* or the covariances Σ_{yw} and Σ_{xw} have no effect on the conditional distribution of Y_* given X_*.

Example 8.3.5 Consider parameterization (IIIa) in Table 8.3.1. Suppose $\text{vech}(\Sigma_{ww})$ changes. Then *ceteris paribus* (i.e. holding all other parameters in this column constant), $f(y_*|x_*, w_*)$ remains unaffected by this change because $\alpha_{y\cdot xw}$, $B_{yx\cdot w}$, $B_{yw\cdot x}$, and $\Sigma_{yy\cdot xw}$ are unchanged. Hence, $f(y_*|x_*, w_*)$ is structural with respect to such changes.

Because $\text{vech}(\Sigma_{xx})$ and Σ_{xw} are unchanged, B_{wx} in (8.3.21) is unchanged, and in light of (8.3.19) B_{yx} must also be unchanged. Because (8.3.9) and (8.3.10) imply $\alpha_{y\cdot x}$ and $\Sigma_{yy\cdot x}$ are also unchanged when $\text{vech}(\Sigma_{ww})$ changes, $f(y_*|x_*)$ is also structural.

If $\Sigma_{xw} \neq 0$, then a change in $\text{vech}(\Sigma_{ww})$ results in a change in $B_{xw} = [\Sigma_{ww}]^{-1}\Sigma'_{xw}$, and hence (8.3.20) implies B_{yw} must also change. Therefore, $f(y_*|w_*)$ is *not* structural. If $\Sigma_{xw} = 0$, then a change in $\text{vech}(\Sigma_{ww})$ does not change B_{xw} nor B_{yw}. In this case $E(y_*|x_*, w_*)$, $E(y_*|x_*)$ and $E(y_*|w_*)$ are all unaffected by a change in $\text{vech}(\Sigma_{ww})$. $f(y_*|w_*)$ is still *not* structural in this case because $\text{Var}(y_*|w_*)$ changes.

Example 8.3.6 Consider parameterization (IIIb) in Table 8.3.1. Then $E(y_*|x_*)$ is structural with respect to changes in $\alpha_{y\cdot xw}$, μ_w, Σ_{ww}, $B_{yw\cdot x}$, B_{wx}, and $\Sigma_{yy\cdot xw}$. In particular, changes in the slope coefficient $B_{yw\cdot x}$ of W_* in the multiple regression of Y_* on X_* and W_* has no effect on the coefficients in the regression of Y_* on X_*. Nonetheless, $f(y_*|x_*)$ is *not* structural since Exercise 8.3.7(f) implies $\Sigma_{yy\cdot x} = \Sigma_{yy\cdot xw} + B'_{yw\cdot x}\,\text{Var}(W)B_{yw\cdot x}$ changes with changes in $B_{yw\cdot x}$. However, $f(y_*|x_*)$ *is* structural with respect to changes in $B_{yw\cdot x}$ *and* $\Sigma_{yy\cdot xw}$, which leave $\Sigma_{yy\cdot xw}$ unchanged.

The validity of the window for in-sample observations rests on its goodness-of-fit and the compellingness of the theoretical arguments upon which it is built. (More will be said on this point in Chapter 10.) In the out-of-sample context, there are initially no observations for determining goodness-of-fit, and so the extrapolation must rest on the theory behind the window, and possibly, the experimental design generating the in-sample data. In the case of observational studies, which characterize most of econometrics, experimental design is a moot point. Compelling theory can sometimes provide confidence to take an inductive leap. The structural approach is appealing, however, only when its assumptions are credible.

In summary, if tomorrow is like today, then prediction is relatively easy. If tomorrow is different, perhaps because policy makers intervene in the economy, then prediction becomes substantially more difficult. Such considerations are most obvious when moving from a situation in which the in-sample data are passively observed and it is then desired to predict out-of-sample data in a situation in which control is exerted on some of the variables to be observed (recall the discussion after Example 8.2.8).

Exercises

8.3.1 Verify (8.3.3) through (8.3.37).

8.3.2 Suppose W_* is not observed. Since $W_*|X_* \sim N(\mu_{W\cdot x}, \Sigma_{w\cdot x})$, where

$$\mu_{w\cdot x} = \alpha_{w\cdot x} + B'_{wx}x, \tag{8.3.38}$$

$$B_{wx} = [\Sigma_{xx}]^{-1}\Sigma'_{xw}, \tag{8.3.39}$$

$$\alpha_{w\cdot x} = \mu_w - B'_{wx}\mu_x, \tag{8.3.40}$$

$$\Sigma_{ww\cdot x} = \Sigma_{ww} - \Sigma'_{xw}[\Sigma_{xx}]^{-1}\Sigma_{xw}, \tag{8.3.41}$$

consider substituting $E(W_*|X_*)$ for W_* in (8.3.15) obtaining the predictor

$$\hat{Y}_* = \mu_{y\cdot xw} + B_{yw\cdot x}X + B_{yw\cdot x}E(W|X). \tag{8.3.42}$$

Show: $\hat{Y}_* = E(Y_*|X_*)$.

8.3.3 Consider the predictive errors:

$$\hat{U}_{*y} = \mu_y - Y_*, \tag{8.3.43}$$

$$\hat{U}_{*y\cdot x} = \mu_{y\cdot x} - Y_*, \tag{8.3.44}$$

$$\hat{U}_{*y\cdot w} = \mu_{y\cdot w} - Y_*, \tag{8.3.45}$$

$$\hat{U}_{*y\cdot xw} = \mu_{y\cdot xw} - Y_*. \tag{8.3.46}$$

Given X_* and W_*, find the predictive mean square errors of each.

8.3.4 Consider (8.3.19). Interpret the conditions under which $B_{yx\cdot w} = B_{yx}$.

8.3.5 Let Y denote daughter's height and let X denote father's height. Suppose you were asked to adapt regression results from the overall population to the subpopulation consisting of families in which the father has played professional basketball. Is $E(Y|X)$ or $E(X|Y)$ more likely to be the same in the overall population or the subpopulation? Why (Goldberger 1991, p. 345)?

8.3.6 Using (8.3.19) and (8.3.20), show:

(a) $B_{yx\cdot w} = [I_{K_x} + B_{wx}B_{xw}]^{-1}[B_{yx} - B_{wx}B_{yw}]$

(b) $B_{yw\cdot x} = [I_{K_w} + B_{xw}B_{wx}]^{-1}[B_{yw} - B_{xw}B_{yx}]$

8.3.7 Show each of the following:

(a) $\text{Var}(Y) = E_{x,w}[\text{Var}(Y|X, W)] + \text{Var}_{x,w}[E(Y|X, W)]$

(b) $\text{Var}_{x,w}[E(Y|X, W)] = E_x\{\text{Var}_w[E(Y|X, W)|X]\} + \text{Var}_x[E(Y|X)]$

(c) If $E(Y|X)$ is linear in X, then $\text{Var}_x[E(Y|X)] = B'_{yx}\,\text{Var}(X)B_{yx}$.

(d) If $E(Y|X, W)$ is linear in X and W, then $\text{Var}_x[E(Y|X, W)|X] = B'_{yw\cdot x}\,\text{Var}(W)B_{yw\cdot x}$.

(e) If $E(Y|X)$ is linear in X and $E(Y|X, W)$ is linear in X and W, then $\text{Var}(Y) = E_{x,w}[\text{Var}(Y|X, W)] + B'_{yw\cdot x}\,\text{Var}(W)B_{yw\cdot x} + B'_{yw}\,\text{Var}(X)B_{yw}$.

(f) If $E(Y|X)$ is linear in X and $E(Y|X, W)$ is linear in X and W, then $\text{Var}(Y|X) = E_{x,w}[\text{Var}(Y|X, W)] + B'_{yw\cdot x}\,\text{Var}(W)B_{yw\cdot x}$.

8.3.8 Suppose Y measures cardiovascular well-being, X_1 is a binary variable equal to 1 for smokers and equal to 0 otherwise, X_2 is height, X_3 is a measure of diet, and X_4 is weight. The question of interest is: what is the effect on Y of giving up smoking? Assuming that X_2 serves solely as a proxy for X_4, compare and contrast $Y|X_1, X_2, X_3$ and $Y|X_1, X_2, X_3, X_4$ as DOIs. (Cox 1984, p. 31).

8.4 Predictive Likelihood

... a riddle wrapped in a mystery inside an enigma.
—Winston Churchill

A distinguishing feature of prediction, compared to estimation and hypothesis testing, is that it involves *two* unknown quantities: θ and Y_*. The future observable Y_* is the quantity of interest, and the entire parameter vector θ consists of nuisance parameters. As seen in Chapter 6, classical statistics struggles with nuisance parameters, and as a result, numerous solutions have been presented (e.g., see the surveys of Butler 1986; Bjørnstad 1990, 1992; and Geisser 1993, Chapter 2). Essentially all these suggestions amount to using at least one of three operations on $f(y, y_*|\theta)$: integration, maximization, or conditioning.

The origins of predictive likelihood lie in some vague remarks of Fisher (1956) for the binomial case. The seminal papers were by Lauritzen (1974) in the discrete case and Hinkley (1979) who introduced the term "predictive likelihood."

The crux of the predictive problem is finding a satisfactory distribution for future observables, given past observables, when θ is unknown. One obvious solution is to replace the nonoperational $f(y_*|y,\theta)$ by $f(y_*|y,\hat{\theta})$, where $\hat{\theta}$ is, say, the ML estimator. Plugging $\hat{\theta}$ into the formula for a point estimator of Y_* such as in (8.2.4), known as the *certainty equivalence* or *plug-in* approach, often performs admirably for point predictors. It is wholly unsatisfactory, however, for purposes of interval forecasts or in obtaining the overall distribution of Y_* given $Y = y$ because it understates the researcher's uncertainty. In fact, use of $f(y_*|y,\hat{\theta})$ is a correct substitute for $f(y_*|y,\theta)$ only if it is known that $\theta = \hat{\theta}$. This amounts to assuming we are back in the case of Section 8.2.

As seen in Chapter 6, classical statistics deals with nuisance parameters best when sufficient statistics are available. Suppose $W = W(Y)$ is a sufficient statistic for θ based on Y, and suppose that $W_+ = W_+(Y, Y_*)$ is a minimal sufficient statistic for θ based on the expanded data set Y and Y_*. In addition suppose that $W_* = W_*(Y_*, W)$ is such that W_+ is determined by W and W_*, and that the minimum sufficient reduction of Y_* is determined by W and W_*. Finally, suppose that $W_+(W, W_*)$ has a unique inverse $W_*(W_+, W)$ for each value of W. Realized values of W, W_* and W_+ are denoted by w, w_* and w_+, respectively.

The sufficiency of W_+ implies (see Definition 6.1.2) that $f(y, y_*|w_+, \theta) = f(y, y_*|w_+)$ does not depend on θ. In turn this implies that the joint density for $W = W(Y)$ and Y_*, given $W_+ = w_+$ and θ,

$$f(w, y_*|w_+, \theta) = f(w, y_*|w_+) = f(y_*|w, w_+)f(w|w_+), \tag{8.4.1}$$

also, fortuitously, does not depend on θ. This observation leads to the following definition (see Hinkley 1979, p. 722 for Equation 8.4.1).

Definition 8.4.1 The *predictive likelihood* of $Y_* = y_*$, denoted $\mathscr{L}_*(y_*; y)$, is

$$\mathscr{L}_*(y_*; y) = f(w, y_*|w_+) = f(y_*|w, w_*)f(w|w_+), \tag{8.4.2}$$

Most importantly, note that $\mathscr{L}_*(y_*; y)$ does *not* depend on θ.

$\mathscr{L}_*(y_*; y)$ measures the relative plausibility of the observed $Y = y$ for different values of y_*. In this regard it is similar to the ordinary likelihood $\mathscr{L}(\theta; y)$. Like ordinary likelihood, (8.4.2) does *not* integrate to unity with respect to y_* as does a density.

Example 8.4.1 Reconsider Example 8.2.2 with $\sigma_o^2 = 1$. Let $Y = [Y_1,$

$Y_2, \ldots, Y_T]'$. Then $W = \overline{Y}_T$ (the sample mean based on the first T observations), $W_* = Y_*$, and $W_+ = \overline{Y}_{T+1}$ (the sample mean based on all $T+1$ observations). Noting that

$$\begin{bmatrix} W \\ W_+ \\ Y_* \end{bmatrix} = \begin{bmatrix} T^{-1}\iota_T' & 0 \\ (T+1)^{-1}\iota_T' & \dfrac{1}{T+1} \\ 0_T' & 1 \end{bmatrix} \begin{bmatrix} Y \\ Y_* \end{bmatrix}, \tag{8.4.3}$$

it follows from Theorem 3.4.7(a) that

$$\begin{bmatrix} W \\ W_+ \\ Y_* \end{bmatrix} \sim N_3\left[\mu_o \iota_3, \frac{1}{T+1}\begin{bmatrix} \dfrac{(T+1)}{T} & 1 & 0 \\ 1 & 1 & 1 \\ 0 & 1 & T+1 \end{bmatrix}\right]. \tag{8.4.4}$$

Using Theorem 3.4.6, (8.4.4) implies $f(y_*|w, w_+) = \phi(y_*|[T+1]w_+ - Tw, 1 - T^{-1})$ and $f(w|w_+) = \phi(w|w_+, [T(T+1)]^{-1})$. Finally, noting

$$w - w_+ = \frac{\bar{y}_T - y_*}{T+1}, \tag{8.4.5}$$

it follows from (8.4.2) that

$$\mathscr{L}_*(y_*; y) \propto \phi(y_*|\bar{y}_T, [1 + T^{-1}]). \tag{8.4.6}$$

Example 8.4.2 (Hinkley 1979, pp. 722–723) Suppose Y_t $(t = 1, 2, \ldots, T, T+1) \sim$ i.i.d. $U(0, \theta)$, where $Y_* = Y_{T+1}$. Let $W = \max\{Y_1, Y_2, \ldots, Y_T\}$, $W_* = Y_{T+1}$ if $Y_{T+1} > W$, and $W_* = 0$ if $Y_{T+1} \leq W$. Then W is sufficient, and $W_+ = W_+(W, W_*) = \max\{Y_1, Y_2, \ldots, Y_{T+1}\}$ is minimal sufficient. Therefore:

$$\mathscr{L}(y_*; y) = \begin{cases} \dfrac{T}{(T+1)w}, & \text{if } y_* \leq w \\ \dfrac{Tw^T}{(T+1)y_*}, & \text{if } y_* > w \end{cases}. \tag{8.4.7}$$

Note that the predictive likelihood is uniform over the observed range $(0, w)$.

Numerous difficulties with (8.4.2) have been noted. For example, although one-to-one transformations of the minimal sufficient statistic W_+ are also minimally sufficient, (8.4.2) is not necessarily invariant to the choice of W_+. Another shortcoming with Definition 8.4.1 is that it applies only when sufficient statistics are available. As Cox and Hinkley (1974, p. 307) note, however, the ML estimator is asymptotically sufficient, and this fact led Cooley and Parke (1987, 1990) to extend Definition 8.4.1 along the following lines by replacing the sufficient statistics W, W_* and W_+ by the corresponding ML estimates $\hat{\theta}$, $\hat{\theta}_*$ and $\hat{\theta}_+$.

Definition 8.4.2 The *asymptotic predictive likelihood* of $Y_* = y_*$ is

$$\mathscr{L}_*^a(y_*; y) = f(y_*|\hat{\theta})\exp[\omega_1(y_*;\hat{\theta}) + \omega_2(y_*;\hat{\theta})], \tag{8.4.8}$$

where

$$\omega_1(y_*;\hat{\theta}) = -\frac{1}{2}\left[\frac{\partial \ln[f(y_*|\hat{\theta})]}{\partial \theta'}\right]\left[\frac{\partial \ln[f(\mathscr{L}(\hat{\theta}; y, y_*)]}{\partial \theta\, \partial \theta'}\right]^{-1}\left[\frac{\partial \ln[f(y_*|\hat{\theta})]}{\partial \theta}\right], \tag{8.4.9}$$

$$\omega_2(y_*;\hat{\theta}) = \exp\left[-\frac{1}{2}\operatorname{tr}\left(\left[\frac{\partial \ln[\mathscr{L}(\hat{\theta}; y)]}{\partial \theta\, \partial \theta'}\right]^{-1}\left[\frac{\partial \ln[f(y_*|\hat{\theta})]}{\partial \theta\, \partial \theta'}\right]\right)\right]. \tag{8.4.10}$$

In a sense, (8.4.8) amounts to $f(y_*|\hat{\theta})$ adjusted for parameter uncertainty. Derivation of (8.4.8) from (8.4.2) is given in Cooley and Parke (1990, Appendix A).

Hinkley (1979) discusses use of predictive likelihood (8.4.2) to form a predictive region with given probability content, like (8.2.8). Maximizing (8.4.2) or (8.4.8) with respect to y_* is one way of generating point predictions. We do not explore these possibilities, however, because predictive likelihood seems to have generated as many questions as answers in the statistics literature, reminiscent of Fisher's fiducial inference. Section 8.5 will provide a Bayesian interpretation of predictive likelihood. The development of predictive likelihood has not been fully accepted even in non-Bayesian/likelihood circles. Evidence of this fact is provided by the fourteen candidates for the title "predictive likelihood" discussed in the review article by Bjørnstad (1990). Winston Churchill's quote (about the Soviet Union) at the beginning of this section seems an accurate assessment of predictive likelihood as well.

Exercises

8.4.1 (Hinkley 1979, p. 724) Predictive likelihood (8.4.2) does *not* satisfy the Likelihood Principle. Demonstrate this fact for (8.4.2) by contrasting binomial versus negative binomial sampling.

8.4.2 Suppose Y_t $(t = 1, 2, \ldots, T)$, $Y_* \sim \text{EXP}(\theta)$. Let $W = (Y_1 + Y_2 + \cdots + Y_T)$.

(a) Show that the predictive density for Y_* is

$$\mathscr{L}(y_*; y) = \frac{Tw^{T-1}}{(w + y_*)^T} \tag{8.4.11}$$

(b) Show that (8.4.7) does not integrate to unity with respect to y_*.

8.4.3 Suppose Y_t $(t = 1, 2, \ldots, T)$, $Y_* \sim \text{Po}(\theta)$. Let $W = (Y_1 + Y_2 + \cdots + Y_T)$.

(a) Show that the predictive density for Y_* is

$$\mathscr{L}_*(y_*; y) = \binom{y_* + w}{y_*}\frac{T^w}{(T+1)^{w+y_*}} \tag{8.4.12}$$

(b) Show that (8.4.8) does not integrate to unity.

8.5 Classical Point and Interval Prediction

Ex ante (sampling inferences) are the backbone of classical statistics, whereas *ex post* (posterior inferences) are the backbone of Bayesian statistics. Prediction involves both *ex ante* and *ex post* perspectives (after seeing some data, predict other data yet to be observed). It is the *ex post* aspect that causes problems for sampling theorist.

Rather than striving for a full predictive distribution in the face of unknown parameters, suppose instead we content ourselves merely with point and interval forecasts. The most common frequentist approach to point prediction when θ is unknown is perhaps also the most obvious, namely, replace θ in the formulas of Section 8.2 by an estimator obtained from Chapter 6. Often this provides sensible point predictors; rarely, however, does it provide sensible prediction intervals.

Analogous to MSE estimation in Chapter 6, in the face of unknown parameters, no operational minimum MSEP exists without further restricting the class of potential predictors. The sampling theory approach recommends that the consequences of using a procedure should be evaluated by averaging over the sample space $\mathscr{S}_T$. These considerations suggest augmenting criterion function (8.2.1) by averaging over both $\mathscr{S}_T$ and $\mathscr{S}_*$, that is, by

$$E_{Y|\theta_o}[E_{Y_*|Y,\theta_o}(C[\hat{Y}_*(Y), Y_*])], \tag{8.5.1}$$

where $\hat{Y}_* = \hat{Y}_*(Y)$ is an arbitrary operational predictor. Consider the case of quadratic predictive loss (8.2.3), and the optimal, but not operational, point prediction $\hat{Y}_{**} = E(Y_*|Y,\theta)$ given in (8.2.4). Given an estimator $\hat{\theta} = \hat{\theta}(Y)$ of θ, an operational (but not necessarily optimal in an unrestricted sense) point predictor is $\hat{Y}_* = \hat{Y}_*[Y,\hat{\theta}(Y)] = \hat{Y}_*(Y) = E(Y_*|Y,\hat{\theta})$. The sampling properties of $\hat{Y}_*$ can be evaluated by computing (8.5.1):

$$\begin{aligned} &E_{Y_*|Y,\theta_o}(C[\hat{Y}_*(Y), Y_*]) \\ &\quad = E_{Y|\theta_o}(\mathrm{tr}[A_* E_{Y_*|Y,\theta_o}([\hat{Y}_*(Y) - Y_*][\hat{Y}_*(Y) - Y_*]')]) \\ &\quad = E_{Y|\theta_o}(\mathrm{tr}[A_* \mathrm{MSEP}[\hat{Y}_*(Y)|Y,\theta_o)]) \\ &\quad = \mathrm{tr}(A_*[E_{Y|\theta_o}(\mathrm{MSEP}[\hat{Y}_*(Y)|Y,\theta_o])]). \end{aligned} \tag{8.5.2}$$

If the predictor $\hat{Y}_*(Y)$ is unbiased in the sense Definition 8.2.1, then (8.5.2) simplifies to

$$E_{Y_*|Y,\theta_o}(C[\hat{Y}_*(Y), Y_*]) = \mathrm{tr}(A_*[E_{Y|\theta_o}(\mathrm{Var}[\hat{U}_*(Y, Y_*)|Y,\theta_o])]), \tag{8.5.3}$$

where the prediction error is

$$\tilde{U}_* = \tilde{U}_*(Y, Y_*) = \tilde{Y}_*(Y) - Y_*. \tag{8.5.4}$$

In order to demonstrate this development, consider Examples 8.2.2 and 8.2.4 with unknown means but known variances.

Example 8.5.1 Recall Example 8.2.2, where Y_t $(t = 1, 2, \ldots, T, T + 1) \sim$ i.i.d. $N(\mu, \sigma_o^2)$, with σ_o^2 known, but μ unknown. An unbiased estimator of μ is $\hat{Y} = \bar{Y}$ (the sample mean based on the first T observations). Hence $\bar{Y}$ provides an unbiased predictor of Y_* with prediction error $\tilde{U}_* = \bar{Y} - Y_*$. The joint distribution of $\bar{Y}$ and Y_* is $N_2(\mu\iota_2, \Omega)$, where

$$\Omega = \begin{bmatrix} \sigma_o^2/T & 0 \\ 0 & \sigma_o^2 \end{bmatrix}. \tag{8.5.5}$$

Hence, it follows from Theorem 3.4.7(a) that $\hat{U}_*|\mu, \sigma_o^2 \sim N_2(0_2, [1 + T^{-1}]\sigma_o^2)$. Therefore, the expected loss (8.5.1) of using the predictor $\bar{Y}$ is

$$E_{Y_*, Y|\mu, \sigma_o^2}[C(\bar{Y}, Y_*)] = (1 + T^{-1})\sigma_o^2. \tag{8.5.6}$$

Comparing (8.5.6) with (8.2.7), the extra predictive loss of not knowing μ is seen to be $T^{-1}\sigma_o^2 > 0$.

Example 8.5.2 Recall Example 8.2.4 in which Z_t $(t = 1, 2, \ldots, T, T + 1) \sim$ i.i.d. $N_M(\mu, \Sigma_o)$, but now with Σ_o known and μ unknown. Preceding analogously to Example 8.5.1, it follows that $\bar{Y}$ is an unbiased predictor of $Y_* = Y_{T+1}$, the prediction error $\hat{U}_* = \bar{Y} - Y_*$ satisfies $\hat{U}_*|\mu, \Sigma_o \sim N_M(0_M, [1 + T^{-1}]\Sigma_o)$, and the expected loss (8.5.1) of using the predictor $\bar{Y}$ is

$$E_{Y_*, Y|\mu, \Sigma_o}[C(\bar{Y}, Y_*)] = (1 + T^{-1})\,\text{tr}[A_*\Sigma_o]. \tag{8.5.7}$$

Comparing (8.5.7) with (8.2.8), the extra predictive loss of not knowing μ is seen to be $T^{-1}\,\text{tr}[A_*\Sigma_o] > 0$.

Examples 8.5.1 and 8.5.2 deal with point prediction. The next two examples consider interval prediction.

Example 8.5.3 In Example 8.5.1, $\hat{U}_* = \bar{Y} - Y_*$ serves as a pivotal quantity, and a $1 - \alpha$ prediction (forecast) interval for Y_* is given by $\mathscr{S}_* = \{Y_*|\theta_o - z_{\alpha/2}\sigma_o[1 + T^{-1}]^{1/2} < Y_* < \theta_o + z_{\alpha/2}\sigma_o[1 + T^{-1}]^{1/2}\}$, where $z_{\alpha/2}$ satisfies $\Phi(z_{\alpha/2}) = 1 - \alpha$.

Example 8.5.4 In Example 8.5.2, $\hat{U}_* = \hat{Y} - Y_*$ serves as a pivotal quantity, and Theorem 4.5.1 implies that a $1 - \alpha$ prediction (forecast) ellipsoid for Z_* is given by $\mathscr{S}_* = \{Z_*|(Z_* - \mu_o)'\Sigma_o^{-1}(Z_* - \mu_o) \le c_\alpha[1 + T^{-1}]\}$, where c_α cuts off $1 - \alpha$ probability in the righthand tail of the chi-squared distribution with M degrees of freedom.

Generalization of Examples 8.5.1 and 8.5.2 to cover the case where both mean and variance are unknown is trivial because the predictors do not depend on variances; nothing changes except that the predicted losses themselves are now unknown. Examples 8.5.3 through 8.5.4 are slightly different since the quantities $\hat{U}_*$ in each are no longer pivotal since their distributions involve the unknown variances. As noted in Section 6.9, there is no generally agreed upon classical strategy for interval estimation due to the problems of nuisance parameters. The same is true for prediction intervals, and the response is similar: Limit the discussion to cases in which there is a pivotal quantity (recall Definition 6.9.2) involving Y_*, which can be inverted to yield a probabilistic forecast statement like (8.2.6).

Suppose $Q[\hat{Y}_*(Y), Y_*]$ is a pivotal quantity, that is, it has a known distribution free of any unknown parameters. Then for any fixed $0 \le 1 - \alpha \le 1$, there exists $q_1 = q_1(1-\alpha)$ and $q_2 = q_2(1-\alpha)$ such that $P_{Y_*, Y|Y_o}(q_1 \le Q[\hat{Y}_*(Y), Y_*] \le q_2) = 1 - \alpha$.[7] If it is possible to invert $Q[\hat{Y}_*(Y), Y_*]$ and solve for $\hat{Y}_*$, then it will be possible to construct a prediction (forecast) region for Y_*. The appropriate generalizations of Examples 8.5.3 and 8.5.4 are given in the next two examples.

Example 8.5.5 Consider Example 8.5.3, but with *both* mean and variance unknown. Let

$$S^2 = \frac{1}{T-1}\sum_{t=1}^{T}(Y_t - \bar{Y})^2. \tag{8.5.8}$$

Because (i) $\tilde{U}_*/[1 + T^{-1}]^{1/2}\sigma_o \sim N_M(0_M, 1)$, (ii) $\tilde{U}_*/[1 + T^{-1}]^{1/2}\sigma_o$ and S^2 are independent (Exercise 8.5.2), and are independent, and (iii) $(T-1)S^2/\sigma_o^2 \sim \chi^2(T-1)$, by Theorem 5.3.5(b), it follows from Theorem 3.4.16 that

$$\tau_* \equiv \frac{\dfrac{\hat{U}_*}{([1 + T^{-1}]\sigma_o^2)^{1/2}}}{\left[\dfrac{(T-1)S^2}{T-1}\right]^{1/2}} = \frac{\dfrac{\bar{Y} - Y_*}{S}}{[1 + T^{-1}]^{1/2}} \sim t(0, 1, T-1). \tag{8.5.9}$$

Hence, τ_* is a pivotal quantity. Therefore, a $1 - \alpha$ prediction (forecast) interval for Y_* is given by $\mathscr{S}_* = \{Y_* | \bar{Y} - \tau_{\alpha/2, T-1}s[1 + T^{-1}]^{1/2} < Y_* < \bar{Y} + \tau_{\alpha/2, T-1}s[1 + T^{-1}]^{1/2}\}$, where $\tau_{\alpha/2, T-1}$ cuts off $1 - (\alpha/2)$ probability in the righthand tail of a Student-t distribution with $T - 1$ degrees of freedom.

Example 8.5.6 Consider Example 8.5.4, but with *both* μ and Σ unknown. Using Exercise 6.9.11(b) it is easy to show that a $1 - \alpha$ prediction (forecast) ellipsoid for Z_* is given by $\mathscr{S}_* = \{Z_* | (Z_* - \mu_o)'\Sigma_o^{-1}(Z_* - \mu_o) \le c_\alpha[1 + T^{-1}]\}$, where c_α cuts off $1 - \alpha$ probability in the righthand tail of the $F(M, T - M)$ distribution.

7. This statement need not be true in the case of finite samples from discrete distributions. As in section 6.9, throughout this section we will consider only samples from continuous distributions.

Comparison of Examples 8.5.3 and 8.5.4 with Examples 8.2.5 and 8.2.7 demonstrates that forecast regions are wider as the result of the unknown means in Exercises 8.5.3 and 8.5.4. Similarly, comparison of Examples 8.5.5 and 8.5.6 with Example 8.5.3 and 8.5.4 demonstrates the increased uncertainty arising from unknown variances—Student ts and Fs have fatter tails than standard normal and chi-squared distribution.

Even when no nuisance parameters are present, the classical approach to interval estimation can run into problems. Consider the following example.

Example 8.5.7 Recall Example 8.2.3, which corresponded to the Gaussian AR(1) process of Example 6.10.6 with quadratic cost. An operational counterpart to $\hat{Y}_{**} = \theta_o y_T$ is $\hat{Y}_* = \hat{\theta} Y_T$, where $\hat{\theta}$ is the MLE given by (6.10.7). Calculation of the expected posterior loss associated with $\hat{Y}_{**}$, however, is difficult due to the lack of a convenient sampling distribution: $\hat{\theta}$ is a *nonlinear* function of Y_t $(t = 1, 2, \ldots, T)$. Furthermore, in contrast to Example 8.5.3, it is not possible to form an exact prediction interval for Y_* in this case because there is no tractable sampling distribution in finite samples for the MLE $\hat{\theta}$. The introduction of nuisance parameters only further complicates the problem.

Exercises

8.5.1 Derive the joint distribution of $\hat{Y}$ and Y_* in Example 8.5.1.

8.5.2 Verify (ii) in Example 8.5.5, that is, $\tilde{U}_*/[1 + T^{-1}]^{1/2}\sigma_o$ and S^2 are independent.

8.5.3 Rigorously derive the forecast interval in Example 8.5.6.

8.5.4 Suppose Y_t $(t = 1, 2, \ldots, T + m) \sim$ i.i.d. $N(\mu, \sigma^2)$, where both μ and σ^2 are both unknown. Define $Z = [Z_1, Z_2, \ldots, Z_m]'$, where $Z_t = Y_{T+t}/[(T-1)S^2]^{1/2}$ $(t = 1, 2, \ldots, m)$. Show: $Z \sim t_m(0_m, I_m + T^{-1}\iota_m\iota_m', T - 1)$.

8.6 Bayesian Point and Interval Prediction

The approaches of the last two sections can be viewed as attempts to get back to the ideal situation of Section 8.2. The predictive likelihood of Section 8.4 is an attempt to obtain a satisfactory analogue of the usual likelihood of Chapter 6 so that the prediction question can be recast into the estimation question of Chapter 6. The naive certainty equivalence approach of Section 8.5 is based on the treating the estimate $\hat{\theta}$ as if it were θ, and then proceeding as in Section 8.2. This procedure was seen, however, to be particularly unsatisfactory for producing prediction intervals because it understates the researcher's uncertainty. It accounts for the inherent predictive uncertainty reflected in $\text{Var}(Y_*|y, \theta)$, but completely ignores the estimative uncertainty in $\hat{\theta}$. Only when a pivotal quantity was available was it possible to obtain a satisfactory procedure for producing prediction intervals that reflect both types of uncertainty.

The Bayesian approach discussed in this section, already summarized in (8.2.2), also is motivated by the desire to return to the ideal situation of the known predictive density of Section 8.2. The path for the Bayesian, however, is straightforward and conceptually simple: If $f(y_*|y,\theta)$ is not operational because θ is unknown, then remove this nuisance parameter from the problem by integrating it out (i.e., marginalizing) using the posterior density of θ to obtain the operational counterpart $f(y_*|y)$ given in (8.2.2). Once again, *the ability to deal with nuisance parameters in a general setting distinguishes the Bayesian approach from its competitors.*

The next two examples are the Bayesian analogs of Examples 8.5.1 through 8.5.4.

Example 8.6.1 Consider Example 8.5.1. Suppose σ^2 is known, and that the prior distribution for μ is $N(\underline{\mu}, \sigma^2/\underline{T})$. Then according to Example 6.7.2, the posterior distribution for μ is $N(\overline{\mu}, \sigma^2/\overline{T})$, where

$$\overline{\mu} = \frac{\underline{T}\underline{\mu} + T\overline{y}}{\overline{T}}, \tag{8.6.1}$$

$$\overline{T} = \underline{T} + T. \tag{8.6.2}$$

Using (A.14.16) with $x = \mu$, $a = y_*$, $A = 1$, $b = \overline{\mu}$, $B = \overline{T}$ and $c = (1 + T^{-1})(y_* + \overline{T}\overline{\mu})$, it follows that

$$(y_* - \mu)^2 + \overline{T}(\mu + \overline{\mu})^2 = (1 + T^{-1})(\mu - c)^2 + (1 + T^{-1})(y_* - \overline{\mu})^2. \tag{8.6.3}$$

Therefore, the predictive density is

$$\begin{aligned} f(y_*|y) &= \int_{\Re} f(y_*|y,\mu)f(\mu|y)\,d\mu \\ &= \int_{\Re} \phi(y_*|\mu,\sigma^2)\phi(\mu|\overline{\mu},\sigma^2/\overline{T})\,d\mu \\ &= \phi(y_*|\overline{\mu},\sigma^2[1 + \overline{T}^{-1}])\int_{\Re} \phi(\mu|c,\sigma^2[1 + \overline{T}^{-1}])\,d\mu \\ &= \phi(y_*|\overline{\mu},\sigma^2[1 + \overline{T}^{-1}]). \end{aligned} \tag{8.6.4}$$

Under squared error loss, the Bayesian point forecast of Y_* is $\overline{\mu}$. A $1 - \alpha$ prediction (forecast) interval for Y_* is given by $\mathscr{S}_* = \{Y_*|\overline{\mu} - z_{\alpha/2}\sigma_o[1 + \overline{T}^{-1}]^{1/2} < Y_* < \overline{\mu} + z_{\alpha/2}\sigma_o[1 + \overline{T}^{-1}]^{1/2}\}$, where $z_{\alpha/2}$ satisfies $\Phi(z_{\alpha/2}) = 1 - \alpha$.

Example 8.6.2 Consider Example 8.5.2. Suppose Σ is known, and that the prior distribution for μ is $N_M(\underline{\mu}, \Sigma/\underline{T})$. Then according to Table 6.7.2 and Exercise 6.7.28(a), the posterior distribution of μ is $N_M(\overline{\mu}, \Sigma/\overline{T})$, where

$$\bar{\mu} = \frac{\underline{T}\underline{\mu} + T\bar{y}}{\bar{T}}, \tag{8.6.5}$$

$$\bar{T} = \underline{T} + T. \tag{8.6.6.}$$

Using (A.14.16) with $x = \mu$, $a = y_*$, $A = \Sigma^{-1}$, $b = \bar{\mu}$, $B = \bar{T}\Sigma^{-1}$ and $c = (1 + T^{-1})(y_* + \bar{T}\bar{\mu})$, it follows that

$$\begin{aligned}(y_* - \mu)'\Sigma^{-1}(y_* - \mu) + \bar{T}(\mu - \bar{\mu})'\Sigma^{-1}(\mu - \bar{\mu})\\ = (1 + \bar{T}^{-1})(\mu - c)'\Sigma^{-1}(\mu - c) + (1 + T^{-1})(y_* - \bar{\mu})'\Sigma^{-1}(y_* - \bar{\mu}).\end{aligned} \tag{8.6.7}$$

It is a straightforward exercise to show that the predictive density is

$$\begin{aligned} f(y_*|y) &= \int_{\Re^M} f(y_*|y,\mu)f(\mu|y)\,d\mu \\ &= \int_{\Re^M} \phi_M(y_*|\mu,\Sigma)\phi_M(\mu|\bar{\mu},\Sigma/\bar{T})\,d\mu \\ &= \phi_M(y_*|\bar{\mu},[1 + T^{-1}]\Sigma)\int_{\Re^M} \phi_M(\mu|c,[1 + T^{-1}]\Sigma)\,dy \\ &= \phi_M(y_*|\bar{\mu},[1 + \bar{T}^{-1}]\Sigma). \end{aligned} \tag{8.6.8}$$

Under squared error loss, the Bayesian point forecast of Y_* is $\bar{\mu}$. Theorem 4.5.1 implies that a $1 - \alpha$ prediction (forecast) ellipsoid for Z_* is given by $\bar{\mathscr{S}}_* = \{Z_*|(Z_* - \bar{\mu})'\Sigma^{-1}(Z_* - \bar{\mu}) \leq c_\alpha[1 + \bar{T}^{-1}]\}$, where c_α cuts off $1 - \alpha$ probability in the righthand tail of the chi-squared distribution with M degrees of freedom.

Note that in Examples 8.6.1 through 8.6.2, the classical results of Examples 8.5.1 through 8.5.4 emerge as $\underline{T} \to 0$. The next two examples consider the case of unknown variances with conjugate priors.

Example 8.6.3 Consider Example 8.5.1 with both μ and σ^2 unknown. Suppose the prior distribution for μ and σ^{-2} is the natural conjugate normal-gamma prior $NG(\underline{\mu}, \underline{T}^{-1}, \underline{s}^{-2}, \underline{v})$ introduced in Example 6.7.4. Then the posterior distribution for μ and σ^{-2} is $NG(\bar{\mu}, \bar{T}^{-1}, \bar{s}^{-2}, \bar{v})$, where $\bar{\mu}$, $\bar{q}$, $\bar{s}^2$, and $\bar{v}$ are given by (6.7.34), (6.7.33), (6.7.35), and (6.7.31), respectively. Under quadratic loss, the optimal point predictor of Y_* is $\bar{\mu}$. It is a straightforward exercise to show that the predictive density is

$$\begin{aligned} f(y_*|y) &= \int_0^\infty \int_{-\infty}^\infty f(y_*|y,\mu)f(\mu|y)\,d\mu\,d\sigma^{-2} \\ &= \int_0^\infty \left[\int_{-\infty}^\infty \phi(y_*|\mu,\sigma^2)\phi(\mu|\bar{\mu},\sigma^2/\bar{T})\,d\mu\right]\gamma(\sigma^{-2}|\bar{s}^{-2},\bar{v})\,d\sigma^{-2} \\ &= \int_0^\infty \phi(y_*|\bar{\mu},\sigma^2[1 + \bar{T}^{-1}])\gamma(\sigma^{-2}|\bar{s}^{-2},\bar{v})\,d\sigma^{-2} \\ &= t(y_*|\bar{\mu},\bar{s}^2[1 + \bar{T}^{-1}],\bar{v}). \end{aligned} \tag{8.6.9}$$

The inner integral in (8.6.9) follows from (8.6.3); the outer integral follows from Theorem 3.4.13(a). Under squared error loss, the Bayesian point forecast of Y_* is $\bar{\mu}$. A $1-\alpha$ prediction (forecast) interval for Y_* is given by $\mathcal{S}_* = \{Y_* | \bar{\mu} - t_{\alpha/2,\bar{\nu}}\bar{s}_o[1 + \bar{T}^{-1}]^{1/2} < Y_* < \bar{\mu} + t_{\alpha/2,\bar{\nu}}\bar{s}_o[1 + \bar{T}^{-1}]^{1/2}\}$, where $t_{\alpha/2,\bar{\nu}}$ cuts off $1-(\alpha/2)$ probability in the righthand tail of a Student-t distribution with $T-1$ degrees of freedom.

Example 8.6.4 Consider Example 8.5.6 with both μ and Σ unknown. Suppose the prior distribution for μ and Σ^{-1} is the natural conjugate normal-Wishart prior $NW_M(\underline{\mu}, \underline{T}\underline{S}^{-1}, \underline{\omega})$ introduced in Exercise 6.8.5(a), implying $\mu|\Sigma^{-1} \sim N_M(\underline{\mu}, \underline{T}^{-1}\Sigma)$ and $\Sigma^{-1} \sim W_M(\underline{S}^{-1}, \underline{\omega})$. Then the posterior distribution for μ and Σ^{-1} is $NW_M(\bar{\mu}', \bar{T}\bar{S}^{-1}, \bar{\omega})$, where $\bar{\mu}$ and $\bar{T}$ are given by (8.6.1) and (8.6.2), respectively, and

$$\bar{S}^{-1} = \underline{S}^{-1} + S^{-1}, \tag{8.6.10}$$

$$\bar{\omega} = \underline{\omega} + T, \tag{8.6.11}$$

that is, $\mu|\Sigma^{-1}, y \sim N_M(\bar{\mu}, \bar{T}^{-1}\Sigma)$ and $\Sigma^{-1}|y \sim W_M(\bar{S}, \bar{\omega})$. Under quadratic loss, the optimal point predictor of Y_* is $\bar{\mu}$. Letting $\Sigma^{-1} > 0$ denote that Σ^{-1} is positive definite, it is a straightforward exercise to show that the predictive density is

$$\begin{aligned} f(y_*|y) &= \int_{\Sigma^{-1}>0}\int_{\Re^M} f(y_*|y,\mu) f(\mu|y)\, d\mu\, d\,\text{vech}(\Sigma^{-1}) \\ &= \int_{\Sigma^{-1}>0}\left[\int_{\Re^M} \phi_M(y_*|\mu,\Sigma)\phi_M(\mu|\bar{\mu},\bar{T}^{-1}\Sigma)\, d\mu\right] \\ &\quad f_W(\Sigma^{-1}|\bar{S},\bar{\omega})\, d\,\text{vech}(\Sigma^{-1}) \\ &= \int_{\Sigma^{-1}>0} \phi_M(y_*|\bar{\mu},[1+\bar{T}^{-1}]\Sigma) f_W(\Sigma^{-1}|\bar{S}^{-1},\bar{\omega})\, d\,\text{vech}(\Sigma^{-1}) \\ &= t_M(y_*|\bar{\mu},[1+\bar{T}^{-1}]\bar{S},\bar{\omega}). \end{aligned} \tag{8.6.12}$$

A $1-\alpha$ prediction (forecast) ellipsoid for Z_* is given by $\mathcal{S}_* = \{Z_* | (Z_* - \bar{\mu})'\bar{S}^{-1}(Z_* - \bar{\mu}) \le c_\alpha[1 + \bar{T}^{-1}]\}$, where c_α cuts off $1-\alpha$ probability in the righthand tail of the $F(M, \bar{\omega} - M)$ distribution.

Taking $\underline{T} \to 0$ in Examples 8.5.3 and 8.5.5 does *not* produce the classical results in Examples 8.5.3 through 8.5.4. Using "noninformative" priors (6.8.7) and (6.8.27), however, will do it.

Bayesian analysis of the troublesome Gaussian AR(1) process of Example 8.5.7 is strikingly straightforward.

Example 8.6.5 Recall Example 8.5.7. To emphasize that differences that arise are due to informative prior specification, we adopt the improper uniform prior for θ. As noted in Example 6.10.6, the exact posterior distribution of θ in this case is simply $\theta|y \sim N(\hat{\theta}, w^{-1})$, where $\hat{\theta}$ is the MLE given by (6.10.7), and w is given by (6.10.9). Proceeding analogously to (8.6.4), the predictive distributive of Y_* is

$$f(y_*|y) = \phi(y_*|\hat{\theta}y_T, 1 + w). \tag{8.6.13}$$

Under quadratic cost, the optimal Bayesian point predictor of Y_* is the posterior mean of (8.6.13), that is, $\hat{Y}_{**} = \hat{\theta}y_T$. A $1 - \alpha$ prediction (forecast) interval for Y_* is given by $\mathscr{S}_* = \{Y_*|\hat{\theta}y_T - z_{\alpha/2}[1 + w]^{1/2} < Y_* < \hat{\theta}y_T + z_{\alpha/2}[1 + w]^{1/2}\}$, where $\Phi(z_{\alpha/2}) = 1 - (\alpha/2)$. The fact that $\hat{\theta}$ is a nonlinear function of Y_t $(t = 1, 2, \ldots, T)$ is immaterial to whether θ has a tractable posterior distribution, and hence whether the predictive distribution is tractable. Furthermore, the introduction of nuisance parameters (e.g., by assuming the variance is unknown) poses no complications. The striking difference in this problem compared to classical analysis boils down to conditioning, that is, $\theta|y$ versus $Y|\theta$.

Bayesian predictive p.f. (8.2.2) can also shed some light on the predictive likelihood developed in Section 8.4. We proceed in two steps. First, following Hinkley (1979, pp. 723–724) consider the statistics $W(Y)$, $W_+(Y, Y_*) = W_+(Y, Y_*)$, and $W_*(W, Y_*)$ introduced in Section 8.4. The predictive p.f. of W_*, given $W = w$, is

$$f(w_*|w) = \frac{\int_\Theta f(w, w_*|\theta)f(\theta)\,d\theta}{\int_\Theta f(w|\theta)f(\theta)\,d\theta}. \tag{8.6.14}$$

The sufficiency of W_+, implies $f(w, w_*|\theta) = f(w, w_*|w_+)f(w_+|\theta)$, and hence (8.6.14) implies

$$f(w_*|w) = f(w, w_*|w_+)\left[\frac{f(w_+)}{f(w)}\right], \tag{8.6.15}$$

where

$$f(w_+) = \int_\Theta f(w_+|\theta)f(\theta)\,d\theta, \tag{8.6.16}$$

$$f(w) = \int_\Theta f(w|\theta)f(\theta)\,d\theta. \tag{8.6.17}$$

But $f(w, w_*|w_+) = f(w_*|w, w_+)f(w|w_+) = f(w|w_+)$, because W_* is assumed to be completely determined by W and W_+. Therefore, (8.6.15) can be written as

$$\begin{aligned} f(w_*|w) &= f(w|w_+)\left[\frac{f(w_+)}{f(w)}\right] \\ &\propto f(w|w_+)f(w_+). \end{aligned} \tag{8.6.18}$$

Hinkley (1979, p. 722) refers to $f(w|w_+)$, denoted here by $\mathscr{L}(y_*; y)$, as the predictive likelihood of the statistic w_+ given the statistic w. Note that (8.6.18) is a predictive analog to the parametric Bayesian paradigm: $f(w_+)$ in (8.6.18) plays the role of a prior density, and the "posterior" $f(w_*|w)$ is proportional to the (predictive) likelihood times $f(w_+)$. In general, the prior on θ may render $f(w_+)$ informative about w_*. Using this terminology, (8.6.18) implies the Bayesian predictive density $f(w_*|w)$ is proportional to the predictive likelihood $\mathscr{L}_*(w_*; w)$ iff the marginal density $f(w_+)$, not $f(\theta)$, is constant.

Second, we need to extend the preceding development involving sufficient statistics for Y and Y_*. Davison (1986, p. 326) provides the necessary connection between the Bayesian predictive density $f(y|y)$ and the predictive likelihood $\mathscr{L}(y_*; y)$:

$$f(y_*|y) = \mathscr{L}_*(y_*; y)\left[\frac{f(y|w, y_*)}{f(y|w)}\right]\left[\frac{f(w_+)}{f(w)}\right]. \tag{8.6.19}$$

Note (8.4.2) implies

$$\mathscr{L}_*(y_*; y) = \mathscr{L}_*(w_*; w)f(y_*|w, w_+). \tag{8.6.20}$$

Substituting (8.6.20) into (8.6.18) relates the Bayesian predictive density $f(y_*|y)$ to the predictive likelihood $\mathscr{L}_*(w_*; w)$ of w_* given w.

Note that predictive density (8.2.2) can be written as

$$f(y_*|y) = E_{\theta|y}[f(Y_*|y, \theta)]. \tag{8.6.21}$$

Since $f(y_*|y, \theta) > 0$, predictive density (8.6.20) is ideally suited to approximation by the method of Tierney and Kadane (1986) discussed in Section 6.7. Define $a_D(\theta; y) \equiv \ln[f(\theta)] + L(\theta; y)]$ and $a_N(\theta; y, y_*) \equiv \ln[f(y_*|y, \theta)] + a_D(\theta; y)$. Let $\hat{\theta}_D(y)$ and $\hat{\theta}_N(y, y_*)$ denote their respective modes, and $H_D(\theta; y) \equiv \partial^2 a_D(\theta)/\partial\theta\,\partial\theta'$ and $H_N(\theta; y, y_*) \equiv \partial^2 a_N(\theta)/\partial\theta\,\partial\theta'$, their respective Hessians. Then the Tierney-Kadane approximation to the predictive density is

$$\begin{aligned}\hat{f}(y_*|y) &= \frac{\exp(a_N[\hat{\theta}_N(y, y_*); y, y_*])|-H_N[\hat{\theta}_N(y, y_*); y, y_*]|^{-1/2}}{\exp(a_D[\hat{\theta}_D(y); y])|-H_D[\hat{\theta}_D(y); y]|^{-1/2}}\\ &= f[y_*|y, \hat{\theta}_N(y, y_*)]\left[\frac{f(\hat{\theta}_N(y, y_*)]\mathscr{L}[\hat{\theta}_N(y, y_*); y]}{f[\hat{\theta}_D(y)]\mathscr{L}[\hat{\theta}_D(y); y]}\right]\\ &\quad\times\left[\frac{|-H_N[\hat{\theta}_n(y, y_*); y, y_*]|^{-1/2}}{|-H_D[\hat{\theta}_D(y); y]|^{-1/2}}\right].\end{aligned} \tag{8.6.22}$$

In the case $T_* = 1$, Davison (1986) shows:

$$f(y_*|y) = \hat{f}(y_*|y)[1 + O(T^{-2})]. \tag{8.6.23}$$

Also note that replacing $\hat{\theta}_N(y, y_*)$ in (8.6.22) by the one-step estimate

$$\tilde{\theta}(y, y_*) \equiv \hat{\theta}_D(y) - (H_N[\hat{\theta}_D(y); y, y_*])^{-1}\left[\frac{\partial a_N[\hat{\theta}_D(y); y, y_*]}{\partial \theta}\right] \tag{8.6.24}$$

does not change the quality of the approximation.

Exercises

8.6.1 Suppose $f(y|\lambda) = \text{Po}(\lambda)$ and $f(\lambda) = G(\alpha, \beta)$. Show:

$$f(y_*|y) = \frac{\Gamma(\alpha + Y_* + y)}{y!\,\Gamma(\alpha + y)}\left[\frac{y}{\beta^{-1} + 1 + y}\right]^{y_*}\left[1 - \frac{1}{\beta^{-1} + 1 + y}\right]^{\alpha + y}. \tag{8.6.25}$$

8.6.2 Show (Besag 1989):

$$f(y_*|y) = \frac{f(y_*|y, \theta)f(\theta|y)}{f(\theta|y, y_*)}. \tag{8.6.26}$$

8.6.3 Suppose Y_t $(t = 1, 2, \ldots, T)|\alpha, \theta \sim$ i.i.d. $G(\alpha, \theta^{-1})$, where $\theta \sim G(\underline{a}, \underline{b}^{-1})$ and α, $\underline{a}$, and $\underline{b}$ are known.

(a) Show: $\theta|y \sim G(\bar{a}, \bar{b}^{-1})$, where $\bar{a} = \underline{a} + T\alpha$ and $\bar{b} = \underline{b}^{-1} + T\bar{y}$.

(b) Suppose $Y_*|\delta, \theta \sim G(\delta, \theta)$. Show: $Y_*|y \sim \beta^{-1}(\delta, \bar{a}, \bar{b})$, i.e.

$$f(y_*|y) = \frac{\bar{b}^{\bar{a}} y_*^{\delta - 1}}{B(\delta, \bar{a})(\bar{b} + y_*)^{\bar{a} + \delta}}. \tag{8.6.27}$$

8.6.4 Suppose $Y|\theta \sim t(\theta, 1, 1)$ and $y_*|\theta \sim t(\theta, 1, 1)$ are independent, and θ has an improper uniform distribution over $\Re$. Show:

$$f(y_*|y) = (2\pi[1 + \tfrac{1}{4}(y_* - y)^2])^{-1}, \quad -\infty < y_* < \infty. \tag{8.6.28}$$

8.6.5 Suppose Y and Y_* are independent double exponential random variables (recall Exercise 3.3.22) with location parameter θ (i.e., $Y - \theta \sim \text{EPF}(1)$ and $Y_* - \theta \sim \text{EPF}(1)$ are independent). Then the respective p.d.f.s are:

$$f(y|\theta) = \tfrac{1}{2}\exp(-|y - \theta|), \quad -\infty < y < \infty, \tag{8.6.29}$$

$$f(y_*|\theta) = \tfrac{1}{2}\exp(-|y_* - \theta|), \quad -\infty < y_* < \infty. \tag{8.6.30}$$

Suppose θ has an improper uniform prior over $\Re$. Show:

$$f(y_*|y) = \tfrac{1}{4}(1 + |y_* - y|)\exp(-|y_* - y|), \quad -\infty < y_* < \infty. \tag{8.6.31}$$

8.6.6 Derive (8.6.19).

8.6.7 How does (8.6.19) simplify when $f(y_*|y, \theta) = f(y_*|\theta)$?

8.6.8 Consider Example 8.6.1. Compute $E_{Y_*|Y, \mu, \Sigma}[(\bar{\mu} - Y_*)^2]$.

8.6.9 Consider Example 8.6.2. Compute $E_{Y_*|Y, \mu, \Sigma}[(\bar{\mu} - Y_*)' A_*(\bar{\mu} - Y_*)]$.

8.6.10 Verify the statement in the text that using "noninformative" priors (6.8.7) and (6.8.27) produces prediction regions numerically identical to their classical counterparts Examples 8.5.3 through 8.5.4.

8.6.11 Verify (8.6.13).

8.7 Combination of Forecasts

There is a long tradition in the forecasting literature that addresses the issue of what to do when more than one forecast (prediction) of some future observable is available. The general message of this literature is that it is better to combine the forecasts rather than use only one of the forecasts. Indeed, a simple averaging of forecasts often behaves better than any single forecast, and the simple average is often close to being the optimal forecast combination. Such simple averages are often used in reporting aggregate economic forecast based on forecasts from competing firms. Much of this literature appears in two journals, the *Journal of Forecasting* and the *International Journal of Forecasting*, which are not mainstream econometrics or statistics journals. As a result, this literature often does not receive its due attention in econometrics and statistics texts. This section attempts to remedy that situation. A good review article, including an annotated bibliography, is Clemen (1989).

Although the seminal work in this area is Bates and Granger (1969), the wisdom of the advice to combine forecasts is best appreciated in a Bayesian framework, and so we will begin there. Suppose that the permissible parameter space Θ is partitioned into J mutually exclusive subsets Θ_j $(j = 1, 2, \ldots, J)$ such that $\Theta = \Theta_1 \cup \Theta_2 \cup \cdots \Theta_J$. This partitioning gives rise to J hypotheses H_j: $\theta \in \Theta_j$ $(j = 1, 2, \ldots, J)$. Also suppose that the likelihood $\mathscr{L}(\theta; y)$, prior probabilities $\underline{\pi}_j = \text{Prob}(H_j)$ $(j = 1, 2, \ldots, J)$, and conditional prior p.d.f.s $f(\theta|H_j)$ $(j = 1, 2, \ldots, J)$ are given. Conditional on hypothesis H_j, and given data y leading to the posterior p.d.f. $f(\theta|y, H_j)$, the jth conditional predictive density of Y_* is

$$f(y_*|y, H_j) = \int_{\mathscr{S}_*} f(y_*|\theta, y, H_j) f(\theta|y, H_j)\, d\theta. \tag{8.7.1}$$

Using the posterior probabilities $\overline{\pi}_j = \text{Prob}(H_j|y)$ $(j = 1, 2, \ldots, J)$, the unconditional (marginal) predictive density of Y_* is the mixture

$$\begin{aligned} f(y_*|y) &= \sum_{j=1}^{J} f(y_*, H_j|y) \\ &= \sum_{j=1}^{J} \overline{\pi}_j f(y_*|y, H_j). \end{aligned} \tag{8.7.2}$$

Predictive density (8.7.2) is the basis for constructing prediction intervals and point forecasts unconditional of the competing hypotheses. For example, under quadratic loss it was seen in Section 8.6 that the optimal Bayesian point estimate is the predictive mean $E(Y_*|y)$, which by (8.7.2) is

$$E(Y_*|y) = \sum_{j=1}^{J} \bar{\pi}_j E(Y_*|y, H_j). \tag{8.7.3}$$

Since (8.7.3) is a weighted average of the optimal point forecasts $E(Y_*|y, H_j)$ under these hypotheses, the Bayesian motivation for combining forecasts is straightforward. Furthermore, the weights in this case, the posterior probabilities $\bar{\pi}_j$ $(j = 1, 2, \ldots, J)$ of the respective hypotheses, have an intuitive appeal: the forecasts of more probable hypotheses *a posteriori* receive more weight. The "optimality" of these weights is self-evident to the Bayesian: given the likelihood, hypotheses and priors, (8.7.2) is the unique predictive distribution for future observables. To use any other distribution would be "incoherent."

The preceding development is fairly formal, requiring point forecasts derived from explicit predictive distributions, and it is Bayesian in development. Much of the literature on combining forecasts is less formal, and often non-Bayesian in motivation. Suppose there are J point forecasts $\hat{Y}_{j*}$ available for predicting Y_*, yielding the forecast errors $U_{*j} \equiv \hat{Y}_{*j} - Y_*$ $(j = 1, 2, \ldots, J)$. For example, Y_* may be next quarter's U.S. gross national product, and $\hat{Y}_{j*}$ may be its forecast from forecasting firm j. Let $\hat{Y}_* = [\hat{Y}_{*1}, \hat{Y}_{*2}, \ldots, \hat{Y}_{*J}]'$ and $X_* = [U_{*1}, U_{*2}, \ldots, U_{*J}]' = \hat{Y}_* - Y_* \iota_J$. Often it is difficult to model the generation of forecasts (e.g., when dealing with the point forecasts of interviewees). Instead, suppose the forecast errors themselves are taken as the primitive objects of the modeling exercise. Specifically, suppose

$$X_*|\theta, \Sigma \sim N_J(\theta, \Sigma), \tag{8.7.4}$$

where θ denotes the bias of the forecasts $\hat{Y}_*$, and $\Sigma = [\sigma_{ij}]$ is positive definite.[8] The corrected forecasts $\hat{Y}_* - \theta$ are unbiased, that is $E[(\hat{Y}_* - \theta) - Y_*] = 0_J$, and $\hat{Y}_* - \theta \sim N_J(0_J, \Sigma)$. Before discussing the case of unknown θ and Σ, we first consider the case where θ and Σ are known.

Let $w = [w_1, w_2, \ldots, w_J]'$ be a vector of nonrandom weights satisfying $\iota_J' w = 1$, i.e. the weights sum to unity. Consider the combined univariate forecast error corrected for bias:

$$U_*(\theta) \equiv w'(\hat{Y}_* - \theta) - Y_* \sim N(0_J, w'\Sigma w). \tag{8.7.5}$$

One appealing criterion for finding weights is to choose w so as to minimize $\text{Var}[U_*(\theta)] = E([U_*(\theta)]^2) = w'\Sigma w$, subject to $\iota_J' w = 1$. This can be

8. Biased forecasts occur quite naturally when using asymmetric loss functions (e.g., see Zellner 1986c and the references cited therein). Asymmetric loss functions were studied in (6.7.50) and (6.7.81) (also see Aigner et al. 1976; Britney and Winkler 1968; Newey and Powell 1987; and Poirier 1976, Chapter 9).

achieved by minimizing the Lagrangian $l(w, \mu) = w'\Sigma w - \mu(\iota_J' w - 1)$, leading to the first-order conditions

$$\frac{\partial l(w^*, \mu^*)}{\partial w} = 2\Sigma w^* - \mu^* \iota_J = 0_J, \tag{8.7.6}$$

$$\frac{\partial l(w^*, \mu^*)}{\partial \mu} = -(\iota_J' w^* - 1) = 0, \tag{8.7.7}$$

for the optimal weights w^* and the Lagrange multiplier μ^*. Solving (8.7.6) for w^* yields

$$w^* = \tfrac{1}{2}\mu^* \Sigma^{-1} \iota_J, \tag{8.7.8}$$

and together with (8.7.7) this implies

$$\mu^* = \frac{2}{\iota_J' \Sigma^{-1} \iota_J}. \tag{8.7.9}$$

Substituting (8.7.9) into (8.7.6) yields the optimal weights (verification of second-order conditions is straightforward):

$$w^* = \frac{\Sigma^{-1} \iota_J}{\iota_J' \Sigma^{-1} \iota_J}. \tag{8.7.10}$$

Substituting (8.7.10) into the criterion function yields the achievable expected squared forecast error:

$$E([U_*(\theta)]^2 | w = w^*) = (\iota_J' \Sigma^{-1} \iota_J)^{-1}. \tag{8.7.11}$$

Simply using $\hat{Y}_{j*}$ alone corresponds to setting $w = e_{j,J}$ [$e_{j,J}$ is a $J \times 1$ vector with all elements equalling zero except the jth which equals unity], and yields expected squared forecast error:

$$E([U_*(\theta)^2 | w = e_{j,J}) = \sigma_{jj} \geq E([U_*(\theta)]^2 | w = w^*). \tag{8.7.12}$$

Again, combining forecasts is seen to be optimal compared to using a single forecast. If the equal weights $w = J^{-1}\iota_J$ are used, then the achievable expected squared forecast error is:

$$E([U_*(\theta)]^2 | w = J^{-1}\iota_J) = \frac{\iota_J' \Sigma^{-1} \iota_J}{J^2} \geq E([U_*(\theta)]^2 | w = w^*). \tag{8.7.13}$$

The moral at this point is clear: in either the full model-based Bayesian analysis or in the case of a known forecast error distribution, it is optimal from the standpoint of expected squared forecast error to combine forecasts. As in Section 6.2, there is little disagreement about this recommendation when there are no unknowns. Rational arguments against combining forecasts are usually premised on the inapplicability of either of these settings, due to the heroic assumption of the absence of unknowns.

As seen in Section 8.6, in the presence of unknown parameters the Bayesian solution to predictive questions is to use priors to integrate-out these "nuisances" and obtain a known predictive distribution. A similar strategy can be adopted with forecast error distribution (8.7.5) when θ and/or Σ are unknown: specify a distribution for the unknown parameters, use it to integrate-out the unknown parameters from (8.7.5) in order to obtain a known forecast error distribution, and then proceed as above to obtain optimal weights (e.g., see Winkler 1981 and Palm and Zellner 1990). Such Bayesian analysis is straightforward under two convenient priors (see Exercises 8.7.4 and 8.7.5). Furthermore, if past data is available on forecast errors, the such data can be used to update these priors to obtain posterior distributions to be used in obtaining a known predictive distributions (see Exercises 8.7.6 and 8.7.7). In short, the Bayesian moral remains: Optimally combined forecasts are expected to outperform individual forecasts.

Two minor qualifiers to this Bayesian advice, however, should be noted. First, while improper priors usually yield proper predictive distributions, well-defined posterior probabilities on sharp hypotheses require proper priors, and hence weighted prediction (8.7.5) also requires proper priors. Second, Min and Zellner (1993), Zellner and Min (1992a), and Palm and Zellner (1990) have noted that if a Bayesian researcher entertains a non-exhaustive set of hypotheses, then it need not be optimal to combine the forecasts in the usual manner over the hypotheses explicitly considered. Both these qualifiers are directed at clarifying the requirements for prior information needed for unknown parameters or unknown hypotheses that warrant positive prior probability.

From the classical perspective, when θ and Σ are unknown in (8.7.5), then data on previous forecast errors are required in order to estimate θ and Σ before seeking optimal weights. MLEs for the unknown mean and covariance matrix of a multivariate normal distribution, based on a random sample X_t $(t = 1, 2, \ldots, T) \sim$ i.i.d. $N_J(\theta, \Sigma)$, were obtained in Example 6.6.6. When θ is unknown, but Σ is known, then the MLE $\overline{Y}$ can be used to form $U_*(\overline{Y}) = w'(\hat{Y}_* - \overline{Y}) - Y_* \sim N[0, (1 + T^{-1})\Sigma]$. It is straightforward to show that choosing w to minimize $\text{Var}[U_*(\overline{Y})] = E([U_*(\overline{Y})]^2) = (1 + T^{-1})w'\Sigma w$, subject to $\iota_J' w = 1$, once again yields the optimal weights (8.7.10). The achievable expected squared error forecast errors analogous to (8.7.11)–(8.7.13) are slightly larger:

$$E([U_*(\overline{X})]^2 | w = w^*) = \frac{1 + T^{-1}}{\iota_J' \Sigma^{-1} \iota_J}, \tag{8.7.14}$$

In the case of unknown Σ, the analysis is not so simple.

$$E([U_*(\bar{X})]^2|w = e_{j,J}) = (1 + T^{-1})\sigma_{jj} \geq E([U_*(\bar{X})]^2|w = w^*), \tag{8.7.15}$$

$$E([U_*(\bar{X})]^2|w = J^{-1}\iota_J) = \frac{\iota_J'\Sigma^{-1}\iota_J}{J^2} \geq E([U_*(\bar{X})]^2|w = w^*). \tag{8.7.16}$$

Exercises

8.7.1 Let $\hat{Y}_1 = Y + \varepsilon_1$ and $\hat{Y}_2 = \theta + Y + \varepsilon_2$ be two forecasts of the scalar random variable Y, where $E(\varepsilon_1) = E(\varepsilon_2) = 0$, $\text{Var}(\varepsilon_1) = \text{Var}(\varepsilon_2) = \sigma^2$, $\text{Corr}(\varepsilon_1, \varepsilon_2) = \rho$, and θ is the bias associated with forecast $\hat{Y}_2$. Consider the combined forecast $\hat{Y}(w) = w\hat{Y}_1 + (1 - w)\hat{Y}_2$, where w is a fixed weight and $0 < w < 1$.

(a) Find $E\{[\hat{Y}(w) - Y]^2\}$.

(b) Find w so as to minimize (a) when it is known that $\theta = 0$.

(c) Let w^* be the optimal weight obtained in (b). Compare $E\{[\hat{Y}(w^*) - Y]^2\}$ and $E\{[\hat{Y}_1 - Y]^2\}$ when $\theta \neq 0$.

8.7.2 Verify algebraically the inequality in (8.7.12).

8.7.2 Verify algebraically the inequality in (8.7.13).

8.7.4 Suppose θ and Σ in forecast error distribution (8.7.4) are unknown, but there are data U_t $(t = 1, 2, \ldots, T) \sim$ i.i.d. $N_J(\theta, \Sigma)$ on forecast errors in T previous periods. Consider the "noninformative" improper prior:

$$f(\theta, \Sigma^{-1}) \propto |\Sigma^{-1}|^{-(J+1)/2}. \tag{8.7.17}$$

Show that the predictive distribution of U_* [cf. (8.7.5)] is the univariate t-distribution $t(w'\bar{x}, w'\Sigma w, T - 1)$.

8.7.5 Suppose θ and Σ in forecast error distribution (8.7.5) are unknown, but there are data U_t $(t = 1, 2, \ldots, T) \sim$ i.i.d. $N_J(\theta, \Sigma)$ on forecast errors in T previous periods. Consider the informative conjugate Normal-Wishart prior, where $\mu|\Sigma^{-1} \sim N(\underline{\mu}, \underline{T}^{-1}\Sigma)$ and $\Sigma^{-1} \sim W_M(\underline{S}^{-1}, \underline{\omega})$. Show that the predictive distribution of U_* [cf. (8.7.5)] is the univariate t-distribution $t(w'\bar{\mu}, w'\bar{S}w/T, T - 1)$, where $\bar{\mu}$ and $\bar{S}^{-1}$ are given by (8.6.15) and (8.6.10), respectively.

9 The Linear Regression Model

Econometricians have found their Philosophers' Stone; it is called regression analysis and is used for transforming data into significant results.
—Hendry (1980)

9.1 A Tale of Two Regressions

The basic concepts of regression and correlation arose from the work of Sir Francis Galton (1822–1911), cousin of Charles Darwin, in the nineteenth century. In his studies of hereditary traits, Galton noted that unusually tall men tend to have sons shorter than themselves, and unusually short men tend to have sons taller than themselves. This suggested a "regression toward mediocrity" in height from generation to generation, hence the term "regression." Although such an observation is best interpreted as the result of low probability of genetic factors causing unusual height or lack thereof being passed on to offspring, rather than as a "regression toward mediocrity," the terminology used by Galton has persisted. The mathematical interpretation of this phenomenon underlies Exercise 9.1.1.

When analyzing data by "regression analysis," there are two distinct formulations that can be entertained: the explanatory variables may be viewed as constants (Case I) or as random variables (Case II). Case I is a mechanical extension of the univariate location problem of Chapter 6 in which the location parameter is specified to be a function of observable constants and unknown parameters. Case II is an extension along the lines of the multivariate problem in Example 6.6.6, and corresponds to the motivation behind the discussion of population regression functions in Section 2.7. Choices between the two approaches should ideally be made based on the problem at hand, and in economics, Case II is usually the most appropriate. Unfortunately, consideration of the convenience of presentation favors the former, at least as far as immediate pedagogical concerns. Later pedagogical concerns suggest otherwise (see Binkley and Abbott 1987). Most econometrics texts focus attention on Case I at the expense of Case II. Spanos (1986) and Goldberger (1991) provide refreshingly more balanced treatments. Both cases are discussed simultaneously here.

Case I may be attractive for natural sciences in which designed experiments are possible and the "explanatory" variables are under the control of the experimenter. In such instances the explanatory variables are set (i.e., fixed) at various values and the dependent variable is then observed. Such a viewpoint is not realistic in most social sciences where controlled experimentation is seldom possible, and all variables are passively observed as draws from some underlying joint distribution as in Case II. The conceptual differences between the two cases are important, yet in some situations, random explanatory variables can be viewed "as if" they are fixed.

We begin by introducing notation. The heavy use of matrix algebra in the following development necessitates some changes in previous notation in order to not unduly clutter things. Specifically, we do not distinguish any more between a random variable and its realization; the context should make the distinction clear. This greatly simplifies notational matters. As long as the reader keeps in mind the case under discussion at any moment, no problems should arise. Also unless stated otherwise, all random variables are assumed to have finite second moments.

Let the $m \times 1$ vector $z_t = [y_t', \tilde{x}_t']$ $(t = 1, 2, \ldots, T)$ comprise the observable variables under consideration. The presumed goal is to "explain" the behavior of the $m \times 1$ random variable y_t (the *regressands*) in terms of the $(K - 1) \times 1$ random variables in $\tilde{x}_t$ (the *regressors*).[1] Let $y = [y_1', y_2', \ldots, y_T']'$ and $\tilde{X} = [\tilde{x}_1, \tilde{x}_2, \ldots, \tilde{x}_T]'$ denote T observations on the *m regressands* and the $K - 1$ *regressors*. The "~" notation is used to differentiate the vector $\tilde{x}_t$ from the $K \times 1$ vector $x_t \equiv [1, \tilde{x}_t']'$. The vector x_t is useful in models which contain an intercept term. Analogous to the $T \times (K - 1)$ matrix $\tilde{X}$, define the $T \times K$ matrix $X \equiv [\iota_T, \tilde{X}] = [x_1', x_2', \ldots, x_T']'$. Under both Cases I and II, y is random. In contrast, $\tilde{X}$ is random under Case II, but not random under Case I.

For simplicity, first we consider the case of a single regressand (i.e., $m = 1$). (Situations with $m > 1$ are briefly discussed later.) Both Cases I and II amount to a decomposition of y_t into two components:

$$y_t = \mu_t + u_t \; (t = 1, 2, \ldots, T).$$

When y_t $(t = 1, 2, \ldots, T)$ comprise a random sample from a parametric: "location family" (recall Definition 3.1.1), then $\mu_t = \mu$ $(t = 1, 2, \ldots, T)$, where μ is the common location parameter, and u_t $(t = 1, 2, \ldots, T)$ are random draws from a population with a location parameter equal to zero. For example, in the prototypical case $y_t|\mu, \sigma^2 \sim$ i.i.d. $N(\mu, \sigma^2)$ $(t = 1, 2, \ldots, T)$, $u_t \sim$ i.i.d. $N(0, \sigma^2)$. The two cases of regression analysis studied in this chapter both specify μ_t to be a function of $\tilde{x}_t$ and a vector of unknown parameters β. The component $\mu_t = \mu_t(\tilde{x}_t, \beta)$ is referred to as a *systematic*

1. Formally, consider the experiment characterized by the probability space $(\mathscr{S}, \tilde{A}, P(\cdot))$, where $\mathscr{S}$ is the sample space, $\tilde{A}$ is a σ-field of events (recall Definition 2.1.3), and $P(\cdot)$ assigns probabilities to events in $\tilde{A}$. Let z be a M-dimensional random variable mapping from $\mathscr{S}$ into $\Re^M$, enabling the construction of an equivalent probability space $(\Re^K, \mathring{A}, P_z(\cdot))$, which is easier to handle mathematically, and where $P_z(\cdot)$ is defined over the Borel field $\mathring{A}$ consisting of intervals of the form $(-\infty, z]$. The functions $P(\cdot)$, $P_z(\cdot)$ and the c.d.f. $F(\cdot)$ are related by $P(s|z(s) \in (-\infty, z], s \in \mathscr{S}) = P_z(-\infty, z] = F(z)$.

component and u_t is referred to as a *nonsystematic component*.[2] The competing cases differ in terms of the information set and the question of whether $\tilde{x}_t$ $(t = 1, 2, \ldots, T)$ are random variables or known constants. Both cases specify sufficient structure to define a unique decomposition, and both interpret variation (across observations) in the systematic component as a vehicle for "explaining" variation in y_t.

As previously noted, Case I is a fairly mechanical generalization of the location parameter model. It allows for non-identically distributed observations y_t $(t = 1, 2, \ldots, T)$ to depend on known constants $\tilde{x}_t$ $(t = 1, 2, \ldots, T)$ and an unknown parameter vector β. Given its simplicity, we discuss Case I first.

Case I (Fixed Regressors) $\tilde{x}_t$ $(t = 1, 2, \ldots, T)$ are fixed constants observed without error, satisfying

$$\operatorname{rank}(X) = K, \tag{9.1.1}$$

and y_t $(t = 1, 2, \ldots, T)$ are uncorrelated random variables such that

$$E(y_t) = \beta_1 + \tilde{x}_t'\tilde{\beta}_2 = x_t'\beta \; (t = 1, 2, \ldots, T), \tag{9.1.2}$$

$$\operatorname{Var}(y_t) = \sigma^2 \; (t = 1, 2, \ldots, T), \tag{9.1.3}$$

where $\sigma^2 > 0$ and

$$\beta = [\beta_1, \tilde{\beta}_2']'. \tag{9.1.4}$$

In matrix notation, uncorrelatedness, (9.1.2) and (9.1.3) can be summarized by

$$E(y) = X\beta, \tag{9.1.5}$$

$$\operatorname{Var}(y) = \sigma^2 I_T. \tag{9.1.6}$$

Case I gives rise to the decomposition

$$y_t = x_t'\beta + u_t \; (t = 1, 2, \ldots, T), \tag{9.1.7}$$

where the "systematic component" $x_t'\beta$ is nonstochastic, and the stochastic "nonsystematic component" (*disturbance term*) $u_t \equiv y_t - x_t'\beta$ satisfies

2. Let $\kappa_t \subseteq \tilde{A}$ be a sub-σ-field that depends on $\tilde{x}_t$ and possibly lagged values of both y_t and $\tilde{x}_t$. Intuitively, κ_t serves as an *information set*, the contents of which determine the nature of the "explanation" of y provided by $\tilde{x}$. The choice of an information set is of the utmost importance. It reflects an interplay between theory, data availability and the sampling process. The terms "systematic" and "non-systematic" are relative to this information set. By choosing $\mu_t = E(y_t|A_t)$, the non-systematic component u_t, conditional on the information set κ_t, has zero mean and is orthogonal to the systematic component:

$$E(u_t|\kappa_t) = E([y_t - E(y_t|\kappa_t)]|\kappa_t) = 0,$$

$$E(\mu_t u_t|\kappa_t) = \mu_t E(u_t|\kappa_t) = 0.$$

These properties hold by construction (as opposed to "by assumption"). Many of the models considered in econometrics can be generated from this framework by appropriate choice of the σ-field κ_t and the stochastic process $\{z_t, t \in \mathfrak{F}\}$.

$$E(u_t) = 0 \ (t = 1, 2, \ldots, T), \tag{9.1.8}$$

$$\mathrm{Var}(u_t) = \sigma^2 \ (t = 1, 2, \ldots, T), \tag{9.1.9}$$

$$E(u_t u_j) = 0 \ (t \neq j; t, j = 1, 2, \ldots, T). \tag{9.1.10}$$

Letting $u = [u_1, u_2, \ldots, u_T]'$, (9.1.8)–(9.1.10) can be summarized by

$$y = X\beta + u, \tag{9.1.11}$$

$$E(u) = 0_T, \tag{9.1.12}$$

$$\mathrm{Var}(u) = \sigma^2 I_T. \tag{9.1.13}$$

This leads to the following terminology.

Definition 9.1.1 The model described under Case I, (9.1.1) through (9.1.13) with $m = 1$, is the *standard multiple linear regression model with fixed regressors.* If in addition, Case I is augmented by the assumption that y has a multivariate normal distribution, then Case I corresponds to the *standard multiple linear normal regression model with fixed regressors*, that is,

$$y \sim N_T(x_t'\beta, \sigma^2 I_T), \tag{9.1.14}$$

$$u \sim N_T(0_T, \sigma^2 I_T). \tag{9.1.15}$$

When the regression has a nonzero intercept and only one regressor (i.e., $K = 2$), then "multiple" is replaced by "simple."

Figure 9.1.1 depicts the standard linear normal regression model with fixed regressors in the case of simple regression with a single nonconstant regressor $\tilde{x}$ (i.e., $K = 2$).

We now turn attention to Case II, which was previewed in Section 2.7.

Case II (Stochastic Regressors) Let z_t $(t = 1, 2, \ldots, T)$ be a random sample from a multivariate process with

$$\mu \equiv E(z) = \begin{bmatrix} \mu_y \\ \mu_x \end{bmatrix}, \tag{9.1.16}$$

$$\Sigma \equiv \mathrm{Var}(z) = \begin{bmatrix} \sigma_{yy} & \sigma_{xy}' \\ \sigma_{xy} & \Sigma_{xx} \end{bmatrix}, \tag{9.1.17}$$

where Σ is positive definite. Suppose that the conditional mean of y_t, given the random variable $\tilde{x}_t$, is linear in the conditioning variables $\tilde{x}_t$:[3]

$$E(y_t|\tilde{x}_t) = \beta_1 + \tilde{x}_t'\tilde{\beta}_2 = x_t'\beta \ (t = 1, 2, \ldots, T), \tag{9.1.18}$$

where by Theorem 2.7.1:

3. If $E(y_t|\tilde{x}_t)$ is *not* linear in $\tilde{x}_t$, a simple generalization of Theorem 2.7.6 implies that (9.1.18) is the best [in the sense of minimizing $E(u_t^2)$] linear approximation to $E(y_t|\tilde{x}_t)$.

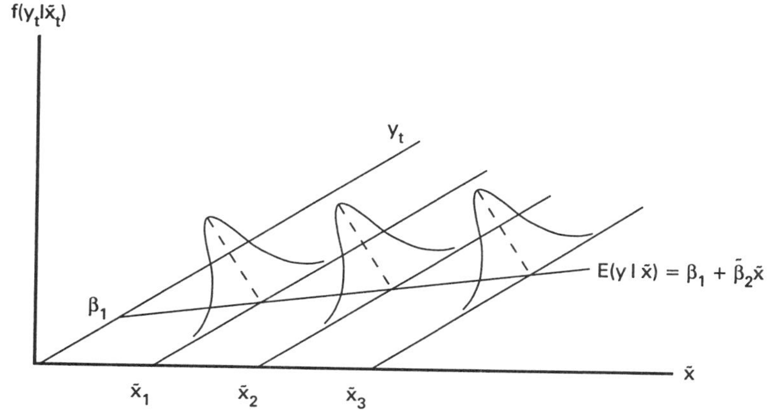

Figure 9.1.1
Standard simple linear normal regression model with $K = 2$

$$\tilde{\beta}_2 = \Sigma_{xx}^{-1}\sigma_{xy}, \tag{9.1.19}$$

$$\beta_1 = \mu_y - \mu_x'\tilde{\beta}_2. \tag{9.1.20}$$

Also suppose that y_t is variance-independent of $\tilde{x}_t$ (recall Exercise 2.7.12):

$$\mathrm{Var}(y_t|\tilde{x}_t) = \sigma^2 \ (t = 1, 2, \ldots, T), \tag{9.1.21}$$

where $\sigma^2 > 0$ is an unknown parameter. In matrix notation, independence, (9.1.18) and (9.1.21) can be summarized:

$$E(y|\tilde{X}) = X\beta, \tag{9.1.22}$$

$$\mathrm{Var}(y|\tilde{X}) = \sigma^2 I_T. \tag{9.1.23}$$

Finally, we assume $E[(X'X)^{-1}]$ exists.

Case II gives rise to the decomposition

$$y_t = x_t'\beta + u_t, \tag{9.1.24}$$

where both the systematic component $x_t'\beta$ and the nonsystematic component (*disturbance term*) $u_t \equiv y_t - x_t'\beta$ are random variables, and the latter satisfies[4]

4. Note that the conditioning in (9.1.25)–(9.1.26) is on the entire regressor matrix $\tilde{X}$ and not just on its corresponding row $\tilde{x}_t'$ or $\tilde{x}_i'$. This total conditionality is required in order for results in subsequent sections to go through. While clearly, for $t = 1, 2, \ldots, T$:

$E(u_t|\tilde{X}) = 0$ implies $E(u_t|\tilde{x}_t) = 0$,

$E(u_t^2|\tilde{X}) = \sigma^2$ implies $E(u_t^2|\tilde{x}_t) = \sigma^2$,

$E(u_t u_i|\tilde{X}) = 0$ implies $E(u_t|u_i|\tilde{x}_t, \tilde{x}_i) = 0$,

the converses are not necessarily true. If, however, $\tilde{x}_t$ $(t = 1, 2, \ldots, T)$ are i.i.d. as in the case at hand, then the converses hold.

$$E(u_t|\tilde{X}) = 0 \; (t = 1, 2, \ldots, T), \tag{9.1.25}$$

$$\text{Var}(u_t|\tilde{X}) = \sigma^2 \; (t = 1, 2, \ldots, T), \tag{9.1.26}$$

$$E(u_t u_j|\tilde{X}) = 0 \; (t \neq j; t, j = 1, 2, \ldots, T). \tag{9.1.27}$$

In matrix notation (9.1.25)–(9.1.27) can be written

$$y = X\beta + u, \tag{9.1.28}$$

$$E(u|\tilde{X}) = 0_T, \tag{9.1.29}$$

$$\text{Var}(u|\tilde{X}) = \sigma^2 I_T. \tag{9.1.30}$$

Because disturbance term properties (9.1.25) through (9.1.27) or (9.1.28) through (9.1.30) covering the conditional distribution $u|\tilde{X}$ do not involve $\tilde{X}$, they hold unconditionally as well, that is, u satisfies (9.1.12) through (9.1.13) (see Exercise 9.1.3). These assumptions stop short of asserting that u and $\tilde{X}$ are statistically independent; instead they assert a sufficient degree of weakness in the relationship between u and $\tilde{X}$ in order for most of the results in the fixed regressor case to carry over to the stochastic regressor case. Using iterated expectations (recall Theorem 2.6.8), or simply (9.1.16) and (9.1.17), the first two moments of y, unconditional of $\tilde{X}$, are

$$E(y) = \mu_y \iota_T, \tag{9.1.31}$$

$$\text{Var}(y) = \sigma_{yy} I_T. \tag{9.1.32}$$

Our discussion of Case II leads to the following terminology.

Definition 9.1.2 Under Case II, the model described by (9.1.16) through (9.1.32) is the *standard multiple linear regression model with stochastic regressors*. If in addition, Case II is augmented by the assumption that y has a multivariate normal distribution given $\tilde{X}$, then Case II corresponds to the *standard multiple linear normal regression model with stochastic regressors*, that is,

$$y|\tilde{X} \sim N_T(X\beta, \sigma^2 I_T), \tag{9.1.33}$$

$$u|\tilde{X} \sim N_T(0_T, \sigma^2 I_T), \tag{9.1.34}$$

where

$$\sigma^2 = \sigma_{yy} - \sigma'_{xy}[\Sigma_{xx}]^{-1}\sigma_{xy} = \sigma_{yy} - \tilde{\beta}'_2 \Sigma_{xx} \tilde{\beta}_2. \tag{9.1.35}$$

When the regression has a nonzero intercept and only one regressor (i.e. $K = 2$), then "multiple" is replaced by "simple." Note that no particular distributional family for the stochastic regressors is asserted.

There are many similarities and differences in Cases I and II. The following points are worth keeping in mind:

a. In contrast to Case I, Case II treats all observables as random variables.

b. Our discussion of Cases I and II has given priority emphasis to observables, using any assumptions concerning their stochastic nature to *derive* properties for unobservable disturbances. This emphasis on observables goes back to the seminal work of Haavelmo (1944), but was lost in subsequent econometric pedagogy. Today it has received somewhat of a resurgence in the British school of econometrics (see Spanos 1986). Of course emphasis on observables is also natural in the Bayesian approach.

c. Case I assumes only uncorrelated sampling, whereas Case II is predicated on independent sampling. Of course, if multivariate normality is also assumed in Case I, then independent sampling also occurs (Theorem 3.4.8d).

d. In Case I, assumption (9.1.1) implies $T \geq K$, that $X'X$ is positive definite (see Theorem A.8.3a), and hence that $(X'X)^{-1}$ exists. In contrast, while the assumed existence of $E[(X'X)^{-1}]$ (which goes beyond the assumed positive definiteness of Σ) in Case II does not guarantee the positive definiteness of $(X'X)^{-1}$ in every finite sample, under fairly weak additional assumptions the probability that $(X'X)^{-1}$ is positive definite approaches unity as $T \to \infty$.

e. The chief link between the two cases occurs in the specification of the conditional distribution of y_t given x_t in Case II. Note, however, that the conditioning in (9.1.18) defining the systematic component for Case II is on the random variable $\tilde{x}_t$, and is not just evaluated at a particular realization of $\tilde{x}_t$.[5] If this systematic component is defined only for the realized value of $\tilde{x}_t$, then Case II essentially reduces to Case I.

f. The randomness of the systematic component in Case II allows computation of the marginal moments of y. Equations (9.1.5) through (9.1.6) are in sharp contrast to (9.1.31) through (9.1.32). In Case I, y_t $(t = 1, 2, \ldots, T)$ are *not* identically distributed; in Case II, y_t $(t = 1, 2, \ldots, T)$ are identically distributed.

g. Both Cases I and II require the disturbance u_t to have constant variance. Such disturbances are said to be *homoskedastic*; otherwise the disturbances are said to be *heteroskedastic*.[6]

5. More carefully, the conditioning in Case II is on the "minimal σ-field generated by the random variable $\tilde{x}_t$" (see Spanos 1986, pp. 48–54, 412–415). Intuitively, conditioning y_t on the minimal σ-field generated by the random variable $\tilde{x}_t$ corresponds to considering the part of the random variable y_t associated with *all* events generated by the random variable $\tilde{x}_t$, and not just on the events corresponding to the realized value of $\tilde{x}_t$.

6. Alternative spellings are homoscedastic and heteroscedastic, respectively.

h. In Case II the independent sampling assumption together with *variance-independence* assumption (9.1.21) imply (9.1.30). In this case u_t and u_i are *covariance-independent* of $\tilde{X}$.

i. By Definition 2.7.1 a regression function focus attention on one particular aspect of the conditional distribution of $y_t|\tilde{x}_t$, namely, its mean. In contrast *quantile regression* focuses attention on particular quantiles of this conditional distribution (e.g., its median), and in situations where normality assumptions are suspect, quantile regression can be an attractive alternative (e.g., see Koenker and Bassett 1978 and Koenker 1982).

j. Independent sampling from a multivariate normal distribution, that is, (i.e., $z_t|\mu, \Sigma \sim$ i.i.d. $N_K(\mu_z, \Sigma_{zz})$ is sufficient to imply all assumptions characterizing the standard multiple linear normal regression model with stochastic regressors, and in addition, implies $\tilde{x}_t|\mu, \Sigma \sim$ i.i.d. $N_{K-1}(\mu_x, \Sigma_{xx})$. This multivariate normal sampling model plays a crucial role in the distributional theory of Section 9.4 underlying confidence intervals and hypothesis tests in Case II models.

Expanding on (j), assessing the incremental impact of the assumptions of linearity in the conditioning variables, variance independence and multivariate normality enhances understanding of Case II. As previously noted (see Theorem 2.7.5), simply choosing to decompose y_t into its conditional mean and u_t is enough to obtain (9.1.25), mean-independence of u_t from $\tilde{x}_t$, and $\text{Cov}(\tilde{x}_t, u_t) = 0$. The independent sampling assumption of Case II implies

$$\begin{aligned}
E(u_t u_i|\tilde{x}_t) &= \int_{-\infty}^{\infty}\int_{-\infty}^{\infty} u_t u_i f(u_t, u_i|\tilde{x}_t, \tilde{x}_i)\, du_t\, du_i \\
&= \int_{-\infty}^{\infty}\int_{-\infty}^{\infty} u_t u_i \left[\frac{f(u_t, \tilde{x}_t) f(u_i, \tilde{x}_i)}{f(\tilde{x}_t) f(\tilde{x}_i)}\right] du_t\, du_i \\
&= \left[\int_{-\infty}^{\infty} u_t f(u_t|\tilde{x}_t)\, du_t\right]\left[\int_{-\infty}^{\infty} u_i f(u_i|\tilde{x}_i)\, du_i\right] \\
&= E(u_t|\tilde{x}_t) E(u_i|\tilde{x}_i) = 0 \qquad (9.1.36)
\end{aligned}$$

for $t \neq i$, (9.1.26) and

$$E(y_t y_i|\tilde{X}) = 0 (t \neq i). \qquad (9.1.37)$$

Linearity in the conditioning variables implies the disturbance can be written

$$\begin{aligned}
u_t &= y_t - \beta_1 - \tilde{x}_t'\tilde{\beta}_2 \\
&= (y_t - \mu_y) - (\tilde{x}_t - \mu_x)'\tilde{\beta}_2. \qquad (9.1.38)
\end{aligned}$$

Independent sampling and linearity together imply the conditional variance

$$\begin{aligned}\operatorname{Var}(y_t|\tilde{X}) &= \operatorname{Var}(u_t|\tilde{X}) = \operatorname{Var}(y_t|\tilde{x}_t) = \operatorname{Var}(u_t|\tilde{x}_t)\\ &= E(u_t^2|\tilde{x}_t) = E[(y_t - \mu_y)^2|\tilde{x}_t] - 2\tilde{\beta}'(\tilde{x}_t - \mu_x)[E(y_y|\tilde{x}_t) - \mu_y]\\ &\quad + \tilde{\beta}_2'(\tilde{x}_t - \mu_x)(\tilde{x}_t - \mu_x)'\tilde{\beta}_2\\ &= E[(y_t - \mu_y)^2|\tilde{x}_t] - \tilde{\beta}_2'(\tilde{x}_t - \mu_x)(\tilde{x}_t - \mu_x)'\tilde{\beta}_2. \end{aligned} \tag{9.1.39}$$

From (9.1.39) it follows [see Exercise 9.1.6(a)] that the unconditional variance is

$$\begin{aligned}E[\operatorname{Var}(y_t|\tilde{x}_t)] &= E[\operatorname{Var}(u_t|\tilde{x}_t)]\\ &= \sigma_{yy} - \tilde{\beta}_2'\Sigma_{xx}\tilde{\beta}_2. \end{aligned} \tag{9.1.40}$$

Equation (9.1.40) implies that independent sampling and linearity of the conditional mean of y_t given $\tilde{x}_t$ imply a disturbance u_t which on *average* (averaging over $\tilde{x}_t$) has variance (9.1.40). This does not imply, however, that $\operatorname{Var}(u_t|\tilde{x}_t)$ equals some constant σ^2 not depending on $\tilde{x}_t$ as homoskedasticity condition (9.1.21) asserts. For example, a random sample drawn from a multivariate t-distribution with $v > 2$ yields a *linear* regression curve for y_t given $\tilde{x}_t$, but a conditional variance for y_t given $\tilde{x}_t$ that involves a *quadratic* form in $\tilde{x}_t$ (recall Theorem 3.4.10). A sufficient, and nearly necessary, condition that rationalizes (9.1.18) and (9.1.21) is random sampling from a multivariate normal distribution (Theorem 3.4.6). One of the most striking assumptions embodied in the windows discussed in this chapter is that the effects of $\tilde{x}_t$ on y_t are confined to the first moment of y_t. Weakening this assumption is discussed in Chapter 10, but for now, note that in the Case I (fixed regressors), there are few guidelines available on exactly how to incorporate dependency of $\operatorname{Var}(y_t)$ on $\tilde{x}_t$. In the stochastic regressor Case II, however, a distributional assumption on $z_t = [y_t, \tilde{x}_t']'$ not only implies $\operatorname{Var}(y_t|\tilde{x}_t)$, but also it often implies very parsimonious structures for $\operatorname{Var}(y_t|\tilde{x}_t)$.

The preceding developments presuppose that attention focuses on the distribution of one element in z_t, y_t, given all remaining elements $\tilde{x}_t$. This is not so in all cases. Suppose there are $m = 2$ potential regressands: $y_t = [y_{t1}, y_{t2}]'$. There are many ways of factoring the joint density $f(y_{t1}, y_{t2}, \tilde{x}_t)$, two of which are:

$$f(y_{t1}, y_{t2}, \tilde{x}_t) = f(y_{t1}|y_{t2}, \tilde{x}_t)f(y_{t2}, \tilde{x}_t) \tag{9.1.41a}$$

$$= f(y_{t1}, y_{t2}|\tilde{x}_t)f(\tilde{x}_t). \tag{9.1.41b}$$

Which factorization to choose depends on the purposes of the analysis as embodied in the *distribution of interest* (DOI) (recall Definition 8.1.1). The DOI reflects the goals of the analysis. Even if all distributions are fully known, and so no estimation or testing problems are present, there still remains the question of prediction of future observables. Often the researcher casts such predictive questions in the form of *scenario forecasts* describing the distribution of some subset of y_{t1}, y_{t2}, and $\tilde{x}_t$, given the remaining elements. For example, (9.1.41a) suggests the DOI corresponds to the density $f(y_{t1}|y_{t2}, \tilde{x}_t)$, whereas (9.1.41b) suggests the DOI corresponds to $f(y_{t1}, y_{t2}|\tilde{x}_t)$. The decision as to the DOI also leads to a choice of a systematic component, and hence, to a choice for the disturbance u_t. In each case properties of u_t are *derived* from more fundamental assumptions regarding the fundamental entity $f(y_{t1}, y_{t2}, \tilde{x}_t)$. To illustrate the issues involved, consider the following example developed along the lines of Case II.

Example 9.1.1 Suppose $K = 2$ and $z_t = [y_{t1}, y_{t2}, \tilde{x}_t]'$ has a trivariate normal distribution. The density $f(y_{t1}, y_{t2}|\tilde{x}_t)$ is given by the bivariate normal density

$$\phi_2(y_t|E[y_t|\tilde{x}_t], \Lambda), \tag{9.1.42}$$

where

$$E[y_t|\tilde{x}_t] = \alpha + \pi\tilde{x}_t, \tag{9.1.43}$$

$$\pi = \begin{bmatrix} \pi_1 \\ \pi_2 \end{bmatrix} = \begin{bmatrix} \sigma_{y_1x}/\sigma_{xx} \\ \sigma_{y_2x}/\sigma_{xx} \end{bmatrix}, \tag{9.1.44}$$

$$\alpha = \begin{bmatrix} \alpha_1 \\ \alpha_2 \end{bmatrix} = \begin{bmatrix} \mu_{y_1} \\ \mu_{y_2} \end{bmatrix} - \pi\mu_x, \tag{9.1.45}$$

$$\begin{aligned} \Lambda = \begin{bmatrix} \lambda_{11} & \lambda_{12} \\ \lambda_{12} & \lambda_{22} \end{bmatrix} &= \text{Var}(y_t|\tilde{x}_t) \\ &= \begin{bmatrix} \sigma_{y_1y_1} & \sigma_{y_1y_2} \\ \sigma_{y_1y_2} & \sigma_{y_2y_2} \end{bmatrix} - \frac{1}{\sigma_{xx}}\begin{bmatrix} \sigma_{y_1x} \\ \sigma_{y_2x} \end{bmatrix}[\sigma_{y_1x}, \sigma_{y_2x}]'. \end{aligned} \tag{9.1.46}$$

Define

$$v_t = [v_{t1}, v_{t2}]' = y_t - E(y_t|\tilde{x}_t). \tag{9.1.47}$$

Then (9.1.42) through (9.1.47) implies the multivariate regression

$$\begin{aligned} \begin{bmatrix} y_{t1} \\ y_{t2} \end{bmatrix} &= \alpha + \pi\tilde{x}_t + v_t \\ &= \begin{bmatrix} \alpha_1 \\ \alpha_2 \end{bmatrix} + \begin{bmatrix} \pi_1 \\ \pi_2 \end{bmatrix}\tilde{x}_t + \begin{bmatrix} v_{t1} \\ v_{t2} \end{bmatrix}, \end{aligned} \tag{9.1.48}$$

with the disturbance

$$v_t|\tilde{x}_t \sim N_2(0_2, \Lambda). \tag{9.1.49}$$

Now let $\Gamma = [1, -\gamma]'$, where γ is an unspecified parameter, and form the linear combination $\Gamma' y_t$. Then using Theorem 3.4.7(a):

$$\Gamma' y_t | \tilde{x}_t \sim N(\Gamma'[\alpha + \pi \tilde{x}_t], \Gamma' \Lambda \Gamma), \tag{9.1.50}$$

or equivalently,

$$y_{t1} = [1, y_{t2}, \tilde{x}_t]\delta + \varepsilon_t, \tag{9.1.51}$$

where

$$\begin{aligned} \delta &= [\Gamma'\alpha, \gamma, \Gamma'\pi]' \\ &= [\alpha_1 - \gamma\alpha_2, \gamma, (\sigma_{y_1 x} - \gamma\sigma_{y_2 x})/\sigma_{xx})', \end{aligned} \tag{9.1.52}$$

$$\varepsilon_t = v_{t1} - \gamma v_{t2}. \tag{9.1.53}$$

$$\varepsilon_t | \tilde{x}_t \sim N_2(0_2, \Gamma' \Lambda \Gamma). \tag{9.1.54}$$

Although (9.1.51) may superficially resemble (9.1.24), there are important differences. As derived, δ is not identifiable since γ is totally arbitrary in the absence of additional restrictions. Furthermore, unlike the disturbance u_t in (9.1.24), which satisfies (9.1.25), ε_t in (9.1.54) does not. In particular, although $\text{Cov}(\varepsilon_t, \tilde{x}_t) = 0$,

$$\begin{aligned} \text{Cov}(\varepsilon_t, y_{t2}) &= E(\varepsilon_t y_{t2}) = E[\varepsilon_t(\alpha_2 + \pi_2 \tilde{x}_t + v_{t2})] \\ &= E(\varepsilon_t v_{t2}) = E[(v_{t1} - \gamma v_{t2})v_{t2}] \\ &= \text{Cov}(v_{t1}, v_{t2}) - \gamma \,\text{Var}(v_{t2}) \end{aligned} \tag{9.1.55}$$

which in general is nonzero. Thus (9.1.25) does *not* hold in general. For the particular value $\gamma = \text{Cov}(v_{t1}, v_{t2})/\text{Var}(v_{t2})$, (9.1.25) holds and in fact $\delta = \beta$.

An example when the density $f(y_{t1}, y_{t2} | \tilde{x}_t)$ would be of interest is the following. Confronted with price-quantity market data, the conditional distribution of quantity given price, or price given quantity, is *not* of primary interest since price and quantity are jointly determined by the market mechanism. In such cases interest is more appropriately directed toward the *joint* distribution of price and quantity, given other variables, and falls in the realm of simultaneous equations models. The following example elaborates on this point.[7]

Example 9.1.2 Consider a market equilibrium in period t ($t = 1, 2, \ldots, T$) in which $y_{t1} \equiv$ equilibrium quantity exchanged on the market, $y_{t2} \equiv$ equilibrium price, and $\tilde{x}_t \equiv$ wealth of consumers. For purposes of simplicity we condition on $\tilde{x}_t$, and focus interest on the distribution of y_{t1} and y_{t2}, which are jointly determined in the marketplace. Under the assumptions

7. Also see Exercise 9.1.7, which introduces a classic errors-in-variables problem in which the distribution of interest is the conditional distribution of y_t given an unobserved regressor $\tilde{x}_t^*$ and not the conditional distribution of y_t given the observed measurement-error-plagued regressor $\tilde{x}_t$.

of Example 9.1.1, we are led to the two equations in (9.1.48). These equations do not correspond to "demand" or "supply" curves since each contains only one of the jointly determined variables. To draw on the theoretical constructs "demand" and "supply" we first form two linear combinations of (9.1.48) analogous to the single linear combination in (9.1.51). Letting

$$\Gamma' = \begin{bmatrix} 1 & -\gamma_1 \\ 1 & -\gamma_2 \end{bmatrix}, \tag{9.1.56}$$

we can obtain analogous to (9.1.51) the two equations:

$$y_{t1} = [1, y_{t2}, \tilde{x}_t]\delta_1 + \varepsilon_{t1}, \tag{9.1.57}$$

$$y_{t1} = [1, y_{t2}, \tilde{x}_t]\delta_2 + \varepsilon_{t2}, \tag{9.1.58}$$

where

$$\delta_1 = \left[\alpha_1 - \gamma_1\alpha_2, \gamma_1, \frac{\sigma_{y_1x} - \gamma_1\sigma_{y_2x}}{\sigma_{xx}}\right]', \tag{9.1.59}$$

$$\delta_2 = \left[\alpha_1 - \gamma_2\alpha_2, \gamma_2, \frac{\sigma_{y_1x} - \gamma_2\sigma_{y_2x}}{\sigma_{xx}}\right]', \tag{9.1.60}$$

$$\varepsilon_t \equiv [\varepsilon_{t1}, \varepsilon_{t2}]' = \Gamma' v_t = [v_{t1} - \gamma_1 v_{t2}, v_{t1} - \gamma_2 v_{t2}]', \tag{9.1.61}$$

$$\varepsilon_t | z_t \sim N_2(0_2, \Gamma'\Lambda\Gamma). \tag{9.1.62}$$

Becuase γ_1 and γ_2 are arbitrary, the parameters in (9.1.57) and (9.1.58) are not identified. Suppose, however, the researcher asserts based on prior information that wealth $\tilde{x}_t$ does not enter the supply curve. This belief is held dogmatically. Without loss of generality suppose the supply curve is (9.1.58). Then $\delta_{23} = 0$. The parameters of supply curve are then identified, but the parameters of demand curve (9.1.57) remain unidentified.

Insight into these issues can be obtained from Figure 9.1.2. All observations are assumed randomly distributed around market equilibrium, that is, the point of intersection of the demand and supply curves. As wealth $\tilde{x}$ varies across the sample observations, say $\tilde{x} = w_j$ $(j = 1, 2, 3)$, the demand curve shifts, but by assumption the supply curve remains fixed (since $\delta_{23} = 0$). Therefore, shifting of the demand curve traces out the supply curve.

Examples 9.1.1 and 9.1.2 are intended to emphasize the importance of clear articulation of the distribution of interest, before considering a linear stochastic equation like (returning to the case $m = 1$)

$$y_t = \beta_1 + \tilde{x}_t'\tilde{\beta}_2 + u_t = x_t'\beta + u_t. \tag{9.1.63}$$

The disturbance u_t is *defined* to be $y_t - x_t'\beta$, and it inherits its statistical properties from the assumptions made regarding the systematic part $x_t'\beta$. Regression is intended to address problems where $f(y_t|\tilde{x}_t)$ is the DOI. Cases involving the joint distribution of y_t and some subset of the elements

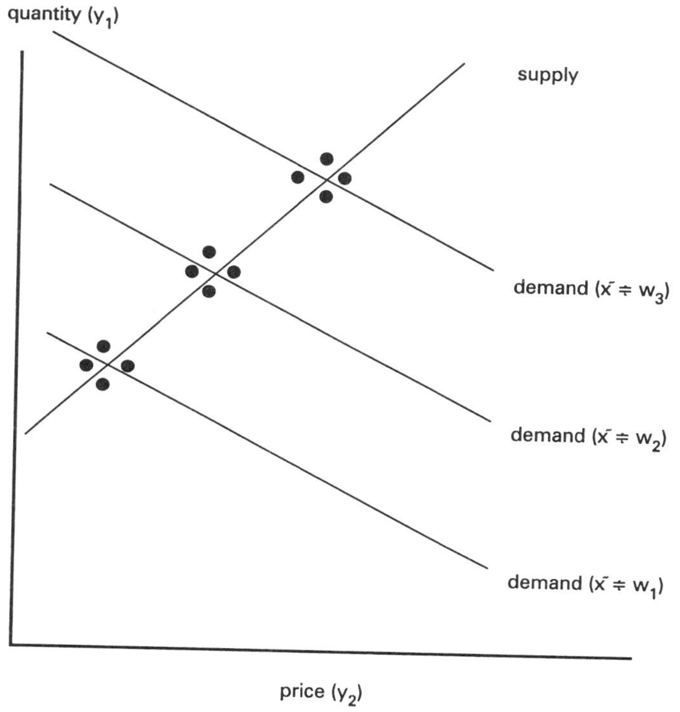

Figure 9.1.2
Example 9.1.2: Demand and supply

in $\tilde{x}_t$, given the remaining elements in $\tilde{x}_t$, are *not* (in general) best addressed by regression methods. The theorist's thought experiment and the goals of the analysis *dictate* the distribution of interest. Treating $\tilde{x}_t$ as a fixed constant necessitates interest in the *marginal* distribution of $f(y_t)$ and rules-out a host of econometric issues.

Under Case II just writing down (9.1.63) does not permit identification of β nor assessment of the properties of u_t unless additional information is available. For example, consider the simple regression ($K = 2$)

$$y_t = \beta_1 + \tilde{\beta}_2 \tilde{x}_t + u_t. \tag{9.1.64}$$

Without identifying $\tilde{\beta}_2$ or interpreting u_t, the assertion $E(u_t|\tilde{x}_t) = 0$ has no bite. Imposing $E(u_t|\tilde{x}_t) = 0$ in (9.1.64) implies that $E(u_t^*|\tilde{x}_t) \neq 0$ in

$$y_t = \beta_1 + \tilde{\beta}_2^* \tilde{x}_t + u_t^*, \tag{9.1.65}$$

where $\tilde{\beta}_2^* \equiv \tilde{\beta}_2 + 1$ and $u_t^* \equiv u_t - \tilde{x}_t$. Similarly, imposing $E(u_t^*|\tilde{x}_t) = 0$ in (9.1.65) implies $E(u_t|\tilde{x}_t) \neq 0$ in (9.1.64). Which assumption is more reasonable requires identifying more precisely $\tilde{\beta}_2$ and u_t.

Finally, the use of the term "linearity" in this section warrants some explanation. The "linearity" refers to the linearity of $E(y_t|\tilde{x}_t)$ in the unknown regression coefficients β, not in the regressors $\tilde{x}_t$, which also appear linearly. For example, there may exist a variable r such that $\tilde{x}_t = [r_t, r_t^2]'$ and

$$E(y_t|\tilde{x}_t) = \beta_1 + \tilde{x}_t'\tilde{\beta}_2 = \beta_1 + \beta_2 r_t + \beta_3 r_t^2, \tag{9.1.66}$$

where $\tilde{\beta}_2 = [\beta_2, \beta_3]'$. Although (9.1.66) is quadratic in r_t, it is linear in the regression coefficients $\beta = [\beta_1, \beta_2, \beta_3]'$, and hence (9.1.66) is still considered a linear regression although it constitutes a nonlinear relationship between y_t and r_t. In such cases, r_t alone is often referred to as the *explanatory variable*, and r_t and r_t^2 together are referred to as the regressors.

Models that are not themselves linear in parameters, but which can be transformed into models of the form (9.1.25) are said to be *intrinsically linear*. For example,

$$\tilde{y}_t = \exp(\beta_1 + \tilde{x}_t'\tilde{\beta}_2 + u_t) \tag{9.1.67}$$

is intrinsically linear since it can be transformed into the semi-logarithmic form

$$y_t = \ln(\tilde{y}_t) = \beta_1 + \tilde{x}_t'\tilde{\beta}_2 + u_t. \tag{9.1.68}$$

In contrast, the model

$$\tilde{y}_t = [\exp(\beta_1 + \tilde{x}_t'\tilde{\beta}_2)] + u_t \tag{9.1.69}$$

is *intrinsically nonlinear*.

Exercises

9.1.1 Consider (9.1.25) in the case $K = 2$. Show that the standardized value of $E(y_t|\tilde{x}_t)$, that is, $[E(y_t|\tilde{x}_t) - \mu_y]/\sigma_{yy}^{1/2}$, is closer to zero than the standardized value of $[\tilde{x}_t - E(\tilde{x}_t)]/\sigma_{xx}^{1/2}$. Relate this fact to Galton's studies of heredity. Can a similar statement be made regarding $[E(\tilde{x}_t|y_t) - \mu_x]/\sigma_{xx}^{1/2}$ and $[y_t - E(y_t)]/\sigma_{yy}^{1/2}$?

9.1.2 Consider two random variables x and y with joint p.d.f.: $f(x, y) = y^2 \exp[-y(x + 1)]$ for $x \geq 0$, $y \geq 0$, and equalling zero otherwise.

(a) Show that the marginal p.d.f. of x is: $f_x(x) = 2(x + 1)^{-3}$ for $x \geq 0$, and equalling zero otherwise.

(b) Show that the marginal p.d.f. of y is: $f_y(y) = y[\exp(-y)]$ if $y \geq 0$, and equalling zero otherwise.

(c) Using $\Gamma(4) = \int_0^\infty v^3 \exp(-v)\,dv = 3! = 6$, show $E(y|x) = 3/(x + 1)$. Graph $E(y|x)$.

(d) Show that the best linear approximation to $E(y|x)$ has $\beta_1 = 2$ and $\beta_2 = 0$. Note: $\text{Var}(x) = \infty$.

(e) Show that $E(x|y) = y^{-1}$.

(f) Show that the best linear approximation to $E(x|y)$ has $\beta_1 = 2$, $\beta_2 = -\frac{1}{2}$.

9.1.3 Show that (9.1.29) and (9.1.30) imply (9.1.12) through (9.1.13).

9.1.4 Suppose $z = [y, \tilde{x}]'$ has a bivariate normal distribution with zero means, unit variances, and correlation ρ. Show each of the following:

(a) $E(y^2|\tilde{x}^2) = 1 + \rho^2(\tilde{x}^2 - 1)$.

(b) $E(y|\tilde{x}^2) = 0$.

9.1.5 Let x and y be random variables such that $z_1 \equiv \ln x$ and $z_2 \equiv \ln y$ have a bivariate normal distribution which means μ_1 and μ_2, variances σ_1^2 and σ_2^2, and correlation ρ.

(a) Find $E(y|x)$.

(b) Find $\mathrm{Var}(y|x)$.

9.1.6 Suppose $E(y|\tilde{x}) = \beta_1 + \beta_2\tilde{x}$.

(a) Show that $E[\mathrm{Var}(y|\tilde{x})] = \mathrm{Var}(y) - [\mathrm{Cov}(y, \tilde{x})]^2/\mathrm{Var}(\tilde{x})$.

(b) Suppose in addition that $\mathrm{Var}(y|\tilde{x})$ does not depend on $\tilde{x}$. Then show that $\mathrm{Var}(y|\tilde{x}) = \mathrm{Var}(y) - [\mathrm{Cov}(y, \tilde{x})]^2/\mathrm{Var}(\tilde{x})$.

(c) Relate (a) and (b) to the case in which it is also known that y and $\tilde{x}$ have a bivariate normal distribution.

9.1.7 Let x^* and y be random variables such that $E(y|x^*) = \beta x^*$. Define $u \equiv y - E(y|x^*)$. Suppose that x^* is not observed, but rather only the proxy variable $\tilde{x} = x^* + v$. Assume that u, v and x^* are independent normal random variables with zero means and variances σ_u^2, σ_v^2, and σ_*^2, respectively.

(a) Show that $y = \beta\tilde{x} + w$, where $w \equiv u - \beta v$.

(b) Find the joint distribution of $\tilde{x}$ and w.

(c) Find $E(y|\tilde{x})$.

9.1.8 Consider the trivariate density $f(y_t, w_t, z_t)$. Express $E(y_t|z_t)$ as a function of $E(y_t|w_t, z_t)$.

9.1.9 Suppose two random variables X and Y have the bivariate Pareto p.d.f.:

$$f(y, x) = \theta(\theta + 1)(c_1c_2)^{\theta+1}[c_2y + c_1x - c_1c_2]^{-(\theta+2)}, \tag{9.1.70}$$

where $y > c_1 > 0$, $x > c_2 > 0$ and $\theta > 0$.

(a) Find $E(y|x)$.

(b) Find $\mathrm{Var}(y|x)$.

9.1.10 Suppose two random variables X and Y have a bivariate logistic p.d.f.:

$$f(y, x) = 2[1 + \exp(-y) + \exp(-x)]^{-3}\exp[-(y + x)], \tag{9.1.71}$$

where $y > 0$, $x > 0$.

(a) Find $E(y|x)$.

(b) Find $\mathrm{Var}(y|x)$.

9.1.11 Suppose X and Y have Gumbel's bivariate exponential c.d.f.:

$$F(y, x) = 1 - \exp(-y) - \exp(-x) + \exp[-(y + x + \theta yx)], \tag{9.1.72}$$

where $y > 0$, $x > 0$ and $0 \le \theta \le 1$.

(a) Find $E(y|x)$.

(b) Find $\mathrm{Var}(y|x)$.

9.1.12 Which of the following is intrinsically linear? If intrinsically linear, then show it. Also compute the derivative $d[E(y_t|\tilde{x}_t)]/d\tilde{x}_t$ and the elasticity $\{d[E(y_t|\tilde{x}_t)]/d\tilde{x}_t\} \times \{\tilde{x}_2/[E(y_t|\tilde{x}_t)]\}$.

(a) $y_t = \beta_1\tilde{x}_{t2}^{\beta_2}u_t$

(b) $y_t = [\beta_1 + \beta_2\tilde{x}_{t2}]u_t$

(c) $y_t = \beta_1 + \beta_{t2}\tilde{x}_{t2}^{-1} + u_t$

(d) $y_t^{-1} = \alpha + \beta\tilde{x}_2^{-1} + u_t$

(e) $y_t = \exp[\beta_1 + \beta_2\tilde{x}_{t2} + u_t]$

(f) $y_t = \exp[\beta_1 + \beta_2\tilde{x}_{t2}] + u_t$

(g) $y_t = \dfrac{1}{1 + \exp(\beta_1 + \beta_2\tilde{x}_{t2} + u_t)}$

9.2 Classical Estimation in Multiple Linear Normal Regression

This section and the next depart somewhat from the likelihood based approach of this text, and consider the sampling properties of estimators of coefficients in regression models that do not depend on explicit distributional assumptions. Although the standard multiple linear normal regression model with fixed or stochastic regressor is used to suggest the estimators, these two sections only consider sampling properties that do not depend on the multivariate normality assumption embodied in the standard multiple linear normal regression model with fixed or stochastic regressors. Further distributional results for these frameworks are addressed in Section 9.4.

Consider the standard multiple linear normal regression model with fixed or stochastic regressors

$$y = X\beta + u. \tag{9.2.1}$$

The parameters of interest, defined as $\lambda = [\beta', \sigma^2]'$, are assumed to be those of the conditional distribution of y_t, given the $K - 1$ regressors $\tilde{x}_t$.

Under the assumption of fixed regressors, $u \sim N(0_T, \sigma^2 I_T)$ and $y \sim N(X\beta, \sigma^2 I_T)$.[8] Hence, the log-likelihood function of the sample is

$$\begin{aligned} L(\beta, \sigma^2 | y) &\equiv \ln[(2\pi)^{-T/2}|\sigma^2 I_T|^{-1/2}\exp\{-\tfrac{1}{2}(y - X\beta)'(\sigma^2 I_T)^{-1}(y - X\beta)\}] \\ &= -(T/2)\ln(2\pi\sigma^2) - (y - X\beta)'(y - X\beta)/2\sigma^2. \end{aligned} \tag{9.2.2}$$

In contrast, under stochastic regressors $u|X \sim N(0_T, \sigma^2 I_T)$, $y|X \sim N(X\beta, \sigma^2 I_T)$, and the log-likelihood of the data $z \equiv [y, \tilde{X}]$ is

$$\begin{aligned} L(\lambda, \xi | z) &= \ln[f(y|\tilde{X}, \lambda)g(\tilde{X}|\theta)] \\ &= L(\beta, \sigma^2 | y) + \ln[g(\tilde{X}|\theta)], \end{aligned} \tag{9.2.3}$$

where $g(\tilde{X}|\theta)$ denotes the marginal p.d.f. of $\tilde{X}$ and $\theta = [\lambda', \xi']'$. If the nuisance parameters ξ fully characterize the marginal distribution of

8. Note that although u_t $(t = 1, 2, \ldots, T)$ are i.i.d., y_t $(t = 1, 2, \ldots, T)$ are i.n.i.d. because the latter have different means.

$\tilde{X}$ (i.e. $g(\tilde{X}|\theta) = g(\tilde{X}|\xi)$] and there are no restrictions across ξ and the parameters of interest λ, then λ and ξ are said to be *variation-free*, and $\tilde{X}$ is said to be *weakly exogenous* in the sense of Engle, Hendry and Richard (1983). In this case it is clear that maximizing (9.2.3) with respect to λ and ξ yields the same maximum likelihood (ML) estimator of β and σ^2 and obtained from maximizing (9.2.2). In addition maximizing (9.2.3) yields the ML estimator of ξ, which depends on the postulated p.d.f. $g(\tilde{X}|\xi)$. This section is only concerned with estimation of β and σ^2.

Direct inspection of (9.2.2) suggests the estimator of β, which maximizes (9.2.2) can also be viewed as the estimator that minimizes the *least squares criterion*:

$$\mathrm{SSE}(\beta) \equiv \sum_{t=1}^{T} (y_t - x_t'\beta)^2 = (y - X\beta)'(y - X\beta). \tag{9.2.4}$$

Even without reference to a normality assumption and likelihood (9.2.2), an intuitively reasonable way to proceed in choosing an estimator $\hat{\beta} = [\hat{\beta}_1, \hat{\beta}_2, \ldots, \hat{\beta}_K]'$ is to make the observed errors $y_t - x_t'\hat{\beta}_t$ $(t = 1, 2, \ldots, T)$ as small as possible. Although there are many competing metrics in which to define "small," the most popular choice is the squared Euclidean length of $\hat{u} = y - \hat{y} = y - X\hat{\beta}$, that is, the sum of squared errors in (9.2.4).[9] Sections 9.2 and 9.3 consider the first two moments of the sampling distribution of the *ordinary least squares* (OLS) estimator $b = [b_1, b_2, \ldots, b_K]'$, defined as an estimator that minimizes (9.2.4), based solely on the multiple linear regression model with either fixed or stochastic regressors, without invoking a multivariate normality assumption. In addition, this section also investigates the sampling moments of estimators of σ^2.

The method of least squares appears to have been proposed independently by Gauss and Legendre. Supposedly, the basic idea occurred to Gauss in the autumn of 1794 when he was seventeen years old, but the first published account was in an astronomy book published in 1805 by Legendre. In 1806 Gauss completed a book but it was not published until 1809 because of difficulty in finding a publisher. In his book Gauss referred to his "discovery" of least squares which led to a heated debate

9. For example, one prominent competitor to (9.2.4) is based on minimizing the sum of absolute values of the errors. Although the resulting estimator, known as the *minimum (or least) absolute deviation (MAD or LAD) estimator*, can be motivated as the MLE based on a Laplace distribution (see Exercise 6.6.2d), it is usually motivated by its general robustness of sampling properties across a variety of underlying data distributions—including those with tails much thicker than the normal distribution. See Bassett and Koenker (1978) for a discussion of MAD estimators.

between himself and Legendre over the priority of discovery. For an interesting account of the debate, see Plackett (1972).

The estimate $\hat{\beta} = b$ that minimizes (9.2.4) can be found by solving the first-order conditions (commonly called the *normal equations*) using the differentiation rules of Appendix B:

$$\frac{\partial \, \mathrm{SSE}(b)}{\partial \beta} = -2X'(y - Xb) = 0_K, \tag{9.2.5a}$$

or equivalently,

$$(X'X)b = X'y. \tag{9.2.5b}$$

If the regressors are fixed, then (9.1.1) implies that $X'X$ is positive definite, and hence $(X'X)^{-1}$ exists. Hence, (9.2.5b) can be solved to yield the OLS estimator

$$b = (X'X)^{-1}X'y. \tag{9.2.6}$$

Because

$$\frac{\partial^2 \, \mathrm{SSE}(\beta)}{\partial \beta \, \partial \beta'} = 2(X'X) \tag{9.2.7}$$

is positive definite for all β, b given by (9.2.6) corresponds to the unique minimum of (9.2.4). If the regressors are random, then $X'X$ is not guaranteed to be positive definite in the realized sample, but it is expected to be since the population counterpart $E[(X'X)]$ is assumed to be positive definite. In fact the weak law of large numbers implies $T^{-1}X'X$ approaches $E[(X'X)]$ in probability as $T \to \infty$.

It should be noted that in the case of fixed regressors the OLS solution (9.2.6) corresponds to the least squares approximate solution defined in Definition A.5.1. In that setting we are trying to find an approximate solution to the *inconsistent* (i.e. over-determined) set of equations $y = X\beta$. According to Theorem A.5.3(i), the generalized inverse of X is $X^+ = (X'X)^{-1}X'$ and Theorem A.5.6(c) implies $b = X^+y = (X'X)^{-1}X'y$ is the unique minimum norm least squares approximate solution. Thus, although not mentioned explicitly, generalized inverses are relevant to the present discussion. It will be seen later that generalized inverses are especially relevant when discussing situations involving violation of (9.1.1), that is, perfect multicollinearity.

The *sampling error* of b is

$$b - \beta = (X'X)^{-1}X'(X\beta + u) - \beta = (X'X)^{-1}X'u. \tag{9.2.8}$$

Using (9.2.8) as a basis, the following theorem gives the first two sampling moments of b under both Cases I and II. Because these cases describe different sampling schemes, they give rise to two different sampling distributions. These two distributions have the same first moments, but different second moments. The differences reflect the importance placed on the sample space in frequentist statistics. Because the sample spaces are different for Cases I and II, it is not surprising that different sampling results are obtained.[10] Choice between these sampling distributions is a question of fundamental importance in classical regression analysis (recall Section 6.10), but it receives little attention in econometrics textbooks.

The appropriate classical solution would seem to be that of the "conditional frequentist." Because the weak exogeneity assumption for $\tilde{x}_t$ implies that $\tilde{X}$ is ancillary (i.e., its distribution does not depend on the parameters of interest β and σ^2 [Definition 5.2.2]), conditional frequentists advocate investigating the sampling properties of estimators conditional on these ancillary statistics—in other words, treating the regressors "as if" they are fixed—essentially Case I (recall note 10). From a pedagogical standpoint this can be confusing because in many econometric windows beyond regression analysis (e.g., Example 9.1.2), the regressors are no longer ancillary for the parameters of interest, and the fixed regressor Case I serves as a poor prototype for sampling analysis. Furthermore, whether the actual sampling process that gave rise to the data involved fixing $\tilde{X}$ and then drawing y conditional on these fixed values $\tilde{X}$, is immaterial from this viewpoint.

In order to offer a pedagogically complete analysis of the frequentist perspective, the discussion here will cover both Case I and Case II. Readers who are uncomfortable with these details of the sampling perspective and the need to keep track of two different sampling distributions might be comforted to know that the distinction between Case I and Case II will be immaterial in Sections 9.9 and 9.10. Those sections, however, discuss Bayesian analysis of regression models, and therefore condition on all the data (as recommended by the LP), treating y and $\tilde{x}$ symmetrically. These differences reinforce the point made in Section 6.10 that *conditioning lies at the basis of most debates in statistics.*

The following theorem provides the first two sampling moments of the OLS estimator under Cases I and II.

10. In fact there is a third possible sampling distribution of interest, namely, Case II but where the conditional sampling distribution of y_t given $\tilde{x}_t$ is sought. Because this amounts to random regressors but for which conditional sampling properties are sought, this case reduces in all practical aspects back to the fixed regressors in Case I, and so it will not be treated separately.

Theorem 9.2.1 Let b be the OLS estimator (9.2.6).

(a) Consider the multiple linear regression model with fixed regressors (Case I).[11] Then the following results hold:

(i) $E_{y|\lambda}(b) = \beta$,

(ii) $\text{Var}_{y|\lambda}(b) = \sigma^2(X'X)^{-1}$.

(b) Consider the multiple linear regression model with stochastic regressors (Case II). Then the following results hold:

(i) $E_{y,\tilde{X}|\theta}(b) = \beta$,

(ii) $\text{Var}_{y,\tilde{X}|\theta}(\text{b}) = \sigma^2 E_{\tilde{X}|\theta}(X'X)^{-1}$.

Proof

(a) Taking the appropriate sampling expectation (under Case I) of sampling error (9.2.8):

$$E_{y|\lambda}(b - \beta) = (X'X)^{-1}X'E_{y|\lambda}(u) = 0_K.$$

Hence, $E_{y|\lambda}(b) = \beta$. Similarly,

$$\begin{aligned}\text{Var}_{y|\lambda}(b) &= E_{y|\lambda}[(b - \beta)(b - \beta)'] = (X'X)^{-1}X'\{E_{y|\lambda}(uu')\}X(X'X)^{-1}\\ &= (X'X)^{-1}X'\{\sigma^2 I_T\}X(X'X)^{-1} = \sigma^2(X'X)^{-1}.\end{aligned}$$

(b) Taking the appropriate sampling expectation (under Case II) of sampling error (9.2.8):

$$E_{y|\tilde{X},\lambda}(b - \beta) = (X'X)^{-1}X'E_{y|\tilde{X},\lambda}(u) = 0_K.$$

Thus the conditional mean of b is $E_{y|\tilde{X},\lambda}(b) = \beta$, which is constant, and hence the unconditional mean is

$$E_{y|\tilde{X},\theta}(b) = E_{\tilde{X}|\theta}[E_{y|\tilde{X},\lambda}(b)] = E_{\tilde{X}|\theta}(\beta) = \beta.$$

Similarly,

$$\begin{aligned}\text{Var}_{y|\tilde{X},\lambda}(b|\tilde{X}) &= E_{y|\tilde{X},\lambda}[(b - \beta)(b - \beta)']\\ &= (X'X)^{-1}X'\{E_{y|\tilde{X},\lambda}(uu')\}X(X'X)^{-1}\\ &= (X'X)^{-1}X'\{\sigma^2 I_T\}X(X'X)^{-1} = \sigma^2(X'X)^{-1}.\end{aligned}$$

Hence using variance decomposition (2.7.25),

$$\begin{aligned}\text{Var}_{y,\tilde{X}|\theta}(b) &= E_{\tilde{X}|\theta}[\text{Var}(b|\tilde{X})] + \text{Var}_{\tilde{X}|\theta}[E_{y|\tilde{X},\lambda}(b)]\\ &= E_{\tilde{X}|\theta}[\sigma^2(X'X)^{-1}] + 0\\ &= \sigma^2 E_{\tilde{X}|\theta}[(X'X)^{-1}].\end{aligned}$$

11. Jensen (1979) considers the Case I linear model with u following a spherical distribution (see Exercise 3.4.27), which does not necessarily possess any positive moments. Maxwell (1860) showed that the only member of the spherical class in which the elements in u are independent, is the case of the multivariate normal distribution. Jensen (1979) shows that the OLS estimator is a "median unbiased" estimator of β, and within the class of such "median unbiased" estimators, the OLS estimator is at least as "concentrated around β" as any other median unbiased estimator.

In other words, according to Theorem 9.2.1, the OLS estimator is unconditionally unbiased under both Case I and Case II. Note that these results depend only on first-moment assumptions (9.1.2) and (9.1.18), and not on assumptions (9.1.3) and (9.1.21) regarding variances, nor on the uncorrelatedness or independence assumptions of the Cases I and II, respectively. Derivation of the unconditional sampling variances in each case, however, depend on these latter assumptions concerning second moments.

To illustrate the results so far, the following two examples will consider the cases in which $K = 2$ (simple regression) and $K = 3$, respectively.

Example 9.2.1 Consider the standard simple linear regression model

$$y_t = \beta_1 + \beta_2 \tilde{x}_t + u_t \; (t = 1, 2, \ldots, T). \tag{9.2.9}$$

In this case normal equations (9.2.5b) can be written

$$\begin{bmatrix} T & \sum_{t=1}^{T} \tilde{x}_t \\ \sum_{t=1}^{T} \tilde{x}_t & \sum_{t=1}^{T} \tilde{x}_t^2 \end{bmatrix} \begin{bmatrix} b_1 \\ b_2 \end{bmatrix} = \begin{bmatrix} \sum_{t=1}^{T} y_t \\ \sum_{t=1}^{T} \tilde{x}_t y_t \end{bmatrix}, \tag{9.2.10}$$

and solved to yield

$$\begin{aligned} b_2 &= \frac{\sum_{t=1}^{T} \tilde{x}_t y_t - T\bar{\tilde{x}}\bar{y}}{\sum_{t=1}^{T} \tilde{x}_t^2 - T\bar{\tilde{x}}^2} = \frac{\sum_{t=1}^{T} (\tilde{x} - \bar{\tilde{x}})(y_t - \bar{y})}{\sum_{t=1}^{T} (\tilde{x}_t - \bar{\tilde{x}})^2} \\ &= \frac{\sum_{t=1}^{T} y_t(\tilde{x}_t - \bar{x})}{\sum_{t=1}^{T} (\tilde{x}_t - \bar{\tilde{x}})^2} = \frac{\sum_{t=1}^{T} (y_t - \bar{y})\tilde{x}_t}{\sum_{t=1}^{T} (\tilde{x}_t - \bar{\tilde{x}})^2}, \end{aligned} \tag{9.2.11}$$

$$b_1 = \bar{y} - b_2 \bar{\tilde{x}}. \tag{9.2.12}$$

Furthermore, from Theorem 9.2.1(a) the covariance matrix of b is

$$\operatorname{Var}(b) = \frac{\sigma^2}{\sum_{t=1}^{T} (\tilde{x}_t - \bar{\tilde{x}})^2} \begin{bmatrix} \frac{1}{T} \sum_{t=1}^{T} \tilde{x}_t^2 & -\bar{\tilde{x}} \\ -\bar{\tilde{x}} & 1 \end{bmatrix}. \tag{9.2.13}$$

Note that $\operatorname{Var}(b_2)$ is smaller the smaller is σ^2 and the larger is the variation in $\tilde{x}$ around its mean. Note also that $\operatorname{Cov}(b_1, b_2) = 0$ iff $\bar{\tilde{x}} = 0$, in which case $\operatorname{Var}(b_1) = \sigma^2/T$ as in the case of estimating the mean in the simple location problem studied in Chapter 6.

Example 9.2.2 Consider the two-regressor model

$$y_t = \beta_1 + \beta_2 \tilde{x}_{t2} + \beta_3 \tilde{x}_{t3} + u_t \; (t = 1, 2, \ldots, T). \tag{9.2.14}$$

In this case normal equations (9.2.5b) can be written

$$\begin{bmatrix} T & \sum_{t=1}^{T} \tilde{x}_{t2} & \sum_{t=1}^{T} \tilde{x}_{t3} \\ \sum_{t=1}^{T} \tilde{x}_{t2} & \sum_{t=1}^{T} \tilde{x}_{t2}^2 & \sum_{t=1}^{T} \tilde{x}_{t2}\tilde{x}_{t3} \\ \sum_{t=1}^{T} \tilde{x}_{t3} & \sum_{t=1}^{T} \tilde{x}_{t2}\tilde{x}_{t3} & \sum_{t=1}^{T} \tilde{x}_{t3}^2 \end{bmatrix} \begin{bmatrix} b_1 \\ b_2 \\ b_3 \end{bmatrix} = \begin{bmatrix} \sum_{t=1}^{T} y_t \\ \sum_{t=1}^{T} \tilde{x}_{t2} y_t \\ \sum_{t=1}^{T} \tilde{x}_{t3} y_t \end{bmatrix}. \tag{9.2.15}$$

Denoting the sample moments (uncorrected for sample size) around the sample means as

$$m_{ij} = \sum_{t=1}^{T} (\tilde{x}_{ti} - \bar{\tilde{x}}_i)(\tilde{x}_{tj} - \bar{\tilde{x}}_j)\ (i,j = 1,2), \tag{9.2.16}$$

$$m_{yj} = \sum_{t=1}^{T} (y_t - \bar{y})(\tilde{x}_{tj} - \bar{\tilde{x}})\ (j = 1,2), \tag{9.2.17}$$

normal equations (9.2.15) may be solved to yield the OLS estimators

$$b_2 = \frac{m_{y2}m_{23} - m_{y3}m_{23}}{m_{22}m_{33} - m_{23}^2}, \tag{9.2.18}$$

$$b_3 = \frac{m_{y3}m_{22} - m_{y2}m_{23}}{m_{22}m_{33} - m_{23}^2}, \tag{9.2.19}$$

$$b_1 = \bar{y} - b_2\bar{\tilde{x}}_2 - b_3\bar{\tilde{x}}_3. \tag{9.2.20}$$

The OLS solutions in Examples 9.2.1 and 9.2.2 suggest that estimates of the slopes can be obtained in terms of sample moments around sample means, and then estimates of the intercept can be obtained by (9.2.12) and (9.2.20). This result can be generalized as follows. Write regressor matrix (9.1.19) as

$$X = [\iota_T, \tilde{X}], \tag{9.2.21}$$

where ι_T is a T-dimensional column vector with each element equal to unity, and $\tilde{X}$ is a $T \times (K-1)$ matrix of observations on the nonconstant regressors. Partition

$$b = [b_1, \tilde{b}_2']' \tag{9.2.22}$$

according to (9.2.21), and define the idempotent matrix

$$A = I_T - T^{-1}\iota_T\iota_T' \tag{9.2.23}$$

introduced in Exercise A.6.2. Note $X_* \equiv A\tilde{X}$ and $y_* = Ay$ convert $\tilde{X}$ and y to deviation form. It is straightforward to show (see Exercise A.4.2 and Theorem A.4.4):

$$(X'X)^{-1} = \begin{bmatrix} T & \iota_T'\tilde{X} \\ \tilde{X}'\iota_T & \tilde{X}'\tilde{X} \end{bmatrix}^{-1}$$

$$= \begin{bmatrix} T^{-1} + T^{-2}\iota_T'\tilde{X}(\tilde{X}'A\tilde{X})^{-1}\tilde{X}'\iota_T & -T^{-1}\iota_T'\tilde{X}(\tilde{X}A\tilde{X})^{-1} \\ -T^{-1}(\tilde{X}'A\tilde{X})^{-1}\tilde{X}'\iota_T & (\tilde{X}'A\tilde{X})^{-1} \end{bmatrix}$$

$$= \begin{bmatrix} T^{-1} + \bar{\bar{x}}'(X_*'X_*)^{-1}\bar{\bar{x}} & -\bar{\bar{x}}'(X_*'X_*)^{-1} \\ -(X_*'X_*)^{-1}\bar{\bar{x}} & (X_*'X_*)^{-1} \end{bmatrix}, \tag{9.2.24}$$

$$X'y = \begin{bmatrix} T\bar{y} \\ \tilde{X}'y \end{bmatrix} = \begin{bmatrix} T\bar{y} \\ X_*'y_* + T\bar{\bar{x}}\bar{y}_* \end{bmatrix}, \tag{9.2.25}$$

where

$$\bar{\bar{x}} = [\bar{\bar{x}}_2, \bar{\bar{x}}_3, \ldots, \bar{\bar{x}}_K]'. \tag{9.2.26}$$

Thus, post-multiplying (9.2.24) by (9.2.25) implies that the OLS estimator $b = [b_1, \tilde{b}_2']' = (X'X)^{-1}X'y$ reduces to

$$\tilde{b}_2 = (X_*'X_*)^{-1}X_*'y_*, \tag{9.2.27}$$

$$b_1 = \bar{y} - \bar{\bar{x}}'\tilde{b}_2. \tag{9.2.28}$$

For example, in the case $K = 3$ considered in Example 9.2.2,

$$(X_*'X_*)^{-1} = \begin{bmatrix} m_{22} & m_{23} \\ m_{23} & m_{33} \end{bmatrix}^{-1} = \frac{1}{m_{22}m_{33} - m_{23}^2}\begin{bmatrix} m_{33} & -m_{23} \\ -m_{23} & m_{22} \end{bmatrix}, \tag{9.2.29}$$

and (9.2.18) through (9.2.20) follows directly from (9.2.27) through (9.2.29). Furthermore, from (9.2.8), (9.2.24) and (9.2.29) it follows that the covariance matrix of b in Example 9.2.2 is

$$\mathrm{Var}(b) = \frac{\sigma^2}{m_{22}m_{33} - m_{23}^2} \times \begin{bmatrix} q & \bar{\bar{x}}_3 m_{23} - \bar{\bar{x}}_2 m_{33} & \bar{\bar{x}}_2 m_{23} - \bar{\bar{x}}_3 m_{22} \\ \bar{\bar{x}}_3 m_{23} - \bar{\bar{x}}_2 m_{22} & m_{33} & -m_{23} \\ \bar{\bar{x}}_2 m_{23} - \bar{\bar{x}}_3 m_{22} & -m_{23} & m_{22} \end{bmatrix}, \tag{9.2.30}$$

where

$$q = \frac{1}{T(m_{22}m_{33} - m_{23}^2)}) + \bar{\bar{x}}_2^2 m_{33} + 2\bar{\bar{x}}_2\bar{\bar{x}}_3 m_{23} + \bar{\bar{x}}_3^2 m_{22}. \tag{9.2.31}$$

Finally, it is clear from (9.2.24), or (9.2.30) and (9.2.31), that when the initial data are centered at the origin (i.e., $\bar{\bar{x}} = 0_{K-1}$), then

$$\mathrm{Cov}(b_1, \tilde{b}_2) = 0_{K-1}, \tag{9.3.32}$$

$$\mathrm{Var}(b_1) = \sigma^2/T. \tag{9.2.33}$$

Given the OLS estimator b, consider the predictions

$$\hat{y} \equiv Xb = X(X'X)^{-1}X'y = (I_T - M)y, \tag{9.2.34}$$

and the OLS residuals

$$\hat{u} \equiv y - \hat{y} = My \tag{9.2.35a}$$

$$= X\beta + u - X[\beta + (X'X)^{-1}X'u] = Mu, \tag{9.2.35b}$$

where M is the $T \times T$ idempotent matrix [see Exercise A.6.1]:

$$M \equiv I_T - X(X'X)^{-1}X'. \tag{9.2.36}$$

As noted in Exercise A.6.1, $I_T - M = X(X'X)^{-1}X'$ in (9.2.34) is known as a *projection matrix* because it "projects" the observed T-dimensional vector y down into the K-dimensional vector space spanned by the columns of X. Rewriting normal equations (9.2.5b) as

$$X'\hat{u} = 0_K, \tag{9.2.37}$$

it is seen that the OLS residuals are orthogonal to this K-dimensional space, and hence orthogonal to $\hat{y}$, that is,

$$\hat{y}'\hat{u} = 0. \tag{9.2.38}$$

To illustrate this geometrical interpretation, we turn to the following example.

Example 9.2.3 Consider the standard multiple linear regression with $T = 3$, $K = 2$,

$$y = \begin{bmatrix} 0 \\ 5 \\ 4 \end{bmatrix}, X = \begin{bmatrix} 1 & -4 \\ 1 & 1 \\ 1 & 3 \end{bmatrix}.$$

As shown in Figure 9.2.1, OLS yields a prediction vector $\hat{y} = [\hat{y}_1, \hat{y}_2, \hat{y}_3]'$, which lies in the plane defined by the column vectors $\iota_3 = [1, 1, 1]'$ and $x_2 = [-4, 1, 3]'$. Note also that the residual vector $\hat{u} = [\hat{u}_1, \hat{u}_2, \hat{u}_3]'$ is perpendicular to this plane.

Using normal equations (9.2.5), the minimized error sum of squares equals

$$\text{SSE} \equiv \text{SSE}(b) = \hat{u}'\hat{u} = (y - Xb)'(y - Xb) \tag{9.2.39a}$$

$$= y'y - 2b'X'y + b'X'Xb \tag{9.2.39b}$$

$$= y'y - 2b'X'y + b'X'y \tag{9.2.39c}$$

$$= y'y - b'X'y \tag{9.2.39d}$$

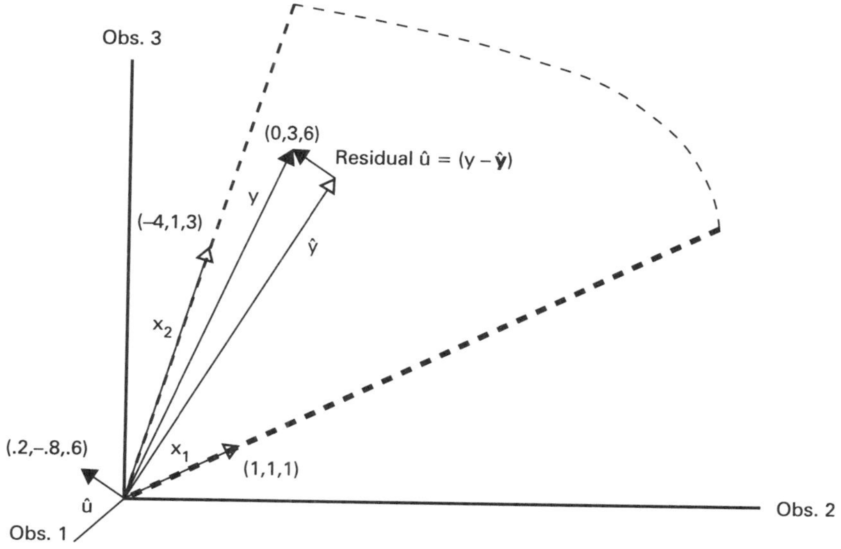

Figure 9.2.1
The geometry of least squares with three observations

$$= y'y - \hat{y}'y \tag{9.2.39e}$$

$$= (y - \hat{y})'y \tag{9.2.39f}$$

$$= \hat{u}'y \tag{9.2.39g}$$

$$= y'y - 2b'X'Xb + b'X'Xb \tag{9.2.39h}$$

$$= y'y - b'X'Xb \tag{9.2.39i}$$

$$= y'y - \hat{y}'\hat{y}. \tag{9.2.39j}$$

Because the second raw moment (not corrected for sample size) of y around the origin, $y'y$, is given, it follows from (9.2.39j) that the least squares objective of minimizing the sum of squared errors can also be interpreted as maximizing $\hat{y}'\hat{y}$. Rearranging (9.2.39j) yields the decomposition

$$y'y = \hat{y}'\hat{y} + \hat{u}'\hat{u}, \tag{9.2.40}$$

which motivates the following measure of relative goodness-of-fit:

$$R^2_{\text{raw}} \equiv \frac{\hat{y}'\hat{y}}{y'y} = 1 - \frac{\hat{u}'\hat{u}}{y'y}. \tag{9.2.41}$$

Note that $0 \leq R^2_{\text{raw}} \leq 1$.

Usually, the regression model includes an intercept (or more generally, Xc is constant for some $K \times 1$ nonzero vector c), and this gives rise to some special properties which have not yet been exploited. For example, the normal equation in (9.2.37) corresponding to the intercept implies that the OLS residuals sum to zero, that is,

$$\iota_T'\hat{u} = \sum_{t=1}^{T} \hat{u}_t = \sum_{t=1}^{T} y_t - \hat{y}_t = 0. \tag{9.2.42}$$

Conditional (9.2.42) implies in turn that the mean predicted value equals the observed sample mean of y, that is,

$$\bar{\hat{y}} = \bar{y}. \tag{9.2.43}$$

Denoting the total variation in the dependent variable around its sample mean as SST, it follows that

$$\begin{aligned} \text{SST} &= \sum_{t=1}^{T} (y_t - \bar{y})^2 = y'Ay = (\hat{y} + \hat{u})'A(\hat{y} + \hat{u}) \\ &= \hat{y}'A\hat{y} + 2\hat{y}'A\hat{u} + \hat{u}'A\hat{u}, \end{aligned} \tag{9.2.44}$$

where A is the idempotent matrix given by (9.2.23). Because (9.2.42) implies $A\hat{u} = \hat{u}$, it follows from (9.2.38) that the middle term in (9.2.44) equals zero. Hence, (9.2.44) implies

$$\text{SST} = \text{SSR} + \text{SSE}, \tag{9.2.45}$$

where

$$\begin{aligned} \text{SSR} &= \hat{y}'A\hat{y} = \sum_{t=1}^{T} (\hat{y} - \bar{\hat{y}})^2 = \sum_{t=1}^{T} (\hat{y} - \bar{y})^2 \\ &= \hat{y}'A(y - \hat{u}) = \hat{y}'Ay - \hat{y}'A\hat{u} = \hat{y}'Ay - \hat{y}'\hat{u} = \hat{y}'Ay \\ &= b'(X'AX)b = \tilde{b}_2'(X_*'X_*)\tilde{b}_2 \end{aligned} \tag{9.2.46}$$

is referred to as the *regression sum-of-squares*. From (9.2.45) arises the following familiar measure of goodness-of-fit known as the *coefficient of determination*:

$$R^2 \equiv \frac{\text{SSR}}{\text{SST}} = 1 - \frac{\text{SSE}}{\text{SST}}. \tag{9.2.47}$$

Provided the model includes an intercept, $0 \le R^2 \le 1$. It is clear from (9.2.45) through (9.2.47), minimizing SSE is equivalent to maximizing SSR or R^2.

The population counterpart of (9.2.47) in the case where the regressors are stochastic is the squared correlation between y_t and $\beta_1 + \tilde{x}_t\tilde{\beta}_2$, where β_1 and $\tilde{\beta}_2$ are defined by (9.1.19) and (9.1.20), respectively (recall Exercise 2.7.19):

$$R^2_{\text{pop}} = \frac{\sigma'_{xy}\Sigma^{-1}_{xx}\sigma_{xy}}{\sigma_{yy}} = \frac{\tilde{\beta}'_2\Sigma_{xx}\tilde{\beta}_2}{\sigma_{yy}}. \tag{9.2.48a}$$

The numerator in (9.2.48a) corresponds to $\text{Var}_x[E(y|\tilde{x})]$. Using variance decomposition (2.7.25), it follows that

$$\text{Var}(y_t) = E_x[\text{Var}(y_t|\tilde{x}_t)] + \tilde{\beta}'_2\Sigma_{xx}\tilde{\beta}_2. \tag{9.2.49}$$

This correspondence does not depend on the multivariate normality assumption, nor even on the assumption that $E(y_t|\tilde{x}_t)$ is linear in $\tilde{x}_t$. Under variance independence assumption (9.1.21), as implied by a multivariate normality assumption, however, the first term in (9.2.49) does not depend on $\tilde{x}_t$, and hence (9.2.48a) corresponds to the proportion of the unconditional variance σ_{yy} in y "explained" by $\tilde{X}$. Wishart (1931) showed that R^2 was a biased estimator of R^2_{pop}, and in fact

$$E(R^2) = R^2_{\text{pop}} + T^{-1}(1 - R^2_{\text{pop}})(K - 1 - 2R^2_{\text{pop}}). \tag{9.2.50}$$

In the case of fixed regressors, the population counterpart of R^2 is (see Barten 1962):

$$R^2_{\text{pop}} = \frac{\tilde{\beta}'_2\tilde{X}'\tilde{X}\tilde{\beta}_2}{\tilde{\beta}'_2\tilde{X}'\tilde{X}\tilde{\beta}_2 + T\sigma^2} = \frac{\tilde{\beta}'_2(T^{-1}\tilde{X}'\tilde{X})\tilde{\beta}_2}{\tilde{\beta}'_2(T^{-1}\tilde{X}'\tilde{X})\tilde{\beta}_2 + \sigma^2}. \tag{9.2.48b}$$

So far nothing has been said concerning estimation of σ^2. In fact, least squares criterion function (9.2.4) is not even a function of σ^2. Under a multivariate normality assumption, the likelihood equations (first-order conditions) are

$$\frac{\partial L(\hat{\beta}, \hat{\sigma}^2|y)}{\partial \beta} = \hat{\sigma}^{-2}X'(y - X\hat{\beta}) = 0_K, \tag{9.2.51}$$

$$\frac{\partial L(\hat{\beta}, \hat{\sigma}^2|y)}{\partial \sigma^2} = \frac{-T}{2\hat{\sigma}^2} + \frac{1}{2\hat{\sigma}^4}(y - X\hat{\beta})'(y - X\hat{\beta}) = 0. \tag{9.2.52}$$

From (9.2.51) the earlier noted point that the MLE of β corresponds to the OLS estimator follows immediately. Solving (9.2.52) for $\hat{\sigma}^2$ implies the MLE of σ^2 is

$$\hat{\sigma}^2 = T^{-1}(y - Xb)'(y - Xb) = T^{-1}\hat{u}'\hat{u}. \tag{9.2.53}$$

To aid in investigating the sampling properties of (9.2.53) consider (see Equation 9.2.34)

$$\text{SSE} = \text{SSE}(b) = \hat{u}'\hat{u} = y'My = u'Mu. \tag{9.2.54}$$

Noting that SSE is a scalar and using Theorem A.1.4(c) and Exercise A.6.1, it follows from (9.2.54) that in the case of fixed regressors (Case I):

$$E_{y|\lambda}(\text{SSE}) = E_{y|\lambda}[\text{tr}(u'Mu)] = E_{y|\lambda}[\text{tr}(Muu')]$$
$$= \text{tr}[ME_{y|\lambda}(uu')] = \sigma^2\,\text{tr}(M)$$
$$= (T - K)\sigma^2. \tag{9.2.55}$$

In the case of stochastic regressors (Case II):

$$E_{y,\tilde{X}|\theta}(\text{SSE}) = E_{\tilde{X}|\theta}[E_{y|\tilde{X},\lambda}(\text{SSE})]$$
$$= E_{\tilde{X}|\theta}[(T - K)\sigma^2]$$
$$= (T - K)\sigma^2. \tag{9.2.56}$$

Hence, from (9.2.55) and (9.2.56) it follows, under either Case I or Case II, $\hat{\sigma}^2$ is a biased estimator of σ^2 with

$$\text{Bias}(\hat{\sigma}^2) = -\frac{K}{T}\sigma^2. \tag{9.2.57}$$

An obvious unbiased estimator σ^2 is $s^2 \equiv (T - K)^{-1}\hat{u}'\hat{u}$. Comparison of $\hat{\sigma}^2$ and s^2 in the case $K = 1$, corresponds to the investigation of Exercises 6.3.4 and 6.3.5.

Whether s^2 has other optimal properties besides unbiasedness has been investigated by Hsu (1938) and Rao (1952, 1971) in the case of fixed regressors. Both authors considered unbiased quadratic estimators of the form $y'Gy$. Hsu (1938) also imposed the condition that $\text{Var}(y'Gy)$ is independent of β, and Rao (1952, 1981) imposed the condition that $y'Gy$ is nonnegative. In either case it can be shown that s^2 has a minimum variance within the respective class provided the u_t ($t = 1, 2, \ldots, T$) are i.i.d. with a distribution having a Pearsonian measure of kurtosis $E(u_t^4)/\sigma^4 = 3$ (the same as that of the normal distribution).

In the case of fixed regressors, b has the desirable property of being BLUE. This result is given in the following celebrated theorem. If $\tilde{X}$ is stochastic, then b is not a linear function of the data $z = [y, \tilde{X}]$ because the weights attached to y_t ($t = 1, 2, \ldots, T$) are stochastic, and hence, b is not a candidate for being BLUE. Shafer (1991) develops an analog of Theorem 9.2.2 in this case.

Theorem 9.2.2 (Gauss-Markov Theorem) Given Case I, the OLS estimator b is BLUE in the following sense. Any other unbiased estimator of β which is also linear in the vector y, has a covariance matrix which exceeds that of b by a positive semi-definite matrix.

Proof Let $\hat{\beta} = Dy$ be any linear unbiased estimator of β. Define $A = D - (X'X)^{-1}X'$ to be the difference between the linear weights for $\hat{\beta}$ and the weights for the OLS estimator b. Then

$$\hat{\beta} = Dy = (A + (X'X)^{-1}X')(X\beta + u)$$
$$= (AX + I_K)\beta + [A + (X'X)^{-1}X']u. \tag{9.2.58}$$

Because $E_{y|X,\lambda}(\hat{\beta}) = (AX + I_K)\beta$, in order for $\hat{\beta}$ to be unbiased, it is necessary that

$$AX = 0. \tag{9.2.59}$$

The sampling error of $\hat{\beta}$ is $\hat{\beta} - \beta = [A + (X'X)^{-1}X']u$. Hence, the variance-covariance matrix of $\hat{\beta}$ is

$$E[(\hat{\beta} - \beta)(\hat{\beta} - \beta)'] = E[(A + (X'X)^{-1}X')uu'(A' + X(X'X)^{-1})]$$
$$= [A + (X'X)^{-1}X']E(uu')[A' + X(X'X)^{-1}]$$
$$= \sigma^2[A + (X'X)^{-1}X'][A' + X(X'X)^{-1}]$$
$$= \sigma^2[AA' + AX(X'X)^{-1} + (X'X)^{-1}X'A' + (X'X)^{-1}]$$
$$= \sigma^2 AA' + \sigma^2(X'X)^{-1}, \tag{9.2.60}$$

where the last line of (9.2.60) follows as a result of (9.2.59). By Theorem A.7.11(b) AA' is positive semi-definite, which completes the proof.

Corollary 1 Consider an arbitrary linear combination $w'\beta$ (with a fixed weight vector w) of the elements of the parameter vector β; also consider the corresponding combination $w'b$ of the OLS estimator b. Then under the assumptions of the Gauss-Markov Theorem, the sampling variance of $w'b$ is less than or equal to the sampling variance of the corresponding combination of any other linear unbiased estimator of β.

Proof

$$\text{Var}(w'\hat{\beta}) = E_{Y|\lambda}(w'\hat{\beta} - w'\beta)^2 = E_{Y|\lambda}[w'(\hat{\beta} - \beta)]^2$$
$$= E_{Y|\lambda}[w'(\hat{\beta} - \beta)(\hat{\beta} - \beta)'w]$$
$$= w'[\sigma^2 AA' + \sigma^2(X'X)^{-1}]w$$
$$= \sigma^2(A'w)'(A'w) + \sigma^2 w'(X'X)^{-1}w$$
$$\geq \sigma^2 w'(X'X)^{-1}w \equiv \text{Var}(w'b).$$

In the special case in which w is a vector with all elements equalling zero except for the kth which equals unity, the preceding Corollary implies that $\text{Var}(b_k)$ is less than that of any linear unbiased estimator of β. Furthermore, the following can also be proved.

Corollary 2 Under the assumptions of the Gauss-Markov Theorem, the OLS estimator minimizes the expected value of any nonnegative definitive quadratic form in the sampling errors within the class of linear unbiased estimators.

Proof Let G be a nonnegative definite matrix of order K. It follows that for any linear unbiased estimator $\hat{\beta}$ of β with covariance matrix Ω,

$$E_{Y|\lambda}[(\hat{\beta} - \beta)'G(\hat{\beta} - \beta)] = E_{Y|\lambda}[\mathrm{tr}\{(\hat{\beta} - \beta)'G(\hat{\beta} - \beta)\}] = \mathrm{tr}(G\Omega). \quad (9.2.61)$$

Using (9.2.60), if follows that

$$\begin{aligned}\mathrm{tr}(G\Omega) &= \sigma^2\,\mathrm{tr}(GAA') + \sigma^2\,\mathrm{tr}[G(X'X)^{-1}]\\ &= \sigma^2\,\mathrm{tr}(A'GA) + \sigma^2\,\mathrm{tr}[G(X'X)^{-1}]\\ &\geq \sigma^2\,\mathrm{tr}[G(X'X)^{-1}],\end{aligned}$$

which proves Corollary 2.

Although the Gauss-Markov Theorem and its two corollaries are in a sense independent of any distributional assumption on u, in a more subtle sense they are not independent. Although the OLS estimator is the BLUE of β, this does *not* mean that b is necessarily a good estimator in an absolute sense. The relative optimality of the OLS estimator within the class of linear unbiased estimators is an important property only if this class contains estimators that are optimal in some absolute sense. For example, does the class of linear estimators ever include the maximum likelihood estimator which in a wide variety of circumstances has desirable properties in large samples? If the disturbances are i.i.d., then the ML estimator is linear iff the disturbances are normal random variables.[12] Thus, *although normality is not necessary to prove the Gauss-Markov Theorem, it is necessary to make the Gauss-Markov Theorem a result of practical importance.*

Example 9.2.4 The analysis to this point is sufficiently flexible to also encompass the case in which (9.1.13) is replaced by

$$E(uu') = \sigma^2\Omega, \quad (9.2.62)$$

or (9.1.30) is replaced by

$$E(uu'|\tilde{X}) = \sigma^2\Omega, \quad (9.2.63)$$

where Ω is a positive definite matrix. Such extensions with Ω unknown are known as the *general multiple linear regression model*, and they are briefly discussed in Section 10.3. When appropriate the words "normal," "fixed" and "stochastic" are added as needed. When Ω is *known*, then the specification can be transformed into a standard multiple linear regression. To see this, let $\Lambda^{-1/2}$ be the diagonal matrix with the reciprocals of the square roots of the characteristic roots of Ω on its main diagonal, let C be the orthogonal matrix with columns equalling the corresponding characteristic vectors of Ω, and define $P \equiv \Lambda^{-1/2}C'$. Note that (using Theorem A.7.2b)

$$P\Omega P' = \Lambda^{-1/2}C'\Omega C\Lambda^{-1/2} = \Lambda^{-1/2}\Lambda\Lambda^{-1/2} = I_T, \quad (9.2.64)$$

12. This need not be the case when the i.i.d. assumption does not hold. See Exercise 9.4.2.

and (using Theorem A.7.2c)

$$\Omega^{-1} = (C\Lambda C')^{-1} = C\Lambda^{-1}C' = C\Lambda^{-1/2}\Lambda^{-1/2}C' = P'P. \tag{9.2.65}$$

Premultiplying $y = X\beta + u$ by P yields

$$y_\dagger = X_\dagger\beta + u_\dagger, \tag{9.2.66}$$

where $y_\dagger \equiv Py$, $X_\dagger \equiv PX$ and $u_\dagger \equiv Pu$. Using (9.2.64) it follows that

$$E(u_\dagger u_\dagger') = E(Puu'P') = \sigma^2 P\Omega P' = \sigma^2 I_T. \tag{9.2.67}$$

Thus transformed model (9.2.66) satisfies all the assumptions of the standard multiple linear regression model. Note that the OLS estimator of β based on (9.2.66) is

$$b_\dagger \equiv (X_\dagger' X_\dagger)^{-1} X_\dagger' y_\dagger \tag{9.2.68a}$$

$$= (X'P'PX)^{-1}X'P'Py = (X^{-1}\Omega^{-1}X)^{-1}X'\Omega^{-1}y. \tag{9.2.68b}$$

For Case I, the Gauss-Markov Theorem applied to (9.2.66) implies $b_\dagger$ is the BLUE of β.

Example 9.2.5 Finally, another transformation of the standard multiple linear regression model that is sometimes used is the following. Let Ψ denote the diagonal matrix whose diagonal elements are the characteristic roots of the positive definite matrix $X'X$, let W be the corresponding orthogonal matrix whose columns are the corresponding characteristic vectors, and define $G \equiv W\Psi^{-1/2}Wy'$. Then the standard multiple linear regression model can be transformed as follows:

$$y = X\beta + u$$

$$= XGG^{-1}\beta + u = Z\gamma + u, \tag{9.2.69}$$

where

$$Z \equiv XG, \tag{9.2.70}$$

$$\gamma \equiv G^{-1}\beta, \tag{9.2.71}$$

$$G^{-1} = W\Psi^{1/2}W'. \tag{9.2.72}$$

Using Theorem A.7.3 it follows that

$$\begin{aligned} Z'Z &= G'X'XG \\ &= W\Psi^{-1/2}W'(X'X)W\Psi^{-1/2}W' \\ &= W\Psi^{-1/2}\Psi\Psi^{-1/2}W' \\ &= WW' = I_K, \end{aligned} \tag{9.2.73}$$

$$(X'X)^{-1} = (W\Psi W')^{-1} = W\Psi^{-1}W'. \tag{9.2.74}$$

The transformation in (9.2.69) is known as a *canonical reduction*. Unlike transformation (9.2.66), the stochastic properties of the original model are unchanged in (9.2.69), but the latter does involve a reparameterization from β to γ. The OLS estimator of γ in (9.2.69) is

$$\hat{\gamma} = (Z'Z)^{-1}Z'y = Z'y \tag{9.2.75a}$$
$$= G'X'y = G^{-1}GG'X'y$$
$$= G^{-1}[W\Psi^{-1/2}W'W\Psi^{-1/2}W']X'y$$
$$= G^{-1}(W\Psi^{-1}W')X'y = G^{-1}b, \tag{9.2.75b}$$

and its covariance matrix is

$$\text{Var}(\hat{\gamma}) = \sigma^2(Z'Z)^{-1} = \sigma^2 I_K. \tag{9.2.76}$$

Unlike b_k $(k = 1, 2, \ldots, K)$, $\hat{\gamma}_k$ $(k = 1, 2, \ldots, K)$ are uncorrelated.

Exercises

9.2.1 Show that (9.2.4) can be written

$$\min_{\hat{\beta}} \text{SSE}(\hat{\beta}) = \min_{\hat{\beta}} \{y'My + (\hat{\beta} + b)'X'X(\hat{\beta} - b)\}, \tag{9.2.77}$$

where M and b are given by (9.2.36) and (9.2.6), respectively, and argue directly that the solution is $\hat{\beta} = b$.

9.2.2 Consider the standard multiple linear regression with fixed regressors: $y = X\beta + u$. Premultiplying by the idempotent matrix A defined by (9.2.23) yields the deviation model

$$y_* = \tilde{X}_*\tilde{\beta}_2 + u_*, \tag{9.2.78}$$

where $y_* \equiv Ay$, $\tilde{X}_* \equiv A\tilde{X}$ and $u_* \equiv Au$. Assuming fixed regressors, does this transformed model satisfy assumptions of the standard multiple linear regression with fixed regressors?

9.2.3 Consider the two standard simple linear regressions

$$y_t = \beta_1 + \beta_2 x_t + u_t \ (t = 1, 2, \ldots, T),$$

$$x_t = \gamma_1 + \gamma_2 y_t + v_t \ (t = 1, 2, \ldots, T),$$

and let $\hat{\beta}_2$ and $\hat{\gamma}_2$ denote the OLS estimators of their respective slopes. Does $\hat{\beta}_2 = (\hat{\gamma}_2)^{-1}$?

9.2.4 Suppose you need to estimate

$$y_t = \beta_1 + \beta_2 x_{t2} + \beta_3 x_{t3} + \beta_4 x_{t4} + \varepsilon_t \ (t = 1, 2, \ldots, T),$$

where y_t = total consumption, x_{t2} = total income, x_{t3} = total wage income, and x_{t4} = total nonwage income. What difficulties are you likely to encounter in estimating this model?

9.2.5 Find the Hessian matrix corresponding to log-likelihood (9.2.2).

9.2.6 In the classical linear model the X-variables are often called the *independent* variables, the columns of X are assumed to be *linearly independent*, and the elements of u are assumed to be *independently distributed* random variables. What is meant by "independent" in each of these three contexts?

9.2.7 Consider a standard simple linear regression model in which the regressand is aggregate savings and the regressors are a constant and an interest rate. Would you rather sample during a period of fluctuating interest rates or during a period in which interest rates are relatively constant?

9.2.8 Consider the standard multiple linear regression $y = X\beta + u$, where $T = 5$, $K = 3$, $y = [0, 2, 5, 7, 6]'$, $\beta = [\beta_1, \beta_2, \beta_3]'$, and

$$X = \begin{bmatrix} 1 & 0 & 0 \\ 1 & 1 & 0 \\ 1 & 2 & 2 \\ 1 & 3 & 3 \\ 1 & 4 & 0 \end{bmatrix}.$$

(a) Compute $(X'X)$, $(X'X)^{-1}$ and $X'y$.

(b) Let $X = [\iota_5, \tilde{X}]$ and $A = I_5 - (.2)\iota_5\iota_5'$, where $\iota_5 = [1, 1, 1, 1, 1]'$. Compute $(\tilde{X}'A\tilde{X})$, $(\tilde{X}'A\tilde{X})^{-1}$ and $\tilde{X}'Ay$.

(c) Compute $b = (X'X)^{-1}X'y$ and $(\tilde{X}'A\tilde{X})^{-1}\tilde{X}'Ay$.

(d) Compute $\hat{y} = Xb$, $\hat{u} = y - \hat{y}$, $\hat{u}'\hat{u}$ and $s^2 = \hat{u}'\hat{u}/(T - K)$.

(e) Compute $M = I_5 - X(X'X)^{-1}X'$ and $y'My$

(f) Compute $\iota_5'\hat{u}$ and $X'\hat{u}$.

(g) Compute $y'y$, $y'\hat{y}$, $\hat{y}'\hat{y}$, $y'Ay$, $\hat{y}'A\hat{y}$ and $y'A\hat{y}$.

(h) Let $w = [1, 5, 0]'$. Compute $w(X'X)^{-1}w$.

9.2.9 Suppose that the original observation are x_{tj} $(j = 1, 2, \ldots, K)$, y_t $(t = 1, 2, \ldots, T)$ and we wish to undertake computations in terms of the scaled observations

$x_{tj}^* = p_j x_{tj}$ $(j = 1, 2, \ldots, K)$, $y_t^* = py_t$, $(t = 1, 2, \ldots, T)$.

Then in matrix notation

$X^* = XP$, $y^* = py$,

where P is the diagonal matrix of order K with p_j's $(j = 1, 2, \ldots, K)$ on the diagonal and zeroes elsewhere. Express each of the following quantities in terms of the scaled observations: $(X'X)^{-1}$, $X'y$, b, SST, SSR, SSE, s^2, R^2.

9.2.10 Although the OLS estimator b is BLUE and hence has the smallest MSE within the class of linear unbiased estimators, there are other linear estimators which are biased and have a smaller MSE. As noted by Kmenta (1986, p. 219), any attempt to find the linear estimator with the smallest MSE breaks down because the minimization problem yields the "estimator" (for the case of *simple* regression)

$$\hat{\beta} = \left[\frac{\beta^2 \sum_{t=1}^{T} (\tilde{x} - \bar{\tilde{x}})^2}{\sigma^2 + \beta^2 \sum_{t=1}^{T} (\tilde{x}_t - \bar{\tilde{x}})^2}\right] b. \tag{9.2.79}$$

$\hat{\beta}$ is *not* a legitimate estimator since it depends on unknown parameters, namely, β and σ^2. The analogous "estimator" for the case of standard multiple linear regression is (see Theil 1971, p. 125):

$$\hat{\theta} = \left[\frac{\beta' X' y}{\sigma^2 + \beta' X' X \beta}\right] \beta. \tag{9.2.80}$$

Now consider again the case of standard simple linear regression $y = \beta\tilde{x} + u$ and suppose we decide to choose the linear estimator $\hat{\beta}$, which minimizes

$$C(\hat{\beta}, \beta) = h\left[\frac{\mathrm{Var}(\hat{\beta})}{\sigma^2}\right] + (1 - h)\left[\frac{\mathrm{Bias}(\hat{\beta})}{\beta}\right]^2 \quad (0 < h < 1). \tag{9.2.81}$$

Find $\hat{\beta}$. Is $\hat{\beta}$ a legitimate estimator?

9.2.11 Consider the Cobb-Douglas production function

$$Q = \beta_1 K^{\beta_2} L^{\beta_3} u. \tag{9.2.82}$$

Discuss the use of OLS to obtain BLUE estimators of β_1, β_2 and β_3. Explicitly state any assumptions you make concerning u. If some of the parameters can only be estimated with bias, then state the direction of bias.

9.2.12 Consider a scatter diagram of x, y observations with y measured on the vertical axis and x on the horizontal axis. The OLS regression line with slope and intercept

$$b_v = \frac{m_{xy}}{m_{xx}}, \; a_v = \bar{y} - b_v \bar{x}, \tag{9.2.83}$$

is characterized by the fact that it is the straight line that minimizes the sum of squared deviations in the vertical direction. One might also consider the straight line which minimizes the sum of squared deviations measured in the horizontal direction (i.e., the linear sample regression of x on y). The implied estimates from this line are

$$b_h = \frac{m_{yy}}{m_{xy}}, \; a_h = \bar{y} - b_h \bar{x}. \tag{9.2.84}$$

A third alternative, called perpendicular (or orthogonal) regression, is characterized by the fact that it is the straight line which minimizes the sum of squared deviations measured in a direction perpendicular to the line. For perpendicular regression (see Malinvaud 1970, pp. 9–13, 35–39),

$$b_p = \frac{2m_{xy}}{m_{xx} - m_{yy} + [(m_{xx} - m_{yy})^2 + 4m_{xy}^2]^{1/2}}, \; a_p = \bar{y} - b_p \bar{x}. \tag{9.2.85}$$

Show: $|b_v| \le |b_p| \le |b_h|$.

9.2.13 Consider the standard simple linear regression model with fixed regressors with a single fixed regressor

$$y_t = \beta \tilde{x}_t + u_t \; (t = 1, 2, \ldots, T) \tag{9.2.86}$$

Note that there is no intercept in this model. Consider the estimator

$$\hat{\beta} = \frac{\bar{y}}{\bar{\tilde{x}}}. \tag{9.2.87}$$

(a) Is $\hat{\beta}$ an unbiased estimator of β? Justify your answer.

(b) Consider the OLS estimator b for this model. Is $\text{Var}(\hat{\beta}) < \text{Var}(b)$? Justify your answer.

9.2.14 Consider the standard simple linear regression model with a single fixed regressor

$$y_t = \alpha + \beta x_t + u_t \; (t = 1, 2, \ldots, T). \tag{9.2.88}$$

Suppose the observations are ordered according to increasing values of the regressor. Further suppose that T is even, define $\bar{\tilde{x}}_1$, $\bar{\tilde{x}}_2$, $\bar{y}_1$ and $\bar{y}_2$ to be the mean values of the regressor and the regressand over the first $T/2$ and last $T/2$ observations, respectively, and define

$$\tilde{\beta} = \frac{\bar{y}_2 - \bar{y}_1}{\bar{\tilde{x}}_2 - \bar{\tilde{x}}_1}. \tag{9.2.89}$$

(a) Find $E(\tilde{\beta})$.

(b) Find $\text{Var}(\tilde{\beta})$. If $\text{Var}(\tilde{\beta}) < \text{Var}(b)$? Justify your answer.

9.2.15 Consider (9.2.63), where Ω has all diagonal elements equal to unity and all off-diagonal elements to ρ. Also consider Exercise A.8.1.

(a) What constraints must be placed on ρ in order to insure that Ω is positive definite?

(b) Show that $b_\dagger$ given by (9.2.68) reduces to the OLS estimator.

9.2.16 Consider the standard multiple linear regression model with fixed regressors: $y_t = x_t\beta + u_t$ $(t = 1, 2, \ldots, T)$.

(a) Find $\text{Cov}(y_t - \hat{y}_t, \hat{y}_t)$.

(b) Find $\text{Cov}(y_t - \hat{y}_t, y_t)$.

9.2.17 Consider the standard multiple linear regression model with fixed regressors: $y_t = \beta_1 + \tilde{x}_t\tilde{\beta}_2 + u_t$ $(t = 1, 2, \ldots, T)$. What are the properties of OLS estimator of $\tilde{\beta}_2$ in the regression

$$y_t - y_{t-1} = (\tilde{x}_t - \tilde{x}_{t-1})\tilde{\beta}_2 + \varepsilon_t \; (t = 2, 3, \ldots, T), \tag{9.2.90}$$

where $\varepsilon_t = u_t - u_{t-1}$?

9.2.18 Consider the standard multiple linear regression model with fixed regressors

$$y = X\beta + u = X_1\beta_1 + X_2\beta_2 + u_1, \tag{9.2.91}$$

where $X = [X_1, X_2]$, $\beta = [\beta_1', \beta_2]'$, X_i is $T \times K_i$, β_i is $K_i \times 1$ $(i = 1, 2)$, and $K_1 + K_2 = K$.

(a) Show:

$$\begin{aligned}
(X'X)^{-1} &= \begin{bmatrix} X_1'X_1 & X_1'X_2 \\ X_2'X_1 & X_2'X_2 \end{bmatrix}^{-1} \\
&= \begin{bmatrix} Q_1 + Q_1C_1Q_1 & -Q_1'X_1'X_2(X_2'M_1X_2)^{-1} \\ -(X_2'M_1M_2)^{-1}X_2'X_1Q_1 & (X_2'M_1X_2)^{-1} \end{bmatrix} \\
&= \begin{bmatrix} (X_1'M_2X_1)^{-1} & -(X_1'M_2X_1)^{-1}X_1'X_2Q_2 \\ -Q_2X_2'X_1(X_1'M_2X_1)^{-1} & Q_2 + Q_2C_2Q_2 \end{bmatrix},
\end{aligned} \tag{9.2.92}$$

where

$$Q_i = (X_i'X_i)^{-1} \; (i = 1, 2), \tag{9.2.93}$$

$$M_i = I_T - X_i(X_i'X_i)^{-1}X_i' \; (i = 1, 2), \tag{9.2.94}$$

$$C_1 = (X_2'X_1)'(X_2'M_1X_2)^{-1}(X_2'X_1), \tag{9.2.95}$$

$$C_2 = (X_1'X_2)'(X_1'M_2X_1)^{-1}(X_1'X_2). \tag{9.2.96}$$

(b) Show $b = [b_1', \tilde{b}_2']' = (X'X)^{-1}X'y$ can be expressed as either

$$b_1 = (X_1'X_1)^{-1}X_1'(y - X_2b_2), \tag{9.2.97a}$$

$$b_2 = (X_2'M_1X_2)^{-1}X_2'M_1y, \tag{9.2.98a}$$

or

$$b_1 = (X_1'M_2X_1)^{-1}X_1'M_2y, \tag{9.2.97b}$$

$$b_2 = (X_2'X_2)^{-1}X_2'(y - X_1b_1). \tag{9.2.98b}$$

(c) Show:

$$|X'X| = |X_2'X_2| \cdot |X_1'M_2X_1| \tag{9.2.99a}$$

$$= |X_1'X_1| \cdot |X_2'M_1X_2|. \tag{9.2.99b}$$

9.2.19 Consider Exercise 9.2.18. Define $y_* \equiv M_2y$ and $X_* = M_2X_1$. Show that regressing y on either

(a) X_1 and X_2, or

(b) X_*, or

(c) X_* and X_2,

yields in all cases identical estimates of the vector of coefficients associated with X_1 or X_* as found in regressing y_* on X_*. Recalling that M_2 is a projection matrix, interpret this result (see Frisch and Waugh 1933 and Lovell 1963).

9.2.20 Consider the regression model

$$y = X_1\beta_1 + X_2\beta_2 + u \tag{9.2.100}$$

with fixed regressors and $E(u|X_1, X_2) = X_1\gamma$. Let $b = [b_1', b_2']'$ be the OLS estimator applied to (9.2.100).

(a) Find $E(b_1)$.

(b) Find $E(b_2)$.

9.2.21 Find the information matrix corresponding to log-likelihood (9.2.2) (see Exercise 9.2.5).

9.2.22 Consider Case I, $y \sim N(X\beta, \sigma^2\Omega)$, where Ω is a known positive definite matrix. Find the ML estimators of β and σ^2.

9.2.23 Consider Exercise 9.2.23. Find the distribution of the OLS estimator b.

9.2.24 Consider Example 9.2.3 with fixed regressors.

(a) Show: $\text{Var}(b) = \sigma^2(X'X)^{-1}X'\Omega X(X'X)^{-1}$.

(b) Show: $\text{Var}(b_\dagger) = \sigma^2(X'\Omega^{-1}X)^{-1}$.

(c) Show: $(X'X)^{-1}X'\Omega X(X'X)^{-1} - (X'\Omega^{-1}X)^{-1}$ is positive semidefinite.

9.2.25 Consider the standard multiple linear regression model

$$y = X\beta + u, \tag{9.2.101}$$

where y is $T \times 1$, X is $T \times$ K, β is $K \times 1$ and u is $T \times 1$. Let d be a $K \times 1$ vector of known constants and define $y^* = y - Xd$.

(a) Find β^* such that (9.2.101) can be expressed as

$$y^* = X\beta^* + u. \tag{9.2.102}$$

(b) Express the OLS estimator b^* based on (9.2.102) in terms of the OLS estimator b based on (9.2.101).

(c) Express the OLS residuals $\hat{u}^*$ based on (9.2.102) in terms of the OLS residuals $\hat{u}$ based on (9.2.101).

(d) It is often claimed that if the dependent variable includes variables that also appear as explanatory variables, then the R^2 is overstated. Investigate this claim by comparing the R^2's from (9.2.101) and (9.2.102). You may find it useful to express your results in terms of the OLS estimator of the slope in the following simple regression:

$$y = \alpha + \gamma(Xd) + \varepsilon. \tag{9.2.103}$$

9.2.26 Consider the standard multiple linear regression model

$$y_t = \beta_1 + \beta_2\tilde{x}_{t2} + \beta_3 t + u_t \, (t = 1, 2, \ldots, T), \tag{9.2.104}$$

and the statement: "The OLS estimator b_2 is the same as that obtained from a simple regression of y_t on $\tilde{x}_{t2}$ after a linear time trend has been removed from $\tilde{x}_{t2}$." Agree or disagree? Justify your answer.

9.2.27 Consider the standard simple linear regression $y_t = \beta_1 + \beta_2\tilde{x}_t + u_t$ $(t = 1, 2, \ldots, T)$, where $\beta_1 = 2$, $\beta_2 = 5$, u_t are i.i.d. discrete uniform random variables such that $T = 3$,

Table 9.2.1
Possible samples for Exercise 9.2.27

u_1	u_2	u_3	y_1	y_2	y_3	b_1	b_2	$\hat{u}_1$	$\hat{u}_2$	$\hat{u}_3$	s^2
−1	−1	−1	11	21	31	1	5	0	0	0	0
−1	1	−1									
−1	−1	1									
−1	1	1									
1	−1	−1									
1	1	−1									
1	−1	1									
1	1	1									

Table 9.2.2
Data for Exercise 9.2.29

State	X	Y	State	X	Y
Alabama	1820	17.05	Montana	2375	19.50
Arizona	2582	19.80	Nebraska	2332	16.70
Arkansas	1824	15.98	Nevada	4240	23.03
California	2860	22.07	New Jersey	2864	25.95
Connecticut	3110	22.83	New Mexico	2116	14.59
Delaware	3360	24.55	New York	2914	25.02
District of Columbia	4046	27.27	North Dakota	1996	12.12
Florida	2827	23.57	Ohio	2638	21.89
Idaho	2010	13.58	Oklahoma	2344	19.45
Illinois	2791	22.80	Pennsylvania	2378	22.11
Indiana	2618	20.30	Rhode Island	2918	23.68
Iowa	2212	16.59	South Carolina	1806	17.45
Kansas	2184	16.84	South Dakota	2094	14.11
Kentucky	2344	17.71	Tennessee	2008	17.60
Louisiana	2158	25.45	Texas	2257	20.74
Maine	2892	20.94	Utah	1400	12.01
Maryland	2591	26.48	Vermont	2589	21.22
Massachusetts	2692	22.04	Washington	2117	20.34
Michigan	2496	22.72	West Virginia	2125	20.55
Minnesota	2206	14.20	Wisconsin	2286	15.53
Mississippi	1608	15.60	Wyoming	2804	15.92
Missouri	2756	20.98	Alaska	3034	25.88

Prob($u_t = -1$) = Prob($u_t = 1$) = $\frac{1}{2}$ ($t = 1, 2, 3$), $\tilde{x}_1 = 2$, $\tilde{x}_2 = 4$ and $\tilde{x}_3 = 6$. Find each of the following (see Oksanen 1992).

(a) Show: $E(u_t) = 0$ and $\sigma^2 \equiv \text{Var}(u_t) = 1$ ($t = 1, 2, 3$).

(b) Fill out the $8 = 2^3$ equally likely possible samples in Table 9.2.1, where b_1 and b_2 are the OLS estimates, and $\tilde{u}_t$ ($t = 1, 2, 3$) are the OLS residuals. As an aid the first row of Table 9.2.1 has already been completed.

(c) Find the joint sampling distribution of b_1 and b_2.

(d) Find the marginal sampling distribution of b_1, $E(b_1)$ and $\text{Var}(b_1)$.

(e) Find the marginal sampling distribution of b_2, $E(b_2)$ and $\text{Var}(b_2)$.

(f) Find $\text{Cov}(b_1, b_2)$.

(f) Find the marginal sampling distribution of s^2, $E(s^2)$ and $\text{Var}(s^2)$.

(g) Find the marginal sampling distribution of $\hat{u}_1$, $E(\hat{u}_1)$ and $\text{Var}(\hat{u}_1)$.

(h) Find the marginal sampling distribution of $\hat{u}_2$, $E(\hat{u}_2)$ and $\text{Var}(\hat{u}_2)$.

(i) Find the marginal sampling distribution of $\hat{u}_3$, $E(\hat{u}_3)$ and $\text{Var}(\hat{u}_3)$.

(j) Find $\text{Cov}(\hat{u}_1, \hat{u}_2)$, $\text{Cov}(\hat{u}_1, \hat{u}_3)$, and $\text{Cov}(\hat{u}_2, \hat{u}_3)$.

(k) Find the joint sampling distribution of b_2 and $\hat{u}_1$.

9.2.28 Consider Example 9.2.3 with fixed regressors. Then $b_\dagger = b$ provided any of the following conditions hold:

(a) $(X'X)^{-1}X'\Omega X(X'X)^{-1} = (X'\Omega X)^{-1}$.

(b) $\Omega X = XC$ for some nonsingular matrix C.

(c) $(X'X)^{-1}X' = (X'\Omega^{-1}X)^{-1}X'\Omega^{-1}$.

(d) $X = HA$, for some nonsingular matrix A, where the columns of H are K characteristic vectors of Ω.

(e) $X'\Omega Z = 0$ for any Z such that $Z'X = 0$.

(f) $\Omega = X\Gamma X' + ZDZ' + \sigma^2 I_T$ for some Γ, D and Z such that $Z'X = 0$.

Show that (a)–(f) are equivalent (see Amemiya 1985, pp. 182–183).

9.2.29 The data in Table 9.2.2 (taken from Fraumeni 1968) give the cigarettes smoked per person (estimated from cigarette tax revenues) X and the deaths Y per 100,000 population due to lung cancer for the 43 states and the District of Columbia which charged a cigarette tax in 1960. Compute the regression of Y on X (including an intercept).

9.3 Estimation Subject to Exact Linear Restrictions on Regression Coefficients

It is common in applied work to draw on econometric theory for the purpose of imposing nonsample information on the estimation process. This section investigates the case in which this information takes the form of exact linear constraints on the regression coefficients. Such information is dogmatic and is much stronger than the stochastic information considered later in Bayesian analyses.

Formally, we consider restrictions of the form

$$R\beta = r, \tag{9.3.1}$$

where R is a $J \times K$ matrix of known constants with $\text{rank}(R) = J$, and r is a J-dimensional column vector of known constants. If $\text{rank}(R) < J$, then constraints (9.3.1) are either linearly dependent or inconsistent, in which case some constraints must be discarded until an R is obtained for which $\operatorname{rank}(R) = J$.

The *restricted least squares estimator* (equivalently, the restricted maximum likelihood estimator) is defined to be the solution to the problem:

$$\min_{\hat{\beta}} (y - X\beta)'(y - X\beta) \text{ subject to } R\beta = r. \tag{9.3.2}$$

This problem may be obtained by first forming the Lagrangian function

$$\psi(\beta, \omega) \equiv (y - X\beta)'(y - X\beta) - \omega'(r - R\beta), \tag{9.3.3}$$

and then considering the first-order conditions:

$$\frac{\partial\psi(b^*, \omega^*)}{\partial\beta} = -2X'y + 2X'Xb^* + R'\omega^* = 0_K, \tag{9.3.4}$$

$$\frac{\partial\psi(b^*, \omega^*)}{\partial\omega} = r - Rb^* = 0. \tag{9.3.5}$$

Premultiplying both sides of (9.3.4) by $R(X'X)^{-1}$ yields

$$-2R(X'X)^{-1}X'y + 2Rb^* + R(X'X)^{-1}R'\omega^* = 0_K. \tag{9.3.6}$$

Because R has full row rank by assumption, $R(X'X)^{-1}R'$ is nonsingular (see Exercise 9.3.5), and (9.3.6) may be solved for ω^* to yield (after noting Equation 9.3.5):

$$\omega^* = -2[R(X'X)^{-1}R']^{-1}[r - Rb]. \tag{9.3.7}$$

Substituting (9.3.7) into (9.3.4) and premultiplying by $(X'X)^{-1}$, yields (after some algebraic manipulation) the *restricted least squares (RLS) estimator*

$$b^* = b + (X'X)^{-1}R'[R(X'X)^{-1}R']^{-1}(r - Rb), \tag{9.3.8}$$

where b is the OLS (unrestricted) estimator.

Three comments regarding (9.3.8) are in order. First, the difference $b^* - b$ between the restricted and unrestricted least squares estimator is a *linear* function of the difference $r - Rb$ that measures the degree to which the unrestricted OLS estimator b fails to satisfy restrictions (9.3.1). If b satisfies the restrictions, then of course $b^* = b$.

Second, in the case $J = K$, $b^* = R^{-1}r$. Thus the RLS estimator is determined solely by restrictions (9.3.1), and does not depend at all on the data.

Third, the sum of squared residuals corresponding to b^* is seen from Exercise 9.2.1 to be

$$(y - Xb^*)'(y - Xb^*) = (y - Xb)'(y - Xb) + (b^* - b)'X'X(b^* - b). \tag{9.3.9}$$

Noting (9.2.37) and substituting (9.3.8) into (9.3.9) yields

$$(y - Xb^*)'(y - Xb^*) = y'My + (r - Rb)'[R(X'X)^{-1}R']^{-1}(r - Rb), \tag{9.3.10}$$

which cannot be less than the unconstrained sum of squared errors $y'My$ because the matrix of the quadratic form in the second term of (9.3.10) is nonnegative definite.

Before deriving the sampling properties of the restricted least squares estimator, we first turn to the following example.

Example 9.3.1 Consider the following statistical specification of a Cobb-Douglas production function:

$$q_t = L_t^{\beta_2} K_t^{\beta_3} \exp(\beta_1 + u_t) \; (t = 1, 2, \ldots, T), \tag{9.3.11}$$

where q_t, L_t and K_t denote output, labor input and capital input in period t. Taking logarithms of (9.3.11) yields

$$\ln(q_t) = \beta_1 + \beta_2 \ln(L_t) + \beta_3 \ln(K_t) + u_t \; (t = 1, 2, \ldots, T). \tag{9.3.12}$$

Imposing constant returns to scale implies the restriction

$$\beta_2 + \beta_3 = 1, \tag{9.3.13}$$

which in terms of (9.3.1) corresponds to $R = [0, 1, 1]$ and $r = 1$. Although the RLS estimator can be computed in this case according to (9.3.8), it is easier to substitute (9.3.13) directly into (9.3.12) and rearrange terms to get

$$\ln(q_t) - \ln(K_t) = \beta_1 + \beta_2[\ln(L_t) - \ln(K_t)] + u_t \; (t = 1, 2, \ldots, T). \tag{9.3.14}$$

Defining $y_t \equiv \ln(q_t) - \ln(K_t)$ and $X_t \equiv \ln(L_t) - \ln(K_t)$, it follows from Example 9.2.1 that the OLS estimators b_1^* and b_2^* of β_1 and β_2 in (9.3.14) are given by (9.2.11) and (9.2.10). From (9.3.13), it follows that $b_3^* = 1 - b_2^*$. The estimators b_1^*, b_2^*, and b_3^* are identical to those that would be obtained from (9.3.8).

The first two sampling moments of the RLS estimator are given in the following theorem for Case I.

Theorem 9.3.1 Consider standard multiple linear regression model with fixed regressors and RLS estimator (9.3.8). Define

$$\delta \equiv r - R\beta, \tag{9.3.15}$$

$$Q \equiv (X'X)^{-1}. \tag{9.3.16}$$

(a) Using only (9.1.1) and (9.1.2):

$$E(b^*) = \begin{Bmatrix} \beta, & \text{if } \delta = 0_J \\ \beta + QR'[RQR']^{-1}\delta, & \text{if } \delta \neq 0_J \end{Bmatrix}. \tag{9.1.17}$$

(b) Using in addition second moment assumptions, regardless of whether or not β satisfies (9.3.1):

$$\text{Var}(b^*) = \sigma^2[Q - QR'(RQR')^{-1}RQ]. \tag{9.3.18}$$

Proof Substituting (9.3.16) into (9.3.8) gives:

$$b^* = b + QR'[RQR']^{-1}(r - Rb). \tag{9.3.19}$$

(a) From (9.3.19) and Theorem 9.2.1(a), (9.3.17) follows directly.

(b) From (9.3.19) and Theorem 9.2.1(b, ii) it follows that

$$b^* - E(b^*) = [I_K - QR'(RQR')^{-1}R](b - \beta),$$

and hence,

$$\begin{aligned}
\text{Var}(b^*) &\equiv [\{b^* - E(b^*)\}\{b^* - E(b^*)\}'] \\
&= [I_K - QR(RQR')^{-1}R]E[(b - \beta)(b - \beta)'] \\
&\quad \times [I_K - QR'(RQR')^{-1}R]' \\
&= \sigma^2[Q - QR(RQR')^{-1}RQ - QR'(RQR')^{-1}RQ \\
&\quad + QR'(RQR')^{-1}RQR'(RQR')^{-1}RQ] \\
&= \sigma^2[Q - QR'(RQR')^{-1}RQ].
\end{aligned}$$

From (9.3.18) and (9.2.7) it follows that

$$\text{Var}(b) - \text{Var}(b^*) = \sigma^2 QR'(RQR')^{-1}RQ. \tag{9.3.20}$$

Using Exercise 9.3.5, (9.3.20) is seen to be nonnegative definite. Thus the covariance matrix of the RLS estimator is never "larger" than the covariance matrix of the OLS estimator, *regardless of whether the restrictions are in fact valid*. This result does not violate the Gauss Markov Theorem because the RLS estimator is unbiased only if the restrictions are valid, and in that case, more information is being used in computing b^* (namely the restrictions) than is assumed in the Gauss Markov Theorem. What the nonnegative definiteness of (9.3.17) does imply is that there is the possibility that the bias of the RLS estimator noted in (9.3.15) may be offset in the mean square error sense by a reduction in variance.

To be more specific, recall Theorem 6.2.1, which implies that

$$\text{MSE}(b^*) = \sigma^2[Q - QR'(RQR')^{-1}RQ] + QR'(RQR')^{-1}\delta\delta'(RQR')^{-1}RQ. \tag{9.3.21}$$

Because

$$\text{MSE}(b) = \text{Var}(b) = \sigma^2 Q, \tag{9.3.22}$$

it follows from (9.3.21) and (9.3.22) that

$$\text{MSE}(b) - \text{MSE}(b^*) = QR'(RQR')^{-1}[\sigma^2 RQR' - \delta\delta'](RQR')^{-1}RQ. \tag{9.3.23}$$

The mean square error of any linear combination of the b_k's will exceed that of the b_k^*'s iff (9.3.23) is positive definite that, as a result of Exercise 9.3.5, will occur iff

$$\sigma^2 RQR' - \delta\delta' = \sigma^2 RQR' - (R\beta - r)(R\beta - r)' \tag{9.3.24}$$

is positive definite. Because (9.3.24) involves unknown parameters it cannot serve as an operational means for determining whether b or b^* has more desirable mean square error properties. It will be seen in Section 9.8, however, that (9.3.24) evaluated at $\sigma^2 = s^2$ and $\beta = b$ can be used to infer the definiteness of (9.3.24) and give rise in the process to a *pretest estimator*, which chooses between b and b^* based on the outcome of a statistical test.

Next, we consider the problem of estimating σ^2 based on the RLS estimator b^*. Defining

$$y^* \equiv Xb^*, \tag{9.3.25}$$

$$u^* \equiv y - y^*, \tag{9.3.26}$$

it is readily verified that under restriction (9.3.1),

$$u^* = (M + V)u, \tag{9.3.27}$$

where M and V are the idempotent matrices defined by (9.2.34) and in Exercise 9.3.3. Noting the results of Exercise 9.3.3, it follows that

$$(u^*)'u^* = u'(M + V)u, \tag{9.3.28}$$

and hence, analogous to (9.2.47),

$$E[(u^*)'u^*] = \sigma^2 \operatorname{tr}(M + V) = \sigma^2(T - K + J). \tag{9.3.29}$$

Thus we have proved the following theorem.

Theorem 9.3.2 Consider the univariate linear regression model with fixed regressors and suppose the restrictions (9.3.1) are valid. An unbiased estimator of σ^2 is

$$\sigma_*^2 = \frac{u^{*\prime}u^*}{T - K + J}. \tag{9.3.30}$$

Proof Follows directly from (9.3.29).

Finally, if all constraints of the form $R\beta = r$ are allowed, then any value of β is a RLS estimate for some choice of R and r. Let b_0 be a given $K \times 1$ vector. If only constraints with $r = Rb_0$ are considered, then the set of possible RLS estimators is the ellipsoid described in the following theorem of Leamer (1978, pp. 127–128). Although it is difficult to interpret this case from a classical point of view, it will be given an important Bayesian interpretation in Section 8.11 in terms of a prior for $R\beta$ located at Rb_0.

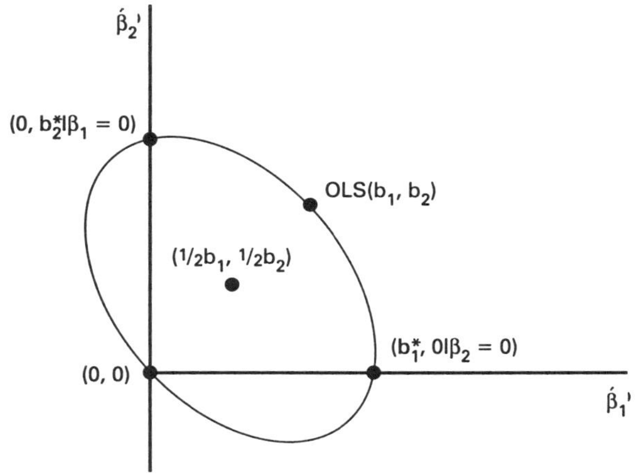

Figure 9.3.1
Ellipsoid (9.3.31)

Theorem 9.3.3 (Feasible Ellipsoid Theorem)

(a) An RLS estimate subject to the constraints $R\beta = Rb_0$ lies on the ellipsoid

$$[\beta - \tfrac{1}{2}(b + b_0)]'X'X[\beta - \tfrac{1}{2}(b + b_0)] = \tfrac{1}{4}(b - b_0)'X'X(b - b_0), \qquad (9.3.31)$$

where b is the OLS estimate.

(b) Any point on ellipsoid (9.3.31) is a RLS estimate for some choice of R.

Proof Leamer (1978).

Example 9.3.2 Put $K = 2$ and $b_0 = 0_2$. Ellipsoid (9.3.31) is depicted in Figure 9.3.1. The point $(\hat{\beta}_1, \hat{\beta}_2)$ lies on this ellipse iff there exists R such that $(\hat{\beta}_1, \hat{\beta}_2)$ is RLS subject to $R\beta = 0$. The axes of the ellipse are $(r\lambda_k^{-1/2})\xi_k$, where λ_1, λ_2 are the eigenvalues of $X'X$, ξ_1 and ξ_2 are the eigenvectors, and $r = \tfrac{1}{4}(b - b_0)'X'X(b - b_0)$.

Exercises

9.3.1 Verify that b^* given by (9.3.8) corresponds to a minimum of (9.3.2) and not a maximum or a saddle point.

9.3.2 Verify the claim in the last sentence of Example 9.3.1.

9.3.3 Show that $V = X(X'X)^{-1}R'[R(X'X)^{-1}R]^{-1}R(X'X)^{-1}X'$ is idempotent and has rank J. Also show $MV = 0$.

9.3.4 Consider the univariate linear regression model with fixed regressors:

$$y_t = \beta_1 + \beta_2 x_{t2} + \beta_3 x_{t3} + \beta_4 x_{t2}^2 + u_t\ (t = 1, 2, \ldots, 7),$$

where $y = [1, 4, 8, 9, 3, 8, 9]'$,

$$X' = \begin{bmatrix} 1 & 1 & 1 & 1 & 1 & 1 & 1 \\ -1 & 1 & -1 & 1 & 0 & 0 & 0 \\ -1 & -1 & 1 & 1 & 0 & 1 & 2 \\ 1 & 1 & 1 & 1 & 0 & 0 & 0 \end{bmatrix},$$

$$X'X = \begin{bmatrix} 7 & 0 & 3 & 4 \\ 0 & 4 & 0 & 0 \\ 3 & 0 & 9 & 0 \\ 4 & 0 & 0 & 4 \end{bmatrix},$$

$$(X'X)^{-1} = \begin{bmatrix} \frac{1}{2} & 0 & -\frac{1}{6} & -\frac{1}{2} \\ 0 & \frac{1}{4} & 0 & 0 \\ -\frac{1}{6} & 0 & \frac{1}{6} & \frac{1}{6} \\ -\frac{1}{2} & 0 & \frac{1}{6} & \frac{3}{4} \end{bmatrix},$$

(a) Find the OLS estimator.

(b) Find the RLS estimator subject to the restrictions:

$$\begin{bmatrix} 0 & 0 & 0 & 1 \\ 0 & 1 & -1 & 0 \\ 0 & 1 & -1 & 1 \\ 0 & 2 & -2 & 93 \end{bmatrix} \begin{bmatrix} \beta_1 \\ \beta_2 \\ \beta_3 \\ \beta_4 \end{bmatrix} = 0_4.$$

9.3.5 Let B be a positive definite matrix of order K and let C be a $K \times N$ matrix such that $\text{rank}(C) = m$. Show that $C'BC$ is positive definite if $m = N$ and that $C'BC$ is positive semidefinite if $m < N$.

9.3.6 Restate and prove the analog of Theorem 9.3.1 for the univariate linear regression model with stochastic regressors (see Binkley and Abbot 1987 and Kinal and Lahiri 1983).

9.3.7 Find the MSE of (9.3.28) when (9.3.1) does not hold.

9.3.8 Let $b^* = [b_1^{*\prime}, b_2^{*\prime}]'$ be the RLS estimator (9.3.8) subject to the restrictions $R\beta = R_1\beta_1 + R_2\beta_2 = r$, where R_2 is a $(K - J) \times (K - J)$ nonsingular matrix. Show that the RLS estimator b_1^* corresponds to the OLS estimator of β_1 in

$$y - X_2 R_2^{-1} r = (X_1 - X_2 R_2^{-1} R_1)\beta_1 + u. \tag{9.3.32}$$

9.3.9 Consider the univariate normal linear regression model with fixed regressors:

$$y = X\beta + u, \tag{9.3.33}$$

where y is $T \times 1$, X is $T \times K$, β is $K \times 1$ and u is $T \times 1$. Let G be a $K \times J$ matrix of known constants with $\text{rank}(G) = J$, let α be a $J \times 1$ vector of unknown parameters, and suppose

$$\beta = G\alpha. \tag{9.3.34}$$

(a) Find the least squares estimator $\hat{\alpha}$ of α and give its sampling distribution.

(b) Find the restricted least squares estimator $\hat{\beta}$ of β subject to (9.3.34) and give its sampling distribution.

9.3.10 Set up the Lagrangian function for the log-likelihood subject to (9.3.1) and find the corresponding first and second derivatives with respect to β and σ^2.

9.3.11 Consider the univariate normal linear regression model with fixed regressors subject to the J restriction $R\beta = r$, where $\text{rank}(R) = J$. Find the ML estimator of β and σ^2.

9.3.12 Suppose you have cross-sectional data on house prices (y) for a large city and you think that the price of a house can be adequately described by a linear function of the size of the house (x_2), the size of the lot (x_3), the age of the house (x_4), the quality of the neighborhood schools (x_5), and the distance from the central core of the city (x_6). Variables x_4 and x_6 are expected, *ceteris paribus*, to have a negative effect on the price; all other variables are expected to have a positive effect. Unfortunately, you only have data on x_2, x_3, and x_4. What, if any, bias does the omission of x_5 and x_6 introduce? Suppose that other evidence suggests that house size and lot size bear no systematic relation to the quality of schools, that older neighborhoods have poorer schools, and that homes in the suburbs tend to be newer, smaller, and on large city lots. To what use can you put this evidence? Clearly state and justify any assumptions you make.

9.3.13 Consider the standard simple linear regression model

$$y_t = \alpha_1 + \alpha_2 \tilde{x}_{t2} + u_t \; (t = 1, 2, \ldots, T). \tag{9.3.35}$$

Suppose you do not have observations on $\tilde{x}_{t2}$, but that you do have observations on a proxy variable $\tilde{x}_{t3}$. Assume $\tilde{x}_{t3}$ is independent conditional on $\tilde{x}_{t2}$. Suppose you estimate the simple linear regression

$$y_t = \gamma_1 + \gamma_2 \tilde{x}_{t3} + v_t \; (t = 1, 2, \ldots, T). \tag{9.3.36}$$

(a) Is the OLS estimator of γ_2 an unbiased estimator of α_2? If yes, then show it; if not, then determine its bias.

(b) Repeat (a) under the assumption that $\tilde{x}_{t2}$ and $\tilde{x}_{t3}$ are perfectly correlated. Hint: Consider this exercise in terms of RLS applied to the multiple regression

$$y_t = \beta_1 + \beta_2 \tilde{x}_{t3} + \beta_3 \tilde{x}_{t3} + u_t \; (t = 1, 2, \ldots, T). \tag{9.3.37}$$

9.3.14 Consider the standard multiple linear regression model

$$y_t = \beta_1 \tilde{x}_{t2} + \beta_2 \tilde{x}_{t2}^2 + u_t \; (t = 1, 2, \ldots, T). \tag{9.3.38}$$

Suppose you estimate the simple linear regression

$$y_t = \beta_1 \tilde{x}_{t2} + v_t \; (t = 1, 2, \ldots, T). \tag{9.3.39}$$

Find the bias of the OLS estimator of β_1 in (9.3.39).

9.3.15 Consider Cobb-Douglas production function (9.3.12) without the constant returns to scale assumption. Economic theory suggests that K_t should be a measure of capital *services*. Suppose, however, you only observe $\tilde{K}_t$ the existing physical stock of capital in period t ($t = 1, 2, \ldots, T$) that does not take into account the extent to which the capital stock is utilized.

(a) Suppose that the capital stock is utilized at a constant rate over the period under investigation. Hence, capital services are proportional to the capital stock. What are the statistical properties of OLS applied to the multiple regression of $\ln(q_t)$ on an intercept, $\ln(L_t)$ and $\ln(\tilde{K}_t)$? Be as specific as possible.

(b) How does your answer in (a) change if the rate of utilization of the capital stock varies across the observations?

9.3.16 Consider a standard multiple linear regression model with fixed regressors. Show that the OLS estimate b_k subject to a single liner constraint must li in the interval $(b_k - \tilde{s}_k|t|, b_k + \tilde{s}_k|t|)$, where b_k is the unconstrained OLS estimate of β_k, $\tilde{s}_k^2$ is the kth diagonal element in $s^2(X'X)^{-1}$, and t is the t-statistic for testing the restriction. In terms of omitting a variable, this result implies there can be no change in sign of any coefficient that is more significant than the coefficient of an omitted variable (Leamer 1975).

9.4 Distribution Theory for Classical Estimation

Without a distributional assumption, it is not possible in finite samples to determine the exact distribution of the OLS estimator, to construct confidence intervals or to test hypotheses. Here multivariate normality is invoked and the full sampling distribution of the ML/OLS estimator b and of s^2 are derived, augmenting the sampling moments derived in Section 9.2. Under multivariate normality and additional assumptions involving the large sample behavior of the matrices $T^{-1}(X'X)$ and $T^{-1}X'u$ these estimators have the expected desired asymptotic properties of consistency, asymptotic normality and asymptotic efficiency within the class of CUAN estimators. Furthermore, the estimators b and s^2 maintain these asymptotic properties in a wide variety of settings where the normality assumption does not hold, and in which b is not the MLE.

The next two sections discuss finite-sample confidence intervals and hypothesis testing in the standard multiple linear normal regression model with fixed or stochastic regressors. The distributional theory upon which those discussions are based is given in the next two theorems.

Theorem 9.4.1 Consider the standard multiple linear normal regression model with fixed regressors. Then the following results hold:

(a) $b \sim N_K(\beta, \sigma^2(X'X)^{-1})$,

(b) $[(T-K)s^2/\sigma^2] \sim \chi^2(T-K)$,

(c) b and s^2 are independent.

Proof Note that $y \sim N(X\beta, \sigma^2 I_T)$.

(a) Because $b = [(X'X)^{-1}X']y$, (a) follows directly from Theorem 3.4.8(a).

(b) Because $(T-K)s^2/\sigma^2 = \text{SSE}(b)\sigma^2 = u'Mu/\sigma^2 = (u/\sigma)'M(u/\sigma)$ and $M = I_T - X(X'X)^{-1}X'$ is an idempotent matrix with rank $T-K$, (b) follows directly from Theorem 4.5.2.

(c) Because $(X'X)^{-1}X'M = (X'X)^{-1}X' - (X'X)^{-1}X'X(X'X)^{-1}X' = 0$, (c) follows directly from Theorem 4.5.6.

Theorem 9.4.2 Consider the standard multiple linear normal regression model with stochastic regressors. Suppose the regressors are random draws from a multivariate normal distribution, i.e. $\tilde{x}_t|\mu, \Sigma \sim N_{K-1}(\mu_x, \Sigma_{xx})$.[13] Then the following results hold:

13. Note also that (a) $b|\tilde{X} \sim N_K(\beta, \sigma^2(X'X)^{-1})$, (b) $[(T-K)s^2/\sigma^2]|\tilde{X} \sim \chi^2(T-K)$, and (c) conditional on $\tilde{X}$, b and s^2 are independent.

(a) $b \sim t_K(\beta, \sigma^2\Sigma_{xx}^{-1}, T - K)$,
(b) $[(T - K)s^2/\sigma^2] \sim \chi^2(T - K)$,
(c) b and s^2 are independent.

Proof See Sampson (1974, pp. 684–685).

In summary, Theorems 9.4.1 and 9.4.2 show that in the standard multiple linear normal regression model with either fixed or stochastic regressors, the ML estimators $\hat{\beta} = b$ and $\hat{\sigma}^2 = T^{-1}\text{SSE}(b)$ of β and σ^2 are the same, $(T - K)s^2/\sigma^2 = T\hat{\sigma}^2/\sigma^2$ has the same distribution, and b and s^2 (also b and $\hat{\sigma}^2$) are independent. The distribution of b differs, however, across the two cases: being multivariate normal in Case I and multivariate-t in Case II. Such differences add to those noted in Section 9.2.

Although Parts (b) of Theorems 9.4.1 and 9.4.2 offer pivotal quantities (recall Definition 6.9.2) for hypothesis testing and confidence intervals involving σ^2, the sampling distributions for b in Parts (a) of these theorems cannot by themselves be used to construct pivotal quantities because they involve the unknown nuisance parameters σ^2 and/or Σ_{xx}.

Keeping in mind the goal of Sections 9.6 and 9.7 to provide confidence intervals and hypothesis testing procedures for linear combinations of regression coefficients, consider the following straightforward extensions of Theorems 9.4.1 and 9.4.2.

Theorem 9.4.3 Let R be a known fixed $J \times K$ matrix with $\text{rank}(R) = J$. In the case of the standard linear normal regression model with fixed regressors.

(a) $Rb \sim N_J(R\beta, \sigma^2 R(X'X)^{-1}R')$,
(b) Rb and s^2 are independent.

Proof Exercise 9.4.3.

Theorem 9.4.4 Let R be a known fixed $J \times K$ matrix with $\text{rank}(R) = J$. Consider the standard multiple linear normal regression model with stochastic regressors with the additional assumption that the regressors are random draws from a multivariate normal distribution, that is, $\tilde{x}_t|\mu, \Sigma \sim N_{K-1}(\mu_x, \Sigma_{xx})$.[14]

(a) $Rb \sim t_J(R\beta, \sigma^2 R\Sigma_{xx}^{-1}R', T - K)$,
(b) Rb and s^2 are independent.

Proof Exercise 9.4.4.

14. It also follows that $Rb|\tilde{X} \sim N(R\beta, \sigma^2 R(X'X)^{-1}R')$, and that conditional on $\tilde{X}$, Rb and s^2 are independent.

Given Theorems 9.4.3 and 9.4.4, it is now possible to construct the required the pivotal quantities needed for developing classical confidence intervals and hypothesis tests involving the linear combinations $R\beta$. Consider first the univariate normal linear regression model with fixed regressors.

Theorem 9.4.5 Consider the standard multiple linear normal regression model with fixed regressors.

(a) $v = [R(b - \beta)]'[\sigma^2 R(X'X)^{-1}R']^{-1}[R(b - \beta)] \sim \chi^2(J)$.

(b) v and s^2 are independent.

(c) $$q = \frac{v/J}{[(T-K)s^2/\sigma^2]/(T-K)} = \frac{(b-\beta)'R'[R(X'X)^{-1}R']^{-1}R(b-\beta)}{Js^2} \sim F(J, T-K). \tag{9.4.1}$$

Proof

(a) This part follows directly from Theorem 4.5.1.

(b) By Theorem 9.4.1(b) and (9.2.48), $(T - K)s^2/\sigma^2 = u'Mu/\sigma^2 \sim \chi^2(T - K)$. Because according to (9.2.6), $b - \beta \equiv (X'X)^{-1}X'u$, v in (a) can be expressed as

$$v = (u/\sigma)'D(u/\sigma), \tag{9.4.2}$$

where

$$D = X(X'X)^{-1}R'[R(X'X)^{-1}R']^{-1}R(X'X)^{-1}X'. \tag{9.4.3}$$

Because $DM = 0_{T \times T}$, where $M = I_T - X(X'X)^{-1}X'$, it follows from Theorem 4.5.4 that v and s^2 are independent.

(c) This part follows directly from (a), (b) and Theorem 9.4.1.

In the case of stochastic regressors (Case II), pivotal quantities do not exist in general for arbitrary distributions of the regressors. Given the nonlinear fashion in which the regressors enter (9.4.3) this should not be surprising. An exceptional case occurs, however, when drawing a random sample from a multivariate normal distribution.

Theorem 9.4.6 Consider the standard multiple linear normal regression model with stochastic regressors with the additional assumption that the regressors are random draws from a multivariate normal distribution, that is, $\tilde{x}_t|\mu, \Sigma \sim N_{K-1}(\mu_x, \Sigma_{xx})$. Then analogous to Theorem 9.4.5, the following results hold.

(a) $v = [R(b - \beta)]'[\sigma^2 R(X'X)^{-1}R']^{-1}[R(b - \beta)] \sim \chi^2(J)$.

(b) v and s^2 are independent.

$$\text{(c)}\quad q = \frac{v/J}{[(T-K)s^2/\sigma^2]/(T-K)} = \frac{(b-\beta)'R'[R(X'X)^{-1}R']^{-1}R(b-\beta)}{Js^2} \sim F(J, T-K). \tag{9.4.4}$$

Proof See Sampson (1974).

Pivotal quantities (9.4.1) and (9.4.4) play central roles in the developments of confidence intervals and hypothesis tests in the next two sections. Finally, the normality assumption also provides the missing conditions for discussing optimality of estimators of σ^2 as seen in the following theorem.

Theorem 9.4.7 Consider the standard multiple linear normal regression model with fixed regressors. Then the OLS estimator s^2 of σ^2 is *best quadratic unbiased* in the following sense. Any other estimator of σ^2 that is also unbiased and quadratic in y has a sampling variance larger than or equal to

$$\text{Var}(s^2) = 2\sigma^4/(T-K). \tag{9.4.5}$$

Under the same assumptions the estimator

$$\tilde{\sigma}^2 = \hat{u}'\hat{u}/(T-K+2) \tag{9.4.6}$$

is the best quadratic (i.e., minimum mean square error) in the sense that any other estimator of the form $y'Cy$, where C is a symmetric $T \times T$ matrix such that $CX = 0$, has a second-order sampling moment around σ^2, which is larger than or equal to[15]

$$E[(\tilde{\sigma}^2 - \sigma^2)^2] = 2\sigma^4/(T-K+2). \tag{9.4.7}$$

Moreover, under these assumptions the bias of $\tilde{\sigma}^2$ is

$$\text{Bias}(\tilde{\sigma}^2) = E[\tilde{\sigma}^2 - \sigma^2) = 2\sigma^2/(T-K+2). \tag{9.4.8}$$

Proof Theil (1971, pp. 128–130).

Exercises

9.4.1 Let b be the OLS estimator of β in (9.3.33) ignoring (9.3.34). Derive the sampling distribution of

$$w = (\hat{\beta} - b)'X'X(\hat{\beta} - b)/\sigma^2 \tag{9.4.9}$$

under (9.3.34), where $\hat{\beta}$ is given in Exercise 9.3.8(b).

9.4.2 (Zellner 1976). Consider the standard multiple linear regression model with fixed regressors. Suppose $u \sim t_T(0, \sigma^2 I, v)$, where $v > 2$ is known.

(a) Show that the ML estimators of β and σ^2 are given by $\hat{\beta} = (X'X)^{-1}X'y$ and $\hat{\sigma}^2 = (y - X\hat{\beta})'(y - X\hat{\beta})/T$.

(b) Assuming v is not known, investigate the use of ML to estimate v.

15. The assumption $CX = 0$ guarantees the distribution of σ^2 does not depend on β.

9.4.3 Prove Theorem 9.4.3.

9.4.4 Prove Theorem 9.4.4.

9.4.5 Consider the standard multiple linear normal regression model with multivariate normal regressors, an intercept and $K \geq 3$. Show the OLS estimator of the intercept, under quadratic loss is admissible conditional on the ancillary statistic $\tilde{X}$, but inadmissible unconditionally (Brown 1990).

9.4.6 Find the ML estimators of μ and Σ in Example 9.1.5. (Hint: Maximize with respect to μ and Σ^{-1}.) How do your answers relate to the ML estimators of β, σ^2 and ξ based on (9.2.3)?

9.5 Confidence Intervals

Let R be a known fixed $J \times K$ matrix with $\text{rank}(R) = J$. For the standard multiple linear normal regression model with either fixed or stochastic regressors it is possible to construct a $100(1-\alpha)$ percent confidence region for the linear combinations $R\beta$. The development depends on the distribution theory embodied in Theorems 9.4.1 through 9.4.6, and is based on the procedures discussed in Section 6.9.

From Theorems 9.4.5(c) or 9.4.6(c) it follows directly that a $100(1-\alpha)$ percent probability region for β is given by

$$\text{Prob}[(b-\beta)'R'[R(X'X)^{-1}R']^{-1}R(b-\beta) \leq J \cdot s^2 F(1-\alpha; J, T-K)] = 1-\alpha, \tag{9.5.1}$$

where $F(1-\alpha; J, T-K)$ denotes the $100(1-\alpha)$ percentile of a F-distribution with J and $T-K$ degrees of freedom in the numerator and denominator, respectively. Note that (9.5.1) is a *probability* region provided b and s^2 denote estimators. Once estimates are plugged into (9.5.1) in order to make it of applied interest, then (9.5.1) becomes a $100(1-\alpha)$ percent *confidence* region.

Probability region (9.5.1) is quite general and serves as the basis for deriving confidence intervals for individual linear combinations of the β_k's $(k = 1, 2, \ldots, K)$. For example, suppose $J = 1$ and R is simply a row vector, which for clarity we will denote as $R = w'$. Then (9.5.1) reduces to

$$\text{Prob}\left[\frac{[w'(b-\beta)]^2}{s^2 w'(X'X)^{-1}w} \leq F(1-\alpha; 1, T-K)\right] = 1-\alpha. \tag{9.5.2}$$

Noting that a F-distribution with one degree of freedom in the numerator corresponds to the square of a t-distribution (Theorem 3.2.16a), it follows from (9.5.2) that

$$\text{Prob}[w'b - t(1-\tfrac{1}{2}\alpha; T-K)\tilde{s} < w'\beta < w'b + t(1-\tfrac{1}{2}\alpha; T-K)\tilde{s}] = 1-\alpha, \tag{9.5.3}$$

where $\tilde{s} = s[w'(X'X)^{-1}w]^{1/2}$. If all elements in w equal zero except for the kth, which equals unity, then (9.5.3) implies

$$\text{Prob}[b_k - t(1 - \tfrac{1}{2}\alpha; T - K)\tilde{s}_k < \beta_k < b_k + t(1 - \tfrac{1}{2}\alpha; T - K)\tilde{s}_k] = 1 - \alpha, \quad (9.5.4)$$

where $\tilde{s}_k^2$ equals s^2 times the kth diagonal element of $(X'X)^{-1}$. Again we emphasize that when estimates are substituted into (9.5.3) and (9.5.4), they become *confidence* intervals and no direct nontrivial probability statements can be made concerning them.

Example 9.5.1 Consider Exercise 9.2.8. Noting that $t(.025; 2) = 4.303$ and

$$\tilde{s}_1 = \left[\frac{7}{71} \cdot \frac{221}{335}\right]^{1/2} = .248, \; \tilde{s}_2 = \left[\frac{7}{71} \cdot \frac{40}{355}\right]^{1/2} = .105,$$

$$\tilde{s}_3 = \left[\frac{7}{71} \cdot \frac{50}{355}\right]^{1/2} = .118,$$

the following confidence intervals can be constructed

$$C[(19/71) - 4.303(.248) < \beta_1 < (19/71) + 4.303(.248)]$$
$$= C[-.800 < \beta_1 < 1.33] = .95,$$
$$C[(103/71) - 4.303(.105) < \beta_2 < (103/71) + 4.303(.105)]$$
$$= C[.499 < \beta_2 < 1.90] = .95,$$
$$C[(59/71) - 4.303(.118) < \beta_3 < (59/71) + 4.303(.118)]$$
$$= C[.323 < \beta_3 < 1.34] = .95.$$

Also, if $w = [0, 2, -1]'$, then

$$w'b = 2b_2 - b_3 = 2(103/71) - (59/71) = 2.07,$$
$$s[w'(X'X)^{-1}w]^{1/2} = [(7/71)\{4(40/355) + (5/355) - 4(-15/355)\}]^{1/2}$$
$$= .274.$$

Hence, a 95 percent confidence interval for $w'\beta = 2\beta_2 - \beta_3$ is

$$C[2.07 - 4.303(.274) < 2\beta_2 - \beta_3 < 2.07 + 4.303(.274)]$$
$$= C[.891 < 2\beta_2 - \beta_3 < 3.25] = .95.$$

K-dimensional confidence regions based on (9.5.1) are not easy to describe, so it is often desired to make a joint confidence statement about a series of univariate confidence intervals

$$b_k - t(1 - \tfrac{1}{2}\alpha; T - K)\tilde{s}_k < \beta_k < b_k + t(1 - \tfrac{1}{2}\alpha; T - K)\tilde{s}_k \; (k = 1, 2, \ldots, K), \quad (9.5.5)$$

or equivalently,

$$|(b_k - \beta_k)/\tilde{s}_k| < t(1 - \alpha/2; T - K) \; (k = 1, 2, \ldots, K). \quad (9.5.6)$$

Taken together, the intervals in (9.5.5)—or (9.5.6)—constitute a K-dimensional polyhedron. The principal question is what is the joint confidence to be assigned to all intervals taken *simultaneously*, as opposed to individually. If the underlying probability intervals are independent, then the joint confidence level is $(1-\alpha)^K$, and the probability of at least one interval failing is $1-(1-\alpha)^K$. In general, however, such intervals are dependent. A bound on the joint confidence level possessed by the polyhedron can be obtained based on the Bonferroni inequality (see Exercise 6.9.7):

$$\text{Prob}(A_1 \cap A_2 \cap \cdots \cap A_K) \geq 1 - \sum_{k=1}^{K} \text{Prob}(A_k^c), \tag{9.5.7}$$

where A_k is an event and A_k^c its complement.[16] Letting A_k denote the event that the kth underlying $1-\alpha_k$ level probability interval contains β_k, it follows that $\text{Prob}(A_k^c) = \alpha$, and hence, the overall joint probability that each of the underlying probability intervals contains its respective β_k is *at least* $1-(\alpha_1 + \cdots + \alpha_K)$. For example, if it is desired to have an overall confidence level of at least 90 percent for $K = 10$ intervals, then it is sufficient to consider a 94.5 percent confidence interval for β_1 and 99.5 percent confidence interval for β_k $(k = 2, 3, \ldots, 10)$ because $.055 + 9(.005) = .10$. Alternatively, one might choose $K = 10$ intervals at 99 percent confidence. For more details see, Miller (1981) and Savin (1980, 1884). In particular it should be noted that neither joint polyhedron (9.5.5) nor region (9.5.1) is entirely contained within the other.

Another classical method applicable to simultaneous confidence intervals is due to Scheffé (1953, 1959, 1977).[17] In order to describe this method, consider Theorem 9.5.2(c) and Theorem A.7.19 [with $z \equiv R(b-\beta)$, $A \equiv R(X'X)^{-1}R'$ and $c = x$]. Then it follows:

$$\frac{[R(b-\beta)]'[R(X'X)^{-1}R']^{-1}[R(b-\beta)]}{Js^2} = \frac{1}{Js^2}\left[\sup_c \frac{[R(b-\beta)'c]^2}{c'[R(X'X)^{-1}R']c}\right], \tag{9.5.8}$$

here c is an arbitrary J-dimensional column vector of constants. Combining (9.5.3) and (9.5.8) implies:

$$\text{Prob}\left[\sup_c \frac{|c'R(b-\beta)|}{\{c'[R(X'X)^{-1}R']c\}^{1/2}} \leq (sJ^{1/2})F(1-\tfrac{1}{2}\alpha; J, T-K)\right] = 1-\alpha, \tag{9.5.9}$$

16. Sidak (1967) has proved a general inequality that gives a slight improvement over the Bonferroni inequality when both are applicable. See also Games (1977).

17. For more details see Dhrymes (1978, pp. 90–97), Rao (1973, pp. 240–244), Savin (1980, 1984), and Seber (1977, Chapter 5).

or equivalently,

$$\text{Prob}(c'Rb - s^* < c'R\beta < c'Rb + s^*) = 1 - , \tag{9.5.10}$$

where $s^* \equiv s[J \cdot F(1 - \frac{1}{2}\alpha; J, T - K)c'\{R(X'X)^{-1}R'\}c]^{1/2}$. Equation (9.5.10) provides *simultaneous* probability intervals *for all* functions of the form $c'(R\beta)$, that is, all linear combinations of the parametric functions $R\beta$, because (9.5.10) holds for the "most extreme" linear combination

$$c_* = A^{-1}z = [R(X'X)^{-1}R']R(b - \beta), \tag{9.5.11}$$

which maximizes the right hand side of (9.5.8). Furthermore, for a particular choice of c, a confidence interval constructed according to (9.5.10) has a confidence coefficient of *at least* $1 - \alpha$.

The so-called S-intervals (9.5.10) can also be related directly to joint probability region (9.5.1). Viewing (9.5.1) as a joint probability region for $R\beta$, consider the question as to whether it contains the known J-dimensional column vector r. This in turn is equivalent to the question of whether the joint probability region

$$\begin{aligned}&\text{Prob}[\{R(b - \beta) - r\}'[R(X'X)^{-1}R']^{-1}\{R(b - \beta) - r\}\\ &\quad \leq Js^2F(1 - \alpha; J, T - K)] = 1 - \alpha\end{aligned} \tag{9.5.12}$$

contains 0_J. The equivalence of (9.5.1) and (9.5.12) follows from merely translating the centers of the two respective confidence ellipses. Subtracting $c'r$ from each term of the interval in (9.5.10) yields

$$\text{Prob}[c'(Rb - r) - s^* < c'(R\beta - r) < c'(Rb - r) + s^*] = 1 - \alpha. \tag{9.5.13}$$

The connection between (9.5.12) and (9.5.13) is given in the following remarkable theorem.

Theorem 9.5.1 Under the assumptions of Theorem 9.4.5, joint probability region (9.5.12) excludes 0_J iff interval (9.5.13) excludes zero for *some* J-dimensional vector c.

Proof Scheffé (1959).

In other words, the ellipse in (9.5.12) excludes the origin (i.e., one would reject H_1: $R\beta = r$ based on Equation 9.5.1, excluding r) iff the univariate Scheffé interval (9.5.13) suggests $c'(R\beta - r)$ is "significantly" different from zero for some vector c. In effect the linear combination $c'(R\beta - r)$ of the constraints (given a choice of c) is responsible for the rejection of H_1.

In closing, two additional topics in any discussion of confidence intervals deserve mention. First, confidence intervals for σ^2 can be constructed based on Theorem 9.4.1(b) in a fashion analogous to Example 6.7.6. It should be noted, however, that such intervals are substantially less robust to departures from normality than intervals constructed for β. Second, suppose for an unknown value of $\tilde{x}_0$, the value y_0 is observed. Point and interval estimation of $\tilde{x}_0$ is known as the *calibration problem.* The resulting confidence interval is known as a tolerance interval. See Graybill (1976, pp. 275–283) and Maddala (1977, pp. 101–102) for details.

Exercises

9.5.1 Prove Theorem 9.5.1.

9.5.2 A production function model is specified as

$$y_t = \beta_1 + \beta_2 x_{t2} + \beta_3 x_{t3} + u_t, (t = 1, 2, \ldots, 23),$$

where y_t = log output, x_{t2} = log labor input, and x_{t3} = log capital input. The subscript t refers to firm t. There are 23 observations in the sample, and the moment matrices (*in terms of deviations from sample means*) are

$$X_*'X_* = \begin{bmatrix} 12 & 8 \\ 8 & 12 \end{bmatrix}, X_*'y_* = \begin{bmatrix} 10 \\ 8 \end{bmatrix}, y_*'y_* = 10.$$

(a) Find the OLS estimates b_2 and b_3, and their estimated standard errors.

(b) Construct a 95 percent confidence interval for returns to scale: $\beta_2 + \beta_3$.

(c) Sketch a 99 percent confidence region for β_2 and β_3.

9.6 Classical Hypothesis Testing

As suggested in Chapter 7 there is a close connection between confidence interval construction and hypothesis testing in classical statistics. Theorem 9.5.2 provided the basis for our discussion of confidence intervals in Section 9.5. Theorems 9.6.1 and 9.6.2 are based on Theorem 9.5.2, and they in turn provide the basic ingredients for testing linear hypotheses about the regression coefficients.

Our approach closely follows the general classical approach to hypothesis testing outlined in Section 7.2. Considering the case of testing a null hypothesis H_1, comprising J sharp linear restrictions on the regression coefficients β, versus a two-sided alternative hypothesis H_2. Specifically, define

$$H_1\colon R\beta = r, \tag{9.6.1a}$$

$$H_2\colon R\beta \neq r, \tag{9.6.2a}$$

where R is a known $J \times K$ constant matrix with rank$(R) = J$, and r is a known J-dimensional column vector of constants. We seek a *test statistic* f and a *critical region* $\mathscr{S}_2$, which is a subset of the sample space, such that for a given *level of significance* α:

$$\text{Prob(Type I error)} = \text{Prob(rejecting } H_1 | H_1) = \text{Prob}(f \in \mathscr{S}_2 | H_1) = \alpha. \tag{9.6.3}$$

In addition among a selected subset of tests that satisfy (9.6.3), we seek a test which maximizes (in some appropriate sense) the *power*:

$$\mathscr{P}(\delta) \equiv 1 - \text{Prob(Type II error} | H_2) = \text{Prob}(f \in \mathscr{S}_2 | H_2), \tag{9.6.4}$$

where the $J \times 1$ vector

$$\delta \equiv r - R\beta \tag{9.6.5}$$

measures the departure from H_1. Note that hypotheses (9.6.1) and (9.6.2) can be equivalently stated in terms of δ as

$$\mathrm{H}_1\colon \delta = 0_J, \tag{9.6.1b}$$

$$H_2\colon \delta \neq 0_J. \tag{9.6.2b}$$

In general, the classical hypothesis tests (Wald, Likelihood Ratio and Lagrange Multiplier/efficient score) yield different results and have a common asymptotic basis only under the null hypothesis and local alternatives $\delta = O(T^{-1/2})$ (see Section 7.3). For the problem at hand, all three procedures are monotonic functions of the F-test developed later in this chapter, and hence once adjusted to have the same finite sample size, each test gives rise to the same critical region (see Engle 1984, pp. 785–786).

An obvious way of constructing a test statistic for H_1 versus H_2 is to consider the following estimator of δ:

$$\hat{\delta} = r - Rb, \tag{9.6.6}$$

where b is the OLS estimator (see Equation 9.2.4). Under the standard multiple linear normal regression model with either fixed or stochastic regressors, it follows from Theorems 9.4.4 and 9.4.4 that

$$\hat{\delta} \sim N_J(\delta, \sigma^2 R[X'X]^{-1}R'). \tag{9.6.7}$$

(The matter of unconditional inference for Case II is addressed later.) The following theorem provides the statistical basis for subsequent analysis in this section.

Theorem 9.6.1 Let

$$\omega_I = \tfrac{1}{2}\delta'[\sigma^2 R(X'X)^{-1}R']^{-1}\delta. \tag{9.6.8a}$$

$$\omega_{II} = \tfrac{1}{2}\delta'[\sigma^2 R\{E_{\tilde{X}|\theta}(X'X)^{-1}\}R']^{-1}\delta. \tag{9.6.8b}$$

Under the univariate normal linear regressor model with fixed or stochastic regressors:

(a) $w = \hat{\delta}'[\sigma^2 R(X'X)^{-1}R']^{-1}\hat{\delta} \sim \chi^2(J, \omega)$.

(b) $$f = \frac{w/J}{[(T-K)s^2/\sigma^2]/(T-K)} = \frac{\hat{\delta}'[R(X'X)^{-1}R']^{-1}\hat{\delta}}{Js^2} \sim F(J, T-K, \omega). \quad (9.6.9a)$$

where $\omega = \omega_I$ or $\omega = \omega_{II}$.

Proof

(a) The result follows directly from (9.6.7) and Theorem 4.5.2.

(b) The independence of b and s^2 in Theorems 9.4.1(c) and 9.4.2(c) implies (Theorem 2.5.1) that w and s^2 are independent. By Theorems 9.4.1(b) and 9.4.2(b), $(T-K)s^2/\sigma^2 \sim \chi^2(T-K)$. These two results, together with part (a) and Theorem 4.5.4, imply $f \sim F(J, T-K, \omega)$. Note that f is free of the nuisance parameter σ^2.

Corollary 9.6.1 Under the assumptions of Theorem 9.6.1 and the null hypothesis H_1 given by (9.6.1), $f \sim F(J, T-K)$.

Proof Under H_1: $\delta = 0_J$, noncentrality parameter (9.6.8) is $\omega = 0$. Therefore, f has a central F-distribution with J and $T-K$ degrees of freedom by Theorem 9.6.1(b).

Note that the distribution of the test statistic f under H_1 is identical to the distribution in Theorems 9.4.5(c) and 9.4.6(c), which served as a basis for constructing confidence intervals. Here f serves as a pivotal quantity under the null hypothesis because it is a statistic and its null distribution does *not* depend on any unknown parameters. As a test statistic for the null hypothesis H_1: $\delta = 0_J$, clearly large values of f favor H_2: $\delta \neq 0_J$.[18] This suggests the α-level critical region:

$$\mathscr{S}_2 \equiv \{f \mid f \geq F(1-\alpha; J, T-K)\}, \quad (9.6.10)$$

where $F(1-\alpha; J, T-K)$ denotes the $100(1-\alpha)$ percentile of an F-distribution with J and $T-K$ degrees of freedom in the numerator and denominator, respectively. Therefore, the following testing procedure will be adopted: Reject H_1: $R\beta = r$ iff the realized value of f falls in (9.6.10), that is, iff $f \geq F(1-\alpha; J, T-K)$. Critical region (9.6.10) comprises the complement of probability region (9.5.3). Hence, a realized confidence region based on (9.5.3) can be interpreted as the set of all null hypotheses that the data cannot reject.

18. As noted in Table 4.5.1(II), $E_{y|X,\beta,\sigma^{-2}}(f) = [(T-K)(J+\omega)]/[J(T-K-2)]$ if $T-K > 2$, which is clearly monotonically increasing in the noncentrality parameter ω.

Calculation of f is facilitated by the following algebraic equivalences.

Theorem 9.6.2 Consider the test statistic f defined in (9.6.9a). Then:

$$f = \frac{(Rb - r)'[R(X'X)^{-1}R']^{-1}(Rb - r)}{Js^2} \tag{9.6.9b}$$

$$= \frac{(b^* - b)'X'X(b^* - b)}{Js^2} \tag{9.6.9c}$$

$$= \frac{[\text{SSE}(b^*) - \text{SSE}(b)]/J}{\text{SSE}(b)/(T - K)} \tag{9.6.9d}$$

$$= \frac{(R^2_{\text{raw}} - R^2_{*\text{raw}})/J}{(1 - R^2_{\text{raw}})/(T - K)} \tag{9.6.9e}$$

$$= \frac{(R^2 - R^2_*)/J}{(1 - R^2)/(T - K)}, \tag{9.6.9f}$$

where $R^2_{*\text{raw}} = 1 - [\text{SSE}(b^*)/y'y]$, b and b^* are the OLS and RLS estimators given by (9.2.4) and (9.3.8), respectively, and (9.6.9f) holds only if the model contains an intercept under both H_1 and H_2.

Proof The validity of (9.6.9b) follows from simply substituting (9.6.5) directly into (9.6.9a). The equivalence of (9.6.9c) and (9.6.9b) follows from substituting (9.3.8) directly into (9.6.9c). Alternative formulation (9.6.9d) follows directly from either (9.3.9) or (9.3.10). Finally, formulations (9.6.9e) and (9.6.9f) following directly by using (9.2.39) and (9.2.45).

Using (9.6.4), the *power* of the test corresponding to critical region (9.6.10) is

$$\mathscr{P} = \mathscr{P}(\omega) = \text{Prob}(\text{rejecting } H_1 | H_2)$$

$$= \int_{F(1-\alpha;J,T-K;0)}^{\infty} f_2(z|J, T - K, \omega)\, dz, \tag{9.6.11}$$

where $f_2(z|J, T - K, \omega)$ denotes the noncentral f density with J and $T - K$ degrees of freedom and non-centrality parameter ω. Kendall and Stuart (1979, p. 270) provide a reference list of various tables and charts for evaluating (9.6.11). A simple approximation to (9.6.11) can be made by noting the fact that if $f \sim F(J, T - K; \omega)$, then

$$\tilde{f} \equiv [(J + \omega)/J]f \sim F(v_1, T - K), \tag{9.6.12}$$

where

$$v_1 \equiv (J + \omega)^2/(J + 2\omega). \tag{9.6.13}$$

Thus (9.6.11) can be approximated by

$$\mathscr{P}(\omega) \doteq \int_{F(1-\alpha;J,T-K)}^{\infty} f_1(z|v_1, T-K)\,dz, \tag{9.6.14}$$

where $f_1(z|v_1, T-K)$ denotes the density of a *central* F-distribution with v_1 and $T-K$ degrees of freedom. Patnaik (1949) shows that the power function calculated from (9.6.14) is generally accurate to two significant digits. See Kendall and Stuart (1979, pp. 270–271) for more details.

Statistical properties of the standard F-test based on f are discussed in some detail by Seber (1980, pp. 34–39). Clearly, critical region (9.6.10) is a *similar region* because the size of the test is α under H_1 for all values of the nuisance parameters. This result holds because the test statistic is free of all nuisance parameters under the null hypothesis H_1. The power of the test depends on the unknown values of δ and σ^2 under H_2 only through the value of the noncentrality parameter ω defined by (9.6.8). Furthermore, it can be shown that $\mathscr{P}(\omega)$ is (1) decreasing in v_1, holding v_2 and ω constant; (2) increasing in v_2, holding v_1 and ω constant; and (3) an increasing function of ω, holding v_1 and v_2 constant. This last fact implies that $\mathscr{P}(\omega) > \mathscr{P}(0)$ for all $\omega > 0$. Becauce $\omega = 0$ only under the null hypothesis H_1: $\delta = 0_J$ (because the matrix of the quadratic form in (9.6.8) is positive definite under Assumption 3), it follows that $\mathscr{P}(\omega) > \alpha$, and hence, that the test is *unbiased*. From the optimality standpoint, critical region (9.6.10) is UMP (uniformly most powerful) among all unbiased tests. Also the test is UMP invariant among all tests whose power depends only on the non-centrality parameter ω. Furthermore, it is UMP among all tests that are invariant to transformations of the form $y \to c_0 y + Xc_1$, where $c_0 > 0$ and c_1 is $K \times 1$. Finally, all these properties, as well as the confidence intervals derived in Section 9.5, continue to hold when the normality assumption is generalized to other members of the spherical family of distributions (see Ullah and Zinde-Walsh 1985).

We will now illustrate the wide applicability of Theorem 9.6.1 by a series of examples.

Example 9.6.1 Consider the standard linear normal regression model of Exercise 9.2.18:

$$y = X\beta + u \tag{9.6.15a}$$

$$= X_1\beta_1 + X_2\beta_2 + u, \tag{9.6.15b}$$

where $X = [X_1, X_2]$, $\beta = [\beta_1', \beta_2']'$, X_i is a $T \times K_i$ $(i = 1, 2)$, β_i is a $K_i \times 1$ $(i = 1, 2)$ and $\operatorname{rank}(X) = K_1 + K_2 = K$. Consider the hypotheses

$$H_1\colon \beta_2 = 0, \tag{9.6.16}$$

$$H_2\colon \beta_2 \neq 0. \tag{9.6.17}$$

H_1 asserts that the regressors in X_2 have no impact on $E(y|X_1, X_2)$. The RLS estimator under H_1 is $b^* = [(b_1^*)', 0']'$, where $b_1^* = (X_1'X_1)^{-1}X_1'y$,

$\text{SSE}(b^*) = y'M_1y$ and M_1 is defined in (9.2.94). Substituting these values into (9.6.9a) through (9.6.9e), the F-statistic may be computed and H_1 tested. If X_1 contains an intercept, then (9.6.9f) may also be used. If $J = K - 1$ and X_1 contains only an intercept, then

$$f = \left(\frac{\text{SSR}}{\text{SSE}}\right)\left(\frac{T-K}{K-1}\right) = \left(\frac{R^2}{1-R^2}\right)\left(\frac{T-K}{K-1}\right), \tag{9.6.18}$$

and noncentrality parameter (9.6.8) reduces to

$$\omega = \delta' X_2' A X_2 \delta / 2\sigma^2, \tag{9.6.19}$$

where A is the now familiar idempotent matrix $A = I_T - T^{-1}\iota_T\iota_T'$.

Example 9.6.2 In order to see the connection between individual t-tests and a joint F-test in the standard linear normal regression model, let τ_k $(k = 2, 3, \ldots, K)$ be the t-statistic for testing $\beta_k = 0$, let f be the F-statistic in (9.6.18) for testing $\beta_2 = \beta_3 = \cdots = \beta_K = 0$, let r_{kj} be the simple correlation between the kth and jth regressors, and let m^{kk} be the kth diagonal element of the inverse of the correlation matrix. Then Duchan (1969) showed that

$$\begin{aligned} f &= \frac{1}{K-1}\sum_{k=2}^{K}\sum_{j=2}^{K} r_{kj}\tau_k\tau_j[m^{kk}m^{jj}]^{1/2} \\ &= \frac{1}{K-1}\sum_{k=2}^{K}\sum_{j=2}^{K} \frac{\tau_{kj}\tau_k\tau_j}{[(1-R_k^2)(1-R_j^2)]^{1/2}}, \end{aligned} \tag{9.6.20}$$

where R_k^2 is the coefficient of determination in the regression of the kth regressor variable on all other regressors (including a constant regressor). In the case $K = 3$ (see Example 8.2.2), (9.6.20) reduces to

$$f = \frac{\tau_2^2 + \tau_3^2 + 2\tau_2\tau_3 r_{23}}{2(1 - r_{23}^2)}. \tag{9.6.21}$$

If r_{23} is not far from unity, then f will be large even if both τ_2 and τ_3 are small. Thus neither b_2 nor b_3 may be significantly different from zero and yet the value of f may be highly significant. As Kmenta (1986, pp. 415–416) notes, if $T = 20$, $\tau_2 = \tau_3 = 1.444$ and $r_{23} = .95$, then $f = 41.5$. Similarly, it is possible for f to be "small" and both τ_2 and τ_3 to be large. For example, consider $T = 63$, $\tau_2 = \tau_3 = 2$ and $r_{23} = -1/3$. Then $f = 3$ and the corresponding $\alpha = .05$ critical values for the t-test and F-tests are approximately 1.96 and 3.15.

Example 9.6.3 The general case in Theorem 9.6.1 of testing the null hypothesis $R\beta = r$ can always be recast into a test of a null hypothesis of the form $\gamma_2 = r$ in a reparameterized regression of the form:

$$y = Z\gamma + u = Z_1\gamma_1 + Z_2\gamma_2 + u. \tag{9.6.22}$$

If $r = 0_J$, then the recast problem is similar to that in Example 9.6.1. If $r \neq 0_J$, then transforming the dependent variable y to $y - X_2 r$ recasts the problem into one similar to Example 9.6.1. To see this fact, partition the regressor and restriction matrices as $X = [X_1, X_2]$ and $R = [R_1, R_2]$, where X_1 is $T \times (K - J)$, X_2 is $T \times J$, R_1 is $J \times (K - J)$ and R_2 is $J \times J$. Also partition coefficient vector as $\beta = [\beta_1', \beta_2']'$, where β_1 is $(K - J) \times 1$ and β_2 is $J \times 1$. Define the $K \times K$ matrix

$$A = \begin{bmatrix} I_{K-J} & 0_{(K-J)\times J} \\ R_1 & R_2 \end{bmatrix}, \tag{9.6.23}$$

and reparameterize the original model (9.6.15a) as follows:

$$\begin{aligned} y &= (XA^{-1})(A\beta) + u \\ &= Z\gamma + u, \end{aligned} \tag{9.6.24}$$

where

$$\begin{aligned} Z &\equiv [Z_1, Z_2] = XA^{-1} \\ &= [X_1 - X_2R_2^{-1}R_1, X_2R_2^{-1}], \end{aligned} \tag{9.6.25}$$

$$A^{-1} = \begin{bmatrix} I_{K-J} & O_{(K-J)\times J} \\ -R_2^{-1}R_1 & R_2^{-1} \end{bmatrix}, \tag{9.6.26}$$

$$\gamma = [\gamma_1', \gamma_2']' = A\beta = [\beta_1', (R\beta)'] . \tag{9.6.27}$$

From (9.6.27) it is clear that testing $R\beta = r$ is equivalent to testing $\gamma_2 = r$ in (9.6.22).

Example 9.6.4 A test of particular interest in applied work is the following. Consider a set of N mutually independent standard linear normal regression models:

$$y_n = X_n\beta_n + u_n \; (n = 1, 2, \ldots, N). \tag{9.6.28}$$

We will assume that model n contains $T_n > K$ observations, K regressors, and that

$$u_n \sim N_{T_n}(0_{T_n}, \sigma^2 I_{T_n}) \; (n = 1, 2, \ldots, N) \tag{9.6.29}$$

under Case I, or

$$u_n | X_n \sim N_{T_n}(0_{T_n}, \sigma^2 I_{T_n}) \; (n = 1, 2, \ldots, N) \tag{9.6.30}$$

under Case II. Note that (9.6.29) and (9.6.30) imply homoskedasticity across models.[19] Defining

$$y \equiv [y_1', y_2', \ldots, y_N']', \tag{9.6.31}$$

$$X = \begin{bmatrix} X_1 & 0_{T_1\times K} & \cdots & 0_{T_1\times K} \\ 0_{T_2\times K} & X_2 & \cdots & 0_{T_2\times K} \\ \vdots & \vdots & & \vdots \\ 0_{T_N\times K} & 0_{T_N\times K} & \cdots & X_N \end{bmatrix}, \tag{9.6.32}$$

19. The case $T_1 = T_2 = 1 \cdots = T_N$, $E(u_n u_i') = \sigma_{ni} I_T$ $(i, n = 1, 2, \ldots, N)$, and $X_1 = X_2 = \cdots = X_N$ is referred to as the *multivariate regression model.* When there are no restrictions on X_n $(n = 1, 2, \ldots, N)$, including their column dimensions, the case is known as the *Seemingly Unrelated Regression (SUR)* model. The literatures in both cases are quite extensive.

$$\beta = [\beta_1', \beta_2', \ldots, \beta_N']', \tag{9.6.33}$$

$$u = [u_1', u_2', \ldots, u_N']', \tag{9.6.34}$$

(9.6.28) can be conveniently written as

$$y = X\beta + u, \tag{9.6.35}$$

where $T \equiv T_1 + T_2 + \cdots + T_N$, y is $T \times 1$, X is $T \times NK$, β is $NK \times 1$ and $u \sim N_T(0_T, \sigma^2 I_T)$. The hypotheses of interest are

$$H_1\colon \beta_1 = \beta_2 = \cdots = \beta_N, \tag{9.6.36}$$

$$H_2\colon \beta_i \neq \beta_j \text{ for some } i \neq j. \tag{9.6.37}$$

The $(N-1)K$ constraints in null hypothesis (9.6.36) can alternatively be expressed

$$H_1\colon \beta_n = \beta_N \ (n = 1, 2, \ldots, N-1), \tag{9.6.38}$$

or

$$H_1\colon R\beta = 0_{(N-1)K}, \tag{9.6.39}$$

where R is the $(N-1)K \times NK$ matrix

$$R = \begin{bmatrix} I_K & 0_{K\times K} & \cdots & 0_{K\times K} & -I_K \\ 0_{K\times K} & I_K & \cdots & 0_{K\times K} & -I_K \\ \vdots & \vdots & & \vdots & \vdots \\ 0_{K\times K} & 0_{K\times K} & \cdots & I_K & -I_K \end{bmatrix}. \tag{9.6.40}$$

Estimation under H_1 may be performed by applying OLS to

$$y = [X_1', X_2', \ldots, X_N']'\beta_N + u, \tag{9.6.41}$$

to obtain

$$b_N^* = \left[\sum_{n=1}^{N} X_n'X_n\right]^{-1}\left[\sum_{n=1}^{N} X_n'y_n\right], \tag{9.6.42}$$

$$\hat{u}^{*\prime}\hat{u}^* = \sum_{n=1}^{N} (y_n - X_n b_n^*)'(y - X_n b_N^*). \tag{9.6.43}$$

Estimation under H_2 involves applying OLS separately to each of the N models in (9.6.28) to yield

$$b_n = (X_n'X_n)^{-1}X_n'y_n \ (n = 1, 2, \ldots, N), \tag{9.6.44}$$

$$\hat{u}_n'\hat{u}_n = (y_n - X_n b_n)'(y_n - X_n b_n) \ (n = 1, 2, \ldots, N), \tag{9.6.45}$$

$$b = [b_1', b_2', \ldots, b_N']', \tag{9.6.46}$$

$$\hat{u}'\hat{u} = \sum_{n=1}^{N} \hat{u}_n'\hat{u}_n. \tag{9.6.47}$$

Hence it follows from (9.6.9d) of Theorem 9.6.2 that under H_1,

$$f = \left[\frac{(\hat{u}^{*\prime}\hat{u}^* - \hat{u}'\hat{u})/(N-1)K}{\hat{u}'\hat{u}/(T - NK)}\right] \sim F[(N-1)K, T - NK]. \tag{9.6.48}$$

The case where $N = 2$ and $T_2 < K$, considered in Exercise 9.6.4, is referred to as a *Chow test* after Chow (1960). Dufour (1982) considers the Chow test when $N > 2$ and the X_n's have arbitrary ranks. Cantrell et al. (1991) derive the noncentrality parameter for the test proposed by Dufour (1982). In the case $N = 2$, Rea (1978) points out that the Chow test has no power over certain regions of the parameter space in which $\beta_1 \neq \beta_2$. A helpful survey of these and related models is Pesaran et al. (1985). Exercises 9.6.4 through 9.6.8 consider related cases.

It may come somewhat as a surprise to the reader that replacing two-sided alternative hypothesis (9.6.2) by the one sided alternative

$$H_3\colon R\beta \geq r \text{ and } R\beta \neq r \tag{9.6.49}$$

results in substantial complications when $J > 1$, unlike in the case $J = 1$.[20] Few finite sample results are available, and those available are exceedingly complicated. For a recent detailed exposition of the problem, see Wolak (1989).[21] We do not devote more space here to this problem, not because it is lacking in relevance, but rather because the Bayesian solution is so strikingly simple and straightforward, as will be seen in Section 9.10 and as demonstrated in Geweke (1986).

The case of unconditional inference in the presence of stochastic regressors (as opposed to conditional inference on $\tilde{X}$) is both similar and different. It is similar in the sense that the distribution of f under H_1, provided the regressors are i.i.d. $N_{K-1}(\mu_x, \Sigma_{xx})$, is the same central F-distribution with J and $T - K$ degrees of freedom as given in Corollary 9.6.1. Thus the confidence levels of Section 9.5 and the type I error probabilities of this section remain unchanged. Under the alternative hypothesis H_2, however, the conditional (on $\tilde{X}$) noncentral F-distribution for the test statistic f found in Theorem 9.6.1(a) depends on $\tilde{X}$ through noncentrality parameter (9.6.8). Hence widths of confidence intervals, type II errors and the power of tests depend on $\tilde{X}$ and hence differ from those studied here. See Graybill (1976, pp. 384–385) for details.

All of the preceding examples involve sharp null hypotheses. The relevance of the question of the exact "truth" of a sharp null hypothesis has long been a topic of debate in statistics (e.g., see Berkson 1938 and Hodges and Lehmann 1954) and Section 7.6. As Kadane and Dickey (1980) note:

> Nearly every model used in econometrics is known a priori to be literally false. Because of this, although a typical statistical test with a small sample will rarely

20. If a and b are $J \times 1$ vectors, then $a \geq b$ denotes $a_j \geq b_j$ $(j = 1, 2, \ldots, J)$.

21. One simple, but not necessarily powerful test, is suggested by King and Smith (1986) who reparameterize the model as in (9.6.22), and then propose a *univariate* t-test of $\psi = 0$ versus $\psi \geq 0$ in the regression $y = X_1\gamma_1 + (X_2\gamma_2^*)\psi + u$, where γ_2^* is a pre-selected vector (say, $\gamma_2^* = \iota_J$). The test is UMP in the neighborhood of $\gamma_2 = \psi\gamma_2^*$, $\psi > 0$, against tests invariant with respect to transformations of the form $y \rightarrow c_0 y + X_1 c_1$, where $c_0 > 0$ and c_1 is a $(K - J) \times 1$ vector.

reject, for large enough samples it will nearly always reject. Consequently, whether a test rejects a null hypothesis appears to have more to do with the sample size than with how true the null hypothesis is. For these reasons we find methods based on classical tests of hypotheses to be most unsatisfactory. A purist may object, saying that the level of a test should be set in consideration of the power that can be achieved with that sample size, but after all these years there is no satisfactory theory of how to decide what level of test to set, and most practitioners use .05 or .01 in an automatic way, without justification.

Kadane and Dickey (1980) further argue that the fundamental problem with the test of a hypothesis lies not in the failure to jiggle the level of significance satisfactorily, but rather with the underlying fact of having asked a poor question. Usually, the important practical question is not, say, whether the true effect of a regressor is nonzero, since it is already known not to be exactly zero, but rather: "How large is the effect?" A point estimate and a confidence interval around it provide one answer. A hypothesis test goes beyond this question in that it attempts to give guidance as to the appropriate actions to be taken based on an answer to this question. Satisfactory guidance can only be given with reference to the utility function of the concerned scientist, however, hence an explicit decision theoretic analysis seems more appropriate.

Exercises

9.6.1 Define $\hat{y}^* = Xb^*$, where b^* is the RLS estimator subject to $R\beta = r$. Verify or disprove each of the following decompositions analogous to (9.2.38) and (9.2.43):

$$y'y = (\hat{y}^*)'\hat{y}^* + \mathrm{SSE}(b^*), \tag{9.6.50}$$

$$\mathrm{SST} = (\hat{y}^*)'A(\hat{y}^*) + \mathrm{SSE}(b^*). \tag{9.6.51}$$

9.6.2 Consider Exercise 9.2.8. Test $H_1\colon \beta_2 = \beta_3 = 0$ versus $H_2\colon \beta_2 \neq 0$ or $\beta_3 \neq 0$ at the ten percent level of significance.

9.6.3 Consider Exercise 9.3.4. Test the restrictions at the five percent level of significance.

9.6.4 (Chow Test) Consider Example 9.6.4 in the case $N = 2$, $T_1 > K$ and $T_2 < K$. Let $\hat{u}^*$ be the vector of calculated residuals from restricted regression (9.6.41), and let $\hat{u}_n$ $(n = 1, 2)$ be the vector of calculated residuals from unrestricted regression (9.6.28). Then $\hat{u}^* = M^*u$ and $\hat{u}_1 = M_1 u$, where $M^* \equiv I_T - X^*[(X^*)'X^*]^{-1}(X^*)'$, $X^* \equiv [X_1', X_2']'$ and $M_1 \equiv I_T - X_1(X_1'X_1)^{-1}X_1'$.

(a) Show that $\hat{u}_2 = 0$, and hence using (9.6.47), $\hat{u}'\hat{u} = \hat{u}_1'\hat{u}_1 = u'Mu$, where

$$M = \begin{bmatrix} M_1 & 0_{T_1 \times T_2} \\ 0_{T_2 \times T_1} & 0_{T_2 \times T_2} \end{bmatrix}. \tag{9.6.52}$$

(b) Show: $\mathrm{tr}(M^*) = T_1 + T_2 - K$ and $\mathrm{tr}(M) = T_1 - K$.

(c) Using Theorem 4.5.10, show that under $H_1\colon \beta_1 = \beta_2$,

$$f = \left[\frac{(\hat{u}^{*\prime}\hat{u}^* - \hat{u}'\hat{u})/T_2}{(\hat{u}'\hat{u})/(T_1 - K)}\right] \sim F(T_2, T_1 - K). \tag{9.6.53}$$

9.6.5 Consider Example 9.6.4 with a structure reminiscent of Example 9.6.1:

$$y_1 = X_1\beta_1 + u_1 = X_{11}\beta_{11} + X_{12}\beta_{12} + u_1, \tag{9.6.54}$$

$$y_2 = X_2\beta_2 + u_2 = X_{21}\beta_{21} + X_{22}\beta_{22} + u_2, \tag{9.6.55}$$

where X_{ni} is $T_n \times K_i$ $(n, i = 1, 2)$, $u \equiv [u_1', u_2']' \sim N_T(0, \sigma^2 I_T)$, $T = T_1 + T_2$ and let $K = K_1 + K_2$. Consider the null hypotheses H_1: $\beta_{11} = \beta_{21}$ and the restricted pooled model

$$\begin{bmatrix} y_1 \\ y_2 \end{bmatrix} = \begin{bmatrix} X_{11} & X_{12} & 0_{T_1 \times K_2} \\ X_{21} & 0_{T_2 \times K_1} & X_{22} \end{bmatrix} \begin{bmatrix} \beta_{11} \\ \beta_{12} \\ \beta_{22} \end{bmatrix} + \begin{bmatrix} u_1 \\ u_2 \end{bmatrix} \tag{9.6.56}$$

with OLS residuals $\hat{u}^*$. Assuming $T_1 > K$ and $T_2 > K$, show that

$$f = \left[\frac{(\hat{u}^{*\prime}\hat{u}^* - \hat{u}'\hat{u})/K_1}{(\hat{u}'\hat{u})/(T - 2K)}\right] \sim F(K_1, T - 2K), \tag{9.6.57}$$

where $\hat{u}$ is the vector of OLS residuals from the unrestricted pooled model given by (9.6.54) and (9.6.55).

9.6.6 Consider Exercise 9.6.5 with $T_1 > K$ and $K_2 < T_2 \le K$. Under H_1: $\beta_{11} = \beta_{21}$, show:

$$f = \left[\frac{(\hat{u}^{*\prime}\hat{u}^* - \hat{u}'\hat{u})/(T_2 + K_2)K_1}{(\hat{u}'\hat{u})/(T - K_1)}\right] \sim F(T_2 - K_2, T_1 - K). \tag{9.6.58}$$

9.6.7 Derive the appropriate test of H_1: $\beta_{11} = \beta_{21}$ in Exercise 9.6.5 with the maintained hypothesis $\beta_{12} = \beta_{22}$.

9.6.8 Derive the appropriate test of H_1: $\beta_{11} = \beta_{21}$ in Exercise 9.6.6 with the maintained hypothesis $\beta_{12} = \beta_{22}$.

9.6.9 Consider your homework problem Exercise 9.2.18 involving the standard multiple linear normal regression model with fixed regressors: $y = X_1\beta_1 + X_2\beta_2 + u$.

(a) In part (b) of Exercise 9.2.18 you showed that the OLS estimator of β_2 was $b_2 = (X_2'M_1X_2)^{-1}X_2'M_1y$, where $M_1 = I_T - X_1(X_1'X_1)^{-1}X_1'$. Give a geometrical interpretation of b_2.

(b) Define $W \equiv b_2'(X_2'M_1X_2)b_2/K_2s^2$. Find the distribution of W.

9.6.10 Verify (9.6.19) using Example 9.5.1.

9.6.11 Let X and X_* be $T \times K_1$ and $T \times K_2$ matrices such that $X = X_*A$, where A is $K_2 \times K_1$. Show that $MM_* = M_*$, where $M = I_T - X(X'X)^{-1}X'$ and $M_* = I_T - X_*(X_*X_*)^{-1}X_*'$. Relate your result to Theorem 4.5.10 and the hypothesis tests of Section 9.6.

9.6.12 Demonstrate (9.6.26).

9.6.13 *Purchasing-power parity* (PPP) is an economic theory that states that the exchange rate between two currencies is in long-run "equilibrium" when the prices of identical bundles of traded goods and services in both countries are equalized. As an indication of the empirical validity of this famous theory, *The Economist* (April 17, 1993, p. 79) published data on the price of McDonald's Big Mac in 24 countries. Table 9.6.1 contains the actual exchange rate $\tilde{x}_t$ on April 13, 1993 for the currencies of $T = 24$ countries in terms of the \$US (i.e., local currency units per \$US), and the implied PPP of the \$US, y_t (i.e., local price divided by price in the United States—actually an average of the prices in Atlanta, Chicago, New York, and San Francisco). For example, the price of a Big Mac in the United States was \$2.28 (\$US) (including sales taxes) and \$2.76 (\$CN) in Canada, implying the PPP of the \$US in terms of \$CN is 2.76/2.28 = 1.21. In other words, the \$CN is undervalued by 4% = [(126 − 121) × 100%]/

Table 9.6.1
Data for Exercise 9.6.14

Country	Actual exchange rate ($\tilde{x}_t$)	Implied PPP of the $US ($y_t$)
Argentina	1.00	1.58
Australia	1.39	1.07
Belgium	32.45	47.81
Brazil	27521	33772
Britain	.641	.787
Canada	1.26	1.21
China	5.68	3.73
Denmark	6.06	11.29
France	5.34	8.11
Germany	1.58	2.02
Holland	1.77	2.39
Hong Kong	7.73	3.95
Hungary	88.18	68.86
Ireland	.649	.649
Italy	1523	1974
Japan	113	171
Malaysia	2.58	1.47
Mexico	3.10	3.11
Russia	686	342
South Korea	796	1009
Spain	114	143
Sweden	7.43	11.18
Switzerland	1.45	2.50
Thailand	25.16	21.05

121 versus the $US. Using the data of Table 9.6.1, and assuming the validity of the standard normal linear regression model, estimate the regression $y_t = \beta_1 + \beta_2 \tilde{x}_t + u_t$, and test H_1: $\beta_1 = 0$ and $\beta_2 = 1$ versus H_2: $\beta_1 \neq 0$ or $\beta_2 \neq 1$ at the .05 level of significance.

9.7 Dummy Variables

Let us remember the unfortunate econometrician who, in one of the major functions of his system, had to use a proxy for risk and a dummy for sex.
—Machlup (1974, p. 892)

We begin with a simple definition.

Definition 9.7.1 A *dummy (or binary) variable* is a variable that can take on only two values, usually either zero or one.

Dummy variables can be used to represent *qualitative* effects such as race, gender, or religious affiliation. Dummy variables can also be used to represent underlying quantitative effects that have been classified (e.g., income, age, and education classes). Obviously, there is a loss of information in using a dummy variable classification of an inherently continuous variable.

To illustrate the use of dummy variables we consider a series of simple examples which for purposes of exposition omit non-binary variables from the conditioning set.

Example 9.7.1 (Formulation I) Consider a sample of T recent university job market candidates who successfully obtained their first full-time job. For $t = 1, 2, \ldots, T$ define the following variables:

y_t = starting earnings of candidate t,

$$z_{t1} = \left\{\begin{matrix} 1, & \text{if the highest degree achieved by candidate } t \text{ is a bachelors} \\ 0, & \text{otherwise} \end{matrix}\right\},$$

$$z_{t2} = \left\{\begin{matrix} 1, & \text{if the highest degree achieved by candidate } t \text{ is a masters} \\ 0, & \text{otherwise} \end{matrix}\right\},$$

$$z_{t3} = \left\{\begin{matrix} 1, & \text{if the highest degree achieved by candidate } t \text{ is a PhD} \\ 0, & \text{otherwise} \end{matrix}\right\},$$

Suppose the T observations are ordered so that the first T_1 have $z_{t1} = 1$, the next T_2 have $z_{t2} = 1$, and the last T_3 have $z_{t3} = 1$, where $T = T_1 + T_2 + T_3$. Under the standard multiple linear normal regression model with fixed regressors, consider

$$y_t = \beta_1 + \beta_2 z_{t2} + \beta_3 z_{t3} + u_t \; (t = 1, 2, \ldots, T), \tag{9.7.1a}$$

or

$$y = Z_I \beta + u, \tag{9.7.1b}$$

where

$$Z_I = \begin{bmatrix} \iota'_{T_1} & \iota'_{T_2} & \iota'_{T_3} \\ 0'_{T_1} & \iota'_{T_2} & 0'_{T_3} \\ 0'_{T_1} & 0'_{T_2} & \iota'_{T_3} \end{bmatrix}', \tag{9.7.2}$$

$$Z'_I Z_I = \begin{bmatrix} T & T_2 & T_3 \\ T_2 & T_2 & 0 \\ T_3 & 0 & T_3 \end{bmatrix}, \tag{9.7.3}$$

$$(Z'_I Z_I)^{-1} = \begin{bmatrix} \frac{1}{T_1} & -\frac{1}{T_1} & -\frac{1}{T_1} \\ -\frac{1}{T_1} & \frac{T_1 + T_2}{T_1 T_2} & \frac{1}{T_1} \\ -\frac{1}{T_1} & \frac{1}{T_1} & \frac{T_1 + T_3}{T_1 T_3} \end{bmatrix}, \tag{9.7.4}$$

$$Z_I'y = [T\bar{y}, T_2\bar{y}_2, T_3\bar{y}_3]'. \tag{9.7.5}$$

The OLS estimator is given by

$$b = [\bar{y}_1, \bar{y}_2 - \bar{y}_1, \bar{y}_3 - \bar{y}_1]', \tag{9.7.6}$$

where $\bar{y}_1$, $\bar{y}_2$, and $\bar{y}_3$ are the mean earnings corresponding to the first T_1, the next T_2, and the last T_3 observations.

To aid in the interpretation of the parameters, consider:

$$E(y_t|z_{t1} = 1, z_{t2} = 0, z_{t3} = 0) = \beta_1, \tag{9.7.7}$$

$$E(y_t|z_{t1} = 0, z_{t2} = 1, z_{t3} = 0) = \beta_1 + \beta_2, \tag{9.7.8}$$

$$E(y_t|z_{t1} = 0, z_{t2} = 0, z_{t3} = 1) = \beta_1 + \beta_3. \tag{9.7.9}$$

Then β_1 is the expected earnings of a candidate with only a bachelors degree, β_2 is the expected masters/bachelors earnings differential, and β_3 is expected Ph.D./bachelors earnings differential. A variety of hypothesis tests may be of interest. Under the null hypothesis

$$H_1\colon \beta_2 = 0, \tag{9.7.10}$$

holders of a masters as their highest degree earn the same starting earnings as those with a bachelors as their highest degree. Under the null hypothesis

$$H_2\colon \beta_3 = 0, \tag{9.7.11}$$

holders of a Ph.D. as their highest degree earn the same starting earnings as those with a bachelors degree as their highest degree. Under the null hypothesis

$$H_3\colon \beta_2 = \beta_3, \tag{9.7.12}$$

holders of a masters as their highest degree earn the same starting earnings as those with a Ph.D. as their highest degree. Under the null hypothesis

$$H_4\colon \beta_2 = \beta_3 = 0, \tag{9.7.13}$$

all three educational groups have the same expected starting earnings. Against two-sided alternatives, tests of null hypotheses (9.7.10) through (9.7.12) are t-tests, and a test of joint null hypothesis (9.7.13) is an F-test with 2 degrees of freedom in the numerator. One-sided alternatives involving $\beta_2 > 0$, $\beta_3 > 0$, $\beta_3 > \beta_2$, however, seem more appropriate in the present context. In the case of (9.7.10) through (9.7.12), these one-sided alternatives require standard one-sided t-tests. As noted in Section 9.6, however, in the case of (9.7.13) a joint one-sided alternative is difficult to handle.

Generalization of Example 9.7.1 to the case of G mutually exclusive groups is straightforward. It requires use of $G - 1$ dummies in addition to the unitary regressor corresponding to the intercept. If all G dummies are used together with an intercept, then the regressor matrix will not have full column rank, violating (9.1.1), because adding together the G columns corresponding to the mutually exclusive dummies yields ι_T. The coefficients of the $G - 1$ dummies measure deviations in the conditional means of y_t for the respective groups from the conditional mean for the omitted group.

An alternative parameterization is to omit the intercept term and include dummy variables for every group. This change results in the orthogonal model described in Example 9.7.2.

Example 9.7.2 (Formulation II) Consider

$$y_t = \beta_1 z_{t1} + \beta_2 z_{t2} + \beta_3 z_{t3} + u_t \ (t = 1, 2, \ldots, T) \tag{9.7.14}$$

or

$$y = Z_{\text{II}}\beta + u, \tag{9.7.15}$$

where

$$Z_{\text{II}} = \begin{bmatrix} \iota'_{T_1} & 0'_{T_2} & 0'_{T_3} \\ 0'_{T_1} & \iota'_{T_2} & 0'_{T_3} \\ 0'_{T_1} & 0'_{T_2} & \iota'_{T_3} \end{bmatrix}', \tag{9.7.16}$$

$$Z'_{\text{II}}Z_{\text{II}} = \begin{bmatrix} T_1 & 0 & 0 \\ 0 & T_2 & 0 \\ 0 & 0 & T_3 \end{bmatrix}, \tag{9.7.17}$$

$$(Z'_{\text{II}}Z_{\text{II}})^{-1} = \begin{bmatrix} \frac{1}{T_1} & 0 & 0 \\ 0 & \frac{1}{T_2} & 0 \\ 0 & 0 & \frac{1}{T_3} \end{bmatrix}, \tag{9.7.18}$$

$$Z'_{\text{II}}y = [T_1\bar{y}_1, T_2\bar{y}_2, T_3\bar{y}_3]'. \tag{9.7.19}$$

The OLS estimator is given by

$$b = [\bar{y}_1, \bar{y}_2, \bar{y}_3]', \tag{9.7.20}$$

In Parameterization II levels are estimated directly:

$$E(y_t | z_{t1} = 1, z_{t2} = 0, z_{t3} = 0) = \beta_1, \tag{9.7.21}$$

$$E(y_t | z_{t1} = 0, z_{t2} = 1, z_{t3} = 0) = \beta_2, \tag{9.7.22}$$

$$E(y_t | z_{t1} = 0, z_{t2} = 0, z_{t3} = 1) = \beta_3. \tag{9.7.23}$$

Unlike Formulation I, null hypotheses (9.7.10) and (9.7.11) are of little concern in Formulation II because zero starting earnings for any of the groups do *not* constitute interesting assertions. Null hypothesis (9.7.12) remains of interest and has the same interpretation as in Formulation I. Null hypothesis (9.7.13) in Formulation I, all three educational groups have the same mean starting earnings, becomes

$$H_5\colon \beta_1 = \beta_2 = \beta_3 \tag{9.7.24}$$

in Formulation II.

Formulations I and II are essentially the same except that in I deviations from the omitted class are estimated, whereas the actual means are estimated in II.

Example 9.7.3 (Formulation III) Consider

$$y_t = \beta_1 z_{t1} + \beta_2 z_{t2} + \beta_3 z_{t3} + \beta_4 + u_t, (t = 1, 2, \ldots, T), \tag{9.7.25}$$

subject to

$$\beta_1 + \beta_2 + \beta_3 = 0. \tag{9.7.26}$$

Using (9.7.26) to substitute-out β_3 in (9.7.25) yields

$$\begin{aligned} y_t &= \beta_1 z_{t1} + \beta_2 z_{t2} + (-\beta_1 - \beta_2) z_{t3} + \beta_4 + u_t \\ &= \beta_1(z_{t1} - z_{t3}) + \beta_2(z_{t2} - z_{t3}) + \beta_4 + u_t, \end{aligned} \tag{9.7.27}$$

where β_4 is a "pure" intercept. To aid in the interpretation of the parameters in this model, consider

$$E(y_t | z_{t1} = 1, z_{t2} = 0, z_{t3} = 0) = \beta_1 + \beta_4, \tag{9.7.28}$$

$$E(y_t | z_{t1} = 0, z_{t2} = 1, z_{t3} = 0) = \beta_2 + \beta_4, \tag{9.7.29}$$

$$E(y_t | z_{t1} = 0, z_{t2} = 0, z_{t3} = 1) = \beta_3 + \beta_4. \tag{9.7.30}$$

Also consider the marginal mean of y_t for a candidate who is equally likely to have each of the three possible terminal degrees. Then averaging across (9.7.28) through (9.7.30) and noting (9.7.26) yields

$$E(y_t) = \beta_4. \tag{9.7.31}$$

Comparison of (9.7.28) through (9.7.30) with (9.7.31) implies that β_k corresponds to deviation of the expected starting earnings for education group k ($k = 1, 2, 3$) from that of the "grand mean" in (9.7.31). Null hypotheses (9.7.10) through (9.7.12) remain interesting in the case of Formulation III, however, they now correspond to deviations from the grand mean rather than the mean of the omitted group as in Formulation I.

Formulations I, II, and III are equivalent formulations of the familiar *one-way analysis of variance model* involving the single "factor" education. By adding a second factor (e.g., gender) the model becomes a *two-way ANOVA model.* The following two examples generalize Examples 9.7.1 and 9.7.2 to include this factor.

Example 9.7.4 Define $z_t = [z_{t1}, z_{t2}, z_{t3}, z_{t4}]'$, where

$$z_{t4} = \begin{Bmatrix} 1, & \text{if candidate } t \text{ is female} \\ 0, & \text{otherwise} \end{Bmatrix}. \tag{9.7.32}$$

Consider modeling the conditional mean $E(y_t | z_t)$ by adding z_{t4} to Formulation I:

$$y_t = \beta_1 + \beta_2 z_{t2} + \beta_3 z_{t3} + \beta_4 z_{t4} + u_t, (t = 1, 2, \ldots, T). \tag{9.7.33}$$

The interpretation of parameters can be obtained by considering

$$E(y_t | z_{t1} = 1, z_{t2} = 0, z_{t3} = 0, z_{t4} = 0) = \beta_1, \tag{9.7.34}$$

$$E(y_t | z_{t1} = 0, z_{t2} = 1, z_{t3} = 0, z_{t4} = 0) = \beta_1 + \beta_2, \tag{9.7.35}$$

$$E(y_t | z_{t1} = 0, z_{t2} = 0, z_{t3} = 1, z_{t4} = 0) = \beta_1 + \beta_3, \tag{9.7.36}$$

$$E(y_t | z_{t1} = 1, z_{t2} = 0, z_{t3} = 0, z_{t4} = 1) = \beta_1 + \beta_4, \tag{9.7.37}$$

$$E(y_t | z_{t1} = 0, z_{t2} = 1, z_{t3} = 0, z_{t4} = 1) = \beta_1 + \beta_2 + \beta_4, \tag{9.7.38}$$

$$E(y_t | z_{t1} = 0, z_{t2} = 0, z_{t3} = 1, z_{t4} = 1) = \beta_1 + \beta_3 + \beta_4. \tag{9.7.39}$$

The interpretation of β_1, β_2 and β_3 is the same as in Example 9.7.1 for males. In addition, β_4 is the additive female differential which is constant across the three educational groups. An obvious null hypothesis of interest is

$$H_6: \beta_4 = 0. \tag{9.7.40}$$

Example 9.7.5 Consider the following two-way ANOVA model with interaction terms:

$$y_t = \beta_1 + \beta_2 z_{t2} + \beta_3 z_{t3} + \beta_4 z_{t4} + \beta_5 (z_{t2} z_{t4}) + \beta_6 (z_{t3} z_{t4}) + u_t \quad (t = 1, 2, \ldots, T). \tag{9.7.41}$$

To help interpret the parameters, consider:

$$E(y_t | z_{t1} = 1, z_{t2} = 0, z_{t3} = 0, z_{t4} = 0) = \beta_1, \tag{9.7.42}$$

$$E(y_t | z_{t1} = 0, z_{t2} = 1, z_{t3} = 0, z_{t4} = 0) = \beta_1 + \beta_2, \tag{9.7.43}$$

$$E(y_t | z_{t1} = 0, z_{t2} = 0, z_{t3} = 1, z_{t4} = 0) = \beta_1 + \beta_3, \tag{9.7.44}$$

$$E(y_t | z_{t1} = 1, z_{t2} = 0, z_{t3} = 0, z_{t4} = 1) = \beta_1 + \beta_4, \tag{9.7.45}$$

$$E(y_t | z_{t1} = 0, z_{t2} = 1, z_{t3} = 0, z_{t4} = 1) = \beta_1 + \beta_2 + \beta_4 + \beta_5, \tag{9.7.46}$$

$$E(y_t | z_{t1} = 0, z_{t2} = 0, z_{t3} = 1, z_{t4} = 1) = \beta_1 + \beta_3 + \beta_4 + \beta_6. \tag{9.7.47}$$

The interpretation of β_1, β_2 and β_3 is the same as in Example 9.7.1, except that it now applies only to males. Null hypotheses (9.7.10) through (9.7.12) are of interest for males. Unlike Example 9.7.4, in which the female-male earnings differential is constant across the three educational groups, in Example 9.7.5 the female-male earnings differential varies across the three educational groups. Specifically, β_4 is the additive female-male expected earnings differential for those candidates having a bachelors as the highest degree, β_5 is the additive female-male expected earnings differential on top of the bachelors differential for those candidates having a masters as the highest degree, and β_6 is the additive female-male expected earnings differential on top of the bachelors differential for those candidates having a Ph.D. as the highest degree. Also, $\beta_2 + \beta_5$ and $\beta_3 + \beta_6$ are the masters-bachelors and Ph.D.-bachelors expected earnings differentials for females. In addition to null hypothesis (9.7.40), it is also interesting to test:

$$H_7\colon \beta_5 = 0, \tag{9.7.48}$$

$$H_8\colon \beta_6 = 0. \tag{9.7.49}$$

The null hypothesis that there is no female/male expected earnings differential at any educational level corresponds to

$$H_9\colon \beta_4 = \beta_5 = \beta_6 = 0. \tag{9.7.50}$$

Finally, the test that the expected starting earnings is the same for all candidates is

$$H_{10}\colon \beta_2 = \beta_3 = \beta_4 = \beta_5 = \beta_6 = 0. \tag{9.7.51}$$

Example 9.7.6 Consider the following alternative formulation of Example 9.7.5:

$$y_t = \beta_1 z_{t1} + \beta_2 z_{t2} + \beta_3 z_{t3} + \beta_4(z_{t1}z_{t4}) + \beta_5(z_{t2}z_{t4}) + \beta_6(z_{t3}z_{t4}) + u_t \quad (t = 1, 2, \ldots, T). \tag{9.7.52}$$

The interpretation of parameters can be obtained by considering

$$E(y_t|z_{t1} = 1, z_{t2} = 0, z_{t3} = 0, z_{t4} = 0) = \beta_1, \tag{9.7.53}$$

$$E(y_t|z_{t1} = 0, z_{t2} = 1, z_{t3} = 0, z_{t4} = 0) = \beta_2, \tag{9.7.54}$$

$$E(y_t|z_{t1} = 0, z_{t2} = 0, z_{t3} = 1, z_{t4} = 0) = \beta_3, \tag{9.7.55}$$

$$E(y_t|z_{t1} = 1, z_{t2} = 0, z_{t3} = 0, z_{t4} = 1) = \beta_1 + \beta_4, \tag{9.7.56}$$

$$E(y_t|z_{t1} = 0, z_{t2} = 1, z_{t3} = 0, z_{t4} = 1) = \beta_2 + \beta_5, \tag{9.7.57}$$

$$E(y_t|z_{t1} = 0, z_{t2} = 0, z_{t3} = 1, z_{t4} = 1) = \beta_3 + \beta_6. \tag{9.7.58}$$

In (9.7.52) expected earnings levels for males β_k $(k = 1, 2, 3)$ are estimated directly. Null hypotheses (9.7.10) and (9.7.11) are of little interest because zero expected starting earnings for any of the groups do *not* constitute interesting positions. Null hypothesis (9.7.12) remains of interest and has the same interpretation as in Formulation I, except that it holds only for males. Null hypothesis (9.7.13), all three male educational groups have the same expected starting earnings, becomes

$$H_{11}\colon \beta_1 = \beta_2 = \beta_3. \tag{9.7.59}$$

The parameters β_k $(k = 4, 5, 6)$ correspond to female/male earnings differentials at each of the educational levels. Null hypotheses (9.7.40) and (9.7.48) through (9.7.50) remain interesting. Finally, the null hypothesis that the starting earnings is the same for all candidates is

$$H_{12}\colon \beta_1 = \beta_2 = \beta_3, \text{ and } \beta_4 = \beta_5 = \beta_6 = 0. \tag{9.7.60}$$

Next we move to a different context.

Example 9.7.7 Consider the regression model

$$y_t = \beta_1 + \beta_2 x_t + \beta_3 z_t + u_t \; (t = 1, 2, \ldots, T), \tag{9.7.61}$$

where y_t and x_t are real aggregate personal consumption and disposable income, and

$$z_t = \begin{cases} 1, & \text{if year } t \text{ is a war year} \\ 0, & \text{otherwise} \end{cases}. \tag{9.7.62}$$

Note that this model can also be expressed as

$$y_t = \beta_1 + \beta_2 x_t + u_t \; (\text{peacetime}), \tag{9.7.63}$$

$$y_t = (\beta_1 + \beta_3) + \beta_2 x_t + u_t \; (\text{wartime}). \tag{9.7.64}$$

Equations (9.7.63) and (9.7.64) imply the marginal propensity to consume is the same in peacetime and wartime, but that there is a shift β_3 in consumption level. An obvious null hypothesis of interest is

$$H_{13}\colon \beta_3 = 0. \tag{9.7.65}$$

Ordering the observations so that the first m correspond to war years, the normal equations are

$$\frac{\partial \,\text{SSE}}{\partial \beta_1} = \sum_{t=1}^{T} \hat{u}_t = 0, \tag{9.7.66}$$

$$\frac{\partial \,\text{SSE}}{\partial \beta_2} = \sum_{t=1}^{T} x_t \hat{u}_t = 0, \tag{9.7.67}$$

Letting p denote peacetime and w denote wartime, it is easy to see that

$$\frac{\partial \,\text{SSE}}{\partial \beta_3} = \sum_{t=1}^{m} \hat{u}_t = 0, \tag{9.7.68}$$

$$\bar{y}_m = \bar{\hat{y}}_w \text{ and } \bar{y}_p = \bar{\hat{y}}_p. \tag{9.7.69}$$

Example 9.7.8 As an alternative to Example 9.7.7, consider

$$y_t = \beta_1 + \beta_2 x_t + \beta_3 (x_t z_t) + u_t \; (t = 1, 2, \ldots, T), \tag{9.7.70}$$

or equivalently,

$$y_t = \beta_1 + \beta_2 x_t + u_t \; (\text{peacetime}), \tag{9.7.71}$$

$$y_t = \beta_1 + (\beta_2 + \beta_3) x_t + u_t \; (\text{wartime}). \tag{9.7.72}$$

Equations (9.7.71) and (9.7.72) imply the mpc increases by β_3 from peacetime to wartime, but that the intercept remains the same. An obvious null hypothesis of interest is again (9.7.65), but where now the wartime shift refers to the mpc.

Example 9.7.9 Corresponding to both Examples 9.7.7 and 9.7.8, consider the model

$$y_t = \beta_1 + \beta_2 x_t + \beta_3 z_t + \beta_4 (x_t z_t) + u_t \qquad (t = 1, 2, \ldots, T), \tag{9.7.73}$$

or equivalently,

$$y_t = \beta_1 + \beta_2 x_t + u_t \qquad (\text{peacetime}), \tag{9.7.74}$$

$$y_t = (\beta_1 + \beta_3) + (\beta_2 + \beta_4)x_t + u_t \qquad \text{(wartime)}. \tag{9.7.75}$$

In the case of (9.7.74) and (9.7.75) the intercept and the slope of consumption are permitted to shift between peacetime and wartime. An obvious hypothesis of interest is

$$H_{14}: \beta_3 = \beta_4 = 0. \tag{9.7.76}$$

Finally, note that one implication of Example 9.7.9 is that the observations from peacetime years have no effect on the regression coefficient estimates for wartime, and vice versa (see Exercise 9.7.6). The peacetime and wartime models are still tied together, however, in the sense if the errors are assumed to have the same variance in the two models, then all the observations should be pooled together to estimate σ^2 efficiently, that is,

$$s^2 = \frac{1}{T-4}\sum_{t=1}^{T} \hat{u}_t^2. \tag{9.7.77}$$

In this case Example 9.7.9 is a special case of Example 9.7.4.

Exercises

9.7.1 Suppose you have observations on $T = 100$ Canadians for the following regression:

$$y = \beta_1 z_1 + \beta_2 z_2 + \cdots + \beta_{10} z_{10} + X\gamma + u, \tag{9.7.78}$$

where

$y = \ln$ wage rate,

$z_1 =$ intercept,

$z_2 = 1$, if female; $=0$, if male,

$z_3 = 1$, if French-speaking; $=0$, otherwise,

$z_4 = 1$, if lives in Ontario; $=0$, otherwise,

$z_5 = 1$, if lives in Quebec; $=0$, otherwise,

$z_6 = z_2 z_3$,

$z_7 = z_2 z_4$,

$z_8 = z_2 z_5$,

$z_9 = z_3 z_4$,

$z_{10} = z_3 z_5$.

X is a $T \times (K - 10)$ matrix of relevant socioeconomic-demographic variables. State clearly and explicitly the null and two-sided alternative hypotheses for the following tests. State whether a t-test or a F-test is appropriate and the corresponding degrees of freedom.

(a) Test whether (everything else being equal) females have the same wage rates as males.

(b) Test whether (everything else being equal) wage rates are the same in all regions of Canada.

(c) Test whether (everything else being equal) French-speaking females in Quebec have the same wage rates than French-speaking males in Ontario.

(d) Test whether (everything else being equal) a non-French-speaking male living outside of Ontario and Quebec has the same wage rate as a non-French-speaking female living outside of Ontario and Quebec.

9.7.2 In estimating a money demand equation from annual data over the period from 1920 to 1957 (inclusive), it was felt that the relationship might have changed. When breaking up the sample into two groups, 1920 to 1939 and 1940 to 1957, based on a priori theory, it was found that the error sums of squares for the two periods were .281 and .419, respectively. For the "pooled" model the error sum of squares was .801. If there are three explanatory variables (besides the constant), would you conclude at the .05 level of significance that the two subsamples come from different models?

9.7.3 Consider Exercise 9.6.4 and suppose X_2 corresponds to a $T \times 4$ matrix of quarterly dummy variables. Define $y_s = y - X_2\hat{\beta}_2$, where $\hat{\beta}_2 = (X_2'X_2)^{-1}X_2'y$. Contrast the use of $y^* = M^*y$ in Exercise 9.6.4 versus y_s as a "deseasonalized series." See Johnston (1972, pp. 186–192), Jorgenson (1964) and Lovell (1963) for more details.

9.7.4 Consider Example 9.7.1 in the general case of G mutually exclusive groups. Partition Z_I into two parts corresponding to the intercept and the $G - 1$ dummies, and find:

(a) $Z_I'Z_I$

(b) $(Z_I'Z_I)^{-1}$.

9.7.5 Consider the standard linear normal regression model $y = X_1\beta_1 + X_2\beta_2 + u$, where $X_1 = Z_I$ as defined in Exercise 9.7.4. Use Exercise 8.2.18 to obtain expressions for the OLS of β_1 and β_2. Interpret your results.

9.7.6 Show that the OLS estimates of β_k $(k = 1, 2, 3, 4)$ in Example 9.7.9 can be obtained by running OLS on peacetime and wartime observations separately.

9.7.7 Compare and contrast Example 9.7.6 with the formulation

$$y_t = \beta_1[z_{t1}(1 - z_{t4})] + \beta_2[z_{t2}(1 - z_{t4})] + \beta_3[z_{t3}(1 - z_{t4})] + \beta_4(z_{t1}z_{t4}) + \beta_5(z_{t2}z_{t4}) + \beta_6(z_{t3}z_{t4}) + u_t \qquad (t = 1, 2, \ldots, T). \tag{9.7.79}$$

9.7.8 Redefine z_{ti} $(i = 1, 2, 3)$ in Example 9.7.1 as follows:

$$z_{t1} = \begin{cases} 1, & \text{if candidate } t \text{ has a bachelors} \\ 0, & \text{otherwise} \end{cases},$$

$$z_{t2} = \begin{cases} 1, & \text{if candidate } t \text{ has a masters} \\ 0, & \text{otherwise} \end{cases},$$

$$z_{t3} = \begin{cases} 1, & \text{if candidate } t \text{ has a PhD} \\ 0, & \text{otherwise} \end{cases}.$$

Assume that all candidates with masters also have a bachelors degree, and that all Ph.D.s have both a bachelors and a masters degree. Rework Examples 9.7.1 through 9.7.3 paying particular attention to parameter interpretation in this new parameterization.

9.7.9 Consider two researchers working with the same data and similar models that differ only in the use of G mutually exclusive and exhaustive dummies. Researcher A excludes the first group and estimates a model containing an intercept, $G - 1$ dummies for groups 2 through G, and other regressors denoted Z. Researcher B excludes the Gth group and estimates a model containing an intercept, $G - 1$ dummies for groups 1 through $G - 1$, and Z. Researcher A claims that the t-ratios of the coefficients of each of the $G - 1$ dummy variables 2 through G are mostly all significant at the .05 level. Researcher A, however, refuses to show these results to Researcher B. Suppose the $G - 1$ coefficients of the $G - 1$ dummies in researcher B's model mostly have low t-ratios. Is this possible? Explain your answer.

9.7.10 Consider the standard linear multiple regression with fixed regressors:

$$y = X\beta + z\gamma + u, \tag{9.7.80}$$

where X is a $T \times K$ matrix (including a constant regressor), β is $K \times 1$, z is a $T \times 1$ vector of observations on a binary variable. Let b and $\hat{\gamma}$ be the OLS estimators of β and γ, and let R^2 be the estimated coefficient of determination. Define $w = Xb$, and consider the regression

$$w = \alpha\iota_T + \delta y + \gamma^* z + u^*. \tag{9.7.81}$$

Let $\hat{\gamma}^*$ be the OLS estimator of γ^* in (9.7.81). Show [see Greene (1993, pp. 264–265)]

$$\hat{\gamma}^* = \frac{(\bar{y}_1 - \bar{y})(1 - R^2)}{(1 - \bar{z})(1 - r^2)}, \tag{9.7.82}$$

where $\bar{y}_1$ is the mean of y for observations with $z_t = 1$, $\bar{y}$ and $\bar{z}$ are the means of y and z over all observations, and r^2 is the squared correlation between y and z.

9.8 Pretest Estimators

Pretest estimators are used all the time.... Unfortunately, the properties of pretest estimators are, in practice, very difficult to know.... In practice, there is often not very much we can do about the problems caused by pretesting, except to recognize that pretesting adds an additional element of uncertainty to most problems of statistical inference.... In the remainder of this book, we entirely ignore the problems caused by pretesting, not because they are unimportant, but because, in practice, they are generally intractable.
—Davidson and MacKinnon (1993, pp. 97–98)

The discussion of hypothesis testing in Section 9.6 focused around essentially a "truth search" involving one of two actions: "reject" or "not reject" the null hypothesis H_1. Although intellectual curiosity may suggest such a binary objective, observed behavior of researchers suggests that they often employ the methodology of Section 9.6 to choose among data analytic procedures. Many researchers act as if hypotheses tests are a stepping stone toward obtaining "improved" estimators, predictors, or subsequent hypothesis tests. For example, in estimation rarely do researchers use the OLS estimator b in (9.2.5) or the RLS estimator b^* in (9.3.8). Instead the more commonly used estimator is defined by a procedure which chooses between b and b^* based on the outcome of a test of H_1: $R\beta = r$ versus H_2: $R\beta \neq r$. Such behavior gives rise to the *pretest estimator*:

$$\tilde{\beta}_{PT} = \begin{Bmatrix} b^*, & \text{if } f < c \\ b, & \text{if } f \geq c \end{Bmatrix} = b - [I_{(0,c)}(f)](b - b^*), \tag{9.8.1}$$

where $c = c(\alpha) = F(1 - \alpha; J, T - K)$ and the indicator function is defined by

$$I_{(a,d)}(f) = \begin{Bmatrix} 1, & \text{if } a < f < d \\ 0, & \text{otherwise} \end{Bmatrix}. \tag{9.8.2}$$

In words, (9.8.1) suggests that if the null hypothesis cannot be rejected, then the restricted estimator b^* is used, whereas if the null is rejected, then the unrestricted estimator b is used. From the frequentist standpoint, the appropriate way to evaluate (9.8.1) is based on the resulting sampling properties of the pretest estimator $\tilde{\beta}_{PT}$.

Before discussing the sampling properties of the pretest estimator, let us review the properties of its constituent parts b and b^*, consider the standard multiple linear normal regression model with fixed regressors

$$y = X\beta + u. \tag{9.8.3}$$

Let $\hat{\beta}$ be an arbitrary estimator of β and recall the general quadratic loss function $C(\hat{\beta}; \beta, G) \equiv (\hat{\beta} - \beta)'G(\hat{\beta} - \beta)$, where G is a positive definite matrix. Sampling theorists are concerned with the risk function

$$\rho(\hat{\beta}; \beta, G) \equiv E_{Y|\lambda}[C(\hat{\beta}; \beta, G)] = \mathrm{tr}[G\{\mathrm{MSE}(\hat{\beta}; \beta)\}], \tag{9.8.4}$$

where $\lambda = [\beta', \sigma^{-2}]'$ and $\mathrm{MSE}(\hat{\beta}; \beta) \equiv E_{y|\lambda}[(\hat{\beta} - \beta)(\hat{\beta} - \beta)']$. Exercise 9.8.2 provides a detailed comparison of b and b^* using $\rho(\hat{\beta}; \beta, G)$ for various choices of G. As expected the risk functions of b and b^* cross, and each dominates over different subsets of the parameter space. The RLS estimator is preferred if the constraints $R\beta = r$ are "close" to being valid; otherwise, OLS is preferred. The definition of "close" depends on the choice of G. Pretest estimator (9.8.1) attempts to make an "enlightened" choice by testing whether the parameters fall in a particular parameter subspace.

The "truth search" motivation of Section 9.6 (i.e., is H_1: $R\beta = r$ valid?) is equivalent to the assertion that the RLS estimator b^* has no bias. This in turn is equivalent to the assertion that noncentrality parameter (9.6.8) satisfies $\omega = 0$. Under the alternative hypothesis H_2: $R\beta \neq r$, $\omega > 0$. If biased estimators are entertained, then a MSE error criterion can be used to trade-off bias with decreased variance. Exercise 9.8.2(b) provides a critical value ω_0 of the noncentrality parameter ω which delineates the dominance of b^* over b in terms of their MSE matrices, and Exercise 9.8.2(c) considers the in-sample predictive case of (9.8.4) with $G = X'X$. A sufficient (but not necessary) condition for dominance of b^* for arbitrary positive definite G, in terms of the noncentrality parameter (9.6.8), is provided by Exercise 9.8.2(d). A necessary and sufficient condition for the dominance of b^*, in terms of a different measure than (9.3.8) is provided by Exercise 9.8.2(e). These last four cases are *not* concerned with the literal "truth" of the restrictions, but rather, whether imposition of the restrictions yields a "better" estimator of β in the sense of risk function (9.8.4).

These considerations suggest a more general class of pretest estimators defined by

$$\tilde{\beta}_{PT} = \tilde{\beta}_{PT}[c(\alpha, \omega_0)] = \begin{cases} b^*, & \text{if } f < c(\alpha, \omega_0) \\ b, & \text{if } f \geq c(\alpha, \omega_0) \end{cases}$$

$$= b - [I_{(0, c[\alpha, \omega_0])}(f)](b - b^*), \tag{9.8.5}$$

where $c(\alpha, \omega_0)$ is a scalar critical value for a test of

$$H_4\colon \omega_0 \leq \omega_0 \text{ versus } H_5\colon \omega > \omega_0 \tag{9.8.6}$$

satisfying

$$\alpha = \int_{c(\alpha, \omega_0)}^{\infty} f_2(z|J, T-K, \omega_0)\, dz, \tag{9.8.7}$$

and $f_2(z|J, T-K, \omega_0)$ is a noncentral F-density with J and $T-K$ degrees of freedom and noncentrality parameter ω_0. A rejection region of size α for (9.8.6) is $\{f|f > c(\alpha, \omega_0)\}$. The "truth search" motivation of Section 9.6 suggests $\omega_0 = 0$ and $c(\alpha, \omega_0) = F(1-\alpha; J, T-K)$ (see Exercise 9.8.2a). Dominance of b^* over b in terms of their MSE matrices motivates test (9.8.6) with $\omega_0 = \frac{1}{2}$ (see Exercise 9.8.2b). Exercise 9.8.2(c) motivates test (9.8.6) with $\omega_0 = J/2$. Finally, Exercise 9.8.2(d) provides yet another choice of ω_0. In each case, the choice of significance level α (usually made in a cavalier manner) plays a crucial role in determining the sampling performance of the estimator.[22]

The pretest estimator equals neither the OLS nor RLS estimators. Derivation of its sampling distribution is complicated because it is a stochastic mixture of the sampling distributions of b and b^*. Even calculating the moments and risk function of $\tilde{\beta}_{PT}$ is a non-trivial task (see Judge and Bock 1978). The following theorem provides conditions under which $\tilde{\beta}_{PT}$ is "better" than b or b^*.[23]

Theorem 9.8.1 Let $v_0 \equiv c(\omega_0)/[c(\omega_0) + (T-K)/J]$.

(a) $\text{MSE}(b) - \text{MSE}(\tilde{\beta}_{PT})$ is p.s.d. if $\omega \leq [2(2-v_0)]^{-1}$ and $T-K > 1$.

(b) $\text{MSE}(\tilde{\beta}_{PT}) - \text{MSE}(b^*)$ is p.s.d. if $\omega \leq \frac{1}{2}$.

(c) $\rho(b; \beta, X'X) > \rho(\tilde{\beta}_{PT}; \beta, X'X)$ if $\omega \leq \frac{1}{4}$.

(d) Given the positive definite matrix G, define $V \equiv RQGQR'[RQR']^{-1}$. Let ξ_S and ξ_L denote the smallest and

22. For discussions of the "optimal" level of significance at which to do a pretest, see Kennedy and Bancroft (1971), Sawa and Hiromatsu (1973), Farebrother (1975), Brook (1976), and Toyoda and Wallace (1976).

23. For a similar discussion involving estimators restricted by linear inequality constraints, see Judge and Bock (1983, pp. 612–614). The orthogonal case is considered by Judge et al. (1985, pp. 78–82).

largest characteristic roots of V. (Note: if $G = X'X$, then $V = I_J$ and $\xi_S = \xi_L = 1$.) Then $\rho(b;\beta, G) > \rho(\tilde{\beta}_{PT};\beta, G)$ if

$\omega < \mathrm{tr}[V\{2\xi_L(2 - v_0)\}]$ and $T - K \geq 2$;

and $\rho(b;\beta, G) < \rho(\tilde{\beta}_{PT};\beta, G)$ if

$\omega > \mathrm{tr}[V/\{2\xi_S[2 - \min\{1, v_0(1 + [T - K - 2]/[J + 4])\}]\}]$

and $T - K \geq 2$.

(e) Given the definitions in Part (d):

(1) $\rho(\tilde{\beta}_{PT};\beta, G) \geq \rho(b^*;\beta, G)$ if $\omega \leq \mathrm{tr}[V/2\xi_L]$,

(2) $\rho(\tilde{\beta}_{PT};\beta, G) \leq \rho(b^*;\beta, G)$ if $\omega \geq \mathrm{tr}[V]/\{2\xi_S \mathrm{Prob}[\{X^2(J)/X^2(T - K)\} \geq c_0 J/(T - K)]\}$.

(f) Bias $(\tilde{\beta}_{PT}) \leq$ Bias(b^*).

Proof See Judge and Bock (1978): (a) pp. 112–113, (b) pp. 117–118, (c) pp. 118–119, (d) pp. 95–98, (e) pp. 98–99, (f) p. 79.

The pretest estimator $\tilde{\beta}_{PT}$ is a discontinuous function of the data y because a small change in y can bring about a switch from b^* to b. This discontinuity has been shown by Cohen (1965) to imply that the pretest estimator is inadmissible with respect to quadratic loss, although he did not suggest a superior estimator.[24] Schlove et al. (1972) proposed an estimator which uniformly dominated $\tilde{\beta}_{PT}$ under squared error loss, although it also was inadmissible. To a conscientious frequentist, inadmissibility under such a standard loss function is deeply disturbing. Proponents of pretesting wishing to rescue it from these inadmissibility results should direct their attention to alternative loss structures. For example, it seems necessary to consider discontinuous loss structures in order to rescue this discontinuous estimator from inadmissibility. Such loss structures might reflect rewards for parsimony arising when the restricted estimator is chosen and the dimensionality of the problem is reduced. Progress in this regard has been made by Meeden and Arnold (1979), but quantifying "parsimony" remains a daunting task.

Despite the devastating nature of this criticism, pretest estimators remain in wide-spread use. Indeed they are the logical outcome of the increased "diagnostic testing" of assumptions advocated in many econometric circles. Adams (1991), Freedman (1983), Lovell (1983), Miller

24. For discussion of risk properties of various types of pretest estimators, see Judge and Bock (1983, pp. 617–627). For a discussion of the inadmissibility of various pretest estimators, see Judge and Bock (1983, pp. 631–634). For a similar discussion involving the risk merits of the mixed estimator of Theil and Goldberger (1961) corresponding to stochastic linear constraints, see Judge and Bock (1983, pp. 610–612). Such discontinuity can be eliminated by employing a continuous mixing scheme such as proposed by Huntsberger (1955) and Feldstein (1973).

(1990), and Rencher and Pun (1980), to name a few, have documented that even when there is no relationship between the regressand and any of the potential regressors, if there are many possible regressors to search over via pretests, then the chances of obtaining a specification that looks "significant" (judged by standard nominal levels of significance that ignore the pretesting) is very high. Furthermore, unless the level of significance is chosen to be a decreasing function of sample size in order that the probability of *both* type I and type II errors go to zero asymptotically, pretesting affects the asymptotic distribution theory as well (see Pötscher 1983). The resiliency of users to such damning results explains the label "the teflon factor" bestowed by Poirier (1988c; also see Hendry et al. 1990, pp. 220–225).

Exercises

9.8.1 In a seminar a speaker remarked: "I failed to reject an auxiliary hypothesis on nuisance parameters, and so I re-estimated with that restriction imposed in order to increase the efficiency of estimation of the parameters of interest." Critically evaluate this comment. What alternative procedures might you suggest?

9.8.2 Consider the standard multiple linear normal regression model with fixed regressors. Let $\hat{\beta}$ be an arbitrary estimator of β and consider the *weighted squared error* loss function $C(\hat{\beta};\beta,G) \equiv (\hat{\beta}-\beta)'G(\hat{\beta}-\beta)$ defined in Definition 6.3.6, where G is a positive definite matrix. Sampling theorists are concerned with the *risk function*

$$\rho(\hat{\beta};\beta,G) \equiv E_{Y|\lambda}[C(\hat{\beta};\beta,G)] = \mathrm{tr}[G\{\mathrm{MSE}(\hat{\beta};\beta)\}], \tag{9.8.8}$$

where $\lambda = [\beta', \sigma^{-2}]'$ and $\mathrm{MSE}(\hat{\beta};\beta) \equiv E_{y|\lambda}[(\hat{\beta}-\beta)(\hat{\beta}-\beta)']$. The case $G = I_K$, known as *squared error loss*, often warrants special attention because

$$\rho(\hat{\beta};\beta,I_K) = \mathrm{tr}[\mathrm{MSE}(\hat{\beta};\beta)] = E_{Y|\lambda}[(\hat{\beta}-\beta)'(\hat{\beta}-\beta)] \tag{9.8.9}$$

corresponds to the expected squared Euclidean length of sampling error. The case $G = X'X$ yields the in-sample predictive criterion:

$$\rho(\hat{\beta};\beta,X'X) = E_{y|\lambda}\{[\hat{y}-E(y)]'[\hat{y}-E(y)]\}, \tag{9.8.10}$$

where $\hat{y} = X\hat{\beta}$ and $E(y) = X\beta$. Since $\rho(\hat{\beta};\beta,G)$ depends in general on β, it cannot be used to provide an "optimal" estimator. It can, however, be used to compare two given estimators $\hat{\beta}_1$ and $\hat{\beta}_2$.

Consider the noncentrality parameter $\omega = \delta'[R(X'X)^{-1}R']\delta/2\sigma^2$ given by (9.6.8). Show each of the following (see Judge and Bock 1978, pp. 27–34):

(a) $\mathrm{Bias}(b^*) = 0$ iff $\omega = 0$.

(b) $\mathrm{MSE}(b) - \mathrm{MSE}(b^*)$ is p.s.d. iff $\omega \le \frac{1}{2}$.

(c) $\rho(b;\beta,X'X) - \rho(b^*;\beta,X'X) \ge 0$ iff $\omega \le J/2$.

(d) $\rho(b;\beta,G) - \rho(b^*;\beta,G) \ge 0$ if (but *not* only if) $\omega \le \mathrm{tr}[FG/2\xi]$, where ξ is the largest characteristic root of $D'GD$ and

$$F = (X'X)^{-1}R'[R(X'X)^{-1}R']^{-1}R(X'X)^{-1}, \tag{9.8.11}$$

$$D = (X'X)^{-1}R[R(X'X)^{-1}R']^{-1/2}. \tag{9.8.12}$$

(e) A necessary and sufficient formulation of (d) is as follows: $\rho(b;\beta,G) - \rho(b^*;\beta,G) \ge 0$ iff $\gamma \le \mathrm{tr}[\frac{1}{2}FG)]$, where

$$\gamma \equiv \delta' A' G A \delta / 2\sigma^2, \tag{9.8.13}$$

$$A = (X'X)^{-1}R'[R(X'X)^{-1}R']^{-1}. \tag{9.8.14}$$

9.8.3 Let $\hat{\theta}_i$ $(i = 1, 2)$ be two estimators of a scalar parameter θ, and let Z be a statistic such that $\text{Prob}(Z > c) = w$, where c is a constant. Define the pretest estimator:

$$\hat{\theta}_{PT} = \begin{Bmatrix} \hat{\theta}_1, & \text{if } Z > c \\ \hat{\theta}_2, & \text{if } Z \leq c \end{Bmatrix}. \tag{9.8.15}$$

Also define the estimator $\hat{\theta} = w\hat{\theta}_1 + (1 - w)\hat{\theta}_2$. Show (see Zellner 1983, p. 139):

$$E[(\hat{\theta}_{PT} - \theta)^2] - E[(\hat{\theta} - \theta)^2] = w(1 - w)E[(\hat{\theta}_1 - \theta) - (\hat{\theta}_2 - \theta)]^2 > 0. \tag{9.8.16}$$

9.8.4 Consider the following statement. "If there are any data imaginable that would lead to abandonment of the current regression specification, then a pretesting situation exists. Whether the actual data fall in the acceptable region is immaterial." Explain this statement (see Hill 1985–1986).

9.9 Bayesian Estimation in Multiple Linear Normal Regression

It is my impression that rather generally, not just in econometrics, it is considered decent to use judgement in choosing a functional form but indecent to use judgment in choosing a coefficient. If judgment about important things is quite all right, why should it not be used for less important ones as well?
—Tukey (1978, p. 52)

The distinction made in Section 9.1 between Case I (fixed regressors) and Case II (stochastic regressors) is crucial in classical analysis of the standard linear normal regression model because it determines the appropriate sample space over which to consider sampling properties. For example, the sampling distribution of the pivotal quantity q in Theorem 9.5.2(c), which is fundamental in constructing confidence intervals in Section 9.5 and test statistics in Section 9.6, is the same in the fixed and stochastic (unconditional) regressor case only when the stochastic regressors are i.i.d. draws from a multivariate normal distribution. In fact, the distribution of q appears tractable in the face of stochastic regressors only in this case.

In contrast, for the Bayesian both y and $\tilde{X}$ constitute data, and posterior analysis conditions on both. In particular consider the case where $\tilde{X}$ is weakly exogenous for $\lambda = [\beta', \sigma^{-2}]'$, then provided prior beliefs concerning the parameters $\xi \in \Xi$ governing the distribution of $\tilde{X}$ (not necessarily i.i.d. multivariate normal) are independent of prior beliefs concerning λ, the posterior density of λ is the same in the case of both stochastic and fixed regressors, regardless of the distribution of $\tilde{X}$ in the former case. Hence, in sharp contrast to Theorem 9.5.2, Bayesian inference is identical in both cases.

The Bayesian analysis is remarkably straightforward. Consider likelihood corresponding to (9.2.3):

$$\mathscr{L}(\beta, \sigma^{-2}, \xi; y, X) = f(y|\tilde{X}, \lambda)f(\tilde{X}|\xi)$$
$$= \phi(y|X\beta, \sigma^2 I_T)f(\tilde{X}|\xi). \tag{9.9.1}$$

Provided there are no constraints tying ξ to the presumed parameter of interest β, then in the terminology of Definition 9.1.2, $\tilde{x}_t$ is said to be weakly exogenous for β. Assuming further that prior beliefs concerning β, σ^{-2} and ξ are independent, that is,

$$f(\beta, \sigma^{-2}, \gamma) = f(\beta, \sigma^{-2})f(\xi), \tag{9.9.2}$$

then it follows directly from Bayes Theorem that

$$f(\beta, \sigma^{-2}, \xi|y, \tilde{X}) = \frac{f(y, \tilde{X}|\beta, \sigma^{-2}, \xi)f(\beta, \sigma^{-2}, \xi)}{f(y, \tilde{X})} \tag{9.9.3a}$$
$$= \frac{f(y|\tilde{X}, \beta, \sigma^{-2}, \xi)f(\tilde{X}|\beta, \sigma^{-2}, \xi)f(\beta, \sigma^{-2})f(\xi)}{f(y|\tilde{X})f(\tilde{X})} \tag{9.9.3b}$$
$$= \left[\frac{\phi_T(y|X\beta, \sigma^2 I_T)f(\beta, \sigma^{-2})}{f(y|\tilde{X})}\right]\left[\frac{f(\tilde{X}|\xi)f(\xi)}{f(\tilde{X})}\right] \tag{9.9.3c}$$
$$= f(\beta, \sigma^{-2}|y)f(\xi|\tilde{X}), \tag{9.9.3d}$$

and hence,

$$f(\beta, \sigma^{-2}|y, \tilde{X}) = \int_{\Xi} f(\beta, \sigma^{-2}, \xi|y, \tilde{X})\, d\xi$$
$$= f(\beta, \sigma^{-2}|y). \tag{9.9.4}$$

Because the first factor in (9.9.3d) is the same as (9.9.4), it follows that in the case considered (i.e., weak exogeneity of $\tilde{x}_t$ for β and prior independence condition; (see Equation 9.9.2) the distinction between fixed and stochastic regressors is immaterial in Bayesian analysis.[25]

Bayesian point estimation of β and σ^{-2} is based on posterior density (9.9.4). The general principles outlined in Section 6.7 apply directly here as well: minimize expected posterior loss (see Definition 6.7.2). Under weighted squared error loss (i.e. $C(\hat{\beta}, \beta) = (\hat{\beta} - \beta)'G(\hat{\beta} - \beta)$, where G is an arbitrary positive definite matrix), the Bayesian point estimate of β is the posterior mean $E(\beta|y)$ (recall Theorem 6.7.2). Under "all-or-nothing" loss, the Bayesian point estimate of β is the posterior mode. The remainder of this section concerns posterior density (9.9.4) for various choices of priors.

25. Note that the unobservables β, σ^{-2} and $u \equiv y - X\beta$ are all treated similarly in the sense that distributions are assigned to them: a prior density $f(\beta, \sigma^{-2})$ for the parameters β and σ^{-2}, and a $N(0_T, \sigma^2 I_T)$ distribution for the disturbance u. Although classical analysis treats u in the same fashion, the unobservables β and σ^{-2} are treated as unknown constants.

Consider posterior density (9.9.4) in the case in which prior density $f(\beta, \sigma^{-2})$ corresponds to the natural conjugate prior. The case $K = 1$ was studied in Example 6.7.4. As in Example 6.7.4, the conjugate prior in the case $K > 1$ is also the normal-gamma distribution (recall Definition 3.4.5). Specifically, the conjugate prior distribution of β and σ^{-2} is the normal-gamma distribution $NG(\underline{b}, \underline{Q}, \underline{s}^{-2}, \underline{\nu})$ with p.d.f.

$$f(\beta, \sigma^{-2}) = f(\beta, \sigma^{-2} | \underline{b}, \underline{Q}, \underline{s}^2, \underline{\nu})$$

$$= \phi_K(\beta | \underline{b}, \sigma^2 \underline{Q}) \gamma(\sigma^{-2} | \underline{s}^{-2}, \underline{\nu}), \tag{9.9.5}$$

where $\phi_K(\cdot)$ denotes a K-dimensional multivariate normal p.d.f. and $\gamma(\cdot)$ denotes a gamma p.d.f. (Definition 3.3.4). In words, (9.9.5) asserts that the joint prior distribution of β and σ^{-2} is such that the conditional distribution of β given σ^{-2} is multivariate normal with mean $\underline{b}$ and variance-covariance matrix $\sigma^2 \underline{Q}$, and the prior distribution of σ^{-2} is gamma with mean $E(\sigma^{-2}) = \underline{s}^{-2}$ and variance $\mathrm{Var}(\sigma^{-2}) = 2/\underline{\nu}\underline{s}^4$ (see Theorem 3.3.4).[26] Furthermore, it follows from Theorem 3.3.16 that the marginal prior distribution of β is the multivariate t-distribution (see Definition 3.4.4) $t(\underline{b}, \underline{s}^2 \underline{Q}, \underline{\nu})$ with mean and variance:

$$E(\beta) = \underline{b}, \text{ if } \underline{\nu} > 1, \tag{9.9.6}$$

$$\mathrm{Var}(\beta) = [\underline{\nu}/(\underline{\nu} - 2)]\underline{s}^2 \underline{Q}, \text{ if } \underline{\nu} > 2. \tag{9.9.7}$$

Given this normal-gamma prior, we can now state the following theorem describing the posterior distribution in the natural conjugate case.

Theorem 9.9.1 Consider the standard linear normal model and the normal-gamma prior $NG(\underline{b}, \underline{Q}, \underline{s}^{-2}, \underline{\nu})$. Then the posterior distribution of β and σ^{-2} is the normal-gamma distribution $NG(\bar{b}, \bar{Q}, \bar{s}^{-2}, \bar{\nu})$, where

$$\bar{b} = \bar{Q}(\underline{Q}^{-1}\underline{b} + X'Xb), \tag{9.9.8}$$

$$\bar{Q} = (\underline{Q}^{-1} + X'X)^{-1}, \tag{9.9.9}$$

$$\bar{\nu} = \underline{\nu} + T, \tag{9.9.10}$$

$$\bar{\nu}\bar{s}^2 = \underline{\nu}\underline{s}^2 + \nu s^2 + (b - \underline{b})'[(X'X)\bar{Q}\underline{Q}^{-1}](b - \underline{b}) \tag{9.9.11a}$$

$$= \underline{\nu}\underline{s}^2 + \nu s^2 + (b - \underline{b})'[\underline{Q} + (X'X)^{-1}]^{-1}(b - \underline{b}) \tag{9.9.11b}$$

$$= \underline{\nu}\underline{s}^2 + \nu s^2 + (b - \underline{b})'[X'X - (X'X)\bar{Q}(X'X)](b - \underline{b}) \tag{9.9.11c}$$

$$= \underline{\nu}\underline{s}^2 + \nu s^2 + (\bar{b} - b)'X'X(\bar{b} - b) + (\bar{b} - \underline{b})'\underline{Q}^{-1}(\bar{b} - \underline{b}) \tag{9.9.11d}$$

$$= \underline{\nu}\underline{s}^2 + (y - X\bar{b})'(y - X\bar{b}) + (\bar{b} - \underline{b})'\underline{Q}^{-1}(\bar{b} - \underline{b}) \tag{9.9.11e}$$

$$= \underline{\nu}\underline{s}^2 + (y - X\underline{b})'(I_T + X\underline{Q}X')(y - X\underline{b}). \tag{9.9.11f}$$

26. The implied prior distribution for σ^2 is the inverted-gamma distribution of Table 3.3.1(e) (also see Zellner 1971, pp. 371–373).

Proof Using Bayes Theorem (6.7.1b) implies that the posterior density of β and σ^{-2} is

$$f(\beta, \sigma^{-2}|y) \propto f(\beta, \sigma^{-2})\mathscr{L}(\beta, \sigma^{-2}; y)$$
$$\propto \phi_K(\beta|\underline{b}, \sigma^2\underline{Q})\gamma(\sigma^{-2}|\underline{s}^{-2}, \underline{v})\phi_T(y|X\beta, \sigma^2 I_T)$$
$$\propto [\sigma^{-2}]^{1/2(\bar{v}+K-2)}\exp[-\tfrac{1}{2}\sigma^{-2}(\underline{v}\underline{s}^2 + a)], \tag{9.9.12a}$$

where $\bar{v} = \underline{v} + T$ and

$$a = a(\beta) = (y - X\beta)'(y - X\beta) + (\beta - \underline{b})'\underline{Q}^{-1}(\beta - \underline{b}). \tag{9.9.13a}$$

Letting $vs^2 = (y - Xb)'(y - Xb)$ and using Exercise A.4.10(a, b) (with $W = I_T$, $Z = X$, $\underline{d} = \underline{b}$, $d = b$, $\bar{d} = \bar{b}$, $\underline{C} = \underline{Q}$ and $\bar{C} = \bar{Q}$), it follows from (9.9.13a) that

$$a = a(\beta) = vs^2 + (\beta - b)'X'X(\beta - b) + (\beta - \underline{b})'\underline{Q}^{-1}(\beta - \underline{b}) \tag{9.9.13b}$$
$$= vs^2 + (b - \underline{b})'X'X\bar{Q}\underline{Q}^{-1}(b - \underline{b}) + (\beta - \bar{b})'\bar{Q}^{-1}(\beta - \bar{b}), \tag{9.9.13c}$$

where $\bar{b}$ and $\bar{Q}$ are given by (9.9.8) and (9.9.9), respectively. Substituting (9.9.13c) into (9.9.12a) implies

$$f(\beta, \sigma^{-2}|y) \propto [\sigma^{-2}]^{1/2(\bar{v}+K-2)}\exp[-\tfrac{1}{2}\sigma^{-2}\{vs^2 + (\beta - \bar{b})'\bar{Q}^{-1}(\beta - \bar{b})\}], \tag{9.9.12b}$$

where $\bar{v}\bar{s}^2$ is given by (9.9.11a). From (9.9.12b) it follows immediately—compare to (9.9.12a)—that the posterior distribution of β and σ^{-2} is $NG(\bar{b}, \bar{Q}, \bar{s}^{-2}, \bar{v})$. The various forms of expression for $\bar{v}\bar{s}^2$ in (9.9.11a) through (9.9.11f) follow from Exercise A.4.10.

As in the conjugate analysis of Section 6.7, Theorem 9.9.1 has an interpretation in which the prior is viewed as arising from a fictitious sample from the same underlying population. The matrix weighted average of prior location $\underline{b}$ and sample location b in (9.9.8) is precisely the way a classicist would combine two samples from the same distribution: the first a fictitious sample yielding an OLS estimate $\underline{b}$ with $\text{Var}(\underline{b}|\sigma^2) = \sigma^2\underline{Q}$, and an actual sample yielding the OLS estimate b with $\text{Var}(b|\sigma^2) = \sigma^2(X'X)^{-1}$. To be more specific, let $[\underline{y}, \underline{X}]$ be fictitious observations such that $(\underline{X}'\underline{X})^{-1} = \underline{Q}$ and $(\underline{X}'\underline{X})^{-1}\underline{X}'\underline{y} = \underline{b}$. Then applying OLS to

$$\begin{bmatrix} \underline{y} \\ y \end{bmatrix} = \begin{bmatrix} \underline{X} \\ X \end{bmatrix}\beta + \begin{bmatrix} \underline{u} \\ u \end{bmatrix}, \tag{9.9.14}$$

yields the OLS estimate

$$(\underline{X}'\underline{X} + X'X)^{-1}(\underline{X}'\underline{y} + X'y) = (\underline{Q}^{-1} + X'X)^{-1}(\underline{Q}^{-1}\underline{b} + X'Xb) = \bar{b}, \tag{9.9.15}$$

which is identical to posterior mean (9.9.8).

The assessment of informative conjugate prior distributions for β and σ^{-2} has been discussed by Chen (1979), Kadane (1980), Kadane et al. (1980), Oman (1985), Pilz (1991, pp. 33–36), Winkler (1967, 1977), Winkler et al. (1978), and Zellner (1972).[27] Such procedures, however, have not been used much in applied econometrics.[28]

Leamer (1978, p. 79) notes that the posterior distribution of β under a normal-gamma prior is both unimodal and (from Equation 9.9.8) located at a *fixed* matrix-weighted average of the sample location b and the prior location $\underline{b}$. Because a conjugate prior treats prior information as if it were a previous sample of the *same* process, the normal-gamma prior does not distinguish sample information from prior information, no matter how strong their apparent conflict. Leamer argues that most prior information is distinctly different from sample information, and when they are apparently in conflict, the posterior distribution should be *multimodal* with modes at both the sample location and the prior location.[29]

One prior that permits a multimodal posterior is the *Student-gamma* prior discussed by Dickey (1975), Leamer (1978, pp. 79–80) and Judge et al. (1985, pp. 111–112). The Student-gamma prior specifies that β has a multivariate t-distribution $t_K(\beta|\underline{b}, \underline{Q}, \underline{\omega})$ *independent* of σ^{-2}, which has a gamma prior distribution $\gamma(\sigma^{-2}|\underline{s}^2, \underline{\nu})$. This independence between β and σ^{-2} is in sharp contrast to the normal-gamma prior in which β and σ^{-2} must be *dependent*. In the case of the Student-gamma prior the marginal posterior density of β is proportional to the product of two t-densities:

$$f(\beta|y) \propto t_K(\beta|b, s^2(X'X)^{-1}, \bar{\nu}) t_K(\beta|\underline{b}, \underline{Q}, \underline{\omega}), \tag{9.9.16}$$

where

$$\bar{\nu} \equiv \underline{\nu} + \nu, \tag{9.9.17}$$

$$\bar{s}^2 \equiv \bar{\nu}^{-1}(\underline{\nu s}^2 + \nu s^2), \tag{9.9.18}$$

$\nu = T - K$ and $\nu s^2 = \text{SSE}(b)$.[30] Posterior (9.9.16) is an example of what is commonly referred to as a *poly-t density* (see Drèze 1977), and it unfortunately is not very tractable in the sense that closed-form expressions for its integrating constant and moments are not available. Although the

27. In particular Chen (1979) demonstrates that the normal-gamma prior is consistent with the natural conjugate prior analysis of i.i.d. sampling from the multivariate normal distribution using a normal-Wishart prior distribution (see Section 3.5) for the mean and precision matrix.

28. There are of course exceptions. For example, see Leamer (1972) or Exercise 9.9.5.

29. Mixtures of natural conjugate priors produce posteriors that are mixtures of the posteriors corresponding to each of the priors in the mixture. Such mixed posteriors can be multimodal and they have excellent approximation properties as well as being computationally attractive. See Dalal and Hall (1983) and Diaconis and Ylvisaker (1985) for more details. Unfortunately, mixtures tend to be "parameter rich" because they require the setting of many prior hyperparameters.

30. Alternatively (9.9.16) can be written as a one-dimensional mixture of t-distributions. See Dickey (1975) for details.

normal-gamma prior was observed to be equivalent to a fictitious sample drawn from the same regression process, the Student-gamma prior is equivalent to a fictitious sample drawn from a regression process with the same regression coefficients but a different variance. In fact the posterior mode of (9.9.16) can be obtained by solving the following system of equations for $\tilde{\beta}$:[31]

$$\tilde{\beta} = [X'X + q\underline{Q}^{-1}]^{-1}(X'Xb + q\underline{Q}^{-1}\underline{b}), \tag{9.9.19}$$

$$q = q(\tilde{\beta}) = \frac{(\underline{\omega} + K)[\underline{\nu}\underline{s}^2 + \mathrm{SSE}(b) + (\tilde{\beta} - b)'X'X(\tilde{\beta} - b)]}{(\underline{\nu} + T)[\underline{\omega} + (\tilde{\beta} - \underline{b})'\underline{Q}^{-1}(\tilde{\beta} - \underline{b})]}. \tag{9.9.20}$$

Following in the footsteps of Hill (1969), Leamer (1978, pp. 81–84) extends these results for normal-gamma and Student-gamma priors to cases where both the prior and the data likelihood belong to the class of *spherically symmetric distributions* (recall Exercise 3.4.19). A continuous random vector z is said to have a spherically symmetric distribution iff its p.d.f. depends only on the length of z, that is, $f(z) = cg(z'z)$ where c is a constant and $g(\cdot)$ is an appropriately chosen function. Suppose that for some matrix A, $A\beta$ and u have independent, spherically symmetric densities:

$$f(y|\beta) \propto g_u[w_1(\beta)], \tag{9.9.21}$$

$$f(\beta) \propto g_\beta[w_2(\beta)], \tag{9.9.22}$$

where

$$\begin{aligned} w_1(\beta) &\equiv (y - X\beta')(y - X\beta) \\ &= \mathrm{SSE}(b) + (\beta - b)'X'X(\beta - b), \end{aligned} \tag{9.9.23}$$

$$w_2(\beta) = (\beta - \underline{b})'\tilde{Q}\underline{Q}^{-1}(\beta - \underline{b}), \tag{9.9.24}$$

and $\tilde{Q}^{-1} = A'A$. Because the posterior density of β is given by

$$\begin{aligned} f(\beta|y) &\propto f(y|\beta)f(\beta) \\ &\propto g_u[w_1(\beta)]g_\beta[w_2(\beta)], \end{aligned} \tag{9.9.25}$$

it is straightforward to show that the posterior mode $\tilde{\beta}$ of (9.9.25) satisfies

$$\begin{aligned} \frac{\partial \ln[f(\beta|y)]}{\partial\beta} &= \left[\frac{\partial g_u[w_1(\tilde{\beta})]/\partial w_1(\tilde{\beta})}{g_u[w_1(\tilde{\beta})]}\right] \\ &= 2X'X(\tilde{\beta} - b) + \left[\frac{\partial g_\beta[w_2(\tilde{\beta})]/\partial w_2(\tilde{\beta})}{g_\beta[w_2(\tilde{\beta})]}\right] 2\underline{Q}^{-1}(\tilde{\beta} - b) = 0_K. \end{aligned} \tag{9.9.26}$$

31. See Leamer (1978, pp. 82–83).

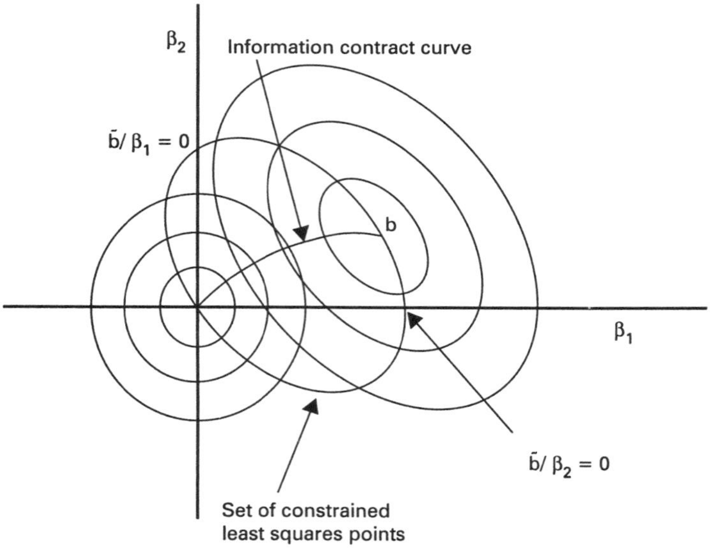

Figure 9.9.1
Information contract curve and ellipsoid bound

"Solving" (9.9.26) for $\tilde{\beta}$ yields

$$\tilde{\beta} = (q\underline{Q}^{-1} + X'X)^{-1}(q\underline{Q}^{-1}\underline{b} + X'Xb), \tag{9.9.27}$$

where

$$q = q(\tilde{\beta}) = \frac{g_u[w_1(\tilde{\beta})][\partial g_\beta[w_2(\tilde{\beta})]/\partial w_2(\tilde{\beta})]}{g_\beta[w_2(\tilde{\beta})][\partial g_u[w_1(\tilde{\beta})]/\partial w_1(\tilde{\beta})]} \tag{9.9.28}$$

depends in general, as does (9.9.20), on $\tilde{\beta}$.

As q varies from zero to infinity, (9.9.27) sweeps out a curve in K-dimensional Euclidean space, called the *curve décolletage* by Dickey (1975) and the *information contract curve* by Leamer (1978), which connects $\underline{b}$ and b. Choice of a point along the curve depends on the actual densities $g_u(\cdot)$ and $g_\beta(\cdot)$, but spherical symmetry is sufficient to imply the curve.

Figure 9.9.1 gives an example of a curve décolletage in the case $K = 2$. Ellipses around the OLS estimator b are isolikelihood ellipses of the form $(\beta - b)'X'X(\beta - b) = c$. The data prefer most the OLS estimate b and are indifferent among points on a given likelihood ellipse. The prior prefers $\underline{b}$, and is indifferent among points on the isodensity ellipse $(\beta - \underline{b})'\underline{\tilde{Q}}^{-1}(\beta - \underline{b}) = \underline{c}$. The curve décolletage contains all the points jointly preferred by the prior and the data. Reminiscent of a Edgeworth-Bowley diagram, given any point not on the curve, there is a point on the curve in which neither the likelihood value nor the prior density is less, and at least one is greater.

Because construction of a multidimensional prior is at best a difficult task, it is natural to investigate robustness of the posterior with respect to changes in the prior. For example, in the case of posterior mean (9.9.8) under a normal-gamma prior:

$$\frac{\partial \bar{b}}{\partial \underline{v}} = \frac{\partial \bar{b}}{\partial \underline{s}^2} = 0_K, \tag{9.9.29}$$

$$\frac{\partial \bar{b}}{\partial \underline{b}} \equiv \begin{bmatrix} \frac{\partial \bar{b}_1}{\partial \underline{b}_1} & \frac{\partial \bar{b}_1}{\partial \underline{b}_2} & \cdots & \frac{\partial \bar{b}_1}{\partial \underline{b}_K} \\ \frac{\partial \bar{b}_2}{\partial \underline{b}_1} & \frac{\partial \bar{b}_2}{\partial \underline{b}_2} & \cdots & \frac{\partial \bar{b}_2}{\partial \underline{b}_K} \\ \vdots & \vdots & & \vdots \\ \frac{\partial \bar{b}_K}{\partial \underline{b}_1} & \frac{\partial \bar{b}_K}{\partial \underline{b}_2} & \cdots & \frac{\partial \bar{b}_K}{\partial \underline{b}_K} \end{bmatrix} = \bar{Q}\underline{Q}^{-1}. \tag{9.9.30}$$

See Exercise 9.9.7 for additional derivatives of $\bar{b}$ and $\bar{Q}$ with respect to prior hyperparameters.

More interestingly, Chamberlain and Leamer (1976) and Leamer (1978) show that if only the prior location $\underline{b}$ and the sample location b are known, then the posterior mean (9.9.8) may lie essentially anywhere.[32] Knowledge of the sample ellipsoid, or in other words $X'X$, shrinks the set of possible values for posterior mean (9.9.8) to fall in the ellipsoid given in the following theorem.

Theorem 9.9.2 (Ellipsoid Bound Theorem) Consider Theorem 9.9.1. Given the prior and sample location vectors $\underline{b}$ and b, the midpoint on the line segment joining $\underline{b}$ and b is

$$c_1 = \tfrac{1}{2}(\underline{b} + b). \tag{9.9.31}$$

Let

$$A_1 = X'X, \tag{9.9.32}$$

$$a_1 = \tfrac{1}{4}(b - \underline{b})'A_1(b - \underline{b}). \tag{9.9.33}$$

Then for any choice of prior covariance matrix $\underline{Q}$, the posterior mean $\bar{b}$ of the regression coefficients is constrained to lie in the ellipsoid

$$(\bar{b} - c_1)'A_1(\bar{b} - c_1) \leq a_1. \tag{9.9.34}$$

Proof Leamer (1978, pp. 185–186) or Polasek (1984, pp. 236–237).

32. This contrasts sharply with the analogous one dimensional result—see (6.7.34)—that constrains the posterior mean to be algebraically between the scalar prior and sample means.

It was noted in Theorem 9.3.3 that the boundary of ellipsoid (9.9.34) is the set of all restricted least squares (RLS) estimates of the form (9.3.8) with constraints of the form

$$R(\beta - \underline{b}) = 0_J, \tag{9.9.35}$$

that is, every RLS estimate with constraints of the form (9.9.35) lies on the boundary of (9.9.34) and any point on the boundary of (9.9.34) is an RLS estimate for an appropriate choice of R. Ellipsoid (9.9.34) implies that the posterior mean must lie everywhere within an ellipsoid from the sample family of ellipsoids with center at the midpoint c_1 of the line segment joining $\underline{b}$ to b and with boundary including $\underline{b}$ and b (see Figure 9.9.1). Conversely, any point in this ellipsoid is a posterior mean for some $\underline{Q}$. Thus the bound is minimal. Knowledge of the major axes of the prior ellipse further restricts the feasible region for posterior mean (9.9.8) to a weighted average of the 2^K constrained regressions formed be omitting variables in all different combinations.[33]

Often interest focuses on particular linear combinations of the regression coefficients, rather than the coefficients themselves. In such cases, ellipsoid (9.9.34) implies bounds on the linear combinations of interest. The following theorem deals with this case.

Theorem 9.9.3 Consider Theorem 9.9.2, and suppose interest focuses on the linear combinations $\delta \equiv \psi'\beta$, where ψ is a known $K \times 1$ vector of constants. Then

$$\delta_{\min,1} \leq E(\delta|y) \leq \delta_{\max,1}, \tag{9.9.36}$$

where

$$\delta_{\min,1} = \psi'c_1 - [a_1\psi'A_1^{-1}\psi]^{1/2}, \tag{9.9.37}$$

$$\delta_{\max,1} = \psi'c_1 + [a_1\psi'A_1^{-1}\psi]^{1/2}. \tag{9.9.38}$$

Proof Leamer (1982, Lemma 3, pp. 731–732).

If the researcher is willing to restrict the set of possible prior covariance matrices $\underline{Q}$, then the set of feasible posterior means $\bar{b}$ for the regression coefficient vector β can be reduced further than (9.9.34). Mathematically, tractable results are available if prior covariance matrix $\underline{Q}$ is bounded above and below in the sense there exists known $K \times K$ positive definite matrices $\underline{Q}_1$ and $\underline{Q}_2$ such that

$$\underline{Q} - \underline{Q}_1 \text{ is positive semidefinite,} \tag{9.9.39}$$

and

33. All weighted averages of these 2^K points are, however, not necessarily feasible.

$$\underline{Q}_2 - \underline{Q} \text{ is positive semidefinite.} \tag{9.9.40}$$

Relationships (9.9.39) and (9.9.40) are commonly denoted by

$$\underline{Q} \geq \underline{Q}_1, \tag{9.9.41}$$

$$\underline{Q}_2 \geq \underline{Q}, \tag{9.9.42}$$

respectively, and taken together, they imply[34]

$$\underline{Q}_1 \leq \underline{Q} \leq \underline{Q}_2. \tag{9.9.43}$$

Under (9.9.43), Theorems 9.9.2 and 9.9.3 can be strengthened as follows.

Theorem 9.9.4 Consider Theorem 9.9.2 together with bounds (9.9.43). Then the posterior mean $\bar{b}$ lies in the ellipsoid

$$(\bar{b} - c_2)'A_2(\bar{b} - c_2) \leq a_2, \tag{9.9.44}$$

where

$$c_2 = \tfrac{1}{2}(A_1 + \underline{Q}_2^{-1})^{-1}(I_K + \underline{Q}_1^{-1} - \underline{Q}_2^{-1})(A_1 + \underline{Q}_2^{-1})^{-1}A_1(b - \underline{b}), \tag{9.9.45}$$

$$A_2 = (A_1 + \underline{Q}_2^{-1})(\underline{Q}_1^{-1} - \underline{Q}_2^{-1})^{-1}(A_1 + \underline{Q}_2^{-1}) + (A_1 + \underline{Q}_2^{-1}), \tag{9.9.46}$$

$$a_2 = \tfrac{1}{4}(b - \underline{b})'[A_1(A_1 + \underline{Q}_2^{-1})^{-1}(\underline{Q}_1^{-1} - \underline{Q}_2^{-1})^{-1}(A_1 + \underline{Q}_1^{-1})^{-1}A_1](b - \underline{b}). \tag{9.9.47}$$

Proof Leamer (1982, Theorem 4, p. 729).

As in Figure 9.9.1, Figure 9.9.2 depicts prior and sample ellipsoids as well as ellipsoid (9.9.34). The boundary of (9.9.34) is generated by priors that assign zero prior variance to a linear combinations of parameters but are otherwise diffuse, that is, RLS estimates satisfying (9.9.35) for some R. These boundary points are not obtainable if $\underline{Q}$ is bounded from above or below, with the exception of the prior mean $\underline{b}$ in the former case and the OLS estimate b in the latter case. Ellipsoid (9.9.44) is also depicted in Figure 9.9.2, as well as its limiting cases in which one of the bounds in (9.9.42) is non binding.[35]

In addition to the generalization of Theorem 9.9.2 to Theorem 9.9.4 when prior variance bounds (9.9.43) are taken into account, Theorem 9.9.3 can be generalized as follows.

Theorem 9.9.5 Consider Theorem 9.9.2 and suppose interest focuses on the linear combination $\delta = \psi'\beta$, where ψ is a known $K \times 1$ vector of

34. One-sided bounds can be imposed by considering the limiting cases in which $\underline{Q}_1 \rightarrow 0$ or $\underline{Q}_2^{-1} \rightarrow 0$.

35. For an analogous discussion in terms of the sensitivity of HPD regions to changes in $\underline{Q}$, see Pötzelberger and Polasek (1991).

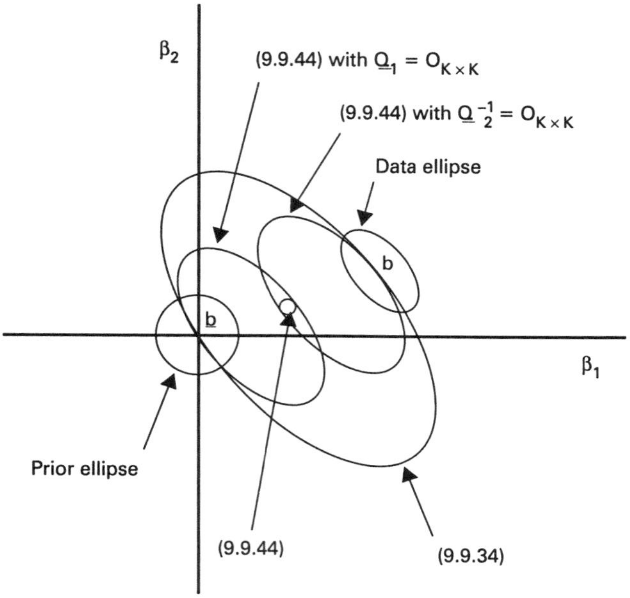

Figure 9.9.2
Ellipsoid bounds subject to prior covariance bounds

constants. Then under prior variance bounds (9.9.43), the posterior mean of δ satisfies

$$\delta_{\min,2} \leq E(\delta|y) \leq \delta_{\max,2}, \tag{9.9.48}$$

where

$$\delta_{\min,2} = \psi' c_2 - [a_2 \psi' A_2^{-1} \psi]^{1/2}, \tag{9.9.49}$$

$$\delta_{\max,2} = \psi' c_2 + [a_2 \psi' A_2^{-1} \psi]^{1/2}. \tag{9.9.50}$$

Proof Apply Leamer (1982, Lemma 3, pp. 731–732) to Theorem 9.9.4.

Many researchers are reluctant even to specify the prior location $\underline{b}$ in Theorems 9.9.2 through 9.9.5. Hence, diffuse (noninformative) priors have received attention. As noted in Section 6.8, the use of diffuse priors has been one of the most controversial issues within the Bayesian literature. One type of diffuse prior can be obtained from the normal-gamma family by considering the limiting case in which $\underline{Q}^{-1} \to 0_{K \times K}$ and $\underline{v} \to 0$. (Obviously, the matrix $\underline{Q}^{-1}$ is singular in this limiting case and hence $(\underline{Q}^{-1})^{-1}$ does not exist.) In this case normal-gamma prior (9.9.5) reduces to

$$f(\beta, \sigma^{-2}) \propto \sigma^{-K}, \tag{9.9.51}$$

which is obviously improper. Given this diffuse prior, the posterior distribution reduces to the $NG(b,(X'X)^{-1}, \hat{\sigma}^{-2}, T)$ distribution, where $\hat{\sigma}^2$ is the

ML estimate of σ^2 given by (9.4.4). The marginal posterior distribution for β, $\beta|y \sim t(b, s^2(X'X)^{-1}, T)$, mimics the classical result except for the degrees of freedom parameter.

Many authors (e.g., Box and Tiao 1973; DeGroot 1970; Jeffreys 1961; Lindley 1965; and Zellner 1971) prefer the diffuse prior

$$f(\beta, \sigma^{-2}) \propto \sigma^2, \tag{9.9.52}$$

which, unlike in the conjugate case, is predicated on the *independence* of prior beliefs concerning β and σ^{-2}. Prior (9.9.52) corresponds to independent improper uniform priors for β and $\ln \sigma$.[36] Given (9.9.52) the independent marginal posterior distributions $\beta|y \sim t(b, s^2(X'X)^{-1}, T-K)$ and $\sigma^{-2}|y \sim \chi^2(T-K)$ mimic the classical results.

An improper prior distribution is often considered as an approximation to a proper prior distribution in the sense that the posterior distribution can be obtained as the limit of the posterior distribution defined by the proper prior. In many situations the researcher is neither in a state of "total ignorance" nor able to specify an entire conjugate prior as in Theorem 9.9.1. Furthermore, the partial prior information demanded of Theorems 9.9.2 through 9.9.5 may also be more than the researcher feels confident in specifying. In such instances the following "middle ground" position may be attractive.

Suppose prior information is available for only $J \le K$ linear combinations of the regression coefficients, say,

$$\mathrm{R}\beta|\sigma^2 \sim N_J(r, \sigma^2 \underline{V}). \tag{9.9.53}$$

The following theorem gives the posterior density of β and σ^{-2} in the presence of such partial prior information.

Theorem 9.9.6 Under (9.9.53), the posterior density of β and σ^{-2} is

$$\beta, \sigma^{-2}|y \sim \mathrm{NG}(\tilde{b}, \tilde{Q}, \tilde{s}^2, \tilde{v}), \tag{9.9.54}$$

where

$$\tilde{b} = \tilde{Q}(R'\underline{V}^{-1}r + X'Xb), \tag{9.9.55}$$

$$\tilde{Q} = (R'\underline{V}^{-1}R + X'X)^{-1}, \tag{9.9.56}$$

$$\tilde{v} = T, \tag{9.9.57}$$

$$\tilde{v}\tilde{s}^2 = vs^2 + (\tilde{b} - b)'X'X(\tilde{b} - b) + (Rb - r)'\underline{V}^{-1}(Rb - r). \tag{9.9.58}$$

Proof Exercise 9.9.6.

Next suppose interest focuses on a linear combination of the regression coefficients and that the prior variance matrix $\underline{V}$ can be bounded analogously to (9.9.43):

36. In terms of β and σ, prior (9.9.52) implies $f(\beta, \sigma) \propto \sigma^{-1}$.

$$\underline{V}_1 \leq \underline{V} \leq \underline{V}_2. \tag{9.9.59}$$

Then analogous to Theorem 9.9.5, the following result is available.[37]

Theorem 9.9.7 Consider Theorem 9.9.6 and suppose interest focuses on the linear combination $\delta = \psi'\beta$, where ψ is a known $K \times 1$ vector of constants. Then under prior variance bounds (9.9.59), the posterior mean of δ satisfies

$$\delta_{\min,3} \leq E(\delta|y) \leq \delta_{\max,3}, \tag{9.9.60}$$

where

$$\delta_{\min,3} = \psi'\hat{\beta} - [a_3\psi' A_3^{-1}\psi]^{1/2}, \tag{9.9.61}$$

$$\delta_{\max,3} = \psi'\hat{\beta} + [a_3\psi' A_3^{-1}\psi]^{1/2}, \tag{9.9.62}$$

with b^* denoting the RLS estimate in (9.3.8),

$$\hat{\beta} = b^* + (X'X)^{-1}R'A_4A_5A_4(Rb - r), \tag{9.9.63}$$

$$A_3 = (X'X)^{-1}R'A_4A_6A_4R(X'X)^{-1}, \tag{9.9.64}$$

$$A_4 = [R(X'X)^{-1}R']^{-1}, \tag{9.9.65}$$

$$A_5 = (A_4 + \underline{V}_1^{-1})^{-1} + \tfrac{1}{2}(A_4 + \underline{V}_1^{-1})(\underline{V}_1^{-1} - \underline{V}_2^{-1})^{-1}(A_4 + \underline{V}_2^{-1}), \tag{9.9.66}$$

$$A_6 = (A_4 + \underline{V}_2^{-1}) + (A_4 + \underline{V}_2^{-1})(\underline{V}_1^{-1} - \underline{V}_2^{-1})^{-1}(A_4 + \underline{V}_2^{-1}), \tag{9.9.67}$$

$$a_3 = \tfrac{1}{4}(Rb - r)'[A_4(A_4 + \underline{V}_2^{-1})^{-1}(\underline{V}_1^{-1} - \underline{V}_2^{-1})(A_4 + \underline{V}_1^{-1})^{-1}A_4](Rb - r). \tag{9.9.68}$$

Proof Leamer (1982, Theorem 7, pp. 732–733).

The results of Theorems 9.9.2 through 9.9.7 comprise the *extreme bounds analysis* (EBA) advocated by Leamer (1978, 1982, 1983, 1984, 1985, 1992). Applications of EBA can be found in Cooley (1982), Cooley and LeRoy (1981), Leamer (1983, 1985, 1992), Leamer and Leonard (1983), Levine and Renelt (1992), and McManus (1985). Criticism of EBA by McAleer et al. (1985), McAleer et al. (1986), (to which Cooley and LeRoy 1986 and Leamer 1985 responded) and Hendry and Mizon (1990) has been vehement.

Finally, inferences regarding the R^2_{pop} can also be made. In the fixed regressor case, Press and Zellner (1978) consider R^2_{pop} as defined by (9.2.48b), and denote it by

37. Leamer (1992) discusses prior elicitation procedures that utilize (9.9.59) and Theorem 9.9.7. He chooses $\underline{V}_2$ so that an affirmative answer to the question "Is $V \leq \underline{V}_2$?" implies that working as if $V = 0$ is acceptable, and he chooses $\underline{V}_1$ so that an affirmative answer to the question "Is $V \geq \underline{V}_1$?" implies that working as if $V^{-1} = 0$ is acceptable. In other words, an affirmative answer to the first question implies imposing the $R\beta = r$, and an affirmative answer to the second question implies behaving as is $R\beta \neq r$. If neither question is answered affirmatively, then the prior distribution needs to be elicited more carefully.

$$P^2 \equiv \frac{\tilde{\beta}_2' X_*' X_* \tilde{\beta}_2}{\tilde{\beta}_2' X_*' X_* \tilde{\beta}_2 + T\sigma^2}, \tag{9.9.69}$$

where $\tilde{X}^*$ denotes $\tilde{X}$ in deviation form and $\tilde{\beta}_2$ are its associated regression coefficients. If the regressors are stochastic, then as $T \to \infty$, $P^2 \to R^2_{\text{pop}}$ (as defined by Exericse 9.2.48a). In the case of "noninformative prior" (9.9.51), Press and Zellner (1978) derive the posterior distribution of P^2:

$$f(P^2|y) = \frac{(1 - R^2)^{(T-K)/2} \exp\left[\dfrac{-TP^2}{2(1 - P^2)}\right]}{\pi^{1/2}\Gamma(v/2)P^2(1 - P^2)} \sum_{r=0}^{\infty} c_r \left[\frac{TP^2}{2(1 - P^2)}\right], \tag{9.9.70}$$

for $0 \leq P^2 < 1$, where

$$c_r = \frac{(2R)^{2r}\Gamma(r + \frac{1}{2})\Gamma(r + \frac{1}{2}v)}{(2r)!\,\Gamma(r + \frac{1}{2}K)}. \tag{9.9.71}$$

The posterior mean of P^2 is approximately [see Press and Zellner (1978, p. 314)]:

$$E(P^2|y) = R^2 + (K/T)(1 - R^2)(1 - 2R^2). \tag{9.9.72}$$

Posterior density (9.9.70) depends on R^2, K, and T. Press and Zellner (1978, p. 317, Figure 1) show that (9.9.70) is often remarkably close to a normal density.

Exercises

9.9.1 Consider the standard linear normal regression model and the diffuse prior $p(\beta, \sigma) \propto \sigma^{-1}$. Suppose one is interested in estimating the ratio $\theta \equiv \beta_i/\beta_j$ of the regression coefficients. Given the relative squared error loss function $C(\hat{\theta}, \theta) = [(\hat{\theta} - \theta)\beta_j]^2$, show that the Bayesian point estimate $\hat{\theta}$ of θ is

$$\hat{\theta} = \left[\frac{b_i}{b_j}\right]\left[\frac{1 + \dfrac{vs^2 q_{ij}}{(v-2)b_i b_j}}{1 + \dfrac{vs^2 q_{jj}}{(v-2)b_j^2}}\right], \tag{9.9.73}$$

where $N \equiv T - K > 2$, b_i and b_j are the OLS estimators of β_i and β_j, $Q \equiv [q_{ij}] = (X'X)^{-1}$, and $vs^2 = \text{SSE}(b)$.

9.9.2 Consider the standard linear normal regression model with a conjugate prior. The posterior distribution in this case is given by Theorem 9.9.1.

(a) Letting $\mu = E_{y|\lambda}(b)$, show that

$$\begin{aligned}\text{MSE}(\bar{b}) &\equiv E_{y|\lambda}[\{\bar{b} - \mu\}\{\bar{b} - \mu\}'] \\ &= \sigma^2\bar{Q}'X\bar{Q} + \bar{Q}\underline{Q}^{-1}(\underline{b} - \beta)(\underline{b} - \beta)'\underline{Q}^{-1}\bar{Q}.\end{aligned}$$

(b) (Giles and Rayner 1979) Show: $\text{MSE}(\bar{b}) - \text{MSE}(b)$ is negative semidefinite iff $(\underline{b} - \beta)'[(X'X)^{-1} + 2\underline{Q}]^{-1}(\underline{b} - \beta) \leq \sigma^2$.

9.9.3 (Judge et al. 1988, pp. 288–294) Consider the standard linear normal regression

$$y_t = \beta_1 + \beta_2 x_{t2} + \beta_3 x_{t3} + u_t,$$

where y_t, x_{t2} and x_{t3} represent output, labor and capital, respectively, all measured in logarithms. Suppose that your prior beliefs concerning $\beta \equiv [\beta_1, \beta_2, \beta_3]'$ and $\sigma^2 \equiv \mathrm{Var}(u_t)$ can be represented by a conjugate prior. You feel confident that returns to scale $\beta_2 + \beta_3$ is close to unity, but you are rather uncertain about the relative contributions of labor and capital. You represent such beliefs quantitatively as follows:

$$E(\beta_2) = E(\beta_3) = .5,$$

$$E(\beta_2 + \beta_3) = 1.0,$$

$$\mathrm{Prob}(.9 < \beta_2 + \beta_3 < 1.1 | \sigma = .3) = .9,$$

$$\mathrm{Prob}(.2 < \beta_2 < .8 | \sigma = .3) = .9,$$

$$\mathrm{Prob}(.2 < \beta_3 < .8 | \sigma = .3) = .9.$$

You also feel that your beliefs concerning β_1 are a priori independent of β_2 and β_3 and that

$$E(\beta_1) = 5,$$

$$\mathrm{Prob}(-10 < \beta_1 < 20 | \sigma = .3) = .9.$$

Finally, suppose that a priori σ^{-2} has a gamma distribution with parameters $\underline{\nu} = 4$ and $\underline{s}^2 = .0754$.

(a) Find the prior distribution of β given σ^2. Note that, because of the nature of the normal-gamma conjugate prior, once $\mathrm{Var}(\beta^2 | \sigma^2)$ is found conditional on one value of σ (say $\sigma = .03$), this is sufficient to specify it for all σ.

(b) Suppose that based on $T = 20$ observations the following quantities are computed.

$$(X'X)^{-1} = \begin{bmatrix} .65660 & -.15312 & -.29171 \\ -.15312 & .11049 & -.01443 \\ -.29171 & -.01443 & .24824 \end{bmatrix},$$

$$b = [9.770, .524, .693]', \; y'y = 2632.54, \; s^2 = .07953,$$

$$(\underline{Q}^{-1} + X'X)^{-1} = \begin{bmatrix} .12264 & -.03549 & -.01391 \\ -.03549 & .07106 & -.05907 \\ -.01391 & -.05907 & .08340 \end{bmatrix}.$$

Using only this sample information, compute a .90 confidence interval for returns to scale $\beta_2 + \beta_3$.

(c) Find the marginal posterior distribution of $\beta = [\beta_1, \beta_2, \beta_3]'$.

(d) Using your answer (c), construct a .90 HPD interval for returns to scale.

(e) Carefully contrast your answers in parts (b) and (d).

(f) Using your answer in part (c) find the probability that decreasing returns to scale exist. Explain any numerical approximation that you make.

9.9.4 Consider the standard linear normal regression model with fixed regressors: $y = X\beta + u$. Suppose you are given the natural conjugate *g-prior* $NG(\underline{b}, \underline{Q}, \underline{s}^{-2}, \underline{\nu})$ [see Zellner (1986a)], where $\underline{Q} = (gX'X)^{-1}$, g is a known positive scalar, and $\underline{\nu} > 2$.

(a) Find the mean of the marginal posterior distribution of β. Geometrically, describe the contract curve in terms of g.

(b) Let w be a $K \times 1$ vector of known constants, and suppose attention centers on estimating $\hat{\theta} \equiv w'\beta$. Given the loss function $C(\hat{\theta}, \theta) = (\hat{\theta} - \theta)^2$, find the Bayesian point estimate $\hat{\theta}$ of θ.

(c) Your answer $\hat{\theta}$ in (b) is a function of y. A non-Bayesian would judge its quality by investigating its properties in repeated samples. Find MSE $(\hat{\theta}) = E_{y|\theta}[(\hat{\theta} - \theta)^2]$.

(d) Suppose w is a normalized characteristic vector of $X'X$ associated with the characteristic root λ. Define $\varepsilon \equiv w'(\underline{b} - \beta)$. Under what circumstances will MSE$(w'b) >$ MSE$(\hat{\theta})$?

9.9.5 Using Exercise A.4.10, show the equivalence of 9.9.11(a) through 9.9.11(f) in Theorem 9.9.1.

9.9.6 Prove Theorem 9.9.6. Hint: Use Example 9.6.3 to reparameterize the model in terms of $\gamma = [\gamma_1', \gamma_2']'$ defined in (9.6.27), apply a standard natural conjugate prior, and then let the prior precision matrix for γ_1 approach the zero matrix.

9.9.7 Suppose $y|\beta \sim N_T(y|X\beta, \Omega)$, $\beta \sim N_K(\underline{b}, \underline{Q})$ and Ω is known. Define $\overline{Q} = [\underline{Q}^{-1} + X'\Omega^{-1}X]^{-1}$. Letting D_T and D_K be the Duplication matrix introduced in Appendix B. Show:

(a) $\partial\overline{b}/\partial\,\text{vech}(\Omega^{-1}) = [(y - X\overline{b})' \otimes \overline{Q}X']D_T$

(b) $\partial\overline{b}/\partial\,\text{vec}(X) = \overline{Q} \otimes (y - X\overline{b})'\Omega^{-1} - \overline{b}' \otimes \overline{Q}X'\Omega$

(c) $\partial\overline{b}/\partial\underline{b} = \overline{Q}\underline{Q}^{-1}$

(d) $\partial\overline{b}/\partial\,\text{vech}(\underline{Q}) = [(\overline{b} - \underline{b})'\underline{Q}^{-1} \otimes \overline{Q}\underline{Q}^{-1}]D_K$

(e) $\partial\,\text{vech}(\underline{Q})/\partial\,\text{vech}(\Omega^{-1}) = D_K + (\overline{Q}X' \otimes \overline{Q}X')D_T$

(f) $\partial\,\text{vech}(\underline{Q})/\partial\,\text{vec}(X) = -2D_K + (\overline{Q} \otimes \overline{Q}X'\Omega^{-1})$

(g) $\partial\,\text{vech}(\overline{Q})/\partial\,\text{vech}(\underline{Q}) = D_K + \overline{Q}(\overline{Q}\underline{Q}^{-1} \otimes \overline{Q}\underline{Q}^{-1})D_K$

9.9.8 (Linear Hierarchical Models: Lindley and Smith 1972) Let y, θ_1, θ_2, and θ_3 be $T \times 1$, $K_1 \times 1$, $K_2 \times 1$, and $k_3 \times 1$ vectors, respectively. Let A_1, A_2, and A_3 be known matrices of dimension $T \times K_1$, $K_1 \times K_2$, and $K_2 \times K_3$, respectively. Finally, let C_1, C_2 and C_3 are known positive definite matrices of dimensions $T \times T$, $K_1 \times K_1$ and $K_2 \times K_1$, respectively. Suppose:

$$y|\theta_1, \theta_2, \theta_3 \sim N_T(A_1\theta_1, C_1), \tag{9.9.74}$$

$$\theta_1|\theta_2, \theta_3 \sim N_{K_1}(A_2\theta_2, C_2), \tag{9.9.75}$$

$$\theta_2|\theta_3 \sim N_{K_2}(A_3\theta_3, C_3). \tag{9.9.76}$$

(a) What is the likelihood function? What is the prior distribution?

(b) Find $\theta_1|y, \theta_3$.

(c) Find the limiting distribution in (b) as $[C_3]^{-1} \to 0$.

(d) Write the mean in (c) as a function of the two statistics:

$$\hat{\theta}_1 = (A_1'C_1^{-1}A_1)^{-1}A_1'C_1^{-1}y, \tag{9.9.77}$$

$$\hat{\theta}_2 = [(A_1A_2)(C_1 + A_1'C_2^{-1}A_1')^{-1}A_1A_2]^{-1}[C_1 + A_1C_2A_1']^{-1}y. \tag{9.9.78}$$

9.9.9 Consider Theorem 9.9.7. Let $V = G'$ and $A_4^{1/2}$ be the unique symmetric matrix $A_4^{1/2}A_4^{1/2} = A_4$, and define $W = A_4^{-1/2}G'$. Also let $z_1 = A_4^{1/2}R(X'X)^{-1}\psi$ and $z_2 = A_4^{1/2}(Rb - r)$. Assume $\underline{V}_1 = 0$ and $(\underline{V}_2)^{-1} = 0$. Show each of the following (Breusch 1990):

(a) $b^* = \psi'b - z_1'z_2$

(b) $E(\delta|y) = \psi'b - z_1'W[I + W'W]^{-1}W'z_2$

(c) $\delta_{\min,3} = \psi'b - \frac{1}{2}z_1'z_2 - \frac{1}{2}[z_1'z_1z_2'z_2]^{1/2}$

(d) $\delta_{\max,3} = \psi'b - \frac{1}{2}z_1'z_2 + \frac{1}{2}[z_1'z_1z_2'z_2]^{1/2}$

(e) $z_1'z_2 = \psi'b - \psi'b^*$

(f) $z_1'z_1 = \text{Var}(\psi'b) - \text{Var}(\psi'b^*)$

(g) The chi-squared statistic for testing $R\beta = r$ is $z_2'z_2$.

9.9.10 Show that (9.9.8) can be written as

$$\bar{b} = \underline{b} + [I_K - (\underline{Q}^{-1} + X'X)^{-1}](b - \underline{b}). \tag{9.9.79}$$

9.9.11 Using "noninformative" prior (9.9.52), show (see Press and Zellner 1978, p. 310) that the implied prior (improper) density for P^2 (see Equation 9.9.69) is

$$f(P^2) \propto (P^2)^{-1}(1 - P^2)^{-1}, 0 \le P^2 < 1. \tag{9.9.80}$$

Graph (9.9.80).

9.9.12 Consider the standard multiple linear normal regression model with fixed regressors:

$$y = X\beta + u, \tag{9.9.81}$$

where $u \sim N_T(0_T, \sigma^2 I_T)$. The loss function is:

$$C(\hat{\beta}, \beta, \sigma^{-2}) = \frac{(\hat{\beta} - \beta)'X'X(\hat{\beta} - \beta)}{\sigma^2}. \tag{9.9.82}$$

(a) Find the risk function of the OLS estimator b, that is, find the sampling expectation of (2) with $\hat{\beta} = b$.

(b) Suppose β and σ^{-2} have a conjugate prior distribution in which $\beta|\sigma^{-2} \sim N_K(0_K, \sigma^2[gX'X]^{-1})$ and $\sigma^{-2} \sim \gamma(\underline{s}^{-2}, \underline{\nu})$. Find the Bayesian point estimate $\tilde{\beta}$ of β.

(c) Find the risk function for $\tilde{\beta}$.

(d) For what values of g does the risk of b exceed the risk of $\tilde{\beta}$?

9.9.13 Consider (9.9.81) and the prior given in Exercise 9.9.12(b). Define $\lambda = \beta'X'X\beta/\sigma^2$ and $P^2 = \lambda/(\lambda + T)$.

(a) Find the distribution of $g\lambda$ given σ^{-2}.

(b) Find the distribution of P^2 given σ^{-2}.

(c) Suppose $E(\beta|\sigma^{-2}) = \underline{b} \neq 0$ in Exercise 9.9.12(b), but that the prior in Exercise 9.9.12(b) holds otherwise. Repeat (a) and (b).

9.10 Bayesian Hypothesis Testing

The people who don't know they are Bayesians are called non-Bayesians.
—I. J. Good (1983)

The principles of Bayesian hypothesis testing developed in Section 7.4 are completely general given the parametric likelihood. This section applies these general principles to tests of linear restrictions on regression coefficients. "All-or-nothing" loss structure of Table 7.4.1 is assumed throughout.

Consider the standard linear normal model

$$y = X\beta + u, \tag{9.10.1}$$

and the hypotheses

$$H_1: R\beta = r, \tag{9.10.2}$$

$$H_2: \mathrm{R}\beta \neq r, \tag{9.10.3}$$

where r and R are known matrices of dimensions $J \times 1$ and $J \times K$, respectively, with $1 \leq J < K$. Without loss of generality, partition R and β as in Example 9.6.3: $R = [R_1, R_2]$ where R_1 is $J \times K_1$, $K_1 = K - J$, R_2 is $J \times J$, $\mathrm{rank}(R_2) = J$, $\beta = [\beta_1', \beta_2']'$, β_1 is $K_1 \times 1$, β_2 is $K_2 \times 1$ and $K_2 = J$. Under H_2, (9.10.1) can be written as

$$w_2 = Z_2\delta_2 + u, \tag{9.10.4}$$

where

$$w_2 = y, \tag{9.10.5}$$

and changing notation slightly from (9.6.25) and (9.6.27):

$$Z_2 = XA^{-1} = [X_1 - X_2R_2^{-1}R_1, X_2R_2^{-1}], \tag{9.10.6}$$

$$\delta_2 \equiv [\delta_{21}', \delta_{22}']' = [\beta_1', (\mathrm{R}\beta)']', \tag{9.10.7}$$

with A and A^{-1} are given by (9.6.23) and (9.6.26). Under H_1, (9.10.1) reduces to

$$w_1 = Z_1\delta_1 + u, \tag{9.10.8}$$

where

$$w_1 = y - X_2R_2^{-1}r, \tag{9.10.9}$$

$$Z_1 = X_1 - X_2R_2^{-1}R_1, \tag{9.10.10}$$

$$\delta_1 = \beta_1. \tag{9.10.11}$$

In order to make comparisons between H_1 and H_2 an interesting exercise, it is necessary to assign an atom of positive prior probability to each:

$$\underline{\pi}_j = \mathrm{Prob}(H_j) \qquad (j = 1, 2), \tag{9.10.12}$$

where $\underline{\pi}_1 + \underline{\pi}_2 = 1$, and employ the mixed prior

$$f(\beta, \sigma^{-2}) = \begin{Bmatrix} \underline{\pi}_1 f(\beta, \sigma^{-2}|H_1), & \text{if } R\beta = r \\ \underline{\pi}_2 f(\beta, \sigma^{-2}|H_2), & \text{if } R\beta \neq r \end{Bmatrix}. \tag{9.10.13}$$

As noted in Section 7.4, the crucial quantity for deciding whether to reject H_1 in favor of H_2 is the Bayes factor

$$B_{21} = \frac{f(y|H_2)}{f(y|H_1)}, \tag{9.10.14}$$

where using the convenient notation defined by (9.10.4) through (9.10.12),

$$f(y|H_j) = \int_0^\infty \int_{\Re^{K_j}} f(y|\delta_j, \sigma^{-2}, H_j) f(\delta_j, \sigma^{-2}|H_j)\, d\delta_j\, d\sigma^{-2}$$

$$= \int_0^\infty \int_{\Re^{K_j}} \phi_T(w_j|Z_j\delta_j, \sigma^2 I_T) f(\delta_j, \sigma^{-2}|H_j)\, d\delta_j\, d\sigma^{-2}. \tag{9.10.15}$$

Integral (9.10.15) has an analytical closed form in the case of the natural conjugate (normal-gamma) prior density

$$f(\delta_j, \sigma^{-2}|H_j) = \phi(\delta_j|\underline{d}_j, \sigma^2\underline{D}_j)\gamma(\sigma^{-2}|\underline{s}_j^{-2}, \underline{v}_j) \qquad (j = 1, 2), \tag{9.10.16}$$

where $\underline{s}_j^2 > 0$, $\underline{v}_j > 0$, $\underline{d}_j$ is $K_j \times 1$ and $\underline{D}_j$ is a $K_j \times K_j$ positive definite matrix. In terms of the original parameters β, (9.10.16) implies the prior densities

$$f(\beta_1, \sigma^{-2}|H_1) = \phi(\beta_1|\underline{b}_1, \sigma^2\underline{Q}_1)\gamma(\sigma^{-2}|\underline{s}_1^2, \underline{v}_1), \tag{9.10.17}$$

where $\underline{b}_1 = \underline{d}_1$, $\underline{Q}_1 = \underline{D}_1$, and

$$f(\beta, \sigma^{-2}|H_2) = \phi(\beta|\underline{b}_2, \sigma^2\underline{Q}_2)\gamma(\sigma^{-2}|\underline{s}_2^2, \underline{v}_2), \tag{9.10.18}$$

where

$$\underline{d}_2 \equiv [\underline{d}_{21}', \underline{d}_{22}']', \tag{9.10.19}$$

$$\underline{b}_2 \equiv [\underline{b}_{21}', \underline{b}_{22}']'$$

$$= A^{-1}\underline{d}_2 = \begin{bmatrix} \underline{d}_{21} \\ R_2^{-1}(\underline{d}_{22} - R_1\underline{d}_{21}) \end{bmatrix}, \tag{9.10.20}$$

$$\underline{D}_2 = \begin{bmatrix} \underline{D}_{211} & \underline{D}_{212} \\ \underline{D}_{212}' & \underline{D}_{222} \end{bmatrix}, \tag{9.10.21}$$

In the case $j = 2$, density (9.10.16) is not defined for $\delta_{22} = r$, nor is (9.10.18)

$$\underline{Q}_2 = \begin{bmatrix} \underline{Q}_{211} & \underline{Q}_{212} \\ \underline{Q}_{212}' & \underline{Q}_{222} \end{bmatrix} = A^{-1}\underline{D}_2(A^{-1})'$$

$$= \begin{bmatrix} \underline{D}_{211} & [R_2^{-1}(\underline{D}_{212}' - R_1\underline{D}_{211})]' \\ R_2^{-1}(\underline{D}_{212}' - R_1\underline{D}_{211}) & ([R_2^{-1}[-R_1, I_J])\underline{D}_2(R_2^{-1}[-R_1, I_J])' \end{bmatrix}. \tag{9.10.22}$$

defined for any β satisfying $R\beta = r$. Under prior (9.10.16), the data density (9.10.15) under H_j has the closed form

$$f(y|H_j) = \int_0^\infty \int_{\Re^{K_j}} \phi_T(w_j|Z_j\delta_j, \sigma^{-2}I_T)\phi_{K_j}(\delta_j|\underline{d}_j, \sigma^2\underline{D}_j)\gamma(\sigma^{-2}|\underline{s}_j^2, \underline{\nu}_j)\, d\delta_j\, d\sigma^{-2}$$
$$= t_T(w_j|Z_j\underline{d}_j, \underline{s}_j^2(I_T + Z_J\underline{D}_jZ_j'), \underline{\nu}_j)$$
$$= c_j[|\overline{D}_j|/|\underline{D}_j|]^{1/2}[\overline{\nu}_j\overline{s}_j^2]^{-\overline{\nu}_j/2} \qquad (j = 1, 2), \tag{9.10.23}$$

where

$$c_j = \frac{\Gamma(\overline{\nu}_j/2)[\underline{\nu}_j\underline{s}_j^2]^{\underline{\nu}_j/2}}{\Gamma(\underline{\nu}_j/2)\pi^{T/2}}, \tag{9.10.24}$$

$$\overline{d}_j = \overline{D}_j[\underline{D}_j^{-1}\underline{d}_j + (Z_j'Z_j)d_j]^{-1}, \tag{9.10.25}$$

$$\overline{D}_j = [\underline{D}_j^{-1} + Z_j'Z_j]^{-1}, \tag{9.10.26}$$

$$d_j = (Z_j'Z_j)^{-1}Z_j'w_j, \tag{9.10.27}$$

$$\overline{\nu}_j = \underline{\nu}_j + T, \tag{9.10.28}$$

$$\overline{\nu}_j\overline{s}_j^2 = \underline{\nu}\underline{s}_j^2 + (w_j - Z_jd_j)'(w_j - Z_jd_j) + (\overline{d}_j - d_j)'Z_j'Z_j(\overline{d}_j - d_j)$$
$$+ (\overline{d}_j - \underline{d}_j)'\underline{D}_j^{-1}(\overline{d}_j - \underline{d}_j). \tag{9.10.29}$$

Therefore, substituting (9.10.23) into (9.10.14), Bayes factor (9.10.14) reduces to

$$B_{21} = \left[\frac{\Gamma(\overline{\nu}_2/2)/\Gamma(\underline{\nu}_2/2)}{\Gamma(\overline{\nu}_1/2)/\Gamma(\underline{\nu}_1/2)}\right]\left[\frac{[\underline{\nu}_2\underline{s}_2^2]^{\underline{\nu}_2/2}}{[\underline{\nu}_1\underline{s}_1^2]^{\underline{\nu}_1/2}}\right]\left[\frac{|\overline{D}_2^{-1}|/|\underline{D}_2^{-1}|}{|\overline{D}_1^{-1}|/|\underline{D}_1^{-1}|}\right]^{-1/2}\left[\frac{[\overline{\nu}_2\overline{s}_2^2]^{-\overline{\nu}_2/2}}{[\overline{\nu}_1\overline{s}_1^2]^{-\overline{\nu}_1/2}}\right]. \tag{9.10.30}$$

In general, neither prior densities $f(\delta_j, \sigma^{-2}|H_j)$ $(j = 1, 2)$, nor prior densities (9.10.17) and (9.10.18), need be related in any formal way. Often, however, researchers choose to impose ties across these densities to reflect the common unrestricted parameters, or to center the prior for $\delta_{22} = R\beta$ under H_2 over r.

To illustrate such restrictions, first write

$$f(\delta_2, \sigma^{-2}|H_2) = f(\delta_{21}, \sigma^{-2}|\delta_{22}, H_2)f(\delta_{22}|H_2)$$
$$= [f(\delta_{21}|\sigma^{-2}, \delta_{22}, H_2)f(\sigma^{-2}|\delta_{22}, H_2)]f(\delta_{22}|H_2)$$
$$= [\phi(\delta_{21}|\underset{\sim}{g}, \sigma^2\underset{\sim}{G})\gamma(\sigma^{-2}|\underset{\sim}{s}_2^2, \underset{\sim}{\nu}_2)]t(\delta_{22}|\underline{d}_{22}, \underline{s}^2\underline{D}_{222}, \underline{\nu}_2)$$
$$= [\phi(\delta_{21}, \underset{\sim}{g}, \sigma^2\underset{\sim}{G})\gamma(\sigma^{-2}|\underset{\sim}{s}_2^2, \underset{\sim}{\nu}_2)]t(R\beta|\underline{d}_{22}, \underline{s}^2\underline{D}_{222}, \underline{\nu}_2), \tag{9.10.31}$$

where using properties of the normal-gamma distribution given in Raiffa and Schlaifer (1961, p. 344),

$$\underset{\sim}{g} = \underline{d}_{21} - \underline{D}_{212}\underline{D}_{222}^{-1}(\delta_{22} - \underline{d}_{22}), \tag{9.10.32}$$

$$\underset{\sim}{G} = \underline{D}_{211} - \underline{D}_{212}\underline{D}_{222}^{-1}\underline{D}_{212}', \tag{9.10.33}$$

$$\underset{\sim}{v}_2 = \underline{v}_2 + J, \tag{9.10.34}$$

$$\underset{\sim}{v}_2 \underset{\sim}{s}_2^2 = \underline{v}_2\underline{s}_2^2 + (\delta_{22} - \underline{d}_{22})'\underline{D}_{222}^{-1}(\delta_{22} - \underline{d}_{22}). \tag{9.10.35}$$

Given values of $\underline{d}_2$ (with $\underline{d}_{22} = r$), $\underline{D}_2$, $\underline{s}_2^2$ and $\underline{v}_2$ for the prior $f(\delta_2, \sigma^{-2}|H_2)$ in (9.10.16), corresponding values of $\underline{b}_2$ [with $\underline{b}_{22} = R_2^{-1}(r - R_1\underline{d}_{21})$], $\underline{Q}_2$, $\underline{s}_2^2$ and $\underline{v}_2$ for the prior $f(\beta, \sigma^{-2}|H_2)$ in (9.10.18) are readily available using (9.10.20) and (9.10.22). There remains, however, the specification of $f(\delta_1, \sigma^{-2}|H_1)$, or equivalently, $f(\beta_1, \sigma^{-2}|H_1)$. Following Dickey (1976) and Poirier (1985), one possibility is to use $f(\delta_{21}, \sigma^{-2}|\delta_{22}, H_2)$ in (9.10.31) to induce $f(\delta_1, \sigma^{-2}|H_1)$ by evaluating the former at $\delta_{22} = R\beta = r$. Evaluating (9.10.32), (9.10.33) and (9.10.35) at this value implies

$$\underset{\sim}{g} = \underline{d}_{21} = \underline{b}_{21}, \tag{9.10.36}$$

$$\underset{\sim}{G} = \underline{D}_{211} = \underline{Q}_{211}, \tag{9.10.37}$$

$$\underset{\sim}{v}_2 \underset{\sim}{s}_2^2 = \underline{v}_2\underline{s}_2^2, \tag{9.10.38}$$

and $\underset{\sim}{v}_2$ given by (9.10.34). Therefore, with these conventions the need to specify the

$$(K - J) + \tfrac{1}{2}(K - J)(K - J + 1) + K + \tfrac{1}{2}K(K + 1) + 4 \tag{9.10.39}$$

quantities $\underline{d}_j$, $\underline{D}_j$, $\underline{s}_j^2$, $\underline{v}_j$ $(j = 1, 2)$ is reduced to simply specifying the

$$K - J + \tfrac{1}{2}K(K + 1) + 2 \tag{9.10.40}$$

values $\underline{d}_{21}$, $\underline{D}_2$, $\underline{s}_2^2$, $\underline{v}_2$ under H_2.

As was found in Section 7.4, Bayesian analysis of sharp hypotheses tends toward trivial results in noninformative settings (e.g., never reject the sharp hypothesis as in the case of Equation 7.4.77b). One explanation for the problem is that the dimensionality of the parameter space is different under the two hypotheses ($K + 1$ under H_1 and $K = K_1 + J + 1$ under H_2), and it is unclear how to be equally-diffuse in spaces of different dimension. For example, consider the natural conjugate case and Bayes factor (9.10.30). Interpreting "noninformative" as the limiting case $\underline{D}_j^{-1} \to 0$ $(j = 1, 2)$, one is confronted with indeterminate forms involving the ratio $|\underline{D}_1^{-1}|/|\underline{D}_2^{-1}|$. To demonstrate the inherent problems involved, consider the alternative specifications

$$\underline{D}_j^{-1} = \varepsilon I_{K_j} \qquad (j = 1, 2), \tag{9.10.41}$$

$$\underline{D}_j^{-1} = [\varepsilon^{1/K_j}]I_{K_j} \qquad (j = 1, 2), \tag{9.10.42}$$

$$\underline{D}_j^{-1} = [\varepsilon^{1/K_j}](Z_j'Z_j) \qquad (j = 1, 2), \tag{9.10.43}$$

where ε is a positive scalar. Assuming $\underline{v}_j \to 0$ ($j = 1, 2$), and letting $\varepsilon \to 0$ in (9.10.41), Leamer (1978, pp. 111–112) notes that Bayes factor (9.10.30) satisfies

$$B_{21} \to \begin{Bmatrix} 0, & \text{if } K_2 > K_1 \\ \left[\dfrac{|Z_2'Z_2|}{|Z_1'Z_1|}\right]^{-1/2}\left[\dfrac{\text{SSE}(b_2)}{\text{SSE}(b_1)}\right]^{-1/2T}, & \text{if } K_2 = K_1 \\ \infty, & \text{if } K_2 < K_1 \end{Bmatrix}. \tag{9.10.44}$$

In contrast, taking this same limit using (9.10.42) implies

$$B_{21} \to \left[\frac{|Z_2'Z_2|}{|Z_1'Z_1|}\right]^{-1/2}\left[\frac{\text{SSE}(b_2)}{\text{SSE}(b_1)}\right]^{-1/2T}, \tag{9.10.45}$$

and taking this limit using (9.10.43) implies

$$B_{21} \to \left[\frac{\text{SSE}(b_2)}{\text{SSE}(b_1)}\right]^{-1/2T}. \tag{9.10.46}$$

In the standard nested hypothesis testing situation, the smaller model is always chosen under (9.10.44), the larger model is always chosen under (9.10.46), and under (9.10.45), the second factor favors the larger model and the first factor is indeterminate. Note that (9.10.45) and (9.10.44) in the case $K_1 = K_2$ depend on the units of measurement. If the hypotheses are non-nested, then all three are cases are indeterminate.

Prior specifications (9.10.41) through (9.10.43) reflect different definitions of "diffuseness" and there are no obvious criteria for choosing among them. Thus the Bayes factor is indeterminate in the face of diffuse prior information. Note, however, that the posterior distribution of β_j ($j = 1, 2$) is proper and the same under all three definitions of diffuseness. This indeterminacy has attracted the attention of numerous authors (e.g., Smith and Spiegelhalter 1980, and Spiegelhalter and Smith 1982). Notably, Pericchi (1984) identifies the important role of the third factor in (9.10.30) involving prior and posterior precision matrices, relates it to the expected gains in information (from sampling) about the unknown parameters in each model, and relates it to both Lindley's Paradox (see Lindley 1957) and "noninformative priors."

When the regressors are stationary, then for large finite T, Leamer (1978, p. 112) argues in favor of the limiting form

$$B_{21} = T^{1/2(K_1 - K_2)}\left(\frac{\text{SSE}(b_2)}{\text{SSE}(b_1)}\right)^{-1/2T}. \tag{9.10.47}$$

Rather than derive (9.10.47) from a diffuse prior, Leamer uses a proper prior that is "dominated" in large samples. Klein and Brown (1984) derive

(9.10.47) from a different perspective in which the "Shannon information" content of the prior is minimized. The consistency of posterior probabilities as $T \to \infty$ for identifying a "true" hypothesis has been studied by Lempers (1971) and Poirier (1981).

Approximate posterior odds (9.10.47) are most interesting in the case where the two hypotheses are nested. Specifically, suppose $R = [O_{J \times (K-J)}, I_J]$, $r = 0_J$, and we wish to test H_1: $\beta_2 = 0$ versus H_2: $\beta_2 \neq 0$. A classical econometrician computes

$$f = \frac{[\mathrm{SSE}(b_1) - \mathrm{SSE}(b_2)]/(K - K_1)}{\mathrm{SSE}(b_2)/(T - K)} = \left(\frac{\mathrm{SSE}(b_1)}{\mathrm{SSE}(b_2)} - 1\right)\left(\frac{T - K}{K - K_1}\right), \tag{9.10.48}$$

and then rejects H_1: $\beta_2 = 0$ if the test statistic f is "significantly" large. "How large" is "large" depends on the level of significance chosen, and as noted in Section 9.6, while ideally this level should be chosen as a function of sample size, classical statistics provides few guidelines for the choice. Interestingly, the Bayesian perspective may provide the classical econometrician some help.

Assuming equal prior odds and all-or-nothing loss function (7.3.43), a Bayesian rejects H_1: $\beta_2 = 0$ in favor of H_2: $\beta_2 \neq 0$ iff $B_{21} > 1$. In other words, H_1 is rejected iff $\mathrm{Prob}(H_2|y) > \mathrm{Prob}(H_1|y)$. Solving (9.10.48) for

$$\frac{\mathrm{SSE}(b_1)}{\mathrm{SSE}(b_2)} = \left(\frac{K_2 - K_1}{T - K_2}\right)f + 1, \tag{9.10.49}$$

and substituting into (9.10.47) gives

$$B_{21} = T^{(K_1 - K_2)/2}\left[\left(\frac{K_2 - K_1}{T - K_2}\right)f + 1\right]^{1/2T}. \tag{9.10.50}$$

Therefore, $B_{21} > 1$ (i.e., reject H_1) iff

$$f > \left(\frac{T - K_2}{K_2 - K_1}\right)[T^{(K_2 - K_1)/T} - 1]. \tag{9.10.51}$$

The right hand side of inequality (9.10.51) provides a critical value for the classical F-test that is an *increasing function of sample size.* Use of (9.10.51) implies that it is more difficult to reject sharp null hypotheses in larger samples—a situation most classical econometricians seek, but find difficult to formalize.

Table 9.10.1 compares critical values from (9.10.51) with .01 level standard critical values for various combinations of T, K, and J. The message is clear. In the standard procedure for fixed K and J, critical values fall as T increases. The critical values obtained from (9.10.51) increase as T

Table 9.10.1
Critical values for (9.10.51) and corresponding to $\alpha = .01$ level of significance

	$T = 100$			$T = 1{,}000$			$T = 10{,}000$		
	$J = 1$	$J = 5$	$J = 10$	$J = 1$	$J = 5$	$J = 10$	$J = 1$	$J = 5$	$J = 10$
$K_2 = 5$	4.48	4.92	*	6.90	6.99	*	9.21	9.23	*
$\alpha = .01$	6.91	3.22	*	6.66	3.04	*	6.63	3.02	*
$K_2 = 10$	4.24	4.66	5.26	6.86	6.96	7.08	9.20	9.22	9.24
$\alpha = .01$	6.93	3.23	2.52	6.66	3.04	2.34	6.63	3.02	2.32
$K_2 = 25$	3.53	3.88	4.39	6.76	6.85	6.97	9.19	9.21	9.23
$\alpha = .01$	6.99	3.27	2.57	6.66	3.04	2.34	6.63	3.02	2.32

Note: $J \equiv K_2 - K_1$ is the number of restrictions.

increases. Furthermore, the discrepancy is most pronounced when J and K are both large, i.e. in models involving many restrictions and many parameters.[38]

This section has implicitly assumed that the posterior odds summarize all the information contained in the data for a Bayesian to make a decision that minimizes expected posterior loss. Kadane and Dickey (1980) have noted that this is the case only under highly restrictive loss structures: In particular the loss resulting from choosing H_1 when H_2 holds must be constant over the entire parameter space in which H_2 is valid. In most situations this is unreasonable. For more discussion, see Kadane and Dickey (1980).

Finally, note that estimation questions can arise in the presence of hypotheses like (9.10.2) and (9.10.3). For example, let us continue with the case $R = [O_{J\times(K-J)}, I_J]$ and the test of H_1: $\beta_2 = 0$ versus H_2: $\beta_2 \neq 0$. Pretest estimator (9.9.1) arises in just such a case when β_1 is the parameter of interest and the researcher entertains imposing H_1 in the hope of getting a "better" estimator of β_1. Under H_2, the posterior density of β_1 is

$$\beta_1 | y, H_2 \sim t(\beta_1 | \bar{d}_{21}, \bar{s}_2^2 \bar{D}_{211}, \bar{v}_2), \tag{9.10.52}$$

where $\bar{d}_{21}$ corresponds to the first K_1 elements of (9.10.25), $\bar{s}_2^2$ is given in (9.10.29), $\bar{D}_{211}$ corresponds to the upper left $K_1 \times K_1$ block of (9.10.26) and $\bar{v}_2$ is given by (9.10.28). Under H_1, the posterior density of β_1 is

$$\beta_1 | y, H_1 \sim t(\beta_1 | \bar{d}_1, \bar{s}_1^2 \bar{D}_1, \bar{v}), \tag{9.10.53}$$

38. Similar results have also been obtained by Zellner and Siow (1980). Building on earlier work of Jeffreys (1967), Zellner and Siow (1980) employ an informative multivariate Cauchy prior distribution for the regression coefficients divided by σ, and a standard "noninformative" prior for the precision. The former informative prior also depends on the regressor matrix X. Although exact closed form expressions for the resulting Bayes factors are not available, Zellner and Siow (1980) provide approximate Bayes factors that are functions of the data only through the classical f statistic.

where (using $j = 1$) $\bar{d}_1$, $\bar{s}_1^2$, $\bar{D}_1$, $\bar{v}_1$ are given by (9.10.25), (9.10.29), (9.10.26), and (9.10.28), respectively. If β_1 is the parameter of interest, then the hypotheses H_1 and H_2 amount to nuisance parameters themselves. The Bayesian way of dealing with nuisance parameters is straightforward: marginalize them from the problem. In the present case this recommendation amounts to considering the unconditional posterior density for β_1:

$$\begin{aligned} f(\beta_1|y) &= \sum_{j=1}^{2} f(\beta_1, H_j|y) = \sum_{j=1}^{2} f(\beta_1|y, H_j)P(H_j|y) \\ &= \bar{\pi}_1 f(\beta_1|y, H_1) + [1 - \bar{\pi}_1]f(\beta_1|y, H_2) \\ &= \bar{\pi}_1 f_t(\beta_1|\bar{d}_1, \bar{s}_1^2\bar{D}_1, \bar{v}) + [1 - \bar{\pi}_1]f_t[\beta_1|\bar{d}_{21}, \bar{s}_2^2\bar{D}_{211}, \bar{v}_2), \end{aligned} \tag{9.10.54}$$

where $f_t(\cdot)$ denotes p.d.f. (3.4.32) of the multivariate t-distribution, and $\bar{\pi}_1 = \text{Prob}(H_1|y) = \{1 + B_{21}(\underline{\pi}_1/\underline{\pi}_2)]^{-1}$ as given by (7.4.23). In words, posterior density (9.10.54) is a mixture of (9.10.52) and (9.10.53) with the posterior probabilities $\bar{\pi}_1$ and $\bar{\pi}_2 = 1 - \bar{\pi}_1$ as weights. Under weighted squared error loss, the Bayesian point estimate of β_1 is the posterior mean of (9.10.54):

$$E(\beta_1|y) = \bar{\pi}_1 E(\beta_1|y, H_1) + [1 - \bar{\pi}_1]E(\beta_1|y, H_2) \tag{9.10.55a}$$

$$= \bar{\pi}_1 \bar{d}_1 + [1 - \bar{\pi}_1]\bar{d}_{21} \tag{9.10.55b}$$

$$= \bar{d}_1 + [1 - \bar{\pi}_1](\bar{d}_{21} - \bar{d}_1). \tag{9.10.55c}$$

Unlike pretest estimator (9.9.1), (9.10.55) is a continuous function of the data. Posterior mean (9.10.55) is optimal under posterior squared error loss, and admissible under quadratic risk.

The EBA of the previous section has an analog in hypothesis testing. Iwata (1992) provides the following development. Let G be a $(K - J) \times K$ matrix such that $[R', G']'$ is nonsingular and $RG' = 0$. Iwata (1992) assumes $G\beta$ and σ to be independent and "noninformative" under both H_1 and H_2:

$$f(Q\beta|R\beta, \sigma) \propto \text{constant} \tag{9.10.56}$$

$$f(\sigma) \propto \sigma^{-1}. \tag{9.10.57}$$

The prior density of $R\beta$ given σ and H_1 is simply a mass point, and under H_2, the prior density $f(R\beta|\sigma, H_2)$ is the item toward which a sensitivity analysis is directed. Iwata (1992) considers three classes of prior densities for $f(R\beta|\sigma, H_2)$ over which he conducts a sensitivity analysis:

$$\mathscr{F}_S = \{\text{all symmetric distributions around } r\}, \tag{9.10.58}$$

$$\mathscr{F}_{US} = \{\text{all unimodal and elliptically symmetric distributions around } r\}, \tag{9.10.59}$$

$$\mathscr{F}_N = \{\text{all normal distributions with mean } r \text{ and variance } \sigma^2 V, \text{ where } V \text{ is some } J \times J \text{ n.n.d. matrix}\}, \tag{9.10.60}$$

$$\mathscr{F}_N(A) = \{\text{mixtures of the form } \underline{\pi}_1\phi(R\beta|r, \sigma^2 A) + \underline{\pi}_2\phi(R\beta|r, \sigma^2[A + U]), \text{ where } U \text{ is a } J \times J \text{ n.n.d. matrix}\}. \tag{9.10.61}$$

The major results of Iwata (1992) are summarized in the following theorem that provides lower bounds $\underline{B}_{12}$ for Bayes factor B_{12}.

Theorem 9.10.1 Let SSE denote the sum of squared errors for OLS, and define

$$q_0 = (Rb - r)'[R(X'X)^{-1}R']^{-1}(Rb - r), \tag{9.10.62}$$

$$g_0 = \frac{(v-1)q_0}{\text{SSE}}. \tag{9.10.63}$$

Then the following results can be shown:

(a) Suppose $f(R\beta|\sigma, H_2) \in \mathscr{F}_S$. If $g_0 \leq 1$, then $\underline{B}_{12} = 1$. If $g_0 > 1$, then B_{12} is minimized by choosing $f(R\beta|\sigma, H_2)$ such that half mass is assigned at the two points $r - \gamma_*(Rb - r)$ and $r + \gamma_*(Rb - r)$ symmetric about r, where γ_* satisfies

$$\int_0^\infty \sigma^{-v-1} h(\gamma_*)\, d\sigma = 0, \tag{9.10.64}$$

$$h(\gamma) = \exp\left[\frac{-(1-\gamma)^2 q_0}{2\sigma^2}\right] - \exp\left[\frac{-(1+\gamma)^2 q_0}{2\sigma^2}\right] - \gamma\left(\exp\left[\frac{-(1-\gamma)^2 q_0}{2\sigma^2}\right] + \exp\left[\frac{-(1+\gamma)^2}{2\sigma^2}\right]\right), \tag{9.10.65}$$

and $B_{12} \geq \underline{B}_{12}(\mathscr{F}_S)$, where

$$\underline{B}_{12}(\mathscr{F}_S) = \frac{2(\text{SSE} + q_0)^{-v/2}}{([\text{SSE} + (1-\gamma_*)q_0]^{-v/2} + [\text{SSE} + (1+\gamma_*)q_0]^{-v/2})}. \tag{9.10.66}$$

(b) Suppose $f(R\beta|\sigma, H_2) \in \mathscr{F}_{US}$. If $g_0 \leq 1$, then $\underline{B}_{12}(\mathscr{F}_{US}) = 1$. If $g_0 > 1$, then B_{12} is minimized by choosing $f(R\beta|\sigma, H_2)$ such that its mass is uniform over the line segment joining $r - \delta_*(Rb - r)$ and $r + \delta_*(Rb - r)$, where $\delta = \delta_*$ satisfies

$$F_t[g_0^{1/2}(1+\delta), v-1] - F_t[g_0^{1/2}(1-\delta), v-1] = \delta g_0^{1/2}(f_t[g_0^{1/2}(1+\delta), v-1] + f_t[g_0^{1/2}(1-\delta), v-1]), \tag{9.10.67}$$

$F_t(\cdot, v-1)$ and $f_t(\cdot, v-1)$ denote the distribution and density, respectively, of the Student-t distribution with $\nu - 1$ degrees of freedom, and $B_{12} \geq \underline{B}_{12}(\mathscr{F}_{US})$, where

$$\underline{B}_{12}(\mathscr{F}_{US}) = \frac{2(\mathrm{SSE} + q_0)^{-\nu/2}}{([\mathrm{SSE} + (1 - \delta_*)^2 q_0]^{-\nu/2} + [\mathrm{SSE} + (1 + \delta_*)^2 q_0]^{-\nu/2})}. \tag{9.10.68}$$

(c) Suppose $f(R\beta|\sigma, H_2) \in \mathscr{F}_N$. If $g_0 \leq 1$, then $\underline{B}_{12}(\mathscr{F}_N) = 1$. If $g_0 > 1$, then $B_{12}(\mathscr{F}_N)$ is minimized by choosing $R\beta|\sigma^2 \sim N(r, \sigma^2 V_*)$, where V_* is given by

$$V_* = \lambda_*(Rb - r)(Rb - r)', \tag{9.10.69}$$

$$\lambda_* = \max\left\{0, \left(\frac{\nu - 1}{\mathrm{SSE}} - \frac{1}{q_0}\right)\right\}, \tag{9.10.70}$$

and $B_{12} \geq \underline{B}_{12}(\mathscr{F}_N)$, where

$$\underline{B}_{12}(\mathscr{F}_N) = g_0^{1/2}\left[1 - \frac{1 - g_0}{\nu}\right]^{-\nu/2}. \tag{9.10.71}$$

(d) Define

$$q_A = (Rb - r)'[A + R(X'X)^{-1}R']^{-1}(Rb - r), \tag{9.10.72}$$

$$g_A = \frac{(\nu - 1)q_A}{\mathrm{SSE}}, \tag{9.10.73}$$

$$V_{*A} = A + \lambda_{*A}(Rb - r)(Rb - r)', \tag{9.10.74}$$

$$\lambda_{*A} = \max\left\{0, \left(\frac{\nu - 1}{\mathrm{SSE}} - \frac{1}{q_A}\right)\right\}. \tag{9.10.75}$$

Suppose $f(R\beta|\sigma, H_2) \in \mathscr{F}_N(A)$. If $g_0 \leq 1$, then $\underline{B}_{12}[\mathscr{F}_N(A)] = 1$. If $g_A > 1$, then B_{12} is minimized by choosing $f(R\beta|\sigma, H_2) = \phi_J(R\beta|r, \sigma^2 V_{*A})$, and $B_{12} \geq \underline{B}_{12}[\mathscr{F}_N(A)]$, where

$$\underline{B}_{12}[\mathscr{F}_N(A)] = g_A^{1/2}\left[1 - \left(\frac{1 - g_A}{\nu}\right)\right]^{-\nu/2}. \tag{9.10.76}$$

Proof Iwata (1992).

If $B_{12} > 1$, then this suggests the data favor H_1 over H_2. If the lower bound $\underline{B}_{12}(\cdot)$ exceeds unity, then this is indeed impressive evidence in favor of H_1. For all the prior families considered by Iwata (1992), the lower bound $\underline{B}_{12}(\cdot)$ cannot strictly exceed unity because $f(y|H_2)$ can be made at least as large as $f(y|H_1)$ just by letting the scale become arbitrarily small. There remains, however, the question of whether $\underline{B}_{12}$ can equal exactly unity. The following theorem resolves the issue.

Theorem 9.10.2

(a) For $\mathscr{F} = \mathscr{F}_S$, $\mathscr{F}_{US}$ and $\mathscr{F}_N$, $\underline{B}_{12}(\mathscr{F}) < 1$ if

$$f > \frac{(T-K)}{J(v-1)}, \tag{9.10.77}$$

and $\underline{B}_{12}(\mathscr{F}) = 1$, otherwise.

(b) Rewrite q_A as

$$q_A = q_0 - (\bar{r} - r)'([R(X'X)^{-1}R']^{-1} + A^{-1})(\bar{r} - r), \tag{9.10.78}$$

where

$$\bar{r} = ([R(X'X)^{-1}R']^{-1} + A^{-1})([R(X'X)^{-1}R']^{-1}Rb + A^{-1}r), \tag{9.10.79}$$

is the posterior mean of $R\beta$ when the prior is $f(R\beta|\sigma, H_2) = \phi_J(R\beta|r, \sigma^2 A)$. Define

$$f^* = \frac{(T-K)(\bar{r} - r)'([R(X'X)^{-1}R'] + A^{-1})(\bar{r} - r)}{J \cdot \mathrm{SSE}}. \tag{9.10.80}$$

Then $\underline{B}_{12}[\mathscr{F}_N(A)] < 1$, if

$$f > f^* + \frac{(T-K)}{J(v-1)}, \tag{9.10.81}$$

and $\underline{B}_{12}[\mathscr{F}_N(A)] = 1$, otherwise.

In closing, we note as does Iwata (1992) that "posterior f-statistic" f^* in (9.10.80) is identical to the "compatibility statistic" of Theil (1963) for checking the compatibility of the prior and sample information.

Exercises

9.10.1 Compute the MSE of (9.10.55).

9.10.2 Verify (9.10.23) through (9.10.30).

9.11 Prediction

Given the standard multiple linear normal regression model

$$y = X\beta + u, \tag{9.11.1}$$

consider T_* out-of-sample observations yet to be observed from the same process:

$$y_* = X_*\beta + u_*, \tag{9.11.2}$$

where y_* and u_* are $T_* \times 1$, X_* is $T_* \times K$, $X_* = [\imath_*, \tilde{X}_*]$ and $\imath_*$ is a $T_* \times 1$ vector with each element equal to unity. The assumptions of the standard multiple linear regression model with either fixed or stochastic regressors are maintained for (9.11.1) and (9.11.2) stacked together. The assumed goal is to predict y_*. An issue that arises immediately is whether $\tilde{X}_*$ is known.

Under Case I in which $\tilde{X}$ is assumed fixed, it seems natural to assume $\tilde{X}_*$ is fixed and known, as when the regressor values are under the control of the researcher. To treat $\tilde{X}_*$ as fixed but unknown is awkward under Case I because nothing has been assumed concerning how these fixed unknown $\tilde{X}_*$ are generated.

Under Case II in which $\tilde{X}$ is stochastic, two possibilities arise. One is to engage in "scenario" forecasts in which the researcher envisions predicting y_* given circumstances in which assumed values of $\tilde{X}_*$ are realized. For all practical purposes this reduces to the case above in which $\tilde{X}_*$ is fixed and known. More realistically is the case in which one wishes to forecast y_* unconditional of $\tilde{X}_*$. In this case the marginal distribution of the regressors is important. Because this chapter has not addressed (at least not in much detail) the problem of estimating the parameters of the marginal distribution of the regressors, in this section we investigate the prediction problem conditional on $\tilde{X}$ and $\tilde{X}_*$.[39] Scenario forecasts lose their appeal when X_* depends on lagged values of y. In the terminology of Engle et al. (1983), we are implicitly assuming *strong exogeneity* in our assumed independent sampling. Note also that the simple case we consider here does not address the quintessential question of econometrics, namely, prediction in the face of policy intervention. In other words, we contemplate choosing X_* without fear of the structure (as captured by λ) changing. We are therefore assuming we have identified a "structural" property of the world which has held in the past and will hold in the future under policy intervention. Engle et al. (1983) use the terminology *super exogeneity* to describe such a situation.[40]

When parameters are known there is little disagreement about how to engage in prediction: Pick point predictions to minimize expected costs (see Section 8.2). Given independent sampling, the optimal point prediction is given by the solution to the problem:

$$\min_{\hat{y}_*} E_{y_*|\tilde{X}_*,\lambda}[C(\hat{y}_*, y_*)], \tag{9.11.3}$$

where $\lambda = [\beta', \sigma^2]'$ and $C(\hat{y}_*, y_*)$ is the relevant predictive loss function. If forecast loss is quadratic, then the optimal point estimate according to (9.11.3) is

$$\hat{y}^* = E(y_*|\tilde{X}_*, \lambda) = X_*\beta. \tag{9.11.4}$$

39. One exception is Exercise 9.11.6.

40. From a philosophical standpoint, strong exogeneity rationalizes inductive inference and guarantees that "tomorrow will be like today" so that we can learn from history.

The preceding approach to point estimation is widely supported by both Bayesians and non-Bayesians. Both would also find it meaningful to make a probability statement like

$$\text{Prob}(y_* \in S_* | \tilde{X}_*, \lambda) = 1 - \alpha, \tag{9.11.5}$$

where S_* is a subset of the sample space for y_*. Furthermore, (9.11.5) can be used in either of two ways: Given S_*, find α; or given α, find the smallest region S_*. Of course proponents of each camp interpret these probability statements differently.

Differences arise, however, once θ is unknown.[41] We first discuss the classical approach. Because point prediction is conceptually easier to address we consider it first.

Point prediction in the face of unknown parameters is essentially a matter of estimation, that is, estimate the function of unknown parameters in (9.11.4). As we have seen, Bayesians and non-Bayesians go about estimation in different ways. Nothing new occurs by casting the estimation problem into point prediction terms. To simplify the following discussion, we consider the case of $T_* = 1$, and therefore write (9.11.2) simply as:

$$y_{T+1} = x'_{T+1}\beta + u_{T+1}. \tag{9.11.6}$$

From the frequentist perspective, under the standard multiple linear regression model with fixed regressors, Corollary 9.2.1 to the Gauss-Markov Theorem 9.2.2 implies that $\hat{y}_{T+1} = x'_{T+1}b$ is the BLUE of $x'_{T+1}\beta$, and

$$\text{Var}(x'_{T+1}b | \tilde{x}_{T+1}) = \sigma^2 x'_{T+1}(X'X)^{-1}x_{T+1}. \tag{9.11.7}$$

Assuming an intercept in the model, then (9.11.7) can also be written in deviation form (using Exercise A.4.2) as

$$\text{Var}(x'_{T+1}b | \tilde{x}_{T+1}) = \sigma^2[T^{-1} + \underline{x}'_{T+1}(\tilde{X}'A\tilde{X})^{-1}\underline{x}_{T+1}], \tag{9.11.8}$$

where $\underline{x}_{T+1} = [x_{T+1,2} - \bar{x}_2, \ldots, x_{T+1,K} - \bar{x}_K]'$ is a $(K-1) \times 1$ vector of deviations of the regressors of the new observation from the corresponding in-sample means, and $A = I_T - T^{-1}\iota_T\iota'_T$.

Example 9.11.1 Consider the simple regression: $y_t = \beta_1 + \beta_2 x_{t2} + u_t$ with $x_{T+1} = [1, x_{T+1,2}]'$. Then (9.11.8) becomes:

$$x'_{T+1}(X'X)^{-1}x_{T+1} = \frac{1}{T} + \frac{(x_{T+1,2} - \bar{x}_2)^2}{m_{22}}, \tag{9.11.9}$$

41. From the standpoint of prediction all parameters are nuisance parameters. We have seen the manner in which nuisance parameters are addressed delineates competing paradigms of statistical thinking, and so it is not surprising that the preceding agreement quickly vanishes in the case of unknown parameters.

where

$$m_{22} = \sum_{t=1}^{T} (x_{t2} - \bar{x}_2)^2. \tag{9.11.10}$$

The sampling uncertainty in using the estimator $\hat{y}_{T+1}$ of $x'_{T+1}\beta$ is described in the following theorem.

Theorem 9.11.1 Consider the standard multiple linear regression model with either fixed or stochastic regressors. Then

$$\left[\frac{\hat{y}_{T+1} - E(y_{T+1}|x_{T+1}, \lambda)}{s_{T+1}}\right]|x_{T+1}, \lambda \sim t(v), \tag{9.11.11}$$

$$C(\hat{y}_{T+1} - t(1 - \tfrac{1}{2}\alpha; v)s_{T+1} < E(y_{T+1}|x_{T+1}, \lambda) < \hat{y}_{T+1} + t(1 - \tfrac{1}{2}\alpha; v)s_{T+1}) = 1 - \alpha, \tag{9.11.12}$$

where $v = T - K$ and

$$\hat{y}_{T+1} = x'_{T+1}b, \tag{9.11.13}$$

$$s_{T+1} = [s^2 x'_{T+1}(X'X)^{-1}x_{T+1}]^{1/2}. \tag{9.11.14a}$$

$$= [s^2\{T^{-1} + \underline{x}'_{T+1}(\tilde{X}'A\tilde{X})^{-1}\underline{x}_{T+1}\}]^{1/2}. \tag{9.11.14b}$$

Proof Follows directly from Theorems 9.5.1 and 9.5.2.

The frequentist approach to point prediction just described views the problem as essentially one of estimation. Interval prediction of y_{T+1}—as opposed to $E(y_{T+1}|x_{T+1}, \lambda)$—is different. As noted in (9.11.5), when λ is known, forecast regions can be constructed using $f(y_{T+1}|x_{T+1}, \lambda)$. Naive use of $f(y_{T+1}|x_{T+1}, \lambda = \hat{\lambda})$, for some estimator $\hat{\lambda}$ of λ, ignores the sampling uncertainty of $\hat{\lambda}$.

In the absence of a generally agreed upon strategy for classical analysis of (9.11.14), the most popular approach is to seek a pivotal quantity involving y_{T+1} which can then be solved to yield a probabilistic forecast statement like (9.11.5). The strategy is similar to that used for confidence intervals in Sections 6.9 and 9.5. Its generality, however, is limited.

In order to produce a forecast interval for y_{T+1}, as opposed to a confidence for its mean $E(y_{T+1}|x_{T+1}, \lambda)$ as in (9.11.12), consider the predictor $\hat{y}_{T+1} = x'_{T+1}b$ and the *forecast error* (or *prediction error*)

$$\hat{e}_{T+1} \equiv y_{T+1} - \hat{y}_{T+1} = x'_{T+1}(\beta - b) + u_{T+1}. \tag{9.11.15}$$

Then $E(\hat{e}_{T+1}) = 0$. The variance of forecast error (9.11.15),

$$\mathrm{Var}(\hat{e}_{T+1}) = \sigma^2 x'_{T+1}(X'X)^{-1}x_{T+1} + \sigma^2 \tag{9.11.16a}$$

$$= \sigma^2[1 + T^{-1} + \underline{x}'_{T+1}(\tilde{X}'A\tilde{X})^{-1}\underline{x}_{T+1}] \tag{9.11.16b}$$

exceeds the variance of the sampling error given in (9.11.7) and (9.11.8) as a result of the additional randomness from u_{T+1} in (9.11.15).

Consider the following theorem.

Theorem 9.11.2 Consider the standard multiple linear regression model with either fixed or stochastic regressors. Then

$$\left[\frac{\hat{y}_{T+1} - y_{T+1}}{s_e}\right] | x_{T+1}, \lambda \sim t(\nu), \tag{9.11.17}$$

$$P(\hat{y}_{T+1} - t(1 - \tfrac{1}{2}\alpha; \nu)s_e < y_{T+1} < \hat{y}_{T+1} + t(1 - \tfrac{1}{2}\alpha; \nu)s_e | x_{T+1}, \lambda) = 1 - \alpha, \tag{9.11.18}$$

where $\hat{y}_{T+1} = x'_{T+1}b$, $\nu = T - K$ and

$$s_e = [s^2 + s^2 x'_{T+1}(X'X)^{-1}x_{T+1}]^{1/2} \tag{9.11.19a}$$

$$= [s^2\{1 + T^{-1} + \underline{x}'_{T+1}(\tilde{X}'A\tilde{X})^{-1}\,\underline{x}_{T+1}\}]^{1/2}. \tag{9.11.19b}$$

Proof Proceed analogous to the proof of Theorem 9.11.1.

Unlike confidence interval (9.11.12), (9.11.18) is a *prediction* or *forecast* interval. Interval (9.11.18) is wider than (9.11.12) because it takes into account the forecast uncertainty of u_{T+1} as well as the estimation uncertainty in estimating β by b. Because y_{T+1} is random, unlike $E(y_{T+1})$, a frequentist *probability* statement can be made about (9.11.18) even after evaluated at the OLS *estimate* b and s^2, whereas only a *confidence* statement can be made about (9.11.12). Both (9.11.12) and (9.11.18) will be narrower: (i) the larger the sample size T, (ii) the greater the "dispersion" in the regressors, and (iii) the smaller the distance between x_{T+1} and the vector of in-sample means of the regressors.

In contrast to the classical approach, the Bayesian approach to prediction is conceptually simple and straightforward. The Bayesian marginalizes $f(y_{T+1}|x_{T+1}, \lambda, y, \tilde{X})$ with respect to the unknown parameters using the posterior distribution for these parameters given the observed data. The *predictive density* is simply:

$$f(y_{T+1}|x_{T+1}, y, \tilde{X}) = \int_{\Lambda} f(y_{T+1}|x_{T+1}, y, \tilde{X}, \lambda) f(\lambda|x_{T+1}, y, \tilde{X})\, d\lambda. \tag{9.11.20}$$

Under independent sampling, $f(y_{T+1}|x_{T+1}, \lambda, y, \tilde{X}) = f(y_{T+1}|x_{T+1}, \theta)$, and so (9.11.20) reduces to

$$f(y_{T+1}|x_{T+1}, y, \tilde{X}) = \int_0^{\infty} \int_{\Re^K} \phi(y_{T+1}|x'_{T+1}\beta, \sigma^2) f(\beta, \sigma^{-2}|y)\, d\beta\, d\sigma^{-2}. \tag{9.11.21}$$

Extension to the case where y_{T+1} is a vector and/or $T_* > 1$ is immediate. If the prior $f(\theta)$ is given, then (9.11.20) is "known," and we proceed in a manner identical to that of "known" parameters. If, as is usually the case, there is some ambiguity as to the most appropriate prior within some class of priors, then (9.12.21) gives rise to a corresponding class of predictive densities. In such cases sensitivity analysis is in order. The following theorem gives predictive density (9.11.21) in the case of natural conjugate and noninformative priors.

Theorem 9.11.3 Consider the standard multiple linear regression model with either fixed or stochastic regressors.

(a) Under the natural conjugate prior $NG(\underline{b}, \underline{Q}, \underline{s}^{-2}, \underline{\nu})$, the predictive density for y_{T+1} is the univariate-t density:

$$f(y_{T+1}|x_{T+1}, y, \tilde{X}) = t(y_{T+1}|x'_{T+1}, \bar{b}, \bar{s}^2[1 + x'_{T+1}\bar{Q}^{-1}x_{T+1}], \bar{\nu}), \tag{9.11.22}$$

where $\bar{b}$, $\bar{Q}$, $\bar{\nu}$ and $\bar{s}^2$ are given by (9.9.8)–(9.9.11).

(b) Under the non-informative prior $f(\beta, \sigma^{-2}) \propto \sigma^2$, the predictive density for y_{T+1} is the univariate-t density:[42]

$$f(y_{T+1}|x_{T+1}, y, \tilde{X}) = t(y_{T+1}|x'_{T+1}b, \bar{s}^2[1 + x'_{T+1}(X'X)^{-1}x_{T+1}], T - K). \tag{9.11.23}$$

Proof Left to the reader.

Predictive density (9.11.21) is the relevant distribution to use when minimizing expected forecast loss when the parameters are unknown since (9.11.3) is inoperative in that case. The optimal point prediction is given by the solution to the problem:

$$\min_{\hat{y}_*} E_{y_*|\tilde{X}_*, y, \tilde{X}}[C(\hat{y}_*, y_*)]. \tag{9.11.24}$$

Note that unlike (9.11.3), the observed data y and $\tilde{X}$ are relevant in (9.11.24) because they contain information regarding the parameters which are now treated as unknown. If forecast loss is quadratic, then the optimal point estimate according to (9.11.24) is

$$\hat{y}_* = E(y_*|\tilde{X}_*, y, \tilde{X}) = X_* E(\beta|y, \tilde{X}, x_{T+1}). \tag{9.11.25}$$

In the present context, (9.11.25) reduces to $\hat{y}_* = x'_{T+1}\bar{b}$ in the case of a natural conjugate prior, and to $\hat{y}_* = x'_{T+1}b$ in the case of a noninformative prior. Also note that the sensitivity of the former can be readily investigated using Theorems 9.9.3, 9.9.5, and 9.9.7.

Bayesian forecast intervals can be obtained directly using predictive density (9.11.21). In the case of a natural conjugate prior, a $1 - \alpha$ forecast interval is given by

42. This result is robust within the class of elliptical distributions that contain multivariate normality as a special case (see Chib et al. 1988).

$$P(\hat{y}_{T+1} - t(1 - \tfrac{1}{2}\alpha; \bar{v})\bar{s}_e < y_{T+1} < \hat{y}_{T+1} + t(1 - \tfrac{1}{2}\alpha; \bar{v})\bar{s}_e | x_{T+1}, \lambda) = 1 - \alpha, \tag{9.11.26}$$

where $\hat{y}_{T+1} = x'_{T+1}\bar{b}$ and $\bar{s}_e^2 = \bar{s}^2[1 + x'_{T+1}\bar{Q}^{-1}x_{T+1}]$. In the case of a noninformative prior, an interval numerically identical to (9.11.18) is obtained.

Finally, we note the predictive implications of pretesting as discussed in Section 9.9. The predictive pretest analog of (9.8.5) is:

$$\hat{y}_{T+1}^{PT} = \begin{Bmatrix} x'_{T+1}b^*, & \text{if } f < c(\alpha, \omega_0) \\ x'_{T+1}b, & \text{if } f \geq c(\alpha, \omega_0) \end{Bmatrix}, \tag{9.11.27}$$

where b_* is the RLS estimator subject to H_1: $R\beta = r$, b is the OLS estimator under H_2: $R\beta \neq r$, f is the standard f-statistic (9.6.9), $c(\alpha, \omega_0)$ is an appropriately chosen critical value for testing H_3: $\omega \leq \omega_0$ versus H_4: $\omega > \omega_0$, and ω is noncentrality parameter (9.6.8). These cases cover both testing the "truth" of $\omega = 0$ and testing the "approximate truth" of $\omega = 0$. As noted in Section 9.10, (9.11.27) is an inadmissible estimator of $x'_{T+1}\beta$ under quadratic loss.

For the Bayesian who assigns prior probability $\underline{\pi}_j$ to H_j $(j = 1, 2)$, $\underline{\pi}_1 + \underline{\pi}_2 = 1$, predictive density (9.11.21) becomes the mixture density:

$$\begin{aligned} f(y_{T+1}|x_{T+1}, y, \tilde{X}) &= \bar{\pi}_1 f(y_{T+1}|x_{T+1}, y, \tilde{X}, H_1) \\ &\quad + (1 - \bar{\pi}_1) f(y_{T+1}|x_{T+1}, y, \tilde{X}, H_2) \\ &= \bar{\pi}_1 t(y_{T+1}|\hat{y}_{T+1,1}, \bar{s}_1^2\bar{Q}_1, \bar{v}_1) \\ &\quad + (1 - \bar{\pi}_1) t(y_{T+1}|\hat{y}_{T+1,2}, \bar{s}^2\bar{Q}_2, \bar{v}_2), \end{aligned} \tag{9.11.28}$$

where

$$\bar{\pi}_1 = [1 + B_{21}(\underline{\pi}_1/\underline{\pi}_2)]^{-1}, \tag{9.11.29}$$

$$\hat{y}_{T+1,j} = x'_{T+1}E(\beta|x_{T+1}, y, \tilde{X}, H_1) = x'_{T+1}\bar{b}_j, \tag{9.11.30}$$

$$\bar{b}_1 = \bar{d}_1, \tag{9.11.31}$$

$$\bar{b}_2 = A^{-1}\bar{d}_2, \tag{9.11.32}$$

$$\bar{Q}_j = A^{-1}\bar{D}_j(A^{-1})', \tag{9.11.33}$$

and A^{-1}, $\bar{d}_j$, $\bar{D}_j$, $\bar{v}_j$ and $\bar{s}_j^2$ $(j = 1, 2)$ are given by (9.6.25), (9.10.24), (9.10.25), (9.10.27) and (9.10.28), respectively. The optimal predictor of y_{T+1} under quadratic loss is the posterior mean of (9.11.27), which can be written as a convex combination of the optimal predictors under each hypothesis:

$$\hat{y}_{T+1} = \bar{\pi}_1\hat{y}_{T+1,1} + (1 - \bar{\pi}_1)\hat{y}_{T+1,2} \tag{9.11.34a}$$

$$= \hat{y}_{T+1,1} + (1 - \bar{\pi}_1)(\hat{y}_{T+1,2} - \hat{y}_{T+1,1}) \tag{9.11.34b}$$

$$= x'_{T+1}[\bar{\pi}_1\bar{b}_1 + (1 - \bar{\pi}_1)\bar{b}_2]. \tag{9.11.34c}$$

Note that this Bayesian predictive analysis generalizes readily to more than two hypotheses and to arbitrary restrictions in models other than regression models. See Poirier (1991c) for examples. In effect the Bayesian's *specification uncertainty* reflected in the competing hypotheses H_j $(j = 1, 2)$ is treated as a nuisance parameter for purposes of prediction, just like it was for estimation toward the end of Section 9.10. If one is interested in prediction, why must one choose between $\hat{y}_{T+1,1}$ and $\hat{y}_{T+1,2}$? The preceding analysis suggests that such a forced choice is non-optimal with respect to expected posterior forecast loss relative to use of weighted prediction (9.11.34).

Exercises

9.11.1 Consider the projection matrix $H = [h_{ij}] = X(X'X)^{-1}X' = I_T - M$, sometimes called the "hat" matrix. Leaving a more detailed discussion to Hoaglin and Welsch (1978), answer each of the following.

(a) Interpret h_{ti} $(t, i = 1, 2, \ldots, T)$.

(b) Show: $0 \leq h_{tt} \leq 1$ $(t = 1, 2, \ldots, T)$.

(c) Show: the average size of a diagonal element in H is K/T.

(d) Give examples for which $h_{tt} = 0$ and $h_{tt} = 1$.

(e) Find h_{ti} in the case of simple regression (i.e., a constant regressor and a single nonconstant regressor).

9.11.2 Delete observation x_T from X leaving the $(T-1) \times K$ matrix X_{T-1}. Show:

$$(X'_{T-1}X_{T-1})^{-1} = (X'X)^{-1} + \frac{(X'X)^{-1}x_T x'_T(X'X)^{-1}}{1 - h_{TT}}.$$

When will deleting an observation likely increase the variance of the OLS estimators?

9.11.3 Prove Theorem 9.11.1.

9.11.4 Prove Theorem 9.11.2.

9.11.5 Show that a regression estimated from an augmented data set obtained by (a) combining T sample points with J forecast points, and (b) including J dummy variables (each equalling one only for the corresponding forecast point), yield J dummy variable coefficients and variances equal to the corresponding prediction errors and prediction error variances, respectively. See Salkever (1976) for help.

9.11.6 Suppose x_{T+1} is unknown, but there exists an unbiased forecast $\hat{x}_{T+1}$ (i.e., $E(\hat{x}_{T+1} - x_{T+1}) = 0$ and $E[\hat{x}'_{T+1}(b - \beta)|\tilde{X}, \tilde{x}_{T+1}, \lambda] = 0$). Let $\Sigma \equiv E[(\hat{x}_{T+1} - x_{T+1})(\hat{x}_{T+1} - x_{T+1})'|\tilde{X}, \tilde{x}_{T+1}, \lambda]$ and $\tilde{u}_{T+1} \equiv y_{T+1} - \hat{x}'_{T+1}b$. Show:

$$\text{Var}(\tilde{u}_{T+1}) = \sigma^2[1 + x'_{T+1}(X'X)^{-1}x_{T+1} + \sigma^{-2}\beta'\Sigma\beta + \text{tr}\{(X'X)^{-1}\Sigma\}]. \quad (9.11.35)$$

9.11.7 Consider the standard linear regression (9.11.1), and the point predictors $\hat{y}_{T+1} = x'_{T+1}b$ and $\hat{y}_{T+2} = x'_{T+2}b$, where x_{T+1} and x_{T+2} are nonstochastic vectors at which predictions are to be made, and b is the OLS estimator. Define the forecast errors $\hat{u}_{T+1} = y_{T+1} - \hat{y}_{T+1}$ and $\hat{u}_{T+2} = y_{T+2} - \hat{y}_{T+2}$.

(a) Find the variance of the average of the two forecast errors: $\text{Var}[\frac{1}{2}(\hat{u}_{T+1} + \hat{u}_{T+2})]$.

(b) Suppose the first regressor identically equals unity. Let $x_{T+1} = [1, x_{T+1,2}, \ldots, x_{T+1,K}]'$ and $x_{T+2} = [1, x_{T+2,2}, \ldots, x_{T+2,K}]'$. Given x_{T+1}, for what values of $x_{T+2,k}$ $(k = 2, 3, \ldots, K)$ is the variance in (a) minimized? Interpret your answer.

9.11.8 Verify that (9.11.3) solves (9.11.1).

9.11.9 Consider the standard linear normal regression model $y = X\beta + u$, together with the normal-gamma prior $NG(\underline{b}, \underline{Q}, \underline{s}^{-2}, \underline{\nu})$. Suppose you wish to predict y_{T+1}, given x_{T+1} and quadratic predictive loss. Finally, suppose that while $\underline{b}$, $\underline{s}^2$, $\underline{\nu}$ and x_{T+1} are all known, you are unable to specify $\underline{Q}$ other than to say it is positive semidefinite. Can you determine a finite range of possible values for your optimal Bayesian point estimate $\hat{y}_*$ regardless of the choice of $\underline{Q}$? If so, do it. If not, why not?

9.12 Goodness-of-Fit

Recall the R^2 as defined by (9.2.46) and assume the model contains an intercept. R^2 is often referred to as the *coefficient of determination*. The following points are worth noting.

a. R^2 is the proportion of variation in y "explained" by the regressors.

b. $0 \leq R^2 \leq 1$.

c. As R^2 approaches unity, the "fit" of the model becomes perfect, i.e., $\hat{u}'\hat{u} = 0$.

d. Picking $\hat{\beta}$ to minimize $\hat{u}'\hat{u}$ is equivalent to picking $\hat{\beta}$ to maximize R^2.

e. $R \equiv +(R^2)^{1/2}$ is known as the *coefficient of multiple correlation* and is sometimes denoted $R_{1\cdot 23\ldots K}$.

f. R^2 is also the square of the coefficient of correlation between y and $\hat{y}$.

g. If $R^2 = 0$, then $\tilde{b}_2 = 0_{K-1}$. Why? If $\tilde{b}_2 = 0$ and SST $\neq 0$, then $R^2 = 0$.

h. $\tilde{b}_2 = 0$ for the simple regressions cases (a) and (b) depicted in Figure 9.12.1. Clearly, $R^2 = 0$ does not require that y and $\tilde{x}$ are unrelated. It only means that y and $\tilde{x}$ are not related in a *linear* fashion. In case (c) y and $\tilde{x}$ related exactly by a horizontal line, SST = SSR = SSE = 0, and R^2 is indeterminate.

Cases in which the regression does not include an intercept warrant special attention because the decomposition SST = SSR + SSE in (9.2.45) is not longer guaranteed to hold. Five candidate "R^2" measures are introduced in the following example.

Example 9.12.1 Suppose the assumptions of the standard multiple linear normal regression model with either fixed or stochastic regressors: $y = X\beta + u$. Define

$$m_{yy} = \text{SST},\ m_{\hat{y}\hat{y}} = \text{SSR},\ m_{\hat{u}\hat{u}} = \sum_{t=1}^{T} (\hat{u}_t - \bar{\hat{u}})^2, \tag{9.12.1}$$

$$m_{jy} = \sum_{t=1}^{T} (x_{tj} - \bar{x}_j)(y_t - \bar{y}),\ m_{xy} = [m_{2y}, m_{3y}, \ldots, m_{Ky}]', \tag{9.12.2}$$

$$R^2_{m\hat{y}} = \frac{m_{\hat{y}\hat{y}}}{m_{yy}},\ R^2_{m\hat{u}} = 1 - \frac{m_{\hat{u}\hat{u}}}{m_{yy}},\ R^2_{mF} = \frac{\tilde{b}_2' m_{xy}}{m_{yy}}, \tag{9.12.3}$$

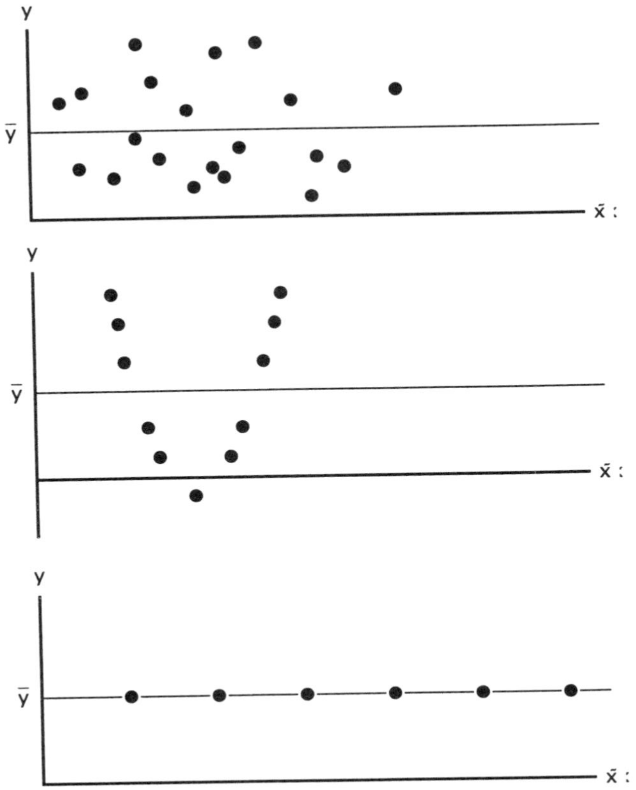

Figure 9.12.1
Data configurations yielding zero slopes

$$R^2_{\text{raw}} = \frac{\hat{y}'\hat{y}}{yy} = \frac{\hat{y}'y}{y'y} = 1 - \frac{\hat{u}'\hat{u}}{y'y}, \; R^2_{mG} = 1 - \frac{\hat{u}'\hat{u}}{m_{yy}}. \tag{9.12.4}$$

If X contains a constant term, then

$$R^2_{m\hat{y}} = R^2_{m\hat{u}} = R^2_{mF}, \tag{9.12.5}$$

and there is no ambiguity in the definition of "R^2". If, however, X does *not* contain a constant term (implicitly or explicitly), then none of these "R^2"—measures need be equal.[43] Also, R^2_{mF} and R^2_{my} may be greater than unity when X does not contain an intercept, and R^2_{mF} and R^2_{mu} may be negative when X does not contain an intercept.

Example 9.12.2 Suppose $y = [1, 0, 1]'$ and $X = [0, 2, 1]'$. Then $b = 1/5$

43. For discussions of "R^2—measures" in models without intercepts, see Aigner (1971, pp. 85–90), Barten (1987), Heijmans and Neudecker (1987), and Theil (1971, p. 178).

and

$R^2_{m\hat{y}} = .12,\ R^2_{m\hat{u}} = -.72,\ R^2_{mF} = -.3.$

Example 9.12.3 Suppose $y = [1, 1, 2]'$ and $X = [0, 1, 2]'$. Then $b = 1$ and $R^2_{m\hat{y}} = 3,\ R^2_{m\hat{u}} = 0,\ R^2_{mF} = 1.5.$

Example 9.12.4 If β_1 corresponds to an intercept, then $H_0\colon \beta_1 = 0$ can be tested (based on Theorem 9.6.1) by constructing the test statistic,

$$f = \frac{(T-K)[R^2_m - R^2_{mG}]}{1 - R^2_m}, \tag{9.12.6}$$

where

$R^2_m = R^2_{m\hat{y}} = R^2_{m\hat{u}} = R^2_{m\hat{u}} = R^2_{mF}.$

Compare (9.12.6) to (9.6.9e) and (9.6.9f).

Although R^2 is the most commonly used measure of goodness-of-fit, it is by no means the only measure. The role of different goodness-of-fit measures in model selection problems will become clear later. Here we will only discuss one very popular alternative measure.

Definition 9.12.1 The *corrected coefficient of determination*, commonly referred to as $\bar{R}^2$ (R-bar-squared), is defined as

$$\bar{R}^2 = R^2 - \left(\frac{K-1}{T-K}\right)(1 - R^2), \tag{9.12.7}$$

or equivalently,

$$1 - \bar{R}^2 = \left(\frac{T-1}{T-K}\right)(1 - R^2) = \frac{\text{SSE}/(T-K)}{\text{SST}/(T-1)}. \tag{9.12.8}$$

$\bar{R}^2$ is basically a loss function which "penalizes" the inevitable non-decrease in R^2, resulting from adding variables to a model, for its using up of degrees of freedom. Although $s^2 = \text{SSE}/(T-K)$ is an unbiased estimator of σ^2, and while $\text{SST}/(T-1)$ is an unbiased estimator of σ_{yy}, their ratio, $1 - \bar{R}^2$, is *not* an unbiased estimator of $1 - R^2_{\text{pop}}$. Also note: (i) $\bar{R}^2$ may be negative, and (ii) $\bar{R}^2 \le R^2$ and $\bar{R}^2 = R^2$ iff $R^2 = 1$.

Finally, recall

$$f = \left(\frac{R^2 - R^2_*}{1 - R^2}\right)\left(\frac{T-K}{J}\right), \tag{9.6.9f}$$

where R^2 refers to the model with K unrestricted coefficients and R^2_* refers to the model with $K - J$ unrestricted coefficients. Let $\bar{R}^2_*$ and $\bar{R}^2$ denote the corrected coefficients of determination for a restricted and a unrestricted model. Test statistic (9.6.9f) can be expressed in terms of $\bar{R}^2$ and $\bar{R}^2_*$ as

$$f = \frac{J + (T - K)\overline{R}^2 - (T - K + J)\overline{R}_*^2}{(T - K)(1 - \overline{R}^2)}. \tag{9.12.9}$$

Then $\overline{R}^2 > \overline{R}_*^2$ iff $f > 1$.

Exercises

9.12.1 Consider a standard simple liner regression model with fixed regressors through the origin: $y_t = \beta x_t + u_t$ $(t = 1, 2, \ldots, T)$. Because there is no intercept in the model, we know that the OLS residuals need not sum to zero, and hence the "appropriate" definition of R^2 is unclear. To circumvent this problem suppose that you decide to pick β such that it minimizes the error sum of squares subject to the constraint that the estimated residuals sum to zero.

(a) Find β. What assumption do you need to add to ensure its existence?

(b) If β an unbiased estimator of β? How does the MSE of β compare to the MSE of the OLS estimator b?

9.12.2 Let (x_t, y_t) $(t = 1, 2, \ldots, T)$ be the observation pairs of two variables x and y. Prove that the correlation coefficient of any linear function of x and any linear function of y equals the same r if the two functions are both increasing or both decreasing, and that this correlation coefficient equals $-r$ if one of these functions is increasing and the other is decreasing.

9.12.3 Prove each of the following

(a) $1 = 1 - R_{mu}^2 - R_{my}^2 + 2R_{mF}^2$

(b) $1 = 1 - R_{mu}^2 + R_{my}^2 + 2(R_{mf}^2 - R_{my}^2)$

(c) $R_{mF}^2 = R_{my}^2$ iff $(\overline{y}, \overline{x}')$ lies on the regression line through the origin

(d) $R_{mu}^2 = 0$ does *not* imply $R_{my}^2 = 0$.

(e) $R_{mF}^2 = 1$ does *not* imply $R_{my}^2 = 1$.

9.12.4 Suppose Researcher A and Researcher B estimate the simple regression model, $y_t = \alpha + \beta x_t + u_t$ $(t = 1, 2, \ldots, T)$, based on two different samples. Suppose that both samples are the same size and that $R_A^2 > R_B^2$. Let b_A and b_B denote their respective OLS estimators. Does it necessarily follow that the estimated variance of b_A is less than the estimated variance of b_B? Explain your answer.

9.12.5 Prove that the coefficient of determination is in fact the square of the coefficient of correlation between y and $\hat{y}$.

9.12.6 Consider a simple regression model with data observations (y_t, x_t) $(t = 1, 2, \ldots, T)$. Suppose the ranks $1, 2, \ldots, R$ are assigned to the x_t's arranged in ascending order, the y_t's are arranged in similar fashion, and that in either case there are no ties. Show that the correlation between these two ranks can be written as

$$r_S = 1 - \frac{6 \sum_{t=1}^{T} d_t^2}{T(T^2 - 1)}, \tag{9.12.10}$$

where d_t is the difference between the ranks assigned to x_t and y_t. r_s is known as the *coefficient of rank correlation* or as *Spearman's rank correlation coefficient*.

9.12.7 Consider a standard multiple linear normal regression model with fixed regressors including an intercept term. Show: the correlation between the OLS b_i and b_j $(i \neq j)$ equals minus the partial correlation between the ith and jth regressors.

9.12.8 In what follows, the coefficient of determination is calculated as one minus the ratio of the sum of squared errors to the total sum of squares. Consider the four-point scatter plots in Figure 9.12.2. For each of the questions below indicate the letter of the

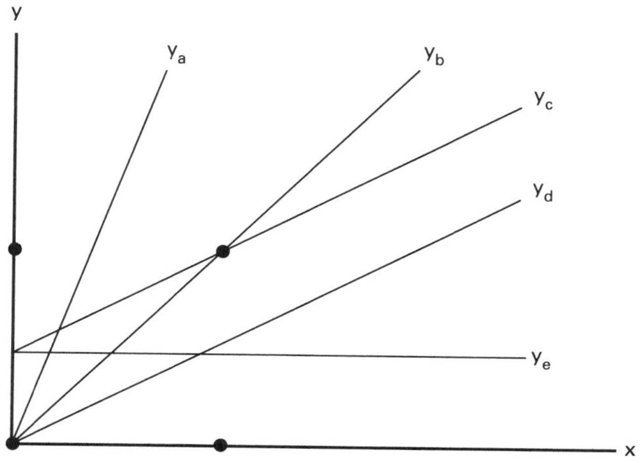

Figure 9.12.2
Data for Exercise 9.12.8

most correct response and give a brief explanation for your reasoning. Note the point (0, 0) is one of the observations (see Becker and Kennedy 1992).

(a) For the four sample points, which line best represents the regression line? (1) y_a, (2) y_b, (c) y_c, (d) y_d, (e) y_e.

(b) The coefficient of determination for the regression line in (a) is: (1) <0, (2) 0, (3) between 0 and $\frac{1}{2}$, (4) $\frac{1}{2}$, (5) $>\frac{1}{2}$

(c) If the regression line is forced to pass through the origin, which line best represents the regression line incorporating this zero intercept constraint? (1) y_a, (2) y_b, (3) y_c, (4) y_d, (5) y_e

(d) The coefficient of determination for the regression line in (c) is: (1) <0, (2) 0, (3) between 0 and $\frac{1}{2}$, (4) $\frac{1}{2}$, (5) $>\frac{1}{2}$

9.12.9 Consider the estimated regression

$$\hat{y}_t = \underset{(25.0)}{100} - \underset{(9.0)}{12}\tilde{x}_{t2} + \underset{(10.0)}{6}\tilde{x}_{t3} + \underset{(9.0)}{8}\tilde{x}_{t4}, \tag{9.12.11}$$

where the values in parentheses are estimated standard errors. Consider the regression model obtained by omitting $\tilde{x}_{t4}$ from (9.12.11), that is,

$$\hat{y}_t = \hat{\beta}_1 + \hat{\beta}_2\tilde{x}_{t2} + \hat{\beta}_3\tilde{x}_{t3}. \tag{9.12.12}$$

(a) Which model has the higher value of $\overline{R}^2$? Explain your answer.

(b) Suppose the coefficients of $\tilde{x}_{t2}$ and $\tilde{x}_{t3}$ in (9.12.11) have the "wrong" signs, but your theory assures you that they belong in the model. Furthermore, suppose your *a priori* feelings concerning $\tilde{x}_{t4}$ were that it was unimportant and that the sample evidence confirmed this; and so you chose to estimate (9.12.12) in the hope of obtaining "correct" signs for $\hat{\beta}_2$ and $\hat{\beta}_3$. What can you expect *t* find? Explain your answer.

9.13 Sample Partial Correlation

On occasion it is convenient to augment the standard regression notation introduced in Section 9.1 to emphasize not only with which regressor each regression coefficient is associated, but also to emphasize the dependent variable of the equation and all other regressors included in the equation.[44] Using the subscript "1" to denote the dependent variable y_t and the subscripts "2", "3", ..., "K" to denote the nonconstant regressors, express the standard multiple linear normal regression model with stochastic regressors as

$$y_t = \alpha_{1\cdot 2\ldots K} + \beta_{12\cdot 3\ldots K}x_{t2} + \beta_{13\cdot 24\ldots K}x_{t3} + \cdots + \beta_{1K\cdot 23\ldots(K-1)}x_{tK} + u_t \tag{9.13.1}$$

for $t = 1, 2, \ldots, T$, where $\alpha_{1\cdot 23\ldots K}$ denotes the intercept in a regression of y_t on x_{tk} $(k = 2, 3, \ldots, K)$, and $\beta_{1j\cdot 23\ldots(j-1)(j+1)\ldots K}$ denotes the regression coefficient of x_{tj} in this regression. The OLS estimators of the elements in (9.13.1) are denoted $a_{1\cdot 2\ldots K}$, $b_{12\cdot 3\ldots K}$, $b_{13\cdot 24\ldots K}, \ldots, b_{1K\cdot 3\ldots(K-1)}$. The variance of the disturbance u_t in (9.13.1) is denoted $\sigma^2_{1\cdot 2\ldots K}$ and its unbiased estimator is denoted $s^2_{1\cdot 2\ldots K}$.

In Section 2.7 we introduced the idea of a population partial correlation (see Definition 2.7.3) and Exercise 3.4.38 demonstrated its close connection to the regression coefficients in (9.13.1). We now introduce sample analogs of these partial correlations and show their intimate connection to OLS estimators.

Definition 9.13.1 The *sample partial correlation* between y and x_j controlling for x_k $(k = 2, 3, \ldots, K; k \neq j)$, denoted $r_{1j\cdot 23\ldots(j-1)(j+1)\ldots K}$, is the simple sample correlation between the OLS residuals from a regression of y_t on x_{tk} $(k = 2, 3, \ldots, K; k \neq j)$ and the OLS residuals of a regression of x_{tj} on x_{tk} $(k = 2, 3, \ldots, K; k \neq j)$, where both regressions include a constant term.

Geometrically, in the case $K = 3$ the partial correlation between y and x_3, controlling for x_2, is the cosine of the angle between the orthogonal projection of y and x_3 on x_2 (e.g., see Thomas and O'Quigley 1993). In contrast, the multiple correlation coefficient R between y and x_2 and x_3 is the cosine of the angle between y and its orthogonal projection on x_2 and x_3.

Theorem 9.13.1

$$b_{1j\cdot 23\ldots(j-1)(j+1)\ldots K} = \left[\frac{s_{1\cdot 2\ldots(j-1)(j+1)\ldots K}}{s_{j\cdot 2\ldots(j-1)(j+1)\ldots K}}\right] r_{1j\cdot 2\ldots(j-1)(j+1)\ldots K}. \tag{9.13.2}$$

Proof Johnston (1972, pp. 132–135).

44. This notation appears to be due to Yule (1907). It was introduced earlier in Exercise 3.4.38.

Partial correlations are helpful in deciding whether to include additional explanatory variables into a regression. For example, r_{1K}^2 may be high, but $r_{1K\cdot 23\ldots(K-1)}^2$ may be low. This implies that if the Kth regressor alone is used to explain the dependent variable, however, after regressors 2 through $K-1$ are included, the Kth regressor explains little of the residual variation. The following theorem relates the t-ratio for testing that the Kth regression coefficient is zero to the partial correlation coefficient $r_{1K\cdot 23\ldots(K-1)}$.

Theorem 9.13.2 Let $\tau_{1K\cdot 23\ldots(K-1)}$ be the calculated t-statistic for testing H_1: $\beta_{1K\cdot 23\ldots(K-1)} = 0$. Then

$$\tau_{1K\cdot 23\ldots(K-1)} = \left[\frac{(T-K)r_{1K\cdot 23\ldots(K-1)}^2}{1 - r_{1K\cdot 23\ldots(K-1)}^2}\right]^{1/2}. \tag{9.13.3}$$

Proof Left to the reader.

To explore the connection between OLS estimators and simple correlations, consider the following. The simple correlation matrix of x_{tk} ($k = 1, 2, \ldots, K$) is denoted:

$$\mathbb{R} = \begin{bmatrix} r_{11} & r_{12} & \cdots & r_{1K} \\ r_{12} & r_{22} & \cdots & r_{2K} \\ \vdots & \vdots & & \vdots \\ r_{1K} & r_{2K} & \cdots & r_{KK} \end{bmatrix}, \tag{9.13.4}$$

and the cofactor of the element in row i and column j is denoted R_{ij}. Also let s_k^2 ($k = 1, 2, \ldots, K$) denote the unbiased sample variance estimators of the variables y_t and x_{tk} ($k = 1, 2, \ldots, K$). The normal equations of least squares corresponding to all the slope parameters can be written:

$$\begin{bmatrix} r_{22} & r_{23} & \cdots & r_{2K} \\ r_{23} & r_{33} & \cdots & r_{3K} \\ \vdots & \vdots & & \vdots \\ r_{2K} & r_{3K} & \cdots & r_{KK} \end{bmatrix} \begin{bmatrix} b_{12\cdot 34\ldots K}s_2 \\ b_{13\cdot 24\ldots K}s_3 \\ \vdots \\ b_{1K\cdot 23\ldots(K-1)}s_K \end{bmatrix} \begin{bmatrix} r_{12}s_1 \\ r_{13}s_1 \\ \vdots \\ r_{1K}s_1 \end{bmatrix}. \tag{9.13.5}$$

Using Cramer's Rule (Theorem A.5.1), (9.13.5) implies that the OLS estimators of the slopes can be written as:

$$b_{1j\cdot 23\ldots(j-1)(j+1)\ldots K} = -\left(\frac{s_1}{s_j}\right)\left(\frac{R_{1j}}{R_{11}}\right). \tag{9.13.6}$$

Furthermore, the optimized sum of squared errors is

$$\mathrm{SSE} = \mathrm{SSE}(b) = \frac{(T-1)s_1^2|\mathbb{R}|}{R_{11}}, \tag{9.13.7}$$

and the coefficient of determination (9.2.46) (also referred to as the *multiple correlation coefficient squared*) can be expressed in the present notation as

$$R^2_{1\cdot 23\ldots K} = 1 - \frac{\text{SSE}}{\text{SST}} = 1 - \frac{|\mathbb{R}|}{R_{11}}. \tag{9.13.8}$$

For details concerning the derivation of (9.13.3) through (9.13.6) see Johnston (1972, pp. 132–134).

Exercises

9.13.1 Consider the standard regression

$$y_t = \beta_1 + \beta_2 x_{t2} + \cdots + \beta_K x_{tK} + u_t \qquad (t = 1, 2, \ldots, T),$$

and the "normalized" model in which each variable is normalized by subtracting its mean and divided by its estimated standard deviation:

$$\frac{y_t - \bar{y}}{s_1} = \beta_2^*\left(\frac{x_{t2} - \bar{x}_2}{s_2}\right) + \cdots + \beta_K^*\left(\frac{x_{tK} - \bar{x}_K}{s_K}\right) + \left(\frac{u_t - \bar{u}}{s_1}\right). \tag{9.13.9}$$

Then $\beta_k^* = (\beta_k s_k)/s_1$ $(k = 1, 2, \ldots, K)$ are known as *beta coefficients* or *standardized regression coefficients*. β_k^* is the effect, ceteris paribus, of a unit standard deviation change from the mean of x_k on a unit standard deviation change from the mean of y.

(a) Show:

$$R^2 = \sum_{k=2}^{K} b_k^* r_{1k}, \tag{9.13.10}$$

where $b_k^* = b_k s_k / s_1$.

(b) Does (a) provide a "useful" breakdown of R^2 into contributions of each of the regressors? Explain your answer.

9.13.2 The principal minors of a square matrix A are all positive, and if the nondiagonal elements of A are all negative, then all elements of A^{-1} are positive. Show:

(a) If the simple correlations of a set of variables are negative, then all partial correlation coefficients of all orders of the set are also negative.

(b) If all partial correlation coefficients of highest order of as et of variables are positive, all partial correlation coefficients of lower orders are also positive, and all simple correlation coefficients are positive.

9.13.3 Consider the standard linear regression with $K = 3$. Verify each of the following:

(a) $r^2_{12\cdot 3} = (R^2_{1\cdot 23} - r^2_{13})/(1 - r^2_{13})$

(b) $1 - R^2_{1\cdot 23} = (1 - r^2_{13})(1 - r^2_{12\cdot 3})$

(c) $r^2_{13\cdot 2} = (R^2_{1\cdot 23} - r^2_{12})/(1 - r^2_{12})$

(d) $1 - R^2_{1\cdot 23} = (1 - r^2_{12})(1 - r^2_{13\cdot 2})$

(e) $R^2_{1\cdot 23} = r^2_{12} + r^2_{13\cdot 2}(1 - r^2_{12})$

(f) $R^2_{1\cdot 23} = r^2_{12} + r^2_{13}$, if $r_{23} = 0$.

9.13.4 Verify the following population recurrence relationships:

$$\text{(a)} \quad \rho_{12\cdot 34\ldots K} = \frac{\rho_{12\cdot 34\ldots(K-1)} - \rho_{1K\cdot 34\ldots(K-1)}\rho_{2K\cdot 34\ldots(K-1)}}{[1 - \rho^2_{1K\cdot 34\ldots(K-1)}]^{1/2}[1 - \rho^2_{K2\cdot 34\ldots(K-1)}]^{1/2}} \tag{9.13.11}$$

$$\text{(b)} \quad \beta_{12\cdot 34\ldots K} = \frac{\beta_{12\cdot 34\ldots(K-1)} - \beta_{1K\cdot 34\ldots(K-1)}\beta_{2K\cdot 34\ldots(K-1)}}{1 - \beta_{1K\cdot 34\ldots(K-1)}\beta_{K2\cdot 34\ldots(K-1)}} \tag{9.13.12}$$

9.13.5 Verify the following sample recurrence relationships:

$$\text{(a)} \quad r_{12\cdot 34\ldots K} = \frac{r_{12\cdot 34\ldots(K-1)} - r_{1K\cdot 34\ldots(K-1)}r_{2K\cdot 34\ldots(K-1)}}{[1 - r^2_{1K\cdot 34\ldots(K-1)}]^{1/2}[1 - r^2_{K2\cdot 34\ldots(K-1)}]^{1/2}} \tag{9.13.13}$$

$$\text{(b)} \quad r_{12\cdot 34\ldots K} = \frac{b_{12\cdot 34\ldots(K-1)} - b_{1K\cdot 34\ldots(K-1)}b_{2K\cdot 34\ldots(K-1)}}{[1 - b_{1K\cdot 34\ldots(K-1)}b_{K2\cdot 34\ldots(K-1)}} \tag{9.13.14}$$

9.13.6 Show (see Johnston 1972, p. 135):

$$r_{1i\cdot 2,\ldots,i-1,i+1,\ldots,K} = -\frac{R_{1i}}{(R_{11}R_{ii})^{1/2}}. \tag{9.13.15}$$

9.14 Multicollinearity

Many applied econometricians view multicollinearity as something akin to original sin. Holders of this view appear to believe that as a result of Adam and Eve's biting into the apple, God decided to inflict the empiricists among their descendants with a plague that would prevent them from finding their nirvana in life: "significant" coefficients. Among an embarrassingly large proportion of applied econometricians, multicollinearity has become the scapegoat for their too-often unsatisfactory empirical results.

This section is intended to eliminate some of the confusion that surrounds the concept of multicollinearity. An extensive literature has evolved dealing with the detection of the existence, severity and location of the "multicollinearity problem." Leaving a survey of this literature to Smith (1974) and Judge et al. (1985, pp. 620–624), the discussion here focuses on the more important question: In what sense is multicollinearity a problem? A natural place to begin is with its definition.

Definition 9.14.1 *Multicollinearity* is present whenever one or more regressors are "highly" correlated with another regressor or a linear combination of regressors. If any such correlation equals ± 1, then *perfect multicollinearity* exists.

The existence of perfect multicollinearity does not necessarily mean that the correlation between any two explanatory variables must be perfect, or even particularly high, when the total number of explanatory variables is greater than two. In other words, perfect correlation between two explanatory variables is a sufficient, but not a necessary, condition for the presence of perfect multicollinearity when the number of explanatory variables exceeds two. For example, Kmenta (1986, p. 434) considers a case in which $K = 4$, $x_{t2} = x_{t3} + x_{t4}$, $m_{33} = m_{44}$, $r_{23} = r_{24} = .5$ and $r_{34} = -.5$.

Although perfect multicollinearity does not usually occur in practice except by mistake (e.g., as the result of including both an intercept and all G dummy variables when dealing with G groups), it is nonetheless helpful to study this extreme case before discussing the variety of collinearity problems usually encountered in practice. We begin by first studying the existence of OLS estimators when the full column rank condition on X in (9.1.1) is violated.

Theorem 9.14.1 Consider the standard multiple linear regression model with fixed regressors less (9.1.1), that is $\text{rank}(X) < K$.

(a) The normal equations $(X'X)\beta = X'y$ are consistent, that is, there exists a solution.

(b) Any solution to the normal equations yields the same unique value for SSE.

Proof

(a) Let $r = \text{rank}(X'X, X'y) = \text{rank}(X'[X, y])$. By Theorem A.3.5(b), $r \le \text{rank}(X') = \text{rank}(X'X)$. Since adjoining the column $X'y$ to the matrix $X'X$ cannot decrease the rank of the resultant matrix, that is, $\text{rank}(X'X) \ge \text{rank}(X'X, X'y) = r$, it follows that $r = \text{rank}(X'X) = \text{rank}(X'X, X'y)$. Hence, by Theorem A.5.4(a) there exists a solution to $(X'X)\beta = X'y$.

(b) Let $\hat{\beta}_i$ $(i = 1, 2)$ be solutions to $(X'X)\hat{\beta}_i = X'y$ $(i = 1, 2)$. Then

$$\begin{aligned}\text{SSE}(\hat{\beta}_1) &= (y - X\hat{\beta}_1)'(y - X\hat{\beta}_1)\\ &= [(y - X\hat{\beta}_2) + X(\hat{\beta}_2 - \hat{\beta}_1)]'[(y - X\hat{\beta}_2) + X(\hat{\beta}_2 - \hat{\beta}_1)]\\ &= \text{SSE}(\hat{\beta}_2) + (y - X\hat{\beta}_2)'X(\hat{\beta}_2 - \hat{\beta}_1)\\ &\quad + (\hat{\beta}_2 - \hat{\beta}_1)'X'(y - X\hat{\beta}_2) + (\hat{\beta}_2 - \hat{\beta}_1)'X'X(\hat{\beta}_2 - \hat{\beta}_1).\end{aligned} \tag{9.14.1}$$

Each of the last three terms in (9.14.1) are zero because the normal equations imply $X'(y - X\hat{\beta}_i) = 0_K$ $(i = 1, 2)$ and $X'X(\hat{\beta}_2 - \hat{\beta}_1) = X'y - X'y = 0_K$. Therefore, $\text{SSE}(\hat{\beta}_1) = \text{SSE}(\hat{\beta}_2)$.

In other words, Theorem 9.14.1 implies that when X has less than full column rank, the normal equations still have a solution, and although a unique solution does not exist, all solutions yield the same sum of squared errors. To illustrate the nonuniqueness of the solution consider the following example.

Example 9.14.1 Consider the standard linear regression model

$$y_t = \beta_1 + \beta_2 x_{t2} + \beta_3 x_{t3} + \beta_4 x_{t4} + u_t \qquad (t = 1, 2, \ldots, T),$$

and suppose assumption (9.1.1) is violated due to

$$x_{t2} = x_{t3} + x_{t4} \qquad (t = 1, 2, \ldots, T).$$

Using the notation introduced in (9.2.15) and (9.2.16), suppose $m_{33} = m_{44} = 1$ and $m_{34} = 0$. After removing the intercept, the normal equations imply:

$$\begin{bmatrix} 2 & 1 & 1 \\ 1 & 1 & 0 \\ 1 & 0 & 1 \end{bmatrix} \begin{bmatrix} b_2 \\ b_3 \\ b_4 \end{bmatrix} = \begin{bmatrix} m_{y2} \\ m_{y3} \\ m_{y4} \end{bmatrix}. \tag{9.14.2}$$

Clearly, (9.14.2) constitutes a singular system. Solving for b_3 and b_4 in terms of b_2 yields

$$b_3 = m_{y3} - b_2, \tag{9.14.3}$$

$$b_4 = m_{y4} - b_2. \tag{9.14.4}$$

For alternative values of b_2, (9.14.3) and (9.14.4) generate alternative solutions to (9.14.2).

Generalizing Example 9.14.1 leads to the following example.

Example 9.14.2 Following-up Example 9.14.1, consider a standard multiple linear normal regression model with fixed regressors such that

$$x_{tK} = c_1 x_{t1} + c_2 x_{t2} + \cdots + c_{K-1} x_{t,K-1} \qquad (t = 1, 2, \ldots, T). \tag{9.14.5}$$

Then for any scalar δ,

$$\begin{aligned} \beta_K x_{tK} &= (1 - \delta)\beta_K x_{tK} + \delta \beta_K x_{tK} \\ &= (1 - \delta)\beta_K x_{tK} + \delta \beta_K (c_1 x_{t1} + c_2 x_{t2} + \cdots + c_{K-1} x_{t,K-1}) \end{aligned}$$

and

$$\begin{aligned} E(y_t | x_t) &= x_t'\beta \\ &= (\beta_1 + \delta c_1 \beta_K) x_{t1} + \cdots + (\beta_{K-1} + \delta c_{K-1} \beta_K) x_{t,K-1} + (1 - \delta)\beta_K x_{tK} \\ &= x_t'\beta^*, \end{aligned} \tag{9.14.6}$$

for $t = 1, 2, \ldots, T$, where

$$\beta_k^* = \beta_k + \delta c_k \beta_K \qquad (k = 1, 2, \ldots, K - 1), \tag{9.14.7}$$

$$\beta_K^* = (1 - \delta)\beta_K. \tag{9.14.8}$$

An important implication of (9.14.6) is $f(y_t|\tilde{x}_t, \beta, \sigma^2) = f(y_t|\tilde{x}_t, \beta^*, \sigma^2)$ $(t = 1, 2, \ldots, T)$, and hence by Definition 6.3.2, β is not identified if constraint (9.14.5) always holds. In other words, no sample drawn from the conditional distribution of y given $\tilde{x}$, subject to (9.14.5), will enable the researcher to discriminate between β and β^*. Therefore, the parameter vector β is not estimable. In this case, $E(y_t|\tilde{x}_t) = x_t'\beta$ and $E(y_t|\tilde{x}_t) = x_t'\beta^*$ are *observationally equivalent*.

If $X'X$ is singular, then at least one of its characteristic roots is zero. The characteristic vector c associated with this root must satisfy

$$(X'X)c = 0_K, \tag{9.14.9}$$

which in turn implies

$$c'(X'X)c = (Xc)'(Xc) = 0. \tag{9.14.10}$$

Because (9.14.10) comprises a sum of squares, it can only equal zero if each element equals zero, and thus $Xc = 0_T$. Therefore the characteristic vector of $X'X$ associated with a zero characteristic root give a linear combination of the columns of X, which are the "cause" of the perfect multicollinearity.

Having established multiple OLS estimators under perfect multicollinearity, attention now turns toward the sampling properties of such estimators. To this end we define and characterize situations in which unbiased estimators of linear functions of the regression coefficients can be unbiasedly estimated.

Definition 9.14.2 Let w be a K-dimensional column vector of constants. If an unbiased linear estimator of $w'\beta$ exists, then $w'\beta$ is said to be *estimable*.[45]

Theorem 9.14.2 Let w be a K-dimensional column vector of constants. Then $w'\beta$ is estimable:

(a) iff w' is a linear combination of the rows of X, or equivalently,

(b) iff w (or w') is a linear combination of the rows or columns of $X'X$, or equivalently,

(c) iff w' is a linear combination of the characteristic vectors of $X'X$ corresponding to the nonzero characteristic roots of $X'X$, or equivalently,

(d) iff $w'c = 0$ for all $K \times 1$ vectors c satisfying $Xc = 0_T$.

Proof

(a) Consider the linear estimator $d'y$ of $w'\beta$ where d is a T-dimensional column vector of constants. Then

$$E(d'y) = d'E(y) = d'X\beta. \tag{9.14.11}$$

Thus, $E(d'y) = w'\beta$ for all β iff $w' = d'X$.

(b) Rao (1973, p. 223).

(c) Silvey (1969).

(d) Leamer (1978, p. 189).

45. For a more general characterization of estimability, see Alalouf and Styan (1979).

To illustrate the concept of estimability and its determination via Theorem 9.14.2(a), consider the following example.

Example 9.14.3 Suppose $K = 3$, $\text{rank}(X) = 2$ and $Xc = 0_T$, where $c = [0, -\alpha, 1]'$ and α is a known scalar. Thus, the third column of X is α times the second column. For $w'\beta$ to be estimable it is necessary, according to Theorem 9.14.2(d), that $w'c = -w_2\alpha + w_3 = 0$ or $w_3 = \alpha w_2$. Therefore, $[0, 1, 0]\beta = \beta_2$ and $[0, 0, 1]\beta = \beta_3$ are *not* estimable, but $[1, 0, 0]\beta = \beta_1$ and $[0, 1, \alpha]\beta = \beta_2 + \alpha\beta_3$ are estimable.

With the introduction of the concept of estimability, we can begin to address our primary question of interest, that is, in what sense is multicollinearity a problem? Clearly, perfect multicollinearity is a problem if parametric functions of interest are not estimable. An important lesson has thus been uncovered. *The issue of whether multicollinearity (perfect or otherwise) is a problem* cannot *be answered without a clear statement of the goals of the researcher.* This text emphasizes clear articulation of the *distribution of interest*. Besides knowing that interest lies in the conditional distribution of y_t given $\tilde{x}_t$, further elaboration is required in terms of parametric functions of interest. In the context of Example 9.14.3, if the researcher is interested in β_2 or β_3, then multicollinearity is a problem.

Given that $w'\beta$ is of interest and is estimable, the question immediately arises as to finding an unbiased estimator. This is answered in the following theorem.

Theorem 9.14.3 Suppose $w'\beta$ is estimable, and let $\hat{\beta}_1$ and $\hat{\beta}_2$ be solutions to the normal equations.

(a) $w'\hat{\beta}_1 = w'\hat{\beta}_2$.

(b) $E(w'\hat{\beta}_1) = E(w'\hat{\beta}_2) = w'\beta$.

Proof

(a) Given that $w'\beta$ is estimable, it follows from Theorem 9.14.2(b) that there exists a K-dimensional column vector d such that $w = X'Xd$. Then

$$w'(\hat{\beta}_1 - \hat{\beta}_2) = d'X'X(\hat{\beta}_1 - \hat{\beta}_2) = d(X'y - X'y) = 0.$$

Therefore, $w'\hat{\beta}_1 = w'\hat{\beta}_2$.

(b) $E(w'\hat{\beta}_1) = E(d'X'X\hat{\beta}_1) = E(d'X'y) = d'X'X\beta = w'\beta$.

Theorem 9.14.3 provides the fortuitous result that although there exist distinct solutions to the normal equations, they all provide identical estimates of the estimable function. Theorem 9.14.4 serves as a generalized Gauss-Markov theorem stating that all such estimators are BLUE.

Theorem 9.14.4 Consider the standard multiple linear normal regression model with fixed regressors and suppose $w'\beta$ is estimable and let $\hat{\beta}$ be any solution to the normal equations. Then $w'\hat{\beta}$ is the BLUE of $w'\beta$.

Proof As noted in the proof of Theorem 9.14.4 (a), there exists a K-dimensional column vector d such that $w = X'Xd$. Thus, $w'\hat{\beta} = d'X'X\hat{\beta} = (d'X')y$, which is clearly linear in y. Theorem 9.14.3(b) guarantees that $w'\hat{\beta}$ is an unbiased estimator or $w'\beta$. If $c'y$ is any linear unbiased estimator of $w'\beta$, then $c'X = w'$, and

$$\begin{aligned}\operatorname{Var}(c'y) &= \operatorname{Var}(c'y - d'X'y + d'X'y)\\ &= \operatorname{Var}(c'y - d'X'y) + \operatorname{Var}(w'\hat{\beta}),\end{aligned} \tag{9.14.12}$$

because $\operatorname{Cov}[(c' - d'X')y, w'\hat{\beta}] = 0$. From (9.14.12) it follows that $\operatorname{Var}(c'y) \geq \operatorname{Var}(w'\hat{\beta})$, and hence, $w'\hat{\beta}$ is the BLUE of $w'\beta$.

Taken together, Theorems 9.14.1 through 9.14.4 suggest that even when $\operatorname{rank}(X) < K$, and hence $X'X$ is singular, a BLUE exists for estimable functions of the regression coefficients. The next two examples consider cases of "multicollinearity" that are not necessarily "perfect multicollinearity."

Example 9.14.4 Consider the two-regressor model in Example 9.2.2 written in the standardized form (9.12.13) of Exercise 9.12.1:

$$y_t^* = \beta_2^* x_{t2}^* + \beta_3^* x_{t3}^* + u_t^*, \tag{9.14.13}$$

where $y_t^* = (y_t - \bar{y})/s_y$, $x_{tj}^* = (x_{tj} - \bar{x}_j)/s_j$ $(j = 1, 2)$, $\beta_j^* = \beta_j(s_j/s_y)$ $(j = 1, 2)$, $u_t^* = (u_t - \bar{u})/s_y$, and

$$s_y^2 = \frac{1}{T-1}\sum_{t=1}^{T}(y_t - \bar{y})^2, \tag{9.14.14}$$

$$s_j^2 = \frac{1}{T-1}\sum_{t=1}^{T}(x_{tj} - \bar{x}_j)^2, \qquad (j = 1, 2), \tag{9.14.15}$$

$$\bar{y} = \frac{1}{T}\sum_{t=1}^{T} y_t,\ \bar{x}_j = \frac{1}{T}\sum_{t=1}^{T} x_{tj}\ (j = 1, 2),\ \bar{u} = \frac{1}{T}\sum_{t=1}^{T} u_t. \tag{9.14.16}$$

It follows immediately that

$$\operatorname{Var}\begin{bmatrix} b_2^* \\ b_3^* \end{bmatrix} = \frac{\sigma^2}{1 - r^2}\begin{bmatrix} 1 & -r \\ -r & 1 \end{bmatrix}, \tag{9.14.17}$$

where

$$r = \frac{1}{T}\sum_{t=1}^{T} x_{t2}^* x_{t3}^*, \tag{9.14.18}$$

is the correlation between x_2 and x_3. Suppose the researcher is primarily interested in $\beta_2^* + \beta_3^*$. The variance of the OLS estimator $b_2^* + b_3^*$ is

$$\text{Var}(b_2^* + b_3^*) = \frac{2\sigma^2}{1 - r^2} - \frac{2r\sigma^2}{1 - r^2} = \frac{2(1 - r)\sigma^2}{1 - r^2} = \frac{2\sigma^2}{1 + r}. \tag{9.14.19}$$

Note that as $r \to 1$, $\text{Var}(b_2^*) = \text{Var}(b_3^*) = \sigma^2/(1 - r^2)$ increases, but that $\text{Var}(b_2^* + b_3^*)$ *decreases.* Is multicollinearity a problem? The answer depends on the parameters of interest. Is the researcher interested in $\beta_2^* + \beta_3^*$, or β_2^* and β_3^* individually?

Example 9.14.5 Consider the effects of rearranging the regressors in Example 9.14.4. Since a linear transformation of the regressors does not affect the implicit estimates of any estimable parameters, the initial arrangement of the variables is totally arbitrary and therefore should not affect a measure of the severity of the collinearity problem. For example, consider

$$y_t^* = \gamma_2 w_{t2} + \gamma_3 w_{t3} + u_t^*, \tag{9.14.20}$$

where

$$w_{t2} = \frac{x_{t2}^* + x_{t3}^*}{\sqrt{2}}, \quad w_{t3} = \frac{x_{t2}^* - x_{t3}^*}{\sqrt{2}}, \tag{9.14.21}$$

$$\gamma_2 = \frac{\beta_2^* + \beta_3^*}{\sqrt{2}}, \quad \gamma_3 = \frac{\beta_2^* - \beta_3^*}{\sqrt{2}}. \tag{9.14.22}$$

Then the variance-covariance matrix of the OLS estimator $\hat{\gamma} = [\hat{\gamma}_2, \hat{\gamma}_3]'$ applied to (9.14.20) is given by

$$\text{Var}(\hat{\gamma}) = \sigma^2 \begin{bmatrix} \dfrac{1}{1 + r} & 0 \\ 0 & \dfrac{1}{1 - r} \end{bmatrix}. \tag{9.14.23}$$

Comparing (9.14.17) with (9.14.23) it is seen that high collinearity in (9.14.13), arising from collinearity between x_{t2}^* and x_{t3}^*, can also be interpreted as low variability of w_{t2} or w_{t3} in (9.14.20). Both are symptoms of the problem of "multicollinearity."

In other words, any statement of high correlation can be equally well expressed in terms of low variation. For example, one could speak of the high correlation between two interest rates, or alternatively, of the stability of the rate differential. Note also the moment matrix or covariance matrix cannot alone convey the seriousness of the collinearity problem since variances can be made arbitrarily large or small simply by changing the units of measurement of the regressors (and hence their coefficients). A seemingly large variance may be of little concern if the parameter itself is large or uninteresting.

Recall that in the case of perfect multicollinearity, only certain linear combinations of the regression coefficients are estimable. If $w'\beta$ is estimable, then Theorem 9.14.2(c) implies that w can be written

$$w = \alpha_1 c_1 + \alpha_2 c_2 + \cdots + \alpha_{K-J} c_{K-J}, \tag{9.14.24}$$

where rank$(X) = K - J$, $0 < J < K$, α_i $(i = 1, 2, \ldots, K - J)$ are constants and c_i $(i = 1, 2, \ldots, K - J)$ are characteristic vectors corresponding to the nonzero roots λ_i $(i = 1, 2, \ldots, K - J)$ of $X'X$. By Theorem 9.14.2, $c_i'\beta$ $(i = 1, 2, \ldots, K - J)$ are estimable. Noting that

$$(X'X)\hat{\beta} = X'y, \tag{9.14.25}$$

$$(X'X)c_i = \lambda_i c_i \qquad (i = 1, 2, \ldots, K - J), \tag{9.14.26}$$

$$c_i'c_j = \begin{cases} 1, & \text{if } i = j \\ 0, & \text{if } i \neq j \end{cases} \qquad (i, j = 1, 2, \ldots, K - J), \tag{9.14.27}$$

it follows from (9.14.25)–(9.14.27) that

$$\begin{aligned} \text{Var}(c_i'\hat{\beta}) &= \text{Var}(\lambda_i^{-1} c_i' X'X\hat{\beta}) \\ &= \text{Var}(\lambda_i^{-1} c_i' X'y) \\ &= \lambda_i^{-2} c_i' X'[\text{Var}(y)] X c_i \\ &= \sigma^2 \lambda_i^{-2} (c_i' X' X c_i) \\ &= \sigma^2/\lambda_i \qquad (i = 1, 2, \ldots, K - J). \end{aligned} \tag{9.14.28}$$

Hence,

$$\begin{aligned} \text{Var}(w'\hat{\beta}) &= \text{Var}\left[\sum_{i=1}^{K-J} \alpha_i c_i'\hat{\beta}\right] \\ &= \text{Var}\left[\sum_{i=1}^{K-J} \alpha_i \lambda_i^{-1} c_i' X'X\hat{\beta}\right] \\ &= \text{Var}\left[\sum_{i=1}^{K-J} \alpha_i \lambda_i^{-1} c_i' X'y\right] \\ &= \sigma^2 \sum_{i=1}^{K-J} \left(\frac{\alpha_i}{\lambda_i}\right)^2 c_i' X' X c_i + 2\sigma^2 \sum_{i=1}^{K-J-1} \sum_{j=i+1}^{K-J} \left(\frac{\alpha_i \alpha_j}{\lambda_i \lambda_j}\right) c_i' X' X c_j \\ &= \sigma^2 \sum_{i=1}^{K-J} \left(\frac{\alpha_i}{\lambda_i}\right)^2 \lambda_i + 0 \\ &= \sigma^2 \sum_{i=1}^{K-J} \left(\frac{\alpha_i^2}{\lambda_i}\right). \end{aligned} \tag{9.14.29}$$

Thus, $w'\beta$ is relatively less precisely estimated if w in (9.14.24) has large weights α_i attached to characteristic vectors c_i corresponding to small characteristic roots λ_i $(i = 1, 2, \ldots, K - J)$. The smaller those roots, the more imprecise is estimation. In contrast, relatively precise estimation is possible in directions of characteristic vectors corresponding to large characteristic roots. Note that (9.14.29) also holds if $J = 0$, that is, $\text{rank}(X) = K$.

If the researcher is interested in prediction, rather than estimation, then multicollinearity is even less likely to be a problem. Because $w = x_t$ is a trivial linear combination of the rows of X, $E(y_t|\tilde{x}_t) = x_t'\beta$ is estimable (Theorem 9.14.2a) and any estimator $\hat{\beta}$ that solves the normal equations provides the same prediction of y_t (Theorem 9.14.3a). Furthermore, for those who value BLUE estimators, Theorem 9.14.4 implies that $x_t'\hat{\beta}$ is the BLUE of $E(y_t|\tilde{x}_t) = x_t'\beta$.

In addition, (9.14.29) implies that prediction need not be affected if performed at regressor values similar to those satisfying the restrictions of the original X matrix. This fact is illustrated in the following example taken from G. Smith (1974). Indeed, prediction at out-of-sample values exhibiting less correlation can be more difficult than predicting at multicollinearity-plagued in-sample values.

Example 9.14.6 Suppose the objective of the model is to forecast the dependent variable accurately in an out-of-sample context. Suppose the T_* out-of-sample values of y are generated by

$$y_* = X_*\beta + u_*, \tag{9.14.30}$$

where

$$E\left(\begin{bmatrix} u \\ u_* \end{bmatrix}[u', u_*']\right) = \begin{bmatrix} \sigma^2 I_T & 0_{T \times T_*} \\ 0_{T_* \times T} & \sigma_*^2 I_{T_*} \end{bmatrix}. \tag{9.14.31}$$

The forecast will be denoted by $\hat{y}_* = X_* b$, where b is the OLS estimator using only the in-sample data. Using the average value of the mean squared forecasting error as a loss function, we have in the two-regressor case:

$$\begin{aligned} \text{AMSE} &\equiv E[T_*^{-1}(\hat{y}_* - y_*)'(\hat{y}_* - y_*)] \\ &= \sigma_*^2 + \frac{\sigma^2}{T}\left[\frac{h_2^2 + h_3^2 + 2rr_* h_2 h_3}{1 - r^2}\right], \end{aligned} \tag{9.14.32}$$

where $h_j = \sigma_{*j}/\sigma_j$ $(j = 2, 3)$ is the square root of the ratio of out-of-sample variability to in-sample variability of the jth regressor. It is ambiguous whether or not an increase in the squared correlation coefficient is harmful. For example, when $h_2 = h_3 = h$, (9.14.32) reduces to

$$\text{AMSE} = \sigma_*^2 + \frac{\sigma^2}{T} 2h^2 \left[\frac{1 - rr_*}{1 - r^2}\right]. \tag{9.14.33}$$

If the out-of-sample and in-sample correlations are $r_* = .9$ and $r = 0$, respectively, then $[(1 - rr_*)/(1 - r^2)] = 1.0$. If on the other hand the in-sample correlation $r = \frac{1}{2}$, then $[(1 - r_*)/(1 - r^2)] = .55/.75 < 1$. In general, a value of r^2 close to one need not be serious if the correlation persists out-of-sample, if there is very little out-of-sample variation of the regressors relative to the in-sample variation, if the in-sample variation of the disturbance term is small, or if there is a great deal of sample data.

The discussion so far has characterized multicollinearity problems as essentially "weak data" problems for the parametric quantities of interest: Either unbiased estimators do not exist, or if they do, sampling variances are unfortunately large. The latter problem can also be the result of small samples size or large σ^2. The solution to weak data is augment the data with additional information. Two sources are possible: more data (assuming the additional data is not also subject to the collinearity problem), or nondata-based prior information. If it is possible to collect one additional observation and interest focuses on $w'\beta$, then the following theorem gives the optimal location of regressors at which to observe y_{T+1}.

Theorem 9.14.5 Consider the standard linear model and suppose we wish to take a new observation at x_{T+1} for which the new error term is uncorrelated with errors in the original sample and has the same variance as each of them. In order to rule out picking an observation arbitrarily far from the existing data, suppose $x'_{T+1}x_{T+1} = r$. Then the optimum direction of x_{T+1} for improving the precision of estimation of the estimable function $w'\beta$ is that of the vector $x^*_{T+1}\ (I_K + r^{-2}X'X)^{-1}w$.

Proof Silvey (1969).

Note that Theorem 9.14.5 holds even when there is a rank deficiency in X. Thus, even if $w'\beta$ cannot be initially estimated, x^*_{T+1} is still the optimal direction in which to break the perfect multicollinearity. For further discussion see Judge et al. (1985, pp. 624–625).

It most situations readily available additional data would have already been collected, and therefore, non-data based (i.e., prior) information must be used. The existence of prior information is a fact that cannot be easily denied. Prior information is conveniently classified as *dogmatic* or *nondogmatic* (i.e., *certain* and *uncertain*). Classical statistics has trouble incorporating anything other than dogmatic prior information. With dogmatic prior information the weak data problem can often be readily overcome, however, rarely do such dogmatic beliefs carry widespread support among other researchers. An exception is the definitional form of exact restriction (9.7.26) in Example 9.7.3. Leamer (1978, p. 170) insightfully observes that if prior knowledge of parameter values is completely certain *or* "completely uncertain," many of the troubling aspects of the multicollinearity problem (e.g., "wrong" signs, or interval estimates overlap "unlikely" regions of the parameter space) would disappear. Problems exist because there exists potentially useful *uncertain* prior information, which complicates the simple interpretation of the data.

As is often the case, a Bayesian analysis of the problem provides insights into the ad hoc solutions suggested in a non-Bayesian tradition. The use of uncertain prior information to aid in interpreting empirical research is discussed in detail by Leamer (1973; 1978, especially Chapter 5). Indeed many of the "solutions" to multicollinearity available in the classical literature are presented without making clear the prior information that lies behind the "solution." Whether a "solution" is appropriate depends on whether the implicit prior information being employed is reasonable for the problem at hand. For example, use of a RLS estimate (e.g., dropping preselected regressors from the regression) should be evaluated in terms of the plausibility of the restrictions involved. Leamer (1978, pp. 148–160) shows that spherical priors make it "natural" to omit orthogonal variables in the order of their variance (as suggested in principle components analysis), whereas priors that are uniform on hyperbolas are associated with strategies that omit insignificant variables in a pretest fashion. Shrinkage estimators (e.g., ridge and Stein estimators), which modify the OLS estimator in the direction of some preselected point, are often suggested as solutions to multicollinearity, and they also have Bayesian interpretations (see Leamer 1978, pp. 136–139).

Of course if inference regarding previously nonestimable parameters of interest is possible after augmenting the data, then such inferences are completely dependent on the prior information invoked. For example, reconsider Example 9.7.3, which involved the use of an intercept together with an exhaustive list of dummy variables. Without any additional restrictions, the coefficients β_k $(k = 1, 2, 3)$ of the dummy variables in regression (9.7.25) are not individually estimable, although $\beta_k + \beta_4$ $(k = 1, 2, 3)$ are estimable. Imposition of the prior information embodied in restriction (9.7.26) that $\beta_1 + \beta_2 + \beta_3 = 0$, however, identifies β_k $(k = 1, 2, 3)$. Although in this case the additional information is basically definitional in nature, the point remains that the "solution" lies in augmenting the data with additional information.

If the additional information is in the form of a subjective prior distribution, then a Bayesian analysis is straightforward. If the prior distribution is proper, then so will be the posterior distribution even in the presence of perfect multicollinearity. For example, in the natural conjugate case, the posterior variance-covariance matrix of β is (see from Equation 9.9.9)

$$\mathrm{Var}(\beta|y) = \left[\frac{\nu}{\nu - 2}\right]\bar{s}^2(\underline{Q}^{-1} + X'X)^{-1}, \tag{9.14.34}$$

which is nonsingular if $\underline{Q}$ is nonsingular, regardless of the singularity of $X'X$. Thus, in the presence of perfect multicollinearity a Bayesian with a proper prior can make inferences about all coefficients individually. If the prior is improper and $X'X$ is singular, then the Bayesian is in a similar situation to the classical econometrician.

Of course there is no "free lunch." Perfect multicollinearity can cause even informative Bayesians some problems. One problem in particular is indicated in the following theorem adapted from Malinvaud (1970, pp. 246–249).

Theorem 9.14.6 Consider the standard linear normal regression model, but with $Xc = 0_T$ for some nonzero K-dimensional column vector c. Let $NG(\underline{b}, \underline{Q}, \underline{s}^{-2}, \underline{\nu})$ denote the natural conjugate normal-gamma prior distribution, and consider the following linear combination of the regression coefficients:

$$\alpha \equiv c'\underline{Q}^{-1}\beta. \tag{9.14.35}$$

Then, given σ^2, the prior and posterior distributions of α are both identically $N(c'\underline{Q}^{-1}\underline{b}, \sigma^2 c'\underline{Q}^{-1}c)$.

Proof Because $\beta|\sigma^2 \sim N(\underline{b}, \sigma^2\underline{Q})$, it follows immediately that the prior density for α given σ^2 is $N(c'\underline{Q}^{-1}\underline{b}, \sigma^2 c'\underline{Q}^{-1}c)$. The posterior density of β given σ^2 is $N_K(\bar{b}, \sigma^2\bar{Q})$, where $\bar{b}$ and $\bar{Q}$ are given by (9.9.8) and (9.9.9). Noting that $Xc = 0_T$, the posterior distribution of α given σ^2 is univariate normal with mean

$$\begin{aligned} c'\underline{Q}^{-1}\bar{b} &= c'(\bar{Q}^{-1} - X'X)\bar{Q}(\underline{Q}^{-1}\underline{b} + X'Xb) \\ &= c'\underline{Q}^{-1}\underline{b} + c'X'Xb - c'X'X\bar{Q}(\underline{Q}^{-1}\underline{b} + X'Xb) \\ &= c'\underline{Q}^{-1}\underline{b}, \end{aligned} \tag{9.14.36}$$

and (using Exercise A.4.4a) with $G = \underline{Q}^{-1}$ and $H = X'X$) variance

$$\begin{aligned} c'\underline{Q}^{-1}(\sigma^2\bar{Q})\underline{Q}^{-1}c &= \sigma^2 c'\underline{Q}^{-1}[(\underline{Q}^{-1} + X'X)^{-1}\underline{Q}^{-1}]c \\ &= \sigma^2 c'\underline{Q}^{-1}[I_K - (\underline{Q}^{-1} + X'X)^{-1}X'X]c \\ &= \sigma^2 c'\underline{Q}^{-1}c. \end{aligned} \tag{9.14.37}$$

Therefore, the prior and posterior distributions of α given σ^2 are the same.

The important implication of Theorem 9.14.6 is that there is no learning from the data about the particular linear combination $\alpha \equiv [c'\underline{Q}^{-1}]\beta$. The Bayesian can learn (in the sense that the data update the prior) about most linear combinations, but not all. The linear combinations the Bayesian cannot learn about necessarily depend on the prior state of information as transmitted through $\underline{Q}^{-1}$ and the nature of the collinearity.[46] If the colli-

46. If prior beliefs about β are independent and all with unit variance, then $\underline{Q} = I_K$, and you cannot learn about $\alpha = c'\beta$. Recall also Example 9.14.2.

nearity is high but not perfect, then the result will be approximately true. As always, whether multicollinearity is a problem depends on whether the subspace about which the researcher cannot learn is of any particular interest.

Beyond the weak data problem and the essential role of uncertain prior information, a particularly important feature of multicollinearity emphasized by Leamer (1978, pp. 170–181) is that data evidence *cannot* be interpreted in a parameter-by-parameter basis. In other words, the interpretation of a parameter may depend crucially on the prior information for a different parameter.

Such concerns lead Leamer (1978, p. 175) to quantify the collinearity problem in terms of the difference between the contract curve for a fully specified prior and that formed by setting the off-diagonal elements of $(X'X)$ and $\underline{Q}$ equal to zero. Although in general the contract curve may lie anywhere, the diagonalized contract curve has the property that the posterior mean is necessarily between the prior mean and the sample mean, coefficient by coefficient, as in the location parameter case of Section 6.7. When this occurs it is possible to say whether the data suggest positive or negative revisions to opinions about a coefficient. Note that even with orthogonal data (i.e. $X'X$ diagonal) the contract curve need not have this property unless the prior is also restricted to be diagonal. If $X'X$ and $\underline{Q}$ are proportional, then the contract curve is a straight line.

Finally, when faced with multicollinear data it is often found that addition of small amounts of data can bring about large changes in point estimates. The Bayesian analogy is that the posterior distribution may be highly sensitive to changes in the prior, and apparently innocuous differences in the prior may be amplified into significant differences in the posterior distribution. In the extreme collinearity-free case with both $X'X$ and $\underline{Q}$ diagonal, the posterior distribution of any coefficient is conditionally independent of the prior distributions of the other coefficients. For example, the sensitivity of the posterior mean to variations in the prior mean, *ceteris paribus*, is indicated in Exercise 9.14.9. The off-diagonal elements of (9.14.36) indicate the extent to which the conditional posterior mean of one coefficient depends on the prior mean of others. These elements are zero if $X'X$ and $\underline{Q}$ are diagonal, or if $X'X$ is proportional to $\underline{Q}$, or if $\lambda = 0$, or finally, if $\underline{Q} = 0$.

Because discussion of multicollinearity tends to draw upon rather wide range of issues, in closing it may be helpful to leave the reader with a concise perspective for viewing multicollinearity. Leaving aside what may be valid numerical problems that are associated with multicollinearity, here is a recommended two-step approach to any discussion of multicollinearity. First, state clearly what are the goals of the analysis. As in the case of most areas of statistical analysis, without a clear statement of the quantities of interest, it is not possible to decide if multicollinearity impinges upon them. Second, *the essence of multicollinearity is the data are not as informative as the researcher would like about the quantities of interest. Therefore, any "solution" to multicollinearity should be based on the implicit or explicit non-data information that recommends it.* The fact that nondata information lies at the heart of any solution to multicollinearity suggests that an obvious medium in which to couch the discussion is Bayesian analysis.

Exercises

9.14.1 Consider the standard multiple linear regression model with fixed regressors:

$$y_t = \beta_1 + \beta_2 x_{t2} + \beta_3 x_{t3} + \beta_4 x_{t4} + u_t \qquad (t = 1, 2, \ldots, T).$$

Some authors suggest that partial correlation coefficients between the regressors can serve as measures of the degree of multicollinearity. Investigate this suggestion by considering the following two correlation matrices measuring the simple correlations among x_2, x_3 and x_4:

$$R_1 = \begin{bmatrix} 1.00 & .99 & .99 \\ .99 & 1.00 & .98 \\ .99 & .98 & 1.00 \end{bmatrix}, \quad R_2 = \begin{bmatrix} 1.00 & .00 & .99 \\ .00 & 1.00 & .10 \\ .99 & .10 & 1.00 \end{bmatrix}. \tag{9.14.38}$$

9.14.2 Consider the standard multiple linear regression model with fixed regressors:

$$y_t = \beta_1 + \beta_2 x_{t2} + \beta_3 x_{t3} + u_t \qquad (t = 1, 2, \ldots, T).$$

(a) Suppose that in deviation form:

$$X'_* X_* = \begin{bmatrix} 200 & 150 \\ 150 & 113 \end{bmatrix}, \quad X'_* y_* = \begin{bmatrix} 350 \\ 263 \end{bmatrix}. \tag{9.14.39}$$

Find b_2 and b_3.

(b) Suppose we drop an observation and the following quantities are obtained:

$$X'_* X_* = \begin{bmatrix} 199 & 149 \\ 149 & 112 \end{bmatrix}, \quad X'_* y_* = \begin{bmatrix} 347.5 \\ 261.5 \end{bmatrix}. \tag{9.14.40}$$

Find b_2 and b_3.

(c) Is "multicollinearity" a problem here? If so, why? If not, why not?

9.14.3 Consider the classical linear normal regression model

$$y_t = \beta_1 + \beta_2 x_{t2} + \beta_3 x_{t3} + u_t \qquad (t = 1, 2, \ldots, 60),$$

and suppose that $r_{12}^2 = r_{13}^2 = .95$ and $r_{23}^2 = .97$.

(a) Find $r_{12.3}^2$ and $r_{13.2}^2$.

(b) Find R^2.

(c) Find the t-ratios corresponding to b_2 and b_3.

(d) Is "multicollinearity" a problem?

9.14.4 "A Bayesian with a well-defined prior distribution can have no problem in interpreting sample evidence, even in the face of collinear data. A Bayesian with poorly defined priors or a wide readership may have extreme difficulties in reporting and interpreting evidence." Comment.

9.14.5 Consider the following hypothetical equation to explain long-run price levels:

$$y_t = \beta_1 + \beta_2 C_t + \beta_3 D_t + \beta_4 x_{t4} + \beta_5 x_{t5} + u_t \qquad (t = 1, 2, \ldots, T)$$

where p_t is the price level, C_t is the amount of currency in circulation, D_t is the level of demand deposits, and x_{t4} and x_{t5} are other relevant exogenous variables. Suppose a law requires a *minimum* currency reserve ratio $(C_t/D_t) = \gamma$. What (if any) are the implications of such a law in this problem? Does it imply multicollinearity problems?

9.14.6 Discuss the usefulness of the following measures of "multicollinearity":

(a) $|X'X|$.

(b) The significance of the F-ratios obtained by regressing in turn each regressor on all other regressors.

(c) "R^2 deletes" (defined to be the R^2's obtained by omitting each regressor in turn). If the difference between R^2 and the max "R^2 delete" is small, then this is indicative of multicollinearity.

9.14.7 Let $R = [r_{ij}]$ be the correlation matrix of $X'X$ and let $\lambda_{\min}$ and $\lambda_{\max}$ be the smallest and largest characteristic roots of R. The ratio $(\lambda_{\min}/\lambda_{\max})$ is sometimes used as a measure of multicollinearity.

(a) What are the bounds of this ratio? What does each bound indicate?

(b) Consider

$$R_1 = \begin{bmatrix} 1-\alpha & 0 \\ 0 & 1-\alpha \end{bmatrix}, \; R_2 = \begin{bmatrix} 1 & \alpha \\ \alpha & 1 \end{bmatrix}, \qquad (9.14.41)$$

where $0 \le \alpha \le 1$. Find the determinants of each of these matrices and the above ratio of their characteristic roots. What happens to each of these ratios as $\alpha \to 1$? What do your results suggest?

9.14.8 To get a feel for some of the numerical problems multicollinearity can cause, consider the following. Suppose, for the sake of illustration only, that the level of accuracy for an inverse calculation is accepted at 0.1. That is, for any approximate inverse B of a matrix A we shall accept it if the elements of AB differ from the elements of the identity matrix I by no more than 0.1. Let

$$A = \begin{bmatrix} 1.00 & 1.00 \\ 1.00 & .99 \end{bmatrix}, \qquad (9.14.42)$$

and for its approximate inverse consider

$$B = \begin{bmatrix} -89 & 100 \\ 90 & -100 \end{bmatrix}. \qquad (9.14.43)$$

(a) Compute AB. Is B a good approximate inverse?

(b) Compute BA. Is B still a good approximate inverse?

(c) Find the exact inverse of A.

9.14.9 Consider the two regressor model considered in Example 9.2.2. Show that

$$\mathrm{Var}(b_j) = \left(\frac{\sigma^2}{m_{jj}}\right)\left(\frac{1}{1-r^2}\right) \qquad (j = 2, 3), \qquad (9.14.44)$$

where $r = \{m_{23}/(m_{22}m_{33} - m_{23}^2)]^{1/2}$ is the sample correlation coefficient between x_2 and x_3.

9.14.10 "Multicollinearity is never a problem because it is always possible to transform to an orthogonal model as in (9.2.69)." Comment.

9.14.11 Consider the following regression which attempts to explain heartbeat y_t among cardiac patients in a given hospital by the length x_{t2} of the right leg and the length x_{t3} of the left leg:

$$y_t = \beta_1 + \beta_2 x_{t2} + \beta_3 x_{t3} + u_t \qquad (t = 1, 2, \ldots, T). \tag{9.14.45}$$

(a) If a researcher computes the simple correlation between x_{t2} and x_{t3}, he will observe "high" correlation; he may therefore suspect multicollinearity and hesitate to estimate the equation. If another researcher were to look at a similar equation with x_{t2} and $x_{t4} = x_{t3} - x_{t2}$, he would see a "low" correlation between x_{t2} and x_{t4} and conclude that multicollinearity was not a problem. Yet the implicit estimates are identical whether the second independent variable is x_{t3} of x_{t4}. Why?

(b) Suppose for the sake of argument, heartbeat is a function of the *difference* in lengths of the legs and not the length of either leg. In this case what will you find if you estimate (9.14.45)? Would either b_2 or b_3 likely be "insignificant"? What would happen to the explanatory power if one of the two regressors was omitted?

9.14.12 Consider a classical linear normal regression model with $T = 12$, $y'y = 2$ and where X is assumed fixed.

$$X'y = \begin{bmatrix} 1 \\ -1 \end{bmatrix}, \; X'X = \begin{bmatrix} 1 & -1 \\ -1 & 1 \end{bmatrix}. \tag{9.14.46}$$

(a) Find a vector λ such that $X\lambda = 0_T$.

(b) Find a vector β that is observationally equivalent to $[3, 2]'$.

(c) Is the function $\beta_1 + \beta_2$ estimable?

(d) Suppose your prior is of the natural conjugate variety and the prior covariance matrix of β given σ^2 is proportional to the 2×2 identity matrix. Find a linear combination of β_1 and β_2 about which the experiment is uninformative for you.

9.14.13 Show that the vectors β and $\beta + dc$ are observationally equivalent, where d is an arbitrary scalar and c is a $K \times 1$ vector satisfying $Xc = 0_T$.

9.14.14 Shrinkage estimators (e.g., ridge and Stein-like) are often recommended in the face of multicollinearity because the OLS estimator tends to produce unnaturally large parameter estimates. To see why, show

$$E[(b - \beta)'(b - \beta)] = \sigma^2 \sum_{k=1}^{K} \lambda_k^{-1}, \tag{9.14.47}$$

where λ_k $(k = 1, 2, \ldots, K)$ are the characteristic roots of $X'X$. As we approach perfect multicollinearity, at least one $\lambda_k \to 0^+$ and hence the expected Euclidean distance squared between b and β approaches infinity.

9.14.15 Critically discuss the effects of multicollinearity in the standard multiple linear normal regression model with fixed regressors on the performance of the estimator s^2 of σ^2.

9.14.16 Let X_j be the jth column of X and let X_{*j} be the other $K - 1$ columns.

(a) Show: the jth diagonal element of $(X'X)^{-1}$ is given by $\{X_j[I_T - X_{*j}(X'_{*j}X_{*j})^{-1} X'_{*j}]X_j\}$.

(b) Interpret (a) in terms of a regression sum of squared errors.

(c) Use your answers in (a) and (b) to determine the behavior of $\mathrm{Var}(b_j)$ as the linear relationship between X_j and X_{*j} increases.

9.14.17 Consider the standard linear normal regression model

$$y = X\beta + u$$
$$= x\beta_1 + x\beta_2 + u,$$

where $K = 2$, $\beta = [\beta_1, \beta_2]'$, $X = [x, x]$ and x is a $T \times 1$ vector. Clearly, there exists perfect multicollinearity because both columns of X are identical. Suppose your prior information is given by the normal-gamma distribution $NG(\underline{b}, \underline{Q}, \underline{s}^{-2}, \underline{v})$ with $\underline{b} = [\underline{b}_1, 0]'$ and

$$\underline{Q} = \begin{bmatrix} \underline{q}_1 & 0 \\ 0 & \underline{q}_2 \end{bmatrix}.$$

(a) Find $E(\beta|y)$.

(b) Find $\text{Var}(\beta|y)$.

(c) Find $E(\beta|y)$ as $\underline{q}_1 \to \infty$ and $\underline{v} \to 0$.

(d) Find $\text{Var}(\beta|y)$ as $\underline{q}_1 \to \infty$ and $\underline{v} \to 0$.

(e) In the face of the perfect collinearity and the partially noninformative prior in (c) and (d), is it possible to draw inferences about β_1 and β_2 *separately*? If so, why? If not, why not? What are the "costs" of the collinear data?

9.14.18 Consider the standard multiple linear normal regression model with fixed regressors, but subject to a rank deficiency of one, i.e. $\text{rank}(X) = K - 1$, and $Xc = 0_T$ for some $K \times 1$ known vector c. Let $\hat{\beta}$ be any solution to the normal equations, and let $\hat{\sigma}^2 = (T - K)^{-1}(y - X\hat{\beta})'(y - X\hat{\beta})$. Is $\hat{\sigma}^2$ an unbiased estimator of σ^2? If so, then show it. If not, then why not?

10 Other Windows on the World

"Which way ought I to go to from here?"
"That depends a good deal on where you want to get to," said the Cat.
"I don't much care where—" said Alice.
"Then it doesn't matter which way you go," said the Cat.
—Lewis Carroll, *Alice in Wonderland*

10.1 Introduction

We are socialized to the belief that there is one true model and that it can be discovered or imposed if only you will make the proper assumptions and impute validity to econometric results that are transparently lacking in power. Of course there are holdouts against this routine, bless their hearts.
—Solow (1985, p. 330)

A "true model" is an oxymoron if there ever was one. This chapter adopts the working definition of an *economic model* as an abstract representation of reality that highlights what a researcher deems relevant to a particular economic issue. By definition economic models are literally false, and so questions regarding their truth are trivial.

A subjectivist's *econometric model* expresses probabilistically the researcher's beliefs concerning future observables of interest to economists. It is a special case of what will be defined formally in Section 10.5 as a statistical model, namely, an economist's view of an aspect of the world of interest to economists. A *statistical model* has two components: (i) a window (likelihood) for viewing observables in the world, and (ii) a prior reflecting a professional position of interest. Both components are subjective, and both involve mathematical fictions commonly called *parameters.* Parameters serve to index distributions; any correspondence to physical reality is a rare side bonus. *What distinguishes the two components of a model in the mind of the researcher is the hope that the window has been chosen sufficiently large to obtain interpersonal agreement among a group of researchers to disagree only in terms of the most appropriate prior.* If such intersubjective agreement is obtained, then by definition there is no disagreement among the researchers over the window.[1] Disagreements can be confined to the choice of prior, and the researcher can address such disagreements by a sensitivity analysis of quantities of interest with respect to changes in the prior. Such analysis may be local or global depending on how far away the researcher is willing to wander from a maintained prior. Sensitivity analyses can be performed in reference to all statistical

1. Whether the group itself can be considered as a single Bayesian decision-maker is another story. See Genest and Zidek (1986) and the references cited therein.

activities: design, estimation, testing, and prediction. Often it addresses more than one of these activities (e.g., Ramsay and Novick 1980). Examples and references to prior sensitivity analysis are discussed in Sections 6.8, 7.4, 9.9, and 9.10.

In one sense this dichotomy between prior and likelihood is tautological: If there is no agreement, then presumably the likelihood can always be expanded until agreement is obtained. The resulting window, however, may be hopelessly complex. The "bite" in the statement comes from the assertion that a researcher believes agreement is compelling in the case of a particular window.

In Poirier (1988c) I introduced the metaphor *window* for a likelihood function because it captures the essential role played by the likelihood, namely, as a parametric medium for viewing the observable world. If a researcher's window is soiled, and hence the view of world's data is "murky," then the usefulness of the window is called into question. In such cases the researcher should either "wash" the window so that it can be fruitfully used again, or abandon the window altogether and entertain a different perspective on the world.[2] This chapter is concerned with the first option, that is, the everyday janitorial work of empirical researchers in maintaining their windows on the world. It does not address the gestalt switch that motivates a big change to a fundamentally different perspective on the world. Broken windows require major repair. The concern here is with the routine cleaning of a window, and possible expansion to nearby larger windows. The discussion strives for the "big picture" rather than a detailed description of diagnostic testing.

Such concerns fall under the rubric of *diagnostic checking* or *likelihood diagnostics* in other researcher's taxonomies (e.g., Pettit 1986). Admittedly the distinction between different types of sensitivity analyses and the window checking to be discussed here are often blurred. Diagnostic checking of a window is close to the diagnostic checking that non-Bayesians undertake. Despite differences in language, religion and scripture, sensitivity of results to likelihood specification is of concern to most pedigrees of statisticians.

10.2 The Initial Window

What makes a piece of mathematical economics not only mathematics but also economics is, I believe, this: When we set up a system of theoretical relationships and use

2. Much of the material in this chapter is taken from Poirier (1991e), where the metaphor of "washing windows" for diagnostic checking is developed.

economic names for the otherwise purely theoretical variables involved, we have in mind some actual experiment, *or some* design of an experiment, *which we could at least imagine arranging, in order to measure those quantities in real economic life that we think might obey the laws imposed on their theoretical namesakes.*
—Haavelmo (1944, p. 6)

Before choosing a window it is first important to decide what the researcher hopes to see through this window. Articulation of Haavelmo's experiment involves announcement of a distribution involving the endogenous variables (variables to be explained), the explanatory variables upon which the analysis is conditioned (including lagged values), and the class of interventions to be entertained when describing future observables (see Hendry et al. 1990, pp. 192–195). This articulation should make clear the *distribution of interest (DOI)* (recall Definition 8.1.1), and it is nothing more than a careful description of the questions of interest in statistical terms. Changes in the DOI amount to changes in the goals of the analysis, and these are *not* the topic of discussion in this chapter.

Confusion often arises in econometric discussions because the goals of the analysis are not well articulated. As argued in Chapter 8, ultimately, a statistical model is "used" by drawing inferences about future observables based on past observables. Thus, most goals of econometric research boil down to identifying a DOI under particular experimental conditions as noted by Haavelmo. The DOI is a primitive; it reflects the purpose of doing the analysis. Different researchers may have different DOIs, in which case they are working on different, but possibly related, questions. Fame and fortune await researchers who excel at identifying DOIs and experiments that capture the imagination of their colleagues. No magical guidance is offered here as how to be so creative.

Suppose the DOI involves a random vector for which T observations are available: z_t $(t = 1, 2, \ldots, T)$. Stacking the T observations, let $Z = [z_1, \ldots, z_T]'$ denote the observed data, and let z_{T+1} denote an out-of-sample observation to be predicted. Some of the variables in z_t are the endogenous variables y_t whose future values are the primary predictive goal of the analysis. Other variables x_t (possibly *exogenous* is some sense of term as used by Engle et al. 1983) in describing the environment in which the analysis to apply is intended may also be included in $z_t = [y_t, x_t]'$ $(t = 1, 2, \ldots, T + 1)$.

If economic theory is to do anything for the empirical researcher, then it should at least suggest the relevant variables to include in z_t. Unfortunately, choice of the variables in z_t is rarely clear cut. Early researchers (e.g. Keynes 1939 and Haavelmo 1944, p. 23) struggled with the issue of how to assess whether all possibly relevant factors have been included in a particular study. I do not believe there is a "correct" list of factors. I think the only healthy way to look at the matter is that choice of z_t determines the scope of the analysis. Obviously, analyses of wider scope have potentially larger readerships than those of narrower scope, but at the price of complexity. The scope of the analysis is a matter over which reasonable people may disagree. Rather than thinking in terms of choosing some ambiguous "true" set of variables for z_t, it is better to simply recognize the limits of any analysis at the beginning, and to not pretend to be able to say anything about analyses involving a larger set of unspecified variables. Data limitations or legal restrictions can sometimes restrict the choice of regressors.

For example, starting in Section 2.7 and throughout Chapters 8 and 9, this text has emphasized the population counterpart underlying estimated regression equations. The regression of y_t on x_{t1}, the regression of y_t on x_{t2}, and the regression of y_t on x_{t1} and x_{t2}, are all different regressions. Which regression (if any) is of interest depends on the predictive question of interest. "Omitted variables" can be thought of as suggestions for enlarging the information set, and hence, changing the DOI. Omitting a variable from the DOI that enters the information set requires convincing arguments in favor of the implied conditional independence of endogenous variables and excluded variable given any variables conditioned upon. Generally regression coefficients change as the set of conditioning variables changes. A case in point is Simpson's paradox (Exercise 8.2.6), where it was seen that the effects of a variable on another can differ in sign depending on whether another variable is included in the conditioning set.

Given the DOI, the next issue the choice of parametric window through which to view the DOI. Although economic theory is often useful in choosing the DOI, generally it is fairly silent about many of the details of a parametric window. In choosing the window $\mathscr{L}(\theta; z)$ the researcher is torn in two directions: choosing the dimensionality of θ to be large increases the chances of getting a bevy of researchers *to agree to disagree* (i.e., limit their disagreement) in terms of the appropriate priors for θ, whereas large dimensional θ necessitate increasingly more informative priors if anything useful is to be learned from a finite sample. The DOI reflects the researchers' interests; the window $\mathscr{L}(\theta; z)$ must be a compelling vehicle for relating the DOI to the data at hand. Given any necessary complications, we seek a window that is *sophisticatedly simple*, to borrow a phrase from Arnold Zellner.

The choice of an initial window occurs during what Leamer (1989) calls the *planning stage*. The planning stage defines the statistical playing field. It represents all the anticipated reactions of the researcher to the data.

According to Leamer, "criticism" occurs when the researcher acknowledges that the planned responses are inappropriate in light of the data. Criticism (like discovery) lies outside any current statistical paradigm and it corresponds to a gestalt switch (e.g., a change in the DOI). A theory of criticism would amount to a theory of creativity, and none is offered here. *By assumption the initial window is chosen to be sufficiently broad so that anticipated minor alterations are viewed as unlikely.* This assumption will play a key role in the statistical framework of Sections 10.5 and the attitude toward diagnostic checking articulated in Section 10.7.

It strikes me that in economics researchers are a long way from agreeing on what constitutes a reasonable initial window. Agreement on a window is a subjective matter. Researchers who mistakenly think they have achieved such agreement find few readers for their work. The common discussion (e.g. Hendry 1980 and Mizon 1977, pp. 1228–1229) of "general to specific" versus "specific to general" research strategies reflects the fact that there is not universal agreement on the appropriate size of the initial window. Nor is there agreement over how much economic content the initial window should reflect. In short, discussion of the choice of the initial window is difficult (see Hendry et al. 1990, pp. 237–238, 242, 252–253), possibly reflecting its artistic elements. That econometrics contains an artistic component, like any science, was acknowledged long ago by Haavelmo (1944, p. 10).

Under predictive exercises in which tomorrow is like today, the out-of-sample window can be chosen by simple reference to the in-sample window (likelihood) for viewing past data. As argued in Section 8.3, prediction in the face of intervention, requires in addition a *structural model.* More generally, prediction under circumstances different than those that describe past data is a matter that often requires delicate handling on a case by case basis.[3] All of the issues raised in connection with an in-sample window occur again with respect to the out-of-sample window. Prediction in a changing world in effect doubles the potential problems for the researcher.

Before becoming more specific about the role of the initial window in the modelling process, the next section provides six examples of how the multiple linear normal regression model of Chapter 9 can be expanded. This provides concrete examples in which to imbed subsequent discussion.

3. A common issue in econometrics is attempting to draw inferences about an entire population when the data are drawn from a different population. For example, a researcher may wish to make inferences regarding the labor supply decisions of all women in the labor force (i.e., working women and women looking for work) based only on data for working women. Such problems are commonly called *sample selection* problems.

10.3 Examples of Larger Windows

Savage put it nicely when he said a model should be as big as an elephant.... Much of the asymptotic, nonparametric theory is technicalities out of control.
—Dennis Lindley (1983, p. 62)

Give me four parameters and I shall describe an elephant; with five, it will wave its trunk.
—Attributed to J. Bertrand by Le Cam (1990, p. 165)

No matter how an initial window is chosen, it does not necessarily take great imagination to expand it. In fact it is quite fashionable these days to do so: witness the continually increasing popularity of semiparametric and nonparametric analyses.[4] *It does, however, take a creative mind to choose a parsimonious parametric view of the world that captures the essence of the problem at hand in terms of a few panes (i.e., subsets of a larger parameter space) that facilitate thoughtful communication among interested researchers.*

The expanded windows introduced in this section make no pretence of being of this latter creative variety. Rather, they are routine extensions of the regression model in Chapter 9, which are widely used by applied researchers; in fact many comprise a chapter in standard econometrics texts. Here we merely present them in parametric likelihood form as potential new windows. The reader is free to maximize them or bounce a prior off them. *The virtue of a likelihood analysis, and especially, a Bayesian analysis, is that a general cut at the problem might be taken, rather than a variety of ad hoc techniques that permeate most other econometrics texts.* The notation of Chapter 9 is used. The first example was touched upon in Section 9.2.

Example 10.3.1 (Generalized Least Squares, or GLS) One of the most common parametric expansions of the linear regression window is to replace the second moment assumptions $\text{Var}(y|X) = \text{Var}(u|X) = \sigma^2 I_T$ by

$$\text{Var}(y|X) = \text{Var}(u|X) = \sigma^2\Omega(\alpha), \tag{10.3.1}$$

where Ω is a known matrix function of an unknown $J \times 1$ vector α, and the identifying normalization $\text{tr}[\Omega(\alpha)] = T$ is imposed. As noted in Section 9.2, if α is known, then it is straightforward to transform the data (see Equations 9.2.62 through 9.2.68) so that it satisfies all the original assumptions of the standard linear normal regression model. The case of un-

4. Such analyses amount to using infinite-dimensional windows in the language of this text, but they are not of concern here. Instead we concern ourselves here with traditional finitely-dimensional windows, for example, the regression analysis of Chapter 9.

known α is commonly called the *general multiple linear normal regression model.* The likelihood function in this case is

$$\begin{aligned}\mathscr{L}(\beta, \sigma^2, \alpha; Z) &= \phi[y|X\beta, \sigma^2\Omega(\alpha)]\\ &= (2\pi\sigma^2)^{-T/2}|\Omega(\alpha)|^{-1/2}\\ &\quad\times \exp\left[-\frac{1}{2\sigma^2}(y - X\beta)'[\Omega(\alpha)]^{-1}(y - X\beta)\right]. \qquad (10.3.2)\end{aligned}$$

See Magnus (1978) and Poirier (1988a) for discussions of estimation based on (10.3.2) by maximum likelihood and Bayesian methods, respectively. Provided there exists $\alpha_* \in A$ such that $\Omega(\alpha_*) = I_T$, the multiple linear normal regression model of Chapter 9 arises as a special case of window (10.3.2).

A special case of Example 10.3.1 that captures a commonly encountered additional type of heterogeneity is considered next.

Example 10.3.2 (Heteroskedasticity) The case of Example 10.3.1 in which $\sigma^2\Omega(\alpha)$ is diagonal, but the diagonal elements are not all the same, is known as *heteroskedasticity.* The window of Chapter 9 focused on the conditional distribution of y given X, but permitted X to affect y only through the first moment. An obvious generalization is to permit the second moment of y (i.e., its variance) to also depend on X giving rise to heteroskedasticity in the process. Letting $\Omega(\alpha) = [\omega_{ij}(\alpha)]$, and suppressing its possible dependency on X, likelihood (10.3.2) simplifies slightly to

$$\mathscr{L}(\beta, \sigma^2, \alpha; Z) = (2\pi\sigma^2)^{-T/2}\left[\prod_{t=1}^{T}\omega_{tt}(\alpha)\right]^{-1/2}\exp\left[-\frac{1}{2\sigma^2}\sum_{t=1}^{T}\frac{(y_t - x_t'\beta)^2}{\omega_{tt}(\alpha)}\right]. \qquad (10.3.3)$$

Provided there exists $\alpha_* \in A$ such that $\omega_{tt}(\alpha_*) = 1$ $(t = 1, 2, \ldots, T)$, the multiple linear normal regression model of Chapter 9 arises as a special case of window (10.3.3).

Next we consider a simple framework which introduces *temporal dependence* in the observations generalizing Example 6.10.6 in the process.

Example 10.3.3 (Dynamic Linear Regression) Consider the following first-order dynamic normal simple linear regression:

$$\begin{aligned}y_t &= \beta_1 + \beta_2\tilde{x}_t + \beta_3\tilde{x}_{t-1} + \beta_4 y_{t-1} + u_t\\ &= x_t'\beta + u_t \qquad (t = 1, 2, \ldots, T), \qquad (10.3.4)\end{aligned}$$

where $x_t = [1, \tilde{x}_t, \tilde{x}_{t-1}, y_{t-1}]'$ and $\beta = [\beta_1, \beta_2, \beta_3, \beta_4]'$. Equivalently, (10.3.4) can be rewritten as

$$\begin{aligned}y_t - y_{t-1} &= \beta_1 + \beta_2(x_t - x_{t-1}) + (1 - \beta_4)(x_{t-1} - y_{t-1})\\ &\quad + \delta x_{t-1} + u_t \qquad (t = 1, 2, \ldots, T), \qquad (10.3.5)\end{aligned}$$

where

$$\delta \equiv \beta_2 + \beta_3 + \beta_4 - 1. \tag{10.3.6}$$

The likelihood function for (10.3.4) is built up sequentially—see (6.1.1)—to yield

$$\mathscr{L}(\beta, \sigma^2, \alpha; Z) = (2\pi\sigma^2)^{-T/2} \exp\left[-\frac{1}{2\sigma^2} \sum_{t=1}^{T} (y_t - x_t'\beta)^2 \right]. \tag{10.3.7}$$

Bayesian analysis of (10.3.7) is essentially the same as any regression model with fixed regressors since such analysis conditions on y. Classical analysis of (10.3.4) is complicated by the inclusion of the stochastic lagged dependent variable y_{t-1}, which greatly complicates any attempt (for finite T) at a sampling theory for purposes of interval estimation or hypothesis testing (but see Dufour 1990 and Dufour and Kiviet 1993).

Despite its simplicity (10.3.4) incorporates a large number of common econometric specifications. See Table 10.3.1 for nine instances. Generalizations to more than one regressor is fairly straightforward (see Hendry et al. 1984; Hendry and Richard 1982, 1983; and Spanos 1986, Chapter 23).

Case 9 in Table 10.3.1 is a special case of Example 10.3.1. with $\alpha = \beta_4$ and

$$\Sigma(\alpha) = \frac{1}{1-\alpha^2} \begin{bmatrix} 1 & \alpha & \cdots & \alpha^{T-2} & \alpha^{T-1} \\ \alpha & 1 & \cdots & \alpha^{T-3} & \alpha^{T-2} \\ \vdots & \vdots & & \vdots & \vdots \\ \alpha^{T-2} & \alpha^{T-3} & \cdots & 1 & \alpha \\ \alpha^{T-1} & \alpha^{T-2} & \cdots & \alpha & 1 \end{bmatrix}. \tag{10.3.8}$$

Table 10.3.1
Special cases of (10.3.4)

Case	Name	Specification	Restrictions
1	Static regression	$y_t = \beta_1 + \beta_2 x_t + u_t$	$\beta_3 = \beta_4 = 0$
2	AR(1)	$y_t = \beta_1 + \beta_4 y_{t-1} + u_t$	$\beta_2 = \beta_3 = 0$
3	Growth rate	$y_t - y_{t-1} = \beta_2(x_t - x_{t-1}) + u_t$	$\beta_2 = -\beta_3, \beta_4 = 1$
4	Leading indicator	$y_t = \beta_1 + \beta_3 x_{t-1} + u_t$	$\beta_2 = \beta_4 = 0$
5	Distributed lag	$y_t = \beta_1 + \beta_2 x_t + \beta_3 x_{t-1} + u_t$	$\beta_4 = 0$
6	Partial adjustment	$y_t = \beta_1 + \beta_2 x_t + \beta_4 y_{t-1} + u_t$	$\beta_3 = 0$
7	Error-correction	$y_t - y_{t-1} = \beta_2(x_t - x_{t-1}) + (1 - \beta_4)(x_{t-1} - y_{t-1}) + u_t$	$\beta_2 + \beta_3 + \beta_4 = 1$ or $\delta = 0$
8	"Dead-start"	$y_t = \beta_1 + \beta_3 x_{t-1} + \beta_4 y_{t-1} + u_t$	$\beta_2 = 0$
9	AR(1) error	$y_t = \beta_0 + \beta_1 x_t + \varepsilon_t$	$\beta_4\beta_2 + \beta_3 = 0$ $\varepsilon_t = \beta_4 \varepsilon_{t-1} + u_t$ $\lvert\beta_4\rvert < 1$ $\beta_0 = \beta_1/(1 - \beta_4)$

Although (10.3.8) with $\beta_3 = 0$ and $\alpha \neq 0$ is often presented in its own right as a convenient generalization of the standard multiple linear normal regression model with $\alpha = 0$, (10.3.8) is more usefully thought of as a special case of the dynamic linear regression model (10.3.4)–(10.3.5) (again see Hendry et al. 1984; Hendry and Richard 1982, 1983; and Spanos 1986, Chapter 23).

Example 10.3.4 (Non-normality) Following Box and Tiao (1973), suppose y_t $(t = 1, 2, \ldots, T)$ are independent exponential power family random variables (see Table 3.3.1b) with p.d.f.

$$f_{EPF}(y_t|x_t, \beta, \sigma^{-2}, \alpha) = \frac{\exp(-\frac{1}{2}|(y_t - x_t'\beta)/\sigma|^{[2/(1+\alpha)]})}{\sigma\Gamma\left(1 + \dfrac{1+\alpha}{2}\right)2^{[1+1/2(1+\alpha)]}} \quad -\infty < z < \infty, \tag{10.3.9}$$

where $-1 < \alpha \leq 1$. Density (10.3.9) is symmetric around its mean/mode/median $x_t'\beta$. This family of symmetric distributions includes three notable special cases: $\alpha = 0$ (normal), $\alpha = 1$ (Laplace/double exponential), and $\alpha \to -1$ (uniform). The likelihood function is

$$\mathscr{L}(\beta, \sigma^{-2}, \alpha; Z) = \exp\left(\sum_{t=1}^{T} -\frac{1}{2}|(y_t - x_t'\beta)/\sigma|^{[2/(1+\alpha)]}\right) \cdot \left[\sigma\Gamma\left(1 + \frac{1+\alpha}{2}\right)2^{[1+1/2(1+\alpha)]}\right]^{-T}. \tag{10.3.10}$$

Because $\partial E(y_t|x_t)/\partial x_t' = \beta$ does not depend on α, this window expansion has the attractive property of not changing the interpretation of likely parameters of interest. If the normal family is extended to include asymmetric possibilities, then the parameters of interest may be less clear.

The preceding examples are window expansions of Chapter 9 that do *not* involve changes in the DOI. More imaginative changes involve different DOI's. The next case expands the DOI an the window to include more than one endogenous variable (recall Examples 9.1.1 and 9.1.2). Exercise 10.3.6 demonstrates that this expansion shares the same parametric form as Example 10.3.1.

Example 10.3.5 (Multivariate Regression) Consider the multivariate normal regression

$$Y = XB + U, \tag{10.3.11}$$

where Y is $T \times M$, X is $T \times K$, B is $K \times M$, U is $T \times M$, $U|X \sim MN_{T\times M}(0_{T\times M}, I_T, \Sigma^{-1})$, or equivalently, $\text{vec}(U) \sim N_{TM}(0_{TM}, \Sigma \otimes I_T)$. Then $Y|X$, B, $\Sigma^{-1} \sim MN_{T\times M}(XB, I_T, \Sigma^{-1})$, or equivalently, $\text{vec}(Y) \sim N_{TM}(\text{vec}(XB), \Sigma \otimes I_T)$. *Also, let* $\underline{B}$ be a $K \times M$ matrix, and let $\underline{C}$ be a

$K \times K$ positive definite matrix. Using Exercise 10.3.7, the likelihood function corresponding to (10.3.11) is

$$\mathscr{L}(B, \Sigma^{-1}; Y, X) = \phi_{TM}(\text{vec}[Y] | \text{vec}[XB], \Sigma \otimes I_T) \tag{10.3.12a}$$

$$= \pi^{-TM/2} |\Sigma^{-1}|^{T/2} \exp[-\tfrac{1}{2}(y - XB)'(\Sigma^{-1} \otimes I_T)(Y - XB)] \tag{10.3.12b}$$

$$= \pi^{-TM/2} |\Sigma^{-1}|^{T/2} \times \exp(-\tfrac{1}{2} \text{tr}\{\Sigma^{-1}[S + (B - \hat{B})'X'X(B - \hat{B})]\}), \tag{10.3.12c}$$

where $\hat{B}$ is the OLS estimator given by (10.3.39). ML estimation based on (10.3.11) is covered in Exercises 10.3.6–10.3.7. Two prior densities provide tractable analytical posterior analysis: Jeffreys' prior (Exercises 10.3.8–10.3.9) and the natural conjugate prior (Exercises 10.3.10–10.3.11).

Example 10.3.6 (Simultaneous Equations) Consider the multivariate normal regression (10.3.10), and post-multiply it by the $M \times M$ matrix Γ of unknown constants to obtain

$$Y\Gamma = X\delta + \varepsilon, \tag{10.3.13}$$

where $\delta = B\Gamma$, $\varepsilon = U\Gamma$ and $\text{vec}(\varepsilon) \sim N_{TM}(0_{TM}, \Gamma\Sigma\Gamma' \otimes I_T)$. The likelihood function corresponding to (10.3.13) is obtained by change-of-variable on (10.3.11) to yield

$$\mathscr{L}(B, \Sigma^{-1}; Y) = |\Gamma|^T \pi^{-TM/2} |\Sigma^{-1}|^{T/2} \exp[-\tfrac{1}{2}(y - XB)'(\Sigma^{-1} \otimes I_T)(Y - XB)]. \tag{10.3.14}$$

Both (10.3.11) and (10.3.13) involve modeling the joint distribution of the components of a row in Y given X. Although the individual equations in (10.3.11) contain only one endogenous variable, (10.3.13) permits more than one endogenous variables in an equation, and so is often more easily interpretable from the standpoint of economic theory (e.g., "demand" and "supply" curves).

The crucial issue in (10.3.13) is the identification of the elements in Γ and δ. Examples 9.1.1 and 9.1.2 provide elementary examples of simultaneous equations and identification issues. The hope in (10.3.13) is that zero restrictions on Γ and δ may "identify" an equation and aid in its theoretical interpretation, facilitating a *structural interpretation* of the parameters in Γ and δ, not possible for B in (10.3.11).

Examples 10.3.1 through 10.3.4 are all fairly mechanical expansions of the regression window $\mathscr{L}(\beta, \sigma^2; y) = \phi(y | X\beta, \sigma^2 I_T)$ of Chapter 9 to a more general window $\mathscr{L}(\beta, \sigma^2, \alpha; y)$ in which the original window is a special case for a suitably chosen value of α. Examples 10.3.5 and 10.3.6 are different because they expand the list of endogenous variables, and Example 10.3.6 also changes the parameters of interest from B to Γ and δ.

Exercises

10.3.1 Consider Example 10.3.1. Suppose $\Omega(\alpha)$ is a known twice differentiable parametric function of the $K_\alpha \times 1$ vector α such that $\Omega(\alpha_*) = I_T$.

(a) Show that the likelihood equations imply the MLE's satisfy:

$$\hat{\beta}(\hat{\alpha}) = (X'[\Omega(\hat{\alpha})]^{-1}X)^{-1}X'[\Omega(\hat{\alpha})]^{-1}y, \tag{10.3.15}$$

$$\hat{\alpha}^2(\hat{\alpha}) = T^{-1}[\hat{u}(\hat{\alpha})]'[\Omega(\hat{\alpha})]^{-1}[\hat{u}(\hat{\alpha})], \tag{10.3.16}$$

$$\hat{\sigma}^2 \operatorname{tr}\left[\left(\frac{\partial([\Omega(\hat{\alpha})]^{-1})}{\partial \alpha_j}\right)\Omega(\hat{\alpha})\right] = [\hat{u}(\hat{\alpha})]'\left[\frac{\partial([\Omega(\hat{\alpha})]^{-1})}{\partial \alpha_j}\right][\hat{u}(\hat{\alpha})], \tag{10.3.17}$$

for $j = 1, 2, \ldots, J$, where

$$\hat{u}(\alpha) = y - X\hat{\beta}(\alpha). \tag{10.3.18}$$

(b) Let $\gamma = [\beta', \sigma^{-2}]'$. Show that the elements in the Hessian of the log-likelihood (10.3.2) are:

$$h_{\gamma\gamma}(\gamma, \alpha) = \begin{bmatrix} h_{\beta\beta}(\gamma, \alpha) & h'_{\sigma^{-2}\beta}(\gamma, \alpha) \\ h_{\sigma^{-2}\beta}(\gamma, \alpha) & h_{\sigma^{-2}\sigma^{-2}}(\gamma, \alpha) \end{bmatrix}, \tag{10.3.19}$$

$$h_{\beta\beta}(\gamma, \alpha) = -\sigma^{-2}X'[\Omega(\alpha)]^{-1}X, \tag{10.3.20}$$

$$h_{\sigma^{-2}\beta}(\gamma, \alpha) = (y - X\beta)'[\Omega(\alpha)]^{-1}X, \tag{10.3.21}$$

$$h_{\sigma^{-2}\sigma^{-2}}(\gamma, \alpha) = -\frac{(T-2)}{2\sigma^4}, \tag{10.3.22}$$

$$h_{\alpha\beta}(\gamma, \alpha) = -\sigma^{-2}\left[\frac{\partial \operatorname{vec} \Omega(\alpha)}{\partial \alpha}\right]'([\Omega(\alpha)]^{-1} \otimes [\Sigma(\alpha)]^{-1})[X \otimes u], \tag{10.3.23}$$

$$h_{\alpha\sigma^{-2}}(\gamma, \alpha) = -[\operatorname{vec} \Omega(\alpha)]'([\Omega(\alpha)]^{-1} \otimes [\Omega(\alpha)]^{-1})[u \otimes u], \tag{10.3.24}$$

$$\begin{aligned} h_{\alpha\alpha}(\gamma, \alpha) &= \frac{1}{2}\sum_{i=1}^{T}\sum_{j=1}^{T}\{[\Omega(\alpha)]_{i,j} - \sigma^{-2}u_i u_j\}\left[\frac{\partial^2[\{\Omega(\alpha)\}^{-1}]_{i,j}}{\partial \alpha \, \partial \alpha'}\right] \\ &\quad - \frac{1}{2}\left[\frac{\partial \operatorname{vec} \Omega(\alpha)}{\partial \alpha}\right]'([\Omega(\alpha)]^{-1} \otimes [\Omega(\alpha)]^{-1})\left[\frac{\partial \operatorname{vec} \Omega(\alpha)}{\partial \alpha}\right]. \end{aligned} \tag{10.3.25}$$

(c) Show that the information matrix is given by

$$J(\theta) = \begin{bmatrix} X'[\Omega(\alpha)]^{-1}X & 0_K & 0_{K \times J} \\ 0'_K & \dfrac{T}{2\sigma^4} & J'_{\alpha,\sigma^2} \\ 0_{J \times K} & J_{\alpha,\sigma^2} & J_{\alpha\alpha} \end{bmatrix}, \tag{10.3.26}$$

where for $i, j = 1, 2, \ldots, J$:

$$\begin{aligned} J_{\alpha,\sigma^2} &= J_{\alpha,\sigma^2}(\alpha, \sigma^2) \\ &= \frac{1}{2\sigma^2}[\operatorname{vec}([\Omega(\alpha)]^{-1})]'\left[\frac{\partial \Omega(\alpha)}{\partial \alpha}\right], \end{aligned} \tag{10.3.27}$$

$$\begin{aligned} J_{\alpha\alpha} &= J_{\alpha,\alpha}(\alpha, \sigma^2) \\ &= \frac{1}{2}\left[\frac{\partial \Omega(\alpha)}{\partial \alpha}\right]'([\Omega(\alpha)]^{-1} \otimes [\Omega(\alpha)]^{-1})\left[\frac{\partial \Omega(\alpha)}{\partial \alpha}\right]. \end{aligned} \tag{10.3.28}$$

10.3.2 Evaluate (10.3.15) through (10.3.28) at $\alpha = \alpha_*$, where $\Omega(\alpha_*) = I_T$.

10.3.3 [Heteroskedasticity] Let $x_t = [1, \tilde{x}_t']'$ and suppose $\Omega(\alpha) = \operatorname{diag}\{\Omega_1(\alpha), \ldots, \Omega_T(\alpha)\}$, where $\Omega_t(\alpha) = \exp(\tilde{x}_t'\alpha)$ $(t = 1, 2, \ldots, T)$ and $K_\alpha = K_\gamma - 2$.

(a) Under $H_*: \alpha = \alpha_*$, show that score $s_\alpha(\gamma, \alpha_*) \equiv \partial L(\gamma, \alpha; y)/\partial\alpha$ evaluated at $\alpha = \alpha_*$ is

$$s_\alpha(\gamma, \alpha_*) = \tfrac{1}{2}(\sigma^{-2}u'u - T). \tag{10.3.29}$$

(b) Show that the elements of the Hessian—see (10.3.19) through (10.3.25)—are

$$h_{\gamma\gamma}(\gamma, \alpha_*) = \begin{bmatrix} -\sigma^{-2}X'X & 0_{K_\gamma - 1} \\ 0'_{K_\gamma - 1} & -\dfrac{(T-2)}{2\sigma^4} \end{bmatrix}, \tag{10.3.30}$$

$$h_{\alpha\gamma}(\gamma, \alpha_*) = -\left[\sigma^{-2}\sum_{t=1}^{T} u_t\tilde{x}_t\tilde{x}_t', \sum_{t=1}^{T} u_t^2\tilde{x}_t\right], \tag{10.3.31}$$

$$h_{\alpha\alpha}(\gamma, \alpha_*) = \frac{\partial^2 \ln[f(\alpha_*|H)]}{\partial\alpha\,\partial\alpha'} - \frac{1}{2}\sigma^{-2}\sum_{t=1}^{T} u_t^2\tilde{x}_t\tilde{x}_t'. \tag{10.3.32}$$

10.3.4 [$AR(1)$] Suppose $K_\alpha = 1$ and consider the case of a first-order autoregressive disturbance $u_t = \alpha u_{t-1} + \varepsilon_t$, where ε_t $(t = 1, 2, \ldots, T) \sim$ i.i.d. $N(0, \sigma^2)$, and it is assumed that the process has been running since the infinite past.

(a) Derive covariance matrix (10.3.8).

(b) Show that the inverse of (10.3.8) is

$$[\Omega(\alpha)]^{-1} = \begin{bmatrix} 1 & -\alpha & \cdots & 0 & 0 \\ -\alpha & 1+\alpha^2 & \cdots & 0 & 0 \\ \vdots & \vdots & & \vdots & \vdots \\ 0 & 0 & \cdots & 1+\alpha^2 & -\alpha \\ 0 & 0 & \cdots & -\alpha & 1 \end{bmatrix}. \tag{10.3.33}$$

(c) Show that $[\Omega(\alpha)]^{-1} = PP'$, where

$$P = P(\alpha) = \begin{bmatrix} \sqrt{1-\alpha^2} & 0 & 0 & \cdots & 0 & 0 \\ -\alpha & 1 & 0 & \cdots & 0 & 0 \\ 0 & -\alpha & 1 & \cdots & 0 & 0 \\ \vdots & \vdots & \vdots & & \vdots & \vdots \\ 0 & 0 & 0 & \cdots & 1 & 0 \\ 0 & 0 & 0 & \cdots & -\alpha & 1 \end{bmatrix}. \tag{10.3.34}$$

(d) Suppose $\alpha = \alpha_* = 0$, show that score with respect to α is

$$s_\alpha(\gamma, \alpha_*) = -\frac{1}{2}\sigma^{-2}\sum_{t=1}^{T} u_{t*}u_{t-1,*}, \tag{10.3.35}$$

where $u_* = u_*(\alpha_*) = [u_{1*}, u_{2*}, \ldots, u_{T*}]' = y - X\hat{\beta}(\alpha_*)$.

(e) Show that the elements of the Hessian of the log-likelihood evaluated at $\alpha_* = 0$ are (10.3.30) and

$$h_{\alpha\gamma}(\gamma, \alpha_*) = \left[0'_{K_\gamma - 1}, \sum_{t=2}^{T} u_{t*}u_{t-1,*}\right], \tag{10.3.36}$$

$$h_{\alpha\alpha}(\gamma, \alpha_*) = \frac{\partial^2 \ln[f(\alpha_*|H)]}{\partial\alpha\,\partial\alpha'} - 1 - \sigma^{-2}\sum_{t=2}^{T-1} u_{t*}^2. \tag{10.3.37}$$

10.3.5 [$MA(1)$] Suppose $u_t = \varepsilon_t + \alpha\varepsilon_{t-1}$, $|\alpha| < 1$, where ε_t $(t = 1, 2, \ldots, T) \sim$ i.i.d. $N(0, \sigma_\varepsilon^2)$.

Show that the covariance matrix of $u = [u_1, u_2, \ldots, u_T]'$ is given by:

$$\Omega(\alpha) = \begin{bmatrix} 1+\alpha^2 & \alpha & \cdots & 0 & 0 \\ \alpha & 1+\alpha^2 & \cdots & 0 & 0 \\ \vdots & \vdots & & \vdots & \vdots \\ 0 & 0 & \cdots & 1+\alpha^2 & \alpha \\ 0 & 0 & \cdots & \alpha & 1+\alpha^2 \end{bmatrix}. \tag{10.3.38}$$

10.3.6 Demonstrate that multivariate regression model (10.3.11) can be written in the form of a single GLS regression. Hint: Stack the observations by row of Y. What happens if you stack the observations according to the columns of Y? Show that the MLE of the unknown regression coefficients corresponds to OLS applied to each equation separately.

10.3.7 Consider the multivariate regression model of Example 10.3.5. Define:

$$\hat{B} = (X'X)^{-1}X'Y, \tag{10.3.39}$$

$$S = (Y - X\hat{B})'(Y - X\hat{B}), \tag{10.3.40}$$

$$\overline{B} = \overline{C}^{-1}(\underline{C}\,\underline{B} + X'X\hat{B}), \tag{10.3.41}$$

$$\overline{C} = (\underline{C} + X'X), \tag{10.3.42}$$

where $c_W(\omega, M)$ is given in (3.5.2) and $c_{mt}(K, M, \nu)$ is given in (3.5.13). Show each of the following:

$$[\mathrm{vec}(Y - XB)]'(\Sigma^{-1} \otimes I_T)[\mathrm{vec}(Y - XB)] = \mathrm{tr}[\Sigma^{-1}(Y - XB)'(Y - XB)], \tag{10.3.43}$$

$$(Y - XB)'(Y - XB) = S + (B - \hat{B})'X'X(B - \hat{B}), \tag{10.3.44}$$

$$[\mathrm{vec}(B - \underline{B})]'(\Sigma^{-1} \otimes \underline{C})[\mathrm{vec}(B - \underline{B})] = \mathrm{tr}[\Sigma^{-1}(B - \underline{B})'\underline{C}(B - \underline{B})], \tag{10.3.45}$$

$$(B - \underline{B})'\underline{C}(B - \underline{B}) + (B - \hat{B})'X'X(B - \hat{B})$$

$$= (B - \overline{B})'\overline{C}(B - \overline{B}) + (\hat{B} - \underline{B})'[\underline{C}\,\overline{C}^{-1}X'X](\hat{B} - \underline{B}) \tag{10.3.46a}$$

$$= (B - \overline{B})'\overline{C}(B - \overline{B}) + (\hat{B} - \underline{B})'[\underline{C}^{-1} + (X'X)^{-1}]^{-1}(\hat{B} - \underline{B}), \tag{10.3.46b}$$

$$\int_{Z>0} |Z|^{(\omega - M - 1)/2} \exp\left[-\frac{1}{2}\mathrm{tr}(AZ)\right] dZ = c_W(\omega, M)|A|^{-\omega/2}, \tag{10.3.47}$$

$$\int_{\Re_K \times \Re_M} |I_M + A^{-1}(B - \hat{B})'C(B - \hat{B})|^{-(\nu + K + M - 1)/2}\, dB$$

$$= c_{mt}(K, M, \nu)|A^{-1}|^{-K/2}|C|^{-M/2}, \tag{10.3.48}$$

10.3.8 Consider multivariate regression (10.3.11) in Example 10.3.5.

(a) Show that Jeffreys' prior is:

$$f(B, \Sigma^{-1}) \propto |\Sigma^{-1}|^{-(M+1)/2}. \tag{10.3.49}$$

(b) Show that the corresponding posterior density is

$$f(B, \Sigma^{-1}|Y) \propto |\Sigma^{-1}|^{(T-M-1)/2} \exp(-\tfrac{1}{2}\mathrm{tr}\{\Sigma^{-1}[S + (B - \hat{B})'X'X(B - \hat{B})]\}), \tag{10.3.50}$$

and hence,

$$B, \Sigma^{-1}|Y \sim NW_{K \times M}(\hat{B}, X'X, S, \omega), \tag{10.3.51}$$

where

$$\omega = T - K. \tag{10.3.52}$$

10.3.9 Consider Exercise 10.3.8. Show each of the following:

(a) $B|Y \sim mt_{K\times M}(\hat{B}, X'X, S, \omega)$

(b) Let β_i be the ith column of B, $\hat{\beta}_i$ be the ith column of $\hat{B}$, and $S = [s_{ij}]$. Then

$$\beta_i \sim t_K(\hat{\beta}_i, \nu^{-1}s_{ii}(X'X)^{-1}, \nu), \tag{10.3.53}$$

where

$$\nu = \omega - (M-1) = T - K - M + 1. \tag{10.3.54}$$

(c) Consider the future observation

$$y'_{T+1} = x'_{T+1}B + v_{T+1}. \tag{10.3.55a}$$

Show that $y'_{T+1}|Y \sim mt_{1\times M}(x'_{T+1}\hat{B}, q, S, \omega)$, where

$$q = 1 - x'_{T+1}(X'X + x_{T+1}x'_{T+1})^{-1}x_{T+1} \tag{10.3.56a}$$

$$= 1 + x'_{T+1}(X'X)^{-1}x_{T+1}, \tag{10.3.56b}$$

or equivalently

$$y'_{T+1}|Y \sim t_M([x'_{T+1}\hat{B}]', q\nu^{-1}S, \nu). \tag{10.3.55b}$$

(d) Let $y_{t+1,i}$ be the ith element in y_{T+1}. Then

$$y_{T+1,i}|Y \sim t(x'_{T+1}\hat{\beta}_i, q\nu^{-1}s_{ii}, \nu) \qquad (i = 1, 2, \ldots, M). \tag{10.3.57}$$

10.3.10 The natural conjugate prior for the multivariate regression model of Example 10.3.5 is the *Normal-Wishart prior*, denoted $\text{NW}(\underline{B}, \underline{C}, \underline{A}, \underline{\omega})$:

$$f(B, \Sigma^{-1}) = \phi_{KM}(\text{vec}[B]|\text{vec}[\underline{B}], \Sigma \otimes \underline{C}^{-1}) f_W(\Sigma^{-1}|\underline{A}, \underline{\omega})$$
$$\propto |\Sigma^{-1}|^{(K+\underline{\omega}-M-1)/2} \exp(-\tfrac{1}{2}\text{tr}\{\Sigma^{-1}[\underline{A} + (B - \underline{B})'\underline{C}(B - \underline{B})]\}). \tag{10.3.58}$$

Show each of the following:

(a) $$f(B, \Sigma^{-1}|Y) \propto |\Sigma^{-1}|^{(T+K+\underline{\omega}-M-1)/2} \exp(-\tfrac{1}{2}\text{tr}\{\Sigma^{-1}[\overline{A} + (B - \overline{B})'\overline{C}(B - \overline{B})]\}) \tag{10.3.59a}$$

$$= \phi_{KM}(\text{vec}[B]|\text{vec}[\hat{B}], \Sigma \otimes \overline{C}^{-1}) f_W(\Sigma^{-1}|\overline{A}, \overline{\omega}) \tag{10.3.59b}$$

where

$$\overline{A} = S + \underline{A}, \tag{10.3.60}$$

$$\overline{\omega} = T + \underline{\omega}. \tag{10.3.61}$$

(b) $B, \Sigma^{-1}|Y \sim \text{NW}_{K\times M}(\overline{B}, \overline{C}, \overline{A}, \overline{\omega})$.

10.3.11 Show that the Normal-Wishart posterior (10.3.58) implies the following:

(a) $$B|Y \sim mt_{K\times M}(\overline{B}, \overline{C}, \overline{A}, \overline{\omega}) \tag{10.3.62}$$

(b) Let β_i be the ith column of B, $\overline{\beta}_i$ be the ith column of $\overline{B}$ in (10.3.41), and $\overline{A} = [\overline{a}_{ij}]$. Then

$$\beta_i \sim t_K(\overline{\beta}_i, \overline{\omega}^{-1}\overline{a}_{ii}\overline{C}^{-1}, \overline{\nu}), \tag{10.3.63}$$

where

$$\overline{\nu} = \overline{\omega} - (M-1) = T + \underline{\omega} - K - M + 1. \tag{10.3.64}$$

(c) Consider the future observation (10.3.55a). Then $y'_{T+1}|Y \sim mt_{1\times M}(x_{T+1}\overline{B}, \overline{q}, \overline{A}, \overline{\omega})$, where

$$\bar{q} = 1 - x'_{T+1}(\bar{C} + x_{T+1}x'_{T+1})^{-1}x_{T+1} \quad (10.3.65a)$$

$$= 1 + x'_{T+1}\bar{C}^{-1}x_{T+1}, \quad (10.3.65b)$$

or equivalently,

$$y'_{T+1}|Y \sim t_M(X_{T+1}\bar{B}, \bar{q}\bar{v}^{-1}\bar{A}, \bar{v}). \quad (10.3.66)$$

(d) Let $y_{t+1,i}$ be the ith element in y_{T+1}. Then

$$y_{T+1,i}|Y \sim t(x'_{T+1}\bar{\beta}_i, \bar{q}\bar{v}^{-1}\bar{a}_{ii}, \bar{v}) \qquad (i = 1, 2, \ldots, m). \quad (10.3.67)$$

(e) $Y|\Sigma^{-1} \sim MN_{T\times M}(X\underline{B}, [I_T + X\underline{C}^{-1}X']^{-1}, \Sigma^{-1})$. (10.3.68)

(f) $Y|\Sigma^{-1} \sim MW_{T\times M}(X\underline{B}, [I_T + X\underline{C}^{-1}X']^{-1}, \underline{A}, \underline{\omega})$. (10.3.69)

(g) $Y \sim mt_{T\times M}(X\underline{B}, [I_T + X\underline{C}^{-1}X']^{-1}, \underline{A}, \underline{\omega})$. (10.3.70)

(h) $|\underline{A} + (Y - X\underline{B})'(I_T + X\underline{C}^{-1}X')^{-1}(Y - X\underline{B})|$

$$= |\underline{A} + S + (\hat{B} - \underline{B})'[\underline{C}^{-1} + (X'X)^{-1}]^{-1}(\hat{B} - B)|. \quad (10.3.71)$$

(i) Using prior (10.3.58) show that the marginal prior for the data is

$$f_{mt}(Y|X\underline{B}, [I_T + X\underline{C}^{-1}X']^{-1}, \underline{A}, \underline{\omega}) = [c_{mt}(T, M, \underline{\omega})]^{-1}[|\bar{C}|/|\underline{C}|]^{-M/2}|\underline{A}|^{-T/2}$$
$$|\underline{A} + S + (\hat{B} - \underline{B})'[\underline{C}^{-1} + (X'X)^{-1}]^{-1}(\hat{B} - \underline{B})|^{-(T+M+\underline{\omega}-1)/2}. \quad (10.3.72)$$

Note: (10.3.72) can be computed without resort to determinants of order T:

(j) Suppose $B = [B_1', B_2']'$, where B_1 is $(K - m) \times M$ and B_2 is $M \times 2$. Show:

(1) $B_1|B_2, \Sigma^{-1} \sim N_{(K-m)\times M}(\text{vec}[B_1]|\text{vec}(\mu), \Sigma \otimes [\underline{C}_{1|2}]^{-1})$, where $\underline{C}^{-1} = [\underline{C}^{ij}]$,

$$\text{vec}(\mu) = \text{vec}[\underline{B}_{12} + \underline{C}^{12}(\underline{C}^{22})^{-1}(B_2 - \underline{B}_2)], \quad (10.3.73)$$

$$\underline{C}_{1|2} = \underline{C}^{11} - \underline{C}^{12}(\underline{C}^{22})^{-1}\underline{C}^{21}. \quad (10.3.74)$$

(2) $\Sigma^{-1}|B_2 \sim W_M(\Sigma^{-1}|\bar{A}, \underline{\omega} + m)$, where

$$\bar{A} = \underline{A} + (B_2 - \underline{B}_2)\underline{C}_{22}(\underline{B}_2 - \underline{B}_2)'. \quad (10.3.75)$$

10.3.12 Exercise 10.3.6 noted that the MLE in the Gaussian multivariate regression model involves no pooling of information across equations in (10.3.11). A Bayesian interpretation of this result is offered by Leamer (1978, p. 270) and summarized here.

(a) Exercise 10.3.11 implies that posterior mean (10.3.41) corresponding to the informative natural conjugate prior (10.3.58) has a very different structure than the MLE: The posterior mean for the coefficients in equation j involves data from other equations and prior information on coefficients in other equations. Show this explicitly in the case $M = 2$.

(b) The incentive to pool evidence arises for two reasons: (i) the coincidence of correlated errors across equations, and (ii) prior information about coefficients.

(1) Show: If the errors are uncorrelated across equations (i.e., Σ is diagonal), then the posterior mean of the coefficients in equation j is the posterior mean based only on the data and prior for the jth equation.

(2) Show that as the prior precision matrices $\underline{C}^{-1} \to 0$, the posterior mean approaches MLE and the posterior mean of Jeffreys' prior in Exercise 10.3.9.

The moral is that the pooling phenomena in multivariate regression is very subtly based on prior information about regression coefficients. For example the *seemingly unrelated regression (SUR)* model pioneered by Zellner (1962) involves dogmatic prior information, namely, that some elements in the coefficient vectors are known to be zero with certainty. Interestingly, this additional information greatly complicates the both the posterior and ML analysis.

(c) Show: $f(\beta_j) = f(\beta_j|y_m)$ for $m \neq j$.

10.3.13 Consider Example 10.3.1. Let $\Omega = I_T + \Psi$, $b = (X'X)^{-1}X'y$, $M = I_T - X(X'X)^{-1}X'$ and $\hat{\gamma} = \hat{\gamma}(\Psi) = (M + \Psi^{-1})^{-1}My$. Show: $\hat{\beta}(\Omega) = \hat{\beta}(\Psi) \equiv b - (X'X)^{-1}X'\hat{\gamma}$. Can you interpret this result? See Leamer 1984, p. 868.

10.3.14 Consider Example 10.3.1. Suppose $\Omega(\alpha) = I_T$ iff $\alpha = 0$, and $\Omega(\alpha)$ is positive definite for all $\alpha \in A$. Let $\theta = [\beta', \sigma^{-2}, \alpha']'$. Define $P = P(\alpha)$ by $[\Omega(\alpha)]^{-1} = [P(\alpha)]'[P(\alpha)]$. The likelihood function is

$$\mathscr{L}(\theta; y) = \phi_T(y|X\beta, \sigma^2\Omega(\alpha)). \tag{10.3.76}$$

Prior beliefs concerning α are independent from those concerning β and σ^{-2}. The former are represented by the prior mixed density

$$f(\alpha) = \begin{Bmatrix} \underline{\pi}, & \text{if } H_1 \\ (1 - \underline{\pi})f(\alpha|H_2), & \text{if } H_2 \end{Bmatrix}, \tag{10.3.77}$$

where $H_1\colon \alpha = 0$ and $H_2\colon \alpha \neq 0$, and the latter are represented by the normal-gamma density $\phi_K(\beta|\underline{b}, \sigma^2\underline{Q})\gamma(\sigma^{-2}|\underline{s}^2, \underline{\nu})$, that is,

$$f(\theta) = \phi_K(\beta|\underline{b}, \sigma^2\underline{Q})\gamma(\sigma^{-2}|\underline{s}^2, \underline{\nu})f(\alpha). \tag{10.3.78}$$

Define the following quantities:

$$\hat{\beta}(\alpha) = [X'\{\Omega(\alpha)\}^{-1}X]^{-1}X'\{\Omega(\alpha)\}^{-1}y, \tag{10.3.79}$$

$$\bar{b}(\alpha) = [\bar{Q}(\alpha)][\underline{Q}^{-1}\underline{b} + (X'\{\Omega(\alpha)\}^{-1}X)^{-1}\beta(\alpha)], \tag{10.3.80}$$

$$\bar{Q}(\alpha) = [\underline{Q}^{-1} + X'\{\Omega(\alpha)\}^{-1}X]^{-1}, \tag{10.3.81}$$

$$\nu = \underline{\nu} + T, \tag{10.3.82}$$

$$\begin{aligned}\overline{\nu s}^2(\alpha) = \underline{\nu s}^2 &+ (y - Xb)'[\Omega(\alpha)]^{-1}(y - Xb) \\ &+ (b - \underline{b})'[\underline{Q} + (X'\{\Omega(\alpha)\}^{-1}X)^{-1}]^{-1}(b - \underline{b}),\end{aligned} \tag{10.3.83}$$

$$\hat{u}(\alpha) = y - X[\hat{\beta}(\alpha)], \tag{10.3.84}$$

$$\bar{u}(\alpha) = y - X[\bar{b}(\alpha)]. \tag{10.3.85}$$

Let $\hat{\alpha} = \hat{\alpha}(y)$ be a consistent estimator of α, and let $\underline{\alpha}$ be a preselected constant value for α. Partition the sample space $\mathscr{S} = \Re^T = \mathscr{S}_1 \cup \mathscr{S}_2$, where $\mathscr{S}_1$ and $\mathscr{S}_2$ are disjoint, and $\mathscr{S}_2$ is a rejection region for H_1 such that

$$\text{Prob}(y \in \mathscr{S}_2|H_1, \theta) = .05. \tag{10.3.86}$$

Standard use of (10.3.85) leads to the pretest estimator:

$$\tilde{\beta} = \begin{Bmatrix} \hat{\beta}(0), & \text{if } y \in S_1 \\ \hat{\beta}(\alpha), & \text{if } y \in S_2 \end{Bmatrix}. \tag{10.3.87}$$

(a) Find the sampling distributions of the following estimators of β.

(1) $\hat{\beta}(\alpha)$

(2) $\bar{b}(\alpha)$

(3) $\hat{\beta}(\underline{\alpha})$

(4) $\bar{b}(\underline{\alpha})$

(b) What complications would arise if you were to repeat Part (a) for the estimators $\hat{\beta}(\hat{\alpha})$ and $\bar{b}(\hat{\alpha})$? What would be the standard resolution?

(c) Find each of the following.

(1) $f(y|H_1)$

(2) $f(y|H_2)$

(3) $f(y)$

(d) Find each of the following.

(1) $f(\alpha|y)$

(2) $f(\beta, \sigma^{-2}|y)$

(e) Find $\bar{\pi} = \text{Prob}(H_1|y)$.

(f) Find each of the following.

(1) $E(\beta|y, \alpha)$

(2) $E(\beta|y, H_1)$

(3) $E(\beta|y, H_2)$

(4) $E(\beta|y)$

(g) Find the sampling distributions of the following residuals.

(1) $\hat{u}(\underset{\sim}{\alpha})$

(2) $\bar{u}(\underset{\sim}{\alpha})$

(h) Compare the merits of $\tilde{\beta}$ and $E(\beta|y)$ as estimators/estimates of β.

10.3.15 Consider Exercise 10.3.13 and out-of-sample values y_{T+1}, X_{T+1} and u_{T+1}, where

$$\begin{bmatrix} y \\ y'_{T+1} \end{bmatrix} = \begin{bmatrix} X \\ x'_{T+1} \end{bmatrix} \beta + \begin{bmatrix} u \\ u'_{T+1} \end{bmatrix}, \tag{10.3.88}$$

and the covariance matrix of the disturbances in (10.3.88) is given by

$$E\left(\begin{bmatrix} u \\ u_{T+1} \end{bmatrix} [u', u_{T+1}]\right) = \begin{bmatrix} \Omega(\alpha) & v(\alpha) \\ v(\alpha)' & \omega_{T+1,T+1}(\alpha) \end{bmatrix}. \tag{10.3.89}$$

Find the following predictive distributions.

(a) $f(y_{T+1}|y, H_1)$

(b) $f(y_{T+1}|y, H_2)$

(c) $f(y_{T+1}|y)$

10.3.16 Consider a standard linear normal regression of $y_t^* = x_t'\beta + u_t$, where u_t $(t = 1, 2, \ldots, T) \sim N(0, \sigma^2)$. Suppose the model is censored (recall Exercise 2.2.6) in that y_t^* is not always observed, but rather only

$$y_t = \begin{cases} y_t^*, & \text{if } y_t^* > 0 \\ 0, & \text{if } y_t^* \leq 0 \end{cases}. \tag{10.3.90}$$

In econometrics this model is known as the *Tobit model*.

(a) Graph the p.f. of y_t.

(b) Find the likelihood corresponding to the observed y_t $(t = 1, 2, \ldots, T)$.

(c) Suppose all the observed y_t in a particular sample are positive. What does the Likelihood Principle imply about use of the OLS estimate? (Poirier 1986, 1987).

10.4 Pragmatic Principles of Model Building

I beseech you, in the bowels of Christ, think it possible you may be mistaken.
—Oliver Cromwell to the Church of Scotland (see Lindley 1985, p. 104)

The subjective Bayesian philosophy discussed in this text has suggests a way of thinking that I have tried elsewhere (Poirier 1988c) to capture in simple pragmatic principles of model building (PPMBs). This section provides a brief summary of this philosophy in slightly amended form. The implementation of this framework is discussed in subsequent sections.

PPMB1 (LP): Given the likelihood, inferences regarding its unknown parameters should be made conditional on the observed data rather than averaged over all possible data sets as required by conventional frequentist procedures.

PPMB2: Subjective (possibly nondata-based) prior beliefs have a role to play in scientific research. Bayesian analysis involves *formal* consideration of both prior information and loss, and such concepts play a *central* role. Classical analysis involves only *informal* consideration of such concepts.

PPMB3: Likelihoods and parameters are most usefully viewed as artifacts of the mind rather than intrinsic characteristics of the observable world. They can provide useful windows through which like-minded researchers view the observable world and engage in prediction of future observables based on what has been observed in the past. To the extent that hypothesis testing, interval estimation, simplification, and model selection facilitate such predictions, they have a useful role to play. No matter how noble they may appear, hypothesis testing truth searches have a relatively minor role to play in such analysis.

PPMB4: Given a window through which to view the world, the major task facing the scientific researcher is to conduct a sensitivity (local, and to the extent possible, global) analysis of the DOI with respect to as wide a range of professionally interesting priors as possible.

PPMB5 (Cromwell's Rule): Never assign a literal probability of unity to the window through which you choose to view the world.

Although it may not always be easy to work according to these guidelines, they serve as admirable goals consistent with subjective Bayesian thinking. PPMB5 concludes with an humble acknowledgement of fallibility. The next section builds a statistical framework based on these principles.

10.5 Statistical Framework

For the moment take as given a window (likelihood) $\mathscr{L}(\theta; Z)$. Consider a discrete random quantity μ taking the values $m = 1, 2, \ldots, M$. The random quantity μ serves as an index for selecting among M prior p.f.'s $f(\theta|\mu)$ for the parameters of this window. Following Box (1980), the combination of prior p.f. $f(\theta|\mu = m)$ and the common window $\mathscr{L}(\theta; Z)$ is defined to be a *statistical model m*:

$$f(\theta|\mu = m)\mathcal{L}(\theta; Z) \qquad (m = 1, 2, \ldots, M). \tag{10.5.1}$$

The M models in (10.5.1) share a common parametric window through which they view a common goal—the DOI. The uniqueness of a model m stems from its unique prior p.f. $f(\theta|\mu = m)$. These priors may assign positive probability to hyperplanes in Θ defined by sharp hypotheses, or they may just be different K-dimensional p.f.s for θ.

The empirical implications of model $\mu = m$ are twofold. First, provided all the priors $f(\theta|\mu = m)$ are proper, model m implies a *marginal p.f.* or *expected likelihood* for the observed data:

$$f(Z|\mu = m) = \int_{\Theta} f(\theta|\mu = m)\mathcal{L}(\theta; Z)\,d\theta. \tag{10.5.2}$$

Second, together with an out-of-sample window $\mathcal{L}_*(\theta; Z, z_{T+1}) = f(z_{T+1}|Z, \theta)$, model m implies a proper predictive density (even in the case of improper "noninformative" priors) for out-of-sample data z_{T+1}:

$$f(z_{T+1}|Z, \mu = m) = \int_{\Theta} \mathcal{L}_*(\theta; Z, z_{T+1}) f(\theta|Z, \mu = m)\,d\theta, \tag{10.5.3}$$

where the posterior p.f. for the parameters of model m is according to Bayes Rule:

$$f(\theta|Z, \mu = m) = \frac{f(\theta|\mu = m)\mathcal{L}(\theta; Z)}{f(Z|\mu = m)}. \tag{10.5.4}$$

Conscientious empirical researchers convey to their readers a feel for a variety of models and ways of looking at the data. In the present context this amounts to checking how model m in (10.5.1) fits the observed data in terms of the marginal p.f. (10.5.2), what it has to say about out-of-sample observables through its predictive p.f. (10.5.3), and interpreting posterior p.f. (10.5.4). The task facing the researcher quickly becomes complicated when M is large because it must be performed for each model. Furthermore, the question arises how to "bring together" the results. Is one model is to be chosen after an "enlightened" search of the data? If so, then the question is how to properly express uncertainty that reflects both sampling uncertainty from estimating the unknown parameters in model m and uncertainty over the model.

Substantial simplification and order can arise if a p.m.f. $f(\mu = m) = \underline{\pi}_m$ $(m = 1, 2, \ldots, M)$ for the model indicator μ is available, since then probability theory can be used to derive a variety of easily interpreted summary measures. For example, marginalizing μ out of the conditional prior p.f.s $f(\theta|\mu = m)$ $(m = 1, 2, \ldots, M)$ yields the unconditional prior p.f.

$$f(\theta) = \sum_{m=1}^{M} \underline{\pi}_m f(\theta|\mu = m). \tag{10.5.5}$$

Similarly, marginalizing (10.5.2) and (10.5.3) with respect to μ yields:

$$\begin{aligned} f(Z) &= \sum_{m=1}^{M} \underline{\pi}_m f(Z|\mu = m) \\ &= \sum_{n=1}^{M} \underline{\pi}_m \int_{\Theta} f(\theta|\mu = m)\mathscr{L}(\theta; Z)\, d\theta \\ &= \int_{\Theta} f(\theta)\mathscr{L}(\theta; Z)\, d\theta, \end{aligned} \tag{10.5.6}$$

$$\begin{aligned} f(z_{T+1}|Z) &= \sum_{m=1}^{M} \underline{\pi}_m f(z_{T+1}|Z, \theta, \mu = m) \\ &= \sum_{n=1}^{M} \underline{\pi}_m \int_{\Theta} \mathscr{L}_*(\theta; Z, z_{T+1}) f(\theta|Z, \mu = m)\, d\theta \\ &= \int_{\Theta} \mathscr{L}_*(\theta; Z, z_{T+1}) f(\theta|Z)\, d\theta, \end{aligned} \tag{10.5.7}$$

where the implied posterior for θ marginal of the M models is

$$f(\theta|Z) = \sum_{m=1}^{M} \bar{\pi}_m f(\theta|Z, \mu = m), \tag{10.5.8}$$

the posterior probabilities of each specification model m is

$$\bar{\pi}_m = \frac{\underline{\pi}_m f(Z|\mu = m)}{\sum_{j=1}^{M} \underline{\pi}_j f(Z|\mu = j)} = \left[\frac{1}{\underline{\pi}_m} \sum_{j=1}^{M} \underline{\pi}_j B_{jm}\right]^{-1}, \tag{10.5.9}$$

and the Bayes factors for model j versus model m is

$$B_{jm} = \frac{f(Z|\mu = j)}{f(Z|\mu = m)}. \tag{10.5.10}$$

Posterior analysis using (10.5.7) and (10.5.8) is loyal to PPMB1.

A great advantage of the prior p.m.f. for μ is that it transforms the large modeling problem into a familiar setting involving a single prior (10.5.5), a single posterior (10.5.8), a single marginal p.f. (10.5.6) for the in-sample data, and a single predictive p.f. (10.5.7) for the out-of-sample data. *The primary modeling problem is then how to convey to other researchers the information contained in distributions such as (10.5.5) through (10.5.8), which are mixtures of many components.* This not an easy task, but it is a well-defined task. Measures of location and scale can be derived. For example, the mean and variance of predictive density (10.5.7),

$$E(z_{T+1}|Z) = \sum_{m=1}^{M} \bar{\pi}_m E(z_{T+1}|Z, H_m). \tag{10.5.11}$$

$$\begin{aligned} \mathrm{Var}(z_{T+1}|Z) &= E_\mu[\mathrm{Var}(z_{T+1}|Z, \mu)] + \mathrm{Var}_\mu[E_\mu(z_{T+1}|Z, \mu)] \\ &= \sum_{m=1}^{M} \bar{\pi}_m \mathrm{Var}(z_{T+1}|Z, \mu = m) \\ &\quad + \sum_{m=1}^{M} \bar{\pi}_m [E(z_{T+1}|Z, \mu = m) - E(z_{T+1}|Z)]^2, \end{aligned} \tag{10.5.12}$$

are directly related to the corresponding quantities for each model and posterior probabilities (10.5.9). To the extent that any of (10.5.5) through (10.5.8) are multimodal, then it is important to describe subregions of Θ receiving large posterior probability. If most of the posterior mass is loaded on only a few models, then the results conditional on these model should be highlighted. Analysis of the sensitivity of (10.5.5) through (10.5.8) to changes in the prior inputs amounts to the sensitivity analysis called for in PPMB4. For an example of such analysis involving 147 models for each of forty-seven countries, see Poirier (1991c). A very interesting example involving multiple models of world oil pricing developed in 1980 are discussed by Draper (1993). Draper (1993) also discusses the space shuttle example of Chapter 1.

If most of the posterior mass in (10.5.9) is loaded on only a few models, then the results conditional on these models can be highlighted. In general, however, *the common practice of choosing a single model according to some model selection criterion (e.g. see Judge et al. 1985, Chapter 21)* is difficult to rationalize. For frequentists, the pretesting problems of Section 9.8 are again relevant. Choice of one model from the set of M possible models is usually just assumed to be the primary goal of the analysis. In contrast to (10.3.5) through (10.3.9), classical researchers implicitly assign a weight of unity to one model and weights of zero to all other models. Although such an assignment may be sensible if in fact posterior probabilities (10.5.9) follow such a pattern, in general it is nonoptimal. For example, under quadratic predictive loss, posterior mean (10.5.11) is the optimal point prediction, and it can differ substantially from the predictive mean for any particular model. In fact, it can even differ substantially from the mean of the model receiving the largest posterior probability. If only a small percentage of the models are discarded, then such "sins" may be less disconcerting, provided the remaining models are treated in a weighted fashion analogous to (10.5.5) through (10.5.9).

The most damaging comment on the standard practice of choosing a single model, and then proceeding conditional on it, is that the researcher's uncertainty is understated. Readers are interested in a clear articulation of the researcher's uncertainty because it can serve as a useful gauge or reference point for their own uncertainty. This can be easily seen from (10.5.12), which expresses the predictive variance as the sum of two nonnegative quantities (each of which themselves is a sum): a convex combination of predictive variances for each model, plus a convex combination of the variability of conditional means across models. This second term can be sizeable in analyses that attempt a catholic view of the world involving numerous models reflecting diverse viewpoints.

One argument in favor of working with only one model, or only a small subset of models, is *simplicity* or *parsimony*. The problem with this argument, however, is that quantifying such concepts is at best difficult—possibly even more difficult than the original problem of summarizing (10.5.5) through (10.5.9). Computational considerations may also argue for not working with all models, but again, quantification in order to make the tradeoffs explicit is usually difficult. At the very least, researchers who make arguments along either of these lines should inform their readers of the tradeoffs involved, and the choices made as a result.

In implementing the statistical framework embodied in (10.5.1) through (10.5.10), it is helpful to have a reference point in the space of M models. The output of the creative thinking discussed in Section 10.2, is an initial window. Despite the many arguments in the literature over the wisdom of "general to specific" as opposed to "specific to general modeling," observed behavior suggests researchers start with a finite parameterization of the problem that can be *both simplified and expanded*. The arguments are really over a matter of emphasis rather than kind.

In order to locate the initial window in the space of models under consideration, partition the parameter vector as $\theta = [\gamma', \alpha']' \in \Gamma \times A$, where γ is $K_\gamma \times 1$ and α is $K_\alpha \times 1$. Suppose a researcher chooses a point $\alpha_* \in A$, proposes a specific initial window $\mathscr{L}(\gamma, \alpha_*; Z)$ identified with the *maintained hypothesis* H_*: $\alpha = \alpha_*$, and imbeds it in a larger window $\mathscr{L}(\gamma, \alpha; Z)$, $\alpha \in A$. As noted in Section 10.2, the initial window is formulated during the *planning stage* (see Leamer 1989), which defines the statistical playing field. It reflects all the anticipated reactions of the researcher to the data. The initial window is chosen to be sufficiently broad so that anticipated minor alterations are viewed as unlikely. Statistically, this formulation translates into substantial prior probability $\underline{\pi}_*$ assigned to the maintained hypothesis H_*: $\alpha = \alpha_*$. Although $\underline{\pi}_*$ should be "large," it should not dogmatically be set equal to unity. Rather the researcher should attempt to convince the bevy of Bayesians with nearby windows, identified with the alternative hypothesis H_*: $\alpha \neq \alpha_*$, of the reasonableness of the initial window and the *maintained hypothesis* H_*: $\alpha = \alpha_*$. Members of this skeptical bevy require evidence that the window expansion defined by H is not necessary.[5]

More specifically, let the initial window $\mathscr{L}(\gamma, \alpha_*; Z)$ be parameterized as discussed previously, and let the prior density $f(\gamma|H_*, \mu = M_*)$ for model M_* be assigned a similar central role. Assume:

i. $f(\gamma|H_*, \mu = M_*)$ is an absolutely continuous p.d.f over Γ.

ii. Priors $f(\gamma|H_*, \mu = m)$ $(m = 1, 2, \ldots, M_* - 1)$, are all defined conditional on the maintained hypothesis $H_*: \alpha = \alpha_*$, and assign positive mass to hyperplanes in Θ defined by sharp hypotheses on γ. This formulation implies

$$\underline{\pi}_* \equiv \text{Prob}(H_*) = \sum_{m=1}^{M} \underline{\pi}_m. \tag{10.5.13}$$

iii. Priors $f(\gamma|H, \mu = m)$ $(m = M_* + 1, M_* + 2, \ldots, M)$ are all defined conditional on the alternative hypothesis $H: \alpha \neq \alpha_*$.

In other words, it is asserted that the researcher provides an initial window $\mathscr{L}(\gamma, \alpha_*; Z)$ on the world which is believed to be sufficiently general so as not to require further expansion in the direction of the larger window $\mathscr{L}(\gamma, \alpha; Z)$, $\alpha \in A$. Keeping in mind PPMB5 (Cromwell's Law), the fallibility of the initial window and the unanticipated need for window expansion are reflected in the "small" nonzero probability $1 - \underline{\pi}_*$ assigned to larger windows lingering in the background.

Two possible vulnerabilities of these recommendations are: (i) the presumed success in getting researchers to agree on the reasonableness of the initial window, and (ii) the possibility that some of the models are data-instigated (i.e., models created after looking at the data). The first problem raises the question of whether it is possible to investigate the value of a hypothesis such as H_* without specifying alternative hypotheses, and this problem is discussed in the next section. After a brief discussion of diagnostic checking in Section 10.7, Section 10.8 discusses the data-instigated problem.

10.6 Pure Significance Tests

They are widely used, yet are logically indefensible.
—Lindley (1986, p. 502)

5. Of course this expanded window can always be compared to yet larger windows. To end this infinite regress, we assert an asymmetry about the chosen H_*. This "asymmetry" is interpreted as an implicit favoring of H_* relative to H. We return to this asymmetry in Section 10.7.

... it seems a matter of ordinary human experience that an appreciation that a situation is unusual does not necessarily depend on the immediate availability of an alternative.
—Box (1980, p. 387)

One dimension that quickly divides researchers is whether an explicit alternative hypothesis must always be associated with a diagnostic check of a maintained hypothesis. For example, in Section 10.5 an initial window was imbedded in a larger window giving rise to a maintained hypothesis $H_*: \alpha = \alpha_*$, and the alternative hypothesis $H: \alpha \neq \alpha_*$. Could the window $\mathscr{L}(\gamma, \alpha_*; Z)$ have been introduced alone with reference to $\mathscr{L}(\gamma, \alpha; Z)$, $\alpha \in A$?

There are a variety of attitudes espoused in the diagnostic testing literature toward the role of alternative hypotheses. Many of these attitudes are in direct conflict with the likelihood methods discussed in Chapter 7, which all agree that formal testing of a hypothesis is never done in isolation, but rather only relative to an explicit alternative hypothesis. Nonetheless, many researchers advocate diagnostic checking of a maintained model without an explicit alternative. Such activity is commonly referred to as *pure significance testing.*

Barnard has argued that we may know a model is "false" without knowing what is "true." Barnard (1965, p. 194; 1990, p. 70) provides examples from the natural sciences to buttress this claim (also see Hodges 1990, p. 77). Significance tests are intended to aid in this appreciation, that is, to help assess in the words of Barnard (1972, p. 129), "whether agreement between this hypothesis and the data is so bad that we must begin to exercise our imaginations to try to think of an alternative that fits the facts better." Indeed, PPMB5 (Cromwell's Rule) warns against the arrogance of dogmatically assuming all is well and cannot be made better. Such acknowledgments, however, are different than advocating statistical testing of null hypotheses without explicit alternatives.

The historical record of pure significance tests in econometrics is a telling tale: Researchers do not know what to make of pure significance tests. Researchers ask: For what alternative does the test have noticeable power? Without identifying such alternatives, researchers do not know what to make of "significant" outcomes, that is, they do not know how to respecify the maintained hypothesis. To some this means that respecification can be done in a completely random fashion. Most sensible researchers, however, seek alternatives for which the test has substantial power and use these alternatives as guides in respecification. The resulting test is then no longer a *pure* significance test. Although the failure of a specification to pass a test can be blamed on the failure of a variety of hypotheses besides those actually specifically tested against, the only constructive advice I can offer is to take explicit alternatives seriously.

My criticism of pure significance tests, however, goes beyond their failure to aid in respecification. As Lindley (1982b, p. 81) notes; "actually all observations have something unusual about them: The key question is whether there is a reasonable alternative to explain the observation." Without an alternative hypothesis it is not possible to sensibly interpret a pure significance test. Consider the following simple example provided by Lindley (1980, p. 423) in his discussion of the provocative article by Box (1980): "A statistician judges a sequence of 12 0's and 1's to be Bernoulli (the model). On observing the sequence he sees 010101010101 and a plausible alternative immediately suggests itself. Suppose, however, he had observed 111010100010, then the alternative that trials of prime (composite) order always give a 1(0) is not seriously entertained because it has low probability. Yet both these sequences have the same probability on the model." The point is simple: The implication of data on a maintained hypothesis requires consideration of both alternatives and the prior beliefs attached to such alternatives. Regardless of whether the alternative is implicit or explicit, it is always lurking in the background, and it is best brought into the foreground.

I do not *claim that it is never sensible to abandon an initial window without an explicit alternative window; I claim only that formal statistical diagnostic checking is not designed to do so.* Another researcher may point out a logical contradiction in the underlying theory or offer convincing arguments that the DOI is not so interesting after all, either of which may force abandonment of an initial window. But the researcher in such cases is left in limbo without any constructive advice, and the creative act of restarting the analysis must then begin. If a bolt of lightning strikes and an appealing new idea appears, then by all means use it. But don't expect diagnostic checks to be the source of such bolts of creativity.

10.7 Diagnostic Checking of the Maintained Hypothesis

The phrase diagnostic "checks" is intended to include both formal hypothesis testing procedures, as well as informal exploratory data procedures. As used in this text, "diagnostic checking" is *not* concerned with determining the DOI. Rather it is an aid in deciding how clear is the view of a particular window relative to nearby windows.

It was noted in Section 10.1 that if the researcher cannot achieve agreement on the initial window, then the distinction between the likelihood and the prior runs the risk of becoming vacuous. Diagnostic checking of the maintained hypothesis $H_*\colon \alpha = \alpha_*$ associated with an initial window can help alleviate the situation. The modeling approach recommended here is to choose an initial window and immediately perform diagnostic checks of the maintained hypothesis H_* to see if window expansion is required. If the diagnostic checks indicate window expansion, then rethinking is required, a new window must be introduced, and the diagnostic checking process repeated. To what extent a new window is guided by the checks employed is a matter of great debate.

The potential infinite regress of window expansion can be stopped by recognizing that window expansion should occur together with increasingly more informative priors for the unknown parameters in order that something useful is obtained. The argument in Section 10.2 that choice of an initial window should reflect a belief that further window expansion will no longer be productive, is consistent with this observation.

Most researchers agree that complexity costs, both conceptual and computational, enter into the choice of an initial window. Also, there is agreement among most researchers that diagnostic checks should be relatively easy to produce. These two points of agreement suggest that diagnostic checks should require only computations readily available under the maintained hypothesis H_*. This observation immediately recommends the classical LM/efficient score test as one source for diagnostic tests. For example, the LM test of $H_*\colon \alpha = 0$ in Example 10.3.4 is a test of normality within the Box-Tiao family of distributions (see Poirier et al. 1986). Indeed the multiple linear normal regression model of Chapter 9 can be easily imbedded in Examples 10.3.1 through 10.3.3 as well by appropriately choosing $\alpha = \alpha_*$. In each case an LM test can be derived that is easy to compute and does not require computation under $H\colon \alpha \neq \alpha_*$. Similarly, Bayesian versions of LM tests as approximations to posterior odds are provided by Poirier (1991b) (see Exercise 7.4.9) and one-step Laplace approximations in which the integral corresponding to $H\colon \alpha \neq \alpha_*$ is evaluated at one Newton iteration away from $\alpha = \alpha_*$.

The viewpoint of statistical modelling being recommended here introduces substantive asymmetries into the previous statistical framework that are relevant to diagnostic testing. One asymmetry is that no non-nested alternatives to the maintained hypothesis $H_*\colon \alpha = \alpha_*$ are considered. This again reflects the central role of model M_*, which is nested within models $m = M_* + 1, M_* + 2, \ldots, M$. The $M_* - 1$ smaller models can be nested or non-nested among themselves. The important point is that the researcher's world is partitioned into smaller worlds than $\mathscr{L}(\gamma, \alpha_*; Z)$ and larger worlds than $\mathscr{L}(\gamma, \alpha_*; Z)$.

Another asymmetry present is that model M_* is given a preferred position relative to the larger models $m = M_* + 1, M_* + 2, \ldots, M$. This asymmetry is intended to stop the infinite expansion of windows. By assumption it is not expected that the initial window will require expansion. The initial window is picked large enough to ensure this status. Once it is verified that remaining analysis can be conditioned upon the maintained hypothesis $H_*: \alpha = \alpha_*$, analysis proceeds according to (10.5.1) through (10.5.10) with M_* rather than M models and $\underline{\pi}_m$ replaced by $\underline{\pi}_m/\underline{\pi}_*$. Such conditioning is a pragmatic concession to PPMB5. Because the $M - M_*$ larger models are not expected to add much, this concession to discarding models should not be too offensive to the reader. Furthermore, because the diagnostic checking of model M_* relative to these larger models often proceeds in a relatively informal manner (see Section 10.8), such conditioning may be a necessary evil. This concession, however, does not suggest deviating from the wisdom of averaging over models $m = 1, 2, \ldots, M_*$.

The extent of diagnostic testing depends in part on the size of the initial window. Everything else being equal, small windows require more checking to convince others of their value than large windows. On the other hand, large windows usually require a relatively more informative prior p.f. $f(\gamma | H_*, \mu = m)$ in order for useful results to be obtained. The researcher maintaining H_* looks toward diagnostic checking of H_* to verify that the view from the maintained window is clear and is on a par with those of nearby windows. Reporting that H_* passes diagnostic checks is intended to soothe the concerns of members of the bevy and establish agreement to proceed conditional on H_*. Failure to pass the diagnostic checks suggests to the researcher that the maintained window needs some cleaning.

The main point of this short section is not to discuss the formulation of a variety of diagnostic checks, nor is it to discuss what to do when a diagnostic check suggests that a new initial window is required. Rather, this section is concerned with what to do when the researcher succeeds in choosing an initial window that diagnostic checks support—assuming that this point is eventually reached. This point is emphasized because the response recommended here differs from the response to hypothesis testing recommended elsewhere in the text. Following the standard Bayesian recommendation to average across hypotheses or models [see (10.3.5)–(10.3.9)], may not even be possible here. It is self-defeating if the decision to incur additional complexity from expanding an initial window requires the computation that diagnostic checks are trying to avoid. This is why it has been emphasized that diagnostic checks should require only computations easily undertaken under the maintained hypothesis. This consideration, earlier noted asymmetries, and the fact that often the alternative window is not always as well defined as would be preferred (but is still better formulated than in the case of the pure significance tests of Section 10.6) favor conditioning on the maintained hypothesis that passes diagnostic tests and proceeding with the analysis. It is important not to let aesthetics get in the way of proceeding with empirical analysis, and it is also important not to let any initial compromises translate into further bad habits in subsequent analysis. For better or worse, some sort of conditioning is necessary to get started.

The maintained hypothesis deserves special treatment not afforded to models $m = 1, 2, \ldots, M_* - 1$, which receive the brunt of the specification analysis of most researchers. Researchers often engage in contracting searches of models nested in the initial window. The motivation for such contracting searches are multifold: Leamer (1978) identifies six different types of searches.[6] Instead of such searches, the recommended procedure here is to condition on the accepted maintained hypothesis H_*, and averaging across models $m = 1, 2, \ldots, M_*$ for all other activities. As noted previously, this amounts to replacing M by M_* and $\underline{\pi}_m$ by $\underline{\pi}_m/\underline{\pi}_*$ in (10.3.5) through (10.3.9).

In short, *the role for diagnostic checking is to convince members of a research community that the highest marginal return lies in adopting a particular window defined by a maintained hypothesis H_* and proceeding to the next step in the analysis.* Such checks identify a *locally robust maintained window* (see Hendry and Mizon 1990, p. 122). Researchers are unlikely to put forth a window that diagnostic checks suggest is not robust with respect to local alternative windows. A locally robust window seems close to what Spanos (1990, p. 352) defines as a *tentatively adequate statistical model.* Other characteristics of desirable models (e.g., Hendry and Richard 1982, 1983) can also be viewed in this fashion.[7]

The willingness to adhere to PPMB5 motivates broad tolerance of techniques which purport to critique H_*. Such diagnostic checking fits naturally within the role of a window in intersubjective modeling, that is, a window is a vehicle for getting researchers to agree to disagree in terms of the prior. Casual experience suggests it is often difficult to get such agreement among an audience of economists. Do what is necessary to proceed. But when you achieve agreement to proceed, take the Bayesian path.

6. Here are three of Leamer's searches. An *interpretative search* is intended to integrate into the data analysis uncertain prior information. From the Bayesian standpoint, an interpretative search asks two questions: (i) Does the search lead to a posterior distribution similar to that of some prior, and (ii) is the corresponding prior opinion of public interest? Interpretative searches concentrate probability in subregions of the parameter space. *Hypothesis testing searches* go further in assigning positive probability to hyperplanes in the parameter space; they seek to detect "truth." *Simplification searches* impose sharp hypotheses not because they are "true," nor because they lead to better parameter estimates, but rather because the resulting simplicity enhances the communicability of the results to other researchers.

7. An idea that has played an important spiritual role in British econometrics is *encompassing.* A model that can account for the results obtained by rival explanations is said to be *encompassing* (see Davidson et al. 1978; Hendry and Richard 1989; Mizon 1984; Mizon and Richard 1986). Because larger models always "encompass" smaller models nested within them, an extended concept of *parsimonious encompassing* is required to prevent trivial results.

10.8 Data-Instigated Hypotheses

An experiment not preceded by theory, i.e., by an idea, bears the same relation to scientific research as a child's rattle does to music.
—von Liebig (1863, p. 49)

It's critical that you didn't look at the data before. Acquiring priors from the data and then going back and using the same data does not seem to be right. Such objections are important for me. I think about them all the time but I don't let them stop me.
—Sargent in Klamer (1984, p. 75)

We open the newspaper in the morning and read some data on a topic we had not previously thought about. In order to process the data, we try to think about what our prior distribution would have been before we saw the data so we can calculate our posterior distribution. But we are too late. Who can say what our prior distribution would have been before we saw the data. We lost our virginity when we read the newspaper.
—DeGroot (1980, pp. 311–312)

How does one restore virginity lost? The importance of the question depends on the purity of the researcher. Once the researcher gives up the ideal state of the "single-prior Bayesian" and admits the need for sensitivity analysis in public research, the researcher is left with the usual task of presenting a variety of mappings from "interesting" priors to posteriors and leaving it to the reader to decide whether the priors are sufficiently plausible to warrant serious consideration. Those who prefer "virgin priors" are likely to be "virgin data analysts" themselves.[8]

Numerous researchers have addressed data-instigated hypotheses (e.g., DeGroot 1980, pp. 311–312; Hendry et al. 1990; Hill 1985–1986, 1990; Leamer 1974, 1978, Chapter 9, 1989; Poirier 1988c, pp. 140–141; 1991d). Others (e.g., O'Hagan 1980; Savage et al. 1962, pp. 80–84; or DeGroot 1982, pp. 337–338) have noted that it is always possible when considering the models $m = 1, 2, \ldots, M$ to assign only $1 - \varepsilon$ prior probability to them, and to reserve ε $(0 < \varepsilon < 1)$ probability for model $M + 1$: "something else," that is, we can specify $\underline{\pi}_m = \text{Prob}(\mu = m | \mu = 1 \text{ or } \mu = 2 \text{ or } \ldots \text{ or } \mu = M)$ and update these relative probabilities. Provided the researcher specifies priors for the unknown parameters of each of the well-specified models $m = 1, 2, \ldots, M$, and the relative prior probabilities of these M models, standard posterior odds analysis permits comparison of the *relative* posterior probabilities of these models without specifying ε. If in the

8. I considered titling this section "ARCH," but I feared some readers may be disturbed to discover that it is not about the seminal work of Engle (1982b) on *autoregressive conditional heteroskedasticity*. Instead this section is concerned with "arch," which is an acronym for the ubiquitous fact that "*a*ctual *r*esearchers *c*hange *h*ypotheses" after looking at the data.

process the researcher's creative mind has a new insight leading to specification of "something else," then given interesting sets of values for ε, and priors for the parameters of model $M + 1$, analysis once again proceeds straightforwardly. *The Bayesian moral is simple: Never make anything more than* relative *probability statements about the models explicitly entertained. Be suspicious of those who promise more!*

The attitude espoused in the previous section regarding conditioning on a tentatively acceptable maintained hypothesis easily fits into this framework. Bayesian coherence amounts to agreement at the time of prior formation to update from the prior density $f(\theta|\mu)$ to the posterior density $f(\theta|Z, \mu)$ *if it were to be the case that* $Z = z$. Once $Z = z$ is experienced, it requires an assumption of intertemporal coherence to insure that $f(\theta|Z, \mu)$ serves as a prior for the next round of investigation. If observing $Z = z$ triggers thinking and a "discovery experience," so be it. Bayesian analysis is flexible enough to accommodate such changes.

Although Bayesian analysis can play a limited role, it cannot play a primary role in such discovery; it merely accommodates it. I am not prepared to discuss a theory of discovery, nor do I know of anyone who seriously purports to do so. It is useful to draw lines of demarcation around disciplines. Like A. F. M. Smith (1984), I see Bayesian analysis as outside of the area of discovery. I do not mean to connote disparaging judgment on those researchers who work at pushing the frontiers of a discipline out to cover more and more aspects of our life. I even wish them good luck. If they succeed, then they should be rewarded handsomely—reflecting my assessment of the low probability of such an event.

Differences in opinion regarding the LP (recall PPMB1) amount to differences over the appropriate form of conditioning (recall Section 6.10). Sometimes strange bedfellows arise in the process. For example, David Hendry has argued that *how* one arrives at a model or hypothesis in no way reflects its validity (e.g. Hendry et al. 1990, pp. 186, 204–212 and Hendry and Mizon 1990, p. 124). This position is remarkably close to the Bayesian position on the matter, as well as the position of proponents of the LP. As Hill (1990, p. 60) succinctly puts it: "Once a model has been formulated, whether pre- or post-data, the likelihood function for the parameters of that model, conditional upon the truth of that model, does not in any way depend upon the circumstances under which the model was discovered. This simple logical fact constitutes, I believe, the only truly objective feature of statistical practice." The fact that such a strong opponent (Hendry) to the LP and such a strong proponent (Hill) agree on this matter is indeed remarkable. Unfortunately, I do not understand how a non-Bayesian can consistently maintain this position and at the same time adhere to a frequentist interpretation of probability underlying significance testing (see Hendry et al. 1990, pp. 204–212, 220–225).

Because Bayesians follow the LP and condition on the data when drawing inferences, the major problem confronting the *ex ante* view of sampling theory, in light of *ex post* modeling decisions, is not a problem at all for Bayesians. *The pretesting problem for Bayesians is the appropriate choice of a "post-data prior" when employing a hypothesis suggested by the data.*

"Contamination" of the prior can indeed be a problem for the "single prior Bayesian," but I know few such researchers. Once the researcher gives up the ideal "Savage" state of the single-prior Bayesian and admits the need for sensitivity analysis in public research, the researcher is left with the usual task of presenting a variety of mappings from "interesting" priors to posteriors. It is left to the reader to decide whether the priors are sufficiently plausible to warrant serious consideration. Priors that have been contaminated by data can be presented as such; as always it remains for the reader to assess their plausibility.

If in the process of data analysis the hypothesis $H: \alpha \neq \alpha_*$ is suggested as an expansion of an initial window with the maintained hypothesis H_*: $\alpha = \alpha_*$, then in most cases I would argue that the researcher initially "revealed" an implicit prior for α under H that is "tight" around α_*. I am *not* dogmatic in this regard. Upon rethinking the problem, if the researcher believes that the initial window was poorly chosen, then the sensible thing to do is to go with a prior for α consistent with that belief. In most cases, however, I stand by my first suggestion.

10.9 Reconciliation

I have learned to be wary of those who claim that they would like to reconcile the various opposing views on statistical inference. In my experience, the invariable consequence is, rather, a polarisation of attitudes and a great deal of fruitless apoplexy.
—Dawid (1980, p. 311)

Frequentists search for objective characteristics of this world: "truth," the data generating process, or whatever. Subjective Bayesian econometrics does not purport to deliver unqualified "truths" to the doorsteps of researchers; rather it describes a coherent approach in an uncertain world. Different bases of probability underlie these differences, and they may also explain different attitudes towards diagnostic checking.

Nonetheless, despite such differences and Dawid's warning, it is argued here that the two groups may not be so far apart. Although frequentists may preach searching for the "true" model, when cornered most researchers readily admit that their models are always false. The "words of Wisdom" at the beginning of the book are quotes from notable researchers that admit as much. The PPMBs of Section 10.4 are intended to reach out to a variety of researchers, and I believe they are consistent in spirit with much observed behavior; they differ in terms of statistical techniques. Let me briefly argue the case in the reverse order of their introduction.

PPMB5 (Cromwell's Rule) appeals to the humble side of most seasoned empirical researchers. Once you admit that all "models are false" in a literal sense, it seems necessary to admit that there is always a possibility that some other model, not yet introduced, may be deemed "better" in the future. The essential message is: *Always think critically about the models presently under consideration.*

Nobody has a monopoly on defining what constitutes "better." The statistical framework suggested in Section 10.5 assigns a prior probability $\underline{\pi}_*$ to a currently maintained hypothesis H_*. This maintained hypothesis is conditioned upon in subsequent analysis unless it is in violent conflict with the observed data. I recommend a large window with a fairly tight prior for the corresponding *reference model* M_*: $f(\gamma|H_*, \mu = M_*)\mathscr{L}(\gamma, \alpha_*; y)$. Such a combination generalizes the usual implicit "dogmatic priors" whose users are in the embarrassing position of purporting to have sufficient information to assign a positive atom of probability to $\mu = M_*$, while being "noninformative" on the free parameters γ describing the window $\mathscr{L}(\gamma, \alpha_*; Z)$.

The sensitivity analysis called for by PPMB4 is a hallmark of any good piece of empirical research: Convince the reader that small changes in the analysis will not drastically change the primary results of interest. Sensitivity or robustness in this sense cuts across researchers of a variety of pedigrees. The intensity with which the maintained hypothesis H_*: $\alpha = \alpha_*$ is criticized should be in inverse proportion to the size of the initial window.

The "existence" of the parameters in the researcher's model are at best questionable, and often nonsensical in the social sciences. *I believe most researchers admit when pressed that parameters are meant to be used, not worshipped.* Most empirical researchers also admit they wish to "use" their results for pragmatic purposes like policy analysis. Bad habits can lead to emphasizing parameters more than they should (e.g., by seemingly unending hypothesis testing). On the positive side, the emphasis on parameters is sometimes a crude approximation for summarizing predictive effects. Thus, the primacy of prediction advocated by PPMB3, and the Founders of the Econometric Society as evidenced by their interest in *structural models*, may be palatable to such researchers.

Although many researchers are reluctant to admit that they entertain "subjective" nondata information, they are also likely to argue that they bring valuable "insight" and "wisdom" to data analysis in their field of expertise. The only quarrel such researchers should have with PPMB2 is over whether such information warrants *formal* introduction into the analysis. Note that formal introduction of subjective information is more intellectually "honest" than traditional ways of hiding it from the reader.

Finally, regarding PPMB1, it was already noted in Section 6.1 that most researchers readily accept the Conditionality Principle and Sufficiency Principle, which taken together are logically equivalent to the Likelihood Principle, and hence, also accept PPMB1—until they realize they just renounced their frequentist principles. *Therefore, as I see it, many researchers, Bayesians and non-Bayesians agree on PPMB2 through PPMB5, and disagree in public (but maybe not in private) over the Likelihood Principle espoused by PPMB1.*

Therefore, two fundamental themes of this text emerge: (i) Conditioning is of fundamental importance in comparing competing paradigms and (ii) the Likelihood Principle serves as a litmus test for the most researcher's statistical pedigree. I hope readers will take away PPMB2 through PPMB5s and apply them to their empirical research. Personally, I find adhering to PPMB1 in a Bayesian implementation of PPMB2 through PPMB5, is the only way of living coherently.

Appendix A: Matrix Algebra Review I

This appendix is a concise *review* of the *basic* principles of matrix algebra used throughout the text. It is not intended to be a substitute for an elementary course in linear algebra; rather it is a refresher for such a course. The format is definition and theorem, with no intervening text and only a few scattered remarks and examples. Most proofs are omitted as all results are well known. Exercises, however, are provided. Texts on matrix algebra that provide more detailed development of the topics here are Bellman (1960), Dhrymes (1984), Graybill (1969), Hadley (1961), Magnus (1988), Magnus and Neudecker (1988), Searle (1982), and Yaari (1971).

A.1 Elementary Definitions

Definition A.1.1 A *matrix* $A = [a_{nk}]$ is an arrangement of NK real numbers in N rows and K columns, where a_{nk} denotes the element in row n and column k.

Definition A.1.2 A matrix with only one column is a *column vector*. A matrix with only one row is a *row vector*. When the context is clear, "column" or "row" may be dropped. Unless stated otherwise, all vectors are treated as column vectors.

Definition A.1.3 If $A = [a_{nk}]$ and $B = [b_{nk}]$ are two $N \times K$ matrices, then the *sum* of A and B is the $N \times K$ matrix $A + B = [a_{nk} + b_{nk}]$.

Theorem A.1.1 Let A, B, and C be $N \times K$ matrices.

(a) Commutative property: $A + B = B + A$

(b) Associative property: $A + (B + C) = (A + B) + C$

Definition A.1.4 Let $A = [a_{nk}]$ be a $N \times K$ matrix and let c be a constant. Then the *scalar multiplication* of A by c is $cA \equiv [ca_{nk}]$.

Theorem A.1.2 Let A and B be two $N \times K$ matrices, and let c and d be constants.

(a) $(c + d)A = cA + dA$

(b) $c(A + B) = cA + cB$

Definition A.1.5 Let $A = [a_{nk}]$ be a $N \times K$ matrix and let $B = [b_{kj}]$ be a $K \times J$ matrix. Then the product $C \equiv [c_{nj}] \equiv AB$ is the $N \times J$ matrix with typical element

$$c_{nj} = \sum_{k=1}^{K} a_{nk} b_{kj}.$$

Note: In general matrix multiplication is not commutative, that is, $AB \neq BA$, and in fact BA is not even defined when $N \neq J$.

Theorem A.1.3 Let A, B, and C be matrices such that all of the following operations are defined. Then A, B, and C satisfy the two properties:

(a) Associative property: $A(BC) = (AB)C$,

(b) distributive property: $A(B + C) = AB + AC$.

Definition A.1.6 The *trace* of a square matrix A, denoted $\text{tr}(A)$, equals the sum of the elements on its main diagonal.

Theorem A.1.4 Let A, B, and C be matrices such that all of the following operations are defined.

(a) $\text{tr}(A \pm B) = \text{tr}(A) \pm \text{tr}(B)$,

(b) $\text{tr}(AB) = \text{tr}(BA)$,

(c) $\text{tr}(ABC) = \text{tr}(CAB) = \text{tr}(BCA)$.

Definition A.1.7 The *transpose* of a $N \times K$ matrix $A = [a_{ij}]$, denoted $A' = [a'_{ij}]$, is the $K \times N$ matrix obtained by interchanging the rows and columns of A. Hence, $a'_{ij} = a_{ji}$.

Theorem A.1.5 If A is a $N \times K$ matrix and B is a $K \times L$ matrix, then $(AB)' = B'A'$.

Definition A.1.8 A $N \times K$ *null matrix*, denoted $0_{N \times K}$, is the $N \times K$ matrix with all its elements equal to zero. In the case of a null vector, only the nontrivial subscript is included, e.g., $0_{N \times 1}$ is simply $0_N = [0, 0, \ldots, 0]'$. The subscripts are sometimes deleted altogether when the dimensions are immediately clear from the context.

Definition A.1.9 A $N \times K$ *unitary matrix*, denoted $\iota_{N \times K}$, is the $N \times K$ matrix with all elements equal to unity. In the case of a unitary vector, only the nontrivial subscript is included, for example, $\iota_{N \times 1}$ is simply $\iota_N = [1, 1, \ldots, 1]'$. The subscripts are sometimes deleted altogether when the dimensions are immediately clear from the context.

Definition A.1.10 A *square matrix of order N* is a matrix with N rows and N columns. A *diagonal matrix of order N*, $D = \text{diag}(d_1, d_2, \ldots, d_N)$, is a square matrix with elements along its *main diagonal* (i.e., elements running from the upper left to the lower right) equal to d_n $(n = 1, 2, \ldots, N)$ and all off-diagonal elements equal to zero. The *identity matrix of order N*, denoted by I_N or simply I, is the diagonal matrix of order N with all diagonal elements equal to unity. A square matrix is *lower triangular* iff all elements above the main diagonal are zero. A square matrix is *upper triangular* iff all elements below the main diagonal are zero. A *triangular matrix* is a matrix that is either upper triangular or lower triangular. A square matrix A is *symmetric* iff $A = A'$.

Theorem A.1.6 Let A be a $N \times K$ matrix and let 0_{NK} denote a $N \times K$ null matrix.

(a) $A + 0_{NK} = 0_{NK} + A = A$,

(b) $AI_K = I_N A = A$.

Definition A.1.11 The *inner product* between the $K \times 1$ vectors x and y is the scalar

$$x'y = \sum_{k=1}^{K} x_k y_k.$$

The *length* of the vector x is $(x'x)^{1/2}$. The *outer product* of x and y is the $K \times K$ matrix

$$xy' = \begin{bmatrix} x_1y_1 & x_1y_2 & \cdots & x_1y_K \\ x_2y_1 & x_2y_2 & \cdots & x_2y_K \\ \vdots & \vdots & & \vdots \\ x_Ky_1 & x_Ky_2 & \cdots & x_Ky_K \end{bmatrix}.$$

Exercises

A.1.1 Let A, B and C be three matrices conformable to multiplication. Does $\mathrm{tr}(ABC) = \mathrm{tr}(BAC)$? If yes, then show it. If not, then provide a counter-example.

A.1.2 Let A and B be two symmetric matrices such that $C = AB$ exists. Is C symmetric? If yes, then show it. If not, then provide a counter-example.

A.2 Vector Spaces

A vector space is an important concept in linear algebra. For present purposes it suffices to consider only the case in which elements of the vector space are K-dimensional vectors. See Luenberger (1969) for extensions.

Definition A.2.1 Let F be an algebraic field (e.g., the set $\Re$ of real numbers). Let V_K be the set of all K-dimensional $(0 < K < \infty)$ column vectors with components belonging to F. Then V_K is a *vector space* iff it is closed under scalar multiplication and vector addition and it contains the zero vector, that is, iff,

(a) For all $c \in F$ and $x \in V_K$, $cx \in V_K$.

(b) For all $x, y \in V_K$, $x + y \in V_K$.

(c) $0_K \equiv [0, 0, \ldots, 0]' \in V_K$.

In order to introduce a measure of distance in a vector space, consider the following.

Definition A.2.2 Let V_K be a vector space. A *norm* is a real-valued function defined over all $x \in V_K$, denoted $\|x\|$, satisfying:

(a) $\|x\| \geq 0$ for all $x \in V_K$ and $\|x\| = 0$ iff $x = 0_K$.

(b) $\|x + y\| \leq \|x\| + \|y\|$ for all $x, y \in V_K$. (triangle inequality)

(c) $\|\alpha x\| = |\alpha| \cdot \|x\|$ for all scalars α and each $x \in V_K$.

Example A.2.1 $\|x\| = (x'x)^{1/2}$ is a norm.

Definition A.2.3 Let $x_1, x_2, \ldots, x_K$ be a set of K vectors each of which is a column vector of length N, i.e. $x_k = [x_{1k}, x_{2k}, \ldots, x_{Nk}]'$ $(k = 1, 2, \ldots, K)$. Then this set is *linearly dependent* iff there exists a set of scalars $\alpha_1, \alpha_2, \ldots, \alpha_K$ (not all zero) such that $\alpha_1 x_1 + \alpha_2 x_2 + \cdots + \alpha_K x_K = 0$. If this equation can be satisfied only when $\alpha_1 = \alpha_2 = \cdots = \alpha_K = 0$, then these vectors are *linearly independent.*

Example A.2.2 The vectors $x_1 = [2, 7]'$, $x_2 = [1, 8]'$, and $x_3 = [4, 5]'$ are linearly dependent because for $\alpha_1 = 3$, $\alpha_2 = -2$, and $\alpha_3 = -1$: $\alpha_1 x_1 + \alpha_2 x_2 + \alpha_3 x_3 = 0$.

Example A.2.3 The vectors $x_1 = [0, 1]'$ and $x_2 = [2, 2]'$ are linearly independent because $\alpha_1 x_1 + \alpha_2 x_2 = 0$ implies $\alpha_1 + 2\alpha_2 = 0$ and $2\alpha_2 = 0$, and thus $\alpha_1 = \alpha_2 = 0$.

Definition A.2.4 Let x_n $(n = 1, 2, \ldots, N)$ be a set of vectors in a vector space V_K such that for any $y \in V_K$, there exists constants c_n $(n = 1, 2, \ldots, N)$ such that

$$y = \sum_{n=1}^{N} c_n x_n.$$

Then x_n $(n = 1, 2, \ldots, N)$ *span* the vector space V_K. A *basis* is a minimal set of linearly independent vectors that span V_K. The number of vectors in a basis is the *dimension* of V_K, denoted $\dim(V_K)$. A *subspace* is a subset of V_K, which itself is a vector space.

Example A.2.4 x_1 and x_2 in Example A.2.3 form a basis for V_2, as do $e_1 \equiv [1, 0]'$ and $e_2 \equiv [0, 1]'$.

Remark A.2.1 If a set of vectors spans a vector space, then it contains a subset that forms a basis. Clearly, a basis is not unique, but all bases for a given vector space contain the same number of vectors. If $\dim(V_K) = K$, then any set of $N > K$ vectors in V_K must be linearly dependent, and no set containing less than K vectors can span V_K.

Definition A.2.5 Let x and y be two $K \times 1$ vectors. If the inner product $x'y = 0$, then x and y are *orthogonal vectors.* If in addition both x and y have unit length, that is, $x'x = y'y = 1$, then x and y are *orthonormal.* A vector is *orthogonal to a vector space* if it is orthogonal to every vector in the space.

Example A.2.5 $x = [1, -2]'$ and $y = [2, 1]'$ are orthogonal, but not orthonormal, vectors.

Theorem A.2.1 (Law of Cosines) Let x and y be K-dimensional column vectors. Then the cosine of the angle θ between x and y is

$$\cos\theta = \frac{x'y}{(x'x)^{1/2}(y'y)^{1/2}}. \tag{A.2.1}$$

Remark A.2.2 It follows immediately from (A.2.1) that if x and y are orthogonal, then x and y are perpendicular, that is, $\theta = 90°$. Because $-1 \leq \cos\theta \leq 1$, (A.2.1) also implies the celebrated *Cauchy-Schwarz Inequality* (see Theorem 2.7.2)

$$|x'y| \leq (x'x)^{1/2}(y'y)^{1/2}. \tag{A.2.2}$$

The process for converting an arbitrary set of basis vectors to an orthonormal basis is described in the following theorem.

Theorem A.2.2 (Gram-Schmidt Orthogonalization Process) Let x_k $(k = 1, 2, \ldots, K)$ be a basis for a vector space V_K. Then the vectors y_k $(k = 1, 2, \ldots, K)$, where $y_1 \equiv x_1$ and

$$y_k = x_k - \sum_{i=1}^{k-1}\left[\frac{y_i'x_k}{y_i'y_i}\right]y_i \qquad (k = 2, 3, \ldots, K) \tag{A.2.3}$$

form an orthogonal basis for V_K. Furthermore, $z_k \equiv y_k/(y_k'y_k)^{1/2}$ $(k = 1, 2, \ldots, K)$ form an orthonormal basis for V_K.

The next theorem is one of the most important results in optimization theory. Generalizations to the case of Hilbert spaces (i.e., complete normed vector spaces with associated inner products) are discussed by Leunberger (1969, pp. 49–55).

Theorem A.2.3 (Orthogonal Projection of a Vector) Let V_K be a vector space, and let $y \notin V_K$. Then there exist unique vectors v and e such that $y = v + e$, where $v \in V_K$ and $e \neq 0$ is orthogonal to V_K.

Proof A constructive approach for finding v is given at the end of Section A.5.

Definition A.2.6 The vector v in Theorem A.2.3 is the *orthogonal projection* of the vector y on to the space V_K, and the vector e is the *orthogonal complement* of the projection of y onto V_K.

Theorem A.2.4 Consider Theorem A.2.3, $y = v + e$, and the norm $\|x\| =$

$(x'x)^{1/2}$. The orthogonal projection vector v is closest to the vector y in the sense that for all $x \in V_K$:

$$\|y - v\| \leq \|y - x\|. \tag{A.2.4}$$

Proof Write $(y - x) = (y - v) + (v - x) = e + (v - x)$. Because the orthogonal complement e is orthogonal to both v and x, $(y - x)'(y - x) = e'e + (v - x)'(v - x)$, or in other words, $\|y - x\|^2 = \|e\|^2 + \|y - v\|^2$. Hence, Theorem A.2.4 follows immediately.

Theorem A.2.5 (Gram-Schmidt Triangular Reduction) Let A be a $N \times K$ matrix. Then there exists a $K \times K$ upper triangular matrix C and a $N \times K$ matrix B with orthonormal columns such that $A = BC$.

Remark A.2.3 Consider $Ax = b$. Then Theorem A.2.5 implies $B'(BC)x = Cx = B'b$. Because C is upper triangular, $Cx = B'b$ can be solved recursively starting with the last equation.

Exercises

A.2.1 Prove the Law of Cosines (Theorem A.2.1) in the case $K = 2$.

A.2.2 Let V_K be a vector space with norm $\|\cdot\|$. Show: $\|x\| - \|y\| \leq \|x - y\|$ for all $x, y \in V_K$.

A.3 Determinants and Ranks

Definition A.3.1 The *determinant* of a square matrix $A = [a_{nk}]$ of order K is

$$|A| = \Sigma \pm a_{1i}a_{2j}\dots a_{Km},$$

where the summation is over all $K!$ permutations $(i, j, \dots, m)$ of the elements in $\{1, 2, \dots, K\}$, and s is zero or one depending on whether the number of transpositions required to restore $i, j, \dots, m$ to $1, 2, \dots, K$ is even or odd, respectively.

Remark A.3.1 Geometrically, the absolute value of the determinant of A is the volume of the *paralleltope* formed by the column (or row) vectors of A. If $K = 2$, then a paralleltope is called a *parallelogram.*

Definition A.3.2 Let $A = [a_{ij}]$ be a matrix of order K. The *minor* of the elements a_{ij} is the determinant of the submatrix of A arising when the ith row and jth column of A are deleted, and is denoted $|A_{ij}|$. The *cofactor* of the element a_{ij}, denoted C_{ij}, is $(-1)^{i+j}|A_{ij}|$. A cofactor is a "signed" minor.

Example A.3.1 Let $A = [a_{ij}]$ be a 2×2 matrix. Then $|A| = a_{11}a_{22} - a_{12}a_{21}$, and

$|A_{11}| = a_{22}, |A_{12}| = a_{21}, C_{11} = a_{22}, C_{12} = -a_{21},$

$|A_{21}| = a_{12}, |A_{22}| = a_{11}, C_{21} = -a_{12}, C_{22} = a_{11},$

Theorem A.3.1 Let $A = [a_{ij}]$ be a square matrix of order K. Then

$$|A| = \sum_{j=1}^{K} a_{ij}C_{ij} = \sum_{k=1}^{K} a_{km}C_{km} \qquad (i, m = 1, 2, \ldots, K).$$

Theorem A.3.2 The expansion of a determinant by alien cofactors (cofactors of a "wrong" row or column) yields a value of zero:

$$\sum_{j=1}^{K} a_{ij}C_{nj} = 0 \qquad (i \neq n).$$

Theorem A.3.3 Let A and B be square matrices of order K.

(a) $|A'| = |A|$.

(b) The interchange of two rows (columns) will alter the sign, but not the numerical value, of the determinant.

(c) The multiplication of any one row (column) by a scalar α will change the value of the determinant by a factor of α.

(d) The addition (subtraction) of a multiple of any row to (from) another row will leave the value of the determinant unaltered. The same holds true if "row" is replaced by "column" in this statement.

(e) If one row (column) is a multiple of another row (column), the value of the determinant is zero.

(f) $|AB| = |A| \cdot |B|$

(g) The determinant of a diagonal, an upper triangular, or a lower triangular matrix equals the product of its diagonal elements.

(h) Let c be a scalar. Then $|cA| = c^K|A|$.

(i) In general, $|A + B| \neq |A| + |B|$.

Theorem A.3.4 Let A be a $K \times K$ matrix. The rows (columns) of A are linearly dependent iff $|A| = 0$. The rows (columns) of A are linearly independent iff $|A| \neq 0$.

Definition A.3.3 The *rank* of a matrix A is the maximum number of linearly independent rows (columns) in A, or equivalently, the maximum order of a nonvanishing determinant that can be constructed from rows and columns of A. Note that A need not be square.

Theorem A.3.5 Let A and B be matrices such that the following operations are defined.

(a) $\text{rank}(A + B) \leq \text{rank}(A) + \text{rank}(B)$

(b) $\text{rank}(AB) \leq \min[\text{rank}(A), \text{rank}(B)]$

(c) If A and B are square matrices of order K, then $\text{rank}(A) + \text{rank}(B) - K \leq \text{rank}(AB)$.

A.4 Inverses

Definition A.4.1 Let A be $K \times K$. Then the *inverse* of A, denoted A^{-1}, if it exists, is the unique square matrix of order K such that $AA^{-1} = A^{-1}A = I_K$, where I_K is the identity matrix of order K. If A^{-1} exists, then A is said to be *nonsingular*.

Example A.4.1

Suppose $A = \begin{bmatrix} 3 & 1 \\ 0 & 2 \end{bmatrix}$. Then $A^{-1} = \frac{1}{6}\begin{bmatrix} 2 & -1 \\ 0 & 3 \end{bmatrix}$.

Example A.4.2 Recognition that the following matrices do not have inverses is the key to avoiding common mistakes.

(a) $AB = 0$ does *not* necessarily imply $A = 0$ or $B = 0$. For example, consider:

$$AB = \begin{bmatrix} 2 & 4 \\ 1 & 2 \end{bmatrix}\begin{bmatrix} -2 & 4 \\ 1 & -2 \end{bmatrix} = \begin{bmatrix} 0 & 0 \\ 0 & 0 \end{bmatrix}.$$

(b) $CD = CE$ does *not* necessarily imply $D = E$. Let

$$C = \begin{bmatrix} 2 & 3 \\ 6 & 9 \end{bmatrix}, D = \begin{bmatrix} 1 & 1 \\ 1 & 2 \end{bmatrix}, E = \begin{bmatrix} -2 & 1 \\ 3 & 2 \end{bmatrix}.$$

Then

$$CD = CE = \begin{bmatrix} 5 & 8 \\ 15 & 24 \end{bmatrix}.$$

Theorem A.4.1 Suppose A and B are nonsingular square matrices of order K. Then

(a) $(A^{-1})^{-1} = A$.

(b) $(AB)^{-1} = B^{-1}A^{-1}$.

(c) $(A')^{-1} = (A^{-1})'$.

(d) $|A^{-1}| = |A|^{-1}$.

Definition A.4.2 An *orthogonal matrix* is a nonsingular matrix A such that $A^{-1} = A'$.

Remark A.4.1

(a) The columns of A are orthonormal if A is orthogonal.

(b) The determinant of an orthogonal matrix equals ± 1.

(c) If $N = K$ in Theorem A.2.5, then the matrix B is an orthogonal matrix.

Definition A.4.3 Let A be a $K \times K$ matrix with cofactors C_{ij} $(i,j = 1, 2, \ldots, K)$. Then the matrix $C = [C_{ij}]$ is the *cofactor matrix*. The *adjoint of* A, denoted $A^{\#}$, is $A^{\#} \equiv C'$.

Theorem A.4.2 Let A be a nonsingular matrix. Then $A^{-1} = |A|^{-1}A^{\#}$.

Remark A.4.2 The inversion of a matrix using Theorem A.4.2 is usually a difficult task. The following two theorems often facilitate the task.

Theorem A.4.3 Let A and C be nonsingular matrices of orders K and N, respectively. Let B be a $K \times N$ matrix and let D be a $N \times K$ matrix.

(a) $|A + BCD| = |A| \cdot |C| \cdot |C^{-1} + B'A^{-1}D|$ (A.4.1)

(b) Provided the inverses exist,

$$(A + BCD)^{-1} = A^{-1} - A^{-1}B[DA^{-1}B + C^{-1}]^{-1}DA^{-1}. \tag{A.4.2}$$

Theorem A.4.4 Consider the nonsingular matrix

$$A = \begin{bmatrix} A_{11} & A_{12} \\ A_{21} & A_{22} \end{bmatrix},$$

where A_{11} and A_{22} are nonsingular.

(a) $|A| = |A_{22}| \cdot |A_{11} - A_{12}A_{22}^{-1}A_{21}| = |A_{11}| \cdot |A_{22} - A_{21}A_{11}^{-1}A_{12}|$ (A.4.3)

(b) Let $A^{-1} = [A^{ij}]$ be partitioned corresponding to A. Then

$$\begin{aligned} A^{11} &= [A_{11} - A_{12}A_{22}^{-1}A_{21}]^{-1} \\ &= A_{11}^{-1} - A_{11}^{-1}A_{12}[A_{21}A_{11}^{-1}A_{12} - A_{22}]^{-1}A_{21}A_{11}^{-1} \\ &= A_{11}^{-1} + A_{11}^{-1}A_{12}A^{22}A_{21}A_{11}^{-1}, \end{aligned} \tag{A.4.4}$$

$$\begin{aligned} A^{22} &= [A_{22} - A_{21}A_{11}^{-1}A_{12}]^{-1} \\ &= A_{22}^{-1} - A_{22}^{-1}A_{21}[A_{12}A_{22}^{-1}A_{21} - A_{11}]^{-1}A_{12}A_{22}^{-1} \\ &= A_{22}^{-1} + A_{22}^{-1}A_{21}A^{11}A_{12}A_{22}^{-1}, \end{aligned} \tag{A.4.5}$$

$$A^{12} = -A_{11}^{-1}A_{12}A^{22}, \tag{A.4.6}$$

$$A^{21} = -A_{22}^{-1}A_{21}A^{11}. \tag{A.4.7}$$

Exercises

A.4.1 Find A^{-1} for each of the following matrices. What restrictions (if any) must you place on α? Use your answers to (a) and (b) to make an educated guess in part (c), and then verify your conjecture.

(a) $A = \begin{bmatrix} 1 & \alpha \\ \alpha & 1 \end{bmatrix}$.

(b) $A = \begin{bmatrix} 1 & \alpha & \alpha^2 \\ \alpha & 1 & \alpha \\ \alpha^2 & \alpha & 1 \end{bmatrix}$.

(c) $A = (1 - \alpha^2)^{-1} \begin{bmatrix} 1 & -\alpha & 0 & 0 \\ -\alpha & 1 + \alpha^2 & -\alpha & 0 \\ 0 & -\alpha & 1 + \alpha^2 & -\alpha \\ 0 & 0 & -\alpha & 1 \end{bmatrix}$.

A.4.2 Let X be a $T \times K$ matrix with $\text{rank}(X) = K$, and suppose the first column of X consists entirely of 1s, that is, $X = [\iota_T, Z]$ where $\iota_T = [1, 1, \ldots, 1]'$. Let

$$B = \begin{bmatrix} T^{-1} + T^{-2}\iota_T' Z(Z'AZ)^{-1}Z'\iota_T & -T^{-1}\iota_T' Z(Z'AZ)^{-1} \\ -T^{-1}(Z'AZ)^{-1}Z'\iota_T & (Z'AZ)^{-1} \end{bmatrix}, \tag{A.4.8}$$

where $A = I_T - T^{-1}\iota_T\iota_T'$ (also see Exercise A.6.2).

(a) Show that $B = (X'X)^{-1}$.

(b) What interpretation can you give $(Z'AZ)$?

A.4.3 Let A be $N \times K$, B be $K \times N$, and C be $K \times K$.

(a) Show: $|I_N + AB| = |I_K + BA|$.

(b) Suppose $\text{rank}(A) = \text{rank}(B) = K$. Show:

$$|I_N + AC^{-1}A'| = |C + A'A| \cdot |C^{-1}|. \tag{A.4.9}$$

(c) Suppose $\text{rank}(A) = K$. Show:

$$(I_N + AA)^{-1} = I_N - A(I_N + A'A)^{-1}A'. \tag{A.4.10}$$

A.4.4 Suppose G and H are square matrices of order K such that $(G + H)^{-1}$ exists.

(a) Show: $(G + H)^{-1}H = I_K - (G + H)^{-1}G$.

(b) Suppose in addition G, H and $G^{-1} + H^{-1}$ are non-singular. Show:

$$(G + H)^{-1} = G^{-1}(G^{-1} + H^{-1})^{-1}H^{-1}. \tag{A.4.11}$$

(c) Under the assumptions in (b), show:

$$G^{-1} - (G + H)^{-1} = G^{-1}(G^{-1} + H^{-1})^{-1}H^{-1}. \tag{A.4.12}$$

A.4.5 Let C be the $NK \times NK$ matrix partitioned into N^2 square blocks of order K:

$$C = \begin{bmatrix} A & B & \cdots & B \\ B & A & \cdots & B \\ \vdots & \vdots & \cdots & \vdots \\ B & B & \cdots & A \end{bmatrix}, \tag{A.4.13}$$

where A and B are square matrices of order K.

(a) Show that $|C| = |A - B|^{N-1}|A + (N - 1)B|$.

(b) Find C^{-1}.

A.4.6 Consider the symmetric nonsingular matrix

$$H = \begin{bmatrix} A & B & C \\ B' & D & 0 \\ C' & 0 & E \end{bmatrix}. \tag{A.4.14}$$

Let $Q = [A - BD^{-1}B' - CE^{-1}C']^{-1}$. Show (Magnus and Neudecker 1988, p. 12):

$$H^{-1} = \begin{bmatrix} Q & -QBD^{-1} & -QCE^{-1} \\ -D^{-1}B'Q & D^{-1} + D^{-1}B'QBD^{-1} & D^{-1}B'QCE^{-1} \\ -E^{-1}C'Q & E^{-1}C'QBD - 1 & E^{-1} + E^{-1}C'QCE^{-1} \end{bmatrix}. \qquad \text{(A.4.15)}$$

A.4.7 Let x, a and b be N-dimensional column vectors, and let A and B be symmetric matrices of order N such that $A + B$ is nonsingular. Show:

$$(x - a)'A(x - a) + (x - b)'B(x - b) = (x - c)'(A + B)(x - c)$$

$$+ (a - b)'A(A + B)^{-1}B(a - b), \qquad \text{(A.4.16)}$$

where $c \equiv (A + B)^{-1}(Aa + Bb)$ (see Box and Tiao 1973, pp. 418–419).

A.4.8 Let X and X_* be $T \times K$ and $m \times K$ matrices, respectively. Define $B = X'X + X_*'X_*$ and $H = I_m - X_*B^{-1}X_*'$, where rank$(X) = K$. Show that $H^{-1} = I_m + X_*(X'X)^{-1}X_*'$.

A.4.9 If x is scalar, $x \neq 1$, then a well-known result in algebra implies, for a positive integer n: $1 + x + x^2 + \cdots + x^n = (x^n - 1)/(x - 1)$. Letting A be a square matrix such that $(A - I)^{-1}$ exists, show:

$$I + A + A^2 + \cdots + A^{n-1} = (A^n - I)(A - I)^{-1} \qquad \text{(A.4.17a)}$$

$$= (A - I)^{-1}(A^n - I). \qquad \text{(A.4.17b)}$$

A.4.10 Consider the following matrices with given dimensions: y $(T \times 1)$, Z $(T \times K)$, $\underline{d}$ $(K \times 1)$, $\underline{C}$ $(K \times K)$ and W $(T \times T)$. Assume rank$(Z) = K$ and rank$(W) = T$. Let:

$$d = (Z'W^{-1}Z)^{-1}Z'W^{-1}y, \qquad \text{(A.4.18)}$$

$$\bar{C} = (\underline{C}^{-1} + Z'W^{-1}Z)^{-1}, \qquad \text{(A.4.19)}$$

$$\bar{d} = \bar{C}[\underline{C}^{-1}\underline{d} + (Z'W^{-1}Z)d]. \qquad \text{(A.4.20)}$$

Let δ be an arbitrary $K \times 1$ vector. Show each of the following:

(a) $(y - Z\delta)'W^{-1}(y - Z\delta) = (y - Zd)'W^{-1}(y - Zd) + (\delta - d)'Z'W^{-1}Z(\delta - d).$ (A.4.21)

(b) $\bar{d}'\bar{C}^{-1}\bar{d} = -(\underline{d} - d)'\underline{C}^{-1}\bar{C}(Z'W^{-1}Z)(\underline{d} - d) + \underline{d}'\underline{C}^{-1}\underline{d} + \underline{d}'(Z'W^{-1}Z)d.$ (A.4.22)

(c) $(\delta - \underline{d})'\underline{C}^{-1}(\delta - \underline{d}) + (\delta - d)'Z'W^{-1}Z(\delta - d)$

$= (\delta - \bar{d})'\bar{C}^{-1}(\delta - \bar{d}) + (\underline{d} - d)'\underline{C}^{-1}\bar{C}(Z'W^{-1}Z)(\underline{d} - d).$ (A.4.23)

(d) Using (a) through (c) in this exercise and Exercise A.4.4(b), show:

$$(y - Z\underline{d})'(W + Z\underline{C}Z')^{-1}(y - Z\underline{d})$$

$$= (y - Zd)'W^{-1}(y - Zd) + (d - \underline{d})'Z'W^{-1}Z(d - \underline{d})$$

$$- (d - \underline{d})'(Z'W^{-1}Z)\bar{C}(Z'W^{-1}Z)(d - \underline{d}) \qquad \text{(A.4.24)}$$

$$= (y - Zd)'W^{-1}(y - Zd) + (d - \underline{d})'[\underline{C} + (Z'W^{-1}Z)^{-1}]^{-1}(d - \underline{d}) \qquad \text{(A.4.25)}$$

$$= (y - Zd')'W^{-1}(y - Zd) + (d - \underline{d})'(Z'W^{-1}Z)\bar{C}\underline{C}^{-1}(d - \underline{d}) \qquad \text{(A.4.26)}$$

$$= (y - Zd)'W^{-1}(y - Zd) + (\bar{d} - d)'Z'W^{-1}Z(\bar{d} - d) + (\bar{d} - \underline{d})'\underline{C}^{-1}(\bar{d} - \underline{d}) \qquad \text{(A.4.27)}$$

$$= (y - Z\bar{d})'W^{-1}(y - Z\bar{d}) + (\bar{d} - \underline{d})'\underline{C}^{-1}(\bar{d} - \underline{d}). \qquad \text{(A.4.28)}$$

A.5 Systems of Linear Equations and Generalized Inverses

Let A be a $N \times K$ matrix, z a $K \times 1$ vector, and d a $N \times 1$ vector. Consider the system of N equations in K unknowns:

$$Az = d. \tag{A.5.1}$$

A question of considerable importance is determining when (A.5.1) is *consistent* (i.e., has a solution), and if so, when the solution is unique. Also, when (A.5.1) is *not* consistent, it may be of interest to determine a value of z, which minimizes the inconsistency in some sense. The concept of a pseudoinverse (Definition A.5.1) addresses these questions. Before doing so, however, we will consider the case of (A.5.1) when $N = K$ and A is nonsingular.

Theorem A.5.1 (Cramer's Rule) Consider (A.5.1) with $N = K$ and where A is a nonsingular square matrix. Then $z = A^{-1}d$. To find the solution value for the jth variable z_j, replace the jth column of the determinant $|A|$ by the constant terms $d_1, d_2, \ldots, d_K$ to get a new determinant $|A_j|$, and then set $z_j = |A_j|/|A|$.

Proof From Theorem A.4.2, $A^{-1} = |A|^{-1}A^{\#}$. Hence, $z = |A|^{-1}(A^{\#}d) = |A|^{-1}(C'd)$ implies (using Theorem A.3.1)

$$z_j = |A|^{-1} \sum_{i=1}^{N} d_i C_{ij} = |A|^{-1}|A_j|.$$

The case of (A.5.1) in which $d = 0_N$ is known as the *homogeneous* case. In this case (A.5.1) is always consistent, since $z = 0$ is an obvious solution. The next theorem considers situations in which other solutions may also exist.

Theorem A.5.2 Consider the homogeneous case (A.5.1) where $d = 0_N$.

(a) The system has a nontrivial solution $z \neq 0$ iff $\text{rank}(A) < K$.

(b) Suppose $N = K$. Then the system has a nontrivial solution $z \neq 0$ iff $|A| = 0$.

Before addressing whether (A.5.1) has a solution in the general case $N \neq K$, we first introduce one more concept and properties for it.

Definition A.5.1 Let A be a $N \times K$ matrix. Consider a $K \times N$ matrix A^+ and the following properties:

(a) $AA^+A = A$,

(b) AA^+ is symmetric,

(c) $A^+AA^+ = A^+$,

(d) A^+A is symmetric.

If A^+ satisfies (a) through (d), then A^+ is called the *generalized inverse* (or *g-inverse* or *Moore-Penrose* inverse) of A. If A^+ satisfies (a), then A^+ is called the *conditional inverse* (or *c-inverse*) of A, and is denoted by A^c. If A^+

satisfies (a) and (b), then A^+ is called the *least squares inverse* (or *s-inverse*) of A, and is denoted by A^s. Generally speaking, c-inverses, s-inverses and g-inverses are referred to as *pseudoinverses*.

Remark A.5.1 For extensions of Theorems A.4.3 and A.4.4 to cover cases in which generalized inverses are required, see Henderson and Searle (1981).

Theorem A.5.3 Let A be a $N \times K$ matrix.

(a) A^c, A^s and A^+ always exist.

(b) A^c and A^s are not unique. A^+ is unique.

(c) If A is nonsingular, then $A^+ = A^{-1}$.

(d) $(A')^+ = (A^+)'$.

(e) $(A^+)^+ = A$.

(f) $\text{rank}(A^+) = \text{rank}(A) = \text{rank}(AA^+) = \text{rank}(A^+A) = \text{rank}(A^+AA^+) = \text{rank}(AA^+A)$.

(g) If A is symmetric, then A^+ is symmetric.

(h) If $\text{rank}(A) = N$, then $A^+ = A'(AA')^{-1}$ and $AA^+ = I_N$.

(i) If $\text{rank}(A) = K$, then $A^+ = (A'A)^{-1}A'$ and $A^+A = I_K$.

(j) $A'(I_N - AA^+) = 0_K$.

(k) If B is $K \times J$ and $\text{rank}(A) = \text{rank}(B) = K$, then $(AB)^+ = B^+A^+$. In general, $(AB)^+ \neq B^+A^+$.

(l) If y is $N \times 1$, then $y^+ = y'/(y'y)$ provided $y \neq 0$.

We are now prepared to delineate situations in which system (A.5.1) is consistent.

Theorem A.5.4 The system (A.5.1) is consistent iff one of the following holds:

(a) $\text{rank}(A) = \text{rank}(A \vdots d)$.

(b) For any c-inverse A^c of A, $AA^cd = d$.

(c) $AA^+d = d$.

Theorem A.5.5 Suppose (A.5.1) is consistent and let A^c be any c-inverse of A.

(a) For any $K \times 1$ vector b, a solution to (A.5.1) is

$$z^* = A^cd + (I_K - A^cA)b. \tag{A.5.2}$$

Also, every solution can be written in the form (A.5.2) for some $K \times 1$ vector b.

(b) For any $K \times 1$ vector b, a solution to (A.5.1) is

$$z_* = A^+ d + (I_K - A^+ A)b. \tag{A.5.3}$$

Also, every solution can be written in the form (A.5.3) for some $K \times 1$ vector b.

(c) The solution is unique iff $A^+ A = I_N$, or iff $\text{rank}(A) = N$.

(d) If a unique solution exists to (A.5.1), then $A^+ d = A^c d$ for any c-inverse A^c.

(e) Suppose $r \equiv \text{rank}(A)$, $0 < r \leq K$ and $d \neq 0$. Then there are $K - r + 1$ linearly independent solutions.

Definition A.5.2 Consider (A.5.1) and define the residual vector

$$e \equiv e(z) = d - Az. \tag{A.5.4}$$

A $K \times 1$ vector z_* is a *least squares approximate (LS) solution* iff for all $K \times 1$ vectors z,

$$[e(z)]'e(z) \geq [e(z_*)]'e(z_*). \tag{A.5.5}$$

Furthermore, z_* is a *minimum norm least squares approximate (MNLS) solution* iff (A.5.5) holds for all z, and for those z for which (A.5.5) holds with equality, $z'z > z_*'z_*$.

Remark A.5.2 If (A.5.1) is consistent, then a least squares approximate solution z_* is a solution in the usual sense and $e(z_*) = 0$.

Theorem A.5.6 Consider system (A.5.1)

(a) Let A^s be any s-inverse of A. Then $z_* \equiv A^s d$ is "a LS solution."

(b) z_* is a LS solution to (A.5.1) iff z_* is a solution to $Az = AA^+ d$.

(c) $z_* \equiv A^+ d$ is the unique MNLS solution to (A.5.1).

We are now prepared to provide a constructive proof of the Orthogonal Projection Theorem. Using (A.5.4) and Theorem A.5.6(c.), the MNLS satisfies

$$d = Az_* + e_* = v_* + e_*, \tag{A.5.6}$$

where $v_* \equiv Az_* = A(A^+ d)$ and $e_* \equiv e(z_*)$. Consider the column space V_K of A, i.e. the K-dimensional vector space spanned by the columns of A. Clearly, $v_* \in V_K$. If x is any vector in V_K, then there exists a $K \times 1$ vector w such that $x = Aw$. By Theorem A.5.3(j),

$$x'e_* = w'A'(d - v_*) = w'A'(I_N - AA^+)d = 0. \tag{A.5.7}$$

Hence e_* is orthogonal to V_K as required by Theorem A.2.3. The matrix AA^+ is a *projection matrix* because it "projects" the vector d onto the space spanned by the columns of A. If $\text{rank}(A) = K$, then by Theorem A.5.3(i), $AA^+ = A(A'A)^{-1}A'$.

Exercises

A.5.1 Demonstrate each of the following:

(a) Let B be $M \times K$ and let C be $N \times K$ matrices such that $BC' = 0$. Define $A = [B', C']'$. Then $A^+ = [B^+, C^+]$.

(b) Let $A = \begin{bmatrix} B & 0 \\ 0 & C \end{bmatrix}$, where B and C are arbitrary matrices. Then

$$A^+ = \begin{bmatrix} B^+ & 0 \\ 0 & C^+ \end{bmatrix}.$$

A.5.2 Prove each of the following:

(a) If e_k is the kth column of I_K, then $(e_K)^+ = e_K'$.

(b) If $\imath_K = [1, 1, \ldots, 1]'$, then $\imath_K^+ = K^{-1}\imath_K'$.

A.5.3 Let A be a nonsingular matrix of order K and let B be a $N \times K$ matrix with $\text{rank}(B) = K$. Define $C = BAB'$. Show: $B'C^+B = A^{-1}$.

A.5.4 Let A be 2×2 with $\text{rank}(A) = 1$. Show: $A^+ = A'/(a_{11}^2 + a_{12}^2 + a_{21}^2 + a_{22}^2)$.

A.5.5 Suppose $X = [X_1, X_2]$ where X_1 is of full column rank. Let $(X'X)^c$ be the c-inverse of $X'X$. Show: $X(X'X)^c = X_1(X_1'X_1)^{-1}X_1'$.

A.5.6 Suppose $p_1 + p_2 + \cdots + p_K = 1$, $P = \text{diag}\{p_1, p_2, \ldots, p_K\}$, $p = [p_1, p_2, \ldots, p_K]'$, and $= I_K - K^{-1}\imath_K\imath_K'$. Show: $(P - pp')^+ = AP^{-1}A$.

A.6 Idempotent Matrices

Definition A.6.1 *A symmetric matrix A is idempotent iff $A^2 = A$.*

Example A.6.1

$A = \begin{bmatrix} 1 & 0 \\ 0 & 0 \end{bmatrix}$ is idempotent.

Remark A.6.1 Some authors do not require idempotent matrices to be symmetric. Since all idempotent matrices considered here are symmetric, it is included in Definition A.6.1.

Example A.6.2 The projection matrix AA^+ is idempotent [because $(AA^+)^2 = AA^+AA^+ = AA^+$ by Definition A.5.1(a), and AA^+ is symmetric by Definition A.5.1(b)]. Geometrically speaking, the idempotency of AA^+ implies that once AA^+ has projected a vector onto the column space of A, subsequent application of AA^+ leaves the projected vector unchanged.

Exercises

A.6.1 Let X be a $T \times K$ matrix with $\text{rank}(X) = K$. Show that $X(X'X)^{-1}X'$ and $M = I_T - X(X'X)^{-1}X'$ are idempotent and find their ranks.

A.6.2 Let X be a $T \times K$ matrix and define $A = I_T - T^{-1}\iota_T\iota_T'$, where ι_T is a $T \times 1$ column vector of 1s.

(a) Show that A is idempotent.

(b) Find AX.

A.6.3 Let A be a $N \times N$ idempotent matrix. Let c_1 and c_2 be nonzero scalars. Show: $[c_1 A + c_2(I_N - A)]^{-1} = c_1^{-1}A + c_2^{-1}(I - A)$.

A.6.4 Let A be a $K \times N$ matrix. Prove each of the following:

(a) $AA^+, A^+A, I_K - AA^{+\prime}$, and $I_N - A^+A$ are idempotent. Demonstrate your results by applying them to Exercise A.5.2.

(b) Suppose $\text{rank}(A) = N$ and let B be a $N \times K$ matrix with $\text{rank}(B) = N$. Then $(AB)^+ = B^+A^+$.

(c) $(A'A)^+ = A^+(A')^+$

(d) $(AA^+)^+ = AA^+$

(e) $(A^+A)^+ = A^+A$

(f) $AB = AA^+$ iff $ABA = A$ and AB is symmetric.

(g) Write $A = [A_1, A_2]$. Then $AA^+ = A_1A_1^+ + [(I - A_1A_1^+)A_2][(I - A_1A_1^+)A_2]^+$.

A.6.5 Let A^c and B^c denote the c-inverses of the matrices A and B, and suppose AB is conformable. Show: B^cA^c is the c-inverse of AB iff A^cABB^c is idempotent.

A.7 Characteristic Roots and Vectors

Definition A.7.1 The *characteristic value problem* is defined as that of finding values of a (possibly complex) number λ and associated column vector x, $x \neq 0$, satisfying

$$Ax = \lambda x \quad \text{or} \quad (A - \lambda I)x = 0_K \tag{A.7.1}$$

for a given square matrix A of order K. A solution value is an *eigenvalue*, a *characteristic root*, or a *latent root*. A corresponding column vector x is an *eigenvector*, a *characteristic vector*, or a *latent vector*.

Remark A.7.1 (A.7.1) will have a nonzero solution if $(A - \lambda I)$ is singular, that is, $|A - \lambda I| = 0$. This condition yields a polynomial equation, called the *characteristic equation of A*, of degree at most K in the unknown λ. If out of the roots of this equation, a root appears m times, then m is the *multiplicity* of the root. If A is symmetric, then the eigenvalues are all real numbers and complex solutions can be ruled out. Eigenvectors are not unique [e.g. if x solves (A.7.1) for some λ, then so does cx for any constant c], but can be made unique (up to sign) when A is symmetric by normalizing their Euclidean lengths to unity and requiring roots corresponding to the same multiple root to also be orthogonal.

Example 8.7.1 Consider

$$A = \begin{bmatrix} 4 & 2 \\ 2 & 1 \end{bmatrix}.$$

Then the characteristic equation of A is

$|A - \lambda I_2| = (4 - \lambda)(1 - \lambda) - 4 = \lambda(\lambda - 5) = 0,$

which has roots $\lambda_1 = 0$ and $\lambda_2 = 5$. The eigenvector x_1 corresponding to $\lambda_1 = 0$ solves $Ax_1 = 0$, or equivalently, $2x_{11} + x_{21} = 0$. Subject to the normalization $x_1'x_1 = x_{11}^2 + x_{21}^2 = 1$, this implies $x_1 = [5^{-1/2}, -2(5^{-1/2})]'$. Similarly, the eigenvector x_2 corresponding to $\lambda_2 = 5$ solves $(A - 5I_2)x_2 = 0$, or equivalently, $2x_{12} - 4x_{22} = 0$. Subject to the normalization $x_2'x_2 = x_{12}^2 + x_{22}^2 = 1$, this implies $x_2 = [2(5^{-1/2}), 5^{-1/2}]'$.

Theorem A.7.1 Let A be a square *symmetric* matrix.

(a) The characteristic roots of A are real numbers.

(b) The sum of the characteristic roots of A equals the trace of A.

(c) The product of the characteristic roots of A equals the determinant of A.

(d) The number of nonzero roots of A equals the rank of A.

(e) Characteristic vectors corresponding to distinct characteristic roots are orthogonal.

(f) The characteristic roots of A equal those of A'.

(g) The characteristic roots of A^{-1} (if it exists) are the reciprocals of those of A.

(h) If B is a square matrix of the same order as A, then the characteristic roots of AB are the same as the characteristic roots of BA.

Theorem A.7.2 Let A be a symmetric matrix of order N with characteristic roots λ_n $(n = 1, 2, \ldots, N)$. Let x_n $(n = 1, 2, \ldots, N)$ be mutually orthogonal characteristic vectors normalized to have unit length. Define $\Lambda \equiv \text{diag}(\lambda_1, \lambda_2, \ldots, \lambda_N)$ and $X \equiv [x_1, x_2, \ldots, x_N]$ (i.e., X is an orthogonal matrix).

(a) $X'X = I_N = XX' = x_1x_1' + x_2x_2' + \cdots + x_Nx_N'$.

(b) $X'AX = \Lambda$ (diagonalization of A).

(c) $A = X\Lambda X' = \lambda_1 x_1 x_1' + \lambda_2 x_2 x_2' + \cdots + \lambda_N x_N x_N'$ (spectral decomposition of A).

(d) $|A - \lambda I_N| = |\Lambda - \lambda I_N| = \prod_{n=1}^{N} (\lambda_n - \lambda)$.

Remark A.7.2

(a) Suppose all the characteristic roots λ_n $(n = 1, 2, \ldots, N)$ of A are nonnegative. Define $\Lambda^{1/2} \equiv \text{diag}(\lambda_1^{1/2}, \lambda_2^{1/2}, \ldots, \lambda_N^{1/2})$ and $B = \Lambda^{1/2}X'$. Then B serves as a factorization of A in the sense that $A = B'B$ (using Theorem A.7.2b).

(b) If in addition the matrix A in (a) is nonsingular, then $A^{-1} = C'C$, where $C = \Lambda^{-1/2}X'$ (using Theorem A.7.2c).

Theorem A.7.3 Let A_k $(k = 1, 2, \ldots, K)$ be square matrices of order N and define $A = A_1 + A_2 + \cdots + A_K$. Consider the following statements:

(a) $A_k^2 = A_k$ $(k = 1, 2, \ldots, K)$

(b) $A_i A_j = 0$ $(i,j = 1, 2, \ldots, K; i \neq j)$ and $\text{rank}(A_k^2) = \text{rank}(A_k)$ $(k = 1, 2, \ldots, K)$.

(c) $A^2 = A$.

(d) $\text{rank}(A) = \text{rank}(A_1) + \text{rank}(A_2) + \cdots + \text{rank}(A_k)$.

Then any two of (a) through (c) imply all four. Furthermore, (c) and (d) imply (a) and (b).

Theorem A.7.4 Let A be an idempotent matrix.

(a) The latent roots of A are all either zero or one.

(b) $\text{Rank}(A) = \text{tr}(A)$.

(c) If A is nonsingular, then $A = I$.

(d) $I - A$ is idempotent.

(e) $A^+ = A$.

Definition A.7.2 Let A be a square matrix of order K, and let Q be a nonsingular matrix of order K. Then A and $B \equiv Q^{-1}AQ$ are *similar matrices*. A is *diagonalizable* iff it is similar to a diagonal matrix.

Theorem A.7.5 Let A, Q and B be defined as in Definition A.7.2. Then B has the same characteristic roots as A, and if x is a characteristic vector of A, then $A^{-1}x$ is a characteristic vector of B.

Remark A.7.3

(a) Theorem A.7.5 provides one motivation for the concept of similar matrices: given a square matrix A, we immediately have a great deal of information about a class of matrices, namely, those matrices that are similar to A, because the characteristic roots of any member of this class are the same as the characteristic roots of A.

(b) From Theorem A.7.2(b) it follows that all symmetric matrices are diagonalizable.

Theorem A.7.6 (Simultaneous Diagonalizations) Let A and B be two symmetric matrices of order N. Then there exists an orthogonal matrix Q such that

$$Q'AQ = D_1 \text{ and } Q'BQ = D_2, \tag{A.7.2}$$

where D_1 and D_2 are diagonal matrices iff

$$AB = BA. \tag{A.7.3}$$

Corollary Let A and B be two symmetric matrices of order N such that $AB = 0$. Then there exists an orthogonal matrix Q such that $Q'AQ = D_1$ and $Q'BQ = D_2$, where D_1 and D_2 are diagonal matrices. Moreover, $D_1 D_2 = 0$.

Theorem A.7.8 Let A be a symmetric matrix of order K and rank r. Let λ_i $(i = 1, 2, \ldots, r)$ be the nonzero roots of A and let x_i $(i = 1, 2, \ldots, r)$ be the associated characteristic vectors normalized to be of unit length and pairwise orthogonal.

(a) The nonzero roots of A^+ are λ_i^{-1} $(i = 1, 2, \ldots, r)$.

(b) $A^+ = \sum_{i=1}^{r} \lambda_i^{-1} x_i x_i'$.

(c) A and A^+ have the same characteristic vectors.

Exercises

A.7.1 Let A be defined as in Exercise A.4.1(a).

(a) Find the eigenvalues λ_1 and λ_2 of A.

(b) Find the normalized eigenvectors x_1 and x_2 of A.

(c) Repeat (a) and (b) for the matrix cA, where c is a positive scalar. How do the answers compare?

(d) Find an orthogonal matrix B such that

$$B'AB = \begin{bmatrix} \lambda_1 & 0 \\ 0 & \lambda_2 \end{bmatrix}.$$

(e) Verify Theorem A.7.1, parts (a)–(g), for the matrix A.

A.7.2 Let

$$B = \begin{bmatrix} (1-\alpha^2)^{1/2} & 0 & 0 & 0 \\ -\alpha & 1 & 0 & 0 \\ 0 & -\alpha & 1 & 0 \\ 0 & 0 & -\alpha & 1 \end{bmatrix},$$

and let A be defined as in Exercise A.4.1(c). Compute $B'B$ and express it in terms of A. Compute $BA^{-1}B'$ and simplify your answer.

A.7.3 Let A, X and Λ be defined as in Theorem A.7.2. Show: $A^j = X\Lambda^j X'$ for any positive integer j.

A.7.4 Prove Theorem A.7.4.

A.7.5 Let $A = [a_{ij}]$ be the $N \times N$ *tridiagonal matrix* defined by

$$a_{ij} = \begin{Bmatrix} c, & \text{if } i = j \\ d, & \text{if } i = j - 1 \text{ or } i = j + 1 \\ 0, & \text{otherwise} \end{Bmatrix}.$$

Show that the latent roots of A are $\lambda_n = c + 2d\cos[n\pi/(N + 1)]$ $(n = 1, 2, \ldots, N)$, and the associated characteristic vectors are $[\sin\{n\pi/(N + 1)\}, \sin\{2n\pi/(N + 1)\}, \ldots, \sin\{Nn\pi/(N + 1)\}]'$ $(n = 1, 2, \ldots, N)$.

A.7.6 Let x and y be two linearly independent $K \times 1$ vectors. Show that the nonzero eigenvalues of $A = xx' - yy'$ are

$$\lambda = \tfrac{1}{2}\{-(x'x - y'y) \pm [(x'x - y'y)^2 + 4x'xy'y - 4(x'y)^2]^{1/2}\}.$$

A.7.7 Let A be a square matrix of order N with all eigenvalues equal to zero or one. Show that A need not be idempotent.

A.8 Quadratic Forms and Definite Matrices

Definition A.8.1 *A quadratic form* in N variables x_n $(n = 1, 2, \ldots, N)$ is a homogeneous quadratic function of the form

$$q = \sum_{i=1}^{N} \sum_{j=1}^{N} a_{ij} x_i x_j = x'Ax, \tag{A.8.1}$$

where $x \equiv [x_1, x_2, \ldots, x_N]'$ and $A \equiv [\tfrac{1}{2}(a_{ij} + a_{ji})]$ is a symmetric matrix of order N known as the *matrix of the quadratic form.*

Definition A.8.2 *A* quadratic form $x'Ax$ or its matrix A is said to be

(a) *positive definite (p.d.)* iff $x'Ax > 0$ for all nonzero x;

(b) *negative definite (n.d.)* iff $-x'Ax$ is positive definite;

(c) *positive semidefinite (p.s.d.)* iff $x'Ax \geq 0$ for all x, and $x'Ax = 0$ for some $x \neq 0$;

(d) *negative semidefinite (n.s.d.)* iff $-x'Ax$ is positive semidefinite;

(e) *indefinite* iff it is none of the above;

(f) *nonnegative definite (n.n.d.)* iff $x'Ax$ is either p.d. or p.s.d;

(g) *nonpositive definite (n.p.d.)* iff $x'Ax$ is either n.d. or n.s.d.

Definition A.8.3 Let A be a symmetric matrix of order K. The *minors* of order k $(1 \leq k \leq K)$ are the determinants of all $k \times k$ matrices obtained by deleting $(K - k)$ rows and $(K - k)$ columns. The *principal minors* of order k $(1 \leq k \leq K)$ are determinants of all the $k \times k$ matrices obtained by deleting the *same* $(K - k)$ rows and columns of A. The *leading principal minor* of order k $(1 \leq k \leq K)$ is the determinant of the $k \times k$ matrix that consists of the *first* k rows and the *first* k columns of A.

Theorem A.8.1 Let A be a symmetric matrix. A necessary and sufficient condition for positive definiteness is that all leading principal minors be positive. A necessary and sufficient condition for negative definiteness is that the leading principal minors of A alternate in sign starting with negative, that is, all odd-numbered principal minors are negative and all even-numbered ones are positive. A necessary (but *not* sufficient) condition for positive semidefiniteness is that all leading principal minors are non-negative.

Example A.8.1 Consider the following matrices:

$$A = \begin{bmatrix} 5 & 1 \\ 1 & 2 \end{bmatrix}, B = \begin{bmatrix} -1 & 1 \\ 1 & -2 \end{bmatrix}, C = \begin{bmatrix} -1 & 3 \\ 3 & -1 \end{bmatrix}.$$

A is positive definite, B is negative definite, and C is indefinite.

Theorem A.8.2 Let A be a square matrix.

(a) A is p.d. iff all its characteristic roots are positive.

(b) A is n.d. iff all its characteristic roots are negative.

(c) A is p.s.d. iff all its characteristic roots are non-negative, and at least one is zero.

(d) A is n.s.d iff all its characteristic roots are non-positive, and at least one is zero.

(e) A is indefinite iff some of its characteristic roots are positive and some are negative.

Theorem A.8.3 Let A be an $N \times K$ matrix of rank r.

(a) If $r = K$, then $A'A$ is p.d., and if $N > r$, then AA' is p.s.d.

(b) If $r = N$, then AA' is p.d., and if $K > r$, then $A'A$ is p.s.d.

(c) If $r < K$ and $r < N$, then both $A'A$ and AA' are p.s.d and neither is p.d..

Theorem A.8.4 Let A be a symmetric matrix of order K with characteristic roots $\lambda_1 \leq \lambda_2 \leq \cdots \leq \lambda_K$. Then for any $K \times 1$ vector z, $z \neq 0$:

$$\lambda_1 \leq \frac{z'Az}{z'z} \leq \lambda_K. \tag{A.8.2}$$

Theorem A.8.5 Let $A = [a_{ij}]$ be a $N \times N$ positive definite matrix, and let $A^{-1} = [a^{ij}]$.

(a) $a^{ii} \geq (a_{ii})^{-1}$ with equality iff $a_{ij} = 0$ for $i, j = 1, 2, \ldots, N$; $i \neq j$.

(b) $a^{ii} = (a_{ii})^{-1}$ for all i implies $a_{ij} = 0$; $i \neq j$.

Theorem A.8.6 (Cholesky Decomposition) Let A be a positive definite matrix of order N. Then there exists a lower triangular matrix T of order N such that $A = TT'$.

Remark A.8.1

(a) The lower triangular matrix T in Theorem A.8.6 is *not* unique. The matrix T can be rendered unique by specifying all diagonal elements to be positive.

(b) T' is upper triangular.

(c) $A^{-1} = (T')^{-1}T^{-1}$ (This representation is often computationally attractive.)

(d) Theorem A.8.6 may be extended to show the existence of an upper triangular matrix T_* such that $A = T_* T_*'$.

Theorem A.8.7 Let A and B be symmetric matrices or order N and suppose that B is positive definite. Let ω_n $(n = 1, 2, \ldots, N)$ be the roots of $|A - \lambda B| = 0$ and define $\Omega \equiv \text{diag}(\omega_1, \omega_2, \ldots, \omega_n)$. Then there exists a nonsingular square matrix W or order N with columns w_n $(n = 1, 2, \ldots, N)$ such that:

(a) $Aw_n = Bw_n$ $(n = 1, 2, \ldots, N)$

(b) $W'AW = \Omega$

(c) $W'BW = I_n$

(d) $A = (W^{-1})'\Omega W^{-1}$

(e) $B = (W^{-1})'W^{-1}$

(f) $A = \omega_1 w^1(w^1)' + \omega_2 w^2(w^2)' + \cdots + \omega_N w^N(w^N)'$, where w^n is column n of W^{-1} $(n = 1, 2, \ldots, N)$.

(g) $B = w^1(w^1)' + w^2(w^2)' + \cdots + w^N(w^N)'$

Theorem A.8.8 Let A and B be positive definite matrices.

(a) $|A| + |B| \le |A + B|$ with equality only if A if proportional to B.

(b) $|A| > |B|$ if $A - B$ is positive definite.

(c) $B^{-1} - A^{-1}$ is positive definite if $A - B$ is positive definite.

(d) Let $A = [a_{ij}]$ be $K \times K$. Then $|A| \le \prod_{k=1}^{K} a_{kk}$.

Theorem A.8.9 Let A and B be symmetric matrices of order N such that $A - B$ is nonnegative definite. Then $\lambda_n(A) \ge \lambda_n(B)$ $(n = 1, 2, \ldots, N)$, where $\lambda_n(\cdot)$ denotes the nth smallest characteristic root defined in Theorem A.7.12.

Theorem A.8.10 Let A be a positive definite matrix of order K and let x and z be $K \times 1$ vectors. Then

$$\sup_x \frac{(z'x)^2}{x'Ax} = z'A^{-1}z, \tag{A.8.3}$$

where the supremum occurs at $x_* = A^{-1}z$

Theorem A.8.11 Let A be a given positive definite matrix of order K, let c be a given $K \times 1$ vector, let z be a $K \times 1$ vector and let r be a positive scalar.

(a) The extreme values of $c'z$ over all z on the ellipsoid $z'Az = r^2$ occur at

$$z_* = \pm \left[\frac{r^2}{c'A^{-1}c}\right]^{1/2} A^{-1}c. \tag{A.8.4}$$

with $c'z_* = r(c'A^{-1}c)^{1/2}$.

(b) Let $A^{-1} \equiv [a^{ij}]$. The orthogonal projection of $z'Az = r^2$ onto the kth axis is the interval $-r(a^{kk})^{1/2} \leq z_k \leq r(a^{kk})^{1/2}$.

Remark A.8.2 Let A be a positive definite matrix of order K, z be a $K \times 1$ vector, and r be a positive scalar. Denote characteristic roots of A by λ_k $(k = 1, 2, \ldots, K)$ and let c_k $(k = 1, 2, \ldots, K)$ be an associated set of orthonormal characteristic vectors. The equation $z'Az = r^2$ describes a K-dimensional ellipsoid centered at the origin with axes equal to $(r\lambda_k^{-1/2})c_k$ $(k = 1, 2, \ldots, K)$. The directions of tangency between the unit sphere $z'z = 1$ and this ellipse are given by the characteristic vectors of A. The

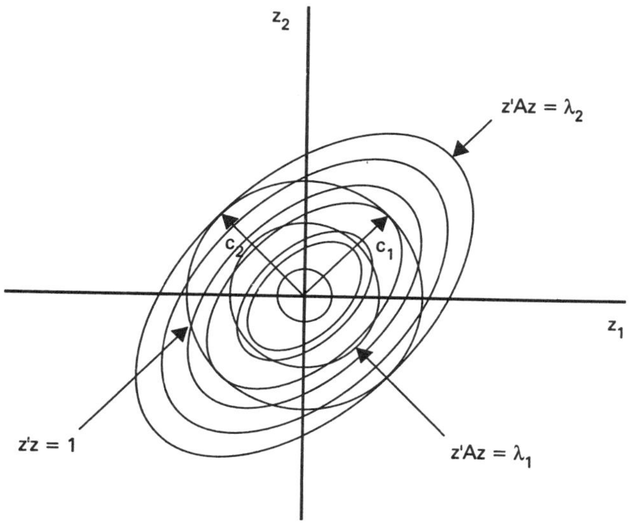

Figure A.1
Characteristic roots and vectors

characteristic roots of A are the values of r^2 needed to produce tangency between the unit sphere and the ellipsoid. This is illustrated in Figure A.1 for $K = 2$. See Leamer (1978, pp. 328–331) for more details.

Exercises

A.8.1 Consider Theorem A.4.3.

(a) Let A be nonsingular of order K, and u and v be $K \times 1$ vectors. Show:

$$(A + uv')^{-1} = A^{-1} - \frac{A^{-1}uv'A^{-1}}{1 + v'A^{-1}u}. \tag{A.8.5}$$

(b) Suppose Ω is a $K \times K$ matrix with all diagonal elements equal to c and all off-diagonal elements equal to d, where c and d are real numbers such that $d > -c/(K-1)$. Use Part (a) to show that

$$\Omega^{-1} = \frac{1}{c-d}\left[I_K - \frac{d\iota_K\iota_K'}{c + (K-1)d}\right]. \tag{A.8.6}$$

(c) Suppose $A = \alpha I_K$. Show that $K - 1$ characteristic roots are equal to α, and one root equals $\alpha + u'v$.

(d) Show that the latent roots of Ω in Part (b) are $\lambda_k = c - d$ $(k = 1, 2, \ldots, K-1)$ and $\lambda_K = c + (K-1)d$.

(e) Consider Part(b).

(1) Show: Ω is positive definite iff $-(K-1)^{-1} < d/c < 1$.

(2) Show: Ω is positive semidefinite iff $-(K-1)^{-1} = d/c$ or $d/c = 1$.

(3) Show: $|\Omega| < 0$ if $d/c < -(K-1)^{-1}$.

A.8.2 Let $A = [A_1, A_2]$ be $N \times K$ with rank K. Define $A_{2*} = [I_N - A_1(A_1'A_1)^{-1}A_1']A_2$. Show: $A(A'A)^{-1}A' = A_1(A_1'A_1)^{-1}A_1' + A_{2*}(A_{2*}'A_{2*})^{-1}A_{2*}'$.

A.8.3 Consider the $(m+n) \times (m+n)$ matrix

$$C = \begin{bmatrix} a_1 I_m & a_2\iota_m\iota_n' \\ a_2\iota_n\iota_m' & a_3 I_n \end{bmatrix}, \tag{A.8.7}$$

where $a_3 \neq 0$. Show C^{-1} exists if $a_1 \neq 0$ and $a_1 \neq mna_2^2/a_3$. Furthermore,

$$C^{-1} = \begin{bmatrix} a_1^{-1}I_m + b_1\iota_m\iota_m' & b_2\iota_m\iota_n' \\ b_2\iota_n\iota_m' & a_3^{-1}I_n + b_3\iota_n\iota_n' \end{bmatrix}, \tag{A.8.8}$$

where

$$b_1 = -\frac{na_2^2}{a_1(mna_2^2 - a_3a_1)}, \tag{A.8.9}$$

$$b_2 = -\frac{a_2}{mna_2^2 - a_3a_1}, \tag{A.8.10}$$

$$b_3 = -\frac{ma_2^2}{a_3(mna_2^2 - a_3a_1)}. \tag{A.8.11}$$

A.8.4 Let A be a $K \times K$ positive definite matrix and let C be a $K \times N$ matrix with $\text{rank}(C) = N$. Show that $C'AC$ is positive definite.

A.8.5 Let A be a positive definite matrix of order K. Let B be a diagonal matrix of order K

with diagonal elements equal to those on the main diagonal of A. Suppose $A \neq B$. Show: $|A| < |B|$ (see Carlstein et al. 1985). Hint: use mathematical induction.

A.8.6 Consider the spectral decomposition in Theorem A.7.2(c) of a p.d. matrix: $A = X\Lambda X'$. Define $C = X\Lambda^{1/2}X'$. Show: $A = C^2$. (Unlike $B = \Lambda^{1/2}X'$ in Remark A.7.2, C is symmetric.)

A.8.7 Suppose A and B are symmetric and A is p.d.. Show that there exists an orthogonal matrix C such that $C'AC = I$ and $C'BC$ is diagonal.

A.8.8 Let A be a p.d. matrix of order N. Show that the lower triangular matrix $T = [t_{ij}]$ of the Cholesky decomposition (see Golub 1969 or Quandt 1983, pp. 704–705) $A = TT'$ (Theorem A.8.6) is given by:

$$t_{11} = \sqrt{a_{11}}, \tag{A.8.12}$$

$$t_{j1} = \frac{a_{ji}}{t_{11}} \qquad (j = 1, 2, \ldots, N), \tag{A.8.13}$$

$$t_{ii} = \sqrt{a_{ii} - \sum_{k=1}^{i-1} t_{iK}^2} \qquad (i > 1), \tag{A.8.14}$$

$$t_{ji} = \frac{a_{ji} - \sum_{k=1}^{i-1} t_{ik}t_{jk}}{t_{ii}} \qquad (j > i), \tag{A.8.15}$$

$$t_{ji} = 0 \qquad (i > j). \tag{A.8.16}$$

A.8.9 Let A be an arbitrary $T \times K$ matrix. Then the *singular value decomposition* of A (e.g., see Golub 1969 and Magnus and Neudecker 1988, p. 18) is $A = XYZ'$, where the columns of X and Z are orthonormal eigenvectors of AA' and $A'A$, respectively, and Y is diagonal and contains the positive square roots of the eigenvalues of $A'A$ and AA'. If $\text{rank}(A) = r < K$, then X, Y and Z' can be chosen to be $T \times r$, $r \times r$ and $r \times K$, respectively. Show that the generalized inverse of A is given by $A^+ = ZY^+X'$, where Y^+ is the same as Y but with its diagonal elements equal to the reciprocals of the nonzero diagonal elements of Y (Quandt 1983, p. 706).

Appendix B: Matrix Algebra Review II

This appendix is a concise review of more advanced topics in matrix algebra than contained in Appendix A. The format is the same as in Appendix A. Appeal to the results of this appendix are made only infrequently in the text. Their mastery, however, will be important in subsequent studies of econometrics. A good reference sources for proofs and extensions of the material in this section are Graham (1981) and Magnus and Neudecker (1988).

B.1 Kronecker Products

A matrix operation that often arises in multivariate statistics is given in the following definition.

Definition B.1.1 Let $A = [a_{nk}]$ be a $N \times K$ matrix and let B be a $M \times J$ matrix. Then the *Kronecker product* of A and B, denoted $A \otimes B$, is the $NM \times KJ$ matrix

$$A \otimes B = \begin{bmatrix} a_{11}B & a_{12}B & \cdots & a_{1K}B \\ a_{21}B & a_{22}B & \cdots & a_{2K}B \\ \vdots & \vdots & & \vdots \\ a_{N1}B & a_{N2}B & \cdots & a_{NK}B \end{bmatrix}. \tag{B.1.1}$$

Example B.1.1 Suppose $N = 2$, $K = 3$, $M = J = 2$ and $B = I_2$. Then

$$A \otimes B = \begin{bmatrix} a_{11} & 0 & a_{12} & 0 & a_{13} & 0 \\ 0 & a_{11} & 0 & a_{12} & 0 & a_{13} \\ a_{21} & 0 & a_{22} & 0 & a_{33} & 0 \\ 0 & a_{21} & 0 & a_{22} & 0 & a_{23} \end{bmatrix}.$$

Properties of Kronecker products in relationship to other matrix operations are given in the following theorem.

Theorem B.1.1

(a) $(A_1 \otimes B_1)(A_2 \otimes B_2)\cdots(A_K \otimes B_K) = (A_1 A_2 \cdots A_K) \otimes (B_1 B_2 \cdots B_K)$ provided all products are conformable.

(b) $(A \otimes B)^{-1} = A^{-1} \otimes B^{-1}$ provided both A and B are square and nonsingular.

(c) $(A \otimes B)' = A' \otimes B'$.

(d) $A \otimes (B + C) = (A \otimes B) + (A \otimes C)$.

(e) $(B + C) \otimes A = B \otimes A + C \otimes A$.

(f) $A \otimes (B \otimes C) = (A \otimes B) \otimes C$.

(g) $|A \otimes B| = |A|^N \cdot |B|^K$, where A is $N \times N$ and B is $K \times K$.

(h) $\text{tr}(A \otimes B) = (\text{tr}\, A)(\text{tr}\, B)$.

(i) $\text{rank}\,(A \otimes B) = (\text{rank}\, A)(\text{rank}\, B)$.

(j) Suppose A is $K \times K$ and B is $N \times N$. Let $\lambda_1, \ldots, \lambda_K$ and $\mu_1, \ldots, \mu_n$ be the characteristic roots of the matrices A and B, and let $x_1, x_2, \ldots, x_K$ and $y_1, y_2, \ldots, y_N$ be the corresponding characteristic vectors. Then the characteristic roots of $A \otimes B$ are of the form $\lambda_i \cdot \mu_j$ with characteristic vectors of the form $x_i \otimes y_j$.

(k) $\alpha A \otimes \beta b = \alpha\beta(A \otimes B)$, where α and β are scalars.

(l) $0 \otimes A = A \otimes 0 = 0 \otimes 0$

(m) $(A \otimes B)^+ = A^+ \otimes B^+$

Exercises

B.1.1 Suppose $Y \sim N_K(0_K, I_K)$. Show: $\text{Cov}(Y, Y \otimes Y) = 0$.

B.2 Vectorization of Matrices

Rearranging matrices into vectors is often a convenient operation, and the following definition provides standard notation.

Definition B.2.1 Let A be a $N \times K$ matrix with columns a_k $(k = 1, 2, \ldots, K)$. Then vec(A) is defined to be the $NK \times 1$ vector formed by stacking the columns of A, that is, $\text{vec}(A) = [a_1', a_2', \ldots, a_K']'$.

Rules for vectorization of products and sums of matrices are given in the following theorem.

Theorem B.2.1 Let A be $N \times M$, B be $M \times J$, C be $J \times K$, and D be $J \times K$.

(a) $\text{vec}(AB) = (B' \otimes I_N)\,\text{vec}(A) = (I_J \otimes A)\,\text{vec}(B)$,

(b) $\text{vec}(ABC) = (I_K \otimes AB)\,\text{vec}(C) = (C' \otimes A)\,\text{vec}(B) = (C'B' \otimes I_M)\,\text{vec}(A)$,

(c) $\text{vec}(A + B) = \text{vec}(A) + \text{vec}(B)$,

(d) $\text{vec}[(A + B)(C + D)] = [(I \otimes A) + (I \otimes B)][\text{vec}(C) + \text{vec}(D)] = [C' \otimes I) + (D' \otimes I)][\text{vec}(A) + \text{vec}(B)]$.

The vec$(\cdot)$ notation and Kronecker product notation have many uses in economics. For example, let Y be a $M \times N$ matrix, B be a $M \times J$ matrix, X be a $J \times K$ matrix and A be a $N \times K$ matrix. Then the matrix equation

$$Y = BXA' \tag{B.2.1}$$

can be equivalently written as in standard form as (using Theorem B.2.1b)

$$\text{vec}(Y) = (A \otimes B)\,\text{vec}(X) \tag{B.2.2}$$

Kronecker product and vec(·) notation is also useful in matrix differentiation as will be seen in Section B.3.4

The interaction between the vec(·) and the tr(·) operators are given in the next theorem.

Theorem B.2.2 Let A be $N \times M$, B be $M \times J$, and C be $J \times N$.

(a) $\text{tr}(AB) = [\text{vec}(A')]'\,\text{vec}(B)$
$= [\text{vec}(B')]'\,\text{vec}(A).$

(b) $\text{tr}(ABC) = [\text{vec}(A')]'(C' \otimes I_M)\,\text{vec}(B)$
$= [\text{vec}(A')]'(I_N \otimes B)\,\text{vec}(C)$
$= [\text{vec}(B')]'(I_M \otimes C)\,\text{vec}(A)$
$= [\text{vec}(B')]'(A' \otimes I_J)\,\text{vec}(C)$
$= [\text{vec}(C')]'(B' \otimes I_N)\,\text{vec}(A)$
$= [\text{vec}(C')]'(I_J \otimes A)\,\text{vec}(B).$

Clearly, the vectors vec(A) and vec(A') contain the same elements but in different order. In order to be able to go back and forth between vec(A) and vec(A'), the following matrix is introduced.

Definition B.2.2 Let A be $N \times J$. The *commutation matrix*, denoted K_{NJ} is the unique $NJ \times NJ$ matrix consisting of 0's and 1's such that

$$K_{NJ}\,\text{vec}(A) = \text{vec}(A'). \tag{B.2.3}$$

If $N = K$, then K_{NN} is often denoted simply as K_N.

Some elementary properties of the commutation matrix are given in the following theorem.

Theorem B.2.3 Commutation matrices satisfy the following properties:

(a) K_{NJ} is a orthogonal matrix, that is, $(K_{NJ})^{-1} = K'_{NJ}$.

(b) $K_{JN} = (K_{NJ})^{-1} = K'_{NJ}$.

(c) $K_{N1} = K_{1N} = I_N$.

One key property of the commutation matrix is that it enables us to "commute" the two matrices in a Kronecker product. The next theorem demonstrates this fact.

Theorem B.2.4 Let A be $N \times M$, B be $J \times q$, and b be $J \times 1$.

(a) $K_{JN}(A \otimes B) = (B \otimes A)K_{qM}$.

(b) $K_{JN}(A \otimes B)K_{Mq} = (B \otimes A)$.

(c) $K_{JN}(A \otimes b) = (b \otimes A)$.

(d) $K_{NJ}(b \otimes A) = A \otimes b$.

Another key property of the commutation matrix is that it enables transforming the "vec" of a Kronecker product into the Kronecker product of "vecs." This proves important in the differentiation of Kronecker products.

Theorem B.2.5 Let A be $N \times J$ and B be $p \times q$. Then

$$\text{vec}(A \otimes B) = (I_M \otimes K_{qN} \otimes I_J)[\text{vec}(A) \otimes \text{vec}(B)]. \tag{B.2.4}$$

When A is symmetric, vec(A) contains numerous redundant elements. The following matrix eliminates redundant elements when vectorizing a symmetric matrix.

Definition B.2.3 Let A be $N \times N$. vech(A) is the $\frac{1}{2}N(N+1)$ vector obtained from vec(A) by eliminating all supradiagonal elements of A.

Example B.2.1 Suppose $N = 3$ and $A = [a_{ij}]$. Then

$\text{vec}(A) = [a_{11}, a_{21}, a_{31}, a_{12}, a_{22}, a_{23}, a_{31}, a_{32}, a_{33}]'$,

$\text{vech}(A) = [a_{11}, a_{21}, a_{31}, a_{22}, a_{23}, a_{33}]'$.

Because the elements of vec(A) are those of vech(A) with some repetitions, vec(A) is simply a linear transformation of vec(A). The matrix that performs this transformation is now defined.

Definition B.2.4 Let A be a symmetric matrix of order N. The *duplication matrix*, denoted D_N, is the $N^2 \times [\frac{1}{2}N(N+1)]$ matrix such that

$$D_N \,\text{vech}(A) = \text{vec}(A). \tag{B.2.5}$$

Some elementary properties of the duplication matrix are given in the following theorem.

Theorem B.2.6 Let A be a square matrix of order N, and let b be $N \times 1$. Then the duplication matrix D_N has the following properties.

(a) D_N has full column rank, that is, $\text{rank}(D_N) = \frac{1}{2}N(N+1)$.

(b) $D^+ = (D_N' D_N)^{-1} D_N$.

(c) $\text{vech}(A) = D_N^+ \,\text{vec}(A)$.

(d) $K_N D_N = D_N$.

(e) $D_N D_N^+ = \frac{1}{2}(I_{N^2} + K_N)$.

(f) $D_N D_N^+ (b \otimes A) = \frac{1}{2}[b \otimes A + A \otimes b]$.

(g) If A is nonsingular, then $[D_N^+(A \otimes A)D_N]^{-1} = D_N^+(A^{-1} \otimes A^{-1})D_N$.

(h) If A is nonsingular, then $[D_N'(A \otimes A)D_N]^{-1} = D_N^+(A^{-1} \otimes A^{-1})D_N^{+\prime}$.

(i) $D_N' \operatorname{vec}(A) = \operatorname{vech}[A + A' - \operatorname{diag}(A)]$.

(j) $|D_N^+(A \otimes A)D_N^+| = 2^{-1/2N(N-1)}|A|^{N+1}$.

B.3 Matrix Differentiation

Various notations and conventions exist for matrix differentiation. This text adopts conventions largely consistent with Magnus and Neudecker (1988).

In this section all derivatives are assumed to exist and be continuous. Let $g(x)$ be a scalar function of the $K \times 1$ vector x. Define:

$$\frac{\partial g(x)}{\partial x} \equiv \begin{bmatrix} \frac{\partial g(x)}{\partial x_1} \\ \frac{\partial g(x)}{\partial x_2} \\ \vdots \\ \frac{\partial g(x)}{\partial x_K} \end{bmatrix}, \tag{B.3.1}$$

$$\frac{\partial g(x)}{\partial x'} \equiv \left[\frac{\partial g(x)}{\partial x_1}, \frac{\partial g(x)}{\partial x_2}, \ldots, \frac{\partial g(x)}{\partial x_K}\right], \tag{B.3.2}$$

$$\frac{\partial^2 g(x)}{\partial x\,\partial x'} \equiv \begin{bmatrix} \frac{\partial^2 g(x)}{\partial x_1^2} & \frac{\partial^2 g(x)}{\partial x_1\,\partial x_2} & \cdots & \frac{\partial^2 g(x)}{\partial x_1\,\partial x_K} \\ \frac{\partial^2 g(x)}{\partial x_2\,\partial x_1} & \frac{\partial^2 g(x)}{\partial x_2^2} & \cdots & \frac{\partial^2 g(x)}{\partial x_2\partial x_K} \\ \vdots & \vdots & & \vdots \\ \frac{\partial^2 g(x)}{\partial x_K\,\partial x_1} & \frac{\partial^2 g(x)}{\partial x_K\,\partial x_2} & \cdots & \frac{\partial^2 g(x)}{\partial x_K^2} \end{bmatrix}. \tag{B.3.3}$$

Let $f(A)$ be a scalar function of the $N \times K$ matrix A. Define

$$\frac{\partial f(A)}{\partial A} \equiv \begin{bmatrix} \frac{\partial f(A)}{\partial a_{11}} & \frac{\partial f(A)}{\partial a_{12}} & \cdots & \frac{\partial f(A)}{\partial a_{1K}} \\ \frac{\partial f(A)}{\partial a_{21}} & \frac{\partial f(A)}{\partial a_{22}} & \cdots & \frac{\partial f(A)}{\partial a_{2K}} \\ \vdots & \vdots & & \vdots \\ \frac{\partial f(A)}{\partial a_{N1}} & \frac{\partial f(A)}{\partial a_{N2}} & \cdots & \frac{\partial f(A)}{\partial a_{NK}} \end{bmatrix}. \tag{B.3.4}$$

Finally, if $y(x) = [y_1(x), y_2(x), \ldots, y_N(x)]'$ is a $N \times 1$ vector function of the

$K \times 1$ vector x, then define

$$\frac{\partial y}{\partial x'} = \begin{bmatrix} \frac{\partial y_1}{\partial x_1} & \frac{\partial y_1}{\partial x_2} & \cdots & \frac{\partial y_1}{\partial x_K} \\ \frac{\partial y_2}{\partial x_1} & \frac{\partial y_2}{\partial x_2} & \cdots & \frac{\partial y_2}{\partial x_K} \\ \vdots & \vdots & & \vdots \\ \frac{\partial y_N}{\partial x_1} & \frac{\partial y_N}{\partial x_2} & \cdots & \frac{\partial y_N}{\partial x_K} \end{bmatrix}, \tag{B.3.5}$$

and

$$\frac{\partial y'}{\partial x} \equiv \left[\frac{\partial y}{\partial x'}\right]'. \tag{B.3.6}$$

A basic ingredient to deriving rules of matrix differentiation is the following extension of the familiar chain rule from calculus.

Theorem B.3.1 (Chain Rule for Vector Differentiation) Let x be $J \times 1$ and z be $N \times 1$. Suppose $h(z)$ is $N \times 1$ and $z = g(x)$. Then the $N \times K$ matrix $\partial h[g(x)]/\partial x'$ is given by:

$$\frac{\partial h[g(x)]}{\partial x'} = \left[\frac{\partial h(z)}{\partial z'}\right]\left[\frac{\partial g(x)}{\partial x'}\right]. \tag{B.3.7}$$

Using Theorem B.3.1, the following results are straightforwardly shown.

Theorem B.3.2

(a) Suppose x is $M \times 1$, $w(x) = [w_1(x), w_2(x), \ldots, w_N(x)]'$ is $N \times 1$, $z(x) = [z_1(x), z_2(x), \ldots, z_J(x)]'$ is $J \times 1$, and A is $N \times J$ and does not depend on x. Then:

$$\frac{\partial[w(x)'Az(x)]}{\partial x'} = z(x)'A'\left[\frac{\partial w(x)}{\partial x'}\right] + w(x)'A\left[\frac{\partial z(x)}{\partial x'}\right]. \tag{B.3.8}$$

(b) Suppose x is $M \times 1$, $A(x)$ is $N \times J$, and $B(x)$ is $J \times q$. Then

$$\frac{\partial \operatorname{vec}(AB)}{\partial x'} = (I_q \otimes A)\left[\frac{\partial \operatorname{vec}(B)}{\partial x'}\right] + (B' \otimes I_N)\left[\frac{\partial \operatorname{vec}(A)}{\partial x'}\right]. \tag{B.3.9}$$

(c) Suppose x is $M \times 1$, $A(x)$ is $N \times J$, and $B(x)$ is $r \times q$. Then

$$\frac{\partial[\operatorname{vec}(A \otimes B)]}{\partial x'} = (I_J \otimes G)\left[\frac{\partial \operatorname{vec}(A)}{\partial x'}\right] + (H \otimes I_r)\left[\frac{\partial \operatorname{vec}(B)}{\partial x'}\right]. \tag{B.3.10}$$

Commonly encountered applications of these two theorems are provided in the following theorem.

Theorem B.3.3 Let x and y be column vectors of length J and N, respectively.

(a) If $y = Ax$ where A is a $N \times J$ matrix not depending on x, then

$$\frac{\partial y}{\partial x} = A. \tag{B.3.11}$$

(b) If $y = x'Ax$ and A is a $N \times N$ matrix not depending on x, then

$$\frac{\partial y}{\partial x} = (A + A')x. \tag{B.3.12}$$

If A is symmetric, then

$$\frac{\partial y}{\partial x} = 2Ax. \tag{B.3.13}$$

(c) If $Q = x'Ax$ and A is a $N \times N$ matrix not depending on x, then

$$\frac{\partial^2 Q}{\partial x\, \partial x'} = A + A'. \tag{B.3.14}$$

If A is symmetric, then

$$\frac{\partial^2 Q}{\partial x\, \partial x'} = 2A. \tag{B.3.15}$$

(d) If $Q = z'Az$, where A is a $N \times N$ matrix not depending on the $J \times 1$ vector x, but z is a $N \times 1$ vector depending on x, then

$$\frac{\partial Q}{\partial x} = 2\left[\frac{\partial z(x)}{\partial x}\right]' Az(x). \tag{B.3.16}$$

Furthermore, in this case

$$\frac{\partial^2 Q}{\partial x\, \partial x'} = 2\left[\frac{\partial z(x)}{\partial x}\right]' A\left[\frac{\partial z(x)}{\partial x'}\right] + 2[z(x)'A \otimes I_J]\left[\frac{\partial\, \mathrm{vec}(\partial z(x)/\partial x)}{\partial x'}\right]. \tag{B.3.17}$$

Theorem B.3.4

(a) Suppose x is $J \times 1$, $B(x)$ is $N \times M$, A is $J \times N$, C is $M \times q$, and A and C do not depend on x. Then

$$\frac{\partial\, \mathrm{vec}(ABC)}{\partial x'} = (C' \otimes A)\left[\frac{\partial\, \mathrm{vec}(B)}{\partial x'}\right]. \tag{B.3.18}$$

(b) Suppose x is $J \times 1$, $A(x)$ is $N \times M$, $D(x)$ is $J \times q$, C is $M \times q$, and C does not depend on x. Then

$$\frac{\partial\, \mathrm{vec}(ACD)}{\partial x'} = (I_q \otimes AC)\left[\frac{\partial\, \mathrm{vec}(D)}{\partial x'}\right] + (D'C' \otimes I_N)\left[\frac{\partial\, \mathrm{vec}(A)}{\partial x'}\right]. \tag{B.3.19}$$

Theorem B.3.5 Let A be a nonsingular matrix of order N with adjoint $A^{\#}$. Then:

(a) $$\frac{\partial \operatorname{vec}(A^{-1})}{\partial \operatorname{vec}(A)} = -(A^{-1})' \otimes A^{-1}. \tag{B.3.20}$$

(b) $$\frac{\partial \operatorname{tr}(A)}{\partial A} = I_N. \tag{B.3.21}$$

(c) $$\frac{\partial |A|}{\partial A} = A^{\#\prime}. \tag{B.3.22}$$

(d) $$\frac{\partial \ln|A|}{\partial A} = (A')^{-1}. \tag{B.3.23}$$

Theorem B.3.6 Suppose A is $N \times M$, B is $N \times N$, C is $M \times N$ and D is $M \times N$. Then:

(a) $$\frac{\partial \operatorname{tr}(AD)}{\partial A} = D' \tag{B.3.24}$$

(b) $$\frac{\partial \operatorname{tr}(BAC)}{\partial A} = B'C' \tag{B.3.25}$$

Theorem B.3.7 Suppose A is a symmetric matrix of order N.

$$\frac{\partial \ln|A|}{\partial A} = 2A^{-1} - |A|^{-1} \operatorname{diag}\{a_{11}, a_{22}, \ldots, a_{NN}\}. \tag{B.3.26}$$

Exercises

B.3.1 Given the $N \times N$ matrix A and the $M \times M$ matrix B, define the *Kronecker sum*, denoted $A \oplus B$, by

$$A \oplus B \equiv (A \otimes I_M) + (I_N \otimes B). \tag{B.3.27}$$

Let X be a $N \times M$ matrix, and consider the equations

$$AX + XB = C \tag{B.3.28}$$

where C is a known $N \times M$ matrix.

(a) Show that (B.3.28) can be written $(B' \oplus A)\operatorname{vec}(X) = \operatorname{vec}(C)$.

(b) Show that (B.3.28) has a unique solution iff A and $-B$ have no eigenvalues in common (Graham 1981, pp. 38–39).

B.3.2 Suppose y is $T \times 1$, Ω is $T \times T$, X is $T \times K$ and β is $K \times 1$. Define

$$S(\beta) = (y - X\beta)'\Omega(y - X\beta). \tag{B.3.29}$$

Show:

(a) $$\frac{\partial S(\beta)}{\partial \beta} = -2X'\Omega(y - X\beta). \tag{B.3.30}$$

(b) $$\frac{\partial^2 S(\beta)}{\partial \beta\, \partial \beta'} = -2X'\Omega X. \tag{B.3.31}$$

Appendix C: Computation

Computers are useless. They can only give you answers.
—Pablo Picasso

This appendix provides some helpful discussion of maximization and integration of functions. For good general discussions of numerical technique in statistics, see Quandt (1983) and Thisted (1988).

C.1 Maximization

Consider the problem of maximizing a continuous twice-differentiable function $g(\theta)$ with respect to the $K \times 1$ vector $\theta \in \Theta$. For example, $g(\theta)$ may be a likelihood or log-likelihood function in which case the point at which it is maximized is the MLE, or $g(\theta)$ may be a posterior distribution in which case the point at which it is maximized is the posterior mode. To simplify notation, the dependency of $g(\theta)$ on data or sample size is suppressed. Rather than work with likelihoods or posterior densities, it is usually preferable to work with their logarithms. Under suitable regularity conditions, the asymptotic normality of the ML estimator or a posterior distribution implies that as $T \to \infty$, T^{-1} times the log-likelihood or log-posterior will be quadratic in θ.

Given an initial value $\theta_{(n-1)}$, consider the Taylor series of $g(\theta)$ around $\theta_{(n-1)}$:

$$g(\theta) = g[\theta_{(n-1)}] + \left[\frac{\partial g[\theta_{(n-1)}]}{\partial \theta}\right][\theta - \theta_{(n-1)}] + \frac{1}{2}[\theta - \theta_{(n-1)}]'\left[\frac{\partial^2 g[\theta_{(n-1)}]}{\partial \theta \, \partial \theta'}\right][\theta - \theta_{(n-1)}] + r, \tag{C.1.1}$$

where r is the remainder. Dropping r and maximizing the quadratic approximation with respect to θ yields the "solution"

$$\theta_{(n)} = \theta_{(n-1)} - \left[\frac{\partial^2 g[\theta_{(n-1)}]}{\partial \theta \, \partial \theta'}\right]^{-1}\left[\frac{\partial g[\theta_{(n-1)}]}{\partial \theta}\right]. \tag{C.1.2}$$

If $g(\theta)$ is exactly quadratic, say $g(\theta) = \theta' A \theta + b'\theta + c$, where A is $K \times K$ negative definite matrix, b is $K \times 1$ and c is a scalar, then (C.1.2) does in fact correspond to the point at which $g(\theta)$ achieves its unique maximum. In general, however, (C.2.2) represents only a "step" in the direction of the solution. Most numerical optimization routines are spinoffs on iterative procedures like (C.2.2), with a variety of choices to replace the hessian matrix. See Judge et al. (1985, pp. 951–979), Quandt (1983) and the references cited therein for details.

Despite the widespread availability of nonlinear maximization options in standard econometric software, nonlinear optimization will always have an artistic side to it as the result of problem-specific complications like multi-modality, poorly chosen parameterizations and side-conditions (see Judge et al. 1985, pp. 969–975).

C.2 Monte Carlo Integration

Integration plays a crucial computational role in Bayesian analysis involving continuous random variables. For example, it arises in computing normalizing constants, marginalization, and expectation.

The computer has transformed what were once many hopeless integration tasks into feasible problems. The breakthroughs have resulted from the emergence of simulation techniques. Older, purely numerical methods, are playing ever smaller roles.[1] This section discusses Monte Carlo integration techniques. The next section discusses Gibbs sampling techniques.

A seminal contribution on Monte Carlo integration is Hammeraly and Handscomb (1964, Section 5.4). Kloek and van Dijk (1978) first introduced the idea of Monte Carlo integration with importance functions (explained later) into econometrics. Using Monte Carlo integration, Geweke (1986) provided a valuable pedagogical demonstration of the straightforward Bayesian analysis of regression models subject to inequality restrictions on the regression coefficients. Geweke (1989) tied together some loose asymptotic strings and describes a valuable class of importance functions. Other important and helpful sources on Monte Carlo integration are Bauwens (1984), Bauwens and Richard (1985), Geweke (1988), Oh and Berger (1991), van Dijk and Kloek (1985), van Dijk et al. (1985), and Zellner and Rossi (1984).

A wide range of quantities of interest in Bayesian analysis amount to the computation of integrals of the form

$$G \equiv E[g(\theta)|y] = \int_{\Theta} g(\theta) f(\theta|y)\, d\theta$$

$$= \frac{\int_{\Theta} g(\theta) f(\theta) \mathscr{L}(\theta; y)\, d\theta}{\int_{\Theta} f(\theta) \mathscr{L}(\theta; y)\, d\theta}, \tag{C.2.1}$$

1. For example, consider the Gauss-Hermite product rule methods discussed by Naylor and Smith (1982) and Smith et al. (1985). Such procedures are fairly attractive when the integrand of the integral of interest can be well-approximated by a polynomial multiplied by a normal density function in the variable to be integrated. These techniques work fairly well when the dimensionality is less than four, and are rarely useful when it exceeds seven.

where $\theta \in \Theta$ is K-dimensional, and $g(\theta)$ is an appropriately chosen function. For example, (i) if $K = 1$ and $g(\theta) = \theta^r$, then G is the rth posterior moment of θ around the origin. (ii) If A is a subset of Θ and $g(\theta)$ is an indicator function equaling unity when $\theta \in A$ and equaling zero when $\theta \notin A$, then $G = E[g(\theta)|y] = \text{Prob}(A|y)$. (iii) If $g(\theta) = f(y_*|y, \theta)$ for some out-of-sample vector y_*, then $G = E[f(y_*|y, \theta)] = f(y_*|y)$ (i.e. the predictive density at y_* (see Section 8.6). A sufficient condition for the existence of G is that all integrals required are defined on bounded regions and have integrands of bounded variation.

If it is possible to generate pseudo random draws (see Davidson and MacKinnon 1993, Chapter 21; Devroye 1986; and Quandt 1983, pp. 755–760) from the posterior distribution of θ, say $\theta^{(n)}$ $(n = 1, 2, \ldots, N)$, then the sample mean

$$\hat{G}_N = \frac{1}{N} \sum_{n=1}^{N} g(\theta^{(n)}) \tag{C.2.2}$$

provides an unbiased estimator of the population mean (C.2.1). Provided the strong law of large numbers is applicable, $\hat{G}_N$ converges almost surely to G as $N \to \infty$. Furthermore, if a central limit theorem can be invoked so that

$$\sqrt{N}(\hat{G}_N - G) \xrightarrow{d} N(0, \sigma^2), \tag{C.2.3}$$

then the numerical accuracy of the approximation can be evaluated. Note $\sigma^2 \equiv \text{Var}(g(\theta)|y)$ can also be estimated by Monte Carlo integration. The conditions that $f(\theta|y)$ must satisfy for these results to hold are fairly innocuous (see Sections 5.6 and 5.7). *Most importantly, the asymptotics in N (the number of draws) is under the control of the researcher, that is, the researcher can make the asymptotic theory relevant to the case at hand.*

When it is not possible to generate random draws directly from the posterior distribution, then an alternative strategy is necessary. Let $I(\theta)$ be a density that mimics the shape of $f(\theta|y)$ and for which it is possible to generate random draws. $I(\theta)$ is known as an *importance function.* Define

$$h(\theta) = \frac{f(\theta)\mathscr{L}(\theta; y)}{I(\theta)}, \qquad I(\theta) > 0. \tag{C.2.4}$$

Using (C.2.4) rewrite (C.2.1) as

$$\begin{aligned} G &= \frac{\displaystyle\int_\Theta g(\theta)\left(\frac{f(\theta)\mathscr{L}(\theta; y)}{I(\theta)}\right) I(\theta)\, d\theta}{\displaystyle\int_\Theta \left(\frac{f(\theta)\mathscr{L}(\theta; y)}{I(\theta)}\right) I(\theta)\, d\theta} \\ &= \frac{E_{I(\theta)}[g(\theta)h(\theta)]}{E_{I(\theta)}[h(\theta)]}. \end{aligned} \tag{C.2.5}$$

Using Monte Carlo integration with a simulated sample $\theta^{(n)}$ $(n = 1, 2, \ldots, N)$ from the distribution with p.d.f. $I(\theta)$ to compute both the numerator and denominator of (C.2.5) yields the approximation

$$\hat{G}_N = \frac{\hat{G}_{1N}}{\hat{G}_{2N}}, \tag{C.2.6}$$

where

$$\hat{G}_{1N} = \frac{1}{N}\sum_{n=1}^{N} g(\theta^{(n)})h(\theta^{(n)}), \tag{C.2.7}$$

$$\hat{G}_{2N} = \frac{1}{N}\sum_{n=1}^{N} h(\theta^{(n)}). \tag{C.2.8}$$

Although (C.2.6) is not an unbiased estimator of (C.2.1), it will possess desirable asymptotic properties as $N \to \infty$ under fairly mild conditions. In stating these results it proves useful to define the kernel $I^*(\theta) = d^{-1}I(\theta)$ of $I(\theta)$, where d is the integrating constant for $I(\theta)$, and define

$$w(\theta) = \frac{f(\theta)\mathscr{L}(\theta; y)}{I^*(\theta)}. \tag{C.2.9}$$

Then rewrite approximation (C.2.6) as

$$\hat{G}_N = \frac{\sum_{n=1}^{N} g(\theta^{(n)})w(\theta^{(n)})}{\sum_{n=1}^{N} w(\theta^{(n)})}. \tag{C.2.10}$$

The following two theorem of Geweke (1989) provide the asymptotics (in the number N of replications) covering Monte Carlo integration with importance sampling.

Theorem C.2.1 Suppose the following conditions hold:

i. $c \equiv \int_\Theta f(\theta)\mathscr{L}(\theta; y)\,d\theta < \infty$.

ii. $\{\theta^{(n)}\}$ $(n = 1, 2, \ldots, N)$ are i.i.d. with density $I(\theta)$.

iii. The support of $I(\theta)$ includes the "true value" θ_o.

iv. $E[g(\theta)|y]$ exists.

Then $\hat{G}_N \xrightarrow{a.s.} G$ as $N \to \infty$, where $\hat{G}_N$ is given by (C.2.10).

Proof Because $w(\theta) > 0$, $E_{I(\theta)}[g(\theta)w(\theta)] = cdG$. By Khinchine's SLLN:

$$\frac{1}{N}\sum_{n=1}^{N} g(\theta^{(n)})w(\theta^{(n)}) \xrightarrow{a.s.} cdG, \tag{C.2.11}$$

$$\frac{1}{N}\sum_{n=1}^{N} w(\theta^{(n)}) \xrightarrow{a.s.} cd. \tag{C.2.12}$$

Therefore, taking the ratio of (C.2.11) to (C.2.12), $\hat{G}_N \xrightarrow{a.s.} G$ as $N \to \infty$, where $\hat{G}_N$ is given by (C.2.6).

Theorem C.2.2 Define

$$\sigma^2 \equiv \frac{1}{cd} E([g(\theta) - G]^2 w(\theta)|y). \tag{C.2.13}$$

In addition to the four assumptions in Theorem C.2.1, also assume:

(v) $E[w(\theta)|y]$ and $E[w(\theta)\{g(\theta)\}|y]$ exist and are finite.

Then

(a) $N^{1/2}(\hat{G}_N - G) \xrightarrow{d} N(0, \sigma^2)$ as $N \to \infty$.

(b) $N\hat{\sigma}_N^2 \xrightarrow{a.s.} \sigma^2$ as $N \to \infty$, where

$$\hat{\sigma}_N^2 = \frac{\sum_{n=1}^{N} [g(\theta^{(n)}) - \hat{G}_N]^2 [w(\theta^{(n)})]^2}{\left[\sum_{n=1}^{N} w(\theta^{(n)})\right]^2}. \tag{C.2.14}$$

Proof Geweke (1989, p. 1321, Theorem 2).

Note that a sufficient condition for (iv) is that $g(\theta)$ is bounded. Either of the following is sufficient for (v): (1) $w(\theta) < w_* < \infty$ for all $\theta \in \Theta$, some $w_* \in \Re$, and $\text{Var}[g(\theta)|y] < \infty$, and (2) Θ is compact and $I(\theta) > \varepsilon > 0$ for all $\theta \in \Theta$.

The expression for σ^2 in (C.2.13) indicates that the numerical standard error is adversely affected by large $\text{Var}[g(\theta)|y]$ and large relative values of the weight function $w(\theta)$. Although the former is inherent in the problem at hand, the latter can be controlled by the choice of an importance function. As a benchmark for comparing the adequacy of an importance function, note that if the importance function was proportional to the posterior density itself, then $\sigma^2 = \text{Var}[g(\theta)|y]$. In this case the number of replications controls the numerical standard error relative to the posterior standard deviation $\sigma/N^{1/2}$ of the function of interest (e.g., $N = 10{,}000$ implies the numerical standard error will be one percent of the posterior standard deviation of the function of interest). Geweke (1989, p. 1322) notes that when it is not possible to construct an importance function proportional to the posterior density, it is still possible to see what the numerical variance would have been by computing

$$\text{RNE} \equiv \frac{\text{Var}[g(\theta)|y]}{d^{-1}E([g(\theta) - \hat{G}_N]^2 w(\theta))} = \frac{\text{Var}[g(\theta|y)]}{\sigma^2}. \tag{C.2.15}$$

The *relative numerical efficiency* (RNE) as defined by (C.2.15) is the ratio of the number of replications required to achieve any specified numerical standard error using the importance density $I(\theta)$, to the number required using the posterior density as the importance density. The numerical standard error for $\hat{G}_N$ is the fraction $(\text{RNE} \cdot N)^{-1/2}$ of the posterior standard deviation.

Low values of RNE motivate further looking into the choice of an importance function. In general, it is desired to pick an importance function that mimics the shape of the posterior density, but with slightly larger tails than the posterior density. This choice is not always an easy task, but Geweke (1989, pp. 1323–1326) has some valuable suggestions. Kass and Raferty (1993) have a good discussion of Monte Carlo integration methods applied to the computation of Bayes factors.

An important advantage of Monte Carlo integration over some other methods is that a large number of posterior moments can be estimated from a single generation of pseudo random variables. Also note that unlike using an asymptotic (in T, not N) approximation such as Laplace's method, an estimate of the numerical accuracy of the result is obtained fairly easily. The resulting error is $O(N^{-1/2})$, where N is the number of Monte Carlo replications. Priors are no longer bound by computational considerations like natural conjugacy.

Exercises

C.2.1 Suppose it is possible to easily generate a random sample from a distribution with p.d.f. $g(\theta)$, $\theta \in \Theta$, but that what is required is a sample from a density $h(\theta)$ absolutely continuous with respect to $g(\theta)$. Let $f(\theta)$ be the kernel of $h(\theta)$, where

$$h(\theta) = \frac{f(\theta)}{\int_{\theta \in \Theta} f(\theta)\, d\theta}, \tag{C.2.16}$$

and suppose there exists a constant c such that $f(\theta)/g(\theta) \leq c$ for all $\theta \in \Theta$. Consider the following *rejection method* for generating a sample from $h(\theta)$:

(i) Generate from $g(\theta)$.

(ii) Generate Z from $U(0, 1)$.

(iii) If $Z \leq f(\theta)/[cg(\theta)]$, then accept θ. Otherwise repeat steps (i)–(iii).

Show (see Ripley 1986, p. 60):

(a) Any accepted θ is a random variate from $h(\theta)$.

(b) If T observations are generated in (i), then the expected number N of accepted observations in the sample from $h(\theta)$ is

$$N = \frac{T}{C}\int_{-\infty}^{\infty} f(\theta)\, d\theta. \tag{C.2.17}$$

C.2.2 Consider Exercise C.2.1 but suppose c is unavailable. Given θ_t $(t = 1, 2, \ldots, T)$ be a sample from the distribution with p.d.f. $g(\theta)$. Define $w_t = f(\theta_t)/g(\theta_t)$ and

$$q_t = \frac{w_t}{\sum_{i=1}^{T} w_i} \qquad (t = 1, 2, \ldots, T). \tag{C.2.18}$$

Draw θ^* from the discrete distribution over θ_t $(t = 1, 2, \ldots, T)$ placing mass q_t on θ_t. Show that θ^* converges in distribution to the distribution with density $g(\theta)$ as $T \times \infty$ (Smith and Gelfand 1992).

C.2.3 Use Exercise 6.4.4 to derive and approximation to the variance of (C.2.10).

C.3 Gibbs Sampling

It is interesting to see that the Gibbs sampler is turning so many statisticians into Bayesians. A computer algorithm seems to be achieving what philosophical arguments could not. Maybe it is a healthy sign of our profession that we are more interested in tools that work rather than in philosophy.
—Taylor and Segal (1992, p. 628)

The Gibbs sampler is a technique or generating random variables from a (marginal) distribution indirectly, without having to calculate the density. By simulating a large enough sample, moments and other characteristics of the marginal distribution can also be computed. The observation generated by the Gibbs sampler are not independent, but rather they form a Markov chain. Although its ancestry can be traced back to Metropolis et al. (1953), Hastings (1970), and Peskun (1973), it received substantial attention from the study of image-processing by Geman and Geman (1984). Its potential usefulness in statistics was not fully appreciated, however, until introduced by Gelfand and Smith (1990). Although it has flourished recently in Bayesian circles, it also has applications in classical statistics when likelihood functions are difficult to calculate (see Tanner 1991). *Gibbs sampling proves especially attractive in situations in which it is not possible to generate samples from the joint or marginal distributions of interest, but in which it is easy to generate samples from all possible conditional distributions.*

The Gibbs sampling algorithm proceeds as follows. Let X_k $(k = 1, 2, \ldots, K)$ be random variables so that there joint density is characterized by all the conditional densities and for which it is desired to draw inferences regarding the marginal distributions. Given arbitrary starting values $X^{(0)} = [X_1^{(0)}, X_2^{(0)}, \ldots, X_K^{(0)}]'$, draw $X_1^{(1)}$ from the conditional distribution with p.f. $f(x_1|x_2^{(0)}, x_3^{(0)}, \ldots, x_K^{(0)})$, draw $X_2^{(1)}$ from the distribution with p.f. $f(x_2|x_1^{(1)}, x_3^{(0)}, \ldots, x_K^{(0)})$, $\ldots$, and draw $X_K^{(1)}$ from the distribution with p.f. $f(x_K|x_1^{(1)}, x_2^{(1)}, \ldots, x_{K-1}^{(1)})$. After N such iterations we would arrive at $X^{(N)} = [x_1^{(N)}, x_2^{(N)}, \ldots, x_K^{(N)}]'$. Geman and Geman (1984) show under mild conditions that $X^{(N)}$ converges in distribution as $N \to \infty$ to a random variable with the desired joint distribution. Repeating this process R times produces the i.i.d. $K \times 1$ vectors $X_r^{(N)}$ $(r = 1, 2, \ldots, R)$. The marginal density of

X_k can be estimated by:

$$\hat{f}(x_k) = \frac{1}{R} \sum_{r=1}^{R} f(x_{k-1}^{(r)} | x_{r1}^{(N)}, \ldots, x_{r,k-1}^{(N)}, \ldots, x_{r,k+1}^{(N)}, \ldots, x_{rK}^{(N)}). \qquad \text{(C.3.1)}$$

The dependency of the observations arising from the Gibbs sampler make it more difficult to detect convergence and to obtain numerical standard errors. Detecting the convergence of the Gibbs sampler remains a current research issue. See Besag and Green (1993), Gelfand and Smith (1990), Gelfand et al. (1990), Gelman and Rubin (1992), Geweke (1992b), Gilks (1992), Raferty and Lewis (1992), G. O. Roberts (1992), Smith and Roberts (1993), Tanner (1991), Tierney (1991a, 1991b), and Zellner and Min (1992b). Related to the Gibbs sampler are the data-augmentation techniques of Tanner and Wong (1987) and Tanner (1991), and the importance sampling algorithm suggested by Rubin (1987, 1988). An excellent introduction to the Gibbs sampler is Casella and George (1992).

Exercises

C.3.1 Suppose the random variables X and Y have the following joint distribution:

$$f(x, y|\alpha, \delta) = \binom{n}{x} y^{x+\alpha-1}(1-y)^{n-x+\delta-1} \qquad (x = 0, 1, \ldots, n; 0 \le y \le 1),$$

and we are interested in calculation some characteristic of the marginal distribution of X (see Casella and George 1992). Note that

$$X|Y = y \sim B(n, y), \qquad \text{(C.3.2)}$$

$$Y|X = x \sim \beta(x + \alpha, n - x + \delta) \qquad \text{(C.3.3)}$$

Given a starting value y_0, x_0 can be generated from (C.3.2). Then x_0 can be used in (C.3.3) to generate y_1, which can in turn be substituted into (C.3.2) to generate x_1. This process may be repeated a large number of times yielding the sample (x_t, y_t) $(t = 1, 2, \ldots, T)$. Note that because the marginal distribution in this case is known to be the beta-binomial distribution (see Exercise 3.3.13), it is possible to check the accuracy of results.

(a) Generate a Gibbs sample of size $N = 10$ following the above procedure.

(b) The $E(X)$ can be approximated by $\overline{X}$, or if $E(X|Y = y_t)$ is available, by

$$\tilde{X} = \frac{1}{T} \sum_{t=1}^{T} E(X|y_t).$$

Demonstrate this calculation with the sample generated in (a).

C.3.2 Let X and Y be two random variables with conditional densities $f_{y|x}(y|x)$ and $f_{x|y}(x|y)$. Show that the marginal density $f_x(x)$ satisfies the fixed point integral equation:

$$f_x(x) = \int_{-\infty}^{\infty} \left[\int_{-\infty}^{\infty} f_{x|y}(x|y) f_{y|x}(y|t)\, dy\right] f_x(t)\, dt.$$

Appendix D: Statistical Tables

Table D.1
Cumulative normal distribution

$$\Phi(y) = \int_{-\infty}^{y} \frac{1}{\sqrt{2\pi}} \exp\left[-\frac{1}{2}t^2\right] dt$$

y	.00	.01	.02	.03	.04	.05	.06	.07	.08	.09
.0	.5000	.5040	.5080	.5120	.5160	.5199	.5239	.5279	.5319	.5359
.1	.5398	.5438	.5478	.5517	.5557	.5596	.5636	.5675	.5714	.5753
.2	.5793	.5832	.5871	.5910	.5948	.5987	.6026	.6064	.6103	.6141
.3	.6179	.6217	.6255	.6293	.6331	.6368	.6406	.6443	.6480	.6517
.4	.6554	.6591	.6628	.6664	.6700	.6736	.6772	.6808	.6884	.6879
.5	.6915	.6950	.6985	.7019	.7054	.7088	.7123	.7157	.7190	.7224
.6	.7257	.7291	.7324	.7357	.7389	.7422	.7454	.7486	.7517	.7549
.7	.7580	.7611	.7642	.7673	.7704	.7734	.7764	.7794	.7823	.7852
.8	.7881	.7910	.7939	.7967	.7995	.8023	.8051	.8078	.8106	.8133
.9	.8159	.8186	.8212	.8238	.8264	.8289	.8315	.8340	.8365	.8389
1.0	.8413	.8438	.8461	.8485	.8508	.8531	.8554	.8577	.8599	.8621
1.1	.8643	.8665	.8686	.8708	.8729	.8749	.8770	.8790	.8810	.8830
1.2	.8849	.8869	.8888	.8907	.8925	.8944	.8962	.8980	.8997	.9015
1.3	.9032	.9049	.9066	.9082	.9099	.9115	.9131	.9147	.9162	.9177
1.4	.9192	.9207	.9222	.9236	.9251	.9265	.9279	.9292	.9306	.9319
1.5	.9332	.9345	.9357	.9370	.9382	.9394	.9406	.9418	.9429	.9441
1.6	.9452	.9463	.9474	.9484	.9495	.9505	.9515	.9525	.9535	.9545
1.7	.9554	.9564	.9573	.9582	.9591	.9599	.9608	.9616	.9625	.9633
1.8	.9641	.9649	.9656	.9664	.9671	.9678	.9686	.9693	.9699	.9706
1.9	.9713	.9719	.9726	.9732	.9738	.9744	.9750	.9756	.9761	.9767
2.0	.9772	.9778	.9783	.9788	.9793	.9798	.9803	.9808	.9812	.9817
2.1	.9821	.9826	.9830	.9834	.9838	.9842	.9846	.9850	.9854	.9857
2.2	.9861	.9864	.9868	.9871	.9875	.9878	.9881	.9884	.9887	.9890
2.3	.9893	.9896	.9898	.9901	.9904	.9906	.9909	.9911	.9913	.9916
2.4	.9918	.9920	.9922	.9922	.9927	.9929	.9931	.9932	.9934	.9936
2.5	.9938	.9940	.9941	.9943	.9945	.9946	.9948	.9949	.9951	.9952
2.6	.9953	.9955	.9956	.9957	.9959	.9960	.9961	.9962	.9963	.9964
2.7	.9965	.9966	.9967	.9968	.9969	.9970	.9971	.9972	.9973	.9974
2.8	.9974	.9975	.9976	.9977	.9977	.9978	.9979	.9979	.9980	.9981
2.9	.9981	.9982	.9982	.9983	.9984	.9984	.9985	.9985	.9986	.9986
3.0	.9987	.9987	.9987	.9988	.9988	.9989	.9989	.9989	.9990	.9990
3.1	.9990	.9991	.9991	.9991	.9992	.9992	.9992	.9992	.9993	.9993
3.2	.9993	.9993	.9994	.9994	.9994	.9994	.9994	.9995	.9995	.9995
3.3	.9995	.9995	.9995	.9996	.9996	.9996	.9996	.9996	.9996	.9997
3.4	.9997	.9997	.9997	.9997	.9997	.9997	.9997	.9997	.9997	.9998

y	1.282	1.645	1.960	2.326	2.576	3.090	3.291	3.891	4.417
$\Phi(y)$	.90	.95	.975	.99	.995	.999	.9995	.99995	.99999
$2[1 - \Phi(y)]$	.20	.10	.05	.02	.01	.002	.001	.0001	.00001

Table D.2
Cumulative chi-squared distribution

$$F_\chi(y|v) = \int_0^y \frac{t^{(v-2)/2}\exp(-t/2)}{2^{v/2}\Gamma(v/2)}\,dt$$

	$F_\chi(y\|v)$												
v	.005	.010	.025	.050	.100	.250	.500	.750	.900	.950	.975	.990	.995
1	$.0^4393$	$.0^4157$	$.0^3982$	$.0^2393$	.0158	.102	.455	1.32	2.71	3.84	5.02	6.63	7.88
2	.0100	.0201	.0506	.103	.211	.575	1.39	2.77	4.61	5.99	7.38	9.21	10.6
3	.0717	.115	.216	.352	.584	1.21	2.37	4.11	6.25	7.81	9.35	11.3	12.8
4	.207	.297	.484	.711	1.06	1.92	3.36	5.39	7.78	9.49	11.1	13.3	14.9
5	.412	.554	.831	1.15	1.61	2.67	4.35	6.63	9.24	11.1	12.8	15.1	16.1
6	.676	.872	1.24	1.64	2.20	3.45	5.35	7.84	10.6	12.6	14.4	16.8	18.5
7	.989	1.24	1.69	2.17	2.83	4.25	6.35	9.04	12.0	14.1	16.0	18.5	20.3
8	1.34	1.65	2.18	2.73	3.49	5.07	7.34	10.2	13.4	15.5	17.5	20.1	22.0
9	1.73	2.09	2.70	3.33	4.17	5.90	8.34	11.4	14.7	16.9	19.0	21.7	23.6
10	2.16	2.56	3.25	3.94	4.87	6.74	9.34	12.5	16.0	18.3	20.5	23.2	25.2
11	2.60	3.05	3.82	4.57	5.58	7.58	10.3	13.7	17.3	19.7	21.9	24.7	26.8
12	3.07	3.57	4.40	5.23	6.30	8.44	11.3	14.8	18.5	21.0	23.3	26.2	28.3
13	3.57	4.11	5.01	5.89	7.04	9.30	12.3	16.0	19.8	22.4	24.7	27.7	29.8
14	4.07	4.66	5.63	6.57	7.79	10.2	13.3	17.1	21.1	23.7	26.1	29.1	31.3
15	4.60	5.23	6.26	7.26	8.55	11.0	14.3	18.2	22.3	25.0	27.5	30.6	32.8
16	5.14	5.81	6.91	7.96	9.31	11.9	15.3	19.4	23.5	26.3	28.8	32.0	34.3
17	5.70	6.41	7.56	8.67	10.1	12.8	16.3	20.5	24.8	27.6	30.2	33.4	35.7
18	6.26	7.01	8.23	9.39	10.9	13.7	17.3	21.6	26.0	28.9	31.5	34.8	37.2
19	6.84	7.63	8.91	10.1	11.7	14.6	18.3	22.7	27.2	30.1	32.9	36.2	38.6
20	7.43	8.26	9.59	10.9	12.4	15.5	19.3	23.8	28.4	31.4	34.2	37.6	40.0
21	8.03	8.90	10.3	11.6	13.2	16.3	20.3	24.9	29.6	32.7	35.5	38.9	41.4
22	8.64	9.54	11.0	12.3	14.0	17.2	21.3	26.0	30.8	33.9	36.8	40.3	42.8
23	9.26	10.2	11.7	13.1	14.8	18.1	22.3	27.1	32.0	35.2	38.1	41.6	44.2
24	9.89	10.9	12.4	13.8	15.7	19.0	23.3	28.2	33.2	36.4	39.4	43.0	45.6
25	10.5	11.5	13.1	14.6	16.5	19.9	24.3	29.3	34.4	37.7	40.6	44.3	46.9
26	11.2	12.2	13.8	15.4	17.3	20.8	25.3	30.4	35.6	38.9	41.9	45.6	48.3
27	11.8	12.9	14.6	16.2	18.1	21.7	26.3	31.5	36.7	40.1	43.2	47.0	49.6
28	12.5	13.6	15.3	16.9	18.9	22.7	27.3	32.6	37.9	41.3	44.5	48.3	51.0
29	13.1	14.3	16.0	17.7	19.8	23.6	28.3	33.7	39.1	42.6	45.7	49.6	52.3
30	13.8	15.0	16.8	18.5	20.6	24.5	29.3	34.8	40.3	43.8	47.0	50.9	53.7

Table D.3
Cumulative F-distribution (ν_1 = degrees of freedom in numerator, ν_2 = degrees of freedom in denominator)

$$F_F(y|\nu_1, \nu_2) = \int_0^y \frac{\Gamma[(\nu_1+\nu_2)/2]\nu_1^{\nu_1/2}\nu_2^{\nu_1/2}t^{(\nu_1-2)/2}(\nu_2+\nu_1 t)^{-(\nu_1+\nu_2)/2}}{\Gamma(\nu_1/2)\Gamma(\nu_2/2)}dt$$

		ν_1																
$F_F(y)$	ν_2	1	2	3	4	5	6	7	8	9	10	12	15	20	30	60	120	∞
.90	1	39.9	49.5	53.6	55.8	57.2	58.2	58.9	59.4	59.9	60.2	60.7	61.2	61.7	62.3	62.8	63.1	63.3
.95		161	200	216	225	230	234	237	239	241	242	244	246	248	250	252	253	254
.975		648	800	864	900	922	937	948	957	963	969	977	985	993	1,000	1,010	1,010	1,020
.99		4,050	5,000	5,400	5,620	5,760	5,860	5,930	5,980	6,020	6,060	6,110	6,160	6,210	6,260	6,310	6,340	6,370
.995		16,200	20,000	21,600	22,500	23,100	23,400	23,700	23,900	24,100	24,200	24,400	24,600	24,800	25,000	25,000	25,400	25,500
.90	2	8.53	9.00	9.16	9.24	9.29	9.33	9.95	9.37	9.38	9.39	9.41	9.42	9.44	9.46	9.47	9.48	9.49
.95		18.5	19.0	19.2	19.2	19.3	19.3	19.4	19.4	19.4	19.4	19.4	19.4	19.5	19.5	19.5	19.5	19.5
.975		38.5	39.0	39.2	39.2	39.3	39.3	39.4	39.4	39.4	39.4	39.4	39.4	39.4	39.5	39.5	39.5	39.5
.99		98.5	99.0	99.2	99.2	99.3	99.3	99.4	99.4	99.4	99.4	99.4	99.4	99.4	99.5	99.5	99.5	9.5
.995		199	199	199	199	199	199	199	199	199	199	199	199	199	199	199	199	199
.90	3	5.54	5.46	5.39	5.34	5.31	5.28	5.27	5.25	5.24	5.23	5.22	5.20	5.18	5.17	5.15	5.14	5.13
.95		10.1	9.55	9.28	9.12	9.01	8.94	8.89	8.85	8.81	8.79	8.74	8.70	8.66	8.62	8.57	8.55	8.53
.975		17.4	16.0	15.4	15.1	14.9	14.7	14.6	14.5	14.5	14.4	14.3	14.3	14.2	14.1	14.0	13.9	13.9
.99		34.1	30.8	29.5	28.7	28.2	27.9	27.7	27.5	27.3	27.2	27.1	26.9	26.7	26.5	26.3	26.2	26.1
.995		55.6	49.8	47.5	46.2	45.4	44.8	44.4	44.1	43.9	43.7	43.4	43.1	42.8	42.5	42.1	42.0	41.8
.90	4	4.54	4.32	4.19	4.11	4.05	4.01	3.98	3.95	3.93	3.92	3.90	3.87	3.84	3.82	3.79	3.78	3.76
.95		7.71	6.94	6.59	6.39	6.26	6.16	6.09	6.04	6.00	5.96	5.91	5.86	5.80	5.75	5.69	5.66	5.63
.975		12.2	10.6	9.98	9.60	9.36	9.20	9.07	8.98	8.90	8.84	8.75	8.66	8.56	8.46	8.36	8.31	8.26
.99		21.2	18.0	16.7	16.0	15.5	15.2	15.0	14.8	14.7	14.5	14.4	14.2	14.0	13.8	13.7	13.6	13.5
.995		31.3	26.3	24.3	23.2	22.5	22.0	21.6	21.4	21.1	21.0	20.7	20.4	20.2	19.9	19.6	19.5	19.3
.90	5	4.06	3.78	3.62	3.52	3.45	3.40	3.37	3.34	3.32	3.30	3.27	3.24	3.21	3.17	3.14	3.12	3.11
.95		6.61	5.79	5.41	5.19	5.05	4.95	4.88	4.82	4.77	4.74	4.68	4.62	4.56	4.50	4.43	4.40	4.37
.975		10.0	8.43	7.76	7.39	7.15	6.98	6.85	6.76	6.68	6.62	6.52	6.43	6.33	6.23	6.12	6.07	6.02
.99		16.3	13.3	12.1	11.4	11.0	10.7	10.5	10.3	10.2	10.1	9.89	9.72	9.55	9.38	9.20	9.11	9.02
.995		22.8	18.3	16.5	15.6	14.9	14.5	14.2	14.0	13.7	13.6	13.4	13.1	12.9	12.7	12.4	12.3	12.1

Table D.3 (cont.)

$F_F(y)$	ν_2	ν_1: 1	2	3	4	5	6	7	8	9	10	12	15	20	30	60	120	∞
.90	6	3.78	3.46	3.29	3.18	3.11	3.05	3.01	2.98	2.96	2.94	2.90	2.87	2.84	2.80	2.76	2.74	2.72
.95		5.99	5.14	4.76	4.53	4.39	4.28	4.21	4.15	4.10	4.06	4.00	3.94	3.87	3.81	3.74	3.70	3.67
.975		8.81	7.26	6.60	6.23	5.99	5.82	5.70	5.60	5.52	5.46	5.37	5.27	5.17	5.07	4.96	4.90	4.85
.99		13.7	10.9	9.78	9.15	8.75	8.47	8.26	8.10	7.98	7.87	7.72	7.56	7.40	7.23	7.06	6.97	6.88
.995		18.6	14.5	12.9	12.0	11.5	11.1	10.8	10.6	10.4	10.2	10.0	9.81	9.59	9.36	9.12	9.00	8.88
.90	7	3.59	3.26	3.07	2.96	2.88	2.83	2.78	2.75	2.72	2.70	2.67	2.63	2.59	2.56	2.51	2.49	2.47
.95		5.59	4.74	4.35	4.12	3.97	3.87	3.79	3.73	3.68	3.64	3.57	3.51	3.44	3.38	3.30	3.27	3.23
.975		8.07	6.54	5.89	5.52	5.29	5.12	4.95	4.90	4.82	4.76	4.67	4.57	4.47	4.36	4.25	4.20	4.14
.99		12.2	9.55	8.45	7.85	7.46	7.19	6.95	6.84	6.72	6.62	6.47	6.31	6.16	5.99	5.82	5.74	5.65
.995		16.2	12.4	10.9	10.1	9.52	9.16	8.89	8.68	8.51	8.38	8.18	7.97	7.75	7.53	7.31	7.19	7.08
.90	8	3.46	3.11	2.92	2.81	2.73	2.67	2.62	2.59	2.56	2.54	2.50	2.46	2.42	2.38	2.34	2.31	2.29
.95		5.32	4.46	4.07	3.84	3.69	3.58	3.50	3.44	3.39	3.35	3.28	3.22	3.15	3.08	3.01	2.97	..93
.975		7.57	6.06	5.42	5.05	4.82	4.65	4.53	4.43	4.36	4.30	4.20	4.10	4.00	3.89	3.78	3.73	3.67
.99		11.3	8.65	7.59	7.01	6.63	6.37	6.18	6.03	5.91	5.81	5.67	5.52	5.36	5.20	5.03	4.95	4.86
.995		14.7	11.0	9.60	8.81	8.30	7.95	7.69	7.50	7.34	7.21	7.01	6.81	6.61	6.40	6.18	6.06	5.95
.90	9	3.26	3.01	2.81	2.69	2.61	2.55	2.51	2.47	2.44	2.42	2.38	2.34	2.30	2.25	2.21	2.18	2.16
.95		5.12	4.26	3.86	3.63	3.48	3.37	3.29	3.23	3.18	3.14	3.07	3.01	2.94	2.86	2.79	2.75	2.71
.975		7.21	5.71	5.08	4.72	4.48	4.32	4.20	4.10	4.03	3.96	3.87	3.77	3.67	3.56	3.45	3.39	3.33
.99		10.6	8.02	6.99	6.42	6.06	5.80	5.61	5.47	5.35	5.26	5.11	4.96	4.81	4.65	4.48	4.40	4.31
.995		13.6	10.1	8.72	7.96	7.47	7.13	6.88	6.69	6.54	6.42	6.23	6.03	5.83	5.62	5.41	5.30	5.19
.90	10	3.29	2.92	2.73	2.61	2.52	2.46	2.41	2.38	2.35	2.32	2.28	2.24	2.20	2.15	2.11	2.08	2.06
.95		4.96	4.10	3.71	3.48	3.33	3.22	3.14	3.07	3.02	2.98	2.91	2.84	2.77	2.70	2.62	2.58	2.54
.975		6.94	5.46	4.83	4.47	4.24	4.07	3.95	3.85	3.78	3.72	3.62	3.52	3.42	3.31	3.20	3.14	3.08
.99		10.0	7.56	6.55	5.99	5.64	5.39	5.20	5.06	4.94	4.85	4.71	4.56	4.41	4.25	4.08	4.40	4.31
.995		12.8	9.43	8.08	7.34	6.87	6.54	6.30	6.12	5.97	5.85	5.66	5.47	5.27	5.07	4.86	4.75	4.64
.90	12	3.18	2.81	2.61	2.48	2.39	2.33	2.28	2.24	2.21	2.19	2.15	2.10	2.06	2.01	1.96	1.93	1.90
.95		4.75	3.89	3.49	3.26	3.11	3.00	2.91	2.82	2.80	2.75	2.69	2.62	2.54	2.47	2.38	2.34	2.30
.975		6.55	5.10	4.47	4.12	3.89	3.73	3.61	3.51	3.44	3.37	3.28	3.18	3.07	2.96	2.85	2.79	2.72
.99		9.33	6.93	5.95	5.41	5.06	4.82	4.64	4.50	4.39	4.30	4.16	4.01	3.86	3.70	3.54	3.45	3.36
.995		11.8	8.51	7.23	6.52	6.07	5.76	5.52	5.35	5.20	5.09	4.91	4.72	4.53	4.33	4.12	4.01	3.90

.90	15	3.07	2.70	2.49	2.36	2.27	2.21	2.16	2.12	2.09	2.06	2.02	1.97	1.92	1.87	1.82	1.79	1.76
.95		4.54	3.68	3.29	3.06	2.90	2.79	2.71	2.64	2.59	2.54	2.48	2.40	2.33	2.25	2.16	2.11	2.07
.975		6.20	4.77	4.15	3.80	3.58	3.41	3.29	3.20	3.12	3.06	2.96	2.86	2.76	2.64	2.52	2.46	2.40
.99		8.68	6.36	5.42	4.89	4.56	4.32	4.14	4.00	3.89	3.80	3.67	3.52	3.37	3.21	3.05	2.96	2.87
.995		10.8	7.70	6.48	5.80	5.37	5.07	4.85	4.67	4.54	4.42	4.25	4.07	3.88	3.69	3.48	3.37	3.26
.90	20	2.97	2.95	2.38	2.25	2.16	2.09	2.04	2.00	1.96	1.94	1.89	1.84	1.79	1.74	1.68	1.64	1.63
.95		4.35	3.49	3.10	2.87	2.71	2.60	2.51	2.45	2.39	2.35	2.28	2.20	2.12	2.04	1.95	1.90	1.84
.975		5.87	4.46	3.86	3.51	3.29	3.13	3.01	2.91	2.84	2.77	2.68	2.57	2.46	2.35	2.22	2.16	2.09
.99		8.10	5.85	4.94	4.43	4.10	3.87	3.70	3.56	3.46	3.37	3.23	3.09	2.94	2.78	2.61	2.52	2.42
.995		9.94	6.99	5.82	5.17	4.76	4.47	4.26	4.09	3.96	3.85	3.68	3.50	3.32	3.12	2.92	2.81	2.69
.90	30	2.88	2.49	2.28	2.14	2.05	1.98	1.93	1.88	1.85	1.82	1.77	1.72	1.67	1.61	1.54	1.50	1.46
.95		4.17	3.32	2.92	2.69	2.53	2.42	2.33	2.27	2.21	2.16	2.09	2.01	1.93	1.84	1.74	1.68	1.62
.975		5.57	4.18	3.59	3.25	3.03	2.87	2.75	2.65	2.57	2.51	2.41	2.31	2.20	2.07	1.94	1.87	1.79
.99		7.56	5.39	4.51	4.02	3.70	3.47	3.30	3.17	3.07	2.98	2.94	2.70	2.55	2.39	2.21	2.11	2.01
.995		9.18	6.35	5.24	4.62	4.23	3.95	3.74	3.58	3.45	3.34	3.18	3.01	2.82	2.63	2.42	2.30	2.18
.90	60	2.79	2.39	2.18	2.04	1.95	1.87	1.82	1.77	1.74	1.71	1.66	1.60	1.54	1.48	1.40	1.35	1.29
.95		4.00	3.15	2.76	2.53	2.37	2.25	2.17	2.10	2.04	1.99	1.92	1.84	1.75	1.65	1.53	1.47	1.39
.975		5.29	3.93	3.34	3.01	2.79	2.63	2.51	2.41	2.33	2.27	2.17	2.06	1.94	1.82	1.67	1.58	1.48
.99		7.08	4.98	4.13	3.65	3.34	3.12	2.95	2.82	2.72	2.63	2.50	2.35	2.20	2.03	1.84	1.73	1.60
.995		8.49	5.80	4.73	4.14	3.76	3.49	3.29	3.13	3.01	2.90	2.74	2.57	2.39	2.19	1.96	1.83	1.69
.90	120	2.75	2.35	2.13	1.99	1.90	1.82	1.77	1.72	1.68	1.65	1.60	1.54	1.48	1.41	1.32	1.26	1.19
.95		3.92	3.07	2.68	2.45	2.29	2.18	2.09	2.02	1.96	1.91	1.83	1.75	1.66	1.55	1.43	1.35	1.25
.975		5.15	3.80	3.23	2.89	2.67	2.52	2.39	2.30	2.22	2.16	2.05	1.94	1.82	1.69	1.53	1.43	1.31
.99		6.85	4.79	3.95	3.48	3.17	2.96	2.79	2.66	2.56	2.47	2.34	2.19	1.98	1.86	1.66	1.53	1.38
.995		8.18	5.54	4.50	3.92	3.55	3.28	3.09	2.93	2.81	2.71	2.54	2.37	2.19	1.98	1.75	1.61	1.43
.90	∞	2.71	2.30	2.08	1.94	1.85	1.77	1.72	1.67	1.63	1.60	1.55	1.49	1.42	1.34	1.24	1.17	1.00
.95		3.84	3.00	2.60	2.37	2.21	2.10	2.01	1.94	1.88	1.83	1.75	1.37	1.57	1.46	1.32	1.22	1.00
.975		5.02	3.69	3.12	2.79	2.57	2.41	2.29	2.19	2.11	2.05	1.94	1.83	1.71	1.57	1.39	1.27	1.00
.99		6.63	4.61	3.78	3.32	3.02	2.80	2.64	2.51	2.41	2.32	2.18	2.04	1.88	1.70	1.47	1.32	1.00
.995		7.88	5.30	4.28	3.72	3.35	3.09	2.90	2.74	2.62	2.52	2.36	2.19	2.00	1.79	1.53	1.36	1.00

Table D.4
Cumulative Student t-distribution

$$F_t(y|v) = \int_{-\infty}^{y} \frac{\Gamma[(v+1)/2]}{\sqrt{\pi v}\,\Gamma(v/2)} \left[1 + \frac{t^2}{v}\right]^{-(v+1)/2} dt$$

	$F_t(y\|v)$						
v	.75	.90	.95	.975	.99	.995	.9995
1	1.000	3.078	6.314	12.706	31.821	63.657	636.619
2	.816	1.886	2.920	4.303	6.965	9.925	31.598
3	.765	1.638	2.353	3.182	4.541	5.841	12.941
4	.741	1.533	2.132	2.776	3.747	4.604	8.610
5	.727	1.476	2.015	2.571	3.365	4.032	6.859
6	.718	1.440	1.943	2.447	3.143	3.707	5.959
7	.711	1.415	1.895	2.365	2.998	3.499	5.405
8	.706	1.397	1.860	2.306	2.896	3.355	5.041
9	.703	1.383	1.833	2.262	2.821	3.250	4.781
10	.700	1.372	1.812	2.228	2.764	3.169	4.587
11	.697	1.363	1.796	2.201	2.718	3.106	4.437
12	.695	1.356	1.782	2.179	2.681	3.055	4.318
13	.694	1.350	1.771	2.160	2.650	3.012	4.221
14	.692	1.345	1.761	2.145	2.624	2.977	4.140
15	.691	1.341	1.753	2.131	2.602	2.947	4.073
16	.690	1.337	1.746	2.120	2.583	2.921	4.015
17	.689	1.333	1.740	2.110	2.567	2.898	3.965
18	.688	1.330	1.734	2.101	2.552	2.878	3.922
19	.688	1.328	1.729	2.093	2.539	2.861	3.883
20	.687	1.325	1.725	2.086	2.528	2.845	3.850
21	.686	1.323	1.721	2.080	2.518	2.831	3.819
22	.686	1.321	1.717	2.074	2.508	2.819	3.792
23	.685	1.319	1.714	2.069	2.500	2.807	3.767
24	.685	1.318	1.711	2.064	2.492	2.797	3.745
25	.684	1.316	1.708	2.060	2.485	2.787	3.725
26	.684	1.315	1.706	2.056	2.479	2.779	3.707
27	.684	1.314	1.703	2.052	2.473	2.771	3.690
28	.683	1.313	1.701	2.048	2.467	2.763	3.674
29	.683	1.311	1.699	2.045	2.462	2.756	3.659
30	.683	1.310	1.697	2.042	2.457	2.750	3.646
40	.681	1.303	1.684	2.021	2.423	2.704	3.551
60	.679	1.296	1.671	2.000	2.390	2.660	3.460
120	.677	1.289	1.658	1.980	2.358	2.617	3.373
∞	.674	1.282	1.645	1.960	2.326	2.576	3.291

References

Achcar, J. A., and A. F. M. Smith. 1990. Aspects of reparameterization in approximate Bayesian inference. In *Bayesian and Likelihood Methods in Statistics and Econometrics*, eds. S. Geisser, J. S. Hodges, S. J. Press, and A. Zellner. Amsterdam: North-Holland, pp. 439–452.

Adams, J. L. 1991. A computer experiment to evaluate regression strategies. *Proceedings of the American Statistical Association, Section on Statistical Computing*, pp. 55–62.

Agresti, A. 1992. A survey of exact inference for contingency tables (with discussion). *Statistical Science* 7:131–177.

Aigner, D. J. 1971. *Basic Econometrics*. Englewood Cliffs: Prentice-Hall.

Aigner, D. J., T. Amemiya, and D. J. Poirier. 1976. On the estimation of production functions: Maximum likelihood estimation of the parameters of a discontinuous density function. *International Economic Review* 17:377–396.

Aitchison, J., and I. R. Dunsmore. 1975. *Statistical Prediction Analysis*. Cambridge: Cambridge University Press.

Aitchison, J., and S. M. Shen. 1980. Logistic-normal distributions: Some properties and uses. *Biometrika* 67:261–272.

Aitchison, J., and S. D. Silvey. 1958. Maximum-likelihood estimation of parameters subject to restrictions. *Annals of Mathematical Statistics* 29:813–828.

Aitkin, M. 1991. Posterior Bayes factors. *Journal of the Royal Statistical Society [B]* 53:111–142.

Akaike, H. 1973. Information theory and the extension of the maximum likelihood principle. In *2nd International Symposium on Information Theory*, eds. B. N. Petrov and F. Csáki. Budapest: Akadémia Kiadó, pp. 267–281.

Akaike, H. 1980. Ignorance prior distribution of a hyperparameter and Stein's estimator. *Annals of the Institute of Mathematical Statistics* 32:171–179.

Alalouf, I. S., and G. P. H. Styan. 1979. Characterizations of estimability in the general linear model. *Annals of Statistics* 7:194–200.

Aldous, D. J. 1983. Exchangeability and related topics. In *Ecole d'Etre de Probabilites de Saint-Flour XIII*, eds. A. Dold and B. Echman. New York: Springer-Verlag, pp. 1–198.

Aldrich, J. 1989. Autonomy. *Oxford Economic Papers* 41:15–34.

Allais, M. 1953. Le comportement de l'homme rationnel devant le risque: Critique des postulats et axioms de l'ecole americane. *Econometrica* 21:503–546.

Amemiya, T. 1973. Regression analysis when the dependent variable is truncated normal. *Econometrica* 42:999–1012.

Amemiya, T. 1985. *Advanced Econometrics*. Cambridge, MA: Harvard University Press.

Anderson, G. J., and G. E., Mizon. 1989. What can statistics contribute to the analysis of economic structural change? In *Statistical Analysis and Forecasting of Economic Structural Change*, ed. P. Hackl. New York: Springer-Verlag, pp. 3–21.

Anderson, T. W. 1959. On asymptotic distributions of estimates of parameters of stochastic difference equations. *Annals of Mathematical Statistics* 30:676–687.

Anderson, T. W. 1984. *An Introduction to Multivariate Statistical Analysis*, 2d ed. New York: Wiley.

Andrews, D. W. K. 1988. Laws of large numbers for dependent non-identically distributed random variables. *Econometric Theory* 4:458–467.

Anscombe, F. J. 1954. Fixed sample-size analysis of sequential trials. *Biometrics* 10:89–100.

Anscombe, F. J., and R. J. Aumann. 1963. A definition of subjective probability. *Annals of Mathematical Statistics* 34:199–205.

Arnold, B. C., N. Balakrishnan, and H. N. Nagaraja. 1992. *A First Course in Order Statistics*. New York: Wiley.

Arnold, B. C., E. Castillo, and J.-M. Sarabia. 1992. *Conditionally Specified Distributions*. New York: Springer-Verlag.

Arrow, K. 1960. Decision theory and the choice of a level of significance for the t-test. In *Contributions to Probability and Statistics: Essays in Honor of Harold Hotelling*, eds. I. Olkin et al. Stanford: Stanford University Press, pp. 70–78.

Bahadur, R. R. 1958. Examples of inconsistency of maximum likelihood estimates. *Sankhā* 20:207–210.

Bahadur, R. R. 1960. Stochastic comparisons of tests. *Annals of Mathematical Statistics* 31:276–295.

Balanda, K. P., and H. L. MacGillivray. 1987. Kurtosis: A critical review. *American Statistician* 42:111–119.

Balanda, K. P., and H. L. MacGillivray. 1990. Kurtosis and spread. *Canadian Journal of Statistics* 18:17–30.

Barnard, G. A. 1947a. The meaning of significance level. *Biometrika* 34:179–182.

Barnard, G. A. 1947b. A review of *Sequential Analysis* by Abraham Wald. *Journal of the American Statistical Association* 42:658–669.

Barnard, G. A. 1949. Statistical inference (with discussion). *Journal of the Royal Statistical Society [B]* 11:115–139.

Barnard, G. A. 1965. Comment. *Journal of the Royal Statistical Society [B]* 27:193–195.

Barnard, G. A. 1972. Review of I. Hacking, *The Logic of Statistical Inference*. *British Journal for the Philosophy of Science* 23:123–190.

Barnard, G. A. 1977. Pivotal inference. *Encyclopedia of Statistics* 7:743–747.

Barnard, G. A. 1980a. Discussion. *Journal of the Royal Statistical Society [A]* 143:404–406.

Barnard, G. A. 1980b. Pivotal inference and the Bayesian controversy (with discussion). In *Bayesian Statistics*, eds. J. M. Bernardo, M. H. DeGroot, D. V. Lindley, and A. F. M. Smith. Valencia: University Press, pp. 295–318.

Barnard, G. A. 1981. A coherent view of statistical inference. Presented at the Symposium on Statistical Inference and Applications, University of Waterloo.

Barnard, G. A. 1990. Comment. *Statistical Science* 5:65–71.

Barndorff-Nielson, O. E. 1976. Plausibility inference (with discussion). *Journal of the Royal Statistical Society [B]* 38:103–131.

Barndorff-Nielson, O. E. 1978. *Information and Exponential Families in Statistical Theory*. New York: Wiley.

Barndorff-Nielson, O. E. 1991. Likelihood theory. In *Statistical Theory and Modelling: In Honour of Sir David Cox, FRS*, eds. D. V. Hinkley, N. Reid, and E. J. Snell. London: Chapman & Hall, pp. 232–264.

Barnett, V. 1982. *Comparative Statistical Inference*, 2d ed. New York: Wiley.

Barten, A. P. 1962. Note on the unbiased estimation of the squared multiple correlation coefficient. *Statistica Neerlandica* 16:151–163.

Barten, A. P. 1987. The coefficient of determination for regression without a constant term. In *The Practice of Econometrics*, eds. R. D. H. Heijmans and H. Neudecker. Dordrecht: Martinus Nijhoff Publishers, pp. 180–189.

Bartle, R. G. 1976. *The Elements of Real Analysis*. New York: Wiley.

Bartlett, M. S. 1957. Comment on D. V. Lindley's statistical paradox. *Biometrika* 44:533–534.

Bassett, G. 1989. Learning about Simpson's paradox. Unpublished manuscript, Department of Economics, University of Illinois at Chicago.

Bassett, G., and R. Koenker. 1978. The asymptotic theory of least absolute error regression. *Journal of the American Statistical Association* 73:618–622.

Basu, D. 1955. An inconsistency of the method maximum likelihood. *Annals of Mathematical Statistics* 26:144–145.

Basu, D. 1959. The family of ancillary statistics. *Sankhyā* 21:247–256.

Basu, D. 1964. Recovery of ancillary information. *Sankhyā* 26:3–16.

Basu, D. 1975. Statistical information and likelihood (with discussion). *Sankhyā* 37:1–71.

Basu, D. 1988. *Statistical Information and Likelihood: A Collection of Critical Essays.* Vol. 45, *Lecture Notes in Statistics.* New York: Springer-Verlag.

Basu, D. 1992. Learning statistics from counter examples: ancillary information. In *Bayesian Analysis in Statistics and Econometrics*, eds. P. K. Goel and N. S. Iyengar. New York: Springer-Verlag, pp. 217–223.

Bates, J. M., and C. W. J. Granger. 1969. The combination of forecasts. *Operations Research Quarterly* 20:451–468.

Bauer, P., B. M. Pötscher, and P. Hackl. 1988. Model selection by multiple test procedures. *Statistics* 19:39–44.

Bauwens, W. 1984. *Bayesian Full Information Analysis of Simultaneous Equation Models Using Integration by Monte Carlo.* Berlin: Springer-Verlag.

Bauwens, W., and J.-F. Richard. 1985. A 1-1 poly-*t* random variable generator with application to Monte Carlo integration. *Journal of Econometrics* 29:19–46.

Bayarri, M. J., M. H. DeGroot, and J. B. Kadane. 1988. What is the likelihood function? (with discussion). In *Statistical Decision Theory and Related Topics IV*, vol. 1, eds. S. Gupta and J. O. Berger. New York: Springer-Verlag, pp. 1–27.

Bayes, T. 1763. An essay towards solving a problem in the doctrine of chance. In *Studies in the History of Statistics and Probability*, eds. E. S. Pearson and M. G. Kendall. London: Griffen, 1970.

Becker, W., and P. Kennedy. 1992. A lesson in least squares and R squared. *American Statistician* 46:282–283.

Bellman, R. 1960. *Introduction to Matrix Analysis.* New York: McGraw-Hill.

Berger, J. O. 1980. *Statistical Decision Theory: Foundations, Concepts and Methods.* New York: Springer-Verlag.

Berger, J. O. 1984. The robust Bayesian viewpoint (with discussion). In *Robustness of Bayesian Analysis*, ed. J. B. Kadane. Amsterdam: Elsevier, pp. 63–144.

Berger, J. O. 1985. *Statistical Decision Theory and Bayesian Analysis*, 2d ed. New York: Springer-Verlag.

Berger, J. O. 1986. Are *P*-values reasonable measures of accuracy? In *Pacific Statistical Congress*, eds. I. S. Francis, B. F. J. Manly and F. C. Lam. Amsterdam: North-Holland, pp. 21–27.

Berger, J. O. 1990. Robust Bayesian analysis: Sensitivity to the prior. *Journal of Statistical Planning and Inference* 25:303–328.

Berger, J. O., and J. M. Bernardo. 1989. Estimating a product of means: Bayesian analysis with reference priors. *Journal of the American Statistical Association* 84:200–207.

Berger, J. O., and J. M. Bernardo. 1992a. On the development of the reference prior method. In *Bayesian Statistics 4*, eds. J. M. Bernardo, J. O. Berger, A. P. Dawid, and A. F. M. Smith. Oxford: Oxford University Press, pp. 35–60.

Berger, J. O., and J. M. Bernardo. 1992b. Ordered group reference priors with application to multinomial problems. *Biometrika* 79:25–37.

Berger, J. O., and D. A. Berry. 1988. The relevance of stopping rules in statistical inference (with discussion). In *Statistical Decision Theory and Related Topics IV*, vol. 1, eds. S. S. Gupta and J. O. Berger. New York: Springer Verlag, pp. 29–72.

Berger, J. O., and M. Delampady. 1987. Testing precise hypotheses (with discussion). *Statistical Science* 2:317–352.

Berger, J. O., and J. Mortera. 1991. Interpreting the stars in precise hypothesis testing. *International Statistical Review* 59:337–353.

Berger, J. O., and T. Sellke. 1987. Testing a point null hypothesis: The irreconcilability of *p*-values and evidence (with discussion). *Journal of the American Statistical Association* 82: 112–139.

Berger, J. O., and R. L. Wolpert. 1988. *The Likelihood Principle*, 2d ed. Haywood, CA: Institute of Mathematical Statistics.

Berkson, J. 1938. Some difficulties of interpretation encountered in the application of the chi-square test. *Journal of the American Statistical Association* 33:526–542.

Berkson, J. 1980. Minimum chi-square, not maximum likelihood. *Annals of Statistics* 81: 457–469.

Bernardo, J. M. 1979. Reference posterior distributions for Bayesian inference (with discussion). *Journal of the Royal Statistical Society [B]* 41:113–147.

Bernardo, J. M., and A. F. M. Smith. 1994. *Bayesian Theory*. New York: Wiley.

Berndt, E. R., B. H. Hall, R. E. Hall, and J. A. Hausman. 1974. Estimation and inference in nonlinear structural models. *Annals of Economic and Social Measurement* 3:653–665.

Berry, A. C. 1941. The accuracy of the Gaussian approximation to the sum of independent variates. *Transactions of the American Mathematical Society* 48:122–136.

Besag, J. 1989. A candidate's formula: A curious result in Bayesian prediction. *Biometrika* 76:183.

Besag, J., and P. J. Green. 1993. Spatial statistics and Bayesian computation. *Journal of the Royal Statistical Society [B]* 55:25–37.

Bhansali, R. J., and D. Y. Downham. 1977. Some properties of the order of an autoregression model selected by a generalization of Akaike's EPF criterion. *Biometrika* 64:547–551.

Bhattacharya, R. N. 1977. Refinements of the multidimensional central limit theorem and Applications. *Annals of Probability* 5:1–27.

Bickel, P. J. 1965. On some robust estimates of location. *Annals of Mathematical Statistics* 36:847–858.

Billingsley, P. 1986. *Probability and Measure*, 2d ed. New York: Wiley.

Binkley, J. K., and P. C. Abbott. 1987. The fixed X assumption in econometrics: Can the textbooks be trusted?. *American Statistician* 41:206–214.

Birnbaum, A. 1962. On the foundations of statistical inference. *Journal of the American Statistical Association* 57:269–306.

Birnbaum, A. 1977. The Neyman-Pearson theory as decision theory, and as inference theory; with a criticism of the Lindley-Savage argument for Bayesian theory. *Synthese* 36:19–49.

Bjørnstad, J. F. 1990. Predictive likelihood: A review (with discussion). *Statistical Science* 5:242–265.

Bjørnstad, J. F. 1992. Introduction to "On the foundations of statistical inference." In *Breakthroughs in Statistics*, vol. I, eds. In S. Kotz and N. L. Johnson. New York: Springer-Verlag, pp. 461–477.

Blackwell, D., and L. Dubins. 1962. Merging of opinions with increasing information. *Annals of Mathematical Statistics* 33:882–886.

Blyth, C. R. 1972. On Simpson's paradox and the sure-thing principle. *Journal of the American Statistical Association* 67:364–366.

Blyth, C. R. 1993. Restrict estimates to the possible values? *American Statistician* 47:73–75.

Blyth, C. R., and P. K. Pathak. 1985. Does an estimator's distribution suffice? In *Proceedings of the Berkeley Conference in Honor of Jerzy Neyman and Jack Kiefer*, vol. 1, eds. L. M. LeCam and R. A. Olshen. Pacific Grove, CA: Wadsworth pp. 45–51.

Boland, L. A. 1979. A critique of Friedman's critics. *Journal of Economic Literature* 17:503–522.

Border, K., and U. Segal. 1990. Dutch book arguments and subjective probability. Working Paper No. 9020, Department of Economics and Institute for Policy Analysis, University of Toronto.

Bowden, R. 1973. The theory of parametric identification. *Econometrica* 34:585–612.

Box, G. E. P. 1980. Sampling and Bayes' inference in scientific modelling (with discussion). *Journal of the Royal Statistical Society [A]* 143:383–430.

Box, G. E. P., and G. C. Tiao. 1973. *Bayesian Inference in Statistical Analysis*. Reading, MA: Addison-Wesley.

Breusch, T. S. 1990. Simplified extreme bounds. In *Modelling Economic Series: Readings in Econometric Methodology*, ed. C. W. J. Granger. Oxford: Clarendon Press, pp. 72–81.

Breusch, T. S., and A. R. Pagan. 1980. The Lagrange multiplier test and its applications to model specification in econometrics. *Review of Economic Studies* 47:239–253.

Britney, R. R., and R. L. Winkler. 1968. Bayesian point estimation under various loss functions. *Proceedings of the American Statistical Association*, pp. 356–364.

Brook, R. J. 1976. On the use of regret function to set significance points in prior tests of estimation. *Journal of the American Statistical Association* 71:126–131.

Brown, L. D. 1967. The conditional level of student's *t*-test. *Annals of Mathematical Statistics* 38:1068–1071.

Brown, L. D. 1990. An ancillarity paradox which appears in multiple linear regression (with discussion). *Annals of Statistics* 18:471–538.

Buehler, R. J. 1982. Some ancillary statistics and their properties (with discussion). *Journal of the American Statistical Association* 77:581–594.

Burguette, J. F., A. R. Gallant, and G. Souza. 1982. On unification of the asymptotic theory of nonlinear econometric models (with discussion). *Econometric Reviews* 1:151–211.

Buse, A. 1982. The likelihood ratio, Wald, and Lagrange multiplier tests: An expository note. *American Statistician* 36:153–157.

Butler, R. W. 1986. Predictive likelihood inference with applications (with discussion). *Journal of the Royal Statistical Society [B]* 48:1–38.

Cabanis, S., and G. Simons. 1977. Measure theory in probability and statistics. *Encyclopedia of Statistics* 5:409–417.

Cantrell, R. S., P. M. Burrows, and Q. H. Vuong. 1991. Interpretations and use of generalized Chow tests. *International Economic Review* 32:725–741.

Carlstein, E., D. Richards, and D. Ruppert. 1985. Letter to the editor. *American Statistician* 39:326–327.

Carnap, R. 1962. *Logical Foundations of Probability*, 2d ed. Chicago, Chicago University Press.

Cartwright, N. 1983. *How the Laws of Physics Lie*. Oxford: Clarendon Press.

Casella, G., and R. L. Berger. 1987. Reconciling Bayesian and frequentist evidence in the one-sided testing problem. *Journal of the American Statistical Association* 82:106–111.

Casella, G., and R. L. Berger. 1990. *Statistical Inference*. Pacific Grove, CA: Wadsworth.

Casella, G., and E. I. George. 1992. Explaining the Gibbs sampler. *American Statistician* 46:167–174.

Chamberlain, G. 1987. Asymptotic efficiency in estimation with conditional moment restrictions. *Journal of Econometrics* 34:305–334.

Chamberlain, G., and E. E. Leamer. 1976. Matrix weighted averages and posterior bounds. *Journal of the Royal Statistical Society [B]* 38:73–84.

Chen, C.-F. 1979. Bayesian inference for a normal dispersion matrix and its application to stochastic multiple regression. *Journal of the Royal Statistical Society [B]* 41:235–248.

Chen, C.-F. 1985. On asymptotic normality of limiting density functions with Bayesian implications. *Journal of the Royal Statistical Society [B]* 47:540–546.

Chib, S., R. C. Tiwari, and S. R. Jammalamadaka. 1988. Bayes prediction in regression with elliptical errors. *Journal of Econometrics* 38:349–360.

Chow, G. C. 1960. Tests of equality between sets of coefficients in two linear regressions. *Econometrica* 28:591–605.

Chow, G. C. 1981. A comparison of the information and posterior probability criteria in model selection. *Journal of Econometrics* 16:21–33.

Chow, Y. S., and H. Teicher. 1988. *Probability Theory: Independence, Interchangeability, Martingales*, 2d ed. New York: Springer-Verlag.

Christ, C. 1985. Early progress in estimating quantitative economic relationships in America. Supplement, *American Economic Review* 75:39–52.

Chung, K. L. 1974. *A Course in Probability Theory*, 2d ed. New York: Academic Press.

Clemen, R. T. 1989. Combining forecasts: A review and annotated bibliography. *International Journal of Forecasting* 5:559–583.

Cohen, A. 1965. Estimates of linear combinations of the parameters in the mean vector of multivariate distribution. *Annals of Mathematical Statistics* 36:78–87.

Conniffe, D. 1990. Applying estimated score tests in econometrics. Paper presented at the Fifth World Congress of the Econometric Society, Barcelona.

Cook, T., and D. Campbell. 1979. *Quasi-Experimentation: Design and Analysis Issues for Field Studies*. Chicago: Rand McNally.

Cooley, T. F. 1982. Specification analysis with discriminating priors: An application to the concentration profits debate (with discussion). *Econometric Reviews* 1:97–128.

Cooley, T. F., and S. F. Leroy. 1981. Identification and estimation of money demand. *American Economic Review* 71:825–844.

Cooley, T. F., and S. F. Leroy. 1986. What will take the con out of econometrics? A reply to McAleer, Pagan and Volker. *American Economic Review* 76:504–507.

Cooley, T. F., and W. R. Parke. 1987. Likelihood and other approaches to prediction in dynamic models. *Journal of Econometrics* 35:119–142.

Cooley, T. F., and W. R. Parke. 1990. Asymptotic likelihood-based prediction methods. *Econometrica* 58:1215–1234.

Cornfield, J. 1966a. A Bayesian test of some classical hypotheses: With applications to sequential clinical trials. *Journal of the American Statistical Association* 61:577–594.

Cornfield, J. 1966b. Sequential trials, sequential analysis and the likelihood principle. *American Statistician* 20:18–22.

Cornfield, J. 1969. The Bayesian outlook and its application (with discussion). *Biometrics* 25:617–657.

Cornfield, J. 1970. The frequency theory of probability, Bayes theorem, and sequential clinical trials. In *Bayesian Statistics*, eds. D. L. Meyer and R. O. Collier, Jr. Itasca, IL: F. E. Peacock, pp. 1–28.

Cox, D. R. 1958a. *Planning of Experiments*. New York: Wiley.

Cox, D. R. 1958b. Some problems connected with statistical inference. *Annals of Mathematical Statistics* 29:357–372.

Cox, D. R. 1984. Design of experiments and regression. *Journal of the Royal Statistical Society [A]* 147:306–315.

Cox, D. R., and D. V. Hinkley. 1974. *Theoretical Statistics*. London: Chapman & Hall.

Cox, D. R., and N. Reid. 1987. Parameter orthogonality and approximate conditional inference. *Journal of the Royal Statistical Society [B]* 49:1–39.

Coyle, C. A., and C. Wang. 1993. Wanna bet? On gambling strategies that may or may not work in a casino. *American Statistician* 47:108–111.

Cramer, H. 1946, *Mathematical Methods of Statistics*. Princeton: Princeton University Press.

Crowder, M. J. 1976. Maximum likelihood estimation for dependent observations. *Journal of the Royal Statistical Society [B]* 38:45–53.

Crowder, M. 1992. Bayesian priors based on a parameter transformation using the distribution function. *Annals of the Institute of Statistics and Mathematics* 44:405–416.

Dagenais, M. G., and J.-M. Dufour. 1991. Invariance, nonlinear models, and asymptotic tests. *Econometrica* 59:1601–1615.

Dalal, S. R., and J. H. Hall. 1983. Approximating priors by mixtures of natural conjugate priors. *Journal of the Royal Statistical Society [B]* 45:278–286.

Dalal, S. R., E. B. Fowlkes, and B. Hoadley. 1989. Risk analysis of the space shuttle: Pre-*Challenger* prediction of failure. *Journal of the American Statistical Association* 84:945–957.

Das Peddada, S. 1985. A short note on Pitman's measure of nearness. *American Statistician* 39:298–299.

David, F. N. 1962. *Games, Gods and Gambling: A History of Probability and Statistical Ideas.* London: Griffin.

Davidson, J. E. H., D. F. Hendry, F. Srba, and S. Yeo. 1978. Econometric modelling of the time-series relationship between consumers' expenditure and income in the United Kingdom. *Economic Journal* 88:661–692.

Davidson, R., and J. G. MacKinnon. 1993. *Estimation and Inference in Econometrics.* Oxford: Oxford University Press.

Davison, A. C. 1986. Approximate predictive likelihood. *Biometrika* 73:323–332.

Dawid, A. P. 1970. On the limiting normality of posterior distributions. *Proceedings of the Cambridge Philosophical Society* 67:625–633.

Dawid, A. P. 1977a. Discussion of Wilkinson: On resolving the controversy in statistical inference. *Journal of the Royal Statistical Society [B]* 37:248–258.

Dawid, A. P. 1977b. Invariant prior distributions. *Encyclopedia of Statistics* 4:228–236.

Dawid, A. P. 1979. Conditional independence in statistical theory (with discussion). *Journal of the Royal Statistical Society [B]* 41:1–31.

Dawid, A. P. 1980. Discussion. In *Bayesian Statistics*, eds. J. Bernardo, M. DeGroot, D. V. Lindley, and A. F. M. Smith. Valencia: Valencia Press, p. 311.

Dawid, A. P. 1982. Intersubjective statistical models. In *Exchangeability in Probability and Statistics*, eds. G. Koch and F. Spizzichino. Amsterdam: North-Holland.

Dawid, A. P., M. Stone, and J. V. Zidek. 1973. Marginalization paradoxes in Bayesian and structural inference. *Journal of the Royal Statistical Society [B]* 34:189–233.

DeBruijn, N. G. 1961. *Asymptotic Methods in Analysis*, 2d ed. Amsterdam: North-Holland.

de Finetti, B. 1937. Foresight: Its logical laws, its subjective sources. Translated from French, in *Studies in Subjective Probability*, eds. H. E. Kyburg Jr., and H. E. Smokler. New York: Wiley. 1964.

de Finetti, B. 1972. *Probability, Induction, and Statistics.* New York: Wiley.

de Finetti, B. 1974. *Theory of Probability*, vol. 1. New York: Wiley.

de Finetti, B. 1975. *Theory of Probability*, vol. 2. New York: Wiley.

DeGroot, M. H. 1970. *Optimal Statistical Decisions.* New York: McGraw-Hill.

DeGroot, M. H. 1980. Discussion. In *Bayesian Statistics*, eds. J. Bernardo, M. DeGroot, D. V. Lindley and A. F. M. Smith. Valencia: Valencia Press, pp. 311–312.

DeGroot, M. H. 1982. Comment. *Journal of the American Statistical Association* 77:336–339.

DeGroot, M. H. 1987. *Probability and Statistics.* Reading, MA: Addison-Wesley.

Delampady, M. 1989a. Lower bounds on Bayes factors for interval hypotheses. *Journal of the American Statistical Association* 84:120–124.

Delampady, M. 1989b. Lower bounds on Bayes factors for invariant testing situations. *Journal of Multivariate Analysis* 28:227–246.

Delampady, M., and J. O. Berger. 1990. Lower bounds on posterior probabilities for multinomial and chi-squared tests. *Annals of Statistics* 18:1295–1316.

De Marchi, N., and C. Gilbert. eds. 1989. History and Methodology of Econometrics. *Oxford Economic Papers* 41.

Dempster, A. P. 1968. Upper and lower probabilities induced by a multi-valued mapping. *Annals of Mathematical Statistics* 38:325–339.

Dempster, A. P. 1990. Causality and Statistics. *Journal of Statistical Planning and Inference* 25:261–278.

Devroye, L. 1986. *Non-Uniform Random Variate Generalization.* New York: Springer-Verlag.

Dhrymes, P. J. 1974. *Econometrics: Statistical Foundations and Applications.* New York: Springer-Verlag.

Dhrymes, P. J. 1978. *Introductory Econometrics.* New York: Springer-Verlag.

Dhrymes, P. J. 1984. *Mathematics for Econometrics*, 2d ed. New York: Springer-Verlag.

Dhrymes, P. J. 1989. *Topics in Advanced Econometrics: Probability Foundations*. New York: Springer-Verlag.

Diaconis, P. 1977. Finite forms of de Finetti's theorem on exchangeability. *Synthese* 36:271–281.

Diaconis, P. 1988. Recent progress on de Finetti's notions of exchangeability. In *Bayesian Statistics 3*, eds. J. M. Bernardo, M. H. DeGroot, D. V. Lindley, and A. F. M. Smith. Oxford: Oxford University Press, pp. 111–125.

Diaconis, P., and D. Freedman. 1980. Finite exchangeable sequences. *Annals of Probability* 8:745–764.

Diaconis, P., and D. Freedman. 1984. Partial exchangeability and sufficiency. Technical Report, Department of Statistics, Stanford University.

Diaconis, P., and D. Ylvisaker. 1979. Conjugate priors for exponential families. *Annals of Mathematical Statistics* 7:269–281.

Diaconis, P., and D. Ylvisaker. 1985. Quantifying prior opinions. In *Bayesian Statistics 2*, eds. J. M. Bernardo, M. H. DeGroot, D. V. Lindley, and A. F. M. Smith. Amsterdam: North-Holland, pp. 133–156.

Diaconis, P., and S. Zabell. 1982. Updating subjective probability. *Journal of the American Statistical Association* 77:822–830.

Diaconis, P. W., M. L. Eaton and S. L. Lauritzen. 1990. Finite de Finetti theorems in linear models and multivariate analysis. Institute for Electronic Systems Report 90–30, University of Aalborg.

Dickey, J. M. 1967. Matricvariate generalizations of the multivariate t distribution and the inverted multivariate t distribution. *Annals of Mathematical Statistics* 38:511–518.

Dickey, J. M. 1971. The weighted likelihood ratio, linear hypotheses on normal location parameters. *Annals of Mathematical Statistics* 7:269–281.

Dickey, J. M. 1975. Bayesian alternatives to the F-test and least-squares estimates in the normal linear model. In *Bayesian Studies in Econometrics and Statistics*, eds. S. E. Fienberg and A. Zellner. Amsterdam: North-Holland.

Dickey, J. M. 1976. Approximate posterior distributions. *Journal of the American Statistical Association* 71:680–689.

Dickey, J. M. 1977. Is the tail area useful as an approximate Bayes factor? *Journal of the American Statistical Association* 72:138–142.

Dickey, J. M., and P. R. Freeman. 1975. Population-distributed personal probabilities. *Journal of the American Statistical Association* 70:362–364.

Draper, D. 1993. Assessment and propagation of model uncertainty. Unpublished Manuscript, Department of Mathematics, University of California at Los Angeles.

Draper, D., J. S. Hodges, C. L. Mallows, and D. Pregibon. 1993. Exchangeability and data analysis (with discussion). *Journal of the Royal Statistical Society [A]* 156:9–37.

Drèze, J. 1977. Bayesian regression analysis using poly-t densities. *Journal of Econometrics* 6:329–354.

Driscoll, M. F., and W. R. Gundberg Jr. 1986. A history of the development of Craig's theorem. *American Statistician* 40:65–70.

Duchan, A. I. 1969. A relationship between the F and t statistics and simple correlation coefficients in classical least squares regression. *American Statistician* 23:27–28.

Dufour, J.-M. 1982. Generalized Chow tests for structural change: A coordinate free approach. *International Economic Review* 23:565–575.

Dufour, J.-M. 1990. Exact tests and confidence tests in linear regressions with autocorrelated errors. *Econometrica* 58:479–494.

Dufuor, J.-M., and M. Hallin. 1992. Improved Berry-Esseen Chebychev bounds with statistical applications. *Econometric Theory* 8:223–240.

Dufour, J.-M., and J. F. Kiviet. 1993. Exact inference methods for first-order auto regressive distributed lag models. Paper presented at the Canadian Econometric Study Group Meeting, University of Toronto.

Duncan, O. 1975. *Introduction to Structural Models*. New York: Academic Press.

Durbin, J. 1970a. On Birnbaum's theorem on the relation between sufficiency, conditionality and likelihood. *Journal of the American Statistical Association* 65:395–398.

Durbin, J. 1970b. Testing for serial correlation in least squares regression when some of the regressors are lagged dependent variables. *Econometrica* 38:410–421.

Earman, J. 1992. *Bayes or Bust? A Critical Examination of Bayesian Confirmation Theory*. Cambridge: MIT Press.

Edwards, A. W. F. 1972. *Likelihood*. Cambridge: Cambridge University Press.

Edwards, A. W. F. 1974. The history of likelihood. *International Statistical Review* 42:9–15.

Edwards, W., H. Lindman, and L. J. Savage. 1963. Bayesian statistical inference for psychological research. *Psychological Review* 70:450–499.

Eells, E. 1991. *Rational Decision and Causality*. Cambridge: Cambridge University Press.

Efron, B., and D. Feldman. 1991. Compliance as an explanatory variable in clinical trials (with discussion). *Journal of the American Statistical Association* 86:9–26.

Efron, B., and D. V. Hinkley. 1978. Assessing the accuracy of the maximum likelihood estimator: Observed versus expected Fisher information. *Biometrika* 65:457–482.

Ellsberg, D. 1961. Risk, ambiguity, and the Savage axiom. *Quarterly Journal of Economics* 75:643–699.

Engle, R. F. 1982a. A general approach to Lagrange multiplier diagnostics. *Journal of Econometrics* 20:83–104.

Engle, R. F. 1982b. Autoregressive conditional heteroskedasticity with estimates of the variance of UK inflation. *Econometrica* 38:410–421.

Engle, R. F. 1984. Wald, likelihood ratio, and Lagrange multiplier tests in econometrics. In *Handbook of Econometrics*, vol. 2, eds. Z. Griliches and M. D. Intriligator. Amsterdam: North-Holland, pp. 775–826.

Engle, R. F., D. F. Hendry, and J.-F. Richard. 1983. Exogeneity. *Econometrica* 51:277–304.

Epstein, R. J. 1987. *A History of Econometrics*. Amsterdam: North-Holland.

Esseen, C. G. 1945. Fourier analysis of distribution functions. *Acta Mathematica* 77:1–125.

Evans, M. J., D. A. S. Fraser, and G. Monette. 1986. On principles and arguments to likelihood (with discussion). *Canadian Journal of Statistics* 14:181–199.

Farebrother, R. W. 1975. The minimum mean square error linear estimator and ridge regression. *Technometrics* 17:127–128.

Favero, C., and D. F. Hendry. 1992. Testing the Lucas critique: A review (with discussion). *Econometric Reviews* 11:265–318.

Feldstein, M. 1973. Multicollinearity and the mean square error criterion. *Econometrica* 41:337–346.

Feller, W. 1968. *An Introduction to Probability Theory and Its Applications*, vol. 1, 3d ed. New York: Wiley.

Feller, W. 1971. *An Introduction to Probability Theory and Its Applications*, vol. 2, 2d ed. New York: Wiley.

Ferguson, T. S. 1982. An inconsistent maximum likelihood estimate. *Journal of the American Statistical Association* 77:831–834.

Fine, T. 1973. *Theories of Probability: An Examination of Foundations*. New York: Academic Press.

Fishburn, P. C. 1981. Subjective expected utility: A review of normative theories. *Theory and Decision* 13:139–199.

Fishburn, P. C. 1982. *The Foundations of Expected Utility*. Dordrecht, The Netherlands: Reidel.

Fishburn, P. C. 1986. The Axioms of Subjective Probability. *Statistical Science* 1:335–358.

Fisher, F. M. 1970. Tests of equality between sets of coefficients in two linear regressions. *Econometrica* 38:361–366.

Fisher, R. A. 1921. On the "probable error" of the coefficient of correlation deduced from a small sample. *Metron I*, 4:3–32.

Fisher, R. A. 1922. On the mathematical foundations of theoretical statistics. *Philosophical Transactions of the Royal Society London [A]* 222:309–368.

Fisher, R. A. 1925. Theory of Statistical Estimation. *Proceedings of the Cambridge Philosophical Society* 22:700–725.

Fisher, R. A. 1934. Two New Properties of Mathematical Likelihood. *Proceedings of the Royal Statistical Society, [A]* 144:285–307.

Fisher, R. A. 1951. *The Design of Experiments.* Edinburgh: Oliver and Boyd.

Fisher, R. A. 1956. *Statistical Methods and Scientific Inference.* Edinburgh: Oliver and Boyd.

Florens, J.-P., and M. Mouchart. 1993. Bayesian testing and testing Bayesians. In *Econometrics, Handbook of Statistics*, vol. 11, eds. G. S. Maddala, C. R. Rao, and H. D. Vinod. Amsterdam: North-Holland.

Fraser, D. A. S. 1963. On the sufficiency and likelihood principles. *Journal of the American Statistical Association* 58:641–647.

Fraser, D. A. S. 1968. *The Structure of Inferences.* New York: Wiley.

Fraser, D. A. S. 1972. Bayes, likelihood, or structural. *Annals of Mathematical Statistics* 43:777–790.

Fraser, D. A. S. 1979. *Inference and Linear Models.* New York: McGraw-Hill.

Fraser, D. A. S., G. Monette, and K.-W. Ng. 1985. Marginalization, likelihood and structural models. In *Multivariate Analysis 6*, ed. P. R. K. Krishnaiah. Amsterdam: North-Holland, pp. 209–217.

Fraumeni, J. F., Jr. 1968. Cigarette smoking and cancers of the urinary tract: Geographical variation in the United States. *Journal of the National Cancer Institute* 41:1205–1211.

Fréchet, M. 1951. Sur les tableaux de corrélation dont les marges sont données. *Annales de l'Université de Lyon, [3]* section A, 14:53–77.

Freedman, D. A. 1983. A note on screening regression equations. *American Statistician* 37: 152–155.

Friedman, M. 1953. The methodology of economics. In *Essays in Positive Economics.* Chicago: University of Chicago Press, pp. 3–46.

Frisch, R. 1933. Editorial. *Econometrica* 1:1–4.

Frisch, R. 1938. Statistical versus theoretical relations in economic macrodynamics. Memorandum prepared for the Business Cycle Conference at Cambridge, England.

Frisch, R., and F. V. Waugh. 1933. Partial time regressions as compared with individual trends. *Econometrica* 1:387–401.

Games, P. A. 1977. An improved *t* table for simultaneous control of *g* contrasts. *Journal of the American Statistical Association* 72:531–534.

Gardenfors, P., and N.-E. Sahlin. 1988. *Decision, Probability, and Utility: Suggested Readings.* Cambridge: Cambridge University Press.

Gauss, C. F., 1823. *Theoria Combinationis Observationum Erroibus Minimis Obnoxiae.* Göttingen: Dieterich.

Geisser, S. 1971. The inferential use of predictive distributions. In *Foundations of Statistical Inference*, eds. B. P. Godambe and D. A. Sprott. Toronto: Holt, Rinehart and Winston, pp. 456–469.

Geisser, S. 1980. A predictivistic primer. In *Bayesian Analysis in Econometrics and Statistics: Essays in Honor of Harold Jeffreys*, ed. A. Zellner. Amsterdam: North-Holland, pp. 363–381.

Geisser, S. 1982. Aspects of the predictive and estimative approaches in the determination of probabilities (with discussion). Supplement, *Biometrics* 58:75–93.

Geisser, S. 1984. On prior distributions for binary trials (with discussion). *American Statistician* 38:244–251.

Geisser, S. 1985. On the prediction of observables: A selective update (with discussion). In

Bayesian Statistics 2, eds. J. M. Bernardo, M. H. DeGroot, D. V. Lindley and A. F. M. Smith. Amsterdam: North-Holland, pp. 203–230.

Geisser, S. 1993. *Predictive Inference: An Introduction.* London: Chapman & Hall.

Gelfand, A. E., and D. K. Dey. 1992. Bayesian model choice: Asymptotics and exact calculations. Unpublished Manuscript, Department of Statistics, University of Connecticut.

Gelfand, A. E., and A. F. M. Smith. 1990. Sampling based approaches to calculating marginal densities. *Journal of the American Statistical Association* 85:398–409.

Gelfand, A. E., S. E. Hills, A. Racine-Poon, and A. F. M. Smith. 1990. Illustration of Bayesian inference in normal data problems. *Journal of the American Statistical Association* 85:972–985.

Gelman, A., and X.-L. Meng. 1991. A note on bivariate distributions that are conditionally normal. *American Statistician* 45:125–126.

Gelman, A., and D. Rubin. 1992. A single series from the Gibbs sample provides a false sense of security. In *Bayesian Statistics 4*, eds. J. O. Berger, J. M. Bernardo, A. P. Dawid, and A. F. M. Smith. Oxford: Clarendon Press, pp. 627–631.

Geman, S., and D. Geman. 1984. Stochastic relaxation, Gibbs distributions, and the Bayesian restoration of images. *IEEE Transactions on Pattern Analysis and Machine Intelligence* 6: 721–741.

Genest, C., and J. V. Zidek. 1986. Combining probability distributions: A critique and annotated bibliography (with discussion). *Statistical Science* 1:114–148.

Geweke, J. 1986. Exact inference in the inequality constrained normal linear regression model. *Journal of Applied Econometrics* 1:127–141.

Geweke, J. 1988. Antithetic acceleration of Monte Carlo integration in Bayesian inference. *Journal of Econometrics* 38:73–90.

Geweke, J. 1989. Bayesian inference in econometric models using Monte Carlo integration. *Econometrica* 57:1317–1339.

Geweke, J.. ed. 1992a. *Decision Making Under Risk and Uncertainty: New Models and Empirical Findings.* Dordrecht: Kluwer.

Geweke, J. 1992b. Evaluating the accuracy of sampling-based approaches to the calculation of posterior moments (with discussion). In *Bayesian Statistics 4*, eds. J. O. Berger, J. M. Bernardo, A. P. Dawid, and A. F. M. Smith. Oxford: Clarendon Press, pp. 169–193.

Gigerenzer, G. 1987. Probabilistic thinking and the fight against subjectivity. In *The Probabilistic Revolution*, vol. 2, eds. L. Krüger, G. Gigerenzer, and M. S. Morgan. Cambridge, MA: MIT Press, pp. 1–33.

Giles, D. E., and A. C. Rayner. 1979. The mean squared errors of the maximum likelihood and the natural-conjugate Bayes regression estimators. *Journal of Econometrics* 11:319–334.

Gilks, W. R. 1992. Derivative-free adaptive rejection sampling for Gibbs sampling. In *Bayesian Statistics 4*, eds. J. O. Berger, J. M. Bernardo, A. P. Dawid, and A. F. M. Smith. Oxford: Clarendon Press, pp. 641–649.

Gleser, L. J. 1990. Discussion of "An ancillarity paradox which appears in multiple linear regression." *Annals of Statistics* 18:507–513.

Glymour, C. 1980. *Theory and Evidence.* Princeton: Princeton University Press.

Goddard, M. J. 1991. Constructing some categorical anomalies. *American Statistician* 45: 129–134.

Godfrey, L. G. 1988. *Misspecification Tests in Econometrics.* Cambridge: Cambridge University Press.

Goel, P. K. 1988. Software for Bayesian analysis: Current status and additional needs. In *Bayesian Statistics 3*, eds. J. M. Bernardo, M. H. DeGroot, D. V. Lindley, and A. F. M. Smith. Oxford: Oxford University Press, pp. 173–188.

Gokhale, D. V. 1976. On partial and multiple correlation. *Journal of the Indian Statistical Association* 14:17–22.

Goldberger, A. S. G. 1968. *Topics in Regression.* New York: Macmillan.

Goldberger, A. S. 1989. ET interview by Nicholas M. Kiefer. *Econometric Theory* 5:133–160.

Goldberger, A. S. 1991. *A Course in Econometrics*. Cambridge, MA: Harvard University Press.

Goldstein, M. 1985. Temporal coherence (with discussion). In *Bayesian Statistics 2*, eds. J. M. Bernardo, M. H. DeGroot, D. V. Lindley, and A. F. M. Smith. Amsterdam: North-Holland, pp. 231–248.

Golub, G. H. 1969. Matrix decompositions and statistical calculations. In *Statistical Computation*, eds. R. C. Milton and J. A. Nelder. New York: Academic Press, pp. 365–397.

Good, I. J. 1950. *Probability and Weighing of Evidence*. London: Griffin.

Good, I. J. 1958. Significance tests in parallel and in series. *Journal of the American Statistical Association* 53:799–813.

Good, I. J. 1962. Subjective probability as a measure of a nonmeasurable set. In *Logic, Methodology and Philosophy of Science*, eds. E. Nagel, P. Suppes, and A. Tarski. Stanford: Stanford University Press.

Good, I. J. 1967. A Bayesian significance test for the multinomial distribution. *Journal of the Royal Statistical Society [B]* 29:399–431.

Good, I. J. 1983. *Good Thinking: The Foundations of Probability and Its Applications*. Minneapolis: University of Minnesota Press.

Good, I. J. 1985. Weight of evidence: A brief survey (with discussion). In *Bayesian Statistics 2*, eds. J. M. Bernardo, M. H. DeGroot, D. V. Lindley, and A. F. M. Smith. Amsterdam: North-Holland, pp. 249–269.

Gourieroux, C., and A. Monfort. 1979. On the characterization of a joint probability distribution by conditional distributions. *Journal of Econometrics* 10:115–118.

Graham, A. 1981. *Kronecker Products and Matrix Calculus: with Applications*. New York: Wiley.

Granger, C. W. J., ed. 1990a. *Modelling Economic Series: Readings in Econometric Methodology*. Oxford: Clarendon Press.

Granger, C. W. J., ed. 1990b. Where are the controversies in econometric methodology? In *Modelling Economic Series: Readings in Econometric Methodology*. Oxford: Clarendon Press.

Graybill, F. A. 1969. *Introduction to Matrices with Applications in Statistics*. Belmont, CA: Wadsworth.

Graybill, F. A. 1976. *Theory and Applications of the Linear Model*. Boston: Duxbury.

Greene, W. H. 1993. *Econometric Analysis*, 2d ed. New York: Macmillan.

Haavelmo, T. 1944. The probability approach in econometrics. Supplement, *Econometrica* 12:1–115.

Hacking, I. 1975. *The Emergence of Probability*. New York: Cambridge University Press.

Hadley, G. 1961. *Linear Algebra*. Reading, MA: Addison Wesley.

Hald, A. 1971. The size of Bayes and minimax tests as a function of the sample size and the loss ratio. *Skandinavisk Aktuarietidskrift* 54:53–73.

Hamilton, J. D. 1994. *Time Series Analysis*. Princeton: Princeton University Press.

Hammersly, J. M., and D. C. Handscomb. 1964. *Monte Carlo Methods*. London: Metheun.

Hannan, E. J., and B. G. Quinn. 1979. The determination of the order of an autoregression. *Journal of the Royal Statistical Society [B]* 41:190–195.

Hansen, L. 1982. Large sample properties of generalized method of moments. *Econometrica* 50:1029–1054.

Hartigan, J. A. 1964. Invariant prior distributions. *Annals of Mathematical Statistics* 35:836–845.

Hartigan, J. A. 1965. The asymptotically unbiased prior distributions. *Annals of Mathematical Statistics* 36:1137–1152.

Hastings, W. K. 1970. Monte Carlo sampling methods using Markov chains and their applications. *Biometrika* 57:97–109.

Haughton, D. M. A. 1988. On the choice of a model to fit data from an exponential model. *Annals of Statistics* 16:342–355.

Heath, D. C., and W. D. Sudderth. 1976. De Finetti's theorem on exchangeable variables. *American Statistician* 30:188–189.

Heath, D. C., and W. D. Sudderth. 1978. On finitely additive priors, coherence, and extended admissibility. *Annals of Statistics* 6:333–345.

Heckman, J. J. 1992. Randomization and social policy evaluation. In *Evaluating Welfare and Training Programs*, eds. C. F. Manski and I. Garfinkel. Cambridge, MA: Harvard University Press, pp. 201–230.

Heckman, J. J., and V. J. Hotz. 1989. Choosing among alternative nonexperimental methods for estimating the impact of social programs: The case of manpower training (with discussion). *Journal of the American Statistical Association* 84:862–880.

Heijmans, R. D. H., and H. Neudecker. 1987. The coefficient of determination revisited. In *The Practice of Econometrics*, eds. R. D. H. Heijmans and H. Neudecker. Dordrecht: Martinus Nijhoff Publishers, pp. 193–204.

Henderson, H. V., and S. R. Searle. 1981. On deriving the inverse of a sum of matrices. *SIAM Review* 23:53–60.

Hendry, D. F. 1980. Econometrics: Alchemy or science? *Economica* 47:387–406.

Hendry, D. F., and G. E. Mizon. 1990. Procrustean econometrics: Or stretching and squeezing data. In *Modelling Economic Series: Readings in Econometric Methodology*, ed. C. W. J. Granger. Oxford: Clarendon Press, pp. 121–136.

Hendry, D. F., and J.-F. Richard. 1982. On the formulation of empirical models in dynamic econometrics. *Journal of Econometrics* 20:3–33.

Hendry, D. F., and J.-F. Richard. 1983. The econometric analysis of economic time series (with discussion). *International Statistical Review* 51:111–163.

Hendry, D. F., and J.-F. Richard. 1989. Recent developments in the theory of encompassing. In *Contributions to Operations Research and Economics: The Twentieth Anniversary of CORE*, eds. B. Cornet and H. Tulkens. Cambridge, MA: MIT Press, pp. 393–440.

Hendry, D. F., E. E. Leamer, and D. J. Poirier. 1990. A conversation on econometric methodology. *Econometric Theory* 6:171–261.

Hendry, D. F., A. R. Pagan, and J. D. Sargan. 1984. Dynamic Specification. In *Handbook of Econometrics*, vol. 2, eds. Z. Griliches and M. D. Intriligator. Amsterdam: North-Holland, pp. 1023–1100.

Hesse, M. 1974. *The Structure of Scientific Inference*. Berkeley: University of California Press.

Hewitt, E., and L. J. Savage. 1955. Symmetric measures on Cartesian products. *Transactions of the American Statistical Society* 80:470–501.

Heyde, C. C., and I. M. Johnson. 1979. On asymptotic posterior normality for stochastic processes. *Journal of the Royal Statistical Society [B]* 41:184–189.

Hill, B. M. 1969. Foundations for the theory of least squares. *Journal of the Royal Statistical Society [B]* 31:89–97.

Hill, B. M. 1985–1986. Some subjective Bayesian considerations in the selection of models (with discussion). *Econometric Reviews* 4:191–288.

Hill, B. M. 1987. The validity of the likelihood principle. *American Statistician* 41:95–100.

Hill, B. M. 1990. A theory of Bayesian data analysis. In *Bayesian and Likelihood Methods in Statistics and Econometrics*, eds. S. Geisser, J. S. Hodges, S. J. Press, and A. Zellner. Amsterdam: North-Holland, pp. 49–73.

Hill, B. M. 1992. Bayesian tests of hypotheses and the forecasting of economic time series. Unpublished Manuscript, University of Michigan.

Hill, B. M., and D. Lane. 1986. Conglomerability and countable additivity. In *Bayesian Inference and Decision Techniques: Essays in Honor of Bruno de Finetti*, eds. P. K. Goel and A. Zellner. Amsterdam: North-Holland, pp. 45–57.

Hillier, G. 1987. Classes of similar regions and their power properties for some econometric models. *Econometric Theory* 3:1–44.

Hills, S. E., and A. F. M. Smith. 1992. Parameterization issues in Bayesian inference. In *Bayesian Statistics 4*, eds. J. O. Berger, J. M. Bernardo, A. P. Dawid, and A. F. M. Smith. Oxford: Clarendon Press, pp. 227–246.

Hills, S. E., and A. F. M. Smith. 1993. Diagnostic plots for improved parameterization in Bayesian inference. *Biometrika* 80:61–74.

Hinkley, D. V. 1979. Predictive likelihood. *Annals of Statistics* 7:718–728.

Hinkley, D. V. 1980. Likelihood. *Canadian Journal of Statistics* 8:151–164.

Hinkley, D. V. 1983. Can frequentist inferences be very wrong? A conditional "yes". In *Scientific Inference, Data Analyzing and Robustness*, eds. G. E. P. Box, T. Leonard, and C.-F. Wu. New York: Academic Press, pp. 85–103.

Hoadley, B. 1971. Asymptotic properties of maximum likelihood estimators for the independent not identically distributed case. *Annals of Mathematical Statistics* 42:72–84.

Hoaglin, D. C., and R. E. Welsch. 1975. The hat matrix in regression and ANOVA. *American Statistician* 32:17–22.

Hocking, R. R. 1985. *The analysis of linear models*. Belmont, CA: Wadsworth.

Hodges, J. S. 1990. Can/May Bayesians do pure test of significance? In *Bayesian and Likelihood Methods in Statistics and Econometrics*, eds. S. Geisser, J. S. Hodges, S. J. Press, and A. Zellner. Amsterdam: North-Holland, pp. 75–90.

Hodges, J. S. 1992. Who knows what alternative lurks in the hearts of significance tests? (with discussion). In *Bayesian Statistics 4*, eds. J. M. Bernardo, J. O. Berger, A. P. Dawid, and A. F. M. Smith. Oxford: Oxford University Press, pp. 247–263.

Hodges, J. L., and E. L. Lehmann. 1954. Testing the approximate validity of statistical hypotheses. *Journal of the Royal Statistical Society [B]* 16:261–268.

Hogarth, R. H. 1975. Cognitive processes and the assessment of subjective probability distributions. *Journal of the American Statistical Association* 70:271–294.

Hogg, R. V., and A. T. Craig. 1978. *Introduction to Mathematical Statistics*, 4th ed. New York: Macmillan.

Holly, A. 1982. A remark on Hausman's specification test. *Econometrica* 50:749–759.

Howson, C., and P. Urbach. 1990. *Scientific Reasoning: The Bayesian Approach*. La Salle, Illinois: Open Court.

Hsiao, C. 1983. Identification. In *Handbook of Econometrics*, vol. 1, eds. Z. Griliches and M. D. Intriligator. Amsterdam: North-Holland, 225–283.

Hsu, P. L. 1938. On the best unbiased quadratic estimate of the variance. *Statistical Research Memorandum* 2:91–104.

Huber, P. J. 1964. Robust estimation of a location parameter. *Annals of Mathematical Statistics* 35:73–101.

Huber, P. J. 1967. The behavior of maximum likelihood estimates under nonstandard conditions. *Proceedings of the Fifth Berkeley Symposium on Mathematical Statistics and Probability* 1:221–233.

Huber, P. J. 1981. *Robust Statistics*. New York: Wiley.

Huntsberger, D. V. 1955. A generalization of preliminary testing procedure for pooling data. *Annals of Mathematical Statistics* 26:734–743.

Huzurbazar, V. S. 1948. The likelihood equation, consistency and the maxima of the likelihood function. *Annals of Eugenics* 14:185–200.

Huzurbazar, V. S. 1955. On the certainty of an inductive inference. *Proceedings of the Cambridge Philosophical Society* 51:761–762.

Huzurbazar, V. S. 1976. *Sufficient Statistics: Selected Contributions*. New York: Marcel Dekker.

Ibragimov, I. A., and Y. V. Linnik. 1971. *Independent and Stationary Sequences of Random Variables*, ed. J. E. C. Kingman. Gronigen: Wolters-Noordhoff Publishers.

Iwata, S. 1992. Lower bounds on Bayes factors for a linear regression model. Unpublished Manuscript, Department of Economics, University of Kansas.

James, W., and C. Stein. 1961. Estimation with quadratic loss. In *Fourth Berkeley Symposium on Mathematical Statistics and Probability*, ed. J. Neyman. Berkeley, CA: University of California Press.

Jaynes, E. T. 1968. Prior probabilities. *IEEE Transactions on Systems Science and Cybernetics*, SSC-4:227–241.

Jaynes, E. T. 1980. Marginalization and prior probabilities (with discussion). In *Bayesian Analysis in Econometrics and Statistics*, ed. A. Zellner. Amsterdam: North-Holland, pp. 43–87.

Jaynes, E. T. 1986. Some applications and extensions of the de Finetti representation theorem. In *Bayesian Inference and Decision Techniques: Essays in Honor of Bruno de Finetti*, eds. P. K. Goel and A. Zellner. Amsterdam: North-Holland, pp. 31–42.

Jeffrey, R. C. 1983. *The Logic of Decision*, 2d ed. New York: McGraw-Hill.

Jeffreys, H. 1946. An invariant form for the prior probability in estimation problems. *Proceedings of the Royal Statistical Society of London [A]* 186:453–461.

Jeffreys, H. 1961. *Theory of Probability*, 3d ed. Oxford: Clarendon Press.

Jeffreys, H. 1980. Some general points in probability theory. In *Bayesian Analysis in Probability and Statistics*, ed. A. Zellner. Amsterdam: North-Holland, pp. 451–453.

Jensen, D. R. 1979. Linear models without moments. *Biometrika* 66:611–618.

Johnson, N. L., and S. Kotz. 1969. *Distributions in Statistics: Discrete Distributions*. Boston: Houghton Mifflin.

Johnson, N. L., and S. Kotz. 1970a. *Distributions in Statistics: Continuous Distributions*, vol. 1. Boston: Houghton Mifflin.

Johnson, N. L., and S. Kotz. 1970b. *Distributions in Statistics: Continuous Distributions*, vol. 2. Boston: Houghton Mifflin.

Johnson, N. L., and S. Kotz. 1972. *Distributions in Statistics: Continuous Multivariate Distributions*. New York: Wiley.

Johnson, N. L., S. K. Kotz, and A. W. Kemp. 1992. *Distributions in Statistics: Univariate Discrete Distributions*, 2d ed. New York: Wiley.

Johnson, R. A. 1970. Asymptotic expansions associated with posterior distributions. *Annals of Mathematical Statistics* 41:851–864.

Johnston, J. 1972. *Econometric Methods*, 2d ed. New York: McGraw-Hill.

Johnston, J. 1991. Econometrics retrospect and prospect. *Economic Journal* 101:51–56.

Johnstone, D. 1987. On the interpretation of hypothesis tests following Neyman and Pearson. In *Probability and Bayesian Statistics*, ed. R. Viertl. New York: Plenum Press, pp. 267–277.

Jones, G. 1982. Scientific consistency, two-stage priors and the true value of a parameter. *British Journal of the Philosophy of Science* 33:133–160.

Jorgenson, D. W. 1964. Minimum variance linear unbiased seasonal adjustment of economic time series. *Journal of the American Statistical Association* 59:681–724.

Judge, G. G., and M. E. Bock. 1978. *Statistical Implications of Pre-Test and Stein Rule Estimators in Econometrics*. Amsterdam: North-Holland.

Judge, G. G., and M. E. Bock. 1983. Biased estimation. In *Handbook of Econometrics*, vol. 1, eds. Z. Griliches and M. D. Intriligator. Amsterdam: North-Holland, pp. 599–649.

Judge, G. G., W. E. Griffiths, R. C. Hill, H. Lütkepohl, and T.-C. Lee. 1985. *The Theory and Practice of Econometrics*, 2d ed. New York: Wiley.

Judge, G. G., R. C. Hill, W. E. Griffiths, H. Lütkepohl, and T.-C. Lee. 1988. *Introduction to the Theory and Practice of Econometrics*, 2d ed. New York: Wiley.

Kadane, J. B. 1980. Predictive and structural methods for eliciting prior distributions. In *Bayesian Analysis in Econometrics and Statistics: Essays in Honor of Harold Jeffreys*, ed. A. Zellner. Amsterdam: North-Holland, pp. 89–93.

Kadane, J. B. 1992. Healthy scepticism as an expected-utility explanation of the phenomena of Allais and Ellsberg. In *Decision Making Under Risk and Uncertainty: New Models and Empirical Findings*, ed. J. Geweke. Dordrecht: Kluwer.

Kadane, J. B., and J. M. Dickey. 1980. Bayesian decision theory and the simplification of models. In *Evaluation of Econometric Models*, eds. J. Kmenta and J. B. Ramsey. New York: Academic Press, pp. 245–268.

Kadane, J. B., and T. Seidenfeld. 1990. Randomization in a Bayesian perspective. *Journal of Statistical Planning and Inference* 25:329–345.

Kadane, J. B., and R. L. Winkler. 1988. Separating probability elicitation from utilities. *Journal of the American Statistical Association* 83:357–363.

Kadane, J. B., M. J. Schervish, and T. Seidenfeld. 1986. Statistical implications of finitely additive probability. In *Bayesian Inference and Decision Techniques: Essays in Honor of Bruno de Finetti*, eds. P. K. Goel and A. Zellner. Amsterdam: Elsevier, pp. 59–76.

Kadane, J. B., J. M. Dickey, R. L. Winkler, W. S. Smith, and S. C. Peters. 1980. Interactive elicitation of opinion for a normal linear normal model. *Journal of the American Statistical Association* 75:845–854.

Kaigh, W. D. 1989. A category representation paradox (with discussion). *American Statistician* 43:92–97.

Kalbfleisch, J. D. 1975. Sufficiency and conditionality (with discussion). *Biometrika* 62:251–268.

Karni, E. 1985. *Decision Making Under Uncertainty*. Cambridge, MA: Harvard University Press.

Karni, E., D. Schmeidler, and K. Vinod. 1983. On state dependent preferences and subjective probability. *Econometrica* 51:1021–1031.

Kass, R. E. 1982. A comment on "Is Jeffreys a 'necessarist'?" *American Statistician* 36:390–391.

Kass, R. E. 1990. Data-translated likelihood and Jeffrey's rules. *Biometrika* 77:107–114.

Kass, R. E., and A. E. Raftery. 1993. Bayes factors and model uncertainty. Technical Report No. 571, Department of Statistics, Carnegie-Mellon University.

Kass, R. E., and E. H. Slate. 1990. Some diagnostics of maximum likelihood and posterior non-normality. Forthcoming, *Annals of Statistics.*

Kass, R. E., and E. H. Slate. 1992. Reparameterization and diagnostics of posterior normality. In *Bayesian Statistics 4*, eds. J. O. Berger, J. M. Bernardo, A. P. Dawid, and A. F. M. Smith. Oxford: Clarendon Press, pp. 289–305.

Kass, R. E., and S. K. Vaidyanathan. 1992. Approximate Bayes factors and orthogonal parameters, with application to testing equality of two binomial proportions. *Journal of the Royal Statistical Society [B]* 54:129–144.

Kass, R. E., L. Tierney, and J. B. Kadane. 1988. Asymptotics in Bayesian computation. In *Bayesian Statistics 3*, eds. J. M. Bernardo, M. H. DeGroot, D. V. Lindley, and A. F. M. Smith. Oxford: Oxford University Press, pp. 263–278.

Kass, R. E., L. Tierney, and J. B. Kadane. 1989. Approximate methods for assessing influence and sensitivity in Bayesian analysis. *Biometrika* 76:663–674.

Kass, R. E., L. Tierney, and J. B. Kadane. 1990. The validity of posterior expansions based on Laplace's method. In *Bayesian and Likelihood Methods in Statistics and Econometrics*, eds. S. Geisser, J. S. Hodges, S. J. Press, and A. Zellner. Amsterdam: North-Holland, pp. 473–488.

Kendall, M., and A. Stuart. 1979. *The Advanced Theory of Statistics*, vol. 2, 4th ed. London: Griffin.

Kendall, M., A. Stuart, and J. K. Ord. 1983. *The Advanced Theory of Statistics*, vol. 3, 4th ed. London: Griffin.

Kennedy, W. J., and T. A. Bancroft. 1971. Model building for predicting in regression based upon repeated significance tests. *Annals of Mathematical Statistics* 42:1273–1284.

Keynes, J. M. 1921. *A Treatise on Probability*. London: Macmillan.

Keynes, J. M. 1939. Professor Tinbergen's method. *Economic Journal* 49:8–68.

Kiefer, J. C. 1977a. Conditional confidence statements and confidence estimators. *Journal of the American Statistical Association* 72:789–827.

Kiefer, J. C. 1977b. Conditional inference. *Encyclopedia of Statistics* 2:103–109.

Kinal, T., and K. Lahiri. 1983. Specification error analysis with stochastic regressors. *Econometrica* 51:1209–1219.

King, M. L., and M. D. Smith. 1986. Joint one-sided tests of linear regression coefficients. *Journal of Econometrics* 32:367–383.

Kingman, J. F. C. 1978. The uses of exchangeability. *Annals of Probability* 16:183–197.

Kiviet, J., and G. Ridder. 1987. On the rationale for the scope of regression models in econometrics. In *The Practice of Econometrics*, eds. R. D. H. Heijmans and H. Neudecker. Dordrecht: Martinus Nijhoff Publishers, pp. 223–246.

Klamer, A. 1984. *Conversations with Economists*. Ropwman & Allanheld.

Klein, I. 1993. Comment. *American Statistician* 47:82–83.

Klein, L. 1991. The statistics seminar, MIT, 1942–1943. *Statistical Science* 6:320–338.

Klein, R., and S. Brown. 1984. Model selection when there is "minimal" prior information. *Econometrica* 52:1291–1312.

Kloek, T., and Y. Haitovsky. eds. 1988. Competing statistical paradigms in econometrics. *Journal of Econometrics* 37.

Kloek, T., and H. K. van Dijk. 1978. Bayesian estimates of equation system parameters: An application of integration by Monte Carlo. *Econometrica* 46:1–19.

Kmenta, J. 1986. *Elements of Econometrics*, 2d ed. New York: Macmillan.

Knight, F. H. 1921. *Risk, Uncertainty and Profit*. Boston: Houghton Mifflin.

Koch, C. G. 1985. A basic demonstration of the $[-1, 1]$ range for the correlation coefficient. *American Statistician* 39:201–202.

Koch, G., and F. Spizzichino. eds. 1982. *Exchangeability in Probability and Statistics*. Amsterdam: North-Holland.

Koenker, R. W. 1982. Robust methods in econometrics (with discussion). *Econometric Reviews* 1:213–289.

Koenker, R. W., and G. W. Bassett. 1978. Regression quantiles. *Econometrica* 46:33–50.

Kolomogorov, A. N. 1950. *Foundations of the Theory of Probability*, translated from German. New York: Chelsea; originally published 1933.

Koop, G., and D. J. Poirier. 1990. Wagner's hypothesis: Is it a "law"? Forthcoming, *Journal of the Royal Statistical Society [A]*.

Koop, G., and D. J. Poirier. 1991. Rank-ordered logit models: An empirical analysis of Ontario voter preferences before the 1988 Canadian federal election. Forthcoming, *Journal of Applied Econometrics*.

Koop, G., and D. J. Poirier. 1993. Bayesian analysis of logit models using natural conjugate priors. *Journal of Econometrics* 56:323–340.

Koopman, B. O. 1940. The bases of probability. *Bulletin of the American Mathematical Society* 46:763–774.

Koopmans, T. C. 1949. A Reply. *Review of Economics and Statistics* 31:86–91.

Kotz, S., and D. F. Stroup. 1983. *Educated Guessing: How to Cope in an Uncertain World*. New York: Marcel Dekker.

Kowalski, C. J. 1973. Non-normal bivariate distributions with normal marginals. *American Statistician* 27:103–106.

Kraft, C., and L. Le Cam. 1956. A remark on the roots of the likelihood equation. *Annals of Mathematical Statistics* 27:1174–1177.

Krutchkoff, R. G. 1970. *Probability and Statistical Inference*. New York: Gordon and Breach.

Kunte, S. 1992. Jeffreys-Lindley paradox and a related problem. In *Bayesian Analysis in Statistics and Econometrics*, eds. P. K. Goel and N. S. Iyengar. New York: Springer-Verlag, pp. 249–255.

Kyburg, H. 1980. Conditionalization. *Journal of Philosophy* 77:98–114.

Kyburg, H. E., Jr., and H. E. Smokler. eds. 1964. *Studies in Subjective Probability*. New York: Wiley.

Laha, R. G., and V. K. Rohatgi. 1979. *Probability Theory*. New York: Wiley.

Laplace, P. S. 1774. Memoir sur la probabilitié des causes par les envénements. *Memoirs de l'Académie Royale des Sciences* 6:621–656.

Laplace, P. S. 1847. *Oeuvres* vol. 7. Paris: Imprimerie Royale.

Lauritzen, S. L. 1974. Sufficiency, prediction and extreme models. *Scandinavian Journal of Statistics* 2:23–33.

Lauritzen, S. L. 1984. Extreme point models in statistics. *Scandinavian Journal of Statistics* 11:65–91.

Lavine, M. 1991a. An approach to robust Bayesian analysis in multidimensional parameter spaces. *Journal of the American Statistical Association* 86:400–403.

Lavine, M. 1991b. Problems in extrapolation illustrated with space shuttle o-ring data (with discussion). *Journal of the American Statistical Association* 86:919–922.

Lavine, M. 1991c. Sensitivity in Bayesian statistics: The prior and the likelihood. *Journal of the American Statistical Association* 86:396–399.

Lawrance, A. J. 1976. On conditional and partial correlation. *American Statistician* 30:146–149.

Lawson, T. 1989. Realism and instrumentalism in the development of econometrics. *Oxford Economic Papers* 41:236–258.

Leamer, E. E. 1972. A class of informative priors and distributed lag analysis. *Econometrica* 40:1059–1081.

Leamer, E. E. 1973. Multicollinearity: A Bayesian interpretation. *Review of Economic Statistics* 55:371–380.

Leamer, E. E. 1974. False models and post-data model construction. *Journal of the American Statistical Association* 69:122–130.

Leamer, E. E. 1975. A result on the sign of a restricted least squares estimate. *Journal of Econometrics* 3:387–390.

Leamer, E. E. 1978. *Specification Searches: Ad Hoc Inference with Nonexperimental Data*. New York: Wiley.

Leamer, E. E. 1982. Sets of posterior means with bounded variance priors. *Econometrica* 50:725–736.

Leamer, E. E. 1983. Let's take the con out of econometrics. *American Economic Review* 73:31–43.

Leamer, E. E. 1984. Global sensitivity results for generalized least squares estimates. *Journal of the American Statistical Association* 79:867–870.

Leamer, E. E. 1985. Sensitivity analyses would help. *American Economic Review* 75:300–313.

Leamer, E. E. 1989. Planning, criticism and revision. Supplement, *Journal of Applied Econometrics* 4:5–27.

Leamer, E. E. 1991. Testing trade theory. Working Paper No. 3957. Cambridge, MA: National Bureau of Economic Research.

Leamer, E. E. 1992. Bayesian elicitation diagnostics. *Econometrica* 60:919–942.

Leamer, E. E., and H. B. Leonard. 1983. Reporting the fragility of regression estimates. *Review of Economics and Statistics* 65:306–317.

Le Cam, L. 1986. *Asymptotic Methods in Statistical Decision Theory*. New York: Springer-Verlag.

Le Cam, L. 1990. Maximum likelihood: An introduction. *International Statistical Review* 58:153–171.

Lee, P. M. 1989. *Bayesian Statistics: An Introduction*. New York: Oxford University Press.

Leemis, L. M. 1986. Relationships among common distributions. *The American Statistician* 40:144–146.

Lehmann, E. L. 1981. An interpretation of completeness and Basu's Theorem. *Journal of the American Statistical Association* 76:335–340.

Lehmann, E. L. 1983. *Theory of Point Estimation.* New York: Wiley.

Lehmann, E. L. 1986. *Testing Statistical Hypotheses*, 2d ed. New York: Wiley.

Lehmann, E. L. 1993. The Fisher, Neyman-Pearson theories of testing hypotheses: One theory or two? *Journal of the American Statistical Association* 88:1242–1249.

Lehmann, E. L., and H. Scheffé. 1950. Completeness, similar regions, and unbiased estimation. *Sankhyā* 10:305–304.

Lehmann, E. L., and F. W. Scholz. 1992. Ancillarity. In *Current Issues in Statistical Inference: Essays in Honor of D. Basu*, eds. M. Ghosh and P. K. Pathak. Hayward, CA: Institute of Mathematical Statistics, pp. 32–51.

Lempers, F. B. 1971. *Posterior Probabilities of Alternative Linear Models.* Rotterdam: University Press.

Leonard, T. 1982. Comment on "A simple predictive density function." *Journal of the American Statistical Association* 77:657–685.

Leonard, T., J. S. J. Hsu, and K.-W. Tsui. 1989. Bayesian marginal inference. *Journal of the American Statistical Association* 84:1051–1058.

LeRoy, S. F., and L. D. Singell. 1987. Knight on risk and uncertainty. *Journal of Political Economy* 95:394–406.

Levi, I. 1978. Confirmational conditionalization. *Journal of Philosophy* 75:730–737.

Levine, R., and D. Renelt. 1992. A sensitivity analysis of cross-country growth regressions. *American Economic Review* 82:942–963.

Lewis, M. C., and G. P. H. Styan. 1981. Equalities and inequalities for conditional and partial correlation coefficients. In *Statistics and Related Topics*, eds. M. Csörgö, D. A. Dawson, J. N. K. Rao, and A. K. M. E. Saleh. Amsterdam: North-Holland, pp. 57–65.

Lindley, D. V. 1957. A statistical paradox. *Biometrika* 44:187–192.

Lindley, D. V. 1961. The use of prior probability distributions in statistical inferences and decisions. In *Proceedings of the Fourth Berkeley Symposium*, vol. 1, ed. J. Neyman. Berkeley: University of California, pp. 453–468.

Lindley, D. V. 1965. *Introduction to Probability and Statistics from a Bayesian Viewpoint*, parts 1 and 2. Cambridge: Cambridge University Press.

Lindley, D. V. 1980a. Discussion. *Journal of the Royal Statistical Society [A]* 143:423.

Lindley, D. V. 1980b. Approximate Bayesian methods. In *Bayesian Statistics 2*, eds. J. M. Bernardo, M. H. DeGroot, D. V. Lindley, and A. F. M. Smith. Amsterdam: North-Holland.

Lindley, D. V. 1982a. The Bayesian approach to statistics. In *Some Recent Advances in Statistics*, eds. J. Tiago de Oliveira and B. Epstein. New York: Academic Press, pp. 65–87.

Lindley, D. V. 1982b. Scoring rules and the inevitability of probability (with discussion). *International Statistical Review* 50:1–26.

Lindley, D. V. 1983. Comment. *Journal of the American Statistical Association* 78:61–62.

Lindley, D. V. 1985. *Making Decisions*, 2d ed. London: Wiley.

Lindley, D. V. 1986. Discussion. *The Statistician* 35:502–504.

Lindley, D. V., and M. Novick. 1981. The role of exchangeability in inference. *Annals of Statistics* 9:45–58.

Lindley, D. V., and L. D. Phillips. 1976. Inference for a Bernoulli Process (a Bayesian view). *American Statistician* 30:112–119.

Lindley, D. V., and A. F. M. Smith. 1972. Bayes estimates for the linear model (with discussion). *Journal of the Royal Statistical Society [B]* 34:1–41.

Loéve, M. 1963. *Probability Theory.* New York: D. van Nostrand, 3d ed.

Lovell, M. C. 1963. Seasonal adjustment of economic time series and multiple regression analysis. *Journal of the American Statistical Association* 58:993–1010.

Lovell, M. C. 1983. Data mining. *Review of Economics and Statistics* 65:1–12.

Lucas, Jr., R. E. 1976. Econometric policy evaluation: a critique. In *The Phillips Curve and Labor Markets*, eds. K. Brunner and A. M. Meltzer, *Carnegie-Rochester Conference on Public Policy* 1:19–46.

Lucas, R. E. 1980. Methods and problems in business cycle theory. *Journal of Money, Credit and Banking* 12:696–715.

Luenberger, D. 1969. *Optimization by Vector Space Methods.* New York: Wiley.

Lukacs, E. 1975. *Stochastic Convergence.* Lexington, MA: Heath.

McAleer, M., A. R. Pagan, and I. Visco. 1986. A further result on the sign of restricted least squares estimates. *Journal of Econometrics* 32:287–290.

McAleer, M., A. R. Pagan, and P. A. Volker. 1985. What will take the con out of econometrics? *American Economic Review* 75:293–307.

McCall, J. J. 1991. Exchangeability and Its Economic Applications. *Journal of Economic Dynamics and Control* 15:549–568.

McCloskey, D. 1985. The loss function has been mislaid: The rhetoric of significance tests. *American Economic Review, Papers and Proceedings* 75:201–205.

McCulloch, R. E. 1989. Local model influence. *Journal of the American Statistical Association* 84:473–478.

McCulloch, R., and P. E. Rossi. 1991. A Bayesian approach to testing the arbitrage pricing theory. *Journal of Econometrics* 49:141–168.

Machina, M. 1987. Choice under uncertainty: Problems solved and unresolved. *Journal of Economic Perspectives* 1(1): 121–154.

Machina, M., and D. Schmeidler. 1992. A more robust definition of subjective probability. *Econometrica* 60:745–780.

Machlup, F. 1974. Proxies and dummies. *Journal of Political Economy* 82:892.

MacKinnon, J. G., and H. White. 1985. Some heteroskedasticity consistent covariance matrix estimators with improved finite sample properties. *Journal of Econometrics* 29:305–325.

McManus, W. S. 1985. Estimates of the deterrent effect of capital punishment: The importance of the researcher's prior beliefs. *Journal of Political Economy* 93:417–425.

Maddala, G. S. 1977. *Econometrics.* New York: McGraw-Hill.

Magnus, J. R. 1978. Maximum likelihood estimation of the GLS model with unknown parameters in the disturbance covariance matrix. *Journal of Econometrics* 7:281–312; Corrigenda. *Journal of Econometrics* 10:261.

Magnus, J. R. 1988. *Linear Structures.* London: Griffin.

Magnus, J. R., and H. Neudecker. 1988. *Matrix Differential Calculus with Applications in Statistics and Econometrics.* New York: Wiley.

Maher, P. 1993. *Betting on Theories.* Cambridge: Cambridge University Press.

Maistrov, L. E. 1974. *Probability Theory: A Historic Sketch.* New York: Academic Press.

Malinvaud, E. 1970. *Statistical Methods in Econometrics*, 2nd ed. Amsterdam: North-Holland.

Mann, H. B., and A. Wald. 1943. On the statistical treatment of linear stochastic difference equations. *Econometrica* 11:173–220.

Manski, C. F. 1984. Adaptive estimation of non-linear regression models (with discussion). *Econometric Reviews* 3:145–210.

Manski, C. F. 1988. *Analogy Estimation Methods in Econometrics.* London: Chapman & Hall.

Manski, C. F. 1991. Regression. *Journal of Economic Literature* 29:34–50.

Mardia, K. V. 1970. *Families of Bivariate Distributions.* London: Griffin.

Martz, H. F., and W. J. Zimmer. 1992. The risk of catastrophic failure of the solid rocket boosters on the space shuttle. *American Statistician* 46:42–47.

Marschak, J. 1953. Economic measurements for policy and prediction. In *Studies in Econometric Method*, eds. W. C. Hood and T. C. Koopmans. New York: Wiley, pp. 1–26.

Mathai, A. M., and S. B. Provost. 1992. *Quadratic Forms in Random Variables*. New York: Marcel Dekker.

Maxwell, J. C., 1860. Illustrations of the dynamical theory of gases, part 1: On the motion and collision of perfectly elastic spheres. *Phil. Mag.* 19:19–32.

Meeden, G., and B. C. Arnold. 1979. The admissibility of a preliminary test estimator when the loss incorporates a complexity cost. *Journal of the American Statistical Association* 74: 872–873.

Meier, P., and L. C. DiNardo. 1990. Simpson's Paradox in employment litigation. Unpublished Manuscript, Department of Statistics, University of Chicago.

Melnick, E. L., and A. Tenenbein. 1982. Misspecifications of the Normal Distribution. *American Statistician* 36:372–373.

Metropolis, N., A. W. Rosenbluth, M. N. Rosenbluth, A. H. Teller, and E. Teller. 1953. Equations of state calculations by fast computing machines. *Journal of Chemical Physics* 21:1087–1091.

Miller, A. J. 1990. *Subset Selection in Regression*. London: Chapman & Hall.

Miller, R. G. 1981. *Simultaneous Statistical Inference*, 2d ed. New York: Springer-Verlag.

Min, C.-K., and A. Zellner. 1993. Bayesian and non-Bayesian methods for combining models and forecasts with applications to forecasting international growth rates. *Journal of Econometrics* 56:89–118.

Mittal, Y. 1991. Homogeneity of subpopulations and Simpson's paradox. *Journal of the American Statistical Association* 86:167–172.

Mizon, G. E. 1977. Inferential procedures in nonlinear models: an application in a UK industrial cross section study of factor substitution and returns to scale. *Econometrica* 45: 1221–1242.

Mizon, G. E. 1984. The encompassing approach in econometrics. In *Econometrics and Quantitative Analysis*, eds. D. F. Hendry and K. F. Wallis. Oxford: Basil Blackwell, pp. 135–172.

Mizon, G. E., and J.-F. Richard. 1986. The encompassing principle and its application to testing non-nested hypotheses. *Econometrica* 54:657–678.

Mood, A. M., F. A. Graybill, and D. C. Boes. 1974. *Introduction to the Theory of Statistics*, 3d ed. McGraw-Hill.

Moors, J. J. A. 1981. Inadmissibility of linearly invariant estimators in truncated parameter spaces. *Journal of the American Statistical Association* 76:910–915.

Morgan, J. P., N. R. Chaganty, R. C. Dahiya, and M. J. Doviak. 1991. Let's make a deal: The player's dilemma (with discussion). *American Statistician* 45:284–289.

Morgan, M. S. 1987. Statistics without probability and Haavelmo's revolution in econometrics. In *The Probabilistic Revolution*, vol. 2, eds. L. Krüger, G. Gigerenzer, and M. S. Morgan. Cambridge, MA: MIT Press.

Morgan, M. S. 1989. *The History of Econometric Ideas*. Cambridge University Press.

Morgenbesser, S. 1969. The Realist-Instrumentalist controversy. In *Philosophy, Science, and Method*, eds. S. Morgenbesser, P. Suppes and M. White. New York: St. Martin's Press, pp. 200–218.

Mosteller, F., and D. L. Wallace. 1964. *Applied Bayesian and Classical Inference: The Case of the Federalist Papers*. Reading, MA: Addison-Wesley.

Muirhead, R. J. 1982. *Aspects of Multivariate Statistical Theory*. New York: Wiley.

Mullen, K. 1967. A note on the ratio of two independent random variables. *American Statistician* 21:30–31.

Nalebuff, B. 1987. Choose a curtain, duel-ity, two point conversions, and more. *Journal of Economic Perspectives* 1(2): 157–163.

Nalebuff, B. 1990. Puzzles: Slot machines, zomepirac, squash, and more. *Journal of Economic Perspectives* 4:179–187.

Naylor, J. C., and A. F. M. Smith. 1982. Applications of a method for the efficient computation of posterior distributions. *Applied Statistics* 31:214–225.

Nelder, J., and R. W. M. Wedderburn. 1972. Generalized linear models. *Journal of the Royal Statistical Society [A]* 135:370–384.

Newey, W. K., and D. McFadden. 1993. Estimation in large samples. In *Handbook of Econometrics*, vol. 4, eds. R. F. Engle and D. McFadden. Amsterdam: North-Holland, Forthcoming.

Newey, W. K., and J. L. Powell. 1987. Asymmetric least squares estimation and testing. *Econometrica* 5:819–847.

Neyman, J. 1959. Optimal asymptotic tests of composite statistical hypotheses. In *Probability and Statistics, the Harald Cramer Volume*, ed. U. Grenander. New York: Wiley.

Neyman, J., and E. S. Pearson. 1933. On the problem of the most efficient test of statistical hypotheses. *Philosophical Transactions of the Royal Society [A]* 231:289–337.

Neyman, J., and E. S. Scott. 1948. Consistent estimates based on partially consistent observations. *Econometrica* 16:1–32.

Norden, R. H. 1972. A survey of maximum likelihood estimation. *International Statistical Review* 40:329–354.

Norden, R. H. 1973. A survey of maximum likelihood estimation. *International Statistical Review* 41:39–58.

Novick, M. R., and J. E. Grizzle. 1965. A Bayesian approach to the analysis of data from clinical trials. *Journal of the American Statistical Association* 60:81–96.

Nunnikhoven, T. S. 1992. A birthday problem solution for nonuniform birth frequencies. *American Statistician* 46:270–274.

Oh, M.-S., and J. O. Berger. 1991. Integration of multimodal functions by monte carlo importance sampling. Technical Report No. 91-31C, Department of Statistics, Purdue University.

O'Hagan, A. 1980. Discussion. In *Bayesian Statistics*, eds. J. Bernardo, M. DeGroot, D. V. Lindley, and A. F. M. Smith. Valencia: Valencia Press, pp. 373–376.

Oksanen, E. H. 1992. Simple sampling schemes for calculating joint distributions of least squares coefficients and least squares residuals. Unpublished Manuscript, Department of Economics, McMaster University.

Oman, S. D. 1985. Specifying a prior distribution in structured regression problems. *Journal of the American Statistical Association* 80:190–195.

Ord, J. K. 1972. *Families of Frequency Distributions*. New York: Hafner.

Pagan, A. R. 1982. Estimation and control of linear econometric models. *IHS—Journal* 6:247–268.

Page, S. E. 1991. We'd rather fight than switch: Trying to understand "Let's Make a Deal." Discussion Paper No. 968, Department of Managerial Economics and Decision Sciences, Northwestern University.

Palm, F. C., and A. Zellner. 1990. To combine or not to combine? Issues of combining forecasts. Forthcoming, *Journal of Forecasting*.

Patnaik, P. B. 1949. The non-central chi-squared and F distribution and their applications. *Biometrika* 36:202–232.

Pearson, E. S. 1955. Statistical concepts in their relation to reality. *Journal of the Royal Statistical Society [B]* 17:204–207.

Pearson, K. 1920a. Notes on the history of correlation. *Biometrika* 13:25–45.

Pearson, K. 1920b. The fundamental problem of practical statistics. *Biometrika* 13:1–16.

Pelloni, G. 1991. A note on Friedman and the neo-Bayesian approach. *Manchester School of Economics and Social Studies* 55:407–418.

Pericchi, L. R. 1984. An alternative to the standard Bayesian procedure for discrimination between normal models. *Biometrika* 71:575–586.

Pericchi, L. R., and A. F. M. Smith. 1992. Exact and approximate posterior moments for a normal location parameter. *Journal of the Royal Statistical Society [B]* 54:793–804.

Pericchi, L. R., and P. Walley. 1991. Robust Bayesian credible intervals and prior ignorance. *International Statistical Review* 58:1–23.

Perks, F. J. A. 1947. Some observations on inverse probability including a new indifference rule. *Journal of the Institute of Actuaries* 73:285–334.

Pesaran, M. H., R. P. Smith, and J. S. Yeo. 1985. Testing for structural stability and predictive failure: A review. *Manchester School* 53:280–295.

Peskun, P. H. 1973. Optimum Monte Carlo sampling using Markov chains. *Biometrika* 60:607–612.

Pettit, L. I. 1986. Diagnostics in Bayesian model choice. *The Statistician* 35:183–190.

Phillips, P. C. B. 1977. A general theorem in the theory of asymptotic expansions as approximations to the finite sample distributions of econometric estimators. *Econometrica* 45:1517–1534.

Phillips, P. C. B. 1983. Marginal densities of instrumental variable estimators in the general single equation case. *Advances in Econometrics* 2:1–24.

Phillips, P. C. B. 1987. Time series with a unit root. *Econometrica* 55:305–325.

Phillips, P. C. B. 1988. Reflections on econometric methodology. *Economic Record* 64:344–359.

Phillips, P. C. B. 1991. To criticize the critics: An objective Bayesian analysis of stochastic trends (with discussion). *Journal of Applied Econometrics* 6:333–364.

Pierce, D. A., and R. L. Dykstra. 1969. Independence and the normal distribution. *American Statistician* 23:39.

Pilz, J. 1991. *Bayesian estimation and experimental design in linear regression models.* New York: Wiley.

Pitman, E. J. G. 1937. The closest estimates of statistical parameters. *Proceedings of the Cambridge Philosophical Society* 33:212–222.

Pitman, E. J. G. 1939. The estimation of location and scale parameters of a continuous population of any given form. *Biometrika* 30:391–421.

Plackett, R. L. 1965. A class of bivariate distributions. *Journal of the American Statistical Association* 60:516–522.

Plackett, R. L. 1972. The discovery of the method of least squares. *Biometrika* 59:239–251.

Planck, M. 1949. *Scientific Autobiography and Other Papers.* New York: Greenwood Press.

Pocock, S. J. 1977. Group sequential methods in the design and analysis of clinical trials. *Biometrika* 64:191–199.

Poirier, D. J. 1976. *The Econometrics of Structural Change.* Amsterdam: North-Holland. Published in Russian. 1981.

Poirier, D. J. 1981. Posterior odds analysis when all competing models are false. *Economics Letters* 8:135–140.

Poirier, D. J. 1985. Bayesian hypothesis testing in linear models with continuously induced conjugate priors across hypotheses. In *Bayesian Statistics 2*, eds. J. M. Bernardo, M. H. DeGroot, D. V. Lindley, and A. F. M. Smith. Amsterdam: North-Holland, pp. 711–722.

Poirier, D. J. 1986. Contrast in inferences based on sampling distributions and posterior distributions. *Econometric Theory* 2:289.

Poirier, D. J. 1987. Solution to "Contrast in inferences based on sampling distributions and posterior distributions." *Econometric Theory* 3:464–466.

Poirier, D. J. 1988a. Bayesian diagnostic testing in the general linear normal regression model. In *Bayesian Statistics 3*, eds. J. M. Bernardo, M. H. DeGroot, D. V. Lindley, and A. F. M. Smith. Oxford: Oxford University Press, pp. 725–732.

Poirier, D. J. 1988b. Causal relationships and replicability. *Journal of Econometrics* 39:213–234; errata. 1989. *Journal of Econometrics* 42:381.

Poirier, D. J. 1988c. Frequentist and subjectivist perspectives on the problems of model building in economics (with discussion). *Journal of Economic Perspectives* 2:121–170.

Poirier, D. J. 1989. Report from the battlefront. *Journal of Business & Economics Statistics* 7:137–139.

Poirier, D. J., ed. 1991a. *Bayesian empirical studies in economics and finance, Annals of the Journal of Econometrics* 49(1,2).

Poirier, D. J. 1991b. Bayesian scores. Unpublished Manuscript, Department of Economics, University of Toronto.

Poirier, D. J. 1991c. A Bayesian view of nominal money and real output through a new classical macroeconomic window (with discussion). *Journal of Business & Economic Statistics* 9:125–161.

Poirier, D. J. 1991d. A comment on "to criticize the critics: An objective Bayesian analysis of stochastic trends." *Journal of Applied Econometrics* 6:381–386.

Poirier, D. J. 1991e. Window washing: A Bayesian perspective on diagnostic checking. In *Volume in Honor of Arnold Zellner*, eds. D. Berry, K. Chalone, and J. Geweke. Forthcoming.

Poirier, D. J. 1992a. Answer: Hopefully the user; A discussion of "Who knows what alternative lurks in the hearts of significance tests." In *Bayesian Statistics 4*, eds. J. O. Berger, J. M. Bernardo, A. P. Dawid, and A. F. M. Smith. Oxford: Clarendon Press, pp. 254–256.

Poirier, D. J. 1994a. Jeffreys' prior for logit models. *Journal of Econometrics* 63:327–339.

Poirier, D. J., ed. 1994b. Introduction. In *The Methodology of Econometrics*, Edward Elgar Publishing, pp. xi–xxii.

Poirier, D. J., ed. 1994. *The Methodology of Econometrics*, vols. 1 and 2. Edward Elgar Publishing.

Poirier, D. J., and S. Klepper. 1981. Model occurrence and model selection in panel data sets. *Journal of Econometrics* 17:333–350.

Poirier, D. J., M. Tello, and S. Zin. 1986. A diagnostic test for normality within the power exponential family. *Journal of Business & Economic Statistics* 4:359–373.

Polasek, W. 1984. Multivariate regression systems: Estimation and sensitivity analysis of two dimensional data. In *Robustness of Bayesian Analysis*, ed. J. B. Kadane. Amsterdam: North-Holland.

Pollock, D. S. G. 1979. *The Algebra of Econometrics*. New York: Wiley.

Popper, K. R. 1959. The propensity interpretation of probability. *British Journal for the Philosophy of Science* 10:25–42.

Pötscher, B. M. 1983. Order estimation in ARMA-models by Lagrange multiplier tests. *Annals of Statistics* 11:872–875.

Pötscher, B. M. 1991. Effects of model selection on inference. *Econometric Theory* 7:163–185.

Pötzelberger, K., and W. Polasek. 1991. Robust HPD regions in Bayesian regression models. *Econometrica* 59:1581–1589.

Pratt, J. W. 1965. Bayesian interpretation of standard inference statements (with discussion). *Journal of the Royal Statistical Society [B]* 27:169–203.

Pratt, J. W., H. Raiffa, and R. Schlaifer. 1964. The foundations of decision under uncertainty: An elementary exposition. *Journal of the American Statistical Association* 59:353–375.

Presidential Commission on the Space Shuttle *Challenger* Accident. 1986. *Report of the Presidential Commission on the Space Shuttle Challenger Accident*, 2 vols. Washington, D.C.: Author.

Press, S. J. 1980. Bayesian computer programs. In *Bayesian Analysis in Econometrics and Statistics*, ed. A. Zellner. Amsterdam: North-Holland, pp. 429–442.

Press, S. J. 1982. *Applied Multivariate Analysis*. Malabar, FL: Krieger Publishing.

Press, S. J. 1989. *Bayesian Statistics: Principles, Models, and Applications*. New York: Wiley.

Press, S. J., and A. Zellner. 1978. Posterior distribution for the multiple correlation coefficient with fixed regressors. *Journal of Econometrics* 8:307–321.

Qin, D. 1989. *History of Econometric Thought: the Formation of Econometrics (1930–1960)*. PhD dissertation, Oxford University.

Quandt, R. E. 1983. Computational problems and methods. In *Handbook of Econometrics*, vol. 1, eds. Z. Griliches and M. D. Intriligator. Amsterdam: North-Holland, pp. 699–764.

Quenouille, M. H. 1956. Notes on bias in estimation. *Biometrika* 43:353–360.

Raferty, A. E., and S. M. Lewis. 1992. How many iterations in the Gibbs sampler? In *Bayesian Statistics 4*, eds. J. O. Berger, J. M. Bernardo, A. P. Dawid, and A. F. M. Smith. Oxford: Clarendon Press, pp. 763–773.

Raiffa, H., and R. Schlaifer. 1961. *Applied Statistical Decision Theory*. Cambridge, MA: Harvard University Press.

Ramsay, J. O., and M. R. Novick. 1980. PLU robust Bayesian decision theory: point estimation. *Journal of the American Statistical Association* 75:901–907.

Ramsey, F. P. 1931. Truth and probability. In *The Foundations of Mathematics and Other Logical Essays*, ed. R. B. Braithwaite. London: Routledge & Keegan Paul, pp. 156–198.

Reprint (1964) in *Studies in Subjective Probability*, eds. H. E. Kyburg Jr., and H. E. Smokler. New York: Wiley, pp. 61–92.

Rao, C. R. 1948. Large sample tests of statistical hypotheses concerning several parameters with applications to problems of estimation. *Proceedings of the Cambridge Philosophical Society* 44:50–57.

Rao, C. R. 1952. Some theorems on minimum variance estimation. *Sankhyā* 12:27–42.

Rao, C. R. 1973. *Linear Statistical Inference and Its Applications*, 2d ed. New York: Wiley.

Rao, C. R. 1981. Some comments on the minimum mean square error as a criterion of estimation. In *Statistics and Related Topics*, eds. M. Csörgö, D. A. Dawson, J. N. K. Rao, and A. K. M. E. Saleh. Amsterdam: North-Holland, pp. 123–143.

Rao, C. R. 1989. *Statistics and Truth: Putting Chance to Work*. New Delhi: Council of Scientific and Industrial Research.

Rao, C. R., J. P. Keating, and R. L. Mason. 1986. The Pitman nearness criterion and its determination. *Communications in Statistics [A]* 15:3173–3191.

Rao, M. M. 1989. Paradoxes in conditional probability. In *Multivariate Statistics and Probability: Essays in Memory of Paruchuri R. Krishnaiah*, eds. C. R. Rao and M. M. Rao. New York: Academic Press, pp. 434–446.

Rea, J. D. 1978. Indeterminacy of the Chow test when the number of observations is insufficient. *Econometrica* 46:229.

Rencher, A. C., and F. C. Pun. 1980. Inflation of R^2 in best subset regression. *Technometrics* 80:49–53.

Rényi, A. 1970. *Probability Theory*. New York: Elsevier.

Ripley, B. 1966. *Stochastic Simulation*. New York: Wiley.

Robbins, H. 1952. Some aspects of the sequential design of experiments. *Bulletin of the American Mathematical Society* 58:527–536.

Roberts, G. O. 1992. Convergence diagnostics of the Gibbs sampler. In *Bayesian Statistics 4*, eds. J. O. Berger, J. M. Bernardo, A. P. Dawid, and A. F. M. Smith. Oxford: Clarendon Press, pp. 775–782.

Roberts, H. V. 1965. Probabilistic prediction. *Journal of the American Statistical Association* 60:50–62.

Roberts, H. V. 1976. For what use are tests of hypotheses and tests of significance. *Communications in Statistics: Theory and Methods* A5:753–761.

Rothenberg, T. J. 1971. Identification in linear models. *Econometrica* 39:577–592.

Rothenberg, T. J. 1984. Approximating the distribution of econometric estimators and test statistics. In *Handbook of Econometrics*, vol. 2, eds. Z. Griliches and M. D. Intriligator. Amsterdam: North-Holland, pp. 881–935.

Rothenberg, T. J., and C. T. Leenders. 1964. Efficient estimation of simultaneous equation systems. *Econometrica* 32:57–76.

Rubin, D. 1987. Comment on "The calculation of posterior distribution by data augmentation." *Journal of the American Statistical Association* 82:543–546.

Rubin, D. 1988. Using the SIR algorithm to simulate posterior distributions. In *Bayesian Statistics 3*, eds. J. M. Bernardo, M. H. DeGroot, D. V. Lindley, and A. F. M. Smith. Oxford: Oxford University Press, pp. 395–402.

Rubin, H. 1987. A weak system of axioms for "rational" behavior and the nonseparability of utility from prior. *Statistics and Decisions* 5:47–58.

Ruppert, D. 1987. What is kurtosis? An influence function approach. *American Statistician* 41:1–5.

Ruud, P. 1984. Tests of specification in econometrics (with discussion). *Econometric Reviews* 3:211–276.

Salkever, D. S. 1976. The use of dummy variables to compute predictions, prediction errors and confidence intervals. *Journal of Econometrics* 4:393–397.

Salop, S. C. 1987. Evaluating uncertain evidence with Sir Thomas Bayes: A note for teachers. *Journal of Economic Perspectives* 1(1): 155–160.

Sampson, A. R. 1974. A tale of two regressions. *Journal of the American Statistical Association* 69:682–689.

Samuels, M. L. 1993. Simpson's paradox and related phenomena. *Journal of the American Statistical Association* 88:81–88.

Sargan, J. D. 1976. Econometric estimators and the Edgeworth approximations. *Econometrica* 42:421–448; erratum 45:272.

Sargan, J. D., and F. Mehta. 1983. A generalization of Durbin's significance test and its application to dynamic specification. *Econometrica* 51:1551–1567.

Savage, L. J. 1954. *The Foundations of Statistics*. New York: Wiley. Second revised edition, New York: Dover Publications. 1972.

Savage, L. J. 1971. Elicitation of personal probabilities and expectations. *Journal of the American Statistical Association* 66:783–801.

Savage, L. J. 1981. *The Writings of Leonard Jimmie Savage: A Memorial Selection*. Haywood, CA: American Statistical Association and Institute of Mathematical Statistics.

Savage, L. J. et al. 1962. *The Foundations of Statistical Inference*. London: Metheun.

Savin, N. E. 1980. The Bonferroni and Scheffé multiple comparison procedures. *Review of Economic Studies* 47:255–273.

Savin, N. E. 1984. Multiple hypothesis testing. In *Handbook of Econometrics*, vol. 2, eds. Z. Griliches and M. D. Intriligator. Amsterdam: North-Holland, pp. 827–879.

Sawa, T., and T. Hiromatsu. 1973. Minimax regret significance points for a preliminary test in regression analysis. *Econometrica* 41:1093–1101.

Scheffé, H. 1953. A method of judging all contrasts in the analysis of variance. *Biometrika* 40:87–104.

Scheffé, H. 1959. *The Analysis of Variance*. New York: Wiley.

Scheffé, H. 1977. A note on a reformulation of the *S*-method of multiple comparisons (with discussion). *Journal of the American Statistical Association* 72:143–146.

Schervish, M. J., and T. Seidenfeld, and J. B. Kadane. 1984. The extent of non-conglomerability of finitely-additive probabilities. *Z. Wahrscheinlichkeitstheorie verw. Gebiete* 66:205–226.

Schervish, M. J., and T. Seidenfeld, and J. B. Kadane. 1990. State dependent utilities. *Journal of the American Statistical Association* 85:840–847.

Schervish, M. J., and T. Seidenfeld, and J. B. Kadane. 1992. Small worlds and state dependent utilities (with discussion). In *Bayesian Analysis in Statistics and Econometrics*, eds. P. K. Goel and N. S. Iyengar. New York: Springer-Verlag, pp. 207–215.

Schwarz, G. 1978. Estimating the dimension of a model. *Annals of Statistics* 6:461–464.

Sclove, S. L., C. Morris, and R. Radhakrishnan. 1972. Non-optimality of preliminary-test estimators for the multinormal mean. *Annals of Mathematical Statistics* 43:1481–1490.

Searle, S. R. 1982. *Matrix Algebra Useful for Statistics.* New York: Wiley.

Seber, G. A. F. 1977. *Linear Regression Analysis.* New York: Wiley.

Seber, G. A. F. 1980. *The Linear Hypothesis: A General Theory.* London: Griffin.

Sen, P. K. 1992. The Pitman closeness of statistical estimators: Latent years and the renaissance. In *Current Issues in Statistical Inference: Essays in Honor of D. Basu,* eds. M. Ghosh and P. K. Pathak. Hayward, CA: Institute of Mathematical Statistics, pp. 52–74.

Serfling, R. J. 1980. *Approximation Theorems of Mathematical Statistics.* New York: Wiley.

Seshadri, V., and G. P. Patil. 1964. A characterization of a bivariate distribution by the marginal and conditional distributions of the same component. *Annals of Mathematical Statistics* 15:215–221.

Shafer, G. 1982. Lindley's paradox (with discussion). *Journal of the American Statistical Association* 77:325–351.

Shafer, G. 1985. Conditional probability (with discussion). *International Statistical Review* 53:261–277.

Shafer, J. P. 1991. The Gauss-Markov theorem and random regressors. *American Statistician* 45:269–273.

Shephard, N. G. 1991. From characteristic function to distribution function: A simple framework for the theory. *Econometric Theory* 7:519–529.

Shuttle Criticality Review Hazard Analysis Audit Committee. 1988. *Post-Challenger Evaluation of Space Shuttle Risk Assessment and Management.* Washington, D. C.: National Academy of Sciences Press.

Sidák, Z. 1967. Rectangular confidence regions for the means of multivariate normal distributions. *Journal of the American Statistical Association* 62:626–633.

Silvey, S. D. 1959. The Lagrange multiplier test. *Annals of Mathematical Statistics* 30:387–407.

Silvey, S. D. 1969. Multicollinearity and imprecise estimation. *Journal of the Royal Statistical Society [B]* 35:65–75.

Silvey, S. D. 1975. *Statistical Inference.* New York: Wiley.

Simpson, E. H. 1951. The interpretation of interaction contingency tables. *Journal of the Royal Statistical Society [B]* 13:238–241.

Sims, C. A., and H. Uhlig. 1991. Understanding unit rooters: A helicopter tour. *Econometrica* 59:1591–1599.

Skyrms, B. 1984. *Pragmatism and Empiricism.* New Haven: Yale University Press.

Smith, A. F. M. 1981. On radom sequences with centred spherical symmetry. *Journal of the Royal Statistical Society [B]* 43:208–209.

Smith, A. F. M. 1984. Present position and potential developments: Some personal views of Bayesian statistics. *Journal of the Royal Statistical Society [A]* 147:245–259.

Smith, A. F. M. 1992. Bayesian computational methods. *Philosophical Transactions of the Royal Society London [A]* 337:369–386.

Smith, A. F. M., and A. E. Gelfand. 1992. Bayesian statistics without tears: A sampling-resampling perspective. *American Statistician* 46:84–88.

Smith, A. F. M., and G. O. Roberts. 1993. Bayesian computation via the Gibbs sampler and related Markov chain Monte Carlo methods. Forthcoming, *Journal of the Royal Statistical Society [B].*

Smith, A. F. M., and D. J. Spiegelhalter. 1980. Bayes factors and choice criteria for linear models. *Journal of the Royal Statistical Society [B]* 42:213–220.

Smith, A. F. M., A. M. Skene, J. E. H. Shaw, J. C. Naylor, and M. Dransfield. 1985. The implementation of the Bayesian paradigm. *Communications in Statistics* 14:1079–1102.

Smith, C. A. B. 1961. Consistency and statistical inference and decision. *Journal of the Royal Statistical Society [B]* 23:1–25.

Smith, G. 1974. Multicollinearity and forecasting. Cowles Foundation Discussion Paper No. 33, Yale University.

Solow, R. M. 1985. Economic history and economics. *AEA Papers and Proceedings* 75:328–331.

Spanos, A. 1986. *Statistical Foundations of Econometric Modelling.* Cambridge: Cambridge University Press.

Spanos, A. 1990. The simultaneous-equations model revisited: statistical adequacy and identification. *Journal of Econometrics* 90:87–105.

Spiegelhalter, D. J., and A. F. M. Smith. 1982. Bayes factors for linear and log-linear models with vague prior information. *Journal of the Royal Statistical Society [B]* 44:377–387.

Stein, C. 1956. Inadmissibility of the usual estimator for the mean of a multivariate normal distribution. In *Proceedings of the Third Berkeley Symposium*, eds. J. Neyman and E. L. Scott. Berkeley: University of California, pp. 197–206.

Stigler, S. M. 1973a. The asymptotic distribution of the trimmed mean. *Annals of Statistics* 1:472–477.

Stigler, S. M. 1973b. Simon Newcomb, Percy Daniell, and the history of robustness. *Journal of the American Statistical Association* 68:872–879.

Stigler, S. M. 1982. Thomas Bayes' Bayesian inference. *Journal of the Royal Statistical Society [A]* 145:250–258.

Stigler, S. M. 1986. *The History of Statistics: The Measurement of Uncertainty Before 1900.* Chicago: Chicago University Press.

Stigum, B. P. 1990. *Toward a Formal Science of Economics: The Axiomatic Method in Economics and Econometrics.* Cambridge, MA: MIT Press.

Stone, M. 1964. Comments on a posterior distribution of Geisser and Cornfield. *Journal of the Royal Statistical Society [B]* 26:274–276.

Stone, M. 1977. An asymptotic equivalence of choice of model by cross-validation and Akaike's criterion. *Journal of the Royal Statistical Society [B]* 39:44–47.

Stone, M. 1979. Comments on model selection criteria of Akaike and Schwarz. *Journal of the Royal Statistical Society [B]* 41:276–278.

Stuart, A., and J. K. Ord. 1987. *Kendall's Advanced Theory of Statistics*, vol. 1, 5th ed. London: Griffin.

Sverdrup, E. 1967. *Laws and Chance Variations: Basic Concepts of Statistical Inference.* Vol. 2, *More Advanced Treatment.* Amsterdam: North-Holland.

Swamy, P. A. V. B., R. K. Conway, and P. von zur Muehlen. 1985. The foundation of econometrics—Are there any? (with discussion). *Econometric Reviews* 4:1–119.

Sweeting, T. J. 1980. Uniform asymptotic normality of the maximum likelihood estimator. *Annals of Statistics* 8:1375–1381.

Sweeting, T. J., and A. O. Adekola. 1987. Asymptotic posterior normality for stochastic processes revisited. *Journal of the Royal Statistical Society [B]* 49:215–222.

Tanner, M. 1991. *Tools for Statistical Inference: Observed Data and Data Augmentation.* New York: Springer-Verlag.

Tanner, M., and W. Wong. 1987. The calculation of posterior distribution by data augmentation (with discussion). *Journal of the American Statistical Association* 82:528–550.

Taylor, J. M. G., and M. R. Segal. 1992. Comment. *Journal of the American Statistical Association* 87:628–631.

Taylor, W. E. 1983. On the relevance of finite sample distribution theory (with discussion). *Econometric Reviews* 2:1–84.

Theil, H. 1963. On the use of incomplete prior information in regression analysis. *Journal of the American Statistical Association* 58:401–14.

Theil, H. 1971. *Principles of Econometrics.* Amsterdam: North Holland.

Theil, H., and A. S. Goldberger. 1961. On pure and mixed estimation in economics. *International Economic Review* 2:65–78.

Thisted, R. A. 1988. *Elements of Statistical Computing: Numerical Computation.* London: Chapman & Hall.

Thomas, G., and J. O'Quigley. 1993. A geometric interpretation of partial correlation using spherical triangles. *American Statistician* 47:30–32.

Tierney, L. 1991a. Exploring posterior distributions using Markov chains. *Computer Science and Statistics: 23rd Symposium on the Interface*. Alexander, VA: American Statistical Association, pp. 579–585.

Tierney, L. 1991b. Markov chains for exploring posterior distributions. Technical Report No. 560, School of Statistics, University of Minnesota.

Tierney, L., and J. B. Kadane. 1986. Accurate approximations for posterior moments and marginal posterior densities. *Journal of the American Statistical Association* 81:82–86.

Tierney, L., R. E. Kass, and J. B. Kadane. 1989a. Approximate marginal densities of nonlinear functions. *Biometrika* 76:425–433; errata, *Biometrika* 78:233–234.

Tierney, L., R. E. Kass, and J. B. Kadane. 1989b. Fully exponential Laplace approximations to expectations and variances of nonpositive functions. *Journal of the American Statistical Association* 84:710–716.

Tintner, G. 1953. The definition of econometrics. *Econometrica* 21:31–40.

Tong, Y. L. 1980. *Probability Inequalities in Multivariate Distributions*. New York: Academic Press.

Toyoda, T., and D. W. Wallace. 1976. Optimal critical values for pre-testing in regression. *Econometrica* 44:365–375.

Tukey, J. W. 1960. Conclusions vs decisions. *Technometrics* 2:423–433.

Tukey, J. W. 1962. *Annals of Mathematical Statistics* 33:1–67.

Tukey, J. W. 1978. Discussion of Granger on seasonality. In *Seasonal Analysis of Economic Time Series*, ed. A. Zellner. Washington, DC: U. S. Government Printing Office, pp. 50–53).

Ullah, A., and V. Zinde-Walsh. 1985. On robustness of tests of linear restrictions in regression models with elliptical error distributions. In *Time Series and Econometric Modelling*, eds. I. V. MacNeil and G. J. Umphrey. Dordrecht, The Netherlands: Reidel.

van Beeck, P. 1972. An application of Fourier methods to the problem of sharpening the Berry-Esseen inequality. *Z. Wahrscheinlichkeitstheorie und Verw. Gebiete* 23:187–196.

van Dijk, H. K., and T. Kloek. 1985. Experiments with some alternatives for simple importance sampling in Monte Carlo integration. In *Bayesian Statistics 2*, eds. J. M. Bernardo, M. H. DeGroot, D. V. Lindley, and A. F. M. Smith. Amsterdam: North-Holland, pp. 511–530.

van Dijk, H. K., T. Kloek, and C. G. E. Boender. 1985. Posterior moments computed by mixed integration. *Journal of Econometrics* 29:3–18.

van Fraassen, B. C. 1980. *The Scientific Image*. Oxford: Clarendon Press.

Varian, H. R. 1975. A Bayesian approach to real estate assessment. In *Studies in Bayesian Econometrics and Statistics*, eds. S. E. Fienberg and A. Zellner. Amsterdam: North-Holland. pp. 197–208.

Villegas, C. 1977. On the representation of ignorance. *Journal of the American Statistical Association* 72:651–652.

von Liebig, J., 1863. *Uber Francis Bacon von Verulam und die Methode der Naturforschung*. Munich: Literausch-Artistisde Anstalt.

von Mises, R. 1928. *Wahrscheinlichkeit, Statistik, und Wahrheit*. Wien: J. Springer. English reprint, *Probability, Statistics, and Truth*, 2d ed. New York: Macmillan, 1954.

Wagner, C. H. 1982. Simpson's paradox in real life. *American Statistician* 36:46–48.

Wald, A. 1943. Tests of statistical hypotheses concerning several parameters when the number of observations is large. *Transactions of the American Mathematical Society* 54:426–482.

Wald, A. 1949. A note on the consistency of the maximum likelihood estimate. *Annals of Mathematical Statistics* 20:595–601.

Wald, A. 1950. *Statistical Decision Functions*. New York: Wiley.

Walley, P. 1991. *Statistical Reasoning with Imprecise Probabilities*. London: Chapman & Hall.

Walker, A. M. 1969. On the asymptotic behaviour of posterior distributions. *Journal of the Royal Statistical Society [B]* 31:80–88.

Wang, Y. H., J. Stoyanov, and Q.-M. Shao. 1993. On independence and dependence properties of a set of events. *American Statistician* 47:112–115.

Wasserman, L. 1992. Recent methodological advances in robust Bayesian inference (with discussion). In *Bayesian Statistics 4*, eds. J. O. Berger, J. M. Bernardo, A. P. Dawid, and A. F. M. Smith. Oxford: Clarendon Press, pp. 483–502.

Wasserman, L., and J. B. Kadane. 1992. Computing bounds on expectations. *Journal of the American Statistical Association* 87:516–522.

Watts, D. W. 1991. Why is introductory statistics difficult to learn? And what can we do to make it easier?. *American Statistician* 45:290–291.

Welsch, B. L., and H. W. Peters. 1963. On formulae for confidence points based on integrals of weighted likelihoods. *Journal of the Royal Statistical Society [B]* 25:318–329.

West, M., and J. Harrison. 1989. *Bayesian Forecasting and Dynamic Models.* New York: Springer-Verlag.

White, H. 1984. *Asymptotic Theory for Econometricians.* New York: Academic Press.

White, J. S. 1958. The limiting distribution of the serial correlation coefficient in the explosive case. *Annals of Mathematical Statistics* 29:1188–1197.

Wilkinson, G. N. 1977. On resolving the controversy in scientific inference (with discussion). *Journal of the Royal Statistical Society [B]* 39:119–171.

Wilks, S. 1938. The large sample distribution of the likelihood ratio for testing composite hypotheses. *Annals of Mathematical Statistics* 9:60–62.

Williams, P. M. 1976. Indeterminate probabilities. In *Formal Methods in the Methodology of Empirical Sciences*, eds. M. Przelecki, K. Szaniawski, and R. Wojciki. Dordrecht, The Netherlands: Reidel, pp. 229–246.

Winkler, R. L. 1967. The assessment of prior distributions in Bayesian analysis. *Journal of the American Statistical Association* 62:776–800.

Winkler, R. L. 1972. *Introduction to Bayesian Inference and Decision.* New York: Holt, Rinehart and Winston.

Winkler, R. L. 1977. Prior distributions and model-building in regression analysis. In *New Developments in the Applications of Bayesian Methods*, eds. A. Aykac and C. Brumat. Amsterdam: North-Holland, pp. 233–242.

Winkler, R. L. 1981. Combining probability distributions from dependent information. *Management Science* 27:479–488.

Winkler, R. L., W. S. Smith, and R. B. Kulkarni. 1978. Adaptive forecasting models based on predictive distributions. *Management Science, Theory and Application* 24:977–986.

Winkler, R. L., and L. A. Franklin. 1979. Warner's randomized response model: a Bayesian approach. *Journal of the American Statistical Association* 74:207–214.

Wishart, J. 1931. The mean and second moment coefficient of the multiple correlation coefficient in samples from a normal population. *Biometrika* 22:353.

Wolak, F. A. 1989. Testing of inequality constraints in linear econometric models. *Journal of Econometrics* 41:205–236.

Wong, R. 1989. *Asymptotic Approximation of Integrals.* New York: Academic Press.

Wong, W. H., and B. Li. 1992. Laplace expansion for posterior densities of nonlinear functions of parameters. *Biometrika* 79:393–398.

Wonnacott, R. J., and T. H. Wonnacott. 1980. *Econometrics.* New York: Wiley.

Yaari, M. E. 1971. *Linear Algebra for Social Sciences.* Englewood Cliffs, NJ: Prentice-Hall.

Yamada, S., and H. Miromoto. 1992. Sufficiency. In *Current Issues in Statistical Inference: Essays in Honor of D. Basu*, eds. M. Ghosh and P. K. Pathak. Hayward, CA: Institute of Mathematical Statistics, pp. 86–98.

Yule, G. U. 1897. On the theory of correlation. *Journal of the Royal Statistical Society* 60:812–854.

Yule, G. U. 1907. On the theory of correlation for any number of variables treated by a new system of notation. *Proceedings of the Royal Statistical Society [A]* 79:182, 192–193.

Zacks, S. 1971. *The Theory of Statistical Inference*. New York: Wiley.

Zellner, A. 1962. An efficient method of estimating seemingly unrelated regressions and tests for aggregation bias. *Journal of the American Statistical Association* 58:977–992.

Zellner, A. 1971. *An Introduction to Bayesian Inference in Econometrics*. New York: Wiley.

Zellner, A. 1972. On assessing informative prior distributions for regression coefficients. Unpublished Manuscript, University of Chicago.

Zellner, A. 1976. Bayesian and non-Bayesian analysis of the regression model with multivariate student t error terms. *Journal of the American Statistical Association* 71:400–405.

Zellner, A. 1977. Maximal data information prior distributions. In *New Developments in the Applications of Bayesian Methods*, eds. A. Aykac and C. Brumat. Amsterdam: North-Holland, pp. 211–231.

Zellner, A. 1978. Estimation of functions of population means and regression coefficients including structural coefficients: A minimal expected loss (MELO) approach. *Journal of Econometrics* 8:127–158.

Zellner, A. 1982a. "Is Jeffreys a "necessarist"? *American statistician* 36:28–30.

Zellner, A. 1982b. "Reply to a comment on "Is Jeffreys a 'necessarist'?" *American Statistician* 36:392–393.

Zellner, A. 1983. Statistical theory and econometrics. In *Handbook of Econometrics*, vol. 1, eds. Z. Griliches and M. D. Intriligator. Amsterdam: North-Holland, pp. 67–178.

Zellner, A. 1986a. On assessing prior distributions and Bayesian regression analysis with g-prior distributions. In *Bayesian Inference and Decision Techniques: Essays in Honor of Bruno de Finetti*, eds. P. K. Goel and A. Zellner. Amsterdam: North-Holland, pp. 233–243.

Zellner, A. 1986b. Bayesian estimation and prediction using asymmetric loss functions. *Journal of the American Statistical Association* 81:446–451.

Zellner, A. 1994. Bayesian and non-Bayesian estimation using balanced loss functions. In: S. S. Gupta and J. O. Berger. *Statistical Decision Theory and Related Topics V*. New York: Springer-Verlag, pp. 377–390.

Zellner, A., and C.-K. Min. 1992a. Bayesian analysis, model selection and prediction. Unpublished Manuscript, Graduate School of Business, University of Chicago.

Zellner, A., and C.-K. Min. 1992b. Gibbs sampler convergence criteria (GSC^2). Unpublished Manuscript, Graduate School of Business, University of Chicago.

Zellner, A., and P. E. Rossi. 1984. Bayesian analysis of dichotomous quantal response models. *Journal of Econometrics* 25:365–394.

Zellner, A., and A. Siow. 1980. Posterior odds ratios for selected regression hypotheses (with discussion). In *Bayesian Statistics*, eds. J. M. Bernardo, M. H. DeGroot, D. V. Lindley, and A. F. M. Smith. Valencia: University Press, pp. 585–603, 618–647.

Author Index

Abbott, P. C., 445, 488
Achcar, J. A., 316
Adams, J. L., 522
Adekola, A. O., 306
Agresti, A., 251
Aigner, D. J., 440, 560
Aitchison, J., 135, 370, 411
Aitkin, M., 394
Akaike, H., 321, 394
Alalouf, I. S., 570
Aldous, D. J., 215
Aldrich, J., 4, 419
Allais, M., 27
Amemiya, T., 195–197, 202, 252, 256, 278, 287, 440
Anderson, G. J., xi
Anderson, T. W., 135, 136, 281, 347
Andrews, D. W. K., 201
Anscombe, F. J., 20
Arnold, B. C., 117, 121, 181, 522
Arrow, K., 363
Aumann, R. J., 20

Bahadur, R. R., 277, 368
Balakrishnan, N., 181
Balanda, K. P., 41
Bancroft, T. A., 521
Barnard, G. A., 219, 227, 228, 608
Barndorff-Nielson, O. E., 113, 219
Barnett, V., 1, 16, 19, 219, 290, 321
Barten, A. P., 560
Bartle, R. G., 187
Bartlett, M. S., 390
Bassett, G., 416, 452, 461
Basu, D., 185, 228, 230, 231, 277, 346, 400
Bates, J. M., 439
Bauer, P., 363, 367
Bauwens, L., 654
Bayarri, M. J., 220, 226
Bayes, T., 18, 20, 214, 405
Becker, W., 563
Bellman, R., 619
Berger, J. O., 217, 227, 230–232, 306, 307, 318, 321, 328–330, 334, 336, 344–346, 364, 366, 376, 398–400, 402, 654
Berger, R. L., 80, 114, 175, 190, 224, 230, 269, 270, 315, 342, 398
Berkson, J., 286, 506
Bernardo, J. M., 21, 215, 217, 219, 318, 321, 325, 328
Berndt, E. R., 281, 370
Bernoulli, J., 16, 18
Berry, A. C., 208
Berry, D. A., 232, 364
Bertrand, J., 590
Besag, J., 660
Bhansali, R. J., 394
Bhattacharya, R. N., 207
Bickel, P. J., 255
Billingsley, P., 12, 61
Binkley, J. K., 445, 448
Birnbaum, A., 23, 227, 230, 319
Bjørnstad, J. F., 230, 425, 428
Blackwell, D., 322
Blyth, C. R., 244, 245, 416
Bock, M. E., 284, 521–523
Boender, C. G. E., 654
Boes, D. C., 87–89, 91, 109, 145, 177, 182, 202, 244, 266, 267, 335, 356
Boland, L. A., 2
Border, K., 22
Bowden, R., 235
Box, G. E. P., xi, 99, 139, 295, 321, 323, 324, 535, 593, 608, 609, 629
Breusch, T. S., 539
Britney, R. R., 440
Brook, R. J., 521
Brown, L. D., 113, 349, 494
Brown, S., 545
Buehler, R. J., 346
Burguette, J. F., 274, 278
Burrows, P. M., 506
Buse, A., 371
Butler, R. W., 425

Cabanis, S., xiv
Campbell, D., 410
Cantrell, R. S., 506
Cardano, G., 16
Carlstein, E., 643
Carnap, R., 15, 19
Carroll, L., 585
Cartwright, N., 1
Casella, G., 80, 114, 175, 190, 224, 230, 269, 270, 315, 342, 398, 660
Castillo, E., 117, 121, 181
Chaganty, N. R., 26
Chamberlain, G., 274
Chen, C.-F., 306, 527, 528
Chib, S., 556
Chow, G. C., 394, 505
Chow, Y. S., 208
Christ, C., 1
Chung, K. L., 40, 195, 201, 209
Churchill, W., 425, 428
Cicero, 9
Clemen, R. T., 439
Cohen, A., 522
Conniffe, D., 373
Conway, R. K., 1
Cook, T., 410
Cooley, T. F., 427, 536
Cornfield, J., 232, 288, 366, 391, 392
Cox, D. R., 219, 244, 317, 340, 355, 359–361, 366, 405, 408, 425, 427
Coyle, C. A., 29
Craig, A. T., 48, 152, 161, 194, 202, 223
Cramér, H., xiv, 205, 278, 281
Crowder, M. J., 278, 281, 320, 372

Dagenais, M. G., 372
Dahiya, R. C., 26

Dalal, S. R., 4, 5, 7, 8, 528
Darwin, C., 445
Das Peddada, S., 245
David, F. N., 16
Davidson, J. E. H., 612
Davidson, R., 185, 372, 373, 375, 579, 654
Davison, A. C., 437
Dawid, A. P., 14, 55, 215, 306, 318, 321, 416, 615
DeBruijn, N. G., 316
deFermat, P., 16
de Finetti, B., 9, 13, 16, 19, 20, 21, 27, 86, 168, 211–215, 216, 219
DeGroot, M. H., 9, 20, 42, 55, 99, 128, 220, 223, 244, 250, 321, 332, 342, 535, 613
Delampady, M., 330, 398, 400, 402
De Marchi, N., 1
de Moirves, A., 16
de Morgan, A., 20
Dempster, A. P., 2, 24
Devroye, L., 654
Dey, D. K., 396
Dhrymes, P. J., 12, 40, 46, 61, 194, 197–199, 201, 205, 207, 209, 275, 496, 619
Diaconis, P., 22, 215, 291, 528
Dickey, J. M., 139, 298, 320, 352, 384, 400, 506, 507, 527, 528, 530, 544, 547
DiNardo, L. C., 416
Doviak, M. J., 26
Downham, D. Y., 394
Dransfield, M., 654
Draper, D., 215, 605
Drèze, J., 528
Driscoll, M. F., 159
Dubins, L., 322
Duchan, A. I., 503
Dufour, J.-M., 208, 372, 505, 506, 592
Duncan, O., 418, 419
Dunsmore, I. R., 411
Durbin, J., 230, 373
Dykstra, R. L., 131

Earman, J., xii, 22
Eaton, M. L., 215
Edwards, A. W. F., 232, 322, 329, 351, 398–400
Edwards, W., 220
Eells, E., 22
Efron, B., 281, 410
Ellsberg, D., 27
Engle, R. F., 368, 373, 461, 499, 552, 587, 613
Epstein, R. J., 1
Esseen, C. G., 208
Evans, M. J., 230

Farebrother, R. W., 521
Favero, C., 419
Feldman, D., 410
Feldstein, M., 522
Feller, W., 93
Ferguson, T. S., 277
Fine, T., 16
Fishburn, P. C., 20, 22
Fisher, F. M., 161
Fisher, R. A., xiii, 13, 219–221, 227, 251, 275, 290, 400, 408, 426
Florens, J.-P., 376
Fowlkes, E. B., 4, 5, 7, 8
Franklin, L. A., 285
Fraser, D. A. S., 228, 230, 321
Fraumeni, J. F., Jr., 482
Fréchet, M., 118, 131
Freedman, D. A., 215, 522
Freeman, P. R., 76, 320
Friedman, M., 2, 23
Frisch, R., 1, 3, 418, 419, 480

Gallant, A. R., 274, 278
Galton, F., 445
Games, P. A., 496
Gardenfors, P., 22
Gauss, C. F., 242, 461
Geisser, S., 325, 411, 425
Gelfand, A. E., 396, 659, 660
Gelman, A., 131, 660
Geman, D., 659
Geman, S., 659
Genest, C., 585
George, E. I., 660
Geweke, J., 22, 326, 506, 654, 656–658, 660
Gigerenzer, G., xiii
Gilbert, C., 1
Giles, D. E., 537
Gilks, W. R., 660
Gleser, L. J., 349
Glymour, C., 28
Goddard, M. J., 416
Godfrey, L. G., 368, 373
Goel, P. K., 309
Gokhale, D. V., 72
Goldberger, A. S. G., xii, 64, 65, 69, 72, 75, 366, 405, 425, 445, 522
Goldstein, M., 23
Golub, G. H., 643
Good, I. J., 24, 329, 381, 400, 540
Gourieroux, C., 117
Graham, A., 645, 652
Granger, C. W. J., 1–3, 415, 439
Graybill, F. A., 87–89, 91, 109, 135, 145, 177, 182, 202, 244, 266, 267, 335, 356, 498, 506, 619
Green, P. J., 660
Greene, W. H., 519
Griffiths, W. E., 528, 538, 567, 576, 605, 653, 654
Grizzle, J. E., 376
Gundberg, W. R., Jr., 159

Haavelmo, T., xi, 1, 3, 24, 418, 451, 587, 589
Hacking, I., 16
Hackl, P., 363, 366

Hadley, G., 619
Haitovsky, Y., 1
Hald, A., 363, 366
Hall, B. H., 281, 370
Hall, J. H., 370, 528
Hall, R. E., 281
Hallin, M., 208
Hamilton, J. D., 201, 209, 274, 317
Hammersly, J. M., 654
Handscomb, D. C., 654
Hannan, E. J., 394
Hansen, L., 273, 274
Harrison, J., xi
Hartigan, J. A., 323
Hastings, W. K., 659
Haughton, D. M. A., 394
Hausman, J. A., 281, 370
Heath, D. C., 213, 215, 333
Heckman, J. J., 410
Heijmans, R. D. H., 560
Henderson, H. V., 631
Hendry, D. F., xi, 227, 354, 363, 419, 461, 523, 536, 552, 587, 589, 592, 612–614
Hesse, M., 28
Hewitt, E., 215
Heyde, C. C., 306
Hill, B. M., 14, 227, 230, 391, 392, 524, 613, 614
Hill, R. C., 528, 538, 567, 576, 605, 653, 654
Hillier, G., 361
Hills, S. E., 316, 660
Hinkley, D. V., 165, 219, 220, 244, 281, 340, 343, 349, 355, 359–361, 426–428, 436, 437
Hiromatsu, T., 521
Hoadley, B., 4, 5, 7, 8, 278
Hoaglin, D. C., 558
Hocking, R. R., 156, 158, 159, 162
Hodges, J. L., 506
Hodges, J. S., 608
Hogarth, R. H., 320
Hogg, R. V., 48, 152, 161, 194, 202, 223
Holly, A., 373
Hotz, V. J., 410
Howson, C., 16
Hsiao, C., 235
Hsu, J. S. J., 308
Hsu, P. L., 472
Huber, P. J., 256, 274, 278
Huntsberger, D. V., 522
Huygens, C., 16
Huzurbazar, V. S., 278

Ibragimov, I. A., 208
Iwata, S., 548–551

James, W., 283
Jammalamadaka, S. R., 556
Jaynes, E. T., 215, 321, 333
Jeffrey, R. C., 23
Jeffreys, H., 16, 19, 27, 219, 321–323, 325, 376–377, 380, 396, 535, 547
Jensen, D. R., 464
Johnson, I. M., 306
Johnson, N. L., 91, 103, 105, 113, 116–118, 133, 155, 156, 158, 160, 306
Johnson, R. A., 306
Johnston, J., xiii, 518, 564, 566
Johnstone, D., 397
Jones, G., 216
Jorgenson, D. W., 518
Judge, G. G., 284, 521–523, 528, 538, 567, 576, 605, 653, 654

Kadane, J. B., xi, 13, 14, 22, 55, 220, 306–309, 315, 316, 320, 330, 333, 352, 384, 393, 394, 506, 507, 527, 547
Kaigh, W. D., 416
Kalbfleisch, J. D., 230
Karni, E., 20, 22
Kass, R. E., 19, 306, 308, 316, 321, 330, 333, 378, 393–395, 658
Keating, J. P., 245
Kemp, A. W., 91
Kendall, M., 75, 244, 274, 276, 359, 361, 501, 502
Kennedy, P., 563
Kennedy, W. J., 521
Keynes, J. M., 19, 24, 219, 329, 587
Kiefer, J. C., 219
Kinal, T., 488
King, M. L., 506
Kingman, J. F. C., 215
Kiviet, J., 64, 592
Klamer, A., 318, 613
Klein, I., 26
Klein, L., 76
Klein, R., 545
Klepper, S., 378
Kloek, T., 1, 654
Kmenta, J., 245, 477, 503
Knight, F. H., 16
Koch, C. G., 175
Koch, G., 215
Koenker, R. W., 256, 452, 461
Kolmogorov, A. N., xiv, 12, 13, 55, 200, 201
Koop, G., 329, 378
Koopman, B. O., 24
Koopmans, T. C., 210, 405, 418
Kotz, S. K., 91, 103, 105, 113, 116–118, 133, 155, 156, 158, 160, 416
Kowalski, C. J., 118
Kraft, C., 277
Krutchkoff, R. G., 268
Kulkarni, R. B., 320, 528
Kunte, S., 363
Kyburg, H. E., Jr., 16, 23

Laha, R. G., 79
Lahiri, K., 488
Lakatos, I., xi
Lane, D., 14
Laplace, P. S., 16–18, 214, 316, 405, 461

Lauritzen, S. L., 215, 426
Lavine, M., 330
Lawrance, A. J., 72
Lawson, T., 2, 3
Leamer, E. E., 219, 227, 233, 244, 320, 321, 330, 351, 352, 354, 363, 487, 489, 523, 525, 534, 536, 545, 570, 576, 577, 579, 587–589, 599, 600, 606, 612–614, 642
Le Cam, L., 185, 277, 306, 590
Lee, P. M., 328
Lee, T.-C., 528, 538, 567, 576, 605, 653, 654
Leemis, L. M., 114
Legendre, A. M., 461
Lehmann, E. L., 43, 78, 113, 116, 208, 224, 225, 242, 244, 250, 252–256, 258, 267–269, 275–278, 281, 286, 287, 315, 346, 355, 356, 359, 360, 398, 506
Lempers, F. B., 546
Leonard, H. B., 536
Leonard, T., 308
Leontieff, W., 1
LeRoy, S. F., 16, 536
Levi, I., 23
Levine, R., 536
Lewis, M. C., 70, 72
Lewis, S. M., 660
Li, B., 308
Lindley, D. V., 20, 21, 26, 29, 42, 215, 308, 321, 322, 323, 331, 364, 376, 408, 410, 415, 416, 535, 539, 545, 590, 601, 607, 609
Lindman, H., 232, 322, 329, 351, 398–400
Linnik, Y. V., 208
Loéve, M., 195, 205, 209
Lovell, M. C., 480, 518, 522
Lucas, R. E., Jr., 351, 419
Luenberger, D., 621, 623
Lukacs, E., 78, 79, 188–192, 198
Lütkepohl, H., 528, 538, 567, 576, 605, 653, 654

MacGillivray, H. L., 42
Machina, M., 20, 22
Machlup, F., 509
MacKinnon, J. G., 185, 281, 372, 375, 519, 654
Maddala, G. S., 498
Magnus, J. R., 281, 591, 619, 628, 643, 645, 649
Maher, P., 22
Maistrov, L. E., 16
Malinvaud, E., 227, 478, 578
Mallows, C. L., 215
Mann, H. B., 193, 195
Manski, C. F., xi, 272, 274
Mardia, K. V., 118
Martz, H. F., 4, 8
Marschak, J., 419
Mason, R. L., 245
Mathai, A. M., 155, 163
Maxwell, J. C., 464
McAleer, M., 536
McCall, J. J., 211
McCloskey, D., 363
McCulloch, R. E., 320, 330
McFadden, D., 197, 256, 274, 278, 287, 288
McManus, W. S., 536
Meeden, G., 522
Meier, P., 416
Melnick, E. L., 131
Mehta, F., 373
Meng, X.-L., 131
Metropolis, N., 659
Miller, A. J., 522, 523
Miller, R. J., 496, 522
Min, C.-K., 442, 660
Miromoto, H., 222
Mittal, Y., 416
Mizon, G. E., xi, 536, 589, 612, 614
Monette, G., 230, 321
Monfort, A., 117
Mood, A. M., 87–89, 91, 109, 145, 177, 182, 202, 244, 266, 267, 335, 356
Moors, J. J. A., 285
Morgan, J. P., 26
Morgan, M. S., 1
Morgenbesser, S., 1
Mortera, J., 400
Mosteller, F., 308
Mouchart, M., 376
Muirhead, R. J., 122, 133, 134, 136, 158, 180, 366
Mullen, K., 79

Nagaraja, H. N., 181
Nalebuff, B., 26, 27
Naylor, J. C., 654
Nelder, J., 354
Neudecker, H., 281, 560, 619, 628, 643, 645, 649
Newey, W. K., 197, 256, 274, 278, 287, 288, 440
Newton, I., 25
Neyman, J., xiii, 277, 356, 373, 397, 398
Ng, K.-W., 321
Norden, R. H., 275
Novick, M. R., 215, 330, 376, 408, 415, 416, 586
Nunnikhoven, T. S., 25

O'Hagan, A., 613
O'Quigley, J., 564
Oh, M.-S., 654
Oksanen, E. H., 482
Oman, S. D., 527
Orcutt, G., xi
Ord, J. K., 47, 118

Pagan, A. R., 370, 374, 536, 592
Page, S. E., 26
Palm, F. C., 442
Parke, W. R., 427
Pascal, B., 16

Pathak, P. K., 245
Patil, G. P., 118
Patnaik, P. B., 113
Pearson, E. S., xiii, 356, 398
Pearson, K., 70, 115, 405
Pelloni, G., 16
Pepys, S., 25
Pericchi, L. R., 315, 321, 330, 545
Perks, F. J. A., 322
Pesaran, M. H., 506
Peskun, P. H., 659
Peters, H. W., 323
Peters, S. C., 320, 527
Pettit, L. I., 586
Phillips, L. D., 364
Phillips, P. C. B., 208, 227, 308, 323, 324, 347
Pierce, D. A., 131
Pilz, J., 320, 527
Pitman, E. J. G., 245, 270
Plackett, R. L., 118, 462
Planck, M., xi
Pocock, S. J., 364
Poirier, D. J., 1, 2, 4, 227, 289, 324, 325, 329, 330, 352, 354, 363, 378, 402, 403, 419, 440, 523, 544, 546, 558, 586, 587, 589, 591, 601, 605, 610, 613, 614
Poisson, S. D., 17
Polasek, W., 531, 533
Pollock, D. S. G., 194
Popper, K. R., 18, 28
Pötscher, B. M., 363, 366, 523
Pötzelberger, K., 533
Powell, J. L., 440
Pratt, J. W., 20, 351
Pregibon, D., 215
Presidential Commission on the Space Shuttle *Challenger* Accident, 4
Press, S. J., 20, 129, 136, 179, 180, 309, 536, 537, 540
Provost, S. B., 155, 163
Pun, F. C., 523

Qin, D., 1
Quandt, R. E., 643, 653, 654
Quenouille, M. H., 248
Quinn, B. G., 394

Racine-Poon, A., 660
Raferty, A. E., 380, 394, 658, 660
Raiffa, H., 20, 320, 543
Ramsay, J. O., 330, 586
Ramsey, F. P., 20, 21
Rao, C. R., 79, 191, 192, 195, 200, 201, 206, 209, 210, 245, 248, 253, 370, 472, 496, 570
Rao, M. M., 47
Rayner, A. C., 537
Rea, J. D., 506
Reid, N., 219, 317
Rencher, A. C., 523
Renelt, D., 536
Rényi, A., 13
Richard, J.-F., 461, 552, 587, 592, 612, 654
Richards, D., 643
Ridder, G., 64
Ripley, B., 658
Robbins, H., 365
Roberts, G. O., 660
Roberts, H. V., 351, 411
Rohatgi, V. K., 79
Rosenbluth, A. W., 659
Rosenbluth, M. N., 659
Rossi, P. E., 320, 654
Rothenberg, T. J., 208, 235, 372, 373
Rubin, D., 660
Rubin, H., 22
Ruppert, D., 42, 643
Ruud, P., 373

Sahlin, N.-E., 22
Salkever, D. S., 558
Salop, S. C., 15
Sampson, A. R., 491
Samuels, M. L., 416
Sarabia, J.-M., 117, 121, 181
Sargan, J. D., 708, 373, 592
Sargent, T., 613
Savage, L. J., xi, 9, 13, 16, 20–22, 215, 219, 227, 232, 320, 322, 329, 351, 362, 398–400, 613
Savin, N. E., 496
Sawa, T., 521
Scheffé, H., 224, 268, 269, 495, 497
Schervish, M. J., 13, 14, 22, 55, 306
Schlaifer, R., 20, 320, 543
Schmeidler, D., 20
Scholz, F. W., 346
Schwarz, G., 394
Sclove, S. L., 522
Scott, E. S., 277
Searle, S. R., 619, 631
Seber, G. A. F., 134, 496, 502
Segal, M. R., 659
Segal, U., 22
Seidenfeld, T., xi, 13, 14, 22, 55, 306, 315
Sellke, T., 330, 398–400
Sen, P. K., 245
Serfling, R. J., 194, 199, 209, 286
Seshadri, V., 118
Shafer, G., 23, 391
Shafer, J. P., 472
Shao, Q.-M., 14
Shaw, J. E. H., 654
Shen, S. M., 135
Shephard, N. G., 42
Shuttle Criticality Review Hazard Analysis Audit Committee, 4
Siddák, Z., 496
Silvey, S. D., 270, 370–372, 570, 576
Simons, G., xiv
Simpson, E. H., 416
Sims, C. A., 346–349
Singell, L. D., 16
Siow, A., 547

Skene, A. M., 654
Skyrms, B., 215
Slate, E. H., 316
Smith, A. F. M., xii, 1, 21, 215, 217, 219, 309, 315, 316, 331, 394, 539, 545, 614, 654, 659
Smith, C. A. B., 24
Smith, G., 567
Smith, M. D., 506
Smith, R. P., 506
Smith, W. S., 320, 527
Smokler, H. E., 16
Solow, R. M., 318, 585
Souza, G., 274, 278
Spanos, A., 188, 201, 205, 209, 278, 445, 451, 592, 612
Spiegelhalter, D. J., 394, 545
Spizzichino, F., 215
Srba, F., 612
Stein, C., 283
Stigler, S. M., 16, 255, 256, 405
Stigum, B. P., 1
Stone, M., 321, 394
Stoyanov, J., 14
Stroup, D. F., 416
Stuart, A., 47, 75, 244, 274, 276, 359, 361, 501, 502
Styan, G. P. H., 70, 72, 570
Sudderth, W. D., 213, 215, 333
Sverdrup, E., 70
Swamy, P. A. V. B., 1
Sweeting, T. J., 306

Tanner, M., 659, 660
Taylor, J. M. G., 659
Taylor, W. E., 251
Teicher, H., 208
Teller, A. H., 659
Teller, E., 659
Tello, M., 610
Tenenbein, A., 131
Theil, H., 207, 245, 493, 522, 551, 560
Thisted, R. A., 653
Thomas, G., 564
Tiao, G. C., 99, 139, 295, 321, 323, 324, 535, 593, 629
Tierney, L., 306–309, 316, 330, 333, 393, 394, 660
Tintner, G., 1
Tiwari, R. C., 556
Tong, Y. L., 134
Toyoda, T., 521
Tsui, K.-W., 308
Tukey, J. W., xi, 23, 319, 524

Uhlig, H., 346–349
Ullah, A., 502
Urbach, P., 16

Vaidyanathan, S. K., 394
van Beeck, P., 208
van Dijk, H. K., 654
van Fraassen, B. C., 26
Varian, H. R., 312
Venn, J., 17
Villegas, C., 324
Vinod, K., 20
Visco, I., 536
Volker, P. A., 536
von Liebig, J., 613
von Mises, R., 17
von zur Muehlen, P., 1
Vuong, Q. H., 506

Wagner, C. H., 416
Wald, A., 193, 195, 227, 305, 369
Walker, A. M., 306
Wallace, D. L., 308
Wallace, D. W., 521
Walley, P., 13, 16, 23, 24, 46, 55, 215, 314, 319–321, 329, 330, 333
Wang, C., 29
Wang, Y. H., 14
Wasserman, L., 330, 395
Watts, D. W., 29
Waugh, F. V., 480
Wedderburn, R. W. M., 394
Welsch, B. L., 323
Welsch, R. E., 558
West, M., xi
White, H., 188, 193, 195, 196, 201, 209, 281
White, J. S., 347
Wilkinson, G. N., 219
Wilks, S., 370
Williams, P. M., 24
Winkler, R. L., 22, 285, 321, 320, 440, 442, 527, 528
Wishart, J., 471
Wolak, F. A., 506
Wolpert, R. L., 227, 230–232, 334, 344–346, 366
Wong, R., 316
Wong, W., 660
Wong, W. H., 308
Wonnacott, R. J., 202
Wonnacott, T. H., 202

Yaari, M. E., 619
Yamada, S., 222
Yeo, J. S., 506, 612
Ylvisaker, D., 291, 528
Yule, G. U., 70, 564

Zabell, S., 22
Zacks, S., 250
Zellner, A., 19, 107, 127, 128, 136, 227, 297, 311, 312, 314, 321–323, 325, 440, 442, 526, 528, 535–538, 540, 547, 588, 599, 654, 660
Zidek, J. V., 321, 585
Zimmer, W. J., 4, 8
Zin, S., 610
Zinde-Walsh, V., 502

Subject Index

Absolutely continuous, 45
Adjoint of a matrix, 651, 652
Admissibility, 238, 314. *See also* Inadmissible estimator
Akaike's criterion, 394
Algebra, 10
Analog principle, 272
Analysis of variance, 513, 514
Ancillary statistic, 169, 185, 225, 269, 281, 315, 344–346, 349
 maximal, 346, 349
Assumption, 3
Asymmetry, 41
Asymptotic
 distribution (limiting), 201–210, 252–258, 273, 274, 278, 280, 282, 283, 347, 369, 371
  Bayesian, 322, 393, 394
 efficiency, 253, 490
 expectation, 252
 moments, 194
 test, 367–376, 390
 variance, 252
Asymptotically
 normal, 252, 253
 unbiased, 247, 252
Asymptotics, 185–210, 225, 247, 250–258, 260, 270, 272–274, 277–283, 287, 306, 347, 367–376, 428, 490, 499, 523, 590
 Bayesian, 306–309, 393–395
Atom, 31, 32, 541, 548, 549
Autoregression (AR), 346–349, 431, 591–593, 596, 613

BAN estimators, 253
Banach's match problem, 93
Bartlett's paradox, 390
Basu's theorem, 269, 345
Bayesian
 Bayes theorem
  for densities, 216, 290, 323
  for events, 15, 333, 379
 estimation, 288–318, 524–540, 548
 factor, 380–385, 388, 389, 393–395, 400, 541–543, 545, 547, 549, 550, 551, 604
 hypothesis testing, 376–396, 540–551
 inference, 319
  necessarists, 219
  subjectivists, 219, 220
 objective, 289, 290, 321, 351
 prediction, 213, 432–433, 551–559
 score, 373, 395, 585, 602
 subjective, 289, 351, 362
 viewpoint, xi–xii, 3, 23, 219, 230, 231, 236, 408, 428, 463, 486, 599, 601–617
Behrens-Fisher problem, 340
Bernoulli distribution, 84, 92, 93, 114, 116, 177, 180, 184, 192, 198, 200, 211–213, 215, 225, 276, 285, 286, 293, 299, 303, 344, 345, 373, 416, 609
Bernoulli trials, 84, 85, 405
Berry-Esseen theorem, 208
Best asymptotically normal estimators. *See* BAN estimators
Best linear unbiased estimators. *See* BLUE
Best quadratic unbiased, 493
Beta coefficients, 566
Beta-binomial distribution, 114, 116, 660
Beta distribution, 104–106, 109, 114, 116, 130, 210, 292, 293, 324
Beta function, 104, 214
Bias, 234, 242, 243, 247–250, 276, 284, 477, 522
Binomial distribution, 84, 85, 88, 92, 114, 116, 118, 153, 181, 1827 199, 214, 233, 363, 364, 407
Binomial theorem, 42, 84
Birthday problem, 25
Bivariate distributions, 43, 118
 exponential, 459
 logistic, 459
 normal, 118, 121, 122, 129, 130, 452, 459
 normal mixture, 130, 155
 Pareto, 132, 459
 Poisson, 133
BLUE, 245, 247, 248, 272, 472, 473, 477, 478, 558, 571, 572, 575. *See also* Gauss-Markov theorem
Bonferroni method, 342, 496
Bootstrap, 220
Borel field, 12, 26, 30, 31, 446
Borel-Kolmogorov paradox, 55
Borel sets, 12, 26
Bounded, 193, 199, 236, 657
Burr distribution, 110

Calibration problem, 498
CAN estimator, 253
Canonical
 form, 113
 reduction, 475
Cauchy distribution
 multivariate, 126
 univariate, 106, 112, 114–116, 130, 153, 155, 178, 198, 209, 275, 396, 547
Causality, 2, 26, 409
Censored random variable, 36, 324, 601
Central limit theorems, 201–210, 278, 281
 Lindeberg-Feller, 205, 206
 Lindeberg-Levy, 202, 204, 273
Certainty equivalence, 426, 432
CES production function, 286
Chain rule of differentiation, 149, 650
Change-of-variable technique, 149–155
Characteristic function, 40, 178, 179, 194, 202
Characteristic root, 163, 474, 487, 522, 539, 570, 574, 575, 581, 582, 634–639, 646
Characteristic value problem, 634
Characteristic vector, 474, 482, 487, 539, 570, 574, 575, 634–638, 646
Chebyshev's theorem, 200

Chi-squared distribution, 100, 101, 107, 109, 113, 114, 130, 136, 137, 147, 150–152, 155, 156, 160–163, 180, 247, 337–339, 369–371, 430, 431, 434, 500, 540
Cholesky decomposition, 639
Chow test, 505, 506
Classical viewpoint, 219, 356, 364, 365
Cobb-Douglas production function, 478, 484, 489, 498
Cochran' s theorem, 161
Coefficient of determination. *See* R^2
Coefficient of multiple correlation, 559. *See* Population R^2 and R^2
Coefficient of variation, 248
Coherent beliefs, 21, 25, 27, 216
Collective, 17, 18
Collector's problem, 25
Combination of forecasts, 439–443
Combinations, 82, 83, 87
Compact set, 253, 287, 657
Complement of a set, 10
Complete statistics, 267, 269, 345
 boundedly, 345, 361
 jointly, 267
Completing the square, 122
Compliance, 410
Computation, 372, 653–660
Concave, 78, 79
Conditional distribution, 46, 450, 452
Conditional event, 13
Conditional expectation, 59, 60
Conditional frequentist inference, 219, 344–346, 463, 506
Conditional inverse, 630–631
Conditional lilkelihood inference, 219
Conditional mean, 64, 127, 453
Conditional probability, 46, 47
Conditional variance, 65, 127, 134, 452
Conditionally independent events, 14, 15
Conditionally independent random variables, 55, 168, 215, 216, 332, 490, 579
Conditioning, 343–349, 425, 451, 452, 455, 463, 614, 617
Confidence
 coefficient, 334
 ellipsoid, 343, 494
 intervals, 173, 334–343, 349, 414, 493, 494–498, 506, 538, 555
  and hypothesis tests, 361, 398, 498
 limits, 334
 set, 344
Conglomerability, 13, 14
Conjugate prior distribution. *See* Prior distribution, conjugate
Consistent asymptotically normal estimator. *See* CAN estimator
Consistent equations, 568
Consistent estimator, 251–253, 274, 277, 280, 281, 287, 370
Consistent test, 367, 371
Consistent uniform asymptotically normal estimator. *See* CUAN estimator
Continuity theorem, 194
Continuous function, 187, 192
Continuous random variable, 33, 93–142
Convergence
 almost surely (strongly, everywhere or with probability one), 189, 193, 214, 655–657
 in distribution (law), 189, 192–194, 196, 201–210, 252–258
 in mean-square, 189, 191, 198
 in *r*th moment, 189, 193, 194
 weakly in probability, 188, 192, 193, 198
Convex, 78, 236
 loss functions, 267
Convolution theorem, 144, 145
Correlation, 56, 70, 74, 77, 123–125, 130, 131, 562, 565, 566, 572, 573, 575, 576, 581, 582
Correlation matrix, 58, 59, 71, 503, 581
Cost function. *See* Loss function
Covariance, 56–58, 63, 64, 66–68, 452, 445, 459, 465, 467, 479
Covariance matrix, 58, 66, 70, 77, 597
Craig's theorem, 158
Cramer's Rule, 565, 630
Cramér-Rao lower bound, 243, 266, 283
Cramér-Wold theorem, 51, 117
Critical region, 355–360, 366, 378–382, 384, 385, 388–392, 397, 498, 500, 501
Critical value, 358, 365, 385, 546, 547
 Bayesian, 383, 384, 390, 546, 547
Criticism, 589
Cromwell's Rule, 602, 607, 608, 616
CUAN estimator, 253, 490
Cumulant generating function, 39
Cumulative distribution function (c.d.f.), 31, 43, 44, 189, 192, 208, 214, 215
Cumulative distribution function technique, 143–147
Curve décolletage. *See* Information contract curve

Data augmentation, 660
Data generating process (DGP), 210, 288, 401
Decision
 optimal, 377, 379–381
 space, 377
 theory, 8, 20, 23
de Finetti representation theorem, 212–217, 289, 290
Degenerate
 estimator, 234, 235
 random variable, 63, 215
Degrees of freedom, 100, 106, 108, 140, 156, 178
Demand curve, 456, 457, 594
δ-method, 207
Dependent events, 14
Determinants, 624–625
Diffuse prior. *See* Prior, noninformative
Digamma function, 271

Dirichlet
multivariate, 132
univariate distribution, 116
Discrete random variable, 32, 33, 44, 81–93, 202–204, 230
Discrete waiting time distribution. *See* Geometric distribution
Disjoint (pairwise) events, 11
Distributed lag, 592
Distribution function. *See* Cumulative distribution function
Distribution of interest (DOI), 405–407, 410, 422, 454, 456, 571, 587, 588, 593, 602, 603, 609
Disturbance term, 446, 449, 450
Double exponential distribution. *See* Laplace distribution
Dummy (binary) variables, 509–519, 558, 568, 577
Duplication matrix, 539, 648
Dutch book, 21–23
Dynamic linear regression, 591–593

Econometric Society, 1, 418, 616
Econometrics, xi, xii, xiv, 1–3, 65, 66, 118, 226, 439
Edgeworth expansion, 208, 372
Eigenvalue. *See* Characteristic root
Eigenvector. *See* Characteristic vector
Elementary event, 11
Ellipsoid bound theorems, 486, 487, 531–536
Elliptically symmetric distribution, 127, 133, 134, 154, 549, 556
Empirical distribution function, 184, 195, 210, 215
Encompassing, 612
Endogenous, 594
Entropy, 333
Equicorrelated case, 130
Error correction, 592
Error possibility frontier, 362
Errors-in-variables, 445
Estimability, 570–571, 573–575, 577, 582
Estimate, 169, 234
Estimation, 219–349, 460–489, 519–540, 567–583. *See also* Ordinary least squares, Maximum likelihood estimation
Bayesian
generalized Bayes, 305
interval, 340–341
point, 301–330, 524–540, 577–580
classical
point, 219–288, 466–489, 567–583
interval, 219, 334–340, 494–498
efficient, 274
extremal, 288
least squares, 277, 461
minimum chi-squared, 286
robust, 202
Estimator, 169, 234–288
jackknife, 249, 250
linear, 245
Event, 11
Evidence, 228, 397, 398. *See also* Weight of evidence
Ex ante, 166–169, 356, 365, 407, 429
Ex post, 166, 168, 173, 429
Exchangeability, 86, 168, 211–217, 292, 408, 412, 417, 418
Exogenous variable, 587. *See also* Strong, Super, and Weak exogeneity
Expectation
asymptotic, 252
multivariate, 55–64
univariate, 36–43
Expected posterior loss, 301–330, 377, 379, 381–385, 432, 525
Experiment, 9, 10, 29, 167, 227, 228, 230, 347, 364, 406, 409, 410, 416, 445, 587, 613
design, 166, 167, 211
mixed, 228, 229
social, 167, 407, 410
Explanatory variable, 458
Exponential distribution, 100, 101, 110, 112, 114–116, 146, 147, 154, 176, 180, 309, 316
bivariate, 459
translated, 287
Exponential family of distributions, 112, 116, 117, 132, 154, 180, 222, 223, 224, 267, 286, 291, 309, 310, 359
curved, 394
Exponential power family, 110, 593, 610
Extreme bounds analysis (EBA), 536, 548. *See also* Ellipsoid bound theorems and Feasible ellipsoid theorem
Extreme value distribution, 110

F-distribution, 108, 109, 113, 114, 116, 130, 179, 339, 432, 494, 500–508
Factorial moment, 41
Factorial moment generating function, 41
Factorization theorem, 223
Falsification, 401, 402
Fat-tailed distribution, 178
Feasible ellipsoid theorem, 486, 487
Fictitious sample, 292, 298, 299, 325, 527, 529
Fiducial inference, 219, 221, 290, 428
Field. *See* Algebra
Final precision, 220, 234, 236, 305, 336
Finite population correction factor, 87
Finite sample distribution theory, 251
Fixed point, 660
Fixed regressors. *See* Regressors, fixed
Forecast interval. *See* Prediction interval
Forecasting. *See* Prediction
Fourier transform, 40
Frame of reference, 13

Frequency interpretation of probability, 200
Frequentist viewpoint, xiii, 3, 173, 200, 219, 220, 230, 336, 346, 351, 397, 614, 615, 617. *See also* Classical viewpoint
Fully exponential, 307, 393
Function, 29
Fundamental Theorem of Calculus, 34

Gambler's fallacy, 167
Gambler's ruin, 26
Gamma distribution, 98–101, 103, 105, 106, 114–116, 128, 136, 148, 176, 177, 209, 313, 438, 526, 528
Gamma function, 97–99, 214
Gauss-Hermite product rule, 654
Gaussian distribution, 202. *See also* Normal distribution
Gauss-Markov theorem, 472–475, 485, 553, 571, 578. *See also* BLUE
Generalized least squares, 590, 591, 597
Generalized variance, 58
General multiple linear regression model, 474
Geometric distribution, 88, 89, 114, 147, 226
Gibbs sampling, 659, 660
g-inverse, 630. *See also* Matrices, generalized inverse
Glivenko-Cantelli theorem, 195
Goodness-of-fit, 559–563
Gramm-Schmidt orthogonalization process, 623
Gramm-Schmidt triangular reduction, 624
Gumbel distribution. *See* Extreme value distribution

Hat matrix, 558
Hawthorne effects, 410
Hazard rate, 115
Hell-Bray theorem, 193, 194
Hessian matrix, 78, 260, 261, 280, 287, 307, 308, 368, 375, 476
Heteroskedasticity, 127, 128, 451, 591, 596, 613
Hierarchical model, 315, 331, 332, 539
Highest posterior density (HPD) interval, 340–343, 376, 377, 533, 538
Hilbert space, 623
Homogeneous system, 630
Homoskedasticity, 127, 451, 453, 504
Hotelling's T^2 statistic, 180, 343
Hypergeometric distribution, 86, 87, 92, 114
Hyperparameter, 300, 327, 378
Hypothesis
  alternative, 113, 354–359, 371, 372, 520, 608, 609
    local, 368, 371, 375, 499
  composite, 353
  data-instigated, 613–615
  maintained, 606, 608–612, 615, 616
  nonexhaustive, 442
  nonlinear, 375
  non-nested, 545
  null, 113, 354–358, 361, 366, 371, 372, 389, 391, 396, 498, 500, 502, 505–507, 511–517, 519, 520
  one-sided, 358, 359, 385, 386, 389, 506, 511
  parametric, 353
  posterior probability, 379–383, 388, 390–392, 396, 398–400, 557, 604
  prior probability, 378, 390, 391, 541, 548, 557, 604, 606, 607, 613
  sharp, 353, 379, 381–383, 391, 402, 498, 506, 544, 601, 612
  simple, 353, 356–358, 363, 366, 381, 385, 389
  statistical, 353
  test, 113, 351–403, 498–509, 511–518, 602, 716. *See also* Asymptotic, Bayesian, Chow, Confidence intervals, Consistent, Jeffreys' prior, Lagrange multiplier, Level-α, Likelihood ratio, Power, Pretest estimator, Pretesting, Sampling approach, Significance, Size, and Wald
  biased, 359
  diagnostic, 522, 523, 586, 609–612
  incidence, 314
  invariant, 360, 361
  local, 359
  locally most powerful (LMP), 361
  most powerful, 356, 357
  pure significance, 607–609
  specificity, 314
  two-sided, 361, 389, 390, 498
  unbiased, 359, 360
  uniformly most powerful (UMP), 356, 358–361, 502, 506
  uniformly most powerful unbiased (UMPU), 360, 361, 502

Identification, 235, 250, 456, 569, 591, 594
i.i.d., 166, 474
Image, 29
Imelda's problem, 93
Importance function, 654–658
Inadmissible estimator, 237–240, 246, 250, 283, 352, 522, 523, 557
Incoherent beliefs, 29
Incomplete beta function, 104
Incomplete gamma function, 98
Inconsistent equations, 462, 482, 630–632
Inconsistent estimator, 277
Independent events
  mutual, 14, 25, 198
  pairwise, 14, 24, 25, 131
Independent random variables. *See* Stochastically independent random variables
Indicator function, 181, 215, 655
Indifference curves, 362
Induction, 2, 10, 28, 403

Inequalities
Bonferroni, 342, 496
Cauchy-Schwarz, 77, 623
Chebyshev, 76, 77, 79
Holder, 77
information, 287
Jensen, 78–80, 286, 287
Liapounov, 80, 208–210
Markov, 76, 191
Minkowski, 79
multivariate Chebyshev, 80
Inequality restriction, 506, 521
Inference, 319, 615
Information contract curve, 530, 534, 538, 579
Information matrix, 261–264, 271, 287, 306, 323, 368, 375, 480, 595
Information set, 406, 408, 414, 422, 446
i.n.i.d., 166, 208, 209, 460
Initial precision, 220, 221, 234–288, 306, 336
Instrumentalism, 1–3, 17, 19, 24
Integrating constants, 98, 100, 106, 126, 131, 136, 140, 291
Interquartile range, 37
Intervention, 3, 411, 418
Intrinsically linear, 458, 459
Iterated expectation, 61, 65, 163
Invariance, 3, 282, 322, 332, 360
Inverse gaussian distribution, 110
Inverse image, 29
Inverse mapping/transformation, 149, 152, 153
Inverted gamma distribution, 111, 297, 312, 526
Inverted-Wishart distribution, 137, 138, 154
Isodensity ellipse, 123
Isomorphism, 215

Jackknife estimator, 249, 250
Jacobian, 149–153, 273, 332
Jeffreys' paradox, 391
Jeffreys' prior
estimation, 317, 322–324, 332, 333, 342, 597
testing, 396
Jeffreys' rule, 323–325

Kernel, 656
Kurtosis, 37, 41, 92, 115, 472

Lagged dependent variable. *See* Autoregression
Lagrange multiplier, 370, 441
Lagrange multiplier (LM) test, 368–375, 395, 499, 610
Laplace approximation, 307, 316, 393, 395, 396, 610, 658
Laplace distribution, 110, 112, 114, 117, 152, 438, 593
Laplace transform, 39
Law of cosines, 623
Law of iterated logarithm, 208–209
Laws of large numbers, 76, 199, 200, 201, 204, 214, 278, 279, 281, 287, 655, 656
Leading indicator, 592
Least absolute deviation (LAD) estimator, 461
Least squares inverse, 631
Lehmann-Scheffé theorem, 268
Leptokurtic, 41
Level-α test, 355, 356
Level of significance. *See* Significance level
Lexicographic preference, 355, 363
Likelihood
approaches, 220, 460, 590, 608
concentrated (profile), 287
equations, 275, 278
function, 216, 220, 221, 227, 275, 343, 344, 347, 378, 379, 382–386, 393, 402, 408, 439, 524, 525, 527, 539, 594, 602
marginal, 290, 373, 379, 603
predictive, 411
Principle (LP), 221, 227, 229–233, 236, 290, 324, 344, 346, 364, 365, 397, 428, 614, 615, 617
corollary, 230
formal, 228
informal, 227
ratio (LR), 356, 357, 381, 382
test, 356, 357, 368–375, 394, 499
Limit, 186
Limiting distribution, 189, 194, 252. *See also* Asymptotic distribution
Lindeberg condition, 205, 206
Lindeberg-Feller central limit theorem, 205, 206
Lindeberg-Levy central limit theorem, 202, 204
Lindley's Paradox, 391, 545
Linear combination, 126, 128, 147
Linear estimator, 245
Linear exponential family, 113, 131, 132
Linear regression, 120, 123, 124, 127, 128, 133, 135, 139, 458, 460–583
Linear system of equations, 629–633
consistent, 631
Location family, 81, 185, 446
Location parameter, 81, 185, 335
Location-scale family, 81, 210, 271
Logistic distribution, 111, 112, 459
Logistic-normal distribution, 135
Logistic transformation, 135
Lognormal distribution
multivariate, 129, 130
univariate, 111, 114
Loss function, 235, 236–238, 301–305, 318, 319, 332, 383, 547, 561, 602
absolute value, 43, 236
all-or-nothing, 302–304, 326, 384, 388, 396, 525, 540, 546
asymmetric, 302, 440

Loss function (cont.)
balanced, 314
bounded, 236
convex, 236
LINEX, 312
quadratic, 40, 66, 236, 237, 302, 313, 314, 393, 411–414, 434, 484, 522, 523, 538, 552, 556, 559, 605
predictive, 411–413, 440, 442, 552, 605
squared error, 238, 239, 304, 311, 433, 442, 522, 548, 575
strictly convex, 236
symmetric, 302, 415
weighted squared error, 238, 239, 310, 523, 525
Lower bound, 243
Lucas critique, 403, 419

MacLaurin series, 39
Marginal distribution, 44
Markov chain, 659
Martingales, 201
Mass point. *See* Atom
Matric-normal distribution, 138, 139, 593
Matric-normal-Wishart distribution, 139
Matric-t distribution, 139–142, 598
Matrices, 619–643
adjoint, 627
cofactors, 624, 625, 627
commutation matrix, 138, 647
definite matrix, 423, 451, 462, 473, 475, 480, 485, 488, 502, 520, 542, 594, 600, 638–643
determinant, 599, 624–627
diagonal, 579, 620
diagonalizable, 636
differentiation, 649–652
generalized inverse, 462, 630–633
idempotent, 156, 159, 161, 179, 633, 634, 466, 468, 476, 486, 487, 490, 503
identity, 620
inner product, 621
inverse, 581, 626–629
Kronecker product, 138, 645, 646
lower triangular, 620, 643
matrix multiplication, 619
minor, 624
nonsingular, 626
null matrix, 620, 621
orthogonal, 134, 482, 626
complement, 623
projection theorem, 564, 623, 632, 641
regression, 478
transformation, 217
outer product, 370, 621
projection matrix, 468, 480
quadratic forms, 638–643
rank, 568, 572, 576, 583, 624–626, 628, 631
scalar multiplication, 619
semidefinite, 480, 532, 533, 537, 559
simultaneous diagonalization, 636–637
singular value decomposition, 643
square, 620
symmetric, 539, 638–643
trace, 590, 619, 647, 652
transpose, 619
triangular, 620, 643
tridiagonal, 637, 638
unitary matrix, 620
upper triangular, 620
Maximization, 653–654
Maximum entropy, 333
Maximum likelihood estimation (MLE), 246, 275, 280–285, 287, 305, 306, 315, 322, 328, 347, 368, 369, 374, 394, 399, 402, 426, 427, 432, 442, 461, 490, 591, 595, 599
Maxwell distribution, 154
Mean-independence, 67–69, 73–76, 124, 135
Mean squared error (MSE), 234, 238–250, 271, 283, 285, 313, 319, 359, 366, 429, 477, 520, 523, 537, 539, 551, 562
matrix, 238–240, 243, 485, 488, 520
Measurable function, 29, 30
Measurable space, 11, 12
Measure, 12, 215
Measure theory, xiv
Median, 35, 37, 42, 64, 182, 185, 208, 209, 236
Median unbiased, 244, 245, 464
Memoryless property, 89, 101, 103
Mesokurtic, 41
Method of moments (MM), 170, 272–274, 273, 284, 288
Methodology, xiii, 1–4
Midrange, 182–184
Minimal representation, 113
Minimal sigma algebra, 11, 26, 31
Minimal sufficient statistic, 222, 224, 225, 226, 269, 426
Minimax
estimator, 311
principle, 242
Minimum, 185
Minimum absolute deviation (MAD) estimator, 461
Minimum norm least squares approximate solution, 632
Minimum variance bound (MVB) estimators, 264–268, 472
Mixed random variable, 36
Mixing processes, 201
Mixture distribution, 291, 528, 548, 549
bivariate normal, 130, 155
Mode, 35, 37, 92, 105, 107–112, 157, 528, 529
Model occurrence, 378
Model selection, 352, 396, 602–607, 611, 612
Models, xi, 2, 3, 351, 405, 418, 585, 590, 602–607, 614, 616

Moment, 37
 asymptotic, 194
 existence, 37
 mean, 37, 58
 moment generating function (m.g.f.), 308
  joint, 62, 147, 148
  not existing, 106, 109, 111
  technique, 147, 148, 155, 395
  univariate, 38–40, 194, 199, 202
 nonexistent, 245
 precision, 37
 problem of moments, 38, 43
 sample, 176
 sample mean, 204, 427, 655
 standard deviation, 37
 variance, 37, 58
Monotone likelihood ratio, 359
Monte Carlo integration, 654–659
Moore-Penrose inverse, 630
Moving average (MA) error, 596,
Multicollinearity, 503, 513, 567–583
Multimodal distribution, 131, 528
Multinomial distribution, 118–120, 128, 148
Multiplication rule, 15
Mutually exclusive events, 11, 14

Natural conjugate distribution, 292, 312, 320, 434
Natural parameter space, 113, 220, 221
Negative binomial distribution, 88, 114, 116, 233, 250, 324, 333, 364, 407
Neyman-Pearson Lemma, 356–358
n.i.i.d, 166
n.i.n.i.d, 166
Non-Bayesian inference, 219
 conditional frequentist, 219
 conditional likelihood, 219
 fiducial, 219
 frequentist, 230, 234–288
 pivotal, 219, 228
 plausibility, 219
 structural, 219, 228
Noncentral distributions
 chi-squared, 156–161, 163, 372, 500
 doubly noncentral F-distribution, 158
 F, 157, 158, 162, 500, 501, 506, 521
 t, 157, 160, 162
 Wishart, 179
Noncentrality parameter, 113, 156, 161, 163, 343, 500–503, 506, 520–523, 557
Nondegenerate random variable, 202, 252
Noninformative experiment, 231
Noninformative prior. *See* Prior, improper, or Prior, noninformative
Nonlinear estimator, 246
Non-nested hypotheses, 545, 610
Nonparametric methods, 181, 225, 590
Nonsingular matrix, 187
Nonstationarity, 323
Nonsystematic component. *See* Disturbance term

Norm, 236, 623
Normal distribution. *See also* Truncated
 bivariate, 121, 123–125, 129–132, 341, 345, 454, 459
 contaminated or mixture, 130, 155
 multivariate, 121–124, 126–131, 133, 135, 136, 141, 155–163, 246, 247, 300–301, 313, 326, 343, 374, 375, 395, 413, 414, 420–424, 430, 433, 435, 440, 442, 443, 451–453, 460, 464, 474, 492, 494, 508, 525, 526, 539, 549, 550, 556, 578, 591
 split, 386, 387
 trivariate, 129, 132, 454
 univariate, 95–98, 103, 107, 112, 114–116, 130, 131, 148, 152–154, 177, 178, 185, 217, 220, 226, 247–250, 293, 295, 303–304, 309, 310, 314, 316, 326, 335–339, 341, 342, 346, 349, 353, 357, 366, 375, 384, 385, 412, 430, 432, 433, 435, 442, 443, 459, 578, 593, 596
Normal equations, 462, 465, 565, 568, 569, 571
Normal-gamma distribution, 128, 129, 298, 313, 325, 434, 526–529, 531–538, 542, 543, 556, 559, 583, 600
Normal-Wishart distribution, 141, 282, 298, 332, 435, 443, 528, 598, 597, 599
Nuisance parameter, 302, 306, 340, 353, 361, 383, 384, 425, 431, 433, 436, 442, 460, 500, 502, 548, 553, 558

o(•), 187, 188
O(•), 187, 188, 308, 309, 391, 394, 395, 437, 499
o_p(•), 196, 371
O_p(•), 196, 282, 371
Objectivist viewpoint, 362. *See also* Classical, Frequentist, and Sampling theory viewpoints
Observational studies, 409, 424
Observationally equivalent, 569, 582
Omitted variable, 489
One-to-one transformation, 149, 150, 152, 153
Order of magnitude, 187
Order statistics, 181–185, 207, 267
Ordinary least squares (OLS), 277, 461, 464–482, 490–494, 519, 524, 555, 557, 558, 562, 564, 565, 568, 570, 573, 577

Paradox, 13, 55, 92
Parameter, 81, 165, 210, 211, 401, 585. *See also* Noncentrality parameter
 of interest, 353, 547, 548, 571, 571, 576, 579, 580
 space
  natural, 113
  permissible, 234
Parametric family, 81
Pareto, 111, 139, 154, 309, 459
Parsimony. *See* Simplicity

Partial adjustment, 592
Partial correlation
 populatlon, 70–72, 75, 135
 sample, 563–567, 580
Partition of a set, 11, 439
Partitioned inverse, 122, 368, 369, 627
Pascal distribution. *See* Negative binomial distribution
Pearson family of distributions, 115–117
Permutations, 82, 211
Pitman drift, 371
Pivotal
 inference, 219
 quantity, 335, 336, 341, 430, 431, 433, 491, 493, 500, 524
Planning stage, 588, 589, 606
Platykurtic, 42
Plausibility inference, 219
Pointwise continuity, 187
Poisson distribution, 41, 89–92, 101, 114, 115, 116, 118, 148, 154, 156, 163, 177, 199, 210, 269, 331, 438
Policy analysis, 406, 419, 552, 616
Polya urn, 181
Poly-t density, 528
Population, 166
Population R^2, 75, 124, 135, 471, 536, 537, 561
Population regression, 64–76, 566, 567, 588
Positive definite matrix, 238, 239, 253
Posterior
 density, 216, 290–334, 388, 525, 527–529, 535, 537, 547, 548, 597
 distribution, 216, 290, 292–296, 298–309, 340, 341, 377, 433, 434, 655–658
 mean, 299, 303, 315, 331, 409, 526, 527, 531–537, 548, 551, 554, 579, 599, 601
 mode, 303, 326, 393–395, 529, 530
 odds, 365, 376–396, 546, 547, 613
 quantile, 303
 variance, 657
Power (function) of a test, 355–360, 367, 499, 501, 502, 506, 507, 608
 asymptotic, 371
Power set, 10
Pragmatic Principles of Model Building (PPMB), 329, 601–602, 605, 607, 608, 611, 612, 614–617
Precision
 final, 220, 234
 initial, 220, 221, 234
 parameter, 293
Prediction, 2, 3, 6–8, 66, 75, 402–443, 551–559, 575, 576, 589, 598, 601, 602
 error, 411–413, 424, 429, 430, 440, 443, 554, 558
 interval (region), 411, 413–415, 430–433, 435, 438, 439, 553, 554, 557
 point, 412–415, 429, 434, 439, 552, 554–558
 unbiased, 440, 558
Predictive
 bias, 412, 440
 covariance matrix, 412
 density, 428, 433, 434, 437–439, 555–557, 604
 distribution, 396, 406–409, 429, 436
 likelihood, 425–428, 436, 437
  asymptotic, 428
 loss, 430
 mean, 604, 605
 mean square error (MSEP), 412, 425, 575
 variance, 605
Predictivist, 351, 411
Pretest estimator, 486, 519–524, 547, 548, 600
Pretesting, 352, 353, 615
Principle of Cogent Reason, 17
Principle of Insufficient Reason, 17, 321
Principle of Stable Estimation, 322
Prior, 586, 613, 615, 616
 choice, 318–331
 conjugate, 291, 295–301, 320, 328, 526–529, 531–538, 540, 544
 density, 216, 290–334, 382, 383, 386–389, 393, 394, 400, 525, 547
 distribution, 215, 216, 290, 378, 433, 442, 443
 elicitation, 320, 378, 392, 527, 528
 g-prior, 538
 improper, 305, 306, 315, 323, 328, 334, 347, 435, 438, 442, 443, 603
 induced, 544
 information, 219, 576–580
 mixed, 600
 natural conjugate, 291–300, 303, 304, 320, 528, 556, 577, 578, 582, 598, 599
 noninformative, 318, 321–329, 332, 376, 390, 438, 443, 535–537, 540, 544, 545, 547, 548, 556, 557, 583, 603. *See also* Prior, improper
 odds, 546
 proper, 305
Probability, 9–29
 density function (p.d.f.), 33
 function, 34
  countable infinite, 12, 13, 27
  finitely additive, 12, 13
 integral transform, 150
 interpretation
  classical, 16, 18, 20
  logical, 16, 18–20
  objective, 3, 8, 16–19, 165, 334
  propensity, 18
  subjective, 3, 8, 16, 18–20, 165, 210–217, 335
 interval, 334
 mass function, 33, 34, 83–93
 of nearness criterion, 245
 space
  countable additive, 12, 14
  finitely additive, 12, 14

Pseudo-random samples, 172, 655
Purchasing power parity, 508, 509
P-value, 396–400

Quadratic form, 122, 155–163, 453
Quadratic form technique, 155–163
Quantile, 35, 207
 regression, 452

R^2, 75, 470, 480, 501, 519, 559–564, 566
R^2 deletes, 581
$\bar{R}^2$, 561–563
R^2_{raw}, 469, 501, 560
Raleigh distribution, 154
Random portfolio, 93
Random sample, 166 171, 200, 210, 211, 221, 231, 412
Random variable, 30–33
Randomized response, 285
Rao-Blackwell theorem, 266, 268
Realism, 1–3, 17, 19, 24, 210, 216
Recognizable subsets, 18
Reference set, 345
Regressand, 446, 476
Regression, 445–583
 multiple, 447, 450
 multivariate, 455, 504, 593, 597–599
 simple, 447, 450, 465, 476, 477, 480, 489
 sum of squared (SSR), 470, 477, 559
 toward mediocracity, 445
Regressors, 446
 fixed (Case I), 445–447, 451, 453, 460, 462–465, 471, 486–488, 499, 504, 524, 540, 551, 552, 554, 555, 559, 580, 582, 583
 stochastic (Case II), 445, 448–451, 453, 454, 457, 460, 462–465, 470, 488, 499, 504, 506, 425, 551, 552, 554, 555, 559
Regularity conditions, 259, 260, 278, 279, 281, 306, 322, 374
Rejection method, 658
Rejection region. *See* Critical region
Relative frequency, 17
Relative numerical efficiency (RNE), 657
Relatively more efficient, 237, 239, 245
Reparameterization, 99, 322, 372, 421, 475, 503, 504, 511–515, 539
Restricted least squares (RLS), 482–489, 501–505, 507, 508, 520, 521, 532, 536, 577
Ridge regression, 577, 582
Riemann integral, 42
Riemann-Stieltjes integral, 42, 378
Risk (risk function), 237–244, 246, 283, 284, 304, 305, 314, 520
Robustness, 8, 97, 202, 318, 392, 497, 612, 616. *See also* Sensitivity analysis

Sample, 165
 correlation, 175
 maximum, 144, 146
 mean, 80, 234, 245, 246, 254
 median, 182, 208, 209, 254
 minimum, 146
 moments, 168, 169
 range, 182–185
 selection, 589
 random size, 146, 147, 231
 space, 9, 29, 30, 234, 600
  predictive, 406
 variance, 169, 176
Sampling
 approach to hypothesis testing, 354–367
 distribution, 166–172, 176–181, 244, 294, 432, 482, 488, 493, 600, 601
 error, 186, 236, 238, 251, 462, 464, 554
 to a foregone conclusion, 363, 365, 391
 properties, 233–250
 with replacement, 86, 165
 without replacement, 86, 87, 165, 180
 theory, xiii (*See also* Frequentist viewpoint and Classical viewpoint)
Savage density ratio, 393
Scale
 family, 81, 176
 matrix, 127
 parameter, 81, 176, 335
Scenario forecast, 454
Scheffé intervals, 496, 497
Schwarz's criterion, 394, 395
Score
 function, 260, 261, 264, 276, 373, 499, 596, 610
 test. *See* Lagrange multiplier test
Scoring rule, 29
Seemingly unrelated regressions (SUR), 504, 599
Sensitivity analysis, 329–331, 531, 548–551, 579, 585, 586, 612, 615, 616. *See also* Ellipsoid bound theorems, Extreme bounds analysis, and Feasible ellipsoid theorem
Sequences, 186–217, 251
Series expansions, 117
Shadow price. *See* Lagrange multiplier
Shrinkage estimator, 246
Sigma algebra/sigma field, 11, 29–31, 446, 451
Sigma partition, 11
Significance
 level, 355–358, 363, 366, 367, 389–391, 396, 397, 498, 499, 507, 520, 523
 test, 354
Similar critical regions, 361, 502
Simplicity, 400, 402, 522, 588, 590, 602, 606, 612
Simpson' s paradox, 415–418
Simultaneous equations, 594
Size of a test, 355
Skewness, 3 7, 41, 92, 115, 349
Slutsky's theorem, 195
Space shuttle, 4–8

Spearman's rank correlation coefficient, 562
Specification
 searches, 352, 612
 uncertainty, 558
Spherically symmetric distribution, 134, 154, 155, 464, 502, 529
Standard error, 402
Standard multiple linear regression model, 447, 460–583
 fixed regressors, 447, 476, 490–492, 494
 stochastic regressors, 450
Standard multiple linear normal regression model, 448, 460–583
 fixed regressors, 447, 460, 490–494
 stochastic regressors, 450, 452, 460
Standardized distribution, 97, 98, 106, 112, 121–124, 130, 132, 136
States of nature, 21, 235, 242
Stationarity, 323
Statistic, 169, 222
Statistical significance, 363–365
Statistically independent. *See* Stochastically independent random variables
Statistics, xii, xiii, 1, 4, 439
Stein-like estimators, 246, 283–285, 334
Stieltjes integral, 42, 213
Stochastic continuity, 197
Stochastic convergence, 185–199, 251
Stochastic processes, 201
Stochastically dependent random variables, 53
Stochastically greater, 117
Stochastically increasing, 117
Stochastically independent random variables, 52–54, 57, 132, 135, 137, 144, 154, 165, 178, 450
 mutually independent, 52–54, 131
 pairwise independent, 53, 54, 126, 131
St. Petersburg paradox, 92
Stirling's series, 99
Stopping rule, 231
 principle (SRP), 232, 364, 365
 proper, 231
Strictly concave, 78
Strictly convex, 78, 236, 250
Strong convergence, 189, 214
Strong exogeneity, 552
Structure, 3, 411, 418–425
Structural, 552, 589, 594, 616
 distribution, 418
 equation, 3
 inference, 219
 parameters, 418
Student-gamma distribution, 528, 529
Student t-distribution, 106, 112–114, 158, 326, 336–338, 431, 432, 435, 438, 443, 549, 550, 599
Subjectivist viewpoint. *See* Bayesian, subjective
Subsequence, 190
Sufficiency Principle, 346, 617
Sufficient statistic, 222, 226, 227, 267–269, 294, 315, 345, 361, 436
 jointly sufficient statistics, 222, 223, 224, 226
 minimal, 346, 427
Sum of squared errors (SSE), 468–472, 476, 477, 559, 561, 562, 565, 568
Super efficient estimator, 253
Super exogeneity, 552
Supply curve, 456, 457, 594
Support, 35, 113, 225
Suppressible statistic, 315, 316
Symmetric
 beliefs, 217
 density/distribution, 36, 41, 98, 349, 399, 400, 548, 550, 593
 matrix, 648, 651, 635
Systematic component, 446–447

Tail behavior, 112
Taylor series, 39, 90, 204, 278, 286, 316, 654
t-distribution
 multivariate, 126–128, 135, 298, 453, 526, 528, 547, 548
 univariate, 106, 107, 109, 112, 113, 116, 130, 556
Testimation. *See* Pretesting
Testing. *See* Hypothesis, test
Theory, xi, 1, 6, 7, 205
Tierney-Kadane method, 307–309, 316, 317, 333, 437
Tobit model, 601
Total sum of squares (SST), 470, 477, 559, 561, 562
Trace of a matrix, 647
Transformations, 117, 143–163
 Box-Mueller, 154
 differences, 144, 145
 logistic, 135
 products, 145
 square, 147
 ratios, 144–146
 quadratic, 155–163
 sums, 145, 148
 variance stabilizing, 210
Trigamma function, 271
Trimmed mean, 255, 256
Trinomial distribution, 129
Trivariate normal, 129
Truncated
 bivariate normal, 132
 normal distribution, 115, 327, 386
 univariate distribution, 36
Truth, xi, 2, 3, 210, 211, 216, 352, 353, 375, 402, 506, 520, 546, 557, 585, 588, 608, 612, 613, 615
Type I error, 354, 366, 388, 390, 398, 499, 506
Type II error, 354, 366, 388, 390, 398, 499, 506

Unbiased estimator, 242–248, 250–252, 266–268, 285, 315, 343, 412, 472, 473, 561, 565, 572, 583, 655. *See also* Asymptotically, unbiased
Uncorrelated random variables, 57, 58, 63, 67, 68, 74, 75, 126, 131, 135, 170, 175, 180, 200, 201, 446
Uniform continuity, 187, 199, 287
Uniform convergence, 253, 278
Uniform distribution
 continuous, 93–95, 103, 105, 110, 113, 114, 146, 150, 153, 176, 177, 183, 185, 190, 198, 217, 225, 226, 248, 274, 309, 312, 314, 315, 324, 333, 336, 438, 547, 548, 593
 discrete, 83, 333, 480, 481
Uniform minimum variance unbiased (UMVU) estimators, 266, 271, 502
Uniformly most powerful (UMP), 356, 358–360, 502, 506
Unimodal, 36, 41
Urn model, 180
Utility, 22, 23, 29

Variance, 37, 58, 63, 248, 249, 459, 465, 467, 471, 477, 478, 484, 554, 558, 572–574
Variance-covariance matrix, 58, 66, 77, 243, 590, 591
Variance-independence, 68, 75, 449, 452
Variance stabilizing transformation, 210
Variation-free, 422, 461
Vec operator, 646–652
Vech operator, 136, 421, 423, 648
Vector, 619. *See also* Matrices
 linearly dependent, 622, 625
 linearly independent, 476, 622, 625
 orthogonal, 622
 orthonormal, 622
Vector space, 621–624
 dimension, 622

Wald test, 368–376, 499
Weak Conditionality Principle (WCP), 227–230, 290, 617
Weak convergence in probability, 187
Weak exogeneity, 461, 524, 525
Weak Sufficiency Principle (WSP), 227–230
Weibull distribution, 112, 114, 115, 154
Weight of evidence, 380
Window, 289, 292, 320, 321, 402, 409, 410, 414, 419, 585–617
 expansion, 590–601, 606, 607, 610, 611
 initial, 586–590, 606–611
 out-of-sample, 603
Wishart distribution, 136–138, 154, 179, 332